WILEY

John Wiley & Sons, Inc.

Professional C++, Second Edition

Published by
John Wiley & Sons, Inc.
10475 Crosspoint Boulevard
Indianapolis, IN 46256
www.wiley.com

Copyright © 2011 by John Wiley & Sons, Inc., Indianapolis, Indiana

Published simultaneously in Canada

ISBN: 978-0-470-93244-5
ISBN: 978-1-118-16995-7 (ebk)
ISBN: 978-1-118-16994-0 (ebk)
ISBN: 978-1-118-16993-3 (ebk)
Manufactured in the United States of America

10 9 8 7 6 5 4 3 2

For general information on our other products and services please contact our Customer Care Department within the United States at (877) 762-2974, outside the United States at (317) 572-3993 or fax (317) 572-4002.

Wiley also publishes its books in a variety of electronic formats and by print-on-demand. Not all content that is available in standard print versions of this book may appear or be packaged in all book formats. If you have purchased a version of this book that did not include media that is referenced by or accompanies a standard print version, you may request this media by visiting http://booksupport.wiley.com. For more information about Wiley products, visit us at www.wiley.com.

Library of Congress Control Number: 2011932278

Dedicated to my parents, who are always there for me.

—MARC GREGOIRE

To Sonja, for her unconditional love and support; and to my son Kai, whose frequent interruptions reminded me what's important in life.

—NICHOLAS A. SOLTER

To Fletch, whose unpredictable cuteness reminds me of someone . . .

—SCOTT J. KLEPER

CREDITS

ABOUT THE AUTHORS

 **MARC GREGOIRE** is a software engineer from Belgium. He graduated from the Catholic University of Leuven, Belgium, with a degree in "Burgerlijk ingenieur in de computer wetenschappen" (equivalent to a master of science in engineering in computer science). The year after, he received the cum laude degree of master in artificial intelligence at the same university. After his studies, Marc started working for a big software consultancy company called Ordina Belgium. As a consultant, he worked for Siemens and Nokia Siemens Networks on critical 2G and 3G software running on Solaris for big telecom operators. This required working in international teams stretching from South America and USA to EMEA and Asia. Now, Marc is working for Nikon Metrology on 3D scanning software. His main expertise is C/C++, and specifically Microsoft VC++ and the MFC framework. Next to C/C++, Marc also likes C# and uses PHP for creating web pages. In addition to his main interest for Windows development, he also has experience in developing C++ programs running 24x7 on Linux platforms; for example, EIB home automation controlling and monitoring software. Since April 2007, he received the yearly Microsoft MVP (Most Valuable Professional) award for his Visual C++ expertise. Marc is an active member on the CodeGuru forum (as Marc G) and wrote some articles and FAQ entries for CodeGuru. He also creates freeware and shareware programs that are distributed through his website at www.nuonsoft.com, and maintains a blog on www.nuonsoft.com/blog/.

 NICHOLAS A. SOLTER is a computer programmer with experience developing a range of software including systems software, games, web services, and more. His work on high availability clusters at Sun Microsystems led to three patents and a publication at the International Parallel and Distributed Processing Symposium. Also at Sun, he enjoyed the opportunity to be involved in OpenSolaris, and was the lead author of the *OpenSolaris Bible* (Wiley, 2009). Now back in the world of web development, Nick is thrilled to be working with Scott again at Context Optional.

Nick studied computer science at Stanford University, where he earned bachelor and master of science degrees, with a concentration in systems. In addition to his industry experience, he taught C++ for one year at Fullerton Community College.

Nick lives with his wife and two children in beautiful Colorado, where he enjoys playing in the snow (having been deprived of winters growing up in southern California).

SCOTT J. KLEPER began his programming career in elementary school, writing adventure games in BASIC for the Tandy TRS-80. As the resident Mac geek at his high school, Scott moved to higher-level languages and released several award-winning shareware applications.

Scott attended Stanford University, where he earned bachelor and master of science degrees in computer science, with a concentration in Human-Computer Interaction. While in college, Scott served as a teaching assistant for classes involving introductory programming, object-oriented design, data structures, GUI frameworks, group projects, and Internet programming. He later adapted "Professional C++" for a course at Stanford.

Since graduating, Scott has served as a lead engineer on the founding teams of several companies. In 2006, Scott co-founded Context Optional, Inc., a leading provider of Social Marketing technology.

Outside of work, Scott is a compulsive online shopper, an avid reader, and an awful guitarist.

ABOUT THE TECHNICAL EDITOR

JOSEPH M. NEWCOMER received his PhD in Computer Science from Carnegie Mellon University (CMU). Since then, he has been faculty at CMU, done a high-tech compiler startup, been one of the founding scientists at the Software Engineering Institute at CMU, and been an independent software developer. He has been a Microsoft MVP in the C/C++/MFC area for 16 years. He is co-author of two books on Microsoft Windows programming, *Win32 Programming* (with Brent Rector, Addison-Wesley, 1997) and *Developing Windows NT Device Drivers* (with Ed Dekker, Addison-Wesley, 1999). He is one of the pioneers in desktop publishing and publish-from-database technolgy, in the early 1970s.

ACKNOWLEDGMENTS

I THANK THE JOHN WILEY & SONS and Wrox Press editorial and production teams for their support. Especially, thank you to Robert Elliott, executive editor at Wiley, for giving me a chance to write this book, and Adaobi Obi Tulton, senior project editor at Wiley, for managing this project.

I also thank the authors of the first edition, Nicholas A. Solter and Scott J. Kleper, for doing such a great job on which I could base this second edition.

A very special thank you to my technical editor, Joseph M. Newcomer, for his meticulous technical review. His many constructive comments and ideas have certainly made this book better.

Also, a big thank you to Ordina Belgium (`www.ordina.be`), the company for which I was working while writing this book, for the generous support they provided me.

Of course, the support and patience of my girlfriend, Zulija N., and my nearest family, my parents and my brother, were very important in finishing this book.

Finally, I thank you, as readers, for trying this approach to professional C++ software development.

CONTENTS

INTRODUCTION   *XXV*

PART I: INTRODUCTION TO PROFESSIONAL C++

CHAPTER 1: A CRASH COURSE IN C++   3

The Basics of C++   3
  The Obligatory Hello, World   4
  Namespaces   7
  Variables   8
  Operators   11
  Types   13
  Conditionals   16
  Loops   19
  Arrays   20
  Functions   22
  Those Are the Basics   24
Diving Deeper into C++   24
  Pointers and Dynamic Memory   24
  Strings in C++   28
  References   29
  Exceptions   30
  The Many Uses of const   31
C++ as an Object-Oriented Language   33
  Declaring a Class   33
The Standard Library   35
Your First Useful C++ Program   37
  An Employee Records System   37
  The Employee Class   37
  The Database Class   41
  The User Interface   44
  Evaluating the Program   47
Summary   47

CHAPTER 2: DESIGNING PROFESSIONAL C++ PROGRAMS   49

What Is Programming Design?   50
The Importance of Programming Design   50
What's Different about C++ Design?   52
Two Rules for C++ Design   53
  Abstraction   54
  Reuse   55

Reusing Code   **57**

A Note on Terminology   57
Deciding Whether or Not to Reuse Code   58
Strategies for Reusing Code   60
Bundling Third-Party Applications   65
Open-Source Libraries   66
The C++ Standard Library   67

Designing with Patterns and Techniques   **68**
Designing a Chess Program   **69**

Requirements   69
Design Steps   69

Summary   **75**

CHAPTER 3: DESIGNING WITH OBJECTS   **77**

Am I Thinking Procedurally?   **78**
The Object-Oriented Philosophy   **78**

Classes   78
Components   79
Properties   79
Behaviors   80
Bringing It All Together   80

Living in a World of Objects   **81**

Overobjectification   81
Overly General Objects   82

Object Relationships   **83**

The Has-A Relationship   83
The Is-A Relationship (Inheritance)   84
The Fine Line between Has-A and Is-A   86
The Not-A Relationship   89
Hierarchies   90
Multiple Inheritance   91
Mix-in Classes   92

Abstraction   **92**

Interface versus Implementation   93
Deciding on an Exposed Interface   93
Designing a Successful Abstraction   95

Summary   **96**

CHAPTER 4: DESIGNING FOR REUSE   **97**

The Reuse Philosophy   **97**
How to Design Reusable Code   **98**

Use Abstraction   99
Structure Your Code for Optimal Reuse   100
Design Usable Interfaces   104
Reconciling Generality and Ease of Use   109

Summary   **110**

CHAPTER 5: CODING WITH STYLE — 111

The Importance of Looking Good — 111
Thinking Ahead — 112
Elements of Good Style — 112
Documenting Your Code — 112
Reasons to Write Comments — 112
Commenting Styles — 116
Comments in This Book — 120
Decomposition — 120
Decomposition through Refactoring — 121
Decomposition by Design — 121
Decomposition in This Book — 122
Naming — 122
Choosing a Good Name — 122
Naming Conventions — 123
Using Language Features with Style — 125
Use Constants — 125
Use References Instead of Pointers — 125
Use Custom Exceptions — 126
Formatting — 126
The Curly Brace Alignment Debate — 126
Coming to Blows over Spaces and Parentheses — 128
Spaces and Tabs — 128
Stylistic Challenges — 128
Summary — 129

PART II: C++ CODING THE PROFESSIONAL WAY

CHAPTER 6: GAINING PROFICIENCY WITH CLASSES AND OBJECTS — 133

Introducing the Spreadsheet Example — 134
Writing Classes — 134
Class Definitions — 134
Defining Methods — 137
Using Objects — 141
Object Life Cycles — 142
Object Creation — 143
Object Destruction — 160
Assigning to Objects — 162
Distinguishing Copying from Assignment — 165
Summary — 167

CHAPTER 7: MASTERING CLASSES AND OBJECTS — 169

Dynamic Memory Allocation in Objects — 169
The Spreadsheet Class — 170

Freeing Memory with Destructors — 172
Handling Copying and Assignment — 172

Different Kinds of Data Members — **181**

static Data Members — 181
const Data Members — 183
Reference Data Members — 184
const Reference Data Members — 185

More about Methods — **186**

static Methods — 186
const Methods — 186
Method Overloading — 188
Default Parameters — 190
Inline Methods — 191

Nested Classes — **192**

Enumerated Types Inside Classes — **194**

Friends — **195**

Operator Overloading — **197**

Example: Implementing Addition for SpreadsheetCells — 197
Overloading Arithmetic Operators — 202
Overloading Comparison Operators — 204
Building Types with Operator Overloading — 206

Building Stable Interfaces — **206**

Using Interface and Implementation Classes — 206

Summary — **210**

CHAPTER 8: DISCOVERING INHERITANCE TECHNIQUES — **211**

Building Classes with Inheritance — **211**

Extending Classes — 212
Overriding Methods — 215

Inheritance for Reuse — **219**

The WeatherPrediction Class — 219
Adding Functionality in a Subclass — 220
Replacing Functionality in a Subclass — 222

Respect Your Parents — **223**

Parent Constructors — 223
Parent Destructors — 224
Referring to Parent Names — 226
Casting Up and Down — 229

Inheritance for Polymorphism — **230**

Return of the Spreadsheet — 230
Designing the Polymorphic Spreadsheet Cell — 231
The Spreadsheet Cell Base Class — 231
The Individual Subclasses — 233
Leveraging Polymorphism — 236
Future Considerations — 237

Multiple Inheritance   **239**

Inheriting from Multiple Classes   239
Naming Collisions and Ambiguous Base Classes   240

Interesting and Obscure Inheritance Issues   **243**

Changing the Overridden Method's Characteristics   243
Inherited Constructors   247
Special Cases in Overriding Methods   251
Copy Constructors and the Equals Operator in Subclasses   258
The Truth about virtual   259
Run Time Type Facilities   263
Non-Public Inheritance   264
Virtual Base Classes   265

Summary   **266**

CHAPTER 9: UNDERSTANDING C++ QUIRKS AND ODDITIES   **267**

References   **268**

Reference Variables   268
Reference Data Members   271
Reference Parameters   271
Reference Return Values   273
Deciding between References and Pointers   273
Rvalue References   277

Keyword Confusion   **282**

The const Keyword   282
The static Keyword   288
Order of Initialization of Nonlocal Variables   292

Types and Casts   **292**

typedefs   292
typedefs for Function Pointers   294
Type Aliases   295
Casts   296

Scope Resolution   **300**

C++11   **301**

Uniform Initialization   302
Alternative Function Syntax   304
Null Pointer Constant   304
Angle Brackets   305
Initializer Lists   306
Explicit Conversion Operators   306
Attributes   308
User Defined Literals   308

Header Files   **310**

C Utilities   **312**

Variable-Length Argument Lists   312
Preprocessor Macros   314

Summary   **316**

CHAPTER 10: HANDLING ERRORS — 317

Errors and Exceptions — 317
What Are Exceptions, Anyway? — 318
Why Exceptions in C++ Are a Good Thing — 318
Why Exceptions in C++ Are a Bad Thing — 320
Our Recommendation — 320
Exception Mechanics — 320
Throwing and Catching Exceptions — 321
Exception Types — 324
Throwing and Catching Multiple Exceptions — 326
Uncaught Exceptions — 329
Throw Lists — 331
Exceptions and Polymorphism — 336
The Standard Exception Hierarchy — 336
Catching Exceptions in a Class Hierarchy — 337
Writing Your Own Exception Classes — 339
Nested Exceptions — 342
Stack Unwinding and Cleanup — 344
Use Smart Pointers — 346
Catch, Cleanup, and Rethrow — 346
Common Error-Handling Issues — 347
Memory Allocation Errors — 347
Errors in Constructors — 350
Function-Try-Blocks for Constructors — 352
Errors in Destructors — 354
Putting It All Together — 355
Summary — 359

CHAPTER 11: DELVING INTO THE STANDARD LIBRARY — 361

Coding Principles — 362
Use of Templates — 362
Use of Operator Overloading — 366
Overview of the C++ Standard Library — 366
Strings — 366
I/O Streams — 366
Localization — 367
Smart Pointers — 367
Exceptions — 367
Mathematical Utilities — 368
Time Utilities — 368
Random Numbers — 368
Compile-Time Rational Arithmetic — 369
Tuples — 369
Regular Expressions — 369
The Standard Template Library — 369

STL Algorithms 376
What's Missing from the STL 384
Summary **384**

CHAPTER 12: UNDERSTANDING CONTAINERS AND ITERATORS 385

Containers Overview **386**
Requirements on Elements 387
Exceptions and Error Checking 388
Iterators 388
C++11 Changes 391
Sequential Containers **393**
vector 393
The vector<bool> Specialization 412
deque 413
list 413
array 418
forward_list 418
Container Adapters **421**
queue 421
priority_queue 424
stack 427
Associative Containers **428**
The pair Utility Class 428
map 430
multimap 438
set 441
multiset 444
Unordered Associative Containers/Hash Tables **444**
Hash Functions 444
unordered_map 445
unordered_map Example: Phone Book 448
unordered_multimap 449
unordered_set/unordered_multiset 449
Other Containers **450**
Standard C-Style Arrays 450
strings 451
Streams 451
bitset 452
Summary **456**

CHAPTER 13: MASTERING STL ALGORITHMS 457

Overview of Algorithms **457**
The find and find_if Algorithms 458
The accumulate Algorithms 461
C++11 Move Semantics with Algorithms 462

Lambda Expressions   **463**

Syntax   463
Capture Block   465
Lambda Expressions as Return Type   465
Lambda Expressions as Parameters   467
Examples   467

Function Objects   **469**

Arithmetic Function Objects   470
Comparison Function Objects   471
Logical Function Objects   472
Bitwise Function Objects   473
Function Object Adapters   473
Writing Your Own Function Objects   480

Algorithm Details   **481**

Utility Algorithms   482
Non-Modifying Algorithms   483
Modifying Algorithms   490
Sorting Algorithms   499
Set Algorithms   501

Algorithms Example: Auditing Voter Registrations   **503**

The Voter Registration Audit Problem Statement   503
The auditVoterRolls Function   504
The getDuplicates Function   505
Testing the auditVoterRolls Function   506

Summary   **507**

CHAPTER 14: USING STRINGS AND REGULAR EXPRESSIONS   **509**

Dynamic Strings   **510**

C-Style Strings   510
String Literals   512
The C++ string Class   513
Raw String Literals   516

Localization   **517**

Localizing String Literals   518
Wide Characters   518
Non-Western Character Sets   519
Locales and Facets   521

Regular Expressions   **523**

ECMAScript Syntax   524
The regex Library   530
regex_match()   531
regex_search()   534
regex_iterator   536
regex_token_iterator   537
regex_replace()   540

Summary   **543**

CHAPTER 15: DEMYSTIFYING C++ I/O — 545

Using Streams — 546
What Is a Stream, Anyway? — 546
Stream Sources and Destinations — 547
Output with Streams — 547
Input with Streams — 552
Input and Output with Objects — 559
String Streams — 560
File Streams — 562
Jumping around with seek() and tell() — 563
Linking Streams Together — 565
Bidirectional I/O — 566
Summary — 567

CHAPTER 16: ADDITIONAL LIBRARY UTILITIES — 569

std::function — 569
Ratios — 571
The Chrono Library — 574
Duration — 574
Clock — 578
Time Point — 580
Random Number Generation — 581
Random Number Engines — 582
Random Number Engine Adapters — 584
Predefined Engines and Engine Adapters — 584
Generating Random Numbers — 585
Random Number Distributions — 587
Tuples — 590
Summary — 594

CHAPTER 17: CUSTOMIZING AND EXTENDING THE STL — 595

Allocators — 596
Iterator Adapters — 596
Reverse Iterators — 596
Stream Iterators — 598
Insert Iterators — 599
Move Iterators — 600
Extending the STL — 602
Why Extend the STL? — 602
Writing an STL Algorithm — 602
Writing an STL Container — 605
Summary — 641

PART III: MASTERING ADVANCED FEATURES OF C++

CHAPTER 18: OVERLOADING C++ OPERATORS — 645

Overview of Operator Overloading	**646**
Why Overload Operators?	646
Limitations to Operator Overloading	646
Choices in Operator Overloading	647
Operators You Shouldn't Overload	649
Summary of Overloadable Operators	650
Rvalue References	653
Overloading the Arithmetic Operators	**654**
Overloading Unary Minus and Unary Plus	654
Overloading Increment and Decrement	655
Overloading the Bitwise and Binary Logical Operators	**656**
Overloading the Insertion and Extraction Operators	**657**
Overloading the Subscripting Operator	**659**
Providing Read-Only Access with operator[]	662
Non-Integral Array Indices	663
Overloading the Function Call Operator	**664**
Overloading the Dereferencing Operators	**666**
Implementing operator*	667
Implementing operator->	668
What in the World Is operator ->* ?	669
Writing Conversion Operators	**669**
Ambiguity Problems with Conversion Operators	671
Conversions for Boolean Expressions	672
Overloading the Memory Allocation and Deallocation Operators	**675**
How new and delete Really Work	675
Overloading operator new and operator delete	677
Overloading operator new and operator delete with Extra Parameters	679
Explicitly Deleting/Defaulting operator new and operator delete	681
Summary	**682**

CHAPTER 19: WRITING GENERIC CODE WITH TEMPLATES — 683

Overview of Templates	**684**
Class Templates	**684**
Writing a Class Template	685
How the Compiler Processes Templates	693
Distributing Template Code between Files	694
Template Parameters	695
Method Templates	698
Template Class Specialization	703
Subclassing Template Classes	706

Inheritance versus Specialization 708
Template Aliases 708
Alternative Function Syntax 709
Function Templates **710**
Function Template Specialization 711
Function Template Overloading 712
Friend Function Templates of Class Templates 713
Summary **714**

CHAPTER 20: ADVANCED TEMPLATES **715**

More about Template Parameters **715**
More about Template Type Parameters 715
Introducing Template Template Parameters 719
More about Non-Type Template Parameters 721
Template Class Partial Specialization **724**
Another Form of Partial Specialization 726
Emulating Function Partial Specialization with Overloading **729**
More on Deduction 730
Template Recursion **731**
An N-Dimensional Grid: First Attempt 731
A Real N-Dimensional Grid 733
Type Inference **738**
The auto Keyword 738
The decltype Keyword 739
auto and decltype with Templates 739
Variadic Templates **742**
Type-Safe Variable-Length Argument Lists 743
Variable Number of Mix-In Classes 745
Metaprogramming **746**
Factorial at Compile Time 746
Loop Unrolling 747
Printing Tuples 749
Type Traits 751
Conclusion 757
Summary **757**

CHAPTER 21: EFFECTIVE MEMORY MANAGEMENT **759**

Working with Dynamic Memory **759**
How to Picture Memory 760
Allocation and Deallocation 761
Arrays 763
Working with Pointers 769
Array-Pointer Duality **771**
Arrays Are Pointers! 772
Not All Pointers Are Arrays! 773

Low-Level Memory Operations   **774**
Pointer Arithmetic   774
Custom Memory Management   775
Garbage Collection   775
Object Pools   776
Function Pointers   776
Pointers to Methods and Members   778
Smart Pointers   **779**
The Old Deprecated auto_ptr   780
The New C++11 Smart Pointers   781
Writing Your Own Smart Pointer Class   784
Common Memory Pitfalls   **790**
Underallocating Strings   790
Memory Leaks   791
Double-Deleting and Invalid Pointers   794
Accessing Out-of-Bounds Memory   795
Summary   **796**

CHAPTER 22: MULTITHREADED PROGRAMMING WITH C++   **797**

Introduction   **798**
Race Conditions and Deadlocks   799
Atomic Operations Library   **802**
Atomic Type Example   803
Atomic Operations   805
Threads   **806**
Thread with Function Pointer   806
Thread with Function Object   808
Thread with Lambda   810
Thread with Member Function   811
Thread Local Storage   811
Cancelling Threads   812
Retrieving Results from Threads   812
Copying and Rethrowing Exceptions   812
Mutual Exclusion   **815**
Mutex Classes   815
Locks   817
std::call_once   819
Mutex Usage Examples   820
Condition Variables   **823**
Futures   **825**
Example: Multithreaded Logger Class   **827**
Thread Pools   **833**
Threading Design and Best Practices   **834**
Summary   **835**

PART IV: C++ SOFTWARE ENGINEERING

CHAPTER 23: MAXIMIZING SOFTWARE ENGINEERING METHODS — 839

The Need for Process — 840
Software Life Cycle Models — 841
The Stagewise Model and Waterfall Model — 841
The Spiral Model — 843
The Rational Unified Process — 845
Software Engineering Methodologies — 847
Agile — 847
Scrum — 848
Extreme Programming (XP) — 850
Software Triage — 854
Building Your Own Process and Methodology — 854
Be Open to New Ideas — 854
Bring New Ideas to the Table — 855
Recognize What Works and What Doesn't Work — 855
Don't Be a Renegade — 855
Source Code Control — 855
Summary — 857

CHAPTER 24: WRITING EFFICIENT C++ — 859

Overview of Performance and Efficiency — 859
Two Approaches to Efficiency — 860
Two Kinds of Programs — 860
Is C++ an Inefficient Language? — 860
Language-Level Efficiency — 861
Handle Objects Efficiently — 862
Use Inline Methods and Functions — 866
Design-Level Efficiency — 866
Cache as Much as Possible — 866
Use Object Pools — 867
Profiling — 871
Profiling Example with gprof — 872
Profiling Example with Visual C++ 2010 — 880
Summary — 882

CHAPTER 25: DEVELOPING CROSS-PLATFORM AND CROSS-LANGUAGE APPLICATIONS — 883

Cross-Platform Development — 884
Architecture Issues — 884
Implementation Issues — 886
Platform-Specific Features — 888

Cross-Language Development	**888**
Mixing C and C++	889
Shifting Paradigms	889
Linking with C Code	892
Mixing C# with C++	894
Mixing Java and C++ with JNI	896
Mixing C++ with Perl and Shell Scripts	898
Mixing C++ with Assembly Code	902
Summary	**903**

CHAPTER 26: BECOMING ADEPT AT TESTING   **905**

Quality Control	**906**
Whose Responsibility Is Testing?	906
The Life Cycle of a Bug	906
Bug-Tracking Tools	907
Unit Testing	**909**
Approaches to Unit Testing	909
The Unit Testing Process	910
Unit Testing in Action	914
Higher-Level Testing	**921**
Integration Tests	921
System Tests	923
Regression Tests	923
Tips for Successful Testing	**924**
Summary	**925**

CHAPTER 27: CONQUERING DEBUGGING   **927**

The Fundamental Law of Debugging	**928**
Bug Taxonomies	**928**
Avoiding Bugs	**928**
Planning for Bugs	**929**
Error Logging	929
Debug Traces	930
Asserts	943
Static Asserts	944
Debugging Techniques	**945**
Reproducing Bugs	945
Debugging Reproducible Bugs	946
Debugging Nonreproducible Bugs	947
Debugging Memory Problems	948
Debugging Multithreaded Programs	952
Debugging Example: Article Citations	953
Lessons from the ArticleCitations Example	966
Summary	**966**

CHAPTER 28: INCORPORATING DESIGN TECHNIQUES AND FRAMEWORKS — **967**

"I Can Never Remember How to . . ." — **968**
  . . . Write a Class — 968
  . . . Subclass an Existing Class — 969
  . . . Throw and Catch Exceptions — 970
  . . . Read from a File — 971
  . . . Write to a File — 971
  . . . Write a Template Class — 972
There Must Be a Better Way — **973**
  Double Dispatch — 973
  Mix-In Classes — 979
Object-Oriented Frameworks — **981**
  Working with Frameworks — 982
  The Model-View-Controller Paradigm — 982
Summary — **983**

CHAPTER 29: APPLYING DESIGN PATTERNS — **985**

The Iterator Pattern — **986**
The Singleton Pattern — **987**
  Example: A Logging Mechanism — 987
  Implementation of a Singleton — 987
  Using a Singleton — 991
  Singletons and Multithreading — 992
The Factory Pattern — **995**
  Example: A Car Factory Simulation — 995
  Implementation of a Factory — 996
  Using a Factory — 998
  Other Uses of Factories — 1000
The Proxy Pattern — **1000**
  Example: Hiding Network Connectivity Issues — 1000
  Implementation of a Proxy — 1001
  Using a Proxy — 1002
The Adapter Pattern — **1002**
  Example: Adapting a Logger Class — 1002
  Implementation of an Adapter — 1003
  Using an Adapter — 1004
The Decorator Pattern — **1004**
  Example: Defining Styles in Web Pages — 1004
  Implementation of a Decorator — 1005
  Using a Decorator — 1006
The Chain of Responsibility Pattern — **1007**
  Example: Event Handling — 1008
  Implementation of a Chain of Responsibility — 1008
  Using a Chain of Responsibility — 1009

The Observer Pattern   **1009**
   Example: Event Handling   1009
   Implementation of an Observer   1009
   Using an Observer   1011
Summary   **1012**

APPENDIX A: C++ INTERVIEWS   1013

APPENDIX B: ANNOTATED BIBLIOGRAPHY   1035

APPENDIX C: STANDARD LIBRARY HEADER FILES   1045

INDEX   *1053*

INTRODUCTION

FOR MANY YEARS, C++ has served as the de facto language for writing fast, powerful, and enterprise-class object-oriented programs. As popular as C++ has become, the language is surprisingly difficult to grasp in full. There are simple, but powerful, techniques that professional C++ programmers use that don't show up in traditional texts, and there are useful parts of C++ that remain a mystery even to experienced C++ programmers.

Too often, programming books focus on the syntax of the language instead of its real-world use. The typical C++ text introduces a major part of the language in each chapter, explaining the syntax and providing an example. *Professional C++* does not follow this pattern. Instead of giving you just the nuts and bolts of the language with little real-world context, this book will teach you how to use C++ in the real world. It will show you the little-known features that will make your life easier, and the reusable coding patterns that separate novice programmers from professional programmers.

WHO THIS BOOK IS FOR

Even if you have used the language for years, you might still be unfamiliar with the more-advanced features of C++ or might not be using the full capabilities of the language. Perhaps you write competent C++ code, but would like to learn more about design in C++ and good programming style. Or maybe you're relatively new to C++, but want to learn the "right" way to program from the start. This book will meet those needs and bring your C++ skills to the professional level.

Because this book focuses on advancing from basic or intermediate knowledge of C++ to becoming a professional C++ programmer, it assumes that you have some knowledge of the language. Chapter 1 covers the basics of C++ as a refresher, but it is not a substitute for actual training and use of the language. If you are just starting with C++, but you have significant experience in C, you should be able to pick up most of what you need from Chapter 1.

In any case, you should have a solid foundation in programming fundamentals. You should know about loops, functions, and variables. You should know how to structure a program, and you should be familiar with fundamental techniques such as recursion. You should have some knowledge of common data structures such as hash tables and queues, and useful algorithms such as sorting and searching. You don't need to know about object-oriented programming just yet — that is covered in Chapter 3.

You will also need to be familiar with the compiler you will be using to develop your code. This book does not provide directions for using individual compilers. Refer to the documentation that came with your compiler for a refresher.

WHAT THIS BOOK COVERS

Professional C++ is an approach to C++ programming that will both increase quality of your code and improve your programming efficiency. This second edition of *Professional C++* includes discussions on the new C++11 features throughout the whole book. The new C++11 features are not just isolated to a few chapters or sections, instead, almost all examples have been updated to use those new features when appropriate.

 C++11, the full ISO name of which is ISO/IEC 14882:2011(E), is the latest C++ standard. The C++11 standardization process started around the beginning of the millennium. During this process, the draft standard was known as C++0x.

Professional C++ teaches more than just the syntax and language features of C++. It also emphasizes programming methodologies, reusable design patterns, and good programming style. The *Professional C++* methodology incorporates the entire software development process — from designing and writing code, to testing, debugging, and working in groups. This approach will enable you to master the C++ language and its idiosyncrasies, as well as take advantage of its powerful capabilities for large-scale software development.

Imagine someone who has learned all of the syntax of C++ without seeing a single example of its use. He knows just enough to be dangerous! Without examples, he might assume that all code should go in the `main()` function of the program, or that all variables should be global — practices that are generally not considered hallmarks of good programming.

Professional C++ programmers understand the correct way to use the language, in addition to the syntax. They recognize the importance of good design, the theories of object-oriented programming, and the best ways to use existing libraries. They have also developed an arsenal of useful code and reusable ideas.

By reading and understanding this book, you will become a professional C++ programmer. You will expand your knowledge of C++ to cover lesser-known and often misunderstood language features. You will gain an appreciation for object-oriented design, and acquire top-notch debugging skills. Perhaps most important, you will finish this book armed with a wealth of reusable ideas that can be applied to your actual daily work.

There are many good reasons to make the effort to be a professional C++ programmer, as opposed to a programmer who knows C++. Understanding the true workings of the language will improve the quality of your code. Learning about different programming methodologies and processes will help you to work better with your team. Discovering reusable libraries and common design patterns will improve your daily efficiency and help you stop reinventing the wheel. All of these lessons will make you a better programmer and a more valuable employee. While this book can't guarantee you a promotion, it certainly won't hurt.

HOW THIS BOOK IS STRUCTURED

This book is made up of five parts.

Part I, "Introduction to Professional C++," begins with a crash course in C++ basics to ensure a foundation of C++ knowledge. Following the crash course, Part I explores C++ design methodologies. You will read about the importance of design, the object-oriented methodology, the importance of code reuse, and how to write *readable* C++ code.

Part II, "C++ Coding the Professional Way," provides a technical tour of C++ from the Professional point of view. You will read about how to create reusable classes, and how to leverage important language features such as inheritance. You will also learn about the unusual and quirky parts of the language, techniques for input and output, professional-grade error handling, and how to work with strings and regular expressions. This part also explains the C++ Standard Library, including containers, iterators, algorithms, and how to customize and extend the library to your needs. You will also read about some additional libraries available in the standard such as the libraries to work with time and random numbers.

Part III, "Mastering Advanced Features of C++," demonstrates how you can get the most out of C++. This part of the book exposes the mysteries of C++ and describes how to use some of its more-advanced features. You will read about the best ways to manage memory in C++, how to implement advanced operator overloading, how to write templates, and how to use multithreaded programming to take advantage of multiprocessor and multicore systems.

Part IV, "C++ Software Engineering," focuses on writing enterprise-quality software. You'll read about the engineering practices being used by programming organizations today; software testing concepts, such as unit testing and regression testing; techniques used to debug C++ programs; how to write efficient C++ code; solutions for cross-language and cross-platform code; and how to incorporate design techniques, frameworks, and conceptual object-oriented design patterns into your own code.

The book concludes with a useful chapter-by-chapter guide to succeeding in a C++ technical interview, an annotated bibliography, and a summary of the C++ header files available in the standard. You will also find a practical reference guide to the C++ Standard Library on the supplemental website for this book at www.wrox.com. This reference guide is called "the Standard Library Reference resource on the website" throughout this book.

WHAT YOU NEED TO USE THIS BOOK

All you need to use this book is a computer with a C++ compiler. This book focuses only on parts of C++ that have been standardized, and not on vendor specific compiler extensions.

`C++11`

This book includes new features introduced in the C++11 standard. At the time of this writing, there were no compilers yet supporting all new C++11 features. GCC 4.6 running on Linux and Microsoft Visual C++ 2010 running on Windows were used for testing code samples. GCC 4.6

supports a lot of new features, but not yet all. Examples using the following C++11 features could not be tested with the version of GCC 4.6 that was available:

➤ The `final` and `override` keywords

➤ User defined literals

➤ In-class non-`static` data member initialization

➤ Template aliases

➤ Delegating constructors

➤ Inheriting constructors

The second compiler used for testing was Microsoft Visual C++ 2010, however, it supports less C++11 features than GCC 4.6. Notably missing from VC++ 2010 are range-based `for` loop, uniform initialization, variadic templates, and the threading library, among others.

The supplemental website for this book at www.wrox.com *contains an extra appendix that lists all C++11 features and whether a compiler supports a feature or not.*

CONVENTIONS

To help you get the most from the text and keep track of what's happening, we've used a number of conventions throughout the book.

Boxes like this one hold important, not-to-be-forgotten information that is directly relevant to the surrounding text.

Tips, hints, tricks, and asides to the current discussion are placed in boxes like this one.

As for styles in the text:

We *highlight* important words when we introduce them.

We show keyboard strokes like this: Ctrl+A.

We show filenames and code within the text like so: `monkey.cpp`.

We show URLs like this: www.wrox.com.

We present code in two different ways:

In code examples we highlight new and important code like this.

```
Code that's less important in the present context or that has been shown before is
formatted like this.
```

 Paragraphs, sections, or chapters that are specific to the new C++11 standard have a little C++11 icon on the left, just as this paragraph does.

SOURCE CODE

As you work through the examples in this book, you may choose either to type in all the code manually or to use the source code files that accompany the book. All of the source code used in this book is available for download at www.wrox.com. Once at the site, locate the book's title (either by using the Search box or by using one of the title lists), and click the Download Code link on the book's details page to obtain all the source code for the book.

> *Because many books have similar titles, you may find it easiest to search by ISBN; for this book the ISBN is 978-0-470-93244-5.*

Alternatively, you can go to the main Wrox code download page at www.wrox.com/dynamic/books/download.aspx to see the code available for this book and all other Wrox books.

Once you've downloaded the code, just decompress it with your favorite decompression tool.

ERRATA

We make every effort to ensure that there are no errors in the text or in the code. However, no one is perfect, and mistakes do occur. If you find an error in one of our books, such as a spelling mistake or faulty piece of code, we would be very grateful for your feedback. By sending in errata you may save another reader hours of frustration, and at the same time you will be helping us provide even higher-quality information.

To find the errata page for this book, go to www.wrox.com and locate the title by using the Search box or one of the title lists. Then, on the book details page, click the Book Errata link. On this page you can view all errata that has been submitted for this book and posted by Wrox editors. A complete book list including links to each book's errata is also available at www.wrox.com/misc-pages/booklist.shtml.

If you don't spot "your" error on the Book Errata page, go to www.wrox.com/contact/techsupport.shtml and complete the form there to send us the error you have found. We'll check the information and, if appropriate, post a message to the book's errata page and fix the problem in subsequent editions of the book.

P2P.WROX.COM

For author and peer discussion, join the P2P forums at p2p.wrox.com. The forums are a web-based system for you to post messages relating to Wrox books and related technologies, and interact with other readers and technology users. The forums offer a subscription feature to e-mail you topics of interest of your choosing when new posts are made to the forums. Wrox authors, editors, other industry experts, and your fellow readers are present on these forums.

At p2p.wrox.com you will find a number of different forums that will help you not only as you read this book, but also as you develop your own applications. To join the forums, just follow these steps:

1. Go to p2p.wrox.com and click the Register link.

2. Read the terms of use and click Agree.

3. Complete the required information to join as well as any optional information you wish to provide and click Submit.

4. You will receive an e-mail with information describing how to verify your account and complete the joining process.

 You can read messages in the forums without joining P2P, but in order to post your own messages, you must join.

Once you've joined, you can post new messages and respond to messages other users post. You can read messages at any time on the web. If you would like to have new messages from a particular forum e-mailed to you, click the Subscribe to this Forum icon by the forum name in the forum listing.

For more information about how to use the Wrox P2P, be sure to read the P2P FAQs for answers to questions about how the forum software works, as well as many common questions specific to P2P and Wrox books. To read the FAQs, click the FAQ link on any P2P page.

PART I
Introduction to Professional C++

▶ **CHAPTER 1:** A Crash Course in C++

▶ **CHAPTER 2:** Designing Professional C++ Programs

▶ **CHAPTER 3:** Designing with Objects

▶ **CHAPTER 4:** Designing for Reuse

▶ **CHAPTER 5:** Coding with Style

1

A Crash Course in C++

WHAT'S IN THIS CHAPTER?

➤ A brief overview of the most important parts and syntax of the
C++ language

The goal of this chapter is to cover briefly the most important parts of C++ so that you
have a base of knowledge before embarking on the rest of the book. This chapter is not a
comprehensive lesson in the C++ programming language. The basic points (such as what
a program is and the difference between = and ==) are not covered. The esoteric points
(Remember what a `union` is? How about the `volatile` keyword?) are also omitted. Certain
parts of the C language that are less relevant in C++ are also left out, as are parts of C++ that
get in-depth coverage in later chapters.

This chapter aims to cover the parts of C++ that programmers encounter every day. For
example, if you've been away from C++ for a while and you've forgotten the syntax of a
`for` loop, you'll find that syntax in this chapter. Also, if you're fairly new to C++ and don't
understand what a reference variable is, you'll learn about that kind of variable here as well.

If you already have significant experience with C++, skim this chapter to make sure that there
aren't any fundamental parts of the language on which you need to brush up. If you're new
to C++, read this chapter carefully and make sure you understand the examples. If you need
additional introductory information, consult the titles listed in Appendix B.

THE BASICS OF C++

The C++ language is often viewed as a "better C" or a "superset of C." Many of the annoyances
or rough edges of the C language were addressed when C++ was designed. Because C++ is
based on C, much of the syntax you'll see in this section will look familiar to you if you are
an experienced C programmer. The two languages certainly have their differences, though. As
evidence, *The C++ Programming Language* by C++ creator Bjarne Stroustrup (Third Edition;
Addison-Wesley Professional, 2000), weighs in at 1030 pages, while Kernighan and Ritchie's

The C Programming Language (Second Edition; Prentice Hall, 1988) is a scant 274 pages. So if you're a C programmer, be on the lookout for new or unfamiliar syntax!

The Obligatory Hello, World

In all its glory, the following code is the simplest C++ program you're likely to encounter.

```cpp
// helloworld.cpp
#include <iostream>
int main()
{
    std::cout << "Hello, World!" << std::endl;
    return 0;
}
```

Code snippet from helloworld\helloworld.cpp

This code, as you might expect, prints the message "Hello, World!" on the screen. It is a simple program and unlikely to win any awards, but it does exhibit the following important concepts about the format of a C++ program.

➤ Comments

➤ Preprocessor Directives

➤ The `main()` Function

➤ I/O Streams

These concepts are briefly explained in the next sections.

Comments

The first line of the program is a *comment*, a message that exists for the programmer only and is ignored by the compiler. In C++, there are two ways to delineate a comment. In the preceding and following examples, two slashes indicate that whatever follows on that line is a comment.

```cpp
// helloworld.cpp
```

The same behavior (this is to say, none) would be achieved by using a *C-style comment*, which is also valid in C++. C-style comments start with /* and end with */. In this fashion, C-style comments are capable of spanning multiple lines. The following code shows a C-style comment in action (or, more appropriately, inaction).

```cpp
/* this is a multiline
 * C-style comment. The
 * compiler will ignore
 * it.
 */
```

Comments are covered in detail in Chapter 5.

Preprocessor Directives

Building a C++ program is a three-step process. First, the code is run through a *preprocessor*, which recognizes meta-information about the code. Next, the code is *compiled*, or translated into machine-readable object files. Finally, the individual object files are *linked* together into a single application. Directives aimed at the preprocessor start with the # character, as in the line `#include <iostream>` in the previous example. In this case, an include directive tells the preprocessor to take everything from the `<iostream>` header file and make it available to the current file. The most common use of header files is to declare functions that will be defined elsewhere. Remember, a *declaration* tells the compiler how a function is called. A *definition* contains the actual code for the function. The `<iostream>` header declares the input and output mechanisms provided by C++. If the program did not include it, it would be unable to perform its only task of outputting text.

> *In C, included files usually end in .h, such as* `<stdio.h>`*. In C++, the suffix is omitted for standard library headers, such as* `<iostream>`*. Your favorite standard headers from C still exist in C++, but with new names. For example, you can access the functionality from* `<stdio.h>` *by including* `<cstdio>`*.*

The following table shows some of the most common preprocessor directives.

PREPROCESSOR DIRECTIVE	FUNCTIONALITY	COMMON USES
`#include [file]`	The specified file is inserted into the code at the location of the directive.	Almost always used to include header files so that code can make use of functionality defined elsewhere.
`#define [key] [value]`	Every occurrence of the specified key is replaced with the specified value.	Often used in C to define a constant value or a macro. C++ provides a better mechanism for constants. Macros are often dangerous so `#define` is rarely used in C++. See Chapter 9 for details.
`#ifdef [key]` `#ifndef [key]` `#endif`	Code within the `ifdef` ("if defined") or `ifndef` ("if not defined") blocks are conditionally included or omitted based on whether the specified key has been defined with `#define`.	Used most frequently to protect against circular includes. Each included file defines a value initially and surrounds the rest of its code with a `#ifndef` and `#endif` so that it won't be included multiple times, see example after this table.
`#pragma [xyz]`	xyz varies from compiler to compiler. Often allows the programmer to display a warning or error if the directive is reached during preprocessing.	See example after this table.

One example of using preprocessor directives is to avoid multiple includes. For example:

```
#ifndef MYHEADER_H
#define MYHEADER_H
// ... the contents of this header file
#endif
```

If your compiler supports the `#pragma once` directive, this can be rewritten as follows:

```
#pragma once
// ... the contents of this header file
```

Chapter 9 discusses this in more details.

The main() Function

`main()` is, of course, where the program starts. An `int` is returned from `main()`, indicating the result status of the program. The `main()` function either takes no parameters, or takes two parameters as follows:

```
int main(int argc, char* argv[])
```

`argc` gives the number of arguments passed to the program, and `argv` contains those arguments. Note that the first argument is always the name of the program itself.

I/O Streams

If you're new to C++ and coming from a C background, you're probably wondering what `std::cout` is and what has been done with trusty old `printf()`. While `printf()` can still be used in C++, a much better input/output facility is provided by the streams library.

I/O streams are covered in depth in Chapter 15, but the basics of output are very simple. Think of an output stream as a laundry chute for data. Anything you toss into it will be output appropriately. `std::cout` is the chute corresponding to the user console, or *standard out*. There are other chutes, including `std::cerr`, which outputs to the error console. The << operator tosses data down the chute. In the preceding example, a quoted string of text is sent to standard out. Output streams allow multiple data of varying types to be sent down the stream sequentially on a single line of code. The following code outputs text, followed by a number, followed by more text.

```
std::cout << "There are " << 219 << " ways I love you." << std::endl;
```

`std::endl` represents an end-of-line sequence. When the output stream encounters `std::endl`, it will output everything that has been sent down the chute so far and move to the next line. An alternate way of representing the end of a line is by using the \n character. The \n character is an *escape character*, which refers to a new-line character. Escape characters can be used within any quoted string of text. The following table shows the most common escape characters.

\n	new line
\r	carriage return
\t	tab
\\	the backslash character
\"	quotation mark

Streams can also be used to accept input from the user. The simplest way to do this is to use the `>>` operator with an input stream. The `std::cin` input stream accepts keyboard input from the user. User input can be tricky because you can never know what kind of data the user will enter. See Chapter 15 for a full explanation of how to use input streams.

Namespaces

Namespaces address the problem of naming conflicts between different pieces of code. For example, you might be writing some code that has a function called `foo()`. One day, you decide to start using a third-party library, which also has a `foo()` function. The compiler has no way of knowing which version of `foo()` you are referring to within your code. You can't change the library's function name, and it would be a big pain to change your own.

Namespaces come to the rescue in such scenarios because you can define the context in which names are defined. To place code in a namespace, enclose it within a namespace block:

```
namespace mycode {
    void foo();
}
```

Code snippet from namespaces\namespaces.h

The implementation of a method or function can also be handled in a namespace:

```
#include <iostream>
#include "namespaces.h"
namespace mycode {
    void foo() {
        std::cout << "foo() called in the mycode namespace" << std::endl;
    }
}
```

Code snippet from namespaces\namespaces.cpp

By placing your version of `foo()` in the namespace "mycode," it is isolated from the `foo()` function provided by the third-party library. To call the namespace-enabled version of `foo()`, prepend the namespace onto the function name by using `::` also called the *scope resolution operator* as follows.

```
mycode::foo();    // Calls the "foo" function in the "mycode" namespace
```

Any code that falls within a "mycode" namespace block can call other code within the same namespace without explicitly prepending the namespace. This implicit namespace is useful in making the code more precise and readable. You can also avoid prepending of namespaces with the `using` directive. This directive tells the compiler that the subsequent code is making use of names in the specified namespace. The namespace is thus implied for the code that follows:

```
#include "namespaces.h"
using namespace mycode;
int main()
{
    foo();  // Implies mycode::foo();
    return 0;
}
```

Code snippet from namespaces\usingnamespaces.cpp

A single source file can contain multiple `using` directives, but beware of overusing this shortcut. In the extreme case, if you declare that you're using every namespace known to humanity, you're effectively eliminating namespaces entirely! Name conflicts will again result if you are using two namespaces that contain the same names. It is also important to know in which namespace your code is operating so that you don't end up accidentally calling the wrong version of a function.

You've seen the namespace syntax before — you used it in the Hello, World program, where `cout` and `endl` are actually names defined in the `std` namespace. You could have written Hello, World with the `using` directive as shown here:

```
#include <iostream>
using namespace std;
int main()
{
    cout << "Hello, World!" << endl;
    return 0;
}
```

The `using` directive can also be used to refer to a particular item within a namespace. For example, if the only part of the `std` namespace that you intend to use is `cout`, you can refer to it as follows:

```
using std::cout;
```

Subsequent code can refer to `cout` without prepending the namespace, but other items in the `std` namespace will still need to be explicit:

```
using std::cout;
cout << "Hello, World!" << std::endl;
```

Variables

In C++, *variables* can be declared just about anywhere in your code and can be used anywhere in the current block below the line where they are declared. Variables can be declared without being given a value. These uninitialized variables generally end up with a semi random value based on whatever is in memory at the time and are the source of countless bugs. Variables in C++ can alternatively be assigned an initial value when they are declared. The code that follows shows both flavors of variable declaration, both using ints, which represent integer values.

```
int uninitializedInt;
int initializedInt = 7;
cout << uninitializedInt << " is a random value" << endl;
cout << initializedInt << " was assigned an initial value" << endl;
```

Code snippet from hellovariables\hellovariables.cpp

When run, this code will output a random value from memory for the first line and the number 7 for the second. This code also shows how variables can be used with output streams.

 Most compilers will issue a warning when code is using uninitialized variables, and some C++ environments may report a run time error when uninitialized variables are being accessed.

The table that follows shows the most common variable types used in C++.

TYPE	DESCRIPTION	USAGE
int	Positive and negative integers, range depends on compiler	int i = 7;
short (int)	Short integer (usually 2 bytes)	short s = 13;
long (int)	Long integer (usually 4 bytes)	long l = -7;
long long (int)	Long long integer, range depends on compiler, but at least the same as long (usually 8 bytes)	long long ll = 14;

unsigned int
unsigned short (int)
unsigned long (int)
unsigned long long (int)
	Limits the preceding types to values >= 0	unsigned int i = 2;
		unsigned short s = 23;
		unsigned long l = 5400;
		unsigned long long ll = 140;

float	Floating-point numbers	float f = 7.2f;

C++11 (appears to the left of the "long long (int)" row)

C++11 (appears to the left of the "unsigned long long (int)" row)

continues

(continued)

TYPE	DESCRIPTION	USAGE
`double`	Double precision numbers, precision is at least the same as for `float`	`double d = 7.2;`
`long double`	Long double precision numbers, precision is at least the same as for `double`	`long double d = 16.98L;`
`char`	A single character	`char ch = 'm';`
`char16_t`	A single 16-bit character	`char16_t c16 = u'm';`
`char32_t`	A single 32-bit character	`char32_t c32 = U'm';`
`wchar_t`	A single wide-character size depends on compiler	`wchar_t w = L'm';`
`bool`	true or false (same as non-0 or 0)	`bool b = true;`
`auto`	The compiler will decide the type automatically	`auto i = 7; // i will be an int`
`decltype(expr)`	The type will be the type of the expression `expr`	`int i = 7;` `decltype(i) j = 8; // j will also be an int`

(C++11 markers appear beside the `char16_t`, `char32_t`, `auto`, and `decltype(expr)` rows.)

> *C++ does not provide a basic string type. However, a standard implementation of a string is provided as part of the standard library as described later in this chapter and in Chapter 14.*

Variables can be converted to other types by *casting* them. For example, an `int` can be cast to a `bool`. C++ provides three ways of explicitly changing the type of a variable. The first method is a holdover from C, but is still the most commonly used. The second method seems more natural at first but is rarely seen. The third method is the most verbose, but often considered the cleanest.

```
bool someBool = (bool)someInt;                 // method 1
bool someBool = bool(someInt);                 // method 2
bool someBool = static_cast<bool>(someInt);    // method 3
```

The result will be `false` if the integer was 0 and `true` otherwise. Chapter 9 describes the different casting methods in more detail. In some contexts, variables can be automatically cast, or *coerced*. For example, a `short` can be automatically converted into a `long` because a `long` represents the same type of data with additional precision.

```
long someLong = someShort;        // no explicit cast needed
```

When automatically casting variables, you need to be aware of the potential loss of data. For example, casting a `float` to an `int` throws away information (the fractional part of the number). Many compilers will issue a warning if you assign a `float` to an `int` without an explicit cast. If you are certain that the left-hand side type is fully compatible with the right-hand side type, it's okay to cast implicitly.

Operators

What good is a variable if you don't have a way to change it? The following table shows the most common *operators* used in C++ and sample code that makes use of them. Note that operators in C++ can be *binary* (operate on two variables), *unary* (operate on a single variable), or even *ternary* (operate on three variables). There is only one ternary operator in C++ and it is covered in the section "Conditionals."

OPERATOR	DESCRIPTION	USAGE

=	Binary operator to assign the value on the right to the variable on the left.	`int i;`
		`i = 3;`
		`int j;`
		`j = i;`

!	Unary operator to complement the true/false (non-0/0) status of a variable.	`bool b = !true;` `bool b2 = !b;`

+	Binary operator for addition.	`int i = 3 + 2;`
		`int j = i + 5;`
		`int k = i + j;`

−
*
/
	Binary operators for subtraction, multiplication, and division.	`int i = 5-1;`
		`int j = 5*2;`
		`int k = j / i;`

%	Binary operator for remainder of a division operation. Also referred to as the *mod* operator.	`int remainder = 5 % 2;`
++	Unary operator to increment a variable by 1. If the operator occurs after the variable or *post-increment*, the result of the expression is the unincremented value. If the operator occurs before the variable or *pre-increment*, the result of the expression is the new value.	`i++;` `++i;`
−−	Unary operator to decrement a variable by 1.	`i--;` `--i;`

continues

(continued)

OPERATOR	DESCRIPTION	USAGE
+=	Shorthand syntax for i = i + j	i += j;

-=
*=
/=
%=
	Shorthand syntax for
	i = i - j;
	i = i * j;
	i = i / j;
	i = i % j;
		i -= j;
		i *= j;
		i /= j;
		i %= j;

& &=	Takes the raw bits of one variable and performs a bitwise "AND" with the other variable.	i = j & k; j &= k;
| |=	Takes the raw bits of one variable and performs a bitwise "OR" with the other variable.	i = j | k; j |= k;

<<
>>
<<=
>>=
	Takes the raw bits of a variable and "shifts" each bit left (<<) or right (>>) the specified number of places.	i = i << 1;
		i = i >> 4;
		i <<= 1;
		i >>= 4;

^ ^=	Performs a bitwise "exclusive or" operation on the two arguments.	i = i ^ j; i ^= j;

The following program shows the most common variable types and operators in action. If you're unsure about how variables and operators work, try to figure out what the output of this program will be, and then run it to confirm your answer.

```cpp
#include <iostream>
using namespace std;
int main()
{
    int someInteger = 256;
    short someShort;
    long someLong;
    float someFloat;
    double someDouble;

    someInteger++;
    someInteger *= 2;
    someShort = (short)someInteger;
    someLong = someShort * 10000;
```

```
        someFloat = someLong + 0.785;
        someDouble = (double)someFloat / 100000;
        cout << someDouble << endl;

        return 0;
    }
```

Code snippet from typetest\typetest.cpp

The C++ compiler has a recipe for the order in which expressions are evaluated. If you have a complicated line of code with many operators, the order of execution may not be obvious. For that reason, it's probably better to break up a complicated statement into several smaller statements or explicitly group expressions by using parentheses. For example, the following line of code is confusing unless you happen to know the C++ operator precedence table by heart:

```
    int i = 34 + 8 * 2 + 21 / 7 % 2;
```

Adding parentheses makes it clear which operations are happening first:

```
    int i = 34 + (8 * 2) + ( (21 / 7) % 2 );
```

Breaking up the statement into separate lines makes it even clearer:

```
    int i = 8 * 2;
    int j = 21 / 7;
    j %= 2;
    i = 34 + i + j;
```

For those of you playing along at home, all three approaches are equivalent and end up with i equal to 51. If you assumed that C++ evaluated expressions from left to right, your answer would have been 1. In fact, C++ evaluates /, *, and % first (in left-to-right order), followed by addition and subtraction, then bitwise operators. Parentheses let you explicitly tell the compiler that a certain operation should be evaluated separately.

Types

In C++, you can use the basic types (int, bool, etc.) to build more complex types of your own design. Once you are an experienced C++ programmer, you will rarely use the following techniques, which are features brought in from C, because classes are far more powerful. Still, it is important to know about the two most common ways of building types so that you will recognize the syntax.

Enumerated Types

An integer really represents a value within a sequence — the sequence of numbers. *Enumerated types* let you define your own sequences so that you can declare variables with values in that sequence. For example, in a chess program, you *could* represent each piece as an int, with constants for the piece types, as shown in the following code. The integers representing the types are marked const to indicate that they can never change.

```
const int kPieceTypeKing = 0;
const int kPieceTypeQueen = 1;
const int kPieceTypeRook = 2;
const int kPieceTypePawn = 3;
//etc.
int myPiece = kPieceTypeKing;
```

This representation is fine, but it can become dangerous. Since the piece is just an int, what would happen if another programmer added code to increment the value of the piece? By adding one, a king becomes a queen, which really makes no sense. Worse still, someone could come in and give a piece a value of -1, which has no corresponding constant.

Enumerated types solve these problems by tightly defining the range of values for a variable. The following code declares a new type, PieceT, which has four possible values, representing four of the chess pieces.

```
typedef enum { kPieceTypeKing, kPieceTypeQueen, kPieceTypeRook,
               kPieceTypePawn } PieceT;
```

Behind the scenes, an enumerated type is just an integer value. The real value of kPieceTypeKing is zero. However, by defining the possible values for variables of type PieceT, your compiler can give you a warning or error if you attempt to perform arithmetic on PieceT variables or treat them as integers. The following code, which declares a PieceT variable, and then attempts to use it as an integer, results in a warning or error on most compilers.

```
PieceT myPiece;
myPiece = 0;
```

It's also possible to specify the integer values for members of an enumeration. The syntax is as follows.

```
typedef enum { kPieceTypeKing = 1, kPieceTypeQueen, kPieceTypeRook = 10,
               kPieceTypePawn } PieceT;
```

In this example, kPieceTypeKing has the integer value 1, kPieceTypeQueen has the value 2 assigned by the compiler, kPieceTypeRook has the value 10 and kPieceTypePawn has the value 11 assigned automatically by the compiler.

C++11 ## Strongly Typed Enumerations

Enumerations as explained above are not strongly typed, meaning they are not type-safe. Basically, they are always interpreted as integers and thus you can compare enumeration values from completely different enumeration types. C++11 introduces the enum class to solve these problems. For example:

```
enum class MyEnum
{
    EnumValue1,
    EnumValue2 = 10,
    EnumValue3
};
```

Code snippet from StronglyTypedEnums\StronglyTypedEnums.cpp

This is a type-safe enumeration called MyEnum. The enumeration values are not automatically converted to integers and the enumeration names are not automatically exported to the enclosing scope. Because of this, the following is not legal in C++11:

```
if (MyEnum::EnumValue3 == 11) {...}
```

By default, the underlying type of an enumeration value is an integer, but this can be changed as follows:

```
enum class MyEnumLong : unsigned long
{
    EnumValueLong1,
    EnumValueLong2 = 10,
    EnumValueLong3
};
```

Code snippet from StronglyTypedEnums\StronglyTypedEnums.cpp

Structs

Structs let you encapsulate one or more existing types into a new type. The classic example of a struct is a database record. If you are building a personnel system to keep track of employee information, you will need to store the first initial, last initial, middle initial, employee number, and salary for each employee. A struct that contains all of this information is shown in the header file that follows.

```
typedef struct {
    char    firstInitial;
    char    middleInitial;
    char    lastInitial;
    int     employeeNumber;
    int     salary;
} EmployeeT;
```

Code snippet from structtest\employeestruct.h

A variable declared with type EmployeeT will have all of these *fields* built-in. The individual fields of a struct can be accessed by using the "." character. The example that follows creates and then outputs the record for an employee.

```
#include <iostream>
#include "employeestruct.h"
using namespace std;
int main()
{
    // Create and populate an employee.
    EmployeeT anEmployee;
    anEmployee.firstInitial = 'M';
    anEmployee.middleInitial = 'R';
    anEmployee.lastInitial = 'G';
    anEmployee.employeeNumber = 42;
    anEmployee.salary = 80000;
    // Output the values of an employee.
    cout << "Employee: " << anEmployee.firstInitial <<
                            anEmployee.middleInitial <<
                            anEmployee.lastInitial << endl;
    cout << "Number: " << anEmployee.employeeNumber << endl;
    cout << "Salary: $" << anEmployee.salary << endl;
    return 0;
}
```

Code snippet from structtest\structtest.cpp

Conditionals

Conditionals let you execute code based on whether or not something is true. As shown in the following sections, there are three main types of conditionals in C++.

if/else Statements

The most common conditional is the `if` statement, which can be accompanied by `else`. If the condition given inside the `if` statement is true, the line or block of code is executed. If not, execution continues to the `else` case if present, or to the code following the conditional. The following pseudocode shows a *cascading if statement*, a fancy way of saying that the `if` statement has an `else` statement that in turn has another `if` statement, and so on.

```
if (i > 4) {
    // Do something.
} else if (i > 2) {
    // Do something else.
} else {
    // Do something else.
}
```

The expression between the parentheses of an `if` statement must be a Boolean value or evaluate to a Boolean value. Conditional operators, described later, provide ways of evaluating expressions to result in a `true` or `false` Boolean value.

switch Statements

The `switch` statement is an alternate syntax for performing actions based on the value of a variable. In `switch` statements, the variable must be compared to a constant, so the greater-than `if` statements above cannot be converted to `switch` statements. Each constant value represents a "case." If the variable matches the case, the subsequent lines of code are executed until the `break` statement is reached. You can also provide a `default` case, which is matched if none of the other cases match.

`switch` statements are generally used when you want to do something based on the specific value of a variable, as opposed to some test on the variable. The following pseudocode shows a common use of the `switch` statement.

```
switch (menuItem) {
    case kOpenMenuItem:
        // Code to open a file
        break;
    case kSaveMenuItem:
        // Code to save a file
        break;
    default:
        // Code to give an error message
        break;
}
```

If you omit the `break` statement, the code for the subsequent case will be executed whether or not it matches. This is sometimes useful, but more frequently a source of bugs.

The Ternary Operator

C++ has one operator that takes three arguments, known as the *ternary operator*. It is used as a shorthand conditional expression of the form "if [*something*] then [*perform action*], otherwise [*perform some other action*]." The ternary operator is represented by a `?` and a `:`. The following code will output "yes" if the variable `i` is greater than 2, and "no" otherwise.

```
std::cout << ((i > 2) ? "yes" : "no");
```

The advantage of the ternary operator is that it can occur within almost any context. In the preceding example, the ternary operator is used within code that performs output. A convenient way to remember how the syntax is used is to treat the question mark as though the statement that comes before it really is a question. For example, "Is `i` greater than 2? If so, the result is 'yes': if not, the result is 'no.'"

Unlike an `if` statement or a `switch` statement, the ternary operator doesn't execute code blocks based on the result. Instead, it is used *within* code, as shown in the preceding example. In this way, it really is an operator (like + and -) as opposed to a true conditional, such as `if` and `switch`.

Conditional Operators

You have already seen a *conditional operator* without a formal definition. The > operator compares two values. The result is "true" if the value on the left is greater than the value on the right. All conditional operators follow this pattern — they all result in a `true` or `false`.

The following table shows common conditional operators (op).

OP	DESCRIPTION	USAGE
 `<` `<=` `>` `>=`	Determines if the left-hand side is less than, less than or equal to, greater than, or greater than or equal to the right-hand side.	```if (i < 0) {` ` std::cout << "i is negative";` `}```
`==`	Determines if the left-hand side equals the right-hand side. Don't confuse this with the = (assignment) operator!	```if (i == 3) {` ` std::cout << "i is 3";` `}```
`!=`	Not equals. The result of the statement is true if the left-hand side does *not* equal the right-hand side.	```if (i != 3) {` ` std::cout << "i is not 3";` `}```
`!`	Logical NOT. Complements the true/false status of a Boolean expression. This is a unary operator.	```if (!someBoolean) {` ` std::cout << "someBoolean is false";` `}```
`&&`	Logical AND. The result is true if both parts of the expression are true.	```if (someBoolean && someOtherBoolean) {` ` std::cout << "both are true";` `}```
`||`	Logical OR. The result is true if either part of the expression is true.	```if (someBoolean || someOtherBoolean) {` ` std::cout << "at least one is true";` `}```

C++ uses *short-circuit logic* when evaluating an expression. That means that once the final result is certain, the rest of the expression won't be evaluated. For example, if you are performing a logical OR operation of several Boolean expressions as shown below, the result is known to be `true` as soon as one of them is found to be `true`. The rest won't even be checked.

```
bool result = bool1 || bool2 || (i > 7) || (27 / 13 % i + 1) < 2;
```

In this example, if `bool1` is found to be `true`, the entire expression must be `true`, so the other parts aren't evaluated. In this way, the language saves your code from doing unnecessary work. It can, however, be a source of hard-to-find bugs if the later expressions in some way influence the state of the program (for example, by calling a separate function). The following code shows a statement using `&&` that will short-circuit after the second term because 0 always evaluates to `false`.

```
bool result = bool1 && 0 && (i > 7) && !done;
```

Loops

Computers are great for doing the same thing over and over. C++ provides three types of looping structures and C++11 adds one new looping mechanism.

The while Loop

The `while` loop lets you perform a block of code repeatedly as long as an expression evaluates to `true`. For example, the following completely silly code will output "This is silly." five times.

```
int i = 0;
while (i < 5) {
    std::cout << "This is silly." << std::endl;
    i++;
}
```

The keyword `break` can be used within a loop to immediately get out of the loop and continue execution of the program. The keyword `continue` can be used to return to the top of the loop and reevaluate the `while` expression. Both are often considered poor style because they cause the execution of a program to jump around somewhat haphazardly, so they should be used sparingly. The only place where you have to use `break` is in the context of the `switch` statement as seen earlier.

The do/while Loop

C++ also has a variation on the `while` loop called `do/while`. It works similarly to the `while` loop, except that the code to be executed comes first, and the conditional check for whether or not to continue happens at the end. In this way, you can use a loop when you want a block of code to always be executed at least once and possibly additional times based on some condition. The example that follows will output "This is silly." once even though the condition will end up being false.

```
int i = 100;
do {
    std::cout << "This is silly." << std::endl;
    i++;
} while (i < 5);
```

The for Loop

The `for` loop provides another syntax for looping. Any `for` loop can be converted to a `while` loop and vice versa. However, the `for` loop syntax is often more convenient because it looks at a loop in terms of a starting expression, an ending condition, and a statement to execute at the end of every iteration. In the following code, i is initialized to 0; the loop will continue as long as i is less than 5; and at the end of every iteration, i is incremented by 1. This code does the same thing as the `while` loop example, but to some programmers, it is easier to read because the starting value, ending condition, and per-iteration statement are all visible on one line.

```
for (int i = 0; i < 5; i++) {
    std::cout << "This is silly." << std::endl;
}
```

The Range-Based for Loop

C++11 The *range-based* for loop is a fourth way of looping which has been added to the C++11 standard. It allows for easy iteration over elements of a list. This type of loop will work for C-style arrays, initializer lists (discussed in Chapter 9) and any type that has a begin() and end() function returning iterators. Since all containers in the STL have these begin() and end() functions, they will all work with this new range-based for loop. STL containers and iterators are explained in more details in Chapter 12.

The following example first defines a list of four integers. The range-based for loop will then iterate over every element in this list and increment its value by 2.

```
int arr[] = {1, 2, 3, 4};
for(auto& i : arr) {
    i += 2;
}
```

Arrays

Arrays hold a series of values, all of the same type, each of which can be accessed by its position in the array. In C++, you must provide the size of the array when the array is declared. You cannot give a variable as the size — it must be a constant value. C++11 relaxes this requirement a little by allowing the size of the array to be a *constant expression* or *constexpr*, which is discussed in Chapter 9. The code that follows shows the declaration of an array of 10 integers followed by a for loop that initializes each integer to zero.

```
int myArray[10];
for (int i = 0; i < 10; i++) {
    myArray[i] = 0;
}
```

The preceding example uses a for loop to initialize every element to zero. This can also be accomplished with the following one-liner.

```
int myArray[10] = {0};
```

Note that this is only possible if you want to initialize all values to zero. For example:

```
int myArray[10] = {2};
```

This line will only fill the first element in the array with the value 2 and will fill all the other elements in the array with the value 0.

The preceding example shows a one-dimensional array, which you can think of as a line of integers, each with its own numbered compartment. C++ allows multi-dimensional arrays. You might think of a two-dimensional array as a checkerboard, where each location has a position along the x-axis and a position along the y-axis. Three-dimensional and higher arrays are harder to picture and are rarely used. The following code shows the syntax for allocating a two-dimensional array of characters for a Tic-Tac-Toe board and then putting an "o" in the center square.

```
char ticTacToeBoard[3][3];
ticTacToeBoard[1][1] = 'o';
```

Figure 1-1 shows a visual representation of this board with the position of each square.

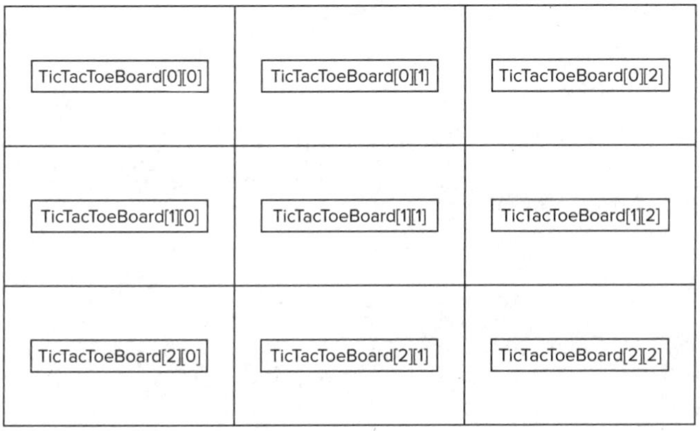

TicTacToeBoard[0][0]	TicTacToeBoard[0][1]	TicTacToeBoard[0][2]
TicTacToeBoard[1][0]	TicTacToeBoard[1][1]	TicTacToeBoard[1][2]
TicTacToeBoard[2][0]	TicTacToeBoard[2][1]	TicTacToeBoard[2][2]

FIGURE 1-1

 In C++, the first element of an array is always at position 0, not position 1! The last position of the array is always the size of the array minus 1!

std::array

C++11

C++11 introduces a new type of container called `std::array`, defined in the `<array>` header file. This is a replacement for the previously discussed standard C-style arrays. If you wanted a more secure type of array before C++11, you would use the `std::vector`. The `std::vector` will automatically grow in size when you add new elements to it. However, sometimes you don't need this flexibility because you know the exact size. The only way to avoid the `std::vector` overhead before C++11 was to switch to standard C-style arrays as explained in the previous section. With C++11 you can switch to the more secure `std::array` instead, which does not have the same overhead as `std::vector`; it's basically a tiny wrapper around standard arrays. There are a number of advantages in using `std::arrays` instead of standard C-style arrays. They always know their own size, do not automatically get cast to a pointer to avoid certain types of bugs and have iterators to easily loop over the elements. Because of the support for iterators, the STL algorithms also work on `std::arrays`. STL algorithms are explained in detail in Chapter 13.

The following example demonstrates how to use the `std::array` container.

Available for
download on
Wrox.com

```cpp
#include <iostream>
#include <array>
using namespace std;
int main()
{
    array<int, 3> arr = {9, 8, 7};
    cout << "Array size = " << arr.size() << endl;
    for (auto i : arr)
        cout << i << endl;
        cout << *iter << endl;
    return 0;
}
```

Code snippet from std_array\std_array.cpp

Both the standard arrays and the new `std::arrays` have a fixed size, which should be known at compile time. They cannot grow or shrink at run time.

Functions

For programs of any significant size, placing all the code inside of `main()` is unmanageable. To make programs easy to understand, you need to break up, or *decompose*, code into concise functions.

In C++, you first declare a function to make it available for other code to use. If the function is used inside a particular file of code, you generally declare and define the function in the source file. If the function is for use by other modules or files, you generally put the declaration in a header file and the definition in a source file.

Function declarations are often called "function prototypes" or "signatures" to emphasize that they represent how the function can be accessed, but not the code behind it.

A function declaration is shown below. This example has a return type of void, indicating that the function does not provide a result to the caller. The caller must provide two arguments for the function to work with — an integer and a character.

```
void myFunction(int i, char c);
```

Without an actual definition to match this function declaration, the link stage of the compilation process will fail because code that makes use of the function myFunction() will be calling nonexistent code. The following definition prints the values of the two parameters.

```
void myFunction(int i, char c)
{
    std::cout << "the value of i is " << i << std::endl;
    std::cout << "the value of c is " << c << std::endl;
}
```

Elsewhere in the program, you can make calls to myFunction() and pass in constants or variables for the two parameters. Some sample function calls are shown here:

```
myFunction(8, 'a');
myFunction(someInt, 'b');
myFunction(5, someChar);
```

 In C++, unlike C, a function that takes no parameters just has an empty parameter list. It is not necessary to use void *to indicate that no parameters are taken. However, you should still use* void *to indicate when no value is returned.*

C++ functions can also *return* a value to the caller. The following function declaration and definition is for a function that adds two numbers and returns the result.

```
int addNumbers(int number1, int number2);
int addNumbers(int number1, int number2)
{
    int result = number1 + number2;
    return result;
}
```

In C++11, every function has a local predefined variable __func__ that looks as follows:

```
static const char __func__[] = "function-name";
```

This variable can for example be used for logging purposes:

```
int addNumbers(int number1, int number2)
{
```

```
        std::cout << "Entering function " << __func__ << std::endl;
        int result = number1 + number2;
        return result;
}
```

Those Are the Basics

At this point, you have reviewed the basic essentials of C++ programming. If this section was a breeze, skim the next section to make sure that you're up to speed on the more-advanced material. If you struggled with this section, you may want to obtain one of the fine introductory C++ books mentioned in Appendix B before continuing.

DIVING DEEPER INTO C++

Loops, variables, and conditionals are terrific building blocks, but there is much more to learn. The topics covered next include many features designed to help C++ programmers with their code as well as a few features that are often more confusing than helpful. If you are a C programmer with little C++ experience, you should read this section carefully.

Pointers and Dynamic Memory

Dynamic memory allows you to build programs with data that is not of fixed size at compile time. Most nontrivial programs make use of dynamic memory in some form.

The Stack and the Heap

Memory in your C++ application is divided into two parts — the *stack* and the *heap*. One way to visualize the stack is as a deck of cards. The current top card represents the current scope of the program, usually the function that is currently being executed. All variables declared inside the current function will take up memory in the top stack frame, the top card of the deck. If the current function, which we'll call `foo()` calls another function `bar()`, a new card is put on the deck so that `bar()` has its own *stack frame* to work with. Any parameters passed from `foo()` to `bar()` are copied from the `foo()` stack frame into the `bar()` stack frame. Figure 1-2 shows what the stack might look like during the execution of a hypothetical function `foo()` that has declared two integer values.

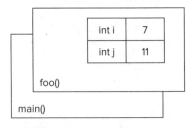

FIGURE 1-2

Stack frames are nice because they provide an isolated memory workspace for each function. If a variable is declared inside the `foo()` stack frame, calling the `bar()` function won't change it unless you specifically tell it to. Also, when the `foo()` function is done running, the stack frame goes away, and all of the variables declared within the function no longer take up memory.

The *heap* is an area of memory that is completely independent of the current function or stack frame. You can put variables on the heap if you want them to exist even when the function in which they were declared has completed. The heap is less structured than the stack. You can think of it as just a pile of bits. Your program can add new bits to the pile at any time or modify bits that are already in the pile.

Dynamically Allocated Arrays

Due to the way that the stack works, the compiler must be able to determine at compile time how big each stack frame will be. Since the stack frame size is predetermined, you cannot declare an array with a variable size. The following code will not compile because the arraySize is a variable, not a constant.

```
int arraySize = 8;
int myVariableSizedArray[arraySize];    // This won't compile!
```

Because the entire array must go on the stack, the compiler needs to know exactly what size it will be, so variables aren't allowed. However, it is possible to specify the size of an array at run time by using *dynamic memory* and placing the array in the heap instead of the stack.

 Some C++ compilers actually do support the preceding declaration, but this syntax is currently not part of the C++ specification. Most compilers offer a "strict" mode that will turn off these nonstandard extensions to the language.

To allocate an array dynamically, you first need to declare a *pointer*:

```
int* myVariableSizedArray;
```

The * after the int type indicates that the variable you are declaring refers to some integer memory in the heap. Think of the pointer as an arrow that points at the dynamically allocated heap memory. It does not yet point to anything specific because you haven't assigned it to anything; it is an uninitialized variable.

To initialize the pointer to new heap memory, you use the new command:

```
myVariableSizedArray = new int[arraySize];
```

This allocates memory for enough integers to satisfy the arraySize variable. Figure 1-3 shows what the stack and the heap both look like after this code is executed. As you can see, the pointer variable still resides on the stack, but the array that was dynamically created lives on the heap.

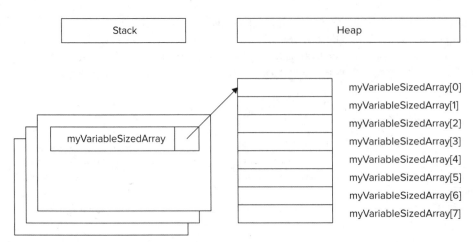

FIGURE 1-3

Now that the memory has been allocated, you can work with `myVariableSizedArray` as though it were a regular stack-based array:

```
myVariableSizedArray[3] = 2;
```

When your code is done with the array, it should remove it from the heap so that other variables can use the memory. In C++, you use the `delete` command to do this.

```
delete [] myVariableSizedArray;
```

The brackets after `delete` indicate that you are deleting an array!

 The C++ commands new *and* `delete` *are similar to* `malloc()` *and* `free()` *from C. The syntax of* `new` *and* `delete` *is simpler because you don't need to know how many bytes of memory are required.*

 In C++, every call to `new` *or* `new[]` *should be paired with a call to* `delete` *or* `delete[]` *to prevent memory leaks. Similarly, every call to* `malloc()` *should be paired with a call to* `free()`. *Memory leaks are discussed in Chapter 21.*

To avoid common memory problems, you should use *smart pointers* instead of normal pointers. Smart pointers will automatically deallocate memory when the smart pointer object goes out of scope. Instead of writing the following:

```
int* myVariableSizedArray = new int[arraySize];
```

You should use the C++11 `unique_ptr` defined in the `<memory>` header:

```
unique_ptr<int[]> myVariableSizedArray(new int[arraySize]);
```

This `unique_ptr` version does not require you to deallocate the memory; it will be deallocated automatically when the `unique_ptr` pointing to that memory goes out of scope. You can use the `myVariableSizedArray` smart pointer the same way as a normal pointer. Smart pointers are discussed in detail in Chapter 21, but as the preceding example showed, they are very easy to use and highly recommended as a replacement for normal pointers to avoid certain memory problems.

Working with Pointers

There are other reasons to use heap memory besides dynamically allocating arrays. You can put any variable in the heap by using a similar syntax:

```
int* myIntegerPointer = new int;
```

In this case, the pointer points to the address of just a single integer value. To access this value, you need to *dereference* the pointer. Think of dereferencing as following the pointer's arrow to the actual value in the heap. To set the value of the newly allocated heap integer, you would use code like the following:

```
*myIntegerPointer = 8;
```

Notice that this is not the same as setting `myIntegerPointer` to the value 8. You are not changing the pointer; you are changing the memory that it points to. If you were to reassign the pointer value, it would point to the memory address 8, which is probably random garbage that will eventually make your program crash.

 A pointer must be valid before dereferencing it. A null or uninitialized pointer will cause a crash if dereferenced.

Pointers don't always point to heap memory. You can declare a pointer that points to a variable on the stack, even another pointer. To get a pointer to a variable, you use the `&` "address of" operator:

```
int i = 8;
int* myIntegerPointer = &i;  // Points to the variable with the value 8
```

C++ has a special syntax for dealing with pointers to structures. Technically, if you have a pointer to a structure, you can access its fields by first dereferencing it with `*`, then using the normal `.` syntax, as in the code that follows, which assumes the existence of a function called `getEmployee()`.

```
EmployeeT* anEmployee = getEmployee();
cout << (*anEmployee).salary << endl;
```

This syntax is a little messy. The -> (arrow) operator lets you perform both the dereference and the field access in one step. The following code is equivalent to the preceding code, but is easier to read.

```
EmployeeT* anEmployee = getEmployee();
cout << anEmployee->salary << endl;
```

Normally, when you pass a variable into a function, you are *passing by value*. If a function takes an integer parameter, it is really a copy of the integer that you pass in. Pointers to stack variables are often used in C to allow functions to modify variables in other stack frames, essentially *passing by reference*. By dereferencing the pointer, the function can change the memory that represents the variable even though that variable isn't in the current stack frame. This is less common in C++ because C++ has a better mechanism, called *references*, which is covered later in this chapter.

Strings in C++

There are three ways to work with strings of text in C++. There is the C-style, which represents strings as arrays of characters; the C++ style, which wraps that representation in an easier-to-use string type; and the general class of nonstandard approaches.

C-Style Strings

A string of text like "Hello, World" is internally represented as an array of characters with the character '\0' representing the end of the string. As you've seen, arrays and pointers are sometimes related. You could use either one to represent a string, as shown here:

```
char arrayString[20] = "Hello, World";
char* pointerString = "Hello, World";
```

For the arrayString, the compiler allocates space for 20 characters on the stack. The first 13 characters in the array are filled in with 'H', 'e', etc., ending with the character '\0'. The characters in positions 13 to 19 contain whatever random values happen to be in memory. The '\0' character tells code that uses the string where the content of the string ends. Even though the array has a length of 20, functions that process or output the string should ignore everything after the '\0' character.

For the pointerString, the compiler allocates enough memory on the stack just to hold the pointer. The pointer points to an area of memory that the compiler has set aside to hold the constant string "Hello, World". In this string, there is also a '\0' character after the 'd' character.

The C language provides a number of standard functions for working with strings, which are described in the <cstring> header file. The details of the standard library are not covered here because C++ provides a much cleaner and simpler way of working with strings.

C++ Strings

C-style strings are important to understand because they are still frequently used by C++ programmers. However, C++ includes a much more flexible string type. The string type, described by the <string> header file, acts just like a basic type. Just like I/O streams, the string type lives in the "std" namespace. The example that follows shows how strings can be used just like character arrays.

```
string myString = "Hello, World";
cout << "The value of myString is " << myString << endl;
```

The magic of C++ `strings` is that you can use standard operators to work with them. Instead of using a function, like `strcat()` in C to concatenate two strings, you can simply use +. If you've ever tried to use the == operator to compare two C-style strings, you've discovered that it doesn't work. == when used on C-style strings is actually comparing the address of the character arrays, not their contents. With C++ `strings`, == actually compares two `strings`. The example that follows shows some of the standard operators in use with C++ `strings`.

```
string str1 = "Hello";
string str2 = "World";
string str3 = str1 + " " + str2;
cout << "str1 is " << str1 << endl;
cout << "str2 is " << str2 << endl;
cout << "str3 is " << str3 << endl;
if (str3 == "Hello World") {
    cout << "str3 is what it should be." << endl;
} else {
    cout << "Hmmm . . . str3 isn't what it should be." << endl;
}
```

The preceding examples show just a few of the many features of C++ `strings`. Chapter 14 goes into further detail.

Nonstandard Strings

There are several reasons why many C++ programmers don't use C++-style strings. Some programmers simply aren't aware of the `string` type because it was not always part of the C++ specification. Others have discovered over the years that the C++ `string` doesn't provide the behavior they need and have developed their own string type. Perhaps the most common reason is that development frameworks and operating systems tend to have their own way of representing strings, such as the `CString` class in Microsoft's MFC. Often, this is for backward compatibility or legacy issues. When starting a project in C++, it is very important to decide ahead of time how your group will represent strings.

References

The pattern for most functions is that they take in zero or more parameters, do some calculations, and return a single result. Sometimes, however, that pattern is broken. You may be tempted to return two values, or you may want the function to be able to change the value of one of the variables that were passed in.

In C, the primary way to accomplish such behavior is to pass in a pointer to the variable instead of the variable itself. The only problem with this approach is that it brings the messiness of pointer syntax into what is really a simple task. In C++, there is an explicit mechanism for "pass-by-reference." Attaching & to a type indicates that the variable is a reference. It is still used as though it was a normal variable, but behind the scenes, it is really a pointer to the original variable. Below are two implementations of an addOne() function. The first will have no effect on the variable that is passed in because it is passed by value. The second uses a reference and thus changes the original variable.

```
void addOne(int i)
{
    i++;   // Has no real effect because this is a copy of the original
}
void addOne(int& i)
{
    i++;   // Actually changes the original variable
}
```

The syntax for the call to the addOne() function with an integer reference is no different than if the function just took an integer.

```
int myInt = 7;
addOne(myInt);
```

There is a subtle difference between the two addOne() *implementations. The version using pass-by-value will accept constants without a problem; for example* "addOne(3);" *is legal. However, doing the same with the pass-by-reference version of* addOne() *will result in a compiler error. This can be solved by using rvalue references, which are explained in Chapter 9.*

Exceptions

C++ is a very flexible language, but not a particularly safe one. The compiler will let you write code that scribbles on random memory addresses or tries to divide by zero (computers don't deal well with infinity). One of the language features that attempts to add a degree of safety back to the language is *exceptions*.

An exception is an unexpected situation. For example, if you are writing a function that retrieves a web page, several things could go wrong. The Internet host that contains the page might be down, the page might come back blank, or the connection could be lost. In many programming languages, you would handle this situation by returning a special value from the function, such as nullptr (NULL in pre-C++11) or an error code. Exceptions provide a much better mechanism for dealing with problems.

Exceptions come with some new terminology. When a piece of code detects an exceptional situation, it *throws* an exception. Another piece of code *catches* the exception and takes appropriate action. The following example shows a function, divideNumbers(), that throws an exception if the caller passes in a denominator of zero.

```
#include <stdexcept>
double divideNumbers(double inNumerator, double inDenominator)
{
    if (inDenominator == 0) {
        throw std::exception();
    }
    return inNumerator / inDenominator;
}
```

When the throw line is executed, the function will immediately end without returning a value. If the caller surrounds the function call with a try/catch block, as shown in the following code, it will receive the exception and be able to handle it.

```
#include <iostream>
#include <stdexcept>
int main()
{
    try {
        std::cout << divideNumbers(2.5, 0.5) << std::endl;
        std::cout << divideNumbers(2.3, 0) << std::endl;
    } catch (const std::exception& exception) {
        std::cout << "An exception was caught!" << std::endl;
    }
    return 0;
}
```

The first call to divideNumbers() executes successfully, and the result is output to the user. The second call throws an exception. No value is returned, and the only output is the error message that is printed when the exception is caught. The output for the preceding block of code is:

```
5
An exception was caught!
```

Exceptions can get tricky in C++. To use exceptions properly, you need to understand what happens to the stack variables when an exception is thrown, and you have to be careful to properly catch and handle the necessary exceptions. The preceding example used the built-in std::exception exception type, but it is preferable to write your own exception types that are more specific to the error being thrown. Unlike the Java language, the C++ compiler doesn't force you to catch every exception that might occur. If your code never catches any exceptions but an exception is thrown, it will be caught by the program itself, which will be terminated. These trickier aspects of exceptions are covered in much more detail in Chapter 10.

The Many Uses of const

The keyword const can be used in several different ways in C++. All of its uses are related, but there are subtle differences. One of the authors has discovered that the subtleties of const make for excellent interview questions! In Chapter 9, you will learn all of the ways that `const` can be used. The following sections outline the most frequent uses.

const Constants

If you assumed that the keyword `const` has something to do with constants, you have correctly uncovered one of its uses. In the C language, programmers often use the preprocessor `#define` mechanism to declare symbolic names for values that won't change during the execution of the program, such as the version number. In C++, programmers are encouraged to avoid `#define` in favor of using `const` to define constants. Defining a constant with `const` is just like defining a variable, except that the compiler guarantees that code cannot change the value.

```
const float kVersionNumber = 2.0f;
const string kProductName = "Super Hyper Net Modulator";
```

const to Protect Parameters

In C++, you can cast a non-`const` variable to a `const` variable. Why would you want to do this? It offers some degree of protection from other code changing the variable. If you are calling a function that a coworker of yours is writing, and you want to ensure that the function doesn't change the value of a parameter you pass in, you can tell your coworker to have the function take a `const` parameter. If the function attempts to change the value of the parameter, it will not compile.

In the following code, a `char*` is automatically cast to a `const char*` in the call to `mysteryFunction()`. If the author of `mysteryFunction()` attempts to change the values within the character array, the code will not compile. There are ways around this restriction, but using them requires conscious effort. C++ only protects against accidentally changing `const` variables.

```
void mysteryFunction(const char* myString);
int main()
{
    char* myString = new char[2];
    myString[0] = 'a';
    myString[1] = '\0';
    mysteryFunction(myString);
    return 0;
}
void mysteryFunction(const char* myString)
{
    myString[0] = 'b';  // Will not compile.
}
```

Code snippet from ConstArg\ConstArg.cpp

const References

You will often find code that uses `const` reference parameters. At first, that seems like a contradiction. Reference parameters allow you to change the value of a variable from within another context. `const` seems to prevent such changes.

The main value in `const` reference parameters is efficiency. When you pass a value into a function, an entire copy is made. When you pass a reference, you are really just passing a pointer to the original so the computer doesn't need to make the copy. By passing a `const` reference, you get the best of both worlds — no copy is made but the original variable cannot be changed.

`const` references become more important when you are dealing with objects because they can be large and making copies of them can have unwanted side effects. Subtle issues like this are covered in Chapter 9.

C++ AS AN OBJECT-ORIENTED LANGUAGE

If you are a C programmer, you may have viewed the features covered so far in this chapter as convenient additions to the C language. As the name C++ implies, in many ways the language is just a "better C." There is one major point that this view overlooks. Unlike C, C++ is an object-oriented language.

Object-oriented programming (OOP) is a very different, arguably more natural, way to write code. If you are used to procedural languages such as C or Pascal, don't worry. Chapter 3 covers all the background information you need to know to shift your mindset to the object-oriented paradigm. If you already know the theory of OOP, the rest of this section will get you up to speed (or refresh your memory) on basic C++ object syntax.

Declaring a Class

A *class* defines the characteristics of an object. In C++, classes are usually declared in a header file and fully defined in a corresponding source file.

A basic class definition for an airline ticket class is shown below. The class can calculate the price of the ticket based on the number of miles in the flight and whether or not the customer is a member of the "Elite Super Rewards Program." The definition begins by declaring the class name. Inside a set of curly braces, the *data members* (properties) of the class and its *methods* (behaviors) are declared. Each data member and method is associated with a particular access level: `public`, `protected`, or `private`. These labels can occur in any order and can be repeated.

```cpp
#include <string>
class AirlineTicket
{
    public:
        AirlineTicket();
        ~AirlineTicket();
        int         calculatePriceInDollars() const;
        std::string getPassengerName() const;
        void        setPassengerName(std::string inName);
        int         getNumberOfMiles() const;
        void        setNumberOfMiles(int inMiles);
        bool        getHasEliteSuperRewardsStatus() const;
        void        setHasEliteSuperRewardsStatus(bool inStatus);
```

```
    protected:
        std::string   mPassengerName;
        int           mNumberOfMiles;
        bool          bHasEliteSuperRewardsStatus;
};
```

Code snippet from AirlineTicket\AirlineTicket.h

The method that has the same name as the class with no return type is a *constructor.* It is automatically called when an object of the class is created. The method with a tilde (~) character followed by the class name is a *destructor.* It is automatically called when the object is destroyed.

> To follow the const-*correctness principle, it's always a good idea to declare member functions that do not change any data member of the object as being* const. *These member functions are also called "inspectors," compared to "mutators" for non-*const *member functions.*

The sample program that follows makes use of the class declared in the previous example. This example shows the creation of a stack-based `AirlineTicket` object as well as a heap-based object.

Available for download on Wrox.com

```
AirlineTicket myTicket;  // Stack-based AirlineTicket
myTicket.setPassengerName("Sherman T. Socketwrench");
myTicket.setNumberOfMiles(700);
int cost = myTicket.calculatePriceInDollars();
cout << "This ticket will cost $" << cost << endl;

// heap-based AirlineTicket with smart pointer
shared_ptr<AirlineTicket> myTicket2(new AirlineTicket());
myTicket2->setPassengerName("Laudimore M. Hallidue");
myTicket2->setNumberOfMiles(2000);
myTicket2->setHasEliteSuperRewardsStatus(true);
int cost2 = myTicket2->calculatePriceInDollars();
cout << "This other ticket will cost $" << cost2 << endl;
// No need to delete myTicket2, happens automatically

// heap-based AirlineTicket without smart pointer
AirlineTicket* myTicket3 = new AirlineTicket();
// ... Use ticket 3
delete myTicket3;  // delete the heap object
```

Code snippet from AirlineTicket\AirlineTicketTest.cpp

The definitions of the `AirlineTicket` class methods are shown below.

Available for download on Wrox.com

```
AirlineTicket::AirlineTicket()
{
    // Initialize data members
    bHasEliteSuperRewardsStatus = false;
    mPassengerName = "Unknown Passenger";
```

```cpp
    mNumberOfMiles = 0;
}
AirlineTicket::~AirlineTicket()
{
    // Nothing much to do in terms of cleanup
}
int AirlineTicket::calculatePriceInDollars() const
{
    if (getHasEliteSuperRewardsStatus()) {
        // Elite Super Rewards customers fly for free!
        return 0;
    }
    // The cost of the ticket is the number of miles times
    // 0.1. Real airlines probably have a more complicated formula!
    return static_cast<int>(getNumberOfMiles() * 0.1);
}
string AirlineTicket::getPassengerName() const
{
    return mPassengerName;
}
void AirlineTicket::setPassengerName(string inName)
{
    mPassengerName = inName;
}
// Other get and set methods omitted for brevity.
```

Code snippet from AirlineTicket\AirlineTicket.cpp

The preceding example exposes you to the general syntax for creating and using classes. Of course, there is much more to learn. Chapters 6 and 7 go into more depth about the specific C++ mechanisms for defining classes.

THE STANDARD LIBRARY

C++ comes with a standard library, which contains a lot of useful classes that can easily be used in your code. The benefit of using classes from the standard library is that you don't need to reinvent certain classes and you don't need to waste time on implementing things that have already been implemented for you. Another benefit is that the classes available in the standard library are heavily tested and verified for correctness by thousands of users. The standard library classes are also tuned for high performance, so using them will most likely result in better performance compared to making your own implementation.

The amount of functionality available to you in the standard library is pretty big. Chapter 11 and later chapters provide more details about the standard library. When you start working with C++ it is a good idea to grasp immediately what the standard library can do for you. This is especially important if you are a C programmer. As a C programmer, you might try to solve problems in C++ the same way you would solve them in C. However, in C++ there is probably an easier and safer solution to the problem by using standard library classes.

You already saw some standard library classes earlier in this chapter; for example, the std::string and std::cout classes. Another example of functionality provided by the standard library is the concept of containers, which will be used further in this chapter. Take the std::vector, as an example. The vector replaces the concept of C arrays with a much more flexible and safer mechanism. As a user, you need not worry about memory management, as the vector will automatically allocate enough memory to hold its elements. A vector is dynamic, meaning that elements can be added and removed at run time. To make it easy to loop over the contents of containers, the standard library provides a concept called *iterators*. Chapter 12 goes into more details regarding containers and iterators.

The following example demonstrates the basic functionality of the std::vector class and the concept of iterators.

```cpp
#include <string>
#include <vector>
#include <iostream>
using namespace std;
int main()
{
    // Create a vector of strings, using C++11 uniform initialization
    vector<string> myVector = {"A first string", "A second string"};
    // Add some strings to the vector using push_back
    myVector.push_back("A third string");
    myVector.push_back("The last string in the vector");
    // Iterate over the elements in the vector and print them
    for (auto iterator = myVector.cbegin();
        iterator != myVector.cend(); ++iterator) {
        cout << *iterator << endl;
    }
    // Print the elements again using C++11 range-based for loop
    for (auto& str : myVector)
        cout << str << endl;
    return 0;
}
```

Code snippet from vectortest\vectortest.cpp

As you can see, myVector is declared as vector<string>. The angled brackets are required to specify the template parameters. A vector is a generic container. It can contain almost any kind of object; but, you have to specify the type of object you want in your vector between those brackets. Templates are discussed in more detail in Chapters 19 and 20.

To add elements to the vector, you can use the push_back() method and the C++11 uniform initialization.

The preceding example uses a new C++11 feature called auto type deduction using the auto keyword to let the compiler automatically decide the type of the variable iterator. If your compiler does not yet understand this new feature, you can write the for loop as follows:

```cpp
for (vector<string>::const_iterator iterator = myVector.begin();
    iterator != myVector.end(); ++iterator) {
    cout << *iterator << endl;
}
```

YOUR FIRST USEFUL C++ PROGRAM

The following program builds on the employee database example used earlier when discussing structs. This time, you will end up with a fully functional C++ program that uses many of the features discussed in this chapter. This real-world example includes the use of classes, exceptions, streams, `vectors`, iterators, namespaces, references, and other language features.

An Employee Records System

A program to manage a company's employee records needs to be flexible and have useful features. The feature set for this program includes the following.

> ➤ The ability to add an employee

> ➤ The ability to fire an employee

> ➤ The ability to promote an employee

> ➤ The ability to view all employees, past and present

> ➤ The ability to view all current employees

> ➤ The ability to view all former employees

The design for this program divides the code into three parts. The `Employee` class encapsulates the information describing a single employee. The `Database` class manages all the employees of the company. A separate `UserInterface` file provides the interactivity of the program.

The Employee Class

The `Employee` class maintains all the information about an employee. Its methods provide a way to query and change that information. `Employees` also know how to display themselves on the console. Methods also exist to adjust the employee's salary and employment status.

Employee.h

The `Employee.h` file declares the behavior of the `Employee` class. The sections of this file are described individually in the material that follows.

The first few lines of the file include a comment indicating the name of the file and the inclusion of the `string` functionality.

This code also declares that the subsequent code, contained within the curly braces, will live in the `Records` namespace. `Records` is the namespace that is used throughout this program for application-specific code.

```
// Employee.h
#include <string>
namespace Records {
```

Code snippet from EmployeeDB\Employee.h

The following constant, representing the default starting salary for new employees, lives in the `Records` namespace. Other code that lives in `Records` can access this constant as `kDefaultStartingSalary`. Elsewhere, it must be referenced as `Records::kDefaultStartingSalary`.

```
const int kDefaultStartingSalary = 30000;
```

Code snippet from EmployeeDB\Employee.h

The `Employee` class is declared, along with its public methods. The `promote()` and `demote()` methods both have integer parameters that are specified with a default value. In this way, other code can omit the integer parameters and the default will automatically be used.

A number of accessors provide mechanisms to change the information about an employee or query the current information about an employee.

```
class Employee
{
    public:
        Employee();
        void      promote(int inRaiseAmount = 1000);
        void      demote(int inDemeritAmount = 1000);
        void      hire();      // Hires or rehires the employee
        void      fire();      // Dismisses the employee
        void      display() const;// Outputs employee info to console
        // Accessors and setters
        void          setFirstName(std::string inFirstName);
        std::string   getFirstName() const;
        void          setLastName(std::string inLastName);
        std::string   getLastName() const;
        void          setEmployeeNumber(int inEmployeeNumber);
        int           getEmployeeNumber() const;
        void          setSalary(int inNewSalary);
        int           getSalary() const;
        bool          getIsHired() const;
```

Code snippet from EmployeeDB\Employee.h

Finally, the data members are declared as `protected` so that other parts of the code cannot modify them directly. The accessors provide the only public way of modifying or querying these values.

```
    protected:
        std::string   mFirstName;
        std::string   mLastName;
        int           mEmployeeNumber;
        int           mSalary;
        bool          bHired;
    };
}
```

Code snippet from EmployeeDB\Employee.h

Employee.cpp

This section discusses the implementations for the `Employee` class methods. The `Employee` constructor sets the initial values for the `Employee`'s data members. By default, new employees have no name, an employee number of -1, the default starting salary, and a status of not hired.

```cpp
#include <iostream>
#include "Employee.h"
using namespace std;
namespace Records {
    Employee::Employee()
        : mFirstName("")
        , mLastName("")
        , mEmployeeNumber(-1)
        , mSalary(kDefaultStartingSalary)
        , bHired(false)
    {
    }
```

Code snippet from EmployeeDB\Employee.cpp

The `promote()` and `demote()` methods simply call the `setSalary()` method with a new value. Note that the default values for the integer parameters do not appear in the source file. They only need to exist in the header.

```cpp
void Employee::promote(int inRaiseAmount)
{
    setSalary(getSalary() + inRaiseAmount);
}
void Employee::demote(int inDemeritAmount)
{
    setSalary(getSalary() - inDemeritAmount);
}
```

Code snippet from EmployeeDB\Employee.cpp

The `hire()` and `fire()` methods just set the `bHired` data member appropriately.

```cpp
void Employee::hire()
{
    bHired = true;
}
void Employee::fire()
{
    bHired = false;
}
```

Code snippet from EmployeeDB\Employee.cpp

The display() method uses the console output stream to display information about the current employee. Because this code is part of the Employee class, it *could* access data members, such as mSalary, directly instead of using the getSalary() accessor. However, it is considered good style to make use of accessors when they exist, even within the class.

Available for
download on
Wrox.com

```cpp
void Employee::display() const
{
    cout << "Employee: " << getLastName() << ", " << getFirstName() << endl;
    cout << "-------------------------" << endl;
    cout << (bHired ? "Current Employee" : "Former Employee") << endl;
    cout << "Employee Number: " << getEmployeeNumber() << endl;
    cout << "Salary: $" << getSalary() << endl;
    cout << endl;
}
```

Code snippet from EmployeeDB\Employee.cpp

A number of accessors and setters perform the task of getting and setting values. Even though these methods seem trivial, it's better to have trivial accessors and setters than to make your data members public. In the future, you may want to perform bounds checking in the setSalary() method, for example.

Available for
download on
Wrox.com

```cpp
// Accessors and setters
void Employee::setFirstName(string inFirstName)
{
    mFirstName = inFirstName;
}
string Employee::getFirstName() const
{
    return mFirstName;
}
// ... other accessors and setters omitted for brevity
}
```

Code snippet from EmployeeDB\Employee.cpp

EmployeeTest.cpp

As you write individual classes, it is often useful to test them in isolation. The following code includes a main() function that performs some simple operations using the Employee class. Once you are confident that the Employee class works, you should remove or comment-out this file so that you don't attempt to compile your code with multiple main() functions.

Available for
download on
Wrox.com

```cpp
#include <iostream>
#include "Employee.h"
using namespace std;
using namespace Records;
int main()
{
    cout << "Testing the Employee class." << endl;
```

```
            Employee emp;
            emp.setFirstName("Marni");
            emp.setLastName("Kleper");
            emp.setEmployeeNumber(71);
            emp.setSalary(50000);
            emp.promote();
            emp.promote(50);
            emp.hire();
            emp.display();
            return 0;
        }
```

The Database Class

The Database class uses the std::vector class from the standard library to store Employee objects.

Database.h

Because the database will take care of automatically assigning an employee number to a new employee, a constant defines where the numbering begins.

Available for
download on
Wrox.com

```
        #include <iostream>
        #include <vector>
        #include "Employee.h"
        namespace Records {
            const int kFirstEmployeeNumber = 1000;
```

The database provides an easy way to add a new employee by providing a first and last name. For convenience, this method will return a reference to the new employee. External code can also get an employee reference by calling the getEmployee() method. Two versions of this method are declared. One allows retrieval by employee number. The other requires a first and last name.

Available for
download on
Wrox.com

```
        class Database
        {
            public:
                Database();
                ~Database();
                Employee& addEmployee(std::string inFirstName,
                    std::string inLastName);
                Employee& getEmployee(int inEmployeeNumber);
                Employee& getEmployee(std::string inFirstName,
                    std::string inLastName);
```

Because the database is the central repository for all employee records, it has methods that will output all employees, the employees who are currently hired, and the employees who are no longer hired.

```
void        displayAll() const;
void        displayCurrent() const;
void        displayFormer() const;
```

Code snippet from EmployeeDB\Database.h

`mEmployees` contains the `Employee` objects. The `mNextEmployeeNumber` data member keeps track of what employee number will be assigned to a new employee.

```
    protected:
        std::vector<Employee>  mEmployees;
        int            mNextEmployeeNumber;
};
}
```

Code snippet from EmployeeDB\Database.h

Database.cpp

The `Database` constructor takes care of initializing the next employee number member to its starting value.

```
#include <iostream>
#include <stdexcept>
#include "Database.h"
using namespace std;
namespace Records {
    Database::Database()
    {
        mNextEmployeeNumber = kFirstEmployeeNumber;
    }
    Database::~Database()
    {
    }
```

Code snippet from EmployeeDB\Database.cpp

The `addEmployee()` method creates a new `Employee` object, fills in its information and adds it to the `vector`. Note that the `mNextEmployeeNumber` data member is incremented after its use so that the next employee will get a new number.

```
Employee& Database::addEmployee(string inFirstName, string inLastName)
{
    Employee theEmployee;
    theEmployee.setFirstName(inFirstName);
```

```
        theEmployee.setLastName(inLastName);
        theEmployee.setEmployeeNumber(mNextEmployeeNumber++);
        theEmployee.hire();
        mEmployees.push_back(theEmployee);
        return mEmployees[mEmployees.size()-1];
    }
```

Code snippet from EmployeeDB\Database.cpp

Only one version of getEmployee() is shown. Both versions work in similar ways. The methods loop over all employees in mEmployees using an iterator and check to see if each Employee is a match for the information passed to the method. If no match is found, an error is output and an exception is thrown. If your compiler does not support the auto feature, you should replace auto with vector<Employee>::iterator.

Available for
download on
Wrox.com

```
    Employee& Database::getEmployee(int inEmployeeNumber)
    {
        for (auto iter = mEmployees.begin();
            iter != mEmployees.end(); ++iter) {
            if (iter->getEmployeeNumber() == inEmployeeNumber)
                return *iter;
        }

        cerr << "No employee with number " << inEmployeeNumber << endl;
        throw exception();
    }
```

Code snippet from EmployeeDB\Database.cpp

The display methods all use a similar algorithm. They loop through all employees and tell each employee to display itself to the console if the criterion for display matches. If your compiler does not support the auto feature, you should replace auto with vector<Employee>::const_iterator because these are const member functions.

Available for
download on
Wrox.com

```
    void Database::displayAll() const
    {
        for (auto iter = mEmployees.begin();
            iter != mEmployees.end(); ++iter) {
            iter->display();
        }
    }
    void Database::displayCurrent() const
    {
        for (auto iter = mEmployees.begin();
            iter != mEmployees.end(); ++iter) {
            if (iter->getIsHired())
                iter->display();
        }
    }
```

Code snippet from EmployeeDB\Database.cpp

DatabaseTest.cpp

A simple test for the basic functionality of the database follows:

```cpp
#include <iostream>
#include "Database.h"
using namespace std;
using namespace Records;
int main()
{
    Database myDB;
    Employee& emp1 = myDB.addEmployee("Greg", "Wallis");
    emp1.fire();
    Employee& emp2 = myDB.addEmployee("Scott", "Kleper");
    emp2.setSalary(100000);
    Employee& emp3 = myDB.addEmployee("Nick", "Solter");
    emp3.setSalary(10000);
    emp3.promote();
    cout << "all employees: " << endl;
    cout << endl;
    myDB.displayAll();
    cout << endl;
    cout << "current employees: " << endl;
    cout << endl;
    myDB.displayCurrent();
    cout << endl;
    cout << "former employees: " << endl;
    cout << endl;
    myDB.displayFormer();
    return 0;
}
```

Code snippet from EmployeeDB\DatabaseTest.cpp

The User Interface

The final part of the program is a menu-based user interface that makes it easy for users to work with the employee database.

UserInterface.cpp

The main() function is a loop that displays the menu, performs the selected action, then does it all again. For most actions, separate functions are defined. For simpler actions, like displaying employees, the actual code is put in the appropriate case.

```cpp
#include <iostream>
#include <stdexcept>
#include "Database.h"
using namespace std;
using namespace Records;
int displayMenu();
void doHire(Database& inDB);
```

```cpp
void doFire(Database& inDB);
void doPromote(Database& inDB);
void doDemote(Database& inDB);
int main()
{
    Database employeeDB;
    bool done = false;
    while (!done) {
        int selection = displayMenu();
        switch (selection) {
        case 1:
            doHire(employeeDB);
            break;
        case 2:
            doFire(employeeDB);
            break;
        case 3:
            doPromote(employeeDB);
            break;
        case 4:
            employeeDB.displayAll();
            break;
        case 5:
            employeeDB.displayCurrent();
            break;
        case 6:
            employeeDB.displayFormer();
            break;
        case 0:
            done = true;
            break;
        default:
            cerr << "Unknown command." << endl;
        }
    }
    return 0;
}
```

Code snippet from EmployeeDB\UserInterface.cpp

The `displayMenu()` function outputs the menu and gets input from the user. One important note is that this code assumes that the user will "play nice" and type a number when a number is requested. When you read about I/O in Chapter 15, you will learn how to protect against bad input.

```cpp
int displayMenu()
{
    int selection;
    cout << endl;
    cout << "Employee Database" << endl;
    cout << "-----------------" << endl;
    cout << "1) Hire a new employee" << endl;
    cout << "2) Fire an employee" << endl;
    cout << "3) Promote an employee" << endl;
```

```
        cout << "4) List all employees" << endl;
        cout << "5) List all current employees" << endl;
        cout << "6) List all previous employees" << endl;
        cout << "0) Quit" << endl;
        cout << endl;
        cout << "---> ";
        cin >> selection;
        return selection;
}
```

Code snippet from EmployeeDB\UserInterface.cpp

The doHire() function gets the new employee's name from the user and tells the database to add the employee. It handles errors somewhat gracefully by outputting a message and continuing.

Available for
download on
Wrox.com

```
void doHire(Database& inDB)
{
    string firstName;
    string lastName;
    cout << "First name? ";
    cin >> firstName;
    cout << "Last name? ";
    cin >> lastName;
    try {
        inDB.addEmployee(firstName, lastName);
    } catch (const std::exception&) {
        cerr << "Unable to add new employee!" << endl;
    }
}
```

Code snippet from EmployeeDB\UserInterface.cpp

doFire() and doPromote() both ask the database for an employee by their employee number and then use the public methods of the Employee object to make changes.

Available for
download on
Wrox.com

```
void doFire(Database& inDB)
{
    int employeeNumber;
    cout << "Employee number? ";
    cin >> employeeNumber;
    try {
        Employee& emp = inDB.getEmployee(employeeNumber);
        emp.fire();
        cout << "Employee " << employeeNumber << " terminated." << endl;
    } catch (const std::exception&) {
        cerr << "Unable to terminate employee!" << endl;
    }
}
void doPromote(Database& inDB)
{
    int employeeNumber;
    int raiseAmount;
```

```
    cout << "Employee number? ";
    cin >> employeeNumber;
    cout << "How much of a raise? ";
    cin >> raiseAmount;
    try {
        Employee& emp = inDB.getEmployee(employeeNumber);
        emp.promote(raiseAmount);
    } catch (const std::exception&) {
        cerr << "Unable to promote employee!" << endl;
    }
}
```

Code snippet from EmployeeDB\UserInterface.cpp

Evaluating the Program

The preceding program covers a number of topics from the very simple to the more complex. There are a number of ways that you could extend this program. For example, the user interface does not expose all of the functionality of the Database or Employee classes. You could modify the UI to include those features. You could also change the Database class to remove fired employees from mEmployees.

If there are parts of this program that don't make sense, consult the preceding sections to review those topics. If something is still unclear, the best way to learn is to play with the code and try things out. For example, if you're not sure how to use the ternary operator, write a short main() function that tries it out.

SUMMARY

Now that you know the fundamentals of C++, you are ready to become a professional C++ programmer. The following chapters will introduce you to several important design concepts. By covering design at a high-level without getting into too much actual code, you will gain an appreciation for good program design without getting bogged down in the syntax.

When you start getting deeper into the C++ language later in the book, refer to this chapter to brush up on parts of the language you may need to review. Going back to some of the sample code in this chapter may be all you need to see to bring a forgotten concept back to the forefront of your mind.

2

Designing Professional
C++ Programs

WHAT'S IN THIS CHAPTER?

➤ The definition of programming design

➤ The importance of programming design

➤ The aspects of design that are unique to C++

➤ The two fundamental themes for effective C++ design: abstraction and reuse

➤ The different types of code available for reuse

➤ The advantages and disadvantages of code reuse

➤ General strategies and guidelines for reusing code

➤ Open-source libraries

➤ The C++ standard library

➤ The specific components of C++ program design

Before writing a single line of code in your application, you should design your program. What data structures will you use? What classes will you write? This plan is especially important when you program in groups. Imagine sitting down to write a program with no idea what your coworker, who is working on the same program, is planning! In this chapter, we'll teach you how to use the Professional C++ approach to C++ design.

Despite the importance of design, it is probably the most misunderstood and underused aspect of the software-engineering process. Too often programmers jump into applications without a clear plan: They design as they code. This approach inevitably leads to convoluted and overly complicated designs. It also makes the development, debugging, and maintenance tasks more difficult. Although counterintuitive, investing extra time at the beginning of a project to design it properly actually saves time over the life of the project.

WHAT IS PROGRAMMING DESIGN?

Your *program design*, or *software design*, is the specification of the architecture that you will implement to fulfill the functional and performance requirements of the program. Informally, the design is how you plan to write the program. You should generally write your design in the form of a design document. Although every company or project has its own variation of a desired design document format, most design documents share the same general layout, including two main parts:

1. The gross subdivision of the program into subsystems, including interfaces and dependencies between the subsystems, data flow between the subsystems, input and output to and from each subsystem, and general threading model.

2. The details of each subsystem, including subdivision into classes, class hierarchies, data structures, algorithms, specific threading model, and error-handling specifics.

The design documents usually include diagrams and tables showing subsystem interactions and class hierarchies. The exact format of the design document is less important than the process of thinking about your design.

 The point of designing is to think about your program before you write it.

You should generally try to make your design as good as possible before you begin coding. The design should provide a map of the program that any reasonable programmer could follow in order to implement the application. Of course, it is inevitable that the design will need to be modified once you begin coding and you encounter issues that you didn't think of earlier. Software-engineering processes have been designed to give you the flexibility to make these changes. The Spiral Method proposed by Barry W. Boehm is one example of such an iterative process whereby the application is developed according to cycles with each cycle containing at least a requirements analysis, design and an implementation part. Chapter 23 describes various software-engineering process models in more detail.

THE IMPORTANCE OF PROGRAMMING DESIGN

It's tempting to skip the design step, or to perform it only cursorily, in order to begin programming as soon as possible. There's nothing like seeing code compiling and running to give you the impression that you have made progress. It seems like a waste of time to formalize a design when you already know, more or less, how you want to structure your program. Besides, writing a design document just isn't as much fun as coding. If you wanted to write papers all day, you wouldn't be a computer programmer! As programmers ourselves, we understand this temptation to begin coding immediately, and have certainly succumbed to it on occasion. However, it will most likely lead to problems on all but the simplest projects. Whether or not you succeed without a design prior to the implementation depends on how deep you understand C++, the problem domain and the requirements.

To help you understand the importance of programming design, imagine that you own a plot of land on which you want to build a house. When the builder shows up you ask to see the blueprints. "What blueprints?" he responds, "I know what I'm doing. I don't need to plan every little detail ahead of time. Two-story house? No problem — I did a one-story house a few months ago — I'll just start with that model and work from there."

Suppose that you suspend your disbelief and allow the builder to proceed. A few months later you notice that the plumbing appears to run outside the house instead of inside the walls. When you query the builder about this anomaly he says, "Oh. Well, I forgot to leave space in the walls for the plumbing. I was so excited about this new drywall technology it just slipped my mind. But it works just as well outside, and functionality is the most important thing." You're starting to have your doubts about his approach, but, against your better judgment, you allow him to continue.

When you take your first tour of the completed building, you notice that the kitchen lacks a sink. The builder excuses himself by saying, "We were already two-thirds done with the kitchen by the time we realized there wasn't space for the sink. Instead of starting over we just added a separate sink room next door. It works, right?"

Do the builder's excuses sound familiar if you translate them to the software domain? Have you ever found yourself implementing an "ugly" solution to a problem like putting plumbing outside the house? For example, maybe you forgot to include locking in your queue data structure that is shared between multiple threads. By the time you realized the problem, you decided to just perform the locking manually on all places where the queue is used. Sure, it's ugly, but it works, you said. That is, until someone new joins the project who assumes that the locking is built into the data structure, fails to ensure mutual exclusion in her access to the shared data, and causes a race condition bug that takes three weeks to track down. Note that this locking problem is just given as an example of an ugly workaround. Obviously, a professional C++ programmer would never decide to perform the locking manually on each queue access but would instead directly incorporate the locking inside the queue class, or make the queue class thread-safe in a lock-free manner.

Formalizing a design before you code helps you determine how everything fits together. Just as blueprints for a house show how the rooms relate to each other and work together to fulfill the requirements of the house, the design for a program shows how the subsystems of the program relate to each other and work together to fulfill the software requirements. Without a design plan, you are likely to miss connections between subsystems, possibilities for reuse or shared information, and the simplest ways to accomplish tasks. Without the "big picture" that the design gives, you might become so bogged down in individual implementation details that you lose track of the overarching architecture and goals. Furthermore, the design provides written documentation to which all members of the project can refer. If you use an iterative process like the Spiral Method mentioned earlier, you need to make sure to keep the design documentation up-to-date during each cycle of the process.

If the preceding analogy hasn't convinced you to design before you code, here is an example where jumping directly into coding fails to lead to an optimal design. Suppose that you want to write a chess program. Instead of designing the entire program before you begin programming, you decide to jump in with the easiest parts and move slowly to the more difficult parts. Following the object-oriented perspective introduced in Chapter 1 and covered in more detail in Chapter 3, you decide to model your chess pieces with classes. The pawn is the simplest chess piece, so you opt to start there.

After considering the features and behaviors of a pawn, you write a class with the properties and behaviors shown in the following table:

CLASS	PROPERTIES	BEHAVIORS
Pawn	Location on Board	Move
	Color (Black or White)	Check Move Legality
	Captured	Draw
		Promote (Upon Reaching Opposing Side of the Board)

Of course, you didn't actually write the table. You went straight to the implementation. Happy with that class you move on to the next easiest piece: the bishop. After considering its attributes and functionality, you write a class with the properties and behaviors shown in the next table:

CLASS	PROPERTIES	BEHAVIORS
Bishop	Location on Board	Move
	Color (Black or White)	Check Move Legality
	Captured	Draw

Again, you didn't generate a table, because you jumped straight to the coding phase. However, at this point you begin to suspect that you might be doing something wrong. The bishop and the pawn look similar. In fact, their properties are identical and they share many behaviors. Although the implementations of the move behavior might differ between the pawn and the bishop, both pieces need the ability to move. If you had designed your program before jumping into coding, you would have realized that the various pieces are actually quite similar, and that you should find some way to write the common functionality only once. Chapter 3 explains the object-oriented design techniques for doing that.

Furthermore, several aspects of the chess pieces depend on other subsystems of your program. For example, you cannot accurately represent the location on the board in a chess piece class without knowing how you will model the board. On the other hand, perhaps you will design your program so that the board manages pieces in a way that doesn't require them to know their own locations. In either case, encoding the location in the piece classes before designing the board leads to problems. To take another example, how can you write a draw method for a piece without first deciding your program's user interface? Will it be graphical or text-based? What will the board look like? The problem is that subsystems of a program do not exist in isolation — they interrelate with other subsystems. Most of the design work determines and defines these relationships.

WHAT'S DIFFERENT ABOUT C++ DESIGN?

There are several aspects of the C++ language that make designing for C++ different, and more complicated, than designing for other languages.

➤ C++ has an immense feature set. It is almost a complete superset of the C language, plus classes and objects, operator overloading, exceptions, templates, and many other features. The sheer size of the language makes design a daunting task.

➤ C++ is an object-oriented language. This means that your designs should include class hierarchies, class interfaces, and object interactions. This type of design is quite different from "traditional" design in C or other procedural languages. Chapter 3 focuses on object-oriented design in C++.

➤ C++ has numerous facilities for designing generic and reusable code. In addition to basic classes and inheritance, you can use other language facilities such as templates and operator overloading for effective design. Design techniques for reusable code are discussed in more details further in this chapter.

➤ C++ provides a useful standard library, including a string class, I/O facilities, and many common data structures and algorithms. All of these facilitate coding in C++.

➤ C++ is a language that readily accommodates many *design patterns*, or common ways to solve problems. Design patterns are discussed in Chapter 29.

Because of all of these issues, tackling a design for a C++ program can be overwhelming. One of the authors of this book has spent entire days scribbling design ideas on paper, crossing them out, writing more ideas, crossing those out, and repeating the process. Sometimes this process is helpful, and, at the end of those days (or weeks), leads to a clean, efficient design. Other times it can be frustrating, and leads nowhere. It's important to remain aware of whether or not you are making real progress. If you find that you are stuck, you can take one of the following actions:

➤ **Ask for help.** Consult a coworker, mentor, book, newsgroup, or web page.

➤ **Work on something else for a while.** Come back to this design choice later.

➤ **Make a decision and move on.** Even if it's not an ideal solution, decide on something and try to work with it. An incorrect choice will soon become apparent. However, it may turn out to be an acceptable method. Perhaps there is no clean way to accomplish what you want to with this design. Sometimes you have to accept an "ugly" solution if it's the only realistic strategy to fulfill your requirements. Whatever you decide, make sure you document your decision, so that you and others in the future know why you made it.

 Keep in mind that good design is hard, and getting it right takes practice. Don't expect to become an expert overnight, and don't be surprised if you find it more difficult to master C++ design than C++ coding.

TWO RULES FOR C++ DESIGN

There are two fundamental design rules in C++: *abstraction* and *reuse*. These guidelines are so important that they can be considered themes of this book. They come up repeatedly throughout the text, and throughout effective C++ program designs in all domains.

Abstraction

The principle of *abstraction* is easiest to understand through a real-world analogy. A television is a simple piece of technology found in most homes. You are probably familiar with its features: You can turn it on and off, change the channel, adjust the volume, and add external components such as speakers, VCRs, and DVD players. However, can you explain how it works inside the black box? That is, do you know how it receives signals over the air or through a cable, translates them, and displays them on the screen? We certainly can't explain how a television works, yet we are quite capable of using it. That is because the television clearly separates its internal *implementation* from its external *interface*. We interact with the television through its interface: the power button, channel changer, and volume control. We don't know, nor do we care, how the television works; we don't care whether it uses a cathode ray tube or some sort of alien technology to generate the image on our screen. It doesn't matter because it doesn't affect the interface.

Benefiting from Abstraction

The abstraction principle is similar in software. You can use code without knowing the underlying implementation. As a trivial example, your program can make a call to the sqrt() function declared in the header file <cmath> without knowing what algorithm the function actually uses to calculate the square root. In fact, the underlying implementation of the square root calculation could change between releases of the library, and as long as the interface stays the same, your function call will still work. The principle of abstraction extends to classes as well. As introduced in Chapter 1, you can use the cout object of class ostream to stream data to standard output like this:

```
cout << "This call will display this line of text" << endl;
```

In this line, you use the documented interface of the cout insertion operator (<<) with a character array. However, you don't need to understand how cout manages to display that text on the user's screen. You only need to know the public interface. The underlying implementation of cout is free to change as long as the exposed behavior and interface remain the same. Chapter 15 covers I/O streams in more detail.

Incorporating Abstraction in Your Design

You should design functions and classes so that you and other programmers can use them without knowing, or relying on, the underlying implementations. To see the difference between a design that exposes the implementation and one that hides it behind an interface, consider the chess program again. You might want to implement the chess board with a two-dimensional array of pointers to ChessPiece objects. You could declare and use the board like this:

```
ChessPiece* chessBoard[8][8];
...
ChessBoard[0][0] = new Rook();
```

However, that approach fails to use the concept of abstraction. Every programmer who uses the chess board knows that it is implemented as a two-dimensional array. Changing that implementation to something else, such as an array of vectors, would be difficult, because you would need to change every use of the board in the entire program. There is no separation of interface from implementation.

A better approach is to model the chess board as a class. You could then expose an interface that hides the underlying implementation details. Here is an example of the `ChessBoard` class:

```
class ChessBoard
{
    public:
        // This example omits constructors, destructors, and assignment operator.
        void setPieceAt(ChessPiece* piece, int x, int y);
        ChessPiece& getPieceAt(int x, int y);
        bool isEmpty(int x, int y);
    protected:
        // This example omits data members.
};
```

Note that this interface makes no commitment to any underlying implementation. The `ChessBoard` could easily be a two-dimensional array, but the interface does not require it. Changing the implementation does not require changing the interface. Furthermore, the implementation can provide additional functionality, such as bounds checking.

The `getPieceAt()` function returns a reference, so it is recommended for the underlying implementation to not directly store objects in a collection, but pointers or better yet smart pointers to objects, to avoid bizarre aliasing problems, which can be hard to track down. For example, suppose a client of the `ChessBoard` class stores a reference received by a call to `getPieceAt()`. If the `ChessBoard` class directly stores objects in the underlying collection, this returned reference can become invalid when the `ChessBoard` class needs to reallocate memory for the collection. Storing pointers or smart pointers in the collection avoids this reference-invalidation problem.

This example, hopefully, has convinced you that abstraction is an important technique in C++ programming. Chapter 3 covers abstraction and object-oriented design in more detail, and Chapters 6 and 7 provide all the details about writing your own classes.

Reuse

The second fundamental rule of design in C++ is *reuse*. Again, it is helpful to examine a real-world analogy to understand this concept. Suppose that you give up your programming career in favor of work as a baker. On your first day of work, the head baker tells you to bake cookies. In order to fulfill his orders you find the recipe for chocolate-chip cookies, mix the ingredients, form cookies on the cookie sheet, and place the sheet in the oven. The head baker is pleased with the result.

Now, we are going to point out something so obvious that it will surprise you: you didn't build your own oven in which to bake the cookies. Nor did you churn your own butter, mill your own flour, or form your own chocolate chips. I can hear you think, "That goes without saying." That's true if you're a real cook, but what if you're a programmer writing a baking simulation game? In that case, you would think nothing of writing every component of the program, from the chocolate chips to the oven. Or, you could save yourself time by looking around for code to reuse. Perhaps your office-mate wrote a cooking simulation game and has some nice oven code lying around. Maybe it doesn't do everything you need, but you might be able to modify it and add the necessary functionality.

Something else you took for granted is that you followed a recipe for the cookies instead of making up your own. Again, that goes without saying. However, in C++ programming, it does not go without saying. Although there are standard ways of approaching problems that arise over and over in C++, many programmers persist in reinventing these strategies in each design.

Reusing Code

The idea of using existing code is not new. You've been reusing code from the first day you printed something with `cout`. You didn't write the code to actually print your data to the screen. You used the existing `ostream` implementation to do the work.

Unfortunately, programmers generally do not take advantage of available code. Your designs should take into account existing code and reuse it when appropriate.

Writing Reusable Code

The design theme of reuse applies to code you write as well as to code that you use. You should design your programs so that you can reuse your classes, algorithms, and data structures. You and your coworkers should be able to use these components in both the current project and in future projects. In general, you should avoid designing overly specific code that is applicable only to the case at hand.

One language technique for writing general-purpose code in C++ is the *template*. The following example shows a templatized data structure. If you've never seen this syntax before, don't worry! Chapter 19 explains the syntax in depth.

Instead of writing a specific `ChessBoard` class that stores `ChessPieces`, as shown earlier, consider writing a generic `GameBoard` template that can be used for any type of two-dimensional board game such as chess or checkers. You would need only to change the class declaration so that it takes the piece to store as a template parameter instead of hard-coding it in the interface. The template could look something like this:

```
template <typename PieceType>
class GameBoard
{
    public:
        // This example omits constructors, destructors, and assignment operator.
        void setPieceAt(PieceType* piece, int x, int y);
        PieceType& getPieceAt(int x, int y);
        bool isEmpty(int x, int y);
    protected:
        // This example omits data members.
};
```

With this simple change in the interface, you now have a generic game board class that you can use for any two-dimensional board game. Although the code change is simple, it is important to make these decisions in the design phase, so that you are able to implement the code effectively and efficiently.

Chapter 4 will go into more details on how to design your code with reuse in mind.

Reusing Ideas

As the baker example illustrates, it would be ludicrous to reinvent recipes for every dish that you make. However, programmers often make an equivalent mistake in their designs. Instead of using existing "recipes," or *patterns*, for designing programs, they reinvent these techniques every time they design a program. However, many *design patterns* appear in myriad different C++ applications. As a C++ programmer, you should familiarize yourself with these patterns so that you can incorporate them effectively into your program designs.

For example, you might want to design your chess program so that you have a single `ErrorLogger` object that serializes all errors from different components to a log file. When you try to design your `ErrorLogger` class, you realize that it would be disastrous to have more than one object instantiated from the `ErrorLogger` class in a single program. You also want to be able to access this `ErrorLogger` object from anywhere in your program. These requirements of a single, globally accessible, instance of a class arise frequently in C++ programs, and there is a standard strategy to implement them, called the *singleton*. Thus, a good design at this point would specify that you want to use the singleton pattern. Chapters 28 and 29 cover design patterns and techniques in much more detail.

Because reuse is such an important design aspect, the following section will go into more detail and give practical tips on how to use the reuse principle.

REUSING CODE

Experienced C++ programmers never start a project from scratch. They incorporate code from a wide variety of sources, such as the standard template library, open-source libraries, proprietary code bases in their workplace, and their own code from previous projects. In addition, good C++ programmers reuse approaches or strategies to address various common design issues. These strategies can range from a technique that worked for a past project to a formal *design pattern*. You should reuse code liberally in your designs. In order to make the most of this rule, you need to understand the types of code that you can reuse and the tradeoffs involved in code reuse.

A Note on Terminology

Before analyzing the advantages and disadvantages of code reuse, it is helpful to specify the terminology involved and to categorize the types of reused code. There are three categories of code available for reuse:

➤ Code you wrote yourself in the past

➤ Code written by a coworker

➤ Code written by a third party outside your current organization or company

There are also several ways that the code you use can be structured:

➤ **Stand-alone functions or classes.** When you reuse your own code or coworkers' code, you will generally encounter this variety.

➤ **Libraries.** A *library* is a collection of code used to accomplish a specific task, such as parsing XML, or to handle a specific domain, such as cryptography. Other examples of functionality usually found in libraries include threads and synchronization support, networking, and graphics.

➤ **Frameworks.** A *framework* is a collection of code around which you design a program. For example, the Microsoft Foundation Classes (MFC) provide a framework for creating graphical user interface applications for Microsoft Windows. Frameworks usually dictate the structure of your program.

A program uses a library but fits into a framework. Libraries provide specific functionality, while frameworks are fundamental to your program design and structure.

Another term that arises frequently is *application programming interface*, or *API*. An API is an interface to a library or body of code for a specific purpose. For example, programmers often refer to the sockets API, meaning the exposed interface to the sockets networking library, instead of the library itself.

Although people use the terms API *and* library *interchangeably, they are not equivalent. The* library *refers to the implementation, while the* API *refers to the published interface to the library.*

For the sake of brevity, the rest of this chapter uses the term *library* to refer to any reused code, whether it is really a library, framework, or random collection of functions from your office-mate.

Deciding Whether or Not to Reuse Code

The rule to reuse code is easy to understand in the abstract. However, it's somewhat vague when it comes to the details. How do you know when it's appropriate to reuse code, and which code to reuse? There is always a tradeoff, and the decision depends on the specific situation. However, there are some general advantages and disadvantages to reusing code.

Advantages to Reusing Code

Reusing code can provide tremendous advantages to you and to your project.

➤ You may not know how to, or may not be able to justify the time to write the code you need. Would you really want to write code to handle formatted input and output? Of course not: That's why you use the standard C++ I/O streams.

➤ Your designs will be simpler because you will not need to design those components of the application that you reuse.

➤ The code that you reuse usually requires no debugging. You can often assume that library code is bug-free because it has already been tested and used extensively.

➤ Libraries handle more error conditions than would your first attempt at the code. You might forget obscure errors or edge cases at the beginning of the project, and would waste time fixing these problems later. Library code that you reuse has generally been tested extensively and used by many programmers before you, so you can assume that it handles most errors properly.

➤ Libraries generally are designed to be suspect of bad user inputs. Invalid requests, or requests not appropriate for the current state, usually result in suitable error notifications. For example, a request to seek to a nonexistent record in a database, or to read a record from a database which is not open, would have well-specified behavior from a library.

➤ Reusing code written by domain experts is safer than writing your own code for that area. For example, you should not attempt to write your own security code unless you are a security expert. If you need security or cryptography in your programs, use a library. Many seemingly minor details in code of that nature could compromise the security of the entire program if you got them wrong.

➤ Library code is constantly improving. If you reuse the code, you receive the benefits of these improvements without doing the work yourself. In fact, if the library writers properly separated the interface from the implementation, you can obtain these benefits by upgrading your library version without changing your interaction with the library. A good upgrade modifies the underlying implementation without changing the interface.

Disadvantages to Reusing Code

Unfortunately, there are also some disadvantages to reusing code.

➤ When you use only code that you wrote yourself, you understand exactly how it works. When you use libraries that you didn't write yourself, you must spend time understanding the interface and correct usage before you can jump in and use it. This extra time at the beginning of your project will slow your initial design and coding.

➤ When you write your own code, it does exactly what you want. Library code might not provide the exact functionality that you require.

➤ Even if the library code provides the exact functionality you need, it might not give you the performance that you desire. The performance might be bad in general, poor for your specific use case, or completely undocumented.

➤ Using library code introduces a Pandora's box of support issues. If you discover a bug in the library, what do you do? Often you don't have access to the source code, so you couldn't fix it even if you wanted to. If you have already invested significant time learning the library interface and using the library, you probably don't want to give it up, but you might find it difficult to convince the library developers to fix the bug on your time schedule. Also, if you are using a third-party library, what do you do if the library authors drop support for the library before you stop supporting the product that depends on it? Think carefully about this before you decide to use a library for which you cannot get source code.

number of items to be sorted by a sorting algorithm, the number of elements in a hash table during a key lookup, and the size of a file to be copied between disks.

Note that big-O notation applies only to algorithms whose speed depends on their inputs. It does not apply to algorithms that take no input or whose running time is random. In practice, you will find that the running times of most algorithms of interest depend on their input, so this limitation is not significant.

To be more formal: Big-O notation specifies algorithm run time as a function of its input size, also known as the *complexity* of the algorithm. However, that's not as complicated as it sounds. For example, suppose that a sorting algorithm takes 50 milliseconds to sort 500 elements and 100 milliseconds to sort 1,000 elements. Because it takes twice as long to sort twice as many elements, its performance is *linear* as a function of its input. That is, you could graph the performance versus input size as a straight line. Big-O notation summarizes the sorting algorithm performance like this: $O(n)$. The O just means that you're using big-O notation, while the n represents the input size. $O(n)$ specifies that the sorting algorithm speed is a direct linear function of the input size.

Unfortunately, not all algorithms have performance that is linear with respect to the input size. Computer programs would run a lot faster if that were true. The following table summarizes the common categories of functions, in order of their performance from best to worst:

ALGORITHM COMPLEXITY	BIG-O NOTATION	EXPLANATION	EXAMPLE ALGORITHMS
Constant	$O(1)$	Running time is independent of input size.	Accessing a single element in an array
Logarithmic	$O(\log n)$	The running time is a function of the logarithm base 2 of the input size.	Finding an element in a sorted list using binary search
Linear	$O(n)$	The running time is directly proportional to the input size.	Finding an element in an unsorted list
Linear Logarithmic	$O(n \log n)$	The running time is a function of the linear times the logarithmic function of the input size.	Merge sort
Quadratic	$O(n^2)$	The running time is a function of the square of the input size.	A slower sorting algorithm like selection sort

There are two advantages to specifying performance as a function of the input size instead of in absolute numbers:

1. It is platform independent. Specifying that a piece of code runs in 200 milliseconds on one computer says nothing about its speed on a second computer. It is also difficult to compare two different algorithms without running them on the same computer with the exact same load. On the other hand, performance specified as a function of the input size is applicable to any platform.

2. Performance as a function of input size covers all possible inputs to the algorithm with one specification. The specific time in seconds that an algorithm takes to run covers only one specific input, and says nothing about any other input.

Sometimes the statistical expectations are taken into account when working with big-O notation in which case big-O represents the *expected time*. For example, a linear search is often said to be $O(n/2)$ because statistically about half of the elements need to be searched each time. The number of cases that are found in less than $O(n/2)$ are compensated for by the number of cases that require more than $O(n/2)$ time.

A big-O notation can be expressed using the following formula:

$$O(f(n)) = s + C*f(n) + t$$

In this formula, s is the setup time, C is the constant of proportionality, and t is the teardown time. For some algorithms, s, C or t can be large, and sometimes $s + t$ can completely swamp $C * f(n)$. Going deeper into the mathematics of the big-O notation is outside the scope of this book.

Tips for Understanding Performance

Now that you are familiar with big-O notation, you are prepared to understand most performance documentation. The C++ standard template library in particular describes its algorithm and data structure performance using big-O notation. However, big-O notation is sometimes insufficient or misleading. Consider the following issues whenever you think about big-O performance specifications:

➤   If an algorithm takes twice as long to work on twice as much data, that says nothing about how long it took in the first place! If the algorithm is written badly but scales well, it's still not something you want to use. For example, suppose the algorithm makes unnecessary disk accesses. That probably wouldn't affect the big-O time but would be very bad for performance.

➤   Along those lines, it's difficult to compare two algorithms with the same big-O running time. For example, if two different sorting algorithms both claim to be $O(n \log n)$, it's hard to tell which is really faster without running your own tests.

➤   For small inputs, big-O time can be very misleading. An $O(n^2)$ algorithm might actually perform better than an $O(\log n)$ algorithm on small input sizes. Consider your likely input sizes before making a decision.

In addition to considering big-O characteristics, you should look at other facets of the algorithm performance. Here are some guidelines to keep in mind:

➤   You should consider how often you intend to use a particular piece of library code. Some people find the "90/10" rule helpful: 90 percent of the running time of most programs is spent in only 10 percent of the code (Hennessy and Patterson, Computer Architecture, A Quantitative Approach, Fourth Edition", 2006, Morgan Kaufmann, 2002). If the library code you intend to use falls in the oft-exercised 10 percent category of your code, you should make sure to analyze its performance characteristics carefully. On the other hand, if it falls into the oft-ignored 90 percent of the code, you should not spend much time analyzing its performance because it will not benefit your overall program performance very much.

➤ Don't trust the documentation. Always run performance tests to determine if library code provides acceptable performance characteristics.

Understand Platform Limitations

Before you start using library code, make sure that you understand on which platforms it runs. That might sound obvious, but even libraries that claim to be cross-platform might contain subtle differences on different platforms.

Also, platforms include not only different operating systems but different versions of the same operating system. If you write an application that should run on Solaris 8, Solaris 9, and Solaris 10, ensure that any libraries you use also support all those releases. You cannot assume either forward or backward compatibility across operating system versions. That is, just because a library runs on Solaris 9 doesn't mean that it will run on Solaris 10 and vice versa.

Understand Licensing and Support

Using third-party libraries often introduces complicated licensing issues. You must sometimes pay license fees to third-party vendors for the use of their libraries. There may also be other licensing restrictions, including export restrictions. Additionally, open-source libraries are sometimes distributed under licenses that require any code that links with them to be open source as well.

 Make sure that you understand the license restrictions of any third-party libraries you use if you plan to distribute or sell the code you develop. When in doubt, consult a legal expert.

Using third-party libraries also introduces support issues. Before you use a library, make sure that you understand the process for submitting bugs, and that you realize how long it will take for bugs to be fixed. If possible, determine how long the library will continue to be supported so that you can plan accordingly.

Interestingly, even using libraries from within your own organization can introduce support issues. You may find it just as difficult to convince a coworker in another part of your company to fix a bug in his or her library as you would to convince a stranger in another company to do the equivalent. In fact, you may even find it harder, because you're not a paying customer. Make sure that you understand the politics and organizational issues within your own organization before using internal libraries.

Know Where to Find Help

Using libraries and frameworks can sometimes be daunting at first. Fortunately, there are many avenues of support available. First of all, consult the documentation that accompanies the library.

If the library is widely used, such as the standard template library (STL), or the MFC, you should be able to find a good book on the topic. In fact, for help with the STL, consult Chapters 11 to 17 of this book. If you have specific questions not addressed by books and product documentation, try searching the web. Type your question in your search engine of choice to find web pages that discuss the library. For example, when you search for the phrase "introduction to C++ STL" you will find several hundred websites about C++ and the STL. Also, many websites contain their own private newsgroups or forums on specific topics for which you can register.

 A note of caution: Don't believe everything you read on the web! Web pages do not necessarily undergo the same review process as printed books and documentation, and may contain inaccuracies.

Prototype

When you first sit down with a new library or framework, it is often a good idea to write a quick prototype. Trying out the code is the best way to familiarize yourself with the library's capabilities. You should consider experimenting with the library even before you tackle your program design so that you are intimately familiar with the library's capabilities and limitations. This empirical testing will allow you to determine the performance characteristics of the library as well.

Even if your prototype application looks nothing like your final application, time spent prototyping is not a waste. Don't feel compelled to write a prototype of your actual application. Write a dummy program that just tests the library capabilities you want to use. The point is only to familiarize yourself with the library.

 Due to time constraints, programmers sometimes find their prototypes morphing into the final product. If you have hacked together a prototype that is insufficient as the basis for the final product, make sure that it doesn't get used that way.

Bundling Third-Party Applications

Your project might include multiple applications. Perhaps you need a web server front end to support your new e-commerce infrastructure. It is possible to bundle third-party applications, such as a web server, with your software. This approach takes code reuse to the extreme in that you reuse entire applications. However, most of the caveats and guidelines for using libraries apply to bundling third-party applications as well. Specifically, make sure that you understand the legality and licensing ramifications of your decision.

 Consult a legal expert whose specialty is Intellectual Property before bundling third-party applications with your software distributions.

Also, the support issue becomes more complex. If customers encounter a problem with your bundled web server, should they contact you or the web server vendor? Make sure that you resolve this issue *before* you release the software.

Open-Source Libraries

Open-source libraries are an increasingly popular class of reusable code. The general meaning of *open-source* is that the source code is available for anyone to look at. There are formal definitions and legal rules about including source with all your distributions, but the important thing to remember about open-source software is that anyone (including you) can look at the source code. Note that open-source applies to more than just libraries. In fact, the most famous open-source product is probably the Linux operating system.

The Open-Source Movements

Unfortunately, there is some confusion in terminology in the open-source community. First of all, there are two competing names for the movement (some would say two separate, but similar, movements). Richard Stallman and the GNU project use the term *free software*. Note that the term free does not imply that the finished product must be available without cost. Developers are welcome to charge as much or as little as they want. Instead, the term free refers to the freedom for people to examine the source code, modify the source code, and redistribute the software. Think of the free in free speech rather than the free in free beer. You can read more about Richard Stallman and the GNU project at www.gnu.org.

The Open Source Initiative uses the term *open-source software* to describe software in which the source must be available. As with free software, open-source software does not require the product or library to be available for free. You can read more about the Open Source Initiative at www.opensource.org.

There are several licensing options available for open-source projects. One of them is the GNU Public License (GPL). However, using a library under the GPL might require you to make your own product open-source as well. On the other hand, an open-source project can use a licensing option like Boost, OpenBSD, CodeGuru, CodeProject, Creative Commons License, and so, on which allow using the open-source library in a closed-source product.

Because the name "open-source" is less ambiguous than "free software," this book uses "open-source" to refer to products and libraries with which the source code is available. The choice of name is not intended to imply endorsement of the open-source philosophy over the free software philosophy: It is only for ease of comprehension.

Finding and Using Open-Source Libraries

Regardless of the terminology, you can gain amazing benefits from using open-source software. The main benefit is functionality. There are a plethora of open-source C++ libraries available for varied tasks: from XML parsing to cross-platform error logging.

Although open-source libraries are not required to provide free distribution and licensing, many open-source libraries are available without monetary cost. You will generally be able to save money in licensing fees by using open-source libraries.

Finally, you are often free to modify open-source libraries to suit your exact needs.

Most open-source libraries are available on the web. For example, searching for "open-source C++ library XML parsing" results in a list of links to XML libraries in C and C++. There are also a few open-source portals where you can start your search, including:

➤ www.opensource.org

➤ www.gnu.org

➤ www.sourceforge.net

Guidelines for Using Open-Source Code

Open-source libraries present several unique issues and require new strategies. First of all, open-source libraries are usually written by people in their "free" time. The source base is generally available for any programmer who wants to pitch in and contribute to development or bug fixing. As a good programming citizen, you should try to contribute to open-source projects if you find yourself reaping the benefits of open-source libraries. If you work for a company, you may find resistance to this idea from your management because it does not lead directly to revenue for your company. However, you might be able to convince management that indirect benefits, such as exposure of your company name, and perceived support from your company for the open-source movement, should allow you to pursue this activity.

Second, because of the distributed nature of their development, and lack of single ownership, open-source libraries often present support issues. If you desperately need a bug fixed in a library, it is often more efficient to make the fix yourself than to wait for someone else to do it. If you do fix bugs, you should make sure to put the fixes into the public source base for the library. Even if you don't fix any bugs, make sure to report problems that you find so that other programmers don't waste time encountering the same issues.

The C++ Standard Library

The most important library that you will use as a C++ programmer is the C++ standard library. As its name implies, this library is part of the C++ standard, so any standards-conforming compiler should include it. The standard library is not monolithic: It includes several disparate components, some of which you have been using already. You may even have assumed they were part of the core language. Chapters 11 to 17 will go into more details about the standard library.

C Standard Library

Because C++ is a superset of C, the entire C library is still available. Its functionality includes mathematical functions such as `abs()`, `sqrt()`, and `pow()`, random numbers with `srand()` and `rand()`, and error-handling helpers such as `assert()` and `errno`. Additionally, the C library facilities for manipulating character arrays as strings, such as `strlen()` and `strcpy()`, and the C-style I/O functions, such as `printf()` and `scanf()`, are all available in C++.

C++ provides better strings and I/O support than C. Even though the C-style strings and I/O routines are available in C++, you should avoid them in favor of C++ strings (Chapter 14) and I/O streams (Chapter 15).

This book assumes that you are familiar with the C libraries. If not, consult one of the C reference books listed in Appendix B. Note also that the C header files have different names in C++. These names should be used instead of the more familiar C library names, because they are less likely to result in name conflicts. For details, see the Standard Library Reference resource on the website.

Deciding Whether or Not to Use the STL

The STL was designed with functionality, performance, and orthogonality as its priorities. The benefits of using it are substantial. Think about the number of times you've tracked down pointer errors in linked list or balanced binary tree implementations, or debugged a sorting algorithm that wasn't sorting properly. If you use the STL correctly, you will rarely, if ever, need to perform that kind of coding again. Chapters 11 to 17 provide in-depth information on the STL functionality.

DESIGNING WITH PATTERNS AND TECHNIQUES

Learning the C++ language and becoming a good C++ programmer are two very different things. If you sat down and read the C++ standard, memorizing every fact, you would know C++ as well as anybody else. However, until you gain some experience by looking at code and writing your own programs, you wouldn't necessarily be a good programmer. The reason is that the C++ syntax defines what the language can do in its raw form, but doesn't say anything about how each feature should be used.

As they become more experienced in using the C++ language, C++ programmers develop their own individual ways of using the features of the language. The C++ community at large has also built some standard ways of leveraging the language, some formal and some informal. Throughout this book, the authors point out these reusable applications of the language, known as *design techniques* and *design patterns*. Additionally, Chapters 28 and 29 focus almost exclusively on design techniques and patterns. Some patterns and techniques will seem obvious to you because they are simply a formalization of the obvious solution. Others describe novel solutions to problems you've encountered in the past. Some present entirely new ways of thinking about your program organization.

It is important for you to familiarize yourself with these patterns and techniques so that you can recognize when a particular design problem calls for one of these solutions. There are many more techniques and patterns applicable to C++ than those described in this book. Although the authors feel that the most useful ones are covered, you may want to consult a book on design patterns for more and different patterns and techniques. See Appendix B for suggestions.

DESIGNING A CHESS PROGRAM

This section introduces a systematic approach to designing a C++ program in the context of a simple chess game application. In order to provide a complete example, some of the steps refer to concepts covered in later chapters. You should read this example now, in order to obtain an overview of the design process, but you might also consider rereading it after you have finished later chapters.

Requirements

Before embarking on the design, it is important to possess clear requirements for the program's functionality and efficiency. Ideally, these requirements would be documented in the form of a requirements specification. The requirements for the chess program would contain the following types of specifications, although in more detail and number:

➤ The program will support the standard rules of chess.

➤ The program will support two human players. The program will not provide an artificially intelligent computer player.

➤ The program will provide a text-based interface:

 ➤ The program will render the game board and pieces in plain text.

 ➤ Players will express their moves by entering numbers representing locations on the chessboard.

The requirements ensure that you design your program so that it performs as its users expect.

Design Steps

You should take a systematic approach to designing your program, working from the general to the specific. The following steps do not always apply to all programs, but they provide a general guideline. Your design should include diagrams and tables as appropriate. This example includes sample diagrams and tables. Feel free to follow the format used here or to invent your own.

 There is no "right" way to draw software design diagrams as long as they are clear and meaningful to yourself and your colleagues.

Divide the Program into Subsystems

Your first step is to divide your program into its general functional subsystems and to specify the interfaces and interactions between the subsystems. At this point, you should not worry about specifics of data structures and algorithms, or even classes. You are trying only to obtain a general feel for the various parts of the program and their interactions. You can list the subsystems in a table that expresses the high-level behaviors or functionality of the subsystem, the interfaces exported from the subsystem to other subsystems, and the interfaces consumed, or used, by this subsystem on other subsystems. The best and recommended design for this chess game is to have a clear separation between storing the data and displaying the data by using the *Model-View-Controller* (MVC) paradigm discussed in Chapter 28. That way, you can easily switch between having a text-based interface and a graphical user interface. A table for the chess game subsystems could look like this:

SUBSYSTEM NAME	INSTANCES	FUNCTIONALITY	INTERFACES EXPORTED	INTERFACES CONSUMED
GamePlay	1	Starts game Controls game flow Controls drawing Declares winner Ends game	Game Over	Take Turn (on Player) Draw (on ChessBoardView)
ChessBoard	1	Stores chess pieces Checks for ties and checkmates	Get Piece At Set Piece At	Game Over (on GamePlay)
ChessBoardView	1	Draws the associated ChessBoard	Draw	Draw (on ChessPieceView)
ChessPiece	32	Moves itself Checks for legal moves	Move Check Move	Get Piece At (on ChessBoard) Set Piece At (on ChessBoard)
ChessPieceView	32	Draws the associated ChessPiece	Draw	None
Player	2	Interacts with user: prompts user for move, obtains user's move Moves pieces	Take Turn	Get Piece At (on ChessBoard) Move (on ChessPiece) Check Move (on ChessPiece)
ErrorLogger	1	Writes error messages to log file	Log Error	None

As this table shows, the functional subsystems of this chess game include a GamePlay subsystem, a ChessBoard and ChessBoardView, 32 ChessPieces and ChessPieceViews, two Players, and one ErrorLogger. However, that is not the only reasonable approach. In software design, as in programming itself, there are often many different ways to accomplish the same goal. Not all ways are equal: Some are certainly better than others. However, there are often several equally valid methods.

A good division into subsystems separates the program into its basic functional parts. For example, a Player is a subsystem distinct from the ChessBoard, ChessPieces, or GamePlay. It wouldn't make sense to lump the players into the GamePlay subsystem because they are logically separate subsystems. Other choices might not be as obvious.

In this MVC design, the ChessBoard and ChessPiece subsystems are part of the Model. The ChessBoardView and ChessPieceView are part of the View and the Player is part of the Controller.

Because it is often difficult to visualize subsystem relationships from tables, it is usually helpful to show the subsystems of a program in a diagram where arrows represent calls from one subsystem to another.

Choose Threading Models

In this step, you choose the number of threads in your program and specify their interactions. In multithreaded designs, you should try to avoid shared data as much as possible because it will make your designs simpler and safer. If you cannot avoid shared data, you should specify locking requirements. If you are unfamiliar with multithreaded programs, or your platform does not support multithreading, then you should make your programs single-threaded. However, if your program has several distinct tasks, each of which should work in parallel, it might be a good candidate for multiple threads. For example, graphical user interface applications often have one thread performing the main application work and another thread waiting for the user to press buttons or select menu items. Multithreaded programming is covered in Chapter 22.

The chess program needs only one thread to control the game flow.

Specify Class Hierarchies for Each Subsystem

In this step, you determine the class hierarchies that you intend to write in your program. The chess program needs a class hierarchy, to represent the chess pieces. The hierarchy could work as shown in Figure 2-1.

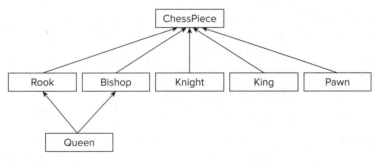

FIGURE 2-1

In this hierarchy, a generic `ChessPiece` class serves as the abstract superclass. The hierarchy uses multiple inheritance to show that the queen piece is a combination of a rook and a bishop. A similar hierarchy is required for the `ChessPieceView` class.

Another class hierarchy can be used for the `ChessBoardView` class to make it possible to have a text-based interface or a graphical user interface for the game. Figure 2-2 shows an example hierarchy that allows the chess board to be displayed as text on a console or as a 2D or 3D rendering.

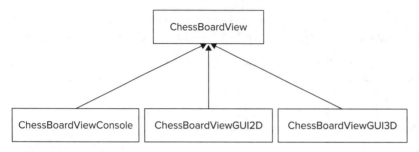

FIGURE 2-2

A similar hierarchy is required for the Player controller and for the individual classes of the `ChessPieceView` hierarchy.

Chapter 3 explains the details of designing classes and class hierarchies.

Specify Classes, Data Structures, Algorithms, and Patterns for Each Subsystem

In this step, you consider a greater level of detail, and specify the particulars of each subsystem, including the specific classes that you write for each subsystem. It may well turn out that you model each subsystem itself as a class. This information can again be summarized in a table:

SUBSYSTEM	CLASSES	DATA STRUCTURES	ALGORITHMS	PATTERNS
GamePlay	GamePlay class	GamePlay object includes one ChessBoard object and two Player objects.	Gives each player a turn to play	None
ChessBoard	ChessBoard class	ChessBoard object stores a two-dimensional representation of 32 ChessPieces.	Checks for win or tie after each move	None

SUBSYSTEM	CLASSES	DATA STRUCTURES	ALGORITHMS	PATTERNS
ChessBoardView	`ChessBoardView` abstract superclass Concrete subclasses `ChessBoardViewConsole`, `ChessBoardViewGUI2D` ...	Stores information on how to draw a chess board	Draws a chess board	Observer
ChessPiece	`ChessPiece` abstract superclass `Rook`, `Bishop`, `Knight`, `King`, `Pawn`, and `Queen` subclasses	Each piece stores its location on the chess board.	Piece checks for legal move by querying chess board for pieces at various locations.	None
ChessPieceView	`ChessPieceView` abstract superclass Subclasses `RookView`, `BishopView` ... and concrete subclasses `RookViewConsole`, `RookViewGUI2D` ...	Stores information on how to draw a chess piece	Draws a chess piece	Observer
Player	`Player` abstract superclass Concrete subclasses `PlayerConsole`, `PlayerGUI2D`, `PlayerGUI3D` ...	Two player objects (black and white)	Take Turn algorithm: Prompt user for move, check if move is legal, and move piece.	Mediator
ErrorLogger	One `ErrorLogger` class	A queue of messages to log	Buffers messages and writes them to a log file	Singleton pattern to ensure only one `ErrorLogger` object

This section of the design document would normally present the actual interfaces for each class, but this example will forgo that level of detail.

Designing classes and choosing data structures, algorithms, and patterns can be tricky. You should always keep in mind the rules of abstraction and reuse discussed earlier in this chapter. For abstraction, the key is to consider the interface and the implementation separately. First, specify the interface from the perspective of the user. Decide *what* you want the component to do. Then decide *how* the component will do it by choosing data structures and algorithms. For reuse, familiarize yourself with standard data structures, algorithms, and patterns. Also, make sure you are aware of the standard library code in C++, as well as any proprietary code available in your workplace.

Specify Error Handling for Each Subsystem

In this design step, you delineate the error handling in each subsystem. The error handling should include both system errors, such as memory allocation failures, and user errors, such as invalid entries. You should specify whether each subsystem uses exceptions. You can again summarize this information in a table:

SUBSYSTEM	HANDLING SYSTEM ERRORS	HANDLING USER ERRORS
GamePlay	Logs an error with the ErrorLogger, shows a message to the user and gracefully shuts down the program if unable to allocate memory for ChessBoard or Players	Not applicable (no direct user interface)
ChessBoard ChessPiece	Logs an error with the ErrorLogger and throws an exception if unable to allocate memory	Not applicable (no direct user interface)
ChessBoardView ChessPieceView	Logs an error with the ErrorLogger and throws an exception if something goes wrong during rendering	Not applicable (no direct user interface)
Player	Logs an error with the ErrorLogger and throws an exception if unable to allocate memory	Sanity-checks user move entry to ensure that it is not off the board; prompts user for another entry. Checks each move legality before moving the piece; if illegal, prompts user for another move.
ErrorLogger	Attempts to log an error, informs user, and gracefully shuts down the program if unable to allocate memory	Not applicable (no direct user interface)

The general rule for error handling is to handle everything. Think hard about all possible error conditions. If you forget one possibility, it will show up as a bug in your program! Don't treat anything as an "unexpected" error. Expect all possibilities: memory allocation failures, invalid user entries, disk failures, and network failures, to name a few. However, as the table for the chess game shows, you should handle user errors differently from internal errors. For example, a user entering an invalid move should not cause your chess program to terminate.

Chapter 10 discusses error handling in more depth.

SUMMARY

In this chapter, you learned about the professional C++ approach to design. We hope it convinced you that software design is an important first step in any programming project. You also learned about some of the aspects of C++ that make design difficult, including its object-oriented focus, its large feature set and standard library, and its facilities for writing generic code. With this information, you are better prepared to tackle C++ design.

This chapter introduced two design themes. The concept of abstraction, or separating interface from implementation, permeates this book and should be a guideline for all your design work.

The notion of reuse, both of code and ideas, also arises frequently in real-world projects, and in this text. You learned that your C++ designs should include both reuse of code, in the form of libraries and frameworks, and reuse of ideas, in the form of techniques and patterns. You should write your code to be as reusable as possible. Also remember about the tradeoffs and about specific guidelines for reusing code, including understanding the capabilities and limitations, the performance, licensing and support models, the platform limitations, prototyping, and where to find help. You also learned about performance analysis and big-O notation. Now that you understand the importance of design and the basic design themes, you are ready for the rest of Part I. Chapter 3 describes strategies for using the object-oriented aspects of C++ in your design.

3

Designing with Objects

WHAT'S IN THIS CHAPTER?

➤ What object-oriented programming design is

➤ How you can define relationships between different objects

➤ The importance of abstraction and how to use it in your designs

Now that you have developed an appreciation for good software design from Chapter 2, it's time to pair the notion of objects with the concept of good design. The difference between programmers who use objects in their code and those who truly grasp object-oriented programming comes down to the way their objects relate to each other and to the overall design of the program.

This chapter begins with the transition from procedural programming to object-oriented programming. Even if you've been using objects for years, you will want to read this chapter for some new ideas regarding how to think about objects. A discussion of the different kinds of relationships between objects includes pitfalls programmers often succumb to when building an object-oriented program. You will also learn how the principal of abstraction relates to objects.

When making the transition from procedural (C-style) coding to object-oriented coding, the most important point to remember is that object-oriented programming (OOP) is just a different way to think about what's going on in your program. Too often, programmers get bogged down in the new syntax and jargon of OOP before they adequately understand what an object is. This chapter is light on code and heavy on concepts and ideas. For specifics on C++ object syntax, see Chapters 6, 7, and 8.

AM I THINKING PROCEDURALLY?

A procedural language, such as C, divides code into small pieces each of which (ideally) accomplishes a single task. Without procedures in C, all your code would be lumped together inside `main()`. Your code would be difficult to read, and your coworkers would be annoyed, to say the least.

The computer doesn't care if all your code is in `main()` or if it's split into bite-sized pieces with descriptive names and comments. Procedures are an abstraction that exists to help you, the programmer, as well as those who read and maintain your code. The concept is built around a fundamental question about your program — *What does this program do?* By answering that question in English, you are thinking procedurally. For example, you might begin designing a stock selection program by answering as follows: First, the program obtains stock quotes from the Internet. Then, it sorts this data by specific metrics. Next, it performs analysis on the sorted data. Finally, it outputs a list of buy and sell recommendations. When you start coding, you might directly turn this mental model into C functions: `retrieveQuotes()`, `sortQuotes()`, `analyzeQuotes()`, and `outputRecommendations()`.

> *Even though C refers to procedures as "functions," C is* not *a functional language. The term* functional *is very different from* procedural *and refers to languages like Lisp, which use an entirely different abstraction.*

The procedural approach tends to work well when your program follows a specific list of steps. In large modern applications, however, there is rarely a linear sequence of events. Often a user is able to perform any command at any time. Procedural thinking also says nothing about data representation. In the previous example, there was no discussion of what a stock quote actually is.

If the procedural mode of thought sounds like the way you approach a program, don't worry. Once you realize that OOP is simply an alternative, more flexible, way of thinking about software, it'll come naturally.

THE OBJECT-ORIENTED PHILOSOPHY

Unlike the procedural approach, which is based on the question *What does this program do?*, the object-oriented approach asks another question: *What real-world objects am I modeling?* OOP is based on the notion that you should divide your program not into tasks, but into models of physical objects. While this seems abstract at first, it becomes clearer when you consider physical objects in terms of their *classes*, *components*, *properties*, and *behaviors*.

Classes

A class helps distinguish an object from its definition. Consider the orange (the Florida Department of Citrus certainly hopes you will). There's a difference between talking about oranges in general as tasty fruit that grows on trees and talking about a specific orange, such as the one that's currently dripping juice on my keyboard.

When answering the question *What are oranges?* you are talking about the *class* of things known as oranges. All oranges are fruit. All oranges grow on trees. All oranges are some shade of orange. All oranges have some particular flavor. A class is simply the encapsulation of what defines a classification of objects.

When describing a specific orange, you are talking about an object. All objects belong to a particular class. Because the object on my desk is an orange, I know that it belongs to the orange class. Thus, I know that it is a fruit that grows on trees. I can further say that it is a medium shade of orange and ranks "mighty tasty" in flavor. An object is an *instance* of a class — a particular item with characteristics that distinguish it from other instances of the same class.

As a more concrete example, reconsider the stock selection application from above. In OOP, "stock quote" is a class because it defines the abstract notion of what makes up a quote. A specific quote, such as "current Microsoft stock quote," would be an object because it is a particular instance of the class.

From a C background, think of classes and objects as analogous to types and variables. In fact, in Chapter 6, you'll see that the syntax for classes is similar to the syntax for C structs.

Components

If you consider a complex real-world object, such as an airplane, it should be fairly easy to see that it is made up of smaller *components*. There's the fuselage, the controls, the landing gear, the engines, and numerous other parts. The ability to think of objects in terms of their smaller components is essential to OOP, just as the breaking up of complicated tasks into smaller procedures is fundamental to procedural programming.

A component is essentially the same thing as a class, just smaller and more specific. A good object-oriented program might have an `Airplane` class, but this class would be huge if it fully described an airplane. Instead, the `Airplane` class deals with many smaller, more manageable, components. Each of these components might have further subcomponents. For example, the landing gear is a component of an airplane, and the wheel is a component of the landing gear.

Properties

Properties are what distinguish one object from another. Going back to the `Orange` class, recall that all oranges are defined as having some shade of orange and a particular flavor. These two characteristics are properties. All oranges have the same properties, just with different values. My orange has a "mighty tasty" flavor, but yours may have a "terribly unpleasant" flavor.

You can also think about properties on the class level. As recognized earlier, all oranges are fruit and grow on trees. These are properties of the fruit class whereas the specific shade of orange is determined by the particular fruit object. Class properties are shared by all members of a class, while object properties are present in all objects of the class, but with different values.

In the stock selection example, a stock quote has several object properties, including the name of the company, its ticker symbol, the current price, and other statistics.

Properties are the characteristics that describe an object. They answer the question *What makes this object different?*

Behaviors

Behaviors answer either of two questions: *What does this object do?* Or, *What can I do to this object?* In the case of an orange, it doesn't do a whole lot, but we can do things to it. One behavior is that it can be eaten. Like properties, you can think of behaviors on the class level or the object level. All oranges can pretty much be eaten in the same way. However, they might differ in some other behavior, such as being rolled down an incline, where the behavior of a perfectly round orange would differ from that of a more oblate one.

The stock selection example provides some more practical behaviors. As you recall, when thinking procedurally, we determined that our program needs to analyze stock quotes as one of its functions. Thinking in OOP, you might decide that a stock quote object can analyze itself. Analysis becomes a behavior of the stock quote object.

In object-oriented programming, the bulk of functional code is moved out of procedures and into objects. By building objects that have certain behaviors and defining how they interact, OOP offers a much richer mechanism for attaching code to the data on which it operates.

Bringing It All Together

With these concepts, you could take another look at the stock selection program and redesign it in an object-oriented manner.

As discussed, "stock quote" would be a fine class to start with. To obtain the list of quotes, the program needs the notion of a group of stock quotes, which is often called a *collection*. So a better design might be to have a class that represents a "collection of stock quotes," which is made up of smaller components that represent a single "stock quote."

Moving on to properties, the collection class would have at least one property — the actual list of quotes received. It might also have additional properties, such as the exact date and time of the most recent retrieval and the number of quotes obtained. As for behaviors, the "collection of stock quotes" would be able to talk to a server to get the quotes and provide a sorted list of quotes. This is the "retrieve quotes" behavior.

The stock quote class would have the properties discussed earlier — name, symbol, current price, and so on. Also, it would have an analyze behavior. You might consider other behaviors, such as buying and selling the stock.

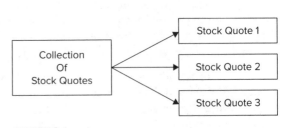

It is often useful to jot down diagrams showing the relationship between components. Figure 3-1 uses multiple lines to indicate that one "collection of stock quotes" contains many "stock quote" objects.

FIGURE 3-1

Another useful way of visualizing classes is to list properties and behaviors when brainstorming the object representation of a program, as in the following table:

CLASS	ASSOCIATED COMPONENTS	PROPERTIES	BEHAVIORS
Orange	Seeds Juice Pulp	Color Flavor	Eat Roll Toss Peel Squeeze
Collection of Stock Quotes	Made up of individual Stock Quote objects	Individual Quotes Timestamp Number of Quotes	Retrieve quotes Sort quotes by various criteria
Stock Quote	None (yet)	Company Name Ticker Symbol Current Price, and so on	Analyze Buy shares Sell shares

LIVING IN A WORLD OF OBJECTS

When programmers make the transition from thinking procedurally to the object-oriented paradigm, they often experience an epiphany about the combination of properties and behaviors into objects. Some programmers find themselves revisiting the design of programs they're working on and rewriting certain pieces as objects. Others might be tempted to throw all the code away and restart the project as a fully object-oriented application.

There are two major approaches to developing software with objects. To some people, objects simply represent a nice encapsulation of data and functionality. These programmers sprinkle objects throughout their programs to make the code more readable and easier to maintain. Programmers taking this approach slice out isolated pieces of code and replace them with objects like a surgeon implanting a pacemaker. There is nothing inherently wrong with this approach. These people see objects as a tool that is beneficial in many situations. Certain parts of a program just "feel like an object," like the stock quote. These are the parts that can be isolated and described in real-world terms.

Other programmers adopt the OOP paradigm fully and turn everything into an object. In their minds, some objects correspond to real-world things, such as an orange or a stock quote, while others encapsulate more abstract concepts, such as a sorter or an undo object. The ideal approach is probably somewhere in between these extremes. Your first object-oriented program might really have been a traditional procedural program with a few objects sprinkled in. Or perhaps you went whole hog and made everything an object, from a class representing an int to a class representing the main application. Over time, you will find a happy medium.

Overobjectification

There is often a fine line between designing a creative object-oriented system and annoying everybody else on your team by turning every little thing into an object. As Freud used to say, sometimes a variable is just a variable. Okay, that's a paraphrase of what he said.

Perhaps you're designing the next bestselling Tic-Tac-Toe game. You're going all-out OOP on this one, so you sit down with a cup of coffee and a notepad to sketch out your classes and objects. In games like this, there's often an object that oversees game play and is able to detect the winner. To represent the game board, you might envision a Grid object that will keep track of the markers and their locations. In fact, a component of the grid could be the Piece object that represents an X or an O.

Wait, back up! This design proposes to have a class that represents an X or an O. That is perhaps object overkill. After all, can't a char represent an X or an O just as well? Better yet, why can't the Grid just use a two-dimensional array of an enumerated type? Does a Piece object just complicate the code? Take a look at the following table representing the proposed piece class:

CLASS	ASSOCIATED COMPONENTS	PROPERTIES	BEHAVIORS
Piece	None	X or O	None

The table is a bit sparse, strongly hinting that what we have here may be too granular to be a full-fledged object.

On the other hand, a forward-thinking programmer might argue that while Piece is a pretty meager class as it currently stands, making it into an object allows future expansion without any real penalty. Perhaps down the road, this will be a graphical application and it might be useful to have the Piece class support drawing behavior. Additional properties could be the color of the Piece or whether the Piece was the most recently moved.

Another solution might be to think about the *state* of a grid square instead of using pieces. The state of a square can be Empty, X or O. To make the design future-proof to support a graphical application, you could design an abstract superclass State with concrete subclasses StateEmpty, StateX and StateO which know how to render themselves.

Obviously, there is no right answer. The important point is that these are issues that you should consider when designing your application. Remember that objects exist to help programmers manage their code. If objects are being used for no reason other than to make the code "more object-oriented," something is wrong.

Overly General Objects

Perhaps a worse annoyance than objects that shouldn't be objects is objects that are too general. All OOP students start with examples like "orange" — things that are objects, no question about it. In real life coding, objects can get pretty abstract. Many OOP programs have an "application object," despite the fact that an application isn't really something you can envision in material form. Yet it may be useful to represent the application as an object because the application itself has certain properties and behaviors.

An overly general object is an object that doesn't represent a particular thing at all. The programmer may be attempting to make an object that is flexible or reusable, but ends up with one that is confusing. For example, imagine a program that organizes and displays media. It can catalog your photos, organize your digital music collection, and serve as a personal journal. The overly general approach is to think of all these things as "media" objects and build a single class that can accommodate all of the formats. It might have a property called "data" that contains the raw bits of the image, song, or journal entry, depending on the type of media. It might have a behavior called "perform" that appropriately draws the image, plays the song, or brings up the journal entry for editing.

The clues that this class is too general are in the names of the properties and behaviors. The word "data" has little meaning by itself — you have to use a general term here because this class has been overextended to three very different uses. Similarly, "perform" will do very different things in the three different cases. Finally, this design is too general because "media" isn't a particular object, not in the user interface, not in real life, and not even in the programmer's mind. A major clue that a class is too general is when many ideas in the programmers mind all unite as a single object, as shown in Figure 3-2.

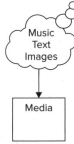

FIGURE 3-2

OBJECT RELATIONSHIPS

As a programmer, you will certainly encounter cases where different classes have characteristics in common, or at least seem somehow related to each other. For example, although creating a "media" object to represent images, music, and text in a digital catalog program is too general, these objects do share characteristics. You may want all of them to keep track of the date and time that they were last modified, or you might want them all to support a delete behavior.

Object-oriented languages provide a number of mechanisms for dealing with such relationships between objects. The tricky part is to understand what the relationship actually is. There are two main types of object relationships — a *has-a* relationship and an *is-a* relationship.

The Has-A Relationship

Objects engaged in a has-a, or *aggregation,* relationship follow the pattern A has a B, or A contains a B. In this type of relationship, you can envision one object as part of another. Components, as defined earlier, generally represent a has-a relationship because they describe objects that are made up of other objects.

A real-world example of this might be the relationship between a zoo and a monkey. You could say that a zoo has a monkey or a zoo contains a monkey. A simulation of a zoo in code would have a zoo object, which has a monkey component.

Often, thinking about user interface scenarios is helpful in understanding object relationships. This is so because even though not all UIs are implemented in OOP (though these days, most are), the visual elements on the screen translate well into objects. One UI analogy for a has-a relationship is a window that contains a button. The button and the window are clearly two separate objects but they are obviously related in some way. Since the button is inside the window, we say that the window has a button.

Figure 3-3 shows various real-world and user interface has-a relationships.

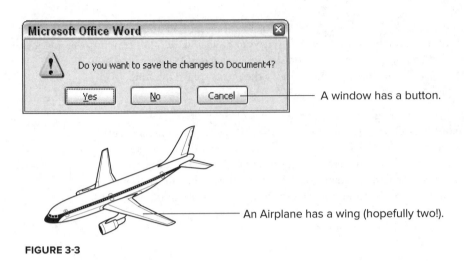

— A window has a button.

— An Airplane has a wing (hopefully two!).

FIGURE 3-3

The Is-A Relationship (Inheritance)

The is-a relationship is such a fundamental concept of object-oriented programming that it has many names, including *subclassing*, *extending*, and *inheriting*. Classes model the fact that the real world contains objects with properties and behaviors. Inheritance models the fact that these objects tend to be organized in hierarchies. These hierarchies indicate is-a relationships.

Fundamentally, inheritance follows the pattern A is a B or A is really quite a bit like B — it can get tricky. To stick with the simple case, revisit the zoo, but assume that there are other animals besides monkeys. That statement alone has already constructed the relationship — a monkey is an animal. Similarly, a giraffe is an animal, a kangaroo is an animal, and a penguin is an animal. So what? Well, the magic of inheritance comes when you realize that monkeys, giraffes, kangaroos, and penguins have certain things in common. These commonalities are characteristics of animals in general.

What this means for the programmer is that you can define an `Animal` class that encapsulates all of the properties (size, location, diet, etc.) and behaviors (move, eat, sleep) that pertain to every animal. The specific animals, such as monkeys, become subclasses of `Animal` because a monkey contains all the characteristics of an animal. Remember, a monkey is an animal plus some additional characteristics that make it distinct. Figure 3-4 shows an inheritance diagram for animals. The arrows indicate the direction of the is-a relationship.

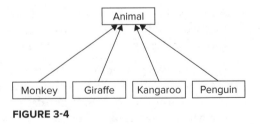

FIGURE 3-4

Just as monkeys and giraffes are different types of animals, a user interface often has different types of buttons. A checkbox, for example, is a button. Assuming that a button is simply a UI element that can be clicked and performs an action, a `Checkbox` extends the `Button` class by adding state — whether the box is checked or unchecked.

When relating classes in an is-a relationship, one goal is to factor common functionality into the *superclass*, the class that other classes extend. If you find that all of your subclasses have code that is similar or exactly the same, consider how you could move some or all of the code into the superclass. That way, any changes that need to be made only happen in one place and future subclasses get the shared functionality "for free."

Inheritance Techniques

The preceding examples cover a few of the techniques used in inheritance without formalizing them. When subclassing, there are several ways that the programmer can distinguish an object from its *parent object* or *superclass*. A subclass may use one or more of these techniques and they are recognized by completing the sentence *A is a B that . . . .*

Adding Functionality

A subclass can augment its parent by adding additional functionality. For example, a monkey is an animal that can swing from trees. In addition to having all of the behaviors of `Animal`, the `Monkey` class also has a `swing from trees` behavior, which is specific to only the `Monkey` class.

Replacing Functionality

A subclass can replace or *override* a behavior of its parent entirely. For example, most animals move by walking, so you might give the `Animal` class a `move` behavior that simulates walking. If that's the case, a kangaroo is an animal that moves by hopping instead of walking. All the other properties and behaviors of the `Animal` superclass still apply, but the `Kangaroo` subclass simply changes the way that the `move` behavior works. Of course, if you find yourself replacing *all* of the functionality of your superclass, it may be an indication that subclassing was not the correct thing to do after all, unless the superclass is an *abstract* superclass. An abstract superclass serves as a baseclass for subclasses to force each of the subclasses to implement a certain behavior. You cannot create instances of an abstract superclass. Abstract classes are discussed in Chapter 8.

Adding Properties

A subclass can also add new properties to the ones that were inherited from the superclass. A penguin has all the properties of an animal but also has a `beak size` property.

Replacing Properties

C++ provides a way of overriding properties similar to the way you can override behaviors. However, doing so is rarely appropriate. It's important not to get the notion of replacing a property confused with the notion of subclasses having different values for properties. For example, all animals have a `diet` property that indicates what they eat. Monkeys eat `bananas` and penguins eat `fish`, but neither of these is replacing the `diet` property — they simply differ in the value assigned to the property.

Polymorphism versus Code Reuse

Polymorphism is the notion that objects that adhere to a standard set of properties and behaviors can be used interchangeably. A class definition is like a contract between objects and the code that interacts with them. By definition, any Monkey object must support the properties and behaviors of the Monkey class.

This notion extends to superclasses as well. Because all monkeys are animals, all Monkey objects support the properties and behaviors of the Animal class as well.

Polymorphism is a beautiful part of object-oriented programming because it truly takes advantage of what inheritance offers. In a zoo simulation, you could programmatically loop through all of the animals in the zoo and have each animal move once. Since all animals are members of the Animal class, they all know how to move. Some of the animals have overridden the move behavior, but that's the best part — our code simply tells each animal to move without knowing or caring what type of animal it is. Each one moves whichever way it knows how.

There is another reason to subclass besides polymorphism. Often, it's just a matter of leveraging existing code. For example, if you need a class that plays music with an echo effect, and your coworker has already written one that plays music without any effects, you might be able to extend the existing class and add in the new functionality. The is-a relationship still applies (an echo music player is a music player that adds an echo effect), but you didn't intend for these classes to be used interchangeably. What you end up with are two separate classes, used in completely different parts of the programs (or maybe even in different programs entirely) that happen to be related only to avoid reinventing the wheel.

The Fine Line between Has-A and Is-A

In the real world, it's pretty easy to classify has-a and is-a relationships between objects. Nobody would claim that an orange has a fruit — an orange *is a* fruit. In code, things sometimes aren't so clear.

Consider a hypothetical class that represents a hash table. A hash table is a data structure that efficiently maps a key to a value. For example, an insurance company could use a Hashtable class to map member IDs to names so that given an ID, it's easy to find the corresponding member name. The member ID is the *key* and the member name is the *value*.

In a standard hash table implementation, every key has a single value. If the ID 14534 maps to the member name "Kleper, Scott", it cannot also map to the member name "Kleper, Marni". In most implementations, if you tried to add a second value for a key that already has a value, the first value would go away. In other words, if the ID 14534 mapped to "Kleper, Scott" and you then assigned the ID 14534 to "Kleper, Marni", then Scott would effectively be uninsured, as shown in the following sequence, which shows two calls to a hypothetical hash table enter() behavior and the resulting contents of the hash table. The notation hash.enter jumps ahead a bit to C++ object syntax. Just think of it as saying "use the enter behavior of the hash object."

```
hash.enter(14534, "Kleper, Scott");
```

KEYS	VALUES
14534	"Kleper, Scott" [string]

```
hash.enter(14534, "Kleper, Marni");
```

KEYS	VALUES
14534	"Kleper, Marni" [string]

It's not difficult to imagine uses for a data structure that's *like* a hash table, but allows multiple values for a given key. In the insurance example, a family might have several names that correspond to the same ID. Because such a data structure is very similar to a hash table, it would be nice to leverage that functionality somehow. A hash table can have only a single value as a key, but that value can be anything. Instead of a string, the value could be a collection (such as an array or a list) containing the multiple values for the key. Every time you add a new member for an existing ID, add the name to the collection. This would work as shown in the following sequence.

```
Collection collection;                   // Make a new collection.
collection.insert("Kleper, Scott");      // Add a new element to the collection.
hash.enter(14534, collection);           // Enter the collection into the table.
```

KEYS	VALUES
14534	{"Kleper, Scott"} [collection]

```
Collection collection = hash.get(14534);// Retrieve the existing collection.
collection.insert("Kleper, Marni");      // Add a new element to the collection.
hash.enter(14534, collection);           // Replace the collection with the updated one.
```

KEYS	VALUES
14534	{"Kleper, Scott", "Kleper, Marni"} [collection]

Messing around with a collection instead of a string is tedious and requires a lot of repetitive code. It would be preferable to wrap up this multiple-value functionality in a separate class, perhaps called a MultiHash. The MultiHash class would work just like Hashtable except that behind the scenes, it would store each value as a collection of strings instead of a single string. Clearly, MultiHash is somehow related to Hashtable because it is still using a hash table to store the data. What is unclear is whether that constitutes an is-a or a has-a relationship.

To start with the is-a relationship, imagine that MultiHash is a subclass of Hashtable. It would have to override the behavior that adds an entry into the table so that it would either create a collection and add the new element or retrieve the existing collection and add the new element. It would also override the behavior that retrieves a value. It could, for example, append all the values for a given key together into one string. This seems like a perfectly reasonable design. Even though it overrides all the behaviors of the superclass, it will still make use of the superclass's behaviors by using the original behaviors within the subclass. This approach is shown in Figure 3-5.

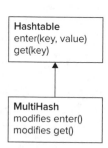

FIGURE 3-5

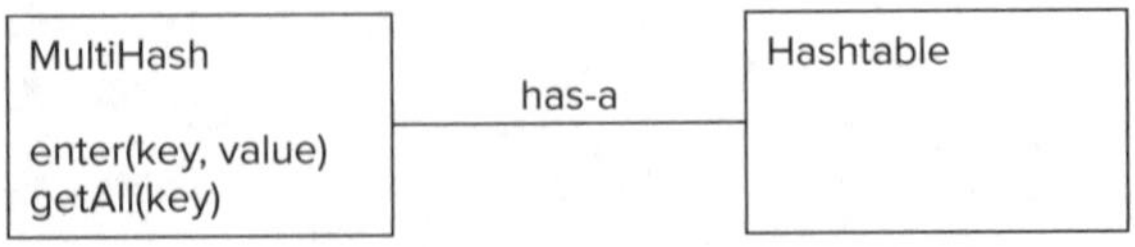

Now consider it as a has-a relationship. `MultiHash` is its own class, but it *contains* a `Hashtable` object. It probably has an interface very similar to `Hashtable`, but it need not be the same. Behind the scenes, when a user adds something to the `MultiHash`, it is really wrapped in a collection and put in a `Hashtable` object. This also seems perfectly reasonable and is shown in Figure 3-6.

FIGURE 3-6

So, which solution is right? There's no clear answer, though one of the authors, who has written a MultiHash class for production use, viewed it as a has-a relationship. The main reason was to allow modifications to the exposed interface without worrying about maintaining hash table functionality. For example, in Figure 3-6, the `get` behavior was changed to `getAll`, making it clear that this would get all the values for a particular key in a `MultiHash`. Additionally, with a has-a relationship, you don't have to worry about any hash table functionality bleeding through. For example, if the hash table class supported a behavior that would get the total number of values, it would report the number of collections unless `MultiHash` knew to override it.

That said, one could make a convincing argument that a `MultiHash` actually is a `Hashtable` with some new functionality, and it should have been an is-a relationship. The point is that there is sometimes a fine line between the two relationships, and you will need to consider how the class is going to be used and whether what you are building just leverages some functionality from another class or really is that class with modified or new functionality.

The following table represents the arguments for and against taking either approach for the `MultiHash` class.

	IS-A	HAS-A
Reasons For	• Fundamentally, it's the same abstraction with different characteristics. • It provides (almost) the same behaviors as `Hashtable`.	• `MultiHash` can have whatever behaviors are useful without needing to worry about what behaviors `Hashtable` has. • The implementation could change to something other than a `Hashtable` without changing the exposed behaviors.
Reasons Against	• A hash table by definition has one value per key. To say `MultiHash` is a hash table is blasphemy! `MultiHash` overrides both behaviors of `Hashtable`, a strong sign that something about the design is wrong. • Unknown or inappropriate properties or behaviors of `Hashtable` could "bleed through" to `MultiHash`.	• In a sense, `MultiHash` reinvents the wheel by coming up with new behaviors. • Some additional properties and behaviors of `Hashtable` might have been useful.

The reasons against using an is-a relationship in this case are pretty strong. In fact, after years of experience, the authors recommend to opt for a has-a relationship over an is-a relationship if you have the choice.

Note that the `Hashtable` and `MultiHash` are used here to demonstrate the difference between the is-a and has-a relationships. In your own code, it is recommended to use one of the standard hash table classes instead of writing your own. The C++11 standard library provides an `unordered_map` class, which you should use instead of the `Hashtable` and an `unordered_multimap` class, which you should use instead of the `MultiHash`. Both of these standard classes are discussed in Chapter 12.

The Not-A Relationship

As you consider what type of relationship classes have, consider whether or not they actually have a relationship at all. Don't let your zeal for object-oriented design turn into a lot of needless class/ subclass relationships.

One pitfall occurs when things are obviously related in the real world but have no actual relationship in code. OO hierarchies need to model *functional* relationships, not artificial ones. Figure 3-7 shows relationships that are meaningful as ontologies or hierarchies, but are unlikely to represent a meaningful relationship in code.

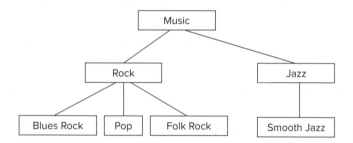

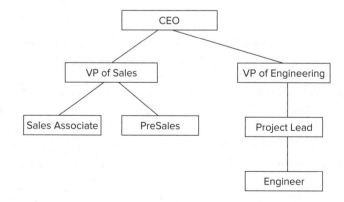

FIGURE 3-7

The best way to avoid needless subclassing is to sketch out your design first. For every class and subclass, write down what properties and behaviors you're planning on putting there. You should rethink your design if you find that a class has no particular properties or behaviors of its own, or if all of those properties and behaviors are completely overridden by its subclasses, except when working with abstract superclasses as mentioned earlier.

Hierarchies

Just as a class A can be a superclass of B, B can also be a superclass of C. Object-oriented hierarchies can model multilevel relationships like this. A zoo simulation with more animals might be designed with every animal as a subclass of a common Animal class as shown in Figure 3-8.

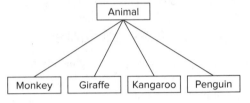

FIGURE 3-8

As you code each of these subclasses, you might find that a lot of them are similar. When this occurs, you should consider putting in a common parent. Realizing that Lion and Panther both move the same way and have the same diet might indicate a possible BigCat class. You could further subdivide the Animal class to include WaterAnimals, and Marsupials. A more hierarchical design that leverages this commonality is shown in Figure 3-9.

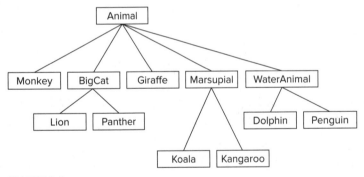

FIGURE 3-9

A biologist looking at this hierarchy may be disappointed — a penguin isn't really in the same family as a dolphin. However, it underlines a good point — in code, you need to balance real-world relationships with shared functionality relationships. Even though two things might be very closely related in the real world, they might have a not-a relationship in code because they really don't share functionality. You could just as easily divide animals into mammals and fish, but that wouldn't factor any commonality to the superclass.

Another important point is that there could be other ways of organizing the hierarchy. The preceding design is organized mostly by how the animals move. If it were instead organized by the animals' diet or height, the hierarchy could be very different. In the end, what matters is how the classes will be used. The needs will dictate the design of the object hierarchy.

A good object-oriented hierarchy accomplishes the following:

➤ Organizes classes into meaningful functional relationships

➤ Supports code reuse by factoring common functionality to superclasses

➤ Avoids having subclasses that override much of the parent's functionality, unless the parent is an abstract class.

Multiple Inheritance

Every example so far has had a single inheritance chain. In other words, a given class has, at most, one immediate parent class. This does not have to be the case. Through multiple inheritance, a class can have more than one superclass.

Figure 3-10 shows a multiple inheritance design. There is still a superclass called Animal, which is further divided by size. A separate hierarchy categorizes by diet, and a third takes care of movement. Each type of animal is then a subclass of all three of these classes, as shown by different lines.

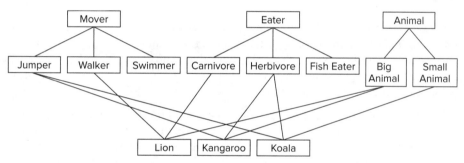

FIGURE 3-10

In a user interface context, imagine an image that the user can click on. This object seems to be both a button and an image so the implementation might involve subclassing both the Image class and the Button class, as shown in Figure 3-11.

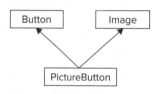

FIGURE 3-11

Multiple inheritance can be very useful in certain cases, but it also has a number of disadvantages that you should always keep in mind. Many programmers dislike multiple inheritance. C++ has explicit support for such relationships, though the Java language does away with them altogether. There are several reasons to which multiple inheritance critics point.

First, visualizing multiple inheritance is complicated. As you saw in Figure 3-10, even a simple class diagram can become very complicated when there are multiple hierarchies and crossing lines. Class hierarchies are supposed to make it easier for the programmer to understand the relationships between code. With multiple inheritance, a class could have several parents that are in no way related to each other. With so many classes contributing code to your object, can you really keep track of what's going on?

Second, multiple inheritance can destroy otherwise clean hierarchies. In the animal example, switching to a multiple inheritance approach means that the `Animal` superclass is less meaningful because the code that describes animals is now separated into three separate hierarchies. While the design illustrated in Figure 3-10 shows three clean hierarchies, it's not difficult to imagine how they could get messy. For example, what if you realize that not only do all `Jumpers` move in the same way, they also eat the same things? Because there are separate hierarchies, there is no way to join the concepts of movement and diet without adding yet another subclass.

Third, implementation of multiple inheritance is complicated. What if two of your superclasses implement the same behavior in different ways? Can you have two superclasses that are themselves a subclass of a common superclass? These possibilities complicate the implementation because structuring such intricate relationships in code is difficult both for the author and a reader.

The reason that other languages can leave out multiple inheritance is that it is usually avoidable. By rethinking your hierarchy or using some of the *design patterns* covered in Chapter 29, you can often avoid introducing multiple inheritance when you have control over the design of a project.

Mix-in Classes

Mix-in classes represent another type of relationship between classes. In C++, a mix-in class is implemented syntactically just like multiple inheritance, but the semantics are refreshingly different. A mix-in class answers the question "What *else* is this class able to do?" and the answer often ends with "-able." Mix-in classes are a way that you can add functionality to a class without committing to a full is-a relationship. You can think of it as a *shares-with* relationship.

Going back to the zoo example, you might want to introduce the notion that some animals are "pettable." That is, there are some animals that visitors to the zoo can pet, presumably without being bitten or mauled. You might want all pettable animals to support the behavior "be pet." Since pettable animals don't have anything else in common and you don't want to break the existing hierarchy you've designed, `Pettable` makes a great mix-in class.

Mix-in classes are used frequently in user interfaces. Instead of saying that a `PictureButton` class is both an `Image` and a `Button`, you might say that it's an `Image` that is `Clickable`. A folder icon on your desktop could be an `Image` that is `Draggable`. Software developers tend to make up lots of fun adjectives.

The difference between a mix-in class and a superclass has more to do with how you think about the class than any code difference. In general, mix-in classes are easier to digest than multiple inheritance because they are very limited in scope. The `Pettable` mix-in class just adds one behavior to any existing class. The `Clickable` mix-in class might just add "mouse down" and "mouse up" behaviors. Also, mix-in classes rarely have a large hierarchy so there's no cross-contamination of functionality.

ABSTRACTION

In Chapter 2, you learned about the concept of abstraction — the notion of separating implementation from the means used to access it. Abstraction is a good idea for many reasons explored earlier. It's also a fundamental part of object-oriented design.

Interface versus Implementation

The key to abstraction is effectively separating the *interface* from the *implementation*. Implementation is the code you're writing to accomplish the task you set out to accomplish. Interface is the way that other people use your code. In C, the header file that describes the functions in a library you've written is an interface. In object-oriented programming, the interface to a class is the collection of publicly accessible properties and behaviors. A good interface contains only public behaviors. Properties/variables of a class should never be made public but can be exposed through public behaviors also called *getters* and *setters*.

Deciding on an Exposed Interface

The question of how other programmers will interact with your objects comes into play when designing a class. In C++, a class's properties and behaviors can each be `public`, `protected`, or `private`. Making a property or behavior `public` means that other code can access it. `protected` means that other code cannot access the property or behavior but subclasses can access them. `private` is a stricter control, which means that not only are the properties or behaviors locked for other code, but also even subclasses can't access them.

Designing the exposed interface is all about choosing what to make `public`. When working on a large project with other programmers, you should view the exposed interface design as a process.

Consider the Audience

The first step in designing an exposed interface is to consider for whom you are designing it. Is your audience another member of your team? Is this an interface that you will personally be using? Is it something that a programmer external to your company will use? Perhaps a customer or an off-shore contractor? In addition to determining who will be coming to you for help with the interface, this should shed some light on some of your design goals.

If the interface is for your own use, you probably have more freedom to iterate on the design. As you're making use of the interface, you can change it to suit your own needs. However, you should keep in mind that roles on an engineering team change and it is quite likely that, some day, others will be using this interface as well.

Designing an interface for other internal programmers to use is slightly different. In a way, your interface becomes a contract with them. For example, if you are implementing the data store component of a program, others are depending on that interface to support certain operations. You will need to find out all of the things that the rest of the team wants your class to do. Do they need versioning? What types of data can they store? As a contract, you should view the interface as slightly less flexible. If the interface is agreed upon before coding begins, you'll receive some groans from other programmers if you decide to change it after code has been written.

If the client is an external customer, you will be designing with a very different set of requirements. Ideally, the target customer will be involved in specifying what functionality your interface exposes. You'll need to consider both the specific features they want as well as what customers might want in the future. The terminology used in the interface will have to correspond to the terms that the customer is familiar with, and the documentation will have to be written with that audience in mind. Inside jokes, codenames, and programmer slang should probably be left out of your design.

Consider the Purpose

There are many reasons for writing an interface. Before putting any code on paper or even deciding on what functionality you're going to expose, you need to understand the purpose of the interface.

Application Programming Interface (API)

An *API* is an externally visible mechanism to extend a product or use its functionality within another context. If an internal interface is a contract, an API is closer to a set-in-stone law. Once people who don't even work for your company are using your API, they don't want it to change unless you're adding new features that will help them. So, care should be given to planning the API and discussing it with customers before making it available to them.

The main tradeoff in designing an API is usually ease of use versus flexibility. Because the target audience for the interface is not familiar with the internal working of your product, the learning curve to use the API should be gradual. After all, your company is exposing this API to customers because the company wants it to be used. If it's too difficult to use, the API is a failure. Flexibility often works against this. Your product may have a lot of different uses, and you want the customer to be able to leverage all the functionality you have to offer. However, an API that lets the customer do anything that your product can do may be too complicated.

As a common programming adage goes, "A good API makes the easy case easy and the hard case *possible*." That is, APIs should have a simple learning curve. The things that most programmers will want to do should be accessible. However, the API should allow for more advanced usage, and it's acceptable to trade off complexity of the rare case for simplicity of the common case.

Utility Class or Library

Often, your task is to develop some particular functionality for general use elsewhere in the application. It could be a random number library or a logging class. In these cases, the interface is somewhat easier to decide on because you tend to expose most or all of the functionality, ideally without giving too much away about its implementation. Generality is an important issue to consider. Since the class or library is general purpose, you'll need to take the possible set of use cases into account in your design.

Subsystem Interface

You may be designing the interface between two major subsystems of the application, such as the mechanism for accessing a database. In these cases, separating the interface from the implementation is paramount because other programmers are likely to start implementing against your interface before your implementation is complete. When working on a subsystem, first think about what its one main purpose is. Once you have identified the main task your subsystem is charged with, think about specific uses and how it should be presented to other parts of the code. Try to put yourself in their shoes and not get bogged down in implementation details.

Component Interface

Most of the interfaces you define will probably be smaller than a subsystem interface or an API. These will be objects that you use within other code that you've written. In these cases, the main pitfall is when your interface evolves gradually and becomes unruly. Even though these interfaces are for your own use, think of them as though they weren't. As with a subsystem interface, consider the one main purpose of each class and be cautious of exposing functionality that doesn't contribute to that purpose.

Consider the Future

As you are designing your interface, keep in mind what the future holds. Is this a design you will be locked into for years? If so, you might need to leave room for expansion by coming up with a plug-in architecture. Do you have evidence that people will try to use your interface for purposes other than what it was designed for? Talk to them and get a better understanding of their use case. The alternative is rewriting it later, or worse, attaching new functionality haphazardly and ending up with a messy interface. Be careful though! Speculative generality is yet another pitfall. Don't design the be-all end-all logging class if the future uses are unclear, because it might unnecessarily complicate the design, the implementation and its public interface.

Designing a Successful Abstraction

Experience and iteration are essential to good abstractions. Truly well-designed interfaces come from years of writing and using other abstractions. As you encounter other abstractions, try to remember what worked and didn't work. What did you find lacking in the Windows file system API you used last week? What would you have done differently if you had written the network wrapper, instead of your coworker? The best interface is rarely the first one you put on paper, so keep iterating. Bring your design to your peers and ask for feedback. If your company uses code reviews, start the code review by doing a review of the interface specifications before the implementation starts. Don't be afraid to change the abstraction once coding has begun, even if it means forcing other programmers to adapt. Hopefully, they'll realize that a good abstraction is beneficial to everyone in the long term.

Sometimes you need to evangelize a bit when communicating your design to other programmers. Perhaps the rest of the team didn't see a problem with the previous design or feels that your approach requires too much work on their part. In those situations, be prepared both to defend your work and to incorporate their ideas when appropriate.

A good abstraction means that the interface has only public behaviors. All code should be in the implementation file and not in the class definition file. This means that the interface files containing the class definitions are stable and will not change.

Beware of single-class abstractions. If there is significant depth to the code you're writing, consider what other companion classes might accompany the main interface. For example, if you're exposing an interface to do some data processing, consider also writing a result object that provides an easy way to view and interpret the results.

When possible, turn properties into behaviors. In other words, don't allow external code to manipulate the data behind your class directly. You don't want some careless or nefarious programmer to set the height of a bunny object to a negative number. Instead, have a "set height" behavior that does the necessary bounds checking.

Iteration is worth mentioning again because it is the most important point. Seek and respond to feedback on your design, change it when necessary, and learn from mistakes.

SUMMARY

In this chapter, you've gained an appreciation for the design of object-oriented programs without a lot of code getting in the way. The concepts you've learned are applicable in almost any object-oriented language. Some of it may have been a review to you, or it may be a new way of formalizing a familiar concept. Perhaps you picked up some new approaches to old problems or new arguments in favor of the concepts you've been preaching to your team all along. Even if you've never used objects in your code, or have used them only sparingly, you now know more about how to design object-oriented programs than many experienced C++ programmers.

The relationships between objects are important to study, not just because well-linked objects contribute to code reuse and reduce clutter, but also because you will be working in a team. Objects that relate in meaningful ways are easier to read and maintain. You may decide to use the "Object Relationships" section as a reference when you design your programs.

Finally, you learned about creating successful abstractions and the two most important design considerations — audience and purpose.

The next chapter continues the design theme by explaining how to design your code with reuse in mind.

Designing for Reuse

WHAT'S IN THIS CHAPTER?

➤ The reuse philosophy: Why you should design code for reuse

➤ How to design reusable code

    ➤ How to use abstraction

    ➤ Three strategies for structuring your code for reuse

    ➤ Six strategies for designing usable interfaces

➤ How to reconcile generality with ease of use

Reusing libraries and other code in your programs is an important design strategy. However, it is only half of the *reuse* strategy. The other half is designing and writing the code that you can reuse in your programs. As you've probably discovered, there is a significant difference between well-designed and poorly designed libraries. Well-designed libraries are a pleasure to use, while poorly designed libraries can prod you to give up in disgust and write the code yourself. Whether you're writing a library explicitly designed for use by other programmers or merely deciding on a class hierarchy, you should design your code with reuse in mind. You never know when you'll need a similar piece of functionality in a subsequent project.

Chapter 2 introduced the design theme of reuse and explained how to apply this theme by incorporating libraries and other code in your designs. This chapter discusses the other side of reuse: designing reusable code. It builds on the object-oriented design principles described in Chapter 3 and introduces some new strategies and guidelines.

THE REUSE PHILOSOPHY

You should design code that both you and other programmers can reuse. This rule applies not only to libraries and frameworks that you specifically intend for other programmers to use, but also to any class, subsystem, or component that you design for a program.

You should always keep in mind the motto, "write once, use often." There are several reasons for this design approach:

➤ **Code is rarely used in only one program.** You can be sure that your code will be used again somehow, so design it correctly to begin with.

➤ **Designing for reuse saves time and money.** If you design your code in a way that precludes future use, you ensure that you or your partners will spend time reinventing the wheel later when you encounter a need for a similar piece of functionality.

➤ **Other programmers in your group must be able to use the code that you write.** You are probably not working alone on a project. Your coworkers will appreciate your efforts to offer them well-designed, functionality-packed libraries and pieces of code to use. Designing for reuse can also be called *cooperative coding.*

➤ **You will be the primary beneficiary of your own work.** Experienced programmers never throw away code. Over time, they build a personal library of evolving tools. You never know when you will need a similar piece of functionality in the future.

When you design or write code as an employee of a company, the company, not you, generally owns the intellectual property rights. It is often illegal to retain copies of your designs or code when you terminate your employment with the company. The same is also true when you are self-employed working for clients.

HOW TO DESIGN REUSABLE CODE

Reusable code fulfills two main goals. First, it is general enough to use for slightly different purposes or in different application domains. Program components with details of a specific application are difficult to reuse in other programs.

Reusable code is also easy to use. It doesn't require significant time to understand its interface or functionality. Programmers must be able to incorporate it readily into their applications.

The means of "delivering" your library to clients is also important. You could deliver it in source form and clients just incorporate your source into their project. Another option is to deliver a static library, which they link into their application, or you could deliver a Dynamic Link Library (DLL). Each of these delivery mechanisms can impose additional constraints on how you code your library.

Note that this chapter uses the term "client" to refer to a programmer who uses your interfaces. Don't confuse clients with "users" who run your programs. The chapter also uses the phrase "client code" to refer to code that is written to use your interfaces.

The most important strategy for designing reusable code is abstraction. Chapter 2 presented the real-world analogy of a television, which you can use through its interfaces without understanding how it works inside. Similarly, when you design code, you should clearly separate the interface from the implementation. This separation makes the code easier to use, primarily because clients do not need to understand the internal implementation details in order to use the functionality.

Abstraction separates code into interface and implementation, so designing reusable code focuses on these two main areas. First, you must structure the code appropriately. What class hierarchies will you use? Should you use templates? How should you divide the code into subsystems?

Second, you must design the *interfaces*, which are the "entries" into your library or code that programmers use to access the functionality you provide.

Use Abstraction

You learned about the principle of abstraction in Chapter 2 and read more about its application to object-oriented design in Chapter 3. To follow the principle of abstraction, you should provide interfaces to your code that hide the underlying implementation details. There should be a clear distinction between the interface and the implementation.

Using abstraction benefits both you and the clients who use your code. Clients benefit because they don't need to worry about the implementation details; they can take advantage of the functionality you offer without understanding how the code really works. You benefit because you can modify the underlying code without changing the interface to the code. Thus, you can provide upgrades and fixes without requiring clients to change their use. With dynamically linked libraries, clients don't even need to rebuild their executables. Finally, you both benefit because you, as the library writer, can specify in the interface exactly what interactions you expect and functionality you support. A clear separation of interfaces and implementations will prevent clients from using the library in ways that you didn't intend, which can otherwise cause unexpected behaviors and bugs.

 When designing your interface, do not expose implementation details to your clients.

Sometimes libraries require client code to keep information returned from one interface in order to pass it to another. This information is sometimes called a *handle* and is often used to keep track of specific instances that require state to be remembered between calls. If your library design requires a handle, don't expose its internals. Make that handle into an *opaque* class, in which the programmer can't access the internal data members. Don't require the client code to tweak variables inside this handle. As an example of a bad design, one of the authors actually used a library that required him to set a specific member of a structure in a supposedly opaque handle in order to turn on error logging.

Unfortunately, C++ is fundamentally unfriendly to the principle of good abstraction when writing classes. The syntax requires you to combine your public *interfaces and non-public (*private *or* protected*) data members and methods together in one class definition, thereby exposing some of the internal implementation details of the class to its clients. Chapter 7 describes some techniques for working around this in order to present clean interfaces.*

Abstraction is so important that it should guide your entire design. As part of every decision you make, ask yourself whether your choice fulfills the principle of abstraction. Put yourself in your clients' shoes and determine whether or not you're requiring knowledge of the internal implementation in the interface. You should rarely, if ever, make exceptions to this rule.

Structure Your Code for Optimal Reuse

You must consider reuse from the beginning of your design. The following strategies will help you organize your code properly. Note that all of these strategies focus on making your code general purpose. The second aspect of designing reusable code, providing ease of use, is more relevant to your interface design and is discussed later in this chapter.

Avoid Combining Unrelated or Logically Separate Concepts

When you design a library or framework, keep it focused on a single task or group of tasks. Don't combine unrelated concepts such as a random number generator and an XML parser.

Even when you are not designing code specifically for reuse, keep this strategy in mind. Entire programs are rarely reused on their own. Instead, pieces or subsystems of the programs are incorporated directly into other applications, or are adapted for slightly different uses. Thus, you should design your programs so that you divide logically separate functionality into distinct components that can be reused in different programs.

This program strategy models the real-world design principle of discrete, interchangeable parts. For example, you could take the tires off an old car and use them on a new car of a different model. Tires are separable components that are not tied to other aspects of the car. You don't need to bring the engine along with the tires!

You can employ the strategy of logical division in your program design on both the macro subsystem level and the micro class hierarchy level.

Divide Your Programs into Logical Subsystems

Design your subsystems as discrete components that can be reused independently. For example, if you are designing a networked game, keep the networking and graphical user interface aspects in separate subsystems. That way you can reuse either component without dragging in the other. For example, you might want to write a non-networked game, in which case you could reuse the graphical interface subsystem, but wouldn't need the networking aspect. Similarly, you could design a peer-to-peer file-sharing program, in which case you could reuse the networking subsystem but not the graphical user interface functionality.

Make sure to follow the principle of abstraction for each subsystem. Think of each subsystem as a miniature library for which you must provide a coherent and easy-to-use interface. Even if you're the only programmer who ever uses these miniature libraries, you will benefit from well-designed interfaces and implementations that separate logically distinct functionality.

Use Class Hierarchies to Separate Logical Concepts

In addition to dividing your program into logical subsystems, you should avoid combining unrelated concepts at the class level. For example, suppose you want to write a balanced binary tree structure for a multithreaded program. You decide that the tree data structure should allow only one thread at a time to access or modify the structure, so you incorporate locking into the data structure itself. However, what if you want to use this binary tree in another program that happens to be single-threaded? In that case, the locking is a waste of time, and might require your program to link with libraries that it could otherwise avoid. Even worse, your tree structure might not compile on a different platform because the locking code might not be cross-platform. Note that C++11 includes a multithreading library which includes locking mechanisms as explained in Chapter 22. The solution is to create a class hierarchy (introduced in Chapter 3) in which a thread-safe binary tree is a subclass of a generic binary tree. That way you can use the binary tree superclass in single-threaded programs without incurring the cost of locking unnecessarily. Figure 4-1 shows this hierarchy.

This strategy works well when there are two logical concepts, such as thread safety and binary trees. It becomes more complicated when there are three or more concepts. For example, suppose you want to provide both an *n*-ary tree and a binary tree, each of which could be thread-safe or not. Logically, the binary tree is a special-case of an *n*-ary tree, and so should be a subclass of an *n*-ary tree. Similarly, thread-safe structures should be subclasses of non-thread-safe structures. You can't provide these separations with a linear hierarchy. One possibility is to make the thread-safe aspect a mix-in class as shown in Figure 4-2.

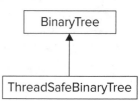

FIGURE 4-1

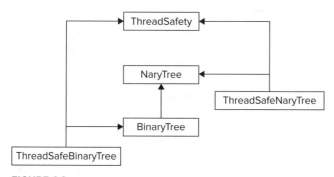

FIGURE 4-2

That hierarchy requires you to write five different classes, but the clear separation of functionality is worth the effort.

Use Aggregation to Separate Logical Concepts

Aggregation, discussed in Chapter 3, models the *has-a* relationship: Objects contain other objects to perform some aspects of their functionality. You can use aggregation to separate unrelated or related but separate functionality when inheritance is not appropriate.

For example, suppose you want to write a `Family` class to store the members of a family. Obviously, a tree data structure would be ideal for storing this information. Instead of integrating the code for the tree structure in your `Family` class, you should write a separate `Tree` class. Your `Family` class can then contain and use a `Tree` instance. To use the object-oriented terminology, the `Family` has-a `Tree`. With this technique, the tree data structure could be reused more easily in another program.

Eliminate User Interface Dependencies

If your library is a data manipulation library, you want to separate data manipulation from the user interface. This means that for those kinds of libraries you should never assume in which type of user interface the library will be used. As such, do not use `cout`, `cerr`, `cin`, `stdout`, `stderr`, or `stdin`, because if the library is used in the context of a graphical user interface these concepts may make no sense. For example, a Windows GUI-based application normally will not have any form of console I/O. If you think your library will only be used in GUI-based applications, you should still never pop up any kind of message box or other kind of notification to the end user; that is the responsibility of the caller to do. These kinds of dependencies not only result in poor reusability, but they prevent the client code from properly responding to an error, and handling it silently.

Use Templates for Generic Data Structures and Algorithms

C++ has a concept called *templates* allowing you to create structures that are generic with respect to a type or class. For example, you might have written code for an array of integers. If you subsequently would like an array of `doubles`, you need to rewrite and replicate all the code to work with `doubles`. The notion of a template is that the type becomes a parameter to the specification, and you can create a single body of code that can work on any type. Templates allow you to write both data structures and algorithms that work on any types.

The simplest example of this is the `std::vector` class which is part of the C++ Standard Template Library (STL), covered in detail in chapters 11 through 17. To create a `vector` of integers, you write `std::vector<int>`; to create a `vector` of `doubles` you write `std::vector<double>`. Template programming is in general extremely powerful but can be very complex. Luckily, it is possible to create rather simple usages of templates that parameterize according to a type. Chapters 19 and 20 explain the techniques to write your own templates, while this section discusses some of their important design aspects.

Whenever possible, you should use a generic design for data structures and algorithms instead of encoding specifics of a particular program. Don't write a balanced binary tree structure that stores only book objects. Make it generic, so that it can store objects of any type. That way you could use it in a bookstore, a music store, an operating system, or anywhere that you need a balanced binary tree. This strategy underlies the standard template library (STL). The STL provides generic data structures and algorithms that work on any types.

Why Templates Are Better Than Other Generic Programming Techniques

Templates are not the only mechanism for writing generic data structures. You can write generic structures in C and C++ by storing `void*` pointers instead of a specific type. Clients can use this structure to store anything they want by casting it to a `void*`. However, the main problem with this approach is that it is not *type-safe*: the containers are unable to check or enforce the types of the stored elements. You can cast any type to a `void*` to store in the structure, and when you remove the pointers from the data structure, you must cast them back to what you think they are. Because there are no checks involved, the results can be disastrous. Imagine a scenario where one programmer stores pointers to `int` in a data structure by first casting them to `void*`, but another programmer thinks they are pointers to `Process` objects. The second programmer will blithely cast the `void*` pointers to `Process*` pointers and try to use them as `Process*`s. Needless to say, the program will not work as expected.

A second approach is to write the data structure for a specific class. Through polymorphism, any subclass of that class can be stored in the structure. Java takes this approach to an extreme: It specifies that every class derives directly or indirectly from the `Object` class. The Java containers store `Object`s, so they can store objects of any type. However, this approach is also not truly type-safe. When you remove an object from the container, you must remember what it really is and down-cast it to the appropriate type.

Templates, on the other hand, are type-safe when used correctly. Each instantiation of a template stores only one type. Your program will not compile if you try to store different types in the same template instantiation.

Problems with Templates

Templates are not perfect. First of all, their syntax is confusing, especially for someone who has not used them before. Second, the parsing is difficult, and not all compilers fully support the entire C++ standard. If your compiler does not fully support the C++ standard regarding templates, your compiler might also not support the entire feature set of the STL. On the other hand, any compiler that fully supports the STL should be sufficiently powerful to support most template programming.

Furthermore, templates require homogeneous data structures, in which you can store only objects of the same type in a single structure. That is, if you write a templatized balanced binary tree, you can create one tree object to store `Process` objects and another tree object to store `int`s. You can't store both `int`s and `Process`es in the same tree. This restriction is a direct result of the type-safe nature of templates. Although type-safety is important, some programmers consider the homogeneity requirement a significant restriction.

Templates versus Inheritance

Programmers sometimes find it tricky to decide whether to use templates or inheritance. Here are some tips to help you make the decision.

Use templates when you want to provide identical functionality for different types. For example, if you want to write a generic sorting algorithm that works on any type, use templates. If you want to create a container that can store any type, use templates. The key concept is that the templatized structure or algorithm treats all types the same.

When you want to provide different behaviors for related types, use inheritance. For example, use inheritance if you want to provide two different, but similar, containers such as a queue and a priority queue.

Note that you can combine inheritance and templates. You could write a templatized queue that stores any type, with a subclass that is a templatized priority queue. Chapter 19 covers the details of the template syntax.

Provide Appropriate Checks and Safeguards

You should always design your programs to be as safe as possible for use by other programmers. The most important aspect of this guideline is to perform error checking in your code. For example, if your random number generator requires a non-negative integer for a seed, don't just trust the user to correctly pass a non-negative integer. Check the value that is passed in, and reject the call if it is invalid. A call can be rejected by returning an error code or by throwing an exception. Your library should never output error messages to a console or show an error in a message box or terminate the calling application.

As an analogy, consider an accountant who prepares income tax returns. When you hire an accountant, you provide him or her with all your financial information for the year. The accountant uses this information to fill out forms from the IRS. However, the accountant does not blindly fill out your information on the form, but instead makes sure the information makes sense. For example, if you own a house, but forget to specify the property tax you paid, the accountant will remind you to supply that information. Similarly, if you say that you paid $12,000 in mortgage interest, but made only $15,000 gross income, the accountant might gently ask you if you provided the correct numbers (or at least recommend more affordable housing).

You can think of the accountant as a "program" where the input is your financial information and the output is an income tax return. However, the value added by an accountant is not just that he or she fills out the forms. You choose to employ an accountant also because of the checks and safeguards that he or she provides. Similarly in programming, you should provide as many checks and safeguards as possible in your implementations.

Under no circumstances should a library decide to terminate the calling program. For the purpose of writing a library, you may safely forget that an `exit()` function or anything resembling its functionality, exist.

There are several techniques and language features that help you incorporate checks and safeguards in your programs. First, you can return an error code or a distinct value like `false` or `nullptr` or throw an exception to notify the client code of an error. Chapter 10 covers exceptions in detail. Second, use smart pointers that help you manage your dynamically allocated memory. Conceptually, a smart pointer is a pointer to dynamically allocated memory that remembers to free the memory when it goes out of scope. Smart pointers are discussed in Chapter 21. Third, use safe memory techniques as discussed in Chapter 21.

Design Usable Interfaces

In addition to abstracting and structuring your code appropriately, designing for reuse requires you to focus on the *interface* with which programmers interact. If you hide an ugly implementation behind a pretty interface, no one needs to know. However, if you provide a beautiful implementation behind a wretched interface, your library won't be much good.

Note that every subsystem and class in your program should have good interfaces, even if you don't intend them to be used in multiple programs. First of all, you never know when something will be reused. Second, a good interface is important even for the first use, especially if you are programming in a group and other programmers must use the code you design and write.

The main purpose of interfaces is to make the code easy to use, but some interface techniques can help you follow the principle of generality as well.

Design Interfaces That Are Easy To Use

Your interfaces should be easy to use. That doesn't mean that they must be trivial, but they should be as simple and intuitive as the functionality allows. You shouldn't require consumers of your library to wade through pages of source code in order to use a simple data structure, or go through contortions in their code to obtain the functionality they need. This section provides four specific strategies for designing interfaces that are easy to use.

Develop Easy-To-Use Interfaces

The best strategy for developing easy-to-use interfaces is to follow standard and familiar ways of doing things. When people encounter an interface similar to something they have used in the past, they will understand it better, adopt it more readily, and be less likely to use it improperly.

For example, suppose that you are designing the steering mechanism of a car. There are a number of possibilities: a joystick, two buttons for moving left or right, a sliding horizontal lever, or a good-old steering wheel. Which interface do you think would be easiest to use? Which interface do you think would sell the most cars? Consumers are familiar with steering wheels, so the answer to both questions is, of course, the steering wheel. Even if you developed another mechanism that provided superior performance and safety, you would have a tough time selling your product, let alone teaching people how to use it. When you have a choice between following standard interface models and branching out in a new direction, it's usually better to stick to the interface to which people are accustomed.

Innovation is important, of course, but you should focus on innovation in the underlying implementation, not in the interface. For example, consumers are excited about the innovative hybrid gasoline-electric engine in some car models. These cars are selling well in part because the interface to use them is identical to cars with standard engines.

Applied to C++, this strategy implies that you should develop interfaces that follow standards to which C++ programmers are accustomed. For example, C++ programmers expect the constructor and destructor of a class to initialize and clean up an object, respectively. When you design your classes, you should follow this standard. If you require programmers to call `initialize()` and `cleanup()` methods for initialization and cleanup instead of placing that functionality in the constructor and destructor, you will confuse everyone who tries to use your class. Because your class behaves differently from other C++ classes, programmers will take longer to learn how to use it and will be more likely to use it incorrectly by forgetting to call `initialize()` or `cleanup()`.

Always think about your interfaces from the perspective of someone using them. Do they make sense? Are they what you would expect?

C++ provides a language feature called *operator overloading* that can help you develop easy-to-use interfaces for your objects. Operator overloading allows you to write classes such that the standard operators work on them just as they work on built-in types like int and double. For example, you can write a Fraction class that allows you to add, subtract, and stream fractions like this:

```
Fraction f1(3,4);
Fraction f2(1,2);
Fraction sum;
Fraction diff;
sum = f1 + f2;
diff = f1 - f2;
cout << f1 << " " << f2 << endl;
```

Contrast that with the same behavior using method calls:

```
Fraction f1(3,4);
Fraction f2(1,2);
Fraction sum;
Fraction diff;
sum = f1.add(f2);
diff = f1.subtract(f2);
f1.print(cout);
cout << " ";
f2.print(cout);
cout << endl;
```

As you can see, operator overloading allows you to provide an easier to use interface for your classes. However, be careful not to abuse operator overloading. It's possible to overload the + operator so that it implements subtraction and the – operator so that it implements multiplication. Those implementations would be counterintuitive. This does not mean that each operator should always implement exactly the same behavior. For example, the string class implements the + operator to concatenate strings, which is an intuitive interface for string concatenation. The string class is discussed in detail in Chapter 14. See Chapters 7 and 18 for details on operator overloading.

Don't Omit Required Functionality

This strategy is twofold. First, include interfaces for all behaviors that clients could need. That might sound obvious at first. Returning to the car analogy, you would never build a car without a speedometer for the driver to view his or her speed! Similarly, you would never design a Fraction class without a mechanism for client code to access the nominator and denominator values.

However, other possible behaviors might be more obscure. This strategy requires you to anticipate all the uses to which clients might put your code. If you are thinking about the interface in one particular way, you might miss functionality that could be needed when clients use it differently. For example, suppose that you want to design a game board class. You might consider only the typical games, such as chess and checkers, and decide to support a maximum of one game piece per spot on the board. However, what if you later decide to write a backgammon game, which allows multiple pieces in one spot on the board? By precluding that possibility, you have ruled out the use of your game board as a backgammon board.

Obviously, anticipating every possible use for your library is difficult, if not impossible. Don't feel compelled to agonize over potential future uses in order to design the perfect interface. Just give it some thought and do the best you can.

The second part of this strategy is to include as much functionality in the implementation as possible. Don't require client code to specify information that you already know in the implementation, or could know if you designed it differently. For example, if your library requires a temporary file, don't make the clients of your library specify that path. They don't care what file you use; find some other way to determine an appropriate temporary file path.

Furthermore, don't require library users to perform unnecessary work to amalgamate results. If your random number library uses a random number algorithm that calculates the low-order and high-order bits of a random number separately, combine the numbers before giving them to the user.

Present Uncluttered Interfaces

In order to avoid omitting functionality in their interfaces, some programmers go to the opposite extreme: They include every possible piece of functionality imaginable. Programmers who use the interfaces are never left without the means to accomplish a task. Unfortunately, the interface might be so cluttered that they never figure out how to do it!

Don't provide unnecessary functionality in your interfaces; keep them clean and simple. It might appear at first that this guideline directly contradicts the previous strategy of avoiding omitting necessary functionality. Although one strategy to avoid omitting functionality would be to include every imaginable interface, that is not a sound strategy. You should include *necessary* functionality and omit useless or counterproductive interfaces.

Consider cars again. You drive a car by interacting with only a few components: the steering wheel, the brake and accelerator pedals, the gearshift, the mirrors, the speedometer, and a few other dials on your dashboard. Now, imagine a car dashboard that looked like an airplane cockpit, with hundreds of dials, levers, monitors, and buttons. It would be unusable! Driving a car is so much easier than flying an airplane that the interface can be much simpler: You don't need to view your altitude, communicate with control towers, or control the myriad components in an airplane such as the wings, engines, and landing gear.

Additionally, from the library development perspective, smaller libraries are easier to maintain. If you try to make everyone happy, then you have more room to make mistakes, and if your implementation is complicated enough so that everything is intertwined, even one mistake can render the library useless.

Unfortunately, the idea of designing uncluttered interfaces looks good on paper, but is remarkably hard to put into practice. The rule is ultimately subjective: You decide what's necessary and what's not. Of course, your clients will be sure to tell you when you get it wrong!

Provide Documentation and Comments

Regardless of how easy to use you make your interfaces, you should supply documentation for their use. You can't expect programmers to use your library properly unless you tell them how to do it. Think of your library or code as a product for other programmers to consume. Your product should have documentation explaining its proper use.

There are two ways to provide documentation for your interfaces: comments in the interfaces themselves and external documentation. You should strive to provide both. Most public APIs provide only external documentation: Comments are a scarce commodity in many of the standard Unix and Windows header files. In Unix, the documentation usually comes in the form of online manuals called *man pages*. In Windows, the documentation usually accompanies the integrated development environment.

Despite the fact that most APIs and libraries omit comments in the interfaces themselves, we actually consider this form of documentation the most important. You should never give out a "naked" header file that contains only code. Even if your comments repeat exactly what's in the external documentation, it is less intimidating to look at a header file with friendly comments than one with only code. Even the best programmers still like to see written language every so often!

Some programmers use tools to create documentation automatically from comments. Chapter 5 discusses this technique in more detail.

Whether you provide comments, external documentation, or both, the documentation should describe the *behavior* of the library, not the *implementation*. The behavior includes the inputs, outputs, error conditions and handling, intended uses, and performance guarantees. For example, documentation describing a call to generate a single random number should specify that it takes no parameters, returns an integer in a previously specified range, and should list all the exceptions that might be thrown when something goes wrong. This documentation should not explain the details of the linear congruence algorithm for actually generating the number. Providing too much implementation detail in interface comments is probably the single most common mistake in interface development. Many developers have seen perfectly good separations of interface and implementation ruined by comments in the interface that are more appropriate for library maintainers than clients.

Of course you should also document your internal implementation, just don't make it publicly available as part of your interface. Chapter 5 provides details on the appropriate use of comments in your code.

Design General-Purpose Interfaces

The interfaces should be general purpose enough that they can be adapted to a variety of tasks. If you encode specifics of one application in a supposedly general interface, it will be unusable for any other purpose. Here are some guidelines to keep in mind.

Provide Multiple Ways to Perform the Same Functionality

In order to satisfy all your "customers," it is sometimes helpful to provide multiple ways to perform the same functionality. Use this technique judiciously, however, because overapplication can easily lead to cluttered interfaces.

Consider cars again. Most new cars these days provide remote keyless entry systems, with which you can unlock your car by pressing a button on a key fob. However, these cars always provide a standard key that you can use to physically unlock the car, for example when the battery in the key fob is empty. Although these two methods are redundant, most customers appreciate having both options.

Sometimes there are similar situations in program interface design. For example, suppose that one of your methods takes a string. You might want to provide two interfaces: one that takes a C++ string object and one that takes a C-style character pointer. Although it's possible to convert between the two, different programmers prefer different types of strings, so it's helpful to cater to both approaches.

Note that this strategy should be considered an exception to the "uncluttered" rule in interface design. There are a few situations where the exception is appropriate, but you should most often follow the "uncluttered" rule.

Provide Customizability

In order to increase the flexibility of your interfaces, provide customizability. Customizability can be as simple as allowing a client to turn on or off error logging. The basic premise of customizability is that it allows you to provide the same basic functionality to every client, but gives clients the ability to tweak it slightly.

You can allow greater customizability through function pointers and template parameters. For example, you could allow clients to set their own error-handling routines. This technique is an application of the decorator pattern described in Chapter 29.

The STL takes this customizability strategy to the extreme and actually allows clients to specify their own memory allocators for containers. If you want to use this feature, you must write a memory allocator object that follows the STL guidelines and adheres to the required interfaces. Each container in the STL takes an allocator as one of its template parameters. Chapter 17 provides the details.

Reconciling Generality and Ease of Use

The two goals of ease of use and generality sometimes appear to conflict. Often, introducing generality increases the complexity of the interfaces. For example, suppose that you need a graph structure in a map program to store cities. In the interest of generality, you might use templates to write a generic map structure for any type, not just cities. That way, if you need to write a network simulator in your next program, you could employ the same graph structure to store routers in the network. Unfortunately, by using templates, you made the interface a little clumsier and harder to use, especially if the potential client is not familiar with templates.

However, generality and ease of use are not mutually exclusive. Although in some cases increased generality may decrease ease of use, it is possible to design interfaces that are both general purpose and straightforward to use. Here are two guidelines you can follow.

Supply Multiple Interfaces

In order to reduce complexity in your interfaces while still providing enough functionality, you can provide two separate interfaces. For example, you could write a generic networking library with two separate facets: One presents the networking interfaces useful for games, and one presents the networking interfaces useful for the HyperText Transport Protocol (HTTP) web browsing protocol.

Make Common Functionality Easy To Use

When you provide a general-purpose interface, some functionality will be used more often than other functionality. You should make the commonly used functionality easy to use, while still providing the option for the more advanced functionality. Returning to the map program, you might want to provide an option for clients of the map to specify names of cities in different languages. English is so predominant that you could make that the default but provide an extra option to change languages. That way most clients will not need to worry about setting the language, but those who want to will be able to do so.

SUMMARY

By reading this chapter, you learned *why* you should design reusable code and *how* you should do it. You read about the philosophy of reuse, summarized as "write once, use often," and learned that reusable code should be both general purpose and easy to use. You also discovered that designing reusable code requires you to use abstraction, to structure your code appropriately, and to design good interfaces.

This chapter presented three specific tips for structuring your code: Avoid combining unrelated or logically separate concepts, use templates for generic data structures and algorithms, and provide appropriate checks and safeguards.

The chapter also presented six strategies for designing interfaces: Develop easy-to-use interfaces, don't omit required functionality, present uncluttered interfaces, provide documentation and comments, provide multiple ways to perform the same functionality, and provide customizability. It concluded with two tips for reconciling the often-conflicting demands of generality and ease of use: Supply multiple interfaces and make common functionality easy to use.

The next (and last) chapter of Part I discusses coding style, which is important especially when working on a project with many people.

5

Coding with Style

If you're going to spend several hours each day in front of a keyboard writing code, you should take some pride in all that work. Writing code that gets the job done is only part of a programmer's work. After all, anybody can learn the fundamentals of coding. It takes a true master to code with style.

This chapter explores the question of what makes good code. Along the way, you'll see several approaches to C++ style. As you will discover, simply changing the style of code can make it appear very different. For example, C++ code written by Windows programmers often has its own style, using Windows conventions. It almost looks like a completely different language than C++ code written by Mac OS programmers. Exposure to several different styles will help you avoid that sinking feeling you get when opening up a C++ source file that barely resembles the C++ you thought you knew.

THE IMPORTANCE OF LOOKING GOOD

Writing code that is stylistically "good" takes time. You could probably whip together a program to parse an XML file in a couple of hours. Writing the same program with functional decomposition, adequate comments, and a clean structure would probably take days. Is it really worth it?

Thinking Ahead

How confident would you be in your code if a new programmer had to work with it a year from now? One of the authors, faced with a growing mess of web application code, encouraged his team to think about a hypothetical intern who would be starting in a year. How would this poor intern ever get up to speed on the code base when there was no documentation and scary multiple-page functions? When you're writing code, imagine that somebody new will have to maintain it in the future. Will you even remember how it works? What if you're not available to help? Well-written code avoids these problems because it is easy to read and understand.

Elements of Good Style

It is difficult to enumerate the characteristics of code that make it "stylistically good." Over time, you'll find styles that you like and notice useful techniques in code that others wrote. Perhaps more important, you'll encounter horrible code that teaches you what to avoid. However, good code shares several universal tenets that will be explored in this chapter.

➤ Documentation

➤ Decomposition

➤ Naming

➤ Use of the Language

➤ Formatting

DOCUMENTING YOUR CODE

In the programming context, documentation usually refers to comments contained in the source files. Comments are your opportunity to tell the world what was going through your head when you wrote the accompanying code. They are a place to say anything that isn't obvious from looking at the code itself.

Reasons to Write Comments

It may seem obvious that writing comments is a good idea, but have you ever stopped to think about why you need to comment your code? Sometimes programmers recognize the importance of commenting without fully understanding why comments are important. There are several reasons, all of which are explored in this chapter.

Commenting to Explain Usage

One reason to use comments is to explain how clients should interact with the code. Each publicly accessible function or method in a header file should have a comment explaining what it does. Some organizations prefer to formalize these comments by explicitly listing the purpose of each method, what its arguments are, what values it returns, and possible exceptions it can throw.

Providing a comment with public methods accomplishes two things. First, you are given the opportunity to state, in English, anything that you can't state in code. For example, there's really no way in C++ code to indicate that the saveRecord() method of a database object can only be called after the openDatabase() method is called. A comment, however, can be the perfect place to note this restriction, as follows.

```
/*
 * saveRecord()
 *
 * Saves the given record to the database.
 *
 * This method will throw a "DatabaseNotOpenedException"
 * if the openDatabase() method was not called first.
 */
```

The second effect of a comment on a public method can be to state usage information. The C++ language forces you to specify the return type of a method, but it does not provide a way for you to say what the returned value actually represents. For example, the declaration of the saveRecord() method may indicate that it returns an int, but the client reading that declaration wouldn't know what the int means. Other ancillary data can be included in a comment as well, as shown in the following.

```
/*
 * saveRecord()
 *
 * Saves the given record to the database.
 *
 * Parameters:
 *     Record& rec: the record to save to the database.
 * Returns: int
 *     An integer representing the ID of the saved record.
 * Throws:
 *     DatabaseNotOpenedException if the openDatabase() method was not
 *     called first.
 */
```

Sometimes, the parameters to, and the return type from a function are generic and can be used to pass all kinds of information. In that case you need to clearly document what exact type is being passed. For example, message handlers in Windows accept two parameters, LPARAM and WPARAM, and can return an LRESULT. All three can be used to pass anything you like, but you cannot change the type of them. By using type casting, they can for example be used to pass a simple integer or to pass a pointer to some object. Your documentation could look as follows.

```
 * Parameters:
 *     WPARAM wParam: (WPARAM)(int): An integer representing an ID.
 *     LPARAM lParam: (LPARAM)(string*): A string representing...
 * Returns: (LRESULT)(Record*)
 *     A pointer to a Record object or nullptr in case of an error.
```

Most editors allow you to bind keystrokes to perform certain actions. You could bind a keystroke so that the editor automatically inserts a standard commenting block which you subsequently fill in with the right information. For example, the keystroke could automatically insert the following comment template.

```
/*
 * func()
 *
 * Description of the function.
 *
 * Parameters:
 *     int param1: parameter 1.
 * Returns: int
 *     An integer representing...
 * Throws:
 *     Exception1 if...
 * Notes:
 *     Additional notes...
 */
```

Commenting to Explain Complicated Code

Good comments are also important inside the actual source code. In a simple program that processes input from the user and writes a result to the console, it is probably easy to read through and understand all of the code. In the professional world, however, you will often need to write code that is algorithmically complex or too esoteric to understand simply by inspection.

Consider the code that follows. It is well written, but it may not be immediately apparent what it is doing. You might recognize the algorithm if you have seen it before, but a newcomer probably wouldn't understand the way the code works.

```
void sort(int inArray[], int inSize)
{
    for (int i = 1; i < inSize; i++) {
        int element = inArray[i];
        int j = i - 1;
        while (j >= 0 && inArray[j] > element) {
            inArray[j+1] = inArray[j];
            j--;
        }
        inArray[j+1] = element;
    }
}
```

A better approach would be to include comments that describe the algorithm that is being used. In the modified function that follows, a thorough comment at the top explains the algorithm at a high level, and inline comments explain specific lines that may be confusing.

```
/*
 * Implements the "insertion sort" algorithm. The algorithm separates the
 * array into two parts--the sorted part and the unsorted part. Each
 * element, starting at position 1, is examined. Everything earlier in the
 * array is in the sorted part, so the algorithm shifts each element over
 * until the correct position is found for the current element. When the
 * algorithm finishes with the last element, the entire array is sorted.
 */
```

```
void sort(int inArray[], int inSize)
{
    // Start at position 1 and examine each element.
    for (int i = 1; i < inSize; i++) {
        int element = inArray[i];
        // j marks the position in the sorted part of the array.
        int j = i - 1;
        // As long as the current slot in the sorted array is higher than
        // the element, shift the slot over and move backwards.
        while (j >= 0 && inArray[j] > element) {
            inArray[j+1] = inArray[j];
            j--;
        }
        // At this point the current position in the sorted array
        // is *not* greater than the element, so this is its new position.
        inArray[j+1] = element;
    }
}
```

The new code is certainly more verbose, but a reader unfamiliar with sorting algorithms would be much more likely to understand it with the comments included. In some organizations, inline comments are frowned upon. In such cases, writing clean code and having good comments at the top of the function becomes vital.

Commenting to Convey Metainformation

Another reason to use comments is to provide information at a higher level than the code itself. This *metainformation* provides details about the creation of the code without addressing the specifics of its behavior. For example, your organization may want to keep track of the original author of each method. You can also use metainformation to cite external documents or refer to other code.

The following example shows several instances of metainformation, including the author of the file, the date it was created, and the specific feature it addresses. It also includes inline comments expressing metadata, such as the bug number that corresponds to a line of code and a reminder to revisit a possible problem in the code later.

```
/*
 * Author:  marcg
 * Date:    110412
 * Feature: PRD version 3, Feature 5.10
 */
int saveRecord(Record& rec)
{
    if (!bDatabaseOpen) {
        throw DatabaseNotOpenedException();
    }
    int id = getDB()->saveRecord(rec);
    if (id == -1) return -1;  // Added to address bug #142 - jsmith 110428
    rec.setId(id);
    // TODO: What if setId() throws an exception? - akshayr 110501
    return id
}
```

A change-log could also be included at the beginning of each file. The following shows a possible example of such a change-log.

```
/*
 * Date      | Change
 *----------+-------------------------------------------------
 * 110413   | REQ #005: <marcg> Do not normalize to maximum
 *          | value if values > 32767.
 * 110417   | REQ #006: <marcg> use nullptr instead of NULL.
 */
```

However, this might not be necessary when you use a source code control solution, discussed in Chapter 23. Every source code control solution, for example CVS, supports check-in comments. You should check-in each change request separately. For example, if you need to implement two change requests in one file, you should check-out the file, implement the first change request and check-in the file with the appropriate change-log comment. Only then you can check-out the file again and work on the second change request. If you want to work on both change requests at the same time, you can branch the source file and start working on the first change request in one branch and work on the second change request in the second branch. When implementation is finished, you can merge both branches back together with appropriate change-log comments for each branch. With this method you don't need to manually keep a change-log in the beginning of each file.

It's easy to go overboard with comments. A good approach is to discuss which types of comments are most useful with your group and form a policy. For example, if one member of the group uses a "TODO" comment to indicate code that still needs work, but nobody else knows about this convention, the code in need could be overlooked.

 If your group decides to use metainformation comments, make sure that you all include the same information or your files will be inconsistent.

Commenting Styles

Every organization has a different approach to commenting code. In some environments, a particular style is mandated to give the code a common standard for documentation. Other times, the quantity and style of commenting is left up to the programmer. The following examples depict several approaches to commenting code.

Commenting Every Line

One way to avoid lack of documentation is to force yourself to overdocument by including a comment for every line. Commenting every line of code should ensure that there's a specific reason for everything you write. In reality, such heavy commenting on a large-scale basis is unscalable, messy, and tedious. For example, consider the following useless comments.

```
int result;                    // Declare an integer to hold the result.
result = doodad.getResult();   // Get the doodad's result.
if (result % 2 ==  0) {        // If the result mod 2 is 0 ...
   logError();                 // then log an error,
```

```
} else {                    // otherwise ...
    logSuccess();           // log success.
}                           // End if/else
return result;              // Return the result
```

The comments in this code express each line as part of an easily readable English story. This is entirely useless if you assume that the reader has at least basic C++ skills. These comments don't add any additional information to code. Specifically, look at this line:

```
if (result % 2 == 0) {      // If the result mod 2 is 0 ...
```

The comment is just an English translation of the code. It doesn't say *why* the programmer has used the mod operator on the result with the value 2. A better comment would be:

```
if (result % 2 == 0) {      // If the result is even ...
```

The modified comment, while still fairly obvious to most programmers, gives additional information about the code. The result is "modded" by 2 because the code needs to check if the result is even.

Despite its tendency to be verbose and superfluous, heavy commenting can be useful in cases where the code would otherwise be difficult to comprehend. The following code also comments every line, but these comments are actually helpful.

```
// Call the calculate method with the default values.
result = doodad.calculate(getDefaultStart(), getDefaultEnd(), getDefaultOffset());
// To determine success or failure, we need to bitwise AND the result with
// the processor-specific mask (see "Doodad API v1.6", page 201).
result &= getProcessorMask();
// Set the user field value based on the "Marigold Formula."
// (see "Doodad API v1.6", page 136)
setUserField((result + kMarigoldOffset) / MarigoldConstant) + MarigoldConstant);
```

This code is taken out of context, but the comments give you a good idea of what each line does. Without them, the calculations involving & and the mysterious "Marigold Formula" would be difficult to decipher.

 Commenting every line of code is usually untenable, but if the code is complicated enough to require it, don't just translate the code to English: explain what's really going on.

Prefix Comments

Your group may decide to begin all of your source files with a standard comment. This is an excellent opportunity to document important information about the program and specific file. Examples of information that you might want to document at the top of every file include the following.

➤   The last-modified date

➤   The original author

➤   A change-log as described earlier

➤ The feature ID addressed by the file

➤ Copyright information

➤ A brief description of the file/class

➤ Incomplete features

➤ Known bugs

Your development environment may allow you to create a template that automatically starts new files with your prefix comment. Some source control systems such as Concurrent Versions System (CVS) can even assist by filling in metadata. For example, if your comment contains the string Id, CVS will automatically expand the comment to include the author, filename, revision, and date.

An example of a prefix comment is shown here:

```
/*
 * $Id: Watermelon.cpp,v 1.6 2004/03/10 12:52:33 klep Exp $
 *
 * Implements the basic functionality of a watermelon. All units are expressed
 * in terms of seeds per cubic centimeter. Watermelon theory is based on the
 * white paper "Algorithms for Watermelon Processing."
 *
 * The following code is (c) copyright 2011, FruitSoft, Inc. ALL RIGHTS RESERVED
 */
```

Fixed-Format Comments

Writing comments in a standard format that can be parsed by external document builders is an increasingly popular programming practice. In the Java language, programmers can write comments in a standard format that allows a tool called JavaDoc to create hyperlinked documentation for the project automatically. For C++, a free tool called Doxygen (available at www.doxygen.org) parses comments to automatically build HTML documentation, class diagrams, UNIX man pages, and other useful documents. Doxygen even recognizes and parses JavaDoc-style comments in C++ programs. The code that follows shows JavaDoc-style comments that are recognized by Doxygen.

```
/**
 * Implements the basic functionality of a watermelon
 * TODO: Implement updated algorithms!
 */
class Watermelon
{
    public:
        /**
         * @param initialSeeds The starting number of seeds
         */
        Watermelon(int initialSeeds);
        /**
         * Computes the seed ratio, using the Marigold algorithm.
         * @param slowCalc Whether or not to use long (slow) calculations
         * @return The marigold ratio
         */
        double calcSeedRatio(bool slowCalc);
};
```

Doxygen recognizes the C++ syntax and special comment directives such as @param and @return to generate customizable output. An example of a Doxygen-generated HTML class reference is shown in Figure 5-1.

Automatically generated documentation like the file shown in Figure 5-1 can be helpful during development because it allows developers to browse through a high-level description of classes and their relationships. Your group can easily customize a tool like Doxygen to work with the style of comments that you have adopted. Ideally, your group would set up a machine that builds documentation on a daily basis.

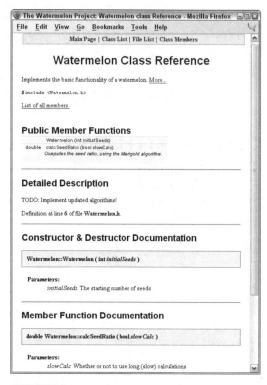

FIGURE 5-1

Ad Hoc Comments

Most of the time, you use comments on an as-needed basis. Here are some guidelines for comments that appear within the body of your code.

➤ Do your best to avoid offensive or derogatory language. You never know who might look at your code some day.

➤ Liberal use of inside jokes is generally considered okay. Check with your manager.

➤ Reference bug numbers or feature IDs when possible.

➤ Include your initials and the date if you think somebody might want to follow up on the comment with you in the future.

➤ Resist the temptation to include somebody *else's* initials and the date to avoid having to take responsibility for the code. This could get you fired.

➤ Remember to update your comments when you update the code. Nothing is more confusing than code that is fully documented with incorrect information.

➤ If you use comments to separate a function into sections, consider whether the function might be broken into multiple, smaller functions.

Self-Documenting Code

Well-written code doesn't always need abundant commenting. The best code is written to be readable. If you find yourself adding a comment for every line, consider whether the code could be rewritten to better match what you are saying in the comments. Remember that C++ is a language. Its main purpose is to tell the computer what to do, but the semantics of the language can also be used to explain its meaning to a reader.

Another way of writing self-documenting code is to break up, or *decompose*, your code into smaller pieces. Decomposition is covered in detail in the material that follows.

 Good code is naturally readable and only requires comments to provide useful additional information.

Comments in This Book

The code examples you will see in this book often use comments to explain complicated code or to point things out to you that may not be evident. We usually omit any prefix comments and fixed-format comments to save space, but we wholeheartedly advocate their inclusion in professional C++ projects.

DECOMPOSITION

Decomposition is the practice of breaking up code into smaller pieces. There is nothing more daunting in the world of coding than opening up a file of source code to find 300-line functions and massive nested blocks of code. Ideally, each function or method should accomplish a single task. Any subtasks of significant complexity should be decomposed into separate functions or methods. For example, if somebody asks you what a method does and you answer "First it does A, then it does B; then, if C, it does D; otherwise, it does E," you should probably have separate helper methods for A, B, C, D, and E.

Decomposition is not an exact science. Some programmers will say that no function should be longer than a page of printed code. That may be a good rule of thumb, but you could certainly find a quarter-page of code that is desperately in need of decomposition. Another rule of thumb is whether the code is long or short, if you squint your eyes and look at the format of the code without reading the actual content, it shouldn't appear too dense in any one area. For example, Figures 5-2 and 5-3 show code that has been purposely blurred so that you can't read the content. It should be obvious that the code in Figure 5-3 has better decomposition than the code in Figure 5-2.

FIGURE 5-2

FIGURE 5-3

Decomposition through Refactoring

Sometimes when you've had a few coffees and you're really in the programming zone, you start coding so fast that you end up with code that does exactly what it's supposed to do, but is far from pretty. All programmers do this from time to time. Short periods of vigorous coding are sometimes the most productive times in the course of a project. Dense code also arises over the course of time as code is modified. As new requirements and bug fixes emerge, existing code is amended with small modifications. The computing term *cruft* refers to the gradual accumulation of small amounts of code that eventually turns a once-elegant piece of code into a mess of patches and special cases.

Refactoring is the act of restructuring your code. The following are a couple of example techniques that you can use to refactor your code. Consult a refactoring book listed in Appendix B to get a more comprehensive list.

➤ Techniques that allow for more abstraction:

➤ **Encapsulate Field:** Make a field protected and give access to it with getter and setter methods.

➤ **Generalize Type:** Create more general types to allow for more code sharing.

➤ Techniques for breaking code apart into more logical pieces:

➤ **Extract Method:** Turn part of a larger method into a new method to make it easier to understand.

➤ **Extract Class:** Move part of the code from an existing class into a new class.

➤ Techniques for improving names and the location of code:

➤ **Move Method or Move Field:** Move to a more appropriate class or source file.

➤ **Rename Method or Rename Field:** Change the name to better reveal its purpose.

➤ **Pull Up:** In OOP, move to a superclass.

➤ **Push Down:** In OOP, move to a subclass.

Whether your code starts its life as a dense block of unreadable cruft or it just evolves that way, refactoring is necessary to periodically purge the code of accumulated hacks. Through refactoring, you revisit existing code and rewrite it to make it more readable and maintainable. Refactoring is an opportunity to revisit the decomposition of code. If the purpose of the code has changed or if it was never decomposed in the first place, when you refactor the code, squint at it and determine if it needs to be broken down into smaller parts.

Decomposition by Design

If you use modular decomposition and approach every module, method, or function by considering what pieces of it you can put off until later, your programs will generally be less dense and more organized than if you implemented every feature in its entirety as you coded.

Of course, we still advocate that you do some design of your program *before* jumping into the code.

Decomposition in This Book

You will see decomposition in many of the examples in this book. In many cases, we refer to methods for which we don't show the implementations because they are not relevant to the example and would take up too much space.

NAMING

Your computer doesn't care at all what you name your variables and functions. The compiler and linker also don't care about how you name things as long as the names don't result in conflicts with other variables or functions. Names exist only to help you and your fellow programmers work with the individual elements of your program. Given this purpose, it is surprising how often programmers use unspecific or inappropriate names in their programs.

Choosing a Good Name

The best name for a variable, method, function, or class accurately describes the purpose of the item. Names can also imply additional information, such as the type or specific usage. Of course, the real test is whether other programmers understand what you are trying to convey with a particular name.

There are no set-in-stone rules for naming other than the rules that work for your organization. However, there are some names that are rarely appropriate. The following table shows some names at the two extreme ends of the naming continuum.

GOOD NAMES	BAD NAMES
`srcName, dstName` Distinguishes two objects	`thing1, thing2` Too general
`gSettings` Conveys global status	`globalUserSpecificSettingsAndPreferences` Too long
`mNameCounter` Conveys data member status	`mNC` Too obscure, concise
`performCalculations()` Simple, accurate	`doAction()` Too general, imprecise
`mTypeString` Easy on the eyes	`_typeSTR256` A name only a computer could love
`mWelshRarebit` Good use of inside joke	`mIHateLarry` Inappropriate inside joke

The previous table mentioned `mNC`. As a member variable this is too obscure and too concise. However, short names are allowed for local variables with a very limited scope. For example:

```
if (bError) {
    CString s;
    s.Format(...);
    AfxMessageBox(s);
}
```

The details of CString, Format, and AfxMessageBox are not important for this discussion. What is important is that the variable name s is very short and not mnemonic, but it has a scope of only three lines. Its use is allowed because it is unlikely to be confused with any other variable in any other context.

Naming Conventions

Selecting a name doesn't always require a lot of thought and creativity. In many cases, you'll want to use standard techniques for naming. Following are some of the types of data for which you can make use of standard names.

Counters

Early in your programming career, you probably saw code that used the variable "i" as a counter. It is customary to use i and j as counters and inner-loop counters, respectively. Be careful with nested loops, however. It's a common mistake to refer to the "ith" element when you really mean the "jth" element. Some programmers prefer using counters like outerLoopIndex and innerLoopIndex instead.

Prefixes

Many programmers begin their variable names with a letter that provides some information about the variable's type or usage. On the other hand, there are as many programmers who frown upon using any kind of prefix because they could make evolving code less maintainable in the future. For example, if a member variable is changed from static to non-static, this would mean that you have to rename all the uses of that name. This is often time consuming and so most programmers don't bother to rename the variables. As the code evolves, the declarations of the variables change but the names do not. This results in names giving the illusion of conveying semantics but in fact they convey the wrong semantics.

However, often you don't have a choice and you need to follow the guidelines for your company. The following table shows some potential prefixes.

PREFIX	EXAMPLE NAME	LITERAL PREFIX MEANING	USAGE
m m_ _	mData m_data _data	"member"	Data member within a class.
s ms ms_	sLookupTable msLookupTable ms_lookupTable	"static"	Static variable or data member.
k	kMaximumLength	"konstant" (German for "constant")	A constant value. Some programmers use all uppercase names to indicate constants.
b	bCompleted	"Boolean"	Designates a Boolean value.
n mNum	nLines mNumLines	"number"	A data member that is also a counter. Since an "n" looks similar to an "m," some programmers instead use mNum as a prefix, as in mNumLines.

Getters and Setters

If your class contains a data member, such as `mStatus`, it is customary to provide access to the member via a getter called `getStatus()` and a setter called `setStatus()`. The C++ language has no prescribed naming for these methods, but your organization will probably want to adopt this or a similar naming scheme.

Capitalization

There are many different ways of capitalizing names in your code. As with most elements of coding style, the most important thing is that your group standardizes on an approach and that all members adopt that approach. One way to get messy code is to have some programmers naming classes in all lowercase with underscores representing spaces (`priority_queue`) and others using capitals with each subsequent word capitalized (`PriorityQueue`). Variables and data members almost always start with a lowercase letter and either use underscores (`my_queue`) or capitals (`myQueue`) to indicate word breaks. Functions and methods are traditionally capitalized in C++, but, as you've seen, in this book we have adopted the style of lowercase functions and methods to distinguish them from class names. We adopt a similar style of capitalizing letters to indicate word boundaries for class and data member names.

Namespaced Constants

Imagine that you are writing a program with a graphical user interface. The program has several menus, including File, Edit, and Help. To represent the ID of each menu, you may decide to use a constant. A perfectly reasonable name for a constant referring to the Help menu ID is `kHelp`.

The name `kHelp` will work fine until one day you add a Help button to the main window. You also need a constant to refer to the ID of the button, but `kHelp` is already taken.

A recommended solution for this is to put your constants in different namespaces, which are discussed in Chapter 1. You create two namespaces: `Menu` and `Button`. Each namespace has a `kHelp` constant and you use them as `Menu::kHelp` and `Button::kHelp`.

Hungarian Notation

Hungarian Notation is a variable and data member naming convention that is popular with Microsoft Windows programmers. The basic idea is that instead of using single-letter prefixes such as `m`, you should use more verbose prefixes to indicate additional information. The following line of code displays the use of Hungarian Notation:

```
char* pszName; // psz means "pointer to a null-terminated string"
```

The term *Hungarian Notation* arose from the fact that its inventor, Charles Simonyi, is Hungarian. Some also say that it accurately reflects the fact that programs using Hungarian Notation end up looking as if they were written in a foreign language. For this latter reason, some programmers tend to dislike Hungarian Notation. In this book, we use prefixes, but not Hungarian Notation. We feel that adequately named variables don't need much additional context information besides the prefix. We think that a data member named `mName` says it all.

Good names convey information about their purpose without making the code unreadable.

USING LANGUAGE FEATURES WITH STYLE

The C++ language lets you do all sorts of terribly unreadable things. Take a look at this wacky code:

```
i++ + ++i;
```

This is unreadable but more importantly, its behavior is undefined by the C++ standard. The problem is that i++ uses the value of i but has a side effect of incrementing it. The standard does not say when this incrementing should be done, only that the side effect (increment) should be visible after the sequence point "; ", but the compiler can do it at any point in time during the execution of that line. It's impossible to know which value of i will be used for the ++i part. Running this code with different compilers and platforms can result in different values. The following is another example of code with undefined behavior which you should avoid.

```
a[i] = i++;
```

With all the power that the C++ language offers, it is important to consider how the language features can be used towards stylistic good instead of evil.

Use Constants

Bad code is often littered with "magic numbers." In some function, the code might be using 2.71828. Why 2.71828? What does that value mean? People with a mathematical background might find it obvious that this represents an approximation of the transcendental value e, but most people don't know this. The language offers constants to give a symbolic name to a value that doesn't change, such as 2.71828.

```
const double kApproximationForE = 2.71828;
```

Use References Instead of Pointers

Traditionally, C++ programmers learn C first. In C, pointers were the only pass-by-reference mechanism, and they certainly worked just fine for many years. Pointers are still required in some cases, but in many situations you can switch to references. If you learned C first, you probably think that references don't really add any new functionality to the language. You might think that they merely introduce a new syntax for functionality that pointers could already provide.

There are several advantages to using references rather than pointers. First, references are safer than pointers because they don't deal directly with memory addresses and cannot be nullptr. Second, references are more stylistically pleasing than pointers because they use the same syntax as stack variables, avoiding symbols such as * and &. They're also easy to use, so you should have no problem adopting references into your style palette. Unfortunately, some programmers think that if they see an & in a function call, they know the called function is going to change the object and if they don't see the & it must be pass-by-value. With references, they say they don't know if the function is going to change the object unless they look at the function prototype. This is a wrong way of thinking. Passing in a pointer does not automatically mean that the object will be modified, because the parameter might be const T*. Both passing a pointer and a reference can modify the object or not depending on whether the function prototype uses const T*, T*, const T& or T&. So, you need to look at the prototype anyway to know if the function might change the object.

Another benefit of references is that they clarify ownership of memory. If you are writing a method and another programmer passes you a reference to an object, it is clear that you can read and modify the object, but you have no easy way of freeing its memory. If you are passed a pointer, this is less clear. Do you need to delete the object to clean up memory? Or will the caller do that? Your group should determine how variable passing techniques imply memory ownership. The preferred way of handling memory is to use smart pointers which are discussed in detail in Chapter 21.

Use Custom Exceptions

C++ makes it easy to ignore exceptions. Nothing about the language syntax forces you to deal with exceptions and you could easily write error-tolerant programs with traditional mechanisms such as returning nullptr or setting an error flag.

Exceptions provide a much richer mechanism for error handling, and custom exceptions allow you to tailor this mechanism to your needs. For example, a custom exception type for a web browser could include fields that specify the web page that contained the error, the network state when the error occurred, and additional context information.

Chapter 10 contains a wealth of information about exceptions in C++.

 Language features exist to help the programmer. Understand and make use of features that contribute to good programming style.

FORMATTING

Many programming groups have been torn apart and friendships ruined over code-formatting arguments. In college, one of the authors got into such a heated debate with a peer over the use of spaces in an if statement that people were stopping by to make sure that everything was okay.

If your organization has standards in place for code formatting, consider yourself lucky. You may not like the standards they have in place, but at least you won't have to argue about it. If everybody on your team is writing code their own way, try to be as tolerant as you can. As you'll see, some practices are just a matter of taste, while others actually make it difficult to work in teams.

The Curly Brace Alignment Debate

Perhaps the most frequently argued-about point is where to put the curly braces that demark a block of code. There are several styles of curly brace use. In this book, we put the curly brace on the same line as the leading statement, except in the case of a function, class, or method name. This style is shown in the code that follows (and throughout the book).

```
void someFunction()
{
    if (condition()) {
        cout << "condition was true" << endl;
    } else {
        cout << "condition was false" << endl;
    }
}
```

This style conserves vertical space while still showing blocks of code by their indentation. Some programmers would argue that preservation of vertical space isn't relevant in real-world coding. A more verbose style is shown below.

```
void someFunction()
{
    if (condition())
    {
        cout << "condition was true" << endl;
    }
    else
    {
        cout << "condition was false" << endl;
    }
}
```

Some programmers are even liberal with use of horizontal space, yielding code like that in the following example.

```
void someFunction()
{
    if (condition())
        {
            cout << "condition was true" << endl;
        }
    else
        {
            cout << "condition was false" << endl;
        }
}
```

Of course, we won't recommend any particular style because we don't want hate mail.

When selecting a style for denoting blocks of code, the important consideration is how well you can see which block falls under which condition simply by looking at the code.

Coming to Blows over Spaces and Parentheses

The formatting of individual lines of code can also be a source of disagreement. Again, we won't advocate a particular approach, but we will show you a few styles that you are likely to encounter.

In this book, we use a space after any keyword, a space before and after any operator, a space after every comma in a parameter list or a call and parentheses to clarify the order of operations, as follows:

```
if (i == 2) {
    j = i + (k / m);
}
```

The alternative, shown next, treats `if` stylistically like a function, with no space between the keyword and the left parenthesis. Also, the parentheses used to clarify the order of operations inside of the `if` statement are omitted because they have no semantic relevance.

```
if( i == 2 ) {
    j = i + k / m;
}
```

The difference is subtle, and the determination of which is better is left to the reader, yet we can't move on from the issue without pointing out that `if` is not a function.

Spaces and Tabs

The use of spaces and tabs is not merely a stylistic preference. If your group does not agree on a convention for spaces and tabs, there are going to be major problems when programmers work jointly. The most obvious problem occurs when Alice uses four spaces to indent code and Bob uses five space tabs; neither will be able to display code properly when working on the same file. An even worse problem arises when Bob reformats the code to use tabs at the same time that Alice edits the same code; many source code control systems won't be able to merge in Alice's changes.

Most, but not all, editors have configurable settings for spaces and tabs. Some environments even adapt to the formatting of the code as it is read in, or always save using spaces even if the tab key is used for authoring. If you have a flexible environment, you have a better chance of being able to work with other people's code. Just remember that tabs and spaces are different because tabs can be any length and a space is always a space. For this reason, we recommend that you use an editor that always translates tabs into spaces.

STYLISTIC CHALLENGES

Many programmers begin a new project by pledging that, this time, they will do everything right. Any time a variable or parameter shouldn't be changed, it'll be marked `const`. All variables will have clear, concise, readable names. Every developer will put the left curly brace on the subsequent line and will adopt the standard text editor and its conventions for tabs and spaces.

For a number of reasons, it is difficult to sustain this level of stylistic consistency. In the case of `const`, sometimes programmers just aren't educated about how to use it. You will eventually come across old code or a library function that isn't `const`-savvy. A good programmer will use `const_cast` to temporarily suspend the `const` property of a variable, but an inexperienced programmer will start to unwind the `const` property back from the calling function, once again ending up with a program that never uses `const`.

Other times, standardization of style comes up against programmers' own individual tastes and biases. Perhaps the culture of your team makes it impractical to enforce strict style guidelines. In such situations, you may have to decide which elements you really need to standardize (such as variable names and tabs) and which ones are safe to leave up to individuals (perhaps spacing and commenting style). You can even obtain or write scripts that will automatically correct style "bugs" or flag stylistic problems along with code errors.

SUMMARY

The C++ language provides a number of stylistic tools without any formal guidelines for how to use them. Ultimately, any style convention is measured by how widely it is adopted and how much it benefits the readability of the code. When coding as part of a team, you should raise issues of style early in the process as part of the discussion of what language and tools to use.

The most important point about style is to appreciate that it is an important aspect of programming. Teach yourself to check over the style of your code before you make it available to others. Recognize good style in the code you interact with and adopt the conventions that you and your organization find useful.

This chapter concludes the first part of this book which focuses on discussing design themes and coding styles on a high level. The next part delves into the implementation phase of the software engineering process with details of C++ coding.

PART II
C++ Coding the Professional Way

▶ **CHAPTER 6:** Gaining Proficiency with Classes and Objects

▶ **CHAPTER 7:** Mastering Classes and Objects

▶ **CHAPTER 8:** Discovering Inheritance Techniques

▶ **CHAPTER 9:** Understanding C++ Quirks and Oddities

▶ **CHAPTER 10:** Handling Errors

▶ **CHAPTER 11:** Delving into the Standard Library

▶ **CHAPTER 12:** Understanding Containers and Iterators

▶ **CHAPTER 13:** Mastering STL Algorithms

▶ **CHAPTER 14:** Using Strings and Regular Expressions

▶ **CHAPTER 15:** Demystifying C++ I/O

▶ **CHAPTER 16:** Additional Library Utilities

▶ **CHAPTER 17:** Customizing and Extending the STL

6

Gaining Proficiency with Classes and Objects

WHAT'S IN THIS CHAPTER?

➤   How to write your own classes with methods and data members

➤   How to control access to your methods and data members

➤   How to use objects on the stack and on the heap

➤   What the life cycle of an object is

➤   How to write code that is executed when an object is created or destroyed

➤   How to write code to copy or assign objects

As an object-oriented language, C++ provides facilities for using objects and for writing object definitions, called classes. You can certainly write programs in C++ without classes and objects, but by doing so, you do not take advantage of the most fundamental and useful aspect of the language; writing a C++ program without classes is like traveling to Paris and eating at McDonald's. In order to use classes and objects effectively, you must understand their syntax and capabilities.

Chapter 1 reviewed the basic syntax of class definitions. Chapter 3 introduced the object-oriented approach to programming in C++ and presented specific design strategies for classes and objects. This chapter describes the fundamental concepts involved in using classes and objects, including writing class definitions, defining methods, using objects on the stack and the heap, writing constructors, default constructors, compiler-generated constructors, constructor initializers (known as *ctor-initializers*), copy constructors, initializer-list constructors, destructors, and assignment operators. Even if you are already comfortable with classes and objects, you should skim this chapter because it contains various tidbits of information with which you might not yet be familiar.

INTRODUCING THE SPREADSHEET EXAMPLE

This chapter and the next present a runnable example of a simple spreadsheet application. A spreadsheet is a two-dimensional grid of "cells," and each cell contains a number or string. Professional spreadsheets such as Microsoft Excel provide the ability to perform mathematical operations, such as calculating the sum of the values of a set of cells. The spreadsheet example in these chapters does not attempt to challenge Microsoft in the marketplace, but is useful for illustrating the issues of classes and objects.

The spreadsheet application uses two basic classes: `Spreadsheet` and `SpreadsheetCell`. Each `Spreadsheet` object contains `SpreadsheetCell` objects. In addition, a `SpreadsheetApplication` class manages a collection of `Spreadsheets`. This chapter focuses on the `SpreadsheetCell`. Chapter 7 develops the `Spreadsheet` and `SpreadsheetApplication` classes.

 This chapter shows several different versions of the `SpreadsheetCell` *class in order to introduce concepts gradually. Thus, the various attempts at the class throughout the chapter do not always illustrate the "best" way to do every aspect of class writing. In particular, the early examples omit important features that would normally be included, but have not yet been introduced. You can download the final version of the class as described in the Introduction.*

WRITING CLASSES

When you write a class you specify the behaviors, or *methods*, that will apply to objects of that class and the properties, or *data members*, that each object will contain.

There are two components in the process of writing classes: defining the classes themselves and defining their methods.

Class Definitions

Here is a first attempt at a simple `SpreadsheetCell` class, in which each cell can store only a single number:

```cpp
class SpreadsheetCell
{
    public:
        void setValue(double inValue);
        double getValue() const;
    protected:
        double mValue;
};
```

Code snippet from SpreadsheetCellNumOnly\SpreadsheetCell.h

As described in Chapter 1, every class definition begins with the keyword `class` and the name of the class. A class definition is a *statement* in C++, so it must end with a semicolon. If you fail to terminate your class definition with a semicolon, your compiler will probably give you several errors, most of which will appear to be completely unrelated.

Class definitions usually go in a file named after the class. For example, the `SpreadsheetCell` class definition can be put in a file called `SpreadsheetCell.h`. This rule is not enforced and you are free to call your file however you like.

Methods and Members

The two lines that look like function prototypes declare the methods that this class supports:

```
void setValue(double inValue);
double getValue() const;
```

Chapter 1 points out that it is always a good idea to declare member functions that do not change the object as `const`.

The line that looks like a variable declaration declares the data member for this class.

```
double mValue;
```

A class defines the methods and members that apply, but the methods and members typically apply only to a specific *instance* of the class, which is an *object*. Classes define concepts; objects contain real bits. So, each object will contain its own value for the `mValue` variable. The implementation of the methods is shared across all objects. Classes can contain any number of methods and members. You cannot give a member the same name as a method.

Access Control

Every method and member in a class is subject to one of three *access specifiers*: `public`, `protected`, or `private`. An access specifier applies to all method and member declarations that follow it, until the next access specifier. In the `SpreadsheetCell` class, the `setValue()` and `getValue()` methods have `public` access, while the `mValue` member has `protected` access.

The default access specifier for classes is `private`: all method and member declarations before the first access specifier have the `private` access specification. For example, moving the `public` access specifier below the `setValue()` method declaration gives the `setValue()` method `private` access instead of `public`:

```
class SpreadsheetCell
{
        void setValue(double inValue); // now has private access
    public:
        double getValue() const;
    protected:
        double mValue;
};
```

Code snippet from SpreadsheetCellNumOnly\AccessControl\SpreadsheetCell.h

In C++, a `struct` and a `union` can have methods just like a `class`. In fact, the only difference is that the default access specifier for a `struct` and `union` is `public` while the default for a `class` is `private`. For example, the `SpreadsheetCell` class can be rewritten using a `struct` as follows:

```
struct SpreadsheetCell
{
        void setValue(double inValue);
        double getValue() const;
    protected:
        double mValue;
};
```

The following table summarizes the meanings of the three access specifiers:

ACCESS SPECIFICATION	MEANING	WHEN TO USE
public	Any code can call a `public` method or access a `public` member of an object.	Behaviors (methods) that you want clients to use. Access methods for `private` and `protected` data members.
protected	Any method of the class can call a `protected` method and access a `protected` member. Methods of a *subclass* (see Chapter 8) can call a `protected` method or access a `protected` member of a *superclass*.	"Helper" methods that you do not want clients to use. Most, or better still, all, data members.
private	Only methods of the class can call a `private` method and access a `private` member. Methods in subclasses *cannot* access `private` methods or members in a superclass.	Only if you want to restrict access from subclasses.

Order of Declarations

You can declare your methods, members, and access control specifiers in any order: C++ does not impose any restrictions, such as methods before members or `public` before `private`. Additionally, you can repeat access specifiers. For example, the `SpreadsheetCell` definition could look like the following:

```
class SpreadsheetCell
{
    public:
        void setValue(double inValue);
    protected:
        double mValue;
    public:
        double getValue() const;
};
```

Code snippet from SpreadsheetCellNumOnly\DeclarationOrder\SpreadsheetCell.h

However, for clarity it is a good idea to group `public`, `protected`, and `private` declarations, and to group methods and members within those declarations.

Defining Methods

The preceding definition for the `SpreadsheetCell` class is enough for you to create objects of the class. However, if you try to call the `setValue()` or `getValue()` methods, your linker will complain that those methods are not defined. That's because the class definition specifies the prototypes for the methods, but does not define their implementations. Just as you write both a prototype and a definition for a stand-alone function, you must write a prototype and a definition for a method. Note that the class definition must precede the method definitions. Usually the class definition goes in a header file, and the method definitions go in a source file that `include`s that header. Here are the definitions for the two methods of the `SpreadsheetCell` class:

Available for download on Wrox.com

```
#include "SpreadsheetCell.h"
void SpreadsheetCell::setValue(double inValue)
{
    mValue = inValue;
}
double SpreadsheetCell::getValue() const
{
    return mValue;
}
```

Code snippet from SpreadsheetCellNumOnly\SpreadsheetCell.cpp

Note that the name of the class followed by two colons precedes each method name:

```
void SpreadsheetCell::setValue(double inValue)
```

The `::` is called the *scope resolution operator*. In this context, the syntax tells the compiler that the coming definition of the `setValue()` method is part of the `SpreadsheetCell` class. Note also that you do not repeat the access specification when you define the method.

If you are using the Microsoft Visual C++ IDE, you will notice that all cpp files start with:

```
#include "stdafx.h"
```

In a VC++ project, every file should start with this line and your own includes must follow this. If you place your own includes before the stdafx.h include, they will appear to have no effect and you will get all kinds of compilation errors. This deals with the concept of precompiled header files, which is outside the scope of this book. Consult the Microsoft documentation on precompiled header files to learn the details.

Accessing Data Members

Most methods of a class, such as `setValue()` and `getValue()`, are always executed on behalf of a specific object of that class (the exceptions are *static* methods, which are discussed later).

Inside the method body, you have access to all the data members of the class for that object. In the previous definition for setValue(), the following line changes the mValue variable inside whatever object calls the method:

```
mValue = inValue;
```

If setValue() is called for two different objects, the same line of code (executed once for each object) changes the variable in two different objects.

Calling Other Methods

You can call methods of a class from inside another method. For example, consider an extension to the SpreadsheetCell class. Real spreadsheet applications allow text data as well as numbers in the cells. When you try to interpret a text cell as a number, the spreadsheet tries to convert the text to a number. If the text does not represent a valid number, the cell value is ignored. In this program, strings that are not numbers will generate a cell value of 0. Here is a first stab at a class definition for a SpreadsheetCell that supports text data:

Available for
download on
Wrox.com

```cpp
#include <string>
using std::string;
class SpreadsheetCell
{
    public:
        void setValue(double inValue);
        double getValue() const;
        void setString(string inString);
        string getString() const;
    protected:
        string doubleToString(double inValue) const;
        double stringToDouble(string inString) const;
        double mValue;
        string mString;
};
```

Code snippet from SpreadsheetCellNumText\SpreadsheetCell.h

This version of the class stores both text and numerical representations of the data. If the client sets the data as a string, it is converted to a double, and a double is converted to a string. If the text is not a valid number, the double value is 0. This class definition shows two new methods to set and retrieve the text representation of the cell and two new protected *helper methods* to convert a double to a string and vice versa. These helper methods use string streams, which are covered in detail in Chapter 15. Here are the implementations of all the methods.

Available for
download on
Wrox.com

```cpp
#include "SpreadsheetCell.h"
#include <iostream>
#include <sstream>
using namespace std;
void SpreadsheetCell::setValue(double inValue)
{
    mValue = inValue;
```

```
        mString = doubleToString(mValue);
}
double SpreadsheetCell::getValue() const
{
    return mValue;
}
void SpreadsheetCell::setString(string inString)
{
    mString = inString;
    mValue = stringToDouble(mString);
}
string SpreadsheetCell::getString() const
{
    return mString;
}
string SpreadsheetCell::doubleToString(double inValue) const
{
    ostringstream ostr;
    ostr << inValue;
    return ostr.str();
}
double SpreadsheetCell::stringToDouble(string inString) const
{
    double temp;
    istringstream istr(inString);
    istr >> temp;
    if (istr.fail() || !istr.eof()) {
        return 0;
    }
    return temp;
}
```

Code snippet from SpreadsheetCellNumText\SpreadsheetCell.cpp

Note that each of the set methods calls a helper method to perform a conversion. With this technique, both mValue and mString are always valid.

The this Pointer

Every normal method call passes a pointer to the object for which it is called as a "hidden" parameter with the name this. You can use this pointer to access data members or call methods, and can pass it to other methods or functions. It is also sometimes useful for disambiguating names. For example, you could have defined the SpreadsheetCell class with a value data member instead of mValue and you could have defined the setValue() method to take a parameter named value instead of inValue. In that case, setValue() would look like this:

```
void SpreadsheetCell::setValue(double value)
{
    value = value; // Ambiguous!
    mString = doubleToString(value);
}
```

Code snippet from SpreadsheetCellThis\ambiguous\SpreadsheetCell.cpp

That line is confusing. Which `value` do you mean: the `value` that was passed as a parameter, or the `value` that is a member of the object?

> *The preceding ambiguous line will compile without any warnings or errors, but it will not produce the results that you are expecting.*

In order to disambiguate the names you can use the `this` pointer:

Available for download on Wrox.com

```cpp
void SpreadsheetCell::setValue(double value)
{
    this->value = value;
    mString = doubleToString(this->value);
}
```

Code snippet from SpreadsheetCellThis\unambiguous\SpreadsheetCell.cpp

However, if you use the naming conventions described in Chapter 5, you will never encounter this type of name collision.

You can also use the `this` pointer to call a function or method that takes a pointer to an object from within a method of that object. For example, suppose you write a `printCell()` stand-alone function (not method) like this:

Available for download on Wrox.com

```cpp
void printCell(SpreadsheetCell* inCellp)
{
    cout << inCellp->getString() << endl;
}
```

Code snippet from SpreadsheetCellThis\unambiguous\SpreadsheetCell.cpp

If you want to call `printCell()` from the `setValue()` method, you must pass `this` as the argument to give `printCell()` a pointer to the `SpreadsheetCell` on which `setValue()` operates:

Available for download on Wrox.com

```cpp
void SpreadsheetCell::setValue(double value)
{
    this->value = value;
    mString = doubleToString(this->value);
    printCell(this);
}
```

Code snippet from SpreadsheetCellThis\unambiguous\SpreadsheetCell.cpp

> *Instead of writing a `printCell()` function, it would be more convenient to overload the `<<` operator, explained in Chapter 18. You can then use the following line to print a `SpreadsheetCell`:*
>
> `cout << *this << endl;`

Using Objects

The previous class definition says that a SpreadsheetCell consists of two member variables, four public methods, and two protected methods. However, the class definition does not actually create any SpreadsheetCells; it just specifies their shape and behavior. In that sense, a class is similar to architectural blueprints. The blueprints specify what a house should look like, but drawing the blueprints doesn't build any houses. Houses must be constructed later based on the blueprints.

Similarly, in C++ you can construct a SpreadsheetCell "object" from the SpreadsheetCell class definition by declaring a variable of type SpreadsheetCell. Just as a builder can build more than one house based on a given set of blueprints, a programmer can create more than one SpreadsheetCell object from a SpreadsheetCell class. There are two ways to create and use objects: on the stack and on the heap.

Objects on the Stack

Here is some code that creates and uses SpreadsheetCell objects on the stack.

Available for
download on
Wrox.com

```cpp
SpreadsheetCell myCell, anotherCell;
myCell.setValue(6);
anotherCell.setString("3.2");
cout << "cell 1: " << myCell.getValue() << endl;
cout << "cell 2: " << anotherCell.getValue() << endl;
```

Code snippet from SpreadsheetCellNumText\SpreadsheetCellTest.cpp

You create objects just as you declare simple variables, except that the variable type is the class name. The . in lines like myCell.setValue(6); is called the "dot" operator; it allows you to call methods on the object. If there were any public data members in the object, you could access them with the dot operator as well.

The output of the program is:

```
cell 1: 6
cell 2: 3.2
```

Objects on the Heap

You can also dynamically allocate objects by using new:

Available for
download on
Wrox.com

```cpp
SpreadsheetCell* myCellp = new SpreadsheetCell();
myCellp->setValue(3.7);
cout << "cell 1: " << myCellp->getValue() <<
        " " << myCellp->getString() << endl;
delete myCellp;
myCellp = nullptr;
```

Code snippet from SpreadsheetCellNumText\SpreadsheetCellHeap.cpp

When you create an object on the heap, you call its methods and access its members through the "arrow" operator:->. The arrow combines dereferencing (*) and method or member access (.). You could use those two operators instead, but doing so would be stylistically awkward:

```
SpreadsheetCell* myCellp = new SpreadsheetCell();
(*myCellp).setValue(3.7);
cout << "cell 1: " << (*myCellp).getValue() <<
        " " << (*myCellp).getString() << endl;
delete myCellp;
myCellp = nullptr;
```

Code snippet from SpreadsheetCellNumText\SpreadsheetCellHeapAlternate.cpp

Just as you must free other memory that you allocate on the heap, you must free the memory for objects that you allocate on the heap by calling `delete` on the objects. To avoid memory problems, it's highly recommended to use smart pointers as follows:

```
shared_ptr<SpreadsheetCell> myCellp(new SpreadsheetCell());
myCellp->setValue(3.7);
cout << "cell 1: " << myCellp->getValue() <<
        " " << myCellp->getString() << endl;
```

Code snippet from SpreadsheetCellNumText\SpreadsheetCellHeapSmartPointer.cpp

With smart pointers you don't need to manually free the memory, it will happen automatically. Smart pointers are discussed in detail in Chapter 21.

 If you allocate an object with new, *free it with* delete *when you are finished with it, or use smart pointers to manage the memory automatically.*

 If you don't use smart pointers, it is always a good idea to reset a pointer to the null pointer after deleting the object to which it pointed. You are not required to do this, but it will make debugging easier in case the pointer is accidently used after deleting the object. In the above example, the pointer is reset to nullptr, *which is a C++11 specific feature. If your compiler does not yet support* nullptr, *use "*myCellp = NULL*" instead.*

OBJECT LIFE CYCLES

The object life cycle involves three activities: creation, destruction, and assignment. It is important to understand how and when objects are created, destroyed, and assigned, and how you can customize these behaviors.

Object Creation

Objects are created at the point you declare them (if they're on the stack) or when you explicitly allocate space for them with `new` or `new[]`. When an object is created, all its embedded objects are also created. For example:

```cpp
#include <string>
class MyClass
{
    protected:
        std::string mName;
};
int main()
{
    MyClass obj;
    return 0;
}
```

The embedded `string` object is created at the point where the `MyClass` object is created in the `main()` function and is destructed when its containing object is destructed.

It is often helpful to give variables initial values as you declare them. For example, you should usually initialize integer variables to `0` like this:

```cpp
int x = 0;
```

Similarly, you should give initial values to objects. You can provide this functionality by declaring and writing a special method called a *constructor*, in which you can perform initialization work for the object. Whenever an object is created, one of its constructors is executed.

 C++ programmers often call a constructor a ctor.

Writing Constructors

Syntactically, a constructor is specified by a method name that is the same as the class name. A constructor never has a return type and may or may not have parameters. A constructor with no parameters is called the *default constructor*. There are many contexts in which you may have to provide a default constructor and you will get compiler errors if you have not provided one. Default constructors will be discussed later in the chapter.

Here is a first attempt at adding a constructor to the `SpreadsheetCell` class:

```cpp
class SpreadsheetCell
{
    public:
        SpreadsheetCell(double initialValue);
        // Remainder of the class definition omitted for brevity
};
```

Code snippet from SpreadsheetCellCtors\SpreadsheetCell.h

Just as you must provide implementations for normal methods, you must provide an implementation for the constructor:

```
SpreadsheetCell::SpreadsheetCell(double initialValue)
{
    setValue(initialValue);
}
```

Code snippet from SpreadsheetCellCtors\SpreadsheetCell.cpp

The `SpreadsheetCell` constructor is a method of the `SpreadsheetCell` class, so C++ requires the normal `SpreadsheetCell::` scope resolution before the method name. The method name itself is also `SpreadsheetCell`, so the code ends up with the funny looking `SpreadsheetCell::SpreadsheetCell`. The implementation simply makes a call to `setValue()` in order to set both the numeric and text representations.

Using Constructors

Using the constructor creates an object and initializes its values. You can use constructors with both stack-based and heap-based allocation.

Constructors on the Stack

When you allocate a `SpreadsheetCell` object on the stack, you use the constructor like this:

```
SpreadsheetCell myCell(5), anotherCell(4);
cout << "cell 1: " << myCell.getValue() << endl;
cout << "cell 2: " << anotherCell.getValue() << endl;
```

Code snippet from SpreadsheetCellCtors\SpreadsheetCellTest.cpp

Note that you do NOT call the `SpreadsheetCell` constructor explicitly. For example, do not use something like the following:

```
SpreadsheetCell myCell.SpreadsheetCell(5); // WILL NOT COMPILE!
```

Similarly, you cannot call the constructor later. The following is also incorrect:

```
SpreadsheetCell myCell;
myCell.SpreadsheetCell(5); // WILL NOT COMPILE!
```

Again, the only correct way to use the constructor on the stack is like this:

```
SpreadsheetCell myCell(5);
```

Constructors on the Heap

When you dynamically allocate a `SpreadsheetCell` object, you use the constructor like this:

```
SpreadsheetCell *myCellp = new SpreadsheetCell(5);
SpreadsheetCell *anotherCellp = nullptr;
anotherCellp = new SpreadsheetCell(4);
// ... do something with the cells
delete myCellp;
myCellp = nullptr;
delete anotherCellp;
anotherCellp = nullptr;
```

Code snippet from SpreadsheetCellCtors\SpreadsheetCellTest.cpp

Note that you can declare a pointer to a `SpreadsheetCell` object without calling the constructor immediately, which is different from objects on the stack, where the constructor is called at the point of declaration.

Whenever you declare a pointer on the stack or in a class, it should be initialized to `nullptr` like in the previous declaration for `anotherCellp`. If you don't assign it to `nullptr`, the pointer is undefined. Accidentally using an undefined pointer will cause unexpected and difficult-to-diagnose memory corruption. If you initialize it to `nullptr`, using that pointer will cause a memory access error in most operating environments, instead of producing unexpected results.

As usual, remember to call `delete` on the objects that you dynamically allocate with `new` or use smart pointers!

Providing Multiple Constructors

You can provide more than one constructor in a class. All constructors have the same name (the name of the class), but different constructors must take a different number of arguments or different argument types. In C++, if you have more than one function with the same name, the compiler will select the one whose parameter types match the types at the call site. This is called *overloading* and is discussed in detail in Chapter 7.

In the `SpreadsheetCell` class, it is helpful to have two constructors: one to take an initial `double` value and one to take an initial `string` value. Here is the class definition with the second constructor:

```
class SpreadsheetCell
{
    public:
        SpreadsheetCell(double initialValue);
        SpreadsheetCell(string initialValue);
        // Remainder of the class definition omitted for brevity
};
```

Code snippet from SpreadsheetCellCtors\SpreadsheetCell.h

Here is the implementation of the second constructor:

```
SpreadsheetCell::SpreadsheetCell(string initialValue)
{
    setString(initialValue);
}
```

Code snippet from SpreadsheetCellCtors\SpreadsheetCell.cpp

And here is some code that uses the two different constructors:

```
SpreadsheetCell aThirdCell("test");   // Uses string-arg ctor
SpreadsheetCell aFourthCell(4.4);     // Uses double-arg ctor
SpreadsheetCell* aThirdCellp = new SpreadsheetCell("4.4"); // string-arg ctor
cout << "aThirdCell: " << aThirdCell.getValue() << endl;
cout << "aFourthCell: " << aFourthCell.getValue() << endl;
cout << "aThirdCellp: " << aThirdCellp->getValue() << endl;
delete aThirdCellp;
aThirdCellp = nullptr;
```

Code snippet from SpreadsheetCellCtors\SpreadsheetCellTest.cpp

When you have multiple constructors, it is tempting to attempt to implement one constructor in terms of another. For example, you might want to call the double constructor from the string constructor as follows:

```
SpreadsheetCell::SpreadsheetCell(string initialValue)
{
    SpreadsheetCell(stringToDouble(initialValue));
}
```

That seems to make sense. After all, you can call normal class methods from within other methods. The code will compile, link, and run, **but will not do what you expect.** The explicit call to the `SpreadsheetCell` constructor actually creates a new temporary unnamed object of type `SpreadsheetCell`. It does not call the constructor for the object that you are supposed to be initializing.

C++11 introduces a new feature called *delegating constructors*, which allows constructors to call another constructor from the same class. This will be discussed later in this chapter.

Default Constructors

A *default constructor* is a constructor that takes no arguments. It is also called a *0-argument constructor*. With a default constructor, you can give initial values to data members even though the client did not specify them.

When You Need a Default Constructor

Consider arrays of objects. The act of creating an array of objects accomplishes two tasks: It allocates contiguous memory space for all the objects and it calls the default constructor on each object. C++ fails to provide any syntax to tell the array creation code directly to call a different constructor. For example, if you do not define a default constructor for the `SpreadsheetCell` class, the following code does not compile:

```
SpreadsheetCell cells[3]; // FAILS compilation without default constructor
SpreadsheetCell* myCellp = new SpreadsheetCell[10]; // Also FAILS
```

You can circumvent this restriction for stack-based arrays by using *initializers* like these:

```
SpreadsheetCell cells[3] = {SpreadsheetCell(0), SpreadsheetCell(23),
    SpreadsheetCell(41)};
```

However, it is usually easier to ensure that your class has a default constructor if you intend to create arrays of objects of that class.

A default constructor is also required for classes that you want to store in an STL container like `std::vector`. STL containers are explained in detail in Chapter 12.

Default constructors are also useful when you want to create objects of that class inside other classes, which is shown later in this chapter under the section *Constructor Initializers*.

Finally, default constructors are convenient when the class serves as a base class of an inheritance hierarchy. In that case, it's convenient for subclasses to initialize superclasses via their default constructors. Chapter 8 covers this issue in more detail.

How To Write a Default Constructor

Here is part of the `SpreadsheetCell` class definition with a default constructor:

Available for
download on
Wrox.com

```
class SpreadsheetCell
{
    public:
        SpreadsheetCell();
        // Remainder of the class definition omitted for brevity
};
```

Code snippet from SpreadsheetCellDefaultCtor\SpreadsheetCell.h

Here is a first crack at an implementation of the default constructor:

Available for
download on
Wrox.com

```
SpreadsheetCell::SpreadsheetCell()
{
    mValue = 0;
    mString = "";
}
```

Code snippet from SpreadsheetCellDefaultCtor\SpreadsheetCell.cpp

You use the default constructor on the stack like this:

```
SpreadsheetCell myCell;
myCell.setValue(6);
cout << "cell 1: " << myCell.getValue() << endl;
```

Code snippet from SpreadsheetCellDefaultCtor\SpreadsheetCellTest.cpp

The preceding code creates a new `SpreadsheetCell` called `myCell`, sets its value, and prints out its value. Unlike other constructors for stack-based objects, you do not call the default constructor with function-call syntax. Based on the syntax for other constructors, you might be tempted to call the default constructor like this:

```
SpreadsheetCell myCell(); // WRONG, but will compile.
myCell.setValue(6);         // However, this line will not compile.
cout << "cell 1: " << myCell.getValue() << endl;
```

Unfortunately, the line attempting to call the default constructor will compile. The line following it will not compile. The problem is that your compiler thinks the first line is actually a function declaration for a function with the name `myCell` that takes zero arguments and returns a `SpreadsheetCell` object. When it gets to the second line, it thinks that you're trying to use a function name as an object!

> *When creating an object on the stack, omit parentheses for the default constructor.*

However, when you use the default constructor with a heap-based object allocation, you are required to use function-call syntax:

```
SpreadsheetCell* myCellp = new SpreadsheetCell(); // Note the function-call syntax
```

Code snippet from SpreadsheetCellDefaultCtor\SpreadsheetCellTest.cpp

Don't waste a lot of time pondering why C++ requires different syntax for heap-based versus stack-based object allocation with a default constructor. It's just one of those things that makes C++ such an exciting language to learn.

Compiler-Generated Default Constructor

The first `SpreadsheetCell` class definition in this chapter looked as follows:

```
class SpreadsheetCell
{
    public:
        void setValue(double inValue);
```

```
        double getValue() const;
    protected:
        double mValue;
};
```

This definition does not declare a default constructor, but still, the code that follows works perfectly.

```
SpreadsheetCell myCell;
myCell.setValue(6);
```

The following definition is the same as the preceding definition except that it adds an explicit constructor, accepting a `double`. It still does not explicitly declare a default constructor.

```
class SpreadsheetCell
{
    public:
        SpreadsheetCell(double initialValue); // No default constructor
        // Remainder of the class definition omitted for brevity
};
```

With this definition, the following code will not compile anymore:

```
SpreadsheetCell myCell;
myCell.setValue(6);
```

What's going on here? The reason is that if you don't specify *any* constructors, the compiler will write one for you that doesn't take any arguments. This *compiler-generated default constructor* calls the default constructor on all object members of the class, but does not initialize the language primitives such as `int` and `double`. Nonetheless, it allows you to create objects of that class. However, if you declare a default constructor, or any other constructor, the compiler no longer generates a default constructor for you.

A default constructor is the same thing as a 0-argument constructor. The term default constructor *does not refer only to the constructor automatically generated if you fail to declare any constructors. It refers to the constructor which is defaulted to if there are no arguments.*

C++11 ## Explicitly Defaulted Constructors

In older versions of C++, if your class required a number of explicit constructors accepting arguments but also a default constructor that does nothing, you had to explicitly write your empty default constructor as follows:

```cpp
class MyClass
{
    public:
        MyClass() {}
        MyClass(int i);
};
```

However, it's recommended that interface files contain only declarations of public methods without any implementations. The preceding class definition violates this. The solution was to define the class as follows:

```cpp
class MyClass
{
    public:
        MyClass();
        MyClass(int i);
};
```

The implementation of the empty default constructor in the implementation file would be:

```cpp
MyClass::MyClass() { }
```

To avoid having to write empty default constructors manually, C++11 introduces the concept of *explicitly defaulted constructors*. This allows you to write the class definition as follows without the need to implement it in the implementation file.

```cpp
class MyClass
{
    public:
        MyClass() = default;
        MyClass(int i);
};
```

MyClass defines a custom constructor that accepts one integer. However, the compiler will still generate a standard compiler generated default constructor due to the use of the default keyword.

C++11 ## Explicitly Deleted Constructors

C++11 also supports the concept of *explicitly deleted constructors*. For example, you can define a class for which you do not want to write any constructors and you also do not want the compiler to generate the default constructor. In that case you need to explicitly delete the default constructor:

```
class MyClass
{
    public:
        MyClass() = delete;
};
```

Constructor Initializers

Up to now, this chapter initialized data members in the body of a constructor, for example:

```
SpreadsheetCell::SpreadsheetCell()
{
    mValue = 0;
    mString = "";
}
```

C++ provides an alternative method for initializing data members in the constructor, called the *constructor initializer or ctor-initializer*. Here is the 0-argument `SpreadsheetCell` constructor rewritten to use the ctor-initializer syntax:

Available for download on Wrox.com

```
SpreadsheetCell::SpreadsheetCell() : mValue(0), mString("")
{
}
```

Code snippet from SpreadsheetCellDefaultCtor\SpreadsheetCellInitList.cpp

As you can see, the ctor-initializer appears syntactically between the constructor argument list and the opening brace for the body of the constructor. The list starts with a colon and is separated by commas. Each element in the list is an initialization of a data member using function notation or a call to a superclass constructor (see Chapter 8).

Initializing data members with a ctor-initializer provides different behavior than does initializing data members inside the constructor body itself. When C++ creates an object, it must create all the data members of the object before calling the constructor. As part of creating these data members, it must call a constructor on any of them that are themselves objects. By the time you assign a value to an object inside your constructor body, you are not actually constructing that object. You are only modifying its value. A ctor-initializer allows you to provide initial values for data members as they are created, which is more efficient than assigning values to them later. Interestingly, the default initialization for `strings` gives them the empty string; so explicitly initializing `mString` to the empty string as shown in the preceding example is superfluous.

If your class has as data member an object without a default constructor, you have to use the ctor-initializer to properly construct that object. For example, take the following `SpreadsheetCell` class:

```
class SpreadsheetCell
{
    public:
        SpreadsheetCell(double d);
};
```

This class only has one explicit constructor accepting a `double` and does not include a default constructor. You can use this class as a data member of another class as follows:

```
class SomeClass
{
    public:
        SomeClass();
    protected:
        SpreadsheetCell mCell;
};
```

And implement the `SomeClass` constructor as follows:

```
SomeClass::SomeClass() { }
```

However, with this implementation, the following line will not compile. The compiler does not know how to initialize the `mCell` data member of `SomeClass` because it does not have a default constructor.

```
SomeClass s;
```

The solution is to initialize the `mCell` data member in the ctor-initializer as follows:

```
SomeClass::SomeClass() : mCell(1.0) { }
```

 Ctor-initializers allow initialization of data members at the time of their creation.

Some programmers prefer to assign initial values in the body of the constructor. However, several data types must be initialized in a ctor-initializer. The following table summarizes them:

DATA TYPE	EXPLANATION
`const` data members	You cannot legally assign a value to a `const` variable after it is created. Any value must be supplied at the time of creation.
Reference data members	References cannot exist without referring to *something*.
Object data members for which there is no default constructor	C++ attempts to initialize member objects using a default constructor. If no default constructor exists, it cannot initialize the object.
Superclasses without default constructors	[Covered in Chapter 8]

There is one important caveat with ctor-initializers: They initialize data members in the order that they appear in the class definition, not their order in the ctor-initializer. Take the following definition for the SpreadsheetCell class:

```
class SpreadsheetCell
{
    public:
        // Code omitted for brevity
    protected:
        // Code omitted for brevity
        double mValue;
        string mString;
};
```

Code snippet from SpreadsheetCellDefaultCtor\SpreadsheetCell.h

Suppose you write your SpreadsheetCell string constructor to use a ctor-initializer like this:

```
SpreadsheetCell::SpreadsheetCell(string initialValue) :
    mString(initialValue), mValue(stringToDouble(mString)) // INCORRECT ORDER!
{
}
```

Code snippet from SpreadsheetCellDefaultCtor\SpreadsheetCellInitListBackward.cpp

The code will compile (although some compilers issue a warning), but the program does not work correctly. You might assume that mString will be initialized before mValue because mString is listed first in the ctor-initializer. But C++ doesn't work that way. The SpreadsheetCell class declares mValue before mString; thus, the ctor-initializer tries to initialize mValue before mString. However, the code to initialize mValue tries to use the value of mString, which is not yet initialized! The solution in this case is to use the initialValue argument instead of mString when initializing mValue. You should also swap their order in the ctor-initializer to avoid confusion:

```
SpreadsheetCell::SpreadsheetCell(string initialValue) :
    mValue(stringToDouble(initialValue)), mString(initialValue)
{
}
```

Code snippet from SpreadsheetCellDefaultCtor\SpreadsheetCellInitList.cpp

 Ctor-Initializers initialize data members in their declared order in the class definition, not their order in the ctor-initializer list.

Copy Constructors

There is a special constructor in C++ called a *copy constructor* that allows you to create an object that is an exact copy of another object. If you don't write a copy constructor yourself, C++ generates one for you that initializes each data member in the new object from its equivalent data member in the source object. For object data members, this initialization means that their copy constructors are called.

Here is the declaration for a copy constructor in the SpreadsheetCell class:

```cpp
class SpreadsheetCell
{
    public:
        SpreadsheetCell(const SpreadsheetCell& src);
        // Remainder of the class definition omitted for brevity
};
```

Code snippet from SpreadsheetCellCopyCtor\SpreadsheetCell.h

The copy constructor takes a const reference to the source object. Like other constructors, it does not return a value. Inside the constructor, you should copy all the data fields from the source object. Technically, of course, you can do whatever you want in the copy constructor, but it's generally a good idea to follow expected behavior and initialize the new object to be a copy of the old one. Here is a sample implementation of the SpreadsheetCell copy constructor:

```cpp
SpreadsheetCell::SpreadsheetCell(const SpreadsheetCell& src) :
    mValue(src.mValue), mString(src.mString)
{
}
```

Code snippet from SpreadsheetCellCopyCtor\SpreadsheetCell.cpp

Note the use of the ctor-initializer. The difference between setting values in the ctor-initializer and in the copy constructor body is examined later in the section on assignment.

> Given a set of member variables, called m1, m2, ... mn, *the compiler-generated copy constructor can be expressed as:*
>
> ```cpp
> classname::classname(const classname& src) :
>   m1(src.m1), m2(src.m2), ... mn(src.mn) { }
> ```
>
> *Therefore, in most circumstances, there is no need for you to specify a copy constructor yourself. However, under certain conditions, this default copy constructor is not sufficient. These conditions are covered in Chapter 7.*

When the Copy Constructor Is Called

The default semantics for passing arguments to functions in C++ is pass-by-value. That means that the function or method receives a copy of the value or object. Thus, whenever you pass an object to a function or method the compiler calls the copy constructor of the new object to initialize it. For example, recall that the definition of the `setString()` method in the `SpreadsheetCell` class looks like this:

```
void SpreadsheetCell::setString(string inString)
{
    mString = inString;
    mValue = stringToDouble(mString);
}
```

Recall, also, that the C++ `string` is actually a class, not a built-in type. When your code makes a call to `setString()` passing a `string` argument, the `string` parameter `inString` is initialized with a call to its copy constructor. The argument to the copy constructor is the `string` you passed to `setString()`. In the following example, the `string` copy constructor is executed for the `inString` object in `setString()` with `name` as its parameter.

```
SpreadsheetCell myCell;
string name = "heading one";
myCell.setString(name); // Copies name
```

When the `setString()` method finishes, `inString` is destroyed. Because it was only a copy of `name`, `name` remains intact.

The copy constructor is also called whenever you return an object from a function or method. In this case, the compiler creates a temporary, unnamed, object through its copy constructor. Chapter 24 explores the impact of temporary objects in more detail. You can avoid the overhead of copy constructors by passing parameters as `const` references, which will be explained in a later section.

Calling the Copy Constructor Explicitly

You can use the copy constructor explicitly as well. It is often useful to be able to construct one object as an exact copy of another. For example, you might want to create a copy of a `SpreadsheetCell` object like this:

```
SpreadsheetCell myCell2(4);
SpreadsheetCell myCell3(myCell2); // myCell3 has the same values as myCell2
```

Code snippet from SpreadsheetCellCopyCtor\SpreadsheetCellTest.cpp

Passing Objects by Reference

In order to avoid copying objects when you pass them to functions and methods you can declare that the function or method takes a *reference* to the object. Passing objects by reference is usually more efficient than passing them by value, because only the address of the object is copied, not the entire contents of the object. Additionally, pass-by-reference avoids problems with dynamic memory allocation in objects, which is discussed in Chapter 7.

When you pass an object by reference, the function or method using the object reference could change the original object. When you're only using pass-by-reference for efficiency, you should preclude this possibility by declaring the object `const` as well. Here is the `SpreadsheetCell` class definition in which string objects are passed as `const` references:

```cpp
class SpreadsheetCell
{
    public:
        SpreadsheetCell();
        SpreadsheetCell(double initialValue);
        SpreadsheetCell(const string& initialValue);
        SpreadsheetCell(const SpreadsheetCell& src);
        void setValue(double inValue);
        double getValue() const;
        void setString(const string& inString);
        string getString() const;
    protected:
        string doubleToString(double inValue) const;
        double stringToDouble(const string& inString) const;
        double mValue;
        string mString;
};
```

Code snippet from SpreadsheetCellCopyCtor\SpreadsheetCell.h

Here is the implementation for `setString()`. Note that the method body remains the same; only the parameter type is different.

```cpp
void SpreadsheetCell::setString(const string& inString)
{
    mString = inString;
    mValue = stringToDouble(mString);
}
```

Code snippet from SpreadsheetCellCopyCtor\SpreadsheetCell.cpp

For performance reasons, it is best to pass objects by `const` *reference instead of by value.*

The `SpreadsheetCell` methods that return a `string` still return it by value. Returning a reference to a data member is risky because the reference is valid only as long as the object is "alive." Once the object is destroyed, the reference is invalid. However, there are sometimes legitimate reasons to return references to data members, as you will see later in this chapter and in subsequent chapters.

C++11 Explicitly Defaulted and Deleted Copy Constructor

You can explicitly default or delete a compiler generated copy constructor as follows:

```
SpreadsheetCell(const SpreadsheetCell& src) = default;
```

or

```
SpreadsheetCell(const SpreadsheetCell& src) = delete;
```

C++11 Initializer-List Constructors

An *initializer-list constructor* is a constructor with `std::initializer_list<T>` as first argument, without any additional arguments or with additional arguments having default values. Before you can use the `std::initializer_list<T>` template you need to include the `<initializer_list>` header. The following class demonstrates its use.

Available for download on Wrox.com

```
class PointSequence
{
    public:
        PointSequence(initializer_list<double> args)
        {
            if (args.size() % 2 != 0) {
                throw invalid_argument("initializer_list should "
                    "contain even number of elements.");
            }
            for (auto iter = args.begin(); iter != args.end(); ++iter)
                mVecPoints.push_back(*iter);
        }
        void dumpPoints() const
        {
            for (auto citer = mVecPoints.cbegin();
                citer != mVecPoints.cend(); citer += 2) {
                cout << "(" << *citer << ", " << *(citer+1) << ")" << endl;
            }
        }
    protected:
        vector<double> mVecPoints;
};
```

Code snippet from InitializerListCtor\InitializerListCtor.cpp

Inside the initializer-list constructor you can access the elements of the initializer-list by using iterators as shown in the previous example. Iterators are discussed in detail in Chapter 12. You can get the number of elements in the initializer-list with the `size()` method.

Objects of `PointSequence` can be constructed as follows:

```
PointSequence p1 = {1.0, 2.0, 3.0, 4.0, 5.0, 6.0};
p1.dumpPoints();
try {
    PointSequence p2 = {1.0, 2.0, 3.0};
} catch (const invalid_argument& e) {
    cout << e.what() << endl;
}
```

Code snippet from InitializerListCtor\InitializerListCtor.cpp

The construction of p2 will throw an exception because it has an odd number of elements in the initializer-list. The preceding equal signs are optional and can be left out, for example:

```
PointSequence p1{1.0, 2.0, 3.0, 4.0, 5.0, 6.0};
```

The C++11 STL has full support for initializer-list constructors. For example, the `std::vector` container can be initialized by using an initializer-list:

```
std::vector<std::string> myVec = {"String 1", "String 2", "String 3"};
```

If you use a compiler that does not yet conform to the C++11 standard, one way to initialize the vector is by using several `push_back()` calls:

```
std::vector<std::string> myVec;
myVec.push_back("String 1");
myVec.push_back("String 2");
myVec.push_back("String 3");
```

Initializer-list constructors are also important in the context of the C++11 *uniform initialization* feature as explained in the section "Uniform Initialization" in Chapter 9.

Initializer lists are not limited to constructors and can also be used with normal functions as explained in Chapter 9.

C++11 In-Class Member Initializers

C++11 allows member variables to be initialized directly in the class definition. For example:

```
#include <string>
class MyClass
{
    protected:
        int mInt = 1;
        std::string mStr = "test";
};
```

The only way you could initialize mInt and mStr before C++11 was within a constructor body, or with a ctor-initializer as follows:

```
#include <string>
class MyClass
{
    public:
        MyClass() : mInt(1), mStr("test") {}
    protected:
        int mInt;
        std::string mStr;
};
```

Before C++11, only static const integral member variables could be initialized in the class definition. For example:

```
#include <string>
class MyClass
{
    protected:
        static const int kI1 = 1;        // OK
        static const std::string kStr = "test"; // Error: not integral type
        static int sI2 = 2;              // Error: not const
        const int kI3 = 3;               // Error: not static
};
```

C++11 Delegating Constructors

Delegating constructors allow constructors to call another constructor from the same class. However, this call cannot be placed in the constructor body; it should be in the constructor initializer. Following is an example:

```
SpreadsheetCell::SpreadsheetCell(const string& initialValue)
    : SpreadsheetCell(stringToDouble(initialValue))
{
}
```

When this string constructor (the delegating constructor) is called, it will first delegate the call to the target, double constructor. When the target constructor returns, the body of the delegating constructor will be executed.

Make sure you avoid constructor recursion while using delegate constructors. For example:

```
class MyClass
{
    MyClass(char c) : MyClass(1.2) { }
    MyClass(double d) : MyClass('m') { }
};
```

The first constructor will delegate to the second constructor, which delegates back to the first one. The behavior of such code is undefined by the standard and depends on the compiler.

Summary of Compiler-Generated Constructors

The compiler will automatically generate a 0-argument constructor and a copy constructor for every class. However, the constructors you define yourself replace these constructors according to the following rules:

IF YOU DEFINE ...	...THEN THE COMPILER GENERATES ...	...AND YOU CAN CREATE AN OBJECT ...

[no constructors]	A 0-argument constructor
	A copy constructor
		With no arguments:
		`SpreadsheetCell cell;`
		As a copy of another object:
		`SpreadsheetCell myCell(cell);`

A 0-argument constructor only	A copy constructor	With no arguments:
		`SpreadsheetCell cell;`
		As a copy of another object:
		`SpreadsheetCell myCell(cell);`

A copy constructor only	No constructors	Theoretically, as a copy of another object. Practically, you can't create any objects.

A single-argument (non-copy constructor) or multi-argument constructor only	A copy constructor	With arguments:
		`SpreadsheetCell cell(6);`
		As a copy of another object:
		`SpreadsheetCell myCell(cell);`

A 0-argument constructor as well as a single-argument constructor (non-copy constructor) or multi-argument constructor	A copy constructor	With no arguments:
		`SpreadsheetCell cell;`
		With arguments:
		`SpreadsheetCell myCell(5);`
		As a copy of another object:
		`SpreadsheetCell anotherCell(cell);`

Note the lack of symmetry between the default constructor and the copy constructor. As long as you don't define a copy constructor explicitly, the compiler creates one for you. On the other hand, as soon as you define *any* constructor, the compiler stops generating a default constructor.

As mentioned before in this chapter, the automatic generation of a default constructor and a default copy constructor can be influenced in C++11 by defining them as explicitly defaulted or explicitly deleted.

Object Destruction

When an object is destroyed, two events occur: The object's *destructor* method is called, and the memory it was taking up is freed. The destructor is your chance to perform any cleanup work for the object, such as freeing dynamically allocated memory or closing file handles. If you don't declare a destructor, the compiler will write one for you that does recursive memberwise destruction and allows the object to be deleted. The section on dynamic memory allocation in Chapter 7 shows you how to write a destructor.

Objects on the stack are destroyed when they go *out of scope*, which means whenever the current function, method, or other execution *block* ends. In other words, whenever the code encounters an ending curly brace, any objects created on the stack within those curly braces are destroyed. The following program shows this behavior:

```
int main()
{
    SpreadsheetCell myCell(5);
    if (myCell.getValue() == 5) {
        SpreadsheetCell anotherCell(6);
    } // anotherCell is destroyed as this block ends.
    cout << "myCell: " << myCell.getValue() << endl;
    return 0;
} // myCell is destroyed as this block ends.
```

Code snippet from Destructors\DestructorExamples.cpp

Objects on the stack are destroyed in the reverse order of their declaration (and construction). For example, in the following code fragment, myCell2 is allocated before anotherCell2, so anotherCell2 is destroyed before myCell2 (note that you can start a new code block at any point in your program with an opening curly brace):

```
{
    SpreadsheetCell myCell2(4);
    SpreadsheetCell anotherCell2(5); // myCell2 constructed before anotherCell2
} // anotherCell2 destroyed before myCell2
```

Code snippet from Destructors\DestructorExamples.cpp

This ordering applies to objects that are data members of other objects. Recall that data members are initialized in the order of their declaration in the class. Thus, following the rule that objects are destroyed in the reverse order of their construction, data member objects are destroyed in the reverse order of their declaration in the class.

Objects allocated on the heap are not destroyed automatically. You must call delete on the object pointer to call its destructor and free the memory. The following program shows this behavior:

```
int main()
{
    SpreadsheetCell* cellPtr1 = new SpreadsheetCell(5);
    SpreadsheetCell* cellPtr2 = new SpreadsheetCell(6);
    cout << "cellPtr1: " << cellPtr1->getValue() << endl;
    delete cellPtr1; // Destroys cellPtr1
    cellPtr1 = nullptr;
    return 0;
} // cellPtr2 is NOT destroyed because delete was not called on it.
```

Code snippet from Destructors\DestructorHeapExamples.cpp

Do not write programs like the preceding example where cellPtr2 *was not deleted. Make sure you always free dynamically allocated memory by calling* delete *or* delete[] *depending on whether the memory was allocated using* new *or* new[] *or better yet, use smart pointers as discussed earlier.*

There are tools that are able to detect unfreed objects. These tools are discussed in Chapter 21.

Assigning to Objects

Just as you can assign the value of one int to another in C++, you can assign the value of one object to another. For example, the following code assigns the value of myCell to anotherCell:

```
SpreadsheetCell myCell(5), anotherCell;
anotherCell = myCell;
```

You might be tempted to say that myCell is "copied" to anotherCell. However, in the world of C++, "copying" only occurs when an object is being initialized. If an object already has a value that is being overwritten, the more accurate term is "assigned" to. Note that the facility that C++ provides for copying is the copy constructor. Since it is a constructor, it can only be used for object creation, not for later assignments to the object.

Therefore, C++ provides another method in every class to perform assignment. This method is called the *assignment operator*. Its name is operator= because it is actually an overloading of the = operator for that class. In the preceding example, the assignment operator for anotherCell is called, with myCell as the argument.

In the C++11 standard, the assignment operator *as explained in this section is sometimes called the* copy assignment operator *because both the left-hand side and the right-hand side object stay alive after the assignment. This distinction is made because C++11 adds a new* move assignment operator *in which the right-hand side object will be destroyed after the assignment for performance reasons. This* move assignment operator *is explained in Chapter 9.*

As usual, if you don't write your own assignment operator, C++ writes one for you to allow objects to be assigned to one another. The default C++ assignment behavior is almost identical to its default copying behavior: It recursively assigns each data member from the source to the destination object. The syntax is slightly tricky, though.

Declaring an Assignment Operator

Here is another attempt at the `SpreadsheetCell` class definition, this time including an assignment operator:

```
class SpreadsheetCell
{
    public:
        // Remainder of the class definition omitted for brevity
        SpreadsheetCell& operator=(const SpreadsheetCell& rhs);
        // Remainder of the class definition omitted for brevity
};
```

Code snippet from SpreadsheetCellAssign\SpreadsheetCell.h

The assignment operator, like the copy constructor, takes a `const` reference to the source object. In this case, we call the source object `rhs`, which stands for "right-hand side" of the equals sign. The object on which the assignment operator is called is the left-hand side of the equals sign.

Unlike a copy constructor, the assignment operator returns a reference to a `SpreadsheetCell` object. The reason is that assignments can be *chained*, as in the following example:

```
myCell = anotherCell = aThirdCell;
```

When that line is executed, the first thing that happens is that the assignment operator for `anotherCell` is called with `aThirdCell` as its "right-hand side" parameter. Next, the assignment operator for `myCell` is called. However, its parameter is not `anotherCell`. Its right-hand side is the *result* of the assignment of `aThirdCell` to `anotherCell`. If that assignment fails to return a result, there is nothing to pass to `myCell`.

You might be wondering why the assignment operator for `myCell` can't just take `anotherCell`. The reason is that using the equals sign is actually just shorthand for what is really a method call. When you look at the line in its full functional syntax, you can see the problem:

```
myCell.operator=(anotherCell.operator=(aThirdCell));
```

Now, you can see that the `operator=` call from `anotherCell` must return a value, which is passed to the `operator=` call for `myCell`. The correct value to return is `anotherCell` itself, so it can serve as the source for the assignment to `myCell`. However, returning `anotherCell` directly would be inefficient, so you can return a reference to `anotherCell`.

You could actually declare the assignment operator to return whatever type you wanted, including void. *However, you should always return a reference to the object on which it is called because that's what clients expect.*

Defining an Assignment Operator

The implementation of the assignment operator is similar to that of a copy constructor, with several important differences. First, a copy constructor is called only for initialization, so the destination object does not yet have valid values. An assignment operator can overwrite the current values in an object. This consideration doesn't really come into play until you have dynamically allocated memory in your objects. See Chapter 7 for details.

Second, it's legal in C++ to assign an object to itself. For example, the following code compiles and runs:

```
SpreadsheetCell cell(4);
cell = cell; // Self-assignment
```

Your assignment operator shouldn't prohibit self-assignment, but also shouldn't perform a full assignment if it happens. Thus, assignment operators should check for self-assignment at the beginning of the method and return immediately.

Here is the definition of the assignment operator for the `SpreadsheetCell` class:

Available for download on Wrox.com

```
SpreadsheetCell& SpreadsheetCell::operator=(const SpreadsheetCell& rhs)
{
    if (this == &rhs) {
```

Code snippet from SpreadsheetCellAssign\SpreadsheetCell.cpp

The previous line checks for self-assignment, but is a bit cryptic. Self-assignment occurs when the left-hand side and the right-hand side of the equals sign are the same. One way to tell if two objects are the same is if they occupy the same memory location — more explicitly, if pointers to them are equal. Recall that `this` is a pointer to an object accessible from any method called on the object. Thus, `this` is a pointer to the left-hand side object. Similarly, `&rhs` is a pointer to the right-hand side object. If these pointers are equal, the assignment must be self-assignment, but because the return type is `SpreadsheetCell&` we must return a correct value. All assignment operators return `*this`, and the self-assignment case is no exception:

```
        return *this;
    }
```

`this` is a pointer to the object on which the method executes, so `*this` is the object itself. The compiler will return a reference to the object to match the declared return value. Now, if it is not self-assignment, you have to do an assignment to every member:

```
    mValue = rhs.mValue;
    mString = rhs.mString;
```

Here the method copies the values.

```
    return *this;
}
```

Finally it returns `*this`, as explained previously.

C++11 Explicitly Defaulted and Deleted Assignment Operator

You can explicitly default or delete a compiler generated assignment operator as follows:

```
SpreadsheetCell& operator=(const SpreadsheetCell& rhs) = default;
```

or

```
SpreadsheetCell& operator=(const SpreadsheetCell& rhs) = delete;
```

Distinguishing Copying from Assignment

It is sometimes difficult to tell when objects are initialized with a copy constructor rather than assigned to with the assignment operator. Essentially, things that look like a declaration are going to be using copy constructors and things that look like assignment statements will be handled by the assignment operator. Consider the following code:

```
SpreadsheetCell myCell(5);
SpreadsheetCell anotherCell(myCell);
```

AnotherCell is constructed with the copy constructor.

```
SpreadsheetCell aThirdCell = myCell;
```

aThirdCell is also constructed with the copy constructor, because this is a declaration. This line does not call operator=! This syntax is just another way to write: SpreadsheetCell aThirdCell(myCell);. However:

```
anotherCell = myCell; // Calls operator= for anotherCell.
```

Here anotherCell has already been constructed, so the compiler calls operator=.

Objects as Return Values

When you return objects from functions or methods, it is sometimes difficult to see exactly what copying and assignment is happening. Recall that the code for getString() looks like this:

```
string SpreadsheetCell::getString() const
{
    return mString;
}
```

Now consider the following code:

```
SpreadsheetCell myCell2(5);
string s1;
s1 = myCell2.getString();
```

When `getString()` returns `mString`, the compiler actually creates an unnamed temporary `string` object by calling a `string` copy constructor. When you assign this result to `s1`, the assignment operator is called for `s1` with the temporary `string` as a parameter. Then, the temporary `string` object is destroyed. Thus, the single line of code invokes the copy constructor and the assignment operator (for two different objects).

In case you're not confused enough, consider this code:

```
SpreadsheetCell myCell3(5);
string s2 = myCell3.getString();
```

In this case, `getString()` still creates a temporary unnamed `string` object when it returns `mString`. But now `s2` gets its copy constructor called, not its assignment operator.

With *move semantics* from C++11, the compiler can use a *move constructor* instead of a copy constructor to return `mString` from `getString()`. This is much more efficient. Move semantics is discussed in Chapter 9.

If you ever forget the order in which these things happen or which constructor or operator is called, you can easily figure it out by temporarily including helpful output in your code or by stepping through it with a debugger.

Copy Constructors and Object Members

You should also note the difference between assignment and copy constructor calls in constructors. If an object contains other objects, the compiler-generated copy constructor calls the copy constructors of each of the contained objects recursively. When you write your own copy constructor, you can provide the same semantics by using a ctor-initializer, as shown previously. If you omit a data member from the ctor-initializer, the compiler performs default initialization on it (a call to the 0-argument constructor for objects) before executing your code in the body of the constructor. Thus, by the time the body of the constructor executes, all object data members have already been initialized.

For example, you could write your copy constructor like this:

```
SpreadsheetCell::SpreadsheetCell(const SpreadsheetCell& src)
    : mString(src.mString)
{
    mValue = src.mValue;
}
```

However, when you assign values to data members in the body of the copy constructor, you are using the assignment operator on them, not the copy constructor, because they have already been initialized, as described previously.

In this example, `mString` is initialized using the copy constructor, while `mValue` is assigned to using the assignment operator.

SUMMARY

This chapter covered the fundamental aspects of C++'s facilities for object-oriented programming: classes and objects. It first reviewed the basic syntax for writing classes and using objects, including access control. Then, it covered object life cycles: when objects are constructed, destructed, and assigned, and what methods those actions invoke. The chapter included details of the constructor syntax, including ctor-initializers and initializer-list constructors, and introduced the notion of copy assignment operators. It also specified exactly which constructors the compiler writes for you, and under what circumstances, and explained that default constructors take no arguments.

For some of you, this chapter was mostly review. For others, it hopefully opened your eyes to the world of object-oriented programming in C++. In any case, now that you are proficient with objects and classes, read Chapter 7 to learn more about their tricks and subtleties.

Mastering Classes and Objects

WHAT'S IN THIS CHAPTER?

➤ How to use dynamic memory allocation in objects

➤ The different kinds of data members you can have (`static`, `const`, `reference`)

➤ The different kinds of methods you can implement (`static`, `const`, `inline`)

➤ The details of method overloading

➤ How to work with default parameters

➤ How to use nested classes

➤ How to make classes friends of other classes

➤ What operator overloading is

➤ How to write separate interface and implementation classes.

Chapter 6 started the discussion on classes and objects. Now it's time to master their subtleties so you can use them to their full potential. By reading this chapter, you will learn how to manipulate and exploit some of the most complicated aspects of the C++ language in order to write safe, effective, and useful classes.

Many of the concepts in this chapter arise in advanced C++ programming, especially in the standard template library.

DYNAMIC MEMORY ALLOCATION IN OBJECTS

Sometimes you don't know how much memory you will need before your program actually runs. As you know, the solution is to dynamically allocate as much space as you need during program execution. Classes are no exception. Sometimes you don't know how much memory an object will need when you write the class. In that case, the object should dynamically allocate memory.

Dynamically allocated memory in objects provides several challenges, including freeing the memory, handling object copying, and handling object assignment.

The Spreadsheet Class

Chapter 6 introduced the `SpreadsheetCell` class. This chapter moves on to write the `Spreadsheet` class. As with the `SpreadsheetCell` class, the `Spreadsheet` class will evolve throughout this chapter. Thus, the various attempts do not always illustrate the best way to do every aspect of class writing. To start, a `Spreadsheet` is simply a two-dimensional array of `SpreadsheetCell`s, with methods to set and retrieve cells at specific locations in the `Spreadsheet`. Although most spreadsheet applications use letters in one direction and numbers in the other to refer to cells, this `Spreadsheet` uses numbers in both directions. Here is a first attempt at a class definition for a simple `Spreadsheet` class:

```cpp
#include "SpreadsheetCell.h"
class Spreadsheet
{
    public:
        Spreadsheet(int inWidth, int inHeight);
        void setCellAt(int x, int y, const SpreadsheetCell& cell);
        SpreadsheetCell getCellAt(int x, int y);
    protected:
        bool inRange(int val, int upper);
        int mWidth, mHeight;
        SpreadsheetCell** mCells;
};
```

Code snippet from Spreadsheet\Spreadsheet.h

The `Spreadsheet` class uses normal pointers for the `mCells` array. This is done throughout this chapter to show the consequences and to explain how you should handle dynamic memory in classes. In production code, you should use one of the standard C++ containers, like `std::vector` which is briefly introduced in Chapter 1 and discussed in detail in Chapter 12.

Note that the `Spreadsheet` class does not contain a standard two-dimensional array of `SpreadsheetCell`s. Instead, it contains a `SpreadsheetCell**`. The reason is that each `Spreadsheet` object might have different dimensions, so the constructor of the class must dynamically allocate the two-dimensional array based on the client-specified height and width. In order to allocate dynamically a two-dimensional array you need to write the following code:

```cpp
#include "Spreadsheet.h"
Spreadsheet::Spreadsheet(int inWidth, int inHeight) :
    mWidth(inWidth), mHeight(inHeight)
{
    mCells = new SpreadsheetCell* [mWidth];
```

```
        for (int i = 0; i < mWidth; i++) {
            mCells[i] = new SpreadsheetCell[mHeight];
        }
    }
```

Code snippet from Spreadsheet\Spreadsheet.cpp

The resultant memory for a `Spreadsheet` called `s1` on the stack with width four and height three is shown in Figure 7-1.

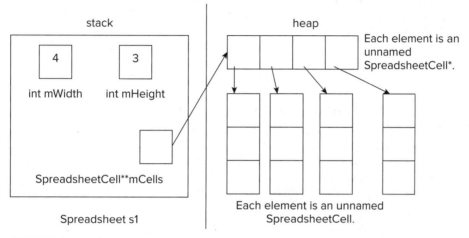

FIGURE 7-1

The implementations of the set and retrieval methods are straightforward:

Available for
download on
Wrox.com

```
void Spreadsheet::setCellAt(int x, int y, const SpreadsheetCell& cell)
{
    if (!inRange(x, mWidth) || !inRange(y, mHeight)) {
        throw std::out_of_range("");
    }
    mCells[x][y] = cell;
}
SpreadsheetCell Spreadsheet::getCellAt(int x, int y)
{
    if (!inRange(x, mWidth) || !inRange(y, mHeight)) {
        throw std::out_of_range("");
    }
    return mCells[x][y];
}
```

Code snippet from Spreadsheet\Spreadsheet.cpp

Note that these two methods use a helper method `inRange()` to check that `x` and `y` represent valid coordinates in the spreadsheet. Attempting to access an array element at an out-of-range index will cause the program to malfunction. This example uses exceptions which are mentioned in Chapter 1 and described in detail in Chapter 10.

Freeing Memory with Destructors

Whenever you are finished with dynamically allocated memory, you should free it. If you dynamically allocate memory in an object, the place to free that memory is in the destructor. The compiler guarantees that the destructor will be called when the object is destroyed. Here is the `Spreadsheet` class definition from earlier with a destructor:

Available for
download on
Wrox.com

```cpp
class Spreadsheet
{
    public:
        Spreadsheet(int inWidth, int inHeight);
        ~Spreadsheet();
        // Code omitted for brevity
};
```

Code snippet from Spreadsheet\Spreadsheet.h

The destructor has the same name as the name of the class (and of the constructors), preceded by a tilde (~). The destructor takes no arguments, and there can only be one of them.

Here is the implementation of the `Spreadsheet` class destructor:

Available for
download on
Wrox.com

```cpp
Spreadsheet::~Spreadsheet()
{
    for (int i = 0; i < mWidth; i++) {
        delete [] mCells[i];
    }
    delete [] mCells;
    mCells = nullptr;
}
```

Code snippet from Spreadsheet\Spreadsheet.cpp

This destructor frees the memory that was allocated in the constructor. However, no rule requires you to free memory in the destructor. You can write whatever code you want in the destructor, but it is a good idea to use it only for freeing memory or disposing of other resources.

Handling Copying and Assignment

Recall from Chapter 6 that, if you don't write a copy constructor and an assignment operator yourself, C++ writes them for you. These compiler-generated methods recursively call the copy constructor or assignment operator on object data members. However, for primitives, such as `int`, `double`, and pointers, they provide *shallow* or *bitwise* copying or assignment: They just copy or assign the data members from the source object directly to the destination object. That presents problems when you dynamically allocate memory in your object. For example, the following code copies the spreadsheet `s1` to initialize `s` when `s1` is passed to the `printSpreadsheet()` function.

Available for
download on
Wrox.com

```cpp
#include "Spreadsheet.h"
void printSpreadsheet(Spreadsheet s)
{
    // Code omitted for brevity.
}
```

```
int main()
{
    Spreadsheet s1(4, 3);
    printSpreadsheet(s1);
    return 0;
}
```

Code snippet from Spreadsheet\SpreadsheetTest.cpp

The `Spreadsheet` contains one pointer variable: `mCells`. A shallow copy of a spreadsheet gives the destination object a copy of the `mCells` pointer, but not a copy of the underlying data. Thus, you end up with a situation where both `s` and `s1` have a pointer to the same data, as shown in Figure 7-2.

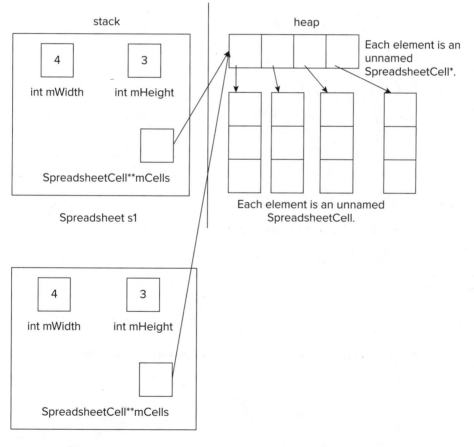

FIGURE 7-2

If s were to change something to which mCells points, that change would show up in s1 too. Even worse, when the printSpreadsheet() function exits, s's destructor is called, which frees the memory pointed to by mCells. That leaves the situation shown in Figure 7-3.

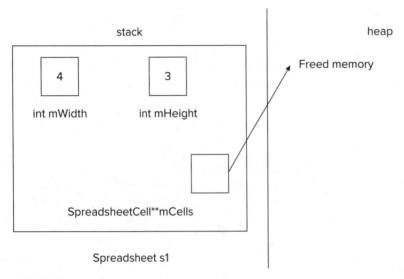

FIGURE 7-3

Now s1 has a pointer which no longer points to valid memory. This is called a *dangling pointer*.

Unbelievably, the problem is even worse with assignment. Suppose that you had the following code:

```
Spreadsheet s1(2, 2), s2(4, 3);
s1 = s2;
```

Code snippet from Spreadsheet\SpreadsheetTest.cpp

After both objects are constructed, you would have the memory layout shown in Figure 7-4.

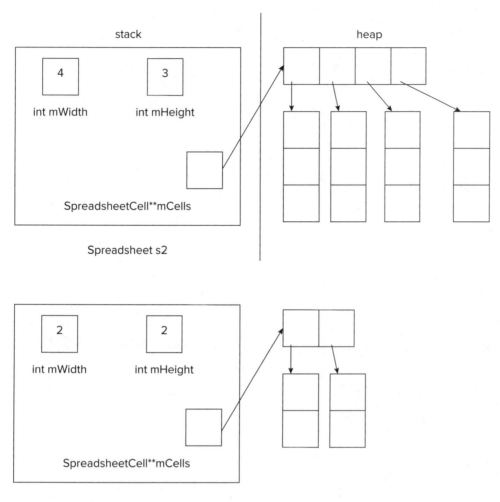

FIGURE 7-4

After the assignment statement, you would have the layout shown in Figure 7-5.

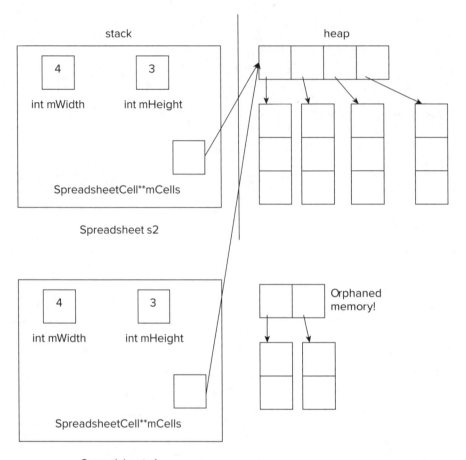

FIGURE 7-5

Now, not only do the `mCells` pointers in `s1` and `s2` point to the same memory, but also you have *orphaned* the memory to which `mCells` in `s1` previously pointed. That is why in assignment operators you must first free the memory referenced by the left-hand side, and then do a deep copy.

As you can see, relying on C++'s default copy constructor or assignment operator is not always a good idea.

 Whenever you have dynamically allocated memory in a class, you should write your own copy constructor and assignment operator to provide a deep copy of the memory.

The Spreadsheet Copy Constructor

Here is a declaration for a copy constructor in the `Spreadsheet` class:

```
class Spreadsheet
{
    public:
        Spreadsheet(int inWidth, int inHeight);
        Spreadsheet(const Spreadsheet& src);
        // Code omitted for brevity
};
```

Code snippet from Spreadsheet\Spreadsheet.h

Here is a first definition of the copy constructor:

```
Spreadsheet::Spreadsheet(const Spreadsheet& src)
{
    mWidth = src.mWidth;
    mHeight = src.mHeight;
    mCells = new SpreadsheetCell* [mWidth];
    for (int i = 0; i < mWidth; i++) {
        mCells[i] = new SpreadsheetCell[mHeight];
    }
    for (int i = 0; i < mWidth; i++) {
        for (int j = 0; j < mHeight; j++) {
            mCells[i][j] = src.mCells[i][j];
        }
    }
}
```

Code snippet from Spreadsheet\SpreadsheetNoCopyFrom.cpp

Note that the copy constructor copies all data members, including `mWidth` and `mHeight`, not just the pointer data members. The rest of the code in the copy constructor provides a deep copy of the `mCells` dynamically allocated two-dimensional array. There is no need to delete the existing `mCells` because this is a copy constructor and therefore there is no existing `mCells` yet in `this` object.

The Spreadsheet Assignment Operator

Here is the definition for the `Spreadsheet` class with an assignment operator:

```
class Spreadsheet
{
    public:
        // Code omitted for brevity
        Spreadsheet& operator=(const Spreadsheet& rhs);
        // Code omitted for brevity
};
```

Code snippet from Spreadsheet\Spreadsheet.h

Here is the implementation of the assignment operator for the `Spreadsheet` class, with explanations interspersed. Note that when an object is assigned to, it already has been initialized. Thus, you must free any dynamically allocated memory before allocating new memory. You can think of an assignment operator as a combination of a destructor and a copy constructor. You are essentially "reincarnating" the object with new life (or data) when you assign to it.

The first lines of code in any assignment operator checks for self-assignment.

```cpp
Spreadsheet& Spreadsheet::operator=(const Spreadsheet& rhs)
{
    // Check for self-assignment.
    if (this == &rhs) {
        return *this;
    }
```

Code snippet from Spreadsheet\SpreadsheetNoCopyFrom.cpp

This self-assignment check is required, not only for efficiency, but also for correctness. If the preceding self-assignment test was removed, the code will most likely crash on self-assignment, because the second step in the code deletes `mCells` for the left-hand side and afterwards copies `mCells` from the right-hand side to the left-hand side. In the case of self-assignment, both sides are the same, so during copying you would access dangling pointers.

Because this is an assignment operator, the object being assigned to already has `mCells` initialized. You need to free these cells up.

```cpp
    // Free the old memory.
    for (int i = 0; i < mWidth; i++) {
        delete [] mCells[i];
    }
    delete [] mCells;
    mCells = nullptr;
```

Code snippet from Spreadsheet\SpreadsheetNoCopyFrom.cpp

This chunk of code is identical to the destructor. You must free all the memory before reallocating it, or you will create a memory leak. The next step is to copy the memory.

```cpp
    // Copy the new memory.
    mWidth = rhs.mWidth;
    mHeight = rhs.mHeight;
    mCells = new SpreadsheetCell* [mWidth];
    for (int i = 0; i < mWidth; i++) {
        mCells[i] = new SpreadsheetCell[mHeight];
    }
    for (int i = 0; i < mWidth; i++) {
        for (int j = 0; j < mHeight; j++) {
            mCells[i][j] = rhs.mCells[i][j];
        }
    }
    return *this;
}
```

Code snippet from Spreadsheet\SpreadsheetNoCopyFrom.cpp

Note that this code looks remarkably like the code in the copy constructor. The following section will explain how you can avoid this code duplication.

The assignment operator completes the "big 3" routines for managing dynamically allocated memory in an object: the **destructor**, the **copy constructor**, and the **assignment operator**. Whenever you find yourself writing one of those methods you should write all of them.

 Whenever a class dynamically allocates memory, write a destructor, copy constructor, and assignment operator.

 C++11 includes a new concept called move semantics, *which requires a* move constructor *and* move assignment operator. *These can be used to increase performance in certain situations and are discussed in detail in Chapter 9.*

Common Helper Routines for Copy Constructor and Assignment Operator

The copy constructor and the assignment operator are quite similar. Thus, it's usually convenient to factor the common tasks into a helper method. For example, you could add a `copyFrom()` method to the `Spreadsheet` class, and rewrite the copy constructor and assignment operator to use it like this:

Available for download on Wrox.com

```
void Spreadsheet::copyFrom(const Spreadsheet& src)
{
    mWidth = src.mWidth;
    mHeight = src.mHeight;
    mCells = new SpreadsheetCell* [mWidth];
    for (int i = 0; i < mWidth; i++) {
        mCells[i] = new SpreadsheetCell[mHeight];
    }
    for (int i = 0; i < mWidth; i++) {
        for (int j = 0; j < mHeight; j++) {
            mCells[i][j] = src.mCells[i][j];
        }
    }
}
Spreadsheet::Spreadsheet(const Spreadsheet& src)
{
    copyFrom(src);
}
```

```
Spreadsheet& Spreadsheet::operator=(const Spreadsheet& rhs)
{
    // Check for self-assignment.
    if (this == &rhs) {
        return *this;
    }
    // Free the old memory.
    for (int i = 0; i < mWidth; i++) {
        delete [] mCells[i];
    }
    delete [] mCells;
    mCells = nullptr;
    // Copy the new memory.
    copyFrom(rhs);
    return *this;
}
```

Code snippet from Spreadsheet\Spreadsheet.cpp

Disallowing Assignment and Pass-By-Value

Sometimes when you dynamically allocate memory in your class, it's easiest just to prevent anyone from copying or assigning to your objects. You can do this by marking your `operator=` and copy constructor `private`. That way, if anyone tries to pass the object by value, return it from a function or method, or assign to it, the compiler will complain. Here is a `Spreadsheet` class definition that prevents assignment and pass-by-value:

Available for download on Wrox.com

```
class Spreadsheet
{
    // Code omitted for brevity
    private:
        Spreadsheet(const Spreadsheet& src);
        Spreadsheet& operator=(const Spreadsheet& rhs);
};
```

Code snippet from SpreadsheetNoCopyAssign\Spreadsheet.h

You don't need to provide implementations for `private` copy constructors and assignment operators. The linker will never look for them because the compiler won't allow code to call them. When you write code to copy or assign to a `Spreadsheet` object, the compiler will complain with a message like:

```
'=' : cannot access private member declared in class 'Spreadsheet'.
```

 Instead of making your `operator=` *and copy constructor* `private`, *you can make them* `protected` *if you want to allow subclasses to use them. Subclasses are discussed in Chapter 8.*

DIFFERENT KINDS OF DATA MEMBERS

C++ gives you many choices for data members. In addition to declaring simple data members in your classes, you can create `static` data members that all objects of the class share, `const` members, reference members, `const` reference members, and more. This section explains the intricacies of these different kinds of data members.

static Data Members

Sometimes giving each object of a class a copy of a variable is overkill or won't work. The data member might be specific to the class, but not appropriate for each object to have its own copy. For example, you might want to give each spreadsheet a unique numerical identifier. You would need a counter that starts at 0 from which each new object could obtain its ID. This spreadsheet counter really belongs to the `Spreadsheet` class, but it doesn't make sense for each `Spreadsheet` object to have a copy of it because you would have to keep all the counters synchronized somehow. C++ provides a solution with *static data members*. A `static` data member is a data member associated with a class instead of an object. You can think of `static` data members as global variables specific to a class. Here is the `Spreadsheet` class definition, including the new `static` counter data member:

Available for download on Wrox.com

```
class Spreadsheet
{
    // Omitted for brevity
    protected:
        static int sCounter = 0;
};
```

Code snippet from SpreadsheetDataMembers\Spreadsheet.h

With C++11, that's all you need to do. If you are using C++ prior to C++11, it is a bit clumsier. In that case, you cannot do initialization in the class definition. In addition to listing `static` class members in the class definition, you will have to allocate space for them in a source file, usually the source file in which you place your class method definitions. You can initialize them at the same time, but note that unlike normal variables and data members, they are initialized to 0 by default. `static` pointers are initialized to `nullptr`. Here is the code to allocate space for and initialize the sCounter member in pre-C++11:

Available for download on Wrox.com

```
int Spreadsheet::sCounter = 0;
```

Code snippet from SpreadsheetDataMembers\Spreadsheet.cpp

This code appears outside of any function or method bodies. It's almost like declaring a global variable, except that the `Spreadsheet::` scope resolution specifies that it's part of the `Spreadsheet` class.

Accessing static Data Members within Class Methods

You can use `static` data members as if they were regular data members from within class methods. For example, you might want to create an `mId` member of the `Spreadsheet` class and initialize it from the `sCounter` member in the `Spreadsheet` constructor. Here is the `Spreadsheet` class definition with an `mId` member:

```
class Spreadsheet
{
    public:
        // Omitted for brevity
        int getId() const;
    protected:
        // Omitted for brevity
        static int sCounter = 0;
        int mId;
};
```

Code snippet from SpreadsheetDataMembers\Spreadsheet.h

Here is an implementation of the `Spreadsheet` constructor that assigns the initial ID:

```
Spreadsheet::Spreadsheet(int inWidth, int inHeight) :
    mWidth(inWidth), mHeight(inHeight)
{
    mId = sCounter++;
    mCells = new SpreadsheetCell* [mWidth];
    for (int i = 0; i < mWidth; i++) {
        mCells[i] = new SpreadsheetCell[mHeight];
    }
}
```

Code snippet from SpreadsheetDataMembers\Spreadsheet.cpp

As you can see, the constructor can access `sCounter` as if it were a normal member. Remember to assign an ID in the copy constructor as well:

```
Spreadsheet::Spreadsheet(const Spreadsheet& src)
{
    mId = sCounter++;
    copyFrom(src);
}
```

Code snippet from SpreadsheetDataMembers\Spreadsheet.cpp

You should not copy the ID in the assignment operator. Once an ID is assigned to an object it should never change.

Accessing static Data Members Outside Methods

Access control specifiers apply to `static` data members: `sCounter` is `protected`, so it cannot be accessed from outside class methods. If `sCounter` was `public`, you could access it from outside class methods by specifying that the variable is part of the Spreadsheet class with the :: scope resolution operator:

```
int c = Spreadsheet::sCounter;
```

However, it's not recommended to have `public` data members. You should grant access through `public` get/set methods. If you want to grant access to a `static` data member, you need to implement `static` get/set methods, which are explained later in this chapter.

const Data Members

Data members in your class can be declared `const`, meaning they can't be changed after they are created and initialized. Constants almost never make sense at the object level, so `const` data members are usually `static` as well. You should use `static const` data members in place of global constants when the constants apply only to the class. For example, you might want to specify a maximum height and width for spreadsheets. If the user tries to construct a spreadsheet with a greater height or width than the maximum, the maximum is used instead. You can make the max height and width `static const` members of the Spreadsheet class:

Available for
download on
Wrox.com

```
class Spreadsheet
{
    public:
        // Omitted for brevity
        static const int kMaxHeight = 100;
        static const int kMaxWidth = 100;
};
```

Code snippet from SpreadsheetDataMembers\Spreadsheet.h

You can use these new constants in your constructor as shown in the following section of code (note the use of the ternary operator):

Available for
download on
Wrox.com

```
Spreadsheet::Spreadsheet(int inWidth, int inHeight) :
    mWidth(inWidth < kMaxWidth ? inWidth : kMaxWidth),
    mHeight(inHeight < kMaxHeight ? inHeight : kMaxHeight)
{
    mId = sCounter++;
    mCells = new SpreadsheetCell* [mWidth];
    for (int i = 0; i < mWidth; i++) {
        mCells[i] = new SpreadsheetCell[mHeight];
    }
}
```

Code snippet from SpreadsheetDataMembers\Spreadsheet.cpp

*Instead of automatically clamping the width and height to their maximum, you could also decide to throw an exception when the width or height exceed their maximum. However, the destructor **will not** be called when you throw an exception from a constructor. So, you need to be careful with this. Details are explained in Chapter 10.*

kMaxHeight and kMaxWidth are public, so you can access them from anywhere in your program as if they were global variables, but with slightly different syntax: You must specify that the variable is part of the Spreadsheet class with the :: scope resolution operator:

```
cout << "Maximum height is: " << Spreadsheet::kMaxHeight << endl;
```

Reference Data Members

Spreadsheets and SpreadsheetCells are great, but they don't make a very useful application by themselves. You need code to control the whole spreadsheet program, which you could package into a SpreadsheetApplication class.

The implementation of this class is unimportant at the moment. For now, consider this architecture problem: How can spreadsheets communicate with the application? The application stores a list of spreadsheets, so it can communicate with the spreadsheets. Similarly, each spreadsheet should store a reference to the application object. The Spreadsheet class must know about the SpreadsheetApplication class and the SpreadsheetApplication class must know about the Spreadsheet class. This is a circular reference and cannot be solved with normal #includes. The solution is to use a *forward declaration* in one of the header files (see Chapter 9 for details). Here is the new Spreadsheet class definition that uses a forward declaration to tell the compiler about the SpreadsheetApplication class:

```cpp
class SpreadsheetApplication; // forward declaration
class Spreadsheet
{
    public:
        Spreadsheet(int inWidth, int inHeight,
            SpreadsheetApplication& theApp);
        // Code omitted for brevity.
    protected:
        // Code omitted for brevity.
        SpreadsheetApplication& mTheApp;
};
```

Code snippet from SpreadsheetDataMembers\Spreadsheet.h

This definition adds a SpreadsheetApplication reference as a data member. It's recommended to use a reference in this case instead of a pointer because a Spreadsheet should always refer to a SpreadsheetApplication. This would not be guaranteed with a pointer.

Note that the application reference is given to each Spreadsheet in its constructor. A reference cannot exist without referring to something, so mTheApp must be given a value in the ctor-initializer of the constructor:

```cpp
Spreadsheet::Spreadsheet(int inWidth, int inHeight,
        SpreadsheetApplication& theApp)
    : mWidth(inWidth < kMaxWidth ? inWidth : kMaxWidth),
```

```
       mHeight(inHeight < kMaxHeight ? inHeight : kMaxHeight), mTheApp(theApp)
{
    // Code omitted for brevity.
}
```

You must also initialize the reference member in the copy constructor:

```
Spreadsheet::Spreadsheet(const Spreadsheet& src) :
    mTheApp(src.mTheApp)
{
    mId = sCounter++;
    copyFrom(src);
}
```

Remember that after you have initialized a reference you cannot change the object to which it refers. Thus, you do not need to attempt to assign to references in the assignment operator.

const Reference Data Members

Your reference members can refer to const objects just as normal references can refer to const objects. For example, you might decide that Spreadsheets should only have a const reference to the application object. You can simply change the class definition to declare mTheApp as a const reference:

```
class Spreadsheet
{
    public:
        Spreadsheet(int inWidth, int inHeight,
            const SpreadsheetApplication& theApp);
        // Code omitted for brevity.
    protected:
        // Code omitted for brevity.
        const SpreadsheetApplication& mTheApp;
};
```

There is an important difference between using a const reference versus a non-const reference. The const reference SpreadsheetApplication data member can only be used to call const methods on the SpreadsheetApplication object. If you try to call a non-const method through a const reference, you will get a compiler error.

It's also possible to have a static reference member or a static const reference member, but you will rarely find the need for something like that.

MORE ABOUT METHODS

C++ also provides myriad choices for methods. This section explains all the tricky details.

static Methods

Methods, like members, sometimes apply to the class as a whole, not to each object. You can write `static` methods as well as members. As an example, consider the `SpreadsheetCell` class from Chapter 6. It has two helper methods: `stringToDouble()` and `doubleToString()`. These methods don't access information about specific objects, so they could be `static`. Here is the class definition with these methods `static`:

```
class SpreadsheetCell
{
    // Omitted for brevity
    protected:
        static string doubleToString(double val);
        static double stringToDouble(const string& str);
        // Omitted for brevity
};
```

Code snippet from SpreadsheetCellMethods\SpreadsheetCell.h

These methods are not declared as `const` anymore because it's not allowed to declare `static` methods as `const`. The non-`static` versions of those methods were marked as `const`.

The implementations of these two methods are identical to the previous implementations. You don't repeat the `static` keyword in front of the method definitions. However, note that `static` methods are not called on a specific object, so they have no `this` pointer, and are not executing for a specific object with access to its non-`static` members. In fact, a `static` method is just like a regular function. The only difference is that it can access `private` and `protected` `static` data members of the class. It can also access `private` and `protected` non-static data members on other objects of the same type, if those other objects are made visible to the `static` method, for example by passing in a reference or pointer to such object.

You call a `static` method just like a regular function from within any method of the class. Thus, the implementation of all methods in `SpreadsheetCell` can stay the same. Outside of the class, you need to qualify the method name with the class name using the scope resolution operator (as for `static` members). Access control applies as usual.

You might want to make `stringToDouble()` and `doubleToString()` `public` so that other code outside the class could make use of them. If so, you could call them from anywhere like this:

```
string str = SpreadsheetCell::doubleToString(5);
```

const Methods

A `const` object is an object whose value cannot be changed. If you have a `const`, reference to `const` or pointer to `const` object, the compiler will not let you call any methods on that object unless those methods guarantee that they won't change any data members. The way you guarantee that a method won't change data members is to mark the method itself with the const keyword. Here is the SpreadsheetCell class with the methods that don't change any data member marked const:

```
class SpreadsheetCell
{
    public:
        // Omitted for brevity
        double getValue() const;
        string getString() const;
        // Omitted for brevity
};
```

Code snippet from SpreadsheetCellMethods\SpreadsheetCell.h

The const specification is part of the method prototype and must accompany its definition as well:

```
double SpreadsheetCell::getValue() const
{
    return mValue;
}
string SpreadsheetCell::getString() const
{
    return mString;
}
```

Code snippet from SpreadsheetCellMethods\SpreadsheetCell.h

Marking a method as const signs a contract with client code guaranteeing that you will not try to change the internal values of the object within the method. If you try to declare a method const that actually modifies a data member, the compiler will complain. You also cannot declare a static method const because it is redundant. Static methods do not have an instance of the class so it would be impossible for them to change internal values. const works by making it appear inside the method that you have a const reference to each data member. Thus, if you try to change the data member the compiler will flag an error.

A non-const object can call const and non-const methods. However, a const object can only call const methods. Here are some examples:

```
SpreadsheetCell myCell(5);
cout << myCell.getValue() << endl;      // OK
myCell.setString("6");                  // OK
const SpreadsheetCell& anotherCell = myCell;
cout << anotherCell.getValue() << endl; // OK
anotherCell.setString("6");             // Compilation Error!
```

Code snippet from SpreadsheetCellMethods\SpreadsheetCellTest.cpp

You should get into the habit of declaring `const` all methods that don't modify the object so that you can use references to `const` objects in your program.

Note that `const` objects can still be destroyed, and their destructor can be called. You shouldn't try to mark the destructor `const`.

mutable Data Members

Sometimes you write a method that is "logically" `const` but happens to change a data member of the object. This modification has no effect on any user-visible data, but is technically a change, so the compiler won't let you declare the method `const`. For example, suppose that you want to profile your spreadsheet application to obtain info about how often data is being read. A crude way to do this would be to add a counter to the `SpreadsheetCell` class that counts each call to `getValue()` or `getString()`. Unfortunately, that makes those methods non-`const` in the compiler's eyes, which is not what you intended. The solution is to make your new counter variable `mutable`, which tells the compiler that it's okay to change it in a `const` method. Here is the new `SpreadsheetCell` class definition:

```
class SpreadsheetCell
{
    // Omitted for brevity
    protected:
        double mValue;
        string mString;
        mutable int mNumAccesses = 0;
};
```

Code snippet from SpreadsheetCellMethods\SpreadsheetCell.h

Here are the definitions for `getValue()` and `getString()`:

```
double SpreadsheetCell::getValue() const
{
    mNumAccesses++;
    return mValue;
}
string SpreadsheetCell::getString() const
{
    mNumAccesses++;
    return mString;
}
```

Code snippet from SpreadsheetCellMethods\SpreadsheetCell.h

Method Overloading

You've already noticed that you can write multiple constructors in a class, all of which have the same name. These constructors differ only in the number or types of their parameters. You can do the same thing for any method or function in C++. Specifically, you can *overload* the function or method name by using it for multiple functions, as long as the number or types of the parameters differ. For example, in the `SpreadsheetCell` class you could rename both `setString()` and `setValue()` to `set()`. The class definition now looks like this:

```
class SpreadsheetCell
{
    public:
        // Omitted for brevity
        void set(double inValue);
        void set(const string& inString);
        // Omitted for brevity
};
```

Code snippet from SpreadsheetCellMethods\SpreadsheetCell.h

The implementations of the `set()` methods stay the same. Note that the double constructor that previously called `setValue()` must now call `set()`. When you write code to call `set()`, the compiler determines which instance to call based on the parameter you pass: If you pass a `string` the compiler calls the `string` instance; if you pass a `double` the compiler calls the `double` instance. This is called *overload resolution*.

You might be tempted to do the same thing for `getValue()` and `getString()`: Rename each of them to `get()`. However, that does not compile. C++ does not allow you to overload a method name based only on the return type of the method because in many cases it would be impossible for the compiler to determine which instance of the method to call. For example, if the return value of the method is not captured anywhere, the compiler has no way to tell which instance of the method you wanted.

Note also that you can overload a method based on `const`. That is, you can write two methods with the same name and same parameters, one of which is declared `const` and one of which is not. The compiler will call the `const` method if you have a `const` object and the non-`const` method if you have a non-`const` object.

C++11 Overloaded methods can be explicitly deleted, which can be used to disallow calling a member function with particular parameters. For example, suppose you have the following class:

```
class MyClass
{
    public:
        void foo(int i);
};
```

The `foo()` method can be called as follows:

```
MyClass c;
c.foo(123);
c.foo(1.23);
```

For the second line, the compiler will convert the `double` value (1.23) to an integer value (1) and then call `foo(int i)`. The compiler might give you a warning, but it will perform this implicit conversion. You can prevent the compiler from performing this conversion by explicitly deleting a double instance of foo():

```
class MyClass
{
    public:
        void foo(int i);
        void foo(double d) = delete;
};
```

With this change, an attempt to call foo() with a double will be flagged as an error by the compiler, instead of performing a conversion to an integer.

Default Parameters

A feature similar to method overloading in C++ is *default parameters*. You can specify defaults for function and method parameters in the prototype. If the user specifies those arguments, the defaults are ignored. If the user omits those arguments, the default values are used. There is a limitation, though: You can only provide defaults for a continuous list of parameters starting from the *rightmost parameter*. Otherwise, the compiler would not be able to match missing arguments to default parameters. Default parameters are most useful in constructors. For example, you can assign default values to the width and height in your Spreadsheet constructor:

```
class Spreadsheet
{
    public:
        Spreadsheet(const SpreadsheetApplication& theApp,
            int inWidth = kMaxWidth, int inHeight = kMaxHeight);
        // Omitted for brevity
};
```

Code snippet from SpreadsheetDefaultParams\Spreadsheet.h

The implementation of the Spreadsheet constructor stays the same. Note that you specify the default parameters only in the method declaration, but not in the definition.

Now you can call the Spreadsheet constructor with one, two, or three arguments even though there is only one non-copy constructor:

```
SpreadsheetApplication theApp;
Spreadsheet s1(theApp);
Spreadsheet s2(theApp, 5);
Spreadsheet s3(theApp, 5, 6);
```

Code snippet from SpreadsheetDefaultParams\SpreadsheetTest.cpp

A constructor with defaults for all its parameters can function as a default constructor. That is, you can construct an object of that class without specifying any arguments. If you try to declare both a default constructor and a multi-argument constructor with defaults for all its parameters, the compiler will complain because it won't know which constructor to call if you don't specify any arguments.

Note that anything you can do with default parameters you can do with method overloading. You could write three different constructors, each of which takes a different number of parameters. However, default parameters allow you to write only one constructor to take three different numbers of arguments. You should use the mechanism with which you are most comfortable.

Inline Methods

C++ gives you the ability to recommend that a call to a method or function should not actually be implemented in the generated code as a call to a separate block of code. Instead, the compiler should insert the method or function body directly into the code where the method or function call is made. This process is called *inlining*, and methods or functions that want this behavior are called `inline` methods or functions. Inlining is safer than using `#define` macros.

You can specify an `inline` method or function by placing the `inline` keyword in front of its name in the function or method definition. For example, you might want to make the accessor methods of the `SpreadsheetCell` class `inline`, in which case you would define them like this:

```cpp
inline double SpreadsheetCell::getValue() const
{
    mNumAccesses++;
    return mValue;
}
inline string SpreadsheetCell::getString() const
{
    mNumAccesses++;
    return mString;
}
```

Code snippet from SpreadsheetCellMethods\SpreadsheetCell.h

Now, the compiler has the option to replace calls to `getValue()` and `getString()` with the actual method body instead of generating code to make a function call.

There is one caveat: Definitions of `inline` methods and functions must be available in every source file in which they are called. That makes sense if you think about it: How can the compiler substitute the function body if it can't see the function definition? Thus, if you write `inline` functions or methods you should place the definitions in a header file along with their prototypes. For methods, this means placing the definitions in the `.h` file that includes the class definition. This placement is perfectly safe: The linker doesn't complain about multiple definitions of the same method.

> *Advanced C++ compilers do not require you to put definitions of `inline` methods in a header file. For example, Microsoft Visual C++ supports Link-Time Code Generation (LTCG) which will automatically inline small function bodies, even if they are not declared as `inline` and even if they are not defined in a header file. When you use such a compiler, make use of it, and don't put the definitions in the header file. This way, your interface files stay clean without any implementation details visible in it.*

C++ provides an alternate syntax for declaring `inline` methods that doesn't use the `inline` keyword at all. Instead, you place the method definition directly in the class definition. Here is a `SpreadsheetCell` class definition with this syntax:

```
class SpreadsheetCell
{
    public:
        // Omitted for brevity
        double getValue() const {mNumAccesses++; return mValue; }
        string getString() const {mNumAccesses++; return mString; }
        // Omitted for brevity
};
```

Code snippet from SpreadsheetCellMethods\SpreadsheetCell.h

 If you single-step with a debugger on a function call that is inlined, some advanced C++ debuggers will jump to the actual source code of the inline function in the header file, giving you the illusion of a function call, but in reality, the code is inlined.

Many C++ programmers discover the `inline` method syntax and employ it without understanding the ramifications of making a method `inline`. First, there are many restrictions on which methods can be `inline`. Compilers will only `inline` the simplest methods and functions. If you define an `inline` method that the compiler doesn't want to `inline`, it may silently ignore the directive. Second, big `inline` methods can lead to code bloat. The body of the methods are reproduced everywhere they are called, increasing the size of your program executable.

Modern compilers like Microsoft Visual C++ will take metrics like code bloat into account before deciding to inline a method, and they will not inline anything that is not cost-effective.

NESTED CLASSES

Class definitions can contain more than just methods and members. You can also write nested classes and `struct`s, declare `typedef`s, or create enumerated types. Anything declared inside a class is in the scope of that class. If it is `public`, you can access it outside the class by scoping it with the `ClassName::` scope resolution syntax.

You can provide a class definition inside another class definition. For example, you might decide that the `SpreadsheetCell` class is really part of the `Spreadsheet` class. You could define both of them like this:

```
class Spreadsheet
{
    public:
        class SpreadsheetCell
        {
            public:
```

```
                SpreadsheetCell();
                SpreadsheetCell(double initialValue);
                // Omitted for brevity
            protected:
                double mValue;
                string mString;
                mutable int mNumAccesses;
        };
        Spreadsheet(const SpreadsheetApplication& theApp,
            int inWidth = kMaxWidth, int inHeight = kMaxHeight);
        Spreadsheet(const Spreadsheet& src);
        ~Spreadsheet();
        // Remainder of Spreadsheet declarations omitted for brevity
};
```

Code snippet from NestedClasses\Spreadsheet.h

Now, the `SpreadsheetCell` class is defined inside the `Spreadsheet` class, so anywhere you refer to a `SpreadsheetCell` outside of the `Spreadsheet` class you must qualify the name with the `Spreadsheet::` scope. This applies even to the method definitions. For example, the default constructor now looks like this:

```
Spreadsheet::SpreadsheetCell::SpreadsheetCell() : mValue(0), mNumAccesses(0)
{
}
```

Code snippet from NestedClasses\Spreadsheet.cpp

This syntax can quickly become clumsy. For example, the definition of the `SpreadsheetCell` assignment operator now looks like this:

```
Spreadsheet::SpreadsheetCell& Spreadsheet::SpreadsheetCell::operator=(
    const SpreadsheetCell& rhs)
{
    if (this == &rhs) {
        return *this;
    }
    mValue = rhs.mValue;
    mString = rhs.mString;
    mNumAccesses = rhs.mNumAccesses;
    return *this;
}
```

Code snippet from NestedClasses\Spreadsheet.cpp

In fact, you must even use the syntax for return types (but not parameters) of methods in the `Spreadsheet` class itself:

```
Spreadsheet::SpreadsheetCell Spreadsheet::getCellAt(int x, int y)
{
    if (!inRange(x, mWidth) || !inRange(y, mHeight)) {
        throw std::out_of_range("");
```

```
        }
        return mCells[x][y];
    }
```

You can avoid the clumsy syntax by using a `typedef` to rename `Spreadsheet::SpreadsheetCell` to something more manageable like `SCell`:

```
typedef Spreadsheet::SpreadsheetCell SCell;
```

This `typedef` should go outside the `Spreadsheet` class definition, or else you will have to qualify the `typedef` name itself with `Spreadsheet::` to get `Spreadsheet::SCell`. That wouldn't do you much good!

Now you can write your constructor like this:

```
SCell::SpreadsheetCell() : mValue(0), mNumAccesses(0)
{
}
```

Normal access control applies to nested class definitions. If you declare a `private` or `protected` nested class, you can only use it inside the outer class.

You should generally use nested class definitions only for trivial classes. It is really too clumsy for something like the `SpreadsheetCell` class.

ENUMERATED TYPES INSIDE CLASSES

If you want to define a number of constants inside a class, you should use an enumerated type instead of a collection of `#define`s. For example, you can add support for cell coloring to the `SpreadsheetCell` class as follows:

```
class SpreadsheetCell
{
    public:
        // Omitted for brevity
        typedef enum {Red=1, Green, Blue, Yellow} Colors;
        void setColor(Colors color);
    protected:
        // Omitted for brevity
        Colors mColor = Red;
};
```

The implementation of the `setColor()` method is straightforward:

```
void SpreadsheetCell::setColor(Colors color)
{
    mColor = color;
}
```

Code snippet from SpreadsheetCellColors\SpreadsheetCell.cpp

The new method can be used as follows:

```
SpreadsheetCell myCell(5);
myCell.setColor(SpreadsheetCell::Blue);
```

Code snippet from SpreadsheetCellColors\SpreadsheetCellTest.cpp

Using an enumerated type is the preferred solution instead of using `#defines` as follows:

```
#define SPREADSHEETCELL_RED 1
#define SPREADSHEETCELL_GREEN 2
#define SPREADSHEETCELL_BLUE 3
#define SPREADSHEETCELL_YELLOW 4
class SpreadsheetCell
{
    public:
        // Omitted for brevity
        void setColor(int color);
    protected:
        // Omitted for brevity
        int mColor;
};
```

When you use `#defines`, you have to use an integer parameter for the `setColor()` function instead of a clear type like the `Colors` enumerated type.

FRIENDS

C++ allows classes to declare that other classes or member functions of other classes or nonmember functions are *friends*, and can access `protected` and `private` data members and methods. For example, the `SpreadsheetCell` class could specify that the `Spreadsheet` class is its "friend" like this:

```
class SpreadsheetCell
{
    public:
        friend class Spreadsheet;
        // Remainder of the class omitted for brevity
};
```

Now all the methods of the `Spreadsheet` class can access the `private` and `protected` data members and methods of the `SpreadsheetCell` class.

If you only want to make a specific member function of the `Spreadsheet` class a `friend`, you can do that as follows:

```
class SpreadsheetCell
{
    public:
        friend void Spreadsheet::setCellAt(int x, int y,
            const SpreadsheetCell& cell);
        // Remainder of the class omitted for brevity
};
```

Code snippet from Friends\FriendMethod\SpreadsheetCell.h

Note that a class needs to know which other classes, methods, or functions wish to be its friends; a class, method or function cannot declare itself to be a friend of some other class and access the non-public names of that class.

You might, for example, want to write a function to verify that the string of a `SpreadsheetCell` object is not empty. You might want this verification routine to be outside the `SpreadsheetCell` class to model an external audit, but the function should be able to access the internal data members of the object in order to check it properly. Here is the `SpreadsheetCell` class definition with a `friend checkSpreadsheetCell()` function:

```
class SpreadsheetCell
{
    public:
        friend bool checkSpreadsheetCell(const SpreadsheetCell& cell);
        // Omitted for brevity
};
```

Code snippet from Friends\SpreadsheetCell.h

The `friend` declaration in the class serves as the function's prototype. There's no need to write the prototype elsewhere (although it's harmless to do so).

Here is the function definition:

```
bool checkSpreadsheetCell(const SpreadsheetCell& cell)
{
    return !(cell.mString.empty());
}
```

Code snippet from Friends\SpreadsheetCell.cpp

You write this function just like any other function, except that you can directly access `private` and `protected` data members of the `SpreadsheetCell` class. You don't repeat the `friend` keyword on the function definition.

`friend` classes and methods are easy to abuse; they allow you to violate the principle of abstraction by exposing internals of your class to other classes or functions. Thus, you should use them only in limited circumstances such as operator overloading because in that case you need access to `protected` and `private` members, as discussed in the next section.

OPERATOR OVERLOADING

You often want to perform operations on objects, such as adding them, comparing them, or streaming them to or from files. For example, spreadsheets are really only useful when you can perform arithmetic actions on them, such as summing an entire row of cells.

Example: Implementing Addition for SpreadsheetCells

In true object-oriented fashion, `SpreadsheetCell` objects should be able to add themselves to other `SpreadsheetCell` objects. Adding a cell to another cell produces a third cell with the result. It doesn't change either of the original cells. The meaning of addition for `SpreadsheetCell`s is the addition of the values of the cells. The string representations are ignored.

First Attempt: The add Method

You can declare and define an `add()` method for your `SpreadsheetCell` class like this:

Available for download on Wrox.com

```
class SpreadsheetCell
{
    public:
        // Omitted for brevity
        const SpreadsheetCell add(const SpreadsheetCell& cell) const;
        // Omitted for brevity
};
```

Code snippet from OperatorOverloading\AddFirstAttempt\SpreadsheetCell.h

This method adds two cells together, returning a new third cell whose value is the sum of the first two. It is declared `const` and takes a reference to a `const SpreadsheetCell` because `add()` does not change either of the source cells. It returns a `const SpreadsheetCell` because you don't want users to change the return value. They should just assign it to another object. `add()` is a method, so it is called on one object and passed another. Here is the implementation:

Available for download on Wrox.com

```
const SpreadsheetCell SpreadsheetCell::add(const SpreadsheetCell& cell) const
{
    SpreadsheetCell newCell;
    newCell.set(mValue + cell.mValue); // update mValue and mString
    return newCell;
}
```

Code snippet from OperatorOverloading\AddFirstAttempt\SpreadsheetCell.cpp

Note that the implementation creates a new `SpreadsheetCell` called `newCell` and returns a *copy* of that cell. You might be tempted to return a reference to the cell instead. However, that will not work because as soon as the `add()` method ends and `newCell` goes out of scope it will be destroyed. The reference that you returned will then be a dangling reference.

You can use the `add()` method like this:

```
SpreadsheetCell myCell(4), anotherCell(5);
SpreadsheetCell aThirdCell = myCell.add(anotherCell);
```

Code snippet from OperatorOverloading\AddFirstAttempt\SpreadsheetCellTest.cpp

That works, but it's a bit clumsy. You can do better.

Second Attempt: Overloaded operator+ as a Method

It would be convenient to be able to add two cells with the plus sign the way that you add two `ints` or two `doubles`. Something like this:

```
SpreadsheetCell myCell(4), anotherCell(5);
SpreadsheetCell aThirdCell = myCell + anotherCell;
```

Code snippet from OperatorOverloading\AddSecondAttempt\SpreadsheetCellTest.cpp

C++ allows you to write your own version of the plus sign, called the addition operator, to work correctly with your classes. To do that you write a method with the name `operator+` that looks like this:

```
class SpreadsheetCell
{
    public:
        // Omitted for brevity
        const SpreadsheetCell operator+(const SpreadsheetCell& cell) const;
        // Omitted for brevity
};
```

Code snippet from OperatorOverloading\AddSecondAttempt\SpreadsheetCell.h

 You are allowed to write spaces between operator *and the plus sign. For example, instead of writing* operator+, *you can write* operator   +. *This is true for all operators. This book adopts the style without spaces.*

The definition of the method is identical to the implementation of the `add()` method:

```
const SpreadsheetCell
SpreadsheetCell::operator+(const SpreadsheetCell& cell) const
{
```

```
        SpreadsheetCell newCell;
        newCell.set(mValue + cell.mValue); // update mValue and mString.
        return newCell;
}
```

Code snippet from OperatorOverloading\AddSecondAttempt\SpreadsheetCell.cpp

Now you can add two cells together using the plus sign as shown previously.

This syntax takes a bit of getting used to. Try not to worry too much about the strange method name operator+ — it's just a name like foo or add. In order to understand the rest of the syntax, it helps to understand what's really going on. When your C++ compiler parses a program and encounters an operator, such as +, -, =, or <<, it tries to find a function or method with the name operator+, operator-, operator=, or operator<<, respectively, that takes the appropriate parameters. For example, when the compiler sees the following line, it tries to find either a method in the SpreadsheetCell class named operator+ that takes another SpreadsheetCell object or a global function named operator+ that takes two SpreadsheetCell objects:

```
        SpreadsheetCell aThirdCell = myCell + anotherCell;
```

Note that there's no requirement that operator+ takes as a parameter an object of the same type as the class for which it's written. You could write an operator+ for SpreadsheetCells that takes a Spreadsheet to add to the SpreadsheetCell. That wouldn't make sense to the programmer, but the compiler would allow it.

Note also that you can give operator+ any return value you want. Operator overloading is a form of function overloading, and recall that function overloading does not look at the return type of the function.

Implicit Conversions

Surprisingly, once you've written the operator+ shown earlier, not only can you add two cells together, you can also add a cell to a string, a double, or an int!

```
        SpreadsheetCell myCell(4), aThirdCell;
        string str = "hello";
        aThirdCell = myCell + str;
        aThirdCell = myCell + 5.6;
        aThirdCell = myCell + 4;
```

Code snippet from OperatorOverloading\AddSecondAttempt\SpreadsheetCellTest.cpp

The reason this code works is that the compiler does more to try to find an appropriate operator+ than just look for one with the exact types specified. The compiler also tries to find an appropriate conversion for the types so that an operator+ can be found. Constructors that take the type in question are appropriate converters. In the preceding example, when the compiler sees a SpreadsheetCell trying to add itself to double, it finds the SpreadsheetCell constructor that takes a double and constructs a temporary SpreadsheetCell object to pass to operator+. Similarly, when the compiler sees the line trying to add a SpreadsheetCell to a string, it calls the string SpreadsheetCell constructor to create a temporary SpreadsheetCell to pass to operator+.

This implicit conversion behavior is usually convenient. However, in the preceding example, it doesn't really make sense to add a `SpreadsheetCell` to a `string`. You can prevent the implicit construction of a `SpreadsheetCell` from a `string` by marking that constructor with the `explicit` keyword:

Available for download on Wrox.com

```
class SpreadsheetCell
{
    public:
        SpreadsheetCell();
        SpreadsheetCell(double initialValue);
        explicit SpreadsheetCell(const string& initialValue);
        SpreadsheetCell(const SpreadsheetCell& src);
        SpreadsheetCell& operator=(const SpreadsheetCell& rhs);
    // Remainder omitted for brevity
};
```

Code snippet from OperatorOverloading\AddSecondAttempt\SpreadsheetCell.h

The `explicit` keyword goes only in the `class` definition, and only makes sense when applied to constructors with exactly one argument.

The selection of an implicit constructor might be inefficient, because temporary objects must be created. To avoid implicit construction for adding a `double`, you could write a second `operator+` as follows:

Available for download on Wrox.com

```
const SpreadsheetCell SpreadsheetCell::operator+(double rhs) const
{
    return SpreadsheetCell(mValue + rhs);
}
```

Code snippet from OperatorOverloading\AddSecondAttempt\SpreadsheetCell.cpp

Note also that this demonstrates that you don't need to create a variable to return a value.

Third Attempt: Global operator+

Implicit conversions allow you to use an `operator+` method to add your `SpreadsheetCell` objects to `int`s and `double`s. However, the operator is not commutative, as shown in the following code:

Available for download on Wrox.com

```
aThirdCell = myCell + 4;   // Works fine.
aThirdCell = myCell + 5.6; // Works fine.
aThirdCell = 4 + myCell;   // FAILS TO COMPILE!
aThirdCell = 5.6 + myCell; // FAILS TO COMPILE!
```

Code snippet from OperatorOverloading\AddSecondAttempt\SpreadsheetCellTest.cpp

The implicit conversion works fine when the `SpreadsheetCell` object is on the left of the operator, but doesn't work when it's on the right. Addition is supposed to be commutative, so something is wrong here. The problem is that the `operator+` method must be called on a `SpreadsheetCell` object, and that object must be on the left-hand side of the `operator+`. That's just the way the C++

language is defined. So, there's no way you can get the above code to work with an `operator+` method.

However, you can get it to work if you replace the in-class `operator+` with a global `operator+` function that is not tied to any particular object. The function looks like this:

```cpp
const SpreadsheetCell operator+(const SpreadsheetCell& lhs,
    const SpreadsheetCell& rhs)
{
    SpreadsheetCell newCell;
    newCell.set(lhs.mValue + rhs.mValue); // update mValue and mString.
    return newCell;
}
```

Code snippet from OperatorOverloading\SpreadsheetCell.cpp

Now all four of the addition lines work as you expect:

```cpp
aThirdCell = myCell + 4;    // Works fine.
aThirdCell = myCell + 5.6;  // Works fine.
aThirdCell = 4 + myCell;    // Works fine.
aThirdCell = 5.6 + myCell;  // Works fine.
```

Code snippet from OperatorOverloading\SpreadsheetCellTest.cpp

Note that the implementation of the global `operator+` accesses `protected` data members of `SpreadsheetCell` objects. Therefore, it must be a `friend` function of the `SpreadsheetCell` class:

```cpp
class SpreadsheetCell
{
    public:
        // Omitted for brevity
        friend const SpreadsheetCell operator+(const SpreadsheetCell& lhs,
            const SpreadsheetCell& rhs);
        //Omitted for brevity
};
```

Code snippet from OperatorOverloading\SpreadsheetCell.h

You might be wondering what happens if you write the following code:

```cpp
aThirdCell = 4.5 + 5.5;
```

Code snippet from OperatorOverloading\SpreadsheetCellTest.cpp

It compiles and runs, but it's not calling the `operator+` you wrote. It does normal `double` addition of 4.5 and 5.5, which results in the following intermediate statement:

```cpp
aThirdCell = 10;
```

To make this assignment work, there should be a `SpreadsheetCell` object on the right-hand side. The compiler will discover a user-defined constructor that takes a `double`, will use this constructor to implicitly convert the `double` value into a temporary `SpreadsheetCell` object, and will then call the assignment operator.

Overloading Arithmetic Operators

Now that you understand how to write `operator+`, the rest of the basic arithmetic operators are straightforward. Here are declarations of `-`, `*`, and `/` (you can also overload `%`, but it doesn't make sense for the `double` values stored in `SpreadsheetCells`):

```cpp
class SpreadsheetCell
{
    public:
        // Omitted for brevity
        friend const SpreadsheetCell operator+(const SpreadsheetCell& lhs,
            const SpreadsheetCell& rhs);
        friend const SpreadsheetCell operator-(const SpreadsheetCell& lhs,
            const SpreadsheetCell& rhs);
        friend const SpreadsheetCell operator*(const SpreadsheetCell& lhs,
            const SpreadsheetCell& rhs);
        friend const SpreadsheetCell operator/(const SpreadsheetCell& lhs,
            const SpreadsheetCell& rhs);
        // Omitted for brevity
};
```

Code snippet from OperatorOverloading\SpreadsheetCell.h

Here are the implementations. The only tricky aspect is remembering to check for division by zero. This implementation throws an exception if division by zero is detected:

```cpp
const SpreadsheetCell operator-(const SpreadsheetCell& lhs,
    const SpreadsheetCell& rhs)
{
    SpreadsheetCell newCell;
    newCell.set(lhs.mValue - rhs.mValue); // update mValue and mString.
    return newCell;
}
const SpreadsheetCell operator*(const SpreadsheetCell& lhs,
    const SpreadsheetCell& rhs)
{
    SpreadsheetCell newCell;
    newCell.set(lhs.mValue * rhs.mValue); // update mValue and mString.
    return newCell;
}
const SpreadsheetCell operator/(const SpreadsheetCell& lhs,
    const SpreadsheetCell& rhs)
{
    if (rhs.mValue == 0)
        throw invalid_argument("Divide by zero.");
    SpreadsheetCell newCell;
```

```
        newCell.set(lhs.mValue / rhs.mValue); // update mValue and mString
        return newCell;
    }
```

Code snippet from OperatorOverloading\SpreadsheetCell.cpp

C++ does not require you to actually implement multiplication in `operator*`, division in `operator/`, and so on. You could implement multiplication in `operator/`, division in `operator+`, and so forth. However, that would be extremely confusing, and there is no good reason to do so except as a practical joke. Whenever possible, stick to the commonly used operator meanings in your implementations.

 *In C++, you cannot change the precedence of operators. For example, * and / are always evaluated before + and -. The only thing user-defined operators can do is specify the implementation once the precedence of operations has been determined.*

Overloading the Arithmetic Shorthand Operators

In addition to the basic arithmetic operators, C++ provides shorthand operators such as += and -=. You might assume that writing `operator+` for your class provides `operator+=` also. No such luck. You have to overload the shorthand arithmetic operators explicitly. These operators differ from the basic arithmetic operators in that they change the object on the left-hand side of the operator instead of creating a new object. A second, subtler, difference is that, like the assignment operator, they generate a result that is a reference to the modified object.

The arithmetic operators always require an object on the left-hand side, so you should write them as methods, not as global functions. Here are the declarations for the `SpreadsheetCell` class:

```
class SpreadsheetCell
{
    public:
        // Omitted for brevity
        SpreadsheetCell& operator+=(const SpreadsheetCell& rhs);
        SpreadsheetCell& operator-=(const SpreadsheetCell& rhs);
        SpreadsheetCell& operator*=(const SpreadsheetCell& rhs);
        SpreadsheetCell& operator/=(const SpreadsheetCell& rhs);
        // Omitted for brevity
};
```

Code snippet from OperatorOverloading\SpreadsheetCell.h

Here are the implementations:

```
SpreadsheetCell& SpreadsheetCell::operator+=(const SpreadsheetCell& rhs)
{
    set(mValue + rhs.mValue); // Call set to update mValue and mString.
    return *this;
}
```

```
SpreadsheetCell& SpreadsheetCell::operator-=(const SpreadsheetCell& rhs)
{
    set(mValue - rhs.mValue); // Call set to update mValue and mString.
    return *this;
}
SpreadsheetCell& SpreadsheetCell::operator*=(const SpreadsheetCell& rhs)
{
    set(mValue * rhs.mValue); // Call set to update mValue and mString.
    return *this;
}
SpreadsheetCell& SpreadsheetCell::operator/=(const SpreadsheetCell& rhs)
{
    if (rhs.mValue == 0)
        throw invalid_argument("Divide by zero.");
    set(mValue / rhs.mValue); // Call set to update mValue and mString.
    return *this;
}
```

Code snippet from OperatorOverloading\SpreadsheetCell.cpp

The shorthand arithmetic operators are combinations of the basic arithmetic and the assignment operators. With the above definitions, you can now write code like this:

```
SpreadsheetCell myCell(4), aThirdCell(2);
aThirdCell -= myCell;
aThirdCell += 5.4;
```

Code snippet from OperatorOverloading\SpreadsheetCellTest.cpp

You cannot, however, write code like this (which is a good thing!):

```
5.4 += aThirdCell;
```

Overloading Comparison Operators

The comparison operators, such as >, <, and ==, are another useful set of operators to define for your classes. Like the basic arithmetic operators, they should be global `friend` functions so that you can use implicit conversion on both the left-hand side and right-hand side of the operator. The comparison operators all return a `bool`. Of course, you can change the return type, but we don't recommend it. Here are the declarations and definitions:

```
class SpreadsheetCell
{
    public:
        // Omitted for brevity
        friend bool operator==(const SpreadsheetCell& lhs,
            const SpreadsheetCell& rhs);
        friend bool operator<(const SpreadsheetCell& lhs,
            const SpreadsheetCell& rhs);
        friend bool operator>(const SpreadsheetCell& lhs,
            const SpreadsheetCell& rhs);
        friend bool operator!=(const SpreadsheetCell& lhs,
```

```
            const SpreadsheetCell& rhs);
        friend bool operator<=(const SpreadsheetCell& lhs,
            const SpreadsheetCell& rhs);
        friend bool operator>=(const SpreadsheetCell& lhs,
            const SpreadsheetCell& rhs);
        // Omitted for brevity
};
```

Code snippet from OperatorOverloading\SpreadsheetCell.h

Available for
download on
Wrox.com

```
bool operator==(const SpreadsheetCell& lhs, const SpreadsheetCell& rhs)
{
    return (lhs.mValue == rhs.mValue);
}
bool operator<(const SpreadsheetCell& lhs, const SpreadsheetCell& rhs)
{
    return (lhs.mValue < rhs.mValue);
}
bool operator>(const SpreadsheetCell& lhs, const SpreadsheetCell& rhs)
{
    return (lhs.mValue > rhs.mValue);
}
bool operator!=(const SpreadsheetCell& lhs, const SpreadsheetCell& rhs)
{
    return (lhs.mValue != rhs.mValue);
}
bool operator<=(const SpreadsheetCell& lhs, const SpreadsheetCell& rhs)
{
    return (lhs.mValue <= rhs.mValue);
}
bool operator>=(const SpreadsheetCell& lhs, const SpreadsheetCell& rhs)
{
    return (lhs.mValue >= rhs.mValue);
}
```

Code snippet from OperatorOverloading\SpreadsheetCell.cpp

The preceding overloaded operators are working with `mValue`, *which is a* `double`. *Most of the time, performing equality or inequality tests on floating point values is not a good idea. You should use an* epsilon test, *but this falls outside the scope of this book.*

In classes with more data members, it might be painful to compare each data member. However, once you've implemented == and <, you can write the rest of the comparison operators in terms of those two. For example, here is a definition of operator>= that uses operator<:

```
bool operator>=(const SpreadsheetCell& lhs, const SpreadsheetCell& rhs)
{
    return !(lhs < rhs);
}
```

You can use these operators to compare `SpreadsheetCells` to other `SpreadsheetCells`, and to doubles and ints:

```
if (myCell > aThirdCell || myCell < 10) {
    cout << myCell.getValue() << endl;
}
```

Code snippet from OperatorOverloading\SpreadsheetCellTest.cpp

Building Types with Operator Overloading

Many people find the syntax of operator overloading tricky and confusing, at least at first. The irony is that it's supposed to make things simpler. As you've discovered, that doesn't mean simpler for the person writing the class, but simpler for the person using the class. The point is to make your new classes as similar as possible to built-in types such as int and double: It's easier to add objects using + than to remember whether the method name you should call is add() or sum().

Provide operator overloading as a service to clients of your class.

At this point, you might be wondering exactly which operators you can overload. The answer is "almost all of them — even some you've never heard of." You have actually just scratched the surface: You've seen the assignment operator in the section on object life cycles, the basic arithmetic operators, the shorthand arithmetic operators, and the comparison operators. Overloading the stream insertion and extraction operators is also useful. In addition, there are some tricky, but interesting, things you can do with operator overloading that you might not anticipate at first. The STL uses operator overloading extensively. Chapter 18 explains how and when to overload the rest of the operators. Chapters 11 to 17 cover the STL.

BUILDING STABLE INTERFACES

Now that you understand all the gory syntax of writing classes in C++, it helps to revisit the design principles from Chapters 3 and 4. Classes are the main unit of abstraction in C++. You should apply the principles of abstraction to your classes to separate the interface from the implementation as much as possible. Specifically, you should make all data members protected or private and provide getter and setter methods for them. This is how the `SpreadsheetCell` class is implemented. `mValue` and `mString` are protected; set(), getValue(), and getString() set and retrieve those values. That way you can keep `mValue` and `mString` in synch internally without worrying about clients delving in and changing those values.

Using Interface and Implementation Classes

Even with the preceding measures and the best design principles, the C++ language is fundamentally unfriendly to the principle of abstraction. The syntax requires you to combine your public interfaces and `private` (or `protected`) data members and methods together in one class definition, thereby exposing some of the internal implementation details of the class to its clients. The downside of this is that if you have to add new non-`public` methods or data members to your class, all the clients of the class have to be recompiled. This can become a burden in bigger projects.

The good news is that you can make your interfaces a lot cleaner and hide all implementation details, resulting in stable interfaces. The bad news is that it takes a bit of hacking. The basic principle is to define two classes for every class you want to write: the *interface class* and the *implementation class*. The implementation class is identical to the class you would have written if you were not taking this approach. The interface class presents `public` methods identical to those of the implementation class, but it only has one data member: a pointer to an implementation class object. The interface class method implementations simply call the equivalent methods on the implementation class object. The result of this is that no matter how the implementation changes, it has no impact on the `public` interface class. This reduces the need for recompilation. None of the clients that use the interface class need to be recompiled if the implementation (and only the implementation) changes.

To use this approach with the `Spreadsheet` class, simply rename the old `Spreadsheet` class to `SpreadsheetImpl`. Here is the new `SpreadsheetImpl` class (which is identical to the old `Spreadsheet` class, but with a different name):

```cpp
#include "SpreadsheetCell.h"
class SpreadsheetApplication; // Forward declaration
class SpreadsheetImpl
{
    public:
        SpreadsheetImpl(const SpreadsheetApplication& theApp,
            int inWidth = kMaxWidth, int inHeight = kMaxHeight);
        SpreadsheetImpl(const SpreadsheetImpl& src);
        ~SpreadsheetImpl();
        SpreadsheetImpl &operator=(const SpreadsheetImpl& rhs);
        void setCellAt(int x, int y, const SpreadsheetCell& inCell);
        SpreadsheetCell getCellAt(int x, int y);
        int getId() const;
        static const int kMaxHeight = 100;
        static const int kMaxWidth = 100;
    protected:
        bool inRange(int val, int upper);
        void copyFrom(const SpreadsheetImpl& src);
        int mWidth, mHeight;
        int mId;
        SpreadsheetCell** mCells;
        const SpreadsheetApplication& mTheApp;
        static int sCounter;
};
```

Code snippet from SeparateImpl\SpreadsheetImpl.h

Then define a new `Spreadsheet` class that looks like this:

```cpp
#include "SpreadsheetCell.h"
// Forward declarations
class SpreadsheetImpl;
```

```
class SpreadsheetApplication;
class Spreadsheet
{
    public:
        Spreadsheet(const SpreadsheetApplication& theApp, int inWidth,
            int inHeight);
        Spreadsheet(const SpreadsheetApplication& theApp);
        Spreadsheet(const Spreadsheet& src);
        ~Spreadsheet();
        Spreadsheet& operator=(const Spreadsheet& rhs);
        void setCellAt(int x, int y, const SpreadsheetCell& inCell);
        SpreadsheetCell getCellAt(int x, int y);
        int getId() const;
    protected:
        SpreadsheetImpl* mImpl;
};
```

Code snippet from SeparateImpl\Spreadsheet.h

This class now contains only one data member: a pointer to a SpreadsheetImpl. The public methods are identical to the old Spreadsheet with one exception: The Spreadsheet constructor with default arguments has been split into two constructors because the values for the default arguments were const members that are no longer in the Spreadsheet class. Instead, the SpreadsheetImpl class will provide the defaults.

The implementations of the Spreadsheet methods, such as setCellAt() and getCellAt(), just pass the request on to the underlying SpreadsheetImpl object:

```
void Spreadsheet::setCellAt(int x, int y, const SpreadsheetCell& inCell)
{
    mImpl->setCellAt(x, y, inCell);
}
SpreadsheetCell Spreadsheet::getCellAt(int x, int y)
{
    return mImpl->getCellAt(x, y);
}
int Spreadsheet::getId() const
{
    return mImpl->getId();
}
```

Code snippet from SeparateImpl\Spreadsheet.cpp

The constructors for the Spreadsheet must construct a new SpreadsheetImpl to do its work, and the destructor must free the dynamically allocated memory. Note that the SpreadsheetImpl class has only one constructor with default arguments. Both normal constructors in the Spreadsheet class call that constructor on the SpreadsheetImpl class:

```
Spreadsheet::Spreadsheet(const SpreadsheetApplication& theApp, int inWidth,
    int inHeight)
{
```

```
    mImpl = new SpreadsheetImpl(theApp, inWidth, inHeight);
}
Spreadsheet::Spreadsheet(const SpreadsheetApplication& theApp)
{
    mImpl = new SpreadsheetImpl(theApp);
}
Spreadsheet::Spreadsheet(const Spreadsheet& src)
{
    mImpl = new SpreadsheetImpl(*(src.mImpl));
}
Spreadsheet::~Spreadsheet()
{
    delete mImpl;
    mImpl = nullptr;
}
```

Code snippet from SeparateImpl\Spreadsheet.cpp

The copy constructor looks a bit strange because it needs to copy the underlying SpreadsheetImpl from the source spreadsheet. Because the copy constructor takes a reference to a SpreadsheetImpl, not a pointer, you must dereference the mImpl pointer to get to the object itself so the constructor call can take its reference.

The Spreadsheet assignment operator must similarly pass on the assignment to the underlying SpreadsheetImpl:

```
Spreadsheet& Spreadsheet::operator=(const Spreadsheet& rhs)
{
    *mImpl = *(rhs.mImpl);
    return *this;
}
```

Code snippet from SeparateImpl\Spreadsheet.cpp

The first line in the assignment operator looks a little strange. You might be tempted to write this line instead:

```
    mImpl = rhs.mImpl; // Incorrect assignment!
```

That code will compile and run, but it doesn't do what you want. It just copies pointers so that the left-hand side and right-hand side Spreadsheets now both possess pointers to the same SpreadsheetImpl. If one of them changes it, the change will show up in the other. If one of them destroys it, the other will be left with a dangling pointer. Therefore, you can't just assign the pointers. You must force the SpreadsheetImpl assignment operator to run, which only happens when you copy direct objects. By dereferencing the mImpl pointers, you force direct object assignment, which causes the assignment operator to be called. Note that you can only do this because you already allocated memory for mImpl in the constructor.

This technique to truly separate interface from implementation is powerful. Although a bit clumsy at first, once you get used to it you will find it natural to work with. However, it's not common practice in most workplace environments, so you might find some resistance to trying it from your coworkers. The most compelling argument in favor of it is not the aesthetic one of splitting out the interface but the cost of a full rebuild if the implementation of the class changes. A full rebuild on a huge project might take hours. With stable interface classes, rebuild time is minimized, and concepts like precompiled headers can further reduce build costs. A discussion on precompiled headers is outside the scope of this book.

SUMMARY

This chapter, along with Chapter 6, provided all the tools you need to write solid, well-designed classes, and to use objects effectively.

You discovered that dynamic memory allocation in objects presents new challenges: You must free the memory in the destructor, copy the memory in the copy constructor, and both free and copy the memory in the assignment operator. You learned how to prevent assignment and pass-by-value by declaring a `private` copy constructor and assignment operator.

You learned more about different kinds of data members, including `static`, `const`, `const` reference, and `mutable` members. You also learned about `static`, `inline`, and `const` methods, method overloading and default parameters. The chapter also described nested class definitions, and `friend` classes, functions and methods.

You encountered operator overloading, and learned how to overload the arithmetic and comparison operators, both as global `friend` functions and as class methods.

Finally, you learned how to take abstraction to an extreme by providing separate interface and implementation classes.

Now that you're fluent in the language of object-oriented programming, it's time to tackle inheritance, which is covered in Chapter 8.

Discovering Inheritance Techniques

WHAT'S IN THIS CHAPTER?

➤ How to extend a class through inheritance

➤ How to employ inheritance to reuse code

➤ How to build interactions between superclasses and subclasses

➤ How to use inheritance to achieve polymorphism

➤ How to work with multiple inheritance

➤ How to deal with unusual problems in inheritance

Without inheritance, classes would simply be data structures with associated behaviors. That alone would be a powerful improvement over procedural languages, but inheritance adds an entirely new dimension. Through inheritance, you can build new classes based on existing ones. In this way, your classes become reusable and extensible components. This chapter will teach you the different ways to leverage the power of inheritance. You will learn about the specific syntax of inheritance as well as sophisticated techniques for making the most of inheritance.

The portion of this chapter relating to polymorphism draws heavily on the spreadsheet example discussed in Chapters 6 and 7. If you have not read Chapters 6 and 7, you may wish to skim the sample code in those chapters to get a background on this example. This chapter also refers to the object-oriented methodologies described in Chapter 3. If you have not read that chapter and are unfamiliar with the theories behind inheritance, you should review Chapter 3 before continuing.

BUILDING CLASSES WITH INHERITANCE

In Chapter 3, you learned that an "is-a" relationship recognizes the pattern that real-world objects tend to exist in hierarchies. In programming, that pattern becomes relevant when you need to write a class that builds on, or slightly changes, another class. One way to accomplish this aim is to copy code from one class and paste it into the other. By changing the relevant parts or amending the code, you can achieve the goal of creating a new class that is slightly different from the original. This approach, however, leaves an OOP programmer feeling sullen and slightly annoyed for the following reasons:

➤ A bug fix to the original class will not be reflected in the new class because the two classes contain completely separate code.

➤ The compiler does not know about any relationship between the two classes, so they are not polymorphic — they are not just different variations on the same thing.

➤ This approach does not build a true is-a relationship. The new class is very similar to the original because it shares code, not because it really *is* the same type of object.

➤ The original code might not be obtainable. It may exist only in a precompiled binary format, so copying and pasting the code might be impossible.

Not surprisingly, C++ provides built-in support for defining a true is-a relationship. The characteristics of C++ is-a relationships are described in the following section.

Extending Classes

When you write a class definition in C++, you can tell the compiler that your class is *inheriting from,* or *extending,* an existing class. By doing so, your class will automatically contain the data members and methods of the original class, which is called the *parent class* or *superclass.* Extending an existing class gives your class (which is now called a *derived* class or a *subclass*) the ability to describe only the ways in which it is different from the parent class.

To extend a class in C++, you specify the class you are extending when you write the class definition. To show the syntax for inheritance, you use two classes called Super and Sub. Don't worry — more interesting examples are coming later. To begin, consider the following definition for the Super class:

```
class Super
{
    public:
        Super();
        void someMethod();
    protected:
        int mProtectedInt;
    private:
        int mPrivateInt;
};
```

If you wanted to build a new class, called Sub, which inherits from Super, you would tell the compiler that Sub derives from Super with the following syntax:

```
class Sub : public Super
{
    public:
        Sub();
        void someOtherMethod();
};
```

Sub itself is a full-fledged class that just happens to share the characteristics of the Super class. Don't worry about the word public for now — its meaning is explained later in this chapter. Figure 8-1 shows the simple relationship between Sub and Super. You can declare objects of type Sub just like any other object. You could even define a third class that subclasses Sub, forming a chain of classes, as shown in Figure 8-2.

Sub doesn't have to be the only subclass of Super. Additional classes can also subclass Super, effectively becoming *siblings* to Sub, as shown in Figure 8-3.

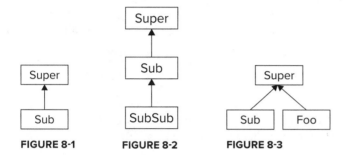

FIGURE 8-1   **FIGURE 8-2**   **FIGURE 8-3**

A Client's View of Inheritance

To a client, or another part of your code, an object of type Sub is also an object of type Super because Sub inherits from Super. This means that all the public methods and data members of Super *and* all the public methods and data members of Sub are available.

Code that uses the subclass does not need to know which class in your inheritance chain has defined a method in order to call it. For example, the following code calls two methods of a Sub object even though one of the methods was defined by the Super class:

```
Sub mySub;
mySub.someMethod();
mySub.someOtherMethod();
```

It is important to understand that inheritance works in only one direction. The Sub class has a very clearly defined relationship to the Super class, but the Super class, as written, doesn't know anything about the Sub class. That means that objects of type Super do not support public methods and data members of Sub because Super is *not* a Sub.

The following code will not compile because the Super class does not contain a public method called someOtherMethod():

```
Super mySuper;
mySuper.someOtherMethod();  // BUG! Super doesn't have a someOtherMethod().
```

From the perspective of other code, an object belongs to its defined class as well as to any superclasses.

A pointer or reference to an object can refer to an object of the declared class or any of its subclasses. This tricky subject is explained in detail later in this chapter. The concept to understand at this point is that a pointer to a Super can actually be pointing to a Sub object. The same is true for a reference. The client can still access only the methods and data members that exist in Super, but through this mechanism, any code that operates on a Super can also operate on a Sub.

For example, the following code compiles and works just fine even though it initially appears that there is a type mismatch:

```
Super* superPointer = new Sub(); // Create sub, store it in super pointer.
```

However, you cannot call methods from the Sub class through the Super pointer. The following will not work:

```
superPointer->someOtherMethod();
```

This will be flagged as an error by the compiler, because, although the object is of type Sub and therefore does have someOtherMethod() defined, the compiler can only think of it as type Super which does not have someOtherMethod() defined. This problem will be addressed later with the discussion of virtual methods.

A Subclass's View of Inheritance

To the subclass itself, nothing much has changed in terms of how it is written or how it behaves. You can still define methods and data members on a subclass just as you would on a regular class. The previous definition of Sub declares a method called someOtherMethod(). Thus, the Sub class augments the Super class by adding an additional method.

A subclass can access public and protected methods and data members declared in its superclass as though they were its own, because technically, they are. For example, the implementation of someOtherMethod() on Sub could make use of the data member mProtectedInt, which was declared as part of Super. The following code shows this implementation. Accessing a superclass data member or method is no different than if the data member or method were declared as part of the subclass.

```
void Sub::someOtherMethod()
{
    cout << "I can access superclass data member mProtectedInt." << endl;
    cout << "Its value is " << mProtectedInt << endl;
}
```

When we introduced access specifiers (public, private, and protected) in Chapter 6, the difference between private and protected may have been confusing. Now that you understand subclasses, the difference should be clear. If a class declares methods or data members as protected, subclasses have access to them. If they are declared as private, subclasses do not have access.

The following implementation of someOtherMethod() will not compile because the subclass attempts to access a private data member from the superclass.

```
void Sub::someOtherMethod()
{
    cout << "I can access superclass data member mProtectedInt." << endl;
    cout << "Its value is " << mProtectedInt << endl;
    cout << "The value of mPrivateInt is " << mPrivateInt << endl; // BUG!
}
```

The `private` access specifier gives you control over how a potential subclass could interact with your class. In practice, most data members are declared as `protected`, and most methods are either `public` or `protected`. The reason is that most of the time, you or someone you work with will be extending the class so you don't want to shut out any potential uses by making methods or members `private`. Occasionally, the `private` specifier is useful to block subclasses from accessing potentially dangerous methods. It is also useful when writing classes that external or unknown parties will extend because you can block access to prevent misuse. For example, in your superclass you can declare `private` data members to prevent anyone, including subclasses from accessing them directly. To allow only subclasses to change those values, you can provide `protected` setter and getter methods.

 From the perspective of a subclass, all `public` *and* `protected` *data members and methods from the superclass are available for use.*

C++11 Preventing Inheritance

C++11 allows you to mark a class as `final`, which means trying to inherit from it will result in a compiler error. A class can be marked as `final` with the `final` keyword right behind the name of the class. For example, the following `Super` class is marked as `final`:

```
class Super final
{
    // Omitted for brevity
};
```

The following `Sub` class tries to inherit from the `Super` class, but this will result in a compiler error because `Super` is marked as `final`.

```
class Sub : public Super
{
    // Omitted for brevity
};
```

Overriding Methods

The main reasons to inherit from a class are to add or replace functionality. The definition of `Sub` adds functionality to its parent class by providing an additional method, `someOtherMethod()`. The other method, `someMethod()`, is inherited from `Super` and behaves in the subclass exactly as it does in the superclass. In many cases, you will want to modify the behavior of a class by replacing, or *overriding*, a method.

How I Learned to Stop Worrying and Make Everything virtual

There is one small twist to overriding methods in C++ and it has to do with the keyword `virtual`. Only methods that are declared as `virtual` in the superclass can be overridden properly by subclasses. The keyword goes at the beginning of a method declaration as shown in the modified version of `Super` that follows:

```
class Super
{
    public:
        Super();
        virtual void someMethod();
    protected:
        int mProtectedInt;
    private:
        int mPrivateInt;
};
```

The `virtual` keyword has a few subtleties and is often cited as a poorly designed part of the language. A good rule of thumb is to just make all of your methods `virtual`. That way, you won't have to worry about whether or not overriding the method will work. The only drawback is a very tiny performance hit. The subtleties of the `virtual` keyword are covered toward the end of this chapter, and performance is discussed further in Chapter 24.

Even though it is unlikely that the `Sub` class will be extended, it is a good idea to make its methods `virtual` as well, just in case.

```
class Sub : public Super
{
    public:
        Sub();
        virtual void someOtherMethod();
};
```

 As a rule of thumb, make all your methods virtual *(including the destructor, but not constructors) to avoid problems associated with omission of the* virtual *keyword.*

Syntax for Overriding a Method

To override a method, you redeclare it in the subclass class definition exactly as it was declared in the superclass. In the subclass's implementation file, you provide the new definition.

For example, the Super class contains a method called someMethod(). The definition of someMethod() is provided in Super.cpp and shown here:

```
void Super::someMethod()
{
    cout << "This is Super's version of someMethod()." << endl;
}
```

Note that you do not repeat the virtual keyword in front of the method definition.

If you wish to provide a new definition for someMethod() in the Sub class, you must first add it to the class definition for Sub, as follows:

```
class Sub : public Super
{
    public:
        Sub();
        virtual void someMethod();  // Overrides Super's someMethod()
        virtual void someOtherMethod();
};
```

The new definition of someMethod() is specified along with the rest of Sub's methods in Sub.cpp.

```
void Sub::someMethod()
{
    cout << "This is Sub's version of someMethod()." << endl;
}
```

Once a method or destructor is marked as virtual, it will be virtual for all subclasses even if the virtual keyword is removed from subclasses. For example, in the following Sub class, someMethod() is still virtual and can still be overridden by subclasses of Sub, because it was marked as virtual in the Super class.

```
class Sub : public Super
{
    public:
        Sub();
        void someMethod();  // Overrides Super's someMethod()
};
```

A Client's View of Overridden Methods

With the preceding changes, other code would still call someMethod() the same way it did before. Just as before, the method could be called on an object of class Super or an object of class Sub. Now, however, the behavior of someMethod() will vary based on the class of the object.

For example, the following code works just as it did before, calling Super's version of someMethod():

```
Super mySuper;
mySuper.someMethod();  // Calls Super's version of someMethod().
```

The output of this code is:

```
This is Super's version of someMethod().
```

If the code declares an object of class Sub, the other version will automatically be called:

```
Sub mySub;
mySub.someMethod();    // Calls Sub's version of someMethod()
```

The output this time is:

```
This is Sub's version of someMethod().
```

Everything else about objects of class Sub remains the same. Other methods that might have been inherited from Super will still have the definition provided by Super unless they are explicitly overridden in Sub.

As you learned earlier, a pointer or reference can refer to an object of a class or any of its subclasses. The object itself "knows" the class of which it is actually a member, so the appropriate method is called as long as it was declared virtual. For example, if you have a Super reference that refers to an object that is really a Sub, calling someMethod() will actually call the subclass's version, as shown next. This aspect of overriding will *not* work properly if you omit the virtual keyword in the superclass.

```
Sub mySub;
Super& ref = mySub;
ref.someMethod();    // Calls Sub's version of someMethod()
```

Remember that even though a superclass reference or pointer knows that it is actually a subclass, you cannot access subclass methods or members that are not defined in the superclass. The following code will not compile because a Super reference does not have a method called someOtherMethod():

```
Sub mySub;
Super& ref = mySub;
mySub.someOtherMethod();   // This is fine.
ref.someOtherMethod();     // BUG
```

The subclass knowledge characteristic is *not* true of nonpointer nonreference objects. You can cast or assign a Sub to a Super because a Sub is a Super. However, the object will lose any knowledge of the subclass at this point:

```
Sub mySub;
Super assignedObject = mySub;    // Assigns a Sub to a Super.
assignedObject.someMethod();     // Calls Super's version of someMethod()
```

One way to remember this seemingly strange behavior is to imagine what the objects look like in memory. Picture a Super object as a box taking up a certain amount of memory. A Sub object is a box that is a little bit bigger because it has everything a Super has plus a bit more. When you have a reference or pointer to a Sub, the box doesn't change — you just have a new way of accessing it.

However, when you cast a `Sub` into a `Super`, you are throwing out all the "uniqueness" of the `Sub` class to fit it into a smaller box.

 Subclasses retain their overridden methods when referred to by superclass pointers or references. They lose their uniqueness when cast to a superclass object. The loss of overridden methods and subclass data is called slicing.

C++11 Preventing Overriding

C++11 allows you to mark a method as `final` which means that the method cannot be overridden in a subclass. Trying to override a `final` method will result in a compiler error. Take the following `Super` class:

```
class Super
{
    public:
        Super();
        virtual void someMethod() final;
};
```

Trying to override `someMethod()`, as in the following `Sub` class, will result in a compiler error because `someMethod()` is marked as `final` in the `Super` class.

```
class Sub : public Super
{
    public:
        Sub();
        virtual void someMethod();   // Error
        virtual void someOtherMethod();
};
```

INHERITANCE FOR REUSE

Now that you are familiar with the basic syntax for inheritance, it's time to explore one of the main reasons that inheritance is an important feature of the C++ language. Inheritance is a vehicle that allows you to leverage existing code. This section presents a real-world application of inheritance for the purpose of code reuse.

The WeatherPrediction Class

Imagine that you are given the task of writing a program to issue simple weather predictions, working with both Fahrenheit and Celsius. Weather predictions may be a little out of your area of expertise as a programmer, so you obtain a third-party class library that was written to make weather predictions based on the current temperature and the present distance between Jupiter and Mars (hey, it's plausible). This third-party package is distributed as a compiled library to protect the intellectual property of the prediction algorithms, but you do get to see the class definition. The class definition for `WeatherPrediction` is as follows:

```cpp
// Predicts the weather using proven new-age techniques given the current
// temperature and the distance from Jupiter to Mars. If these values are
// not provided, a guess is still given but it's only 99% accurate.
class WeatherPrediction
{
    public:
        // Sets the current temperature in fahrenheit
        virtual void setCurrentTempFahrenheit(int inTemp);
        // Sets the current distance between Jupiter and Mars
        virtual void setPositionOfJupiter(int inDistanceFromMars);
        // Gets the prediction for tomorrow's temperature
        virtual int getTomorrowTempFahrenheit();
        // Gets the probability of rain tomorrow. 1 means
        // definite rain. 0 means no chance of rain.
        virtual double getChanceOfRain();
        // Displays the result to the user in this format:
        // Result: x.xx chance. Temp. xx
        virtual void showResult();
        // Returns string representation of the temperature
        virtual std::string getTemperature() const;
    protected:
        int mCurrentTempFahrenheit;
        int mDistanceFromMars;
};
```

Code snippet from WeatherPrediction\WeatherPrediction.h

Note that this class marks all methods as `virtual`, because the class presumes that its methods might be overridden in a subclass.

This class solves most of the problems for your program. However, as is usually the case, it's not *exactly* right for your needs. First, all the temperatures are given in Fahrenheit. Your program needs to operate in Celsius as well. Also, the `showResult()` method might not display the result in a way you require.

Adding Functionality in a Subclass

When you learned about inheritance in Chapter 3, adding functionality was the first technique described. Fundamentally, your program needs something just like the `WeatherPrediction` class but with a few extra bells and whistles. Sounds like a good case for inheritance to reuse code. To begin, define a new class, `MyWeatherPrediction`, that inherits from `WeatherPrediction`.

```cpp
#include "WeatherPrediction.h"
class MyWeatherPrediction : public WeatherPrediction
{
};
```

Code snippet from WeatherPrediction\MyWeatherPrediction.h

The preceding class definition will compile just fine. The `MyWeatherPrediction` class can already be used in place of `WeatherPrediction`. It will provide the same functionality, but nothing new yet.

For the first modification, you might want to add knowledge of the Celsius scale to the class. There is a bit of a quandary here because you don't know what the class is doing internally. If all of the internal calculations are made by using Fahrenheit, how do you add support for Celsius? One way is to use the subclass to act as a go-between, interfacing between the user, who can use either scale, and the superclass, which only understands Fahrenheit.

The first step in supporting Celsius is to add new methods that allow clients to set the current temperature in Celsius instead of Fahrenheit and to get tomorrow's prediction in Celsius instead of Fahrenheit. You will also need protected helper methods that convert between Celsius and Fahrenheit. These methods can be `static` because they are the same for all instances of the class.

```cpp
#include "WeatherPrediction.h"
class MyWeatherPrediction : public WeatherPrediction
{
    public:
        virtual void setCurrentTempCelsius(int inTemp);
        virtual int getTomorrowTempCelsius();
    protected:
        static int convertCelsiusToFahrenheit(int inCelsius);
        static int convertFahrenheitToCelsius(int inFahrenheit);
};
```

Code snippet from WeatherPrediction\MyWeatherPrediction.h

The new methods follow the same naming convention as the parent class. Remember that from the point of view of other code, a `MyWeatherPrediction` object will have all of the functionality defined in both `MyWeatherPrediction` and `WeatherPrediction`. Adopting the parent class's naming convention presents a consistent interface.

We will leave the implementation of the Celsius/Fahrenheit conversion methods as an exercise for the reader — and a fun one at that! The other two methods are more interesting. To set the current temperature in Celsius, you need to convert the temperature first and then present it to the parent class in units that it understands.

```cpp
void MyWeatherPrediction::setCurrentTempCelsius(int inTemp)
{
    int fahrenheitTemp = convertCelsiusToFahrenheit(inTemp);
    setCurrentTempFahrenheit(fahrenheitTemp);
}
```

Code snippet from WeatherPrediction\MyWeatherPrediction.cpp

As you can see, once the temperature is converted, the method calls the existing functionality from the superclass. Similarly, the implementation of `getTomorrowTempCelsius()` uses the parent's existing functionality to get the temperature in Fahrenheit, but converts the result before returning it.

```
int MyWeatherPrediction::getTomorrowTempCelsius()
{
    int fahrenheitTemp = getTomorrowTempFahrenheit();
    return convertFahrenheitToCelsius(fahrenheitTemp);
}
```

Code snippet from WeatherPrediction\MyWeatherPrediction.cpp

The two new methods effectively reuse the parent class because they "wrap" the existing functionality in a way that provides a new interface for using it.

You can also add new functionality completely unrelated to existing functionality of the parent class. For example, you could add a method that will retrieve alternative forecasts from the Internet or a method that will suggest an activity based on the predicted weather.

Replacing Functionality in a Subclass

The other major technique for subclassing is replacing existing functionality. The showResult() method in the WeatherPrediction class is in dire need of a facelift. MyWeatherPrediction can override this method to replace the behavior with its own implementation.

The new class definition for MyWeatherPrediction is as follows:

```
#include "WeatherPrediction.h"
class MyWeatherPrediction : public WeatherPrediction
{
    public:
        virtual void setCurrentTempCelsius(int inTemp);
        virtual int getTomorrowTempCelsius();
        virtual void showResult();
    protected:
        static int convertCelsiusToFahrenheit(int inCelsius);
        static int convertFahrenheitToCelsius(int inFahrenheit);
};
```

Code snippet from WeatherPrediction\MyWeatherPrediction.h

A possible new user-friendly implementation follows:

```
void MyWeatherPrediction::showResult()
{
    cout << "Tomorrow's temperature will be " <<
            getTomorrowTempCelsius() << " degrees Celsius (" <<
            getTomorrowTempFahrenheit() << " degrees Fahrenheit)" << endl;
    cout << "Chance of rain is " << (getChanceOfRain() * 100) << " percent"
         << endl;
    if (getChanceOfRain() > 0.5) {
        cout << "Bring an umbrella!" << endl;
    }
}
```

Code snippet from WeatherPrediction\MyWeatherPrediction.cpp

To clients using this class, it's as if the old version of showResult() never existed. As long as the object is a MyWeatherPrediction object, the new version will be called.

As a result of these changes, MyWeatherPrediction has emerged as a new class with new functionality tailored to a more specific purpose. Yet, it did not require much code because it leveraged its superclass's existing functionality.

RESPECT YOUR PARENTS

When you write a subclass, you need to be aware of the interaction between parent classes and child classes. Issues such as order of creation, constructor chaining, and casting are all potential sources of bugs.

Parent Constructors

Objects don't spring to life all at once; they must be constructed along with their parents and any objects that are contained within them. C++ defines the creation order as follows:

1. If the class has a base class, the default constructor of the base class is executed.

2. Non-static data members of the class are constructed in the order in which they were declared.

3. The body of the class's constructor is executed.

These rules can apply recursively. If the class has a grandparent, the grandparent is initialized before the parent, and so on. The following code shows this creation order. As a reminder, we generally advise against implementing methods directly in a class definition, as we've done in the code that follows. In the interest of readable and concise examples, we have broken our own rule. The proper execution will output the result 123.

```cpp
class Something
{
    public:
        Something() { cout << "2"; }
};
class Parent
{
    public:
        Parent() { cout << "1"; }
};
class Child : public Parent
{
    public:
        Child() { cout << "3"; }
    protected:
        Something mDataMember;
};
int main()
```

```
    {
        Child myChild;
        return 0;
    }
```

When the `myChild` object is created, the constructor for `Parent` is called first, outputting the string `"1"`. Next, `mDataMember` is initialized, calling the `Something` constructor, which outputs the string `"2"`. Finally, the `Child` constructor is called, which outputs `"3"`.

Note that the `Parent` constructor was called automatically. C++ will automatically call the default constructor for the parent class if one exists. If no default constructor exists in the parent class, or if one does exist but you wish to use an alternate constructor, you can *chain* the constructor just as when initializing data members in the constructor initializer.

The following code shows a version of `Super` that lacks a default constructor. The associated version of `Sub` must explicitly tell the compiler how to call the `Super` constructor or the code will not compile.

```
class Super
{
    public:
        Super(int i);
};
class Sub : public Super
{
    public:
        Sub();
};
Sub::Sub() : Super(7)
{
    // Do Sub's other initialization here.
}
```

In the preceding code, the `Sub` constructor passes a fixed value (7) to the `Super` constructor. `Sub` could also pass a variable if its constructor required an argument:

```
Sub::Sub(int i) : Super(i) {}
```

Passing constructor arguments from the subclass to the superclass is perfectly fine and quite normal. Passing data members, however, will not work. The code will compile, but remember that data members are not initialized until *after* the superclass is constructed. If you pass a data member as an argument to the parent constructor, it will be uninitialized.

Parent Destructors

Because destructors cannot take arguments, the language can automatically call the destructor for parent classes. The order of destruction is conveniently the reverse of the order of construction:

1. The body of the class's destructor is called.

2. Any data members of the class are destroyed in the reverse order of their construction.

3. The parent class, if any, is destructed.

Again, these rules apply recursively. The lowest member of the chain is always destructed first. The following code adds destructors to the previous example. The destructors are all declared `virtual`, which is very important and will be discussed right after this example. If executed, this code will output `"123321"`.

```cpp
class Something
{
    public:
        Something() { cout << "2"; }
        virtual ~Something() { cout << "2"; }
};
class Parent
{
    public:
        Parent() { cout << "1"; }
        virtual ~Parent() { cout << "1"; }
};
class Child : public Parent
{
    public:
        Child() { cout << "3"; }
        virtual ~Child() { cout << "3"; }
    protected:
        Something mDataMember;
};
int main()
{
    Child myChild;
    return 0;
}
```

Code snippet from ConstructorChain\ConstructorChain.cpp

Notice that the destructors are all `virtual`. As a rule of thumb, all destructors should be declared `virtual`. If the preceding destructors were not declared `virtual`, the code would continue to work fine. However, if code ever called `delete` on a superclass pointer that was really pointing to a subclass, the destruction chain would begin in the wrong place. For example, the following code is similar to the previous example but the destructors are not `virtual`. This becomes a problem when a `Child` object is accessed as a pointer to a `Parent` and deleted.

```cpp
class Something
{
    public:
        Something() { cout << "2"; }
        ~Something() { cout << "2"; }  // Should be virtual, but will work
};
```

```
class Parent
{
    public:
        Parent() { cout << "1"; }
        ~Parent() { cout << "1"; }  // BUG! Make this virtual!
};
class Child : public Parent
{
    public:
        Child() { cout << "3"; }
        ~Child() { cout << "3"; }   // Should be virtual, but will work
    protected:
        Something mDataMember;
};
int main()
{
    Parent* ptr = new Child();
    delete ptr;
    return 0;
}
```

The output of this code is a shockingly terse "1231". When the `ptr` variable is deleted, only the `Parent` destructor is called because the destructor was not declared `virtual`. As a result, the `Child` destructor is not called and the destructors for its data members are not called.

Technically, you could fix the preceding problem by making the `Parent` destructor `virtual`. The "virtualness" would automatically be used by any children. However, we advocate explicitly making all destructors `virtual` so that you never have to worry about it.

 Always make your destructors `virtual`! *The compiler generated default destructor is not* `virtual`, *so you should define your own* `virtual` *destructor, at least for your parent classes.*

Referring to Parent Names

When you override a method in a subclass, you are effectively replacing the original as far as other code is concerned. However, that parent version of the method still exists and you may want to make use of it. For example, an overridden method would like to keep doing what the superclass implementation does, plus something else. Take a look at the `getTemperature()` method in the `WeatherPrediction` class that returns a `string` representation of the current temperature.

Available for download on Wrox.com

```
class WeatherPrediction
{
    public:
        virtual std::string getTemperature() const;
    // Omitted for brevity
};
```

Code snippet from WeatherPrediction\WeatherPrediction.h

You can override this method in the `MyWeatherPrediction` class as follows:

```
class MyWeatherPrediction : public WeatherPrediction
{
    public:
        virtual std::string getTemperature() const;
    // Omitted for brevity
};
```

Code snippet from WeatherPrediction\MyWeatherPrediction.h

Suppose the subclass wants to add °F to the string by first calling the superclass `getTemperature()` method and then adding °F to the `string`. You might want to try to write this as follows:

```
string MyWeatherPrediction::getTemperature() const
{
    return getTemperature() + "°F";  // BUG
}
```

However, this will not work because, under the rules of name resolution for C++, it first resolves against the local scope, then the class scope, and as a consequence will end up calling `MyWeatherPrediction::getTemperature()`. This will result in an infinite recursion until you run out of stack space (some compilers detect this error and report it at compile time).

To make this work, you need to use the scope resolution operator as follows:

```
string MyWeatherPrediction::getTemperature() const
{
    return WeatherPrediction::getTemperature() + "°F";
}
```

Code snippet from WeatherPrediction\MyWeatherPrediction.cpp

> *Microsoft Visual C++ supports the* __super *keyword (with two underscores). This allows you to write the following:*
>
> ```
> return __super::getTemperature() + "°F";
> ```

Calling the parent version of the current method is a commonly used pattern in C++. If you have a chain of subclasses, each might want to perform the operation already defined by the superclass but add their own additional functionality as well.

As another example, imagine a class hierarchy of types of books. A diagram showing such a hierarchy is shown in Figure 8-4.

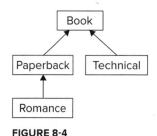

FIGURE 8-4

Since each lower class in the hierarchy further specifies the type of book, a method that gets the description of a book really needs to take all levels of the hierarchy into consideration. This can be accomplished by chaining to the parent method. The following code illustrates this pattern. The code also defines a `virtual getHeight()` method, discussed further after the example.

```cpp
class Book
{
    public:
        virtual string getDescription() { return "Book"; }
        virtual int getHeight() { return 120; }
};
class Paperback : public Book
{
    public:
        virtual string getDescription() {
            return "Paperback " + Book::getDescription();
        }
};
class Romance : public Paperback
{
    public:
        virtual string getDescription() {
            return "Romance " + Paperback::getDescription();
        }
        virtual int getHeight() { return Paperback::getHeight() / 2; }
};
class Technical : public Book
{
    public:
        virtual string getDescription() {
            return "Technical " + Book::getDescription();
        }
};
int main()
{
    Romance novel;
    Book book;
    cout << novel.getDescription() << endl; // Outputs "Romance Paperback Book"
    cout << book.getDescription() << endl;  // Outputs "Book"
    cout << novel.getHeight() << endl;      // outputs "60"
    cout << book.getHeight() << endl;       // outputs "120"
    return 0;
}
```

Code snippet from Book\Book.cpp

The `Book` class defines a `virtual getHeight()` method, returning 120. Only the `Romance` class overrides this by calling `getHeight()` on its parent class (`Paperback`) and dividing the result by two as follows:

```cpp
virtual int getHeight() { return Paperback::getHeight() / 2; }
```

However, `Paperback` does not override `getHeight()`, so C++ will walk up the class hierarchy to find a class that implements `getHeight()`. In the preceding example, `Paperback::getHeight()` will resolve to `Book::getHeight()`.

Casting Up and Down

As you have already seen, an object can be cast or assigned to its parent class. If the cast or assignment is performed on a plain old object, this results in slicing:

```
Super mySuper = mySub;  // SLICE!
```

Slicing occurs in situations like this because the end result is a `Super` object, and `Super` objects lack the additional functionality defined in the `Sub` class. However, slicing does *not* occur if a subclass is assigned to a pointer or reference to its superclass:

```
Super& mySuper = mySub; // No slice!
```

This is generally the correct way to refer to a subclass in terms of its superclass, also called *upcasting*. This is why it's always a good idea to make your methods and functions take references to classes instead of directly using objects of those classes. By using references, subclasses can be passed in without slicing.

 When upcasting, use a pointer or reference to the superclass to avoid slicing.

Casting from a superclass to one of its subclasses, also called *downcasting*, is often frowned upon by professional C++ programmers because there is no guarantee that the object really belongs to that subclass. For example, consider the following code:

```
void presumptuous(Super* inSuper)
{
    Sub* mySub = static_cast<Sub*>(inSuper);
    // Proceed to access Sub methods on mySub.
}
```

If the author of `presumptuous()` also wrote code that called `presumptuous()`, everything would probably be okay because the author knows that the function expects the argument to be of type `Sub*`. However, if other programmers were to call `presumptuous()`, they might pass in a `Super*`. There are no compile-time checks that can be done to enforce the type of the argument, and the function blindly assumes that `inSuper` is actually a pointer to a `Sub`.

Downcasting is sometimes necessary, and you can use it effectively in controlled circumstances. If you're going to downcast, however, you should use a `dynamic_cast`, which uses the object's built-in knowledge of its type to refuse a cast that doesn't make sense. If a `dynamic_cast` fails on a pointer, the pointer's value will be `nullptr` instead of pointing to nonsensical data. If a `dynamic_cast` fails on an object reference, a `std::bad_cast` exception will be thrown. Chapter 9 discusses casting in more detail and Chapter 10 explains more about exceptions.

The previous example should have been written as follows:

```
void lessPresumptuous(Super* inSuper)
{
    Sub* mySub = dynamic_cast<Sub*>(inSuper);
    if (mySub != nullptr) {
        // Proceed to access Sub methods on mySub.
    }
}
```

 Use downcasting only when necessary and be sure to use a `dynamic_cast`.

INHERITANCE FOR POLYMORPHISM

Now that you understand the relationship between a subclass and its parent, you can use inheritance in its most powerful scenario — polymorphism. Chapter 3 discusses how polymorphism allows you to use objects with a common parent class interchangeably, and to use objects in place of their parents.

Return of the Spreadsheet

Chapters 6 and 7 use a spreadsheet program as an example of an application that lends itself to an object-oriented design. A `SpreadsheetCell` represents a single element of data. That element could be either a `double` or a `string`. A simplified class definition for `SpreadsheetCell` follows. Note that a cell can be set either as a `double` or a `string`. The current value of the cell, however, is always returned as a `string` for this example.

```
class SpreadsheetCell
{
    public:
        SpreadsheetCell();
        virtual void set(double inDouble);
        virtual void set(const std::string& inString);
        virtual std::string getString() const;
    protected:
        static std::string doubleToString(double inValue);
        static double stringToDouble(const std::string& inString);
        double      mValue;
        std::string mString;
};
```

The preceding `SpreadsheetCell` class seems to be having an identity crisis — sometimes a cell represents a `double`, sometimes a `string`. Sometimes it has to convert between these formats. To achieve this duality, the class needs to store both values even though a given cell should be able to contain only a single value. Worse still, what if additional types of cells are needed, such as a formula cell or a date cell? The SpreadsheetCell class would grow dramatically to support all of these data types and the conversions between them.

Designing the Polymorphic Spreadsheet Cell

The SpreadsheetCell class is screaming out for a hierarchical makeover. A reasonable approach would be to narrow the scope of the SpreadsheetCell to cover only strings, perhaps renaming it StringSpreadsheetCell in the process. To handle doubles, a second class, DoubleSpreadsheetCell, would inherit from the StringSpreadsheetCell and provide functionality specific to its own format. Figure 8-5 illustrates such a design. This approach models inheritance for reuse since the DoubleSpreadsheetCell would only be subclassing StringSpreadsheetCell to make use of some of its built-in functionality.

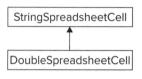

FIGURE 8-5

If you were to implement the design shown in Figure 8-5, you might discover that the subclass would override most, if not all, of the functionality of the base class. Since doubles are treated differently from strings in almost all cases, the relationship may not be quite as it was originally understood. Yet, there clearly is a relationship between a cell containing strings and a cell containing doubles. Rather than using the model in Figure 8-5, which implies that somehow a DoubleSpreadsheetCell "is-a" StringSpreadsheetCell, a better design would make these classes peers with a common parent, SpreadsheetCell. Such a design is shown in Figure 8-6.

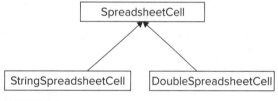

FIGURE 8-6

The design in Figure 8-6 shows a polymorphic approach to the SpreadsheetCell hierarchy. Since DoubleSpreadsheetCell and StringSpreadsheetCell both inherit from a common parent, SpreadsheetCell, they are interchangeable in the view of other code. In practical terms, that means:

➤   Both subclasses support the same interface (set of methods) defined by the base class.

➤   Code that makes use of SpreadsheetCell objects can call any method in the interface without even knowing whether the cell is a DoubleSpreadsheetCell or a StringSpreadsheetCell.

➤   Through the magic of virtual methods, the appropriate instance of every method in the interface will be called depending on the class of the object.

➤   Other data structures, such as the Spreadsheet class described in Chapter 7, can contain a collection of multityped cells by referring to the parent type.

The Spreadsheet Cell Base Class

Since all spreadsheet cells are subclasses of the SpreadsheetCell base class, it is probably a good idea to write that class first. When designing a base class, you need to consider how the subclasses relate to each other. From this information, you can derive the commonality that will go inside the parent class. For example, `string` cells and `double` cells are similar in that they both contain a single piece of data. Since the data is coming from the user and will be displayed back to the user, the value is set as a `string` and retrieved as a `string`. These behaviors are the shared functionality that will make up the base class.

A First Attempt

The `SpreadsheetCell` base class is responsible for defining the behaviors that all `SpreadsheetCell` subclasses will support. In our example, all cells need to be able to set their value as a `string`. All cells also need to be able to return their current value as a `string`. The base class definition declares these methods, but note that it has no data members. The reason will be explained afterwards.

```
class SpreadsheetCell
{
    public:
        SpreadsheetCell();
        virtual ~SpreadsheetCell();
        virtual void set(const std::string& inString);
        virtual std::string getString() const;
};
```

When you start writing the `.cpp` file for this class, you very quickly run into a problem. Since the base class of spreadsheet cell contains neither a `double` nor a `string`, how can you implement it? More generally, how do you write a parent class that declares the behaviors that are supported by subclasses without actually defining the implementation of those behaviors?

One possible approach is to implement "do nothing" functionality for those behaviors. For example, calling the `set()` method on the `SpreadsheetCell` base class will have no effect because the base class has nothing to set. This approach still doesn't feel right, however. Ideally, there should never be an object that is an instance of the base class. Calling `set()` should always have an effect because it should always be called on either a `DoubleSpreadsheetCell` or a `StringSpreadsheetCell`. A good solution will enforce this constraint.

The preceding code declares a `virtual` destructor for the `SpreadsheetCell` class. If you don't do this, the compiler will generate a default destructor for you but a non-`virtual` one. That means if you don't declare the `virtual` destructor yourself, you might encounter problems with destruction of subclasses through pointers or references as explained earlier in this chapter.

Pure Virtual Methods and Abstract Base Classes

Pure virtual methods are methods that are explicitly undefined in the class definition. By making a method pure virtual, you are telling the compiler that no definition for the method exists in the current class. Thus, the class is said to be *abstract* because no other code will be able to instantiate it. The compiler enforces the fact that if a class contains one or more pure virtual methods, it can never be used to construct an object of that type.

There is a special syntax for designating a pure virtual method. The method declaration is followed by =0. No code needs to be written in the `.cpp` file, and any attempt to write code will cause a compiler error.

```
class SpreadsheetCell
{
    public:
        SpreadsheetCell();
        virtual ~SpreadsheetCell();
        virtual void set(const std::string& inString) = 0;
        virtual std::string getString() const = 0;
};
```

Code snippet from PolymorphicSpreadsheet\SpreadsheetCell.h

Now that the base class is an abstract class, it is impossible to create a `SpreadsheetCell` object. The following code will not compile, and will give an error such as `Cannot declare object of type 'SpreadsheetCell' because one or more virtual functions are abstract`:

```
SpreadsheetCell cell; // BUG! Attempts creating abstract class instance
```

However, the following code will compile:

```
SpreadsheetCell* ptr;
```

This works because it will require instantiating a derived class of the abstract superclass, for example:

```
ptr = new StringSpreadsheetCell();
```

> *An abstract class provides a way to prevent other code from instantiating an object directly, as opposed to one of its subclasses.*

Base Class Source Code

There is not much code required for `SpreadsheetCell.cpp`. As the class was defined, most of the methods are pure virtual — there is no definition to give. All that is left is the constructor and destructor. For this example, the constructor is implemented just as a placeholder in case initialization needs to happen in the future. However, the `virtual` destructor is required as was explained earlier.

```
SpreadsheetCell::SpreadsheetCell() { }
SpreadsheetCell::~SpreadsheetCell() { }
```

Code snippet from PolymorphicSpreadsheet\SpreadsheetCell.cpp

The Individual Subclasses

Writing the `StringSpreadsheetCell` and `DoubleSpreadsheetCell` classes is just a matter of implementing the functionality that is *defined* in the parent. Because we want clients to be able to instantiate and work with `string` cells and `double` cells, the cells can't be abstract — they *must* implement all of the pure virtual methods inherited from their parent.

String Spreadsheet Cell Class Definition

The first step in writing the class definition of `StringSpreadsheetCell` is to subclass `SpreadsheetCell`:

```
class StringSpreadsheetCell : public SpreadsheetCell
{
```

Code snippet from PolymorphicSpreadsheet\StringSpreadsheetCell.h

You want to initialize the data value of the `StringSpreadsheetCell` to "#NOVALUE" to indicate that the value has not been set. The compiler generated default constructor will call the default `string` constructor for `mValue` which will set the initial value to the empty string, "". So, you need to provide an explicit default constructor and initialize the value yourself.

```
public:
    StringSpreadsheetCell();
```

Next, the inherited pure virtual methods are overridden, this time without being set to zero:

```
virtual void set(const std::string& inString);
virtual std::string getString() const;
```

Finally, the `string` cell adds a protected data member, `mValue`, which stores the actual cell data:

```
protected:
    std::string mValue;
};
```

String Spreadsheet Cell Implementation

The `.cpp` file for `StringSpreadsheetCell` is a bit more interesting than the base class. In the constructor, `mValue` is initialized to a `string` that indicates that no value has been set.

```
StringSpreadsheetCell::StringSpreadsheetCell() : mValue("#NOVALUE") { }
```

Code snippet from PolymorphicSpreadsheet\StringSpreadsheetCell.cpp

The `set` method is straightforward since the internal representation is already a string. Similarly, the `getString()` method returns the stored value.

```
void StringSpreadsheetCell::set(const string& inString)
{
    mValue = inString;
}
string StringSpreadsheetCell::getString() const
```

```
{
    return mValue;
}
```

Double Spreadsheet Cell Class Definition and Implementation

The `double` version follows a similar pattern, but with different logic. In addition to the `set()` method that takes a `string`, it also provides a new `set()` method that allows a client to set the value with a `double`. Two new `protected` methods are used to convert between a `string` and a `double`. As in `StringSpreadsheetCell`, it has a data member called `mValue`, this time a `double`. Because `DoubleSpreadsheetCell` and `StringSpreadsheetCell` are siblings, no hiding or naming conflicts occur as a result.

```
class DoubleSpreadsheetCell : public SpreadsheetCell
{
    public:
        DoubleSpreadsheetCell ();
        virtual void set(double inDouble);
        virtual void set(const std::string& inString);
        virtual std::string getString() const;
    protected:
        static std::string doubleToString(double inValue);
        static double stringToDouble(const std::string& inValue);
        double mValue;
};
```

The implementation of the `DoubleSpreadsheetCell` constructor is as follows.

```
DoubleSpreadsheetCell::DoubleSpreadsheetCell() : mValue(-1) { }
```

> *To keep this example simple,* `mValue` *is initialized to -1. In production code you would probably initialize it to NaN which stands for "Not a Number." In C++ you could do this with* `std::numeric_limits<double>::quiet_NaN()`.

The `set()` method that takes a `double` is straightforward. The `string` version uses the `protected static` method `stringToDouble()`. The `getString()` method converts the stored `double` value into a `string`:

```
void DoubleSpreadsheetCell::set(double inDouble)
{
    mValue = inDouble;
}
void DoubleSpreadsheetCell::set(const string& inString)
{
    mValue = stringToDouble(inString);
}
string DoubleSpreadsheetCell::getString() const
{
    return doubleToString(mValue);
}
```

Code snippet from PolymorphicSpreadsheet\DoubleSpreadsheetCell.cpp

You may already see one major advantage of implementing spreadsheet cells in a hierarchy — the code is much simpler. You don't need to worry about using two fields to represent the two types of data. Each object can be self-centered and only deal with its own functionality.

Note that the implementations of `doubleToString()` and `stringToDouble()` were omitted because they are the same as in Chapter 6.

Leveraging Polymorphism

Now that the `SpreadsheetCell` hierarchy is polymorphic, client code can take advantage of the many benefits that polymorphism has to offer. The following test program explores many of these features:

```
int main()
{
```

Code snippet from PolymorphicSpreadsheet\SpreadsheetTest.cpp

To demonstrate polymorphism, this test program declares an array of three `SpreadsheetCell` pointers. Remember that since `SpreadsheetCell` is an abstract class, you can't create objects of that type. However, you can still have a pointer or reference to a `SpreadsheetCell` because it would actually be pointing to one of the subclasses. This array, because it is an array of the parent type `SpreadsheetCell`, allows you to store a heterogeneous mixture of the two subclasses. This means that elements of the array could be either a `StringSpreadsheetCell` or a `DoubleSpreadsheetCell`.

```
SpreadsheetCell* cellArray[3];
```

The 0th element of the array is set to point to a new `StringSpreadsheetCell`; the first is also set to a new `StringSpreadsheetCell`, and the second is a new `DoubleSpreadsheetCell`.

```
cellArray[0] = new StringSpreadsheetCell();
cellArray[1] = new StringSpreadsheetCell();
cellArray[2] = new DoubleSpreadsheetCell();
```

Now that the array contains multityped data, any of the methods declared by the base class can be applied to the objects in the array. The code just uses SpreadsheetCell pointers — the compiler has no idea at compile time what types the objects actually are. However, because they are subclasses of SpreadsheetCell, they must support the methods of SpreadsheetCell.

```
cellArray[0]->set("hello");
cellArray[1]->set("10");
cellArray[2]->set("18");
```

When the getString() method is called, each object properly returns a string representation of their value. The important, and somewhat amazing, thing to realize is that the different objects do this in different ways. A StringSpreadsheetCell will return its stored value. A DoubleSpreadsheetCell will first perform a conversion. As the programmer, you don't need to know how the object does it — you just need to know that because the object is a SpreadsheetCell, it *can* perform this behavior.

```
cout << "Array values are [" << cellArray[0]->getString() << "," <<
                                cellArray[1]->getString() << "," <<
                                cellArray[2]->getString() << "]" <<
                                endl;
    return 0;
}
```

Future Considerations

The new implementation of the SpreadsheetCell hierarchy is certainly an improvement from an object-oriented design point of view. Yet, it would probably not suffice as an actual class hierarchy for a real-world spreadsheet program for several reasons.

First, despite the improved design, one feature of the original is still missing: the ability to convert from one cell type to another. By dividing them into two classes, the cell objects become more loosely integrated. To provide the ability to convert from a DoubleSpreadsheetCell to a StringSpreadsheetCell, you could add a typed constructor. It would have a similar appearance to a copy constructor but instead of a reference to an object of the same class, it would take a reference to an object of a sibling class.

```
class StringSpreadsheetCell : public SpreadsheetCell
{
    public:
        StringSpreadsheetCell();
        StringSpreadsheetCell(const DoubleSpreadsheetCell& inDoubleCell);
    // Omitted for brevity
};
```

Code snippet from PolymorphicSpreadsheet\StringSpreadsheetCell.h

With a typed constructor, you can easily create a StringSpreadsheetCell given a DoubleSpreadsheetCell. Don't confuse this with casting, however. Casting from one sibling to another will not work, unless you overload the cast operator as described in Chapter 18.

You can always cast up the hierarchy, and you can sometimes cast down the hierarchy, but you can never cast across the hierarchy unless you have changed the behavior of the cast operator.

The question of how to implement overloaded operators for cells is an interesting one, and there are several possible solutions. One approach is to implement a version of each operator for every combination of cells. With only two subclasses, this is manageable. There would be an `operator+` function to add two `double` cells, to add two `string` cells, and to add a `double` cell to a `string` cell. Another approach is to decide on a common representation. The preceding implementation already standardizes on a `string` as a common representation of sorts. A single `operator+` function could cover all the cases by taking advantage of this common representation. One possible implementation, which assumes that the result of adding two cells is always a `string` cell, is as follows:

Available for
download on
Wrox.com

```
const StringSpreadsheetCell operator+(const StringSpreadsheetCell& lhs,
                                      const StringSpreadsheetCell& rhs)
{
    StringSpreadsheetCell newCell;
    newCell.set(lhs.getString() + rhs.getString());
    return newCell;
}
```

Code snippet from PolymorphicSpreadsheet\SpreadsheetTest.cpp

As long as the compiler has a way to turn a particular cell into a `StringSpreadsheetCell`, the operator will work. Given the previous example of having a `StringSpreadsheetCell` constructor that takes a `DoubleSpreadsheetCell` as an argument, the compiler will automatically perform the conversion if it is the only way to get the `operator+` to work. That means the following code will work, even though `operator+` was explicitly written to work on `StringSpreadsheetCells`:

Available for
download on
Wrox.com

```
DoubleSpreadsheetCell myDbl;
myDbl.set(8.4);
StringSpreadsheetCell result = myDbl + myDbl;
```

Code snippet from PolymorphicSpreadsheet\SpreadsheetTest.cpp

Of course, the result of this addition won't really add the numbers together. It will convert the `double` cells into `string` cells and add the `strings`, resulting in a `StringSpreadsheetCell` with a value of `8.48.4`.

If you are still feeling a little unsure about polymorphism, start with the code for this example and try things out. The `main()` function in the preceding example is a great starting point for experimental code that simply exercises various aspects of the class.

MULTIPLE INHERITANCE

As you read in Chapter 3, multiple inheritance is often perceived as a complicated and unnecessary part of object-oriented programming. We'll leave the decision of whether or not it is useful up to you and your coworkers. This section explains the mechanics of multiple inheritance in C++.

Inheriting from Multiple Classes

Defining a class to have multiple parent classes is very simple from a syntactic point of view. All you need to do is list the superclasses individually when declaring the class name.

```
class Baz : public Foo, public Bar
{
    // Etc.
};
```

By listing multiple parents, the Baz object will have the following characteristics:

➤ A Baz object will support the public methods and contain the data members of both Foo and Bar.

➤ The methods of the Baz class will have access to protected data and methods in both Foo and Bar.

➤ A Baz object can be upcast to either a Foo or a Bar.

➤ Creating a new Baz object will automatically call the Foo and Bar default constructors, in the order that the classes were listed in the class definition.

➤ Deleting a Baz object will automatically call the destructors for the Foo and Bar classes, in the reverse order that the classes were listed in the class definition.

The following example shows a class, DogBird, that has two parent classes — a Dog class and a Bird class. The fact that a dog-bird is a ridiculous example should not be viewed as a statement that multiple inheritance itself is ridiculous. Honestly, we leave that judgment up to you.

Available for download on Wrox.com

```
class Dog
{
    public:
        virtual void bark() { cout << "Woof!" << endl; }
};
class Bird
{
    public:
        virtual void chirp() { cout << "Chirp!" << endl; }
};
class DogBird : public Dog, public Bird
{
};
```

Code snippet from DogBird\DogBird.cpp

The class hierarchy for `DogBird` is shown in Figure 8-7.

Using objects of classes with multiple parents is no different from using objects without multiple parents. In fact, the client code doesn't even have to know that the class has two parents. All that really matters are the properties and behaviors supported by the class. In this case, a `DogBird` object supports all of the `public` methods of `Dog` and `Bird`.

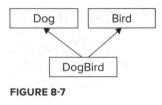

FIGURE 8-7

```
DogBird myConfusedAnimal;
myConfusedAnimal.bark();
myConfusedAnimal.chirp();
```

Code snippet from DogBird\DogBird.cpp

The output of this program is as follows:

```
Woof!
Chirp!
```

Naming Collisions and Ambiguous Base Classes

It's not difficult to construct a scenario where multiple inheritance would seem to break down. The following examples show some of the edge cases that must be considered:

Name Ambiguity

What if the `Dog` class and the `Bird` class both had a method called `eat()`? Since `Dog` and `Bird` are not related in any way, one version of the method does not override the other — they both continue to exist in the `DogBird` subclass.

As long as client code never attempts to call the `eat()` method, that is not a problem. The `DogBird` class will compile correctly despite having two versions of `eat()`. However, if client code attempts to call the `eat()` method on a `DogBird`, the compiler will give an error indicating that the call to `eat()` is ambiguous. The compiler will not know which version to call. The following code provokes this ambiguity error:

```
class Dog
{
    public:
        virtual void bark() { cout << "Woof!" << endl; }
        virtual void eat() { cout << "The dog has eaten." << endl; }
};
class Bird
{
    public:
        virtual void chirp() { cout << "Chirp!" << endl; }
        virtual void eat() { cout << "The bird has eaten." << endl; }
};
class DogBird : public Dog, public Bird
```

```
{
};
int main()
{
    DogBird myConfusedAnimal;
    myConfusedAnimal.eat();    // BUG! Ambiguous call to method eat()
    return 0;
}
```

The solution to the ambiguity is to either explicitly upcast the object, essentially hiding the undesired version of the method from the compiler, or to use a disambiguation syntax. For example, the following code shows two ways to invoke the Dog version of eat():

```
static_cast<Dog>(myConfusedAnimal).eat();  // Slices, calling Dog::eat()
myConfusedAnimal.Dog::eat();                // Calls Dog::eat()
```

Methods of the subclass itself can also explicitly disambiguate between different methods of the same name by using the same syntax used to access parent methods, the :: operator. For example, the DogBird class could prevent ambiguity errors in other code by defining its own eat() method. Inside this method, it would determine which parent version to call.

```
void DogBird::eat()
{
    Dog::eat();  // Explicitly call Dog's version of eat()
}
```

Another way to provoke ambiguity is to inherit from the same class twice. For example, if the Bird class inherited from Dog for some reason, the code for DogBird would not compile because Dog becomes an ambiguous base class.

```
class Dog {};
class Bird : public Dog {};
class DogBird : public Bird, public Dog {};  // BUG! Dog is an ambiguous base class.
```

Most occurrences of ambiguous base classes are either contrived "what-if" examples, as in the preceding, or arise from untidy class hierarchies. Figure 8-8 shows a class diagram for the preceding example, indicating the ambiguity.

Ambiguity can also occur with data members. If Dog and Bird both had a data member with the same name, an ambiguity error would occur when client code attempted to access that member.

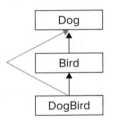

FIGURE 8-8

Ambiguous Base Classes

A more likely scenario is that multiple parents themselves have common parents. For example, perhaps both `Bird` and `Dog` are subclasses of an `Animal` class, as shown in Figure 8-9.

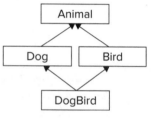

FIGURE 8-9

This type of class hierarchy is permitted in C++, though name ambiguity can still occur. For example, if the `Animal` class has a `public` method called `sleep()`, that method could not be called on a `DogBird` object because the compiler would not know whether to call the version inherited by `Dog` or by `Bird`.

The best way to use these "diamond-shaped" class hierarchies is to make the topmost class an abstract base class with all methods declared as pure virtual. Since the class only declares methods without providing definitions, there are no methods in the base class to call and thus there are no ambiguities at that level.

The following example implements a diamond-shaped class hierarchy with a pure virtual `eat()` method that must be defined by each subclass. The `DogBird` class still needs to be explicit about which parent's `eat()` method it uses, but any ambiguity would be caused by `Dog` and `Bird` having the same method, not because they inherit from the same class.

```
class Animal
{
    public:
        virtual void eat() = 0;
};
class Dog : public Animal
{
    public:
        virtual void bark() { cout << "Woof!" << endl; }
        virtual void eat() { cout << "The dog has eaten." << endl; }
};
class Bird : public Animal
{
    public:
        virtual void chirp() { cout << "Chirp!" << endl; }
        virtual void eat() { cout << "The bird has eaten." << endl; }
};
class DogBird : public Dog, public Bird
{
    public:
        virtual void eat() { Dog::eat(); }
};
```

A more refined mechanism for dealing with the top class in a diamond-shaped hierarchy, *virtual base classes*, is explained at the end of this chapter.

Uses for Multiple Inheritance

At this point, you're probably wondering why programmers would want to tackle multiple inheritance in their code. The most straightforward use case for multiple inheritance is to define a class of objects that is-a something and also is-a something else. As was said in Chapter 3, any real-world objects you find that follow this pattern are unlikely to translate well into code.

One of the most compelling and simple uses of multiple inheritance is for the implementation of mix-in classes. Mix-in classes are explained in Chapter 3. An example implementation using multiple inheritance is shown in Chapter 28.

Another reason that people sometimes use multiple inheritance is to model a component-based class. Chapter 3 gave the example of an airplane simulator. The `Airplane` class has an engine, a fuselage, controls, and other components. While the typical implementation of an `Airplane` class would make each of these components a separate data member, you *could* use multiple inheritance. The airplane class would inherit from engine, fuselage, and controls, in effect getting the behaviors and properties of all of its components. We recommend you stay away from this type of code because it confuses a clear has-a relationship with inheritance, which should be used for is-a relationships. The recommended solution is to have an `Airplane` class which contains data members of type `Engine`, `Fuselage`, and `Controls`.

INTERESTING AND OBSCURE INHERITANCE ISSUES

Extending a class opens up a variety of issues. What characteristics of the class can and cannot be changed? What does the mysterious `virtual` keyword really do? These questions, and many more, are answered in the following sections.

Changing the Overridden Method's Characteristics

For the most part, the reason you override a method is to change its implementation. Sometimes, however, you may want to change other characteristics of the method.

Changing the Method Return Type

A good rule of thumb is to override a method with the exact method declaration, or *method prototype*, that the superclass uses. The implementation can change, but the prototype stays the same.

That does not have to be the case, however. In C++, an overriding method can change the return type as long as the original return type is a pointer or reference to a class, and the new return type is a pointer or reference to a descendent class. Such types are called *covariant return types*. This feature sometimes comes in handy when the superclass and subclass work with objects in a *parallel hierarchy*. That is, another group of classes that is tangential, but related, to the first class hierarchy.

For example, consider a hypothetical cherry orchard simulator. You might have two hierarchies of classes that model different real-world objects but are obviously related. The first is the `Cherry` chain. The base class, `Cherry`, has a subclass called `BingCherry`. Similarly, there is another chain of classes with a base class called `CherryTree` and a subclass called `BingCherryTree`. Figure 8-10 shows the two class chains.

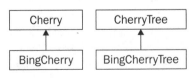

FIGURE 8-10

Now assume that the `CherryTree` class has a method called `pick()` that will retrieve a single cherry from the tree:

```
Cherry* CherryTree::pick()
{
    return new Cherry();
}
```

Code snippet from Cherry\CherryTree.h

In the `BingCherryTree` subclass, you may want to override this method. Perhaps Bing Cherries need to be polished when they are picked (bear with us on this one). Because a `BingCherry` is a `Cherry`, you could leave the method prototype as is and override the method as in the following example. The `BingCherry` pointer is automatically cast to a `Cherry` pointer.

```
Cherry* BingCherryTree::pick()
{
    BingCherry* theCherry = new BingCherry();
    theCherry->polish();
    return theCherry;
}
```

The implementation above is perfectly fine and is probably the way that the authors would write it. However, because you know that the `BingCherryTree` will always return `BingCherry` objects, you could indicate this fact to potential users of this class by changing the return type, as shown here:

```
BingCherry* BingCherryTree::pick()
{
    BingCherry* theCherry = new BingCherry();
    theCherry->polish();
    return theCherry;
}
```

Code snippet from Cherry\BingCherryTree.h

A good way to figure out whether you can change the return type of an overridden method is to consider whether existing code would still work. In the preceding example, changing the return type was fine because any code that assumed that the `pick()` method would always return a `Cherry*` would still compile and work correctly. Because a `BingCherry` is a `Cherry`, any methods that were called on the result of `CherryTree`'s version of `pick()` could still be called on the result of `BingCherryTree`'s version of `pick()`.

You could *not*, for example, change the return type to something completely unrelated, such as `void*`. The following code will not compile because the compiler thinks that you are trying to override `CherryTree::pick()`, but cannot distinguish `BingCherryTree`'s `pick()` method from `CherryTree`'s `pick()` method because return types are not used in method disambiguation:

```
void* BingCherryTree::pick()  // BUG!
{
    BingCherry* theCherry = new BingCherry();
```

```
        theCherry->polish();
        return theCherry;
    }
```

This will generate a compiler error, something like `'BingCherryTree::pick': overriding virtual function return type differs and is not covariant from 'CherryTree::pick'`.

Changing the Method Parameters

If you use the name of a `virtual` method from the parent class in the definition of a subclass, but it uses different parameters than the method of that name uses in the parent class, it is not overriding the method of the parent class — it is creating a new method. Returning to the `Super` and `Sub` example from earlier in this chapter, you could *attempt* to override `someMethod()` in `Sub` with a new argument list as follows:

```
class Super
{
    public:
        Super();
        virtual void someMethod();
};
class Sub : public Super
{
    public:
        Sub();
        virtual void someMethod(int i);  // Compiles, but doesn't override
        virtual void someOtherMethod();
};
```

The implementation of this method could be as follows:

```
void Sub::someMethod(int i)
{
    cout << "This is Sub's version of someMethod with argument " << i
        << "." << endl;
}
```

The preceding class definition will compile, but you have not overridden `someMethod()`. Because the arguments are different, you have created a new method that exists only in `Sub`. If you want a method called `someMethod()` that takes an `int`, and you want it to work only on objects of class `Sub`, the preceding code is correct.

In fact, the C++ standard says that the original method is now hidden as far as `Sub` is concerned. The following sample code will not compile because there is no longer a no-argument version of `someMethod()`.

```
Sub mySub;
mySub.someMethod(); // BUG! Won't compile because original method is hidden.
```

There is a somewhat obscure technique you can use to have your cake and eat it too. That is, you can use this technique to effectively "override" a method in the subclass with a new prototype but continue to inherit the superclass version. This technique uses the `using` keyword to explicitly include the superclass definition of the method within the subclass as follows:

```
class Super
{
    public:
        Super();
        virtual void someMethod();
};
class Sub : public Super
{
    public:
        Sub();
        using Super::someMethod; // Explicitly "inherits" the Super version
        virtual void someMethod(int i); // Adds a new version of someMethod
        virtual void someOtherMethod();
};
```

 It is rare to find a method in a subclass with the same name as a method in the superclass but using a different parameter list.

C++11 ## The override Keyword

Sometimes, it is possible to accidentally create a new `virtual` method instead of overriding a method from the superclass. Take the following `Super` and `Sub` classes where `Sub` is properly overriding `someMethod()`:

```
class Super
{
    public:
        Super();
        virtual void someMethod(double d);
};
class Sub : public Super
{
    public:
        Sub();
        virtual void someMethod(double d);
};
```

You can call `someMethod()` through a reference as follows:

```
Sub mySub;
Super& ref = mySub;
ref.someMethod(1);  // Calls Sub's version of someMethod()
```

This will correctly call the overridden someMethod() from the Sub class. Now, suppose you used an integer parameter instead of a double while overriding someMethod() as follows:

```
class Sub : public Super
{
    public:
        Sub();
        virtual void someMethod(int i);
};
```

As seen in the previous section, this code will **not** override someMethod(), but will instead create a new virtual method. If you try to call someMethod() through a reference as in the following code, someMethod() of Super will be called instead of the one from Sub.

```
Sub mySub;
Super& ref = mySub;
ref.someMethod(1);  // Calls Super's version of someMethod()
```

This type of problem can happen when you start to modify the Super class but forget to update all subclasses. For example, maybe your first version of the Super class had a method called someMethod() accepting an integer. You then wrote the Sub subclass overriding this someMethod() accepting an integer. Later you decide that someMethod() in the Super class needs a double instead of an integer, so you update someMethod() in the Super class. It might happen that at that time, you forget to update the someMethod() methods in subclasses to also accept a double instead of an integer. By forgetting this, you are now actually creating a new virtual method instead of properly overriding the method.

You can prevent this situation by using the override keyword as follows:

```
class Sub : public Super
{
    public:
        Sub();
        virtual void someMethod(int i) override;
};
```

This definition of Sub will generate a compiler error, because with the override keyword you are saying that someMethod() is supposed to be overriding a method from the Super class, but in the Super class there is no someMethod() accepting an integer, only one accepting a double.

C++11 Inherited Constructors

In an earlier section you saw the use of the using keyword to explicitly include the superclass definition of a method within a subclass. This works perfectly for normal class methods, however, prior to C++11, it did not work for constructors. C++11 solves this and allows you to inherit base class constructors in your subclasses. Take a look at the following definition for the Super and Sub classes:

```
class Super
{
    public:
        Super(const std::string& str);
};
class Sub : public Super
{
    public:
        Sub(int i);
};
```

You can construct a Super object only with the provided Super constructor, which requires a string as parameter. On the other hand, constructing a Sub object can happen only with the provided Sub constructor, which requires a single integer as parameter. You cannot construct Sub objects by using the constructor accepting a string defined in the Super class. For example:

```
Super super("Hello"); // OK, calls string based Super ctor
Sub sub1(1);          // OK, calls integer based Sub ctor
Sub sub2("Hello");    // Error, Sub does not inherit string Super ctor
```

If you would like the ability to construct Sub objects using the string based Super constructor, you can explicitly inherit the Super constructors in the Sub class as follows:

```
class Sub : public Super
{
    public:
        using Super::Super;
        Sub(int i);
};
```

Now you can construct Sub objects in the following two ways:

```
Sub sub1(1);          // OK, calls integer based Sub ctor
Sub sub2("Hello");    // OK, calls inherited string based Super ctor
```

The Sub class can define a constructor with the same parameter list as one of the inherited constructors in the Super class. In this case, as with any override, the constructor of the Sub class takes precedence over the inherited constructor. In the following example, the Sub class inherits all constructors from the Super class with the using keyword. However, since the Sub class defines its own constructor with a single argument of type float, the inherited constructor from the Super class with a single argument of type float is overridden.

```
class Super
{
    public:
        Super(const std::string& str);
        Super(float f);
};
class Sub : public Super
```

```
{
    public:
        using Super::Super;
        Sub(float f);          // Overrides inherited float based Super ctor
};
```

With this definition, objects of Sub can be created as follows:

```
Sub sub1("Hello");   // OK, calls inherited string based Super ctor
Sub sub2(1.23);      // OK, calls float based Sub ctor
```

A few restrictions apply to inheriting constructors from a base class with the using clause. When you inherit a constructor from a base class, you inherit all of them. It is not possible to inherit only a subset of the constructors of a base class. A second restriction is related to multiple inheritance. It's not possible to inherit constructors from one of the base classes if another base class has a constructor with the same parameter list, because this will lead to ambiguity. To resolve this, the Sub class needs to explicitly define the conflicting constructors. For example, the following Sub class tries to inherit all constructors from both the Super1 and Super2 class, which results in a compiler error due to ambiguity of the float based constructors.

```
class Super1
{
    public:
        Super1(float f);
};
class Super2
{
    public:
        Super2(const std::string& str);
        Super2(float f);
};
class Sub : public Super1, public Super2
{
    public:
        using Super1::Super1;
        using Super2::Super2;
        Sub(char c);
};
```

The first using clause in Sub inherits the constructors from Super1. This means that Sub will get the following constructor:

```
Sub(float f);    // Inherited from Super1
```

With the second using clause in Sub you are trying to inherit all constructors from Super2. However, this will generate a compiler error because this would mean that Sub gets a second Sub(float f) constructor. The problem is solved by explicitly declaring conflicting constructors in the Sub class as follows:

```
class Sub : public Super1, public Super2
{
    public:
        using Super1::Super1;
```

```
        using Super2::Super2;
        Sub(char c);
        Sub(float f);
};
```

The `Sub` class now explicitly declares a constructor with a single argument of type `float`, solving the ambiguity. If you want, this explicitly declared constructor in the `Sub` class accepting a `float` parameter can still forward the call to the `Super1` and `Super2` constructors in its ctor-initializer as follows:

```
Sub::Sub(float f) : Super1(f), Super2(f) {}
```

When using inherited constructors, make sure that all member variables are properly initialized. For example, take the following new definitions for the `Super` and `Sub` classes. This example does not properly initialize the `mInt` data member in all cases which is a serious error. These cases and a solution will be given after the example.

```
class Super
{
    public:
        Super(const std::string& str) : mStr(str) {}
    protected:
        std::string mStr;
};
class Sub : public Super
{
    public:
        using Super::Super;
        Sub(int i) : Super(""), mInt(i) {}
    protected:
        int mInt;
};
```

You can create a `Sub` object as follows:

```
Sub s1(2);
```

This will call the `Sub(int i)` constructor, which will initialize the `mInt` data member of the `Sub` class and call the `Super` constructor with an empty string to initialize the `mStr` data member.

Because the `Super` constructor is inherited in the `Sub` class, you can also construct a `Sub` object as follows:

```
Sub s2("Hello World");
```

This will call the inherited `Super` constructor in the `Sub` class. However, this inherited `Super` constructor only initializes the `mStr` member variable of the `Super` class and does not initialize the `mInt` member variable of the `Sub` class, leaving it in an uninitialized state. This is usually not recommended.

The solution is to use another C++11 feature called in-class member initializers, which are discussed in Chapter 6. The following code uses an in-class member initializer to initialize mInt to 0. The Sub(int i) constructor can still change this initialization and initialize mInt to the constructor argument i.

```
class Sub : public Super
{
    public:
        using Super::Super;
        Sub(int i) : Super(""), mInt(i) {}
    protected:
        int mInt = 0;
};
```

Special Cases in Overriding Methods

Several special cases require attention when overriding a method. In this section, we have outlined the cases that you are likely to encounter.

The Superclass Method Is static

In C++, you cannot override a static method. For the most part, that's all you need to know. There are, however, a few corollaries that you need to understand.

First of all, a method cannot be both static and virtual. This is the first clue that attempting to override a static method will not do what you intend for it to do. If you have a static method in your subclass with the same name as a static method in your superclass, you actually have two separate methods.

The following code shows two classes that both happen to have static methods called beStatic(). These two methods are in no way related.

```
class SuperStatic
{
    public:
        static void beStatic() {
            cout << "SuperStatic being static." << endl; }
};
class SubStatic : public SuperStatic
{
    public:
        static void beStatic() {
            cout << "SubStatic keepin' it static." << endl; }
};
```

Because a static method belongs to its class, calling the identically named methods on the two different classes will call their respective methods:

```
SuperStatic::beStatic();
SubStatic::beStatic();
```

Will output:

```
SuperStatic being static.
SubStatic keepin' it static.
```

Everything makes perfect sense as long as the methods are accessed by class. The behavior is less clear when objects are involved. In C++, you can call a `static` method using an object, but since the method is `static`, it has no `this` pointer and no access to the object itself, so it is equivalent to calling it by `classname::method()`. Referring to the previous example classes, you can write code as follows, but the results may be surprising.

```
SubStatic mySubStatic;
SuperStatic& ref = mySubStatic;
mySubStatic.beStatic();
ref.beStatic();
```

The first call to `beStatic()` will obviously call the `SubStatic` version because it is explicitly called on an object declared as a `SubStatic`. The second call might not work as you expect. The object is a `SuperStatic` reference, but it refers to a `SubStatic` object. In this case, `SuperStatic`'s version of `beStatic()` will be called. The reason is that C++ doesn't care what the object actually is when calling a `static` method. It cares about only the compile-time type. In this case, the type is a reference to a `SuperStatic`.

The output of the previous example is as follows:

```
SubStatic keepin' it static.
SuperStatic being static.
```

 static methods are scoped by the name of the class in which they are defined, but are not methods that apply to a specific object. A method in a class that calls a static method calls the version determined by normal name resolution. When called syntactically by using an object, the object is not actually involved in the call, except to determine the type.

The Superclass Method Is Overloaded

When you override a method by specifying a name and a set of parameters, the compiler implicitly hides all other instances of the name in the superclass. The idea is that if you have overridden one method of a given name, you might have intended to override all the methods of that name, but simply forgot, and therefore this should be treated as an error. It makes sense if you think about it — why would you want to change some versions of a method and not others? Consider the following subclass, which overrides a method without overriding its associated overloaded siblings:

```
class Super
{
    public:
        virtual void overload() { cout << "Super's overload()" << endl; }
        virtual void overload(int i) {
            cout << "Super's overload(int i)" << endl; }
};
class Sub : public Super
{
    public:
        virtual void overload() { cout << "Sub's overload()" << endl; }
};
```

If you attempt to call the version of overload() that takes an int parameter on a Sub object, your code will not compile because it was not explicitly overridden.

```
mySub.overload(2); // BUG! No matching method for overload(int).
```

It is possible, however, to access this version of the method from a Sub object. All you need is a pointer or a reference to a Super object.

```
Sub mySub;
Super* ptr = &mySub;
ptr->overload(7);
```

The hiding of unimplemented overloaded methods is only skin deep in C++. Objects that are explicitly declared as instances of the subtype will not make the method available, but a simple cast to the superclass will bring it right back.

The using keyword can be employed to save you the trouble of overloading all the versions when you really only want to change one. In the following code, the Sub class definition uses one version of overload() from Super and explicitly overloads the other:

```
class Super
{
    public:
        virtual void overload() { cout << "Super's overload()" << endl; }
        virtual void overload(int i) {
            cout << "Super's overload(int i)" << endl; }
};
class Sub : public Super
{
    public:
        using Super::overload;
        virtual void overload() { cout << "Sub's overload()" << endl; }
};
```

The using clause has certain risks. Suppose a third overload() method is added to Super, which should have been overridden in Sub. This will now not be detected as an error because due to the using clause, the designer of the Sub class has explicitly said "I am willing to accept all other overloads of this method from the parent class."

> *To avoid obscure bugs, you should override all versions of an overloaded method, either explicitly or with the* using *keyword, but keep the risks of the* using *clause in mind.*

The Superclass Method Is private or protected

There's absolutely nothing wrong with overriding a private or protected method. Remember that the access specifier for a method determines who is able to *call* the method. Just because a subclass can't call its parent's private methods doesn't mean it can't override them. In fact, overriding a private or protected method is a common pattern in object-oriented languages. It allows subclasses to define their own "uniqueness" that is referenced in the superclass.

For example, the following class is part of a car simulator that estimates the number of miles the car can travel based on its gas mileage and amount of fuel left:

```cpp
class MilesEstimator
{
    public:
        virtual int getMilesLeft() {
                return getMilesPerGallon() * getGallonsLeft();
        }
        virtual void setGallonsLeft(int inValue) { mGallonsLeft = inValue; }
        virtual int  getGallonsLeft() { return mGallonsLeft; }
    private:
        int mGallonsLeft;
        virtual int getMilesPerGallon() { return 20; }
};
```

Code snippet from MilesEstimator\MilesEstimator.h

The getMilesLeft() method performs a calculation based on the results of two of its own methods. The following code uses the MilesEstimator to calculate how many miles can be traveled with 2 gallons of gas:

```cpp
MilesEstimator myMilesEstimator;
myMilesEstimator.setGallonsLeft(2);
cout << "I can go " << myMilesEstimator.getMilesLeft() << " more miles." << endl;
```

Code snippet from MilesEstimator\TestMilesEstimator.cpp

The output of this code is as follows:

```
I can go 40 more miles.
```

To make the simulator more interesting, you may want to introduce different types of vehicles, perhaps a more efficient car. The existing MilesEstimator assumes that all cars get 20 miles per gallon, but this value is returned from a separate method specifically so that a subclass could override it. Such a subclass is shown here:

```
class EfficientCarMilesEstimator : public MilesEstimator
{
    private:
        virtual int getMilesPerGallon() { return 35; }
};
```

Code snippet from MilesEstimator\EfficientCarMilesEstimator.h

By overriding this one `private` method, the new class completely changes the behavior of existing, unmodified, `public` methods. The `getMilesLeft()` method in the superclass will automatically call the overridden version of the `private` `getMilesPerGallon()` method. An example using the new class is as follows:

```
EfficientCarMilesEstimator myEstimator;
myEstimator.setGallonsLeft(2);
cout << "I can go " << myEstimator.getMilesLeft() << " more miles." << endl;
```

Code snippet from MilesEstimator\TestMilesEstimator.cpp

This time, the output reflects the overridden functionality:

```
I can go 70 more miles.
```

Overriding `private` *and* `protected` *methods is a good way to change certain features of a class without a major overhaul.*

The Superclass Method Has Default Arguments

Subclasses and superclasses can each have different default arguments, but the argument that is used depends on the declared type of the variable, not the underlying object. Following is a simple example of a subclass that provides a different default argument in an overridden method:

```
class Super
{
    public:
        virtual void go(int i = 2) {
            cout << "Super's go with i=" << i << endl; }
};
class Sub : public Super
{
    public:
        virtual void go(int i = 7) {
            cout << "Sub's go with i=" << i << endl; }
};
```

If `go()` is called on a `Sub` object, `Sub`'s version of `go()` will be executed with the default argument of 7. If `go()` is called on a `Super` object, `Super`'s version of `go()` will be executed with the default argument of 2. However (this is the weird part), if `go()` is called on a `Super` pointer or `Super` reference that really points to a `Sub` object, `Sub`'s version of `go()` will be called but it will use the default `Super` argument of 2. This behavior is shown in the following example:

```
Super mySuper;
Sub mySub;
Super& mySuperReferenceToSub = mySub;
mySuper.go();
mySub.go();
mySuperReferenceToSub.go();
```

The output of this code is as follows:

```
Super's go with i=2
Sub's go with i=7
Sub's go with i=2
```

The reason for this behavior is that C++ binds default arguments to the type of the expression describing the object being involved, not by the actual object type. For this same reason, default arguments are not "inherited" in C++. If the `Sub` class above failed to provide a default argument as its parent did, it would be overloading the `go()` method with a new non zero-argument version.

 When overriding a method that has a default argument, you should provide a default argument as well, and it should probably be the same value. It is recommended to use a symbolic constant for default values so that the same symbolic constant can be used in subclasses.

The Superclass Method Has a Different Access Level

There are two ways you may wish to change the access level of a method — you could try to make it more restrictive or less restrictive. Neither case makes much sense in C++, but there are a few legitimate reasons for attempting to do so.

To enforce tighter restriction on a method (or on a data member for that matter), there are two approaches you can take. One way is to change the access specifier for the entire base class. This approach is described later in this chapter. The other approach is simply to redefine the access in the subclass, as illustrated in the `Shy` class that follows:

```
class Gregarious
{
    public:
        virtual void talk() { cout << "Gregarious says hi!" << endl; }
};
class Shy : public Gregarious
```

```
    {
        protected:
            virtual void talk() { cout << "Shy reluctantly says hello." << endl; }
    };
```

The `protected` version of `talk()` in the `Shy` class properly overrides the method. Any client code that attempts to call `talk()` on a `Shy` object will get a compile error:

```
    myShy.talk();   // BUG! Attempt to access protected method.
```

However, the method is not fully protected. One only has to obtain a `Gregarious` reference or pointer to access the method that you thought was protected:

```
    Shy myShy;
    Gregarious& ref = myShy;
    ref.talk();
```

The output of the preceding code is:

```
    Shy reluctantly says hello.
```

This proves that making the method `protected` in the subclass did actually override the method (because the subclass version was correctly called), but it also proves that the `protected` access can't be fully enforced if the superclass makes it `public`.

 There is no reasonable way (or good reason why) to restrict access to a public *parent method.*

It's much easier (and makes a lot more sense) to lessen access restrictions in subclasses. The simplest way is simply to provide a `public` method that calls a `protected` method from the superclass, as shown here:

```
    class Secret
    {
        protected:
            virtual void dontTell() { cout << "I'll never tell." << endl; }
    };
    class Blabber : public Secret
    {
        public:
            virtual void tell() { dontTell(); }
    };
```

A client calling the `public` `tell()` method of a `Blabber` object would effectively access the `protected` method of the `Secret` class. Of course, this doesn't *really* change the access level of `dontTell()`, it just provides a `public` way of accessing it.

You could also override `dontTell()` explicitly in the `Blabber` subclass and give it new behavior with `public` access. This makes a lot more sense than reducing the level of access because it is entirely clear what happens with a reference or pointer to the base class. For example, suppose that `Blabber` actually made the `dontTell()` method public:

```
class Secret
{
    protected:
        virtual void dontTell() { cout << "I'll never tell." << endl; }
};
class Blabber : public Secret
{
    public:
        virtual void dontTell() { cout << "I'll tell all!" << endl; }
};
```

If the `dontTell()` method is called on a `Blabber` object, it will output `I'll tell all!`

```
myBlabber.dontTell(); // Outputs "I'll tell all!"
```

In this case, however, the `protected` method in the superclass stays `protected` because any attempts to call `Secret`'s `dontTell()` method through a pointer or reference will not compile.

```
Blabber myBlabber;
Secret& ref = myBlabber;
Secret* ptr = &myBlabber;
ref.dontTell();  // BUG! Attempt to access protected method.
ptr->dontTell(); // BUG! Attempt to access protected method.
```

 The only truly useful way to change a method's access level is by providing a less restrictive accessor to a protected *method.*

Copy Constructors and the Equals Operator in Subclasses

Chapter 7 says that providing a copy constructor and assignment operator is considered a good programming practice when you have dynamically allocated memory in the class. When defining a subclass, you need to be careful about copy constructors and `operator=`.

If your subclass does not have any special data (pointers, usually) that require a nondefault copy constructor or `operator=`, you don't need to have one, regardless of whether or not the superclass has one. If your subclass omits the copy constructor or `operator=`, a default copy constructor or `operator=` will be provided for the data members specified in the subclass and the superclass copy constructor or `operator=` will be used for the data members specified in the superclass.

On the other hand, if you *do* specify a copy constructor in the subclass, you need to explicitly chain to the parent copy constructor, as shown in the following code. If you do not do this, the default constructor (not the copy constructor!) will be used for the parent portion of the object.

```
class Super
{
    public:
        Super();
        Super(const Super& inSuper);
};
class Sub : public Super
{
    public:
        Sub();
        Sub(const Sub& inSub);
};
Sub::Sub(const Sub& inSub) : Super(inSub)
{
}
```

Similarly, if the subclass overrides operator=, it is almost always necessary to call the parent's version of operator= as well. The only case where you wouldn't do this is if there is some bizarre reason why you only want part of the object assigned when an assignment takes place. The following code shows how to call the parent's assignment operator from the subclass:

```
Sub& Sub::operator=(const Sub& inSub)
{
    if (&inSub == this) {
        return *this;
    }
    Super::operator=(inSub) // Calls parent's operator=.
    // Do necessary assignments for subclass.
    return *this;
}
```

If your subclass does not specify its own copy constructor or operator=, *the parent functionality continues to work. If the subclass does provide its own copy constructor or* operator=, *it needs to explicitly reference the parent versions.*

The Truth about virtual

When you first encountered method overriding earlier in this chapter, we told you that only virtual methods can be properly overridden. The reason we had to add the qualifier *properly* is that if a method is not virtual, you can still attempt to override it but it will be wrong in subtle ways.

Hiding Instead of Overriding

The following code shows a superclass and a subclass, each with a single method. The subclass is attempting to override the method in the superclass, but it is not declared to be virtual in the superclass.

```
class Super
{
    public:
        void go() { cout << "go() called on Super" << endl; }
};
class Sub : public Super
{
    public:
        void go() { cout << "go() called on Sub" << endl; }
};
```

Attempting to call the `go()` method on a `Sub` object will initially appear to work.

```
Sub mySub;
mySub.go();
```

The output of this call is, as expected, `go() called on Sub`. However, since the method was not `virtual`, it was not actually overridden. Rather, the `Sub` class created a new method, also called `go()` that is completely unrelated to the `Super` class's method called `go()`. To prove this, simply call the method in the context of a `Super` pointer or reference.

```
Sub mySub;
Super& ref = mySub;
ref.go();
```

You would expect the output to be, `go() called on Sub`, but in fact, the output will be, `go() called on Super`. This is because the `ref` variable is a `Super` reference and because the `virtual` keyword was omitted. When the `go()` method is called, it simply executes `Super`'s `go()` method. Because it is not `virtual`, there is no need to consider whether a subclass has overridden it.

 Attempting to override a non-`virtual` method will "hide" the superclass definition and will only be used in the context of the subclass.

How virtual Is Implemented

To understand why method hiding occurs, you need to know a bit more about what the `virtual` keyword actually does. When a class is compiled in C++, a binary object is created that contains all of the data members and methods for the class. In the non-`virtual` case, the code to transfer control to the appropriate method is hard-coded directly where the method is called based on the compile-time type.

If the method is declared `virtual`, the correct implementation is called through the use of a special area of memory called the *vtable*, for "virtual table." Each class that has one or more `virtual` methods has a vtable that contains pointers to the implementations of the `virtual` methods. In this way, when a method is called on an object, the pointer is followed into the vtable and the appropriate version of the method is executed based on the actual type of the object.

To better understand how vtables make overriding of methods possible, take the following Super and Sub classes as an example.

```
class Super
{
    public:
        virtual void func1() {}
        virtual void func2() {}
};
class Sub : public Super
{
    public:
        virtual void func2() {}
};
```

For this example, assume that you have the following two instances:

```
Super mySuper;
Sub mySub;
```

Figure 8-11 shows a high-level view of how the vtables for both instances look. The mySuper object contains a pointer to its vtable. This vtable has two entries, one for func1() and one for func2(). Those entries point to the implementations of Super::func1() and Super::func2().

mySub also contains a pointer to its vtable which also has two entries, one for func1() and one for func2(). The func1() entry of the mySub vtable points to Super::func1() because Sub does not override func1(). On the other hand, the func2() entry of the mySub vtable points to Sub::func2().

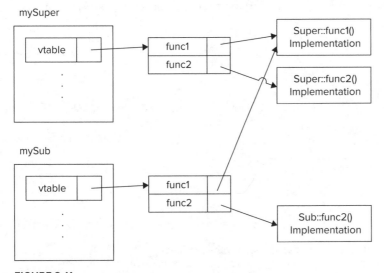

FIGURE 8-11

The Justification for virtual

Given the fact that you are advised to make all methods `virtual`, you might be wondering why the `virtual` keyword even exists. Can't the compiler automatically make all methods `virtual`? The answer is yes, it *could*. Many people think that the language *should* just make everything `virtual`. The Java language effectively does this.

The argument against making everything `virtual`, and the reason that the keyword was created in the first place, has to do with the overhead of the vtable. To call a `virtual` method, the program needs to perform an extra operation by dereferencing the pointer to the appropriate code to execute. This is a miniscule performance hit for most cases, but the designers of C++ thought that it was better, at least at the time, to let the programmer decide if the performance hit was necessary. If the method was never going to be overridden, there was no need to make it `virtual` and take the performance hit. However, with today's CPUs, the performance hit is measured in fractions of a nanosecond and this will keep getting smaller with future CPUs. In most applications, you will not have a measurable performance difference between using `virtual` methods and avoiding them, so you should still follow the advice of making all methods, including destructors, `virtual`.

There is also a tiny hit to code size. In addition to the implementation of the method, each object would also need a pointer, which takes up a tiny amount of space.

The Need for virtual Destructors

Even programmers who don't adopt the guideline of making all methods `virtual` still adhere to the rule when it comes to destructors. The reason is that making your destructors non-`virtual` can easily result in situations in which memory is not freed by object destruction.

For example, if a subclass uses memory that is dynamically allocated in the constructor and deleted in the destructor, it will never be freed if the destructor is never called. As the following code shows, it is easy to "trick" the compiler into skipping the call to the destructor if it is non-`virtual`:

```
class Super
{
    public:
        Super();
        ~Super();
};
class Sub : public Super
{
    public:
        Sub() { mString = new char[30]; }
        ~Sub() { delete [] mString; }
    protected:
        char* mString;
};
int main()
{
    Super* ptr = new Sub();   // mString is allocated here.
    delete ptr;    // ~Super is called, but not ~Sub because the destructor
                   // is not virtual!
    return 0;
}
```

*Unless you have a specific reason not to, we highly recommend making all methods, **including destructors** but not constructors, `virtual`. Constructors cannot and need not be `virtual` because you always specify the exact class being constructed when creating an object.*

Run Time Type Facilities

Relative to other object-oriented languages, C++ is very compile-time oriented. Overriding methods, as you learned above, works because of a level of indirection between a method and its implementation, not because the object has built-in knowledge of its own class.

There are, however, features in C++ that provide a run time view of an object. These features are commonly grouped together under a feature set called *Run Time Type Information*, or *RTTI*. RTTI provides a number of useful features for working with information about an object's class membership. One such feature is `dynamic_cast` to safely convert between types within an OO hierarchy and is discussed earlier in this chapter.

A second RTTI feature is the `typeid` operator, which lets you query an object at run time to find out its type. For the most part, you shouldn't ever need to use `typeid` because any code that is conditionally run based on the type of the object would be better handled with `virtual` methods.

The following code uses `typeid` to print a message based on the type of the object:

```
#include <typeinfo>
void speak(const Animal& inAnimal)
{
    if (typeid(inAnimal) == typeid(Dog&)) {
        cout << "Woof!" << endl;
    } else if (typeid(inAnimal) == typeid(Bird&)) {
        cout << "Chirp!" << endl;
    }
}
```

Anytime you see code like this, you should immediately consider reimplementing the functionality as a `virtual` method. In this case, a better implementation would be to declare a `virtual` method called `speak()` in the `Animal` class. `Dog` would override the method to print `"Woof!"` and `Bird` would override the method to print `"Chirp!"`. This approach better fits object-oriented programming, where functionality related to objects is given to those objects.

In a polymorphic situation, the `typeid` operator will work correctly only if the classes have at least one `virtual` method.

One of the primary values of the `typeid` operator is for logging and debugging purposes. The following code makes use of `typeid` for logging. The `logObject` function takes a "loggable" object as a parameter. The design is such that any object that can be logged subclasses the `Loggable` class and supports a method called `getLogMessage()`. In this way, `Loggable` is a mix-in class.

```
#include <typeinfo>
void logObject(Loggable& inLoggableObject)
{
    logfile << typeid(inLoggableObject).name() << " ";
    logfile << inLoggableObject.getLogMessage() << endl;
}
```

The `logObject()` function first writes the name of the object's class to the file, followed by its log message. This way, when you read the log later, you can see which object was responsible for every line of the file.

 If you are using `typeid` *other than for logging and debugging purposes, consider reimplementing it using* `virtual` *methods.*

Non-Public Inheritance

In all previous examples, parent classes were always listed using the `public` keyword. You may be wondering if a parent can be `private` or `protected`. In fact it can, though neither is as common as `public`.

Declaring the relationship with the parent to be `protected` means that all `public` and `protected` methods and data members from the superclass become `protected` in the context of the subclass. Similarly, specifying `private` access means that all `public`, `protected`, and `private` methods and data members of the superclass become `private` in the subclass.

There are a handful of reasons why you might want to uniformly degrade the access level of the parent in this way, but most reasons imply flaws in the design of the hierarchy. Some programmers abuse this language feature, often in combination with multiple inheritance, to implement "components" of a class. Instead of making an `Airplane` class that contains an engine data member and a fuselage data member, they make an `Airplane` class that is a `protected` engine and a `protected` fuselage. In this way, the `Airplane` doesn't look like an engine or a fuselage to client code (because everything is `protected`), but it is able to use all of that functionality internally.

 Non-public inheritance is rare and we recommend using it cautiously, if for no other reason than because most programmers are not familiar with it.

Virtual Base Classes

Earlier in this chapter, you learned about ambiguous base classes, a situation that arises when multiple parents each have a parent in common, as shown again in Figure 8-12. The solution that we recommended was to make sure that the shared parent doesn't have any functionality of its own. That way, its methods can never be called and there is no ambiguity problem.

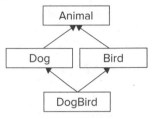

FIGURE 8-12

C++ has another mechanism for addressing this problem in the event that you do want the shared parent to have its own functionality. If the shared parent is a *virtual base class*, there will not be any ambiguity. The following code adds a `sleep()` method to the `Animal` base class and modifies the `Dog` and `Bird` classes to inherit from `Animal` as a virtual base class. Without the `virtual` keyword, a call to `sleep()` on a `DogBird` object would be ambiguous and would generate a compiler error because `DogBird` would have two subobjects of class `Animal`, one coming from `Dog` and one coming from `Bird`. However, when `Animal` is inherited virtually, `DogBird` has only one subobject of class `Animal`, so there will be no ambiguity with calling `sleep()`.

```cpp
class Animal
{
    public:
        virtual void eat() = 0;
        virtual void sleep() { cout << "zzzzz...." << endl; }
};
class Dog : public virtual Animal
{
    public:
        virtual void bark() { cout << "Woof!" << endl; }
        virtual void eat() { cout << "The dog has eaten." << endl; }
};
class Bird : public virtual Animal
{
    public:
        virtual void chirp() { cout << "Chirp!" << endl; }
        virtual void eat() { cout << "The bird has eaten." << endl; }
};
class DogBird : public Dog, public Bird
{
    public:
        virtual void eat() { Dog::eat(); }
};
int main()
{
    DogBird myConfusedAnimal;
    myConfusedAnimal.sleep();  // Not ambiguous because Animal is virtual
    return 0;
}
```

Virtual base classes are a great way to avoid ambiguity in class hierarchies. The only drawback is that many C++ programmers are unfamiliar with the concept.

SUMMARY

This chapter has covered numerous details about inheritance. You have learned about its many applications, including code reuse and polymorphism. You have also learned about its many abuses, including poorly-designed multiple inheritance schemes. Along the way, you've uncovered some cases that require special attention.

Inheritance is a powerful language feature that takes some time to get used to. After you have worked with the examples of this chapter and experimented on your own, we hope that inheritance will become your tool of choice for object-oriented design.

Understanding C++ Quirks and Oddities

WHAT'S IN THIS CHAPTER?

➤ What the different use-cases are for references

➤ Keyword confusion

➤ How to use `typedef`s and type aliases

➤ What scope resolution is

➤ Details of new C++11 features that do not fit elsewhere in this book

Many parts of the C++ language have tricky syntax or quirky semantics. As a C++ programmer, you grow accustomed to most of this idiosyncratic behavior; it starts to feel natural. However, some aspects of C++ are a source of perennial confusion. Either books never explain them thoroughly enough, or you forget how they work and continually look them up, or both. This chapter addresses this gap by providing clear explanations for some of C++'s most niggling quirks and oddities.

Many language idiosyncrasies are covered in various chapters throughout this book. This chapter tries not to repeat those topics, by limiting itself to subjects that are not covered in detail elsewhere in the book. There is a bit of redundancy with other chapters, but the material is "sliced" in a different way in order to provide you with a new perspective.

The topics of this chapter include references, `const`, `constexpr`, `static`, `extern`, `typedef`s, type aliases, casts, scope resolution, uniform initialization, alternative function syntax, null pointer constant, angle brackets, initializer lists, explicit conversion operators, attributes, user-defined literals, header files, variable-length argument lists, and preprocessor macros.

Although this list might appear to be a hodgepodge of topics, it is a carefully selected collection of some of the most confusing, but commonly used, aspects of the language, and of new C++11 features.

REFERENCES

Professional C++ code, including much of the code in this book, uses references extensively. It is helpful to step back and think about what exactly references are, and how they behave.

A *reference* in C++ is an *alias* for another variable. All modifications to the reference change the value of the variable to which it refers. You can think of references as implicit pointers that save you the trouble of taking the address of variables and dereferencing the pointer. Alternatively, you can think of references as just another name for the original variable. You can create stand-alone reference variables, use reference data members in classes, accept references as parameters to functions and methods and return references from functions and methods.

Reference Variables

Reference variables must be initialized as soon as they are created, like this:

```cpp
int x = 3;
int& xRef = x;
```

Code snippet from References\ReferenceVariables.cpp

Subsequent to this assignment, `xRef` is another name for `x`. Any use of `xRef` uses the current value of `x`. Any assignment to `xRef` changes the value of `x`. For example, the following code sets x to 10 through `xRef`:

```cpp
xRef = 10;
```

Code snippet from References\ReferenceVariables.cpp

You cannot declare a reference variable outside of a class without initializing it:

```cpp
int& emptyRef; // DOES NOT COMPILE!
```

Code snippet from References\ReferenceVariables.cpp

> You must always initialize a reference when it is created. Usually, references are created when they are declared, but reference data members need to be initialized in the constructor initializer for the containing class.

You cannot create a reference to an unnamed value such as an integer literal, unless the reference is to a `const` value. In the following example, `unnamedRef1` will not compile because it is a non-`const` reference to a constant. That would mean you could change the value of the constant, 5, which doesn't make sense. `unnamedRef2` works because it's a `const` reference, so you cannot write "unnamedRef2 = 7".

```
int& unnamedRef1 = 5; // DOES NOT COMPILE
const int& unnamedRef2 = 5; // Works
```

Code snippet from References\ReferenceVariables.cpp

Modifying References

A reference always refers to the same variable to which it is initialized; references cannot be changed once they are created. This rule leads to some confusing syntax. If you "assign" a variable to a reference when the reference is declared, the reference refers to that variable. However, if you assign a variable to a reference after that, the variable to which the reference refers is changed to the value of the variable being assigned. The reference is not updated to refer to that variable. Here is a code example:

```
int x = 3, y = 4;
int& xRef = x;
xRef = y; // Changes value of x to 4. Doesn't make xRef refer to y.
```

Code snippet from References\ReferenceVariables.cpp

You might try to circumvent this restriction by taking the address of `y` when you assign it:

```
int x = 3, y = 4;
int& xRef = x;
xRef = &y; // DOES NOT COMPILE!
```

This code does not compile. The address of `y` is a pointer, but `xRef` is declared as a reference to an `int`, not a reference to a pointer.

Some programmers go even further in attempts to circumvent the intended semantics of references. What if you assign a reference to a reference? Won't that make the first reference refer to the variable to which the second reference refers? You might be tempted to try this code:

```
int x = 3, z = 5;
int& xRef = x;
int& zRef = z;
zRef = xRef; // Assigns values, not references
```

Code snippet from References\ReferenceVariables.cpp

The final line does not change `zRef`. Instead, it sets the value of `z` to 3, because `xRef` refers to `x`, which is 3.

You cannot change the variable to which a reference refers after it is initialized; you can only change the value of that variable.

References to Pointers and Pointers to References

You can create references to any type, including pointer types. Here is an example of a reference to a pointer to `int`:

```
int* intP;
int*& ptrRef = intP;
ptrRef = new int;
*ptrRef = 5;
```

Code snippet from References\ReferenceVariables.cpp

The syntax is a little strange: You might not be accustomed to seeing `*` and `&` right next to each other. However, the semantics are straightforward: `ptrRef` is a reference to `intP`, which is a pointer to `int`. Modifying `ptrRef` changes `intP`. References to pointers are rare, but can occasionally be useful, as discussed in the "Reference Parameters" section later in this chapter.

Note that taking the address of a reference gives the same result as taking the address of the variable to which the reference refers. For example:

```
int x = 3;
int& xRef = x;
int* xPtr = &xRef; // Address of a reference is pointer to value
*xPtr = 100;
```

Code snippet from References\ReferenceVariables.cpp

This code sets `xPtr` to point to `x` by taking the address of a reference to `x`. Assigning 100 to `*xPtr` changes the value of `x` to 100. Writing a comparison "`xPtr == xRef`" will not compile because of a type mismatch; `xPtr` is a pointer to an `int` while `xRef` is a reference to an `int`. The comparisons "`xPtr == &xRef`" and "`xPtr == &x`" both compile without errors and are both `true`.

Finally, note that you cannot declare a reference to a reference or a pointer to a reference:

```
int x = 3;
int& xRef = x;
int&& xDoubleRef = xRef; // DOES NOT COMPILE!
int&* refPtr = &xRef; // DOES NOT COMPILE!
```

Code snippet from References\ReferenceVariables.cpp

> **C++11** *In this example `&&` is used in an attempt to declare a reference to a reference which is not possible. However, the C++11 standard assigns a new meaning to `&&`. It now means* rvalue reference *and is discussed later in this chapter.*

Reference Data Members

As Chapter 7 explains, data members of classes can be references. A reference cannot exist without referring to some other variable. Thus, you must initialize reference data members in the constructor initializer, not in the body of the constructor. The following is a quick example:

```cpp
class MyClass
{
    public:
        MyClass(int& ref) : mRef(ref) {}
    protected:
        int& mRef;
};
int main()
{
    int i = 123;
    MyClass m(i);
    return 0;
}
```

Code snippet from References\ReferenceDataMembers.cpp

Consult Chapter 7 for details.

Reference Parameters

C++ programmers do not often use stand-alone reference variables or reference data members. The most common use of references is for parameters to functions and methods. Recall that the default parameter-passing semantics are pass-by-value: Functions receive copies of their arguments. When those parameters are modified, the original arguments remain unchanged. References allow you to specify alternative pass-by-reference semantics for arguments passed to the function. When you use reference parameters, the function receives references to the function arguments. If those references are modified, the changes are reflected in the original argument variables. For example, here is a simple swap function to swap the values of two `int`s:

```cpp
void swap(int& first, int& second)
{
    int temp = first;
    first = second;
    second = temp;
}
```

Code snippet from References\ReferenceParameters.cpp

You can call it like this:

```cpp
int x = 5, y = 6;
swap(x, y);
```

Code snippet from References\ReferenceParameters.cpp

When the function `swap()` is called with the arguments `x` and `y`, the `first` parameter is initialized to refer to `x`, and the `second` parameter is initialized to refer to `y`. When `swap()` modifies `first` and `second`, `x` and `y` are actually changed.

Just as you can't initialize normal reference variables with constants, you can't pass constants as arguments to functions that employ pass-by-reference:

```
swap(3, 4); // DOES NOT COMPILE
```

Code snippet from References\ReferenceParameters.cpp

 C++11 *Using* rvalue references *from C++11, it is possible to pass constants as arguments to functions that employ pass-by-rvalue-reference. Rvalue references are discussed later in this chapter.*

References from Pointers

A common quandary arises when you have a pointer to something that you need to pass to a function or method that takes a reference. You can "convert" a pointer to a reference in this case simply by dereferencing the pointer. This action gives you the value to which the pointer points, which the compiler then uses to initialize the reference parameter. For example, you can call `swap()` like this:

```
int x = 5, y = 6;
int *xp = &x, *yp = &y;
swap(*xp, *yp);
```

Code snippet from References\ReferenceParameters.cpp

Pass-By-Reference versus Pass-By-Value

Pass-by-reference is required when you want to modify the parameter and see those changes reflected in the variable argument to the function or method. However, you should not limit your use of pass-by-reference to only those cases. Pass-by-reference avoids copying the arguments to the function, providing two additional benefits in some cases:

1. **Efficiency:** Large objects and `structs` could take a long time to copy. Pass-by-reference passes only a pointer to the object or `struct` into the function.

2. **Correctness:** Not all objects allow pass-by-value. Even those that do allow it might not support deep copying correctly. As Chapter 7 explains, objects with dynamically allocated memory must provide a custom copy constructor in order to support deep copying.

If you want to leverage these benefits, but do not want to allow the original objects to be modified, you can mark the parameters `const`, giving you pass-by-const-reference. This topic is covered in detail later in this chapter.

These benefits to pass-by-reference imply that you should use pass-by-value only for simple built-in types like `int` and `double` for which you don't need to modify the arguments. Use pass-by-reference in all other cases.

Reference Return Values

You can also return a reference from a function or method. The main reason to do so is efficiency. Instead of returning a whole object, return a reference to the object to avoid copying it unnecessarily. Of course, you can only use this technique if the object in question will continue to exist following the function termination.

 From a function or method, never return a reference to a variable that is locally scoped to that function or method, such as an automatically allocated variable on the stack that will be destroyed when the function ends.

A second reason to return a reference is if you want to be able to assign to the return value directly as an *lvalue* (the left-hand side of an assignment statement).

Several overloaded operators commonly return references. Chapter 7 shows some examples, and you can read about more applications of this technique in Chapter 18.

Deciding between References and Pointers

References in C++ could be considered redundant: almost everything you can do with references, you can accomplish with pointers. For example, you could write the previously shown `swap()` function like this:

```
void swap(int* first, int* second)
{
    int temp = *first;
    *first = *second;
    *second = temp;
}
```

However, this code is more cluttered than the version with references: References make your programs cleaner and easier to understand. References are also safer than pointers: It's impossible to have an invalid reference, and you don't explicitly dereference references, so you can't encounter any of the dereferencing errors associated with pointers. These arguments, saying that references are safer, are only valid in the absence of any pointers. For example, take the following function which accepts a reference to an `int`:

```
void refcall(int& t) { ++t; }
```

You could declare a pointer and initialize it to the null pointer. Then you could dereference this pointer and pass it as the reference argument to `refcall()` as in the following code. This code will compile but will crash when trying to execute it.

```
int main()
{
    int* ptr = nullptr;
    refcall(*ptr);
    return 0;
}
```

Most of the time, you can use references instead of pointers. References to objects even support polymorphism in the same way as pointers to objects. The only case in which you need to use a pointer is when you need to change the location to which it points. Recall that you cannot change the variable to which references refer. For example, when you dynamically allocate memory, you need to store a pointer to the result in a pointer rather than a reference.

Another way to distinguish between appropriate use of pointers and references in parameters and return types is to consider who *owns* the memory. If the code receiving the variable is responsible for releasing the memory associated with an object, it must receive a pointer to the object. If the code receiving the variable should not free the memory, it should receive a reference.

> *Use references instead of pointers unless you need to change to where the reference refers to.*

Strict application of this rule can lead to some unfamiliar syntax. Consider a function that splits an array of `int`s into two arrays: one of even numbers and one of odd numbers. The function doesn't know how many numbers in the source array will be even or odd, so it should dynamically allocate the memory for the destination arrays after examining the source array. It should also return the sizes of the two new arrays. Altogether, there are four items to return: pointers to the two new arrays and the sizes of the two new arrays. Obviously, you must use pass-by-reference. The canonical C way to write the function looks like this:

Available for
download on
Wrox.com

```
void separateOddsAndEvens(const int arr[], int size, int** odds,
    int* numOdds, int** evens, int* numEvens)
{
    // First pass to determine array sizes
    *numOdds = *numEvens = 0;
    for (int i = 0; i < size; i++) {
        if (arr[i] % 2 == 1) {
            (*numOdds)++;
        } else {
            (*numEvens)++;
        }
    }
}
```

```
    // Allocate two new arrays of the appropriate size.
    *odds = new int[*numOdds];
    *evens = new int[*numEvens];
    // Copy the odds and evens to the new arrays
    int oddsPos = 0, evensPos = 0;
    for (int i = 0; i < size; i++) {
        if (arr[i] % 2 == 1) {
            (*odds)[oddsPos++] = arr[i];
        } else {
            (*evens)[evensPos++] = arr[i];
        }
    }
}
```

Code snippet from References\OddsEvensPtrs.cpp

The final four parameters to the function are the "reference" parameters. In order to change the values to which they refer, `separateOddsAndEvens()` must dereference them, leading to some ugly syntax in the function body.

Additionally, when you want to call `separateOddsAndEvens()`, you must pass the address of two pointers so that the function can change the actual pointers, and the address of two `int`s so that the function can change the actual `int`s:

Available for download on Wrox.com

```
int unSplit[10] = {1, 2, 3, 4, 5, 6, 6, 8, 9, 10};
int *oddNums, *evenNums;
int numOdds, numEvens;
separateOddsAndEvens(unSplit, 10, &oddNums, &numOdds, &evenNums, &numEvens);
```

Code snippet from References\OddsEvensPtrs.cpp

If such syntax annoys you (which it should), you can write the same function by using references to obtain true pass-by-reference semantics:

Available for download on Wrox.com

```
void separateOddsAndEvens(const int arr[], int size, int*& odds,
    int& numOdds, int*& evens, int& numEvens)
{
    numOdds = numEvens = 0;
    for (int i = 0; i < size; i++) {
        if (arr[i] % 2 == 1) {
            numOdds++;
        } else {
            numEvens++;
        }
    }
    odds = new int[numOdds];
    evens = new int[numEvens];
    int oddsPos = 0, evensPos = 0;
    for (int i = 0; i < size; i++) {
        if (arr[i] % 2 == 1) {
            odds[oddsPos++] = arr[i];
        } else {
```

```
                    evens[evensPos++] = arr[i];
                }
            }
        }
```

Code snippet from References\OddsEvensRefs.cpp

In this case, the `odds` and `evens` parameters are references to `int*`s. `separateOddsAndEvens()` can modify the `int*`s that are used as arguments to the function (through the reference), without any explicit dereferencing. The same logic applies to `numOdds` and `numEvens`, which are references to `int`s.

With this version of the function, you no longer need to pass the addresses of the pointers or `int`s. The reference parameters handle it for you automatically:

```
int unSplit[10] = {1, 2, 3, 4, 5, 6, 6, 8, 9, 10};
int *oddNums, *evenNums;
int numOdds, numEvens;
separateOddsAndEvens(unSplit, 10, oddNums, numOdds, evenNums, numEvens);
```

Code snippet from References\OddsEvensRefs.cpp

It's recommended to avoid dynamically allocated arrays as much as possible to make your life easier. For example, by using the STL `vector` container, the previous `separateOddsAndEvens()` can be rewritten much more compactly and elegantly, because all memory allocation and deallocation happens automatically.

```
void separateOddsAndEvens(const vector<int>& arr,
    vector<int>& odds, vector<int>& evens)
{
    for (auto& i : arr) {
        if (i % 2 == 1)
            odds.push_back(i);
        else
            evens.push_back(i);
    }
}
```

Code snippet from References\OddsEvensVector.cpp

This version can be used as follows:

```
vector<int> vecUnSplit = {1, 2, 3, 4, 5, 6, 6, 8, 9, 10};
vector<int> odds, evens;
separateOddsAndEvens(vecUnSplit, odds, evens);
```

Code snippet from References\OddsEvensVector.cpp

The STL `vector` container is discussed in more detail in Chapter 12.

C++11 Rvalue References

In C++, an *lvalue* is something of which you can take an address, a named variable for example. The name comes from the fact that they normally appear on the left-hand side of an assignment. An *rvalue* on the other hand is anything that is not an lvalue, a constant value for example or a temporary object or value. Typically an rvalue is on the right-hand side of an assignment operator.

C++11 introduces a new concept, an *rvalue reference*, which is a reference to an rvalue. In particular, it is a concept that is applied when the rvalue is a temporary object. The purpose of an rvalue reference is to allow methods (most particularly, but not restricted to, copy constructors and `operator=`) so that a particular method can be chosen when a temporary object is involved. The consequence of this is that certain operations which normally involve copying large values can be implemented by simply copying pointers to those values, knowing the temporary object will be destroyed.

A method can specify an rvalue reference parameter by using `&&` as part of the parameter specification, e.g., `type&& name`. Normally, a temporary object will be seen as a `const type&`, but when there is a method that uses an rvalue reference, a temporary object can be resolved to this overload.

However, rvalue references are not limited to parameters of functions. You can declare a variable of type rvalue reference, and assign to it, although this usage is uncommon. Consider the following code, which is illegal in C++:

```
int& i = 2;        // Invalid: reference to a constant
int a = 2, b = 3;
int& j = a + b;    // Invalid: reference to a temporary
```

Using rvalue references, the following is perfectly legal:

```
int&& i = 2;
int a = 2, b = 3;
int&& j = a + b;
```

Standalone rvalue references as in the preceding example are rarely used as such. However, they can be useful as parameters to functions or methods as the following example demonstrates. The code first defines two `incr()` functions, one accepting an lvalue reference and one accepting an rvalue reference.

Available for download on Wrox.com

```
// Increment value using lvalue reference parameter.
void incr(int& value)
{
    cout << "increment with lvalue reference" << endl;
    ++value;
}
// Increment value using rvalue reference parameter.
void incr(int&& value)
{
    cout << "increment with rvalue reference" << endl;
```

```
        ++value;
    }
```

You can call the `incr()` function with a named variable as argument as follows. Because `a` is a named variable, the `incr()` function accepting an lvalue reference is called. After the call to `incr()`, the value of `a` will be 11.

```
int a = 10, b = 20;
incr(a);              // Will call incr(int& value)
```

You can also call the `incr()` function with an expression as argument as follows. The `incr()` function accepting an lvalue reference cannot be used, because the expression `a + b` results in a temporary, which is not an lvalue. In this case the rvalue reference version is called. Since the argument is a temporary, the incremented value is actually lost after the call to `incr()`.

```
incr(a + b);          // Will call incr(int&& value)
```

A literal can also be used as argument to the `incr()` call. This will also trigger a call to the rvalue reference version because a literal cannot be an lvalue.

```
incr(3);              // Will call incr(int&& value)
```

If you remove the definition accepting an lvalue reference, `incr(int& value)`, calling `incr()` with a named variable like `incr(b)` will result in a compiler error, because the C++ standard says that an rvalue reference parameter (`int&& value`) will never be bound to an lvalue (`b`). You can force the compiler to call the rvalue reference version of `incr()` by using `std::move()` which converts an lvalue into an rvalue as follows. After the `incr()` call, the value of `b` will be 21.

```
incr(std::move(b)); // Will call incr(int&& value)
```

Move Semantics

C++11 adds the concept of *move semantics* to objects by implementing a *move constructor* and a *move assignment operator*. These will be used by the compiler on places where the second object is a temporary object that will be destroyed after the copy or assignment. Both the move constructor and the move assignment operator copy the member variables from the source object to the new object and then reset the variables of the source object to null values. By doing this, they are actually *moving ownership* of the memory from one object to another object. They basically do a *shallow* copy of the member variables *and* switch ownership of allocated memory to prevent dangling pointers or memory leaks.

Move semantics is implemented by using rvalue references. To add move semantics to a class, a move constructor and a move assignment operator need to be implemented. Following is the `Spreadsheet` class definition from Chapter 7, which now includes a move constructor and a move assignment operator.

```
class Spreadsheet
{
    public:
        Spreadsheet(Spreadsheet&& src); // Move constructor
        Spreadsheet& operator=(Spreadsheet&& rhs);  // Move assignment
        // Remaining code omitted for brevity
};
```

Code snippet from SpreadsheetMoveSemantics\Spreadsheet.h

The implementation is as follows.

```
// Move constructor
Spreadsheet::Spreadsheet(Spreadsheet&& src)
{
    // Shallow copy of data
    mWidth = src.mWidth;
    mHeight = src.mHeight;
    mCells = src.mCells;
    // Reset the source object
    src.mWidth = 0;
    src.mHeight = 0;
    src.mCells = nullptr;
}
// Move assignment operator
Spreadsheet& Spreadsheet::operator=(Spreadsheet&& rhs)
{
    // check for self-assignment
    if (this == &rhs) {
        return *this;
    }
    // free the old memory
    for (int i = 0; i < mWidth; i++) {
        delete [] mCells[i];
    }
    delete [] mCells;
    mCells = nullptr;
    // Shallow copy of data
    mWidth = rhs.mWidth;
    mHeight = rhs.mHeight;
    mCells = rhs.mCells;
```

```
        // Reset the source object
        rhs.mWidth = 0;
        rhs.mHeight = 0;
        rhs.mCells = nullptr;
        return *this;
    }
```

Code snippet from SpreadsheetMoveSemantics\Spreadsheet.cpp

Both the move constructor and the move assignment operator are moving ownership of the memory for mCells from the source object to the new object. They reset the mCells pointer of the source object to a null pointer to prevent the destructor of the source object to deallocate that memory, because now the new object is the owner of that memory.

The preceding move constructor and move assignment operator can be tested with the following code:

Available for
download on
Wrox.com

```
Spreadsheet CreateObject()
{
    return Spreadsheet(3, 2);
}
int main()
{
    vector<Spreadsheet> vec;
    for (int i = 0; i < 2; ++i) {
        cout << "Iteration " << i << endl;
        vec.push_back(Spreadsheet(100, 100));
        cout << endl;
    }
    Spreadsheet s(2,3);
    s = CreateObject();
    Spreadsheet s2(5,6);
    s2 = s;
    return 0;
}
```

Code snippet from SpreadsheetMoveSemantics\SpreadsheetTest.cpp

Chapter 1 introduces the vector. A vector grows dynamically in size to accommodate new objects. This is done by allocating a bigger chunk of memory and then copying or moving the objects from the old vector to the new and bigger vector. If the compiler finds a move constructor, the objects will be moved instead of copied. By moving them there is no need for any deep copying making it much more efficient.

When you add output statements to all constructors and assignment operators of the Spreadsheet class, the output of the preceding test program will be as follows:

```
Iteration 0
Normal constructor      (1)
Move constructor        (2)
```

```
Iteration 1
Normal constructor        (3)
Move constructor          (4)
Move constructor          (5)


Normal constructor        (6)
Normal constructor        (7)
Move assignment operator  (8)
Normal constructor        (9)
Assignment operator       (10)
```

On the first iteration of the loop, the `vector` is still empty. Take the following line of code from the loop:

```
vec.push_back(Spreadsheet(100, 100));
```

With this line, a new `Spreadsheet` object is created which will invoke the normal constructor (1). The `vector` will resize itself to make space for the new object being pushed in. The created `Spreadsheet` object is then moved into the `vector`, invoking the move constructor (2).

On the second iteration of the loop, a second `Spreadsheet` object is created with the normal constructor (3). At this point, the `vector` can hold one element, so it's again resized to make space for a second object. By resizing the `vector`, the previously added elements need to be moved from the old `vector` to the new and bigger `vector`, so this will trigger a call to the move constructor for each previously added element (4). Then, the new `Spreadsheet` object is moved into the vector with its move constructor (5).

The `CreateObject` function creates a temporary `Spreadsheet` object with its normal constructor (7), which is then returned from the function and move-assigned to the variable `s` (8). Because the temporary object will cease to exist after the assignment, the compiler will invoke the move assignment operator instead of the normal copy assignment operator. On the other hand, the assignment `s2 = s` will invoke the copy assignment operator (10) because the right-hand side object is not a temporary object, but a named object.

If the `Spreadsheet` class did not include a move constructor and move assignment operator, the above output would look as follows:

```
Iteration 0
Normal constructor
Copy constructor

Iteration 1
Normal constructor
Copy constructor
Copy constructor


Normal constructor
Normal constructor
Assignment operator
Normal constructor
Assignment operator
```

As you can see, copy constructors are called instead of move constructors and copy assignment operators are called instead of move assignment operators. In the previous example, the Spreadsheet objects have 10.000 (100 x 100) elements. The implementation of the Spreadsheet move constructor and move assignment operator don't require any memory allocation, while the copy constructor and copy assignment operator require 101 allocations. So, using move semantics can increase performance a lot in certain situations.

Move constructors and move assignment operators can also be explicitly deleted or defaulted, just like normal constructors and normal copy assignment operators, as explained in Chapter 6.

As another example where move semantics increases performance, take a swap() function that swaps two objects. Before C++11, a swap() function could be implemented as follows. This example uses templates, which are discussed in detail in Chapter 19.

```
template<typename T>
void swapCopy(T& a, T& b)
{
    T temp(a);
    a = b;
    b = temp;
}
```

This implementation first copies a to temp, then copies b to a and then copies temp to b. If type T is expensive to copy, this swap implementation will hurt performance. With move semantics the swap() function can avoid all copying:

```
template<typename T>
void swapMove(T& a, T& b)
{
    T temp(std::move(a));
    a = std::move(b);
    b = std::move(temp);
}
```

Obviously, move semantics is useful only when you know that the source object will be destroyed.

KEYWORD CONFUSION

Two keywords in C++ appear to cause more confusion than any others: const and static. Both of these keywords have several different meanings, and each of their uses presents subtleties that are important to understand.

The const Keyword

The keyword const is short for "constant" and specifies that something remains unchanged. The compiler will enforce this requirement by marking any attempt to change it as an error. Furthermore, when optimizations are enabled, the compiler can take advantage of this knowledge to produce better code.

The keyword const has two related roles. It can mark variables or parameters, and it can mark methods. This section provides a definitive discussion of these two meanings.

const Variables and Parameters

You can use const to "protect" variables by specifying that they cannot be modified. As Chapters 1 and 5 explain, one important use of this keyword is as a replacement for #define to declare constants. This use of const is its most straightforward application. For example, you could declare the constant PI like this:

```
const double PI = 3.14159;
```

Code snippet from Const\Const.cpp

You can mark any variable const, including global variables and class data members.

You can also use const to specify that parameters to functions or methods should remain unchanged. For example, the following function accepts a const parameter. In the body of the function, you cannot modify the param integer. If you do try to modify it, the compiler will generate an error.

```
void func(const int param)
{
    // Not allowed to change param...
}
```

Code snippet from Const\Const.cpp

The following subsections discuss two special kinds of const variables or parameters in more detail: const pointers and const references.

const Pointers

When a variable contains one or more levels of indirection via a pointer, applying const becomes trickier. Consider the following lines of code:

```
int* ip;
ip = new int[10];
ip[4] = 5;
```

Code snippet from Const\Const.cpp

Suppose that you decide to apply const to ip. Set aside your doubts about the usefulness of doing so for a moment, and consider what it means. Do you want to prevent the ip variable itself from being changed, or do you want to prevent the values to which it points from being changed? That is, do you want to prevent the second line or the third line in the previous example?

In order to prevent the pointed-to value from being modified (as in the third line), you can add the keyword `const` to the declaration of `ip` like this:

```
const int* ip;
ip = new int[10];
ip[4] = 5; // DOES NOT COMPILE!
```

Code snippet from Const\Const.cpp

Now you cannot change the values to which `ip` points.

An alternative, but semantically equivalent way to write this is as follows:

```
int const* ip;
ip = new int[10];
ip[4] = 5; // DOES NOT COMPILE!
```

Code snippet from Const\Const.cpp

Putting the `const` before or after the `int` makes no difference in its functionality.

If you want instead to mark `ip` itself `const` (not the values to which it points), you need to write this:

```
int* const ip = nullptr;
ip = new int[10]; // DOES NOT COMPILE!
ip[4] = 5;   // Error: dereferencing a null pointer
```

Code snippet from Const\Const.cpp

Now that `ip` itself cannot be changed, the compiler requires you to initialize it when you declare it, either with `nullptr` as in the preceding code or with newly allocated memory as follows:

```
int* const ip = new int[10];
ip[4] = 5;
```

Code snippet from Const\Const.cpp

You can also mark both the pointer and the values to which it points `const` like this:

```
int const* const ip = nullptr;
```

Code snippet from Const\Const.cpp

An alternative but equivalent syntax is the following:

```
const int* const ip = nullptr;
```

Code snippet from Const\Const.cpp

Although this syntax might seem confusing, there is actually a very simple rule: the `const` keyword applies to whatever is directly to its left. Consider this line again:

```cpp
int const* const ip = nullptr;
```

Code snippet from Const\Const.cpp

From left to right, the first `const` is directly to the right of the word `int`. Thus, it applies to the `int` to which `ip` points. Therefore, it specifies that you cannot change the values to which `ip` points. The second `const` is directly to the right of the `*`. Thus, it applies to the pointer to the `int`, which is the `ip` variable. Therefore, it specifies that you cannot change `ip` (the pointer) itself.

 `const` *applies to the level of indirection directly to its left.*

The reason this rule becomes confusing is an exception: The first `const` can go before the variable like this:

```cpp
const int* const ip = nullptr;
```

Code snippet from Const\Const.cpp

This "exceptional" syntax is used much more commonly than the other syntax.

You can extend this rule to any number of levels of indirection. For example:

```cpp
const int * const * const * const ip = nullptr;
```

Code snippet from Const\Const.cpp

 Another easy to remember rule to figure out complicated variable declarations: read from right to left. Take for example "`int* const ip`*." Reading this from right to left gives us "*`ip`* is a const pointer to an* `int`*." On the other hand, "*`int const* ip`*" will read as "*`ip`* is a pointer to a const* `int`*."*

const References

`const` applied to references is usually simpler than `const` applied to pointers for two reasons. First, references are `const` by default, in that you can't change to what they refer. So, C++ does not allow you to mark a reference variable explicitly `const`. Second, there is usually only one level of indirection with references. As explained earlier, you can't create a reference to a reference. The only way to get multiple levels of indirection is to create a reference to a pointer.

Thus, when C++ programmers refer to a "const reference," they mean something like this:

```
int z;
const int& zRef = z;
zRef = 4; // DOES NOT COMPILE
```

Code snippet from Const\Const.cpp

By applying `const` to the `int`, you prevent assignment to `zRef`, as shown. Remember that `const int& zRef` is equivalent to `int const& zRef`. Note, however, that marking `zRef const` has no effect on `z`. You can still modify the value of `z` by changing it directly instead of through the reference.

`const` references are used most commonly as parameters, where they are quite useful. If you want to pass something by reference for efficiency, but don't want it to be modifiable, make it a `const` reference. For example:

```
void doSomething(const BigClass& arg)
{
    // Implementation here
}
```

Code snippet from Const\Const.cpp

> *Your default choice for passing objects as parameters should be `const` reference. You should only omit the `const`, if you explicitly need to change the object.*

const Methods

Chapter 7 explains that you can mark a class method `const`. That specification prevents the method from modifying any non-`mutable` data members of the class. Consult Chapter 7 for an example.

C++11 The constexpr Keyword

The `constexpr` keyword is new in C++11. C++ always had the notion of constant expressions and in some circumstances, constant expressions are required. For example when defining an array, the size of the array needs to be a constant expression. Because of this restriction, the following piece of code is not valid in C++.

```
const int getArraySize() { return 32; }
int main()
{
```

```
        int myArray[getArraySize()];    // Invalid in C++
        return 0;
    }
```

Using the new `constexpr` keyword, the `getArraySize()` function can be redefined as follows:

```
constexpr int getArraySize() { return 32; }
int main()
{
    int myArray[getArraySize()];    // OK with C++11
    return 0;
}
```

Code snippet from Constexpr\constexpr.cpp

You can even do something like this:

```
int myArray[getArraySize() + 1];    // OK with C++11
```

The benefit of using `constexpr` is that the compiler can optimize your code much better during the compilation process. Declaring a function as `constexpr` imposes a few limitations on what that function can do.

➤ If the `constexpr` function is a member of a class, the function cannot be `virtual`.

➤ The return type of the function should be a literal type or a reference to a literal type. It cannot be `void`.

➤ All the function arguments should be literal types or references to literal types.

➤ The function body should be in the form `{return expression;}` where `expression` is a constant expression after argument substitution. `expression` is allowed to call other `constexpr` functions.

➤ A `constexpr` function cannot be called until it's defined in the translation unit because the compiler needs to know the complete definition.

These limitations are in place because the compiler must be able to evaluate a `constexpr` function at compile time.

By defining a `constexpr` constructor you can create constant expression variables of user-defined types. A `constexpr` constructor should satisfy the following requirements.

➤ All the constructor arguments should be literal types or references to literal types.

➤ The constructor body cannot be a function-try-block.

➤ The constructor body should be empty.

➤ All data members should be initialized with constant expressions.

For example, the following `Rect` class defines a `constexpr` constructor satisfying the previous requirements and also defines a `constexpr getArea()` method that is performing some calculation.

```cpp
class Rect
{
    public:
        constexpr Rect(int width, int height)
            : mWidth(width), mHeight(height) {}
        constexpr int getArea() const { return mWidth * mHeight; }
    private:
        int mWidth, mHeight;
};
```

Code snippet from Constexpr\constexprClasses.cpp

Using this class to declare a `constexpr` object is straightforward:

```cpp
constexpr Rect r(8, 2);
int myArray[r.getArea()];    // OK with C++11
```

Code snippet from Constexpr\constexprClasses.cpp

The static Keyword

There are several uses of the keyword `static` in C++, all seemingly unrelated. Part of the motivation for "overloading" the keyword was attempting to avoid having to introduce new keywords into the language.

static Data Members and Methods

You can declare `static` data members and methods of classes. `static` data members, unlike non-`static` data members, are not part of each object. Instead, there is only one copy of the data member, which exists outside any objects of that class.

`static` methods are similarly at the class level instead of the object level. A `static` method does not execute in the context of a specific object.

Chapter 7 provides examples of both `static` members and methods.

static Linkage

Before covering the use of the `static` keyword for linkage, you need to understand the concept of *linkage* in C++. C++ source files are each compiled independently, and the resulting object files are linked together. Each name in a C++ source file, including functions and global variables, has a linkage that is either *internal* or *external*. External linkage means that the name is available from other source files. Internal linkage (also called *static linkage*) means that it is not. By default, functions and global variables have external linkage. However, you can specify internal (or static) linkage by prefixing the declaration with the keyword `static`. For example, suppose you have two source files: `FirstFile.cpp` and `AnotherFile.cpp`. Here is `FirstFile.cpp`:

```
void f();
int main()
{
    f();
    return 0;
}
```

Code snippet from Static\FirstFile.cpp

Note that this file provides a prototype for `f()`, but doesn't show the definition.

Here is `AnotherFile.cpp`:

```
#include <iostream>
using namespace std;
void f();
void f()
{
    cout << "f\n";
}
```

Code snippet from Static\AnotherFile.cpp

This file provides both a prototype and a definition for `f()`. Note that it is legal to write prototypes for the same function in two different files. That's precisely what the preprocessor does for you if you put the prototype in a header file that you `#include` in each of the source files. The reason to use header files is that it's easier to maintain (and keep synchronized) one copy of the prototype. However, for this example we don't use a header file.

Each of these source files compiles without error, and the program links fine: because `f()` has external linkage, `main()` can call it from a different file.

However, suppose you apply `static` to the `f()` prototype in `AnotherFile.cpp`. Note that you don't need to repeat the `static` keyword in front of the definition of `f()`. As long as it precedes the first instance of the function name, there is no need to repeat it

```
#include <iostream>
using namespace std;
static void f();
void f()
{
    cout << "f\n";
}
```

Code snippet from Static\AnotherFile.cpp

Now each of the source files compiles without error, but the linker step fails because `f()` has internal (`static`) linkage, making it unavailable from `FirstFile.cpp`. Some compilers issue a warning when `static` methods are defined but not used in that source file (implying that they shouldn't be `static`, because they're probably used elsewhere).

Now that you've learned all about this use of `static`, you will be happy to know that the C++ committee finally realized that `static` was too overloaded, and deprecated this particular use of the keyword. That means that it continues to be part of the standard for now, but is not guaranteed to be in the future. However, much legacy C++ code still uses `static` in this way.

The supported alternative is to employ *anonymous namespaces* to achieve the same affect. Instead of marking a variable or function `static`, wrap it in an unnamed namespace like this:

```cpp
#include <iostream>
using namespace std;
namespace {
    void f();
    void f()
    {
        cout << "f\n";
    }
}
```

Code snippet from AnonymousNamespaces\AnotherFile.cpp

Entities in an anonymous namespace can be accessed anywhere following their declaration in the same source file, but cannot be accessed from other source files. These semantics are the same as those obtained with the `static` keyword.

The extern Keyword

A related keyword, `extern`, seems like it should be the opposite of `static`, specifying external linkage for the names it precedes. It can be used that way in certain cases. For example, `const`s and `typedef`s have internal linkage by default. You can use `extern` to give them external linkage.

However, `extern` has some complications. When you specify a name as `extern`, the compiler treats it as a declaration, not a definition. For variables, this means the compiler doesn't allocate space for the variable. You must provide a separate definition line for the variable without the `extern` keyword. For example:

```cpp
extern int x;
int x = 3;
```

Code snippet from Extern\AnotherFile.cpp

Alternatively, you can initialize x in the `extern` line, which then serves as the declaration and definition:

```cpp
extern int x = 3;
```

Code snippet from Extern\AnotherFile.cpp

The `extern` in this file is not very useful, because x has external linkage by default anyway. The real use of `extern` is when you want to use x from another source file:

```
#include <iostream>
using namespace std;
extern int x;
int main()
{
    cout << x << endl;
}
```

Code snippet from Extern\FirstFile.cpp

Here `FirstFile.cpp` uses an `extern` declaration so that it can use x. The compiler needs a declaration of x in order to use it in `main()`. However, if you declared x without the `extern` keyword, the compiler would think it's a definition and would allocate space for x, causing the linkage step to fail (because there are now two x variables in the global scope). With `extern`, you can make variables globally accessible from multiple source files.

However, we do not recommend using global variables at all. They are confusing and error-prone, especially in large programs. For similar functionality, you should use `static` class members and methods.

static Variables in Functions

The final use of the `static` keyword in C++ is to create local variables that retain their values between exits and entrances to their scope. A `static` variable inside a function is like a global variable that is only accessible from that function. One common use of `static` variables is to "remember" whether a particular initialization has been performed for a certain function. For example, code that employs this technique might look something like this:

```
void performTask()
{
    static bool inited = false;
    if (!inited) {
        cout << "initing\n";
        // Perform initialization.
        inited = true;
    }
    // Perform the desired task.
}
```

Code snippet from Static\StaticsInFunctions.cpp

However, `static` variables are confusing, and there are usually better ways to structure your code so that you can avoid them. In this case, you might want to write a class in which the constructor performs the required initialization.

 Avoid using stand-alone `static` variables. Maintain state within an object instead.

Order of Initialization of Nonlocal Variables

Before leaving the topic of `static` data members and global variables, consider the order of initialization of these variables. All global variables and `static` class data members in a program are initialized before `main()` begins. The variables in a given source file are initialized in the order they appear in the source file. For example, in the following file `Demo::x` is guaranteed to be initialized before `y`:

```cpp
class Demo
{
    public:
        static int x;
};
int Demo::x = 3;
int y = 4;
```

Code snippet from Static\order.cpp

However, C++ provides no specifications or guarantees about the initialization ordering of nonlocal variables in different source files. If you have a global variable x in one source file and a global variable y in another, you have no way of knowing which will be initialized first. Normally, this lack of specification isn't cause for concern. However, it can be problematic if one global or `static` variable depends on another. Recall that initialization of objects implies running their constructors. The constructor of one global object might access another global object, assuming that it is already constructed. If these two global objects are declared in two different source files, you cannot count on one being constructed before the other, and you cannot control the order of initialization. This order may not be the same for different compilers or even different versions of the same compiler, and the order might even change by simply adding another file to your project.

Initialization order of nonlocal variables in different source files is undefined.

TYPES AND CASTS

The basic types in C++ are reviewed in Chapter 1, while Chapter 6 shows you how to write your own types with classes. This section explores some of the trickier aspects of types: `typedefs`, `typedefs` for function pointers, type aliases, and casts.

typedefs

A `typedef` provides a new name for an existing type declaration. You can think of a `typedef` simply as syntax for introducing a synonym for an existing type declaration without creating a new type. The following gives the new name `IntPtr` to the `int*` type declaration:

```cpp
typedef int* IntPtr;
```

You can use the new type name and the definition it aliases interchangeably. For example, the following two lines are valid:

```
int* p1;
IntPtr p2;
```

Variables created with the new type name are completely compatible with those created with the original type declaration. So it is perfectly valid, given the above definitions, to write the following, because they are not just "compatible" types, they are the same type:

```
p1 = p2;
p2 = p1;
```

The most common use of `typedefs` is to provide manageable names when the real type declarations become too unwieldy. This situation commonly arises with templates. For example, Chapter 1 introduces the `std::vector` from the standard library. To declare a `vector` of `strings`, you need to declare it as `std::vector<std::string>`. It's a templated class, and thus requires you to specify the template parameters anytime you want to refer to the type of this `vector`. Templates are discussed in detail in Chapter 19. For declaring variables, specifying function parameters, and so on, you would have to write `std::vector<std::string>`:

Available for download on Wrox.com

```
void processVector(const std::vector<std::string>& vec) { /* omitted */ }
int main()
{
    std::vector<std::string> myVector;
    return 0;
}
```

Code snippet from Typedefs\Typedefs.cpp

With a `typedef`, you can create a shorter, more meaningful, name:

Available for download on Wrox.com

```
typedef std::vector<std::string> StringVector;
void processVector(const StringVector& vec) { /* omitted */ }
int main()
{
    StringVector myVector;
    return 0;
}
```

Code snippet from Typedefs\Typedefs.cpp

`typedefs` can include the scope qualifiers. The preceding example shows this by including the scope `std` for `StringVector`.

The STL uses `typedefs` extensively to provide shorter names for types. For example, `string` is actually a `typedef` that looks like this:

```
typedef basic_string<char> string;
```

typedefs for Function Pointers

The most convoluted use of `typedefs` is when defining function pointers. While function pointers in C++ are uncommon (being replaced by `virtual` methods), there are needs to obtain function pointers in certain cases.

Perhaps the most common example of this is when obtaining a pointer to a function in a dynamic link library. The following example obtains a pointer to a function in a Microsoft Windows DLL. Details of Windows DLLs are outside the scope of this book on platform-independent C++, however, it is so important to Windows programmers that it is worth discussing and it is a good example to explain the details of function pointers in general.

Consider a Dynamic Link Library (DLL) that has a function called `MyFunc()`. You would like to load this library only if you need to call `MyFunc()`. This at run time loading of the library is done with the Windows `LoadLibrary()` kernel call:

```
HMODULE lib = ::LoadLibrary(_T("library name"));
```

The result of this call is what is called a "library handle" and will be NULL if there is an error.

Before you can load the function from the library, you need to know the prototype for the function. Suppose the following is the prototype for the `MyFunc()` function which returns an integer and accepts three parameters: a Boolean, an integer and a C-style string.

```
int __stdcall MyFunc(bool b, int n, const char* p);
```

The `__stdcall` is a Microsoft-specific directive to specify how parameters are passed to the function and cleaned up.

You can now use a `typedef` to define a short name (`MyFuncProc`) for a pointer to a function with the preceding prototype.

```
typedef int (__stdcall *MyFuncProc)(bool b, int n, const char* p);
```

Note that the `typedef` name `MyFuncProc` is embedded in the middle of the syntax. It is clear from this example that these kinds of `typedefs` are rather convoluted. Unfortunately, this is the syntax required by the standard. The following section will show you a new and cleaner C++11 solution to this problem.

Having successfully loaded the library and defined a short name for the function pointer, you can get a pointer to the function in the library as follows:

```
MyFuncProc MyProc = ::GetProcAddress(lib, "MyFunc");
```

If this fails, `MyProc` will be NULL. If it succeeds, you can call the loaded function as follows:

```
MyProc(true, 3, "Hello world");
```

A C programmer might think that you need to dereference the function pointer before calling it as follows:

```
(*MyProc)(true, 3, "Hello world");
```

This was true decades ago, but now, every C and C++ compiler is smart enough to know how to automatically dereference the function pointer before calling it.

C++11 Type Aliases

C++11 adds a new mechanism for creating *type aliases*, which is easier to understand than the old typedefs in certain situations. It is called *template aliases* and allows you to give another name to specific type declarations. For example you could define a new name MyInt as an alias for int as follows:

```
using MyInt = int;
```

This is equivalent to the following old typedef syntax:

```
typedef int MyInt;
```

In both cases, you have given another name to type int and now you can define integers using type MyInt instead of int as follows:

```
MyInt i = 123;
```

Of course, the original type int still exists and can still be used as a type specification.

This new template alias feature is especially useful in cases where the typedef becomes complicated as is the case with typedefs for function pointers as seen in the previous section. For example, the following is the prototype of a function, which returns an integer and accepts a char and a double as parameters:

```
int someFunction(char c, double d);
```

If you would like to define a pointer pFunc to this function, you can do something like this:

```
int (*pFunc)(char, double) = &someFunction;
```

This is pretty hard to read. Before C++11 this could be simplified by using a typedef as explained in the previous section:

```
typedef int (*FuncType)(char, double);
FuncType pFunc = &someFunction;
```

The typedef defines a name FuncType, which specifies the type of a pointer to a function with the given prototype. Once this typedef is defined, using it is straightforward and easy to understand. However, the typedef line itself is convoluted because the name FuncType is somewhere in the middle of the line. Using the C++11 template alias feature this can be rewritten as follows:

```
using FuncType = int (*)(char, double);
FuncType pFunc = &someFunction;
```

This piece of code is doing exactly the same as the one using the `typedef`, but the `using` line is easier to read.

By reading through this section, you might think that the new template alias feature is nothing more than an easier-to-read `typedef`, but there is more. The problem with the old `typedef`s becomes apparent when you want to use it with templates, but that is covered in Chapter 19 because it requires more details about the template feature first.

Casts

The old-style C casts with `()` still work in C++. However, C++ also provides four new casts: `static_cast`, `dynamic_cast`, `const_cast`, and `reinterpret_cast`. You should use the C++ style casts instead of the old C-style casts because they perform more type checking and stand out better syntactically in your code.

This section describes the purposes for each cast and specifies when you would use each of them.

const_cast

The `const_cast` is the most straightforward. You can use it to cast away `const`-ness of a variable. It is the only cast of the four that is allowed to cast away `const`-ness. Theoretically, of course, there should be no need for a `const` cast. If a variable is `const`, it should stay `const`. In practice, however, you sometimes find yourself in a situation where a function is specified to take a `const` variable, which it must then pass to a function that takes a non-`const` variable. The "correct" solution would be to make `const` consistent in the program, but that is not always an option, especially if you are using third-party libraries. Thus, you sometimes need to cast away the `const`-ness of a variable. Here is an example:

Available for download on Wrox.com

```
extern void ThirdPartyLibraryMethod(char* str);
void f(const char* str)
{
    ThirdPartyLibraryMethod(const_cast<char*>(str));
}
```

Code snippet from Casts\ConstCast.cpp

static_cast

You can use the `static_cast` to perform explicitly conversions that are supported directly by the language. For example, if you write an arithmetic expression in which you need to convert an `int` to a `double` in order to avoid integer division, use a `static_cast`:

Available for download on Wrox.com

```
int i = 3;
double result = static_cast<double>(i) / 10;
```

Code snippet from Casts\StaticCast.cpp

You can also use `static_cast` to perform explicitly conversions that are allowed because of user-defined constructors or conversion routines. For example, if class `A` has a constructor that takes an object of class `B`, you can convert a `B` object to an `A` object with a `static_cast`. In most situations where you want this behavior, however, the compiler will perform the conversion automatically.

Another use for the `static_cast` is to perform downcasts in an inheritance hierarchy. For example:

```cpp
class Base
{
    public:
        Base() {};
        virtual ~Base() {}
};
class Derived : public Base
{
    public:
        Derived() {}
        virtual ~Derived() {}
};
int main()
{
    Base* b;
    Derived* d = new Derived();
    b = d; // Don't need a cast to go up the inheritance hierarchy
    d = static_cast<Derived*>(b); // Need a cast to go down the hierarchy
    Base base;
    Derived derived;
    Base& br = derived;
    Derived& dr = static_cast<Derived&>(br);
    return 0;
}
```

Code snippet from Casts\StaticCast.cpp

These casts work with both pointers and references. They do not work with objects themselves.

Note that these casts with `static_cast` do not perform run-time type checking. They allow you to convert any `Base` pointer to a `Derived` pointer or `Base` reference to a `Derived` reference, even if the `Base` really isn't a `Derived` at run time. For example, the following code will compile and execute, but using the pointer `d` can result in potentially catastrophic failure, including memory overwrites outside the bounds of the object.

```cpp
Base* b = new Base();
Derived* d = static_cast<Derived*>(b);
```

To perform the cast safely, with run-time type checking, use the `dynamic_cast` explained in a following section.

`static_cast`s are not all-powerful. You can't `static_cast` pointers of one type to pointers of another unrelated type. You can't `static_cast` directly objects of one type to objects of another type. You can't `static_cast` a const type to a non-const type. You can't `static_cast` pointers to `int`s. Basically, you can't do anything that doesn't make sense according to the type rules of C++.

reinterpret_cast

The `reinterpret_cast` is a bit more powerful, and concomitantly less safe, than the `static_cast`. You can use it to perform some casts that are not technically allowed by C++ type rules, but which might make sense to the programmer in some circumstances. For example, you can cast a pointer type to any other pointer type, even if they are unrelated by an inheritance hierarchy. This is commonly used to cast a pointer to a `void*` and back. Similarly, you can cast a reference to one type to a reference to another type, even if the types are unrelated. Here are some examples:

```cpp
class X {};
class Y {};
int main()
{
    X x;
    Y y;
    X* xp = &x;
    Y* yp = &y;
    // Need reinterpret cast for pointer conversion from unrelated classes
    // static_cast doesn't work.
    xp = reinterpret_cast<X*>(yp);
    // Need reinterpret cast for pointer conversion from unrelated pointers
    void* p = reinterpret_cast<void*>(xp);
    xp = reinterpret_cast<X*>(p);
    // Need reinterpret cast for reference conversion from unrelated classes
    // static_cast doesn't work.
    X& xr = x;
    Y& yr = reinterpret_cast<Y&>(x);
    return 0;
}
```

Code snippet from Casts\ReinterpretCast.cpp

In theory, you could also use `reinterpret_cast` to cast pointers to `int`s and `int`s to pointers, but this is considered erroneous programming, because on many platforms (especially 64-bit platforms) pointers and `int`s are of different sizes. For example, on a 64-bit platform, pointers will be 64 bit, but integers could be 32 bit. Casting a 64-bit pointer to a 32-bit integer will result in losing 32 critical bits!

You should be very careful with the `reinterpret_cast` because it allows you to do conversions without performing any type checking.

dynamic_cast

The `dynamic_cast` provides a run-time check on casts within an inheritance hierarchy. You can use it to cast pointers or references. `dynamic_cast` checks the run-time type information of the underlying object at run time. If the cast doesn't make sense, `dynamic_cast` returns a null pointer (for the pointer version) or throws a `bad_cast` exception (for the reference version).

Note that the run-time type information is stored in the vtable of the object. Therefore, in order to use dynamic_cast, your classes must have at least one virtual method. If your classes don't have a vtable, trying to use dynamic_cast will result in a compiler error which can be a bit obscure. Microsoft VC++ for example will give the error

```
error C2683: 'dynamic_cast' : 'MyClass' is not a polymorphic type.
```

Here are some examples:

```cpp
class Base
{
    public:
        Base() {};
        virtual ~Base() {}
};
class Derived : public Base
{
    public:
        Derived() {}
        virtual ~Derived() {}
};
```

Code snippet from Casts\DynamicCast.cpp

The following example shows a correct usage of dynamic_cast.

```cpp
Base* b;
Derived* d = new Derived();
b = d;
d = dynamic_cast<Derived*>(b);
```

Code snippet from Casts\DynamicCast.cpp

The following dynamic_cast on a reference will cause an exception to be thrown. Chapter 10 covers the details of exception handling.

```cpp
Base base;
Derived derived;
Base& br = base;
try {
    Derived& dr = dynamic_cast<Derived&>(br);
} catch (const bad_cast&) {
    cout << "Bad cast!\n";
}
```

Code snippet from Casts\DynamicCast.cpp

Note that you can perform the same casts down the inheritance hierarchy with a static_cast or reinterpret_cast. The difference with dynamic_cast is that it performs run-time (dynamic) type checking, while static_cast and reinterpret_cast will perform the casting even if they are erroneous.

Summary of Casts

The following table summarizes the casts you should use for difference situations.

SITUATION	CAST
Remove `const`-ness	`const_cast`
Explicit cast supported by language (e.g., `int` to `double`, `int` to `bool`)	`static_cast`
Explicit cast supported by user-defined constructors or conversions	`static_cast`
Object of one class to object of another (unrelated) class	Can't be done
Pointer-to-object of one class to pointer-to-object of another class in the same inheritance hierarchy	`static_cast` or `dynamic_cast`
Reference-to-object of one class to reference-to-object of another class in the same inheritance hierarchy	`static_cast` or `dynamic_cast`
Pointer-to-type to unrelated pointer-to-type	`reinterpret_cast`
Reference-to-type to unrelated reference-to-type	`reinterpret_cast`
Pointer-to-function to pointer-to-function	`reinterpret_cast`

SCOPE RESOLUTION

As a C++ programmer, you need to familiarize yourself with the concept of *scope*. Every name in your program, including variable, function, and class names, is in a certain scope. You create scopes with namespaces, function definitions, and class definitions. When you try to access a variable, function, or class, the name is first looked up in the nearest enclosing scope, then the next scope, and so forth, up to the *global scope*. Any name not in a namespace, function, or class is assumed to be in the global scope. If it is not found in the global scope, at that point the compiler generates an undefined symbol error.

Sometimes names in scopes hide identical names in other scopes. Other times, the scope you want is not part of the default scope resolution from that particular line in the program. If you don't want the default scope resolution for a name, you can qualify the name with a specific scope using the scope resolution operator ::. For example, to access a `static` method of a class, one way is to prefix the method name with the name of the class (its scope) and the scope resolution operator. A second way is to access the `static` method through an object of that class. The following example demonstrates these options. The example defines a class `Demo` with a static get() method, a get() function that is globally scoped, and a get() function that is in the NS namespace.

Available for download on Wrox.com

```
class Demo
{
    public:
        static int get() { return 5; }
};
int get() { return 10; }
namespace NS
{
    int get() { return 20; }
};
```

Code snippet from Scope\Scope.cpp

The global scope is unnamed, but you can access it specifically by using the scope resolution operator by itself (with no name prefix). The different get() functions can be called as follows.

Available for download on Wrox.com

```
Demo* pd = new Demo();
Demo d;
std::cout << pd->get() << std::endl;     // prints 5
std::cout << d.get() << std::endl;       // prints 5
std::cout << NS::get() << std::endl;     // prints 20
std::cout << Demo::get() << std::endl;   // prints 5
std::cout << ::get() << std::endl;       // prints 10
std::cout << get() << std::endl;         // prints 10
```

Code snippet from Scope\Scope.cpp

Note that if the namespace called NS is given as an unnamed namespace, then the following line will give an error about ambiguous name resolution, because you would have a get() defined in the global scope and another get() defined in the unnamed namespace.

```
std::cout << get() << std::endl;
```

This same error occurs if you add the following using clause right before the main() function:

```
using namespace NS;
```

C++11 C++11

C++11 has a lot of new functionality. This section describes a few new features that do not immediately fit elsewhere in this book.

Uniform Initialization

Before C++11, initialization of types was not always uniform. For example, take the following definition of a circle, once as a structure, once as a class:

```cpp
struct CircleStruct
{
    int x, y;
    double radius;
};
class CircleClass
{
    public:
        CircleClass(int x, int y, double radius)
            : mX(x), mY(y), mRadius(radius) {}
    private:
        int mX, mY;
        double mRadius;
};
```

Code snippet from UniformInitialization\UniformInitialization.cpp

In pre-C++11, initialization of a variable of type `CircleStruct` and a variable of type `CircleClass` looks different:

```cpp
CircleStruct myCircle1 = {10, 10, 2.5};
CircleClass myCircle2(10, 10, 2.5);
```

Code snippet from UniformInitialization\UniformInitialization.cpp

For the structure version you can use the `{...}` syntax. However, for the class version you need to call the constructor using function notation `(...)`.

C++11 allows you to more uniformly use the `{...}` syntax to initialize types. Using that, you can rewrite the above as follows:

```cpp
CircleStruct myCircle3 = {10, 10, 2.5};
CircleClass myCircle4 = {10, 10, 2.5};
```

Code snippet from UniformInitialization\UniformInitialization.cpp

The definition of `myCircle4` will automatically call the constructor of `CircleClass`. The use of the equal sign is even optional, so the following is identical.

```cpp
CircleStruct myCircle5{10, 10, 2.5};
CircleClass myCircle6{10, 10, 2.5};
```

Code snippet from UniformInitialization\UniformInitialization.cpp

Using this uniform initialization also prevents *narrowing*. C++ implicitly performs narrowing, for example:

```
void func(int i) { /* ... */ }
int main()
{
    int x = 3.14;
    func(3.14);
    return 0;
}
```

C++ will automatically truncate 3.14 in both cases to 3 before assigning it to x or calling func(). Note that some compilers might issue a warning about this narrowing. This narrowing can be prevented by using uniform initialization:

Available for
download on
Wrox.com

```
void func(int i) { /* ... */ }
int main()
{
    int x = {3.14};     // Error because narrowing
    func({3.14});       // Error because narrowing
    return 0;
}
```

Code snippet from UniformInitialization\UniformInitialization.cpp

Now both the assignment to x and the call to func() will generate a compiler error if your compiler fully conforms to the C++11 standard.

The same new uniform initialization can also be used on STL containers, which are discussed in depth in Chapter 12. For example, initializing a vector of strings used to require code as follows:

```
std::vector<std::string> myVec;
myVec.push_back("String 1");
myVec.push_back("String 2");
myVec.push_back("String 3");
```

With C++11 uniform initialization, this can be rewritten:

Available for
download on
Wrox.com

```
std::vector<std::string> myVec = {"String 1", "String 2", "String 3"};
```

Code snippet from UniformInitialization\UniformInitialization.cpp

Uniform initialization can also be used to initialize dynamically allocated arrays. For example:

Available for
download on
Wrox.com

```
int* pArray = new int[4]{0, 1, 2, 3};
```

Code snippet from UniformInitialization\UniformInitialization.cpp

And last but not least, it can also be used in the constructor initializer to initialize arrays that are members of a class.

```cpp
class MyClass
{
    public:
        MyClass() : mArray{0, 1, 2, 3} {}
    private:
        int mArray[4];
};
```

Code snippet from UniformInitialization\UniformInitialization.cpp

Alternative Function Syntax

C++ is still using the function syntax as it was designed for C. In the meantime, C++ has been extended with quite a lot of new functionality and this exposed a number of problems with the old function syntax. C++11 includes an alternative function syntax as follows. Note that the `auto` keyword in this context has the meaning of starting a function prototype using the new alternative function syntax.

```cpp
auto func(int i) -> int
{
    return i+2;
}
```

Code snippet from AlternativeFunctionSyntax\AlternativeFunctionSyntax.cpp

The return type of the function is no longer at the beginning of the declaration, but placed at the end of the line after the arrow, `->`. The following code demonstrates that calling `func()` remains exactly the same and shows that the `main()` function can also use this alternative syntax:

```cpp
auto main() -> int
{
    cout << func(3) << endl;
    return 0;
}
```

Code snippet from AlternativeFunctionSyntax\AlternativeFunctionSyntax.cpp

This new syntax is not of much use for ordinary functions, but is very useful in the context of specifying the return type of template functions. Templates are studied in detail in Chapters 19 and 20.

Null Pointer Constant

Before C++11, the constant 0 was used to define either the number 0 or a null pointer. This can cause some problems. Take the following example:

```
void func(char* str) {cout << "char* version" << endl;}
void func(int i) {cout << "int version" << endl;}
int main()
{
    func(NULL);
    return 0;
}
```

Code snippet from NullPointerConstant\NullPointerConstant.cpp

The `main()` function is calling the function `func()` with parameter `NULL`, which is supposed to be a null pointer constant. In other words, you are expecting the `char*` version of `func()` to be called with a null pointer as argument. However, since `NULL` is identical to the integer 0, the compiler will actually call the integer version of `func()`, as can be seen in the output of the program:

```
int version
```

You could call the `char*` version by explicitly using a cast:

```
func((char*)NULL);
```

Code snippet from NullPointerConstant\NullPointerConstant.cpp

This will print:

```
char* version
```

C++11 solves this problem more elegantly by introducing a real null pointer constant, `nullptr`, which can be used as follows:

```
func(nullptr);
```

Code snippet from NullPointerConstant\NullPointerConstant.cpp

This will generate the following output:

```
char* version
```

Angle Brackets

Before C++11, the double angle brackets `>>` could only mean one thing: the `>>` operator. Depending on the types involved, this `>>` operator can be a right shift operation or a stream extraction operator. This caused small problems with template code. For example, if you wanted to declare a `vector` for objects of type `basic_string<wchar_t>`, the following would be invalid:

```
vector<basic_string<wchar_t>> vec;
```

This was invalid because of the double angle brackets >> without a space in between. The lexical analyzer would interpret it as the >> operator. Instead, you had to make sure to include a space between the two brackets as follows:

```
vector<basic_string<wchar_t> > vec;
```

C++11 solves this problem, and the first version without the space is perfectly valid now.

Initializer Lists

C++11 adds the concept of initializer lists, defined in the `<initializer_list>` header file, which make it easy to write a function that can accept a variable number of arguments. The difference with variable-length argument lists described later in this chapter is that all the elements in an initializer list should have the same predefined type. Initializer lists are very easy to use as can be seen from the following example.

```cpp
#include <initializer_list>
using namespace std;
int makeSum(initializer_list<int> lst)
{
    int total = 0;
    for (auto iter = lst.begin(); iter != lst.end(); ++iter)
        total += (*iter);
    return total;
}
```

Code snippet from InitializerLists\InitializerLists.cpp

The function `makeSum()` accepts an initializer list of integers as argument. The body of the function uses an iterator to loop over all the elements in the given list and to accumulate the total sum.

This function can be used as follows.

```cpp
int a = makeSum({1,2,3});
int b = makeSum({10,20,30,40,50,60});
```

Initializer lists are type-safe and define which type is allowed to be in the list. For the above `makeSum()` function, calling it with a `double` value is invalid:

```cpp
int c = makeSum({1,2,3.0});
```

The last element is a `double`, which will result in a compiler error.

Explicit Conversion Operators

Chapter 7 discusses the implicit conversion that can happen with single argument constructors and how to prevent the compiler from using those implicit conversions with the `explicit` keyword. The C++ compiler will also perform implicit conversion with custom written conversion operators.

In C++11 it is now possible to apply the `explicit` keyword, not only to constructors, but also to conversion operators.

To explain explicit conversion operators, you need to understand implicit conversion first. Take the following example. It defines a class `IntWrapper` that just wraps an integer and implements an `int()` conversion operator, which the compiler can use to perform implicit conversion from an `IntWrapper` to type `int`.

```cpp
class IntWrapper
{
    public:
        IntWrapper(int i) : mInt(i) {}
        operator int() const { return mInt; }
    private:
        int mInt;
};
```

Code snippet from ExplicitConversionOperators\ExplicitConversionOperators.cpp

The following code demonstrates this implicit conversion; `iC1` will contain the value 123.

```cpp
IntWrapper c(123);
int iC1 = c;
```

Code snippet from ExplicitConversionOperators\ExplicitConversionOperators.cpp

If you want, you can still explicitly tell the compiler to call the `int()` conversion operator as follows. `iC2` will also contain the value 123.

```cpp
int iC2 = int(c);
```

Code snippet from ExplicitConversionOperators\ExplicitConversionOperators.cpp

With C++11, you can use the `explicit` keyword to prevent the compiler from performing the implicit conversion. Below is the new class definition.

```cpp
class IntWrapper
{
    public:
        IntWrapper(int i) : mInt(i) {}
        explicit operator int() const { return mInt; }
    private:
        int mInt;
};
```

Code snippet from ExplicitConversionOperators\ExplicitConversionOperators.cpp

Trying to compile the following lines of code with this new class definition will result in a compiler error because the `int()` conversion operator is marked as `explicit`, so the compiler cannot use it anymore to perform implicit conversion.

```
IntWrapper c(123);
int iC1 = c; // Error, because of explicit int() operator
```

Code snippet from ExplicitConversionOperators\ExplicitConversionOperators.cpp

Once you have an explicit conversion operator, you have to explicitly call it if you want to use it. For example:

```
int iC2 = int(c);
int iC3 = static_cast<int>(c);
```

Code snippet from ExplicitConversionOperators\ExplicitConversionOperators.cpp

Attributes

Attributes are a new mechanism to add optional and/or vendor-specific information into source code. Before C++11, the vendor decided how to specify that information. Examples are `__attribute__`, `__declspec`, and so on. C++11 adds support for attributes by using the double square brackets syntax `[[attribute]]`.

The C++11 standard defines only two standard attributes: `[[noreturn]]` and `[[carries_dependency]]`.

`[[noreturn]]` means that a function never returns control to the call site. Typically, the function either causes some kind of termination (process termination or thread termination) or throws an exception. For example:

```
[[noreturn]] void func()
{
    throw 1;
}
```

The second attribute, `[[carries_dependency]]`, is a rather exotic attribute and is not discussed further.

Most attributes will be vendor-specific extensions. The C++11 standard advises vendors to not use attributes to change the meaning of the program, but to use them to help the compiler to optimize code or detect errors in code. Since attributes of different vendors could clash, vendors are recommended to qualify them. For example:

```
[[microsoft::novtable]]
```

User Defined Literals

C++ has a number of standard literals that you can use in your code. For example:

➤ `'a'`: character

➤ `"character array"`: zero-terminated array of characters, C-style string

➤ `3.14f`: `float` floating point value

➤ `0xabc`: hexadecimal value

C++11 allows you to define your own literals. These user defined literals should start with an underscore and are implemented by writing *literal operators*. A literal operator can work in *raw* or *cooked* mode. In raw mode, your literal operator will receive a sequence of characters, while in cooked mode your literal operator will receive a specific interpreted type. For example, take the C++ literal `123`. Your raw literal operator will receive this as a sequence of characters `'1'`, `'2'`, `'3'`. Your cooked literal operator will receive this as the integer 123. Another example, take the C++ literal `0x23`. The raw operator will receive the characters `'0'`, `'x'`, `'2'`, `'3'`, while the cooked operator will receive the integer 35. One last example, take the C++ literal `3.14`. Your raw operator will receive this as `'3'`, `'.'`, `'1'`, `'4'`, while your cooked operator will receive the floating point value 3.14.

A cooked mode literal operator should have:

➤ one parameter of type `unsigned long long` or `long double` to process numeric values,

➤ or two parameters where the first is a character array and the second is the length of the character array, to process strings. For example: `const char* str, size_t len`.

As an example, the following implements a cooked literal operator for the user defined literal `_i` to define a complex number literal.

Available for download on Wrox.com

```
std::complex<double> operator"" _i(long double d)
{
    return std::complex<double>(0, d);
}
```

Code snippet from UserDefinedLiterals\UserDefinedLiterals.cpp

This `_i` literal can be used as follows:

Available for download on Wrox.com

```
std::complex<double> c1 = 9.634_i;
auto c2 = 1.23_i;            // c2 will have as type std::complex<double>
```

Code snippet from UserDefinedLiterals\UserDefinedLiterals.cpp

A second example implements a cooked operator for a user defined literal `_s` to define `std::string` literals:

Available for download on Wrox.com

```
std::string operator"" _s(const char* str, size_t len)
{
    return std::string(str, len);
}
```

Code snippet from UserDefinedLiterals\UserDefinedLiterals.cpp

This literal can be used as follows:

```
std::string str1 = "Hello World"_s;
auto str2 = "Hello World"_s;    // str2 will have as type std::string
```

Code snippet from UserDefinedLiterals\UserDefinedLiterals.cpp

Without the _s literal, the auto type deduction would be `const char*`:

```
auto str3 = "Hello World";      // str3 will have as type const char*
```

Code snippet from UserDefinedLiterals\UserDefinedLiterals.cpp

A raw mode literal operator requires one parameter of type `const char*`; a zero-terminated C-style string. The following example defines the literal _i but using a raw literal operator:

```
std::complex<double> operator"" _i(const char* p)
{
    // Implementation omitted; it requires parsing the C-style
    // string and converting it to a complex number.
}
```

Code snippet from UserDefinedLiterals\UserDefinedLiterals.cpp

Using this raw mode operator is exactly the same as using the cooked version:

```
std::complex<double> c1 = 9.634_i;
auto c2 = 1.23_i;              // c2 will have as type std::complex<double>
```

Some more examples of useful user defined literals that you could implement:

➤ `1000101110_b`: a binary number

➤ `10_s`: seconds

➤ `100_km`: kilometer

➤ and so on...

HEADER FILES

Header files are a mechanism for providing an abstract interface to a subsystem or piece of code. One of the trickier parts of using headers is avoiding circular references and multiple includes of the same header file. For example, perhaps you are responsible for writing the `Logger` class that performs all error message logging tasks. You may end up using another class, `Preferences`, that keeps track of user settings. The `Preferences` class may in turn use the `Logger` class indirectly, through yet another header.

As the following code shows, the `#ifndef` mechanism can be used to avoid circular and multiple includes. At the beginning of each header file, the `#ifndef` directive checks to see if a certain key has *not* been defined. If the key has been defined, the compiler will skip to the matching `#endif`, which is usually placed at the end of the file. If the key has *not* been defined, the file will proceed to define the key so that a subsequent include of the same file will be skipped. This mechanism is also known as *include guards*.

```
#ifndef __LOGGER__
#define __LOGGER__
#include "Preferences.h"
class Logger
{
    public:
        static void setPreferences(const Preferences& inPrefs);
        static void logError(const char* inError);
};
#endif // __LOGGER__
```

Code snippet from Headers\Logger.h

If your compiler supports the `#pragma once` directive (like Microsoft Visual C++ or GCC), this can be rewritten as follows:

```
#pragma once
#include "Preferences.h"
class Logger
{
    public:
        static void setPreferences(const Preferences& inPrefs);
        static void logError(const char* inError);
};
```

Code snippet from Headers\LoggerPragmaOnce.h

These include guards or `#pragma once` directives also make sure that you don't get duplicate definitions by including a header file multiple times. For example, suppose `A.h` includes `Logger.h` and `B.h` also includes `Logger.h`. If you have a source file called `App.cpp` which includes both `A.h` and `B.h`, the compiler will not complain about a duplicate definition of the `Logger` class because the `Logger.h` header will be included only once, even though `A.h` and `B.h` both include it.

Another tool for avoiding problems with headers is forward declarations. If you need to refer to a class but you cannot include its header file (for example, because it relies heavily on the class you are writing), you can tell the compiler that such a class exists without providing a formal definition through the `#include` mechanism. Of course, you cannot actually use the class in the code because the compiler knows nothing about it, except that the named class will exist after everything is linked together. However, you can still make use of pointers or references to the class in your class definition. In the following code, the `Logger` class refers to the `Preferences` class without including its header file.

```
#ifndef __LOGGER__
#define __LOGGER__
class Preferences;  // forward declaration
```

```
class Logger
{
    public:
        static void setPreferences(const Preferences& inPrefs);
        static void logError(const char* inError);
};
#endif // __LOGGER__
```

Code snippet from Headers\Logger.h

C UTILITIES

Recall that C++ is a superset of C, and thus contains all of its functionality. There are a few obscure C features which can occasionally be useful. This section examines two of these features: variable-length argument lists and preprocessor macros. There is no proper C++ alternative for preprocessor macros. However, C++11 does introduce a proper replacement for the old C-style variable-length argument lists.

Variable-Length Argument Lists

This section explains the old C-style variable-length argument lists. You need to know how these work because you might find them in older code. However, in new code you should use the type-safe C++11 variable-length argument lists using variadic templates, described in Chapter 20.

Consider the C function `printf()` from `<cstdio>`. You can call it with any number of arguments:

Available for
download on
Wrox.com

```
#include <cstdio>
int main()
{
    printf("int %d\n", 5);
    printf("String %s and int %d\n", "hello", 5);
    printf("Many ints: %d, %d, %d, %d, %d\n", 1, 2, 3, 4, 5);
    return 0;
}
```

Code snippet from VarArgs\PrintfDemo.cpp

C/C++ provides the syntax and some utility macros for writing your own functions with a variable number of arguments. These functions usually look a lot like `printf()`. Although you shouldn't need this feature very often, occasionally you run into situations in which it's quite useful. For example, suppose you want to write a quick-and-dirty debug function that prints strings to `stderr` if a debug flag is set, but does nothing if the debug flag is not set. This function should be able to print strings with arbitrary numbers and types of arguments. A simple implementation looks like this:

Available for
download on
Wrox.com

```
#include <cstdio>
#include <cstdarg>
bool debug = false;
void debugOut(char* str, ...)
```

```
{
    va_list ap;
    if (debug) {
        va_start(ap, str);
        vfprintf(stderr, str, ap);
        va_end(ap);
    }
}
```

Code snippet from VarArgs\VarArgs.cpp

First, note that the prototype for `debugOut()` contains one typed and named parameter `str`, followed by `...` (ellipses). They stand for any number and types of arguments. In order to access these arguments, you must use macros defined in `<cstdarg>`. You declare a variable of type `va_list`, and initialize it with a call to `va_start`. The second parameter to `va_start()` must be the rightmost *named* variable in the parameter list. All functions with variable-length argument lists require at least one named parameter. The `debugOut()` function simply passes this list to `vfprintf()` (a standard function in `<cstdio>`). After the call to `vfprintf()` returns, `debugOut()` calls `va_end()` to terminate the access of the variable argument list. You must always call `va_end()` after calling `va_start()` to ensure that the function ends with the stack in a consistent state.

You can use the function in the following way:

```
debug = true;
debugOut("int %d\n", 5);
debugOut("String %s and int %d\n", "hello", 5);
debugOut("Many ints: %d, %d, %d, %d, %d\n", 1, 2, 3, 4, 5);
```

Code snippet from VarArgs\VarArgs.cpp

Accessing the Arguments

If you want to access the actual arguments yourself, you can use `va_arg()` to do so. Unfortunately, there is no way to know what the end of the argument list is unless you provide an explicit way of doing so. For example, you can make the first parameter a count of the number of parameters. Or, in the case where you have a set of pointers, you may require the last pointer to be `nullptr`. There are many ways, but they are all burdensome to the programmer.

The following example demonstrates the technique where the caller specifies in the first named parameter how many arguments are provided. The function accepts any number of `int`s and prints them out.

```
void printInts(int num, ...)
{
    int temp;
    va_list ap;
    va_start(ap, num);
    for (int i = 0; i < num; i++) {
```

```
            temp = va_arg(ap, int);
            cout << temp << " ";
        }
        va_end(ap);
        cout << endl;
    }
```

Code snippet from VarArgs\VarArgs.cpp

You can call `printInts()` as follows. Note that the first parameter specifies how many integers will follow.

```
printInts(5, 5, 4, 3, 2, 1);
```

Code snippet from VarArgs\VarArgs.cpp

Why You Shouldn't Use C-Style Variable-Length Argument Lists

Accessing C-style variable-length argument lists is not very safe. As you can see from the `printInts()` function, there are several risks:

➤   You don't know the number of parameters. In the case of `printInts()`, you must trust the caller to pass the right number of arguments as the first argument. In the case of `debugOut()`, you must trust the caller to pass the same number of arguments after the character array as there are formatting codes in the character array.

➤   You don't know the types of the arguments. `va_arg()` takes a type, which it uses to interpret the value in its current spot. However, you can tell `va_arg()` to interpret the value as any type. There is no way for it to verify the correct type.

 Avoid using C-style variable-length argument lists. It is preferable to pass in an array or vector of values, or to use initializer lists, which are described earlier in this chapter, or to switch to the type-safe C++11 variable-length argument lists using variadic templates, described in Chapter 20.

Preprocessor Macros

You can use the C++ preprocessor to write *macros*, which are like little functions. Here is an example:

```
#define SQUARE(x) ((x) * (x)) // No semicolon after the macro definition!
int main()
{
    cout << SQUARE(5) << endl;
```

```
        return 0;
    }
```

Macros are a remnant from C that are quite similar to `inline` functions, except that they are not type checked, and the preprocessor dumbly replaces any calls to them with their expansions. The preprocessor does not apply true function-call semantics. This behavior can cause unexpected results. For example, consider what would happen if you called the SQUARE macro with 2 + 3 instead of 5, like this:

```
    cout << SQUARE(2 + 3) << endl;
```

You expect SQUARE to calculate 25, which it does. However, what if you left off some parentheses on the macro definition, so that it looks like this?

```
    #define SQUARE(x) (x * x)
```

Now, the call to SQUARE(2 + 3) generates 11, not 25! Remember that the macro is dumbly expanded without regard to function-call semantics. This means that any x in the macro body is replaced by 2 + 3, leading to this expansion:

```
    cout << 2 + 3 * 2 + 3 << endl;
```

Following proper order of operations, this line performs the multiplication first, followed by the additions, generating 11 instead of 25!

Macros also cause problems for debugging because the code you write is not the code that the compiler sees, or that shows up in your debugger (because of the search and replace behavior of the preprocessor). For these reasons, you should avoid macros entirely in favor of inline functions. We show the details here only because quite a bit of C++ code out there employs macros. You need to understand them in order to read and maintain that code.

> *Some compilers can output the preprocessed source to a file. You can use that file to see how the preprocessor is preprocessing your file. For example, with Microsoft VC++ you need to use the /P switch. With GCC you can use the -E switch.*

SUMMARY

This chapter explained some of the aspects of C++ that generate the most confusion. By reading this chapter, you learned a plethora of syntax details about C++. Some of the information, such as the details of references, `const`, scope resolution, the specifics of the C++-style casts, the null pointer constant, and the techniques for header files, you should use often in your programs. Other information, such as the uses of `static` and `extern`, how to write C-style variable-length argument lists, and how to write preprocessor macros, is important to understand, but not information that you should put into use in your programs on a day-to-day basis.

10

Handling Errors

WHAT'S IN THIS CHAPTER?

➤ How to handle errors in C++, including pros and cons of exceptions

➤ The syntax of exceptions

➤ Exception class hierarchies and polymorphism

➤ Stack unwinding and cleanup

➤ Common error-handling situations

Inevitably, your C++ programs will encounter errors. The program might be unable to open a file, the network connection might go down, or the user might enter an incorrect value, to name a few possibilities. The C++ language provides a feature called *exceptions* to handle these *exceptional* but not *unexpected* situations.

The code examples in this book so far have virtually always ignored error conditions for brevity. This chapter rectifies that simplification by teaching you how to incorporate error handling into your programs from their beginnings. It focuses on C++ exceptions, including the details of their syntax, and describes how to employ them effectively to create well-designed error-handling programs.

ERRORS AND EXCEPTIONS

No program exists in isolation; they all depend on external facilities such as interfaces with the operating system, networks and file systems, external code such as third-party libraries, and user input. Each of these areas can introduce situations which require responding to problems which may be encountered. These potential problems can be referred to with the general term *exceptional situations*. Even perfectly written programs encounter errors and exceptional situations. Thus, anyone who writes a computer program must include error-handling capabilities. Some languages, such as C, do not include many specific language facilities for error handling. Programmers using these languages generally rely on return values from functions and other *ad hoc* approaches. Other languages, such as Java, enforce the use of a language feature called *exceptions* as an error-handling mechanism. C++ lies between these extremes. It provides language support for exceptions, but does not require their use. However, you can't ignore exceptions entirely in C++ because a few basic facilities, such as memory allocation routines, use them.

What Are Exceptions, Anyway?

Exceptions are a mechanism for a piece of code to notify another piece of code of an "exceptional" situation or error condition without progressing through the normal code paths. The code that encounters the error *throws* the exception, and the code that handles the exception *catches* it. Exceptions do not follow the fundamental rule of step-by-step execution to which you are accustomed. When a piece of code throws an exception, the program control immediately stops executing code step by step and transitions to the exception handler, which could be anywhere from the next line in the same function to several function calls up the stack. If you like sports analogies, you can think of the code that throws an exception as an outfielder throwing a baseball back to the infield, where the nearest infielder (closest exception handler) catches it. Figure 10-1 shows a hypothetical stack of three function calls. Function A() has the exception handler. It calls function B(), which calls function C(), which throws the exception.

Figure 10-2 shows the handler catching the exception. The stack frames for C() and B() have been removed, leaving only A().

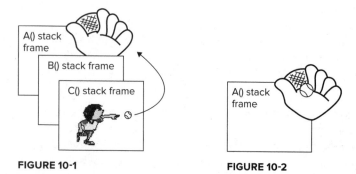

FIGURE 10-1   **FIGURE 10-2**

Some people who have used C++ for years are surprised to learn that C++ supports exceptions. Programmers tend to associate exceptions with languages like Java, in which they are much more visible. However, C++ has full-fledged support for exceptions.

Why Exceptions in C++ Are a Good Thing

As mentioned earlier, run-time errors in programs are inevitable. Despite that fact, error handling in most C and C++ programs is messy and *ad hoc*. The *de facto* C error-handling standard, which was carried over into many C++ programs, uses integer function return codes and the errno macro to signify errors. Each thread has its own errno value. errno acts as a thread-global integer variable that functions can use to communicate errors back to calling functions.

Unfortunately, the integer return codes and `errno` are used inconsistently. Some functions might choose to return 0 for success and –1 for an error. If they return –1, they also set `errno` to an error code. Other functions return 0 for success and nonzero for an error, with the actual return value specifying the error code. These functions do not use `errno`. Still others return 0 for failure instead of for success, presumably because 0 always evaluates to `false` in C and C++.

These inconsistencies can cause problems because programmers encountering a new function often assume that its return codes are the same as other similar functions. That is not always true. On Solaris 9, there are two different libraries of synchronization objects: the POSIX version and the Solaris version. The function to initialize a semaphore in the POSIX version is called `sem_init()`, and the function to initialize a semaphore in the Solaris version is called `sema_init()`. As if that weren't confusing enough, the two functions handle error codes differently! `sem_init()` returns –1 and sets `errno` on error, while `sema_init()` returns the error code directly as a positive integer, and does not set `errno`.

Another problem is that the return type of functions in C++ can only be of one type, so if you need to return both an error and a value, you must find an alternative mechanism. One solution is to return a `std::pair` or `std::tuple`, an object that you can use to store two or more types. They are discussed in later STL chapters. Another choice is to define your own `struct` or class that contains several values, and return an instance of that `struct` or class from your function. Yet another option is to return the value or error through a reference parameter or to make the error code one possible value of the return type, such as a `nullptr` pointer. In all these solutions, the caller is responsible to explicitly check for any errors returned from the function and if it doesn't handle the error itself, it should propagate the error to its caller. Unfortunately, this will often result in the loss of critical details about the error.

C programmers may be familiar with a mechanism known as `setjmp()`/`longjmp()`. This mechanism cannot be used correctly in C++, because it bypasses scoped destructors on the stack. You should avoid it at all cost, even in C programs; therefor this book will not explain the details of how to use it.

Exceptions provide an easier, more consistent, and safer mechanism for error handling. There are several specific advantages of exceptions over the *ad hoc* approaches in C and C++.

➤ When return codes are used as an error reporting mechanism, a defect is that a caller may choose to ignore the return codes, or process them only locally without propagating them upwards, even though higher-level callers need to know there was a lower-level failure. Exceptions cannot be ignored: If your program fails to catch an exception, it will terminate.

➤ When integer return codes are used, they generally do not contain sufficient information. You can use exceptions to pass as much information as you want from the code that finds the error to the code that handles it. Exceptions can also be used to communicate information other than errors, though many programmers consider that an abuse of the exception mechanism.

➤ Exception handling can skip levels of the call stack. That is, a function can handle an error that occurred several function calls down the stack, without error-handling code in the intermediate functions. Return codes require each level of the call stack to clean up explicitly after the previous level.

Why Exceptions in C++ Are a Bad Thing

In some compilers (fewer and fewer these days), exception handling added a tiny amount of overhead to any function that had an exception handler. In modern compilers, this overhead is so small or even non-existing, so that you can ignore it. Do not assume that the urban legend about exceptions introducing serious overhead is true; you have to check it out in your compiler.

Exception handling is not enforced in C++. For example, in Java a function that does not specify a list of possible exceptions that it can throw is not allowed to throw any exceptions. In C++, it is just the opposite: a function that does not specify a list of exceptions can throw any exception it wants! Additionally, the exception list is not enforced at compile time in C++, meaning that the exception list of a function can be violated at run time. Note that some tools, such as using /Analyze with Microsoft VC++, will check exceptions and report potential problems.

Our Recommendation

We recommend exceptions as a useful mechanism for error handling. We feel that the structure and error-handling formalization that exceptions provide outweigh the less desirable aspects. Thus, the remainder of this chapter focuses on exceptions. Also, many popular libraries, such as the STL and Boost use exceptions, so you need to be prepared to handle them. We recommend you read the rest of this chapter, because you should not be surprised by the experience of having an exception thrown.

EXCEPTION MECHANICS

Exceptional situations arise frequently in file input and output. The following is a function to open a file, read a list of integers from the file, and store the integers in the supplied `std::vector` data structure. A `vector` is a dynamic array. You can add elements to it by using the `push_back()` method, and access them with array notation.

Available for download on Wrox.com

```
void readIntegerFile(const string& fileName, vector<int>& dest)
{
    ifstream istr;
    int temp;
    istr.open(fileName.c_str());
    // Read the integers one by one and add them to the vector.
    while (istr >> temp) {
        dest.push_back(temp);
    }
}
```

Code snippet from ReadIntegerFile\NoExceptionHandling.cpp

The following line keeps reading values from the `ifstream` until the end of the file is reached or until an error occurs.

```
while (istr >> temp) {
```

This works because the >> operator returns a reference to the `ifstream` object itself. Additionally, `ifstream` provides a `bool()` conversion operator implemented as follows:

```
return !fail();
```

If the >> operator encounters an error, it will set the fail bit of the `ifstream` object. In that case, the `bool()` conversion operator will return `false` and the `while` loop will terminate. Streams are discussed in more detail in Chapter 15.

You might use `readIntegerFile()` like this:

```cpp
vector<int> myInts;
const string fileName = "IntegerFile.txt";
readIntegerFile(fileName, myInts);
for (size_t i = 0; i < myInts.size(); i++) {
    cout << myInts[i] << " ";
}
cout << endl;
```

Code snippet from ReadIntegerFile\NoExceptionHandling.cpp

The lack of error handling in these functions should jump out at you. The rest of this section shows you how to add error handling with exceptions.

Throwing and Catching Exceptions

Using exceptions consists of providing two parts in your program: a `try/catch` construct, to handle an exception, and a `throw` statement, that throws an exception. Both must be present in some form to make exceptions work. However, in many cases, the `throw` happens deep inside some library (including the C++ run time) and the programmer never sees it, but still has to react to it using a `try/catch` construct.

The `try/catch` construct looks as follows:

```cpp
try {
    // ... code which may result in an exception being thrown
} catch (exception-type1 exception-name) {
    // ... code which responds to the exception of type 1
} catch (exception-type2 exception-name) {
    // ... code which responds to the exception of type 2
}
// ... remaining code
```

The code which may result in an exception being thrown might contain a `throw` directly, or might be calling a function which either directly throws an exception or calls, by some unknown number of layers of calls, a function which throws an exception.

If no exception is thrown, the code in the `catch` blocks is not executed, and the "remaining code" which follows will follow the last statement executed in the `try` block.

If an exception is thrown, any code following the `throw` or following the call which resulted in the `throw`, is not executed, but control immediately goes to the right `catch` block depending on the type of the exception that is thrown.

If the `catch` block does not do a control transfer, for example by returning a value, throwing a new exception or rethrowing the exception, then the "remaining code" is executed after the last statement of that `catch` block.

The simplest example to demonstrate exception handling is avoiding divide-by-zero. This example throws an exception of type `invalid_argument` which requires the `<stdexcept>` header.

```cpp
int SafeDivide(int num, int den)
{
    if (den == 0)
        throw invalid_argument("Divide by zero");
    return num / den;
}
int main()
{
    try {
        cout << SafeDivide(5, 2) << endl;
        cout << SafeDivide(10, 0) << endl;
        cout << SafeDivide(3, 3) << endl;
    } catch (const invalid_argument& e) {
        cout << "Caught exception: " << e.what() << endl;
    }
    return 0;
}
```

Code snippet from SafeDivide\SafeDivide.cpp

The output is as follows:

```
2
Caught exception: Divide by zero
```

`throw` is a keyword in C++, and is the only way to throw an exception. The `invalid_argument()` part of the `throw` line means that you are constructing a new object of type `invalid_argument` to throw.

The `throw` keyword can also be used to rethrow the current exception. For example:

```cpp
void g() { throw 2; }
void f()
{
    try {
        g();
    } catch (int i) {
        cout << "caught in f: " << i << endl;
        throw;  // rethrow
    }
}
```

```
int main()
{
    try {
        f();
    } catch (int i) {
        cout << "caught in main: " << i << endl;
    }
    return 0;
}
```

Code snippet from Rethrow\rethrow.cpp

This example produces the following output:

```
caught in f: 2
caught in main: 2
```

Let's go back to the `readIntegerFile()` function. The most likely problem to occur is for the file open to fail. That's a perfect situation for throwing an exception. This code throws an exception of type `exception` which requires the `<exception>` header. The syntax looks like this:

Available for download on Wrox.com

```
#include <exception>
void readIntegerFile(const string& fileName, vector<int>& dest)
{
    ifstream istr;
    int temp;
    istr.open(fileName.c_str());
    if (istr.fail()) {
        // We failed to open the file: throw an exception.
        throw exception();
    }
    // Read the integers one by one and add them to the vector.
    while (istr >> temp) {
        dest.push_back(temp);
    }
}
```

Code snippet from ReadIntegerFile\BasicExceptions.cpp

If the function fails to open the file and executes the `throw exception();` line, the rest of the function is skipped, and control transitions to the nearest exception handler.

Throwing exceptions in your code is most useful when you also write code that handles them. Exception handling is a way to "try" a block of code, with another block of code designated to react to any problems that might occur. In the following `main()` function the `catch` statement reacts to any exception of type `exception` that was thrown within the `try` block by printing an error message. If the `try` block finishes without throwing an exception, the `catch` block is skipped. You can think of `try`/`catch` blocks as glorified `if` statements. If an exception is thrown in the `try` block, execute the `catch` block. Otherwise, skip it.

```
int main()
{
    vector<int> myInts;
    const string fileName = "IntegerFile.txt";
    try {
        readIntegerFile(fileName, myInts);
    } catch (const exception& e) {
        cerr << "Unable to open file " << fileName << endl;
        return 1;
    }
    for (size_t i = 0; i < myInts.size(); i++) {
        cout << myInts[i] << " ";
    }
    cout << endl;
    return 0;
}
```

Code snippet from ReadIntegerFile\BasicExceptions.cpp

 Although by default, streams do not throw exceptions, you can tell the streams to throw exceptions for error conditions by calling their exceptions( ) *method. However, Bjarne Stroustrup, creator of C++, likes to deal with the stream state directly instead of using exceptions (The C++ Programming Language, third edition). This book follows his style in that regard.*

Exception Types

You can throw an exception of any type. The preceding example throws an object of type `exception`, but exceptions do not need to be objects. You could throw a simple `int` like this:

```
void readIntegerFile(const string& fileName, vector<int>& dest)
{
    // Code omitted
    istr.open(fileName.c_str());
    if (istr.fail()) {
        // We failed to open the file: throw an exception.
        throw 5;
    }
    // Code omitted
}
```

Code snippet from ReadIntegerFile\ThrowInt.cpp

You would then need to change the `catch` statement as well:

```
try {
    readIntegerFile(fileName, myInts);
} catch (int e) {
    cerr << "Unable to open file " << fileName << endl;
    return 1;
}
```

Code snippet from ReadIntegerFile\ThrowInt.cpp

Alternatively, you could throw a `char*` C-style string. This technique is sometimes useful because the string can contain information about the exception.

```
void readIntegerFile(const string& fileName, vector<int>& dest)
{
    // Code omitted
    istr.open(fileName.c_str());
    if (istr.fail()) {
        // We failed to open the file: throw an exception.
        throw "Unable to open file";
    }
    // Code omitted
}
```

Code snippet from ReadIntegerFile\ThrowCharStar.cpp

When you catch the `char*` exception, you can print the result:

```
try {
    readIntegerFile(fileName, myInts);
} catch (const char* e) {
    cerr << e << endl;
    return 1;
}
```

Code snippet from ReadIntegerFile\ThrowCharStar.cpp

 In modern programming, you should avoid using 8-bit `char*` C-style strings. You should use Unicode strings which are discussed in detail in Chapter 14.

Despite the previous examples, you should generally throw objects as exceptions for two reasons:

➤ Objects convey information by their class name.

➤ Objects can store information, including strings that describe the exceptions.

The C++ standard library defines a number of predefined exception classes and you can write your own exception classes. Details are described later in this chapter.

Catching Exception Objects by const and Reference

In the preceding example in which readIntegerFile() throws an object of type exception, the catch line looks like this:

```
} catch (const exception& e) {
```

However, there is no requirement to catch objects by const reference. You could catch the object by value like this:

```
} catch (exception e) {
```

Code snippet from ReadIntegerFile\CatchByValue.cpp

Alternatively, you could catch the object by reference (without the const):

```
} catch (exception& e) {
```

Code snippet from ReadIntegerFile\CatchByNonConstReference.cpp

Also, as you saw in the char* example, you can catch pointers to exceptions, as long as pointers to exceptions are thrown.

It is recommended to catch exceptions by const reference.

Throwing and Catching Multiple Exceptions

Failure to open the file is not the only problem readIntegerFile() could encounter. Reading the data from the file can cause an error if it is formatted incorrectly. Here is an implementation of readIntegerFile() that throws an exception if it cannot either open the file or read the data correctly:

```
void readIntegerFile(const string& fileName, vector<int>& dest)
{
    ifstream istr;
    int temp;
    istr.open(fileName.c_str());
    if (istr.fail()) {
        // We failed to open the file: throw an exception.
        throw exception();
    }
    // Read the integers one by one and add them to the vector.
    while (istr >> temp) {
        dest.push_back(temp);
    }
    if (istr.eof()) {
        // We reached the end-of-file.
        istr.close();
```

```
    } else {
        // Some other error. Throw an exception.
        istr.close();
        throw exception();
    }
}
```

Code snippet from ReadIntegerFile\ThrowingMultipleBasic.cpp

Your code in `main()` does not need to change because it already catches an exception of type `exception`. However, that exception could now be thrown in two different situations, so you should modify the error message accordingly:

Available for download on Wrox.com

```
try {
    readIntegerFile(fileName, myInts);
} catch (const exception& e) {
    cerr << "Unable either to open or to read " << fileName << endl;
    return 1;
}
```

Code snippet from ReadIntegerFile\ThrowingMultipleBasic.cpp

Alternatively, you could throw two different types of exceptions from `readIntegerFile()`, so that the caller can tell which error occurred. Here is an implementation of `readIntegerFile()` that throws an exception object of class `invalid_argument` if the file cannot be opened and an object of class `runtime_error` if the integers cannot be read. Both `invalid_argument` and `runtime_error` are classes defined in the header file `<stdexcept>` as part of the C++ Standard Library.

Available for download on Wrox.com

```
#include <stdexcept>
void readIntegerFile(const string& fileName, vector<int>& dest)
{
    ifstream istr;
    int temp;
    istr.open(fileName.c_str());
    if (istr.fail()) {
        // We failed to open the file: throw an exception.
        throw invalid_argument("");
    }
    // Read the integers one by one and add them to the vector.
    while (istr >> temp) {
        dest.push_back(temp);
    }
    if (istr.eof()) {
        // We reached the end-of-file.
        istr.close();
    } else {
        // Some other error. Throw an exception.
        istr.close();
        throw runtime_error("");
    }
}
```

Code snippet from ReadIntegerFile\ThrowingTwoTypes.cpp

There are no public default constructors for invalid_argument and runtime_error, only string constructors.

Now main() can catch both invalid_argument and runtime_error with two catch statements:

```
try {
    readIntegerFile(fileName, myInts);
} catch (const invalid_argument& e) {
    cerr << "Unable to open file " << fileName << endl;
    return 1;
} catch (const runtime_error& e) {
    cerr << "Error reading file " << fileName << endl;
    return 1;
}
```

Code snippet from ReadIntegerFile\ThrowingTwoTypes.cpp

If an exception is thrown inside the try block, the compiler will match the type of the exception to the proper catch handler. So, if readIntegerFile() is unable to open the file and throws an invalid_argument object, it will be caught by the first catch statement. If readIntegerFile() is unable to read the file properly and throws a runtime_error, then the second catch statement will catch the exception.

Matching and const

The const-ness specified in the type of the exception you want to catch makes no difference for matching purposes. That is, this line matches any exception of type runtime_error.

```
} catch (const runtime_error& e) {
```

The following line also matches any exception of type runtime_error:

```
} catch (runtime_error& e) {
```

Matching Any Exception

You can write a catch line that matches any possible exception with the special syntax shown in the following example:

```
try {
    readIntegerFile(fileName, myInts);
} catch (...) {
    cerr << "Error reading or opening file " << fileName << endl;
    return 1;
}
```

Code snippet from ReadIntegerFile\MatchingAnyException.cpp

The three dots are not a typo. They are a wildcard that match any exception type. When you are calling poorly documented code, this technique can be useful to ensure that you catch all possible exceptions.

However, in situations where you have complete information about the set of thrown exceptions, this technique is considered suboptimal because it handles every exception type identically. It's better to match exception types explicitly and take appropriate, targeted action.

A possible use of a `catch` block matching any exception is as a default `catch` handler. When an exception is thrown, a `catch` handler is looked up in the order that they appear in the code. The following example shows how you can write `catch` handlers that explicitly handle `invalid_argument` and `runtime_error` exceptions and how to include a default `catch` handler for all other exceptions.

```
try {
    // Code that can throw exceptions
} catch (const invalid_argument& e) {
    // Handle invalid_argument exception
} catch (const runtime_error& e) {
    // Handle runtime_error exception
} catch (...) {
    // Handle all other exceptions
}
```

Uncaught Exceptions

If your program throws an exception that is not caught anywhere, the program will terminate. Basically there is a `try/catch` construct around the call to your `main()` function which catches all unhandled exceptions, something as follows:

```
try {
    main(argc, argv);
} catch (...) {
    // issue error message and terminate program
}
```

However, this behavior is not usually what you want. The point of exceptions is to give your program a chance to handle and correct undesirable or unexpected situations.

 Catch and handle all possible exceptions thrown in your programs.

Even if you can't handle a particular exception, you should still write code to catch it and print or show an appropriate error message.

It is also possible to change the behavior of your program if there is an uncaught exception. When the program encounters an uncaught exception, it calls the built-in `terminate()` function, which calls `abort()` from `<cstdlib>` to kill the program. You can set your own `terminate_handler` by calling `set_terminate()` with a pointer to a callback function that takes no arguments and returns no value. `terminate()`, `set_terminate()`, and `terminate_handler` are all declared in the `<exception>` header. The following code shows a high-level overview of how it works.

```
try {
    main(argc, argv);
} catch (...) {
    if (terminate_handler != nullptr) {
        terminate_handler();
        abort();
    } else {
        terminate();
    }
}
// normal termination code
```

Before you get too excited about this feature, you should know that your callback function must still terminate the program, or else `abort()` will be called anyway. It can't just ignore the error. However, you can use it to print a helpful error message before exiting. Here is an example of a `main()` function that doesn't catch the exceptions thrown by `readIntegerFile()`. Instead, it sets the `terminate_handler` to a callback that prints an error message before exiting:

```
void myTerminate()
{
    cout << "Uncaught exception!" << endl;
    exit(1);
}
int main()
{
    vector<int> myInts;
    const string fileName = "IntegerFile.txt";
    set_terminate(myTerminate);
    readIntegerFile(fileName, myInts);
    for (size_t i = 0; i < myInts.size(); i++) {
        cout << myInts[i] << " ";
    }
    cout << endl;
    return 0;
}
```

Code snippet from ReadIntegerFile\TerminateHandler.cpp

Although not shown in this example, `set_terminate()` returns the old `terminate_handler` when it sets the new one. The `terminate_handler` applies program-wide, so it's considered good style to reset the old `terminate_handler` when you have completed the code that needed the new `terminate_handler`. In this case, the entire program needs the new `terminate_handler`, so there's no point in resetting it.

Although it's important to know about `set_terminate()`, it's not a very effective exception-handling approach. We recommend trying to catch and handle each exception individually in order to provide more precise error handling.

Throw Lists

C++ allows you to specify the exceptions a function or method intends to throw. This specification is called the *throw list* or the *exception specification*. Here is the `readIntegerFile()` function from the earlier example with the proper throw list:

```
void readIntegerFile(const string& fileName, vector<int>& dest)
    throw(invalid_argument, runtime_error)
{
    // Remainder of the function is the same as before
}
```

Code snippet from ReadIntegerFile\ThrowList.cpp

The throw list shows the types of exceptions that can be thrown from the function. Note that the throw list must also be provided for the function prototype:

```
void readIntegerFile(const string& fileName, vector<int>& dest)
    throw(invalid_argument, runtime_error);
```

Code snippet from ReadIntegerFile\ThrowList.cpp

You cannot overload a function based solely on different exceptions in the throw list.

If a function or method specifies no throw list, it can throw any exception. You've already seen this behavior in the previous implementation of the `readIntegerFile()` function. If you want to specify that a function or method throws no exceptions, you need to use `noexcept` like this:

```
void readIntegerFile(const string& fileName, vector<int>& dest) noexcept;
```

Code snippet from ReadIntegerFile\noexcept.cpp

> **C++11**
>
> *The `noexcept` keyword is introduced with C++11. If your compiler is not yet C++11 compliant, you should replace the `noexcept` keyword with `throw()`. However, it is important to remember that C++11 has deprecated the empty `throw()` list, which means that it might disappear in future compilers.*

If this behavior seems backward to you, you're not alone. However, it's best just to accept it and move on.

A function without a throw list can throw exceptions of any type. A function with noexcept *or an empty throw list shouldn't throw any exception.*

Unexpected Exceptions

Unfortunately, the throw list is not enforced at compile time in C++. Code that calls readIntegerFile() does not need to catch the exceptions listed in the throw list. This behavior is different from that in other languages, such as Java, which requires a function or method to catch exceptions or declare them in their own function or method throw lists.

Additionally, you could implement readIntegerFile() like this:

Available for download on Wrox.com

```
void readIntegerFile(const string& fileName, vector<int>& dest)
    throw(invalid_argument, runtime_error)
{
    throw 5;
}
```

Code snippet from ReadIntegerFile\UnexpectedExceptions.cpp

Even though the throw list states that readIntegerFile() doesn't throw an int, this code, which obviously throws an int, compiles and runs. However, it won't do what you want. Suppose that you write this main() function which has a catch block for int:

Available for download on Wrox.com

```
int main()
{
    vector<int> myInts;
    const string fileName = "IntegerFile.txt";
    try {
        readIntegerFile(fileName, myInts);
    } catch (int x) {
        cerr << "Caught int" << endl;
    }
    return 0;
}
```

Code snippet from ReadIntegerFile\UnexpectedExceptions.cpp

When this program runs and readIntegerFile() throws the int exception, the program terminates. It does not allow main() to catch the int.

Throw lists don't prevent functions from throwing unlisted exception types, but they prevent the exception from leaving the function, resulting in a run-time error.

> *All versions of Microsoft Visual C++, up to version 2010 at the time of this writing, do not yet support throw lists for functions as explained earlier. As a result, the preceding* main() *function will catch the* int *exception because Visual C++ just ignores the* throw(invalid_argument, runtime_error) *specification and will issue a warning like* "warning C4290: C++ exception specification ignored except to indicate a function is not __declspec(nothrow)". *Maybe future versions will support this.*

You can change this behavior. When a function throws an exception that is not listed in its throw list, C++ calls a special function unexpected(). The built-in implementation of unexpected() calls terminate(). However, just as you can set your own terminate_handler, you can set your own unexpected_handler. Unlike in the terminate_handler, you can actually do something other than just terminate the program in the unexpected_handler. Your version of the function must either throw a new exception or terminate the program — it can't just exit the function normally. If it throws a new exception, that exception will be substituted for the unexpected exception as if the new one had been thrown originally. If this substituted exception is also not listed in the throw list, the program will do one of two things. If the throw list for the function specifies bad_exception, then bad_exception will be thrown. Otherwise, the program will terminate. Custom implementations of unexpected() are normally used to convert unexpected exceptions into expected exceptions. For example, you could write a version of unexpected() like this:

```cpp
void myUnexpected()
{
    cerr << "Unexpected exception!" << endl;
    throw runtime_error("");
}
```

Code snippet from ReadIntegerFile\UnexpectedExceptions.cpp

This code converts an unexpected exception to a runtime_error exception, which the function readIntegerFile() has in its throw list.

You could set this unexpected exception handler in main() with the set_unexpected() function. Like set_terminate(), set_unexpected() returns the current handler. The unexpected() function applies program-wide, not just to this function, so you should reset the handler when you are done with the code that needed your special handler:

```cpp
int main()
{
    vector<int> myInts;
    const string fileName = "IntegerFile.txt";
    unexpected_handler old_handler = set_unexpected(myUnexpected);
    try {
        readIntegerFile(fileName, myInts);
    } catch (const invalid_argument& e) {
        cerr << "Unable to open file " << fileName << endl;
        return 1;
```

```
    } catch (const runtime_error& e) {
        cerr << "Error reading file " << fileName << endl;
        return 1;
    } catch (int x) {
        cerr << "Caught int" << endl;
    }
    set_unexpected(old_handler);
    // Remainder of function omitted
}
```

Now `main()` handles any exception thrown from `readIntegerFile()` by converting it to a `runtime_error`. However, as with `set_terminate()`, we recommend using this capability judiciously.

`unexpected()`, `set_unexpected()`, and `bad_exception` are all declared in the `<exception>` header file.

Changing the Throw List in Overridden Methods

When you override a `virtual` method in a subclass, you can change the throw list as long as you make it *more restrictive* than the throw list in the superclass. The following changes qualify as more restrictive:

➤ Removing exceptions from the list

➤ Adding subclasses of exceptions that appear in the superclass throw list

➤ Making it a `noexcept` method

The following changes do not qualify as more restrictive:

➤ Adding exceptions to the list that are not subclasses of exceptions in the superclass throw list

➤ Removing the throw list entirely

 If you change throw lists when you override methods, remember that any code that called the superclass version of the method must be able to call the subclass version. Thus, you can't add exceptions.

For example, suppose that you have the following superclass:

Available for download on Wrox.com

```
class Base
{
    public:
        virtual void func() throw(exception) { cout << "Base!\n"; }
};
```

You could write a subclass that overrides `func()` and specifies that it doesn't throw any exceptions:

```
class Derived : public Base
{
    public:
        virtual void func() noexcept { cout << "Derived!\n"; }
};
```

Code snippet from ThrowListsVirtualMethods\CorrectOne.cpp

You could also override `func()` such that it throws a `runtime_error` as well as an `exception`, because `runtime_error` is a subclass of `exception`.

```
class Derived : public Base
{
    public:
        virtual void func() throw(exception, runtime_error)
            { cout << "Derived!\n"; }
};
```

Code snippet from ThrowListsVirtualMethods\CorrectTwo.cpp

However, you cannot remove the throw list entirely, because that means `func()` could throw any exception.

As a second example, suppose `Base` looked like this:

```
class Base
{
    public:
        virtual void func() throw(runtime_error) { cout << "Base!\n"; }
};
```

Code snippet from ThrowListsVirtualMethods\Broken.cpp

Then you cannot override `func()` in `Derived` with a throw list like this:

```
class Derived : public Base
{
    public:
        virtual void func() throw(exception) // ERROR!
            { cout << "Derived!\n"; }
};
```

Code snippet from ThrowListsVirtualMethods\Broken.cpp

`exception` is a superclass of `runtime_error`, so you cannot substitute an `exception` for a `runtime_error`.

Are Throw Lists Useful?

Given the opportunity to specify the behavior of a function in its prototype, it seems wasteful not to take advantage of it. The exceptions thrown from a particular function are an important part of its interface, and should be documented as well as possible.

Unfortunately, most of the C++ code in use today, including the Standard Library, does not follow this advice. That makes it difficult for you to determine which exceptions can be thrown when you use this code. Additionally, it is impossible to specify the exception characteristics of templatized functions and methods. When you don't even know what types will be used to instantiate the template, you have no way to determine the exceptions that methods of those types can throw. As a final problem, the throw list syntax and enforcement is somewhat obscure.

Thus, we leave the decision up to you.

EXCEPTIONS AND POLYMORPHISM

As described earlier, you can actually throw any type of exception. However, classes are the most useful types of exceptions. In fact, exception classes are usually written in a hierarchy, so that you can employ polymorphism when you catch the exceptions.

The Standard Exception Hierarchy

You've already seen several exceptions from the C++ standard exception hierarchy: `exception`, `runtime_error`, and `invalid_argument`. Figure 10-3 shows the complete hierarchy:

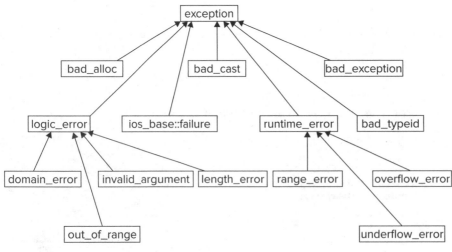

FIGURE 10-3

All of the exceptions thrown by the C++ Standard Library are objects of classes in this hierarchy. Each class in the hierarchy supports a `what()` method that returns a `const char*` string describing the exception. You can use this string in an error message.

All the exception classes except for the base `exception` require you to set in the constructor the string that will be returned by `what()`. That's why you have to specify a string in the constructors for `runtime_error` and `invalid_argument`. Now that you know what the strings are used for, you can make them more useful. Here is an example where the string is used to pass the full error message back to the caller:

```cpp
void readIntegerFile(const string& fileName, vector<int>& dest)
    throw(invalid_argument, runtime_error)
{
    ifstream istr;
    int temp;
    istr.open(fileName.c_str());
    if (istr.fail()) {
        // We failed to open the file: throw an exception.
        string error = "Unable to open file " + fileName;
        throw invalid_argument(error);
    }
    // Read the integers one by one and add them to the vector.
    while (istr >> temp) {
        dest.push_back(temp);
    }
    if (istr.eof()) {
        // We reached the end-of-file.
        istr.close();
    } else {
        // Some other error. Throw an exception.
        istr.close();
        string error = "Unable to read file " + fileName;
        throw runtime_error(error);
    }
}
int main()
{
    // Code omitted
    try {
        readIntegerFile(fileName, myInts);
    } catch (const invalid_argument& e) {
        cerr << e.what() << endl;
        return 1;
    } catch (const runtime_error& e) {
        cerr << e.what() << endl;
        return 1;
    }
    // Code omitted
}
```

Code snippet from ExceptionsAndPolymorphism\UsingWhat.cpp

Catching Exceptions in a Class Hierarchy

The most exciting feature of exception hierarchies is that you can catch exceptions polymorphically. For example, if you look at the two `catch` statements in `main()` following the call to `readIntegerFile()`, you can see that they are identical except for the exception class that they handle. Conveniently, `invalid_argument` and `runtime_error` are both subclasses of `exception`, so you can replace the two `catch` statements with a single `catch` statement for class `exception`:

```
try {
    readIntegerFile(fileName, myInts);
} catch (const exception& e) {
    cerr << e.what() << endl;
    return 1;
}
```

Code snippet from ExceptionsAndPolymorphism\CatchingPolymorphicallyCorrectOne.cpp

The `catch` statement for an `exception` reference matches any subclasses of `exception`, including both `invalid_argument` and `runtime_error`. Note that the higher in the exception hierarchy that you catch exceptions, the less specific is your error handling. You should generally catch exceptions at as specific a level as possible.

> *When you catch exceptions polymorphically, make sure to catch them by reference. If you catch exceptions by value, you can encounter* slicing, *in which case you lose information from the object. See Chapter 8 for details on slicing.*

When more than one `catch` clause is used, the `catch` clauses are matched in syntactic order as they appear in your code; the first one that matches, wins. If one `catch` is more inclusive than a later one, it will match first, and the more restrictive one, which comes later, will not be executed at all. Therefore, you should place your `catch` clauses from most restrictive to least restrictive order. For example, suppose that you want to catch `invalid_argument` from `readIntegerFile()` explicitly, but leave the generic `exception` match for any other exceptions. The correct way to do so is like this:

```
try {
    readIntegerFile(fileName, myInts);
} catch (const invalid_argument& e) { // List exception subclass first.
    // Take some special action for invalid filenames.
} catch (const exception& e) { // Now list exception
    cerr << e.what() << endl;
    return 1;
}
```

Code snippet from ExceptionsAndPolymorphism\CatchingPolymorphicallyCorrectTwo.cpp

The first `catch` statement catches `invalid_argument` exceptions, and the second catches any other exceptions of type `exception`. However, if you reverse the order of the `catch` statements, you don't get the same result:

```
try {
    readIntegerFile(fileName, myInts);
} catch (const exception& e) { // BUG: catching superclass first!
    cerr << e.what() << endl;
    return 1;
} catch (const invalid_argument& e) {
    // Take some special action for invalid filenames.
}
```

Code snippet from ExceptionsAndPolymorphism\CatchingPolymorphicallyIncorrect.cpp

With this order, any exception of a class that subclasses `exception` is caught by the first `catch` statement; the second will never be reached. Some compilers issue a warning in this case, but you shouldn't count on it.

Writing Your Own Exception Classes

There are two advantages to writing your own exception classes.

1. The number of exceptions in the C++ Standard Library is limited. Instead of using an exception class with a generic name, such as `runtime_error`, you can create classes with names that are more meaningful for the particular errors in your program.

2. You can add your own information to these exceptions. The exceptions in the standard hierarchy allow you to set only an error string. You might want to pass different information in the exception.

We recommend that all the exception classes that you write inherit directly or indirectly from the standard `exception` class. If everyone on your project follows that rule, you know that every exception in the program will be a subclass of `exception` (assuming that you aren't using third-party libraries that break this rule). This guideline makes exception handling via polymorphism significantly easier.

For example, `invalid_argument` and `runtime_error` don't capture very well the file opening and reading errors in `readIntegerFile()`. You can define your own error hierarchy for file errors, starting with a generic `FileError` class:

```
class FileError : public runtime_error
{
    public:
        FileError(const string& fileIn)
            : runtime_error(""), mFile(fileIn) {}
        virtual const char* what() const noexcept { return mMsg.c_str(); }
        string getFileName() { return mFile; }
    protected:
        string mFile, mMsg;
};
```

Code snippet from ExceptionsAndPolymorphism\WritingExceptions.cpp

As a good programming citizen, you should make `FileError` a part of the standard exception hierarchy. It seems appropriate to integrate it as a child of `runtime_error`. When you write a subclass of `runtime_error` (or any other exception in the standard hierarchy), you need to override the `what()` method, which has the prototype shown and is supposed to return a `const char*` string that is valid until the object is destroyed. In the case of `FileError`, this string comes from the `mMsg` data member, which is set to `""` in the constructor. Subclasses of `FileError` must set this `mMsg` string to something different if they want a different message.

The generic `FileError` class also contains a filename and an accessor for that filename.

The first exceptional situation in `readIntegerFile()` occurs if the file cannot be opened. Thus, you might want to write a `FileOpenError` subclass of `FileError`:

```cpp
class FileOpenError : public FileError
{
    public:
        FileOpenError(const string& fileNameIn);
};
FileOpenError::FileOpenError(const string& fileNameIn) : FileError(fileNameIn)
{
    mMsg = "Unable to open " + fileNameIn;
}
```

Code snippet from ExceptionsAndPolymorphism\WritingExceptions.cpp

The `FileOpenError` changes the `mMsg` string to represent the file-opening error.

The second exceptional situation in `readIntegerFile()` occurs if the file cannot be read properly. It might be useful for this exception to contain the line number of the error in the file, as well as the filename and the error message string returned from `what()`. Here is a `FileReadError` subclass of `FileError`:

```cpp
class FileReadError : public FileError
{
    public:
        FileReadError(const string& fileNameIn, int lineNumIn);
        int getLineNum() { return mLineNum; }
    protected:
        int mLineNum;
};
FileReadError::FileReadError(const string& fileNameIn, int lineNumIn)
    : FileError(fileNameIn), mLineNum(lineNumIn)
{
    ostringstream ostr;
    ostr << "Error reading " << fileNameIn << " at line " << lineNumIn;
    mMsg = ostr.str();
}
```

Code snippet from ExceptionsAndPolymorphism\WritingExceptions.cpp

Of course, in order to set the line number properly, you need to modify your `readIntegerFile()` function to track the number of lines read instead of just reading integers directly. Here is a new `readIntegerFile()` function that uses the new exceptions:

```cpp
void readIntegerFile(const string& fileName, vector<int>& dest)
    throw(FileOpenError, FileReadError)
{
    ifstream istr;
    int temp;
    string line;
    int lineNumber = 0;
    istr.open(fileName.c_str());
    if (istr.fail()) {
        // We failed to open the file: throw an exception.
        throw FileOpenError(fileName);
    }
    while (!istr.eof()) {
        // Read one line from the file.
        getline(istr, line);
        lineNumber++;
        // Create a string stream out of the line.
        istringstream lineStream(line);
        // Read the integers one by one and add them to the vector.
        while (lineStream >> temp) {
            dest.push_back(temp);
        }
        if (!lineStream.eof()) {
            // Some other error. Close the file and throw an exception.
            istr.close();
            throw FileReadError(fileName, lineNumber);
        }
    }
    istr.close();
}
```

Code snippet from ExceptionsAndPolymorphism\WritingExceptions.cpp

Now, code that calls `readIntegerFile()` can use polymorphism to catch exceptions of type `FileError` like this:

```cpp
try {
    readIntegerFile(fileName, myInts);
} catch (const FileError& e) {
    cerr << e.what() << endl;
    return 1;
}
```

Code snippet from ExceptionsAndPolymorphism\WritingExceptions.cpp

There is one trick to writing classes whose objects will be used as exceptions. When a piece of code throws an exception, the object or value thrown is copied. That is, a new object is constructed from the old object by using the copy constructor. It must be copied because the original could go out of scope (and be destroyed and have its memory reclaimed) before the exception is caught, higher up in the stack. Thus, if you write a class whose objects will be thrown as exceptions, you must make those objects copyable. This means that if you have dynamically allocated memory, you must write a destructor, copy constructor, and assignment operator, as described in Chapter 7.

 Objects thrown as exceptions are always copied by value at least once.

It is possible for exceptions to be copied more than once, but only if you catch the exception by value instead of by reference.

 Catch exception objects by reference to avoid unnecessary copying.

C++11 Nested Exceptions

It could happen that during handling of a first exception, a second exceptional situation is triggered which requires a second exception to be thrown. Unfortunately, when you throw the second exception, all information about the first exception that you are currently trying to handle will be lost. C++11 provides a solution to this problem with the concept of *nested exceptions*, which allow you to nest a caught exception in the context of a new exception. To that end, a mix-in class called std::nested_exception is provided which captures and stores a copy of the exception currently being processed. A catch handler for the second exception can use a dynamic_cast to get access to the nested_exception representing the first exception. The following example will demonstrate the use of nested exceptions. The first thing you need to do is to define your own exception class and at least inherit from the nested_exception mix-in class. This example defines a MyException class which derives from exception and from the mix-in class nested_exception. It also accepts a string in its constructor.

```cpp
class MyException : public std::exception, public std::nested_exception
{
public:
    MyException(const char* msg) : mMsg(msg) {}
    virtual ~MyException() noexcept {}
    virtual const char* what() const noexcept { return mMsg.c_str(); }
protected:
    std::string mMsg;
};
```

Code snippet from NestedException\NestedException.cpp

When you are handling a first exception and you need to throw a second exception with the first one nested inside it, you need to use the std::throw_with_nested() function. This function requires as parameter an instance of a class that inherits from nested_exception, like the MyException class in this example. The following doSomething() function throws a runtime_error which is immediately caught in the catch handler. The catch handler writes a message and then uses the throw_with_nested() function to throw a second exception that has the first one nested inside it. Note that nesting the exception inside the MyException instance happens automatically due to the nested_exception mix-in class.

```cpp
void doSomething()
{
    try {
        throw std::runtime_error("Throwing a runtime_error exception");
    } catch (const std::runtime_error& e) {
        std::cout << __func__ << " caught a runtime_error" << std::endl;
        std::cout << __func__ << " throwing MyException" << std::endl;
        std::throw_with_nested(
            MyException("MyException with nested runtime_error"));
    }
}
```

Code snippet from NestedException\NestedException.cpp

The following main() function demonstrates how to handle the exception with a nested exception. The code calls the doSomething() function and has one catch handler for exceptions of type MyException. When it catches such an exception, it writes a message and then uses a dynamic_cast to get access to the nested exception. If there is no nested exception inside, the result will be a null pointer. If there is a nested exception inside, the rethrow_nested() method on the nested_exception is called. This will cause the nested exception to be rethrown which you can then catch in another try/catch block.

```cpp
int main()
{
    try {
        doSomething();
    } catch (const MyException& e) {
        std::cout << __func__ << " caught MyException: " << e.what()
                  << std::endl;
        const std::nested_exception* pNested =
            dynamic_cast<const std::nested_exception*>(&e);
        if (pNested) {
            try {
                pNested->rethrow_nested();
            } catch (const std::runtime_error& e) {
                // Handle nested exception
                std::cout << "  Nested exception: " << e.what()
                          << std::endl;
            }
        }
    }
    return 0;
}
```

Code snippet from NestedException\NestedException.cpp

The output should be as follows:

```
doSomething caught a runtime_error
doSomething throwing MyException
main caught MyException: MyException with nested runtime_error
   Nested exception: Throwing a runtime_error exception
```

The preceding `main()` function uses a `dynamic_cast` to check for the nested exception. Since you always have to perform this `dynamic_cast` if you want to check for a nested exception, the standard provides a small wrapper called `std::rethrow_if_nested()` that does it for you. This wrapper can be used as follows:

Available for download on Wrox.com

```cpp
int main()
{
    try {
        doSomething();
    } catch (const MyException& e) {
        std::cout << __func__ << " caught MyException: " << e.what()
                << std::endl;
        try {
            std::rethrow_if_nested(e);
        } catch (const std::runtime_error& e) {
            // Handle nested exception
            std::cout << "  Nested exception: " << e.what() << std::endl;
        }
    }
    return 0;
}
```

Code snippet from NestedException\NestedException.cpp

STACK UNWINDING AND CLEANUP

When a piece of code throws an exception, it searches for a catch handler on the stack. This catch handler could be zero or more function calls up the stack of execution. When one is found, the stack is stripped back to the stack level that defines the catch handler by unwinding all intermediate stack frames. *Stack unwinding* means that the destructors for all locally-scoped names are called and all code remaining in each function past the current point of execution is skipped.

However, in stack unwinding, pointer variables are not freed, and other cleanup is not performed. This behavior can present problems, as the following code demonstrates:

Available for download on Wrox.com

```cpp
void funcOne() throw(exception);
void funcTwo() throw(exception);
int main()
{
    try {
        funcOne();
    } catch (const exception& e) {
```

```
            cerr << "Exception caught!" << endl;
            return 1;
        }
        return 0;
    }
    void funcOne() throw(exception)
    {
        string str1;
        string* str2 = new string();
        funcTwo();
        delete str2;
    }
    void funcTwo() throw(exception)
    {
        ifstream istr;
        istr.open("filename");
        throw exception();
        istr.close();
    }
```

Code snippet from StackUnwinding\BadCode.cpp

When `funcTwo()` throws an exception, the closest exception handler is in `main()`. Control then jumps immediately from this line in `funcTwo()`:

```
throw exception();
```

to this line in `main()`:

```
cerr << "Exception caught!" << endl;
```

In `funcTwo()`, control remains at the line that threw the exception, so this subsequent line never gets a chance to run:

```
istr.close();
```

However, luckily for you, the `ifstream` destructor is called because `istr` is a local variable on the stack. The `ifstream` destructor closes the file for you, so there is no resource leak here. If you had dynamically allocated `istr`, it would not be destroyed, and the file would not be closed.

In `funcOne()`, control is at the call to `funcTwo()`, so this subsequent line never gets a chance to run:

```
delete str2;
```

In this case, there really is a memory leak. Stack unwinding does not automatically call `delete` on `str2` for you. However, `str1` is destroyed properly because it is a local variable on the stack. Stack unwinding destroys all local variables correctly.

 Careless exception handling can lead to memory and resource leaks.

This is one reason you should never mix older C models of allocation (even if you are calling `new` so it looks like C++) with modern programming methodologies like exceptions. In C++, this situation should be handled by one of the techniques discussed in the following two sections.

Use Smart Pointers

The first and recommended technique is to use smart pointers. They allow you to write code that automatically prevents memory or resource leaks with exception handling. Chapter 21 discusses smart pointers in detail. Smart pointer objects are allocated on the stack and whenever the smart pointer object is destroyed, it frees the underlying resource. Here is an example of the previous `funcOne()` function but using the `unique_ptr` (C++11) smart pointer:

```cpp
#include <memory>
using namespace std;
void funcOne() throw(exception)
{
    string str1;
    unique_ptr<string> str2(new string("hello"));
    funcTwo();
}
```

Code snippet from StackUnwinding\SmartPointer.cpp

The `str2` pointer of type `string*` will automatically be deleted when you return from `funcOne()` or when an exception is thrown.

With smart pointers, you never have to remember to free the underlying resource: the smart pointer destructor does it for you, whether you leave the function via an exception or leave the function normally.

Catch, Cleanup, and Rethrow

The next technique for avoiding memory and resource leaks is for each function to catch any possible exceptions, perform necessary cleanup work, and rethrow the exception for the function higher up the stack to handle. Here is a revised `funcOne()` with this technique:

```cpp
void funcOne() throw(exception)
{
    string str1;
    string* str2 = new string();
    try {
        funcTwo();
    } catch (...) {
        delete str2;
        throw; // Rethrow the exception.
    }
    delete str2;
}
```

Code snippet from StackUnwinding\CatchAndRethrow.cpp

This function wraps the call to `funcTwo()` with an exception handler that performs the cleanup (calls `delete` on `str2`) and then rethrows the exception. The keyword `throw` by itself rethrows whatever exception was caught most recently. Note that the catch statement uses the ... syntax to catch any exception.

This method works fine, but can be messy. In particular, note that there are now two identical lines that call `delete` on `str2`: one to handle the exception and one if the function exits normally.

 The preferred solution is to use smart pointers instead of the catch, cleanup, and rethrow technique.

COMMON ERROR-HANDLING ISSUES

Whether or not you use exceptions in your programs is up to you and your colleagues. However, we strongly encourage you to formalize an error-handling plan for your programs, regardless of your use of exceptions. If you use exceptions, it is generally easier to come up with a unified error-handling scheme, but it is not impossible without exceptions. The most important aspect of a good plan is uniformity of error handling throughout all the modules of the program. Make sure that every programmer on the project understands and follows the error-handling rules.

This section discusses the most common error-handling issues in the context of exceptions, but the issues are also relevant to programs that do not use exceptions.

Memory Allocation Errors

Despite the fact that all of our examples so far in this book have ignored the possibility, memory allocation can, and will, fail. However, production code must account for memory allocation failures. C++ provides several different ways to handle memory errors.

The default behaviors of `new` and `new[]` are to throw an exception of type `bad_alloc`, defined in the `<new>` header file, if they cannot allocate memory. Your code should catch these exceptions and handle them appropriately.

Thus, all your `new` statements should look something like this:

```cpp
try {
    ptr = new int[numInts];
} catch (const bad_alloc& e) {
    cerr << __FILE__ << "(" << __LINE__
         << "): Unable to allocate memory!" << endl;
    // Handle memory allocation failure.
    return;
}
// Proceed with function that assumes memory has been allocated.
```

Code snippet from NewFailures\Exceptions.cpp

Note that this code uses the predefined preprocessor symbols __FILE__ and __LINE__ which will be replaced with the name of the file and the current line number. This makes debugging easier.

> *This example prints an error message to* cerr. *This assumes your program is running with a console. In GUI applications, you often don't have a console in which case you need to show the error in a GUI specific way to the user.*

You could, of course, bulk handle many possible new failures with a single try/catch block at a higher point in the program, if it will work for your program.

Another consideration is that logging an error might try to allocate memory. If new fails, there might not be enough memory left even to log the error message.

Non-Throwing new

As Chapter 21 explains, if you don't like exceptions, you can revert to the old C model in which memory allocation routines return a null pointer if they cannot allocate memory. C++ provides *nothrow* versions of new and new[], which return nullptr instead of throwing an exception if they fail to allocate memory. This is done by using the syntax new(nothrow) instead of new as shown in the following example.

Available for download on Wrox.com

```
ptr = new(nothrow) int[numInts];
if (ptr == nullptr) {
    cerr << __FILE__ << "(" << __LINE__
        << "): Unable to allocate memory!" << endl;
    // Handle memory allocation failure.
    return;
}
// Proceed with function that assumes memory has been allocated.
```

Code snippet from NewFailures\Nothrow.cpp

The syntax is a little strange: you really do write "nothrow" as if it's an argument to new (which it is).

Customizing Memory Allocation Failure Behavior

C++ allows you to specify a *new handler* callback function. By default, there is no new handler, so new and new[] just throw bad_alloc exceptions. However, if there is a new handler, the memory allocation routine calls the new handler upon memory allocation failure instead of throwing an exception. If the new handler returns, the memory allocation routines attempt to allocate memory again, calling the new handler again if they fail. This cycle could become an infinite loop unless your new handler changes the situation with one of four alternatives. Practically speaking, some of the four options are better than others. Here is the list with commentary:

➤ **Make more memory available.** One trick to expose space is to allocate a large chunk of memory at program start-up, and then to free it in the new handler. A practical example is when you hit an allocation error and you need to save the user state so no work gets lost. The key is to allocate a block of memory at program start-up large enough to allow a complete document save operation. When the new handler is triggered, you free this block, save the document, restart the application and let it reload the saved document.

➤ **Throw an exception.** new and new[] have throw lists that say they will throw exceptions only of type bad_alloc. So, unless you want to create a call to unexpected(), if you throw an exception from the new handler, throw bad_alloc or a subclass. For example, when your new handler is triggered, you can throw a document_recovery_alloc exception which inherits from bad_alloc. You can catch this exception somewhere in your application and trigger the document save operation and restart of the application.

➤ **Set a different new handler.** Theoretically, you could have a series of new handlers, each of which tries to create memory and sets a different new handler if it fails. However, such a scenario is usually more complicated than useful.

➤ **Terminate the program.** Your new handler can log an error message and throw an agreed-upon exception such as PleaseTerminateMe. In your top-level function, for example main(), you catch this exception and handle it by **returning** from the top-level function. Never explicitly terminate the program by using exit() or abort(), only by returning from the top-level function. If there are some memory allocations that can fail but still allow your program to succeed, you can simply set the new handler back to its default of nullptr temporarily before calling new in those cases.

If you don't do one of these four things in your new handler, any memory allocation failure will cause an infinite loop.

You set the new handler with a call to set_new_handler(), declared in the <new> header file. set_new_handler() completes the trio of C++ functions to set callback functions. The other two are set_terminate() and set_unexpected(), which were discussed earlier in this chapter. Here is an example of a new handler that logs an error message and throws an exception:

Available for
download on
Wrox.com

```cpp
class PleaseTerminateMe { };
void myNewHandler()
{
    cerr << __FILE__ << "(" << __LINE__
        << "): Unable to allocate memory." << endl;
    throw PleaseTerminateMe();
}
```

Code snippet from NewFailures\NewHandler.cpp

The new handler must take no arguments and return no value. This new handler throws a PleaseTerminateMe exception like suggested in the fourth bullet in the preceding list.

You can set the new handler like this:

Available for
download on
Wrox.com

```cpp
int main()
{
    try {
        // Set the new new_handler and save the old.
        new_handler oldHandler = set_new_handler(myNewHandler);
        // Generate allocation error
```

```
            int numInts = numeric_limits<int>::max();
            int* ptr = new int[numInts];
            // reset the old new_handler
            set_new_handler(oldHandler);
        } catch (const PleaseTerminateMe&) {
            cerr << __FILE__ << "(" << __LINE__
                << "): Terminating program." << endl;
            return 1;
        }
        return 0;
    }
```

Code snippet from NewFailures\NewHandler.cpp

Note that `new_handler` is a `typedef` for the type of function pointer that `set_new_handler()` takes.

Errors in Constructors

Before C++ programmers discover exceptions, they are often stymied by error handling and constructors. What if a constructor fails to construct the object properly? Constructors don't have a return value, so the standard pre-exception error-handling mechanism doesn't work. Without exceptions, the best you can do is to set a flag in the object specifying that it is not constructed properly. You can provide a method, with a name like `checkConstructionStatus()`, which returns the value of that flag, and hope that clients remember to call the function on the object after constructing it.

Exceptions provide a much better solution. You can throw an exception from a constructor, even though you can't return a value. With exceptions you can easily tell clients whether or not construction of the object succeeded. However, there is one major problem: if an exception leaves a constructor, the destructor for that object will never be called. Thus, you must be careful to clean up any resources and free any allocated memory in constructors before allowing exceptions to leave the constructor. This problem is the same as in any other function, but it is subtler in constructors because you're accustomed to letting the destructors take care of the memory deallocation and resource freeing.

This section describes a `Matrix` class as an example in which the constructor correctly handles exceptions. The definition of the `Matrix` class looks as follows:

Available for download on Wrox.com

```
#include <stdexcept>
#include "Element.h"
class Matrix
{
    public:
        Matrix(unsigned int width, unsigned int height) throw(std::bad_alloc);
        virtual ~Matrix();
    protected:
        unsigned int mWidth;
        unsigned int mHeight;
        Element** mMatrix;
};
```

Code snippet from ConstructorError\Matrix.h

The preceding class uses the `Element` class, which is kept at a bare minimum for this example:

```cpp
class Element
{
    protected:
        int mValue;
};
```

Code snippet from ConstructorError\Element.h

The implementation of the `Matrix` class is as follows. Note that the first call to `new` is not protected with a `try/catch` block. It doesn't matter if the first `new` throws an exception because the constructor hasn't allocated anything else yet that needs freeing. If any of the subsequent `new` calls throw exceptions, though, the constructor must clean up all of the memory already allocated. However, it doesn't know what exceptions the `Element` constructors themselves might throw, so it catches any exception via ... and translates them into a `bad_alloc` exception. It is also important to have index `i` outside the `try` block because this index is needed during cleanup in the `catch` block.

```cpp
Matrix::Matrix(unsigned int width, unsigned int height) throw(bad_alloc)
    : mWidth(width), mHeight(height), mMatrix(nullptr)
{
    mMatrix = new Element*[width];
    unsigned int i = 0;
    try {
        for (i = 0; i < height; ++i)
            mMatrix[i] = new Element[height];
    } catch (...) {
        cout << "Exception caught in constructor, cleaning up..." << endl;
        // Clean up any memory we already allocated, because the destructor
        // will never be called. The upper bound of the for loop is the
        // index of the last element in the mMatrix array that we tried
        // to allocate (the one that failed). All indices before that
        // one store pointers to allocated memory that must be freed.
        for (unsigned int j = 0; j < i; j++) {
            delete [] mMatrix[j];
        }
        delete [] mMatrix;
        mMatrix = nullptr;
        // Translate any exception to bad_alloc.
        throw bad_alloc();
    }
}
Matrix::~Matrix()
{
    for (unsigned int i = 0; i < mHeight; ++i)
        delete [] mMatrix[i];
    delete [] mMatrix;
    mMatrix = nullptr;
}
```

Code snippet from ConstructorError\Matrix.cpp

> *Remember, if an exception leaves a constructor, the destructor for that object will never be called!*

You might be wondering what happens when you add inheritance into the mix. Superclass constructors run before subclass constructors. If a subclass constructor throws an exception, how are the resources that the superclass constructor allocated freed?

> *C++ guarantees that it will run the destructor for any fully constructed "subobjects." Therefore, any constructor that completes without an exception will cause the corresponding destructor to be run.*

Function-Try-Blocks for Constructors

The exception mechanism as discussed up to now in this chapter is perfect to handle exceptions within functions. However, how should you handle exceptions thrown from inside a ctor-initializer of a constructor? This section explains a feature called *function-try-blocks*, which are capable of catching those exceptions. Most C++ programmers, even experienced C++ programmers don't know the existence of this feature, even though it was introduced more than a decade ago.

The following piece of pseudo code shows the basic syntax for a function-try-block for a constructor:

```
MyClass::MyClass()
try
    : <ctor-initializer>
{
    /* ... constructor body ... */
}
catch (const exception& e)
{
    /* ... */
}
```

As you can see, the `try` keyword should be right before the start of the ctor-initializer. The `catch` statements should be after the closing brace for the constructor, actually putting them outside the constructor body. There are a number of restrictions and guidelines that you should keep in mind when using function-try-blocks with constructors:

➤ The `catch` statements will catch any exception either thrown directly or indirectly by the ctor-initializer or by the constructor body.

➤ The `catch` statements have to rethrow the current exception or throw a new exception. If a `catch` statement doesn't do this, the run time will automatically rethrow the current exception.

➤ When a `catch` statement catches an exception in a function-try-block, all objects that have already been constructed by the constructor will be destroyed before execution of the `catch` statement starts.

➤ You should not access member variables for the object inside a function-try-block `catch` statement.

➤ The `catch` statements in a function-try-block cannot use the `return` keyword to return a value from the function enclosed by it. This is not relevant for constructors because they do not return anything.

Based on this list of limitations, function-try-blocks for constructors are useful only in a very limited number of situations:

➤ To convert an exception thrown by the ctor-initializer to another exception.

➤ To log a message to a log file.

Let's see how to use function-try-blocks with an example. The following code defines a class called `SubObject`. It has only one constructor, which throws an exception of type `runtime_error`.

```cpp
class SubObject
{
    public:
        SubObject(int i) throw(std::runtime_error);
};
SubObject::SubObject(int i) throw(std::runtime_error)
{
    throw std::runtime_error("Exception by SubObject ctor");
}
```

Code snippet from FunctionTryBlock\FunctionTryBlocks.cpp

The `MyClass` class has a member variable of type `SubObject`:

```cpp
class MyClass
{
    public:
        MyClass() throw(std::runtime_error);
    protected:
        SubObject mSubObject;
};
```

Code snippet from FunctionTryBlock\FunctionTryBlocks.cpp

The `SubObject` class does not have a default constructor. This means that you need to initialize `mSubObject` in the `MyClass` ctor-initializer. The constructor of the `MyClass` class will use a function-try-block to catch exceptions thrown in its ctor-initializer:

```cpp
MyClass::MyClass() throw(std::runtime_error)
try
    : mSubObject(42)
{
    /* ... constructor body ... */
}
```

```
catch (const std::exception& e)
{
    cout << "function-try-block caught: '" << e.what() << "'" << endl;
}
```

Code snippet from FunctionTryBlock\FunctionTryBlocks.cpp

Remember that `catch` statements in a function-try-block for a constructor have to either rethrow the current exception or throw a new exception. The preceding `catch` statement does not throw anything, so the C++ run time will automatically rethrow the current exception. Following is a simple function that uses the preceding class:

Available for download on Wrox.com

```
int main()
{
    try {
        MyClass m;
    } catch (const std::exception& e) {
        cout << "main() caught: '" << e.what() << "'" << endl;
    }
    return 0;
}
```

Code snippet from FunctionTryBlock\FunctionTryBlocks.cpp

The output of the preceding example is as follows:

```
function-try-block caught: 'Exception by SubObject ctor'
main() caught: 'Exception by SubObject ctor'
```

Function-try-blocks are not limited to constructors. They can be used with ordinary functions as well. However, for normal functions, there is no useful reason to use function-try-blocks because they can just as easily be converted to a simple `try`/`catch` block inside the function body. One notable difference when using a function-try-block on a normal function compared to a constructor is that rethrowing the current exception or throwing a new exception in the `catch` statements is not required and the C++ run time will not automatically rethrow the exception.

Errors in Destructors

You should handle all error conditions that arise in destructors in the destructors themselves. You should not let any exceptions be thrown from destructors, for three reasons:

1. Destructors can run while there is another pending exception, in the process of stack unwinding. If you throw an exception from the destructor in the middle of stack unwinding, the program will terminate. For the brave and curious, C++ does provide the ability to determine, in a destructor, whether you are executing as a result of a normal function exit or delete call, or because of stack unwinding. The function `uncaught_exception()`, declared in the `<exception>` header file, returns `true` if there is an uncaught exception

and you are in the middle of stack unwinding. Otherwise, it returns `false`. However, this approach is messy and should be avoided.

2. What action would clients take? Clients don't call destructors explicitly: they call `delete`, which calls the destructor. If you throw an exception from the destructor, what is a client supposed to do? It can't call `delete` on the object again, and it shouldn't call the destructor explicitly. There is no reasonable action the client can take, so there is no reason to burden that code with exception handling.

3. The destructor is your one chance to free memory and resources used in the object. If you waste your chance by exiting the function early due to an exception, you will never be able to go back and free the memory or resources.

Therefore, be careful to catch in a destructor any exceptions that can be thrown by calls you make from the destructor. Normally, destructors call only `delete` and `delete[]`, which cannot throw exceptions, so there should be no problem.

PUTTING IT ALL TOGETHER

Now that you've learned about error handling and exceptions, let's see it all coming together in a bigger example, a `GameBoard` class. This `GameBoard` class will come back in Chapter 19. First, here is the definition of the class without any exceptions.

```cpp
class GameBoard
{
    public:
        // general-purpose GameBoard allows user to specify its dimensions
        GameBoard(int inWidth = kDefaultWidth,
            int inHeight = kDefaultHeight);
        GameBoard(const GameBoard& src); // Copy constructor
        virtual ~GameBoard();
        GameBoard& operator=(const GameBoard& rhs); // Assignment operator
        void setPieceAt(int x, int y, const GamePiece& inPiece);
        GamePiece& getPieceAt(int x, int y);
        const GamePiece& getPieceAt(int x, int y) const;
        int getHeight() const { return mHeight; }
        int getWidth() const { return mWidth; }
        static const int kDefaultWidth = 100;
        static const int kDefaultHeight = 100;
    protected:
        void copyFrom(const GameBoard& src);
        // Objects dynamically allocate space for the game pieces.
        GamePiece** mCells;
        int mWidth, mHeight;
};
```

Code snippet from GameBoard\NoExceptions\GameBoard.h

And here is the implementation without any exceptions:

```cpp
GameBoard::GameBoard(int inWidth, int inHeight) :
    mWidth(inWidth), mHeight(inHeight)
{
    mCells = new GamePiece* [mWidth];
    for (int i = 0; i < mWidth; i++) {
        mCells[i] = new GamePiece[mHeight];
    }
}
GameBoard::GameBoard(const GameBoard& src)
{
    copyFrom(src);
}
GameBoard::~GameBoard()
{
    // Free the old memory
    for (int i = 0; i < mWidth; i++) {
        delete [] mCells[i];
    }
    delete [] mCells;
    mCells = nullptr;
}
void GameBoard::copyFrom(const GameBoard& src)
{
    mWidth = src.mWidth;
    mHeight = src.mHeight;
    mCells = new GamePiece* [mWidth];
    for (int i = 0; i < mWidth; i++) {
        mCells[i] = new GamePiece[mHeight];
    }
    for (int i = 0; i < mWidth; i++) {
        for (int j = 0; j < mHeight; j++) {
            mCells[i][j] = src.mCells[i][j];
        }
    }
}
GameBoard& GameBoard::operator=(const GameBoard& rhs)
{
    // Check for self-assignment
    if (this == &rhs) {
        return *this;
    }
    // Free the old memory
    for (int i = 0; i < mWidth; i++) {
        delete [] mCells[i];
    }
    delete [] mCells;
    mCells = nullptr;
    // Copy the new memory
    copyFrom(rhs);
    return *this;
}
```

```
void GameBoard::setPieceAt(int x, int y, const GamePiece& inElem)
{
    mCells[x][y] = inElem;
}
GamePiece& GameBoard::getPieceAt(int x, int y)
{
    return mCells[x][y];
}
const GamePiece& GameBoard::getPieceAt(int x, int y) const
{
    return mCells[x][y];
}
```

Code snippet from GameBoard\NoExceptions\GameBoard.cpp

Now, let's retrofit the preceding class to include error handling and exceptions. The constructors, `operator=` and `copyFrom()` can all throw `bad_alloc` because they perform memory allocation. The destructor, `getHeight()`, and `getWidth()` throw no exceptions. `setPieceAt()` and `getPieceAt()` throw `out_of_range` if the caller supplies an invalid coordinate. Here is the retrofitted class definition:

```
#include <stdexcept>
#include <new>
using std::bad_alloc;
using std::out_of_range;
class GameBoard
{
    public:
        GameBoard(int inWidth = kDefaultWidth,
            int inHeight = kDefaultHeight) throw(bad_alloc);
        GameBoard(const GameBoard& src) throw(bad_alloc);
        virtual ~GameBoard() noexcept;
        GameBoard& operator=(const GameBoard& rhs) throw(bad_alloc);
        void setPieceAt(int x, int y, const GamePiece& inPiece)
            throw(out_of_range);
        GamePiece& getPieceAt(int x, int y) throw(out_of_range);
        const GamePiece& getPieceAt(int x, int y) const
            throw(out_of_range);
        int getHeight() const noexcept { return mHeight; }
        int getWidth() const noexcept { return mWidth; }
        static const int kDefaultWidth = 100;
        static const int kDefaultHeight = 100;
    protected:
        void copyFrom(const GameBoard& src) throw(bad_alloc);
        GamePiece** mCells;
        int mWidth, mHeight;
};
```

Code snippet from GameBoard\GameBoard.h

Here are the implementations of the constructor, `copyFrom()`, and `setPieceAt()` methods with exception handling. `getPieceAt()` is not shown because it is similar to `setPieceAt()`. The implementations of the copy constructor and `operator=` did not change except for their throw lists because all the work is in `copyFrom()`, so their implementations are not shown. The destructor also did not change, so its implementation is not shown either.

```cpp
GameBoard::GameBoard(int inWidth, int inHeight) throw(bad_alloc) :
    mWidth(inWidth), mHeight(inHeight)
{
    int i = 0;
    mCells = new GamePiece* [mWidth];
    try {
        for (i = 0; i < mWidth; i++) {
            mCells[i] = new GamePiece[mHeight];
        }
    } catch (...) {
        // Cleanup any memory we already allocated, because the destructor
        // will never get called. The upper bound of the for loop is the
        // index of the last element in the mCells array that we tried
        // to allocate (the one that failed). All indices before that
        // one store pointers to allocated memory that must be freed.
        for (int j = 0; j < i; j++) {
            delete [] mCells[j];
        }
        delete [] mCells;
        mCells = nullptr;
        // Translate any exception to bad_alloc.
        throw bad_alloc();
    }
}
void GameBoard::copyFrom(const GameBoard& src) throw(bad_alloc)
{
    int i = 0;
    mWidth = src.mWidth;
    mHeight = src.mHeight;
    mCells = new GamePiece *[mWidth];
    try {
        for (i = 0; i < mWidth; i++) {
            mCells[i] = new GamePiece[mHeight];
        }
    } catch (...) {
        // Clean up any memory we already allocated.
        // If this function is called from the copy constructor,
        // the destructor will never be called.
        // Use the same loop upper bound as described in the constructor.
        for (int j = 0; j < i; j++) {
            delete [] mCells[j];
        }
        delete [] mCells;
        // Set mCells and mWidth to values that will allow the
        // destructor to run without harming anything.
        // This function is called from operator=, in which case the
        // object was already constructed, so the destructor will be
        // called at some point.
        mCells = nullptr;
        mWidth = 0;
```

```
            throw bad_alloc();
        }
        for (i = 0; i < mWidth; i++) {
            for (int j = 0; j < mHeight; j++) {
                mCells[i][j] = src.mCells[i][j];
            }
        }
    }
void GameBoard::setPieceAt(int x, int y, const GamePiece& inElem)
        throw(out_of_range)
{
    // Check for out of range arguments
    if (x < 0)
        throw out_of_range("GameBoard::setPieceAt: x-coord negative");
    if (x >= mWidth)
        throw out_of_range("GameBoard::setPieceAt: x-coord beyond width");
    if (y < 0)
        throw out_of_range("GameBoard::setPieceAt: y-coord negative");
    if (y >= mHeight)
        throw out_of_range("GameBoard::setPieceAt: y-coord beyond height");

    mCells[x][y] = inElem;
}
```

Code snippet from GameBoard\GameBoard.cpp

SUMMARY

This chapter described the issues related to error handling in C++ programs, and emphasized that you must design and code your programs with an error-handling plan. By reading this chapter, you learned the details of C++ exceptions syntax and behavior. The chapter also covered some of the areas in which error handling plays a large role, including I/O streams, memory allocation, constructors, and destructors. Finally, you saw an example of error handling in a GameBoard class.

Classes and functionality of the C++ standard library have already been used extensively throughout this book, so it's time to go deeper in on that subject. The next few chapters start delving into the C++ standard library.

11

Delving into the Standard Library

WHAT'S IN THIS CHAPTER?

➤ What the coding principles used throughout the Standard Library are

➤ What kind of functionality the Standard Library provides

The most important library that you will use as a C++ programmer is the C++ standard library. As its name implies, this library is part of the C++ standard, so any standards-conforming compiler should include it. The standard library is not monolithic: It includes several disparate components, some of which you have been using already. You may even have assumed they were part of the core language.

The heart of the C++ standard library is its generic *containers* and *algorithms*. This subset of the library is often called the *Standard Template Library*, or *STL* for short, because of its abundant use of templates. The power of the STL is that it provides generic containers and generic algorithms in such a way that most of the algorithms work on most of the containers, no matter what type of data the containers store. Performance is a very important part of the STL. The goal is to make the STL containers and algorithms as fast as or faster than hand written code.

Many programmers who claim to know C++ have never heard of the Standard Template Library. A C++ programmer who wishes to claim language expertise is expected to be familiar with the Standard Template Library. You can save yourself immeasurable time and energy by incorporating the STL containers and algorithms into your programs instead of writing and debugging your own versions. Now is the time to master the standard library.

This first chapter on the standard library starts with a brief explanation on how to use templates and mentions the concept of operator overloading. Both of these concepts are used extensively by the STL. It also provides a general overview of the functionality available in the standard library and in the STL.

The next few chapters go into much more detail on several aspects of the standard library and the STL, including containers, iterators, generic algorithms, predefined function object classes; and customizing and extending the library by writing your own allocators, algorithms, containers, iterators, and using iterator adapters.

Despite the depth of material found in this and the next chapters, the standard library is too large for this book to cover exhaustively. You should read this and the following chapters to learn about the standard library and the STL, but keep in mind that they don't mention every method and member that the various classes provide, or show you the prototypes of every algorithm. Appendix C provides a summary of all the header files in the standard library, while the Standard Library Reference resource on the website (www.wrox.com) presents a reference for the various classes and algorithms in the STL.

CODING PRINCIPLES

The standard library, and definitely the standard template library, make heavy use of the C++ features called *templates* and *operator overloading*. This section will give a brief introduction to both concepts.

Use of Templates

Templates are described in full detail in Chapter 19. This section will give a basic overview of how to use templates to avoid any problems with code samples. Templates are used to allow *generic programming*. They make it possible to write code that can work with all kinds of objects, even objects unknown to the programmer when writing the code. The obligation of the programmer writing the template code is to specify the requirements of the classes that define these objects, for example, that they have an operator for comparison, or a copy constructor, or whatever is deemed appropriate, and then making sure the code that is written uses only those required capabilities. The obligation of the programmer creating the objects is to supply those operators and methods that the template writer requires.

Unfortunately, many programmers consider templates to be the most difficult part of C++ and, for that reason, tend to avoid them. However, even if you never write your own templates, you need to understand their syntax and capabilities in order to use the STL.

Explaining the use of templates is best done with an example. Suppose that you would like to write a small class that wraps a standard fixed-sized array of elements of type int. The class definition could be as follows:

Available for
download on
Wrox.com

```cpp
class MyArray
{
    public:
        MyArray(size_t size);
        virtual ~MyArray();
        size_t getSize() const;
        int& at(size_t index) throw(out_of_range);
    protected:
        size_t mSize;
```

```
            int* mArray;
    };
```

The implementation is pretty straightforward. Note that error checking is omitted to keep the example compact.

Available for
download on
Wrox.com

```
MyArray::MyArray(size_t size) : mSize(size), mArray(nullptr)
{
    mArray = new int[size];
}
MyArray::~MyArray()
{
    if (mArray) {
        delete [] mArray;
        mArray = nullptr;
    }
}
size_t MyArray::getSize() const
{
    return mSize;
}
int& MyArray::at(size_t index) throw(out_of_range)
{
    if (index >= 0 && index < getSize())
        return mArray[index];
    else
        throw out_of_range("MyArray::at: Index out of range.");
}
```

The class defines a constructor that accepts the size of the wrapped array. The constructor allocates the memory for the array while the destructor frees the memory. The `getSize()` method allows you to query the size of the wrapped array. The class also includes an `at()` method to give you access to elements of the wrapped array. Note that the `at()` method returns a reference, so it can also be used to assign values to array elements like in the following example:

Available for
download on
Wrox.com

```
MyArray arr(10);
cout << "Array size: " << arr.getSize() << endl;
arr.at(3) = 42;
cout << "arr[3] = " << arr.at(3) << endl;
try {
    arr.at(10) = 3;
} catch (const exception& e) {
    cout << "Caught exception: '" << e.what() << "'" << endl;
}
```

Now that you have this class, what would you do when you need to wrap an array of type `double`, or `float` or maybe even `std::string`? One possible solution would be to copy/paste the preceding code and edit it so that the type name is changed to type `double`, `float`, or whichever type you need.

By now you should immediately think that this cannot be the best solution to this problem and you are right. Templates allow you to solve exactly this problem without writing any new classes. The only thing you need to do is rewrite the preceding class a little so that it becomes a *generic template class* that you will be able to use with any type you want. What you have to do is specify that the type of the objects is also a parameter to the specification. This is done with a special syntax. Only a few small changes are required, as shown in the following new class definition. Note also that templates require you to put the implementation of the methods in the header file itself, because the compiler needs to know the complete definition, including the definition of methods before it can create an instance of the template. Putting implementations in header files is only acceptable with templates. In all other cases, it's highly recommended to put implementation details in source files, not in header files. Chapters 19 and 20 will go much deeper into all the details about templates.

```cpp
#include <stdexcept>
template<typename T>
class MyArray
{
    public:
        MyArray(size_t size) : mSize(size), mArray(nullptr)
        {
            mArray = new T[size];
        }
        virtual ~MyArray()
        {
            if (mArray) {
                delete [] mArray;
                mArray = nullptr;
            }
        }
        size_t getSize() const { return mSize; }
        T& at(size_t index) throw(std::out_of_range)
        {
            if (index >= 0 && index < getSize())
                return mArray[index];
            else
                throw std::out_of_range("MyArray::at: Index out of range.");
        }
    protected:
        size_t mSize;
        T* mArray;
};
```

Code snippet from TemplateIntroduction\TemplateIntroduction.h

As you can see in the preceding code, instead of using a specific type such as `int`, an unspecified type `T` is used everywhere. Before the `class` keyword, it is stated that this is a template class that accepts just one type, T. You can use any name you want for T, as long as it is not an existing keyword or type.

This generic fixed sized array template class can be used as follows:

```cpp
// Wrap an int array
MyArray<int> arrInt(10);
cout << "Array size: " << arrInt.getSize() << endl;
arrInt.at(3) = 42;
cout << "arr[3] = " << arrInt.at(3) << endl;
try {
    arrInt.at(10) = 3;
} catch (const exception& e) {
    cout << "Caught exception: '" << e.what() << "'" << endl;
}
// Wrap a std::string array
MyArray<string> arrString(5);
cout << "Array size: " << arrString.getSize() << endl;
arrString.at(3) = "This is a test";
cout << "arr[3] = " << arrString.at(3) << endl;
try {
    arrString.at(10) = 3;
} catch (const exception& e) {
    cout << "Caught exception: '" << e.what() << "'" << endl;
}
```

Code snippet from TemplateIntroduction\TemplateIntroductionTest.cpp

The example code first runs a number of tests on an array of type int, which is created as follows:

```cpp
MyArray<int> arrInt(10);
```

With the preceding line, the compiler will *instantiate* a version of the MyArray class where T is substituted by int. Basically, the compiler will copy all the code for the MyArray class and replace every T with int.

After that, the example runs the same number of tests but on an array with elements of type std::string, which is created as follows:

```cpp
MyArray<string> arrString(5);
```

With this line, the compiler will create a second copy of the MyArray code and will replace every T with string.

As you can see, the template parameter between the angled brackets is different. Other than that, using the two arrays is completely the same, independent of the type of the array elements. The output of the preceding example is as follows:

```
Array size: 10
arr[3] = 42
Caught exception: 'MyArray::at: Index out of range.'
```

```
Array size: 5
arr[3] = This is a test
Caught exception: 'MyArray::at: Index out of range.'
```

Use of Operator Overloading

Operator overloading is used extensively by the C++ standard library, including the STL. Chapter 7 has a whole section devoted to operator overloading. Make sure you read that section and understand it before tackling this and subsequent chapters. In addition, Chapter 18 presents much more detail on the subject of operator overloading, but those details are not required to understand the following chapters.

OVERVIEW OF THE C++ STANDARD LIBRARY

This section introduces the various components of the standard library from a design perspective. You will learn what facilities are available for you to use, but you will not learn the coding details. Those details are covered in other chapters throughout the book.

Note that the following overview is not comprehensive. Some details are introduced later in the book where they are more appropriate, and some details are omitted entirely. The standard library is too extensive to cover in its entirety in a general C++ book; there are books with over 800 pages that cover only the standard library.

Strings

C++ provides a built-in `string` class. Although you may still use C-style strings of character arrays, the C++ `string` class is superior in almost every way. It handles the memory management; provides some bounds checking, assignment semantics, and comparisons; and supports manipulations such as concatenation, substring extraction, and substring or character replacement.

 Technically, the C++ `string` *is actually a* `typedef` *name for a* `char` *instantiation of the* `basic_string` *template. However, you need not worry about these details; you can use* `string` *as if it were a bona fide nontemplate class.*

In case you missed it, Chapter 1 briefly reviews the `string` class functionality , and Chapter 14 provides all the details.

I/O Streams

C++ introduces a new model for input and output using *streams*. The C++ library provides routines for reading and writing built-in types from and to files, console/keyboard, and strings. C++ also provides the facilities for coding your own routines for reading and writing your own objects. Chapter 1 reviews the basics of I/O streams. Chapter 15 provides the details of streams.

Localization

C++ also provides support for *localization*. These features allow you to write programs that work with different languages, character formats, and number formats. Chapter 14 discusses localization.

Smart Pointers

One of the problems faced in doing robust programming is knowing when to delete an object. There are several failures that can happen. A first problem is not deleting the object at all (failing to free the storage). This is known as *memory leaks*, where objects accumulate and take up space but are not used. Another problem is where someone deletes the storage but others are still pointing to that storage, resulting in pointers to storage which is either no longer in use or has been reallocated for another purpose. This is known as *dangling pointers*. One more problem is when one piece of code frees the storage, and another piece of code attempts to free the same storage. This is known as *double-freeing*. All of these tend to result in program failures of some sort. Some failures are readily detected; others simply cause the program to produce erroneous results. Most of these errors are difficult to discover and repair.

C++11 introduces two new concepts, the `unique_ptr` and the `shared_ptr`, which attempt to address these problems.

The `unique_ptr` is analogous to an ordinary pointer, except that it will automatically free the memory or resource when the `unique_ptr` goes out of scope or is deleted. One advantage of the `unique_ptr` is that it simplifies coding where storage must be freed when an exception is taken. When the variable leaves its scope, the storage is automatically freed.

`shared_ptr` allows for distributed "ownership" of the data. Each time a `shared_ptr` is assigned, a reference count is incremented indicating there is one more "owner" of the data. When a `shared_ptr` goes out of scope, the reference count is decremented. When the reference count goes to zero it means there is no longer any owner of the data, and the object referenced by the pointer is freed.

Before C++11, the functionality of `unique_ptr` was handled by a type called `auto_ptr`, which is now deprecated and should not be used anymore. There was no equivalent to `shared_ptr` in the earlier STL, although many third-party libraries (for example Boost) did provide this capability.

 If your compiler supports the new C++11 `unique_ptr` *and* `shared_ptr`, *it is highly recommended to use them instead of the deprecated* `auto_ptr`.

Chapter 21 discusses smart pointers in more detail.

Exceptions

The C++ language supports exceptions, which allow functions or methods to pass errors of various types up to calling functions or methods. The C++ standard library provides a class hierarchy of exceptions that you can use in your program as is, or that you can subclass to create your own exception types. Chapter 10 covers the details of exceptions and the standard exception classes.

Mathematical Utilities

The C++ library provides some mathematical utility classes. Although they are templatized so that you can use them with any type, they are not generally considered part of the standard template library. Unless you are using C++ for numeric computation, you will probably not need to use these utilities.

The standard library provides a complex number class, called `complex`, which provides an abstraction for working with numbers that contain both real and imaginary components.

The standard library also contains a class called `valarray`, which is similar to the `vector` class but is more optimized for high performance numerical applications. The library provides several related classes to represent the concept of vector slices. From these building blocks, it is possible to build classes to perform matrix mathematics. There is no built-in matrix class; however, there are third-party libraries like Boost that include matrix support.

C++ also provides a new way to obtain information about numeric limits, such as the maximum possible value for an integer on the current platform. In C, you could access #defines, such as `INT_MAX`. While those are still available in C++, you can also use the new `numeric_limits` template class defined in the `<limits>` header file. Its use is straightforward as is shown in the following code:

Available for
download on
Wrox.com

```
cout << "Max int value: " << numeric_limits<int>::max() << endl;
cout << "Lowest int value: " << numeric_limits<int>::lowest() << endl;
cout << "Max double value: " << numeric_limits<double>::max() << endl;
cout << "Lowest double value: " << numeric_limits<double>::lowest() << endl;
```

Code snippet from numeric_limits\numeric_limits.cpp

C++11 Time Utilities

C++11 adds the Chrono library to the standard. It is defined in the `<chrono>` header file. This library makes it easy to work with time; for example, to time certain durations or to perform actions based on timing. The Chrono library is discussed in detail in Chapter 16.

C++11 Random Numbers

C++ already had support for generating pseudo-random numbers; however, it was only very basic support. For example, you could not change the distribution of the generated random numbers.

C++11 adds a complete random number library, which is much more powerful than the old C++ way of generating random numbers. The new library comes with *uniform random number generators, random number engines, random number engine adaptors,* and *random number distributions.* All of these can be used to give you random numbers more suited to your problem domain, such as normal distributions, negative exponential distributions, etc.

Consult Chapter 16 for all the details on this new library.

`C++11` Compile-Time Rational Arithmetic

The compile-time rational arithmetic library is new to C++11 and provides a `ratio` template class defined in the `<ratio>` header file. This `ratio` class can exactly represent any finite rational number defined by a numerator and denominator. This library is discussed in Chapter 16.

`C++11` Tuples

Tuples are sequences with a fixed size that can have heterogeneous elements and are defined in the `<tuple>` header file. All standard template library containers discussed further in this chapter store *homogenous* elements, meaning that all the elements in a container must have the same type. A `tuple` allows you to store elements of completely unrelated types in one object. The number and type of elements for a `tuple` instantiation is fixed at compile time. Tuples are discussed in Chapter 16.

`C++11` Regular Expressions

C++11 adds the concept of regular expressions to the standard library and are defined in the `<regex>` header file. Regular expressions make it easy to perform so-called *pattern-matching*, often used in text processing. Pattern-matching allows you to search special patterns in strings and optionally replace those with a new pattern. Regular expressions are discussed in Chapter 14.

The Standard Template Library

The standard template library (STL) supports various *containers* and *algorithms*. This section briefly introduces those containers and algorithms. Later chapters will provide the coding details for using them in your programs.

STL Containers

The STL provides implementations of commonly-used data structures such as linked lists and queues. When you use C++, you should not need to write such data structures again. The data structures are implemented using a concept called *containers*, which store information called *elements*, in a way that implements the data structure (linked list, queue, etc.) appropriately. Different data structures have different insertion, deletion, and access behavior and performance characteristics. It is important to be familiar with the data structures available so that you can choose the most appropriate one for any given task.

All the containers in the STL are templates, so you can use them to store any type, from built-in types such as `int` and `double` to your own classes. Each container instance stores only objects of one type, that is, they are *homogeneous collections*. There is a new type in C++11 called *tuples* that allows fixed-sized heterogeneous collections of objects; but for ordinary containers, you need to store objects of one type and one type only. If you need non fixed-sized heterogeneous collections, you could create a class which has multiple subclasses, and each subclass could wrap an object of your required type.

 The C++ STL containers are homogenous: *They allow elements of only one type in each container.*

Note that the C++ standard specifies the *interface*, but not the *implementation*, of each container and algorithm. Thus, different vendors are free to provide different implementations. However, the standard also specifies performance requirements as part of the interface, which the implementations must meet.

This section provides an overview of the various containers available in the STL.

vector

A vector stores a sequence of elements and provides random access to these elements. You can think of a vector as an array of elements that grows dynamically as you insert elements and provides some bounds checking. Like an array, the elements of a vector are stored in contiguous memory.

> *A* vector *in C++ is a synonym for a dynamic array: an array that grows and shrinks automatically in response to the number of elements it stores.*

vectors provide fast element insertion and deletion (amortized constant time) at the end of the vector. Amortized constant time insertion means that most of the time insertions are done in constant time $O(1)$. However, sometimes the vector needs to grow in size to accommodate new elements which has a complexity of $O(N)$. On average this results in $O(1)$ complexity or amortized constant time. Details are explained in Chapter 12. A vector has slow (linear time) insertion and deletion anywhere else, because the operation must move all the elements "down" or "up" by one to make room for the new element or to fill the space left by the deleted element. Like arrays, vectors provide fast (constant time) access to any of their elements.

You should use a vector in your programs when you need fast access to the elements, but do not plan to add or remove elements often. A good rule of thumb is to use a vector whenever you would have used an array. For example, a system-monitoring tool might keep a list of computer systems that it monitors in a vector. Only rarely would new computers be added to the list, or current computers removed from the list. However, users would often want to look up information about a particular computer, so lookup times should be fast.

> *Use a* vector *instead of an array whenever possible.*

There is a template specialization available for vector<bool> to store Boolean values in a vector. This specialization optimizes space allocation for the Boolean elements; however, the standard does not specify how an implementation of vector<bool> should optimize space. The difference between the vector<bool> specialization and the bitset discussed further in this chapter is that the bitset container is of fixed size.

list

An STL list is a *doubly linked list* structure. Like an array or vector, it stores a sequence of elements. However, unlike an array or vector, the elements of a list are not necessarily in contiguous memory. Instead, each element in the list specifies where to find the next and previous elements in the list (usually via pointers), hence the name doubly linked list.

The performance characteristics of a list are the exact opposite of a vector. They provide slow (linear time) element lookup and access, but quick (constant time) insertion and deletion of elements once the relevant position has been found. Thus, you should use a list when you plan to insert and remove many elements, but do not require quick lookup.

deque

The name deque is an abbreviation for a *double-ended queue*, although it behaves more like a vector instead of a queue which is discussed later. A deque provides quick (constant time) element access. It also provides fast (amortized constant time) insertion and deletion at both ends of the sequence, but it provides slow (linear time) insertion and deletion in the middle of the sequence.

You should use a deque instead of a vector when you need to insert or remove elements from either end of the sequence but still need fast access to all elements. However, this requirement does not apply to many programming problems; in most cases a vector or list should suffice.

C++11

array

C++11 introduces a new type of sequential container called std::array. This is a replacement for the standard C-style arrays. Sometimes you know the exact number of elements in your container upfront and you don't need the flexibility of a vector or a list, which are able to grow dynamically to accommodate new elements. The C++11 std::array is perfect for such fixed-sized collections and it does not have the same overhead as vector; it's basically a thin wrapper around standard C-style arrays. There are a number of advantages in using std::arrays instead of standard C-style arrays; they always know their own size, do not automatically get cast to a pointer to avoid certain types of bugs, and have iterators to easily loop over the elements.

std::arrays do not provide insertion or deletion. They have a fixed size. Access to elements is very fast (constant time), just as with vectors.

C++11

forward_list

The forward_list, introduced in C++11, is a *singly linked list*, compared to the list container, which is doubly linked. The forward_list supports forward iteration only. They require less memory than a list; allow constant time insertion and deletion anywhere; and like lists, there is no fast random access to elements.

 The vector, list, deque, array, *and* forward_list *containers are called* sequential containers *because they store a sequence of elements.*

queue

The name queue comes directly from the definition of the English word *queue*, which means a line of people or objects. The queue container provides standard *first in, first out* (or *FIFO*) semantics. A queue is a container in which you insert elements at one end and take them out at the other end. Both insertion (amortized constant time) and removal (constant time) of elements is quick.

You should use a `queue` structure when you want to model real-life "first-come, first-served" semantics. For example, consider a bank. As customers arrive at the bank, they get in line. As tellers become available, they serve the next customer in line, thus providing "first-come, first-served" behavior. You could implement a bank simulation by storing Customer objects in a `queue`. As customers arrive at the bank, they are added to the end of the `queue`. As tellers serve customers, they start with customers at the front of the `queue`. That way, customers are served in the order in which they arrived.

priority_queue

A `priority_queue` provides `queue` functionality in which each element has a priority. Elements are removed from the queue in priority order. In the case of priority ties, the FIFO semantics hold so that the first element inserted is the first removed. `priority_queue` insertion and deletion are generally slower than simple `queue` insertion and deletion, because the elements must be reordered to support the priority ordering.

You can use `priority_queue`s to model "queues with exceptions." For example, in the preceding bank simulation, suppose that customers with business accounts take priority over regular customers. Many real-life banks implement this behavior with two separate lines: one for business customers and one for everyone else. Any customers in the business queue are taken before customers in the other line. However, banks could also provide this behavior with a single line in which business customers move to the front of the line ahead of any nonbusiness customers. In your program, you could use a `priority_queue` in which customers have one of two priorities: business or regular. All business customers would be serviced before all regular customers, but each group would be serviced in first-come, first-served order.

stack

The STL `stack` provides standard *first-in, last-out (FILO)* semantics, also known as *last-in, first-out (LIFO)*. Like a `queue`, elements are inserted and removed from the container. However, in a `stack`, the most recent element inserted is the first one removed. The name `stack` derives from a visualization of this structure as a stack of objects in which only the top object is visible. When you add an object to the stack, you hide all the objects underneath it.

The STL `stack` container provides fast (constant time) insertion and removal of elements. You should use the `stack` structure when you want FILO semantics. For example, an error-processing tool might want to store errors on a `stack` so that the most recent error is the first one available for a human administrator to read. Processing errors in a FILO order is often useful because newer errors sometimes obviate older ones.

 Technically, the `queue`, `priority_queue`, *and* `stack` *containers are* container adapters. *They are simple interfaces built on top of one of the standard sequential containers (*`vector`, `list`, `deque`, `array`, *and* `forward_list`*).*

set and multiset

A `set` in the STL is, as the name suggests, a set of elements, loosely analogous to the notion of a mathematical set: Each element is unique, and there is at most one instance of the element in the set. One difference between the mathematical concept of set, and `set` as implemented in the STL, is that in the STL the elements are kept in an order. The reason for the order is that when the client enumerates the elements, they come out in the ordering imposed by the type's `operator<` or a user defined comparator. The `set` provides logarithmic insertion, deletion, and lookup. This means insertions and deletions are faster than for a `vector` but slower than for a `list`. Lookups are faster than for a `list`, but slower than for a `vector`.

You should use a `set` when you need the elements to be in an order, have equal amounts of insertion/deletion and lookups, and want to optimize performance for both as much as possible. For example, an inventory-tracking program in a busy bookstore might want to use a `set` to store the books. The list of books in stock must be updated whenever books arrive or are sold, so insertion and deletion should be quick. Customers also need the ability to look for a specific book, so the program should provide fast lookup as well.

> *Use a* `set` *instead of a* `vector` *or* `list` *if you need order and want equal performance for insertion, deletion, and lookup.*

Note that a `set` does not allow duplicate elements. That is, each element in the `set` must be unique. If you want to store duplicate elements, you must use a `multiset`.

map and multimap

A `map` stores key/value pairs. A `map` keeps its elements in sorted order, based on the key values, not the object values. In all other respects, it is identical to a `set`. You should use a `map` when you want to associate keys and values. For example, in the preceding bookstore example, you might want to store the books in a `map` where the key is the ISBN number of the book and the value is a `Book` object containing detailed information for that specific book.

A `multimap` has the same relation to a `map` as a `multiset` does to a `set`. Specifically, a `multimap` is a `map` that allows duplicate keys.

Note that you can use a `map` as an *associative array*. That is, you can use it as an array in which the index can be any type, such as a `string`.

> *The* `set` *and* `map` *containers are called* associative containers *because they associate keys and values. This term is confusing when applied to* `set`*s, because in* `set`*s the keys are themselves the values. These containers sort their elements, so they are called* 'sorted *or* ordered *associative containers.*

bitset

C and C++ programmers commonly store a set of flags in a single `int` or `long`, using one bit for each flag. They set and access these bits with the bitwise operators: `&`, `|`, `^`, `~`, `<<`, and `>>`. The C++

standard library provides a `bitset` class that abstracts this bit field manipulation, so you shouldn't need to use the bit manipulation operators anymore.

The `<bitset>` header file defines the `bitset` container, but this is not a container in the normal sense, in that it does not implement a specific data structure in which you insert and remove elements; they have a fixed size and don't support iterators. You can think of them as a sequence of Boolean values that you can read and write. However, unlike the normal way this is handled in C programming, the `bitset` is not limited to the size of an `int` or other elementary data types. Thus, you can have a 40-bit `bitset`, or a 213-bit `bitset`. The implementation will use as much storage as it needs to implement N bits when you declare your `bitset` with `bitset<N>`.

C++11

Unordered Associative Containers / Hash Tables

C++11 adds the concept of *hash tables*, also called *unordered associative containers*. Four hash tables are introduced:

➤ `unordered_map`

➤ `unordered_set`

➤ `unordered_multimap`

➤ `unordered_multiset`

Better names would have been `hash_map`, `hash_set`, and so on. Unfortunately, hash tables were not part of the C++ standard library before C++11, which means a lot of third-party libraries implemented hash tables themselves by using names with a prefix *hash* like `hash_map`. Because of this, the C++ standard committee decided to use the prefix *unordered* instead of *hash* to avoid name clashes.

These unordered associative containers behave similar to their ordered counterparts. An `unordered_map` is similar to a standard `map` except that the standard `map` sorts its elements while the `unordered_map` doesn't sort its elements.

Insertion, deletion, and lookup with these unordered associative containers can be done on average in constant time. In a worst case scenario it will be in linear time. Lookup of elements in an unordered container can be much faster than with a normal `map` or `set`, especially when there are lots of elements in the container.

Chapter 12 explains how these unordered associative containers work and why they are also called hash tables.

Summary of STL Containers

The following table summarizes the containers provided by the STL. It uses the big-O notation introduced in Chapter 2 to present the performance characteristics on a container of *N* elements. An N/A entry in the table means that the operation is not part of the container semantics.

CONTAINER CLASS NAME	CONTAINER TYPE	INSERTION PERFORMANCE	DELETION PERFORMANCE	LOOKUP PERFORMANCE
vector	Sequential	Amortized $O(1)$ at end; $O(N\text{-}p)$ for an insert at position p	Amortized $O(1)$ at end; $O(N\text{-}p)$ for a delete at position p	$O(1)$
When to Use: Need quick lookup. Don't mind slow insertion/deletion. Whenever you would use a standard C-style array that should dynamically grow/shrink in size.				
list	Sequential	$O(1)$	$O(1)$	$O(N)$; Statistically $O(N/2)$
When to Use: Need quick insertion/deletion. Don't mind slow lookup.				
deque	Sequential	Amortized $O(1)$ at beginning or end; $O(\min(N\text{-}p, p))$ for an insert at position p	Amortized $O(1)$ at beginning or end; $O(\min(N\text{-}p, p))$ for a delete at position p	$O(1)$
When to Use: Not usually needed; use a vector or list instead.				
array `C++11`	Sequential	N/A	N/A	$O(1)$
When to Use: When you need a fixed-size array to replace a standard C-style array.				
forward_ list `C++11`	Sequential	$O(1)$	$O(1)$	$O(N)$; Statistically $O(N/2)$
When to Use: When you need the benefits of a list but require only forward iteration.				
queue	Container Adapter	$O(1)$	$O(1)$	N/A
When to Use: When you want a FIFO structure				
priority_ queue	Container Adapter	$O(\log(N))$	$O(\log(N))$	N/A
When to Use: When you want a FIFO structure with priority.				
stack	Container Adapter	$O(1)$	$O(1)$	N/A
When to Use: When you want a FILO/LIFO structure.				

continues

(continued)

CONTAINER CLASS NAME	CONTAINER TYPE	INSERTION PERFORMANCE	DELETION PERFORMANCE	LOOKUP PERFORMANCE
set multiset	Sorted Associative	$O(\log(N))$	$O(\log(N))$	$O(\log(N))$
When to Use: When you want a sorted collection of elements with equal lookup, insertion, and deletion times.				
map multimap	Sorted Associative	$O(\log(N))$	$O(\log(N))$	$O(\log(N))$
When to Use: When you want a sorted collection to associate keys with values with equal lookup, insertion, and deletion times.				
bitset	Special	N/A	N/A	$O(1)$
When to Use: When you want a collection of flags.				
unordered_ map unordered_ multimap	Unordered associative / hash table	Average case $O(1)$; worst case $O(N)$	Average case $O(1)$; worst case $O(N)$	Average case $O(1)$; worst case $O(N)$
When to Use: When you want to associate keys with values with equal lookup, insertion, and deletion times and don't require the elements to be sorted. Performance can be better than with a normal map but that depends on the elements.				
unordered_ set unordered_ multiset	Unordered associative / hash table	Average case $O(1)$; worst case $O(N)$	Average case $O(1)$; worst case $O(N)$	Average case $O(1)$; worst case $O(N)$
When to Use: When you want a collection of elements with equal lookup, insertion, and deletion times and don't require the elements to be sorted. Performance can be better than with a normal set but that depends on the elements.				

C++11 (marks unordered_map / unordered_multimap row)

C++11 (marks unordered_set / unordered_multiset row)

Note that strings are technically containers as well. They can be thought of as vectors of characters. Thus, some of the algorithms described in the material that follows also work on strings.

STL Algorithms

In addition to containers, the STL provides implementations of many generic algorithms. An *algorithm* is a strategy for performing a particular task, such as sorting or searching. These algorithms are also implemented as templates, so they work on most of the different container types. Note that the algorithms are not generally part of the containers. The STL takes the approach of separating the *data* (containers) from the *functionality* (algorithms). Although this approach seems counter to the spirit of object-oriented programming, it is necessary in order to support generic programming in the STL. The guiding principle of *orthogonality* maintains that algorithms and containers are independent, with (almost) any algorithm working with (almost) any container.

Although the algorithms and containers are theoretically independent, some containers provide certain algorithms in the form of class methods because the generic algorithms do not perform well on those particular containers. For example, sets *provide their own* find() *algorithm that is faster than the generic* find() *algorithm. You should use the container-specific method form of the algorithm, if provided, because it is generally more efficient or appropriate for the container at hand.*

Note that the generic algorithms do not work directly on the containers. They use an intermediary called an *iterator*. Each container in the STL provides an iterator that supports traversing the elements in the container in a sequence. The different iterators for the various containers adhere to standard interfaces, so algorithms can perform their work by using iterators without worrying about the underlying container implementation.

This section gives an overview of what kind of algorithms are available in the STL without giving all the fine points. The Standard Library Reference resource on the website (www.wrox.com) contains the exact prototypes of all the algorithms. The following chapters go deeper in on iterators, algorithms, and containers with coding examples.

Iterators mediate between algorithms and containers. They provide a standard interface to traverse the elements of a container in sequence, so that any algorithm can work on any container.

There are approximately 60 algorithms in the STL (depending on how you count them), generally divided into several different categories. In addition, C++11 adds several new algorithms to the STL. The categories tend to vary slightly from book to book. This book uses the following five categories: *utility, non-modifying, modifying, sorting,* and *set.* Some of the categories can be subdivided further. Note that whenever the following algorithms are specified as working on a "sequence" of elements, that sequence is presented to the algorithm via iterators.

When examining the list of algorithms, keep in mind that the STL was designed by a committee. The committee approach tends to add generality that might never be used, but which, if required, would be essential. You may not need every algorithm, or need to worry about the more obscure parameters which are there for anticipated generality. It is important only to be aware of what's available in case you ever find it useful.

Utility Algorithms

Unlike the other algorithms, the utility algorithms do not work on sequences of data. We consider them part of the STL only because they are templatized.

ALGORITHM NAME	ALGORITHM SYNOPSIS
min(), max()	Returns the minimum or maximum of two values. C++11 allows you to use the min() and max() functions to find the minimum and maximum of more than two values.
minmax()	Returns the minimum and maximum of two or more values as a pair.
swap()	Swaps two values.

C++11 (for minmax())

Non-Modifying Algorithms

The non-modifying algorithms are those that look at a sequence of elements and return some information about the elements, or execute some function on each element. As "non-modifying" algorithms, they cannot change the values of elements or the order of elements within the sequence. This category contains four types of algorithms. The following tables list and provide brief summaries of the various non-modifying algorithms. With these algorithms, you should rarely need to write a for loop to iterate over a sequence of values.

Search Algorithms

ALGORITHM NAME	ALGORITHM SYNOPSIS	REQUIRES SORTED SEQUENCE?	COMPLEXITY
find(), find_if()	Finds the first element that matches a value or causes a predicate to return true.	No	Linear
find_if_not()	Finds the first element that causes a predicate to return false.	No	Linear
find_first_ of()	Like find, except searches for one of several elements at the same time.	No	Quadratic

C++11 (for find_if_not())

	ALGORITHM NAME	ALGORITHM SYNOPSIS	REQUIRES SORTED SEQUENCE?	COMPLEXITY
	`adjacent_find()`	Finds the first instance of two consecutive elements that are equal to each other or match a predicate.	No	Linear
	`search()`, `find_end()`	Finds the first (`search()`) or last (`find_end()`) subsequence in a sequence that matches another sequence or whose elements are equivalent as specified by a predicate.	No	Quadratic
	`search_n()`	Finds the first instance of *n* consecutive elements that are equal to a given value or relate to that value according to a predicate.	No	Linear
	`lower_bound()`, `upper_bound()`, `equal_range()`	Finds the beginning, (`lower_bound()`), end (`upper_bound()`), or both sides (`equal_range()`) of the range including a specified element.	Yes	Logarithmic
	`binary_search()`	Finds a value in a sorted sequence.	Yes	Logarithmic
	`min_element()`, `max_element()`	Finds the minimum or maximum element in a sequence.	No	Linear
C++11	`minmax_element()`	Finds the minimum and maximum element in a sequence and returns the result as a `pair`.	No	Linear
C++11	`all_of()`	Returns `true` if the sequence is empty or if the predicate returns `true` for all the elements in the sequence; `false` otherwise.	No	Linear
C++11	`any_of()`	Returns `false` if the sequence is empty or if the predicate returns `false` for all the elements in the sequence; `true` otherwise.	No	Linear
C++11	`none_of()`	Returns `true` if the sequence is empty or if the predicate returns `false` for all the elements in the sequence; `false` otherwise.	No	Linear
C++11	`partition_point()`	Returns an iterator such that all elements before this iterator return `true` for a predicate and all elements after this iterator return `false` for that predicate.	No	Logarithmic

Numerical Processing Algorithms

The following numerical processing algorithms are provided. None of them require the source sequences to be ordered. All of them have a linear complexity.

ALGORITHM NAME	ALGORITHM SYNOPSIS
count(), count_if()	Counts the number of elements matching a value or that cause a predicate to return true.
accumulate()	"Accumulates" the values of all the elements in a sequence. The default behavior is to sum the elements, but the caller can supply a different binary function instead.
inner_product()	Similar to accumulate(), but works on two sequences. Calls a binary function (multiplication by default) on parallel elements in the sequences, accumulating the result using another binary function (addition by default). If the sequences represent mathematical vectors, the algorithm calculates the dot product of the vectors.
partial_sum()	Generates a new sequence in which each element is the sum (or other binary operation) of the parallel element, and all preceding elements, in the source sequence.
adjacent_difference()	Generates a new sequence in which each element is the difference (or other binary operation) of the parallel element, and its predecessor, in the source sequence.

Comparison Algorithms

The following comparison algorithms are provided. None of them require the source sequences to be ordered. All of them have a linear worst case complexity.

ALGORITHM NAME	ALGORITHM SYNOPSIS
equal()	Determines if two sequences are equal by checking if parallel elements are equal or match a predicate.
mismatch()	Returns the first element in each sequence that does not match the element in the same location in the other sequence.
lexicographical_compare()	Compares two sequences to determine their "lexicographical" ordering. Compares each element of the first sequence with its equivalent element in the second. If one element is less than the other, that sequence is lexicographically first. If the elements are equal, compares the next elements in order.

Operational Algorithms

The following operational algorithms are provided. None of them require the source sequences to be ordered. All of them have a linear complexity.

ALGORITHM NAME	ALGORITHM SYNOPSIS
for_each()	Executes a function on each element in the sequence.

Modifying Algorithms

The modifying algorithms modify some or all of the elements in a sequence. Some of them modify elements *in place*, so that the original sequence changes. Others copy the results to a different sequence so that the original sequence is unchanged. All of them have a linear worst case complexity. The following table summarizes the modifying algorithms:

	ALGORITHM NAME	ALGORITHM SYNOPSIS
	transform()	Calls a unary function on each element of a sequence or a binary function on parallel elements of two sequences.
	copy(), copy_backward()	Copies elements from one sequence to another.
C++11	iota()	Sequentially assigns a given value to each element in a sequence and increments the given value after each element assignment.
C++11	copy_if()	Copies elements for which the predicate returns true from one sequence to another.
C++11	copy_n()	Copies n elements from one sequence to another.
C++11	partition_copy()	Copies elements from one sequence to two different sequences. The target sequence is selected based on the result of a predicate, either true or false.
C++11	move()	Moves elements from one sequence to another. This uses the efficient move semantics introduced by C++11.
C++11	move_backward()	Moves elements from one sequence to another starting with the last element. This uses the efficient move semantics introduced by C++11.
	iter_swap(), swap_ranges()	Swaps two elements or sequences of elements.
	replace(), replace_if()	Replaces all elements matching a value or that cause a predicate to return true with a new element.
	replace_copy(), replace_copy_if()	Replaces all elements matching a value or that cause a predicate to return true with a new element, by copying results to a new sequence.

continues

(continued)

ALGORITHM NAME	ALGORITHM SYNOPSIS
`fill()`	Sets all elements in the sequence to a new value.
`fill_n()`	Sets the first n elements in the sequence to a new value.
`generate()`	Calls a specified function to generate a new value and sets all elements in the sequence to the result of that function.
`generate_n()`	Calls a specified function to generate a new value and sets the first n elements in the sequence to the result of that function.
`remove()`, `remove_if()`	Removes elements that match a given value or that cause a predicate to return `true`.
`remove_copy()`, `remove_copy_if()`	Removes elements that match a given value or that cause a predicate to return `true`, by copying results to a different sequence.
`unique()`, `unique_copy()`	Removes consecutive duplicates from the sequence, either in place or by copying results to a different sequence.
`reverse()`, `reverse_copy()`	Reverses the order of the elements in the sequence, either in place or by copying the results to a different sequence.
`rotate()`, `rotate_copy()`	Swaps the first and second "halves" of the sequence, either in place or by copying the results to a different sequence. The two subsequences to be swapped need not be equal in size.
`next_permutation()`, `prev_permutation()`	Modifies the sequence by transforming it into its "next" or "previous" permutation. Successive calls to one or the other will permute the sequence into all possible permutations of its elements. Returns `false` if no more permutations exist.

Sorting Algorithms

Sorting algorithms are a special category of modifying algorithms that sort the elements of a sequence. The STL provides several different sorting algorithms with varying performance guarantees.

ALGORITHM NAME	ALGORITHM SYNOPSIS	COMPLEXITY
`sort()`, `stable_sort()`	Sorts elements in place, either preserving the order of duplicate elements or not.	Linear Logarithmic
`partial_sort()`, `partial_sort_copy()`	Partially sorts the sequence: The first n elements (specified by iterators) are sorted; the rest are not. They are sorted either in place or by copying them to a new sequence.	Linear Logarithmic

ALGORITHM NAME	ALGORITHM SYNOPSIS	COMPLEXITY
nth_element()	Relocates the *n*th element of the sequence such that the element in the position pointed to by *n*th is the element that would be in that position if the whole range were sorted.	Linear
merge()	Merges two sorted sequences by copying them to a new sequence.	Linear
inplace_merge()	Merges two sorted sequences in place.	Linear Logarithmic
make_heap(), is_heap(), is_heap_until()	A *heap* is a standard data structure in which the elements of an array or sequence are ordered in a semi-sorted fashion so that finding the "top" element is quick. Six algorithms allow you to use heap-sort on sequences. is_heap() and is_heap_until() are new since C++11.	Linear
push_heap(), pop_heap()	See previous row.	Logarithmic
sort_heap()	See previous row.	Linear Logarithmic
partition()	Sorts the sequence such that all elements for which a predicate returns true are before all elements for which it returns false, without preserving the original order of the elements within each partition.	Linear
stable_partition()	Sorts the sequence such that all elements for which a predicate returns true are before all elements for which it returns false, while preserving the original order of the elements within each partition.	Linear Logarithmic
random_shuffle()	"Unsorts" the sequence by randomly reordering the elements. In C++11, it is possible to specify the properties of the random number generator used for this.	Linear
is_sorted(), is_sorted_until()	Checks if a sequence is sorted or which subsequence is sorted.	Linear

C++11

Set Algorithms

Set algorithms are special modifying algorithms that perform set operations on sequences. They are most appropriate on sequences from `set` containers, but work on sorted sequences from most containers. All of them have a linear worst case complexity.

ALGORITHM NAME	ALGORITHM SYNOPSIS
`includes()`	Determines if every element from one sequence is in another sequence.
`set_union()`, `set_intersection()`, `set_difference()`, `set_symmetric_difference()`	Performs the specified set operation on two sorted sequences, copying results to a third sorted sequence. See Chapter 13 for an explanation of the set operations.

Choosing an Algorithm

The number and capabilities of the algorithms might overwhelm you at first. It can also be difficult to see how to apply them in the beginning. However, now that you have an idea of the available options, you are better able to tackle your program designs. The next chapters cover the details of how to use these algorithms in your code.

What's Missing from the STL

The STL is powerful, but it's not perfect. Here is a list of omissions and unsupported functionality:

➤ The STL does not guarantee any thread safety for accessing containers simultaneously from multiple threads.

➤ The STL does not provide any generic tree or graph structures. Although `maps` and `sets` are generally implemented as balanced binary trees, the STL does not expose this implementation in the interface. If you need a tree or graph structure for something like writing a parser, you will need to implement your own or find an implementation in another library.

However, it is important to keep in mind that the STL is *extensible*. You can write your own containers or algorithms that will work with existing algorithms or containers. So, if the STL doesn't provide exactly what you need, consider writing your desired code such that it works with the STL. Chapter 17 covers the topic of customizing and extending the STL.

SUMMARY

This chapter provided an overview of the C++ standard library, which is the most important library that you will use in your code. It subsumes the C library and includes additional facilities for strings, I/O, error handling, and other tasks. It also includes generic containers and algorithms, which are together referred to as the standard template library (STL). The next chapters describe the standard template library in more detail.

12

Understanding Containers and Iterators

WHAT'S IN THIS CHAPTER?

➤   What iterators are

➤   What the different container classes are and how to use them

Chapter 11 introduced the STL, described its basic philosophy, and provided an overview of the various containers and algorithms. You should be familiar with Chapter 11 before you tackle Chapter 12.

This chapter begins a tour of the STL by covering the STL containers, including the following:

➤   **Containers Overview:** requirements on elements, general error handling, and iterators

➤   **Sequential Containers:** `vector`, `deque`, `list`, `array`, and `forward_list`

➤   **Container Adapters:** `queue`, `priority_queue`, and `stack`

➤   **Associative Containers:** the `pair` utility, `map`, `multimap`, `set`, and `multiset`

➤   **Unordered Associative Containers/Hash Tables:** `unordered_map`, `unordered_multimap`, `unordered_set`, and `unordered_multiset`

➤   **Other Containers:** standard C-style arrays, `strings`, streams, and `bitset`

A detailed list of available classes and methods can be found in the Standard Library Reference resource on the website.

The next chapters will go deeper in on topics like algorithms, strings, regular expressions, I/O and how you can customize and extend the STL.

CONTAINERS OVERVIEW

Containers in the STL are generic data structures useful for storing collections of data. You should rarely need to use a standard C-style array, write a linked list, or design a stack when you use the STL. The containers are implemented as templates, which allow you to instantiate them for any type that meets certain basic conditions outlined below. Most of the STL containers, except for the `std::array` and `std::bitset`, are flexible in size and will automatically grow or shrink to accommodate more or fewer elements. This is a huge benefit compared to the old standard C-style arrays, which had a fixed size. Because of the fixed-size nature of standard C-style arrays, they are more vulnerable to overruns, which in the simplest cases merely cause the program to crash because data has been corrupted, but in the worst cases allow certain kinds of security attacks. By using STL containers your programs will be less vulnerable to these kinds of problems.

The STL provides 17 containers, divided into five categories.

➤ **Sequential containers:**

    ➤ `vector` (dynamic array)

    ➤ `list`

    ➤ `deque`

    ➤ `array`

    ➤ `forward_list`

➤ **Associative containers:**

    ➤ `map`

    ➤ `multimap`

    ➤ `set`

    ➤ `multiset`

➤ **Unordered associative containers or hash tables:**

    ➤ `unordered_map`

    ➤ `unordered_multimap`

    ➤ `unordered_set`

    ➤ `unordered_multiset`

➤ **Container adapters:**

    ➤ `queue`

    ➤ `priority_queue`

    ➤ `stack`

➤ **bitset**

Additionally, C++ `strings`, and streams can also be used as STL containers to a certain degree.

Everything in the STL is in the `std` namespace. The examples in this book usually use the blanket `using namespace std;` statement in source files (never use this in header files!), but you can be more selective in your own programs about which symbols from `std` to use.

Requirements on Elements

STL containers use *value semantics* on elements. That is, they store a copy of the element that they are given, and return copies of elements when requested. They also assign to elements with the assignment operator and destroy elements with the destructor. Thus, when you write classes that you intend to use with the STL, make sure that it's okay to have multiple copies of an object in the program at the same time.

If you prefer reference semantics, you must implement them yourself by storing pointers to elements instead of the elements themselves. When the containers copy a pointer, the result still refers to the same element.

 If you store pointers in containers, we recommend using reference-counted smart pointers in order to handle the memory management properly. If you use C++11, you can use the new `shared_ptr` *reference counted smart pointer. It's more difficult if your compiler does not yet support* `shared_ptr`. *You cannot use the C++* `auto_ptr` *class in containers because it does not implement copying correctly (as far as the STL is concerned). See Chapter 21 for a* `SuperSmartPointer` *class that you can use in the STL containers without C++11 support.*

The specific requirements on elements in containers are shown in the following table:

METHOD	DESCRIPTION	NOTES
Copy Constructor	Creates a new element that is "equal" to the old one, but that can safely be destructed without affecting the old one	Used every time you insert an element
Move Constructor	Creates a new element by moving all content from a source element to the new element	Used when the source element will be destroyed after the construction of the new element
Assignment Operator	Replaces the contents of an element with a copy of the source element	Used every time you modify an element
Move Assignment Operator	Replaces the contents of an element by moving all content from a source element	Used when the source element will be destroyed after the assignment operation

C++11 (Move Constructor)

C++11 (Move Assignment Operator)

continues

(continued)

METHOD	DESCRIPTION	NOTES
Destructor	Cleans up an element	Used every time you remove an element
Default Constructor	Constructs an element without any arguments	Required only for certain operations, such as the `vector` `resize()` method and the `map` `operator[]` access
`operator==`	Compares two elements for equality	Required only for certain operations, such as `operator==` on two containers
`operator<`	Determines if one element is less than another	Required for keys in associative containers and for certain operations, such as `operator<` on two containers

Chapter 7 shows you how to write these methods. C++11 move semantics is discussed in Chapter 9.

 The STL containers call the copy constructor and assignment operator for elements often, so make those operations efficient. With C++11 it can be made much more efficient by implementing move semantics for your elements, as described in Chapter 9.

Exceptions and Error Checking

The STL containers provide limited error checking. Clients are expected to ensure that their uses are valid. However, some container methods and functions throw exceptions in certain conditions such as out-of-bounds indexing. This chapter mentions exceptions where appropriate. The Standard Library Reference resource on the website attempts to catalog the possible exceptions thrown from each method. However, it is impossible to list exhaustively the exceptions that can be thrown from these methods because they perform operations on user-specified types with unknown exception characteristics.

Iterators

The STL uses the iterator pattern to provide a generic abstraction for accessing the elements of the containers. Each container provides a container-specific iterator, which is a glorified smart pointer that knows how to iterate over the elements of that specific container. The iterators for all the different containers adhere to a specific interface defined in the C++ standard. Thus, even though the containers provide different functionality, the iterators present a common interface to code that wishes to work with elements of the containers.

You can think of an iterator as a pointer to a specific element of the container. Like pointers to elements in an array, iterators can move to the next element with `operator++`. Similarly, you can usually use `operator*` and `operator->` on the iterator to access the actual element or field of the element. Some iterators allow comparison with `operator==` and `operator!=`, and support `operator--` for moving to previous elements. Different containers provide iterators with slightly different capabilities. The standard defines five categories of iterators, summarized in the following table.

ITERATOR CATEGORY	OPERATIONS REQUIRED	COMMENTS

Read (officially called "input" iterator)	`operator++`
	`operator*`
	`operator->`
	copy constructor
	`operator=`
	`operator==`
	`operator!=`
		Provides read-only access, forward-only (no `operator--` to move backward).
		Iterators can be assigned and copied with assignment operator and copy constructor.
		Iterators can be compared for equality.

Write (officially called "output" iterator)	`operator++`
	`operator*`
	copy constructor
		Provides write-only access, forward only.
		Iterators cannot be assigned.
		Iterators cannot be compared for equality.
		Note the absence of `operator->`.

Forward	`operator++`
	`operator*`
	`operator->`
	copy constructor
	default constructor
	`operator=`
	`operator==`
	`operator!=`
		Provides read/write access, forward only.
		Iterators can be assigned and copied with assignment operator and copy constructor.
		Iterators can be compared for equality.

Bidirectional	Capabilities of forward iterators, plus: `operator--`	Provides everything forward iterator provides. Iterators can also move backward to previous element.

Random Access	Bidirectional capability, plus:
	`operator+`
	`operator-`
	`operator+=`
	`operator-=`
	`operator<`
	`operator>`
	`operator<=`
	`operator>=`
	`operator[]`
		Equivalent to dumb pointers: Iterators support pointer arithmetic, array index syntax, and all forms of comparison.

The standard containers that provide iterators all furnish either random access or bidirectional iterators.

Iterators are implemented similarly to smart pointer classes in that they overload the specific desired operators. Consult Chapter 18 for details on operator overloading. See Chapter 17 for a sample iterator implementation.

The basic iterator operations are similar to those supported by dumb pointers, so a dumb pointer is a legitimate iterator for certain containers. In fact, the `vector` iterator is often implemented as simply a dumb pointer. However, as a client of the containers, you need not worry about the implementation details; you can simply use the iterator abstraction.

> *Iterators might not be implemented internally as pointers, so this text uses the term "refers to" instead of "points to" when discussing the elements accessible via an iterator.*

Chapters 13 and 17 delve into more detail about iterators and the STL algorithms that use them. This chapter shows you the basics of using the iterators for each container.

> *Only the sequential containers, associative containers, and unordered associative containers provide iterators. The container adapters and* `bitset` *class do not support iteration over their elements.*

Common Iterator typedefs and Methods

Every container class in the STL that supports iterators provides public `typedefs` for its iterator types called `iterator` and `const_iterator`. Containers that allow you to iterate over its elements in reverse order also provide public `typedefs` called `reverse_iterator` and `const_reverse_iterator`. This way, clients can use the container iterators without worrying about the actual types.

> `const_iterators` *and* `const_reverse_iterators` *provide read-only access to elements of the container.*

The containers also provide a method `begin()` that returns an iterator referring to the first element in the container. The `end()` method returns a reference to the "past-the-end" value of the sequence of elements. That is, `end()` returns an iterator that is equal to the result of applying `operator++` to an iterator referring to the last element in the sequence. Together `begin()` and `end()` provide a *half-open range* that includes the first element but not the last. The reason for this apparent complication is to support empty ranges (containers without any elements), in which case `begin()` is equal to `end()`. The half-open range bounded by iterators `begin()` and `end()` is often written mathematically like this: [begin,end).

Similarly, there are `rbegin()` and `rend()` methods for working with reverse iterators.

 The half-open range concept also applies to iterator ranges that are passed to container methods such as `insert()` and `erase()`. See the specific container descriptions later in this chapter for details.

C++11 C++11 Changes

C++11 introduces several changes to the STL containers. One change is the introduction of the unordered associative containers, also called hash tables, which are discussed later in this chapter.

Other changes are performance related. All STL containers now implement move semantics by including a move constructor and move assignment operator. These use rvalue references as described in Chapter 9. A big benefit of this is that we can easily return an STL container from a function *by value* without performance degradation. Take a look at the following function:

Available for download on Wrox.com

```cpp
vector<int> createVectorOfSize(size_t size)
{
    vector<int> vec(size);
    int contents = 0;
    for (auto& i : vec)
        i = contents++;
    return vec;
}
```

Code snippet from CreateVectorOfSize\CreateVectorOfSize.cpp

Without move semantics, the preceding function will create a local `vector` called `vec`. The return statement will then make a *copy* of `vec` and return it from the function. With the C++11 move semantics support in the STL containers, this copying of the `vector` is avoided. Instead, the return statement will *move* the `vector`. Moving is possible in this case because `vec` will go out of scope.

Similarly, push operations can also make use of move semantics to improve performance in certain situations. For example, suppose you have a `vector` of elements of type `Element` as follows:

Available for download on Wrox.com

```cpp
class Element
{
    public:
        Element(int i, string str) : mI(i), mStr(str) {}
    protected:
        int mI;
        string mStr;
};
```

```
int main()
{
    vector<Element> vec;
    return 0;
}
```

Adding an element to this `vector` can be done as follows:

```
Element myElement(12, "Twelve");
vec.push_back(myElement);
```

However, since `myElement` is not a temporary object, the `push_back()` call will make a copy of `myElement` and put it in the `vector`. This copying can be avoided if you call the `push_back()` method as follows:

```
vec.push_back(Element(12, "Twelve"));
```

The `vector` class defines a `push_back(T&& val)` which is the move equivalent of `push_back(const T& val)`. The preceding call to `vec.push_back()` will trigger a call to the move version because the call to the `Element` constructor results in a temporary object. The `push_back()` method will move this temporary `Element` object into the `vector`, avoiding any copying.

Using C++11 uniform initialization (Chapter 9), the preceding can also be written as follows:

```
vec.push_back({12, "Twelve"});
```

In addition, C++11 adds support for *emplace* operations on most STL containers. Emplace means "to put into place." An example is `emplace_back()` on a `vector` object, which does not copy or move anything. Instead, it makes space in the container and constructs the object *in place*. Following is an example.

```
vec.emplace_back(12, "Twelve");
```

The emplace methods take a variable number of arguments as a variadic template. Variadic templates are discussed in Chapter 20. The difference in performance between `emplace_back()` and `push_back()` using move semantics depends on how your specific compiler implements these operations. In most situations you can pick the one based on the syntax that you prefer.

```
vec.push_back({12, "Twelve"});
// Or
vec.emplace_back(12, "Twelve");
```

SEQUENTIAL CONTAINERS

The `vector`, `deque`, `list`, `array`, and `forward_list` are called the *sequential containers*. The best way to learn about the sequential containers is to jump in with an example of the `vector`, which is the container most commonly used. The next section describes the `vector` in detail as an example of a sequential container, followed by briefer descriptions of the `deque`, `list`, `array`, and `forward_list`. Once you become familiar with the sequential containers, it's trivial to switch between them.

vector

The STL `vector` is similar to a standard C-style array: The elements are stored in contiguous memory, each in its own "slot." You can index into the `vector`, as well as add new elements to the back or insert them anywhere else. Inserting and deleting elements into and from the `vector` generally takes linear time, though these operations actually run in *amortized constant* time at the end of the `vector`, explained in the section "The `vector` Memory Allocation Scheme" later in this chapter. Random access of individual elements has a constant complexity.

vector Overview

The `vector` is defined in the `<vector>` header file as a class template with two type parameters: the element type to store and an *allocator* type.

```
template <class T, class Allocator = allocator<T> > class vector;
```

The `Allocator` parameter specifies the type for a memory allocator object that the client can set in order to use custom memory allocation. This template parameter has a default value.

The default value for the `Allocator` type parameter is sufficient for most applications. Programmers do not usually find it useful to customize allocators, but Chapter 17 provides more details in case you are interested. This chapter assumes that you always use the default allocator.

Fixed-Length vectors

The simplest way to use a `vector` is as a fixed-length array. The `vector` provides a constructor that allows you to specify the number of elements, and provides an overloaded `operator[]` in order to access and modify those elements. The C++ standard states that the result of `operator[]` is undefined when used to access an element outside the `vector` bounds. This means that any compiler can decide how to behave in that case. For example, Microsoft Visual C++ will give a run time error message when your program is compiled in debug mode. In release mode, those checks are disabled for performance reasons. Note that the standard does provide an `at()` method which will perform bounds checking and is discussed later in this chapter.

Like "real" array indexing, the operator[] *on a* vector *does not provide bounds checking.*

For example, here is a small program to "normalize" test scores so that the highest score is set to 100, and all other scores are adjusted accordingly. The program creates a vector of 10 doubles, initializes all elements to 0.0, reads in 10 values from the user, divides each value by the max score (times 100), and prints out the new values. For the sake of brevity, the program forsakes error checking.

Available for download on Wrox.com

```
vector<double> doubleVector(10); // Create a vector of 10 doubles.
// Initialize max to smallest number
double max = numeric_limits<double>::lowest();
for (size_t i = 0; i < 10; i++) {
    doubleVector[i] = 0.0;
}
for (size_t i = 0; i < 10; i++) {
    cout << "Enter score " << i + 1 << ": ";
    cin >> doubleVector[i];
    if (doubleVector[i] > max) {
        max = doubleVector[i];
    }
}
max /= 100.0;
for (size_t i = 0; i < 10; i++) {
    doubleVector[i] /= max;
    cout << doubleVector[i] << " ";
}
```

Code snippet from TestScores\TestScores.cpp

As you can see from this example, you can use a vector just as you would use a standard C-style array.

The operator[] *on a* vector *normally returns a reference to the element, which can be used on the left-hand side of assignment statements. If* operator[] *is called on a* const vector *object, it returns a reference to a* const *element, which cannot be used as the target of an assignment. See Chapter 18 for details on how this trick is implemented.*

Specifying an Initial Element Value

You can specify an initial value for the elements when you create the vector like this:

```
vector<double> doubleVector(10, 0.0); // 10 doubles of value 0.0
// Initialize max to smallest number
double max = numeric_limits<double>::lowest();
// No need to initialize each element: the constructor did it for you.
for (size_t i = 0; i < 10; i++) {
    cout << "Enter score " << i + 1 << ": ";
    cin >> doubleVector[i];
    if (doubleVector[i] > max) {
        max = doubleVector[i];
    }
}
max /= 100.0;
for (size_t i = 0; i < 10; i++) {
    doubleVector[i] /= max;
    cout << doubleVector[i] << " ";
}
```

Code snippet from TestScores\TestScoresInitialElem.cpp

Other vector Element Access Methods

In addition to using `operator[]`, you can access `vector` elements via `at()`, `front()`, and `back()`. The `at()` method is identical to `operator[]`, except that it performs bounds checking, and throws an `out_of_range` exception if the index is out of bounds. `front()` and `back()` return the references to the first and last elements of the `vector`, respectively.

All vector element accesses run in constant complexity.

Dynamic-Length vectors

The real power of the `vector` lies in its ability to grow dynamically. For example, consider the test score normalization program from the previous section with the additional requirement that it should handle any number of test scores. Here is the new version:

```
vector<double> doubleVector; // Create a vector with zero elements.
// Initialize max to smallest number
double max = numeric_limits<double>::lowest();
for (size_t i = 0; true; i++) {
    double temp;
    cout << "Enter score " << i + 1 << " (-1 to stop): ";
    cin >> temp;
    if (temp == -1) {
        break;
    }
    doubleVector.push_back(temp);
    if (temp > max) {
        max = temp;
    }
}
```

```
max /= 100.0;
for (size_t i = 0; i < doubleVector.size(); i++) {
    doubleVector[i] /= max;
    cout << doubleVector[i] << " ";
}
```

Code snippet from TestScores\TestScoresDynamic.cpp

This version of the program uses the default constructor to create a vector with zero elements. As each score is read, it's added to the vector with the push_back() method, which takes care of allocating space for the new element. Note that the last for loop uses the size() method on the vector to determine the number of elements in the container. size() returns an unsigned integer, so the type of i size_t.

vector Details

Now that you've had a taste of vectors, it's time to delve into their details.

Constructors and Destructors

The default constructor creates a vector with 0 elements.

```
vector<int> intVector; // Creates a vector of ints with zero elements
```

Code snippet from VectorCtors\DefaultCtor.cpp

As you've already seen, you can specify a number of elements and, optionally, a value for those elements, like this:

```
vector<int> intVector(10, 100); // Creates vector of 10 ints with value 100
```

Code snippet from VectorCtors\InitialElements.cpp

If you omit the default value, the new objects are zero-initialized. Zero-initialization constructs objects with the default constructor and initializes primitive integer types (such as char, int, etc.) to 0 and primitive floating point types to 0.0.

You can also create vectors of built-in classes like this:

```
vector<string> stringVector(10, "hello");
```

Code snippet from VectorCtors\BuiltInClasses.cpp

User-defined classes can also be used as vector elements:

```
class Element
{
    public:
        Element() {}
        virtual ~Element() {}
};
```

```
int main()
{
    vector<Element> elementVector;
    return 0;
}
```

C++11 adds a new constructor to the `vector` class that accepts an `initializer_list` that contains the initial elements for the `vector`. It can be used as follows:

```
vector<int> intVector({1,2,3,4,5,6});
```

`initializer_lists` can also be used for so-called *uniform initialization* as discussed in Chapter 9. Uniform initialization works on most STL containers. For example, the following code demonstrates this for a `vector`:

```
vector<int> intVector = {1,2,3,4,5,6};
```

The `vector` stores copies of the objects, and its destructor calls the destructor for each of the objects.

You can allocate `vectors` on the heap as well:

```
vector<Element>* elementVector = new vector<Element>(10);
delete elementVector;
```

Remember to call `delete` when you are finished with a `vector` that you allocated with `new` or better yet, use a smart pointer to automatically deallocate the `vector` as follows:

```
shared_ptr<vector<Element>> elementVector(new vector<Element>(10));
```

 Use `delete`, *not* `delete[]`, *to free* `vectors`, *because a* `vector` *is a basic type and not an array type.*

Copying and Assigning vectors

The copy constructor and assignment operator for the `vector` class perform deep copies of all the elements in the `vector`. Thus, for efficiency, you should pass `vector`s by reference or `const` reference to functions and methods. Consult Chapter 19 for the details on writing functions that take template instantiations as parameters.

In addition to normal copying and assignment, `vector`s provide an `assign()` method that removes all the current elements and adds any number of new elements. This method is useful if you want to reuse a `vector`. Here is a trivial example. `intVector` is created with 10 elements with value 0. Then `assign()` is used to remove all 10 elements and replace them with 5 elements with value 100.

```
vector<int> intVector(10, 0);
// Other code . . .
intVector.assign(5, 100);
```

Code snippet from VectorCopyAssign\demo.cpp

With C++11, `assign()` can also accept an `initializer_list` as follows. `intVector` will now have 4 elements with the given values.

```
intVector.assign({1, 2, 3, 4});
```

Code snippet from VectorCopyAssign\demo.cpp

`vector`s also provide a `swap()` method that allows you to swap the contents of two `vector`s. Here is a simple example:

```
vector<int> vectorOne(10, 0);
vector<int> vectorTwo(5, 100);
vectorOne.swap(vectorTwo);
// vectorOne now has 5 elements with the value 100.
// vectorTwo now has 10 elements with the value 0.
```

Code snippet from VectorCopyAssign\demo.cpp

Comparing vectors

The STL provides the usual six overloaded comparison operators for `vector`s: `==`, `!=`, `<`, `>`, `<=`, `>=`. Two `vector`s are equal if they have the same number of elements and all the corresponding elements in the two `vector`s are equal to each other. One `vector` is "less than" another if all elements 0 through $i-1$ in the first `vector` are equal to 0 through $i-1$ in the second `vector`, but element i in the first is less than element i in the second, where i must be in the range $0 \ldots n$ and n must be `<= size()-1`.

> *Comparing two* vectors *with* operator== *or* operator!= *requires the individual elements to be comparable with* operator==. *Comparing two vectors with* operator<, operator>, operator<=, *or* operator>= *requires the individual elements to be comparable with* operator<. *If you intend to store objects of a custom class in a* vector, *make sure to write those operators.*

Here is an example of a simple program that compares vectors of ints:

```cpp
vector<int> vectorOne(10, 0);
vector<int> vectorTwo(10, 0);
if (vectorOne == vectorTwo) {
    cout << "equal!" << endl;
} else {
    cout << "not equal!" << endl;
}
vectorOne[3] = 50;
if (vectorOne < vectorTwo) {
    cout << "vectorOne is less than vectorTwo" << endl;
} else {
    cout << "vectorOne is not less than vectorTwo" << endl;
}
```

Code snippet from VectorCompare\compare.cpp

The output of the program is:

```
equal!
vectorOne is not less than vectorTwo
```

vector Iterators

The section on "Iterators" at the beginning of this chapter explained the basics of container iterators. The discussion can get a bit abstract, so it's helpful to jump in and look at a code example. Here is the test score normalization program from earlier with the for loop previously using size() replaced by a for loop using an iterator:

```cpp
vector<double> doubleVector;
// Initialize max to smallest number
double max = numeric_limits<double>::lowest();
for (size_t i = 0; true; i++) {
    double temp;
    cout << "Enter score " << i + 1 << " (-1 to stop): ";
    cin >> temp;
    if (temp == -1) {
        break;
    }
    doubleVector.push_back(temp);
    if (temp > max) {
```

```
            max = temp;
        }
    }
    max /= 100.0;
    for (vector<double>::iterator iter = doubleVector.begin();
        iter != doubleVector.end(); ++iter) {
        *iter /= max;
        cout << *iter << " ";
    }
```

Code snippet from TestScores\TestScoresIterator.cpp

You see `for` loops like the new one in this example quite a bit in STL code. First, take a look at the `for` loop initialization statement:

```
vector<double>::iterator iter = doubleVector.begin();
```

Recall that every container defines a type named `iterator` to represent iterators for that type of container. `begin()` returns an iterator of that type referring to the first element in the container. Thus, the initialization statement obtains in the variable `iter` an iterator referring to the first element of `doubleVector`. Next, look at the `for` loop comparison:

```
iter != doubleVector.end();
```

This statement simply checks if the iterator is past the end of the sequence of elements in the `vector`. When it reaches that point, the loop terminates. The increment statement, `++iter`, increments the iterator to refer to the next element in the `vector`.

 Use preincrement instead of postincrement when possible because preincrement is at least as efficient, and usually more efficient. `iter++` *must return a new iterator object, while* `++iter` *can simply return a reference to* `iter`. *See Chapter 18 for details on implementing* `operator++`, *and Chapter 17 for details on writing your own iterators.*

The `for` loop body contains these two lines:

```
*iter /= max;
cout << *iter << " ";
```

As you can see, your code can both access and modify the elements over which it iterates. The first line uses `*` to dereference `iter` to obtain the element to which it refers, and assigns to that element. The second line dereferences `iter` again, but this time only to stream the element to `cout`.

With C++11, the syntax of the preceding `for` loop using iterators can be simplified by using the `auto` keyword introduced in Chapter 1. This is shown in the following code fragment:

```
for (auto iter = doubleVector.begin();
     iter != doubleVector.end(); ++iter) {
    *iter /= max;
    cout << *iter << " ";
}
```

Code snippet from TestScores\TestScoresIterator.cpp

In this example, the compiler will automatically derive the type of the variable iter based on the right-hand side of the initializer, which in this case is the result of the call to begin().

Using the *range-based* for loop of C++11, the loop can be simplified even further. The *range-based* for loop is introduced in Chapter 1. The following code does exactly the same as the previous implementations of the loop:

```
for (auto& d : doubleVector) {
    d /= max;
    cout << d << " ";
}
```

Code snippet from TestScores\TestScoresIterator.cpp

This looks much more elegant than the other versions of the loop.

Accessing Fields of Object Elements

If the elements of your container are objects, you can use the -> operator on iterators to call methods or access members of those objects. For example, the following small program creates a vector of 10 strings, then iterates over all of them appending a new string to the old one:

```
vector<string> stringVector(10, "hello");
for (auto it = stringVector.begin(); it != stringVector.end(); ++it) {
    it->append(" there");
}
```

Code snippet from VectorIterators\AccessingFields.cpp

Or, using the *range-based* for loop, it can be written as follows:

```
vector<string> stringVector(10, "hello");
for (auto& str : stringVector) {
    str.append(" there");
}
```

Code snippet from VectorIterators\AccessingFields.cpp

const_iterator

The normal iterator is read/write. However, if you call begin() and end() on a const object, you receive a const_iterator. The const_iterator is read-only; you cannot modify the elements. An `iterator` can always be converted to a `const_iterator`, so it's always safe to write something like this:

```
vector<type>::const_iterator it = myVector.begin();
```

However, a `const_iterator` cannot be converted to an `iterator`. If `myVector` is `const`, the following line doesn't compile:

```
vector<type>::iterator it = myVector.begin();
```

 If you do not need to modify the elements of a `vector`, you should use a `const_iterator`. This rule will make it easier to guarantee correctness of your code and allows compilers to perform certain optimizations.

When using the `auto` keyword of C++11, using `const_iterators` looks a bit different. Suppose you write the following code:

```
vector<string> stringVector(10, "hello");
for (auto iter = stringVector.begin();
    iter != stringVector.end(); ++iter) {
    cout << *iter << endl;
}
```

Because of the `auto` keyword, the compiler will decide the type of the `iter` variable automatically and will make it a normal `iterator`, meaning that you can read and write to the iterator. If you want a read-only `const_iterator` in combination with using `auto`, then you need to use `cbegin()` and `cend()` instead of the normal `begin()` and `end()` as follows:

Available for
download on
Wrox.com

```
vector<string> stringVector(10, "hello");
for (auto iter = stringVector.cbegin();
    iter != stringVector.cend(); ++iter) {
    cout << *iter << endl;
}
```

Code snippet from VectorIterators\ConstIterator.cpp

Now the compiler will use the `const_iterator` as type for the variable `iter` because that's what `cbegin()` returns.

Iterator Safety

Generally, iterators are about as safe as pointers: extremely insecure. For example, you can write code like this:

```
vector<int> intVector;
auto it = intVector.end();
*it = 10; // BUG! it doesn't refer to a valid element.
```

Code snippet from VectorIterators\IteratorSafety.cpp

Recall that the iterator returned by `end()` is past the end of the `vector`. Trying to dereference it results in undefined behavior. However, the iterators themselves are not required to perform any verification.

 Remember that `end()` *returns an iterator past the end of the container, not the iterator referring to the last element of the container.*

Another problem can occur if you use mismatched iterators. For example, the following code initializes an iterator from `vectorTwo` and tries to compare it to the end iterator for `vectorOne`. Needless to say, this loop will not do what you intended, and may never terminate. Dereferencing the iterator in the loop will likely produce undefined results.

```
vector<int> vectorOne(10);
vector<int> vectorTwo(10);
// Fill in the vectors.
// BUG! Infinite loop
for (auto it = vectorTwo.begin(); it != vectorOne.end(); ++it) {
    // Loop body
}
```

Code snippet from VectorIterators\IteratorSafety.cpp

 Some C++ runtimes, for example Microsoft Visual C++, will give an assertion error at run time for both of the preceding problems when running a debug build of your program.

Other Iterator Operations

The `vector` iterator is random access, which means that you can move it backward or forward, or jump around. For example, the following code eventually changes the fifth element (index 4) in the `vector` to the value 4:

```
vector<int> intVector(10, 0);
auto it = intVector.begin();
it += 5;
--it;
*it = 4;
```

Code snippet from VectorIterators\IteratorOps.cpp

Iterators versus Indexing

Given that you can write a `for` loop that uses a simple index variable and the `size()` method to iterate over the elements of the `vector`, why should you bother using iterators? That's a valid question, for which there are three main answers:

➤ Iterators allow you to insert and delete elements and sequences of elements at any point in the container. See the following "Adding and Removing Elements" section.

➤ Iterators allow you to use the STL algorithms, which are discussed in Chapter 13.

➤ Using an iterator to access each element sequentially is often more efficient than indexing the container to retrieve each element individually. This generalization is not true for `vectors`, but applies to `lists`, `maps`, and `sets`.

Adding and Removing Elements

As you have already read, you can append an element to a `vector` with the `push_back()` method. The `vector` provides a parallel remove method called `pop_back()`.

> `pop_back()` *does not return the element that it removed. If you want the element you must first retrieve it with* `back()`.

You can also insert elements at any point in the `vector` with the `insert()` method, which adds one or more elements to a position specified by an iterator, shifting all subsequent elements down to make room for the new ones. There are three different overloaded forms of `insert()`: one that inserts a single element, one that inserts n copies of a single element, and one that inserts elements from an iterator range. Recall that the iterator range is half-open, such that it includes the element referred to by the starting iterator but not the one referred to by the ending iterator. C++11 adds two more `insert()` overloads: one that inserts a single element by *moving* the given element to the `vector` using *move semantics,* and another one that inserts a list of elements into the `vector` where the list of elements is given as an `initializer_list`. The `initializer_list` feature is discussed in Chapter 9.

> `push_back()` *and* `insert()` *take* `const` *references to elements, allocate memory as needed to store the new elements, and store copies of the element arguments. C++11 introduces both a* `push_back()` *and an* `insert()` *method that use move semantics to move ownership of the object to the* `vector` *instead of copying the object.*

You can remove elements from any point in the `vector` with `erase()` and you can remove all elements with `clear()`. There are two forms of `erase()`: single element and range specified by an iterator.

If you want to remove a number of elements that satisfy a certain condition, one solution would be to write a loop iterating over all the elements and erasing every element that matches the condition. However, this solution has quadratic complexity, discussed in Chapter 2, which is very bad for performance. In this case, the quadratic complexity can be avoided by using the *remove-erase-idiom*, which has a linear complexity. The remove-erase-idiom is discussed in Chapter 13.

Here is a small program that demonstrates the methods for adding and removing elements. It uses a helper function `printVector()` that prints the contents of the `vector` to `cout`, but whose implementation is not shown here because it uses algorithms covered in the next chapters. The example also includes demonstrations of the following versions of `insert()`:

➤ `insert(const_iterator pos, const T& x);`
  the value x will be inserted at position pos.

➤ `insert(const_iterator pos, size_type n, const T& x);`
  the value x will be inserted n times at position pos.

➤ `insert(const_iterator pos, InputIterator first, InputIterator last);`
  the elements in the range first, last are inserted at position pos.

```cpp
vector<int> vectorOne = {1,2,3,5};
vector<int> vectorTwo;
// Oops, we forgot to add 4. Insert it in the correct place.
vectorOne.insert(vectorOne.begin() + 3, 4);
// Add elements 6 through 10 to vectorTwo.
for (int i = 6; i <= 10; i++) {
    vectorTwo.push_back(i);
}
printVector(vectorOne);
printVector(vectorTwo);
// Add all the elements from vectorTwo to the end of vectorOne.
vectorOne.insert(vectorOne.end(), vectorTwo.begin(), vectorTwo.end());
printVector(vectorOne);
// Now erase the numbers 2 through 5 in vectorOne.
vectorOne.erase(vectorOne.begin() + 1, vectorOne.begin() + 5);
printVector(vectorOne);
// Clear vectorTwo entirely.
vectorTwo.clear();
// And add 10 copies of the value 100.
vectorTwo.insert(vectorTwo.begin(), 10, 100);
// Decide we only want 9 elements.
vectorTwo.pop_back();
printVector(vectorTwo);
```

Code snippet from VectorAddRemove\AddRemove.cpp

The output of the program is:

```
1 2 3 4 5
6 7 8 9 10
1 2 3 4 5 6 7 8 9 10
1 6 7 8 9 10
100 100 100 100 100 100 100 100 100
```

Recall that iterator pairs represent a half-open range, and `insert()` adds elements before the element referred to by the iterator position. Thus, you can insert the entire contents of `vectorTwo` into the end of `vectorOne`, like this:

```
vectorOne.insert(vectorOne.end(), vectorTwo.begin(), vectorTwo.end());
```

Methods such as `insert()` *and* `erase()` *that take a* `vector` *range as arguments assume that the beginning and ending iterators refer to elements in the same container, and that the end iterator refers to an element at or past the begin iterator. The methods will not work correctly if these preconditions are not met!*

Algorithmic Complexity and Iterator Invalidation

Inserting or erasing elements in a `vector` causes all subsequent elements to shift up or down to make room for, or fill in the holes left by, the affected elements. Thus, these operations take linear complexity. Furthermore, all iterators referring to the insertion or removal point or subsequent positions are invalid following the action. The iterators are not "magically" moved to keep up with the elements that are shifted up or down in the `vector`.

Also keep in mind that an internal `vector` reallocation can cause invalidation of all iterators referring to elements in the `vector`, not just those referring to elements past the point of insertion or deletion. See the next section for details.

The vector Memory Allocation Scheme

The `vector` allocates memory automatically to store the elements that you insert. Recall that the `vector` requirements dictate that the elements must be in contiguous memory, like in standard C-style arrays. Because it's impossible to request to add memory to the end of a current chunk of memory, every time the `vector` allocates more memory it must allocate a new, larger, chunk in a separate memory location and copy/move all the elements to the new chunk. This process is time-consuming, so `vector` implementations attempt to avoid it by allocating more space than needed when they have to perform a reallocation. That way, they can avoid reallocating memory every time you insert an element.

One obvious question at this point is why you, as a client of the `vector`, care how it manages its memory internally. You might think that the principle of abstraction should allow you to disregard the internals of the `vector` memory allocation scheme. Unfortunately, there are two reasons why you need to understand how it works:

1. **Efficiency.** The `vector` allocation scheme can guarantee that an element insert runs in *amortized constant time*: Most of the time the operation is constant, but once in a while (if it requires a reallocation), it's linear. If you are worried about efficiency you can control when the `vector` performs reallocations.

2. **Iterator invalidations.** A reallocation invalidates all iterators referring to elements in the `vector`.

Thus, the `vector` interface allows you to query and control the `vector` reallocations. If you don't control the reallocations explicitly, you should assume that all insertions cause a reallocation and thus invalidate all iterators.

Size and Capacity

The `vector` provides two methods for obtaining information about its size: `size()` and `capacity()`. The `size()` method returns the number of elements in the `vector`, while `capacity()` returns the number of elements that it can hold without a reallocation. Thus, the number of elements that you can insert without causing a reallocation is `capacity() - size()`.

You can query whether a `vector` *is empty with the* `empty()` *method. A* `vector` *can be empty but have nonzero capacity.*

Reserving Capacity

If you don't care about efficiency or iterator invalidations, there is never a need to control the `vector` memory allocation explicitly. However, if you want to make your program as efficient as possible, or want to guarantee that iterators will not be invalidated, you can force the `vector` to preallocate enough space to hold all of its elements. Of course, you need to know how many elements it will hold, which is sometimes impossible to predict.

One way to preallocate space is to call `reserve()`. That method allocates enough memory to hold the specified number of elements. The next section shows an example of the `reserve()` method in action.

Reserving space for elements changes the capacity, but not the size. That is, it doesn't actually create elements. Don't access elements past the `vector` *size.*

Another way to preallocate space is to specify, in the constructor or with the `resize()` method, how many elements you want the `vector` to store. This method actually creates a `vector` of that size (and probably of that capacity).

vector Example: A Round-Robin Class

A common problem in computer science is distributing requests among a finite list of resources. For example, a simple operating system could keep a list of processes and assign a time slice (for example 100ms) to each process to let the process perform some of its work. After the time slice is finished, the OS suspends the process and the next process in the list is given a time slice to perform some of its work. One of the simplest algorithmic solutions to this problem is *round-robin scheduling*. When the time slice of the last process is finished, the scheduler starts over again with the first process. For example, in the case of three processes, the first time slice would go to the first process, the second to the second process, the third to the third process, and the fourth back to the first process. The cycle would continue in this way indefinitely.

Suppose that you decide to write a generic round-robin scheduling class that can be used with any type of resource. The class should support adding and removing resources, and should support cycling through the resources in order to obtain the next one. You could use the STL `vector` directly, but it's often helpful to write a wrapper class that provides more directly the functionality you need for your specific application. The following example shows a `RoundRobin` class template with comments explaining the code. This example uses basic functionality of templates. Templates are introduced in Chapter 11 with a `MyArray` class template example. Make sure you understand that section first before continuing with this `RoundRobin` example. Templates are discussed in much more detail in Chapter 19, but for this example, the brief introduction from Chapter 11 is enough to understand it. First, here is the class definition:

```cpp
// Class template RoundRobin
// Provides simple round-robin semantics for a list of elements.
template <typename T>
class RoundRobin
{
    public:
        // Client can give a hint as to the number of expected elements for
        // increased efficiency.
        RoundRobin(int numExpected = 0);
        virtual ~RoundRobin();
        // Appends elem to the end of the list. May be called
        // between calls to getNext().
        void add(const T& elem);
        // Removes the first (and only the first) element
        // in the list that is equal (with operator==) to elem.
        // May be called between calls to getNext().
        void remove(const T& elem);
        // Returns the next element in the list, starting with the first,
        // and cycling back to the first when the end of the list is
        // reached, taking into account elements that are added or removed.
        T& getNext() throw(std::out_of_range);
    protected:
        std::vector<T> mElems;
        typename std::vector<T>::iterator mCurElem;
    private:
        // Prevent assignment and pass-by-value.
        RoundRobin(const RoundRobin& src);
        RoundRobin& operator=(const RoundRobin& rhs);
};
```

Code snippet from RoundRobin\RoundRobin.h

As you can see, the public interface is straightforward: only three methods plus the constructor and destructor. The resources are stored in the `vector` called `mElems`. The iterator `mCurElem` always refers to the next element in `mElems` that should be used in the round-robin scheme. Note the use of the `typename` keyword in front of the line declaring `mCurElem`. So far, you've only seen that keyword used to specify template parameters, but there is another use for it. You must specify `typename` explicitly whenever you access a type based on one or more template parameters. In this case, the template parameter `T` is used to access the `iterator` type. Thus, you must specify `typename`. This is another example of arcane C++ syntax.

The class also prevents assignment and pass-by-value because of the `mCurElem` data member. To make assignment and pass-by-value work you would have to implement an assignment operator and copy constructor and make sure `mCurElem` is valid in the destination object. This is omitted in this example.

The implementation of the `RoundRobin` class follows with comments explaining the code. Note the use of `reserve()` in the constructor, and the extensive use of the iterator in `add()`, `remove()`, and `getNext()`. The trickiest aspect is keeping `mCurElem` valid and referring to the correct element following calls to `add()` or `remove()`.

```cpp
template <typename T>
RoundRobin<T>::RoundRobin(int numExpected)
{
    // If the client gave a guideline, reserve that much space.
    mElems.reserve(numExpected);
    // Initialize mCurElem even though it isn't used until
    // there's at least one element.
    mCurElem = mElems.begin();
}

template <typename T>
RoundRobin<T>::~RoundRobin()
{
    // nothing to do here -- the vector will delete all the elements
}

// Always add the new element at the end
template <typename T>
void RoundRobin<T>::add(const T& elem)
{
    // Even though we add the element at the end, the vector could
    // reallocate and invalidate the iterator with the push_back call.
    // Take advantage of the random access iterator features to save our
    // spot.
    int pos = mCurElem - mElems.begin();
    // add the element
    mElems.push_back(elem);
    // Reset our iterator to make sure it is valid.
    mCurElem = mElems.begin() + pos;
}

template <typename T>
void RoundRobin<T>::remove(const T& elem)
{
    for (auto it = mElems.begin(); it != mElems.end(); ++it) {
        if (*it == elem) {
            // Removing an element will invalidate our mCurElem iterator if
            // it refers to an element past the point of the removal.
            // Take advantage of the random access features of the iterator
```

```
            // to track the position of the current element after removal.
            int newPos;
            // If current iterator is before or at the one we're removing,
            // the new position is the same as before.
            if (mCurElem <= it) {
                newPos = mCurElem - mElems.begin();
            } else {
                // otherwise, it's one less than before
                newPos = mCurElem - mElems.begin() - 1;
            }
            // erase the element (and ignore the return value)
            mElems.erase(it);
            // Now reset our iterator to make sure it is valid.
            mCurElem = mElems.begin() + newPos;
            // If we were pointing to the last element and it was removed,
            // we need to loop back to the first.
            if (mCurElem == mElems.end()) {
                mCurElem = mElems.begin();
            }
            return;
        }
    }
}

template <typename T>
T& RoundRobin<T>::getNext() throw(std::out_of_range)
{
    // First, make sure there are any elements.
    if (mElems.empty()) {
        throw std::out_of_range("No elements in the list");
    }
    // retrieve a reference to return
    T& retVal = *mCurElem;
    // Increment the iterator modulo the number of elements
    ++mCurElem;
    if (mCurElem == mElems.end()) {
        mCurElem = mElems.begin();
    }
    // return the reference
    return retVal;
}
```

Code snippet from RoundRobin\RoundRobin.h

Here's a simple implementation of a scheduler that uses the RoundRobin class template, with comments explaining the code.

```
// Simple Process class.
class Process
{
    public:
        // Constructor accepting the name of the process.
        Process(const string& name) : mName(name) {}
```

```cpp
            // Implementation of doWorkDuringTimeSlice would let the process
            // perform its work for the duration of a time slice.
            // Actual implementation omitted.
            void doWorkDuringTimeSlice() {
                cout << "Process " << mName
                        << " performing work during time slice." << endl;
            }
            // Needed for the RoundRobin::remove method to work.
            bool operator==(const Process& rhs) {
                return mName == rhs.mName;
            }
        protected:
            string mName;
};
// Simple round-robin based process scheduler.
class Scheduler
{
    public:
        // Constructor takes a vector of processes.
        Scheduler(const vector<Process>& processes);
        // Selects the next process using a round-robin scheduling
        // algorithm and allows it to perform some work during
        // this time slice.
        void scheduleTimeSlice();
        // Removes the given process from the list of processes.
        void removeProcess(const Process& process);
    protected:
        RoundRobin<Process> rr;
};

Scheduler::Scheduler(const vector<Process>& processes)
{
    // Add the processes
    for (auto& process : processes) {
        rr.add(process);
    }
}
void Scheduler::scheduleTimeSlice()
{
    try {
        rr.getNext().doWorkDuringTimeSlice();
    } catch (const out_of_range&) {
        cerr << "No more processes to schedule." << endl;
    }
}
void Scheduler::removeProcess(const Process& process)
{
    rr.remove(process);
}
int main()
{
    vector<Process> processes = {Process("1"), Process("2"), Process("3")};
    Scheduler sched(processes);
    for (int i = 0; i < 4; ++i)
```

```
        sched.scheduleTimeSlice();
    sched.removeProcess(processes[1]);
    cout << "Removed second process" << endl;
    for (int i = 0; i < 4; ++i)
        sched.scheduleTimeSlice();
    return 0;
}
```

Code snippet from RoundRobin\RoundRobinTest.cpp

The output should be as follows.

```
Process 1 performing work during time slice.
Process 2 performing work during time slice.
Process 3 performing work during time slice.
Process 1 performing work during time slice.
Removed second process
Process 3 performing work during time slice.
Process 1 performing work during time slice.
Process 3 performing work during time slice.
Process 1 performing work during time slice.
```

The vector<bool> Specialization

The standard requires a partial specialization of vector for bools, with the intention that it optimizes space allocation by "packing" the Boolean values. Recall that a bool is either true or false, and thus could be represented by a single bit, which can take on exactly two values. C++ does not have a native type that stores exactly one bit. Some compilers represent a Boolean value with a type the same size as a char. Some other compilers use an int. The vector<bool> specialization is supposed to store the "array of bools" in single bits, thus saving space.

> *You can think of the* vector<bool> *as a bit-field instead of a* vector. *The* bitset *container described later in this chapter provides a more full-featured bit-field implementation than does* vector<bool>. *However, the benefit of* vector<bool> *is that it can change size dynamically.*

In a half-hearted attempt to provide some bit-field routines for the vector<bool>, there is one additional method: flip(). This method can be called on either the container, in which case it complements all the elements in the container; or on a single reference returned from operator[] or a similar method, in which case it complements that single element.

At this point, you should be wondering how you can call a method on a reference to bool. The answer is that you can't. The vector<bool> specialization actually defines a class called reference that serves as a proxy for the underlying bool (or bit). When you call operator[], at(), or a similar method, the vector<bool> returns a reference object, which is a proxy for the real bool.

> *The fact that references returned from* vector<bool> *are really proxies means that you can't take their addresses to obtain pointers to the actual elements in the container. The* proxy *design pattern is covered in detail in Chapter 29.*

In practice, the little amount of space saved by packing bools hardly seems worth the extra effort. However, you should be familiar with this partial instantiation because of the additional flip() method, and because of the fact that references are actually proxy objects. Many C++ experts recommend avoiding vector<bool> in favor of the bitset, unless you really need a dynamically sized bit-field.

deque

The deque (abbreviation for double-ended queue) is almost identical to the vector, but is used far less frequently. It is defined in the <deque> header file. The principle differences are:

➤ The implementation is not required to store elements contiguously in memory.

➤ The deque supports constant-time insertion and removal of elements at both the front and the back (the vector supports amortized constant time at just the back).

➤ The deque provides push_front() and pop_front(), which the vector omits.

➤ The deque does not expose its memory management scheme via reserve() or capacity().

deques are rarely used, as opposed to vectors and lists. Thus, we leave the details of the deque methods to the Standard Library Reference resource on the website.

list

The STL list, defined in the <list> header file, is a standard doubly linked list. It supports constant-time insertion and deletion of elements at any point in the list, but provides slow (linear) time access to individual elements. In fact, the list does not even provide random access operations like operator[]. Only through iterators can you access individual elements.

Most of the list operations are identical to those of the vector, including the constructors, destructor, copying operations, assignment operations, and comparison operations. This section focuses on those methods that differ from those of vector. Consult the Standard Library Reference resource on the website for details on the list methods not discussed here.

lists also support the C++11 uniform initialization mechanism as shown in the following example:

```
list<string> lst = {"String 1", "String 2", "String 3"};
```

Code snippet from ListUniformInit\ListUniformInit.cpp

Accessing Elements

The only methods provided by the `list` to access elements are `front()` and `back()`, both of which run in constant time. These methods return a reference to the first and last element in the `list`. All other element access must be performed through iterators.

A `list` supports `begin()`, returning an iterator referring to the first element in the `list`, and `end()`, returning an iterator referring to the last element in the `list`.

 Lists do not provide random access to elements.

Iterators

The `list` iterator is bidirectional, not random access like the `vector` iterator. That means that you cannot add and subtract `list` iterators from each other, or perform other pointer arithmetic on them. For example, if `p` is a `list` iterator, you can traverse through the elements of the `list` by doing `++p` or `--p`, but you cannot use the addition or subtraction operator; `p+n` or `p-n` does not work.

Adding and Removing Elements

The `list` supports the same add element and remove element methods like the `vector`, including `push_back()`, `pop_back()`, the five forms of `insert()`, the two forms of `erase()`, and `clear()`. Like the `deque`, it also provides `push_front()` and `pop_front()`. The amazing thing about the `list` is that all these methods (except for `clear()`) run in constant time, once you've found the correct position. Thus, the `list` is appropriate for applications that perform many insertions and deletions from the data structure, but do not need quick index-based element access.

list Size

Like `deques`, and unlike `vectors`, `lists` do not expose their underlying memory model. Consequently, they support `size()`, `empty()` and `resize()`, but not `reserve()` or `capacity()`.

Special list Operations

The `list` provides several special operations that exploit its quick element insertion and deletion. This section provides an overview and examples. The Standard Library Reference resource on the website gives a thorough reference for all the methods.

Splicing

The linked-list characteristics of the `list` class allow it to *splice*, or insert, an entire `list` at any position in another `list` in constant time. The simplest version of this method works as follows:

```
list<string> dictionary, bWords;
// Add the a words.
dictionary.push_back("aardvark");
dictionary.push_back("ambulance");
// Add the c words.
```

```
dictionary.push_back("canticle");
dictionary.push_back("consumerism");
// Create another list, of the b words.
bWords.push_back("bathos");
bWords.push_back("balderdash");
// splice the b words into the main dictionary.
if (bWords.size() > 0) {
    // Get an iterator to the last b word.
    auto iterLastB = --(bWords.cend());
    // Iterate up to the spot where we want to insert bs.
    list<string>::iterator it;
    for (it = dictionary.begin(); it != dictionary.end(); ++it) {
        if (*it > *iterLastB)
            break;
    }
    // Add in the bwords. This action removes the elements from bWords.
    dictionary.splice(it, bWords);
}
// print out the dictionary
for (auto it = dictionary.cbegin(); it != dictionary.cend(); ++it) {
    cout << *it << endl;
}
```

Code snippet from ListSplice\ListSplice.cpp

The result from running this program looks like this:

```
aardvark
ambulance
bathos
balderdash
canticle
consumerism
```

There are also two other forms of `splice()`: one that inserts a single element from another `list` and one that inserts a range from another `list`. See the Standard Library Reference resource on the website for details.

 Splicing is destructive to the `list` passed as a parameter: It removes the spliced elements from one `list` in order to insert them into the other.

More Efficient Versions of Algorithms

In addition to `splice()`, the `list` class provides special implementations of several of the generic STL algorithms. The generic forms are covered in Chapter 13. Here we discuss only the specific versions provided by `list`.

When you have a choice, use the `list` *methods rather than the generic STL algorithms because the former are more efficient.*

The following table summarizes the algorithms for which `list` provides special implementations as methods. See the Standard Library Reference resource on the website and Chapter 13 for prototypes, details on the algorithms, and their specific running time when called on `list`.

METHOD	DESCRIPTION
`remove()` `remove_if()`	Removes certain elements from the `list`.
`unique()`	Removes duplicate consecutive elements from the `list`, based on `operator==` or a user supplied binary predicate.
`merge()`	Merges two `lists`. Both `lists` must be sorted to start, according to `operator<` or a user defined comparator. Like `splice()`, `merge()` is destructive to the `list` passed as an argument.
`sort()`	Performs a stable sort on elements in the `list`.
`reverse()`	Reverses the order of the elements in the `list`.

The following section demonstrates most of these methods.

list Example: Determining Enrollment

Suppose that you are writing a computer registration system for a university. One feature you might provide is the ability to generate a complete list of enrolled students in the university from lists of the students in each class. For the sake of this example, assume that you must write only a single function that takes a `vector` of `lists` of student names (as `strings`), plus a `list` of students that have been dropped from their courses because they failed to pay tuition. This method should generate a complete `list` of all the students in all the courses, without any duplicates, and without those students who have been dropped. Note that students might be in more than one course.

Here is the code for this method, with comments explaining the code. With the power of STL `lists`, the method is practically shorter than its written description! Note that the STL allows you to "nest" containers: In this case, you can use a `vector` of `lists`.

```
// courseStudents is a vector of lists, one for each course. The lists
// contain the students enrolled in those courses. They are not sorted.
//
// droppedStudents is a list of students who failed to pay their
// tuition and so were dropped from their courses.
//
// The function returns a list of every enrolled (non-dropped) student in
// all the courses.
list<string>
```

```
getTotalEnrollment(const vector<list<string>>& courseStudents,
                   const list<string>& droppedStudents)
{
    list<string> allStudents;
    // Concatenate all the course lists onto the master list
    for (auto& lst : courseStudents) {
        allStudents.insert(allStudents.end(), lst.begin(), lst.end());
    }
    // Sort the master list
    allStudents.sort();
    // Remove duplicate student names (those who are in multiple courses).
    allStudents.unique();
    // Remove students who are on the dropped list.
    // Iterate through the drop list, calling remove on the
    // master list for each student in the dropped list.
    for (auto& str : droppedStudents) {
        allStudents.remove(str);
    }
    // done!
    return allStudents;
}
```

Code snippet from StudentEnrollment\Enrollment.cpp

This example is using C++11 *range-based* `for` loops. If your compiler does not yet support those, you can implement the function as follows:

```
list<string>
getTotalEnrollment(const vector<list<string> >& courseStudents,
                   const list<string>& droppedStudents)
{
    list<string> allStudents;
    // Concatenate all the course lists onto the master list
    for (vector<list<string> >::const_iterator it = courseStudents.begin();
        it != courseStudents.end(); ++it) {
        allStudents.insert(allStudents.end(), (*it).begin(), (*it).end());
    }
    // Sort the master list
    allStudents.sort();
    // Remove duplicate student names (those who are in multiple courses).
    allStudents.unique();
    // Remove students who are on the dropped list.
    // Iterate through the drop list, calling remove on the
    // master list for each student in the dropped list.
    for (list<string>::const_iterator it = droppedStudents.begin();
        it != droppedStudents.end(); ++it) {
        allStudents.remove(*it);
    }
    // done!
    return allStudents;
}
```

Code snippet from StudentEnrollment\Enrollment.cpp

C++11 array

The C++11 `std::array` class, defined in the `<array>` header file, is similar to the `vector` except that it is of a fixed size; it cannot grow or shrink in size. The purpose of this is to allow an `array` to be allocated on the stack, rather than always demanding heap access as `vector` does. Just like `vectors`, `arrays` support random access iterators, and elements are stored in contiguous memory. It has support for `front()`, `back()`, `at()` and `operator[]`. It also supports a `fill()` method to fill the `array` with a specific element. Because it is fixed in size, it does not support `push_back()`, `pop_back()`, `insert()`, `erase()`, `clear()`, `resize()`, `reserve()` and `capacity()`. The following small example demonstrates how to use the `array` class. Note that the `array` declaration requires two template parameters; the first specifies the type of the elements, and the second specifies the fixed number of elements in the `array`.

Available for
download on
Wrox.com

```
// Create array of 3 integers and initialize them
// with the given initializer_list using uniform initialization.
array<int, 3> arr = {9, 8, 7};
// Output the size of the array.
cout << "Array size = " << arr.size() << endl;
// Output the contents of the array using iterators.
for (auto iter = arr.cbegin(); iter != arr.cend(); ++iter)
    cout << *iter << endl;

cout << "Performing arr.fill(3)..." << endl;
// Use the fill method to change the contents of the array.
arr.fill(3);
// Output the contents using the range-based for loop.
for (auto& i : arr)
    cout << i << endl;
```

Code snippet from std_array\std_array.cpp

The output of the preceding code is as follows:

```
Array size = 3
9
8
7
Performing arr.fill(3)...
3
3
3
```

C++11 forward_list

The `forward_list` introduced by C++11, defined in the `<forward_list>` header file, is similar to the `list` except that the `forward_list` is a singly linked list while the `list` is a doubly linked list. This means that the `forward_list` supports only forward iteration and because of this, ranges need to be specified differently compared to a `list`. If you want to modify any list, you need access to the element before the first element of interest. Since a `forward_list` does not have an iterator that supports going backward, there is no easy way to get to the preceding element. For this reason, ranges that will be modified, for example ranges supplied to erase and splice, must be open at the beginning. The begin() function seen earlier returns an iterator to the first element and thus can be used only to construct a range that is closed at the beginning. The forward_list class defines a before_begin() method, which returns an iterator that points to an imaginary element before the beginning of the list. You cannot dereference this iterator as it points to invalid data. However, incrementing this iterator by one will make it the same as the iterator returned by begin(); therefore, it can be used to make a range that is open at the beginning. The following table sums up the differences between a list and a forward_list.

OPERATION	list	forward_list
back()	X	
before_begin()		X
begin()	X	X
cbefore_begin()		X
cbegin()	X	X
cend()	X	X
clear()	X	X
crbegin()	X	
crend()	X	
emplace()	X	
emplace_after()		X
emplace_back()	X	
emplace_front()	X	X
empty()	X	X
end()	X	X
erase()	X	
erase_after()		X
front()	X	X
insert()	X	
insert_after()		X
iterator / const_iterator	X	X

continues

(continued)

OPERATION	list	forward_list
merge()	X	X
pop_back()	X	
pop_front()	X	X
push_back()	X	
push_front()	X	X
rbegin()	X	
remove()	X	X
remove_if()	X	X
rend()	X	
resize()	X	X
reverse()	X	X
reverse_iterator / const_reverse_iterator	X	
size()	X	
sort()	X	X
splice()	X	
splice_after()		X
swap()	X	X
unique()	X	X

Constructors and assignment operators are similar between a `list` and a `forward_list`. The standard says that `forward_lists` should try to use minimal space. That's the reason why there is no `size()` method, because by not providing it, there is no need to store the size of the list. The following example demonstrates the use of `forward_lists`:

```cpp
// Create 3 forward lists and use an initializer_list
// to initialize their elements (uniform initialization).
forward_list<int> lst1 = {5,6};
forward_list<int> lst2 = {1,2,3,4};
forward_list<int> lst3 = {7,8,9};
// Insert lst2 at the front of lst1 using splice.
lst1.splice_after(lst1.before_begin(), lst2);
// Add number 0 at the beginning of the lst1.
```

```
lst1.push_front(0);
// Insert lst3 at the end of lst1.
// For this, we first need an iterator to the last element.
auto iter = lst1.before_begin();
auto iterTemp = iter;
while (++iterTemp != lst1.end())
    ++iter;
lst1.insert_after(iter, lst3.begin(), lst3.end());
// Output the contents of lst1.
for (auto& i : lst1)
    cout << i << ' ';
```

Code snippet from ForwardList\forward_list.cpp

To insert lst3, we need an iterator to the last element in the list. However, since this is a forward_list, we cannot use --(lst1.end()), so we need to iterate over the list from the beginning and stop at the last element. The output of this example is as follows:

```
0 1 2 3 4 5 6 7 8 9
```

CONTAINER ADAPTERS

In addition to the standard sequential containers, the STL provides three container adapters: queue, priority_queue, and stack. Each of these adapters is a wrapper around one of the sequential containers. The intent is to simplify the interface and to provide only those features that are appropriate for the stack or queue abstraction. For example, the adapters don't provide iterators or the capability to insert or erase multiple elements simultaneously.

 The container adapters' interfaces may be too limiting for your needs. If so, you can use the sequential containers directly or write your own, more full-featured, adapters. See Chapter 29 for details on the adapter design pattern.

queue

The queue container adapter, defined in the header file <queue>, provides standard "first-in, first-out" (FIFO) semantics. As usual, it's written as a class template, which looks like this:

```
template <class T, class Container = deque<T> > class queue;
```

The T template parameter specifies the type that you intend to store in the queue. The second template parameter allows you to stipulate the underlying container that the queue adapts. However, the queue requires the sequential container to support both push_back() and pop_front(), so you only have two built-in choices: deque and list. For most purposes, you can just stick with the default deque.

queue Operations

The `queue` interface is extremely simple: There are only eight methods plus the constructor and the normal comparison operators. The `push()` and `emplace()` methods add a new element to the tail of the queue, and `pop()` removes the element at the head of the queue. You can retrieve references to, without removing, the first and last elements with `front()` and `back()`, respectively. As usual, when called on `const` objects, `front()` and `back()` return `const` references; and when called on non-`const` objects they return non-`const` (read/write) references.

 `pop()` *does not return the element popped. If you want to retain a copy, you must first retrieve it with* `front()`.

The queue also supports `size()`, `empty()` and `swap()`. See the Standard Library Reference resource on the website for details.

queue Example: A Network Packet Buffer

When two computers communicate over a network, they send information to each other divided up into discrete chunks called *packets*. The networking layer of the computer's operating system must pick up the packets and store them as they arrive. However, the computer might not have enough bandwidth to process all of them at once. Thus, the networking layer usually *buffers*, or stores, the packets until the higher layers have a chance to attend to them. The packets should be processed in the order they arrive, so this problem is perfect for a `queue` structure. The following is a small `PacketBuffer` class, with comments explaining the code, that stores incoming packets in a `queue` until they are processed. It's a template so that different layers of the networking layer can use it for different kinds of packets, such as IP packets or TCP packets. It allows the client to specify a maximum size because operating systems usually limit the number of packets that can be stored, so as not to use too much memory. When the buffer is full, subsequently arriving packets are ignored.

```cpp
template <typename T>
class PacketBuffer
{
    public:
        // If maxSize is 0, the size is unlimited, because creating
        // a buffer of size 0 makes little sense. Otherwise only
        // maxSize packets are allowed in the buffer at any one time.
        PacketBuffer(size_t maxSize = 0);
        // Stores a packet in the buffer.
        // Returns false if the packet has been discarded because
        // there is no more space in the buffer, true otherwise.
        bool bufferPacket(const T& packet);
        // Returns the next packet. Throws out_of_range
        // if the buffer is empty.
        T getNextPacket() throw(std::out_of_range);
    protected:
        std::queue<T> mPackets;
        int mMaxSize;
};
template <typename T>
```

```
PacketBuffer<T>::PacketBuffer(size_t maxSize/* = 0 */)
    : mMaxSize(maxSize)
{
}
template <typename T>
bool PacketBuffer<T>::bufferPacket(const T& packet)
{
    if (mMaxSize > 0 && mPackets.size() == mMaxSize) {
        // No more space. Drop the packet.
        return false;
    }
    mPackets.push(packet);
    return true;
}
template <typename T>
T PacketBuffer<T>::getNextPacket() throw(std::out_of_range)
{
    if (mPackets.empty()) {
        throw std::out_of_range("Buffer is empty");
    }
    // retrieve the head element
    T temp = mPackets.front();
    // pop the head element
    mPackets.pop();
    // return the head element
    return temp;
}
```

Code snippet from PacketBuffer\PacketBuffer.h

A practical application of this class would require multiple threads. C++11 provides synchronization classes to allow thread-safe access to shared objects. Without explicit synchronization provided by the programmer, no STL class can be used safely in multiple threads. Synchronization is discussed in Chapter 22. However, here is a quick single-threaded example of the PacketBuffer:

```
class IPPacket
{
    public:
        IPPacket(int id) : mID(id) {}
        int getID() const { return mID; }
    protected:
        int mID;
};
int main()
{
    PacketBuffer<IPPacket> ipPackets(3);
    // Add 4 packets
    for (int i = 1; i <= 4; ++i) {
        if (!ipPackets.bufferPacket(IPPacket(i)))
            cout << "Packet " << i << " dropped (queue is full)." << endl;
    }
    while (true) {
        try {
```

```
            IPPacket packet = ipPackets.getNextPacket();
            cout << "Processing packet " << packet.getID() << endl;
        } catch (const out_of_range&) {
            cout << "Queue is empty." << endl;
            break;
        }
    }
    return 0;
}
```

Code snippet from PacketBuffer\PacketBufferTest.cpp

The output of this program is as follows:

```
Packet 4 dropped (queue is full).
Processing packet 1
Processing packet 2
Processing packet 3
Queue is empty.
```

priority_queue

A *priority queue* is a queue that keeps its elements in sorted order. Instead of a strict FIFO ordering, the element at the head of the queue at any given time is the one with the highest priority. This element could be the oldest on the queue or the most recent. If two elements have equal priority, their relative order in the queue is FIFO.

The STL `priority_queue` container adapter is also defined in `<queue>`. Its template definition looks something like this (slightly simplified):

```
template <class T, class Container = vector<T>,
          class Compare = less<T> >;
```

It's not as complicated as it looks. You've seen the first two parameters before: `T` is the element type stored in the `priority_queue` and `Container` is the underlying container on which the `priority_queue` is adapted. The `priority_queue` uses `vector` as the default, but `deque` works as well. `list` does not work because the `priority_queue` requires random access to its elements. The third parameter, `Compare`, is trickier. As you'll learn more about in Chapter 13, `less` is a class template that supports comparison of two objects of type `T` with `operator<`. What this means for you is that the priority of elements in the `queue` is determined according to `operator<`. You can customize the comparison used, but that's a topic for Chapter 13. For now, just make sure that you define `operator<` appropriately for the types stored in the `priority_queue`.

The head element of the `priority_queue` is the one with the "highest" priority, by default determined according to `operator<` such that elements that are "less" than other elements have lower priority.

priority_queue Operations

The `priority_queue` provides even fewer operations than does the `queue`. The `push()` and `emplace()` methods allow you to insert elements, `pop()` allows you to remove elements, and `top()` returns a `const` reference to the head element.

 `top()` returns a `const` reference even when called on a non-`const` object, because modifying the element might change its order, which is not allowed. The `priority_queue` provides no mechanism to obtain the tail element.

 `pop()` does not return the element popped. If you want to retain a copy, you must first retrieve it with `top()`.

Like the `queue`, the `priority_queue` supports `size()`, `empty()` and `swap()`. However, it does not provide any comparison operators. Consult the Standard Library Reference resource on the website for details.

This interface is obviously limited. In particular, the `priority_queue` provides no iterator support, and it is impossible to merge two `priority_queues`.

priority_queue Example: An Error Correlator

Single failures on a system can often cause multiple errors to be generated from different components. A good error-handling system uses *error correlation* to process the most important errors first. You can use a `priority_queue` to write a very simple error correlator. Assume all error events encode their own priority. This class simply sorts error events according to their priority, so that the highest-priority errors are always processed first. Here is the class definition:

```cpp
// Sample Error class with just a priority and a string error description.
class Error
{
    public:
        Error(int priority, const std::string& errMsg
            : mPriority(priority), mError(errMsg) {}
        int getPriority() const { return mPriority; }
        std::string getErrorString() const { return mError; }
        friend bool operator<(const Error& lhs, const Error& rhs);
        friend std::ostream& operator<<(std::ostream& os,
            const Error& err);// See Chapter 18 for details on implementing
            operator<<
    protected:
        int mPriority;
        std::string mError;
};
// Simple ErrorCorrelator class that returns highest priority errors first.
class ErrorCorrelator
{
```

```
public:
    ErrorCorrelator() {}
    // Add an error to be correlated.
    void addError(const Error& error);
    // Retrieve the next error to be processed.
    Error getError() throw(std::out_of_range);
protected:
    std::priority_queue<Error> mErrors;
};
```

Here are the definitions of the functions and methods:

```
bool operator<(const Error& lhs, const Error& rhs)
{
    return (lhs.mPriority < rhs.mPriority);
}
ostream& operator<<(ostream& os, const Error& err)
{
    os << err.mError << " (priority " << err.mPriority << ")";
    return os;
}
void ErrorCorrelator::addError(const Error& error)
{
    mErrors.push(error);
}
Error ErrorCorrelator::getError() throw(out_of_range)
{
    // If there are no more errors, throw an exception.
    if (mErrors.empty()) {
        throw out_of_range("No elements!");
    }
    // Save the top element.
    Error top = mErrors.top();
    // Remove the top element.
    mErrors.pop();
    // Return the saved element.
    return top;
}
```

Here is a simple unit test showing how to use the `ErrorCorrelator`. Realistic use would require multiple threads so that one thread adds errors, while another processes them. As mentioned earlier with the `queue` example, without explicit synchronization provided by the programmer, no STL class can be used safely in multiple threads. Synchronization is discussed in Chapter 22.

```
ErrorCorrelator ec;
ec.addError(Error(3, "Unable to read file"));
ec.addError(Error(1, "Incorrect entry from user"));
ec.addError(Error(10, "Unable to allocate memory!"));
```

```
    while (true) {
        try {
            Error e = ec.getError();
            cout << e << endl;
        } catch (const out_of_range&) {
            cout << "Finished processing errors" << endl;
            break;
        }
    }
}
```

Code snippet from ErrorCorrelatorPqueue\ErrorCorrelatorTest.cpp

The output of this program is as follows:

```
Unable to allocate memory! (priority 10)
Unable to read file (priority 3)
Incorrect entry from user (priority 1)
Finished processing errors
```

stack

The `stack` is almost identical to the `queue`, except that it provides *first-in, last-out* (*FILO*) semantics, also known as *last-in, first-out* (*LIFO*), instead of FIFO. It is defined in the `<stack>` header file. The template definition looks like this:

```
template <class T, class Container = deque<T> > class stack;
```

You can use `vector`, `list`, or `deque` as the underlying model for the `stack`.

stack Operations

Like the `queue`, the `stack` provides `push()`, `emplace()` and `pop()`. The difference is that `push()` adds a new element to the top of the `stack`, "pushing down" all elements inserted earlier, and `pop()` removes the element from the top of the `stack`, which is the most recently inserted element. The `top()` method returns a `const` reference to the top element if called on a `const` object and a non-`const` reference if called on a non-`const` object.

 `pop()` *does not return the element popped. If you want to retain a copy, you must first retrieve it with* `top()`.

The `stack` supports `empty()`, `size()`, `swap()` and the standard comparison operators. See the Standard Library Reference resource on the website for details.

stack Example: Revised Error Correlator

Suppose that you decide to rewrite the previous `ErrorCorrelator` class so that it gives out the most recent errors instead of those with the highest priority. You can substitute a `stack` for the `priority_` queue in the `ErrorCorrelator` class definition. Now, the `Errors` will be distributed from the class in LIFO order instead of priority order. Nothing in the method definitions needs to change because the `push()`, `pop()`, `top()`, and `empty()` methods exist on both the `priority_queue` and `stack`. There is only one change required and only in the `ErrorCorrelator` class.

Available for
download on
Wrox.com

```cpp
// Simple ErrorCorrelator class that returns most recent errors first.
class ErrorCorrelator
{
    public:
        ErrorCorrelator() {}
        // Add an error to be correlated.
        void addError(const Error& error);
        // Retrieve the next error to be processed
        Error getError() throw(std::out_of_range);
    protected:
        std::stack<Error> mErrors;
};
```

Code snippet from ErrorCorrelatorStack\ErrorCorrelator.h

All the rest of the code remains the same. The output of this `stack` version is as follows:

```
Unable to allocate memory! (priority 10)
Incorrect entry from user (priority 1)
Unable to read file (priority 3)
Finished processing errors
```

ASSOCIATIVE CONTAINERS

Unlike the sequential containers, the associative containers do not store elements in a linear configuration. Instead, they provide a mapping of keys to values. They generally offer insertion, deletion, and lookup times that are equivalent to each other.

The four associative containers provided by the STL are `map`, `multimap`, `set`, and `multiset`. Each of these containers stores its elements in a **sorted**, treelike, data structure.

The pair Utility Class

Before learning about the associative containers, you must become familiar with the `pair` class, which is defined in the `<utility>` header file. The `pair` is a class template that groups together two values of possibly different types. The values are accessible through the `first` and `second` public data members. `operator==` and `operator<` are defined for pairs to compare both the `first` and `second` elements. Here are some examples:

Available for
download on
Wrox.com

```cpp
// Two-argument constructor and default constructor
pair<string, int> myPair("hello", 5);
pair<string, int> myOtherPair;
// Can assign directly to first and second
```

```
myOtherPair.first = "hello";
myOtherPair.second = 6;
// Copy constructor
pair<string, int> myThirdPair(myOtherPair);
// operator<
if (myPair < myOtherPair) {
    cout << "myPair is less than myOtherPair" << endl;
} else {
    cout << "myPair is greater than or equal to myOtherPair" << endl;
}
// operator==
if (myOtherPair == myThirdPair) {
    cout << "myOtherPair is equal to myThirdPair" << endl;
} else {
    cout << "myOtherPair is not equal to myThirdPair" << endl;
}
```

Code snippet from Pair\PairTest.cpp

The output is as follows:

```
myPair is less than myOtherPair
myOtherPair is equal to myThirdPair
```

The library also provides a utility function template, make_pair(), that constructs a pair from two values. For example, you could use it like this:

```
pair<int, int> aPair = make_pair(5, 10);
```

Code snippet from Pair\PairTest.cpp

Of course, in this case you could have just used the two-argument constructor. However, make_pair() is more useful when you want to pass a pair to a function. Unlike class templates, function templates can infer types from parameters, so you can use make_pair() to construct a pair without explicitly specifying the types. You can also use make_pair() in combination with the C++11 auto keyword as follows:

```
auto aSecondPair = make_pair(5, 10);
```

Code snippet from Pair\PairTest.cpp

Using plain old pointer types in pairs is risky because the pair copy constructor and assignment operator perform only shallow copies and assignments of pointer types. However, you can safely store smart pointers like shared_ptr in your pair.

map

The map is one of the most useful containers, defined in the `<map>` header file. It stores key/value pairs instead of just a single value. Insertion, lookup, and deletion are all based on the key; the value is just "along for the ride." The term "map" comes from the conceptual understanding that the container "maps" keys to values.

The map keeps elements in sorted order, based on the keys, so that insertion, deletion, and lookup all take logarithmic time. Because of the order, when you enumerate the elements, they come out in the ordering imposed by the type's `operator<` or a user defined comparator. It is usually implemented as some form of balanced tree, such as a red-black tree. However, the tree structure is not exposed to the client.

You should use a map whenever you need to store and retrieve elements based on a "key" value and you would like to have them in a certain order.

Constructing maps

The map template takes four types: the key type, the value type, the comparison type, and the allocator type. As usual, we ignore the allocator in this chapter; see Chapter 17 for details. The comparison type is similar to the comparison type for `priority_queue` described earlier. It allows you to specify a different comparison class than the default. You usually shouldn't need to change the sorting criteria. In this chapter, we use only the default `less` comparison. When using the default, make sure that your keys all respond to `operator<` appropriately.

If you're interested in further detail, Chapter 13 explains how to write your own comparison classes.

If you ignore the comparison and allocator parameters (which we urge you to do), constructing a map is just like constructing a `vector` or `list`, except that you specify the key and value types separately in the template. For example, the following code constructs a map that uses `int`s as the key and stores objects of the Data class:

Available for
download on
Wrox.com

```cpp
class Data
{
    public:
        Data(int val = 0) { mVal = val; }
        int getVal() const { return mVal; }
        void setVal(int val) { mVal = val; }
    protected:
        int mVal;
};
int main()
{
    map<int, Data> dataMap;
    return 0;
}
```

Code snippet from MapBasics\MapInsert.cpp

maps also support the C++11 uniform initialization mechanism as shown in the following example:

```
map<string, int> m = {
    {"Marc G.", 123},
    {"Zulija N.", 456},
    {"John D.", 369}
};
```

Code snippet from MapBasics\MapUniformInit.cpp

Inserting Elements

Inserting an element into the sequential containers such as `vector` and `list` always requires you to specify the position at which the element is to be added. The `map`, along with the other associative containers, is different. The `map` internal implementation determines the position in which to store the new element; you need only to supply the key and the value.

> `map` *and the other associative containers do provide a version of* `insert()` *that takes an iterator position. However, that position is only a "hint" to the container as to the correct position. The container is not required to insert the element at that position.*

When inserting elements, it is important to keep in mind that `maps` support so-called "unique keys": Every element in the `map` must have a different key. If you want to support multiple elements with the same key, you must use `multimaps`, which are described later.

There are two ways to insert an element into the `map`: one clumsy and one not so clumsy.

The insert() Method

The clumsy mechanism to add an element to a `map` is the `insert()` method, but it has the advantage of allowing you to detect if the key already exists. One problem is that you must specify the key/value pair as a `pair` object. The second problem is that the return value from the basic form of `insert()` is a `pair` of an iterator and a `bool`. The reason for the complicated return value is that `insert()` does not overwrite an element value if one already exists with the specified key. The `bool` element of the returned `pair` specifies whether the `insert()` actually inserted the new key/value pair or not. The `iterator` refers to the element in the `map` with the specified key (with a new or old value, depending on whether the insert succeeded or failed). Continuing the `map` example from the previous section, you can use `insert()` as follows:

```
map<int, Data> dataMap;
auto ret = dataMap.insert({1, Data(4)}); // Using C++11 initializer_list
if (ret.second) {
    cout << "Insert succeeded!" << endl;
} else {
    cout << "Insert failed!" << endl;
}
```

```
ret = dataMap.insert(make_pair(1, Data(6)));
if (ret.second) {
    cout << "Insert succeeded!" << endl;
} else {
    cout << "Insert failed!" << endl;
}
```

Code snippet from MapBasics\MapInsert.cpp

The output of the program is:

```
Insert succeeded!
Insert failed!
```

If your compiler does not support the C++11 `auto` keyword, you have to declare the correct type for `ret` yourself as follows:

```
pair<map<int, Data>::iterator, bool> ret;
```

The type of `ret` is a pair. The first element of the `pair` is a `map` iterator for a `map` with keys of type `int` and values of type `Data`. The second element of the `pair` is a Boolean value.

operator[]

The less clumsy way to insert an element into the `map` is through the overloaded `operator[]`. The difference is mainly in the syntax: You specify the key and value separately. Additionally, `operator[]` always succeeds. If no element value with the given key exists, it creates a new element with that key and value. If an element with the key exists already, `operator[]` replaces the element value with the newly specified value. Here is the previous example using `operator[]` instead of `insert()`:

Available for download on Wrox.com

```
map<int, Data> dataMap;
dataMap[1] = Data(4);
dataMap[1] = Data(6); // Replaces the element with key 1
```

Code snippet from MapBasics\MapIndexOperator.cpp

There is, however, one major caveat to `operator[]`: It always constructs a new value object, even if it doesn't need to use it. Thus, it requires a default constructor for your element values, and can be less efficient than `insert()`.

The fact that `operator[]` creates a new element in the `map` if the requested element does not already exist means that this operator is not marked as `const`. This sounds obvious, but might sometimes look counter-intuitive. For example, suppose you have the following function:

Available for download on Wrox.com

```
void func(const map<int, int>& m)
{
    cout << m[1] << endl;  // Error
}
```

Code snippet from MapBasics\MapAsParameter.cpp

This will fail to compile, even though you appear to be just reading the value m[1]. It fails because the variable m is a const reference to a map, and operator[] is not marked as const. Instead, you should use the find() method as follows:

```
void func(const map<int, int>& m)
{
    auto iter = m.find(1);
    if (iter != m.end())
        cout << iter->second << endl;
}
```

Code snippet from MapBasics\MapAsParameter.cpp

Or, if your compiler doesn't support the C++11 auto keyword:

```
void func(const map<int, int>& m)
{
    map<int, int>::const_iterator iter = m.find(1);
    if (iter != m.end())
        cout << iter->second << endl;
}
```

Code snippet from MapBasics\MapAsParameter.cpp

map Iterators

map iterators work similarly to the iterators on the sequential containers. The major difference is that the iterators refer to key/value pairs instead of just the values. In order to access the value, you must retrieve the second field of the pair object. Here is how you can iterate through the map from the previous example:

```
map<int, Data> dataMap;
dataMap[1] = Data(4);
dataMap[1] = Data(6); // Replaces the element with key 1
for (auto iter = dataMap.cbegin(); iter != dataMap.cend(); ++iter) {
    cout << iter->second.getVal() << endl;
}
```

Code snippet from MapBasics\MapIterators.cpp

Take another look at the expression used to access the value:

```
iter->second.getVal()
```

iter refers to a key/value pair, so you can use the -> operator to access the second field of that pair, which is a Data object. You can then call the getVal() method on that data object.

Note that the following code is functionally equivalent:

```
(*iter).second.getVal()
```

You still see a lot of code like that around because the -> operator didn't used to be implemented for iterators.

Using the C++11 *range-based* `for` loop, the loop can be written even more elegantly as follows:

```
for (auto& p : dataMap) {
    cout << p.second.getVal() << endl;
}
```

Code snippet from MapBasics\MapIterators.cpp

If your compiler does not support the preceding C++11 versions, you have to write the loop as follows:

```
for (map<int, Data>::const_iterator iter = dataMap.begin();
    iter != dataMap.end(); ++iter) {
    cout << iter->second.getVal() << endl;
}
```

Code snippet from MapBasics\MapIterators.cpp

> *You can modify element values through non-*const *iterators, but the compiler will generate an error if you try to modify the key of an element, even through a non-*const *iterator, because it would destroy the sorted order of the elements in the* map.

`map` iterators are bidirectional, meaning you can traverse them in both directions.

Looking Up Elements

The `map` provides logarithmic lookup of elements based on a supplied key. If you already know that an element with a given key is in the map, the simplest way to look it up is through `operator[]`. The nice thing about `operator[]` is that it returns a reference to the element that you can use (or modify on a non-`const` map) directly, without worrying about pulling the value out of a `pair` object. Here is an extension to the preceding example to call the `setVal()` method on the `Data` object value at key 1:

```
map<int, Data> dataMap;
dataMap[1] = Data(4);
dataMap[1] = Data(6);
dataMap[1].setVal(100);
```

Code snippet from MapBasics\MapLookup.cpp

However, if you don't know whether the element exists, you may not want to use `operator[]`, because it will insert a new element with that key if it doesn't find one already. As an alternative, the map provides a find() method that returns an iterator referring to the element with the specified key, if it exists, or the end() iterator if it's not in the map. Here is an example using find() to perform the same modification to the Data object with key 1:

```
map<int, Data> dataMap;
dataMap[1] = Data(4);
dataMap[1] = Data(6);
auto it = dataMap.find(1);
if (it != dataMap.end()) {
    it->second.setVal(100);
}
```

Code snippet from MapBasics\MapFind.cpp

As you can see, using find() is a bit clumsier, but it's sometimes necessary. If your compiler does not support the C++11 auto keyword you need to call find() as follows:

```
map<int, Data>::iterator it = dataMap.find(1);
```

Code snippet from MapBasics\MapFind.cpp

If you only want to know whether or not an element with a certain key is in the map, you can use the count() member function. It returns the number of elements in the map with a given key. For maps, the result will always be 0 or 1 because there can be no elements with duplicate keys. The following section shows an example using count().

Removing Elements

The map allows you to remove an element at a specific iterator position or to remove all elements in a given iterator range, in amortized constant and logarithmic time, respectively. From the client perspective, these two erase() methods are equivalent to those in the sequential containers. A great feature of the map, however, is that it also provides a version of erase() to remove an element matching a key. Here is an example:

```
map<int, Data> dataMap;
dataMap[1] = Data(4);
cout << "There are " << dataMap.count(1) << " elements with key 1" << endl;
dataMap.erase(1);
cout << "There are " << dataMap.count(1) << " elements with key 1" << endl;
```

Code snippet from MapBasics\MapErase.cpp

The output should be as follows:

```
There are 1 elements with key 1
There are 0 elements with key 1
```

map Example: Bank Account

You can implement a simple bank account database using a `map`. A common pattern is for the key to be one field of a `class` or `struct` that is stored in the `map`. In this case, the key is the account number. Here are simple `BankAccount` and `BankDB` classes:

```cpp
class BankAccount
{
    public:
        BankAccount(int acctNum, const std::string& name)
            : mAcctNum(acctNum), mClientName(name) {}
        void setAcctNum(int acctNum) { mAcctNum = acctNum; }
        int getAcctNum() const { return mAcctNum; }
        void setClientName(const std::string& name) { mClientName = name; }
        std::string getClientName() const { return mClientName; }
    protected:
        int mAcctNum;
        std::string mClientName;
};
class BankDB
{
    public:
        BankDB() {}
        // Adds acct to the bank database. If an account exists already
        // with that number, the new account is not added. Returns true
        // if the account is added, false if it's not.
        bool addAccount(const BankAccount& acct);
        // Removes the account acctNum from the database.
        void deleteAccount(int acctNum);
        // Returns a reference to the account represented
        // by its number or the client name.
        // Throws out_of_range if the account is not found.
        BankAccount& findAccount(int acctNum) throw(std::out_of_range);
        BankAccount& findAccount(const std::string& name)
            throw(std::out_of_range);
        // Adds all the accounts from db to this database.
        // Deletes all the accounts from db.
        void mergeDatabase(BankDB& db);
    protected:
        std::map<int, BankAccount> mAccounts;
};
```

Code snippet from BankAccount\BankDB.h

Here are the implementations of the `BankDB` methods, with comments explaining the code:

```cpp
bool BankDB::addAccount(const BankAccount& acct)
{
    // Do the actual insert, using the account number as the key
    auto res = mAccounts.insert(make_pair(acct.getAcctNum(), acct));
    // Return the bool field of the pair specifying success or failure
    return res.second;
}
```

```cpp
void BankDB::deleteAccount(int acctNum)
{
    mAccounts.erase(acctNum);
}
BankAccount& BankDB::findAccount(int acctNum) throw(out_of_range)
{
    // Finding an element via its key can be done with find()
    auto it = mAccounts.find(acctNum);
    if (it == mAccounts.end()) {
        throw out_of_range("No account with that number.");
    }
    // Remember that iterators into maps refer to pairs of key/value
    return it->second;
}
BankAccount& BankDB::findAccount(const string& name) throw(out_of_range)
{
    // Finding an element by a non-key attribute requires a linear
    // search through the elements.
    for (auto& p : mAccounts) {
        if (p.second.getClientName() == name) {
            // found it!
            return p.second;
        }
    }
    throw out_of_range("No account with that name.");
}
void BankDB::mergeDatabase(BankDB& db)
{
    // Just insert copies of all the accounts in the old db
    // to the new one.
    mAccounts.insert(db.mAccounts.begin(), db.mAccounts.end());
    // Now delete all the accounts in the old one.
    db.mAccounts.clear();
}
```

Code snippet from BankAccount\BankDB.cpp

Note that this code uses a couple of C++11 features. For example, take the following line from the addAccount() method:

```cpp
auto res = mAccounts.insert(make_pair(acct.getAcctNum(), acct));
```

If your compiler does not support the C++11 auto keyword, this should be written as follows:

```cpp
pair<map<int, BankAccount>::iterator, bool> res;
res = mAccounts.insert(make_pair(acct.getAcctNum(), acct));
```

Code snippet from BankAccount\BankDB.cpp

You can test the `BankDB` class with the following code:

```
BankDB db;
db.addAccount(BankAccount(100, "Nicholas Solter"));
db.addAccount(BankAccount(200, "Scott Kleper"));
try {
    auto acct = db.findAccount(100);
    cout << "Found account 100" << endl;
    acct.setClientName("Nicholas A Solter");
    auto acct2 = db.findAccount("Scott Kleper");
    cout << "Found account of Scott Kelper" << endl;
    auto acct3 = db.findAccount(1000);
} catch (const out_of_range&) {
    cout << "Unable to find account" << endl;
}
```

Code snippet from BankAccount\BankDBTest.cpp

The output should be as follows:

```
Found account 100
Found account of Scott Kelper
Unable to find account
```

multimap

The `multimap` is a `map` that allows multiple elements with the same key. Like `maps`, `multimaps` support the C++11 uniform initialization. The interface is almost identical to the `map` interface, with the following changes:

➤ `multimaps` do not provide `operator[]`. The semantics of this operator does not make sense if there can be multiple elements with a single key.

➤ Inserts on `multimaps` always succeed. Thus, the `multimap insert()` method that adds a single element returns only an `iterator`.

`multimaps` *allow you to insert identical key/value pairs. If you want to avoid this redundancy, you must check explicitly before inserting a new element.*

The trickiest aspect of `multimaps` is looking up elements. You can't use `operator[]`, because it is not provided. `find()` isn't very useful because it returns an `iterator` referring to any one of the elements with a given key (not necessarily the first element with that key).

However, `multimaps` store all elements with the same key together and provide methods to obtain `iterators` for this subrange of elements with the same key in the container. The `lower_bound()` and `upper_bound()` methods each return a single `iterator` referring to the first and one-past-the-last elements matching a given key. If there are no elements matching that key, the `iterators` returned by `lower_bound()` and `upper_bound()` will be equal to each other.

In case you don't want to call two separate methods to obtain the `iterators` bounding the elements with a given key, `multimaps` also provide `equal_range()`, which returns a `pair` of the two `iterators` that would be returned by `lower_bound()` and `upper_bound()`.

The example in the next section illustrates the use of these methods.

> *The* `lower_bound()`, `upper_bound()`, *and* `equal_range()` *methods exist for* `maps` *as well, but their usefulness is limited because a* `map` *cannot have multiple elements with the same key.*

multimap Example: Buddy Lists

Most of the numerous online chat programs allow users to have a "buddy list" or list of friends. The chat program confers special privileges on users in the buddy list, such as allowing them to send unsolicited messages to the user.

One way to implement the buddy lists for an online chat program is to store the information in a `multimap`. One `multimap` could store the buddy lists for every user. Each entry in the container stores one buddy for a user. The key is the user and the value is the buddy. For example, if Harry Potter and Ron Weasley had each other on their individual buddy lists, there would be two entries of the form "Harry Potter" maps to "Ron Weasley" and "Ron Weasley" maps to "Harry Potter." The `multimap` allows multiple values for the same key, so the same user is allowed multiple buddies. Here is the `BuddyList` class definition:

Available for
download on
Wrox.com

```cpp
using std::multimap;
using std::string;
using std::list;
class BuddyList
{
    public:
        BuddyList();
        // Adds buddy as a friend of name
        void addBuddy(const string& name, const string& buddy);
        // Removes buddy as a friend of name
        void removeBuddy(const string& name, const string& buddy);
        // Returns true if buddy is a friend of name, false otherwise.
        bool isBuddy(const string& name, const string& buddy) const;
        // Retrieves a list of all the friends of name
        list<string> getBuddies(const string& name) const;
    protected:
        multimap<string, string> mBuddies;
};
```

Code snippet from BuddyList\BuddyList.h

Here is the implementation, with comments explaining the code. It demonstrates the use of `lower_bound()`, `upper_bound()`, and `equal_range()`:

```cpp
void BuddyList::addBuddy(const string& name, const string& buddy)
{
    // Make sure this buddy isn't already there. We don't want
    // to insert an identical copy of the key/value pair.
    if (!isBuddy(name, buddy)) {
        mBuddies.insert({name, buddy});// Using C++11 initializer_list
    }
}
void BuddyList::removeBuddy(const string& name, const string& buddy)
{
    // Obtain the beginning and end of the range of elements with
    // key 'name'.
    auto start = mBuddies.lower_bound(name);
    auto end = mBuddies.upper_bound(name);
    // Iterate through the elements with key 'name' looking
    // for a value 'buddy'
    for (; start != end; ++start) {
        if (start->second == buddy) {
            // We found a match! Remove it from the map.
            mBuddies.erase(start);
            break;
        }
    }
}
bool BuddyList::isBuddy(const string& name, const string& buddy) const
{
    // Obtain the beginning and end of the range of elements with
    // key 'name'.
    auto start = mBuddies.lower_bound(name);
    auto end = mBuddies.upper_bound(name);
    // Iterate through the elements with key 'name' looking
    // for a value 'buddy'. If there are no elements with key 'name',
    // start equals end, so the loop body doesn't execute.
    for (; start != end; ++start) {
        if (start->second == buddy) {
            // We found a match!
            return true;
        }
    }
    // No matches
    return false;
}
list<string> BuddyList::getBuddies(const string& name) const
{
    // Obtain the pair of iterators marking the range containing
    // elements with key 'name'.
    auto its = mBuddies.equal_range(name);
    // Create a list with all names in the range (all buddies of name).
    list<string> buddies;
```

```
        for (; its.first != its.second; ++its.first) {
            buddies.push_back(its.first->second);
        }
        return buddies;
    }
```

Code snippet from BuddyList\BuddyList.cpp

Note that removeBuddy() can't simply use the version of erase() that erases all elements with a given key, because it should erase only one element with the key, not all of them. Note also that getBuddies() can't use insert() on the list to insert the elements in the range returned by equal_range(), because the elements referred to by the multimap iterators are key/value pairs, not strings. The getBuddies() method must iterate explicitly through the list extracting the string from each key/value pair and pushing it onto the new list to be returned.

Here is a simple test of the BuddyList:

```
BuddyList buddies;
buddies.addBuddy("Harry Potter", "Ron Weasley");
buddies.addBuddy("Harry Potter", "Hermione Granger");
buddies.addBuddy("Harry Potter", "Hagrid");
buddies.addBuddy("Harry Potter", "Draco Malfoy");
// That's not right! Remove Draco.
buddies.removeBuddy("Harry Potter", "Draco Malfoy");

buddies.addBuddy("Hagrid", "Harry Potter");
buddies.addBuddy("Hagrid", "Ron Weasley");
buddies.addBuddy("Hagrid", "Hermione Granger");

auto harryBuds = buddies.getBuddies("Harry Potter");
cout << "Harry's friends: " << endl;
for (auto& name : harryBuds) {
    cout << "\t" << name << endl;
}
```

Code snippet from BuddyList\BuddyListTest.cpp

The output should be as follows:

```
Harry's friends:
        Ron Weasley
        Hermione Granger
        Hagrid
```

set

The set container, defined in the <set> header file, is very similar to the map. The difference is that instead of storing key/value pairs, in sets the value itself is the key. The set containers are useful for storing information in which there is no explicit key, but which you want to have in sorted order with quick insertion, lookup, and deletion.

The interface supplied by set is almost identical to that of the map. The main difference is that the set doesn't provide operator[].

Note that a set also supports the C++11 uniform initialization.

Although the standard doesn't state it explicitly, most implementations make the iterator of a set identical to const_iterator, such that you can't modify the elements of the set through the iterator. Even if your version of the STL permits you to modify set elements through an iterator, you should avoid doing so because modifying elements of the set while they are in the container would destroy the order.

set Example: Access Control List

One way to implement basic security on a computer system is through access control lists. Each entity on the system, such as a file or a device, has a list of users with permissions to access that entity. Users can generally be added to and removed from the permissions list for an entity only by users with special privileges. Internally, the set container provides a nice way to represent the access control list. You could use one set for each entity, containing all the usernames who are allowed to access the entity. Here is a class definition for a simple access control list:

Available for download on Wrox.com

```cpp
using std::set;
using std::string;
using std::list;
using std::initializer_list;
class AccessList
{
    public:
        // Default constructor
        AccessList() {}
        // Constructor to support C++11 uniform initialization.
        AccessList(const initializer_list<string>& initlst);
        // Adds the user to the permissions list.
        void addUser(const string& user);
        // Removes the user from the permissions list.
        void removeUser(const string& user);
        // Returns true if the user is in the permissionns list.
        bool isAllowed(const string& user) const;
        // Returns a list of all the users who have permissions.
        list<string> getAllUsers() const;
    protected:
        set<string> mAllowed;
};
```

Code snippet from AccessControlList\AccessList.h

Here are the method definitions:

```cpp
AccessList::AccessList(const initializer_list<string>& initlst)
{
    for (auto& user : initlst) {
        addUser(user);
    }
}
void AccessList::addUser(const string& user)
{
    mAllowed.insert(user);
}
void AccessList::removeUser(const string& user)
{
    mAllowed.erase(user);
}
bool AccessList::isAllowed(const string& user) const
{
    return (mAllowed.count(user) == 1);
}
list<string> AccessList::getAllUsers() const
{
    list<string> users;
    users.insert(users.end(), mAllowed.begin(), mAllowed.end());
    return users;
}
```

Code snippet from AccessControlList\AccessList.cpp

Finally, here is a simple test program:

```cpp
AccessList fileX = {"nsolter", "klep", "baduser"};
fileX.removeUser("baduser");
if (fileX.isAllowed("nsolter")) {
    cout << "nsolter has permissions" << endl;
}
if (fileX.isAllowed("baduser")) {
    cout << "baduser has permissions" << endl;
}
auto users = fileX.getAllUsers();
for (auto& user : users) {
    cout << user << "  ";
}
```

Code snippet from AccessControlList\AccessListTest.cpp

The output of this program is as follows:

```
nsolter has permissions
klep  nsolter
```

The preceding example uses a few C++11 features. One of the constructors for the `AccessList` class uses an `initializer_list` as parameter so that you can use the C++11 uniform initialization syntax, as demonstrated in the test program for initializing the variable `fileX`. The example also uses the C++11 *range-based* `for` loop and the `auto` keyword.

multiset

The `multiset` is to the `set` what the `multimap` is to the `map`. The `multiset` supports all the operations of the `set`, but it allows multiple elements that are equal to each other to be stored in the container simultaneously. We don't show an example of the `multiset` because it's so similar to `set` and `multimap`.

C++11 UNORDERED ASSOCIATIVE CONTAINERS/ HASH TABLES

C++11 adds new kind of containers to the STL called *unordered associative containers* or *hash tables*. There are four of them: `unordered_map`, `unordered_multimap`, `unordered_set`, and `unordered_multiset`. The `map`, `multimap`, `set`, and `multiset` containers discussed earlier sort their elements while these new unordered variants do not sort their elements. If you don't need ordering, use the new unordered associative containers because on average they have faster insertion, deletion, and lookup.

As mentioned in the container overview in Chapter 11, better names would have been `hash_map`, `hash_set`, and so on. Unfortunately, hash tables were not part of the C++ standard library before C++11, which means a lot of third-party libraries implemented hash tables themselves using names with a prefix *hash* like `hash_map`. Because of this, the C++ standard committee decided to use the prefix *unordered* instead of *hash* to avoid name clashes.

Hash Functions

The new containers are also called *hash tables*. That is because the implementation of these new containers makes use of so called *hash functions*. The implementation will usually consist of some kind of array where each element in the array is called a *bucket*. Each bucket has a specific numerical index like 0, 1, 2 up until the last bucket. A hash function transforms a key into a bucket index. The value associated with that key is then stored in that bucket. The result of a hash function is not always unique. The situation in which two or more keys hash to the same bucket index is called a *collision*. There are many approaches to handling collisions, for example quadratic re-hashing, linear chaining, etc. Those who are interested may consult one of the references in the Algorithms and Data Structures section in Appendix B. The STL standard does not specify which collision handling algorithm is required, but most current implementations have chosen to resolve collisions by linear chaining. With linear chaining, buckets do not directly contain the data values associated with the keys, but contain a pointer to a linked list. This linked list contains all the data values for that specific bucket. Figure 12-1 shows how this works.

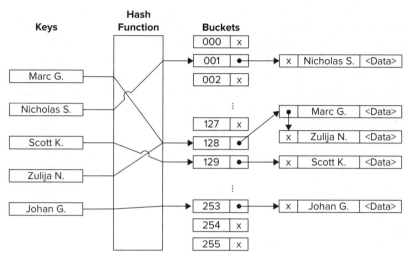

FIGURE 12-1

In Figure 12-1, applying the hash function to the keys "Marc G." and "Zulija N." resulted in the same bucket index 128. This bucket then points to a linked list containing the keys "Marc G." and "Zulija N." together with their associated data values. From Figure 12-1 it is also clear how lookups based on keys work and what the complexity is. A lookup involves a single hash function call to calculate the bucket index and after that one or more equality operations to find the right key in the linked list. This shows that lookups can be much faster compared to lookups with normal maps, but it all depends on how many collisions there are.

The choice of the hash function is very important. A hash function that creates no collisions is known as a "perfect hash." A perfect hash has a lookup time which is constant; a regular hash has a lookup time which is, on average, close to 1, independent of the number of elements. As the number of collisions increases, the lookup time increases, reducing performance. Collisions can be reduced by increasing the basic hash table size, but you need to take cache sizes into account.

Generally, the default hash function is suitable for most purposes. Creating a perfect hash is a nontrivial exercise, even when the set of keys is fixed and known. Even modifying a regular hash is not an exercise for the unwary!

unordered_map

The unordered_map is defined in the `<unordered_map>` header file as a class template as follows:

```
template <class Key,
          class T,
          class Hash = hash<Key>,
          class Pred = std::equal_to<Key>,
          class Alloc = std::allocator<std::pair<const Key, T> > >
    class unordered_map;
```

There are five template parameters: the key type, the value type, the hash type, the equal comparison type, and the allocator type. With the last three parameters you can define your own hash function, equal comparison function, and allocator function, respectively. These parameters can usually be ignored since they have default values. We recommend you keep those default values. For example, it's not trivial to implement your own good hash function. The most important parameters are the first two. As with maps, C++11 uniform initialization can be used to initialize the unordered_map with elements as shown in the following example:

```
unordered_map<int, string> m = {
    {1, "Item 1"},
    {2, "Item 2"},
    {3, "Item 3"},
    {4, "Item 4"}
};
for (auto& p : m)
    cout << p.first << " = " << p.second << endl;
```

Code snippet from unordered_map\unordered_map.cpp

The following table summarizes the differences between a map and an unordered_map.

OPERATION	map	unordered_map
at()	X	X
begin()	X	X
bucket()		X
bucket_count()		X
bucket_size()		X
cbegin()	X	X
cend()	X	X
clear()	X	X
count()	X	X
crbegin()	X	
crend()	X	
emplace()	X	X
emplace_hint()	X	X
empty()	X	X
end()	X	X

OPERATION	map	unordered_map
equal_range()	x	x
erase()	x	x
find()	x	x
insert()	x	x
iterator / const_iterator	x	x
load_factor()		x
local_iterator / const_local_iterator		x
lower_bound()	x	
max_bucket_count()		x
max_load_factor()		x
operator[]	x	x
rbegin()	x	
rehash()		x
rend()	x	
reserve()		x
reverse_iterator / const_reverse_iterator	x	
size()	x	x
swap()	x	x
upper_bound()	x	

As with a normal map, all keys in an unordered_map should be unique. The preceding table includes a number of hash specific methods. For example, load_factor() returns the average number of elements per bucket to give you an indication on the number of collisions. The bucket_count() method returns the number of buckets in the container. It also provides a local_iterator and const_local_iterator allowing you to iterate over the elements in a single bucket; but, these may not be used to iterate across buckets. The bucket(key) method returns the index of the bucket that contains the given key; begin(n) returns a local_iterator referring to the first element in the bucket with index n, and end(n) returns a local_iterator referring to one-past-the-last element in the bucket with index n. The example in the next section will make things more clear on how to use these methods.

unordered_map Example: Phone Book

The following example uses an `unordered_map` to represent a phone book. The name of a person will be the key while the phone number will be the value associated with that key.

```cpp
template<class T>
void printMap(const T& m)
{
    for (auto& p : m) {
        cout << p.first << "(Phone: " << p.second << ")" << endl;
    }
    cout << "-------" << endl;
}
int main()
{
    // Create a hash table.
    unordered_map<string, string> um;
    um.insert({
        {"Marc G.", "123-456789"},
        {"Zulija N.", "987-654321"},
        {"Scott K.", "654-987321"} });
    printMap(um);
    // Add/remove some phone numbers.
    um.insert(make_pair("John D.", "321-987654"));
    um["Johan G."] = "963-258147";
    um["Freddy K."] = "999-256256";
    um.erase("Freddy K.");
    printMap(um);
    // Find the bucket index for a specific key.
    int bucket = um.bucket("Marc G.");
    cout << "Marc G. is in bucket " << bucket
        << " which contains the following "
        << um.bucket_size(bucket) << " elements:" << endl;
    // Get begin and end iterators for the elements in this bucket.
    // 'auto' is being used here. The compiler will derive the type
    // of both iterators as
    // unordered_map<string, string>::const_local_iterator
    auto liter = um.cbegin(bucket);
    auto literEnd = um.cend(bucket);
    while (liter != literEnd) {
        cout << "\t" << liter->first << "(Phone: "
            << liter->second << ")" << endl;
        ++liter;
    }
    cout << "-------" << endl;
    // Print some statistics about the hash table
    cout << "There are " << um.bucket_count() << " buckets." << endl;
    cout << "Average number of elements in a bucket is "
        << um.load_factor() << endl;
    return 0;
}
```

Code snippet from PhoneBook\PhoneBook.cpp

This example uses a lot of C++11 features: `unordered_map`, *range-based* `for` loop, `auto` and `initializer_lists`. The output of this code is as follows:

```
Zulija N.(Phone: 987-654321)
Marc G.(Phone: 123-456789)
Scott K.(Phone: 654-987321)
-------
John D.(Phone: 321-987654)
Zulija N.(Phone: 987-654321)
Marc G.(Phone: 123-456789)
Johan G.(Phone: 963-258147)
Scott K.(Phone: 654-987321)
-------
Marc G. is in bucket 4 which contains the following 1 elements:
    Marc G.(Phone: 123-456789)
  -------
There are 11 buckets.
Average number of elements in a bucket is 0.454545
```

unordered_multimap

The `unordered_multimap` is an `unordered_map` that allows multiple elements with the same key. Their interfaces are almost identical, with the following changes:

➤ `unordered_multimaps` do not provide `operator[]`. The semantics of this operator does not make sense if there can be multiple elements with a single key.

➤ Inserts on `unordered_multimaps` always succeed. Thus, the `unordered_multimap` `insert()` method that adds a single element returns only an `iterator`.

> `unordered_multimaps` *allow you to insert identical key/value pairs. If you want to avoid this redundancy, you must check explicitly before inserting a new element.*

As discussed earlier with `multimaps`, looking up elements in `unordered_multimaps` cannot be done using `operator[]` because it is not provided. You can use `find()` but it will return an iterator referring to any one of the elements with a given key (not necessarily the first element with that key). Instead, it's best to use the `equal_range()` method, which will return a pair of iterators: one referring to the first element matching a given key and one referring to one-past-the-last element matching a given key. The use of `equal_range()` is exactly the same as discussed in the context of the `multimap`, so you can refer to the example given for `multimaps` to see how it works.

unordered_set/unordered_multiset

The `<unordered_set>` header file defines the `unordered_set` and `unordered_multiset` which are very similar to the `set` and `multiset` respectively; except that they do not sort their keys and that they use a hash function. The differences between the `unordered_set` and the `unordered_map` are similar to the differences between the `set` and the `map` as discussed earlier in this chapter, so they are not discussed in details here. The Standard Library Reference resource on the website contains a thorough summary of the `unordered_set` and `unordered_multiset` operations.

OTHER CONTAINERS

There are several other parts of the C++ language that work with the STL to varying degrees, including standard C-style arrays, `strings`, streams, and the `bitset`.

Standard C-Style Arrays

Recall that "dumb" pointers are bona fide iterators because they support the required operators. This point is more than just a piece of trivia. It means that you can treat standard C-style arrays as STL containers by using pointers to their elements as iterators. Standard C-style arrays, of course, don't provide methods like `size()`, `empty()`, `insert()`, and `erase()`, so they aren't true STL containers. Nevertheless, because they do support iterators through pointers, you can use them in the algorithms described in Chapter 13 and in some of the methods described in this chapter.

For example, you could copy all the elements of a standard C-style array into a `vector` using the `insert()` method of a `vector` that takes an iterator range from any container. This `insert()` method prototype looks like this:

```
template <class InputIterator> iterator insert(const_iterator position,
    InputIterator first, InputIterator last);
```

If you want to use a standard C-style `int` array as the source, then the templatized type of `InputIterator` becomes `int*`. Here is the full example:

Available for download on Wrox.com

```
int arr[10];     // standard C-style array
vector<int> vec; // STL vector
// Initialize each element of the array to the value of its index.
for (int i = 0; i < 10; i++) {
    arr[i] = i;
}
// Insert the contents of the array into the end of the vector.
vec.insert(vec.end(), arr, arr + 10);
// Print the contents of the vector.
for (auto& i : vec) {
    cout << i << " ";
}
```

Code snippet from ArrayIterators\ArrayIterators.cpp

Note that the iterator referring to the first element of the array is the address of the first element, which is `arr` in this case. The name of an array alone is interpreted as the address of the first element. The iterator referring to the end must be one-past-the-last element, so it's the address of the first element plus 10, or `arr+10`.

strings

You can think of a `string` as a sequential container of characters. Thus, it shouldn't be surprising to learn that the C++ `string` is a full-fledged sequential container. It contains `begin()` and `end()` methods that return iterators into the `string`, `insert()`, `push_back()` and `erase()` methods, `size()`, `empty()`, and all the rest of the sequential container basics. It resembles a `vector` quite closely, even providing methods `reserve()` and `capacity()`. However, unlike `vectors`, `strings` are not required to store their elements contiguously in memory.

 The C++ `string` *is actually a* `typedef` *of a* char *instantiation of the* `basic_string` *template class. However, we refer to* `string` *for simplicity. The discussion here applies equally to* `wstring` *and other instantiations of the* `basic_string` *template.*

You can use `string` as an STL container just as you would use `vector`. Here is an example:

Available for download on Wrox.com

```cpp
string str1;
str1.insert(str1.end(), 'h');
str1.insert(str1.end(), 'e');
str1.insert(str1.end(), 'l');
str1.insert(str1.end(), 'l');
str1.insert(str1.end(), 'o');
for (auto it = str1.cbegin(); it != str1.cend(); ++it) {
    cout << *it;
}
cout << endl;
for (auto& letter : str1) {
    cout << letter;
}
cout << endl;
```

Code snippet from StringContainers\StringExample.cpp

In addition to the STL sequential container methods, `strings` provide a whole host of useful methods and `friend` functions. The `string` interface is actually quite a good example of a cluttered interface, one of the design pitfalls discussed in Chapter 4. The `string` class is discussed in much more detail in Chapter 14, but this section showed you how `strings` can be used as STL containers.

Streams

Input and output streams are not containers in the traditional sense: They do not store elements. However, they can be considered sequences of elements, and as such share some characteristics with the STL containers. C++ streams do not provide any STL-related methods directly, but the

STL supplies special iterators called `istream_iterator` and `ostream_iterator` that allow you to "iterate" through input and output streams. Chapter 17 explains how to use them.

bitset

The `bitset` is a fixed-length abstraction of a sequence of bits. A bit can represent only two values, 1 and 0, which can be referred to as on/off, true/false, etc. The `bitset` also uses the terminology *set* and *unset*. You can *toggle* or *flip* a bit from one value to the other.

The `bitset` is not a true STL container: It's of fixed size, it's not templatized on an element type, and it doesn't support iteration. However, it's a useful utility, which is often lumped with the containers, so we provide a brief introduction here. The Standard Library Reference resource on the website contains a thorough summary of the `bitset` operations.

bitset Basics

The `bitset`, defined in the `<bitset>` header file, is templatized on the number of bits it stores. The default constructor initializes all fields of the `bitset` to 0. An alternative constructor creates the `bitset` from a `string` of 0 and 1 characters .

You can adjust the values of the individual bits with the `set()`, `reset()`, and `flip()` methods, and you can access and set individual fields with an overloaded `operator[]`. Note that `operator[]` on a non-`const` object returns a proxy object to which you can assign a Boolean value, call `flip()`, or complement with `~`. You can also access individual fields with the `test()` method.

Additionally, you can stream `bitset`s with the normal insertion and extraction operators. The `bitset` is streamed as a `string` of 0 and 1 characters.

Here is a small example:

```cpp
bitset<10> myBitset;
myBitset.set(3);
myBitset.set(6);
myBitset[8] = true;
myBitset[9] = myBitset[3];
if (myBitset.test(3)) {
    cout << "Bit 3 is set!"<< endl;
}
cout << myBitset << endl;
```

Code snippet from BitsetBasics\BitsetBasics.cpp

The output is:

```
Bit 3 is set!
1101001000
```

Note that the leftmost character in the output `string` is the highest numbered bit. This corresponds to our intuitions about binary number representations, where the low-order bit representing $2^0 = 1$ is the rightmost bit in the printed representation.

Bitwise Operators

In addition to the basic bit manipulation routines, the `bitset` provides implementations of all the bitwise operators: &, |, ^, ~, <<, >>, &=, |=, ^=, <<=, and >>=. They behave just as they would on a "real" sequence of bits. Here is an example:

Available for download on Wrox.com

```cpp
auto str1 = "0011001100";
auto str2 = "0000111100";
bitset<10> bitsOne(str1);
bitset<10> bitsTwo(str2);
auto bitsThree = bitsOne & bitsTwo;
cout << bitsThree << endl;
bitsThree <<= 4;
cout << bitsThree << endl;
```

Code snippet from BitsetBasics\BitwiseOperators.cpp

The output of the program is:

```
0000001100
0011000000
```

bitset Example: Representing Cable Channels

One possible use of `bitset`s is tracking channels of cable subscribers. Each subscriber could have a `bitset` of channels associated with his or her subscription, with set bits representing the channels to which he or she actually subscribes. This system could also support "packages" of channels, also represented as `bitset`s, which represent commonly subscribed combinations of channels.

The following `CableCompany` class is a simple example of this model. It uses two `map`s, each of `string`/`bitset`, storing the cable packages as well as the subscriber information.

Available for download on Wrox.com

```cpp
using std::map;
using std::bitset;
using std::string;
using std::out_of_range;
const int kNumChannels = 10;
class CableCompany
{
    public:
        CableCompany() {}
        // Adds the package with the specified channels to the database
        void addPackage(const string& packageName,
            const bitset<kNumChannels>& channels);
        // Removes the specified package from the database
        void removePackage(const string& packageName);
        // Adds customer to database with initial channels found in package
        // Throws out_of_range if the package name is invalid.
        void newCustomer(const string& name, const string& package)
            throw(out_of_range);
        // Adds customer to database with initial channels specified
```

```
        // in channels
        void newCustomer(const string& name,
            const bitset<kNumChannels>& channels);
        // Adds the channel to the customers profile
        void addChannel(const string& name, int channel);
        // Removes the channel from the customers profile
        void removeChannel(const string& name, int channel);
        // Adds the specified package to the customers profile
        void addPackageToCustomer(const string& name,
            const string& package);
        // Removes the specified customer from the database
        void deleteCustomer(const string& name);
        // Retrieves the channels to which this customer subscribes
        // Throws out_of_range if name is not a valid customer
        bitset<kNumChannels>& getCustomerChannels(const string& name)
            throw(out_of_range);
    protected:
        typedef map<string, bitset<kNumChannels> > MapType;
        MapType mPackages, mCustomers;
};
```

Code snippet from CableCompany\CableCompany.h

Here are the implementations of the preceding methods, with comments explaining the code:

```
void CableCompany::addPackage(const string& packageName,
    const bitset<kNumChannels>& channels)
{
    // Just make a key/value pair and insert it into the packages map.
    mPackages.insert({packageName, channels});
}
void CableCompany::removePackage(const string& packageName)
{
    // Just erase the package from the package map.
    mPackages.erase(packageName);
}
void CableCompany::newCustomer(const string& name, const string& package)
    throw(out_of_range)
{
    // Get a reference to the specified package.
    auto it = mPackages.find(package);
    if (it == mPackages.end()) {
        // That package doesn't exist. Throw an exception.
        throw out_of_range("Invalid package");
    } else {
        // Create the account with the bitset representing that package.
        // Note that 'it' refers to a name/bitset pair. The bitset is the
        // second field.
        mCustomers.insert({name, it->second});
    }
}
```

```
void CableCompany::newCustomer(const string& name,
    const bitset<kNumChannels>& channels)
{
    // Just add the customer/channels pair to the customers map.
    mCustomers.insert({name, channels});
}
void CableCompany::addChannel(const string& name, int channel)
{
    // Find a reference to the customer.
    auto it = mCustomers.find(name);
    if (it != mCustomers.end()) {
        // We found this customer; set the channel.
        // Note that 'it' is a reference to a name/bitset pair.
        // The bitset is the second field.
        it->second.set(channel);
    }
}
void CableCompany::removeChannel(const string& name, int channel)
{
    // Find a reference to the customer.
    auto it = mCustomers.find(name);
    if (it != mCustomers.end()) {
        // We found this customer; remove the channel.
        // Note that 'it' is a reference to a name/bitset pair.
        // The bitset is the second field.
        it->second.reset(channel);
    }
}
void CableCompany::addPackageToCustomer(const string& name,
    const string& package)
{
    // Find the package.
    auto itPack = mPackages.find(package);
    // Find the customer.
    auto itCust = mCustomers.find(name);
    if (itCust != mCustomers.end() && itPack != mPackages.end()) {
        // Only if both package and customer found, can we do the update.
        // Or-in the package to the customers existing channels.
        // Note that the iterators are references to name/bitset pairs.
        // The bitset is the second field.
        itCust->second |= itPack->second;
    }
}
void CableCompany::deleteCustomer(const string& name)
{
    // Remove the customer with this name.
    mCustomers.erase(name);
}
bitset<kNumChannels>& CableCompany::getCustomerChannels(const string& name)
    throw(out_of_range)
{
    // Find the customer.
    auto it = mCustomers.find(name);
```

```
    if (it != mCustomers.end()) {
        // Found it!
        // Note that 'it' is a reference to a name/bitset pair.
        // The bitset is the second field.
        return it->second;
    }
    // Didn't find it. Throw an exception.
    throw out_of_range("No customer with that name");
}
```

Code snippet from CableCompany\CableCompany.cpp

Finally, here is a simple program demonstrating how to use the CableCompany class:

Available for download on Wrox.com

```
CableCompany myCC;
auto basic_pkg = "1111000000";
auto premium_pkg = "1111111111";
auto sports_pkg = "0000100111";
myCC.addPackage("basic", bitset<kNumChannels>(basic_pkg));
myCC.addPackage("premium", bitset<kNumChannels>(premium_pkg));
myCC.addPackage("sports", bitset<kNumChannels>(sports_pkg));
myCC.newCustomer("Nicholas Solter", "basic");
myCC.addPackageToCustomer("Nicholas Solter", "sports");
cout << myCC.getCustomerChannels("Nicholas Solter") << endl;
```

Code snippet from CableCompany\CableCompanyTest.cpp

Note that this example uses a lot of C++11 features. For example, the addPackage() method has the following line:

```
mPackages.insert({packageName, channels});
```

This line uses C++11 uniform initialization. If your compiler does not support this you need to write it as follows:

```
mPackages.insert(make_pair(packageName, channels));
```

SUMMARY

This chapter introduced the standard template library containers. It also presented sample code illustrating a variety of uses for these containers. Hopefully, you appreciate the power of the vector, deque, list, array, forward_list, stack, queue, priority_queue, map, multimap, set, multiset, unordered_map, unordered_multimap, unordered_set, unordered_multiset, string, and bitset. Even if you don't incorporate them into your programs immediately, at least keep them in the back of your mind for future projects.

Now that you are familiar with the containers, the next chapter can illustrate the true power of the STL by discussing the generic algorithms.

13

Mastering STL Algorithms

WHAT'S IN THIS CHAPTER?

➤ What algorithms are

➤ What lambda expressions are

➤ What function objects are

➤ The details of the STL algorithms

➤ A larger example: auditing voter registrations

As Chapter 12 shows, the STL provides an impressive collection of generic data structures. Most libraries stop there. The STL, however, contains an additional assortment of generic algorithms that can, with some exceptions, be applied to elements from any container. Using these algorithms, you can find, sort, and process elements in containers, and perform a whole host of other operations. The beauty of the algorithms is that they are independent not only of the types of the underlying elements, but of the types of the containers on which they operate. Algorithms perform their work using only the iterator interfaces.

Many of the algorithms accept *callbacks*, which can be a function pointer or something that behaves like a function pointer, such as an object with an overloaded `operator()` or a C++11 inline lambda expression. Conveniently, the STL provides a set of classes that can be used to create callback objects for the algorithms. These callback objects are called function objects, or just *functors*.

OVERVIEW OF ALGORITHMS

The "magic" behind the algorithms is that they work on iterator intermediaries instead of on the containers themselves. In that way, they are not tied to specific container implementations. All the STL algorithms are implemented as function templates, where the template type parameters are usually iterator types. The iterators themselves are specified as arguments to the function. Templatized functions can usually deduce the template types from the function arguments, so you can generally call the algorithms as if they were normal functions, not templates.

The iterator arguments are usually iterator ranges. As Chapter 12 explains, iterator ranges are half-open for most containers such that they include the first element in the range, but exclude the last. The end iterator is really a "past-the-end" marker.

The C++11 `forward_list` container only supports forward iterators. This means that algorithms requiring bidirectional or random access iterators will not work on a `forward_list`; for example `copy_backward()`, `random_shuffle()`, `stable_sort()`, etc. do not work on a `forward_list`.

Some algorithms require additional template type parameters and arguments, which are sometimes function callbacks. These callbacks can be function pointers, function objects or C++11 lambda expressions.

Most algorithms are defined in the `<algorithm>` header file, while some numerical algorithms are defined in the `<numeric>` header file.

The best way to understand the algorithms is to look at some examples first. After you've seen how a few of them work, it's easy to pick up the others. This section describes the `find()`, `find_if()`, and `accumulate()` algorithms in detail. The next sections present the lambda expressions and function objects, and discusses each of the classes of algorithms with representative samples.

The find and find_if Algorithms

`find()` looks for a specific element in an iterator range. You can use it on elements in any container type. It returns an iterator referring to the element found, or the end iterator of the range in case the element is not found. Note that the range specified in the call to `find()` need not be the entire range of elements in a container; it could be a subset.

 If `find()` *fails to find an element, it returns an iterator equal to the end iterator specified in the function call, not the end iterator of the underlying container.*

Here is an example of `find()`. Note that this example assumes that the user plays nice and enters valid numbers; it does not perform any error checking on the user input. Performing error checking on stream input is discussed in Chapter 15.

```cpp
#include <algorithm>
#include <vector>
#include <iostream>
using namespace std;
int main()
{
    int num;
    vector<int> myVector;
```

```
    while (true) {
        cout << "Enter a number to add (0 to stop): ";
        cin >> num;
        if (num == 0) {
            break;
        }
        myVector.push_back(num);
    }
    while (true) {
        cout << "Enter a number to lookup (0 to stop): ";
        cin >> num;
        if (num == 0) {
            break;
        }
        auto end = myVector.end();
        auto it = find(myVector.begin(), end, num);
        if (it == end) {
            cout << "Could not find " << num << endl;
        } else {
            cout << "Found " << *it << endl;
        }
    }
    return 0;
}
```

Code snippet from AlgorithmOverview\Find.cpp

The call to `find()` is made with `myVector.begin()` and `end` as arguments, where `end` is defined as `myVector.end()` for this example, in order to search all the elements of the `vector`. If you want to search in a sub range, you can change the first argument to the `find()` method and the value of the `end` iterator.

Here is a sample run of the program:

```
Enter a number to add (0 to stop): 3
Enter a number to add (0 to stop): 4
Enter a number to add (0 to stop): 5
Enter a number to add (0 to stop): 6
Enter a number to add (0 to stop): 0
Enter a number to lookup (0 to stop): 5
Found 5
Enter a number to lookup (0 to stop): 8
Could not find 8
Enter a number to lookup (0 to stop): 4
Found 4
Enter a number to lookup (0 to stop): 2
Could not find 2
Enter a number to lookup (0 to stop): 0
```

Some containers, such as `map` and `set`, provide their own versions of `find()` as class methods.

If a container provides a method with the same functionality as a generic algorithm, you should use the method instead, because it's faster. For example, the generic `find()` algorithm runs in linear time, even on a `map` iterator, while the `find()` method on a `map` runs in logarithmic time.

`find_if()` is similar to `find()`, except that it accepts a *predicate function callback* instead of a simple element to match. A predicate returns `true` or `false`. The `find_if()` algorithm calls the predicate on each element in the range until the predicate returns `true`, in which case `find_if()` returns an iterator referring to that element. The following program reads test scores from the user, then checks if any of the scores are "perfect." A perfect score is a score of `100` or higher. The program is similar to the previous example. Only the differences are highlighted.

```cpp
bool perfectScore(int num)
{
    return (num >= 100);
}
int main()
{
    int num;
    vector<int> myVector;
    while (true) {
        cout << "Enter a test score to add (0 to stop): ";
        cin >> num;
        if (num == 0) {
            break;
        }
        myVector.push_back(num);
    }
    auto end = myVector.end();
    auto it = find_if(myVector.begin(), end, perfectScore);
    if (it == end) {
        cout << "No perfect scores" << endl;
    } else {
        cout << "Found a \"perfect\" score of " << *it << endl;
    }
    return 0;
}
```

Code snippet from AlgorithmOverview\FindIf.cpp

This program passes a pointer to the `perfectScore()` function, which the `find_if()` algorithm then calls on each element until it returns `true`.

Here is the same example but using a C++11 lambda expression. It gives you an initial idea about the power of lambda expressions. Don't worry about their syntax. They are explained in detail later in this chapter. Note the absence of the `perfectScore()` function.

```
    int num;
    vector<int> myVector;
    while (true) {
        cout << "Enter a test score to add (0 to stop): ";
        cin >> num;
        if (num == 0) {
            break;
        }
        myVector.push_back(num);
    }
    auto end = myVector.end();
    auto it = find_if(myVector.begin(), end, [](int i){ return i >= 100; });
    if (it == end) {
        cout << "No perfect scores" << endl;
    } else {
        cout << "Found a \"perfect\" score of " << *it << endl;
    }
```

Code snippet from AlgorithmOverview\FindIfLambda.cpp

Unfortunately, the STL provides no `find_all()` or equivalent algorithm that returns all instances matching a predicate. Chapter 17 shows you how to write your own `find_all()` algorithm.

The accumulate Algorithms

It's often useful to calculate the sum, or some other arithmetic quantity, of all the elements in a container. The `accumulate()` function does just that. In its most basic form, it calculates the sum of the elements in a specified range. For example, the following function calculates the arithmetic mean of a sequence of integers in a `vector`. The arithmetic mean is simply the sum of all the elements divided by the number of elements.

```
#include <numeric>
#include <vector>
using namespace std;
double arithmeticMean(const vector<int>& nums)
{
    double sum = accumulate(nums.begin(), nums.end(), 0);
    return sum / nums.size();
}
```

Code snippet from AlgorithmOverview\Accumulate.cpp

Note that `accumulate()` is declared in `<numeric>`, not in `<algorithm>`. The `accumulate()` algorithm takes as its third parameter an initial value for the sum, which in this case should be `0` (the identity for addition) to start a fresh sum.

The second form of `accumulate()` allows the caller to specify an operation to perform instead of the default addition. This operation takes the form of a binary callback. Suppose that you want to calculate the geometric mean, which is the product of all the numbers in the sequence to the power of the inverse of the size. In that case, you would want to use `accumulate()` to calculate the product instead of the sum. You *could* write it like this:

```cpp
#include <numeric>
#include <vector>
#include <cmath>
using namespace std;
int product(int num1, int num2)
{
    return num1 * num2;
}
double geometricMean(const vector<int>& nums)
{
    double mult = accumulate(nums.begin(), nums.end(), 1, product);
    return pow(mult, 1.0 / nums.size());
}
```

Code snippet from AlgorithmOverview\Accumulate.cpp

Note that the `product()` function is passed as a callback to `accumulate()` and that the initial value for the accumulation is `1` (the identity for multiplication) instead of `0`.

To give you a second teaser about the power of C++11 lambda expressions, the `geometricMean()` function *could* be written as follows, without using the `product()` function:

```cpp
double geometricMeanLambda(const vector<int>& nums)
{
    double mult = accumulate(nums.begin(), nums.end(), 1,
        [](int num1, int num2){ return num1 * num2; });
    return pow(mult, 1.0 / nums.size());
}
```

Code snippet from AlgorithmOverview\Accumulate.cpp

Later in this chapter you learn how to use `accumulate()` in the `geometricMean()` function without writing a function callback or lambda expression.

C++11 C++11 Move Semantics with Algorithms

Just like STL containers, STL algorithms are also optimized to use C++11 move semantics at appropriate times. This can greatly speed up certain algorithms, for example `sort()`. For this reason, it is highly recommended that you implement move semantics in your custom element classes that you want to store in containers. Move semantics can be added to any class by implementing a move constructor and a move assignment operator. Consult the "Move Semantics" section in Chapter 9 for details on how to add move semantics to your classes.

C++11 LAMBDA EXPRESSIONS

C++11 adds a new feature called *lambda expressions*. This allows you to write anonymous functions inline, removing the need to write a separate function or to write a function object, and makes code easier to understand.

Syntax

The syntax of a lambda expression is as follows:

```
[capture_block](parameters) mutable exception_specification -> return_type {body}
```

A lambda expression contains the following parts:

➤ **Capture block:** specifies how variables from the enclosing scope are captured and made available in the body of the lambda. Explained in the next section.

➤ **Parameters:** (optional) a list of parameters for the lambda expression. You can only omit this list if you do not need any parameters and you do not specify `mutable`, an exception specification and a return type. Omitting the return type is only allowed in certain cases as explained under the return_type bullet.

For example: `[]{return 10;}`

The parameter list is similar to the parameter list for normal functions with the following differences:

➤ Parameters cannot have default values.

➤ Variable-length argument lists are not allowed.

➤ Unnamed parameters are not allowed.

➤ **Mutable:** (optional) if variables from the enclosing scope are captured by value, a copy of those variables will become available in the body of the lambda expression. Those copies are marked as `const` by default, meaning the lambda body cannot change the value of those copies. If the lambda expression is marked as `mutable`, those copies are not `const` and the body can modify those local copies.

➤ **exception_specification:** (optional) can be used to specify which exceptions the body of the lambda expression can throw.

➤ **return_type:** (optional) the type of the returned value. If the `return_type` part is omitted, the compiler will decide the return type as follows:

➤ If the body of the lambda expression is of the following form:
```
{ return expression; }
```
the type of `expression` will become the `return_type` of the lambda expression.

➤ Otherwise the `return_type` is `void`.

The following example demonstrates that you can create a lambda expression and immediately execute it. The line defines a lambda expression without return type and without any parameters.

It simply prints the string "Hello from Lambda" to the console. Note the parentheses () at the end, which causes the lambda to be executed immediately:

```
[]{cout << "Hello from Lambda" << endl;}();
```

Code snippet from Lambdas\LambdaInvocation.cpp

The output is as follows:

```
Hello from Lambda
```

The following example defines a lambda that accepts a string argument and returns a string. The result is stored in the variable `result`. Again notice the parentheses at the end of the lambda causing the lambda to be executed immediately:

```
string result = [](const string& str) -> string {return "Hello from "
                  + str;}("second Lambda");
cout << "Result: " << result << endl;
```

Code snippet from Lambdas\LambdaInvocation.cpp

The output is as follows:

```
Result: Hello from second Lambda
```

As mentioned before, the return type can be omitted in this case:

```
string result = [](const string& str){return "Hello from "
                  + str;}("second Lambda");
```

Code snippet from Lambdas\LambdaInvocation.cpp

You can also store a pointer to a lambda expression and execute the lambda through the function pointer. Using the C++11 `auto` keyword, this becomes very easy:

```
auto fn = [](const string& str){return "Hello from " + str;};
cout << fn("call 1") << endl;
cout << fn("call 2") << endl;
```

Code snippet from Lambdas\LambdaFunctionPointer.cpp

The preceding code results in the following output:

```
Hello from call 1
Hello from call 2
```

Capture Block

The square brackets part is called the lambda *capture block*. It allows you to specify how you want to *capture* variables from the enclosing scope. *Capturing* a variable means that the variable becomes available inside the body of the lambda. There are two ways to capture all variables from the enclosing scope:

➤ [=] captures all variables by value

➤ [&] captures all variables by reference

Specifying an empty capture block [] means that no variables from the enclosing scope are being captured. It is also possible to selectively decide which variables to capture and how, by specifying a *capture list* with an optional *capture default*. Variables prefixed with & are captured by reference. Variables without a prefix are captured by value. The capture default should be the first element in the capture list and be either & or =. For example:

➤ [&x] captures only x by reference and nothing else.

➤ [x] captures only x by value and nothing else.

➤ [=, &x, &y] captures by value by default, except variables x and y, which are captured by reference.

➤ [&, x] captures by reference by default, except variable x, which is captured by value.

➤ [&x, &x] is illegal because identifiers cannot be repeated.

When you capture a variable by reference, you have to make sure that the reference is still valid at the time the lambda expression is executed. This will be demonstrated with the multiplyBy2Lambda() example in the following section.

Lambda Expressions as Return Type

std::function defined in the <functional> header file is a polymorphic function object wrapper and is similar to a function pointer. It can be bound to anything that can be called (functors, member function pointers, function pointers, and lambdas) as long as the arguments and return type are compatible with those of the wrapper. A wrapper for a function that returns a double and takes two integers as parameters can be defined as follows:

```
function<double(int, int)> myWrapper;
```

By using std::function, lambda expressions can be returned from functions. Take a look at the following definition:

```
function<int(void)> multiplyBy2Lambda(int x)
{
    return [=]()->int{return 2*x;};
}
```

Code snippet from Lambdas\multiplyBy2Lambda.cpp

In this example, the return type and empty parameter list of the lambda expression can be omitted, so the preceding can be written as follows:

```
function<int(void)> multiplyBy2Lambda(int x)
{
    return [=]{return 2*x;};
}
```

Code snippet from Lambdas\multiplyBy2Lambda.cpp

The body of this function creates a lambda expression that captures the variables from the enclosing scope by value and returns an integer, which is two times the value passed to multiplyBy2Lambda(). The return type of the multiplyBy2Lambda() function is function<int(void)>, which is a function accepting no arguments and returning an integer. The lambda expression defined in the body of the function exactly matches this prototype. The variable x is captured by value and thus a copy of the value of x is bound to the x in the lambda expression before the lambda is returned from the function.

The preceding function can be called as follows:

```
function<int(void)> fn = multiplyBy2Lambda(5);
cout << fn() << endl;
```

Code snippet from Lambdas\multiplyBy2Lambda.cpp

You can use the C++11 auto keyword to make this much easier:

```
auto fn = multiplyBy2Lambda(5);
cout << fn() << endl;
```

Code snippet from Lambdas\multiplyBy2Lambda.cpp

The output will be 10.

The multiplyBy2Lambda() example captures the variable x by value, [=]. Suppose the function is rewritten to capture the variable by reference, [&], as follows. This will not work as explained after the code:

```
function<int(void)> multiplyBy2Lambda(int x)
{
    return [&]{return 2*x;};
}
```

The lambda expression captures x by reference. However, the lambda expression will be executed later in the program, not anymore in the scope of the multiplyBy2Lambda() function at which point the reference to x is not valid anymore!

Lambda Expressions as Parameters

You can write your own functions that accept lambda expressions as parameters. This can for example be used to implement callbacks. The following code implements a `testCallback()` function that accepts a `vector` of integers and a callback function. The implementation will iterate over all the elements in the given `vector` and will call the callback function for each element. The callback function accepts the current element in the `vector` as an `int` argument and returns a Boolean. If the callback returns `false`, the iteration is stopped.

Available for download on Wrox.com

```
void testCallback(const vector<int>& vec,
                  const function<bool(int)>& callback)
{
    for (auto i : vec) {
        // Call callback. If it returns false, stop iteration.
        if (!callback(i))
            break;
        // Callback did not stop iteration, so print value
        cout << i << " ";
    }
    cout << endl;
}
```

Code snippet from Lambdas\callback.cpp

The `testCallback()` function can be tested as follows. First a `vector` with 10 elements is created and the `generate()` algorithm is used to fill in those 10 elements. The `generate()` algorithm requires an iterator range and will replace the values in that range with the values returned from the function given as third parameter. The `generate()` algorithm is explained in more detail later in this chapter. The code then outputs all the values of the `vector` using the `for_each()` algorithm in combination with a lambda. The `for_each()` algorithm will call the function given as third parameter for each value in the given iterator range. The last line calls the `testCallback()` function with a small lambda expression as callback function. This lambda expression returns `true` for values that are less than 6.

Available for download on Wrox.com

```
vector<int> vec(10);
int index = 0;
generate(vec.begin(), vec.end(), [&index]{return ++index;});
for_each(vec.begin(), vec.end(), [](int i){cout << i << " ";});
cout << endl;
testCallback(vec, [](int i){return i<6;});
```

Code snippet from Lambdas\callback.cpp

The output of this example is as follows:

```
1 2 3 4 5 6 7 8 9 10
1 2 3 4 5
```

Examples

This section gives a few examples that use STL algorithms in combination with lambda expressions.

count_if

The following example uses the `count_if()` algorithm to count the number of elements in the given `vector` that satisfy a certain condition. The condition is given in the form of a lambda expression, which captures the variables in its enclosing scope by value. This makes the variable `value` available in the body of the lambda. Had the capture clause been the empty capture clause, `[]`, then the variable `value` would not be available in the body of the lambda expression. The lambda expression returns the result of performing the comparison `i>value`, which causes the compiler to automatically make the return type of the lambda a Boolean value. Note that the example initializes the `vector` using C++11 uniform initialization, discussed in Chapter 9.

```
vector<int> vec = {1,2,3,4,5,6,7,8,9};
int value = 3;
int cnt = count_if(vec.cbegin(),vec.cend(),
                   [=](int i){return i>value;});
cout << "Found " << cnt << " values > " << value << endl;
```

Code snippet from Lambdas\count_if.cpp

The output is as follows:

```
Found 6 values > 3
```

The preceding example can be extended to demonstrate capturing variables by reference. The following lambda expression will count the number of times it was called by incrementing a variable in the enclosing scope that was captured by reference.

```
vector<int> vec = {1,2,3,4,5,6,7,8,9};
int value = 3;
int cntLambdaCalled = 0;
int cnt = count_if(vec.cbegin(),vec.cend(),
    [=, &cntLambdaCalled](int i){++cntLambdaCalled; return i>value;});
cout << "The lambda expression was called " << cntLambdaCalled
     << " times." << endl;
cout << "Found " << cnt << " values > " << value << endl;
```

Code snippet from Lambdas\count_if_ref.cpp

The output is as follows:

```
The lambda expression was called 9 times.
Found 6 values > 3
```

generate

The `generate()` algorithm allows you to fill an iterator range with certain values. The following example uses the `generate()` algorithm together with a lambda expression to put the numbers 2, 4, 8, 16, and so on in the `vector`.

```cpp
vector<int> vec(10);
int value = 1;
generate(vec.begin(), vec.end(), [&value]{value*=2; return value;});
for (auto& i : vec)
    cout << i << " ";
```

Code snippet from Lambdas\generate.cpp

The output is as follows:

```
2 4 8 16 32 64 128 256 512 1024
```

for_each

The `for_each()` algorithm can be used to perform a specific action on all elements in the given range. A simple example is to use the `for_each()` algorithm in combination with a lambda expression to print values from a `vector`. This example defines a `vector` of integers. The first two arguments to `for_each()` specify the range in the container on which to apply the lambda expression given as third argument. For each value in the given range, the `for_each()` algorithm will call the lambda expression and will pass that value as argument to the lambda expression. Since the `vector` holds integers, the parameter for the lambda expression is an `int`.

```cpp
vector<int> vec = {11,22,33,44};
int index = 0;
for_each(vec.begin(), vec.end(),
            [&index](int i){cout << "Value " << (index++)
                               << ": " << i << endl;});
```

Code snippet from Lambdas\for_each.cpp

The output of the preceding code is as follows:

```
Value 0: 11
Value 1: 22
Value 2: 33
Value 3: 44
```

FUNCTION OBJECTS

You can overload the function call operator in a class such that objects of the class can be used in place of function pointers. These objects are called *function objects*, or just *functors*.

Many of the STL algorithms, such as `find_if()` and the second form of `accumulate()`, require a function pointer as one of the parameters. When you use these functions, you can pass a functor instead of a lambda or function pointer. C++ provides several predefined functor classes, defined in the `<functional>` header file, that perform the most commonly used callback operations.

Functor classes often consist of simple one-line expressions. The clumsiness of having to create a function or functor class, give it a name that does not conflict with other names, and then use this name is considerable intellectual overhead for what is fundamentally a simple concept. In these cases, using anonymous (unnamed) functions represented by lambda expressions is a big convenience. Their syntax is easier and can make your code easier to understand. They are discussed in the previous sections. However, this section explains functors and how to use the predefined functor classes because you will likely encounter them at some point.

With C++11, it is recommended to use lambda expressions, if possible, instead of function objects because lambdas are easier to use and easier to understand.

Arithmetic Function Objects

C++ provides functor class templates for the five binary arithmetic operators: `plus`, `minus`, `multiplies`, `divides`, and `modulus`. Additionally, unary `negate` is supplied. These classes are templatized on the type of the operands and are wrappers for the actual operators. They take one or two parameters of the template type, perform the operation, and return the result. Here is an example using the `plus` class template:

```cpp
plus<int> myPlus;
int res = myPlus(4, 5);
cout << res << endl;
```

Code snippet from FunctionObjects\Arithmetic.cpp

This example is silly, because there's no reason to use the `plus` class template when you could just use `operator+` directly. The benefit of the arithmetic function objects is that you can pass them as callbacks to algorithms, which you cannot do directly with the arithmetic operators. For example, the implementation of the `geometricMean()` function earlier in this chapter used the `accumulate()` function with a function pointer to the `product()` callback to multiply two integers. You could rewrite it to use the predefined `multiplies` function object:

```cpp
double geometricMean(const vector<int>& nums)
{
    double mult = accumulate(nums.begin(), nums.end(), 1,
        multiplies<int>());
    return pow(mult, 1.0 / nums.size());
}
```

Code snippet from FunctionObjects\Arithmetic.cpp

The expression `multiplies<int>()` creates a new object of the `multiplies` functor class, instantiating it with the `int` type.

The other arithmetic function objects behave similarly.

The arithmetic function objects are just wrappers around the arithmetic operators. If you use the function objects as callbacks in algorithms, make sure that the objects in your container implement the appropriate operation, such as operator* *or* operator+.

Comparison Function Objects

In addition to the arithmetic function object classes, the C++ language provides all the standard comparisons: equal_to, not_equal_to, less, greater, less_equal, and greater_equal. You've already seen less in Chapter 12 as the default comparison for elements in the priority_queue and the associative containers. Now you can learn how to change that criterion. Here's an example of a priority_queue using the default comparison operator: less.

Available for download on Wrox.com

```
priority_queue<int> myQueue;
myQueue.push(3);
myQueue.push(4);
myQueue.push(2);
myQueue.push(1);
while (!myQueue.empty()) {
    cout << myQueue.top() << " ";
    myQueue.pop();
}
```

Code snippet from FunctionObjects\QueueLess.cpp

The output from the program looks like this:

```
4 3 2 1
```

As you can see, the elements of the queue are removed in descending order, according to the less comparison. You can change the comparison to greater by specifying it as the comparison template argument. The priority_queue template definition looks like this:

```
template <class T, class Container = vector<T>, class Compare =
    less<T> >;
```

Unfortunately, the Compare type parameter is last, which means that in order to specify the comparison you must also specify the container. Here is an example of the above program modified so that the priority_queue sorts elements in ascending order using greater:

Available for download on Wrox.com

```
priority_queue<int, vector<int>, greater<int> > myQueue;
myQueue.push(3);
myQueue.push(4);
myQueue.push(2);
myQueue.push(1);
```

```
while (!myQueue.empty()) {
    cout << myQueue.top() << " ";
    myQueue.pop();
}
```

Code snippet from FunctionObjects\QueueGreater.cpp

The output now is as follows:

```
1 2 3 4
```

Due to a syntactic restriction in pre-C++11 versions of C++, it was necessary to put a space between two angle brackets if they were not `operator>>`. This syntactic restriction has been removed in C++11, and spaces are no longer required. This is covered in the "Angle Brackets" section in Chapter 9. Therefore, the declaration of `myQueue` can be written without the formerly-required space, as follows:

```
priority_queue<int, vector<int>, greater<int>> myQueue;
```

Several algorithms that you will learn about later in this chapter require comparison callbacks, for which the predefined comparators come in handy.

Logical Function Objects

C++ provides function object classes for the three logical operations: `logical_not` (operator!), `logical_and` (operator&&), and `logical_or` (operator||).

 Logical operations deal only with the values `true` and `false`. In the original STL, there was no provision for dealing with bitwise operations on integer-type values. C++11 has bitwise function objects (covered in the next section).

Logical functors can for example be used to implement an `allTrue()` function that checks if all the Boolean flags in a container are `true`. This can be implemented as follows:

```
bool allTrue(const vector<bool>& flags)
{
    return accumulate(flags.begin(), flags.end(), true,
        logical_and<bool>());
}
```

Code snippet from FunctionObjects\LogicalFunctors.cpp

Similarly, the `logical_or` functor can be used to implement an `anyTrue()` function that returns `true` if there is at least one Boolean flag in a container `true`:

```
bool anyTrue(const vector<bool>& flags)
{
    return accumulate(flags.begin(), flags.end(), false,
```

```
            logical_or<bool>());
    }
```

C++11 Bitwise Function Objects

C++11 adds function objects for all the bitwise operations: `bit_and` (`operator&`), `bit_or` (`operator|`), and `bit_xor` (`operator^`). These bitwise functors can for example be used together with the `transform()` algorithm (discussed later in this chapter) to perform bitwise operations on all elements in a container.

Function Object Adapters

When you try to use the basic function objects provided by the standard, it often feels as if you're trying to put a square peg into a round hole. For example, you can't use the `less` function object with `find_if()` to find an element smaller than some value because `find_if()` passes only one argument to its callback each time instead of two. The *function adapters* attempt to rectify this problem and others. They provide a modicum of support for *functional composition*, or combining functions together to create the exact behavior you need.

Binders

Binders can be used to *bind* parameters of functions to certain values. C++11 introduces `std::bind()`, which is very flexible and is discussed in the following section. The section afterwards explains the pre-C++11 `bind2nd()` and `bind1st()` adapters, which you have to use if your compiler does not yet support `std::bind()`.

C++11 std::bind

`std::bind()` allows you to bind arguments of a function in a flexible way. You can bind function arguments to fixed values and you can even rearrange function arguments in a different order. It is best explained with an example.

Suppose you have a function called `func()` accepting two arguments:

Available for
download on
Wrox.com

```
void func(int num, const string& str)
{
    cout << "func(" << num << ", " << str << ")" << endl;
}
```

The following code demonstrates how you can use `bind()` to bind the second argument of the `func()` function to a fixed value, `str`. The result is stored in `f1()`. The C++11 `auto` keyword is used to remove the need to specify the exact return type which can become complicated. Arguments that are not bound to specific values should be specified as `_1`, `_2`, `_3` and so on. These are defined in the `std::placeholders` namespace. In the definition of `f1()`, the `_1` specifies where the first argument of `f1()` needs to go when `func()` is called. After this, `f1()` can be called with just a single integer argument as follows:

```
string str = "abc";
auto f1 = bind(func, placeholders::_1, str);
f1(16);
```

Code snippet from FunctionObjects\bind.cpp

The output should be:

```
func(16, abc)
```

`bind()` can also be used to rearrange the arguments as shown in the following code. The `_2` specifies where the second argument of `f2()` needs to go when `func()` is called. In other words, the `f2()` binding means that the first argument to `f2()` will become the second argument to the function `func()` and the second argument to `f2()` will become the first argument to the function `func()`.

```
auto f2 = bind(func, placeholders::_2, placeholders::_1);
f2("Test", 32);
```

Code snippet from FunctionObjects\bind.cpp

The output is as follows:

```
func(32, Test)
```

There is a small issue with binding parameters in combination with overloaded functions. Suppose you have the following two overloaded functions called `overloaded()`. One accepts an integer and the other accepts a floating point number:

```
void overloaded(int num) {}
void overloaded(float f) {}
```

Code snippet from FunctionObjects\bind.cpp

If you want to use `bind()` with these overloaded functions, you need to explicitly specify which of the two overloads you want to bind. The following will not compile:

```
auto f3 = bind(overloaded, placeholders::_1); // ERROR
```

Code snippet from FunctionObjects\bind.cpp

If you want to bind the parameters of the overloaded function accepting a floating point argument, you need the following syntax:

```
auto f4 = bind((void(*)(float))overloaded, placeholders::_1); // OK
```

Code snippet from FunctionObjects\bind.cpp

Another example of the `bind()` function is to use the `find_if()` algorithm to find the first element in a sequence that is greater than or equal to 100. To solve this problem earlier in this chapter, you wrote a function `perfectScore()` and passed a function pointer to it to `find_if()`. Now that you know about the comparison functors, it seems as if you should be able to implement a solution using the `greater_equal` class template.

The problem with `greater_equal` is that it takes two parameters, whereas `find_if()` passes only one parameter to its callback predicate each time. You need the ability to specify that `find_if()` should use `greater_equal`, but should pass 100 as the second argument each time. That way, each element of the sequence will be compared against 100. This can be accomplished with `bind()`. The following code uses `bind()` to bind the second parameter of `greater_equal` to a fixed value of 100:

```cpp
// Code for inputting scores into the vector omitted, similar as earlier.
auto end = myVector.end();
auto it = find_if(myVector.begin(), end,
    bind(greater_equal<int>(), placeholders::_1, 100));
if (it == end) {
    cout << "No perfect scores" << endl;
} else {
    cout << "Found a \"perfect\" score of " << *it << endl;
}
```

Code snippet from FunctionObjects\Binders.cpp

Pre-C++11 bind2nd and bind1st

If your compiler does not support `bind()`, you need to use a method like `bind2nd()`. Unlike `bind()`, `bind2nd()` only works with binary functions and only allows you to bind the second argument. The following example shows that the `bind2nd()` method takes a function and a second argument. Because of `bind2nd()`, the function is then called with one argument passed in by `find_if()` and one argument derived from the `bind2nd()`.

```cpp
// Code for inputting scores into the vector omitted, similar as earlier.
vector<int>::iterator end = myVector.end();
vector<int>::iterator it = find_if(myVector.begin(),end,
    bind2nd(greater_equal<int>(), 100));
if (it == end) {
    cout << "No perfect scores" << endl;
} else {
    cout << "Found a \"perfect\" score of " << *it << endl;
}
```

Code snippet from FunctionObjects\Binders.cpp

The `bind2nd()` function in this code binds the value 100 as the second parameter to `greater_equal`. The result is that `find_if()` compares each element against 100 with `greater_equal`.

There is also an equivalent `bind1st()` function that binds an argument to the first parameter of a binary function. For example, the following finds the first value less than 100 using `bind1st()`, because if the result of `bind1st()` is called with argument x, it returns the value of `100 > x`:

```
find_if(v.begin(), v.end(), bind1st(greater<int>(), 100));
```

Compare this to the following, using `bind2nd()`, which finds the first value greater than 100, because if the result of `bind2nd()` is called with argument x, it returns the value of `x > 100`:

```
find_if(v.begin(), v.end(), bind2nd(greater<int>(), 100));
```

 Both `bind2nd()` *and* `bind1st()` *have been deprecated by C++11. Use lambda expressions or* `bind()` *instead.*

Negators

The *negators* are functions similar to the binders but they simply complement the result of a predicate. For example, if you wanted to find the first element in a sequence of test scores less than 100, you could apply the `not1()` negator adapter to the result of `greater_equal` like this:

```
// Code for inputting scores into the vector omitted, similar as earlier.
auto end = myVector.end();
auto it = find_if(myVector.begin(), end,
    not1(bind2nd(greater_equal<int>(), 100)));
if (it == end) {
    cout << "All perfect scores" << endl;
} else {
    cout << "Found a \"less-than-perfect\" score of " << *it << endl;
}
```

Code snippet from FunctionObjects\Negators.cpp

The function `not1()` complements the result of every call to the predicate it takes as an argument. Of course, you could also just use `less` instead of `greater_equal`. There are cases, often when using nonstandard functors, that `not1()` comes in handy. The "1" in `not1()` refers to the fact that its operand must be a unary function (one that takes a single argument). If its operand is a binary function (takes two arguments), you must use `not2()` instead. Note that you use `not1()` in this case because, even though `greater_equal` is a binary function, `bind2nd()` has already converted it to a unary function, by binding the second argument always to `100`.

As you can see, using functors and adapters can quickly become complicated. Our advice is to use C++11 lambda expressions and use functors sparingly. For example, the previous `find_if()` call using the `not1()` negator can be written more elegantly using a lambda expression:

```
auto it = find_if(myVector.begin(), end, [](int i){ return i < 100; });
```

Code snippet from FunctionObjects\Negators.cpp

Calling Member Functions

If you have a container of objects, you sometimes want to pass a pointer to a class method as the callback to an algorithm. For example, you might want to find the first empty string in a vector of strings by calling empty() on each string in the sequence. However, if you just pass a pointer to string::empty() to find_if(), the algorithm has no way to know that it received a pointer to a method instead of a normal function pointer or functor. The code to call a method pointer is different from that to call a normal function pointer, because the former must be called in the context of an object.

C++11 provides a conversion function called mem_fn() that you can call on a method pointer before passing it to an algorithm. The following example demonstrates this. Note that you have to specify the method pointer as &string::empty. The &string:: part is not optional. See Chapter 21 for details.

Available for download on Wrox.com

```cpp
void findEmptyString(const vector<string>& strings)
{
    auto end = strings.end();
    auto it = find_if(strings.begin(), end, mem_fn(&string::empty));
    if (it == end) {
        cout << "No empty strings!" << endl;
    } else {
        cout << "Empty string at position: " << it - strings.begin() << endl;
    }
}
```

Code snippet from FunctionObjects\EmptyString.cpp

mem_fn() generates a function object that serves as the callback for find_if(). Each time it is called back, it calls the empty() method on its argument.

mem_fn() works exactly the same when you have a container of pointers to objects instead of objects themselves. For example:

Available for download on Wrox.com

```cpp
void findEmptyString(const vector<string*>& strings)
{
    auto end = strings.end();
    auto it = find_if(strings.begin(), end, mem_fn(&string::empty));
    // Remaining of function omitted because it is the same as earlier
}
```

Code snippet from FunctionObjects\EmptyStringPtr.cpp

If your compiler does not yet support the C++11 mem_fn(), you have to use mem_fun_ref() when you have a container of objects as follows:

Available for download on Wrox.com

```cpp
auto it = find_if(strings.begin(), end, mem_fun_ref(&string::empty));
```

Code snippet from FunctionObjects\EmptyString.cpp

However, if you have a container of pointers to objects and you can't use the C++11 mem_fn(), then you have to use mem_fun() as follows:

```
auto it = find_if(strings.begin(), end, mem_fun(&string::empty));
```

Code snippet from FunctionObjects\EmptyStringPtr.cpp

> mem_fun_ref() *and* mem_fun() *work in restricted cases. If the method takes 0 arguments, the result can be used as a callback for a unary function; if it takes 1 argument, the result can be used as a callback for a binary function. C++11* mem_fn() *works for n-ary functions and for both containers of pointers to objects and containers of objects themselves*

mem_fn(), mem_fun_ref(), and mem_fun() are not the most intuitive ways to implement the findEmptyString() function. Using C++11 lambda expressions, it can be implemented in a much more readable and elegant way. Here is the implementation using a lambda expression working on a container of objects:

```
void findEmptyString(const vector<string>& strings)
{
    auto end = strings.end();
    auto it = find_if(strings.begin(), end,
        [](const string& str){ return str.empty(); });
    // Remaining of function omitted because it is the same as earlier
}
```

Code snippet from FunctionObjects\EmptyString.cpp

Similarly, the following uses a lambda expression working on a container of pointers to objects:

```
void findEmptyString(const vector<string*>& strings)
{
    auto end = strings.end();
    auto it = find_if(strings.begin(), end,
        [](const string* str){ return str->empty(); });
    // Remaining of function omitted because it is the same as earlier
}
```

Code snippet from FunctionObjects\EmptyStringPtr.cpp

> *Both* mem_fun_ref() *and* mem_fun() *have been deprecated by C++11. Use lambda expressions instead, or* mem_fn().

Adapting Real Functions

You can't use normal function pointers directly with the function adapters bind1st(), bind2nd(), not1(), or not2(), because these adapters require specific typedefs in the function objects they adapt. For example, not1() can only operate on function objects that include an argument_type typedef, while not2() requires a first_argument_type and second_argument_type typedef. The bind1st() and bind2nd() adapters require similar typedefs.

One last function adapter provided by the C++ standard library, ptr_fun(), allows you to wrap regular function pointers in a way that they can be used with the adapters. The ptr_fun() adapter is only explained here because you might encounter it in older codebases. If you are writing new code and are using a C++11 compiler, you should use lambda expressions.

As an example, suppose that you want to write a function isNumber() that returns true if every character in a string is a digit. The C++ string class provides an iterator. Thus, you can use the find_if() algorithm to search for the first nondigit in the string. If you find one, the string is not a number. The <cctype> header file provides a legacy C function called isdigit(), which returns true if a character is a digit, false otherwise.

 The definition of isdigit() *in* <cctype> *is not the same as* isdigit() *in the more traditional C library* <ctype.h>. *In* <ctype.h>, *the* isdigit() *function is defined as a macro, which makes it completely unsuitable for use in this context. In* <cctype> *it is defined as a function.*

The problem is that you want to find the first character that is not a digit, which requires the not1() adapter. However, because isdigit() is a C function, not a function object, you need to use the ptr_fun() adapter to generate a function object that can be used with not1(). The code looks as follows:

```cpp
bool isNumber(const string& str)
{
    auto end = str.end();
    auto it = find_if(str.begin(), end, not1(ptr_fun(::isdigit)));
    return (it == end);
}
```

Code snippet from FunctionObjects\IsNumber.cpp

Note the use of the :: scope resolution operator to specify that isdigit() should be found in the global scope.

C++11 has deprecated ptr_fun() and you should use a lambda expression instead:

```cpp
bool isNumber(const string& str)
{
    auto end = str.end();
```

```
        auto it = find_if(str.begin(), end, [](char c){return !::isdigit(c);});
        return (it == end);
    }
```

Code snippet from FunctionObjects\IsNumber.cpp

For this example, you can also use the new C++11 `find_if_not()` algorithm as follows:

```
bool isNumber(const string& str)
{
    auto end = str.end();
    auto it = find_if_not(str.begin(), end, ::isdigit);
    return (it == end);
}
```

Code snippet from FunctionObjects\IsNumber.cpp

 `ptr_fun()` *has been deprecated by C++11. Use lambda expressions instead.*

Writing Your Own Function Objects

If your compiler does not yet support the C++11 lambda expressions, you can write your own function objects to perform more specific tasks than those provided by the predefined functors. If you want to be able to use the function adapters with these functors, you must supply certain `typedefs`. The easiest way to do that is to subclass your function object classes from either `unary_function` or `binary_function`, depending on whether they take one or two arguments. These two classes, defined in `<functional>`, are templatized on the parameter and return types of the "function" they provide. For example, instead of using `ptr_fun()` to convert `isdigit()`, you could write a wrapper function object like this:

```
class myIsDigit : public unary_function<char, bool>
{
    public:
        bool operator() (char c) const { return ::isdigit(c); }
};
bool isNumber(const string& str)
{
    auto end = str.end();
    auto it = find_if(str.begin(), end, not1(myIsDigit()));
    return (it == end);
}
```

Code snippet from FunctionObjects\WritingFunctionObject.cpp

Note that the overloaded function call operator of the `myIsDigit` class must be `const` in order to pass objects of it to `find_if()`.

> *The algorithms are allowed to make multiple copies of function object predicates and call different ones for different elements. The function call operator needs to be* const, *thus, you cannot write functors such that they count on any internal state to the object being consistent between calls.*

Before C++11, a class defined locally in the scope of a function could not be used as a template argument. C++11 removes this limitation. The following example is perfectly legal in C++11, but was not legal before C++11:

Available for
download on
Wrox.com

```cpp
bool isNumber(const string& str)
{
    class myIsDigit : public unary_function<char, bool>
    {
        public:
            bool operator() (char c) const { return ::isdigit(c); }
    };
    auto end = str.end();
    auto it = find_if(str.begin(), end, not1(myIsDigit()));
    return (it == end);
}
```

Code snippet from FunctionObjects\WritingFunctionObjectLocal.cpp

> *As you can see from these examples, C++11 lambda expressions allow you to write more readable and more elegant code. We recommend to use simple lambda expressions instead of function objects, and to use function objects only when they need to do more complicated things.*

ALGORITHM DETAILS

This chapter describes the general categories of algorithms, with examples of each. The Standard Library Reference resource on the website (www.wrox.com) contains a summary of *all* the algorithms.

There are five types of iterators: input, output, forward, bidirectional, and random-access. These are described in Chapter 12. There is no formal class hierarchy of these iterators, because the implementations for each container are not part of the standard hierarchy. However, one can deduce a hierarchy based on the functionality they are required to provide. Specifically, every random access iterator is also bidirectional, every bidirectional iterator is also forward, and every forward iterator is also input and output. Figure 13-1 shows such hierarchy. Dotted lines are used because the figure is not a real class hierarchy.

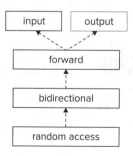

FIGURE 13-1

The standard way for the algorithms to specify what kind of iterators they need is to use the following names for the iterator template arguments: InputIterator, OutputIterator, ForwardIterator, BidirectionalIterator, and RandomAccessIterator. These names are just names: They don't provide binding type checking. Therefore, you could, for example, try to call an algorithm expecting a RandomAccessIterator by passing a bidirectional iterator. The template doesn't do type checking, so it would allow this instantiation. However, the code in the function that uses the random access iterator capabilities would fail to compile on the bidirectional iterator. Thus, the requirement is enforced, just not where you would expect. The error message can therefore be somewhat confusing. For example, attempting to use the generic sort() algorithm, which requires a random access iterator, on a list, which provides only a bidirectional iterator, gives this error in g++:

```
/usr/include/c++/3.2.2/bits/stl_algo.h: In function `void
    std::sort(_RandomAccessIter, _RandomAccessIter) [with _RandomAccessIter =
    std::_List_iterator<int, int&, int*>]':
Sorting.cpp:38:    instantiated from here
/usr/include/c++/3.2.2/bits/stl_algo.h:2178: no match for `
    std::_List_iterator<int, int&, int*>& - std::_List_iterator<int, int&,
    int*>&' operator
```

Most of the algorithms are defined in the <algorithm> header file, but a few algorithms are located in <numeric>. They are all in the std namespace.

Utility Algorithms

The STL provides four utility algorithms implemented as function templates: min(), max(), swap() and the C++11 minmax(). The min() and max() functions compare two elements of any type using operator< or a user-supplied binary predicate, returning a const reference to the smaller or larger element, respectively. The swap() function takes two elements of any type by reference and switches their values. With C++11, the min() and max() algorithms can be used to compare more than two values, while the minmax() algorithm returns a pair containing the minimum and the maximum value of two or more elements.

These utilities do not work on sequences of elements, so they do not take iterator parameters.

The following program demonstrates the four algorithms:

Available for download on Wrox.com

```
int x = 4, y = 5;
cout << "x is " << x << " and y is " << y << endl;
cout << "Max is " << max(x, y) << endl;
cout << "Min is " << min(x, y) << endl;
swap(x, y);
cout << "x is " << x << " and y is " << y << endl;
cout << "Max is " << max(x, y) << endl;
cout << "Min is " << min(x, y) << endl;

// C++11: using max and min on more than two values
int x1 = 2, x2 = 9, x3 = 3, x4 = 12;
cout << "Max of 4 elements is " << max({x1,x2,x3,x4}) << endl;
cout << "Min of 4 elements is " << min({x1,x2,x3,x4}) << endl;
```

```
// C++11: using minmax
auto p2 = minmax({x1,x2,x3,x4});
cout << "Minmax of 4 elements is <"
    << p2.first << "," << p2.second << ">" << endl;
```

Code snippet from UtilityAlgorithms\utilities.cpp

Here is the program output:

```
x is 4 and y is 5
Max is 5
Min is 4
x is 5 and y is 4
Max is 5
Min is 4
Max of 4 elements is 12
Min of 4 elements is 2
Minmax of 4 elements is <2,12>
```

> *The C language also includes a* min() *and* max() *function; however, they are implemented as macros, and will potentially evaluate one of their arguments twice; whereas* std::min() *and* std::max() *evaluate each argument exactly once. Make sure you always use the C++ versions,* std::min() *and* std::max()*, either by explicitly specifying* std:: *or by using a* using namespace std *clause.*

Non-Modifying Algorithms

The non-modifying algorithms include functions for searching elements in a range, generating numerical information about elements in a range, comparing two ranges to each other, and processing each element in a range.

Search Algorithms

You've already seen three examples of using search algorithms: find(), find_if(), and the C++11 find_if_not(). The STL provides several other variations of the basic find() algorithm that work on sequences of elements. The section "Search Algorithms" in Chapter 11 describes the different search algorithms that are available, including their complexity.

All the algorithms use default comparisons of operator== or operator<, but also provide overloaded versions that allow you to specify a comparison callback.

Here are examples of some of the search algorithms:

```
// The list of elements to be searched
vector<int> myVector = {5, 6, 9, 8, 8, 3};
auto begin = myVector.begin();
auto end = myVector.end();
```

```cpp
// Find the min and max elements in the vector
auto it = min_element(begin, end);
auto it2 = max_element(begin, end);
cout << "min is " << *it << " and max is " << *it2 << endl;

// Find the first pair of matching consecutive elements
it = adjacent_find(begin, end);
if (it != end) {
    cout << "Found two consecutive equal elements with value " << *it << endl;
}

// Find the first of two values
vector<int> targets = {8, 9};
it = find_first_of(begin, end, targets.begin(), targets.end());
if (it != end) {
    cout << "Found one of 8 or 9: " << *it << endl;
}

// Find the first subsequence
vector<int> sub = {8, 3};
it = search(begin, end, sub.begin(), sub.end());
if (it != end) {
    cout << "Found subsequence {8,3}" << endl;
} else {
    cout << "Unable to find subsequence {8,3}" << endl;
}

// Find the last subsequence (which is the same as the first in this example)
it2 = find_end(begin, end, sub.begin(), sub.end());
if (it != it2) {
    cout << "Error: search and find_end found different subsequences "
         << "even though there is only one match." << endl;
}

// Find the first subsequence of two consecutive 8s
it = search_n(begin, end, 2, 8);
if (it != end) {
    cout << "Found two consecutive 8s" << endl;
} else {
    cout << "Unable to find two consecutive 8s" << endl;
}
```

Code snippet from NonModifyingAlgorithms\SearchAlgorithms.cpp

Here is the output:

```
min is 3 and max is 9
Found two consecutive equal elements with value 8
Found one of 8 or 9: 9
Found subsequence {8,3}
Found two consecutive 8s
```

There are also several search algorithms that work only on sorted sequences: `binary_search()`, `lower_bound()`, `upper_bound()`, and `equal_range()`. Examples of sorted sequences are `vectors` whose contents are sorted, map, multimap, set, and multiset. The binary_search() algorithm finds a matching element in logarithmic time (see Chapter 2). The other three are similar to their method equivalents on the map and set containers. See Chapter 12 for an example on how to use them.

> *Remember to use equivalent container methods when available instead of generic algorithms, because the methods are more efficient.*

The section "Search Algorithms" in Chapter 11 also describes a number of new C++11 search algorithms: find_if_not(), minmax_element(), all_of(), any_of(), none_of(), and partition_point().

The following example shows these new algorithms in action. This example also demonstrates the use of cbegin() and cend() to get const iterators.

```cpp
vector<int> vec = {0,0,0,1,0,2,0};
auto begin = vec.cbegin();
auto end = vec.cend();

// Find an element != 0
auto it = find_if_not(begin, end, [](int i){return i == 0;});
if (it == end)
    cout << "No element found != 0" << endl;
else
    cout << "Found element " << *it << " != 0" << endl;

// Find min and max with 1 algorithm
auto minmax = minmax_element(begin, end);
cout << "Min = " << *(minmax.first) << " and Max = " << *(minmax.second) << endl;

// all_of()
vector<int> vec2 = {1,1,1,1};
if (all_of(vec2.cbegin(), vec2.cend(), [](int i){return i == 1;}))
    cout << "All elements are == 1" << endl;
else
    cout << "Not all elements are == 1" << endl;

// any_of()
vector<int> vec3 = {0,0,1,0};
if (any_of(vec3.cbegin(), vec3.cend(), [](int i){return i == 1;}))
    cout << "At least one element == 1" << endl;
else
    cout << "No elements are == 1" << endl;

// none_of()
vector<int> vec4 = {0,0,0,0};
if (none_of(vec4.cbegin(), vec4.cend(), [](int i){return i == 1;}))
    cout << "All elements are != 1" << endl;
else
    cout << "Some elements are == 1" << endl;
```

```
// partition_point()
vector<int> vec5 = {1,1,0,4,5,6};
auto ppoint = partition_point(vec5.cbegin(), vec5.cend(),
    [](int i){return i == 1;});
cout << "Partition point at position " << (ppoint-vec5.cbegin()) << endl;
```

Code snippet from NonModifyingAlgorithms\Cpp11SearchAlgorithms.cpp

The output is as follows:

```
Found element 1 != 0
Min = 0 and Max = 2
All elements are == 1
At least one element == 1
All elements are != 1
Partition point at position 2
```

Numerical Processing Algorithms

You've seen an example of one numerical processing algorithm already: `accumulate()`. In addition, the `count()` and `count_if()` algorithms are useful for counting the number of elements of a given value in a container. They function similarly to the `count()` method on the `map` and `set` containers. See section "Numerical Processing Algorithms" in Chapter 11 for a description of all numerical processing algorithms that are available.

As another example, the following calculates the inner product between two `vectors`, which is in this example `(1*9)+(2*8)+(3*7)+(4*6)`:

```
vector<int> v1 = {1,2,3,4};
vector<int> v2 = {9,8,7,6};
cout << inner_product(v1.cbegin(), v1.cend(), v2.cbegin(), 0) << endl;
```

Code snippet from NonModifyingAlgorithms\inner_product.cpp

The output is `70`.

Comparison Algorithms

You can compare entire ranges of elements in three different ways: `equal()`, `mismatch()`, and `lexicographical_compare()`. These algorithms have the advantage that you can compare ranges in different containers. For example, you can compare the contents of a `vector` with the contents of a `list`. In general, these work best with sequential containers. They work by comparing the values in corresponding positions of the two collections to each other.

➤   `equal()` returns `true` if all corresponding elements are equal. It requires both containers to have the same number of elements.

➤   `mismatch()` returns iterators, one iterator for each of the collections, to indicate where in the range the corresponding elements mismatched.

➤ `lexicographical_compare()` deals with the situation where the two ranges may contain different numbers of elements. It returns `true` if all the elements in the first range are less than their corresponding elements in the second range, or, if the first range has fewer elements than the second and all elements in the first range are less than their corresponding initial subsequence in the second set.

"lexicographical_compare" gets its name because it resembles the rules for comparing strings, but extends this set of rules to deal with objects of any type.

> *If you want to compare the elements of two containers of the same type, you can use* `operator==` *or* `operator<` *instead of* `equal()` *or* `lexicographical_compare()`. *The algorithms are useful primarily for comparing sequences of elements from different container types.*

Here are some examples of these algorithms:

```cpp
// Function template to populate a container of ints.
// The container must support push_back().
template<typename Container>
void populateContainer(Container& cont)
{
    int num;
    while (true) {
        cout << "Enter a number (0 to quit): ";
        cin >> num;
        if (num == 0) {
            break;
        }
        cont.push_back(num);
    }
}
int main()
{
    vector<int> myVector;
    list<int> myList;
    cout << "Populate the vector:" << endl;
    populateContainer(myVector);
    cout << "Populate the list:" << endl;
    populateContainer(myList);

    if (myList.size() < myVector.size()) {
        cout << "Sorry, the list is not long enough." << endl;
        return 1;
    }
    // compare the two containers
    if (equal(myVector.begin(), myVector.end(), myList.begin())) {
        cout << "The two containers have equal elements" << endl;
    } else {
```

```
      // If the containers were not equal, find out why not
      auto miss = mismatch(myVector.begin(), myVector.end(),
          myList.begin());
      cout << "The following initial elements are "
          << "the same in the vector and the list:" << endl;
      for (auto i = myVector.begin(); i != miss.first; ++i)
          cout << *i << '\t';
      cout << endl;
   }
   // Now order them.
   if (lexicographical_compare(myVector.begin(), myVector.end(),
      myList.begin(), myList.end())) {
      cout << "The vector is lexicographically first." << endl;
   } else {
      cout << "The list is lexicographically first." << endl;
   }
   return 0;
}
```

Code snippet from NonModifyingAlgorithms\ComparisonAlgorithms.cpp

Here is a sample run of the program:

```
Populate the vector:
Enter a number (0 to quit): 5
Enter a number (0 to quit): 6
Enter a number (0 to quit): 7
Enter a number (0 to quit): 0
Populate the list:
Enter a number (0 to quit): 5
Enter a number (0 to quit): 6
Enter a number (0 to quit): 9
Enter a number (0 to quit): 8
Enter a number (0 to quit): 0
The following initial elements are the same in the vector and the list:
5       6
The vector is lexicographically first.
```

Operational Algorithms

There is only one algorithm in this category: `for_each()`. However, it is one of the most useful algorithms in the STL. It executes a callback on each element of the range. You can use it with simple function callbacks or lambda expressions for things like printing every element in a container. Following is an example using a lambda expression and uniform initialization, printing the elements from the map:

```
map<int, int> myMap = {{4, 40}, {5, 50}, {6, 60}};
for_each(myMap.cbegin(), myMap.cend(), [](const pair<int, int>& p)
    {cout << p.first << "->" << p.second << endl;});
```

Code snippet from NonModifyingAlgorithms\ForEachBasicLambda.cpp

The output is as follows:

```
4->40
5->50
6->60
```

Doing the same thing in pre-C++11 requires a separate function, and a pointer to it is given to
`for_each()`:

Available for
download on
Wrox.com

```
void printPair(const pair<int, int>& elem)
{
    cout << elem.first << "->" << elem.second << endl;
}
int main()
{
    map<int, int> myMap;
    myMap.insert(make_pair(4, 40));
    myMap.insert(make_pair(5, 50));
    myMap.insert(make_pair(6, 60));
    for_each(myMap.begin(), myMap.end(), printPair);
    return 0;
}
```

Code snippet from NonModifyingAlgorithms\ForEachBasic.cpp

A functor could be useful in the context of `for_each()` because `for_each()` returns a copy of
the callback object, so you can accumulate information in your functor that you can retrieve after
`for_each()` has finished processing each element. For example, you could calculate both the
sum and product of elements in one pass by writing a functor `SumAndProd` that tracks both at the
same time:

Available for
download on
Wrox.com

```
// The populateContainer() function is identical to the one shown earlier
// for comparison algorithms, so it is omitted here.
class SumAndProd : public unary_function<int, void>
{
    public:
        SumAndProd() : sum(0), prod(1) {}
        void operator()(int elem);
        // make sum and prod public for easy access
        int sum;
        int prod;
};
void SumAndProd::operator()(int elem)
{
    sum += elem;
    prod *= elem;
}
int main()
{
    vector<int> myVector;
    populateContainer(myVector);
    SumAndProd func;
```

```
        func = for_each(myVector.cbegin(), myVector.cend(), func);
        cout << "The sum is " << func.sum << endl;
        cout << "The product is " << func.prod << endl;
        return 0;
    }
```

Code snippet from NonModifyingAlgorithms\SumAndProd.cpp

You might be tempted to ignore the return value of `for_each()`, yet still try to read information from `func` after the call. However, that doesn't work because `func` is passed-by-value into `for_each()`, so `for_each()` receives a copy of `func`. You must capture the return value in order to ensure correct behavior.

To show the power of C++11 lambda expressions, the preceding example using a functor to calculate the sum and product of a range can be modified to use a small lambda expression as follows. Note that the lambda expression captures all variables in its enclosing scope by reference with `[&]`, otherwise changes made to `sum` and `prod` in the lambda expression would not be visible outside the lambda:

```
// The populateContainer() function is identical to the one shown earlier
// for comparison algorithms, so it is omitted here.
vector<int> myVector;
populateContainer(myVector);
int sum = 0;
int prod = 1;
for_each(myVector.cbegin(), myVector.cend(),
    [&](int i){
        sum += i;
        prod *= i;
});
cout << "The sum is " << sum << endl;
cout << "The product is " << prod << endl;
```

Code snippet from NonModifyingAlgorithms\SumAndProdLambda.cpp

A final point about `for_each()` is that your lambda or callback is allowed to take its argument by reference and modify it. That has the effect of changing values in the actual iterator range. The voter registration example later in this chapter shows a use of this capability.

Modifying Algorithms

The STL provides a variety of *modifying algorithms* that perform tasks such as copying elements from one range to another, removing elements, or reversing the order of elements in a range.

The modifying algorithms all have the concept of *source* and *destination* ranges. The elements are read from the source range and added to or modified in the destination range. The source and destination ranges can often be the same, in which case the algorithm is said to operate *in place*.

Ranges from maps *and* multimaps *cannot be used as destinations of modifying algorithms. These algorithms overwrite entire elements, which in a* map *consist of key/value pairs. However,* maps *and* multimaps *mark the key* const, *so it cannot be assigned to. Similarly, many implementations of* set *and* multiset *provide only* const *iteration over the elements, so you cannot generally use ranges from these containers as destinations of modifying algorithms either. Your alternative is to use an* insert iterator, *described in Chapter 17.*

The section "Modifying Algorithms" in Chapter 11 lists all available modifying algorithms with a description. This section provides code examples for a number of those algorithms.

C++11 iota

C++11 adds an iota() algorithm, defined in the <numeric> header file, which generates a sequence of values in the specified range starting with the specified value and applying operator++ to generate each successive value. The following example shows how to use this new algorithm on a vector of integers, but note that it works on any element type that implements operator++:

Available for download on Wrox.com

```
vector<int> vec(10);
iota(vec.begin(), vec.end(), 5);
for (auto& i : vec) cout << i << " ";
```

Code snippet from ModifyingAlgorithms\iota.cpp

The output is as follows:

```
5 6 7 8 9 10 11 12 13 14
```

transform

The transform() algorithm is similar to for_each(), in that it applies a callback to each element in a range. The difference is that transform() expects the callback to generate a new element for each call, which it stores in the destination range specified. The source and destination ranges can be the same if you want transform() to replace each element in a range with the result from the call to the callback. For example, you could add 100 to each element in a vector like this:

Available for download on Wrox.com

```
// The populateContainer() function is identical to the one shown earlier
// for comparison algorithms, so it is omitted here.
vector<int> myVector;
populateContainer(myVector);
cout << "The vector contents are:" << endl;
for (auto& i : myVector) cout << i << " ";
cout << endl;
transform(myVector.begin(), myVector.end(), myVector.begin(),
    [](int i){return i + 100;});
```

```
cout << "The vector contents are:" << endl;
for (auto& i : myVector) cout << i << " ";
```

Code snippet from ModifyingAlgorithms\TransformLambda.cpp

Another form of `transform()` calls a binary function on pairs of elements in the range. The following example creates two `vectors` and uses `transform()` to calculate the sum of pairs of elements and store the result back in the first `vector`:

```
// The populateContainer() function is identical to the one shown earlier
// for comparison algorithms, so it is omitted here.
vector<int> vec1;
cout << "Vector1:" << endl;
populateContainer(vec1);
cout << "Vector2:" << endl;
vector<int> vec2;
populateContainer(vec2);
if (vec2.size() < vec1.size())
{
    cout << "Vector2 should be at least the same size as vector1." << endl;
    return 1;
}
// Create a lambda to print a vector
auto printVec = [](const vector<int>& vec){
    for (auto& i : vec) cout << i << " ";
    cout << endl;
};
cout << "Vector1: "; printVec(vec1);
cout << "Vector2: "; printVec(vec2);

transform(vec1.begin(), vec1.end(),
    vec2.begin(), vec1.begin(),
    [](int a, int b){return a + b;});

cout << "Vector1: "; printVec(vec1);
cout << "Vector2: "; printVec(vec2);
```

Code snippet from ModifyingAlgorithms\TransformLambdaBinary.cpp

The output could look as follows:

```
Vector1:
Enter a number (0 to quit): 1
Enter a number (0 to quit): 2
Enter a number (0 to quit): 0
Vector2:
Enter a number (0 to quit): 11
Enter a number (0 to quit): 22
Enter a number (0 to quit): 33
Enter a number (0 to quit): 0
Vector1: 1 2
```

```
Vector2: 11 22 33
Vector1: 12 24
Vector2: 11 22 33
```

 `transform()` *and the other modifying algorithms often return an iterator referring to the past-the-end value of the destination range. The examples in this book usually ignore that return value.*

copy

The `copy()` algorithm allows you to copy elements from one range to another, starting with the first element and proceeding to the last element in the range. The source and destination ranges must be different, but they can overlap. Note that `copy()` doesn't **insert** elements into the destination range. It just **overwrites** whatever elements were there already. Thus, you can't use `copy()` directly to insert elements into a container, only to overwrite elements that were previously in a container.

 Chapter 17 describes how to use iterator adapters *to insert elements into a container or stream with* `copy()`.

Here is a simple example of `copy()` that uses the `resize()` method on `vectors` to ensure that there is enough space in the destination container. It copies all elements from `vec1` to `vec2`:

Available for download on Wrox.com

```cpp
// The populateContainer() function is identical to the one shown earlier
// for comparison algorithms, so it is omitted here.
vector<int> vec1, vec2;
populateContainer(vec1);
vec2.resize(vec1.size());
copy(vec1.cbegin(), vec1.cend(), vec2.begin());
for_each(vec2.cbegin(), vec2.cend(), [](int i){cout << i << " ";});
```

Code snippet from ModifyingAlgorithms\Copy.cpp

There is also a `copy_backward()` algorithm, which copies the elements from the source backward to the destination. In other words, it starts with the last element of the source and puts it in the last position in the destination range and moves backward after each copy. The preceding example can be modified to use `copy_backward()` instead of `copy()` as follows. Note that you need to specify `vec2.end()` as third argument instead of `vec2.begin()`:

Available for download on Wrox.com

```cpp
copy_backward(vec1.cbegin(), vec1.cend(), vec2.end());
```

Code snippet from ModifyingAlgorithms\copy_backward.cpp

This will result in exactly the same output.

C++11 adds a few new copy algorithms. These include conditional copy, copy of a specified number of elements (so instead of specifying an ending iterator, only a count is necessary), and a copy that can copy to two different destinations.

The first one is `copy_if()`. It works by having an input range specified by two iterators, an output destination specified by an iterator, and a predicate (function or lambda expression). The function or lambda expression is executed for each element that is a candidate to be copied. If the returned value is `true`, the element is copied and the destination iterator is incremented; if the value is `false` the element is not copied and the destination iterator is not incremented. Thus, the destination may hold fewer elements than the source range. For some containers, because they must have already created space to hold the maximum possible number of elements (remember, copy does not create or extend containers, merely replaces the existing elements), it might be desirable to remove the space "beyond" where the last element was copied to. To facilitate this, `copy_if()` returns an iterator to the one-past-the-last-copied element in the destination range. This can be used to determine how many elements should be removed from the destination container. The following example demonstrates this by copying only the even numbers to vec2:

```cpp
// The populateContainer() function is identical to the one shown earlier
// for comparison algorithms, so it is omitted here.
vector<int> vec1, vec2;
populateContainer(vec1);
vec2.resize(vec1.size());
auto endIterator = copy_if(vec1.cbegin(), vec1.cend(),
        vec2.begin(), [](int i){return i%2==0;});
vec2.erase(endIterator, vec2.end());
for_each(vec2.cbegin(), vec2.cend(), [](int i){cout << i << " ";});
```

Code snippet from ModifyingAlgorithms\copy_if.cpp

Another C++11 addition is `copy_n()`, which copies n elements from the source to the destination. The first parameter of `copy_n()` is the start iterator. The second parameter of `copy_n()` is an integer specifying the number of elements to copy and the third parameter is the destination iterator. The `copy_n()` algorithm does not perform any bounds checking, so you must make sure that the start iterator, incremented by the number of elements to copy, does not exceed the `end()` of the collection or your program will have undefined behavior. Following is an example:

```cpp
// The populateContainer() function is identical to the one shown earlier
// for comparison algorithms, so it is omitted here.
vector<int> vec1, vec2;
populateContainer(vec1);
size_t cnt = 0;
cout << "Enter number of elements you want to copy: ";
cin >> cnt;
cnt = min(cnt, vec1.size());
vec2.resize(cnt);
copy_n(vec1.cbegin(), cnt, vec2.begin());
for_each(vec2.cbegin(), vec2.cend(), [](int i){cout << i << " ";});
```

Code snippet from ModifyingAlgorithms\copy_n.cpp

The last copy-related algorithm added by C++11 is called `partition_copy()`, which copies elements from the source to two different destinations. The specific destination for each element is selected based on the result of a predicate, either `true` or `false`. The returned value of `partition_copy()` is a pair of iterators: one iterator referring to one-past-the-last-copied element in the first destination range, and one iterator referring to one-past-the-last-copied element in the second destination range. These returned iterators can be used in combination with `erase()` to remove excess elements from the two destination ranges, just as with the `copy_if()` example earlier. The following example asks the user to enter a number of integers, which are then *partitioned* into two destination vectors; one for the even numbers and one for the odd numbers:

```cpp
// The populateContainer() function is identical to the one shown earlier
// for comparison algorithms, so it is omitted here.
vector<int> vec1, vecOdd, vecEven;
populateContainer(vec1);
vecOdd.resize(vec1.size());
vecEven.resize(vec1.size());

auto pairIters = partition_copy(vec1.cbegin(), vec1.cend(),
    vecEven.begin(), vecOdd.begin(),
    [](int i){return i%2==0;});

vecEven.erase(pairIters.first, vecEven.end());
vecOdd.erase(pairIters.second, vecOdd.end());
cout << "Even numbers: ";
for_each(vecEven.cbegin(), vecEven.cend(), [](int i){cout << i << " ";});
cout << endl << "Odd numbers: ";
for_each(vecOdd.cbegin(), vecOdd.cend(), [](int i){cout << i << " ";});
```

Code snippet from ModifyingAlgorithms\partition_copy.cpp

```
The output can be as follows:
Enter a number (0 to quit): 11
Enter a number (0 to quit): 22
Enter a number (0 to quit): 33
Enter a number (0 to quit): 44
Enter a number (0 to quit): 0
Even numbers: 22 44
Odd numbers: 11 33
```

Note that the last few examples used the `for_each()` algorithm to print elements of a container. As seen in other examples, you can also print the elements using a C++11 range-based `for` loop. For example, instead of writing the following:

```cpp
for_each(vecOdd.cbegin(), vecOdd.cend(), [](int i){cout << i << " ";});
```

You can write:

```cpp
for (auto& i : vecOdd)
    cout << i << " ";
```

C++11 move

C++11 adds two move related algorithms: `move()` and `move_backward()`. They both use the move semantics introduced in C++11 and discussed in Chapter 9. You have to provide a move assignment operator in your element classes if you want to use these new algorithms on containers with elements of your own types, as demonstrated in the following example. Consult Chapter 9 for details on implementing move assignment operators and the use of `std::move()`. The `MyClass` example defines a move assignment operator. The `main()` function creates a `vector` with three `MyClass` objects and then moves those elements from `vecSrc` to `vecDst`. Note that the code includes two different uses of `move()`. The `move()` function accepting a single argument converts an lvalue into an rvalue (Chapter 9), while `move()` accepting three arguments is the STL `move()` algorithm to move elements between containers.

Available for
download on
Wrox.com

```cpp
class MyClass
{
    public:
        MyClass() {}
        MyClass(const string& str) : mStr(str) {}
        // Move assignment operator
        MyClass& operator=(MyClass&& rhs) {
            if (this == &rhs)
                return *this;
            mStr = std::move(rhs.mStr);
            cout << "Move operator= (mStr=" << mStr << ")" << endl;
            return *this;
        }
        string getString() const {return mStr;}
    protected:
        string mStr;
};
int main()
{
    vector<MyClass> vecSrc = {MyClass("a"), MyClass("b"), MyClass("c")};
    vector<MyClass> vecDst(vecSrc.size());
    move(vecSrc.begin(), vecSrc.end(), vecDst.begin());
    for (auto& c : vecDst) cout << c.getString() << " ";
    return 0;
}
```

Code snippet from ModifyingAlgorithms\move.cpp

The output is as follows:

```
Move operator= (mStr=a)
Move operator= (mStr=b)
Move operator= (mStr=c)
a b c
```

 Chapter 9 explains that source objects in a move operation are reset because the target object takes ownership of the resources of the source object. For the previous example, this means that you should not use the objects from `vecSrc` anymore after the move operation.

`move_backward()` uses the same move mechanism as `move()` but it moves the elements from the last to the first element.

replace

The `replace()` and `replace_if()` algorithms replace elements in a range matching a value or predicate, respectively, with a new value. Take `replace_if()` as an example. Its first and second parameters specify the range of elements in your container. The third parameter is a function or lambda expression that returns `true` or `false`. If it returns `true`, the value in the container is replaced with the value given as fourth parameter; if it returns `false`, it leaves the original value.

For example, you might want to replace all values less than a lower limit with the value of the lower limit and replace all values greater than an upper limit with the value of the upper limit. This is called "clamping" values to a range. In audio applications, this is known as "clipping". For example, audio signals are often limited to integers in the range of -32K to +32K. The following example demonstrates this by first calling `replace_if()` to replace all values less than -32K with -32K and then calling a second `replace_if()` to replace all values greater than 32K with 32K:

Available for download on Wrox.com

```
// The populateContainer() function is identical to the one shown earlier
// for comparison algorithms, so it is omitted here.
vector<int> vec;
populateContainer(vec);
int lowLim = numeric_limits<short>::min();   // = -32768
int upLim = numeric_limits<short>::max();    // = 32767
replace_if(vec.begin(), vec.end(), [=](int i){return i < lowLim;}, lowLim);
replace_if(vec.begin(), vec.end(), [=](int i){return i > upLim;}, upLim);
for_each(vec.cbegin(), vec.cend(), [](int i){cout << i << " ";});
```

Code snippet from ModifyingAlgorithms\Replace.cpp

There are also variants of `replace()` called `replace_copy()` and `replace_copy_if()` that copy the results to a different destination range.

remove

Suppose you have a range of elements and you want to remove elements matching a certain condition. The first solution that you might think of is to check the documentation to see if your container has an `erase()` method and then iterate over all the elements and call `erase()` for each element that matches the condition. The `vector` is an example of a container that has such an `erase()` method. However, if applied to the `vector` container, this solution is very inefficient as it will cause a lot of memory operations to keep the `vector` contiguous in memory, resulting in a quadratic complexity (see Chapter 2), which is very bad. This solution is also error-prone, because you need to be careful that you keep your iterators valid after a call to `erase()`. The correct solution for this problem is the so-called *remove-erase-idiom*, which runs in linear time and is explained in this section.

The `remove()` and `remove_if()` algorithms "remove" certain elements from a range by partitioning the collection into two sets: the elements to be kept and the elements to be removed. The elements to remove can be specified by either a specific value or with a predicate. These elements are not really removed from the underlying container, because the algorithms have access only to the iterator abstraction, not to the container. Instead, elements to be kept are moved or copied to the beginning of the range and elements to be removed are moved or copied to the end of the range. An iterator is returned that points to the first element in the range of elements to be removed. If you want to actually erase these elements from the container, you must use the `remove()` algorithm, then call `erase()` on the container to erase all the elements from the returned iterator up to the end of the range. This is the *remove-erase-idiom.* Here is an example of a function that removes empty strings from a `vector` of strings:

```cpp
void removeEmptyStrings(vector<string>& strings)
{
    auto it = remove_if(strings.begin(), strings.end(),
        [](const string& str){return str.empty();});
    // Erase the removed elements.
    strings.erase(it, strings.end());
}
int main()
{
    vector<string> myVector = {"", "one", "", "two", "three", "four"};
    for (auto& str : myVector) cout << "\"" << str << "\"  ";
    cout << endl;
    removeEmptyStrings(myVector);
    for (auto& str : myVector) cout << "\"" << str << "\"  ";
    cout << endl;
    return 0;
}
```

Code snippet from ModifyingAlgorithms\Remove.cpp

The output is as follows:

```
""   "one"   ""   "two"   "three"   "four"
"one"   "two"   "three"   "four"
```

The `remove_copy()` and `remove_copy_if()` variations of `remove()` do not change the source range. Instead they copy all unremoved/retained elements to a different destination range. They are similar to `copy()`, in that the destination range must already be large enough to hold the new elements.

 The `remove()` *family of functions is* stable *in that it maintains the order of elements remaining in the container even while moving the retained elements toward the beginning.*

unique

The `unique()` algorithm is a special case of `remove()` that removes all duplicate contiguous elements. The `list` container provides its own `unique()` method that implements the same semantics. You should generally use `unique()` on sorted sequences, but nothing prevents you from running it on unsorted sequences.

The basic form of unique() runs in place, but there is also a version of the algorithm called unique_copy() that copies its results to a new destination range.

Chapter 12 showed an example of the list::unique() algorithm, so we omit an example of the general form here.

reverse

The reverse() algorithm reverses the order of the elements in a range. The first element in the range is swapped with the last, the second with the second-to-last, and so on.

The basic form of reverse() runs in place and requires two arguments: a start and end iterator for the range. There is also a version of the algorithm called reverse_copy() that copies its results to a new destination range and requires three arguments: a start and end iterator for the source range and a start iterator for the destination range.

Other Modifying Algorithms

The STL includes several other modifying algorithms, including iter_swap(), swap_ranges(), fill(), fill_n(), generate_n(), rotate(), rotate_copy(), next_permutation(), and prev_permutation(). They are used less frequently, so no examples are given for them. However, if you understand how to use the algorithms explained in this section, you should have no problem using these other algorithms. Consult the section "Modifying Algorithms" in Chapter 11 to get a list of all available modifying algorithms with a brief description.

Sorting Algorithms

The STL provides several variations of sorting algorithms. A "sorting algorithm" will reorder the contents of a container such that an ordering is maintained between sequential elements of the collection. Thus, it applies only to sequential collections. Sorting is not relevant to associative containers because they already maintain elements in a sorted order. Sorting is not relevant to the unordered associative containers either because they have no concept of ordering. Some containers, such as list and forward_list provide their own sorting methods because these can be implemented more efficiently internally than a general sort mechanism. Consequently, the general sorting algorithms are most useful for vectors, deques, and arrays.

Basic Sorting and Merging

The sort() function sorts a range of elements in $O(N \log N)$ time in the general case. Following the application of sort() to a range, the elements in the range are in nondecreasing order (lowest to highest), according to operator<. If you don't like that order, you can specify a different comparison callback such as greater.

A variant of sort(), called stable_sort(), maintains the relative order of equal elements in the range. However, because it needs to maintain relative order of equal elements in the range, it is less efficient than the sort() algorithm.

Once you have sorted the elements in a range, you can apply the binary_search() algorithm to find elements in logarithmic instead of linear time. It requires a start and end iterator specifying the range, a value to search, and optionally a comparison callback. It returns `true` if the value is found in the specified range, `false` otherwise.

The `merge()` function allows you to merge two sorted ranges together, while maintaining the sorted order. The result is a sorted range containing all the elements of the two source ranges. It works in linear time. The following parameters are required:

➤ start and end iterator of first source range

➤ start and end iterator of second source range

➤ start iterator of destination range

➤ optionally, a comparison callback

Without `merge()`, you could still achieve the same effect by concatenating the two ranges and applying `sort()` to the result, but that would be less efficient [$O(N \log N)$ instead of linear].

 Always ensure that you supply a big enough destination range to store the result of the merge!

Here is an example of sorting and merging:

```cpp
// The populateContainer() function is identical to the one shown earlier
// for comparison algorithms, so it is omitted here.
vector<int> vectorOne, vectorTwo, vectorMerged;
cout << "Enter values for first vector:" << endl;
populateContainer(vectorOne);
cout << "Enter values for second vector:" << endl;
populateContainer(vectorTwo);
// Sort both containers
sort(vectorOne.begin(), vectorOne.end());
sort(vectorTwo.begin(), vectorTwo.end());
// Make sure the destination vector is large enough to hold the values
// from both source vectors.
vectorMerged.resize(vectorOne.size() + vectorTwo.size());
merge(vectorOne.cbegin(), vectorOne.cend(), vectorTwo.cbegin(),
    vectorTwo.cend(), vectorMerged.begin());
cout << "Merged vector: ";
for_each(vectorMerged.cbegin(), vectorMerged.cend(),
    [](int i){cout << i << " ";});
cout << endl;
while (true) {
    int num;
    cout << "Enter a number to find (0 to quit): ";
    cin >> num;
    if (num == 0) {
        break;
    }
```

```
if (binary_search(vectorMerged.cbegin(), vectorMerged.cend(), num)) {
    cout << "That number is in the vector." << endl;
} else {
    cout << "That number is not in the vector." << endl;
}
}
```

Code snippet from SortingAlgorithms\SortingAndMerging.cpp

Other Sorting Algorithms

If you need to write your own sort algorithm, which is unlikely, there are several sorting routines that can be used as building blocks, including `partition()`, `partition_copy()` (C++11), `partial_sort()`, `partial_sort_copy()` (C++11), and `nth_element()`. C++11 also introduces `is_sorted()` and `is_sorted_until()` algorithms; `is_sorted()` returns `true` if the given range is sorted, while `is_sorted_until()` returns an iterator in the given range such that everything before this iterator is sorted. However, writing your own sort algorithm is a very exotic problem domain not usually operated in, and therefore we do not discuss these further.

The Standard Library Reference resource on the website contains the details in case the need arises to use one of these algorithms.

random_shuffle

The final "sorting" algorithm is technically more of an "anti-sorting" algorithm; `random_shuffle()` rearranges the elements of a range in a random order with a linear complexity. It's useful for implementing tasks like shuffling a deck of cards. There are two versions of `random_shuffle()`. The first version requires a start and end iterator for the range that you want to shuffle. For this version, the C++ standard does not define which random number generator the implementation has to use. Most compilers use `rand()` from the standard C library. Note that this requires you to seed the random number generator using `srand()`. The second version of `random_shuffle()` requires a start and end iterator for the range to shuffle and also accepts a third parameter which is a random number generator object that can be specified to adapt the randomness to suit your problem domain, for example uniform distribution, binomial distribution, and so on. Random number generators are discussed in detail in Chapter 16.

Set Algorithms

The final class of algorithms in the STL is five functions for performing set operations that work on any sorted iterator range. They do not work on unordered associative containers.

The `includes()` function implements standard subset determination, checking if all the elements of one sorted range are included in another sorted range, in any order.

The `set_union()`, `set_intersection()`, `set_difference()`, and `set_symmetric_difference()` algorithms implement the standard semantics of those operations. In set theory, the result of union is all the elements in either set. The result of intersection is all the elements which are in both sets. The result of difference is all the elements in the first set but not the second. The result of symmetric difference is the "exclusive or" of sets: all the elements in one, but not both, sets.

> *Make sure that your result range is large enough to hold the result of the operations. For* set_union() *and* set_symmetric_difference()*, the result is at most the sum of the sizes of the two input ranges. For* set_intersection() *and* set_difference() *it's at most the maximum of the two sizes.*

> *You can't use iterator ranges from associative containers, including sets, to store the results because they don't allow changes to their keys.*

Here is an example of how to use these algorithms:

```cpp
// The populateContainer() function is identical to the one shown earlier
// for comparison algorithms, so it is omitted here.
vector<int> vec1, vec2, result;
cout << "Enter elements for set 1:" << endl;
populateContainer(vec1);
cout << "Enter elements for set 2:" << endl;
populateContainer(vec2);
// set algorithms work on sorted ranges
sort(vec1.begin(), vec1.end());
sort(vec2.begin(), vec2.end());
cout << "Set 1: ";
for_each(vec1.cbegin(), vec1.cend(), [](int i){cout << i << " ";});
cout << endl;
cout << "Set 2: ";
for_each(vec2.cbegin(), vec2.cend(), [](int i){cout << i << " ";});
cout << endl;

if (includes(vec1.cbegin(), vec1.cend(), vec2.cbegin(), vec2.cend())) {
    cout << "The second set is a subset of the first." << endl;
}
if (includes(vec2.cbegin(), vec2.cend(), vec1.cbegin(), vec1.cend())) {
    cout << "The first set is a subset of the second" << endl;
}

result.resize(vec1.size() + vec2.size());
auto newEnd = set_union(vec1.cbegin(), vec1.cend(), vec2.cbegin(),
    vec2.cend(), result.begin());
cout << "The union is: ";
for_each(result.begin(), newEnd, [](int i){cout << i << " ";});
cout << endl;

newEnd = set_intersection(vec1.cbegin(), vec1.cend(), vec2.cbegin(),
    vec2.cend(), result.begin());
cout << "The intersection is: ";
for_each(result.begin(), newEnd, [](int i){cout << i << " ";});
cout << endl;
```

```
newEnd = set_difference(vec1.cbegin(), vec1.cend(), vec2.cbegin(),
    vec2.cend(), result.begin());
cout << "The difference between set 1 and set 2 is: ";
for_each(result.begin(), newEnd, [](int i){cout << i << " ";});
cout << endl;

newEnd = set_symmetric_difference(vec1.cbegin(), vec1.cend(),
    vec2.cbegin(), vec2.cend(), result.begin());
cout << "The symmetric difference is: ";
for_each(result.begin(), newEnd, [](int i){cout << i << " ";});
cout << endl;
```

Code snippet from SetAlgorithms\Sets.cpp

Here is a sample run of the program:

```
Enter elements for set 1:
Enter a number (0 to quit): 5
Enter a number (0 to quit): 6
Enter a number (0 to quit): 7
Enter a number (0 to quit): 8
Enter a number (0 to quit): 0
Enter elements for set 2:
Enter a number (0 to quit): 8
Enter a number (0 to quit): 9
Enter a number (0 to quit): 10
Enter a number (0 to quit): 0
Set 1: 5 6 7 8
Set 2: 8 9 10
The union is: 5 6 7 8 9 10
The intersection is: 8
The difference between set 1 and set 2 is: 5 6 7
The symmetric difference is: 5 6 7 9 10
```

ALGORITHMS EXAMPLE: AUDITING VOTER REGISTRATIONS

Voter fraud can be a problem everywhere. People sometimes attempt to register and vote in two or more different voting districts. Additionally, some people, for example convicted felons, are ineligible to vote, but occasionally attempt to register and vote anyway. Using your newfound algorithm skills, you could write a simple voter registration auditing function that checks the voter rolls for certain anomalies.

The Voter Registration Audit Problem Statement

The voter registration audit function should audit the voters' information. Assume that voter registrations are stored by district in a map that maps district names to a list of voters. Your audit function should take this map and a list of convicted felons as parameters, and should remove all convicted felons from the lists of voters. Additionally, the function should find all voters who are registered in more than one district and should remove those names from all districts. Voters with duplicate registrations must have all their registrations removed, and therefore become ineligible to vote. For simplicity, assume that the `list` of voters is simply a `list` of `string` names. A real application would obviously require more data, such as address and party affiliation.

The auditVoterRolls Function

The `auditVoterRolls()` function works in three steps:

1. Find all the duplicate names in all the registration `list`s by making a call to `getDuplicates()`.

2. Combine the `set` of duplicates and the `list` of convicted felons.

3. Remove from every voter `list` all the names found in the combined `set` of duplicates and convicted felons. The approach taken here is to use `for_each()` to process each `list` in the `map`, applying a lambda expression to remove the offending names from each `list`.

The following `typedef`s are used in the code:

```cpp
typedef map<string, list<string>> VotersMap;
typedef pair<const string, list<string>> DistrictPair;
```

Code snippet from AuditVoterRolls\AuditVoterRolls.cpp

Here's the implementation of `auditVoterRolls()`:

```cpp
// Expects a map of string/list<string> pairs keyed on district names
// and containing lists of all the registered voters in those districts.
// Removes from each list any name on the convictedFelons list and
// any name that is found on any other list.
void auditVoterRolls(VotersMap& votersByDistrict,
    const list<string>& convictedFelons)
{
    // get all the duplicate names
    set<string> toRemove = getDuplicates(votersByDistrict);

    // combine the duplicates and convicted felons -- we want
    // to remove names on both lists from all voter rolls
    toRemove.insert(convictedFelons.cbegin(), convictedFelons.cend());

    // Now remove all the names we need to remove using
    // nested lambda expressions and the remove-erase-idiom
    for_each(votersByDistrict.begin(), votersByDistrict.end(),
        [&toRemove](DistrictPair& district) {
            auto it = remove_if(district.second.begin(),
                district.second.end(), [&](const string& name) {
                    return (toRemove.count(name) > 0);
                });
            district.second.erase(it, district.second.end());
        });
}
```

Code snippet from AuditVoterRolls\AuditVoterRolls.cpp

The getDuplicates Function

The `getDuplicates()` function must find any name that is on more than one voter registration list. There are several different approaches one could use to solve this problem. To demonstrate the `adjacent_find()` algorithm, this implementation combines the `lists` from each district into one big `list` and sorts it. At that point, any duplicate names between the different `lists` will be next to each other in the big `list`. Now `getDuplicates()` can use the `adjacent_find()` algorithm on the big, sorted, `list` to find all consecutive duplicates and store them in a `set` called `duplicates`. Here is the implementation:

```cpp
// getDuplicates()
//
// Returns a set of all names that appear in more than one list in
// the map.
set<string> getDuplicates(const VotersMap& votersByDistrict)
{
    // Collect all the names from all the lists into one big list
    list<string> allNames;
    for (auto& district : votersByDistrict) {
        allNames.insert(allNames.end(), district.second.begin(),
            district.second.end());
    }

    // sort the list -- use the list version, not the general algorithm,
    // because the list version is faster
    allNames.sort();

    // Now it's sorted, all duplicate names will be next to each other.
    // Use adjacent_find() to find instances of two or more identical names
    // next to each other.
    // Loop until adjacent_find() returns the end iterator.
    set<string> duplicates;
    for (auto lit = allNames.cbegin(); lit != allNames.cend(); ++lit) {
        lit = adjacent_find(lit, allNames.cend());
        if (lit == allNames.cend()) {
            break;
        }
        duplicates.insert(*lit);
    }
    return duplicates;
}
```

Code snippet from AuditVoterRolls\AuditVoterRolls.cpp

In this implementation, `allNames` is of type `list<string>`. That way, this example can show you how to use the `sort()` and `adjacent_find()` algorithms. Another solution is to change the type of `allNames` to `set<string>`, which results in a more compact implementation, because a `set` doesn't allow duplicates. This new solution loops over all lists and tries to insert each name into `allNames`.

When this insert fails, it means that there is already an element with that name in `allNames`, so the name is added to `duplicates`.

```cpp
set<string> getDuplicates(const VotersMap& votersByDistrict)
{
    set<string> allNames;
    set<string> duplicates;
    for (auto& district : votersByDistrict) {
        for (auto& name : district.second) {
            if (!allNames.insert(name).second)
                duplicates.insert(name);
        }
    }
    return duplicates;
}
```

Code snippet from AuditVoterRolls\AuditVoterRolls.cpp

Testing the auditVoterRolls Function

That's the complete implementation of the voter roll audit functionality. Here is a small test program:

```cpp
// Initialize map using uniform initialization
VotersMap voters = {
    {"Orange", {"Amy Aardvark", "Bob Buffalo",
                "Charles Cat", "Dwayne Dog"}},
    {"Los Angeles", {"Elizabeth Elephant", "Fred Flamingo",
                    "Amy Aardvark"}},
    {"San Diego", {"George Goose", "Heidi Hen", "Fred Flamingo"}}
};
list<string> felons = {"Bob Buffalo", "Charles Cat"};

// Local lambda expression to print a district
auto printDistrict = [](const DistrictPair& district) {
    cout << district.first << ":";
    for (auto& str : district.second)
        cout << " {" << str << "}";
    cout << endl;
};

cout << "Before Audit:" << endl;
for_each(voters.cbegin(), voters.cend(), printDistrict);
cout << endl;

auditVoterRolls(voters, felons);

cout << "After Audit:" << endl;
for_each(voters.cbegin(), voters.cend(), printDistrict);
cout << endl;
```

Code snippet from AuditVoterRolls\AuditVoterRolls.cpp

The output of the program is:

Before Audit:

```
Los Angeles: {Elizabeth Elephant} {Fred Flamingo} {Amy Aardvark}
Orange: {Amy Aardvark} {Bob Buffalo} {Charles Cat} {Dwayne Dog}
San Diego: {George Goose} {Heidi Hen} {Fred Flamingo}
```

After Audit:

```
Los Angeles: {Elizabeth Elephant}
Orange: {Dwayne Dog}
San Diego: {George Goose} {Heidi Hen}
```

SUMMARY

This chapter concludes the basic STL functionality. It provided an overview of the various algorithms and function objects available for your use. It also showed you how to use the new C++11 lambda expressions, which make it often easier to understand what your code is doing. We hope that you have gained an appreciation for the usefulness of the STL containers, algorithms, and function objects. If not, think for a moment about rewriting the voter registration audit example without the STL. You would need to write your own linked-list and map classes, and your own searching, removing, iterating, and other algorithms. The program would be much longer, harder to debug, and more difficult to maintain.

If you aren't impressed by the algorithms and function objects, or find them too complex, you obviously don't have to use them. Feel free to pick and choose as well: If the find() algorithm fits perfectly in your program, don't eschew it just because you aren't using the other algorithms. Also, don't take the STL as an all-or-nothing proposition. If you want to use only the vector container and nothing else, that's fine too.

The next chapters discuss a couple of other aspects of the C++ Standard Library. Chapter 14 discusses strings in C++, while Chapter 15 explains the concept of streams for input and output (I/O). Chapter 16 covers a number of additional library utilities that are available for you to use, and Chapter 17 finishes the STL topic with some advanced features, including allocators, iterator adapters, and writing your own algorithms, containers, and iterators.

14

Using Strings and Regular Expressions

WHAT'S IN THIS CHAPTER?

➤ The differences between C-style strings and C++ strings

➤ How you can localize your applications to reach a worldwide audience

➤ How to use regular expressions to do powerful pattern matching

Every program that you write will use strings of some kind. With the old C language there is not much choice but to use a dumb null-terminated character array to represent an ASCII string. Unfortunately, doing so can cause a lot of problems, such as buffer overflows, which can result in security vulnerabilities. The C++ STL includes a safe and easy-to-use `string` class that does not have these disadvantages.

The first section of this chapter discusses strings in more detail. It starts with a discussion of the old C-style strings, explains their disadvantages, and ends with the C++ `string` class. It also mentions raw string literals, which are new in C++11.

The second section discusses localization, which is becoming more and more important these days to allow you to write software that can be localized to different regions around the world.

The last section introduces the new C++11 *regular expressions library*, which makes it easy to perform pattern matching on strings. They allow you to search for sub-strings matching a given pattern, but also to validate, parse, and transform strings. They are really powerful and it's recommended that you start using them instead of manually writing your own string processing code.

DYNAMIC STRINGS

Strings in languages that have supported them as first-class objects tend to have a number of attractive features, such as being able to expand to any size, or have sub-strings extracted or replaced. In other languages, such as C, strings were almost an afterthought; there was no really good "string" data type, just fixed arrays of bytes. The "string library" was nothing more than a collection of rather primitive functions without even bounds checking. C++ provides a string type as a first-class data type, and the strings are implemented using templates and operator overloading.

C-Style Strings

In the C language, strings are represented as an array of characters. The last character of a string is a null character (`'\0'`) so that code operating on the string can determine where it ends. This null character is officially known as NUL, spelled with one L, not two. NUL is not the same as the NULL pointer. Even though C++ provides a better string abstraction, it is important to understand the C technique for strings because they still arise in C++ programming. One of the most common situations is where a C++ program has to call a C-based interface in some third-party library or as part of interfacing to the operating system.

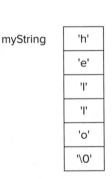

By far, the most common mistake that programmers make with C strings is that they forget to allocate space for the `'\0'` character. For example, the string `"hello"` appears to be five characters long, but six characters worth of space are needed in memory to store the value, as shown in Figure 14-1.

FIGURE 14-1

C++ contains several functions from the C language that operate on strings. As a general rule of thumb, these functions do not handle memory allocation. For example, the `strcpy()` function takes two strings as parameters. It copies the second string onto the first, whether it fits or not. The following code attempts to build a wrapper around `strcpy()` that allocates the correct amount of memory and returns the result, instead of taking in an already allocated string. It uses the `strlen()` function to obtain the length of the string.

Available for download on Wrox.com

```
char* copyString(const char* inString)
{
    char* result = new char[strlen(inString)];   // BUG! Off by one!
    strcpy(result, inString);
    return result;
}
```

Code snippet from CStrings\strcpy.cpp

The copyString() function as written is incorrect. The strlen() function returns the length of the string, not the amount of memory needed to hold it. For the string "hello", strlen() will return 5, not 6. The proper way to allocate memory for a string is to add one to the amount of space needed for the actual characters. It seems a little weird at first to have +1 all over the place, but it quickly becomes natural, and you (hopefully) miss it when it's not there.

Available for download on Wrox.com

```
char* copyString(const char* inString)
{
    char* result = new char[strlen(inString) + 1];
    strcpy(result, inString);
    return result;
}
```

Code snippet from CStrings\strcpy.cpp

One way to remember that strlen() returns only the number of actual characters in the string is to consider what would happen if you were allocating space for a string made up of several others. For example, if your function took in three strings and returned a string that was the concatenation of all three, how big would it be? To hold exactly enough space, it would be the length of all three strings, added together, plus one for the trailing '\0' character. If strlen() included the '\0' in the length of the string, the allocated memory would be too big. The following code uses the strcpy() and strcat() functions to perform this operation.

Available for download on Wrox.com

```
char* appendStrings(const char* inStr1, const char* inStr2, const char* inStr3)
{
    char* result = new char[strlen(inStr1) + strlen(inStr2) + strlen(inStr3) + 1];
    strcpy(result, inStr1);
    strcat(result, inStr2);
    strcat(result, inStr3);
    return result;
}
```

Code snippet from CStrings\strcpy.cpp

Note that sizeof() is not the same as strlen(). You should never use sizeof() to try to get the size of a string. For example:

Available for download on Wrox.com

```
char text1[] = "abcdef";
size_t s1 = sizeof(text1);   // is 7
size_t s2 = strlen(text1);   // is 6
char* text2 = "abcdef";
size_t s3 = sizeof(text2);   // is 4
size_t s4 = strlen(text2);   // is 6
```

Code snippet from CStrings\strlen.cpp

s3 will be 4 when compiled in 32-bit mode and will be 8 when compiled in 64-bit mode because it is returning the size of a char* which is a pointer.

A complete list of C functions to operate on strings can be found in the <cstring> header file.

When you use the C-style string functions with Microsoft Visual Studio, the compiler is likely to give security-related warnings about these functions being deprecated. You can eliminate these warnings by using the new C standard library functions, such as `strcpy_s()` *or* `strcat_s()`*, which are part of the new "secure C library" standard (ISO/IEC TR 24731). However, the best solution is to switch to the C++* `string` *class, which is discussed later in this chapter.*

String Literals

You've probably seen strings written in a C++ program with quotes around them. For example, the following code outputs the string `hello` by including the string itself, not a variable that contains it:

```
cout << "hello" << endl;
```

In the preceding line, `"hello"` is a *string literal* because it is written as a value, not a variable. String literals can be *assigned* to variables, but doing so can be risky. The actual memory associated with a string literal is in a read-only part of memory. This allows the compiler to optimize memory usage by reusing references to equivalent string literals. That is, even if your program uses the string literal `"hello"` 500 times, the compiler can create just one instance of `hello` in memory. This is called *literal pooling.*

The C++ standard officially says that string literals are of type "array of *n* `const char`," however, for backward compatibility with older non-`const` aware code, most compilers do not enforce your program to assign a string literal only to a variable of type `const char*` or `const char[]`. They let you assign a string to a `char*` without `const`, and the program will work fine unless you attempt to change the string. Generally, attempting to change the string will immediately crash your program, as demonstrated in the following code:

```
char* ptr = "hello";      // Assign the string literal to a variable.
ptr[1] = 'a';             // CRASH! Attempts to write to read-only memory
```

A much safer way to code is to use a pointer to `const` characters when referring to string literals. The following code contains the same bug, but because it assigned the literal to a `const` character array, the compiler will catch the attempt to write to read-only memory.

```
const char* ptr = "hello"; // Assign the string literal to a variable.
ptr[1] = 'a';              // BUG! Attempts to write to read-only memory
```

You can also use a string literal as an initial value for a character array (`char[]`). In this case, the compiler creates an array that is big enough to hold the string and copies the string to this array. So, the compiler will not put the literal in read-only memory and will not do any literal pooling.

```
char arr[] = "hello"; // Compiler takes care of creating appropriate sized
                      // character array arr.
arr[1] = 'a';         // The contents can be modified.
```

The C++ string Class

As mentioned earlier, C++ provides a much-improved implementation of the concept of a string as part of the Standard Library. In C++, string is a class (actually an instantiation of the basic_string template class) that supports many of the same functionalities as the <cstring> functions but takes care of memory allocation for you if you use it properly. The string class has already been used on a number of occasions earlier in this book. Now it's time to take a deeper look at it.

What Was Wrong with C-Style Strings?

To understand the necessity of the C++ string class, consider the advantages and disadvantages of C-style strings.

Advantages:

➤ They are simple, making use of the underlying basic character type and array structure.

➤ They are lightweight, taking up only the memory that they need if used properly.

➤ They are low level, so you can easily manipulate and copy them as raw memory.

➤ They are well understood by C programmers — why learn something new?

Disadvantages:

➤ They require incredible efforts to simulate a first-class string data type.

➤ They are unforgiving and susceptible to difficult to find memory bugs.

➤ They don't leverage the object-oriented nature of C++.

➤ They require knowledge of their underlying representation on the part of the programmer.

The preceding lists were carefully constructed to make you think that perhaps there is a better way. As you'll learn, C++ strings solve all the problems of C strings and render most of the arguments about the advantages of C strings over a first-class data type irrelevant.

Using the string Class

Even though string is a class, you can almost always treat it as if it were a built-in type. In fact, the more you think of it as a simple type, the better off you are. Programmers generally encounter the least trouble with string when they forget that strings are objects.

Through the magic of operator overloading, C++ strings are much easier to use than C strings. For example, two strings can be concatenated by using the + operator:

```
string A("abc");
string B("def");
string C;
C = A + B;    // C will become "abcdef"
```

The + operator does not try to "add" the values; the + is redefined as meaning "string concatenation." For example, the following produces 1234, not 46:

```
string A("12");
string B("34");
string C;
C = A + B;
```

The += operator is also overloaded to allow you to easily append a string:

```
string A("12");
string B("34");
A += B;    // A will become "1234"
```

Another problem with C strings was that you could not use == to compare them. Suppose you have the following two strings:

```
char* a = "12";
char b[] = "12";
```

Writing a comparison as follows always returned `false`, because it compared the pointer values, not the contents of the strings:

```
if (a == b)
```

You had to write something as follows:

```
if (strcmp(a, b) == 0)
```

Furthermore, there was no way to use <, <=, >= or > to compare C strings, so `strcmp()` would return -1, 0 or 1 depending on the lexicographic relationship of the strings. This resulted in very clumsy code, which was also error-prone.

With C++ strings, `operator==`, `operator!=`, `operator<`, and so on are all overloaded to work on the actual string characters. Individual characters can still be accessed with `operator[]`.

As the following code shows, when `string` operations require extending the `string`, the memory requirements are automatically handled by the `string` class, so memory overruns are a thing of the past:

```
string myString = "hello";
myString += ", there";
string myOtherString = myString;
if (myString == myOtherString) {
    myOtherString[0] = 'H';
}
cout << myString << endl;
cout << myOtherString << endl;
```

Code snippet from CppStrings\CppStrings.cpp

The output of this code is:

```
hello, there
Hello, there
```

There are several things to note in this example. One point to note is that there are no memory leaks even though strings are allocated and resized left and right. All of these string objects were created as stack variables. While the string class certainly had a bunch of allocating and resizing to do, the string destructors cleaned up this memory when string objects went out of scope.

Another point to note is that the operators work the way you would want them to. For example, the = operator copies the strings, which is most likely what you wanted. If you are used to working with array-based strings, this will either be refreshingly liberating for you or somewhat confusing. Don't worry — once you learn to trust the string class to do the right thing, life gets so much easier.

For compatibility, you can use the c_str() method on a string to get a const character pointer, representing a C-style string. However, the returned const pointer becomes invalid whenever the string has to perform any memory reallocation, or when the string object is destroyed. You should call the method just before using the result so that it accurately reflects the current contents of the string.

The Standard Library Reference resource on the website lists all the operations you can perform on string objects.

C++11 Numeric Conversions

C++11 includes a number of new helper functions making it easier to convert numerical values into strings or strings into numerical values. The following functions are available to convert numerical values into strings:

- ➤ `string to_string(int val);`
- ➤ `string to_string(unsigned val);`
- ➤ `string to_string(long val);`
- ➤ `string to_string(unsigned long val);`
- ➤ `string to_string(long long val);`
- ➤ `string to_string(unsigned long long val);`
- ➤ `string to_string(float val);`
- ➤ `string to_string(double val);`
- ➤ `string to_string(long double val);`

They are pretty straightforward to use. For example, the following code converts a long double value into a string:

```
long double d = 3.14;
string s = to_string(d);
```

There are also wide `string` versions available, which are called `to_wstring` and return a `wstring`. Wide `strings` are discussed later in this chapter.

Converting in the other direction is done by the following set of functions. In these prototypes, `str` is the `string` that you want to convert, `idx` is a pointer that will receive the index of the first non-converted character, and `base` is the mathematical base that should be used during conversion. The `idx` pointer can be a null pointer in which case it will be ignored. They throw `invalid_argument` if no conversion could be performed and throw `out_of_range` if the converted value is outside the range of the return type.

➤   `int stoi(const string& str, size_t *idx=0, int base=10);`

➤   `long stol(const string& str, size_t *idx=0, int base=10);`

➤   `unsigned long stoul(const string& str, size_t *idx=0, int base=10);`

➤   `long long stoll(const string& str, size_t *idx=0, int base=10);`

➤   `unsigned long long stoull(const string& str, size_t *idx=0, int base=10);`

➤   `float stof(const string& str, size_t *idx=0);`

➤   `double stod(const string& str, size_t *idx=0);`

➤   `long double stold(const string& str, size_t *idx=0);`

For example:

```
const string s = "1234";
int i = stoi(s);    // i will be 1234
```

A similar set of functions is available accepting a `wstring` instead of a `string`.

C++11 Raw String Literals

C++11 adds the concept of *raw string literals*, which are string literals where escape sequences like \t and \n are not processed as escape sequences but as normal text. These escape characters are discussed in Chapter 1. If you write the following with a normal string literal, you will get a compiler error, because a normal string literal cannot span multiple lines and the example contains non-escaped quotes in the middle of the string, which are also not allowed:

```
string str = "Line 1
line "2" \t (and)
end";
```

To make the preceding work you need to use a raw string literal, which has the following general format:

```
R"d-char-sequence(r-char-sequence)d-char-sequence"
```

The `d-char-sequence` is an optional delimiter sequence, which should be the same at the beginning and at the end of the raw string. This delimiter sequence can have at most 16 characters.

The `r-char-sequence` is the actual raw string. The preceding example can be modified to use a raw string literal as follows:

```
string str = R"~(Line 1
line "2" \t (and)
end)~";
```

Code snippet from RawStringLiteral\RawStringLiteral.cpp

In this example, the delimiter sequence is a single ~ character, which means the raw string literal has to start with `R"~(` and end with `)~"`. As mentioned before, the delimiter is optional, so the following code is equivalent:

```
string str = R"(Line 1
line "2" \t (and)
end)";
```

Code snippet from RawStringLiteral\RawStringLiteral.cpp

If you write `str` to the console the output will be:

```
Line 1
line "2" \t (and)
end
```

With the raw string literal you do not need to escape quotes in the middle of the string and the `\t` escape character is not replaced with an actual tab character but is taken literally.

You might wonder what the point is of the optional delimiter sequence. It is required for strings that have a character sequence in the middle of the string that could be interpreted as the end of the raw string. For example, the following string is not valid because it contains the `)"` in the middle of the string, which is interpreted by the compiler as the end of the string:

```
string str = R"(The characters )" are embedded in this string)";
```

If you want the preceding string, you need to use a unique delimiter character, for example:

```
string str = R"-(The characters )" are embedded in this string)-";
```

Raw string literals will make life much easier for working with database querying strings, regular expressions, and so on. Regular expressions are discussed later in this chapter.

LOCALIZATION

When you're learning how to program in C or C++, it's useful to think of a character as equivalent to a byte and to treat all characters as members of the ASCII character set (American Standard Code for Information Interchange). ASCII is a 7-bit set usually stored in an 8-bit `char` type. In reality, experienced C++ programmers recognize that successful programs are used throughout the world. Even if you don't initially write your program with international audiences in mind, you shouldn't prevent yourself from *localizing*, or making the software local aware, at a later date.

Localizing String Literals

A critical aspect of localization is that you should never put any native-language literal strings in your source code, except maybe for debug strings targeted at the developer. In Microsoft Windows applications, this is accomplished by putting the strings in STRINGTABLE resources. Most other platforms offer similar capabilities. If you need to translate your application to another language, translating those resources should be all that needs to be done, without requiring any source changes. There are tools available that help you with this translation process.

To make your source code localizable, you should not use cout to compose sentences out of string literals, even if the individual literals can be localized. For example:

```
cout << "Read " << n << " bytes" << endl;
```

This cout statement cannot be localized to Dutch because it requires a reordering of the words. The Dutch translation is as follows:

```
cout << n << " bytes gelezen" << endl;
```

To make sure you can properly localize this cout statement, you could implement something as follows:

```
cout << Format(IDS_TRANSFERRED, n) << endl;
```

IDS_TRANSFERRED is the name of an entry in a string resource table. For the English version, IDS_TRANSFERRED could be defined as "Read $1 bytes", while the Dutch version of the resource could be defined as "$1 bytes gelezen". The Format() function loads the string resource and substitutes $1 with the value of n.

Wide Characters

The problem with viewing a character as a byte is that not all languages, or *character sets*, can be fully represented in 8 bits, or 1 byte. C++ has a built-in type called wchar_t that holds a *wide character*. Languages with non-ASCII (U.S.) characters, such as Japanese and Arabic, can be represented in C++ with wchar_t. However, the C++ standard does not define a size for wchar_t. Some compilers use 16 bits while others use 32 bits. To write portable software, it is not safe to assume that sizeof(wchar_t) is any particular numerical value.

If there is *any* chance that your program will be used in a non-Western character set context (hint: there is!), you should use wide characters from the beginning. When working with wchar_t, string and character literals are prefixed with the letter L to indicate that a wide-character encoding should be used. For example, to initialize a wchar_t character to be the letter m, you would write it like this:

```
wchar_t myWideCharacter = L'm';
```

There are wide-character versions of most of your favorite types and classes. The wide `string` class is `wstring`. The "prefix letter w" pattern applies to streams as well. Wide-character file output streams are handled with the `wofstream`, and input is handled with the `wifstream`. The joy of pronouncing these class names (*woof-stream? whiff-stream?*) is reason enough to make your programs local aware! Streams are discussed in detail in Chapter 15.

In addition to `cout`, `cin`, `cerr`, and `clog` there are wide versions of the built-in console and error streams called `wcout`, `wcin`, `wcerr`, and `wclog`. Using them is no different than using the non-wide versions:

```
wcout << L"I am wide-character aware." << endl;
```

Code snippet from WideStrings\wcout.cpp

Non-Western Character Sets

Wide characters are a great step forward because they increase the amount of space available to define a single character. The next step is to figure out how that space is used. In wide character sets, just like in ASCII, a number corresponds to a particular glyph. The only difference is that each number does not fit in 8 bits. The map of characters to numbers (now called *code points*) is quite a bit larger because it handles many different character sets in addition to the characters that English-speaking programmers are familiar with.

The Universal Character Set (UCS), defined by the International Standard ISO 10646, and Unicode are both standardized sets of characters. They contain around one hundred thousand abstract characters, each identified by an unambiguous name and an integer number called its code point. The same characters with the same numbers exist in both standards. Both have specific *encodings* that you can use. For example, UTF-8 is an example of a Unicode encoding where Unicode characters are encoded using one to four 8-bit bytes. UTF-16 encodes Unicode characters as one or two 16-bit values and UTF-32 encodes Unicode characters as exactly 32 bits.

Different applications can use different encodings. Unfortunately, the C++ standard does not specify a size for wide characters (`wchar_t`). On Windows it is 16 bits, while on other platforms it could be 32 bits. You need to be aware of this when using wide characters for character encoding in cross platform code. To help solve this issue, C++11 introduces two new character types: `char16_t` and `char32_t`. The following list gives an overview of all character types supported by C++11:

➤ `char`: Stores 8 bits. Can be used to store ASCII characters, or as a basic building block for storing UTF-8 encoded Unicode characters, where one Unicode characters is encoded as one to four `char`s.

➤ `char16_t`: Stores 16 bits. Can be used as the basic building block for UTF-16 encoded Unicode characters where one Unicode character is encoded as one or two `char16_t`s.

➤ `char32_t`: Stores 32 bits. Can be used for storing UTF-32 encoded Unicode characters as one `char32_t`.

➤ `wchar_t`: Stores a wide character of a compiler-specific size and encoding.

The benefit of using `char16_t` and `char32_t` instead of `wchar_t` is that the size of `char16_t` and `char32_t` are compiler-independent, whereas the size of `wchar_t` depends on your compiler.

The standard also defines the following two macros:

➤ `__STDC_UTF_32__`: If this is defined, the type `char32_t` represents a UTF-32 encoding. If it is not defined, the type `char32_t` has a compiler dependent encoding.

➤ `__STDC_UTF_16__`: If this is defined, the type `char16_t` represents a UTF-16 encoding. If it is not defined, the type `char16_t` has a compiler dependent encoding.

C++11 defines three new string prefixes in addition to the existing `L` prefix. The complete set of supported string prefixes is as follows:

➤ u8: A `char` string literal with UTF-8 encoding.

➤ u: A `char16_t` string literal, which can be UTF-16 if `__STDC_UTF_16__` is defined.

➤ U: A `char32_t` string literal, which can be UTF-32 if `__STDC_UTF_32__` is defined.

➤ L: A `wchar_t` string literal with a compiler-dependent encoding.

All of these string literals can also be combined with the raw string literal seen earlier in this chapter. For example:

Available for download on Wrox.com

```
const char* s1 = u8R"(Raw UTF-8 encoded string literal)";
const wchar_t* s2 = LR"(Raw wide string literal)";
const char16_t* s3 = uR"(Raw char16_t string literal)";
const char32_t* s4 = UR"(Raw char32_t string literal)";
```

Code snippet from CharTypes\CharTypes.cpp

If you are using Unicode encoding, for example by using u8 UTF-8 string literals or by specifying `__STDC_UTF_16__` or `__STDC_UTF_32__`, you can insert a specific Unicode code point in your non-raw string literal by using the `\uABCD` notation. For example `\u03C0` represents the PI character, and `\u00B2` represents the ² character. The following code prints "π r²":

Available for download on Wrox.com

```
const char* formula = u8"\u03C0 r\u00B2";
cout << formula << endl;
```

Code snippet from CharTypes\CharTypes.cpp

The C++ `string` library has also been extended to include two new `typedef`s to work with the new character types:

➤ `typedef basic_string<char16_t> u16string;`

➤ `typedef basic_string<char32_t> u32string;`

Additionally, the following four new conversion functions related to `char16_t` and `char32_t` are included: `mbrtoc16`, `c16rtomb`, `mbrtoc32` and `c32rtomb`.

Unfortunately, the support for `char16_t` and `char32_t` stops there. For example, the I/O stream classes in the C++11 standard library do not include support for these new character types. This means that there is nothing like a version of `cout` or `cin` that supports `char16_t` and `char32_t` making it difficult to print such strings to a console or to read them from user input. If you want to do more with `char16_t` and `char32_t` strings you will have to resort to third-party libraries.

Locales and Facets

Character sets are only one of the differences in data representation between countries. Even countries that use similar character sets, such as Great Britain and the United States, still differ in how they represent data such as dates and money.

The standard C++ mechanism that groups specific data about a particular set of cultural parameters is called a *locale*. An individual component of a locale, such as date format, time format, number format, etc. is called a *facet*. An example of a locale is U.S. English. An example of a facet is the format used to display a date. There are several built-in facets that are common to all locales. The language also provides a way to customize or add facets.

Using Locales

When using I/O streams, data is formatted according to a particular locale. Locales are objects that can be attached to a stream. They are defined in the `<locale>` header file. Locale names can be implementation-specific. One standard is to separate the language and the area in two-letter sections with an optional encoding. For example, the locale for the English language as spoken in the U.S. is `en_US`, while the locale for the English language as spoken in Great Britain is `en_GB`. The locale for Japanese spoken in Japan with Japanese Industrial Standard encoding is `ja_JP.jis`.

Locale names on Windows follow a different standard, which has the following general format:

```
lang[_country_region[.code_page]]
```

Everything between the square brackets is optional. The following table lists some examples:

	LINUX GCC	WINDOWS
U.S. English	en_US	English_United States
Great Britain English	en_GB	English_Great Britain

Most operating systems have a mechanism to determine the locale as defined by the user. In C++, you can pass an empty string to the `locale` object constructor to create a `locale` from the user's environment. Once this object is created, you can use it to query the `locale`, possibly making programmatic decisions based on it. The following code demonstrates how to use the user's locale by calling the `imbue()` method on a stream. The result is that everything that is send to `wcout` will be formatted according to the formatting rules for your system:

```
wcout.imbue(locale(""));
wcout << 32767 << endl;
```

This means that if your system locale is English United States and you output the number 32767, the number will be displayed as 32,767, but if your system locale is Dutch Belgium, the same number will be displayed as 32.767.

The user's locale is usually *not* the default locale. The default locale is generally the *classic* locale, which uses ANSI C conventions. The classic C locale is similar to U.S. English, but there are slight differences. For example, if you do not set a locale at all, or set the default locale, and you output a number, it will be presented without any punctuation:

```
wcout.imbue(locale("C"));
wcout << 32767 << endl;
```

The output of this code will be as follows:

```
32767
```

The following code manually sets the U.S. English locale, so the number 32767 will be formatted with U.S. English punctuation, independent of your system locale:

```
wcout.imbue(locale("en_US"));
wcout << 32767 << endl;
```

The output of this code will be as follows:

```
32,767
```

A `locale` object allows you to query information about the locale. For example, the following program creates a `locale` matching the user's environment. The `name()` method is used to get a C++ `string` that describes the locale. Then, the `find()` method is used on the `string` object to find a given sub-string, which returns `string::npos` when the given sub-string was not found. The code checks for the Windows name and the Linux GCC name. One of two messages is output, depending on whether the locale appears to be U.S. English or not:

```
locale loc("");
if (loc.name().find("en_US") == string::npos &&
    loc.name().find("United States") == string::npos) {
    wcout << L"Welcome non-U.S. English speaker!" << endl;
} else {
    wcout << L"Welcome U.S. English speaker!" << endl;
}
```

Code snippet from Locales\Locales.cpp

Using Facets

You can use the `std::use_facet()` function to obtain a particular facet in a particular locale. The argument to `use_facet()` is a `locale`. For example, the following expression retrieves the standard monetary punctuation facet of the British English locale using the Linux GCC locale name:

```
use_facet<moneypunct<wchar_t>>(locale("en_GB"));
```

Note that the innermost template type determines the character type to use. This is usually `wchar_t` or `char`. The use of nested template classes is unfortunate, but once you get past the syntax, the result is an object that contains all the information you want to know about British money punctuation. The data available in the standard facets are defined in the `<locale>` header and its associated files.

The following program brings together locales and facets by printing out the currency symbol in both U.S. English and British English. Note that, depending on your environment, the British currency symbol may appear as a question mark, a box, or not at all. If your environment is equipped to handle it, you may actually get the British pound symbol:

Available for download on Wrox.com

```
locale locUSEng("en_US");
locale locBritEng("en_GB");
wstring dollars = use_facet<moneypunct<wchar_t>>(locUSEng).curr_symbol();
wstring pounds = use_facet<moneypunct<wchar_t>>(locBritEng).curr_symbol();
wcout << L"In the US, the currency symbol is " << dollars << endl;
wcout << L"In Great Britain, the currency symbol is " << pounds << endl;
```

Code snippet from Facets\use_facet.cpp

C++11 REGULAR EXPRESSIONS

Regular expressions are a new and powerful addition to the C++11 Standard Library. They are a special mini-language for string processing. They might seem complicated at first, but once you get to know them, they make working with strings easier. Regular expressions can be used for several string-related operations:

- ➤ **Validation:** Check if an input string is well-formed.

  For example: Is the input string a well-formed phone number?

- ➤ **Decision:** Check what kind of string an input represents.

  For example: Is the input string the name of a JPEG or a PNG file?

- ➤ **Parsing:** Extract information from an input string.

  For example: From a full filename, extract the filename part without the full path and without its extension.

- ➤ **Transformation:** Search sub-strings and replace them with a new formatted sub-string.

  For example: Search all occurrences of "C++11" and replace them with "C++."

- ➤ **Iteration:** Search all occurrences of a sub-string.

  For example: Extract all phone numbers from an input string.

- ➤ **Tokenization:** Split a string into sub-strings based on a set of delimiters.

  For example: Split a string on whitespace, commas, periods, and so on to extract its individual words.

Of course you could write your own code to perform any of the preceding operations on your strings, but using the regular expressions feature is highly recommended, because writing correct and safe code to process strings can be tricky.

Before we can go into more details on the regular expressions, there is some important terminology to know. The following terms are used throughout the discussion:

➤ **Pattern:** The actual regular expression is a pattern represented by a string.

➤ **Match:** Determines whether there is a match between a given regular expression and all of the characters in a given sequence [first,last).

➤ **Search:** Determines whether there is some sub-string within a given sequence [first,last) that matches a given regular expression.

➤ **Replace:** Identifies sub-strings in a given sequence, and replaces them with a corresponding new sub-string computed from another pattern, called a *substitution pattern*.

If you look around on the internet you will find out that there are several different grammars for regular expressions. For this reason, C++11 includes support for several of these grammars: *ECMAScript, basic, extended, awk, grep,* and *egrep.* If you already know any of these regular expression grammars, you can use it straight away in C++11 by telling the regular expression library to use that specific syntax (`syntax_option_type`). The default grammar in C++11 is ECMAScript whose syntax is explained in detail in the following section. It is also the most powerful grammar, so it's highly recommended to use ECMAScript instead of one of the other more limited grammars. Explaining the other regular expression grammars falls outside the scope of this book.

If this is the first time you hear anything about regular expressions, just leave the powerful default ECMAScript syntax.

ECMAScript Syntax

A regular expression pattern is a sequence of characters representing what you want to match. Any character in the regular expression matches itself except for the following special characters:

```
^ $ \ . * + ? ( ) [ ] { } |
```

These special characters are explained throughout the following discussion. If you need to match one of these special characters, you need to escape it using the \ character. For example:

```
\[ or \. or \* or \\
```

*Don't forget that you need to escape the back slash in your C++ string literals. For example, if your regular expression needs to match the single * character, you need to escape it for the regular expression engine and for C++, so your C++ string literal should be *.*

Anchors

The special characters ^ and $ are called *anchors*. The ^ character will match the beginning of the string and $ will match the end of the string. For example, ^test$ will match only the string test, and not strings which contain test in the line with anything else like 1test, test2, test abc, and so on.

Wildcards

The *wildcard* character . can be used to match any character except a newline character. For example, the regular expression a.c will match abc, and a5c, but will not match ab5c, ac and so on.

Repetition

Parts of a regular expression can be repeated by using one of four *repeats*:

➤ * matches the preceding part *zero or more* times. For example: a*b will match b, ab, aab, aaab, and so on.

➤ + matches the preceding part *one or more* times. For example: a+b will match ab, aab, aaab, and so on, but not b.

➤ ? matches the preceding part *zero or one* time. For example: a?b will match b and ab, but nothing else.

➤ {...} represents a *bounded repeat*. a{n} will match a repeated *exactly n* times; a{n,} will match a repeated *n times or more*, and a{n,m} will match a repeated *between n and m* times inclusive. For example, ^a{3,4}$ will match aaa and aaaa but not a, aa, aaaaa, and so on.

The repeats described in the previous list are called *greedy* because they will find the longest match. To make them *non-greedy*, a ? can be added behind the repeat as in *?, +?, ?? and {...}?. The following table gives an example. The first column is the string on which the regular expression will be applied. The second column represents the matches found by the regular expression a+ and the third column shows the matches found by the non-greedy a+?.

SOURCE STRING	a+	a+?
" "	no match	no match
a	matches a	matches a
aa	matches aa	matches a
aaa	matches aaa	matches a
aaaa	matches aaaa	matches a

Alternation

The | character can be used to specify the "or" relationship. For example, a|b will match a or b.

Grouping

Parentheses () are used to mark *sub-expressions,* also called *capture groups.* Capture groups can be used for several purposes:

➤ Capture groups can be used to identify individual sub-sequences of the original string; each marked sub-expression (capture group) will be returned in the result. For example, take the following regular expression: (.*)(ab|cd)(.*). It has three marked sub-expressions. Running a regex_search() with this regular expression on 123cd4 will result in a match with four entries. The first entry is the entire match 123cd4 followed by three entries for the three marked sub-expressions. These three entries are 123, cd and 4. The details on how to use the regex_search() algorithm are shown in a later section.

➤ Capture groups can be used during matching for a purpose called *back references* (explained later).

➤ Capture groups can be used to identify components during a *replace operations* (explained later).

Precedence

Just as with mathematical formulas it's important to know the precedence of the regular expression elements. Precedence is as follows:

➤ **Elements:** like a are the basic building blocks of a regular expression.

➤ **Quantifiers:** like +, *, ? and {...} bind tightly to the element on the left, for example b+.

➤ **Concatenation:** like ab+c binds after quantifiers.

➤ **Alternations:** like | binds as last.

For example, take the regular expression ab+c|d. This will match abc, abbc, abbbc, and so on and also d. Parentheses can be used to change these precedence rules. For example ab+(c|d) will match abc, abbc, abbbc, ..., abd, abbd, abbbd, and so on. However, by using parentheses you also mark it as a sub-expression or capture group. It is possible to change the precedence rules without creating a new capture group by using (?:...). For example ab+(?:c|d) matches the same as the preceding ab+(c|d) but does not create an additional capture group.

Character Set Matches

Instead of having to write (a|b|c|...|z) which is clumsy and introduces a capture group, a special syntax for specifying sets of characters or ranges of characters is available. In addition, a "not" form of the match is also available. A *character set* is specified between square brackets, and allows you to write [$c_1c_2c_3$] which will match any of the characters c_1, c_2 or c_3. For example, [abc] will match any character a, b or c. If the first character is ^, it means "any but":

➤ ab[cde] matches abc, abd, and abe.

➤ ab[^cde] matches abf, abp, and so on but not abc, abd, and abe.

If you need to match the ^, [or] characters themselves, you need to escape them, for example: [\[\^\]] matches the characters [, ^ or].

If you want to specify all letters, you could use a character set like `[abcdefghijklmnopqrstuvwxyz ABCDEFGHIJKLMNOPQRSTUVWXYZ]`, however, this is clumsy and doing this several times is awkward, especially if you make a typo and omit one of the letters accidentally. There are two solutions to this.

The *range specification* in square brackets allows you to write `[a-zA-Z]` which recognizes all the letters in the range a to z and A to Z. If you need to match a hyphen, you need to escape it, for example `[a-zA-Z\-]*` matches any word including a hyphenated word.

Another capability is to use one of the *character classes*. These are used to denote specific types of characters and are represented as `[:name:]` where `name` is one of the classes in the following table:

CHARACTER CLASS NAME	DESCRIPTION
alnum	lowercase letters, uppercase letters, and digits
alpha	lowercase letters and uppercase letters
blank	space or tab characters
cntrl	file format escape characters like newlines, form feeds, and so on (`\f`, `\n`, `\r`, `\t` and `\v`)
digit	digits
graph	lowercase letters, uppercase letters, digits, and punctuation characters
lower	lowercase letters
print	lowercase letters, uppercase letters, digits, punctuation characters, and space characters
punct	punctuation characters
space	space characters
upper	uppercase letters
xdigit	digits and 'a', 'b', 'c', 'd', 'e', 'f', 'A', 'B', 'C', 'D', 'E', 'F'
d	same as digit
s	same as space
w	same as alnum

Character classes are used within character sets, for example `[[:alpha:]]*` in English means the same as `[a-zA-Z]*`.

Because certain concepts like matching digits are so common, there are shorthand patterns for them. For example, `[:digit:]` and `[:d:]` mean the same thing as `[0-9]`. Some classes have an even shorter pattern using the escape notation \. For example \d means [:digit:]. Therefore, to recognize a sequence of one or more numbers, you can write any of the following patterns:

➤ `[0-9]+`

➤ `[[:digit:]]+`

➤ `[[:d:]]+`

➤ `\d+`

The following table lists the available escape notations for character classes:

ESCAPE NOTATION	EQUIVALENT TO
\d	[[:d:]]
\D	[^[:d:]]
\s	[[:s:]]
\S	[^[:s:]]
\w	[[:w:]]
\W	[^[:w:]]

Some examples:

➤ `Test[5-8]` will match `Test5`, `Test6`, `Test7`, and `Test8`.

➤ `[[:lower:]]` will match a, b, and so on but not A, B, and so on.

➤ `[^[:lower:]]` will match any character except lowercase letters like a, b, and so on.

➤ `[[:lower:]5-7]` will match any lower case letter like a, b, and so on and will also match the numbers 5, 6, and 7.

Word Boundaries

A *word boundary* can mean the following:

➤ The beginning of the source string if the first character of the source string is one of the word characters [A-Za-z0-9_].

➤ The end of the source string if the last character of the source string is one of the word characters.

➤ The first character of a word, which is one of the word characters, while the preceding character is not a word character.

➤ The end of a word, which is a non-word character after a word, while the preceding character is a word character.

You can use \b to match a word boundary, and \B to match anything except a word boundary.

Back References

Back references allow you to reference a captured group inside the regular expression itself: \n refers to the *n*-th captured group. The 0-th capture group is equal to the complete match. For example the regular expression ^(\d+)-.*-\1$ matches a string that has the following format:

➤ The beginning of the string ^

➤ followed by one or more digits captured in a capture group (\d+)

➤ followed by a dash -

➤ followed by zero or more characters .*

➤ followed by another dash -

➤ followed by exactly the same digits captured by the first capture group \1

➤ followed by the end of the string $

This regular expression will match 123-abc-123, 1234-a-1234, and so on but will not match 123-abc-1234, 123-abc-321, and so on.

Regular Expressions and Raw String Literals

As seen in the preceding sections, regular expressions often use special characters that should be escaped in normal C++ string literals. For example, if you write \d in a regular expression it will match any digit. However, since \ is a special character in C++, you need to escape it in your regular expression string literal as \\d, otherwise your C++ compiler will try to interpret the \d. It can get more complicated if you want your regular expression to match a single back-slash character \. Because \ is a special character in the regular expression syntax itself, you need to escape it as \\. The \ character is also a special character in C++ string literals, so you need to escape it in your C++ string literal, resulting in \\\\.

You can use the new C++11 *raw string literals* to make complicated regular expression easier to read in your C++ source code. Raw string literals are explained earlier in this chapter. For example take the following regular expression:

(|\\n|\\r|\\\\)

This regular expression searches for spaces, newlines, form feeds, and back slashes. As you can see, you need a lot of escape characters. Using raw string literals, this can be replaced with the following more readable regular expression:

R"((|\n|\r|\\))"

The raw string literal starts with R"(and ends with)". Everything in between is the regular expression. Of course we still need a double back slash at the end because the back slash needs to be escaped in the regular expression itself.

This concludes a brief description of the ECMAScript grammar. The following section starts with actually using regular expressions in your C++11 code.

The regex Library

Everything for the C++11 regular expression library is in the `<regex>` header file and in the `std` namespace. The basic templated types defined by the regular expression library are:

➤ `basic_regex`: An object representing a specific regular expression.

➤ `match_results`: A sub-string that matched a regular expression, including all the captured groups. It is a collection of `sub_matches`.

➤ `sub_match`: An iterator pair representing a specific matched capture group.

The library provides three key algorithms: `regex_match()`, `regex_search()` and `regex_replace()`. These are explained in later sections. All of these algorithms have different versions that allow you to specify the source string as an STL `string`, a character array, or as a begin and end iterator pair. The iterators can be any of the following:

➤ `const char*`

➤ `const wchar_t*`

➤ `string::const_iterator`

➤ `wstring::const_iterator`

In fact, any iterator that behaves as a bidirectional iterator can be used. Iterators are discussed in detail in Chapter 12.

The library also defines *regular expression iterators,* which are very important if you want to find all occurrences of a pattern in a source string as you will see in a later section. There are two templated regular expression iterators defined:

➤ `regex_iterator`: iterates over all the occurrences of a pattern in a source string

➤ `regex_token_iterator`: iterates over all the capture groups of all occurrences of a pattern in a source string

To make the library easier to use, the standard defines a number of `typedefs` for the preceding templates:

```
typedef basic_regex<char>    regex;
typedef basic_regex<wchar_t> wregex;

typedef sub_match<const char*>             csub_match;
typedef sub_match<const wchar_t*>          wcsub_match;
typedef sub_match<string::const_iterator>  ssub_match;
typedef sub_match<wstring::const_iterator> wssub_match;

typedef match_results<const char*>             cmatch;
typedef match_results<const wchar_t*>          wcmatch;
typedef match_results<string::const_iterator>  smatch;
typedef match_results<wstring::const_iterator> wsmatch;

typedef regex_iterator<const char*>            cregex_iterator;
typedef regex_iterator<const wchar_t*>         wcregex_iterator;
```

```
typedef regex_iterator<string::const_iterator>  sregex_iterator;
typedef regex_iterator<wstring::const_iterator> wsregex_iterator;

typedef regex_token_iterator<const char*>               cregex_token_iterator;
typedef regex_token_iterator<const wchar_t*>            wcregex_token_iterator;
typedef regex_token_iterator<string::const_iterator>   sregex_token_iterator;
typedef regex_token_iterator<wstring::const_iterator>  wsregex_token_iterator;
```

The following sections explain the `regex_match()`, `regex_search()` and `regex_replace()` algorithms and the `regex_iterator` and `regex_token_iterator`.

regex_match()

The `regex_match()` algorithm can be used to compare a given source string with a regular expression pattern and will return `true` if the pattern matches the entire source string, `false` otherwise. It is very easy to use. There are six versions of the `regex_match()` algorithm accepting different kinds of arguments:

```
template <class BidirectionalIterator, class Allocator, class charT, class traits>
  bool regex_match(BidirectionalIterator first,
                   BidirectionalIterator last,
                   match_results<BidirectionalIterator, Allocator>& m,
                   const basic_regex<charT, traits>& e,
                   regex_constants::match_flag_type flags =
                       regex_constants::match_default);

template <class BidirectionalIterator, class charT, class traits>
  bool regex_match(BidirectionalIterator first,
                   BidirectionalIterator last,
                   const basic_regex<charT, traits>& e,
                   regex_constants::match_flag_type flags =
                       regex_constants::match_default);

template <class charT, class Allocator, class traits>
  bool regex_match(const charT* str,
                   match_results<const charT*, Allocator>& m,
                   const basic_regex<charT, traits>& e,
                   regex_constants::match_flag_type flags =
                       regex_constants::match_default);

template <class ST, class SA, class Allocator, class charT, class traits>
  bool regex_match(const basic_string<charT, ST, SA>& s,
                   match_results<
                       typename basic_string<charT, ST, SA>::const_iterator,
                       Allocator>& m,
                   const basic_regex<charT, traits>& e,
                   regex_constants::match_flag_type flags =
                       regex_constants::match_default);

template <class charT, class traits>
  bool regex_match(const charT* str,
                   const basic_regex<charT, traits>& e,
```

```
                        regex_constants::match_flag_type flags =
                             regex_constants::match_default);

    template <class ST, class SA, class charT, class traits>
      bool regex_match(const basic_string<charT, ST, SA>& s,
                        const basic_regex<charT, traits>& e,
                        regex_constants::match_flag_type flags =
                             regex_constants::match_default);
```

Some of them accept a start and end iterator into a source string where pattern matching should start and end; others accept a simple `string` or a character array as source. All of them require a `basic_regex` as one of their arguments, which represents the regular expression. All variations return `true` when the entire source string matches the pattern, `false` otherwise; and all accept a combination of flags to specify options for the matching algorithm. In most cases this can be left as `match_default`. Consult the Standard Library Reference resource on the website for more details.

Both `regex_match()` and `regex_search()` described in a later section can use an optional `match_results` object. If the algorithms return `false`, you are only allowed to call `match_results::empty()` or `match_results::size()`; anything else is undefined. When the algorithms return `true`, a match is found and you can inspect the `match_results` object for what exactly got matched. How to do this is explained with examples in the following sections.

regex_match() Example

The function prototypes in the previous section might look complicated, but actually using `regex_match()` is not complicated at all.

Suppose you want to write a program that asks the user to enter a date in the following format year/month/day where year is four digits, month is a number between 1 and 12, and day is a number between 1 and 31. You can use a regular expression together with the `regex_match()` algorithm to validate the user input as follows. The details of the regular expression are explained after the code:

```
regex r("^\\d{4}/(?:0?[1-9]|1[0-2])/(?:0?[1-9]|[1-2][0-9]|3[0-1])$");
while (true) {
    cout << "Enter a date (year/month/day) (q=quit): ";
    string str;
    if (!getline(cin, str) || str == "q")
        break;
    if (regex_match(str, r))
        cout << "  Valid date." << endl;
    else
        cout << "  Invalid date!" << endl;
}
```

Code snippet from RegularExpressions\regex_match_dates_1.cpp

The first line creates the regular expression. The expression consists of three parts separated by a forward slash / character, one part for year, one for month, and one for day. The following list explains these parts:

➤ `^\\d{4}`: This will match any combination of four digits, for example 1234, 2010, and so on, at the beginning of the string.

➤ `(?:0?[1-9]|1[0-2])`: This sub part of the regular expression is wrapped inside parentheses to make sure the precedence is correct. We don't need any capture group so `(?:...)` is used. The inner expression consists of an alternation of two parts separated by the `|` character.

  ➤ `0?[1-9]`: This will match any number from 1 to 9 with an optional 0 in front of it. For example it will match 1, 2, 9, 03, 04, and so on. It will not match 0, 10, 11, and so on.

  ➤ `1[0-2]`: This will match 10, 11, or 12, nothing else.

➤ `(?:0?[1-9]|[1-2][0-9]|3[0-1])$`: This sub part is also wrapped inside a non-capture group and consists of an alternation of three parts followed by the end of the string:

  ➤ `0?[1-9]`: This is the same as the first part of the month matcher explained above.

  ➤ `[1-2][0-9]`: This will match any number between 10 and 29 and nothing else.

  ➤ `3[0-1]`: This will match 30 or 31 and nothing else.

The example then enters an infinite loop to ask the user to enter a date. Each date entered is then given to the `regex_match()` algorithm. When `regex_match()` returns `true` the user has entered a date that matches the date regular expression pattern.

This example can be expanded a bit by asking the `regex_match()` algorithm to return captured sub-expressions in a results object. The following code extracts the year, month, and day digits into three separate integer variables.

To understand this code, you have to understand what a capture group does. By specifying a `match_results` object like `smatch` in the call to `regex_match()`, the elements of the `match_results` object are filled in when the regular expression matches the string. To be able to extract these sub-strings, you must create capture groups, so although parentheses are not required for grouping in this example, they are used to define new capture groups.

The first element, `[0]`, in a `match_results` object contains the string that matched the entire pattern. When using `regex_match()` and a match is found, this is the entire source sequence. When using `regex_search()`, discussed in the next section, this is a sub-string in the source sequence that matches the regular expression. Element `[1]` is the sub-string matched by the first capture group, `[2]` by the second capture group, and so on.

The regular expression in the revised example has a few small changes. The first part matching the year is wrapped in a capture group, while the month and day parts are now also capture groups instead of non-capture groups. The call to `regex_match()` includes a `smatch` parameter, which will contain the matched capture groups. Here is the adapted example:

```
regex r("^(\\d{4})/(0?[1-9]|1[0-2])/(0?[1-9]|[1-2][0-9]|3[0-1])$");
while (true) {
    cout << "Enter a date (year/month/day) (q=quit): ";
    string str;
    if (!getline(cin, str) || str == "q")
        break;
```

```
smatch m;
if (regex_match(str, m, r)) {
    int year = atoi(m[1].str().c_str());
    int month = atoi(m[2].str().c_str());
    int day = atoi(m[3].str().c_str());
    cout << "  Valid date: Year=" << year
         << ", month=" << month
         << ", day=" << day << endl;
} else {
    cout << "  Invalid date!" << endl;
}
}
```

Code snippet from RegularExpressions\regex_match_dates_2.cpp

In this example there are four elements in the `smatch` results objects, the full match, and three captured groups:

➤   `[0]`: the string matching the full regular expression, which is the full date in this example

➤   `[1]`: the year

➤   `[2]`: the month

➤   `[3]`: the day

When you execute this example you can get the following output:

```
Enter a date (year/month/day) (q=quit): 2011/12/01
  Valid date: Year=2011, month=12, day=1
Enter a date (year/month/day) (q=quit): 11/12/01
  Invalid date!
```

These date matching examples only check if the date consists of a year (four digits), a month (1-12) and a day (1-31). They do not perform any validation for leap years and so on. If you need that, you have to write code to validate the year, month and day values that are extracted by `regex_match()`. *This validation is not a job for regular expressions, so this is not shown.*

regex_search()

The `regex_match()` algorithm discussed in the previous section returns `true` if the entire source string matches the regular expression, `false` otherwise. It cannot be used to find a matching substring in the source string. The `regex_search()` algorithm allows you to search for a sub-string that matches a certain pattern in a source string. There are six versions of the `regex_search()` algorithm. The difference between them is in the type of arguments, similar to the six versions of `regex_match()`. See the Standard Library Reference resource on the website for more details.

One of the versions of the `regex_search()` algorithm accepts a begin and end iterator into a string that you want to process. You might be tempted to use this version of `regex_search()` in a loop to find all occurrences of a pattern in a source string by manipulating these begin and end iterators for each `regex_search()` call. Never do this! It can cause problems when your regular expression uses anchors (^ or $), word boundaries, and so on. It can also cause an infinite loop due to empty matches. Use the `regex_iterator` or `regex_token_iterator` as explained later in this chapter to extract all occurrences of a pattern from a source string.

> *Never use* `regex_search()` *in a loop to find all occurrences of a pattern in a source string. Instead, use a* `regex_iterator` *or* `regex_token_iterator`*.*

regex_search() Example

The `regex_search()` algorithm can be used to extract matching sub-strings from an input string. The following example extracts code comments from input lines. The regular expression searches for a sub-string that starts with // followed by some optional whitespace \\s* followed by one or more characters captured in a capture group (.+). This capture group will capture only the comment sub-string. The `smatch` object m will contain the search results. To get a string representation of the first capture group, you can write `m[1]` as in the following code or write `m[1].str()`. You can check the `m[1].first` and `m[1].second` iterators to see where exactly the sub-string was found in the source string.

Available for download on Wrox.com

```cpp
regex r("//\\s*(.+)");
while (true) {
    cout << "Enter a string (q=quit): ";
    string str;
    if (!getline(cin, str) || str == "q")
        break;
    smatch m;
    if (regex_search(str, m, r))
        cout << "  Found comment '" << m[1] << "'" << endl;
    else
        cout << "  No comment found!" << endl;
}
```

Code snippet from RegularExpressions\regex_search_comments.cpp

The output of this program can look as follows:

```
Enter a string (q=quit): std::string str;    // Our source string
   Found comment 'Our source string'
Enter a string (q=quit): int a; // A comment with // in the middle
   Found comment 'A comment with // in the middle'
Enter a string (q=quit): float f; // A comment with a        (tab) character
   Found comment 'A comment with a        (tab) character'
```

The `match_results` object also has a `prefix()` and `suffix()` method, which returns the string preceding or following the match respectively.

regex_iterator

As explained in the previous section, you should never use `regex_search()` in a loop to extract all occurrences of a pattern from a source string. Instead, you should use a `regex_iterator` or `regex_token_iterator`. They work similarly like iterators for STL containers which are discussed in Chapter 12.

Internally, both a `regex_iterator` and a `regex_token_iterator` contain a pointer to the regular expression. Because of this, you should not create them with a temporary `regex` object.

Never try to create a `regex_iterator` *or* `regex_token_iterator` *with a temporary* `regex` *object.*

regex_iterator Example

The following example asks the user to enter a source string, extracts every word from that string, and prints it between quotes. The regular expression in this case is `[\\w]+`, which searches for one or more word-letters. This example uses `std::string` as source, so it uses `sregex_iterator` for the iterators. A standard iterator loop is used, but in this case, the end iterator is done slightly differently from the end iterators of ordinary STL containers. Normally, you specify an end iterator for a particular container, but for `regex_iterator`, there is only one "end" value. You can get this end iterator by simply declaring a `regex_iterator` type using the default constructor; it will implicitly be initialized to the end value.

The `for` loop creates a start iterator called `it`, which accepts a begin and end iterator into the source string together with the regular expression. The loop body will be called for every match found, which is every word in this example. The `sregex_iterator` iterates over all the matches. By dereferencing a `sregex_iterator`, you get a `smatch` object. Accessing the first element of this `smatch` object, `[0]`, gives you the matched sub-string:

Available for download on Wrox.com

```
regex reg("[\\w]+");
while (true) {
    cout << "Enter a string to split (q=quit): ";
    string str;
    if (!getline(cin, str) || str == "q")
        break;
    const sregex_iterator end;
    for (sregex_iterator it(str.begin(), str.end(), reg); it != end; ++it) {
        cout << "\"" << (*it)[0] << "\"" << endl;
    }
}
```

Code snippet from RegularExpressions\regex_iterator.cpp

The output of this program can look as follows:

```
Enter a string to split (q=quit): This, is    a test.
"This"
"is"
"a"
"test"
```

As this example demonstrates, even simple regular expressions can do some powerful string manipulation.

regex_token_iterator

The previous section described `regex_iterator` which iterates through every matched pattern. In each iteration of the loop you get a `match_results` object, which you can use to extract sub-expressions for that match captured by capture groups.

A `regex_token_iterator` can be used to automatically iterate over all or selected capture groups across all matched patterns. It has four constructors. The first creates an iterator that only iterates over capture groups with given index `submatch`. The second iterates over all capture groups with an index that appears in the `submatches` vector. The third iterates over all capture groups with an index that appears in the `submatches` initializer list and the fourth iterates over all capture groups with an index that appears in the `submatches` array.

```cpp
regex_token_iterator(BidirectionalIterator a,
                     BidirectionalIterator b,
                     const regex_type& re,
                     int submatch = 0,
                     regex_constants::match_flag_type m =
                         regex_constants::match_default);

regex_token_iterator(BidirectionalIterator a,
                     BidirectionalIterator b,
                     const regex_type& re,
                     const std::vector<int>& submatches,
                     regex_constants::match_flag_type m =
                         regex_constants::match_default);

regex_token_iterator(BidirectionalIterator a,
                     BidirectionalIterator b,
                     const regex_type& re,
                     initializer_list<int> submatches,
                     regex_constants::match_flag_type m =
                         regex_constants::match_default);

template <std::size_t N>
regex_token_iterator(BidirectionalIterator a,
                     BidirectionalIterator b,
                     const regex_type& re,
                     const int (&submatches)[N],
                     regex_constants::match_flag_type m =
                         regex_constants::match_default);
```

When you use the first constructor and use the default value of 0 for submatch, you get an iterator that iterates over all capture groups with index 0, which are the sub-strings matching the full regular expression.

regex_token_iterator Examples

The previous regex_iterator example can be rewritten by using a regex_token_iterator as follows. Since the token iterator will automatically iterate over all capture groups with index 0, you use *iter in the loop body instead of (*iter)[0]. The output of this code is exactly the same as the output generated by the regex_iterator example:

```cpp
regex reg("[\\w]+");
while (true) {
    cout << "Enter a string to split (q=quit): ";
    string str;
    if (!getline(cin, str) || str == "q")
        break;
    const sregex_token_iterator end;
    for (sregex_token_iterator iter(str.begin(), str.end(), reg);
        iter != end; ++iter) {
        cout << "\"" << *iter << "\"" << endl;
    }
}
```

Code snippet from RegularExpressions\regex_token_iterator_1.cpp

The following example asks the user to enter a date and then uses a regex_token_iterator to iterate over the second and third capture group (month and day), which is specified by using a vector<int>. The regular expression used for dates is explained in an earlier section in this chapter:

```cpp
regex reg("^(\\d{4})/(0?[1-9]|1[0-2])/(0?[1-9]|[1-2][0-9]|3[0-1])$");
while (true) {
    cout << "Enter a date (year/month/day) (q=quit): ";
    string str;
    if (!getline(cin, str) || str == "q")
        break;
    vector<int> vec = {2, 3};
    const sregex_token_iterator end;
    for (sregex_token_iterator iter(str.begin(), str.end(), reg, vec);
        iter != end; ++iter) {
        cout << "\"" << *iter << "\"" << endl;
    }
}
```

Code snippet from RegularExpressions\regex_token_iterator_2.cpp

This code prints only the month and day of valid dates. Output generated by this example can look as follows:

```
Enter a date (year/month/day) (q=quit): 2011/1/13
"1"
"13"
Enter a date (year/month/day) (q=quit): 2011/1/32
Enter a date (year/month/day) (q=quit): 2011/12/5
"12"
"5"
```

The `regex_token_iterator` can also be used to perform a so-called *field splitting* or *tokenization*. It is a much safer and more flexible alternative than using the old `strtok()` function. Tokenization is triggered in the `regex_token_iterator` constructor by specifying `-1` as the capture group index to iterate over. When in tokenization mode, the iterator will iterate over all sub-strings of the source string that **do not match** the regular expression. The following code demonstrates this by tokenizing a string on the delimiters , and ; with any number of whitespace characters before or after the delimiters:

```cpp
regex reg("\\s*[,;]+\\s*");
while (true) {
    cout << "Enter a string to split on ',' and ';' (q=quit): ";
    string str;
    if (!getline(cin, str) || str == "q")
        break;
    const sregex_token_iterator end;
    for (sregex_token_iterator iter(str.begin(), str.end(), reg, -1);
         iter != end; ++iter) {
        cout << "\"" << *iter << "\"" << endl;
    }
}
```

Code snippet from RegularExpressions\regex_token_iterator_field_splitting.cpp

The regular expression in this example searches for patterns that match the following:

➤ Zero or more whitespace characters,

➤ followed by 1 or more , or ; characters,

➤ followed by zero or more whitespace characters.

The output can be as follows:

```
Enter a string to split on ',' and ';' (q=quit): This is,    a; test string.
"This is"
"a"
"test string."
```

As you can see from this output, the string is split on , and ; and all whitespace characters around the , or ; are removed, because the tokenization iterator iterates over all sub-strings that do not match the regular expression, and because the regular expression matches , and ; with whitespace around them.

regex_replace()

The `regex_replace()` algorithm requires a regular expression, and a formatting string that will be used to replace matching sub-strings. This formatting string can reference part of the matched sub-strings by using the following escape sequences:

ESCAPE SEQUENCE	REPLACED WITH
$n	the string matching the *n*-th capture group, for example $1 for the first capture group, $2 for the second, and so on
$&	the string matching the whole regular expression, which is the same as $0
$`	the part of the source string that appears to the left of the sub-string matching the regular expression
$'	the part of the source string that appears to the right of the sub-string matching the regular expression
$$	a dollar sign

There are six versions of the `regex_replace()` algorithm. The difference between them is in the type of arguments:

```
template <class OutputIterator, class BidirectionalIterator,
         class traits, class charT, class ST, class SA>
  OutputIterator
    regex_replace(OutputIterator out,
                  BidirectionalIterator first,
                  BidirectionalIterator last,
                  const basic_regex<charT, traits>& e,
                  const basic_string<charT, ST, SA>& fmt,
                  regex_constants::match_flag_type flags =
                      regex_constants::match_default);

template <class OutputIterator, class BidirectionalIterator,
         class traits, class charT>
  OutputIterator
    regex_replace(OutputIterator out,
                  BidirectionalIterator first,
                  BidirectionalIterator last,
                  const basic_regex<charT, traits>& e,
                  const charT* fmt,
                  regex_constants::match_flag_type flags =
                      regex_constants::match_default);

template <class traits, class charT, class ST, class SA, class FST, class FSA>
  basic_string<charT, ST, SA>
    regex_replace(const basic_string<charT, ST, SA>& s,
                  const basic_regex<charT, traits>& e,
                  const basic_string<charT, FST, FSA>& fmt,
                  regex_constants::match_flag_type flags =
```

```
                                     regex_constants::match_default);

        template <class traits, class charT, class ST, class SA>
          basic_string<charT, ST, SA>
            regex_replace(const basic_string<charT, ST, SA>& s,
                          const basic_regex<charT, traits>& e,
                          const charT* fmt,
                          regex_constants::match_flag_type flags =
                              regex_constants::match_default);

        template <class traits, class charT, class ST, class SA>
          basic_string<charT>
            regex_replace(const charT* s,
                          const basic_regex<charT, traits>& e,
                          const basic_string<charT, ST, SA>& fmt,
                          regex_constants::match_flag_type flags =
                              regex_constants::match_default);

        template <class traits, class charT>
          basic_string<charT>
            regex_replace(const charT* s,
                          const basic_regex<charT, traits>& e,
                          const charT* fmt,
                          regex_constants::match_flag_type flags =
                              regex_constants::match_default);
```

regex_replace() Examples

As a first example, take the source HTML string `<body><h1>Header</h1><p>Some text</p>`
`</body>` and the regular expression `<h1>(.*)</h1><p>(.*)</p>`. The following table shows the
different escape sequences and with what they will be replaced with:

ESCAPE SEQUENCE	REPLACED WITH
$1	Header
$2	Some text
$&	<h1>Header</h1><p>Some text</p>
$`	<body>
$'	</body>

The following code demonstrates the use of `regex_replace()`:

```cpp
const string str("<body><h1>Header</h1><p>Some text</p></body>");
regex r("<h1>(.*)</h1><p>(.*)</p>");
const string format("H1=$1 and P=$2");
string result = regex_replace(str, r, format);
cout << "Original string: '" << str << "'" << endl;
cout << "New string      : '" << result << "'" << endl;
```

Code snippet from RegularExpressions\regex_replace_1.cpp

The output of this program is as follows:

```
Original string: '<body><h1>Header</h1><p>Some text</p></body>'
New string     : '<body>H1=Header and P=Some text</body>'
```

The `regex_replace()` algorithm accepts a number of flags that can be used to manipulate how it is working. The most important flags are given in the following table:

FLAG	DESCRIPTION
`format_default`	The default is to replace all occurrences of the pattern, and to also copy everything that does not match the pattern to the result string.
`format_no_copy`	Replace all occurrences of the pattern, but do not copy anything that does not match the pattern to the result string.
`format_first_only`	Replace only the first occurrence of the pattern.

The following example modifies the previous code to use the `format_no_copy` flag:

Available for
download on
Wrox.com

```
const string str("<body><h1>Header</h1><p>Some text</p></body>");
regex r("<h1>(.*)</h1><p>(.*)</p>");
const string format("H1=$1 and P=$2");
string result = regex_replace(str, r, format,
    regex_constants::format_no_copy);
cout << "Original string: '" << str << "'" << endl;
cout << "New string     : '" << result << "'" << endl;
```

Code snippet from RegularExpressions\regex_replace_2.cpp

The output is as follows. Compare this with the output of the previous version.

```
Original string: '<body><h1>Header</h1><p>Some text</p></body>'
New string     : 'H1=Header and P=Some text'
```

Another example is to get an input string and replace each word boundary with a newline so that the target string contains only one word per line. The following example demonstrates this without using any loops to process a given string. The code first creates a regular expression that matches individual words. When a match is found it is replaced by `$1\n` where `$1` will be replaced with the matched word. Note also the use of the `format_no_copy` flag to prevent copying whitespace from the source string to the result string:

Available for
download on
Wrox.com

```
regex reg("([\\w]+)");
const string format("$1\n");
while (true) {
    cout << "Enter a string to split over multiple lines (q=quit): ";
    string str;
```

```
        if (!getline(cin, str) || str == "q")
            break;
        cout << regex_replace(str, reg, format,
            regex_constants::format_no_copy) << endl;
    }
```

Code snippet from RegularExpressions\regex_replace_3.cpp

The output of this program can be as follows:

```
Enter a string to split over multiple lines (q=quit):   This is   a test.
This
is
a
test
```

SUMMARY

This chapter started with a discussion on the C++ `string` class and why you should use it instead of the old plain C-style character arrays. It also explained a number of new helper functions added to C++11 to make it easier to convert numerical values into `strings` and vice versa, and introduced the concept of raw string literals.

The second part of this chapter gave you an appreciation for coding with localization in mind. As anyone who has been through a localization effort will tell you, adding support for a new language or locale is infinitely easier if you have planned ahead, for example by using Unicode characters and being mindful of locales.

The last part of this chapter explained the new C++11 regular expressions library. Once you know the syntax of regular expressions, it becomes much easier to work with strings. Regular expressions allow you to easily validate strings, search for sub-strings inside a source string, perform find-and-replace operations on strings, and so on. It is highly recommended to get to know them and to start using them instead of writing your own string manipulation routines. They will make your life easier.

15

Demystifying C++ I/O

WHAT'S IN THIS CHAPTER?

➤ What streams are

➤ How to use streams for input and output of data

➤ What the available standard streams are in the Standard Library

A program's fundamental job is to accept input and produce output. A program that produces no output of any sort would not be very useful. All languages provide some mechanism for I/O, either as a built-in part of the language or through an OS-specific API. A good I/O system is both flexible and easy to use. Flexible I/O systems support input and output through a variety of devices, such as files and the user console. They also support reading and writing of different types of data. I/O is error-prone because data coming from a user can be incorrect or the underlying file system or other data source can be inaccessible. Thus, a good I/O system is also capable of handling error conditions.

If you are familiar with the C language, you have undoubtedly used `printf()` and `scanf()`. As I/O mechanisms, `printf()` and `scanf()` are certainly flexible. Through escape codes and variable placeholders, they can be customized to read in specially formatted data, or output any value that the formatting codes permit, which is currently limited to integer/character values, floating point values, and strings. However, `printf()` and `scanf()` falter on other measures of good I/O systems. They do not handle errors particularly well, they are not flexible enough to handle custom data types, and, worst of all in an object-oriented language like C++, they are not at all object oriented!

C++ provides a more refined method of input and output through a mechanism known as *streams*. Streams are a flexible and object-oriented approach to I/O. In this chapter, you will learn how to use streams for data output and input. You will also learn how to use the stream mechanism to read from various sources and write to various destinations, such as the user console, files, and even strings. This chapter covers the most commonly used I/O features.

USING STREAMS

The stream metaphor takes a bit of getting used to. At first, streams may seem more complex than traditional C-style I/O, such as printf(). In reality, they seem complicated initially only because there is a deeper metaphor behind streams than there is behind printf(). Don't worry though; after a few examples, you'll never look back.

What Is a Stream, Anyway?

Chapter 1 compares the cout stream like a laundry chute for data. You throw some variables down the stream, and they are written to the user's screen, or *console*. More generally, all streams can be viewed as data chutes. Streams vary in their direction and their associated source or destination. For example, the cout stream that you are already familiar with is an output stream, so its direction is "out." It writes data to the console so its associated destination is "console." There is another standard stream called cin that accepts input from the user. Its direction is "in," and its associated source is "console." Both cout and cin are predefined instances of streams that are defined within the std namespace in C++. The following table gives a brief description of all predefined streams. The difference between *buffered* and *unbuffered* streams is explained in a later section:

STREAM	DESCRIPTION
cin	An input stream, reads data from the "input console."
cout	A buffered output stream, writes data to the "output console."
cerr	An unbuffered output stream, writes data to the "error console," which is often the same as the "output console."
clog	A buffered version of cerr.

Note that graphical user interface applications normally do not have a console; i.e., if you write something to cout, the user will not see it. If you are writing a library, you should never assume the existence of cout, cin, cerr or clog because you never know if your library will be used in a console or in a GUI application.

 Every input stream has an associated source. Every output stream has an associated destination.

Another important aspect of streams is that they include data but also have a so-called *current position*. The current position is the position in the stream where the next read or write operation will take place.

Stream Sources and Destinations

Streams as a concept can be applied to any object that accepts data or emits data. You could write a stream-based network class or stream-based access to a MIDI-based instrument. In C++, there are three common sources and destinations for streams.

You have already read many examples of user, or console, streams. Console input streams make programs interactive by allowing input from the user during run time. Console output streams provide feedback to the user and output results.

File streams, as the name implies, read data from a file system and write data to a file system. File input streams are useful for reading in configuration data and saved files or for batch processing file-based data. File output streams are useful for saving state and providing output. File streams subsume the functionality of the C functions `fprintf()`, `fwrite()`, and `fputs()` for output, and `fscanf()`, `fread()`, and `fgets()` for input.

String streams are an application of the stream metaphor to the string type. With a string stream, you can treat character data just as you would treat any other stream. For the most part, this is merely a handy syntax for functionality that could be handled through methods on the `string` class. However, using stream syntax provides opportunities for optimization and can be far more convenient than direct use of the `string` class. String streams subsume the functionality of `sprintf()`, `sprintf_s()`, and other forms of C string formatting functions.

The rest of this section deals with console streams (`cin` and `cout`). Examples of file and string streams are provided later in this chapter. Other types of streams, such as printer output or network I/O are often platform dependent, so they are not covered in this book.

Output with Streams

Output using streams is introduced in Chapter 1 and is used in almost every chapter in this book. This section will briefly revisit some of the basics and will introduce material that is more advanced.

Output Basics

Output streams are defined in the `<ostream>` header file. Most programmers include `<iostream>` in their programs, which in turn includes the headers for both input streams and output streams. The `<iostream>` header also declares the standard console output stream, `cout`.

The `<<` operator is the simplest way to use output streams. C++ basic types, such as `int`s, pointers, `double`s, and characters, can be output using `<<`. In addition, the C++ `string` class is compatible with `<<`, and C-style strings are properly output as well. Following are some examples of using `<<`:

```cpp
int i = 7;
cout << i << endl;

char ch = 'a';
cout << ch << endl;

string myString = "Marni is adorable.";
cout << myString << endl;
```

Code snippet from OutputBasics\OutputBasics.cpp

The output is as follows:

```
7
a
Marni is adorable.
```

The `cout` stream is the built-in stream for writing to the console, or *standard output*. You can "chain" uses of << together to output multiple pieces of data. This is because the << operator returns a reference to the stream as its result so you can immediately use << again on the same stream. For example:

```
int j = 11;
cout << "On a scale of 1 to cute, Marni ranks " << j << "!" << endl;
```

Code snippet from OutputBasics\OutputBasics.cpp

The output is as follows:

```
On a scale of 1 to cute, Marni ranks 11!
```

C++ streams will correctly parse C-style escape codes, such as strings that contain \n, but it is much more hip to use the built-in `endl` mechanism for this purpose. The following example uses `endl`, which is defined in the `std` namespace to represent an end-of-line character and to flush the output buffer. Several lines of text are output using one line of code.

```
cout << "Line 1" << endl << "Line 2" << endl << "Line 3" << endl;
```

Code snippet from OutputBasics\OutputBasics.cpp

The output is as follows:

```
Line 1
Line 2
Line 3
```

Methods of Output Streams

The << operator is, without a doubt, the most useful part of output streams. However, there is additional functionality to be explored. If you take a peek at the `<ostream>` header file, you'll see many lines of overloaded definitions of the << operator. You'll also find some useful public methods.

put() and write()

`put()` and `write()` are *raw output methods*. Instead of taking an object or variable that has some defined behavior for output, `put()` accepts a single character, while `write()` accepts a character array. The data passed to these methods is output as is, without any special formatting or processing. For example, the following function takes a C-style string and outputs it to the console without using the << operator:

```
void rawWrite(const char* data, int dataSize)
{
    cout.write(data, dataSize);
}
```

Code snippet from Write\Write.cpp

The next function writes the given index of a C-style string to the console by using the `put()` method:

```
void rawPutChar(const char* data, int charIndex)
{
    cout.put(data[charIndex]);
}
```

Code snippet from Put\Put.cpp

flush()

When you write to an output stream, the stream does not necessarily write the data to its destination right away. Most output streams *buffer*, or accumulate data instead of writing it out as it comes in. The stream will *flush*, or write out the accumulated data, when one of the following conditions occurs:

➤ A sentinel, such as the `endl` marker, is reached.

➤ The stream goes out of scope and is destructed.

➤ Input is requested from a corresponding input stream (i.e., when you make use of `cin` for input, `cout` will flush). In the section on file streams, you will learn how to establish this type of link.

➤ The stream buffer is full.

➤ You explicitly tell the stream to flush its buffer.

One way to explicitly tell a stream to flush is to call its `flush()` method, as in the code that follows:

```
cout << "abc";
cout.flush();    // abc is written to the console.
cout << "def";
cout << endl;    // def is written to the console.
```

Code snippet from Flush\flush.cpp

> *Not all output streams are buffered. The `cerr` stream, for example, does not buffer its output.*

Handling Output Errors

Output errors can arise in a variety of situations. Perhaps you are trying to open a non-existing file. Maybe a disk error has prevented a write operation from succeeding, for example because the disk is full. None of the streams' code you have read up until this point has considered these possibilities, mainly for brevity. However, it is vital that you address any error conditions that occur.

When a stream is in its normal usable state, it is said to be "good." The `good()` method can be called directly on a stream to determine whether or not the stream is currently good.

```
if (cout.good()) {
    cout << "All good" << endl;
}
```

The `good()` method provides an easy way to obtain basic information about the validity of the stream, but it does not tell you why the stream is unusable. There is a method called `bad()` that provides a bit more information. If `bad()` returns `true`, it means that a fatal error has occurred (as opposed to any nonfatal condition like end-of-file). Another method, `fail()`, returns `true` if the most recent operation has failed, implying that the next operation will also fail. For example, after calling `flush()` on an output stream, you could call `fail()` to make sure the stream is still usable.

```
cout.flush();
if (cout.fail()) {
    cerr << "Unable to flush to standard out" << endl;
}
```

You can also tell the streams to throw exceptions when a failure occurs. You then write a `catch` handler to catch `ios_base::failure` exceptions on which you can use the `what()` method to get a description of the error and the `code()` method to get the error code. However, whether or not you get useful information is compiler-dependent:

```
cout.exceptions(ios::failbit | ios::badbit | ios::eofbit);
try {
    cout << "Hello World." << endl;
} catch (const ios_base::failure& ex) {
    cerr << "Caught exception: " << ex.what()
         << ", error code = " << ex.code() << endl;
}
```

Code snippet from Exceptions\Exceptions.cpp

To reset the error state of a stream, use the `clear()` method:

```
cout.clear();
```

Error checking is performed less frequently for console output streams than for file output streams or input streams. The methods discussed here apply for other types of streams as well and are revisited later as each type is discussed.

Output Manipulators

One of the unusual features of streams is that you can throw more than just data down the chute. C++ streams also recognize *manipulators*, objects that make a change to the behavior of the stream instead of, or in addition to, providing data for the stream to work with.

You have already seen one manipulator: endl. The endl manipulator encapsulates data and behavior. It tells the stream to output an end-of-line sequence and to flush its buffer. Following are some other useful manipulators, many of which are defined in the <ios> and <iomanip> standard header files. The example after this list shows how to use them:

- **boolalpha** and **noboolalpha**. Tells the stream to output bool values as *true* and *false* (boolalpha) or *1* and *0* (noboolalpha). The default is noboolalpha.

- **hex, oct,** and **dec.** Outputs numbers in hexadecimal, octal, and base 10, respectively.

- **setprecision.** Sets the number of decimal places that are output for fractional numbers. This is a parameterized manipulator (meaning that it takes an argument).

- **setw.** Sets the field width for outputting numerical data. This is a parameterized manipulator.

- **setfill.** Specifies the character that is used to pad numbers that are smaller than the specified width. This is a parameterized manipulator.

- **showpoint** and **noshowpoint.** Forces the stream to always or never show the decimal point for floating point numbers with no fractional part.

- **put_money.** Writes a formatted money amount to a stream.

- **put_time.** Writes a formatted time to a stream.

The following example uses several of these manipulators to customize its output. The example also uses the concept of locales, discussed in Chapter 14.

```
// Boolean values
bool myBool = true;
cout << "This is the default: " << myBool << endl;
cout << "This should be true: " << boolalpha << myBool << endl;
cout << "This should be 1: " << noboolalpha << myBool << endl;

// Simulate "%6d" with streams
int i = 123;
printf("This should be '   123': %6d\n", i);
cout << "This should be '   123': " << setw(6) << i << endl;
// Simulate "%06d" with streams
printf("This should be '000123': %06d\n", i);
cout << "This should be '000123': " << setfill('0') << setw(6) << i << endl;

// Fill with *
cout << "This should be '***123': " << setfill('*') << setw(6) << i << endl;
// Reset fill character
cout << setfill(' ');

// Floating point values
double dbl = 1.452;
double dbl2 = 5;
cout << "This should be ' 5': " << setw(2) << noshowpoint << dbl2 << endl;
cout << "This should be @@1.452: " << setw(7) << setfill('@') << dbl << endl;
```

```
// Format numbers according to your location
cout.imbue(locale(""));
cout << "This is 1234567 formatted according to your location: " << 1234567 << endl;

// C++11 put_money:
cout << "This should be a money amount of 1200, "
     << "formatted according to your location: "
     << put_money("120000") << endl;

// C++11 put_time:
time_t tt;
time(&tt);
tm t;
localtime_s(&t, &tt);
cout << "This should be the current date and time "
     << "formatted according to your location: "
     << put_time(&t, "%c") << endl;
```

Code snippet from Manipulator\Manipulator.cpp

If you don't care for the concept of manipulators, you can usually get by without them. Streams provide much of the same functionality through equivalent methods like `precision()`. For example, take the following line:

```
cout << "This should be '1.2346': " << setprecision(5) << 1.234567 << endl;
```

This can be converted to use a method call as follows:

Available for
download on
Wrox.com

```
cout.precision(5);
cout << "This should be '1.2346': " << 1.23456789 << endl;
```

Code snippet from Manipulator\Manipulator.cpp

See the Standard Library Reference resource on the website for details.

Input with Streams

Input streams provide a simple way to read in structured or unstructured data. In this section, the techniques for input are discussed within the context of `cin`, the console input stream.

Input Basics

There are two easy ways to read data by using an input stream. The first is an analog of the `<<` operator that outputs data to an output stream. The corresponding operator for reading data is `>>`. When you use `>>` to read data from an input stream, the variable you provide is the storage for the received value. For example, the following program reads one word from the user and puts it into a string. Then the string is output back to the console:

```
string userInput;
cin >> userInput;
cout << "User input was " << userInput << endl;
```

Code snippet from Input\string.cpp

By default, the >> operator will *tokenize* values according to white space. For example, if a user runs the previous program and enters `hello there` as input, only the characters up to the first white space character (the space character in this instance) will be captured into the `userInput` variable. The output would be as follows:

```
User input was hello
```

One solution to include white space in the input is to use `get()`, discussed later in this chapter.

The >> operator works with different variable types, just like the << operator. For example, to read an integer, the code differs only in the type of the variable:

```
int userInput;
cin >> userInput;
cout << "User input was " << userInput << endl;
```

Code snippet from Input\int.cpp

You can use input streams to read in multiple values, mixing and matching types as necessary. For example, the following function, an excerpt from a restaurant reservation system, asks the user for a last name and the number of people in their party:

```
void getReservationData()
{
    string guestName;
    int partySize;
    cout << "Name and number of guests: ";
    cin >> guestName >> partySize;
    cout << "Thank you, " << guestName << "." << endl;
    if (partySize > 10) {
        cout << "An extra gratuity will apply." << endl;
    }
}
```

Code snippet from Input\getReservationData.cpp

Note that the >> operator will tokenize values according to white space, so the `getReservationData()` function does not allow you to enter a name with white space. A solution using `unget()` is discussed later in this chapter. Note also that even though the use of `cout` does not explicitly flush the buffer using `endl` or `flush()`, the text will still be written to the console because the use of `cin` immediately flushes the `cout` buffer; they are linked together in this way.

If you get confused between << and >>, just think of the angles as pointing toward their destination. In an output stream, << points toward the stream itself because data is being sent to the stream. In an input stream, >> points toward the variables because data is being stored.

Input Methods

Just like output streams, input streams have several methods that allow a lower level of access than the functionality provided by the more common >> operator.

get()

The get() method allows raw input of data from a stream. The simplest version of get() returns the next character in the stream, though other versions exist that read multiple characters at once. get() is most commonly used to avoid the automatic tokenization that occurs with the >> operator. For example, the following function reads a name, which can be made up of several words, from an input stream until the end of the stream is reached:

Available for
download on
Wrox.com

```cpp
string readName(istream& inStream)
{
    string name;
    while (inStream.good()) {
        int next = inStream.get();
        if (next == EOF)
            break;
        name += next;// Implicitly convert to a char and append.
    }
    return name;
}
```

Code snippet from Get\Get.cpp

There are several interesting observations to make about this readName() function:

➤ Its parameter is a non-const reference to an istream, not a const reference. The methods that read in data from a stream will change the actual stream (most notably, its position), so they are not const methods. Thus, you can't call them on a const reference.

➤ The return value of get() is stored in an int, not in a char. Because get() can return special non-character values such as EOF (end-of-file), ints are used. When next is appended to a string, it is implicitly converted to a char, and when it is appended to a wstring, it is converted to a wchar_t.

readName() is a bit strange because there are two ways to get out of the loop. Either the stream can get into a "not good" state, or the end of the stream is reached. A more common pattern for reading from a stream uses a different version of get() that takes a reference to a character and returns a reference to the stream. This pattern takes advantage of the fact that evaluating an input stream within a conditional context will result in true only if the stream is available for additional reading. Encountering an error or reaching the end-of-file both cause the stream to evaluate to false. The underlying details of the conversion operations required to implement this feature are explained in Chapter 18. The following version of the same function is a bit more concise:

```
string readName(istream& inStream)
{
    string name;
    char next;
    while (inStream.get(next)) {
        name += next;
    }
    return name;
}
```

Code snippet from Get\Get.cpp

unget()

For most purposes, the correct way to think of an input stream is as a one-way chute. Data falls down the chute and into variables. The unget() method breaks this model in a way by allowing you to push data back up the chute.

A call to unget() causes the stream to back up by one position, essentially putting the previous character read back on the stream. You can use the fail() method to see if unget() was successful or not. For example, unget() can fail if the current position is at the beginning of the stream.

The getReservationData() function seen earlier in this chapter did not allow you to enter a name with white space. The following code uses unget() to allow white space in the name. The code reads character by character and checks whether the character is a digit or not. If the character is not a digit, it is added to guestName. If it is a digit, the character is put back into the stream using unget(), the loop is stopped, and the >> operator is used to input an integer, partySize. The meaning of noskipws is discussed later in the section "Input Manipulators."

```
void getReservationData()
{
    string guestName;
    int partySize = 0;
    // Read letters until we find a non-letter
    char ch;
    cin >> noskipws;
    while (cin >> ch) {
        if (isdigit(ch)) {
            cin.unget();
            if (cin.fail())
                cout << "unget() failed" << endl;
            break;
        }
        guestName += ch;
    }
    // Read partysize
```

```
    cin >> partySize;
    cout << "Thank you '" << guestName
        << "', party of " << partySize << endl;
    if (partySize > 10) {
        cout << "An extra gratuity will apply." << endl;
    }
}
```

Code snippet from Unget\Unget.cpp

putback()

putback(), like unget(), lets you move backward by one character in an input stream. The difference is that the putback() method takes the character being placed back on the stream as a parameter:

```
char ch1;
cin >> ch1;
cin.putback(ch1);
// ch1 will be the next character read off the stream.
```

peek()

The peek() method allows you to preview the next value that *would* be returned if you were to call get(). To take the chute metaphor perhaps a bit too far, you could think of it as looking up the chute without a value actually falling down it.

peek() is ideal for any situation where you need to look ahead before reading a value. For example, the following code implements the getReservationData() function that allows white space in the name, but uses peek() instead of unget():

```
void getReservationData()
{
    string guestName;
    int partySize = 0;
    // Read letters until we find a non-letter
    char ch;
    cin >> noskipws;
    while (true) {
        // 'peek' at next character
        ch = cin.peek();
        if (!cin.good())
            break;
        if (isdigit(ch)) {
            // next character will be a digit, so stop the loop
            break;
        }
        // next character will be a non-digit, so read it
        cin >> ch;
        guestName += ch;
    }
    // Read partysize
    cin >> partySize;
    cout << "Thank you '" << guestName
```

```
            << "', party of " << partySize << endl;
        if (partySize > 10) {
            cout << "An extra gratuity will apply." << endl;
        }
    }
}
```

getline()

Obtaining a single line of data from an input stream is so common that a method exists to do it for you. The getline() method fills a character buffer with a line of data up to the specified size. The specified size includes the \0 character. Thus, the following code will read a maximum of kBufferSize-1 characters from cin, or until an end-of-line sequence is read:

```
char buffer[kBufferSize];
cin.getline(buffer, kBufferSize);
```

When getline() is called, it reads a line from the input stream, up to and including the end-of-line sequence. However, the end-of-line character or characters do not appear in the string. Note that the end-of-line sequence is platform dependent. For example, it can be \r\n, or \n, or \n\r.

There is a form of get() that performs the same operation as getline(), except that it leaves the newline sequence in the input stream.

There is also a function called getline() that can be used with C++ strings. It is defined in the <string> header file and is in the std namespace. It takes a stream reference, a string reference, and an optional delimiter as parameters:

```
string myString;
std::getline(cin, myString);
```

Handling Input Errors

Input streams have a number of methods to detect unusual circumstances. Most of the error conditions related to input streams occur when there is no data available to read. For example, the end of stream (referred to as *end-of-file*, even for non-file streams) may have been reached. The most common way of querying the state of an input stream is to access it within a conditional. For example, the following loop will keep looping as long as cin remains in a good state:

```
while (cin) { ... }
```

You can input data at the same time:

```
while (cin >> ch) { ... }
```

You can also call the `good()` method, just like on output streams. There is also an `eof()` method that returns `true` if the stream has reached its end.

You should also get in the habit of checking the stream state after reading data so that you can recover from bad input.

The following program shows the common pattern for reading data from a stream and handling errors. The program reads numbers from standard input and displays their sum once end-of-file is reached. Note that in command-line environments, the end-of-file is indicated by the user typing a particular character. In Unix and Linux, it is `Control+D`, in Windows it is `Control+Z`. The exact character is operating system dependent, so you will need to know what your operating system requires:

```cpp
cout << "Enter numbers on separate lines to add. "
     << "Use Control+D to finish (Control+Z in Windows)." << endl;
int sum = 0;
if (!cin.good()) {
    cerr << "Standard input is in a bad state!" << endl;
    return 1;
}
int number;
while (true) {
    cin >> number;
    if (cin.good()) {
        sum += number;
    } else if (cin.eof()) {
        break; // Reached end of file
    } else {
        // Error!
        cin.clear(); // Clear the error state.
        string badToken;
        cin >> badToken; // Consume the bad input.
        cerr << "WARNING: Bad input encountered: " << badToken << endl;
    }
}
cout << "The sum is " << sum << endl;
```

Code snippet from ErrorCheck\ErrorCheck.cpp

Input Manipulators

The built-in input manipulators, described in the list that follows, can be sent to an input stream to customize the way that data is read.

➤ **boolalpha** and **noboolalpha**. If `boolalpha` is used, the string *false* will be interpreted as a Boolean value `false`; anything else will be treated as the Boolean value `true`. If `noboolalpha` is set, 0 will be interpreted as `false`, anything else as `true`. The default is `noboolalpha`.

➤ **hex, oct,** and **dec**. Reads numbers in hexadecimal, octal, and base 10, respectively.

➤ **skipws** and **noskipws**. Tells the stream to either skip white space when tokenizing or to read in white space as its own token.

➤ **ws.** A handy manipulator that simply skips over the current series of white space at the present position in the stream.

C++11 ➤ **get_money.** Reads a money amount from a stream.

C++11 ➤ **get_time.** Reads a formatted time from a stream.

Input is locale aware. For example, take the following code, which enables your system locale for `cin`. Locales are discussed in Chapter 14:

```
cin.imbue(locale(""));
int i;
cin >> i;
```

If your system locale is U.S. English, you can enter `1,000` and it will be parsed as 1000. On the other hand, if your system locale is Dutch Belgium, you should enter `1.000` to get the value of 1000.

Input and Output with Objects

You can use the `<<` operator to output a C++ `string` even though it is not a basic type. In C++, objects are able to prescribe how they are output and input. This is accomplished by *overloading* the `<<` and `>>` operator to understand a new type or class.

Why would you want to overload these operators? If you are familiar with the `printf()` function in C, you know that it is not flexible in this area. `printf()` knows about several types of data, but there really isn't a way to give it additional knowledge. For example, consider the following simple class:

Available for download on Wrox.com

```
class Muffin
{
    public:
        string  getDescription() const;
        void    setDescription(const string& inDesc);
        int     getSize() const;
        void    setSize(int inSize);
        bool    getHasChocolateChips() const;
        void    setHasChocolateChips(bool inChips);
    protected:
        string  mDesc;
        int     mSize;
        bool    mHasChocolateChips;
};
string Muffin::getDescription() const { return mDesc; }
void Muffin::setDescription(const string& inDesc) { mDesc = inDesc; }
int Muffin::getSize() const { return mSize; }
void Muffin::setSize(int inSize) { mSize = inSize; }
bool Muffin::getHasChocolateChips() const { return mHasChocolateChips; }
void Muffin::setHasChocolateChips(bool inChips) { mHasChocolateChips = inChips; }
```

Code snippet from Muffin\Muffin.cpp

To output an object of class `Muffin` by using `printf()`, it would be nice if you could specify it as an argument, perhaps using `%m` as a placeholder:

```
printf("Muffin output: %m\n", myMuffin); // BUG! printf doesn't understand Muffin.
```

Unfortunately, the `printf()` function knows nothing about the `Muffin` type and is unable to output an object of type `Muffin`. Worse still, because of the way the `printf()` function is declared, this will result in a run-time error, not a compile-time error (though a good compiler will give you a warning).

The best you can do with `printf()` is to add a new `output()` method to the `Muffin` class:

Available for download on Wrox.com

```
class Muffin
{
    public:
        string getDescription() const;
        void   setDescription(const string& inDesc);
        int    getSize() const;
        void   setSize(int inSize);
        bool   getHasChocolateChips() const;
        void   setHasChocolateChips(bool inChips);
        void   output();
    protected:
        string mDesc;
        int    mSize;
        bool   mHasChocolateChips;
};
// Other method implementations omitted for brevity
void Muffin::output()
{
    printf("%s, Size is %d, %s\n", getDescription().c_str(), getSize(),
                (getHasChocolateChips() ? "has chips" : "no chips"));
}
```

Code snippet from Muffin\Muffin.cpp

Using such a mechanism is cumbersome, however. To output a `Muffin` in the middle of another line of text, you'd need to split the line into two calls with a call to `Muffin::output()` in between, as shown in the following:

```
printf("The muffin is ");
myMuffin.output();
printf(" -- yummy!\n");
```

Overloading the `<<` operator lets you output a `Muffin` just like you output a `string` — by providing it as an argument to `<<`. Chapter 18 covers the details of overloading the `<<` and `>>` operators.

STRING STREAMS

String streams provide a way to use stream semantics with `strings`. In this way, you can have an *in-memory stream* that represents textual data. For example, in a GUI application you might want to use streams to build up textual data, but instead of outputting the text to the console or a file, you might want to display the result in a GUI element like a message box or an edit control. Another example could be that you want to pass a string stream around to different functions, while retaining the current read position, so that each function can process the next part of the stream. String streams are also useful for parsing text, because streams have built-in tokenizing functionality.

The `ostringstream` class is used to write data to a `string`, while the `istringstream` class is used to read data from a `string`. They are both defined in the `<sstream>` header file. Because `ostringstream` and `istringstream` inherit the same behavior as `ostream` and `istream`, working with them is pleasantly similar.

The following program requests words from the user and outputs them to a single `ostringstream`, separated by the tab character. At the end of the program, the whole stream is turned into a `string` object using the `str()` method and is written to the console. Input of tokens can be stopped by entering the token "done" or by closing the input stream with `Control+D` (Unix) or `Control+Z` (Windows):

Available for download on Wrox.com

```cpp
cout << "Enter tokens. Control+D (Unix) or Control+Z (Windows) to end" << endl;
ostringstream outStream;
while (cin) {
    string nextToken;
    cout << "Next token: ";
    cin >> nextToken;
    if (nextToken == "done")
        break;
    outStream << nextToken << "\t";
}
cout << "The end result is: " << outStream.str();
```

Code snippet from StringStream\StringStream.cpp

Reading data from a string stream is similarly familiar. The following function creates and populates a `Muffin` object (see earlier example) from a string input stream. The stream data is in a fixed format so that the function can easily turn its values into calls to the `Muffin` setters:

Available for download on Wrox.com

```cpp
Muffin createMuffin(istringstream& inStream)
{
    Muffin muffin;
    // Assume data is properly formatted:
    // Description size chips
    string description;
    int size;
    bool hasChips;
    // Read all three values. Note that chips is represented
    // by the strings "true" and "false"
    inStream >> description >> size >> boolalpha >> hasChips;
    muffin.setSize(size);
    muffin.setDescription(description);
    muffin.setHasChocolateChips(hasChips);
    return muffin;
}
```

Code snippet from Muffin\Muffin.cpp

Turning an object into a "flattened" type, like a string, *is often called* marshalling. *Marshalling is useful for saving objects to disk or sending them across a network.*

The main advantage of a string stream over a standard C++ `string` is that, in addition to data, the object knows where the next read or write operation will take place, also called current position. There may also be performance benefits depending on the particular implementation of string streams. For example, if you need to append a lot of strings together, it might be more efficient to use a string stream, instead of repeatedly calling the += operator on a `string` object.

FILE STREAMS

Files lend themselves very well to the stream abstraction because reading and writing files always involves a position in addition to the data. In C++, the `ofstream` and `ifstream` classes provide output and input functionality for files. They are defined in the `<fstream>` header file.

When dealing with the file system, it is especially important to detect and handle error cases. The file you are working with could be on a network file store that just went offline, or you may be trying to write to a file that is located on a disk that is full. Maybe you are trying to open a file to which the current user does not have permissions to. Error conditions can be detected by using the standard error handling mechanisms described earlier.

The only major difference between output file streams and other output streams is that the file stream constructor can take the name of the file and the mode in which you would like to open it. The default mode is write, `ios_base::out`, which starts writing to a file at the beginning, overwriting any existing data. You can also open an output file stream in append mode by specifying the constant `ios_base::app` as second argument to the file stream constructor. The following table lists the different constants that are available:

CONSTANT	DESCRIPTION
ios_base::app	Open and go to the end before each write operation.
ios_base::ate	Open and go to the end immediately after opening.
ios_base::binary	Perform input and output in binary mode (as opposed to text mode).
ios_base::in	Open for input.
ios_base::out	Open for output.
ios_base::trunc	Open and truncate any existing data.

The following program opens the file `test` and outputs the arguments to the program. The `ifstream` and `ofstream` destructors will automatically close the underlying file, so there is no need to explicitly call `close()`:

```cpp
int main(int argc, char* argv[])
{
    ofstream outFile("test");
    if (!outFile.good()) {
        cerr << "Error while opening output file!" << endl;
        return -1;
    }
    outFile << "There were " << argc << " arguments to this program." << endl;
    outFile << "They are: " << endl;
    for (int i = 0; i < argc; i++) {
        outFile << argv[i] << endl;
    }
    return 0;
}
```

Code snippet from FileStream\FileStream1.cpp

Jumping around with seek() and tell()

The seek() and tell() methods are present on all input and output streams, but they rarely make sense outside of the context of file streams.

The seek() methods let you move to an arbitrary position within an input or output stream. There are several forms of seek(). The methods of seek() within an input stream are actually called seekg() (the g is for *get*), and the versions of seek() in an output stream are called seekp() (the p is for *put*). You might wonder why there is both a seekg() and a seekp() method, instead of one seek() method. The reason is that you can have streams that are both input and output, for example, file streams. In that case, the stream needs to remember both a read position and a separate write position. This is also called bidirectional I/O and is covered later in this chapter.

There are two overloads of seekg() and two of seekp(). One overload accepts a single argument, an absolute position, and seeks to this absolute position. The second overload accepts an offset and a position, and seeks an offset relative to the given position. Positions are of type ios_base::streampos, while offsets are of type ios_base::streamoff, both are measured in bytes. There are three predefined positions available:

POSITION	DESCRIPTION
ios_base::beg	The beginning of the stream
ios_base::end	The end of the stream
ios_base::cur	The current position in the stream

For example, to seek to an absolute position in an output stream, you can use the one-parameter version of seekp(), as in the following case, which uses the constant ios_base::beg to move to the beginning of the stream:

```cpp
outStream.seekp(ios_base::beg);
```

Seeking within an input stream is exactly the same, except that the `seekg()` method is used:

```
inStream.seekg(ios_base::beg);
```

The two-argument versions move to a relative position in the stream. The first argument prescribes how many positions to move and the second argument provides the starting point. To move relative to the beginning of the file, the constant `ios_base::beg` is used. To move relative to the end of the file, `ios_base::end` is used. To move relative to the current position, `ios_base::cur` is used. For example, the following line moves to the second byte from the beginning of the stream. Note that integers are implicitly converted to type `ios_base::streampos` and `ios_base::streamoff`:

```
outStream.seekp(2, ios_base::beg);
```

The next example moves to the third-to-last byte of an input stream.

```
inStream.seekg(-3, ios_base::end);
```

You can also query a stream's current location using the `tell()` method which returns an `ios_base::streampos` that indicates the current position. You can use this result to remember the current marker position before doing a `seek()` or to query whether you are in a particular location. As with `seek()`, there are separate versions of `tell()` for input streams and output streams. Input streams use `tellg()`, and output streams use `tellp()`.

The following code checks the position of an input stream to determine if it is at the beginning.

```
ios_base::streampos curPos = inStream.tellg();
if (ios_base::beg == curPos) {
    cout << "We're at the beginning." << endl;
}
```

Following is a sample program that brings it all together. This program writes into a file called `test.out` and performs the following tests:

1. Outputs the string `12345` to the file.

2. Verifies that the marker is at position 5 in the stream.

3. Moves to position 2 in the output stream.

4. Outputs a `0` in position 2 and closes the output stream.

5. Opens an input stream on the `test.out` file.

6. Reads the first token as an integer.

7. Confirms that the value is `12045`.

```
ofstream fout("test.out");
if (!fout) {
    cerr << "Error opening test.out for writing" << endl;
    return 1;
}
// 1. Output the string "12345".
```

```cpp
fout << "12345";
// 2. Verify that the marker is at position 5.
ios_base::streampos curPos = fout.tellp();
if (5 == curPos) {
    cout << "Test passed: Currently at position 5" << endl;
} else {
    cout << "Test failed: Not at position 5" << endl;
}
// 3. Move to position 2 in the stream.
fout.seekp(2, ios_base::beg);
// 4. Output a 0 in position 2 and close the stream.
fout << 0;
fout.close();
// 5. Open an input stream on test.out.
ifstream fin("test.out");
if (!fin) {
    cerr << "Error opening test.out for reading" << endl;
    return 1;
}
// 6. Read the first token as an integer.
int testVal;
fin >> testVal;
// 7. Confirm that the value is 12045.
const int expected = 12045;
if (testVal == expected) {
    cout << "Test passed: Value is " << expected << endl;
} else {
    cout << "Test failed: Value is not " << expected
         << " (it was " << testVal << ")" << endl;
}
```

Code snippet from FileStream\FileStream2.cpp

Linking Streams Together

A link can be established between any input and output streams to give them *flush-on-access* behavior. In other words, when data is requested from an input stream, its linked output stream will automatically flush. This behavior is available to all streams, but is particularly useful for file streams that may be dependent upon each other.

Stream linking is accomplished with the `tie()` method. To tie an output stream to an input stream, call `tie()` on the input stream, and pass the address of the output stream. To break the link, pass `nullptr`.

The following program ties the input stream of one file to the output stream of an entirely different file. You could also tie it to an output stream on the same file, but bidirectional I/O (covered below) is perhaps a more elegant way to read and write the same file simultaneously:

```cpp
ifstream inFile("input.txt");
ofstream outFile("output.txt");
// Set up a link between inFile and outFile.
inFile.tie(&outFile);
// Output some text to outFile. Normally, this would
```

```
// not flush because std::endl was not sent.
outFile << "Hello there!";
// outFile has NOT been flushed.
// Read some text from inFile. This will trigger flush()
// on outFile.
string nextToken;
inFile >> nextToken;
// outFile HAS been flushed.
```

Code snippet from tie\tie.cpp

The `flush()` method is defined on the `ostream` base class, so you can also link an output stream to another output stream:

```
outFile.tie(&anotherOutputFile);
```

Such a relationship would mean that every time you wrote to one file, the buffered data that had been sent to the other file would be written. You could use this mechanism to keep two related files synchronized.

One example of this stream linking is the link between `cout` and `cin`. Whenever you try to input data from `cin`, `cout` is automatically flushed.

BIDIRECTIONAL I/O

So far, this chapter has discussed input and output streams as two separate but related classes. In fact, there is such a thing as a stream that performs both input and output. A *bidirectional stream* operates as both an input stream and an output stream.

Bidirectional streams are subclasses of `iostream`, which in turn subclasses both `istream` and `ostream`, thus serving as an example of useful multiple inheritance. As you would expect, bidirectional streams support both the `>>` operator and the `<<` operator, as well as the methods of both input streams and output streams.

The `fstream` class provides a bidirectional file stream. `fstream` is ideal for applications that need to replace data within a file because you can read until you find the correct position, then immediately switch to writing. For example, imagine a program that stores a list of mappings between ID numbers and phone numbers. It might use a data file with the following format:

```
123 408-555-0394
124 415-555-3422
164 585-555-3490
100 650-555-3434
```

A reasonable approach to such a program would be to read in the entire data file when the program opens and rewrite the file, with any modifications, when the program closes. If the data set is huge, however, you might not be able to keep everything in memory. With `iostreams`, you don't have to. You can easily scan through the file to find a record, and you can add new records by opening the file for output in append mode. To modify an existing record, you could use a bidirectional stream, as in the following function that changes the phone number for a given ID:

```cpp
bool changeNumberForID(const string& inFileName, int inID,
    const string& inNewNumber)
{
    fstream ioData(inFileName.c_str());
    if (!ioData) {
        cerr << "Error while opening file " << inFileName << endl;
        return false;
    }
    // Loop until the end of file
    while (ioData.good()) {
        int id;
        string number;
        // Read the next ID.
        ioData >> id;
        // Check to see if the current record is the one being changed.
        if (id == inID) {
            // Seek to the current read position
            ioData.seekp(ioData.tellg());
            // Output a space, then the new number.
            ioData << " " << inNewNumber;
            break;
        }
        // Read the current number to advance the stream.
        ioData >> number;
    }
    return true;
}
```

Code snippet from Bidirectional\Bidirectional.cpp

Of course, an approach like this will work properly only if the data is of a fixed size. When the preceding program switched from reading to writing, the output data overwrote other data in the file. To preserve the format of the file, and to avoid writing over the next record, the data had to be the exact same size.

String streams can also be accessed in a bidirectional manner through the `stringstream` class.

Bidirectional streams have separate pointers for the read position and the write position. When switching between reading and writing, you will need to seek to the appropriate position.

SUMMARY

Streams provide a flexible and object-oriented way to perform input and output. The most important message in this chapter, even more important than the use of streams, is the concept of a stream. Some operating systems may have their own file access and I/O facilities, but knowledge of how streams and stream-like libraries work is essential to working with any type of modern I/O system.

16

C++11 Additional Library Utilities

WHAT'S IN THIS CHAPTER?

➤ How you can use std::function for function pointers

➤ How to work with compile time rational numbers

➤ How to work with time

➤ How to generate random numbers

➤ What tuples are and how to use them

C++11 adds a lot more functionality to the C++ standard library not described in previous chapters. These additional library features are combined and explained in this chapter because they don't fit anywhere else.

STD::FUNCTION

std::function, defined in the <functional> header file, can be used to create a type that can point to a function, a function object, or a lambda expression; basically anything that is callable. It can be used as a function pointer or as a parameter for a function to implement callbacks. The template parameters for the std::function template look a bit different than most template parameters. Its syntax is as follows:

```
std::function<R(ArgTypes...)>
```

R is the return value type of the function and ArgTypes is a comma-separated list of argument types for the function.

The following example demonstrates how to use `std::function` to implement a function pointer. It creates a function pointer `f1` to point to the function `func()`. Once `f1` is defined, you can call `func()` by using the name `func` or `f1`:

```cpp
void func(int num, const string& str)
{
    cout << "func(" << num << ", " << str << ")" << endl;
}
int main()
{
    function<void(int, const string&)> f1 = func;
    f1(1, "test");
    return 0;
}
```

Code snippet from Function\function.cpp

Of course, in the preceding example it is possible to use the C++11 `auto` keyword, which removes the need for you to specify the exact type of `f1`. The following works exactly the same and is much shorter:

```cpp
auto f1 = func;
```

Code snippet from Function\function.cpp

Since `std::function` types behave as function pointers, they can be passed to STL algorithms as shown in the following example using the `count_if()` algorithm. STL algorithms are discussed in Chapter 13.

```cpp
bool isEven(int num)
{
    return num % 2 == 0;
}
int main()
{
    vector<int> vec;
    for (int i = 0; i < 10; ++i)
        vec.push_back(i);
    auto f2 = isEven;  // f2 will be of type function<bool(int)>
    int cnt = count_if(vec.cbegin(), vec.cend(), f2);
    cout << cnt << " even numbers" << endl;
    return 0;
}
```

Code snippet from Function\function_count_if.cpp

After the preceding examples, you might think that `std::function` is not really useful; but, where `std::function` really shines, is accepting a function pointer as argument to your own function. The following example defines a function called `process()`, which accepts a reference to a vector and a `std::function`. The `process()` function will iterate over all the elements in the given vector and will call the given function `f` for each element. You can think of the parameter `f` as a callback.

The `print()` function prints a given element to the console. The `main()` function first creates a vector of integers and populates it. It then calls the `process()` function with a function pointer to `print()`. The result will be that each element in the `vector` is printed.

The last part of the `main()` function demonstrates that you can also pass a lambda expression for the `std::function` parameter of the `process()` function, and that's the power of `std::function`. You cannot get this same functionality by using a function pointer `typedef`.

```cpp
void process(const vector<int>& vec, function<void(int)> f)
{
    for (auto& i : vec)
        f(i);
}
void print(int num)
{
    cout << num << "   ";
}
int main()
{
    vector<int> vec;
    for (int i = 0; i < 10; ++i)
        vec.push_back(i);
    process(vec, print);
    cout << endl;
    int sum = 0;
    process(vec, [&sum](int num){sum += num;});
    cout << "sum = " << sum << endl;
    return 0;
}
```

Code snippet from Function\function_callback.cpp

The output of this example is as follows:

```
0  1  2  3  4  5  6  7  8  9
sum = 45
```

RATIOS

The C++11 Ratio library allows you to exactly represent any finite rational number that you can use at compile time. Everything is defined in the `<ratio>` header file and is in the `std` namespace. The numerator and denominator of a rational number are represented as compile time constants of type `std::intmax_t`. Because of the compile time nature of these rational numbers, using them might look a bit complicated and different than usual. You cannot define a `ratio` object the same way as you define normal objects, and you cannot call methods on it. You need to use `typedefs`. For example, the following line defines a rational compile time constant representing 1/60:

```
typedef ratio<1, 60> r1;
```

The numerator and denominator of the `r1` rational number are compile time constants and can be accessed as follows:

```
intmax_t num = r1::num;
intmax_t den = r1::den;
```

Remember that a `ratio` is a **compile time constant**, which means that the numerator and denominator need to be known at compile time. The following will generate a compiler error:

```
intmax_t n = 1;
intmax_t d = 60;
typedef ratio<n, d> r1;     // Error
```

Making n and d constants removes the compilation error:

```
const intmax_t n = 1;
const intmax_t d = 60;
typedef ratio<n, d> r1;     // Ok
```

Rational numbers are always normalized. For a rational number `ratio<n, d>`, the greatest common divisor, `gcd`, is calculated and the numerator, `num`, and denominator, `den`, are defined as follows:

➤   `num = sign(n)*sign(d)*abs(n)/gcd`

➤   `den = abs(d)/gcd`

The library supports adding, subtracting, multiplying, and dividing rational numbers. Because all these operations are also happening at compile time, you cannot use the standard arithmetic operators. Instead, you need to use specific templates in combination with `typedefs`. The following arithmetic `ratio` templates are available: `ratio_add`, `ratio_subtract`, `ratio_multiply`, and `ratio_divide`. These templates calculate the result as a new `ratio` type. This type can be accessed with the embedded `typedef` called `type`. For example, the following code first defines two `ratios`, one representing 1/60 and the other representing 1/30. The `ratio_add` template adds those two rational numbers together to produce the `result` rational number, which, after normalization, will be 1/20:

```
typedef ratio<1, 60> r1;
typedef ratio<1, 30> r2;
typedef ratio_add<r1, r2>::type result;
```

The standard also defines a number of `ratio` comparison templates: `ratio_equal`, `ratio_not_equal`, `ratio_less`, `ratio_less_equal`, `ratio_greater`, and `ratio_greater_equal`. Just like the arithmetic `ratio` templates, the `ratio` comparison templates are all evaluated at compile time. These comparison templates create a new type, `std::integral_constant`, representing the result. An `integral_constant` is a `struct` template that stores a type and a compile time constant value. For example, `integral_constant<bool, true>` stores a Boolean with value `true`, while integral_constant<int, 15> stores an integer with value 15. The result of the ratio comparison templates is either integral_constant<bool, true> or integral_constant<bool, false>. The value associated with an integral_constant can be accessed using the value data member. The following example demonstrates the use of ratio_less. Chapter 15 discusses the use of boolalpha to output true or false for Boolean values:

```
typedef ratio<1, 60> r1;
typedef ratio<1, 30> r2;
typedef ratio_less<r2, r1> res;
cout << boolalpha << res::value << endl;
```

The following example combines everything. Note that since ratios are compile time constants, you cannot do something like cout << r1, you need to get the numerator and denominator and print them separately:

```
// Define a compile time rational number
typedef ratio<1, 60> r1;
cout << "1) " << r1::num << "/" << r1::den << endl;
// Get numerator and denominator
intmax_t num = r1::num;
intmax_t den = r1::den;
cout << "2) " << num << "/" << den << endl;
// Add two rational numbers
typedef ratio<1, 30> r2;
cout << "3) " << r2::num << "/" << r2::den << endl;
typedef ratio_add<r1, r2>::type result;
cout << "4) " << result::num << "/" << result::den << endl;
// Compare two rational numbers
typedef ratio_less<r2, r1> res;
cout << "5) " << boolalpha << res::value << endl;
```

Code snippet from Ratio\ratios.cpp

The output should be as follows:

```
1) 1/60
2) 1/60
3) 1/30
4) 1/20
5) false
```

The library provides a number of SI (*Système International*) typedefs for your convenience. They are as follows:

```
typedef ratio<1, 1000000000000000000000000> yocto; // *
typedef ratio<1,    1000000000000000000000> zepto; // *
typedef ratio<1,       1000000000000000000> atto;
typedef ratio<1,          1000000000000000> femto;
typedef ratio<1,             1000000000000> pico;
typedef ratio<1,                1000000000> nano;
typedef ratio<1,                   1000000> micro;
```

```
typedef ratio<1,                            1000> milli;
typedef ratio<1,                             100> centi;
typedef ratio<1,                              10> deci;
typedef ratio<                           10,   1> deca;
typedef ratio<                          100,   1> hecto;
typedef ratio<                         1000,   1> kilo;
typedef ratio<                      1000000,   1> mega;
typedef ratio<                   1000000000,   1> giga;
typedef ratio<                1000000000000,   1> tera;
typedef ratio<             1000000000000000,   1> peta;
typedef ratio<          1000000000000000000,   1> exa;
typedef ratio<       1000000000000000000000,   1> zetta; // *
typedef ratio<1000000000000000000000000, 1> yotta; // *
```

The SI units with an asterisk at the end are defined only if your compiler can represent the constant numerator and denominator values for those typedefs as an intmax_t. An example on how to use these predefined SI units is given during the discussion of durations later in this chapter.

THE CHRONO LIBRARY

The C++11 Chrono library is a collection of classes to work with times. The library consists of the following components:

➤ Duration

➤ Clock

➤ Time point

Everything is defined in the std::chrono namespace and requires you to include the <chrono> header file. The following sections explain each component.

Duration

A *duration*, which represents an interval between two points in time, is specified by the templatized duration class. The duration class stores a number of *ticks* and a *tick period*. The tick period is the time in seconds between two ticks and is represented as a compile time ratio constant, which means it could be a fraction of a second. Ratios are discussed earlier in this chapter. The duration template accepts two template parameters and is defined as follows:

```
template <class Rep, class Period = ratio<1>> class duration {...}
```

The first template parameter, Rep, is the type of variable storing the number of ticks and should be an arithmetic type, for example long, double, and so on. The second template parameter, Period, is the rational constant representing the period of a tick. If you don't specify the tick period, the default value ratio<1> will be used, which represents a tick period of 1 second.

Three constructors are provided: the default constructor; one that accepts a single value, the number of ticks; and one that accepts another duration. The latter can be used to convert from one duration to another duration, for example from minutes to seconds. An example is given later in this section.

Durations support arithmetic operations such as +, -, *, /, %, ++, --, +=, -=, *=, /= and %=, and support the comparison operators. The class contains the following methods:

METHOD	DESCRIPTION
Rep count() const	Returns the duration value as the number of ticks. The return type is the type specified as parameter to the duration template.
static duration zero()	Returns a duration with a duration value equivalent to 0.
static duration min() static duration max()	Returns a duration with the minimum/maximum possible duration value representable by the type specified as parameter to the duration template.

Let's see how durations can be used in actual code. A duration where each tick is one second can be defined as follows:

```
duration<long> d1;
```

Because ratio<1> is the default tick period, this is the same as writing the following:

```
duration<long, ratio<1>> d1;
```

The following specifies a duration in minutes (tick period = 60 seconds):

```
duration<long, ratio<60>> d2;
```

To define a duration where each tick period is a sixtieth of a second, use the following:

```
duration<double, ratio<1, 60>> d3;
```

As seen earlier in this chapter, the <ratio> header file defines a number of SI rational constants. These predefined constants come in handy for defining tick periods. For example, the following line of code defines a duration where each tick period is one millisecond:

```
duration<long long, milli> d4;
```

The following example demonstrates several aspects of durations. It shows you how to define durations, how to perform arithmetic operations on them, and how to convert one duration into another duration with a different tick period:

Available for download on Wrox.com

```
// Specify a duration where each tick is 60 seconds
duration<long, ratio<60>> d1(123);
cout << d1.count() << endl;
// Specify a duration represented by a double with each tick
// equal to 1 second and assign the largest possible duration to it.
```

```
duration<double> d2;
d2 = d2.max();
cout << d2.count() << endl;
// Define 2 durations:
// For the first duration, each tick is 1 minute
// For the second duration, each tick is 1 second
duration<long, ratio<60>> d3(10);   // = 10 minutes
duration<long, ratio<1>> d4(14);    // = 14 seconds
// Compare both durations
if (d3 > d4)
    cout << "d3 > d4" << endl;
else
    cout << "d3 <= d4" << endl;
// Increment d4 with 1 resulting in 15 seconds
++d4;
// Multiply d4 by 2 resulting in 30 seconds
d4 *= 2;
// Add both durations and store as minutes
duration<double, ratio<60>> d5 = d3 + d4;
// Add both durations and store as seconds
duration<long, ratio<1>> d6 = d3 + d4;
cout << d3.count() << " minutes + " << d4.count() << " seconds = "
    << d5.count() << " minutes or "
    << d6.count() << " seconds" << endl;
// Create a duration of 30 seconds
duration<long> d7(30);
// Convert the seconds of d7 to minutes
duration<double, ratio<60>> d8(d7);
cout << d7.count() << " seconds = " << d8.count() << " minutes" << endl;
```

Code snippet from Chrono\durations.cpp

The output is as follows:

```
123
1.79769e+308
d3 > d4
10 minutes + 30 seconds = 10.5 minutes or 630 seconds
30 seconds = 0.5 minutes
```

 The second line in the output represents the largest possible duration *with type* double. *The exact value might be different depending on your compiler.*

Pay special attention to the following two lines:

```
duration<double, ratio<60>> d5 = d3 + d4;
duration<long, ratio<1>> d6 = d3 + d4;
```

They both calculate d3+d4 but the first one stores it as a floating point value representing minutes while the second one stores the result as an integer representing seconds. Conversion from minutes to seconds or vice versa happens automatically.

The following two lines from the preceding example demonstrate how to convert between different units of time:

```
duration<long> d7(30);              // seconds
duration<double, ratio<60>> d8(d7);  // minutes
```

The first line defines a duration representing 30 seconds. The second line converts these 30 seconds into minutes, resulting in 0.5 minutes. Converting in this direction can result in a non-integral value and thus requires you to use a duration represented by a floating point type; otherwise, you will get some cryptic compiler errors. The following lines, for example, will not compile because d8 is using long instead of a floating point type:

```
duration<long> d7(30);              // seconds
duration<long, ratio<60>> d8(d7);   // minutes    // Error
```

Converting in the other direction does not require floating point types if the source is an integral type, because the result is always an integral value if you started with an integral value. For example, the following lines convert 10 minutes into seconds, both represented by the integral type long:

```
duration<long, ratio<60>> d9(10);   // minutes
duration<long> d10(d9);             // seconds
```

The library also provides the following standard duration types, where X stands for "signed integer type of at least":

```
typedef duration<X 64 bits, nano>      nanoseconds;
typedef duration<X 55 bits, micro>     microseconds;
typedef duration<X 45 bits, milli>     milliseconds;
typedef duration<X 35 bits>            seconds;
typedef duration<X 29 bits, ratio<60>>     minutes;
typedef duration<X 23 bits, ratio<3600>>   hours;
```

The exact type of X depends on your compiler, but the C++ standard requires it to be a signed integer type of at least the specified size. The preceding typedefs make use of the predefined SI ratio typedefs as described earlier in this chapter. The following is an example of how to use these predefined durations. The code first defines a variable t, which is the result of 1 hour + 23 minutes + 45 seconds. The auto keyword is used to let the compiler automatically figure out the exact type of t. The second line uses the constructor of the predefined seconds duration to convert the value of t to seconds and write the result to the console:

```
auto t = hours(1) + minutes(23) + seconds(45);
cout << seconds(t).count() << " seconds" << endl;
```

Code snippet from Chrono\durations.cpp

Because the standard requires that the predefined durations use integer types, there can be compiler errors if a conversion **could** end up with a non-integral value. While integer division normally truncates, in the case of durations, which are implemented by `ratio` types, the compiler declares any computation that could result in a non-zero remainder as a compile-time error. For example, the following will not compile because converting 90 seconds results in 1.5 minutes:

```
seconds s(90);
minutes m(s);
```

However, the following will not compile either, even though 60 seconds is exactly 1 minute. It is flagged as a compile-time error because converting from seconds to minutes could result in non-integral values:

```
seconds s(60);
minutes m(s);
```

Converting in the other direction works perfectly fine because the `minutes` duration is an integral value and converting it to `seconds` always results in an integral value:

```
minutes m(2);
seconds s(m);
```

Clock

A `clock` is a class consisting of a `time_point` and a `duration`. The `time_point` type is discussed in detail in the next section, but those details are not required to understand how `clocks` work. However, `time_points` themselves depend on `clocks`, so it's important to know the details of `clocks` first.

Three `clocks` are defined by the standard. The first is called `system_clock` and represents the wall clock time from the system-wide realtime clock. The second is called `steady_clock`, which is a clock that guarantees its `time_point` will never decrease. The third is the `high_resolution_clock`, which has the shortest possible tick period. Depending on your compiler, it is possible for the `high_resolution_clock` to be a synonym for `steady_clock` or `system_clock`.

Every `clock` has a static `now()` method to get the current time as a `time_point`. The `system_clock` also defines two static helper functions for converting `time_points` to and from the `time_t` C-style time representation. The first is called `to_time_t()` converting a given `time_point` to a `time_t`; the second is called `from_time_t()`, which will return a `time_point` initialized with a given `time_t` value. The `time_t` type is defined in the `<time.h>` header file.

The following example shows a complete program, which gets the current time from the system and outputs the time in a human readable format on the console. The `localtime()` function converts a `time_t` to a local time represented by `tm` and is defined in the `<time.h>` header file. The C++11 `put_time()` stream manipulator, defined in the `<iomanip>` header is discussed in Chapter 15:

```
// Get current time as a time_point
system_clock::time_point tpoint = system_clock::now();
// Convert to a time_t
time_t tt = system_clock::to_time_t(tpoint);
```

```
// Convert to local time
tm* t = localtime(&tt);
// Write the time to the console
cout << put_time(t, "%H:%M:%S") << endl;
```

Code snippet from Chrono\now_put_time.cpp

If your compiler does not yet support the put_time() manipulator, you can use the C-style strftime() function, defined in <time.h>, as follows. Using the old strftime() function, requires you to supply a buffer that is big enough to hold the human readable representation of the given time:

```
// Get current time as a time_point
system_clock::time_point tpoint = system_clock::now();
// Convert to a time_t
time_t tt = system_clock::to_time_t(tpoint);
// Convert to local time
tm* t = localtime(&tt);
// Convert to readable format
char buffer[80] = {0};
strftime(buffer, sizeof(buffer), "%H:%M:%S", t);
// Write the time to the console
cout << buffer << endl;
```

Code snippet from Chrono\now.cpp

> When you compile the preceding examples with Microsoft Visual Studio, you might get a security-related warning on the call to localtime(). You can get rid of that warning by switching to localtime_s(), but this function is not available on other platforms, such as Linux. On Linux for example, you can switch to localtime_r().

The Chrono library can also be used to time how long it takes for a piece of code to execute. The following example shows how you can do this. The actual type of the variables start and end is system_clock::time_point and the actual type of diff is a duration:

```
// Get the start time
auto start = system_clock::now();
// Execute code that you want to time
double d = 0;
for (int i = 0; i < 1000000; ++i)
    d += sqrt(sin(i) * cos(i));
// Get the end time and calculate the difference
auto end = system_clock::now();
auto diff = end - start;
// Convert the difference into milliseconds and print on the console
cout << duration<double, milli>(diff).count() << "ms" << endl;
```

Code snippet from Chrono\timing.cpp

The loop in this example is performing some arithmetic operations with `sqrt()`, `sin()`, and `cos()` to make sure the loop doesn't end too fast. If you get really small values for the difference in milliseconds on your system, those values will not be accurate and you should increase the number of iterations of the loop to make it last longer. Small timings will not be accurate, because, while timers often have a resolution in milliseconds, on most operating systems, this timer is updated infrequently, for example, every 10ms or 15ms. This induces a phenomenon called *gating error*, where any event that occurs in less than 1 timer tick appears to take place in zero units of time; any event between 1 and 2 timer ticks appears to take place in 1 timer unit. For example, on a system with a 15ms timer update, a loop that takes 44ms will appear to take only 30ms. When using such timers to time computations, it is important to make sure that the entire computation takes place across a fairly large number of basic timer tick units so that these errors are minimized.

Time Point

A point in time is represented by the `time_point` class and stored as a `duration` relative to the *epoch*. A `time_point` is always associated with a certain `clock` and the epoch is the origin of this associated `clock`. For example, the epoch for the classic Unix/Linux time is 1st of January 1970, and durations are measured in seconds. The epoch for Windows is 1st of January 1601 and durations are measured in 100 nanosecond units. Other operating systems have different epoch dates and duration units.

The `time_point` class contains a function called `time_since_epoch()`, which returns a `duration` representing the time between the epoch of the associated `clock` and the stored point in time. A `time_point` supports arithmetic operations that make sense for time points such as +, -, += and -=. Comparison operators are also supported to compare two time points. Two static methods are provided: `min()` returning the smallest possible point in time, and `max()` returning the largest possible point in time.

The `time_point` class has three constructors:

➤ `time_point()`: constructs a `time_point` initialized with `duration::zero()`. The resulting `time_point` represents the epoch of the associated `clock`.

➤ `time_point(const duration& d)`: constructs a `time_point` initialized with the given `duration`. The resulting `time_point` represents `epoch + d`.

➤ `template<class Duration2> time_point(const time_point<clock, Duration2>& t)`: constructs a `time_point` initialized with `t.time_since_epoch()`.

Each `time_point` is associated with a `clock`. To create a `time_point`, you specify the `clock` as the template parameter:

```
time_point<steady_clock> tp1;
```

Each `clock` also knows its `time_point` type, so you can also write it as follows:

```
steady_clock::time_point tp1;
```

The following example demonstrates the `time_point` class:

```
// Create a time_point representing the epoch
// of the associated steady clock
time_point<steady_clock> tp1;
// Add 10 minutes to the time_point
tp1 += minutes(10);
// Store the duration between epoch and time_point
auto d1 = tp1.time_since_epoch();
// Convert the duration to seconds and write to console
duration<double> d2(d1);
cout << d2.count() << " seconds" << endl;
```

Code snippet from Chrono\time_point.cpp

The output should be:

```
600 seconds
```

RANDOM NUMBER GENERATION

Generating good random numbers in software is a complex topic. Before C++11, the only way to generate random numbers was to use the C-style srand() and rand() functions. The srand() function needs to be called once in your application and is used to initialize the random number generator, also called *seeding*. Usually the current system time would be used as a seed.

 You need to make sure that you use a good quality seed for your software-based random number generator. If you initialize the random number generator with the same seed every time, you will create the same sequence of random numbers every time. This is why the seed is usually the current system time.

Once the generator is initialized, random numbers can be generated by using rand(). The following example shows how to use srand(), to initialize the generator with the current system time as the seed, and rand(), to generate a random number. The time(nullptr) call returns the system time, and is defined in the <time.h> header file:

```
srand(static_cast<unsigned int>(time(nullptr)));
cout << rand() << endl;
```

Code snippet from Random\old.cpp

A random number within a certain range can be generated by using the following function:

```
int getRandom(int min, int max)
{
    return (rand() % static_cast<int>(max + 1 - min)) + min;
}
```

Code snippet from Random\old.cpp

The old C-style rand() function generates random numbers in the range 0 to RAND_MAX, which is defined by the standard to be at least 32767. Unfortunately, the low-order bits of rand() are often not very random, which means, using the previous getRandom() number to generate a random number in a small range, such as 1 to 6, will not result in very good randomness.

 Software-based random number generators can never generate truly random numbers and are therefore called pseudo-random number generators because they rely on mathematical formulas to give the impression of randomness.

The old srand() and rand() functions don't offer much in terms of flexibility. You cannot, for example, change the distribution of the generated random numbers. C++11 adds a powerful library to generate random numbers by using different algorithms and distributions. The library is defined in the <random> header file. The library has three big components: *engines*, *engine adapters*, and *distributions*. A random number *engine* is responsible for generating the actual random numbers and storing the state for generating subsequent random numbers. The *distribution* determines the range of the generated random numbers and how they are mathematically distributed within that range. A random number *engine adapter* modifies the results of a random number engine you associate it with.

Random Number Engines

C++11 defines the following random number engine templates:

➤ random_device

➤ linear_congruential_engine

➤ Mersenne_twister_engine

➤ subtract_with_carry_engine

The random_device engine is not a software-based generator; it is a special engine that requires a piece of hardware attached to your computer that generates truly non-deterministic random numbers, for example by using the laws of physics. A classic mechanism measures the decay of a radioactive isotope by counting alpha-particles-per-time-interval or something like that, but there are many other kinds of physics-based random-number generators, including measuring the "noise" of reverse-biased diodes (thus eliminating the concerns about radioactive sources in your computer). The details of these mechanisms fall outside the scope of this book.

According to the specification for random_device, if no such device is attached to the computer, the library is free to use one of the software algorithms. The choice of algorithm is up to the library designer.

The quality of a random number generator is referred to as its *entropy* measure. The entropy() method of the random_device class returns 0.0 if it is using a software-based pseudo-random number generator, and returns a nonzero value if there is a hardware device attached. The nonzero value is an estimate of the entropy of the attached device.

Using the `random_device` engine is rather straightforward:

```
random_device rnd;
cout << "Entropy: " << rnd.entropy() << endl;
cout << "Min value: " << rnd.min()
     << ", Max value: " << rnd.max() << endl;
cout << "Random number: " << rnd() << endl;
```

Code snippet from Random\random_device.cpp

A possible output of this program could be as follows:

```
Entropy: 32
Min value: 0, Max value: 4294967295
Random number: 3590924439
```

Next to the `random_device` engine, there are three pseudo-random number engines:

➤ The *linear congruential engine* requires a minimal amount of memory to store its state. The state is a single integer containing the last generated random number or the initial seed if no random number has been generated yet. The period of this engine depends on an algorithmic parameter and can be up to 2^{64} but usually less. For this reason, the linear congruential engine should not be used when you need a high-quality random number sequence.

➤ From the three pseudo-random number engines, the *Mersenne twister* generates the highest quality of random numbers. The period of a Mersenne twister depends on an algorithmic parameter but is much bigger than the period of a linear congruential engine. The memory required to store the state of a Mersenne twister also depends on its parameters but is much higher than the single integer state of the linear congruential engine. For example, the predefined Mersenne twister `mt19937` has a period of 2^{19937}-1, while the state contains 624 integers or around 2.5 kilobytes.

➤ The *subtract with carry engine* requires a state of 25 integers or around 100 bytes, however, the quality of the generated random numbers is less than the numbers generated by the Mersenne twister.

The mathematical details of the engines fall outside the scope of this book, and defining the quality of random numbers requires a mathematical background. If you want to know more about this topic, you can consult a reference from the "Random Numbers" section in Appendix B.

The `random_device` engine is easy to use and doesn't require any parameters. However, creating an instance of one of the three pseudo-random number generators requires you to specify a number of mathematical parameters, which can be complicated. The selection of parameters greatly influences the quality of the generated random numbers. For example, the definition of the `mersenne_twister_engine` class looks as follows:

```
template<class UIntType, size_t w, size_t n, size_t m, size_t r,
        UIntType a, size_t u, UIntType d, size_t s,
        UIntType b, size_t t, UIntType c, size_t l, UIntType f>
    class mersenne_twister_engine {...}
```

It requires 14 parameters. The `linear_congruential_engine` and the `subtract_with_carry_engine` classes also require a number of these mathematical parameters. For this reason, the standard defines a number of predefined engines. One example is the `mt19937` Mersenne twister which is defined as follows:

```
typedef mersenne_twister_engine<uint_fast32_t, 32, 624, 397, 31,
    0x9908b0df, 11, 0xffffffff, 7, 0x9d2c5680, 15, 0xefc60000, 18,
    1812433253> mt19937;
```

These parameters are all magic, unless you understand the details of the Mersenne twister algorithm. In general, you do not want to modify any of these parameters unless you are a specialist in the mathematics of pseudo-random number generators. Instead, it is highly recommended to use one of the predefined `typedefs` such as `mt19937`. A complete list of predefined engines is given in a later section.

Random Number Engine Adapters

A random number engine adapter modifies the result of a random number engine you associate it with, which is called the *base engine*. This is an example of the *adapter pattern* as described in Chapter 29. The following three adapter templates are defined:

```
template<class Engine, size_t p, size_t r> class
    discard_block_engine {...}
template<class Engine, size_t w, class UIntType> class
    independent_bits_engine {...}
template<class Engine, size_t k> class
    shuffle_order_engine {...}
```

The `discard_block_engine` adapter generates random numbers by discarding some of the values generated by its base engine. It requires three parameters: the engine to adapt, the block size p, and the used block size r. The base engine is used to generate p random numbers. The adapter then discards $p-r$ of those numbers and returns the remaining r numbers.

The `independent_bits_engine` adapter generates random numbers with a given number of bits w by combining several random numbers generated by the base engine.

The `shuffle_order_engine` adapter generates the same random numbers that are generated by the base engine, but delivers them in a different order.

The exact working of these adapters depends on mathematics and falls outside the scope of this book.

The standard includes a number of predefined engine adapters. The following section lists the predefined engines and engine adapters.

Predefined Engines and Engine Adapters

As mentioned earlier, it is not recommended to specify your own parameters for pseudo-random number engines or engine adapters, but instead to use one of the standard ones. C++11 defines the following predefined engines and engine adapters, all in the `<random>` header file:

```
typedef linear_congruential_engine<uint_fast32_t, 16807, 0, 2147483647>
    minstd_rand0;
typedef linear_congruential_engine<uint_fast32_t, 48271, 0, 2147483647>
    minstd_rand;
typedef mersenne_twister_engine<uint_fast32_t, 32, 624, 397, 31,
    0x9908b0df, 11, 0xffffffff, 7, 0x9d2c5680, 15, 0xefc60000, 18,
    1812433253> mt19937;
typedef mersenne_twister_engine<uint_fast64_t, 64, 312, 156, 31,
    0xb5026f5aa96619e9, 29, 0x5555555555555555, 17, 0x71d67fffeda60000, 37,
    0xfff7eee000000000, 43, 6364136223846793005> mt19937_64;
typedef subtract_with_carry_engine<uint_fast32_t, 24, 10, 24>
    ranlux24_base;
typedef subtract_with_carry_engine<uint_fast64_t, 48, 5, 12> ranlux48_base;
typedef discard_block_engine<ranlux24_base, 223, 23> ranlux24;
typedef discard_block_engine<ranlux48_base, 389, 11> ranlux48;
typedef shuffle_order_engine<minstd_rand0, 256> knuth_b;
typedef implementation-defined default_random_engine;
```

The `default_random_engine` is compiler dependent.

The following section gives an example of how to use these predefined engines.

Generating Random Numbers

Before you can generate any random number, you first need to create an instance of an engine. If you use a software-based engine, you will also need to define a distribution. A distribution is a mathematical formula describing how numbers are distributed within a certain range. The easiest way to create an engine is to use one of the predefined engines as discussed earlier.

The following example uses the predefined engine called `mt19937`, using a Mersenne twister engine. This is a software-based generator. Just as with the old `srand()`/`rand()` generator, a software-based engine should be initialized with a seed. In this example, the seed is the current system time, which is passed to the constructor of the `mt19937` engine:

```
mt19937 eng(static_cast<unsigned long>(time(nullptr)));
```

Code snippet from Random\basic.cpp

Next, a distribution is defined. This example uses a uniform integer distribution, for the range 1 to 99. Distributions are explained in detail in the next section, but the uniform distribution is easy enough to use for this example:

```
uniform_int_distribution<int> dist(1, 99);
```

Code snippet from Random\basic.cpp

Once the engine and distribution are defined, random numbers can be generated by calling a function whose name is the name of the distribution and passing as a parameter the engine. For this example this is written as `dist(eng)`:

```
cout << dist(eng) << endl;
```

Code snippet from Random\basic.cpp

As you can see, to generate a random number by using a software-based engine, you always need to specify the engine and distribution. The `std::bind()` utility introduced in Chapter 13 and defined in the `<functional>` header file can be used to remove the need to specify both the distribution and the engine when generating a random number. The following example uses the same `mt19937` engine and uniform distribution as the previous example. It then defines `gen()` by using `std::bind()` to bind `eng` to the first parameter of `dist()`. This way, you can call `gen()` without any argument to generate a new random number. The `auto` keyword is used in the definition of `gen()` to avoid having to write the exact type ourselves. The example then demonstrates the use of `gen()` in combination with the `generate()` algorithm to fill a `vector` of 10 elements with random numbers. The `generate()` algorithm is discussed in Chapter 13 and is defined in `<algorithm>`:

```
mt19937 eng(static_cast<unsigned long>(time(nullptr)));
uniform_int_distribution<int> dist(1, 99);
auto gen = std::bind(dist, eng);
vector<int> vec(10);
generate(vec.begin(), vec.end(), gen);
for (auto i : vec)
    cout << i << "  ";
```

Code snippet from Random\generate.cpp

> *Remember that the `generate()` algorithm overwrites existing elements and will not insert new elements. This means that you first need to size the `vector` to hold the number of elements you need, and then call the `generate()` algorithm. The previous example sizes the `vector` by specifying the size as argument to the constructor.*

Even though you don't know the exact type of `gen()`, because of the use of the `auto` keyword, it's still possible to pass `gen()` to another function that wants to use that generator. However, you cannot use a normal function; you need to use a template function. The previous example can be adapted to do the generation of random numbers in a function called `fillVector()`, which is a template function that looks as follows:

```
template<class T>
void fillVector(vector<int>& vec, T rndGen)
{
    generate(vec.begin(), vec.end(), rndGen);
}
```

Code snippet from Random\generate_function.cpp

The previous example can then be adapted as follows:

```
mt19937 eng(static_cast<unsigned long>(time(nullptr)));
uniform_int_distribution<int> dist(1, 99);
auto gen = std::bind(dist, eng);
vector<int> vec(10);
fillVector(vec, gen);
for (auto i : vec)
    cout << i << "   ";
```

Code snippet from Random\generate_function.cpp

Random Number Distributions

A distribution is a mathematical formula describing how numbers are distributed within a certain range. The C++11 random number generator library comes with the following distributions that can be used with pseudo-random number engines to define the distribution of the generated random numbers. It's a compacted representation. The first line of each distribution is the class name and class template parameters, if any. The next lines are a constructor for the distribution. Only one constructor for each distribution is shown to give you an idea of the class. Consult the Standard Library Reference resource on the website (www.wrox.com) for a detailed list of all constructors and methods of each distribution.

Uniform distributions:

```
template<class IntType = int> class uniform_int_distribution
    uniform_int_distribution(IntType a = 0,
                             IntType b = numeric_limits<IntType>::max());
template<class RealType = double> class uniform_real_distribution
    uniform_real_distribution(RealType a = 0.0, RealType b = 1.0);
```

Bernoulli distributions:

```
class bernoulli_distribution
    bernoulli_distribution(double p = 0.5);
template<class IntType = int> class binomial_distribution
    binomial_distribution(IntType t = 1, double p = 0.5);
template<class IntType = int> class geometric_distribution
    geometric_distribution(double p = 0.5);
template<class IntType = int> class negative_binomial_distribution
    negative_binomial_distribution(IntType k = 1, double p = 0.5);
```

Poisson distributions:

```
template<class IntType = int> class poisson_distribution
    poisson_distribution(double mean = 1.0);
template<class RealType = double> class exponential_distribution
    exponential_distribution(RealType lambda = 1.0);
template<class RealType = double> class gamma_distribution
    gamma_distribution(RealType alpha = 1.0, RealType beta = 1.0);
```

```
template<class RealType = double> class weibull_distribution
    weibull_distribution(RealType a = 1.0, RealType b = 1.0);
template<class RealType = double> class extreme_value_distribution
    extreme_value_distribution(RealType a = 0.0, RealType b = 1.0);
```

Normal distributions:

```
template<class RealType = double> class normal_distribution
    normal_distribution(RealType mean = 0.0, RealType stddev = 1.0);
template<class RealType = double> class lognormal_distribution
    lognormal_distribution(RealType m = 0.0, RealType s = 1.0);
template<class RealType = double> class chi_squared_distribution
    chi_squared_distribution(RealType n = 1);
template<class RealType = double> class cauchy_distribution
    cauchy_distribution(RealType a = 0.0, RealType b = 1.0);
template<class RealType = double> class fisher_f_distribution
    fisher_f_distribution(RealType m = 1, RealType n = 1);
template<class RealType = double> class student_t_distribution
    student_t_distribution(RealType n = 1);
```

Sampling distributions:

```
template<class IntType = int> class discrete_distribution
    discrete_distribution(initializer_list<double> wl);
template<class RealType = double> class piecewise_constant_distribution
    template<class UnaryOperation>
        piecewise_constant_distribution(initializer_list<RealType> bl,
            UnaryOperation fw);
template<class RealType = double> class piecewise_linear_distribution
    template<class UnaryOperation>
        piecewise_linear_distribution(initializer_list<RealType> bl,
            UnaryOperation fw);
```

Each distribution requires a set of parameters. Explaining all these mathematical parameters in detail is outside the scope of this book, but the rest of this section gives a couple of examples to explain the impact of a distribution on the generated random numbers.

Distributions are easiest to understand when you look at a graphical representation of them. For example, the following code generates one million random numbers between 1 and 99 and counts how many times a certain number between 1 and 99 is randomly chosen. This is stored in a map where the key is a number between 1 and 99, and the value associated with a key is the number of times that that key has been selected randomly. After the loop, the results are written to a CSV (Comma Separated Values) file, which can be opened in a spreadsheet application to generate a graphical representation:

```
const unsigned int DIST_START = 1;
const unsigned int DIST_END = 99;
const unsigned int ITERATIONS = 1000000;
// Uniform Mersenne Twister
mt19937 eng(static_cast<unsigned long>(time(nullptr)));
uniform_int_distribution<int> dist(DIST_START, DIST_END);
auto gen = bind(dist, eng);
```

```
map<int, int> m;
for (unsigned int i = 0; i < ITERATIONS; ++i) {
    int rnd = gen();
    // Search map for a key = rnd. If found, add 1 to the value associated
    // with that key. If not found, add the key to the map with value 1.
    ++(m[rnd]);
}
// Write to a CSV file
ofstream of("res.csv");
for (unsigned int i = DIST_START; i <= DIST_END; ++i) {
    of << i << ",";
    auto res = m.find(i);
    of << (res != m.end() ? res->second : 0) << endl;
}
```

Code snippet from Random\uniform_int_distribution.cpp

The resulting data can then be used to generate a graphical representation. The graph of the preceding uniform Mersenne twister is shown in Figure 16-1.

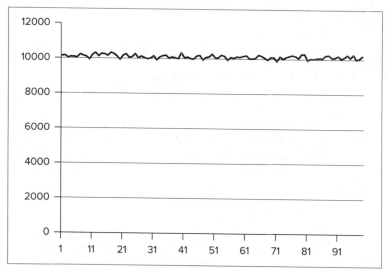

FIGURE 16-1

The horizontal axis represents the range in which random numbers are generated. The graph clearly shows that all numbers between 1 and 99 are randomly chosen around 10,000 times and that the distribution of the generated random numbers is uniform across the entire range.

The example can be modified to generate random numbers according to a normal distribution instead of a uniform distribution. Only two small changes are required. First, the creation of the distribution is modified as follows:

```
normal_distribution<double> dist(50, 10);
```

Because normal distributions use `doubles` instead of integers, you also need to modify the call to `gen()`:

```
int rnd = static_cast<int>(gen());
```

Figure 16-2 shows a graphical representation of the random numbers generated according to the normal distribution.

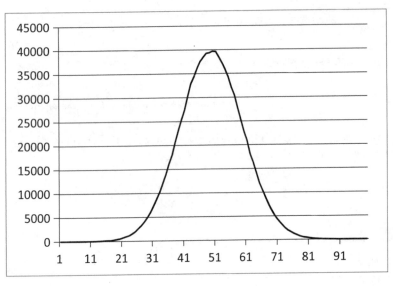

FIGURE 16-2

The graph clearly shows that most of the generated random numbers will be around the center of the range. In this example, the value 50 will be randomly chosen around 40,000 times, while values like 20 or 80 will be chosen randomly only around 500 times.

TUPLES

The `std::pair` class, introduced in Chapter 12, can store two values, each with a specific type. The type of each value should be known at compile time. The following is a short example:

```
pair<int, string> p1(16, "Hello World");
pair<bool, float> p2(true, 0.123f);
cout << "p1 = (" << p1.first << ", " << p1.second << ")" << endl;
cout << "p2 = (" << p2.first << ", " << p2.second << ")" << endl;
```

Code snippet from Tuple\pair.cpp

The output is as follows:

```
p1 = (16, Hello World)
p2 = (1, 0.123)
```

C++11 introduces the `std::tuple` class, defined in the `<tuple>` header file. A `tuple` is a generalization of a `pair`, and allows you to store any number of values, each with its own specific type. Just like a `pair`, a `tuple` has a fixed size and fixed value types, determined at compile time.

A `tuple` can be created with a `tuple` constructor, specifying the template types and specifying the actual values. For example, the following code creates a `tuple` where the first element is an integer, the second element a `string`, and the last element a Boolean:

```cpp
typedef tuple<int, string, bool> MyTuple;
MyTuple t1(16, "Test", true);
```

Code snippet from Tuple\tuple.cpp

`std::get<i>()` is used to get the *i*-th element from a `tuple`, where *i* is a 0-based index; that is `<0>` is the first element of the tuple, `<1>` is the second element of the tuple and so on. The value returned will have the correct type for that index in the `tuple`:

```cpp
cout << "t1 = (" << get<0>(t1) << ", " << get<1>(t1)
     << ", " << get<2>(t1) << ")" << endl;
// Outputs: t1 = (16, Test, 1)
```

Code snippet from Tuple\tuple.cpp

You can check that `get<i>()` returns the correct type by using `typeid()`, from the `<typeinfo>` header. The output of the following code should say that the value returned by `get<1>(t1)` is indeed a `std::string`:

```cpp
cout << "Type of get<1>(t1) = " << typeid(get<1>(t1)).name() << endl;
// Outputs: Type of get<1>(t1) = class std::basic_string<char,
//          struct std::char_traits<char>,class std::allocator<char> >
```

Code snippet from Tuple\tuple.cpp

 The exact string returned by `typeid()` is compiler dependent. The preceding output is from Visual C++ 2010.

The size of a tuple can be queried with the `std::tuple_size` template. Note that `tuple_size` requires you to specify the type of the `tuple` (`MyTuple` in this case) and not an actual `tuple` instance like `t1`:

```cpp
cout << "Tuple Size = " << tuple_size<MyTuple>::value << endl;
// Outputs: Tuple Size = 3
```

Code snippet from Tuple\tuple.cpp

Another way to create a `tuple` is to use the `std::make_tuple()` utility function. This function only needs the actual values and will deduce the types automatically at compile time. Because of the automatic deduction of types, you cannot use `&` to specify a reference. If you want to use `make_tuple()` to generate a `tuple` containing a reference or a constant reference, then you need to use `ref()` or `cref()`, respectively, as is demonstrated in the following example. The `ref()` and `cref()` helpers are defined in the `<functional>` header file. For example, the following `make_tuple()` call will result in a `tuple` of type `tuple<int, double&, string&, const string&>`:

```
double d = 3.14;
string str1 = "Test";
auto t2 = make_tuple(16, ref(d), ref(str1), cref(str1));
```

Code snippet from Tuple\tuple.cpp

To test the `double` reference in the `t2` tuple, the following three lines of code first write the value of the `double` variable to the console. It then uses `get<1>(t2)`, which will actually return a reference because `ref()` was used for the second `tuple` element. The second line changes the value of the variable referenced and the last line shows that the value of `d` is indeed changed through the reference stored in the `tuple`:

```
cout << "d = " << d << endl;
get<1>(t2) *= 2;
cout << "d = " << d << endl;
// Outputs: d = 3.14
//          d = 6.28
```

Code snippet from Tuple\tuple.cpp

The following block of code demonstrates something similar, but uses `strings`. It tries to change the value of the variable referenced by the third element of the `tuple`, which works perfectly because of the use of `ref()`, which results in a `string&`. However, trying to change the variable referenced by the fourth element will fail because that is a `const string&`:

```
cout << "str = " << str1 << endl;
get<2>(t2) = "Hello";
//get<3>(t2) = "Hello";    // ERROR: would be an error because of cref
cout << "str = " << str1 << endl;
// Outputs: str = Test
//          str = Hello
```

Code snippet from Tuple\tuple.cpp

Tuples can also contain other containers. The following line creates a `tuple` where the first element is a `string` and the second element is a `vector` of integers:

```
tuple<string, vector<int>> t1("test", {1,2,3,4});
```

The standard defines a `std::tie()` utility function, which generates a `tuple` of references. The following example first creates a `tuple` consisting of an integer, a `string`, and a Boolean value.

It then creates three variables: an integer, a string, and a Boolean and writes the values of those variables to the console. The `tie(i, str, b)` call will create a tuple containing a reference to i, a reference to str, and a reference to b. The assignment operator is used to assign tuple t1 to the result of `tie()`. Since the result of `tie()` is a tuple of references, the assignment actually changes the values in the three separate variables as is shown by the output of the values after the assignment:

Available for
download on
Wrox.com

```
tuple<int, string, bool> t1(16, "Test", true);
int i = 0;
string str;
bool b = false;
cout << "Before: i = " << i << ", str = \"" << str << "\", b = " << b << endl;
tie(i, str, b) = t1;
cout << "After:  i = " << i << ", str = \"" << str << "\", b = " << b << endl;
```

Code snippet from Tuple\tuple_tie.cpp

The result is as follows:

```
Before: i = 0, str = "", b = 0
After:  i = 16, str = "Test", b = 1
```

You can use `std::tuple_cat()` to concatenate two tuples into one tuple. In the following example, the type of t3 will be `tuple<int, string, bool, double, string>`:

Available for
download on
Wrox.com

```
tuple<int, string, bool> t1(16, "Test", true);
tuple<double, string> t2(3.14, "string 2");
auto t3 = tuple_cat(t1, t2);
```

Code snippet from Tuple\tuple_cat.cpp

Tuples also support the following comparison operators: ==, <, !=, >, <= and >=. For the comparison operators to work, the element types stored in the tuple should support them as well. For example:

Available for
download on
Wrox.com

```
tuple<int, string> t1(123, "def");
tuple<int, string> t2(123, "abc");
if (t1 < t2)
    cout << "t1 < t2" << endl;
else
    cout << "t1 >= t2" << endl;
```

Code snippet from Tuple\tuple_comparison.cpp

The output should be as follows:

```
t1 >= t2
```

Iterating over the values of a tuple is unfortunately not straightforward. You cannot write a simple loop and call something like `get<i>(mytuple)` because the value of i must be known at compile time. A solution is to use template metaprogramming, which is discussed in detail in Chapter 20, together with an example on how to print `tuple` values.

SUMMARY

This chapter gave an overview of additional functionality provided by the C++ standard that did not fit in other chapters. You learned how to use `std::function` to create function pointers. This chapter also gave an overview of the new `ratio` template to define compile time rational numbers, the Chrono library, and the random number generation library. The chapter finished with a discussion on `tuples`, which are a generalization of `pairs`.

Chapter 17 finishes the discussion of the C++ standard library and standard template library by showing you how to customize and extend the functionality provided by the STL.

17

Customizing and Extending the STL

WHAT'S IN THIS CHAPTER?

➤ What allocators are

➤ What iterator adapters are

➤ How to extend the STL

    ➤ How to write your own algorithms

    ➤ How to write your own containers

    ➤ How to write your own iterators

The previous chapters show that the STL is a powerful general-purpose collection of containers and algorithms. The information covered so far should be sufficient for most applications. However, those chapters show only the basic functionality of the library. The STL can be customized and extended however you like. For example, you can apply iterators to input and output streams; write your own containers, algorithms, and iterators; and even specify your own memory allocation schemes for containers to use. This chapter provides a taste of these advanced features, primarily through the development of a new STL container: the hashmap.

This chapter is not for the faint of heart! The contents delve into some of the most complicated and syntactically confusing areas of the C++ language. If you're happy with the basic STL containers and algorithms from the previous chapters, you can skip this one. However, if you really want to understand the STL, not just use it, give this chapter a chance. You should be comfortable with the operator overloading material of Chapter 18, and because this chapter uses templates extensively, you should also be comfortable with the template material in Chapter 19 before continuing!

ALLOCATORS

Every STL container takes an `Allocator` type as a template parameter, for which the default will usually suffice. For example, the `vector` template definition looks like this:

```
template <class T, class Allocator = allocator<T> > class vector;
```

The container constructors then allow you to specify an object of type `Allocator`. These extra parameters permit you to customize the way the containers allocate memory. Every memory allocation performed by a container is made with a call to the `allocate()` method of the `Allocator` object. Conversely, every deallocation is performed with a call to the `deallocate()` method of the `Allocator` object. The standard library provides a default `Allocator` class called `allocator`, which implements these methods as wrappers for `operator new` and `operator delete`.

If you want containers in your program to use a custom memory allocation and deallocation scheme, you can write your own `Allocator` class. There are several reasons for using custom allocators. For example, if the underlying allocator has unacceptable performance, there are alternatives that can be constructed. Or, if memory fragmentation is a problem (lots of different allocations and deallocations leaving unusable small holes in memory), a single "pool" of objects of one type can be created, called a memory pool. When OS specific capabilities, such as shared memory segments, must be allocated, using custom allocators allows the use of STL containers in those shared memory segments. The use of custom allocators is complex, and there are many possible problems if you are not careful, so this should not be approached lightly.

Any class that provides `allocate()`, `deallocate()`, and several other required methods and `typedefs` can be used in place of the default `allocator` class. However, in our experience, this feature is rarely used, so we have omitted the details from this book. For more details, consult one of the books on the C++ Standard Library listed in Appendix B.

ITERATOR ADAPTERS

The Standard Library provides four *iterator adapters*: special iterators that are built on top of other iterators. You'll learn more about the adapter design pattern in Chapter 29. For now, just appreciate what these iterators can do for you. All four iterator adapters are declared in the `<iterator>` header.

You can also write your own iterator adapters. Consult one of the books on the Standard Library listed in Appendix B for details.

Reverse Iterators

The STL provides a `reverse_iterator` class that iterates through a bidirectional or random access iterator in a reverse direction. Every reversible container in the STL, which happens to be every container that's part of the standard, supplies a `typedef reverse_iterator` and methods called rbegin() and rend(). The method rbegin() returns a reverse_iterator starting at the last element of the container, and rend() returns a reverse_iterator starting at the first element of the container. Applying operator++ to a reverse_iterator calls operator-- on the underlying container iterator, and vice versa. For example, iterating over a collection from the beginning to the end can be done as follows:

```
for (auto iter = collection.begin(); iter != collection.end(); ++iter) {}
```

Iterating over the elements in the collection from the end to the beginning can be done using a reverse_iterator by calling rbegin() and rend(). Note that you still call ++iter:

```
for (auto iter = collection.rbegin(); iter != collection.rend(); ++iter) {}
```

The reverse_iterator is useful mostly with algorithms in the STL that have no equivalents that work in reverse order. For example, the basic find() algorithm searches for the first element in a sequence. If you want to find the last element in the sequence, you can use a reverse_iterator instead. Note that when you call an algorithm such as find() with a reverse_iterator, it returns a reverse_iterator as well. You can always obtain the underlying iterator from a reverse_iterator by calling the base() method on the reverse_iterator. However, due to the implementation details of reverse_iterator, the iterator returned from base() always refers to one element past the element referred to by the reverse_iterator on which it's called.

Here is an example of find() with a reverse_iterator:

```
// The implementation of populateContainer() is identical to that shown in
// Chapter 13, so it is omitted here.
vector<int> myVector;
populateContainer(myVector);
int num;
cout << "Enter a number to find: ";
cin >> num;
vector<int>::iterator it1;
vector<int>::reverse_iterator it2;
it1 = find(myVector.begin(), myVector.end(), num);
it2 = find(myVector.rbegin(), myVector.rend(), num);
if (it1 != myVector.end()) {
    cout << "Found " << num << " at position " << it1 - myVector.begin()
         << " going forward." << endl;
    cout << "Found " << num << " at position "
         << it2.base() - 1 - myVector.begin() << " going backward." << endl;
} else {
    cout << "Failed to find " << num << endl;
}
```

Code snippet from IteratorAdapters\ReverseIterators.cpp

One line in this program needs further explanation. The code to print out the position found by the reverse iterator looks like this:

```
cout << "Found " << num << " at position "
     << it2.base() - 1 - myVector.begin() << " going backward." << endl;
```

As noted earlier, `base()` returns an `iterator` referring to one past the element referred to by the `reverse_iterator`. In order to get to the same element, you must subtract one.

A possible output of this program is as follows:

```
Enter a number (0 to quit): 11
Enter a number (0 to quit): 22
Enter a number (0 to quit): 33
Enter a number (0 to quit): 22
Enter a number (0 to quit): 11
Enter a number (0 to quit): 0
Enter a number to find: 22
Found 22 at position 1 going forward.
Found 22 at position 3 going backward.
```

The previous example defined the iterators as follows:

```
vector<int>::iterator it1;
vector<int>::reverse_iterator it2;
it1 = find(myVector.begin(), myVector.end(), num);
it2 = find(myVector.rbegin(), myVector.rend(), num);
```

This is done to show you the exact types of `it1` and `it2`. Of course, using the `auto` keyword, these four lines can be compacted to the following two lines:

```
auto it1 = find(myVector.begin(), myVector.end(), num);
auto it2 = find(myVector.rbegin(), myVector.rend(), num);
```

Stream Iterators

The STL provides adapters that allow you to treat input and output streams as input and output iterators. Using these iterators you can adapt input and output streams so that they can serve as sources and destinations, respectively, in the various STL algorithms. The `ostream_iterator` class is an *output stream iterator*. It is a template class that takes the element type as a type parameter. Its constructor takes an output stream and a `string` to write to the stream following each element. The `ostream_iterator` class writes elements using `operator<<`.

For example, you can use the `ostream_iterator` with the `copy()` algorithm to print the elements of a container with only one line of code. The first parameter of `copy()` is the start iterator of the range to copy, the second parameter is the end iterator of the range, and the third parameter is the destination iterator:

```
vector<int> myVector;
for (int i = 0; i < 10; i++) {
    myVector.push_back(i);
}
// Print the contents of the vector.
copy(myVector.begin(), myVector.end(), ostream_iterator<int>(cout, " "));
```

Code snippet from IteratorAdapters\StreamIterators.cpp

Similarly, you can use the *input stream iterator*, `istream_iterator`, to read values from an input stream using the iterator abstraction. Elements are read using `operator>>`. An `istream_iterator` can be used as sources in the algorithms and container methods. Its usage is less common than that of the `ostream_iterator`, so we don't show an example here.

Insert Iterators

As Chapter 13 mentions, algorithms like `copy()` don't insert elements into a container; they simply replace old elements in a range with new ones. In order to make algorithms like `copy()` more useful, the STL provides three *insert iterator adapters* that actually insert elements into a container. They are templatized on a container type, and take the actual container reference in their constructor. By supplying the necessary iterator interfaces, these adapters can be used as the destination iterators of algorithms like `copy()`. However, instead of replacing elements in the container, they make calls on their container to actually insert new elements.

The basic `insert_iterator` calls `insert(position, element)` on the container, the `back_insert_iterator` calls `push_back(element)`, and the `front_insert_iterator` calls `push_front(element)`.

For example, you can use the `back_insert_iterator` with the `remove_copy_if()` algorithm to populate `vectorTwo` with all elements from `vectorOne` that are not equal to 100:

```cpp
// The implementation of populateContainer() is identical to that shown in
// Chapter 13, so it is omitted here.
vector<int> vectorOne, vectorTwo;
populateContainer(vectorOne);
back_insert_iterator<vector<int>> inserter(vectorTwo);
remove_copy_if(vectorOne.begin(), vectorOne.end(), inserter,
    [](int i){return i==100;});
copy(vectorTwo.begin(), vectorTwo.end(), ostream_iterator<int>(cout, " "));
```

Code snippet from IteratorAdapters\BackInsertIterator.cpp

As you can see, when you use insert iterators, you don't need to size the destination containers ahead of time.

You can also use the `back_inserter()` utility function to create a `back_insert_iterator`. For example, in the previous example, you can remove the line which defines the `inserter` variable and rewrite the `remove_copy_if()` call as follows. The result is exactly the same as the previous implementation:

```cpp
remove_copy_if(vectorOne.begin(), vectorOne.end(),
    back_inserter(vectorTwo), [](int i){return i==100;});
```

The `insert_iterator` and `front_insert_iterator` work similarly, except that the `insert_iterator` also takes an initial iterator position in its constructor, which it passes to the first call to `insert(position, element)`. Subsequent iterator position hints are generated based on the return value from each `insert()` call.

One huge benefit of `insert_iterator` is that it allows you to use associative containers as destinations of the modifying algorithms. Chapter 13 explains that the problem with associative containers is that you are not allowed to modify the elements over which you iterate. By using an `insert_iterator`, you can instead insert elements, allowing the container to sort them properly internally. Associative containers actually support a form of `insert()` that takes an iterator position, and are supposed to use the position as a "hint," which they can ignore. When you use an `insert_iterator` on an associative container, you can pass the `begin()` or `end()` iterator of the container to use as the hint. Here is the previous example modified so that the destination container is a `set` instead of a `vector`:

Available for
download on
Wrox.com

```
// The implementation of populateContainer() is identical to that shown in
// Chapter 13, so it is omitted here.
vector<int> vectorOne;
set<int> setOne;
populateContainer(vectorOne);
insert_iterator<set<int>> inserter(setOne, setOne.begin());
remove_copy_if(vectorOne.begin(), vectorOne.end(), inserter,
    [](int i){return i==100;});
copy(setOne.begin(), setOne.end(), ostream_iterator<int>(cout, " "));
```

Code snippet from IteratorAdapters\InsertIterator.cpp

Note that the `insert_iterator` modifies the iterator position hint that it passes to `insert()` after each call to `insert()`, such that the position is one past the just-inserted element.

C++11 Move Iterators

Chapter 9 discusses a new C++11 feature called *move semantics*, which can be used to prevent unnecessary copying in cases where you know that the source object will be destroyed after an assignment or copy construction. C++11 also introduces a `move_iterator`. The dereferencing operator for a `move_iterator` will automatically convert the value to an *rvalue reference*, which means that the value can be moved to a new destination without the overhead of copying. Before you can use move semantics, you need to make sure your objects are supporting it. The following `MoveableClass` supports move semantics. For more details, see Chapter 9.

Available for
download on
Wrox.com

```
class MoveableClass
{
    public:
        MoveableClass() {
            cout << "Default constructor" << endl;
        }
        MoveableClass(const MoveableClass& src) {
            cout << "Copy constructor" << endl;
        }
        MoveableClass(MoveableClass&& src) {
            cout << "Move constructor" << endl;
        }
        MoveableClass& operator=(const MoveableClass& rhs) {
            cout << "Copy assignment operator" << endl;
            return *this;
        }
```

```
MoveableClass& operator=(MoveableClass&& rhs) {
    cout << "Move assignment operator" << endl;
    return *this;
}
};
```

The constructors and assignment operators are not doing anything useful here, except printing a message to make it easy to see which one is being called. Now that you have this class, you can define a `vector` and store a few `MoveableClass` instances in it as follows:

```
vector<MoveableClass> vecSource;
MoveableClass mc;
vecSource.push_back(mc);
vecSource.push_back(mc);
```

The second line of the code creates a `MoveableClass` instance by using the default constructor. The first `push_back()` call triggers the copy constructor to copy `mc` into the `vector`. After this operation, the vector will have space for one element, the first copy of `mc`.

The second `push_back()` call triggers the `vector` to resize itself, to allocate space for the second element. This resizing causes the move constructor to be called to move every element from the old `vector` to the new resized `vector`. After that, the copy constructor is triggered to copy `mc` a second time into the `vector`. The output should be as follows:

```
Default constructor
Copy constructor
Move constructor
Copy constructor
```

You can create a new `vector` called `vecOne` that contains a copy of the elements from `vecSource` as follows:

```
vector<MoveableClass> vecOne(vecSource.begin(), vecSource.end());
```

Without using `move_iterators`, this code triggers the copy constructor two times, once for every element in `vecSource`:

```
Copy constructor
Copy constructor
```

By using the `make_move_iterator()` function to create `move_iterators`, the move constructor of `MoveableClass` is called instead of the copy constructor:

```
vector<MoveableClass> vecTwo(make_move_iterator(vecSource.begin()),
                            make_move_iterator(vecSource.end()));
```

This generates the following output:

```
Move constructor
Move constructor
```

 Once objects have been moved, you should not access the original objects anymore. For example, in the previous example, you should not access objects in vecSource *after having moved them to* vecTwo. *See Chapter 9 for details on move semantics.*

EXTENDING THE STL

The STL includes many useful containers, algorithms, and iterators that you can use in your applications. It is impossible, however, for any library to include all possible utilities that all potential clients might need. Thus, the best libraries are extensible: They allow clients to adapt and add to the basic capabilities to obtain exactly the functionality they require. The STL is inherently extensible because of its fundamental structure of separating data from the algorithms that operate on them. You can write your own container that can work with the STL algorithms by providing an iterator that conforms to the STL standard. Similarly, you can write a function that works with iterators from the standard containers. This section explains the rules for extending the STL and provides sample implementations of extensions.

Why Extend the STL?

If you sit down to write an algorithm or container in C++, you can either make it adhere to the STL conventions or not. For simple containers and algorithms, it might not be worth the extra effort to follow the STL guidelines. However, for substantial code that you plan to reuse, the effort pays off. First, the code will be easier for other C++ programmers to understand, because you follow well-established interface guidelines. Second, you will be able to use your container or algorithm on the other parts of the STL (algorithms or containers), without needing to provide special hacks or adapters. Finally, it will force you to employ the necessary rigor required to develop solid code.

Writing an STL Algorithm

Chapter 13 describes a useful set of algorithms which are part of the STL, but you will inevitably encounter situations in your programs for which you need new algorithms. When that happens, it is usually not difficult to write your own algorithm that works with STL iterators just like the standard algorithms.

find_all()

Suppose that you want to find all the elements matching a predicate in a given range. The find() and find_if() algorithms are the most likely candidate algorithms, but each returns an iterator referring to only one element. In fact, there is no standard algorithm to find all the elements matching a predicate, but you can write your own version of this functionality called `find_all()`.

The first task is to define the function prototype. You can follow the model established by `find_if()`. It will be a templatized function on two type parameters: the iterator and the predicate. Its arguments will be start and end iterators and the predicate object. Only its return value differs from `find_if()`: Instead of returning a single iterator referring to the matching element, `find_all()` returns a `vector` of iterators referring to all the matching elements. Here is the prototype:

```
template <typename InputIterator, typename Predicate>
vector<InputIterator>
find_all(InputIterator first, InputIterator last, Predicate pred);
```

Code snippet from WritingAlgorithms\FindAll.cpp

Another option would be to return an iterator that iterates over all the matching elements in the container, but that would require you to write your own iterator class.

The next task is to write the implementation. The `find_all()` algorithm can be layered on top of `find_if()` by calling `find_if()` repeatedly. The first call to `find_if()` uses the whole supplied range from `first` to `last`. The second call uses a smaller range, from the element found with the previous call to `last`. The loop continues until `find_if()` fails to find a match. Here is the implementation:

```
template <typename InputIterator, typename Predicate>
vector<InputIterator>
find_all(InputIterator first, InputIterator last, Predicate pred)
{
    vector<InputIterator> res;
    while (true) {
        // Find the next match in the current range.
        first = find_if(first, last, pred);
        // check if find_if failed to find a match
        if (first == last) {
            break;
        }
        // Store this match.
        res.push_back(first);
        // Shorten the range to start at one past the current match
        ++first;
    }
    return res;
}
```

Code snippet from WritingAlgorithms\FindAll.cpp

This `find_all()` implementation creates a local `vector` to store the result. At the end of the function, this local `vector` is returned. In C++ prior to C++11 this would require the local `vector` to be copied. However, since the local `vector` will go out of scope at the end of the function, C++11 will use move semantics to avoid copying. This makes returning the `vector` by value in C++11 very efficient.

Here is some code that tests `find_all()`. The type of the `all` variable will be `vector<vector<int>::iterator>`. After finding iterators to all the elements, the test code counts the number of elements found, which is the number of iterators in `all`. Then, it iterates through the returned iterators, printing each element:

```cpp
vector<int> vec = {3, 4, 5, 4, 5, 6, 5, 8};
auto all = find_all(vec.begin(), vec.end(), [](int i){return i==5;});
cout << "Found " << all.size() << " matching elements: ";
for (auto it : all) {
    cout << *it << " ";
}
```

Code snippet from WritingAlgorithms\FindAll.cpp

The output is as follows:

```
Found 3 matching elements: 5 5 5
```

Iterator Traits

Some algorithm implementations need additional information about their iterators. For example, they might need to know the type of the elements referred to by the iterator in order to store temporary values, or perhaps they want to know whether the iterator is bidirectional or random access.

C++ provides a class template called `iterator_traits` that allows you to find this info. You instantiate the `iterator_traits` class template with the iterator type of interest, and access one of five `typedefs`: `value_type`, `difference_type`, `iterator_category`, `pointer`, and `reference`. For example, the following template function declares a temporary variable of the type to which an iterator of type `IteratorType` refers. Note the use of the `typename` keyword in front of the `iterator_traits` line. Chapter 12 explains that you must specify `typename` explicitly whenever you access a type based on one or more template parameters. In this case, the template parameter `IteratorType` is used to access the `value_type` type:

```cpp
#include <iterator>
template <typename IteratorType>
void iteratorTraitsTest(IteratorType it)
{
    typename std::iterator_traits<IteratorType>::value_type temp;
    temp = *it;
    cout << temp << endl;
}
```

Code snippet from WritingAlgorithms\IteratorTraitsTest.cpp

This function can be tested with the following test code:

```
vector<int> v;
v.push_back(5);
iteratorTraitsTest(v.begin());
```

With this test code, the variable `temp` in the `iteratorTraitsTest()` function will be of type `int`. The output is as follows:

```
5
```

The C++11 `auto` keyword can be used to simplify the previous example. The variable `temp` will still be of type `int`:

Available for download on Wrox.com

```
#include <iterator>
template <typename IteratorType>
void iteratorTraitsTest(IteratorType it)
{
    auto temp = *it;
    cout << temp << endl;
}
```

Code snippet from WritingAlgorithms\IteratorTraitsTest.cpp

Writing an STL Container

The C++ standard contains a list of requirements that any container must fulfill in order to qualify as an STL container.

Additionally, if you want your container to be sequential (like a `vector`), associative (like a `map`), or unordered associative (like an `unordered_map`) it must conform to supplementary requirements.

Our suggestion when writing a new container is to write the basic container first following the general STL rules such as making it a class template, but without worrying too much about the specific details of STL conformity. After you've developed the implementation, you can add the iterator and methods so that it can work with the STL framework. This section takes that approach to develop a *hashmap*.

A Basic Hashmap

C++11 supports *unordered associative containers*, also called *hash tables*. These are discussed in Chapter 12. However, previous versions of C++ did not include hash tables. Unlike the STL `map` and `set`, which provide logarithmic insertion, lookup, and deletion times, a hash table provides constant time insertion, deletion, and lookup in the average case, linear in the worst case. Instead of storing elements in sorted order, it *hashes*, or maps, each element to a particular *bucket*. As long as the number of elements stored isn't significantly greater than the number of buckets, and the *hash function* distributes the elements uniformly between the buckets, the insertion, deletion, and lookup operations all run in constant time.

This section assumes that you are familiar with hashed data structures. If you are not, consult Chapter 12, which includes a discussion on hash tables, or one of the standard data structure texts listed in Appendix B.

This section provides an implementation of a simple, but fully functional, `hashmap` that you can take with you between platforms, in case your compiler does not yet support the standard C++11 hash tables. Like a `map`, a `hashmap` stores key/value pairs. In fact, the operations it provides are almost identical to those provided by the `map`, but with different performance characteristics.

This `hashmap` implementation uses chained hashing (also called open hashing) and does not attempt to provide advanced features like rehashing. Chapter 12 explains the concept of chained hashing in the section on C++11 unordered associative containers.

It is recommended to use the C++11 unordered associative containers, also called hash tables, if your compiler supports them, instead of implementing your own. These C++11 hash tables, explained in Chapter 12, are called `unordered_map`, `unordered_multimap`, `unordered_set` *and* `unordered_multiset`. *The* `hashmap` *in this chapter is used to demonstrate writing STL containers and as a solution in case your compiler does not support the C++11 hash tables.*

The Hash Function

The first choice when writing a `hashmap` is how to handle hash functions. Recalling the adage that a good abstraction makes the easy case easy and the hard case possible, a good `hashmap` interface allows clients to specify their own hash function and number of buckets in order to customize the hashing behavior for their particular workload. On the other hand, clients that do not have the desire, or ability, to write a good hash function and choose a number of buckets should still be able to use the container without doing so. One solution is to allow clients to provide a hash function and number of buckets in the `hashmap` constructor, but also to provide defaults values. It also makes sense to package the hash function and the number of buckets into a hashing class. Our default hash class definition looks like this:

Available for
download on
Wrox.com

```
// Any Hash Class must provide two methods: hash() and numBuckets().
template <typename T>
class DefaultHash
{
    public:
        // Throws invalid_argument if numBuckets is illegal
        DefaultHash(size_t numBuckets = 101) throw (invalid_argument);
        size_t hash(const T& key) const;
        size_t numBuckets() const { return mNumBuckets; }
    protected:
        size_t mNumBuckets;
};
```

Code snippet from Hashmap\BasicHashmap\hashmap.h

Note that the `DefaultHash` class is templatized on the key type that it hashes, in order to support a templatized `hashmap` container. The implementation of the constructor is trivial:

Available for
download on
Wrox.com

```cpp
// Throws invalid_argument if numBuckets is illegal
template <typename T>
DefaultHash<T>::DefaultHash(size_t numBuckets) throw (invalid_argument)
{
    if (numBuckets <= 0) {
        throw invalid_argument("numBuckets must be > 0");
    }
    mNumBuckets = numBuckets;
}
```

Code snippet from Hashmap\BasicHashmap\hashmap.cpp

The implementation of `hash()` is trickier, partially because it must apply to keys of any type. It is supposed to map the key to one of the `mNumBuckets` buckets. The following `hash()` function first computes an integer-sized hash value, then limits the calculated hash value to the number of hash buckets by taking the modulo of the calculated value:

Available for
download on
Wrox.com

```cpp
// Uses the division method for hashing.
// Treats the key as a sequence of bytes, sums the ASCII
// values of the bytes, and mods the total by the number
// of buckets.
template <typename T>
size_t DefaultHash<T>::hash(const T& key) const
{
    size_t bytes = sizeof(key);
    size_t res = 0;
    for (size_t i = 0; i < bytes; ++i) {
        unsigned char b = *((unsigned char*)&key + i);
        res += b;
    }
    return (res % mNumBuckets);
}
```

Code snippet from Hashmap\BasicHashmap\hashmap.cpp

Unfortunately, when using the preceding method on `strings`, the function will calculate the hash of the entire `string` object, and not just of the actual text. The result is that two `string` objects with the same text will generate different hash values, because some fields of the `string` objects will be different. Therefore, it's a good idea to provide a specialization of the `DefaultHash` class for `strings`. Template specialization is discussed in detail in Chapter 19:

Available for
download on
Wrox.com

```cpp
// Specialization for strings
template <>
class DefaultHash<string>
{
    public:
        // Throws invalid_argument if numBuckets is illegal
        DefaultHash(size_t numBuckets = 101) throw (invalid_argument);
        size_t hash(const string& key) const;
        size_t numBuckets() const { return mNumBuckets; }
```

```
    protected:
        size_t mNumBuckets;
};
```

```
// Throws invalid_argument if numBuckets is illegal
DefaultHash<string>::DefaultHash(size_t numBuckets) throw (invalid_argument)
{
    if (numBuckets <= 0) {
        throw invalid_argument("numBuckets must be > 0");
    }
    mNumBuckets = numBuckets;
}
// Uses the division method for hashing after summing the
// ASCII values of all the characters in key.
size_t DefaultHash<string>::hash(const string& key) const
{
    size_t sum = 0;
    for (size_t i = 0; i < key.size(); i++) {
        sum += (unsigned char)key[i];
    }
    return (sum % mNumBuckets);
}
```

If the client wants to use other pointer types or objects as the key, she should write her own hash class for those types.

> *The hash functions shown in this section are examples for the basic* hashmap *implementation. They do not guarantee uniform hashing for all key universes. If you need more mathematically rigorous hash functions, or if you don't know what "uniform hashing" is, consult an algorithms reference from Appendix B.*

The Hashmap Interface

A hashmap supports three basic operations: insertion, deletion, and lookup. Of course, it provides a constructor, destructor, copy constructor, and copy assignment operator as well. With C++11 it should also support a move constructor and move assignment operator. Here is the public portion of the hashmap class template:

```
template <typename Key, typename T, typename Compare = std::equal_to<Key>,
    typename Hash = DefaultHash<Key>>
class hashmap
{
    public:
        typedef Key key_type;
        typedef T mapped_type;
```

```
            typedef pair<const Key, T> value_type;
            // Constructors
            // Throws invalid_argument if the hash object specifies an illegal
            // number of buckets
            explicit hashmap(const Compare& comp = Compare(),
                const Hash& hash = Hash()) throw(invalid_argument);
            // destructor, copy constructor, move constructor,
            // copy assignment operator and move assignment operator
            ~hashmap();
            hashmap(const hashmap<Key, T, Compare, Hash>& src);
            hashmap(hashmap<Key, T, Compare, Hash>&& src);      // C++11
            hashmap<Key, T, Compare, Hash>& operator=(
                const hashmap<Key, T, Compare, Hash>& rhs);
            hashmap<Key, T, Compare, Hash>& operator=(
                hashmap<Key, T, Compare, Hash>&& rhs);          // C++11
            // Inserts the key/value pair x
            void insert(const value_type& x);
            // Removes the element with key x, if it exists
            void erase(const key_type& x);
            // find returns a pointer to the element with key x.
            // Returns nullptr if no element with that key exists.
            value_type* find(const key_type& x);
            // operator[] finds the element with key x or inserts an
            // element with that key if none exists yet. Returns a reference to
            // the value corresponding to that key.
            T& operator[] (const key_type& x);
    protected:
            // Implementation details not shown yet
    };
```

Code snippet from Hashmap\BasicHashmap\hashmap.h

As you can see, the `key` and `value` types are both template arguments like in the STL `map`. The hashmap stores `pair<const Key, T>` as the actual elements in the container. The `insert()`, `erase()`, `find()`, and `operator[]` methods are straightforward. However, a few aspects of this interface require further explanation.

The Template Argument Compare

Like the `map`, `set`, and other standard containers, the `hashmap` allows the client to specify the comparison type as a template parameter and to pass a specific comparison object of that type in the constructor. Unlike the `map` and `set`, the `hashmap` does not sort elements by key, but must still compare keys for equality. Thus, instead of using `less` as the default comparison, it uses `equal_to`. The comparison object is used only to detect attempts to insert duplicate keys into the container.

The Template Argument Hash

When you allow clients to define their own classes, from which they construct objects to pass in the constructor, you must figure out how to specify the type of parameter in the constructor. There are several ways to do it. The STL way, which is on the complicated end of the spectrum, takes the class type as a template parameter, and uses that templatized type as the type in the constructor. We follow that approach for the hash class, as you can see above. Thus, the `hashmap` template takes four template parameters: the key type, the value type, the comparison type, and the hash type.

The typedefs

The `hashmap` class template defines three `typedefs`:

```
typedef Key key_type;
typedef T mapped_type;
typedef pair<const Key, T> value_type;
```

The `value_type`, in particular, is useful for referring to the more cumbersome `pair<const Key, T>`. As you will see, these `typedefs` are also required for STL containers by the standard.

The Implementation

After you finalize the `hashmap` interface, you need to choose the implementation model. The basic hash table structure generally consists of a fixed number of buckets, each of which can store one or more elements. The buckets should be accessible in constant time based on a `bucket-id` (the result of hashing a key). Thus, a `vector` is the most appropriate container for the buckets. Each bucket must store a list of elements, so the STL `list` can be used as the bucket type. Thus, the final structure is a `vector` of lists of `pair<const Key, T>` elements. Here are the `protected` members of the `hashmap` class:

Available for
download on
Wrox.com

```
protected:
    typedef list<value_type> ListType;
    // In this first implementation, it would be easier to use a vector
    // instead of a pointer to a vector, which requires dynamic allocation.
    // However, a pointer to a vector is used so that, in the final
    // implementation, swap() can be implemented in constant time.
    vector<ListType>* mElems;
    size_t mSize;
    Compare mComp;
    Hash mHash;
```

Code snippet from Hashmap\BasicHashmap\hashmap.h

Without the `typedefs` for `value_type` and `ListType`, the line declaring `mElems` would look like this:

```
vector<list<pair<const Key, T>>>* mElems;
```

The `mComp` and `mHash` members store the comparison and hashing objects, respectively, and `mSize` stores the number of elements currently in the container.

The Constructor

The constructor initializes all the fields and allocates a new `vector`. Unfortunately, the template syntax is somewhat dense. As mentioned in the beginning of this chapter, if the syntax confuses you, consult Chapter 19 for details on writing class templates.

Available for
download on
Wrox.com

```
// Construct mElems with the number of buckets.
template <typename Key, typename T, typename Compare, typename Hash>
hashmap<Key, T, Compare, Hash>::hashmap(
    const Compare& comp, const Hash& hash) throw(invalid_argument) :
    mSize(0), mComp(comp), mHash(hash)
```

```
{
    if (mHash.numBuckets() <= 0) {
        throw invalid_argument("Number of buckets must be positive");
    }
    mElems = new vector<ListType>(mHash.numBuckets());
}
```

Code snippet from Hashmap\BasicHashmap\hashmap.cpp

The implementation requires at least one bucket, so the constructor enforces that restriction.

Destructor, Copy Constructor, Move Constructor, Copy Assignment Operator, and Move Assignment Operator

Here are the implementations of the destructor, copy constructor, move constructor, copy assignment operator, and move assignment operator. Their implementations are straightforward. Consult Chapter 9 for more details on how move constructors and move assignment operators work.

```
template <typename Key, typename T, typename Compare, typename Hash>
hashmap<Key, T, Compare, Hash>::~hashmap()
{
    delete mElems;
    mElems = nullptr;
    mSize = 0;
}
// Copy constructor
template <typename Key, typename T, typename Compare, typename Hash>
hashmap<Key, T, Compare, Hash>::hashmap(
    const hashmap<Key, T, Compare, Hash>& src) :
    mSize(src.mSize), mComp(src.mComp), mHash(src.mHash)
{
    // Don't need to bother checking if numBuckets is positive, because
    // we know src checked. Use the vector copy constructor.
    mElems = new vector<ListType>(*(src.mElems));
}
// C++11 move constructor
template <typename Key, typename T, typename Compare, typename Hash>
hashmap<Key, T, Compare, Hash>::hashmap(hashmap<Key, T, Compare, Hash>&& src)
{
    // move ownership
    mElems = src.mElems;
    src.mElems = nullptr;
    mSize = src.mSize;
    src.mSize = 0;
    mComp = src.mComp;
    mHash = src.mHash;
}
// Assignment operator
template <typename Key, typename T, typename Compare, typename Hash>
hashmap<Key, T, Compare, Hash>& hashmap<Key, T, Compare, Hash>::operator=(
    const hashmap<Key, T, Compare, Hash>& rhs)
{
    // Check for self-assignment.
    if (this != &rhs) {
```

```
            delete mElems;
            mSize = rhs.mSize;
            mComp = rhs.mComp;
            mHash = rhs.mHash;
            // Don't need to bother checking if numBuckets is positive, because
            // we know rhs checked. Use the vector copy constructor.
            mElems = new vector<ListType>(*(rhs.mElems));
        }
        return *this;
    }
    // C++11 move assignment operator
    template <typename Key, typename T, typename Compare, typename Hash>
    hashmap<Key, T, Compare, Hash>& hashmap<Key, T, Compare, Hash>::operator=(
        hashmap<Key, T, Compare, Hash>&& rhs)
    {
        // check for self-assignment
        if (this != &rhs) {
            delete mElems;

            // move ownership
            mElems = rhs.mElems;
            rhs.mElems = nullptr;
            mSize = rhs.mSize;
            rhs.mSize = 0;
            mComp = rhs.mComp;
            mHash = rhs.mHash;
        }
        return *this;
    }
```

Code snippet from Hashmap\BasicHashmap\hashmap.cpp

Note that the copy constructor and assignment operator both construct the new `vector` by using its copy constructor with the `vector` from the source `hashmap` as the source.

Element Lookup

Each of the three major operations (lookup, insertion, and deletion) requires code to find an element with a given key. Thus, it is helpful to have a `protected` helper method that performs that task. `findElement()` first uses the hash object to hash the key to a specific bucket. Then, it looks in that bucket for an element with a key matching the given key. The elements stored are key/value pairs, so the actual comparison must be done on the first field of the element. The comparison function object specified in the constructor is used to perform the comparison. `lists` require a linear search to find matching elements, but you could use the `find()` algorithm instead of an explicit `for` loop.

Available for
download on
Wrox.com

```
    template <typename Key, typename T, typename Compare, typename Hash>
    typename list<pair<const Key, T>>::iterator
    hashmap<Key, T, Compare, Hash>::findElement(const key_type& x,
        size_t& bucket) const
    {
        // Hash the key to get the bucket.
        bucket = mHash.hash(x);
```

```
        // Look for the key in the bucket.
        for (auto it = (*mElems)[bucket].begin();
            it != (*mElems)[bucket].end(); ++it) {
            if (mComp(it->first, x)) {
                return it;
            }
        }
        return (*mElems)[bucket].end();
    }
```

Code snippet from Hashmap\BasicHashmap\hashmap.cpp

Note that `findElement()` returns an iterator referring to an element in the `list` representing the bucket to which the key hashed. If the element is found, the iterator refers to that element; otherwise, it is the end iterator for that `list`. The bucket is returned by reference in the `bucket` argument.

The syntax in this method is somewhat confusing, particularly the use of the `typename` keyword. You must use the `typename` keyword whenever you are using a type that is dependent on a template parameter. Specifically, the type `list<pair<const Key, T>>::iterator` is dependent on both the `Key` and `T` template parameters.

Another note on the syntax: `mElems` is a pointer, so it must be dereferenced before you can apply `operator[]` to it to obtain a specific element. Hence the somewhat ugly: `(*mElems)[bucket]`.

You can implement the `find()` method as a simple wrapper for `findElement()`:

Available for
download on
Wrox.com

```
template <typename Key, typename T, typename Compare, typename Hash>
typename hashmap<Key, T, Compare, Hash>::value_type*
hashmap<Key, T, Compare, Hash>::find(const key_type& x)
{
    size_t bucket;
    // Use the findElement() helper.
    auto it = findElement(x, bucket);
    if (it == (*mElems)[bucket].end()) {
        // We didn't find the element--return nullptr.
        return nullptr;
    }
    // We found the element. Return a pointer to it.
    return &(*it);
}
```

Code snippet from Hashmap\BasicHashmap\hashmap.cpp

The `operator[]` method uses the `find()` method, and if it does not find the element, it inserts it:

Available for
download on
Wrox.com

```
template <typename Key, typename T, typename Compare, typename Hash>
T& hashmap<Key, T, Compare, Hash>::operator[] (const key_type& x)
{
    // Try to find the element. If it doesn't exist, add a new element.
    value_type* found = find(x);
    if (found == nullptr) {
```

```
        insert(make_pair(x, T()));
        found = find(x);
    }
    return found->second;
}
```

Code snippet from Hashmap\BasicHashmap\hashmap.cpp

This method is somewhat inefficient, because in the worst case it calls `find()` twice and `insert()` once. However, each of these operations runs in constant time with respect to the number of elements in the `hashmap`, so the overhead is not too significant.

Element Insert

`insert()` must first check if an element with that key is already in the `hashmap`. If not, it can add the element to the `list` in the appropriate bucket. Note that `findElement()` returns by reference the bucket to which the key hashes, even if the element with that key is not found:

```
template <typename Key, typename T, typename Compare, typename Hash>
void hashmap<Key, T, Compare, Hash>::insert(const value_type& x)
{
    size_t bucket;
    // Try to find the element.
    auto it = findElement(x.first, bucket);
    if (it != (*mElems)[bucket].end()) {
        // The element already exists.
        return;
    } else {
        // We didn't find the element, so insert a new one.
        mSize++;
        (*mElems)[bucket].insert((*mElems)[bucket].end(), x);
    }
}
```

Code snippet from Hashmap\BasicHashmap\hashmap.cpp

Element Delete

`erase()` follows the same pattern as `insert()`: It first attempts to find the element by calling `findElement()`. If the element exists, it erases it from the list in the appropriate bucket. Otherwise, it does nothing.

```
template <typename Key, typename T, typename Compare, typename Hash>
void hashmap<Key, T, Compare, Hash>::erase(const key_type& x)
{
    size_t bucket;
    // First, try to find the element.
    auto it = findElement(x, bucket);
    if (it != (*mElems)[bucket].end()) {
        // The element exists--erase it.
```

```
                    (*mElems)[bucket].erase(it);
                    mSize--;
            }
    }
}
```

Code snippet from Hashmap\BasicHashmap\hashmap.cpp

Using the Basic Hashmap

Here is a small test program demonstrating the basic `hashmap` class template:

Available for
download on
Wrox.com

```cpp
hashmap<int, int> myHash;
myHash.insert(make_pair(4, 40));
myHash.insert(make_pair(6, 60));
// x will have type hashmap<int, int>::value_type*
auto x = myHash.find(4);
if (x != nullptr) {
    cout << "4 maps to " << x->second << endl;
} else {
    cout << "cannot find 4 in map" << endl;
}
myHash.erase(4);
auto x2 = myHash.find(4);
if (x2 != nullptr) {
    cout << "4 maps to " << x2->second << endl;
} else {
    cout << "cannot find 4 in map" << endl;
}
myHash[4] = 35;
myHash[4] = 60;
auto x3 = myHash.find(4);
if (x3 != nullptr) {
    cout << "4 maps to " << x3->second << endl;
} else {
    cout << "cannot find 4 in map" << endl;
}
```

Code snippet from Hashmap\BasicHashmap\TestHashmap.cpp

The output is:

```
4 maps to 40
cannot find 4 in map
4 maps to 60
```

 With the Microsoft Visual C++ compiler, at least through Visual Studio 2010, you may see a warning "warning C4290: C++ exception specification ignored except to indicate a function is not __declspec(nothrow)," *because it doesn't support exception throw lists. You can ignore these warnings for this example.*

Making the Hashmap an STL Container

The basic `hashmap` shown in the previous section follows the spirit, but not the letter, of the STL. For most purposes, the preceding implementation is good enough. However, if you want to use the STL algorithms on your `hashmap`, you must do a bit more work. The C++ standard specifies specific methods and `typedef`s that a data structure must provide in order to qualify as an STL container.

typedef Container Requirements

The C++ standard specifies that every STL container must provide the following `public typedef`s:

TYPE NAME	DESCRIPTION
value_type	The element type stored in the container
reference	A reference to the element type stored in the container
const_reference	A reference to a `const` element type stored in the container
iterator	The type for iterating over elements of the container
const_iterator	A version of `iterator` for iterating over `const` elements of the container
size_type	A type that can represent the number of elements in the container; usually just `size_t` (from `<cstddef>`)
difference_type	A type that can represent the difference of two `iterator`s for the container; usually just `ptrdiff_t` (from `<cstddef>`)

Here are the definitions in the `hashmap` class of all these `typedef`s except `iterator` and `const_iterator`. Writing an iterator is covered in detail in a subsequent section. Note that `value_type` (plus `key_type` and `mapped_type`, which are discussed later) was already defined in our previous version of the `hashmap`:

```
template <typename Key, typename T, typename Compare = std::equal_to<Key>,
    typename Hash = DefaultHash<Key>>
class hashmap
{
    public:
        typedef Key key_type;
        typedef T mapped_type;
        typedef pair<const Key, T> value_type;
        typedef pair<const Key, T>& reference;
        typedef const pair<const Key, T>& const_reference;
        typedef size_t size_type;
        typedef ptrdiff_t difference_type;
        // Remainder of class definition omitted for brevity
};
```

Code snippet from Hashmap\FinalHashmap\hashmap.h

Method Container Requirements

In addition to the typedefs, every container must provide the following methods:

	METHOD	DESCRIPTION	WORST CASE COMPLEXITY
	Default Constructor	Constructs an empty container	Constant
	Copy constructor	Performs a deep copy of the container	Linear
C++11	Move constructor	Performs a C++11 move constructing operation	Constant
	Copy Assignment operator	Performs a deep copy of the container	Linear
C++11	Move Assignment operator	Performs a C++11 move assignment operation	Constant
	Destructor	Destroys dynamically allocated memory; calls destructor on all elements left in container	Linear

	`iterator begin();`
	`const_iterator`
	`  begin() const;`
		Returns an iterator referring to the first element in the container	Constant

	`iterator end();`
	`const_iterator`
	`  end() const;`
		Returns an iterator referring to the last+1 element in the container	Constant

C++11	`const_iterator` `  cbegin() const;`	Returns a `const` iterator referring to the first element in the container	Constant
C++11	`const_iterator` `  cend() const;`	Returns a `const` iterator referring to the last+1 element in the container	Constant

	`operator==`
	`operator!=`
	`operator<`
	`operator>`
	`operator<=`
	`operator>=`
		Comparison operators that compare two containers, element by element	Linear

	`void swap(Container&);`	Swaps the contents of the container passed to the method with the object on which the method is called	Constant
	`size_type size() const;`	Returns the number of elements in the container	Constant
	`size_type max_size() const;`	Returns the maximum number of elements the container can hold	Constant
	`bool empty() const;`	Specifies whether the container has any elements	Constant

In this `hashmap` *example, we omit the comparison operators. Implementing them would be a good exercise for the reader.*

The following code extract shows the declarations of all the remaining methods except for `begin()`, `end()`, `cbegin()` and `cend()`. Those are covered in the next section.

```
template <typename Key, typename T, typename Compare = std::equal_to<Key>,
    typename Hash = DefaultHash<Key>>
class hashmap
{
    public:
        // typedefs omitted for brevity
        // Constructors
        explicit hashmap(const Compare& comp = Compare(),
            const Hash& hash = Hash()) throw(invalid_argument);
        // destructor, copy constructor, move constructor,
        // copy assignment operator and move assignment operator
        ~hashmap();
        hashmap(const hashmap<Key, T, Compare, Hash>& src);
        hashmap(hashmap<Key, T, Compare, Hash>&& src);         // C++11
        hashmap<Key, T, Compare, Hash>& operator=(
            const hashmap<Key, T, Compare, Hash>& rhs);
        hashmap<Key, T, Compare, Hash>& operator=(
            hashmap<Key, T, Compare, Hash>&& rhs);             // C++11
        // Size methods
        bool empty() const;
        size_type size() const;
        size_type max_size() const;
        // Other modifying utilities
        void swap(hashmap<Key, T, Compare, Hash>& hashIn);
        // Other methods omitted for brevity
};
```

Code snippet from Hashmap\FinalHashmap\hashmap.h

The implementations of the constructor, destructor, copy constructor, move constructor, assignment operator, and move assignment operator are identical to those shown earlier for the basic `hashmap` implementation.

The implementations of `size()` and `empty()` are easy because the `hashmap` implementation tracks its size in the `mSize` data member. Note that `size_type` is one of the `typedefs` that is defined in the class. Since it is a member of the class, such a return type in the implementation must be fully qualified with `typename hashmap<Key, T, Compare, Hash>`.

```
template <typename Key, typename T, typename Compare, typename Hash>
bool hashmap<Key, T, Compare, Hash>::empty() const
{
    return mSize == 0;
}
```

```
template <typename Key, typename T, typename Compare, typename Hash>
typename hashmap<Key, T, Compare, Hash>::size_type
    hashmap<Key, T, Compare, Hash>::size() const
{
    return mSize;
}
```

`max_size()` is a little trickier. At first, you might think the maximum size of the `hashmap` container is the sum of the maximum size of all the `lists`. However, the worst-case scenario is that all the elements hash to the same bucket. Thus, the maximum size it can claim to support is the maximum size of a single `list`:

```
template <typename Key, typename T, typename Compare, typename Hash>
typename hashmap<Key, T, Compare, Hash>::size_type
    hashmap<Key, T, Compare, Hash>::max_size() const
{
    // In the worst case, all the elements hash to the same
    // list, so the max_size is the max_size of a single list.
    // This code assumes that all the lists have the same max_size.
    return (*mElems)[0].max_size();
}
```

Finally, the implementation of `swap()` uses the `std::swap()` utility function to swap each of the four data members. Note that the `vector` pointers are swapped, which is a constant-time operation:

```
// Just swap the four data members. Use the generic swap template.
template <typename Key, typename T, typename Compare, typename Hash>
void hashmap<Key, T, Compare, Hash>::swap(
    hashmap<Key, T, Compare, Hash>& hashIn)
{
    // Explicitly qualify with std:: so the compiler doesn't think
    // it's a recursive call.
    std::swap(*this, hashIn);
}
```

Writing an Iterator

The most important container requirement is the iterator. In order to work with the generic algorithms, every container must provide an iterator for accessing the elements in the container. Your iterator should generally provide overloaded `operator*` and `operator->`, plus some other operations depending on its specific behavior. As long as your iterator provides the basic iteration operations, everything should be fine.

The first decision to make about your iterator is what kind it will be: forward, bidirectional, or random access. Random access iterators don't make much sense for associative containers, so bidirectional seems like the logical choice for the `hashmap` iterator. That means you must also provide `operator++`, `operator--`, `operator==`, and `operator!=`. Consult Chapter 12 for more details on the requirements for the different iterators.

The second decision is how to order the elements of your container. The `hashmap` is unsorted, so iterating in a sorted order is probably too difficult. Instead, your iterator can just step through the buckets, starting with the elements in the first bucket and progressing to those in the last bucket. This order will appear random to the client, but will be consistent and repeatable.

The third decision is how to represent your iterator internally. The implementation is usually quite dependent on the internal implementation of the container. The first purpose of an iterator is to refer to a single element in the container. In the case of the `hashmap`, each element is in an STL list, so perhaps the `hashmap` iterator can be a wrapper around a `list` iterator referring to the element in question. However, the second purpose of a bidirectional iterator is to allow the client to progress to the next or previous element from the current. In order to progress from one bucket to the next, you need to track also the current bucket and the `hashmap` object to which the iterator refers.

Once you've chosen your implementation, you must decide on a consistent representation for the end iterator. Recall that the end iterator should really be the "past-the-end" marker: the iterator that's reached by applying `++` to an iterator referring to the final element in the container. The `hashmap` iterator can use as its end iterator the end iterator of the `list` of the final bucket in the `hashmap`.

The HashIterator Class

Given the decisions made in the previous section, it's time to define the `HashIterator` class. The first thing to note is that each `HashIterator` object is an iterator for a specific instantiation of the `hashmap` class. In order to provide this one-to-one mapping, the `HashIterator` must also be a class template on the same parameters as the `hashmap` class.

The main question in the class definition is how to conform to the bidirectional iterator requirements. Recall that anything that behaves like an iterator is an iterator. Your class is not required to subclass another class in order to qualify as a bidirectional iterator. However, if you want your iterator to be usable in the generic algorithms functions, you must specify its traits. The discussion on writing STL algorithms earlier in this chapter explains that `iterator_traits` is a class template that defines five `typedefs` for each iterator type. It can be partially specialized for your new iterator type if you want. Alternatively, the default implementation of the `iterator_traits` class template just grabs the five `typedefs` out of the iterator class itself. Thus, you can define those `typedefs` directly in your iterator class. In fact, C++ makes it even easier than that. Instead of defining them yourself, you can just subclass the `iterator` class template, which provides the `typedefs` for you. That way you only need to specify the iterator type and the element type as template arguments to the `iterator` class template. The `HashIterator` is a bidirectional iterator, so you can specify `bidirectional_iterator_tag` as the iterator type. Other legal iterator types are `input_iterator_tag`, `output_iterator_tag`, `forward_iterator_tag`, and `random_access_iterator_tag`. For the `HashIterator`, the element type is `pair<const Key, T>`.

Basically, it all boils down to the fact that you should subclass your iterator classes from the generic `iterator` class template.

Here is the basic `HashIterator` class definition:

```cpp
// HashIterator class definition
template<typename Key, typename T, typename Compare, typename Hash>
class HashIterator : public std::iterator<std::bidirectional_iterator_tag,
    pair<const Key, T>>
{
public:
    HashIterator(); // Bidirectional iterators must supply default ctor
    HashIterator(size_t bucket,
        typename list<pair<const Key, T>>::iterator listIt,
        const hashmap<Key, T, Compare, Hash>* inHashmap);
    pair<const Key, T>& operator*() const;
    // Return type must be something to which -> can be applied.
    // Return a pointer to a pair<const Key, T>, to which the compiler will
    // apply -> again.
    pair<const Key, T>* operator->() const;
    HashIterator<Key, T, Compare, Hash>& operator++();
    const HashIterator<Key, T, Compare, Hash> operator++(int);
    HashIterator<Key, T, Compare, Hash>& operator--();
    const HashIterator<Key, T, Compare, Hash> operator--(int);
    // Don't need to define a copy constructor or operator= because the
    // default behavior is what we want
    // Don't need destructor because the default behavior
    // (not deleting mHashmap) is what we want.
    // The following are ok as member functions because we don't
    // support comparisons of different types to this one.
    bool operator==(const HashIterator& rhs) const;
    bool operator!=(const HashIterator& rhs) const;
protected:
    size_t mBucket;
    typename list<pair<const Key, T>>::iterator mIt;
    const hashmap<Key, T, Compare, Hash>* mHashmap;
    // Helper methods for operator++ and operator--
    void increment();
    void decrement();
};
```

Code snippet from Hashmap\FinalHashmap\hashmap.h

If the definitions and implementations (shown in the next section) of the overloaded operators confuse you, consult Chapter 18 for details on operator overloading.

The HashIterator Method Implementations

The `HashIterator` constructors initialize the three member variables. The default constructor exists only so that clients can declare `HashIterator` variables without initializing them. An iterator constructed with the default constructor does not need to refer to any value, and attempting any operations on it is allowed to have undefined results:

```
// Dereferencing or incrementing an iterator constructed with the
// default ctor is undefined, so it doesn't matter what values we give
// here.
template<typename Key, typename T, typename Compare, typename Hash>
HashIterator<Key, T, Compare, Hash>::HashIterator()
{
    mBucket = 0;
    mIt = list<pair<const Key, T>>::iterator();
    mHashmap = nullptr;
}
template<typename Key, typename T, typename Compare, typename Hash>
HashIterator<Key, T, Compare, Hash>::HashIterator(
    size_t bucket, typename list<pair<const Key, T>>::iterator listIt,
    const hashmap<Key, T, Compare, Hash>* inHashmap) :
    mBucket(bucket), mIt(listIt), mHashmap(inHashmap)
{
}
```

Code snippet from Hashmap\FinalHashmap\hashmap.cpp

The implementations of the dereferencing operators are concise, but can be tricky. Chapter 18 explains that `operator*` and `operator->` are asymmetric; `operator*` returns the actual underlying value, which in this case is the element to which the iterator refers, while `operator->` must return something to which the arrow operator can be applied again. Thus, it returns a pointer to the element. The compiler then applies -> to the pointer, which will result in accessing a field of the element:

```
// Return the actual element
template<typename Key, typename T, typename Compare, typename Hash>
pair<const Key, T>& HashIterator<Key, T, Compare, Hash>::operator*() const
{
    return *mIt;
}
// Return the iterator, so the compiler can apply -> to it to access
// the actual desired field.
template<typename Key, typename T, typename Compare, typename Hash>
pair<const Key, T>*
    HashIterator<Key, T, Compare, Hash>::operator->() const
{
    return &(*mIt);
}
```

Code snippet from Hashmap\FinalHashmap\hashmap.cpp

The increment and decrement operators are implemented as follows, which defer the actual incrementing and decrementing procedures to the `increment()` and `decrement()` helper methods:

```cpp
// Defer the details to the increment() helper.
template<typename Key, typename T, typename Compare, typename Hash>
HashIterator<Key, T, Compare, Hash>&
    HashIterator<Key, T, Compare, Hash>::operator++()
{
    increment();
    return *this;
}
// Defer the details to the increment() helper.
template<typename Key, typename T, typename Compare, typename Hash>
const HashIterator<Key, T, Compare, Hash>
    HashIterator<Key, T, Compare, Hash>::operator++(int)
{
    auto oldIt = *this;
    increment();
    return oldIt;
}
// Defer the details to the decrement() helper.
template<typename Key, typename T, typename Compare, typename Hash>
HashIterator<Key, T, Compare, Hash>&
    HashIterator<Key, T, Compare, Hash>::operator--()
{
    decrement();
    return *this;
}
// Defer the details to the decrement() helper.
template<typename Key, typename T, typename Compare, typename Hash>
const HashIterator<Key, T, Compare, Hash>
    HashIterator<Key, T, Compare, Hash>::operator--(int)
{
    auto oldIt = *this;
    decrement();
    return oldIt;
}
```

Code snippet from Hashmap\FinalHashmap\hashmap.cpp

Incrementing a `HashIterator` tells it to refer to the "next" element in the container. This method first increments the `list` iterator, then checks if it has reached the end of its bucket. If so, it finds the next non-empty bucket in the `hashmap` and sets the `list` iterator equal to the start element in that bucket. Note that it can't simply move to the next bucket, because there might not be any elements in it. If there are no more empty buckets, `mIt` is set, by the convention chosen for this example, to the end iterator of the last bucket in the `hashmap`, which is the special "end" position of the `HashIterator`. Iterators are not required to be any safer than dumb pointers, so error-checking for things like incrementing an iterator already at the end is not required:

```cpp
// Behavior is undefined if mIt already refers to the past-the-end
// element in the table, or is otherwise invalid.
template<typename Key, typename T, typename Compare, typename Hash>
void HashIterator<Key, T, Compare, Hash>::increment()
{
    // mIt is an iterator into a single bucket. Increment it.
```

```
        ++mIt;
        // If we're at the end of the current bucket,
        // find the next bucket with elements.
        if (mIt == (*mHashmap->mElems)[mBucket].end()) {
            for (size_t i = mBucket + 1; i < (*mHashmap->mElems).size(); i++) {
                if (!((*mHashmap->mElems)[i].empty())) {
                    // We found a non-empty bucket.
                    // Make mIt refer to the first element in it.
                    mIt = (*mHashmap->mElems)[i].begin();
                    mBucket = i;
                    return;
                }
            }
            // No more empty buckets. Assign mIt to refer to the end
            // iterator of the last list.
            mBucket = (*mHashmap->mElems).size() - 1;
            mIt = (*mHashmap->mElems)[mBucket].end();
        }
    }
```

Code snippet from Hashmap\FinalHashmap\hashmap.cpp

Decrement is the inverse of increment: It makes the iterator refer to the "previous" element in the container. However, there is an asymmetry because of the asymmetry between the way the start and end positions are represented: Start is the first element, but end is "one past" the last element. The algorithm for decrement checks first if the underlying `list` iterator is at the start of its current bucket. If not, it can just be decremented. Otherwise, the code needs to check for the first nonempty bucket before the current one. If one is found, the `list` iterator must be set to refer to the last element in the bucket, which is the end iterator decremented by one. If no non-empty buckets are found, the decrement is invalid, so the code can do anything it wants (behavior is undefined):

```
// Behavior is undefined if mIt already refers to the first element
// in the table, or is otherwise invalid.
template<typename Key, typename T, typename Compare, typename Hash>
void HashIterator<Key, T, Compare, Hash>::decrement()
{
    // mIt is an iterator into a single bucket.
    // If it's at the beginning of the current bucket, don't decrement it.
    // Instead, try to find a non-empty bucket ahead of the current one.
    if (mIt == (*mHashmap->mElems)[mBucket].begin()) {
        for (size_t i = mBucket - 1; i >= 0; --i) {
            if (!((*mHashmap->mElems)[i].empty())) {
                mIt = (*mHashmap->mElems)[i].end();
                --mIt;
                mBucket = i;
                return;
            }
        }
    }
    // No more non-empty buckets. This is an invalid decrement.
    // Assign mIt to refer to one before the start element of the first
    // list (an invalid position).
    mIt = (*mHashmap->mElems)[0].begin();
    --mIt;
```

```
            mBucket = 0;
        } else {
            // We're not at the beginning of the bucket, so just move down.
            --mIt;
        }
    }
```

                                Code snippet from Hashmap\FinalHashmap\hashmap.cpp

Note that both `increment()` and `decrement()` access `protected` members of the `hashmap` class. Thus, the `hashmap` class must declare `HashIterator` to be a `friend` class.

After `increment()` and `decrement()`, `operator==` and `operator!=` are positively simple. They just compare each of the three data members of the objects:

Available for
download on
Wrox.com

```
template<typename Key, typename T, typename Compare, typename Hash>
bool HashIterator<Key, T, Compare, Hash>::operator==(
    const HashIterator& rhs) const
{
    // All fields, including the hashmap to which the iterators refer,
    // must be equal.
    return (mHashmap == rhs.mHashmap && mBucket == rhs.mBucket &&
        mIt == rhs.mIt);
}
template<typename Key, typename T, typename Compare, typename Hash>
bool HashIterator<Key, T, Compare, Hash>::operator!=(
    const HashIterator& rhs) const
{
    return !(*this == rhs);
}
```

                                Code snippet from Hashmap\FinalHashmap\hashmap.cpp

const Iterators

Technically, you should provide both an iterator and a `const` iterator for your `hashmap` class. The `const` iterator should function like the iterator, but should provide read-only access to the elements. The iterator should always be convertible to a `const` iterator. We omit the details of the `const` iterator and leave its implementation as an exercise for the reader.

Iterator typedefs and Access Methods

The final piece involved in providing iterator support for the `hashmap` is to supply the necessary `typedef`s in the `hashmap` class definition and to write the `begin()` and `end()` methods and the C++11 `cbegin()` and `cend()` methods on the `hashmap`. The `typedef`s and method prototypes look like this:

Available for
download on
Wrox.com

```
template <typename Key, typename T, typename Compare = std::equal_to<Key>,
    typename Hash = DefaultHash<Key>>
class hashmap
{
    public:
        // Other typedefs omitted for brevity
```

```
        typedef HashIterator<Key, T, Compare, Hash> iterator;
        typedef HashIterator<Key, T, Compare, Hash> const_iterator;
        // Iterator methods
        iterator begin();
        iterator end();
        const_iterator begin() const;
        const_iterator end() const;
        const_iterator cbegin() const;  // For C++11
        const_iterator cend() const;    // For C++11
        // Remainder of class definition omitted for brevity
};
```

The trickiest aspect of begin() is to remember to return the end iterator if there are no elements in the container:

```
template <typename Key, typename T, typename Compare, typename Hash>
typename hashmap<Key, T, Compare, Hash>::iterator
    hashmap<Key, T, Compare, Hash>::begin()
{
    if (mSize == 0) {
        // Special case: there are no elements, so return the end iterator
        return end();
    }
    // We know there is at least one element. Find the first element.
    for (size_t i = 0; i < mElems->size(); ++i) {
        if (!((*mElems)[i].empty())) {
            return HashIterator<Key, T, Compare, Hash>(i,
                (*mElems)[i].begin(), this);
        }
    }
    // Should never reach here, but if we do, return the end iterator
    return end();
}
```

end() creates a HashIterator referring to the end iterator of the last bucket:

```
template <typename Key, typename T, typename Compare, typename Hash>
typename hashmap<Key, T, Compare, Hash>::iterator
    hashmap<Key, T, Compare, Hash>::end()
{
    // The end iterator is just the end iterator of the list in last bucket.
    return HashIterator<Key, T, Compare, Hash>(mElems->size() - 1,
        (*mElems)[mElems->size() - 1].end(), this);
}
```

Because we don't provide a `const_iterator`, the implementation of the `const` versions of `begin()` and `end()` are identical to the non-`const` versions of `begin()` and `end()`. The C++11 `cbegin()` and `cend()` methods forward the call to the `const` versions of `begin()` and `end()`:

```cpp
template <typename Key, typename T, typename Compare, typename Hash>
typename hashmap<Key, T, Compare, Hash>::const_iterator
    hashmap<Key, T, Compare, Hash>::cbegin() const
{
    return const_cast<const hashmap<Key, T, Compare, Hash>*>(this)->begin();
}
template <typename Key, typename T, typename Compare, typename Hash>
typename hashmap<Key, T, Compare, Hash>::const_iterator
    hashmap<Key, T, Compare, Hash>::cend() const
{
    return const_cast<const hashmap<Key, T, Compare, Hash>*>(this)->end();
}
```

Code snippet from Hashmap\FinalHashmap\hashmap.cpp

Using the HashIterator

Now that the `hashmap` supports iteration, you can iterate over its elements just as you would on any STL container, and you can pass the iterators to methods and functions:

```cpp
hashmap<string, int> myHash;
myHash.insert(make_pair("KeyOne", 100));
myHash.insert(make_pair("KeyTwo", 200));
myHash.insert(make_pair("KeyThree", 300));
for (auto it = myHash.cbegin(); it != myHash.cend(); ++it) {
    // Use both -> and * to test the operations.
    cout << it->first << " maps to " << (*it).second << endl;
}
// Print elements using C++11 range-based for loop
for (auto& p : myHash)
    cout << p.first << " maps to " << p.second << endl;
// Create a map with all the elements in the hashmap.
map<string, int> myMap(myHash.begin(), myHash.end());
for (auto it = myMap.begin(); it != myMap.end(); ++it) {
    cout << it->first << " maps to " << (*it).second << endl;
}
```

Code snippet from Hashmap\FinalHashmap\TestHashmap.cpp

Note on Allocators

As described earlier in this chapter, all the STL containers allow you to specify a custom memory allocator. A "good citizen" `hashmap` implementation should do the same. However, we omit those details because they obscure the main points of this implementation.

Note on Reversible Containers

If your container supplies a bidirectional or random access iterator, it is considered *reversible*. Reversible containers are supposed to supply two additional `typedefs`:

TYPE NAME	DESCRIPTION
`reverse_iterator`	The type for iterating over elements of the container in reverse order.
`const_reverse_iterator`	A version of `reverse_iterator` for iterating over `const` elements of the container in reverse order.

Additionally, the container should provide `rbegin()` and `rend()` which are symmetric with `begin()` and `end()`; and should provide the C++11 `crbegin()` and `crend()` which are symmetric with `cbegin()` and `cend()`. The usual implementations just use the `reverse_iterator` adapter described earlier in this chapter. We leave them as an exercise for the reader.

Making the Hashmap an Associative Container

In addition to the basic container requirements shown already, you can also make your container adhere to additional requirements for associative, unordered associative, or sequential containers. This example makes the `hashmap` an associative container, so it should conform to the following `typedefs` and methods.

Associative Container typedef Requirements

Associative containers require three additional `typedefs`:

TYPE NAME	DESCRIPTION
`key_type`	The key type with which the container is instantiated
`key_compare`	The comparison class or function pointer type with which the container is instantiated
`value_compare`	Class for comparing two `value_type` elements

This example implementation also throws in a `mapped_type` `typedef`, because that's what the `map` does. The `value_compare` is implemented not as a `typedef`, but as a nested class definition. Alternatively, the class could be a `friend` class of the `hashmap`, but this definition follows the `map` definition found in the standard. The purpose of the `value_compare` class is to call the comparison function on the keys of two elements:

Available for download on Wrox.com

```
template <typename Key, typename T, typename Compare = std::equal_to<Key>,
        typename Hash = DefaultHash<Key>>
class hashmap
{
    public:
        typedef Key key_type;
```

```
    typedef T mapped_type;
    typedef pair<const Key, T> value_type;
    typedef Compare key_compare;
    typedef pair<const Key, T>& reference;
    typedef const pair<const Key, T>& const_reference;
    typedef HashIterator<Key, T, Compare, Hash> iterator;
    typedef HashIterator<Key, T, Compare, Hash> const_iterator;
    typedef size_t size_type;
    typedef ptrdiff_t difference_type;
    // Required class definition for associative containers
    class value_compare :
        public std::binary_function<value_type, value_type, bool>
    {
        friend class hashmap<Key, T, Compare, Hash>;
        public:
            bool operator()(const value_type& x, const value_type& y) const
            {
                return comp(x.first, y.first);
            }
        protected:
            Compare comp;
            value_compare(Compare c) : comp(c) {}
    };
    // Remainder of hashmap class definition omitted for brevity
};
```

Code snippet from Hashmap\FinalHashmap\hashmap.h

Associative Container Method Requirements

The standard prescribes quite a few additional method requirements for associative containers:

METHOD	DESCRIPTION	WORST CASE COMPLEXITY
Constructor taking an iterator range.	Constructs the container and inserts elements in the iterator range. The iterator range need not refer into another container of the same type. Note that all constructors of associative containers must take a comparison object of type `value_compare`. The constructors should provide a default constructed object as the default value.	$n \log n$
C++11 Constructor taking an `initializer_list<value_type>` as parameter.	Constructs the container and inserts the elements from the initializer list into the container.	$n \log n$

continues

(continued)

	METHOD	DESCRIPTION	WORST CASE COMPLEXITY
C++11	Assignment operator with an `initializer_list<value_type>` as right-hand side.	Replaces all elements from the container with the elements from the initializer list	*n* log *n*

	`key_compare key_comp() const;`
	
	`value_compare value_comp() const;`
		Returns the comparison objects for comparing just keys or entire values	constant

	`pair<iterator, bool> insert(value_type&);`
	
	`iterator insert( iterator, value_type&);`
	
	`void insert( InputIterator start, InputIterator end);`
		Three different forms of `insert`.
		The `iterator` position in the second is a hint, which can be ignored.
		The range in the third need not be from a container of the same type.
		Containers that allow duplicate keys return just `iterator` from the first form, because `insert()` always succeeds.
			logarithmic except for the second form, which can be amortized constant if the element is inserted immediately before the given hint.

C++11	`void insert( initializer_list <value_type>);`	Inserts the elements from the initializer list into the container.	logarithmic
C++11 C++11	`pair<iterator, bool> emplace( value_type&&);` `iterator emplace_hint( iterator hint, value_type&&);`	Implements the C++11 emplace operations to construct objects *in-place*. In-place construction is discussed in Chapter 12.	logarithmic, except for the second form, which can be amortized constant if the element is inserted immediately before the given hint.

	`size_type erase(key_type&);`
	
	`void erase(iterator);`
	
	`void erase( iterator start, iterator end);`
		Three different forms of erase.
		The first form returns the number of values erased (0 or 1, in containers that do not allow duplicate keys).
		The second and third forms erase the elements at `iterator` position, or in the range `start` to `end`.
			logarithmic, except for the second form, which should be amortized constant

METHOD	DESCRIPTION	WORST CASE COMPLEXITY
`void clear();`	Erases all elements	linear

`iterator`
`   find(key_type&);`
 	
`const_iterator`
`  find(key_type&)`
`    const;`
	Finds the element with the specified key	logarithmic

`size_type`
`   count(key_type&)`
`     const;`
	Returns the number of elements with the specified key (0 or 1 in containers that do not allow duplicate keys)	logarithmic

`iterator lower_bound(`
`  key_type&);`
 	
`iterator upper_bound(`
`  key_type&);`
 	
`pair<iterator,iterator>`
`  equal_range(`
`    key_type&);`
 	
`const_iterator`
`  lower_bound(`
`    key_type&) const;`
 	
`const_iterator`
`  upper_bound(`
`    key_type&) const;`
 	
`pair<const_iterator,`
`  const_iterator>`
`    equal_range(`
`      key_type&) const;`
	Returns iterators referring to the first element of the specified key, one past the last element of the specified key, or both	logarithmic

Note that the collection methods `lower_bound()`, `upper_bound()`, and `equal_range()` only make sense on sorted containers. Thus the `hashmap` class does not need to provide them.

Here is the complete `hashmap` class definition. Note that the prototypes for `insert()`, `erase()`, and `find()` need to change slightly from the previous versions shown, because those initial versions don't have the right return types required for associative containers:

```cpp
template <typename Key, typename T, typename Compare = std::equal_to<Key>,
    typename Hash = DefaultHash<Key>>
class hashmap
{
    public:
        typedef Key key_type;
        typedef T mapped_type;
        typedef pair<const Key, T> value_type;
        typedef Compare key_compare;
        typedef pair<const Key, T>& reference;
        typedef const pair<const Key, T>& const_reference;
        typedef HashIterator<Key, T, Compare, Hash> iterator;
        typedef HashIterator<Key, T, Compare, Hash> const_iterator;
        typedef size_t size_type;
        typedef ptrdiff_t difference_type;
        // Required class definition for associative containers
        class value_compare :
            public std::binary_function<value_type, value_type, bool>
        {
            friend class hashmap<Key, T, Compare, Hash>;
            public:
                bool operator() (const value_type& x, const value_type& y) const
                {
                    return comp(x.first, y.first);
                }
            protected:
                Compare comp;
                value_compare(Compare c) : comp(c) {}
        };
        // The iterator class needs access to protected members of hashmap
        friend class HashIterator<Key, T, Compare, Hash>;
        // Constructors
        explicit hashmap(const Compare& comp = Compare(),
            const Hash& hash = Hash()) throw(invalid_argument);
        template <class InputIterator>
        hashmap(InputIterator first, InputIterator last,
            const Compare& comp = Compare(), const Hash& hash = Hash())
            throw(invalid_argument);
        // destructor, copy constructor, move constructor,
        // copy assignment operator and move assignment operator
        ~hashmap();
        hashmap(const hashmap<Key, T, Compare, Hash>& src);
        hashmap(hashmap<Key, T, Compare, Hash>&& src);        // C++11
        hashmap<Key, T, Compare, Hash>& operator=(
            const hashmap<Key, T, Compare, Hash>& rhs);
        hashmap<Key, T, Compare, Hash>& operator=(
```

```
            hashmap<Key, T, Compare, Hash>&& rhs);          // C++11
        // C++11 initializer list constructor
        hashmap(initializer_list<value_type> il,
            const Compare& comp = Compare(),
            const Hash& hash = Hash()) throw(invalid_argument);
        // C++11 initializer list assignment operator
        hashmap<Key, T, Compare, Hash>& operator=(
            initializer_list<value_type> il);
    // Iterator methods
    iterator begin();
    iterator end();
    const_iterator begin() const;
    const_iterator end() const;
    const_iterator cbegin() const;   // For C++11
    const_iterator cend() const;     // For C++11
    // Size methods
    bool empty() const;
    size_type size() const;
    size_type max_size() const;
        // Element insert methods
        T& operator[] (const key_type& x);
        pair<iterator, bool> insert(const value_type& x);
        iterator insert(iterator position, const value_type& x);
        template <class InputIterator>
        void insert(InputIterator first, InputIterator last);
        void insert(initializer_list<value_type> il);          // C++11
        // C++11 emplace methods
        pair<iterator, bool> emplace(value_type&& x);
        iterator emplace_hint(iterator hint, value_type&& x);
        // Element delete methods
        void erase(iterator position);
        size_type erase(const key_type& x);
        void erase(iterator first, iterator last);
    // Other modifying utilities
    void swap(hashmap<Key, T, Compare, Hash>& hashIn);
        void clear();
        // Access methods for STL conformity
        key_compare key_comp() const;
        value_compare value_comp() const;
        // Lookup methods
        iterator find(const key_type& x);
        const_iterator find(const key_type& x) const;
        size_type count(const key_type& x) const;
protected:
    typedef list<value_type> ListType;
    typename ListType::iterator findElement(
        const key_type& x, size_t& bucket) const;
    vector<ListType>* mElems;
    size_type mSize;
    Compare mComp;
    Hash mHash;
};
```

Code snippet from Hashmap\FinalHashmap\hashmap.h

hashmap Constructors

The implementation of the default constructor is shown earlier. The second constructor is a method template so that it can take an iterator range from any container, not just other `hashmaps`. If it were not a method template, it would need to specify the `InputIterator` type explicitly as `HashIterator`, limiting it to iterators from `hashmaps`. Despite the syntax, the implementation is uncomplicated: It initializes all the data members, then calls `insert()` to actually insert all the elements in the specified range:

Available for download on Wrox.com

```cpp
// Make a call to insert() to actually insert the elements.
template <typename Key, typename T, typename Compare, typename Hash>
template <class InputIterator>
hashmap<Key, T, Compare, Hash>::hashmap(
    InputIterator first, InputIterator last, const Compare& comp,
    const Hash& hash) throw(invalid_argument) : mSize(0), mComp(comp), mHash(hash)
{
    if (mHash.numBuckets() <= 0) {
        throw invalid_argument("Number of buckets must be positive");
    }
    mElems = new vector<ListType>(mHash.numBuckets());
    insert(first, last);
}
```

Code snippet from Hashmap\FinalHashmap\hashmap.cpp

`C++11`

hashmap Initializer List Constructor

C++11 supports initializer lists, which are discussed in Chapter 9. Following is the implementation of the `hashmap` constructor that takes an initializer list, which is very similar to the implementation of the constructor accepting an iterator range:

Available for download on Wrox.com

```cpp
template <typename Key, typename T, typename Compare, typename Hash>
hashmap<Key, T, Compare, Hash>::hashmap(initializer_list<value_type> il,
    const Compare& comp, const Hash& hash) throw(invalid_argument)
    : mSize(0), mComp(comp), mHash(hash)
{
    if (mHash.numBuckets() <= 0) {
        throw invalid_argument("Number of buckets must be positive");
    }
    mElems = new vector<ListType>(mHash.numBuckets());
    insert(il.begin(), il.end());
}
```

Code snippet from Hashmap\FinalHashmap\hashmap.cpp

With this initializer list constructor, a `hashmap` can be constructed in the following way:

```cpp
hashmap<string, int> myHash = {
    {"KeyOne", 100},
```

```
                {"KeyTwo", 200},
                {"KeyThree", 300}};
```

This is much nicer than using `insert()` and `make_pair()` calls:

```
    myHash.insert(make_pair("KeyOne", 100));
    myHash.insert(make_pair("KeyTwo", 200));
    myHash.insert(make_pair("KeyThree", 300));
```

C++11

hashmap Initializer List Assignment Operator

In C++11, assignment operators can also accept an initializer list on the right-hand side. Following is an implementation of an initializer list assignment operator for the `hashmap`. It deletes all the elements from the `hashmap` and then delegates the work to the `insert()` method accepting an iterator range:

Available for
download on
Wrox.com

```
template <typename Key, typename T, typename Compare, typename Hash>
hashmap<Key, T, Compare, Hash>& hashmap<Key, T, Compare, Hash>::operator=(
    initializer_list<value_type> il)
{
    clear();
    insert(il.begin(), il.end());
    return *this;
}
```

Code snippet from Hashmap\FinalHashmap\hashmap.cpp

With this assignment operator, you can write code as follows:

```
    myHash = {
        {"KeyOne", 100},
        {"KeyTwo", 200},
        {"KeyThree", 300}};
```

hashmap Insertion Operations

In the basic `hashmap` section earlier in this chapter, a simple `insert()` method was given. In this version, four `insert()` versions are provided with additional features:

➤ The simple `insert()` operation returns a `pair<iterator, bool>`, which indicates both where the item is inserted and whether or not it was newly-created.

➤ The version of `insert()` that takes a position is useless for a `hashmap`, but it is provided for symmetry with other kinds of collections. The position is ignored, and it merely calls the first version.

➤ The third form of `insert()` is a method template, so it can be used by algorithms that work on arbitrary containers.

➤ The last form of `insert()` accepts an `initializer_list<value_type>`.

The first two `insert()` methods are implemented as follows:

```
template <typename Key, typename T, typename Compare, typename Hash>
pair<typename hashmap<Key, T, Compare, Hash>::iterator, bool>
    hashmap<Key, T, Compare, Hash>::insert(const value_type& x)
{
    size_t bucket;
    // Try to find the element.
    auto it = findElement(x.first, bucket);
    if (it != (*mElems)[bucket].end()) {
        // The element already exists.
        // Convert the list iterator into a HashIterator, which
        // also requires the bucket and a pointer to the hashmap.
        HashIterator<Key, T, Compare, Hash> newIt(bucket, it, this);
        // Some compilers don't like make_pair here.
        pair<HashIterator<Key, T, Compare, Hash>, bool> p(newIt, false);
        return p;
    } else {
        // We didn't find the element, so insert a new one.
        mSize++;
        auto endIt = (*mElems)[bucket].insert((*mElems)[bucket].end(), x);
        pair<HashIterator<Key, T, Compare, Hash>, bool> p(
            HashIterator<Key, T, Compare, Hash>(bucket, endIt, this), true);
        return p;
    }
}
template <typename Key, typename T, typename Compare, typename Hash>
typename hashmap<Key, T, Compare, Hash>::iterator
    hashmap<Key, T, Compare, Hash>::insert(typename hashmap<Key, T, Compare,
    Hash>::iterator position, const value_type& x)
{
    // Completely ignore position
    return insert(x).first;
}
```

Code snippet from Hashmap\FinalHashmap\hashmap.cpp

The third form of `insert()` is a method template for the same reason as the constructor shown earlier: It should be able to insert elements by using iterators from containers of any type. The actual implementation uses an `insert_iterator`, which is described earlier in this chapter:

```
template <typename Key, typename T, typename Compare, typename Hash>
template <class InputIterator>
void hashmap<Key, T, Compare, Hash>::insert(InputIterator first,
    InputIterator last)
{
    // Copy each element in the range by using an insert_iterator
    // adapter. Give begin() as a dummy position--insert ignores it
    // anyway.
    insert_iterator<hashmap<Key, T, Compare, Hash>> inserter(*this, begin());
    copy(first, last, inserter);
}
```

Code snippet from Hashmap\FinalHashmap\hashmap.cpp

C++11 In C++11, you should implement an insert operation that accepts an initializer list, discussed in Chapter 9. The implementation for the `hashmap` is very straightforward and forwards the work to the `insert()` method accepting an iterator range:

```cpp
template <typename Key, typename T, typename Compare, typename Hash>
void hashmap<Key, T, Compare, Hash>::insert(initializer_list<value_type> il)
{
    insert(il.begin(), il.end());
}
```

Code snippet from Hashmap\FinalHashmap\hashmap.cpp

With this `insert()` method, you can write code as follows:

```cpp
myHash.insert({
    {"KeyFour", 400},
    {"KeyFive", 500}});
```

C++11 ## hashmap Emplace Operations

Emplace operations construct objects in place using the rvalue reference feature and are new to C++11. They are discussed in Chapter 12. Their implementation is straightforward in this case because we can forward the emplace operation to the correct bucket list. The `emplace()` method is implemented exactly the same as the corresponding `insert()` method, except that it calls `emplace()` on the `list` instead of `insert()`:

```cpp
template <typename Key, typename T, typename Compare, typename Hash>
pair<typename hashmap<Key, T, Compare, Hash>::iterator, bool>
    hashmap<Key, T, Compare, Hash>::emplace(value_type&& x)
{
    size_t bucket;
    // Try to find the element.
    auto it = findElement(x.first, bucket);
    if (it != (*mElems)[bucket].end()) {
        // The element already exists.
        // Convert the list iterator into a HashIterator, which
        // also requires the bucket and a pointer to the hashmap.
        HashIterator<Key, T, Compare, Hash> newIt(bucket, it, this);
        // Some compilers don't like make_pair here.
        pair<HashIterator<Key, T, Compare, Hash>, bool> p(newIt, false);
        return p;
    } else {
        // We didn't find the element, so emplace a new one.
        mSize++;
        auto endIt = (*mElems)[bucket].emplace((*mElems)[bucket].end(), x);
        pair<HashIterator<Key, T, Compare, Hash>, bool> p(
            HashIterator<Key, T, Compare, Hash>(bucket, endIt, this), true);
        return p;
    }
}
```

Code snippet from Hashmap\FinalHashmap\hashmap.cpp

The `emplace_hint()` method ignores the hint and forwards the call to the `emplace()` method. This implementation uses `std::forward` to forward x as an rvalue reference to the `emplace()` method. This is required, because a named variable, x, will normally be treated as an lvalue reference, but in this case, you want it to be treated as an rvalue reference:

```
template <typename Key, typename T, typename Compare, typename Hash>
typename hashmap<Key, T, Compare, Hash>::iterator
    hashmap<Key, T, Compare, Hash>::emplace_hint(
    typename hashmap<Key, T, Compare, Hash>::iterator hint, value_type&& x)
{
    // completely ignore hint
    return emplace(forward<value_type>(x)).first;
}
```

Code snippet from Hashmap\FinalHashmap\hashmap.cpp

hashmap Erase Operations

The version of `erase()` in the earlier section "A Basic Hashmap" is not compliant with STL requirements. You need to implement the following versions:

➤ A version that takes as a parameter a `key_type` and returns a `size_type` for the number of elements removed from the collection (for the `hashmap`, there are only two possible return values, 0 and 1)

➤ A version that erases a value at a specific iterator position, as indicated by a `HashIterator`, and returns `void`

➤ A version that erases a range of elements, based on two iterators, and returns `void`

The first version is implemented as follows:

```
template <typename Key, typename T, typename Compare, typename Hash>
typename hashmap<Key, T, Compare, Hash>::size_type
    hashmap<Key, T, Compare, Hash>::erase(const key_type& x)
{
    size_t bucket;
    // First, try to find the element.
    auto it = findElement(x, bucket);
    if (it != (*mElems)[bucket].end()) {
        // The element exists--erase it.
        (*mElems)[bucket].erase(it);
        mSize--;
        return 1;
    } else {
        return 0;
    }
}
```

Code snippet from Hashmap\FinalHashmap\hashmap.cpp

The second form of erase() must remove the element at a specific iterator position. The iterator given is, of course, a HashIterator. Thus, the hashmap must have some ability to obtain the underlying bucket and list iterator from the HashIterator. The approach we take is to make the hashmap class a friend of the HashIterator (not shown in the preceding class definition).

```cpp
template <typename Key, typename T, typename Compare, typename Hash>
void hashmap<Key, T, Compare, Hash>::erase(
    typename hashmap<Key, T, Compare, Hash>::iterator position)
{
    // Erase the element from its bucket.
    (*mElems)[position.mBucket].erase(position.mIt);
    mSize--;
}
```

Code snippet from Hashmap\FinalHashmap\hashmap.cpp

The final version of erase() removes a range of elements. It iterates from first to last, calling erase() on each element, thus letting the previous version of erase() do all the work:

```cpp
template <typename Key, typename T, typename Compare, typename Hash>
void hashmap<Key, T, Compare, Hash>::erase(
    typename hashmap<Key, T, Compare, Hash>::iterator first,
    typename hashmap<Key, T, Compare, Hash>::iterator last)
{
    typename hashmap<Key, T, Compare, Hash>::iterator cur, next;
    // Erase all the elements in the range.
    for (next = first; next != last; ) {
        cur = next++;
        erase(cur);
    }
}
```

Code snippet from Hashmap\FinalHashmap\hashmap.cpp

hashmap Clear Operation

The clear() method uses the for_each() algorithm to call clear() on the list representing each bucket:

```cpp
template <typename Key, typename T, typename Compare, typename Hash>
void hashmap<Key, T, Compare, Hash>::clear()
{
    // Call clear on each list.
    for_each(mElems->begin(), mElems->end(),
        [](ListType& e){e.clear();});
    mSize = 0;
}
```

Code snippet from Hashmap\FinalHashmap\hashmap.cpp

hashmap Accessor Operations

The standard requires access methods for the key comparison and value comparison objects. These methods must be called `key_comp()` and `value_comp()`:

Available for
download on
Wrox.com

```
template <typename Key, typename T, typename Compare, typename Hash>
typename hashmap<Key, T, Compare, Hash>::key_compare
    hashmap<Key, T, Compare, Hash>::key_comp() const
{
    return mComp;
}
template <typename Key, typename T, typename Compare, typename Hash>
typename hashmap<Key, T, Compare, Hash>::value_compare
    hashmap<Key, T, Compare, Hash>::value_comp() const
{
    return value_compare(mComp);
}
```

Code snippet from Hashmap\FinalHashmap\hashmap.cpp

The `find()` method is identical to the version shown earlier for the basic `hashmap`, except for the return code. Instead of returning a pointer to the element, it constructs a `HashIterator` referring to it:

Available for
download on
Wrox.com

```
template <typename Key, typename T, typename Compare, typename Hash>
typename hashmap<Key, T, Compare, Hash>::iterator
    hashmap<Key, T, Compare, Hash>::find(const key_type& x)
{
    size_t bucket;
    // Use the findElement() helper.
    auto it = findElement(x, bucket);
    if (it == (*mElems)[bucket].end()) {
        // We didn't find the element--return the end iterator.
        return end();
    }
    // We found the element--convert the bucket/iterator to a HashIterator.
    return HashIterator<Key, T, Compare, Hash>(bucket, it, this);
}
```

Code snippet from Hashmap\FinalHashmap\hashmap.cpp

The `const` version of `find()` is identical, so its implementation is not shown here.

The implementation of `count()` is a wrapper for `find()`, returning 1 if it finds the element, and 0 if it doesn't. The `find()` method returns the end iterator if it can't find the element. `count()` retrieves an end iterator by calling `end()` in order to compare it. Since this `hashmap` does not allow duplicate keys, `count()` always returns either 0 or 1:

Available for
download on
Wrox.com

```
template <typename Key, typename T, typename Compare, typename Hash>
typename hashmap<Key, T, Compare, Hash>::size_type
    hashmap<Key, T, Compare, Hash>::count(const key_type& x) const
{
    // There are either 1 or 0 elements matching key x.
```

```
          // If we can find a match, return 1, otherwise return 0.
          if (find(x) == end()) {
             return 0;
          } else {
             return 1;
          }
       }
```

Code snippet from Hashmap\FinalHashmap\hashmap.cpp

The final method, `operator[]`, is not required by the standard, but is provided for convenience of the programmer, and to be symmetric with `std::map`. The prototype and implementations are identical to those of the `operator[]` in the STL `map`. The comments explain the potentially confusing one-line implementation:

Available for download on Wrox.com

```
template <typename Key, typename T, typename Compare, typename Hash>
T& hashmap<Key, T, Compare, Hash>::operator[] (const key_type& x)
{
       // This definition is the same as that used by map, according to
       // the standard.
       // It's a bit cryptic, but it basically attempts to insert
       // a new key/value pair of x and a new value. Regardless of whether
       // the insert succeeds or fails, insert() returns a pair of an
       // iterator/bool. The iterator refers to a key/value pair, the
       // second element of which is the value we want to return.
       return ((insert(make_pair(x, T())))).first)->second;
}
```

Code snippet from Hashmap\FinalHashmap\hashmap.cpp

Note on Sequential Containers

The `hashmap` developed in the preceding sections is an *associative container*. However, you could also write a *sequential container*, or an *unordered associative container*, in which case you would need to follow a different set of requirements. Instead of listing them here, it's easier to point out that the `deque` container follows the prescribed sequential container requirements almost exactly. The only difference is that it provides an extra `resize()` method (not required by the standard). An example of an unordered associative container is the `unordered_map`, on which you can model your own unordered associative containers.

SUMMARY

The final example in this chapter showed almost the complete development of a `hashmap` associative container and its iterator. This `hashmap` implementation was given here to teach you how to write your own STL containers and iterators. C++11 includes its own set of unordered associative containers or hash tables. If your compiler supports those standard C++11 hash tables, you should use them instead of your own implementation.

In the process of reading this chapter, you also hopefully gained an appreciation for the steps involved in developing containers. Even if you never write another STL algorithm or container, you understand better the STL's mentality and capabilities, and you can put it to better use.

This chapter concludes the tour of the STL, Chapters 11 to 17. Even with all the details given in this book, there are still features omitted. If this material excited you, consult some of the resources in Appendix B for more information. On the other hand, we realize that the syntax and material in these chapters was dense. Don't feel compelled to use all the features discussed here. Forcing them into your programs without a true need will just complicate your code. However, we encourage you to consider incorporating aspects of the STL into your programs where they make sense. Start with the containers, maybe throw in an algorithm or two, and before you know it, you'll be a convert!

PART III
Mastering Advanced Features of C++

▶ **CHAPTER 18:** Overloading C++ Operators

▶ **CHAPTER 19:** Writing Generic Code with Templates

▶ **CHAPTER 20:** Advanced Templates

▶ **CHAPTER 21:** Effective Memory Management

▶ **CHAPTER 22:** Multithreaded Programming with C++

18

Overloading C++ Operators

WHAT'S IN THIS CHAPTER?

➤ What operator overloading is

   ➤ Rationale for overloading operators

   ➤ Limitations, caveats, and choices in operator overloading

   ➤ Summary of operators you can, cannot, and should not overload

➤ How to overload unary plus, unary minus, increment, and decrement

➤ How to overload the I/O streams operators (`operator<<` and `operator>>`)

➤ How to overload the subscripting (array index) operator

➤ How to overload the function call operator

➤ How to overload the dereferencing operators (`*` and `->`)

➤ How to write conversion operators

➤ How to overload the memory allocation and deallocation operators

C++ allows you to redefine the meanings of operators, such as +, -, and =, for your classes. Many object-oriented languages do not provide this capability, so you might be tempted to disregard its usefulness in C++. However, it can be beneficial for making your classes behave similarly to built-in types such as `ints` and `doubles`. It is even possible to write classes that look like arrays, functions, or pointers.

Chapters 3 and 4 introduce object-oriented design and operator overloading, respectively. Chapters 6 and 7 present the syntax details for objects and for basic operator overloading. This chapter picks up operator overloading where Chapter 7 left off.

This chapter focuses on the syntax and semantics of operator overloading. Practical examples are provided for most of the operators, but for a few of them, you already saw practical examples elsewhere in this book. This chapter does not repeat information which is in Chapter 7.

OVERVIEW OF OPERATOR OVERLOADING

As Chapter 1 explains, operators in C++ are symbols such as +, <, *, and <<. They work on built-in types such as `int` and `double` to allow you to perform arithmetic, logical, and other operations. There are also operators such as -> and * that allow you to dereference pointers. The concept of operators in C++ is broad, and even includes [] (array index), () (function call), casting, and the memory allocation and deallocation routines.

Operator overloading allows you to change the behavior of language operators for your classes. However, this capability comes with rules, limitations, and choices.

Why Overload Operators?

Before learning how to overload operators, you probably want to know why you would ever want to do so. The reasons vary for the different operators, but the general guiding principle is to make your classes behave like built-in types. The closer your classes are to built-in types, the easier they will be for clients to use. For example, if you want to write a class to represent fractions, it's quite helpful to have the ability to define what +, -, *, and / mean when applied to objects of that class.

The second reason to overload operators is to gain greater control over the behavior in your program. For example, you can overload memory allocation and deallocation routines for your classes to specify exactly how memory should be distributed and reclaimed for each new object.

It's important to emphasize that operator overloading doesn't necessarily make things easier for you as the class developer; its main purpose is to make things easier for clients of the class.

Limitations to Operator Overloading

Here is a list of things you cannot do when you overload operators:

> You cannot add new operator symbols. You can only redefine the meanings of operators already in the language. The table in the "Summary of Overloadable Operators" section lists all of the operators that you can overload.

> There are a few operators that you cannot overload, such as . (member access in an object), :: (scope resolution operator), `sizeof`, ?: (the ternary operator), and a few others. The table lists all the operators that you *can* overload. The operators that you can't overload are usually not those you would care to overload anyway, so we don't think you'll find this restriction limiting.

> You cannot change the *arity* of the operator. The arity describes the number of arguments, or *operands*, associated with the operator. Unary operators, such as ++, work on only one operand. Binary operators, such as +, work on two operands. There is only one ternary

operator: ?:. The main place where this limitation might bother you is when overloading []
(array brackets), discussed later in this chapter.

➤ You cannot change the *precedence* or *associativity* of the operator. These rules determine
in which order operators are evaluated in a statement. Again, this constraint shouldn't be
cause for concern in most programs because there are rarely benefits to changing the order
of evaluation.

➤ You cannot redefine operators for built-in types. The operator must be a method in a class, or
at least one of the arguments to a global overloaded operator function must be a user-defined
type (e.g., a class). This means that you can't do something ridiculous such as redefine +
for ints to mean subtraction (though you could do so for your classes). The one exception
to this rule is the memory allocation and deallocation routines; you can replace the global
routines for all memory allocations in your program.

Some of the operators already mean two different things. For example, the – operator can be used
as a binary operator, as in x = y - z; or as a unary operator, as in x = -y;. The * operator can
be used for multiplication or for dereferencing a pointer. The << operator is the insertion operator or
the left-shift operator, depending on the context. You can overload both meanings of operators with
dual meanings.

Choices in Operator Overloading

When you overload an operator, you write a function or method with the name operatorX, where
X is the symbol for some operator. For example, Chapter 7 declares operator+ for SpreadsheetCell
objects like this:

```
friend const SpreadsheetCell operator+(const SpreadsheetCell& lhs,
    const SpreadsheetCell& rhs);
```

You are allowed to put whitespace between operator and the X; "operator   X" is the same as
"operatorX". The following sections describe several choices involved in each overloaded operator
function or method you write.

Method or Global Function

First, you must decide whether your operator should be a method of your class or a global function
(usually a friend of the class). How do you choose? First, you need to understand the difference
between these two choices. When the operator is a method of a class, the left-hand side of the
operator expression must always be an object of that class. If you write a global function, the left-
hand side can be an object of a different type.

There are three different types of operators:

➤ **Operators that must be methods:** The C++ language requires some operators to be methods
of a class because they don't make sense outside of a class. For example, operator= is
tied so closely to the class that it can't exist anywhere else. The table in the "Summary of
Overloadable Operators" section lists those operators that must be methods. For these, the
choice of method or global function is simple. However, most operators do not impose this
requirement.

➤ **Operators that must be global functions:** Whenever you need to allow the left-hand side of the operator to be a variable of a different type than your class, you must make the operator a global function. This rule applies specifically to `operator<<` and `operator>>`, where the left-hand side is the `iostream` object, not an object of your class. Additionally, commutative operators like binary + and – should allow variables that are not objects of your class on the left-hand side. Chapter 7 mentions this problem.

➤ **Operators that can be either methods or global functions:** There is some disagreement in the C++ community on whether it's better to write methods or global functions to overload operators. However, we recommend the following rule: Make every operator a method unless you must make it a global function as described previously. One major advantage to this rule is that methods can be `virtual`, but `friend` functions cannot. Therefore, when you plan to write overloaded operators in an inheritance tree, you should make them methods if possible.

When you write an overloaded operator as a method, you should mark the entire method `const` if it doesn't change the object. That way, it can be called on `const` objects.

Choosing Argument Types

You are somewhat limited in your choice of argument types because you can't usually change the number of arguments (although there are exceptions, which are explained later in this chapter). For example, `operator+` must always have two arguments if it is a global function; one argument if it's a method. The compiler issues an error if it differs from this standard. In this sense, the operator functions are different from normal functions, which you can overload with any number of parameters. Additionally, although you can write the operator for whichever types you want, the choice is usually constrained by the class for which you are writing the operator. For example, if you want to implement addition for class `T`, you wouldn't write an `operator+` that takes two `string`s! The real choice arises when you try to determine whether to take parameters by value or by reference, and whether or not to make them `const`.

The choice of value vs. reference is easy: You should take every parameter by reference. As Chapters 7 and 9 explain, never pass objects by value if you can pass-by-reference instead!

The `const` decision is also trivial: Mark every parameter `const` unless you actually modify it. The table in the "Summary of Overloadable Operators" section shows sample prototypes for each operator, with the arguments marked `const` and reference as appropriate.

Choosing Return Types

C++ doesn't determine overload resolution based on return type. Thus, you can specify any return type you want when you write overloaded operators. However, just because you *can* do something doesn't mean you *should* do it. This flexibility implies that you could write confusing code in which comparison operators return pointers, and arithmetic operators return `bool`s. However, you shouldn't do that. Instead, you should write your overloaded operators such that they return the same types as the operators do for the built-in types. If you write a comparison operator, return a `bool`. If you write an arithmetic operator, return an object representing the result of the arithmetic. Sometimes the return type is not obvious at first. For example, as Chapter 6 mentions, `operator=`

should return a reference to the object on which it's called in order to support nested assignments. Other operators have similarly tricky return types, all of which are summarized in the table in the "Summary of Overloadable Operators" section.

The same choices of reference and `const` apply to return types as well. However, for return values, the choices are more difficult. The general rule for value or reference is to return a reference if you can; otherwise, return a value. How do you know when you can return a reference? This choice applies only to operators that return objects: The choice is moot for the comparison operators that return `bool`; the conversion operators that have no return type; and the function call operator, which may return any type you want. If your operator constructs a new object, then you must return that new object by value. If it does not construct a new object, you can return a reference to the object on which the operator is called, or one of its arguments. The table in the "Summary of Overloadable Operators" section shows examples.

A return value that can be modified as an *lvalue* (the left-hand side of an assignment expression) must be non-`const`. Otherwise, it should be `const`. More operators than you might think at first require that you return lvalues, including all of the assignment operators (`operator=`, `operator+=`, `operator-=`, etc.).

If you are in doubt about the appropriate return type, consult the table in the "Summary of Overloadable Operators" section.

Choosing Behavior

You can provide whichever implementation you want in an overloaded operator. For example, you could write an `operator+` that launches a game of Scrabble. However, as Chapter 4 describes, you should generally constrain your implementations to provide behaviors that clients expect. Write `operator+` so that it performs addition, or something like addition, such as string concatenation.

This chapter explains how you *should* implement your overloaded operators. In exceptional circumstances, you might want to differ from these recommendations, but, in general, you should follow the standard patterns.

Operators You Shouldn't Overload

Some operators should not be overloaded, even though it is permitted. Specifically, the address-of operator (`operator&`) is not particularly useful to overload, and leads to confusion if you do because you are changing fundamental language behavior (taking addresses of variables) in potentially unexpected ways. The entire STL, which uses operator overloading extensively, never overloads the address-of operator.

Additionally, you should avoid overloading the binary Boolean operators `operator&&` and `operator||` because you lose C++'s short-circuit evaluation rules.

Finally, you should not overload the comma operator (`operator,`). Yes, you read that correctly: there really is a comma operator in C++. It's also called the *sequencing operator*, and is used to separate two expressions in a single statement, while guaranteeing that they are evaluated left to right. There is rarely (if ever) a good reason to overload this operator.

Summary of Overloadable Operators

The following table lists the operators that you can overload, specifies whether they should be methods of the class or global `friend` functions, summarizes when you should (or should not) overload them, and provides sample prototypes showing the proper return values.

This table should be a useful reference in the future when you want to sit down and write an overloaded operator. You're bound to forget which return type you should use, and whether or not the function should be a method. We're looking forward to referring to this table ourselves.

In this table, T is the name of the class for which the overloaded operator is written, and E is a different type (not the name of the class).

OPERATOR	NAME OR CATEGORY	METHOD OR GLOBAL FRIEND FUNCTION	WHEN TO OVERLOAD	SAMPLE PROTOTYPE
operator+ operator- operator* operator/ operator%	Binary arithmetic	Global friend function recommended	Whenever you want to provide these operations for your class	`friend const T operator+(const T&, const T&);`
operator- operator+ operator~	Unary arithmetic and bitwise operators	Method recommended	Whenever you want to provide these operations for your class	`const T operator-() const;`
operator++ operator--	Pre-increment and pre-decrement	Method recommended	Whenever you overload binary + and -	`T& operator++();`
operator++ operator--	Post-increment and post-decrement	Method recommended	Whenever you overload binary + and -	`T operator++(int);`
operator=	Assignment operator	Method required	Whenever you have dynamically allocated memory in the object or want to prevent assignment, as described in Chapter 7	`T& operator=(const T&);`

OPERATOR	NAME OR CATEGORY	METHOD OR GLOBAL FRIEND FUNCTION	WHEN TO OVERLOAD	SAMPLE PROTOTYPE

`operator+=`
`operator-=`
`operator*/`
`operator/=`
`operator%=`
	Shorthand arithmetic operator assignments	Method recommended	Whenever you overload the binary arithmetic operators	`T& operator+=(const T&);`

`operator<<`
`operator>>`
`operator&`
`operator|`
`operator^`
	Binary bitwise operators	Global friend function recommended	Whenever you want to provide these operations	`friend const T operator<<(const T&, const T&);`

`operator<<=`
`operator>>=`
`operator&=`
`operator|=`
`operator^=`
	Shorthand bitwise operator assignments	Method recommended	Whenever you overload the binary bitwise operators	`T& operator<<=(const T&);`

`operator<`
`operator>`
`operator<=`
`operator>=`
`operator==`
`operator!=`
	Binary comparison operators	Global friend function recommended	Whenever you want to provide these operations	`friend bool operator<(const T&, const T&);`

`operator<<` `operator>>`	I/O stream operators (insertion and extraction)	Global friend function recommended	Whenever you want to provide these operations	`friend ostream& operator<<(ostream&, const T&);` `friend istream& operator>>(istream&, T&);`
`operator!`	Boolean negation operator	Member function recommended	Rarely; use `bool` or `void*` conversion instead	`bool operator!() const;`

continues

(continued)

OPERATOR	NAME OR CATEGORY	METHOD OR GLOBAL FRIEND FUNCTION	WHEN TO OVERLOAD	SAMPLE PROTOTYPE
operator&& operator||	Binary Boolean operators	Global friend function recommended	Rarely	`friend bool operator&&(const T& lhs, const T& rhs);`
operator[]	Subscripting (array index) operator	Method required	When you want to support subscripting	`E& operator[](int);` `const E& operator[](int) const;`
operator()	Function call operator	Method required	When you want objects to behave like function pointers	Return type and arguments can vary; see examples in this chapter
operator type()	Conversion, or cast, operators (separate operator for each type)	Method required	When you want to provide conversions from your class to other types	`operator type() const;`
operator new operator new[]	Memory allocation routines	Method recommended	When you want to control memory allocation for your classes (rarely)	`void* operator new(size_t size);` `void* operator new[](size_t size);`
operator delete operator delete[]	Memory deallocation routines	Method recommended	Whenever you overload the memory allocation routines	`void operator delete(void* ptr) noexcept;` `void operator delete[](void* ptr) noexcept;`
operator* operator->	Dereferencing operators	Method recommended for operator* Method required for operator->	Useful for smart pointers	`E& operator*() const;` `E* operator->() const;`

OPERATOR	NAME OR CATEGORY	METHOD OR GLOBAL FRIEND FUNCTION	WHEN TO OVERLOAD	SAMPLE PROTOTYPE
operator&	Address-of operator	N/A	Never	N/A
operator->*	Dereference pointer-to-member	N/A	Never	N/A
operator,	Comma operator	N/A	Never	N/A

C++11 Rvalue References

Chapter 9 discusses the new C++11 concept called *rvalue references*, written as `&&` instead of the normal lvalue references, `&`. They are demonstrated in Chapter 9 by defining *move assignment operators*, which are used by the compiler in contexts where the second object is a temporary object that will be destroyed after the assignment. The normal assignment operator from the preceding table has the following prototype:

```
T& operator=(const T&);
```

The move assignment operator has almost the same prototype, but uses an rvalue reference. It will modify the argument so it cannot be passed as `const`. Details are explained in Chapter 9:

```
T& operator=(T&&);
```

The preceding table does not include sample prototypes with rvalue reference semantics. However, for most operators it can make sense to write a version using normal lvalue references and a version using rvalue references, but whether it makes sense depends on implementation details of your class. The `operator=` is one example from Chapter 9. Another example is `operator+` to prevent unnecessary memory allocations. The `std::string` class for example implements an `operator+` using rvalue references as follows (simplified):

```
string operator+(string&& lhs, string&& rhs);
```

The implementation of this operator will reuse memory of one of the arguments because they are being passed as rvalue references, meaning both are temporary objects that will be destroyed when `operator+` is finished. The implementation of the preceding `operator+` has the following effect:

```
return std::move(lhs.append(rhs));
```

or

```
return std::move(rhs.insert(0, lhs));
```

In fact, `std::string` defines several overloaded `operator+` operators with different combinations of lvalue references and rvalue references. The following is a list of all `operator+` operators for `std::string` accepting two `strings` as arguments (simplified):

```
string operator+(const string& lhs, const string& rhs);
string operator+(string&& lhs, const string& rhs);
string operator+(const string& lhs, string&& rhs);
string operator+(string&& lhs, string&& rhs);
```

Reusing memory of one of the rvalue reference arguments is implemented in the same way as it is explained for move assignment operators in Chapter 9.

OVERLOADING THE ARITHMETIC OPERATORS

Chapter 7 shows how to write the binary arithmetic operators and the shorthand arithmetic assignment operators, but it does not cover how to overload the other arithmetic operators.

Overloading Unary Minus and Unary Plus

C++ has several unary arithmetic operators. Two of these are unary minus and unary plus. Here is an example of these operators using `ints`:

Available for
download on
Wrox.com

```
int i, j = 4;
i = -j;     // Unary minus
i = +i;     // Unary plus
j = +(-i); // Apply unary plus to the result of applying unary minus to i.
j = -(-i); // Apply unary minus to the result of applying unary minus to i.
```

Code snippet from ArithmeticOperators\SpreadsheetCellTest.cpp

Unary minus negates the operand, while unary plus returns the operand directly. The result of unary plus or minus is not an lvalue; you can't assign to it. This means you should return a `const` object when you overload them. However, note that you can apply unary plus or unary minus to the result of unary plus or unary minus. Because you're applying these operations to a `const` temporary object, you must make the unary `operator-` and `operator+` themselves `const`; otherwise, the compiler won't let you call them on the `const` temporary.

Here is an example of a `SpreadsheetCell` class definition with an overloaded unary `operator-`. Unary plus is usually an identity operation, so this class doesn't overload it:

Available for
download on
Wrox.com

```
class SpreadsheetCell
{
    public:
        // Omitted for brevity. Consult Chapter 7 for details.
        const SpreadsheetCell operator-() const;
        // Omitted for brevity. Consult Chapter 7 for details.
};
```

Code snippet from ArithmeticOperators\SpreadsheetCell.h

Here is the definition of the unary `operator-`:

```
const SpreadsheetCell SpreadsheetCell::operator-() const
{
    SpreadsheetCell newCell(*this);
    newCell.set(-mValue); // call set to update mValue and mStr
    return newCell;
}
```

Code snippet from ArithmeticOperators\SpreadsheetCell.cpp

`operator-` doesn't change the operand, so this method must construct a new `SpreadsheetCell` with the negated value, and return a copy of it. Thus, it can't return a reference.

Overloading Increment and Decrement

There are four ways to add one to a variable:

```
i = i + 1;
i += 1;
++i;
i++;
```

Code snippet from ArithmeticOperators\SpreadsheetCellTest.cpp

The last two are called the *increment* operators. The first form is *prefix increment*, which adds one to the variable, then returns the newly incremented value for use in the rest of the expression. The second form is *postfix increment*, which returns the old (non-incremented) value for use in the rest of the expression. The decrement operators function similarly.

The two possible meanings for `operator++` and `operator--` (prefix and postfix) present a problem when you want to overload them. When you write an overloaded `operator++`, for example, how do you specify whether you are overloading the prefix or the postfix version? C++ introduced a hack to allow you to make this distinction: The prefix versions of `operator++` and `operator--` take no arguments, while the postfix versions take one unused argument of type `int`.

If you want to overload these operators for your `SpreadsheetCell` class, the prototypes would look like this:

```
class SpreadsheetCell
{
    public:
        // Omitted for brevity. Consult Chapter 7 for details.
        SpreadsheetCell& operator++();     // Prefix
        SpreadsheetCell operator++(int);   // Postfix
        SpreadsheetCell& operator--();     // Prefix
        SpreadsheetCell operator--(int);   // Postfix
        // Omitted for brevity. Consult Chapter 7 for details.
};
```

Code snippet from ArithmeticOperators\SpreadsheetCell.h

The C++ standard specifies that the prefix versions of increment and decrement return an lvalue, so they can't return a `const` value. The return value in the prefix forms is the same as the end value of the operand, so prefix increment and decrement can return a reference to the object on which they are called. The postfix versions of increment and decrement, however, return values that are different from the end values of the operands, so they cannot return references.

Here are the implementations of these operators:

Available for
download on
Wrox.com

```cpp
SpreadsheetCell& SpreadsheetCell::operator++()
{
    set(mValue + 1);
    return *this;
}
SpreadsheetCell SpreadsheetCell::operator++(int)
{
    SpreadsheetCell oldCell(*this); // Save the current value before incrementing
    set(mValue + 1); // Increment
    return oldCell;  // Return the old value.
}
SpreadsheetCell& SpreadsheetCell::operator--()
{
    set(mValue - 1);
    return *this;
}
SpreadsheetCell SpreadsheetCell::operator--(int)
{
    SpreadsheetCell oldCell(*this); // Save the current value before decrementing
    set(mValue - 1); // Decrement
    return oldCell;  // Return the old value.
}
```

Code snippet from ArithmeticOperators\SpreadsheetCell.cpp

Now you can increment and decrement your `SpreadsheetCell` objects to your heart's content:

Available for
download on
Wrox.com

```cpp
SpreadsheetCell c1(4);
SpreadsheetCell c2(4);
c1++;
++c2;
```

Code snippet from ArithmeticOperators\SpreadsheetCellTest.cpp

Increment and decrement also work on pointers. When you write classes that are smart pointers or iterators, you can overload `operator++` and `operator--` to provide pointer incrementing and decrementing. This topic is covered in Chapter 17 in the context of writing your own STL iterator.

OVERLOADING THE BITWISE AND BINARY LOGICAL OPERATORS

The bitwise operators are similar to the arithmetic operators, and the bitwise shorthand assignment operators are similar to the arithmetic shorthand assignment operators. However, they are significantly less common, so we do not show examples here. The table in the "Summary of

Overloadable Operators" section shows sample prototypes, so you should be able to implement them easily if the need ever arises.

The logical operators are trickier. We don't recommend overloading && and ||. These operators don't really apply to individual types: They aggregate results of Boolean expressions. Additionally, you lose the short-circuit evaluation, because both the left-hand side and the right-hand side have to be evaluated before they can be bound to the parameters of your overloaded operator && and ||. Thus, it rarely makes sense to overload them for specific types.

OVERLOADING THE INSERTION AND EXTRACTION OPERATORS

In C++, you use operators not only for arithmetic operations, but also for reading from and writing to streams. For example, when you write `int`s and `string`s to `cout` you use the insertion operator, `<<`:

Available for
download on
Wrox.com

```
int number = 10;
cout << "The number is " << number << endl;
```

Code snippet from StreamOperators\SpreadsheetCellTest.cpp

When you read from streams you use the extraction operator, `>>`:

Available for
download on
Wrox.com

```
int number;
string str;
cin >> number >> str;
```

Code snippet from StreamOperators\SpreadsheetCellTest.cpp

You can write insertion and extraction operators that work on your classes as well, so that you can read and write them like this:

Available for
download on
Wrox.com

```
SpreadsheetCell myCell, anotherCell, aThirdCell;
cin >> myCell >> anotherCell >> aThirdCell;
cout << myCell << " " << anotherCell << " " << aThirdCell << endl;
```

Code snippet from StreamOperators\SpreadsheetCellTest.cpp

Before you write the insertion and extraction operators, you need to decide how you want to stream your class out and how you want to read it in. In this example, the `SpreadsheetCell`s will read and write `string`s.

The object on the left of an insertion or extraction operator is the `istream` or `ostream` (such as `cin` or `cout`), not a `SpreadsheetCell` object. Because you can't add a method to the `istream` or `ostream` class, you should write the insertion and extraction operators as global `friend` functions of the `SpreadsheetCell` class. The declaration of these functions in your `SpreadsheetCell` class looks like this:

```
class SpreadsheetCell
{
    public:
        // Omitted for brevity
        friend ostream& operator<<(ostream& ostr, const SpreadsheetCell&
cell);
        friend istream& operator>>(istream& istr, SpreadsheetCell& cell);
        // Omitted for brevity
};
```

Code snippet from StreamOperators\SpreadsheetCell.h

By making the insertion operator take a reference to an `ostream` as its first parameter, you allow it to be used for file output streams, string output streams, `cout`, `cerr`, and `clog`. See Chapter 15 for details. Similarly, by making the extraction operator take a reference to an `istream`, you can make it work on file input streams, string input streams, and `cin`.

The second parameter to `operator<<` and `operator>>` is a reference to the `SpreadsheetCell` object that you want to write or read. The insertion operator doesn't change the `SpreadsheetCell` it writes, so that reference can be `const`. The extraction operator, however, modifies the `SpreadsheetCell` object, requiring the argument to be a non-`const` reference.

Both operators return a reference to the stream they were given as their first argument so that calls to the operator can be nested. Remember that the operator syntax is shorthand for calling the global `operator>>` or `operator<<` functions explicitly. Consider this line:

```
cin >> myCell >> anotherCell >> aThirdCell;
```

It's actually shorthand for this line:

```
operator>>(operator>>(operator>>(cin, myCell), anotherCell), aThirdCell);
```

As you can see, the return value of the first call to `operator>>` is used as input to the next. Thus, you must return the stream reference so that it can be used in the next nested call. Otherwise, the nesting won't compile.

Here are the implementations for `operator<<` and `operator>>` for the `SpreadsheetCell` class:

```
ostream& operator<<(ostream& ostr, const SpreadsheetCell& cell)
{
    ostr << cell.mString;
    return ostr;
}
istream& operator>>(istream& istr, SpreadsheetCell& cell)
{
    string temp;
```

```
        istr >> temp;
        cell.set(temp);
        return istr;
    }
```

The trickiest part of these functions is that, in order for `mValue` to be set correctly, `operator>>` must remember to call the `set()` method on the `SpreadsheetCell` instead of setting `mString` directly.

OVERLOADING THE SUBSCRIPTING OPERATOR

Pretend for a few minutes that you have never heard of the `vector` template class in the STL, and so you have decided to write your own dynamically allocated array class. This class would allow you to set and retrieve elements at specified indices, and would take care of all memory allocation "behind the scenes." A first stab at the class definition for a dynamically allocated integer array might look like this:

```
class Array
{
    public:
        // Creates an array with a default size that will grow as needed.
        Array();
        virtual ~Array();
        // Returns the value at index x. If index x does not exist in the array,
        // throws an exception of type out_of_range.
        int getElementAt(size_t x) const;
        // Sets the value at index x to val. If index x is out of range,
        // allocates more space to make it in range.
        void setElementAt(size_t x, int val);
    protected:
        static const size_t kAllocSize = 4;
        void resize(size_t newSize);
        // Sets all elements to 0
        void initializeElements();
        int* mElems;
        size_t mSize;
    private:
        // Disallow assignment and pass-by-value
        Array(const Array& src);
        Array& operator=(const Array& rhs);
};
```

In order to present only the salient points, we have omitted exception throw lists and have not made this class a template. The interface supports setting and accessing elements. It provides random-access guarantees: A client could create an array and set elements 1, 100, and 1000 without worrying about memory management.

Here are the implementations of the methods:

```cpp
Array::Array()
{
    mSize = kAllocSize;
    mElems = new int[mSize];
    initializeElements();
}
Array::~Array()
{
    delete [] mElems;
    mElems = nullptr;
}
void Array::initializeElements()
{
    for (size_t i = 0; i < mSize; i++)
        mElems[i] = 0;
}
void Array::resize(size_t newSize)
{
    // Make a copy of the current elements pointer and size
    int* oldElems = mElems;
    size_t oldSize = mSize;
    // Create new bigger array
    mSize = newSize;           // store the new size
    mElems = new int[newSize]; // Allocate the new array of the new size
    initializeElements();      // Initialize all elements to 0

    // The new size is always bigger than the old size
    for (size_t i = 0; i < oldSize; i++) {
        // Copy the elements from the old array to the new one
        mElems[i] = oldElems[i];
    }
    delete [] oldElems; // free the memory for the old array
}
int Array::getElementAt(size_t x) const
{
    if (x < 0 || x >= mSize) {
        throw out_of_range("");
    }
    return mElems[x];
}
void Array::setElementAt(size_t x, int val)
{
    if (x < 0) {
        throw out_of_range("");
    }
    if (x >= mSize) {
        // Allocate kAllocSize past the element the client wants
        resize(x + kAllocSize);
    }
    mElems[x] = val;
}
```

Code snippet from SubscriptOperator\Array.cpp

Here is a small example of how you could use this class:

```
Array myArray;
for (size_t i = 0; i < 10; i++) {
    myArray.setElementAt(i, 100);
}
for (size_t i = 0; i < 10; i++) {
    cout << myArray.getElementAt(i) << " ";
}
```

Code snippet from SubscriptOperator\ArrayTest.cpp

As you can see, you never have to tell the array how much space you need. It allocates as much space as it requires to store the elements you give it. However, it's inconvenient to use the setElementAt() and getElementAt() methods. It would be nice to be able to use conventional array index notation like this:

```
Array myArray;
for (size_t i = 0; i < 10; i++) {
    myArray[i] = 100;
}
for (size_t i = 0; i < 10; i++) {
    cout << myArray[i] << " ";
}
```

Code snippet from SubscriptOperator\ArrayTest.cpp

This is where the overloaded subscripting operator comes in. You can replace getElementAt() and setElementAt() in your class with an operator[] like this:

```
class Array
{
    public:
        Array();
        virtual ~Array();
        int& operator[](size_t x)
    // Omitted for brevity
};
```

Code snippet from SubscriptOperator\Array.h

The preceding code using array index notation on the array now compiles. The operator[] can replace both setElementAt() and getElementAt() because it returns a reference to the element at location x. This reference can be an lvalue, so it can be used to assign to that element. Here is the implementation of the operator:

```
int& Array::operator[](size_t x)
{
    if (x < 0) {
        throw out_of_range("");
    }
```

```
        if (x >= mSize) {
            // Allocate kAllocSize past the element the client wants.
            resize(x + kAllocSize);
        }
        return mElems[x];
    }
```

Code snippet from SubscriptOperator\Array.cpp

When `operator[]` is used on the left-hand side of an assignment statement, the assignment actually changes the value at location x in the `mElems` array.

Providing Read-Only Access with operator[]

Although it's sometimes convenient for `operator[]` to return an element that can serve as an lvalue, you don't always want that behavior. It would be nice to be able to provide read-only access to the elements of the array as well, by returning a `const` value or `const` reference. Ideally, you would provide two `operator[]`s: One returns a reference and one returns a `const` reference. You might try to do this as follows:

Available for
download on
Wrox.com

```
int& operator[](size_t x);
const int& operator[](size_t x);    // BUG! Can't overload based on return type
```

Code snippet from SubscriptOperator\Array.h

However, there is one small problem: You can't overload a method or operator based only on the return type. Thus, the preceding code doesn't compile. C++ provides a way around this restriction: If you mark the second `operator[]` with the attribute `const`, then the compiler can distinguish between the two. If you call `operator[]` on a `const` object, it will use the `const operator[]`, and, if you call it on a non-const object, it will use the non-const `operator[]`. Here are the two operators with the correct prototypes:

Available for
download on
Wrox.com

```
int& operator[](size_t x);
const int& operator[](size_t x) const;
```

Code snippet from SubscriptOperator\Array.h

Here is the implementation of the `const operator[]`. It throws an exception if the index is out of range instead of trying to allocate new space. It doesn't make sense to allocate new space when you're only trying to read the element value:

Available for
download on
Wrox.com

```
const int& Array::operator[](size_t x) const
{
    if (x < 0 || x >= mSize) {
        throw out_of_range("");
    }
```

```
        return mElems[x];
    }
```

Code snippet from SubscriptOperator\Array.cpp

The following code demonstrates these two forms of `operator[]`:

```
void printArray(const Array& arr, size_t size);
int main()
{
    Array myArray;
    for (size_t i = 0; i < 10; i++) {
        myArray[i] = 100; // Calls the non-const operator[] because
                          // myArray is a non-const object.
    }
    printArray(myArray, 10);
    return 0;
}
void printArray(const Array& arr, size_t size)
{
    for (size_t i = 0; i < size; i++) {
        cout << arr[i] << " "; // Calls the const operator[] because arr is
                              // a const object.
    }
    cout << endl;
}
```

Code snippet from SubscriptOperator\ArrayTest.cpp

Note that the `const operator[]` is called in `printArray()` only because `arr` is `const`. If `arr` were not `const`, the non-const `operator[]` would be called, despite the fact that the result is not modified.

Non-Integral Array Indices

It is a natural extension of the paradigm of "indexing" into a collection by providing a key of some sort; a `vector` (or in general, any linear array) is a special case where the "key" is just a position in the array. Think of the argument of `operator[]` as providing a mapping between two domains: the domain of keys and the domain of values.

Thus, you can write an `operator[]` that uses any type as its index. This type does not need to be an integer type. This is done for the STL associative containers, like `std::map`, which are described in Chapter 12.

For example, you could create an *associative array*, in which you use `string` keys instead of integers. Here is the definition for an associative array class that stores `int`s:

```
class AssociativeArray
{
    public:
        AssociativeArray();
        virtual ~AssociativeArray();
        int& operator[](const std::string& key);
```

```
          const int& operator[](const std::string& key) const;
     protected:
          // Implementation details omitted
};
```

Implementing this class would be a good exercise for you. You can also find an implementation of this class in the downloadable source code for this book on www.wrox.com.

> *You cannot overload the subscripting operator to take more than one parameter. If you want to provide subscripting on more than one index, you can use the function call operator explained in the next section.*

OVERLOADING THE FUNCTION CALL OPERATOR

C++ allows you to overload the function call operator, written as operator(). If you write an operator() for your class, you can use objects of that class as if they were function pointers. You can only overload this operator as a non-static method in a class. Here is an example of a simple class with an overloaded operator() and a class method with the same behavior:

```
class FunctionObject
{
    public:
        int operator() (int inParam); // Function-call operator
        int doSquare(int inParam);      // Normal method
};
//Implementation of overloaded function-call operator
int FunctionObject::operator() (int inParam)
{
    return doSquare(inParam);
}
// Implementation of normal method
int FunctionObject::doSquare(int inParam)
{
    return inParam * inParam;
}
```

Here is an example of code that uses the function-call operator, contrasted with the call to a normal method of the class:

```
int x = 3, xSquared, xSquaredAgain;
FunctionObject square;
xSquared = square(x);              // Call the function-call operator
xSquaredAgain = square.doSquare(x); // Call the normal method
```

Code snippet from Functors\Functors.cpp

An object of a class with a function call operator is called a *function object*, or *functor*, for short.

At first, the function call operator probably seems a little strange. Why would you want to write a special method for a class to make objects of the class look like function pointers? Why wouldn't you just write a function or a standard method of a class? The advantage of function objects over standard methods of objects is simple: These objects can sometimes masquerade as function pointers. You can pass function objects as callback functions to routines that expect function pointers, as long as the function pointer types are templatized. This is discussed in Chapter 13.

The advantages of function objects over global functions are more intricate. There are two main benefits:

➤ Objects can retain information in their data members between repeated calls to their function-call operators. For example, a function object might be used to keep a running sum of numbers collected from each call to the function-call operator.

➤ You can customize the behavior of a function object by setting data members. For example, you could write a function object to compare an argument to the function against a data member. This data member could be configurable so that the object could be customized for whatever comparison you want.

Of course, you could implement either of the preceding benefits with global or `static` variables. However, function objects provide a cleaner way to do it, and using global or `static` variables might cause problems in a multithreaded application. The true benefits of function objects are demonstrated with the STL in Chapter 13.

By following the normal method overloading rules, you can write as many `operator()`s for your classes as you want. Specifically, the various `operator()`s must have a different number of parameters or different types of parameters. For example, you could add an `operator()` to the `FunctionObject` class that takes a `string` reference:

```
int operator() (int inParam);
void operator() (string& str);
int doSquare(int inParam);
```

Code snippet from Functors\Functors.cpp

The function call operator can also be used to provide subscripting for multiple indices of an array. Simply write an `operator()` that behaves like `operator[]` but allows more than one parameter. The only problem with this technique is that now you have to use `()` to index instead of `[]`, as in

```
myArray(3, 4) = 6;
```

OVERLOADING THE DEREFERENCING OPERATORS

You can overload three de-referencing operators: *, ->, and ->*. Ignoring ->* for the moment (we'll get back to it later), consider the built-in meanings of * and ->. * dereferences a pointer to give you direct access to its value, while -> is shorthand for a * dereference followed by a . member selection. The following code shows the equivalences:

```
SpreadsheetCell* cell = new SpreadsheetCell;
(*cell).set(5); // Dereference plus member selection
cell->set(5);   // Shorthand arrow dereference and member selection together
```

You can overload the dereferencing operators for your classes in order to make objects of the classes behave like pointers. The main use of this capability is for implementing smart pointers, introduced in Chapter 1 and discussed in detail in Chapter 21. It is also useful for iterators, which the STL uses, discussed in Chapter 12. This chapter teaches you the basic mechanics for overloading the relevant operators in the context of a simple smart pointer template class.

C++11

> *Chapter 21 discusses in detail two standard C++11 smart pointers called* std::shared_ptr *and* std::unique_ptr. *It is highly recommended to use these standard smart pointer classes instead of writing your own. The example here is given only to demonstrate how to write dereferencing operators.*

Here is the example smart pointer template class definition, without the dereference operators filled in yet:

Available for
download on
Wrox.com

```
template <typename T>
class Pointer
{
    public:
        Pointer(T* inPtr);
        virtual ~Pointer();
        // Dereference operators will go here.
    protected:
        T* mPtr;
    private:
        // Prevent assignment and pass by value.
        Pointer(const Pointer<T>& src);
        Pointer<T>& operator=(const Pointer<T>& rhs);
};
```

Code snippet from DereferenceOps\Pointer.h

This smart pointer is about as simple as you can get. All it does is store a dumb pointer, and the storage pointed to by the pointer is deleted when the smart pointer is destroyed. The implementation is equally simple: The constructor takes a real ("dumb") pointer, which is stored as the only data member in the class. The destructor frees the storage referenced by the pointer:

```
template <typename T>
Pointer<T>::Pointer(T* inPtr)
{
    mPtr = inPtr;
}
template <typename T>
Pointer<T>::~Pointer()
{
    delete mPtr;
    mPtr = nullptr;
}
```

Code snippet from DereferenceOps\Pointer.h

You would like to be able to use the smart pointer template like this:

```
Pointer<int> smartInt(new int);
*smartInt = 5; // Dereference the smart pointer.
cout << *smartInt << endl;
Pointer<SpreadsheetCell> smartCell(new SpreadsheetCell);
smartCell->set(5); // Dereference and member select the set method.
cout << smartCell->getValue() << endl;
```

Code snippet from DereferenceOps\PointerTest.cpp

As you can see from this example, you will have to provide implementations of `operator*` and `operator->` for this class. These will be implemented in the next two sections.

> *You should rarely, if ever, write an implementation of just one of* `operator*` *and* `operator->`. *You should almost always write both operators together. It would confuse the users of your class if you failed to provide both.*

Implementing operator*

When you dereference a pointer, you expect to be able to access the memory to which the pointer points. If that memory contains a simple type such as an `int`, you should be able to change its value directly. If the memory contains a more complicated type, such as an object, you should be able to access its data members or methods with the `.` operator.

To provide these semantics, you should return a reference to a variable or object from `operator*`. In the `Pointer` class, the declaration and definition look like this:

```
template <typename T>
class Pointer
{
    public:
        Pointer(T* inPtr);
        virtual ~Pointer();
        T& operator*();
```

```
            const T& operator*() const;
            // Omitted for brevity
    };
    template <typename T>
    T& Pointer<T>::operator*()
    {
        return *mPtr;
    }
```

Code snippet from DereferenceOps\Pointer.h

As you can see, `operator*` returns a reference to the object or variable to which the underlying dumb pointer points. As with overloading the subscripting operators, it's useful to provide both `const` and non-`const` versions of the method, which return a `const` reference and a non-`const` reference, respectively. The `const` version is implemented identically to the non-`const` version, so its implementation is not shown here.

Implementing operator->

The arrow operator is a bit trickier. The result of applying the arrow operator should be a member or method of an object. However, in order to implement it like that, you would have to be able to implement the equivalent of `operator*` followed by `operator.`; C++ doesn't allow you to overload `operator.` for good reason: It's impossible to write a single prototype that allows you to capture any possible member or method selection.

Therefore, C++ treats `operator->` as a special case. Consider this line:

```
    smartCell->set(5);
```

C++ translates this to:

```
    (smartCell.operator->())->set(5);
```

As you can see, C++ applies another `operator->` to whatever you return from your overloaded `operator->`. Therefore, you must return a pointer to an object, like this:

```
template <typename T>
class Pointer
{
    public:
        // Omitted for brevity
        T* operator->();
        const T* operator->() const;
        // Omitted for brevity
};
template <typename T>
T* Pointer<T>::operator->()
{
    return mPtr;
}
```

Code snippet from DereferenceOps\Pointer.h

Again, you should write both `const` and non-`const` versions of the operator. The implementation of the `const` version is identical to the non-`const`, so it is not shown here.

You may find it confusing that `operator*` and `operator->` are asymmetric, but, once you see them a few times, you'll get used to it.

What in the World Is operator ->* ?

It's perfectly legitimate in C++ to take the addresses of class members and methods in order to obtain pointers to them. However, you can't access a non-`static` member or call a non-`static` method without an object. The whole point of class members and methods is that they exist on a per-object basis. Thus, when you want to call the method or access the member via the pointer, you must dereference the pointer in the context of an object. The following example demonstrates this. Chapter 21 discusses the syntactical details in the section called "Pointers to Methods and Members." You can ignore these details for this example; the only important parts for now are the `.*` and the `->*` operators:

```
SpreadsheetCell myCell;
double (SpreadsheetCell::*methodPtr) () const = &SpreadsheetCell::getValue;
cout << (myCell.*methodPtr)() << endl;
```

Note the use of the `.*` operator to dereference the method pointer and call the method. There is also an equivalent `operator->*` for calling methods via pointers when you have a pointer to an object instead of the object itself. The operator looks like this:

```
SpreadsheetCell* myCell = new SpreadsheetCell();
double (SpreadsheetCell::*methodPtr) () const = &SpreadsheetCell::getValue;
cout << (myCell->*methodPtr)() << endl;
```

C++ does not allow you to overload `operator.*` (just as you can't overload `operator.`), but you could overload `operator->*`. However, it is very tricky, and, given that most C++ programmers don't even know that you can access methods and members through pointers, it's probably not worth the trouble. The C++11 `shared_ptr` template in the standard library, for example, does not overload `operator->*`.

WRITING CONVERSION OPERATORS

Going back to the `SpreadsheetCell` example, consider these two lines of code:

```
SpreadsheetCell cell(1.23);
string str = cell; // DOES NOT COMPILE!
```

A `SpreadsheetCell` contains a string representation, so it seems logical that you could assign it to a `string` variable. Well, you can't. The compiler tells you that it doesn't know how to convert a

SpreadsheetCell to a string. You might be tempted to try forcing the compiler to do what you want like this:

```
string str = (string)cell; // STILL DOES NOT COMPILE!
```

First, the preceding code still doesn't compile because the compiler still doesn't know *how* to convert the SpreadsheetCell to a string. It already knew from the first line what you wanted it to do, and it would do it if it could. Second, it's a bad idea in general to add gratuitous casts to your program. Even if the compiler allowed this cast to compile, it probably wouldn't do the right thing at run time. For example, it might try to interpret the bits representing your object as a string.

If you want to allow this kind of assignment, you must tell the compiler how to perform it. Specifically, you can write a conversion operator to convert SpreadsheetCells to strings. The prototype looks like this:

```
class SpreadsheetCell
{
    public:
        // Omitted for brevity
        operator string() const;
        // Omitted for brevity
};
```

Code snippet from Conversions\SpreadsheetCell\SpreadsheetCell.h

The name of the function is operator string. It has no return type because the return type is specified by the name of the operator: string. It is const because it doesn't change the object on which it is called. The implementation looks as follows:

```
SpreadsheetCell::operator string() const
{
    return mString;
}
```

Code snippet from Conversions\SpreadsheetCell\SpreadsheetCell.cpp

That's all you need to do to write a conversion operator from SpreadsheetCell to string. Now the compiler accepts the following lines and does the right thing at run time:

```
SpreadsheetCell cell(1.23);
string str = cell; // Works as expected
```

Code snippet from Conversions\SpreadsheetCell\SpreadsheetCellTest.cpp

You can write conversion operators for any type with this same syntax. For example, here is the prototype for a double conversion operator from SpreadsheetCell:

```
class SpreadsheetCell
{
    public:
        // Omitted for brevity
        operator string() const;
        operator double() const;
        // Omitted for brevity
};
```

Code snippet from Conversions\SpreadsheetCell\SpreadsheetCell.h

The implementation looks as follows:

```
SpreadsheetCell::operator double() const
{
    return mValue;
}
```

Code snippet from Conversions\SpreadsheetCell\SpreadsheetCell.cpp

Now you can write code like the following:

```
SpreadsheetCell cell(1.23);
double d1 = cell;
```

Code snippet from Conversions\SpreadsheetCell\SpreadsheetCellTest.cpp

Ambiguity Problems with Conversion Operators

Note that writing the `double` conversion operator for the `SpreadsheetCell` object introduces an *ambiguity* problem. Consider this line:

```
SpreadsheetCell cell(1.23);
double d2 = cell + 3.3; // DOES NOT COMPILE IF YOU DEFINE operator double()
```

This line now fails to compile. It worked before you wrote `operator double()`, so what's the problem now? The issue is that the compiler doesn't know if it should convert `cell` to a `double` with `operator double()` and perform `double` addition, or convert `3.3` to a `SpreadsheetCell` with the `double` constructor and perform `SpreadsheetCell` addition. Before you wrote `operator double()`, the compiler had only one choice: Convert `3.3` to a `SpreadsheetCell` with the `double` constructor and perform `SpreadsheetCell` addition. However, now the compiler could do either. It doesn't want to make a choice for you, which you might not like, so it refuses to make any choice at all.

The usual pre-C++11 solution to this conundrum is to make the constructor in question `explicit`, so that the automatic conversion using that constructor is prevented. However, we don't want that constructor to be `explicit` because we generally like the automatic conversion of `double`s to `SpreadsheetCell`s, as explained in Chapter 7. You might try to solve the problem by making the `double` conversion operator `explicit`, but this is not allowed in pre-C++11. With C++11, this is allowed, as follows:

```
explicit operator double() const;
```

Code snippet from Conversions\SpreadsheetCell\SpreadsheetCell.h

The following code demonstrates its use:

```
SpreadsheetCell cell = 6.6;                      // [1]
string str = cell;                               // [2]
double d1 = static_cast<double>(cell);           // [3]
double d2 = static_cast<double>(cell + 3.3);     // [4]
```

Code snippet from Conversions\SpreadsheetCell\SpreadsheetCellTest.cpp

The different lines in the preceding code are explained in the following list:

➤   [1] Uses the implicit conversion from a `double` to a `SpreadsheetCell`. Because this is in the declaration, this is done by calling the constructor that accepts a `double`.

➤   [2] Uses the `operator string()` conversion operator.

➤   [3] Uses the `operator double()` conversion operator. Note that because this conversion operator is now declared `explicit`, the cast is required.

➤   [4] Uses the implicit conversion of `3.3` to a `SpreadsheetCell`, followed by `operator+` on two `SpreadsheetCells`, followed by a required explicit cast to invoke `operator double()`.

Conversions for Boolean Expressions

Sometimes it is useful to be able to use objects in Boolean expressions. For example, programmers often use pointers in conditional statements like this:

```
if (ptr != nullptr) { /* Perform some dereferencing action. */ }
```

Sometimes they write shorthand conditions such as:

```
if (ptr) { /* Perform some dereferencing action. */ }
```

Other times, you see code as follows:

```
if (!ptr) { /* Do something. */ }
```

Currently, none of the preceding expressions compile with the `Pointer` smart pointer class defined earlier. However, you can add a conversion operator to the class to convert it to a pointer type. Then, the comparisons to `nullptr`, as well as the object alone in an `if` statement, will trigger the conversion to the pointer type. The usual pointer type for the conversion operator is `void*`. Here is the modified `Pointer` class:

```
template <typename T>
class Pointer
{
    public:
        // Omitted for brevity
        operator void*() const { return mPtr; }
        // Omitted for brevity
};
```

Code snippet from Conversions\Pointer\Pointer.h

Now the following code compiles and does what you expect:

```
void process(Pointer<SpreadsheetCell>& p)
{
    if (p != nullptr) { cout << "not nullptr" << endl; }
    if (p != NULL) { cout << "not NULL" << endl; }
    if (p) { cout << "not nullptr" << endl; }
    if (!p) { cout << "nullptr" << endl; }
}
int main()
{
    Pointer<SpreadsheetCell> smartCell(nullptr);
    process(smartCell);
    cout << endl;
    Pointer<SpreadsheetCell> anotherSmartCell(new SpreadsheetCell(5.0));
    process(anotherSmartCell);
}
```

Code snippet from Conversions\Pointer\PointerTest.cpp

The output is as follows:

```
nullptr

not nullptr
not NULL
not nullptr
```

Another alternative is to overload `operator bool()` instead of `operator void*()`. After all, you're using the object in a Boolean expression; why not convert it directly to a `bool`? You could write your `Pointer` class as follows:

```
template <typename T>
class Pointer
{
    public:
        // Omitted for brevity
        operator bool() const { return mPtr != nullptr; }
        // Omitted for brevity
};
```

Code snippet from Conversions\Pointer\PointerBool.h

Comparing with NULL as shown in the following code still works but might generate a compiler warning because the compiler will convert NULL to a non-pointer type int, 0:

```
if (p != NULL) { cout << "not NULL" << endl; }
```

The following comparison tests also still work as before:

```
if (p) { cout << "not nullptr" << endl; }
if (!p) { cout << "nullptr" << endl; }
```

However, with operator bool(), the following comparison with the C++11 nullptr will result in a compiler error:

```
if (p != nullptr) { cout << "not nullptr" << endl; }  // Error
```

This is correct behavior because nullptr has its own type called nullptr_t which is not automatically converted to 0. The compiler cannot find an operator!= which takes a Pointer object and a nullptr_t object. You could implement such an operator!= as a friend of the Pointer class:

```
template <typename T>
bool operator!=(const Pointer<T>& lhs, const std::nullptr_t& rhs)
{
    return lhs.mPtr != rhs;
}
```

Code snippet from Conversions\Pointer\PointerBool.h

However, after implementing this operator!=, the following comparison stops working, because the compiler doesn't know which operator!= to use: either the operator!= you have just defined, or the built-in C++ operator!=(bool,int):

```
if (p != NULL) { cout << "not NULL" << endl; }
```

From this example, you might conclude that the operator bool() technique seems only appropriate for objects that don't represent pointers and for which conversion to a pointer type really doesn't make sense. Unfortunately, adding a conversion operator to bool presents some other unanticipated consequences. C++ applies "promotion" rules to silently convert bool to int whenever the opportunity arises. Therefore, with the operator bool(), the following code compiles and runs:

```
Pointer<SpreadsheetCell> smartCell(new SpreadsheetCell);
int i = smartCell; // Converts smartCell Pointer to bool to int.
```

That's usually not behavior that you expect or desire. Thus, many programmers prefer operator void*() instead of operator bool(). In fact, Chapter 15 shows the following use of streams:

```
ifstream istr;
// Open istr
```

```
int temp;
while (istr >> temp) { /* Process temp */ }
```

In order to allow stream objects to be used in Boolean expressions, but prohibit their undesired promotion to int, the basic_ios class defines operator void*() instead of operator bool().

As you can see, there is a design element to overloading operators. Your decisions about which operators to overload directly influence the ways in which clients can use your classes.

OVERLOADING THE MEMORY ALLOCATION AND DEALLOCATION OPERATORS

C++ gives you the ability to redefine the way memory allocation and deallocation work in your programs. You can provide this customization both on the global level and the class level. This capability is most useful when you are worried about memory fragmentation, which can occur if you allocate and deallocate a lot of small objects. For example, instead of going to the default C++ memory allocation each time you need memory, you could write a memory pool allocator that reuses fixed-size chunks of memory. This section explains the subtleties of the memory allocation and deallocation routines and shows you how to customize them. With these tools, you should be able to write your own allocator if the need ever arises.

 Unless you know a lot about memory allocation strategies, attempts to overload the memory allocation routines are rarely worth the trouble. Don't overload them just because it sounds like a neat idea. Only do so if you have a genuine requirement and the necessary knowledge.

How new and delete Really Work

One of the trickiest aspects of C++ is the details of new and delete. Consider this line of code:

```
SpreadsheetCell* cell = new SpreadsheetCell();
```

The part "new SpreadsheetCell()" is called the *new-expression*. It does two things. First, it allocates space for the SpreadsheetCell object by making a call to operator new. Second, it calls the constructor for the object. Only after the constructor has completed does it return the pointer to you.

delete functions analogously. Consider this line of code:

```
delete cell;
```

This line is called the *delete-expression*. It first calls the destructor for cell, then calls operator delete to free the memory.

You can overload `operator new` and `operator delete` to control memory allocation and deallocation, but you cannot overload the *new-expression* or the *delete-expression*. Thus, you can customize the actual memory allocation and deallocation, but not the calls to the constructor and destructor.

The New-Expression and operator new

There are six different forms of the *new-expression*, each of which has a corresponding `operator new`. Earlier chapters in this book already show four new-expressions: new, new[], nothrow new, and nothrow new[]. The following list shows the corresponding four `operator new` forms from the `<new>` header file:

```
void* operator new(size_t size);                            // For new
void* operator new[](size_t size);                          // For new[]
void* operator new(size_t size, const nothrow_t&) noexcept;   // For nothrow new
void* operator new[](size_t size, const nothrow_t&) noexcept;// For nothrow new[]
```

There are two special new-expressions that do no allocation, but invoke the constructor on an existing piece of storage. These are called *placement new operators* (including both single and array forms). They allow you to construct an object in preexisting memory like this:

```
void* ptr = allocateMemorySomehow();
SpreadsheetCell* cell = new (ptr) SpreadsheetCell();
```

This feature is a bit obscure, but it's important to realize that it exists. It can come in handy if you want to implement memory pools such that you reuse memory without freeing it in between. The corresponding `operator new` forms look as follows:

```
void* operator new(size_t size, void* p) noexcept;
void* operator new[](size_t size, void* p) noexcept;
```

The Delete-Expression and operator delete

There are only two different forms of the *delete-expression* that you can call: delete, and delete[]; there are no nothrow or placement forms. However, there are all six forms of `operator delete`. Why the asymmetry? The four nothrow and placement forms are used only if an exception is thrown from a constructor. In that case, the `operator delete` is called that matches the `operator new` that was used to allocate the memory prior to the constructor call. However, if you delete a pointer normally, delete will call either `operator delete` or `operator delete[]` (never the nothrow or placement forms). Practically, this doesn't really matter: The C++ standard says that throwing an exception from delete results in undefined behavior, which means delete should never throw an exception anyway, so the nothrow version of `operator delete` is superfluous; and placement delete should be a no-op, because the memory wasn't allocated in placement `operator new`, so there's nothing to free. Here are the prototypes for the `operator delete` forms:

```
void operator delete(void* ptr) noexcept;
void operator delete[](void* ptr) noexcept;
void operator delete(void* ptr, const nothrow_t&) noexcept;
```

```
void operator delete[](void* ptr, const nothrow_t&) noexcept;
void operator delete(void* p, void*) noexcept;
void operator delete[](void* p, void*) noexcept;
```

Overloading operator new and operator delete

You can actually replace the global `operator new` and `operator delete` routines if you want.
These functions are called for every new-expression and delete-expression in the program, unless
there are more specific routines in individual classes. However, to quote Bjarne Stroustrup,
". . . replacing the global `operator new` and `operator delete` is not for the fainthearted." (*The
C++ Programming Language*, Third Edition, Addison-Wesley, 1997). We don't recommend it either!

 If you fail to heed our advice and decide to replace the global `operator new`*,
keep in mind that you cannot put any code in the operator that makes a call to*
new: *this will cause an infinite loop. For example, you cannot write a message
to the console with* cout.

A more useful technique is to overload `operator new` and `operator delete` for specific classes.
These overloaded operators will be called only when you allocate and deallocate objects of that
particular class. Here is an example of a class that overloads the four non-placement forms of
`operator new` and `operator delete`:

```
#include <new>
class MemoryDemo
{
    public:
        MemoryDemo() {}
        virtual ~MemoryDemo() {}
        void* operator new(std::size_t size);
        void operator delete(void* ptr) noexcept;
        void* operator new[](std::size_t size);
        void operator delete[](void* ptr) noexcept;
        void* operator new(std::size_t size, const std::nothrow_t&) noexcept;
        void operator delete(void* ptr, const std::nothrow_t&) noexcept;
        void* operator new[](std::size_t size, const std::nothrow_t&) noexcept;
        void operator delete[](void* ptr, const std::nothrow_t&) noexcept;
};
```

Code snippet from Memory\MemoryDemo.h

Here are simple implementations of these operators that pass the argument through to calls to the
global versions of the operators. Note that `nothrow` is actually a variable of type `nothrow_t`:

```
void* MemoryDemo::operator new(size_t size)
{
    cout << "operator new" << endl;
    return ::operator new(size);
}
```

```cpp
void MemoryDemo::operator delete(void* ptr) noexcept
{
    cout << "operator delete" << endl;
    ::operator delete(ptr);
}
void* MemoryDemo::operator new[](size_t size)
{
    cout << "operator new[]" << endl;
    return ::operator new[](size);
}
void MemoryDemo::operator delete[](void* ptr) noexcept
{
    cout << "operator delete[]" << endl;
    ::operator delete[](ptr);
}
void* MemoryDemo::operator new(size_t size, const nothrow_t&) noexcept
{
    cout << "operator new nothrow" << endl;
    return ::operator new(size, nothrow);
}
void MemoryDemo::operator delete(void* ptr, const nothrow_t&) noexcept
{
    cout << "operator delete nothrow" << endl;
    ::operator delete[](ptr, nothrow);
}
void* MemoryDemo::operator new[](size_t size, const nothrow_t&) noexcept
{
    cout << "operator new[] nothrow" << endl;
    return ::operator new[](size, nothrow);
}
void MemoryDemo::operator delete[](void* ptr, const nothrow_t&) noexcept
{
    cout << "operator delete[] nothrow" << endl;
    ::operator delete[](ptr, nothrow);
}
```

Code snippet from Memory\MemoryDemo.cpp

Here is some code that allocates and frees objects of this class in several ways:

```cpp
MemoryDemo* mem = new MemoryDemo();
delete mem;
mem = new MemoryDemo[10];
delete [] mem;
mem = new (nothrow) MemoryDemo();
delete mem;
mem = new (nothrow) MemoryDemo[10];
delete [] mem;
```

Code snippet from Memory\MemoryDemoTest.cpp

Here is the output from running the program:

```
operator new
operator delete
operator new[]
operator delete[]
operator new nothrow
operator delete
operator new[] nothrow
operator delete[]
```

These implementations of `operator new` and `operator delete` are obviously trivial and not particularly useful. They are intended only to give you an idea of the syntax in case you ever want to implement nontrivial versions of them.

> *Whenever you overload* `operator new`, *overload the corresponding form of* `operator delete`. *Otherwise, memory will be allocated as you specify but freed according to the built-in semantics, which may not be compatible.*

It might seem overkill to overload all of the various forms of `operator new`. However, it's generally a good idea to do so in order to prevent inconsistencies in the memory allocations. If you don't want to provide implementations, you can declare the function as `protected` or `private` in order to prevent anyone from using it.

> *Overload all forms of* `operator new`, *or provide* `private` *declarations without implementations for the forms that you don't want to get used.*

Overloading operator new and operator delete with Extra Parameters

In addition to overloading the standard forms of `operator new`, you can write your own versions with extra parameters. For example, here is the MemoryDemo class showing an additional `operator new` and `operator delete` with an extra integer parameter:

Available for
download on
Wrox.com

```cpp
#include <new>
class MemoryDemo
{
    public:
        // Omitted for brevity
        void* operator new(std::size_t size, int extra);
        void operator delete(void* ptr, int extra) noexcept;
};
```

Code snippet from Memory\MemoryDemo.h

The implementation is as follows:

```cpp
void* MemoryDemo::operator new(size_t size, int extra)
{
    cout << "operator new with extra int arg" << endl;
    return ::operator new(size);
}
void MemoryDemo::operator delete(void* ptr, int extra) noexcept
{
    cout << "operator delete with extra int arg" << endl;
    return ::operator delete(ptr);
}
```

Code snippet from Memory\MemoryDemo.cpp

When you write an overloaded `operator new` with extra parameters, the compiler will automatically allow the corresponding new-expression. So, you can now write code like this:

```cpp
MemoryDemo* memp = new(5) MemoryDemo();
delete memp;
```

Code snippet from Memory\MemoryDemoTest.cpp

The extra arguments to `new` are passed with function call syntax (as in `nothrow new`). These extra arguments can be useful for passing various flags or counters to your memory allocation routines. For example, some runtime libraries use this in debug mode to provide the file name and line number where an object is allocated, so when there is a memory leak, the offending line that did the allocation can be identified.

When you define an `operator new` with extra parameters, you should also define the corresponding `operator delete` with the same extra parameters. You cannot call this `operator delete` with extra parameters yourself, but it will be called only when you use your `operator new` with extra parameters and the constructor of your object throws an exception.

An alternate form of `operator delete` gives you the size of the memory that should be freed as well as the pointer. Simply declare the prototype for `operator delete` with an extra size parameter.

If your class declares two identical versions of `operator delete` *except that one takes the size parameter and the other doesn't, the version without the size parameter will always get called. If you want the version with the size to be used, write only that version.*

You can replace `operator delete` with the version that takes a size for any of the versions of `operator delete` independently. Here is the `MemoryDemo` class definition with the first `operator delete` modified to take the size of the memory to be deleted:

```
#include <new>
class MemoryDemo
{
    public:
        MemoryDemo() {}
        virtual ~MemoryDemo() {}
        void* operator new(std::size_t size);
        void operator delete(void* ptr, std::size_t size) noexcept;
        // Omitted for brevity
};
```

Code snippet from Memory\MemoryDemo.h

The implementation of this `operator delete` calls the global `operator delete` without the size parameter because there is no global `operator delete` that takes the size:

```
void MemoryDemo::operator delete(void* ptr, size_t size) noexcept
{
    cout << "operator delete with size" << endl;
    ::operator delete(ptr);
}
```

Code snippet from Memory\MemoryDemo.cpp

This capability is useful only if you are writing a complicated memory allocation and deallocation scheme for your classes.

C++11 Explicitly Deleting/Defaulting operator new and operator delete

Chapter 6 shows how you can explicitly delete or default a constructor or assignment operator. Explicitly deleting or defaulting is not limited to constructors and assignment operators. For example, the following class deletes the `operator new` and `new[]`, which means that this class cannot be dynamically created by using `new` or `new[]`:

```
#include <new>
class MyClass
{
    public:
        void* operator new(std::size_t size) = delete;
        void* operator new[](std::size_t size) = delete;
};
```

Code snippet from Memory\ExplicitDelete\ExplicitDelete.cpp

Using this class in the following ways will result in compiler errors:

```
int main()
{
    MyClass* p1 = new MyClass;
    MyClass* pArray = new MyClass[2];
    return 0;
}
```

Code snippet from Memory\ExplicitDelete\ExplicitDelete.cpp

SUMMARY

This chapter summarized the rationale for operator overloading and provided examples and explanations for overloading the various categories of operators. We hope that this chapter taught you to appreciate the power that it gives you.

Throughout this book, operator overloading is used to provide abstractions, including iterators in Chapter 17 and smart pointers in Chapter 21.

The next chapter starts an in-depth discussion of another advanced C++ feature called templates.

19

Writing Generic Code with Templates

WHAT'S IN THIS CHAPTER?

- ➤ How to write template classes
- ➤ How the compiler processes templates
- ➤ How to organize template source code
- ➤ How to use non-type template parameters
- ➤ How to write templates of individual class methods
- ➤ How to write customizations of your class templates for specific types
- ➤ How to combine templates and inheritance
- ➤ How to write function templates
- ➤ How to make template functions friends of template classes
- ➤ How to write template aliases

C++ provides language support not only for object-oriented programming, but also for *generic programming*. As discussed in Chapter 4, the goal of generic programming is to write reusable code. The fundamental tools for generic programming in C++ are *templates*. Although not strictly an object-oriented feature, templates can be combined with object-oriented programming for powerful results. Many programmers consider templates to be the most difficult part of C++ and, for that reason, tend to avoid them.

This chapter provides the code details for fulfilling the design principle of generality discussed in Chapter 4 and used during the discussion of the standard template library in Chapters 11 through 17.

The next chapter delves into some of the more advanced template features, including:

➤ The three kinds of template parameters and their subtleties

➤ Partial specialization

➤ Function template deduction

➤ How to exploit template recursion

➤ Variadic templates

➤ Metaprogramming

OVERVIEW OF TEMPLATES

The main programming unit in the procedural paradigm is the *procedure* or *function*. Functions are useful primarily because they allow you to write algorithms that are independent of specific values and can thus be reused for many different values. For example, the sqrt() function in C and C++ calculates the square root of a value supplied by the caller. A square root function that calculated only the square root of one number, like four, would not be particularly useful! The sqrt() function is written in terms of a *parameter*, which is a stand-in for whatever value the caller passes. Computer scientists say that functions *parameterize* values.

The object-oriented programming paradigm adds the concept of *objects*, which group related data and behaviors, but does not change the way functions and methods parameterize values.

Templates take the concept of parameterization a step further to allow you to parameterize on *types* as well as *values*. Types in C++ include primitives such as int and double, as well as user-defined classes such as SpreadsheetCell and CherryTree. With templates you can write code that is independent not only of the values it will be given, but also of the types of those values. For example, instead of writing separate stack classes to store ints, Cars, and SpreadsheetCells, you can write one stack class definition that can be used for any of those types.

Although templates are an amazing language feature, templates in C++ are syntactically confusing, and many programmers overlook or avoid them.

This chapter will teach you about template support in C++ with an emphasis on the aspects that arise in the STL. Along the way, you will learn about some nifty features that you can employ in your programs aside from using the standard library.

CLASS TEMPLATES

Class templates define a class where the types of some of the variables, methods and/or parameters to the methods are specified as parameters. Class templates are useful primarily for containers, or data structures, that store objects. This section uses a running example of a Grid container. In order to keep the examples reasonable in length and simple enough to illustrate specific points, different sections of the chapter will add features to the Grid container that are not used in subsequent sections.

Writing a Class Template

Suppose that you want a generic game board class that you can use as a chessboard, checkers board, Tic-Tac-Toe board, or any other two-dimensional game board. In order to make it general-purpose, you should be able to store chess pieces, checkers pieces, Tic-Tac-Toe pieces, or any type of game piece.

Coding without Templates

Without templates, the best approach to build a generic game board is to employ polymorphism to store generic GamePiece objects. Then, you could subclass the pieces for each game from the GamePiece class. For example, in the chess game, the ChessPiece would be a subclass of GamePiece. Through polymorphism, the GameBoard, written to store GamePieces, can also store ChessPieces. Your class definition might look similar to the Spreadsheet class from Chapter 7, which used a dynamically allocated two-dimensional array as the underlying grid structure:

Available for download on Wrox.com

```
class GameBoard
{
    public:
        // The general-purpose GameBoard allows the user to specify its dimensions
        GameBoard(size_t inWidth = kDefaultWidth,
                  size_t inHeight = kDefaultHeight);
        GameBoard(const GameBoard& src); // Copy constructor
        virtual ~GameBoard();
        GameBoard& operator=(const GameBoard& rhs); // Assignment operator
        void setPieceAt(size_t x, size_t y, const GamePiece& inPiece);
        GamePiece& getPieceAt(size_t x, size_t y);
        const GamePiece& getPieceAt(size_t x, size_t y) const;
        size_t getHeight() const { return mHeight; }
        size_t getWidth() const { return mWidth; }
        static const size_t kDefaultWidth = 10;
        static const size_t kDefaultHeight = 10;
    protected:
        void copyFrom(const GameBoard& src);
        // Objects dynamically allocate space for the game pieces.
        GamePiece** mCells;
        size_t mWidth, mHeight;
};
```

Code snippet from GameBoard\GameBoard.h

getPieceAt() returns a reference to the piece at a specified spot instead of a copy of the piece. The GameBoard serves as an abstraction of a two-dimensional array, so it should provide array access semantics by giving the actual object at an index, not a copy of the object. Returning a reference from getPieceAt() works perfectly in this example. However, you should be careful when you write a method that returns something by reference, to make sure the reference stays valid. For example, if the GameBoard class would support a resize() method, this method would reallocate memory for mCells. By doing this, all references previously returned from getPieceAt() would become invalid. So, client code should not store such a reference for future use, but should call getPieceAt() right before using the returned reference.

> *This implementation of the class provides two versions of* getPieceAt(), *one of which returns a reference and one of which returns a* const *reference.*

Here are the method definitions. The implementation is almost identical to the Spreadsheet class from Chapter 7. Production code would, of course, perform bounds checking in setPieceAt() and getPieceAt(). That code is omitted because it is not the point of this chapter:

Available for
download on
Wrox.com

```cpp
GameBoard::GameBoard(size_t inWidth, size_t inHeight) :
    mWidth(inWidth), mHeight(inHeight)
{
    mCells = new GamePiece* [mWidth];
    for (size_t i = 0; i < mWidth; i++) {
        mCells[i] = new GamePiece[mHeight];
    }
}
GameBoard::GameBoard(const GameBoard& src)
{
    copyFrom(src);
}
GameBoard::~GameBoard()
{
    // Free the old memory
    for (size_t i = 0; i < mWidth; i++) {
        delete [] mCells[i];
    }
    delete [] mCells;
    mCells = nullptr;
}
void GameBoard::copyFrom(const GameBoard& src)
{
    mWidth = src.mWidth;
    mHeight = src.mHeight;
    mCells = new GamePiece* [mWidth];
    for (size_t i = 0; i < mWidth; i++) {
        mCells[i] = new GamePiece[mHeight];
    }
    for (size_t i = 0; i < mWidth; i++) {
        for (size_t j = 0; j < mHeight; j++) {
            mCells[i][j] = src.mCells[i][j];
        }
    }
}
GameBoard& GameBoard::operator=(const GameBoard& rhs)
{
    // Check for self-assignment
    if (this == &rhs) {
        return *this;
    }
    // Free the old memory
    for (size_t i = 0; i < mWidth; i++) {
        delete [] mCells[i];
    }
}
```

```
        delete [] mCells;
        mCells = nullptr;
        // Copy the new memory
        copyFrom(rhs);
        return *this;
    }
    void GameBoard::setPieceAt(size_t x, size_t y, const GamePiece& inElem)
    {
        mCells[x][y] = inElem;
    }
    GamePiece& GameBoard::getPieceAt(size_t x, size_t y)
    {
        return mCells[x][y];
    }
    const GamePiece& GameBoard::getPieceAt(size_t x, size_t y) const
    {
        return mCells[x][y];
    }
```

Code snippet from GameBoard\GameBoard.cpp

This GameBoard class works pretty well. Assuming that you wrote a ChessPiece class, you can create GameBoard objects and use them like this:

```
GameBoard chessBoard(8, 8);
ChessPiece pawn;
chessBoard.setPieceAt(0, 0, pawn);
```

A Template Grid Class

The GameBoard class in the previous section is nice, but insufficient. For example, it's quite similar to the Spreadsheet class from Chapter 7, but the only way you could use it as a spreadsheet would be to make the SpreadsheetCell class a subclass of GamePiece. That doesn't make sense because it doesn't fulfill the is-a principle of inheritance: A SpreadsheetCell is not a GamePiece. It would be nice if you could write a generic Grid class that you could use for purposes as diverse as a Spreadsheet or a ChessBoard. In C++, you can do this by writing a *class template*, which allows you to write a class without specifying one or more types. Clients then *instantiate* the template by specifying the types they want to use.

The Grid Class Definition

In order to understand class templates, it is helpful to examine the syntax. The following example shows how you can tweak your GameBoard class slightly to make a templatized Grid class. Don't let the syntax scare you — it's all explained following the code. Note that the class name has changed from GameBoard to Grid, and setPieceAt() and getPieceAt() have changed to setElementAt() and getElementAt() to reflect the class' more generic nature:

Available for
download on
Wrox.com

```
template <typename T>
class Grid
{
    public:
        Grid(size_t inWidth = kDefaultWidth, size_t inHeight = kDefaultHeight);
```

```
            Grid(const Grid<T>& src);
            virtual ~Grid();
            Grid<T>& operator=(const Grid<T>& rhs);
            void setElementAt(size_t x, size_t y, const T& inElem);
            T& getElementAt(size_t x, size_t y);
            const T& getElementAt(size_t x, size_t y) const;
            size_t getHeight() const { return mHeight; }
            size_t getWidth() const { return mWidth; }
            static const size_t kDefaultWidth = 10;
            static const size_t kDefaultHeight = 10;
        protected:
            void copyFrom(const Grid<T>& src);
            T** mCells;
            size_t mWidth, mHeight;
    };
```

Code snippet from Grid\Grid.h

Now that you've seen the full class definition, take another look at it, one line at a time:

```
template <typename T>
```

This first line says that the following class definition is a template on one type. Both `template` and `typename` are keywords in C++. As discussed earlier, templates "parameterize" types the same way that functions "parameterize" values. Just as you use parameter names in functions to represent the arguments that the caller will pass, you use type names (such as `T`) in templates to represent the types that the caller will specify. There's nothing special about the name `T` — you can use whatever name you want. Traditionally, when a single type is used, it is called `T`, but that's just a historical convention, like calling the integer that indexes an array `i` or `j`.

 For historical reasons, you can use the keyword `class` *instead of* `typename` *to specify template type parameters. Thus, many books and existing programs use syntax like this:* `template <class T>`. *However, the use of the word "class" in this context is confusing because it implies that the type must be a class, which is not true. The type can be a class, a struct, a union, a primitive type of the language like* `int` *or* `double`, *and so on.*

The template specifier holds for the entire statement, which in this case is the class definition.

Several lines further, the copy constructor looks like this:

```
Grid(const Grid<T>& src);
```

As you can see, the type of the `src` parameter is no longer a `const Grid&`, but a `const Grid<T>&`. When you write a class template, what you used to think of as the class name (`Grid`) is actually the *template name*. When you want to talk about actual `Grid` classes or types, you discuss them as *instantiations* of the `Grid` class template for a certain type, such as `int`, `SpreadsheetCell`, or `ChessPiece`. At the point where you define the template, you haven't specified the type it will be instantiated for, so you must use a stand-in template parameter, `T`, for whatever type might be used later. Thus, when you need to refer to a type for a `Grid` object as a parameter to, or return value from, a method you must use `Grid<T>`. You can also see this change with the parameter to, and return value from, the assignment operator, and the parameter to the `copyFrom()` method.

Within a class definition, the compiler will interpret `Grid` as `Grid<T>` where needed. However, it's best to get in the habit of specifying `Grid<T>` explicitly because that's the syntax you use outside the class to refer to types generated from the template. Only for constructors and the destructor, you should use `Grid` and not `Grid<T>`.

The final change to the class is that methods such as `setElementAt()` and `getElementAt()` now take and return parameters and values of type `T` instead of type `GamePiece`:

```
void setElementAt(size_t x, size_t y, const T& inElem);
T& getElementAt(size_t x, size_t y);
const T& getElementAt(size_t x, size_t y) const;
```

This type `T` is a placeholder for whatever type the user specifies. `mCells` is now a `T**` instead of a `GamePiece**` because it will point to a dynamically allocated two-dimensional array of `T`s, for whatever type `T` the user specifies.

The Grid Class Method Definitions

The `template <typename T>` specifier must precede each method definition for the `Grid` template. The constructor looks like this:

Available for download on Wrox.com

```
template <typename T>
Grid<T>::Grid(size_t inWidth, size_t inHeight) : mWidth(inWidth),
mHeight(inHeight)
{
    mCells = new T* [mWidth];
    for (size_t i = 0; i < mWidth; i++) {
        mCells[i] = new T[mHeight];
    }
}
```

Code snippet from Grid\Grid.h

 Templates require you to put the implementation of the methods in the header file itself, because the compiler needs to know the complete definition including the definition of methods before it can create an instance of the template. This is discussed in more details later in this chapter.

Note that the class name before the `::` is `Grid<T>`, not `Grid`. You must specify `Grid<T>` as the class name in all your methods and `static` data member definitions. The body of the constructor is identical to the `GameBoard` constructor except that the placeholder type `T` replaces the `GamePiece` type.

The rest of the method definitions are also similar to their equivalents in the GameBoard class with the exception of the appropriate template and Grid<T> syntax changes:

```cpp
template <typename T>
Grid<T>::Grid(const Grid<T>& src)
{
    copyFrom(src);
}
template <typename T>
Grid<T>::~Grid()
{
    // Free the old memory.
    for (size_t i = 0; i < mWidth; i++) {
        delete [] mCells[i];
    }
    delete [] mCells;
    mCells = nullptr;
}
template <typename T>
void Grid<T>::copyFrom(const Grid<T>& src)
{
    mWidth = src.mWidth;
    mHeight = src.mHeight;
    mCells = new T* [mWidth];
    for (size_t i = 0; i < mWidth; i++) {
        mCells[i] = new T[mHeight];
    }
    for (size_t i = 0; i < mWidth; i++) {
        for (size_t j = 0; j < mHeight; j++) {
            mCells[i][j] = src.mCells[i][j];
        }
    }
}
template <typename T>
Grid<T>& Grid<T>::operator=(const Grid<T>& rhs)
{
    // Check for self-assignment.
    if (this == &rhs) {
        return *this;
    }
    // Free the old memory.
    for (size_t i = 0; i < mWidth; i++) {
        delete [] mCells[i];
    }
    delete [] mCells;
    mCells = nullptr;
    // Copy the new memory.
    copyFrom(rhs);
    return *this;
}
template <typename T>
void Grid<T>::setElementAt(size_t x, size_t y, const T& inElem)
{
    mCells[x][y] = inElem;
}
```

```
template <typename T>
T& Grid<T>::getElementAt(size_t x, size_t y)
{
    return mCells[x][y];
}
template <typename T>
const T& Grid<T>::getElementAt(size_t x, size_t y) const
{
    return mCells[x][y];
}
```

Code snippet from Grid\Grid.h

Using the Grid Template

When you want to create grid objects, you cannot use Grid alone as a type; you must specify the type that will be stored in that Grid. Creating an object of a template class for a specific type is called *instantiating the template*. Here is an example:

Available for
download on
Wrox.com

```
Grid<int> myIntGrid; // declares a grid that stores ints,
                     // using default parameters for the constructor
Grid<double> myDoubleGrid(11, 11); // declares an 11x11 Grid of doubles
myIntGrid.setElementAt(0, 0, 10);
int x = myIntGrid.getElementAt(0, 0);
Grid<int> grid2(myIntGrid);
Grid<int> anotherIntGrid = grid2;
```

Code snippet from Grid\GridTest.cpp

Note that the type of myIntGrid, grid2, and anotherIntGrid is Grid<int>. You cannot store SpreadsheetCells or ChessPieces in these grids; the compiler will generate an error if you try to do so.

The type specification is important; neither of the following two lines compiles:

```
Grid test;    // WILL NOT COMPILE
Grid<> test; // WILL NOT COMPILE
```

The first causes your compiler to complain with something like, "use of class template requires template argument list." The second causes it to say something like, "wrong number of template arguments."

If you want to declare a function or method that takes a Grid object, you must specify the type stored in that grid as part of the Grid type:

Available for
download on
Wrox.com

```
void processIntGrid(Grid<int>& inGrid)
{
    // Body omitted for brevity
}
```

Code snippet from Grid\GridTest.cpp

Instead of writing the full `Grid` *type everytime, for example* `Grid<int>`, *you can use a* `typedef` *to give it an easier name:*

```
typedef Grid<int> IntGrid;
```

Now you can write code as follows:

```
void processIntGrid(IntGrid& inGrid) { }
```

The `Grid` template can store more than just `ints`. For example, you can instantiate a `Grid` that stores `SpreadsheetCells`:

```
Grid<SpreadsheetCell> mySpreadsheet;
SpreadsheetCell myCell;
mySpreadsheet.setElementAt(3, 4, myCell);
```

Code snippet from Grid\GridTest.cpp

You can store pointer types as well:

```
Grid<char*> myStringGrid;
myStringGrid.setElementAt(2, 2, "hello");
```

Code snippet from Grid\GridTest.cpp

The type specified can even be another template type. The following example uses the `vector` template from the standard template library (introduced in Chapter 1):

```
Grid<vector<int>> gridOfVectors;
vector<int> myVector;
gridOfVectors.setElementAt(5, 6, myVector);
```

Code snippet from Grid\GridTest.cpp

You can also dynamically allocate `Grid` template instantiations on the heap:

```
Grid<int>* myGridp = new Grid<int>(); // creates Grid with default width/ height
myGridp->setElementAt(0, 0, 10);
int x = myGridp->getElementAt(0, 0);
delete myGridp;
```

Code snippet from Grid\GridTest.cpp

How the Compiler Processes Templates

In order to understand the intricacies of templates, you need to learn how the compiler processes template code. When the compiler encounters template method definitions, it performs syntax checking, but doesn't actually compile the templates. It can't compile template definitions because it doesn't know for which types they will be used. It's impossible for a compiler to generate code for something like x = y without knowing the types of x and y.

When the compiler encounters an instantiation of the template, such as Grid<int> myIntGrid, it writes code for an int version of the Grid template by replacing each T in the template class definition with int. When the compiler encounters a different instantiation of the template, such as Grid<SpreadsheetCell> mySpreadsheet, it writes another version of the Grid class for SpreadsheetCells. The compiler just writes the code that you would write if you didn't have template support in the language and had to write separate classes for each element type. There's no magic here; templates just automate an annoying process. If you don't instantiate a class template for any types in your program, then the class method definitions are never compiled.

This instantiation process explains why you need to use the Grid<T> syntax in various places in your definition. When the compiler instantiates the template for a particular type, such as int, it replaces T with int, so that Grid<int> is the type.

Selective Instantiation

The compiler generates code only for the class methods that you actually call for a particular type. For example, given the preceding Grid template class, suppose that you write this code (and only this code) in main():

```
Grid<int> myIntGrid;
myIntGrid.setElementAt(0, 0, 10);
```

The compiler generates only the 0-argument constructor, the destructor, and the setElementAt() method for an int version of the Grid. It does not generate other methods like the copy constructor, the assignment operator, or getHeight().

Template Requirements on Types

When you write code that is independent of types, you must assume certain things about those types. For example, in the Grid template, you assume that the element type (represented by T) will have an assignment operator because of this line: mCells[x][y] = inElem. Similarly, you assume it will have a default constructor to allow you to create an array of elements.

If you attempt to instantiate a template with a type that does not support all the operations used by the template in your particular program, the code will not compile, and the error messages will almost always be quite obscure. However, even if the type you want to use doesn't support the operations required by all the template code, you can exploit selective instantiation to use some methods but not others. For example, if you try to create a grid for an object that has no assignment operator, but you never call setElementAt() on that grid, your code will work fine. As soon as you try to call setElementAt(), however, you will receive a compilation error.

Distributing Template Code between Files

Normally you put class definitions in a header file and method definitions in a source file. Code that creates or uses objects of the class #includes the header file and obtains access to the method code via the linker. Templates don't work that way. Because they are "templates" for the compiler to generate the actual methods for the instantiated types, both template class definitions and method definitions must be available to the compiler in any source file that uses them. There are several mechanisms to obtain this inclusion.

Template Definitions in Header Files

You can place the method definitions directly in the same header file where you define the class itself. When you #include this file in a source file where you use the template, the compiler will have access to all the code it needs.

Alternatively, you can place the template method definitions in a separate header file that you #include in the header file with the class definitions. Make sure the #include for the method definitions follows the class definition; otherwise the code won't compile.

Available for download on Wrox.com

```
template <typename T>
class Grid
{
    // Class definition omitted for brevity
};
#include "GridDefinitions.h"
```

Code snippet from Grid\MethodsInSeparateHeader\Grid.h

Any client that wants to use the Grid template needs only to include the Grid.h header file. This division helps keep the distinction between class definitions and method definitions.

Template Definitions in Source Files

Method implementations look strange in header files. If that syntax annoys you, there is a way that you can place the method definitions in a source file. However, you still need to make the definitions available to the code that uses the templates, which you can do by #includeing the method implementation *source* file in the template class definition header file. That sounds odd if you've never seen it before, but it's legal in C++. The header file looks like this:

Available for download on Wrox.com

```
template <typename T>
class Grid
{
    // Class definition omitted for brevity
};
#include "Grid.cpp"
```

Code snippet from Grid\MethodsInSource\Grid.h

When using this technique, make sure you don't add the `Grid.cpp` file to your project, because it is not supposed to be, and cannot be compiled separately; it should only be `#included` in a header file.

You can actually call your file with method implementations anything you want. Some programmers like to give source files that are included an `.inl` extension, for example `Grid.inl`.

The pre-C++11 standard actually defined a way for template method definitions to exist in a source file, which does not need to be `#included` in a header file. You use the `export` keyword to specify that the template definitions should be available in all *translation units* (source files). However, this is not allowed anymore in C++11.

Template Parameters

In the `Grid` example, the `Grid` template has one *template parameter*: the type that is stored in the grid. When you write the class template, you specify the parameter list inside the angle brackets, like this:

```
template <typename T>
```

This parameter list is similar to the parameter list in a function or method. As in functions and methods, you can write a class with as many template parameters as you want. Additionally, these parameters don't have to be types, and they can have default values.

Non-Type Template Parameters

Non-type parameters are "normal" parameters such as `int`s and pointers: the kind of parameters with which you're familiar from functions and methods. However, non-type template parameters can only be integral types (`char`, `int`, `long`...), enumeration types, pointers and references.

In the `Grid` template class, you could use non-type template parameters to specify the height and width of the grid instead of specifying them in the constructor. The principle advantage to specifying non-type parameters in the template list instead of in the constructor is that the values are known before the code is compiled. Recall that the compiler generates code for templatized methods by substituting in the template parameters before compiling. Thus, you can use a normal two-dimensional array in your implementation instead of dynamically allocating it. Here is the new class definition:

Available for download on Wrox.com

```
template <typename T, size_t WIDTH, size_t HEIGHT>
class Grid
{
    public:
        void setElementAt(size_t x, size_t y, const T& inElem);
        T& getElementAt(size_t x, size_t y);
        const T& getElementAt(size_t x, size_t y) const;
        size_t getHeight() const { return HEIGHT; }
        size_t getWidth() const { return WIDTH; }
    protected:
        T mCells[WIDTH][HEIGHT];
};
```

Code snippet from GridNonType\Grid.h

This class is significantly simpler than the old version. Note that the template parameter list requires three parameters: the type of objects stored in the grid and the width and height of the grid. The width and height are used to create a two-dimensional array to store the objects. There is no dynamically allocated memory in the class, so it no longer needs a user-defined copy constructor, destructor, or assignment operator. In fact, you don't even need to write a default constructor; the compiler generated one is just fine. Here are the class method definitions:

```
template <typename T, size_t WIDTH, size_t HEIGHT>
void Grid<T, WIDTH, HEIGHT>::setElementAt(size_t x, size_t y, const T& inElem)
{
    mCells[x][y] = inElem;
}
template <typename T, size_t WIDTH, size_t HEIGHT>
T& Grid<T, WIDTH, HEIGHT>::getElementAt(size_t x, size_t y)
{
    return mCells[x][y];
}
template <typename T, size_t WIDTH, size_t HEIGHT>
const T& Grid<T, WIDTH, HEIGHT>::getElementAt(size_t x, size_t y) const
{
    return mCells[x][y];
}
```

Code snippet from GridNonType\Grid.h

Note that wherever you previously specified `Grid<T>` you must now specify `Grid<T, WIDTH, HEIGHT>` to represent the three template parameters.

You can instantiate this template and use it like this:

```
Grid<int, 10, 10> myGrid;
Grid<int, 10, 10> anotherGrid;
myGrid.setElementAt(2, 3, 45);
anotherGrid = myGrid;
cout << anotherGrid.getElementAt(2, 3);
```

Code snippet from GridNonType\GridTest.cpp

This code seems great. Despite the slightly messy syntax for declaring a `Grid`, the actual `Grid` code is a lot simpler. Unfortunately, there are more restrictions than you might think at first. First, you can't use a non-constant integer to specify the height or width. The following code doesn't compile:

```
size_t height = 10;
Grid<int, 10, height> testGrid; // DOES NOT COMPILE
```

However, if you make `height` const, it compiles:

```
const size_t height = 10;
Grid<int, 10, height> testGrid; // compiles and works
```

A second restriction might be more significant. Now that the width and height are template parameters, they are part of the type of each grid. That means that Grid<int, 10, 10> and Grid<int, 10, 11> are two different types. You can't assign an object of one type to an object of the other, and variables of one type can't be passed to functions or methods that expect variables of another type.

Non-type template parameters become part of the type specification of instantiated objects.

Default Values for Non-Type Parameters

If you continue the approach of making height and width template parameters, you might want to be able to provide defaults for the height and width just as you did previously in the constructor of the Grid<T> class. C++ allows you to provide defaults for template parameters with a similar syntax. Here is the class definition:

```
template <typename T, size_t WIDTH = 10, size_t HEIGHT = 10>
class Grid
{
    // Remainder is identical to the previous version
};
```

Code snippet from GridNonTypeDefault\Grid.h

You do not need to specify the default values for WIDTH and HEIGHT in the template specification for the method definitions. For example, here is the implementation of setElementAt():

```
template <typename T, size_t WIDTH, size_t HEIGHT>
void Grid<T, WIDTH, HEIGHT>::setElementAt(size_t x, size_t y, const T& inElem)
{
    mCells[x][y] = inElem;
}
```

Code snippet from GridNonTypeDefault\Grid.h

Now, you can instantiate a Grid with only the element type, the element type and the width, or the element type, width, and height:

```
Grid<int> myGrid;
Grid<int, 10> anotherGrid;
Grid<int, 10, 10> aThirdGrid;
```

Code snippet from GridNonTypeDefault\GridTest.cpp

The rules for default parameters in template parameter lists are the same as for functions or methods: You can provide defaults for parameters in order starting from the right.

Method Templates

C++ allows you to templatize individual methods of a class. These methods can be inside a class template or in a non-templatized class. When you write a templatized class method, you are actually writing many different versions of that method for many different types. Method templates come in useful for assignment operators and copy constructors in class templates.

 Virtual methods and destructors cannot be method templates.

Consider the original `Grid` template with only one parameter: the element type. You can instantiate grids of many different types, such as `int`s and `double`s:

Available for
download on
Wrox.com

```
Grid<int> myIntGrid;
Grid<double> myDoubleGrid;
```

Code snippet from MethodTemplates\GridTest.cpp

However, `Grid<int>` and `Grid<double>` are two different types. If you write a function that takes an object of type `Grid<double>`, you cannot pass a `Grid<int>`. Even though you know that the elements of an `int` grid could be copied to the elements of a `double` grid, because the `int`s could be coerced into `double`s, you cannot assign an object of type `Grid<int>` to one of type `Grid<double>` or construct a `Grid<double>` from a `Grid<int>`. Neither of the following two lines compiles:

```
myDoubleGrid = myIntGrid;              // DOES NOT COMPILE
Grid<double> newDoubleGrid(myIntGrid); // DOES NOT COMPILE
```

The problem is that the `Grid` template copy constructor and `operator=` prototypes look like this:

```
Grid(const Grid<T>& src);
Grid<T>& operator=(const Grid<T>& rhs);
```

The `Grid` copy constructor and `operator=` both take a reference to a `const Grid<T>`. When you instantiate a `Grid<double>` and try to call the copy constructor and `operator=`, the compiler generates methods with these prototypes:

```
Grid(const Grid<double>& src);
Grid<double>& operator=(const Grid<double>& rhs);
```

Note that there are no constructors or `operator=` that take a `Grid<int>` within the generated `Grid<double>` class. However, you can rectify this oversight by adding templatized versions of the copy constructor and `operator=` to the `Grid` class to generate routines that will convert from one grid type to another. Here is the new `Grid` class definition:

```
template <typename T>
class Grid
{
    public:
        Grid(size_t inWidth = kDefaultWidth, size_t inHeight = kDefaultHeight);
        Grid(const Grid<T>& src);
        template <typename E>
        Grid(const Grid<E>& src);
        virtual ~Grid();
        Grid<T>& operator=(const Grid<T>& rhs);
        template <typename E>
        Grid<T>& operator=(const Grid<E>& rhs);
        // Omitted for brevity
    protected:
        void copyFrom(const Grid<T>& src);
        template <typename E>
        void copyFrom(const Grid<E>& src);
        T** mCells;
        size_t mWidth, mHeight;
};
```

Code snippet from MethodTemplates\Grid.h

Member templates do not replace non-template members with the same name. This rule leads to problems with the copy constructor and `operator=` *because of the compiler-generated versions. If you write templatized versions of the copy constructor and* `operator=` *and omit non-templatized versions, the compiler will not call these new templatized versions for assignments of grids with the same type. Instead, it will generate a copy constructor and* `operator=` *for creating and assigning two grids of the same type, which will not do what you want! Thus, you must keep the old non-templatized copy constructor and* `operator=` *as well.*

Examine the new templatized copy constructor first:

```
template <typename E>
Grid(const Grid<E>& src);
```

You can see that there is another template declaration with a different typename, `E` (short for "element"). The class is templatized on one type, `T`, and the new copy constructor is also templatized on a different type, `E`. This twofold templatization allows you to copy grids of one type to another.

Here is the definition of the new copy constructor:

```
template <typename T>
template <typename E>
Grid<T>::Grid(const Grid<E>& src)
{
    copyFrom(src);
}
```

Code snippet from MethodTemplates\Grid.h

As you can see, you must declare the class template line (with the T parameter) before the member template line (with the E parameter). You can't combine them like this:

```
template <typename T, typename E> // Incorrect for nested template constructor!
Grid<T>::Grid(const Grid<E>& src)
```

The copy constructor uses the protected copyFrom() method, so the class needs a templatized version of copyFrom() as well:

```
template <typename T>
template <typename E>
void Grid<T>::copyFrom(const Grid<E>& src)
{
    mWidth = src.getWidth();
    mHeight = src.getHeight();
    mCells = new T* [mWidth];
    for (size_t i = 0; i < mWidth; i++) {
        mCells[i] = new T[mHeight];
    }
    for (size_t i = 0; i < mWidth; i++) {
        for (size_t j = 0; j < mHeight; j++) {
            mCells[i][j] = src.getElementAt(i, j);
        }
    }
}
```

Code snippet from MethodTemplates\Grid.h

In addition to the extra template parameter line before the copyFrom() method definition, note that you must use public accessor methods getWidth(), getHeight(), and getElementAt() to access the elements of src. That's because the object you're copying to is of type Grid<T>, and the object you're copying from is of type Grid<E>. They will not be the same type, so you must use public methods.

The final templatized method is the assignment operator. Note that it takes a const Grid<E>& but returns a Grid<T>&:

```
template <typename T>
template <typename E>
Grid<T>& Grid<T>::operator=(const Grid<E>& rhs)
{
```

```
    // Free the old memory.
    for (size_t i = 0; i < mWidth; i++) {
        delete [] mCells[i];
    }
    delete [] mCells;
    mCells = nullptr;
    // Copy the new memory.
    copyFrom(rhs);
    return *this;
}
```

Code snippet from MethodTemplates\Grid.h

You do not need to check for self-assignment in the templatized assignment operator, because assignment of the same types still happens in the old, non-templatized, version of `operator=`, so there's no way you can get self-assignment here.

Method Templates with Non-Type Parameters

In the earlier example with integer template parameters for HEIGHT and WIDTH, you see that a major problem is that the height and width become part of the types. This restriction prevents you from assigning a grid with one height and width to a grid with a different height and width. In some cases, however, it's desirable to assign or copy a grid of one size to a grid of a different size. Instead of making the destination object a perfect clone of the source object, you would copy only those elements from the source array that fit in the destination array, padding the destination array with default values if the source array is smaller in either dimension. With method templates for the assignment operator and copy constructor, you can do exactly that, thus allow assignment and copying of different sized grids. Here is the class definition:

Available for download on Wrox.com

```
template <typename T, size_t WIDTH = 10, size_t HEIGHT = 10>
class Grid
{
    public:
        Grid() {}
        template <typename E, size_t WIDTH2, size_t HEIGHT2>
        Grid(const Grid<E, WIDTH2, HEIGHT2>& src);
        template <typename E, size_t WIDTH2, size_t HEIGHT2>
        Grid<T, WIDTH, HEIGHT>& operator=(const Grid<E, WIDTH2, HEIGHT2>& rhs);
        void setElementAt(size_t x, size_t y, const T& inElem);
        T& getElementAt(size_t x, size_t y);
        const T& getElementAt(size_t x, size_t y) const;
        size_t getHeight() const { return HEIGHT; }
        size_t getWidth() const { return WIDTH; }
    protected:
        template <typename E, size_t WIDTH2, size_t HEIGHT2>
        void copyFrom(const Grid<E, WIDTH2, HEIGHT2>& src);
        T mCells[WIDTH][HEIGHT];
};
```

Code snippet from MethodTemplatesNonType\Grid.h

This new definition includes method templates for the copy constructor and assignment operator, plus a helper method `copyFrom()`. When you write a copy constructor, the compiler stops generating a default constructor for you (details can be found in Chapter 6), so you have to add a default constructor as well. Note, however, that you do not need to write non-templatized copy constructor and assignment operator methods because the compiler-generated ones continue to be generated. They simply copy or assign `mCells` from the source to the destination, which is exactly the semantics you want for two grids of the same size.

When you templatize the copy constructor, assignment operator, and `copyFrom()`, you must specify all three template parameters. Here is the templatized copy constructor:

Available for
download on
Wrox.com

```
template <typename T, size_t WIDTH, size_t HEIGHT>
template <typename E, size_t WIDTH2, size_t HEIGHT2>
Grid<T, WIDTH, HEIGHT>::Grid(const Grid<E, WIDTH2, HEIGHT2>& src)
{
    copyFrom(src);
}
```

Code snippet from MethodTemplatesNonType\Grid.h

Here are the implementations of `copyFrom()` and `operator=`. Note that `copyFrom()` copies only `WIDTH` and `HEIGHT` elements in the x and y dimensions, respectively, from `src`, even if `src` is bigger than that. If `src` is smaller in either dimension, `copyFrom()` pads the extra spots with zero-initialized values. `T()` calls the default constructor for the object if `T` is a class type, or generates 0 if `T` is a simple type. This syntax is called the *zero-initialization* syntax. It's a good way to provide a reasonable default value for a variable whose type you don't yet know:

Available for
download on
Wrox.com

```
template <typename T, size_t WIDTH, size_t HEIGHT>
template <typename E, size_t WIDTH2, size_t HEIGHT2>
void Grid<T, WIDTH, HEIGHT>::copyFrom(const Grid<E, WIDTH2, HEIGHT2>& src)
{
    for (size_t i = 0; i < WIDTH; i++) {
        for (size_t j = 0; j < HEIGHT; j++) {
            if (i < WIDTH2 && j < HEIGHT2) {
                mCells[i][j] = src.getElementAt(i, j);
            } else {
                mCells[i][j] = T();
            }
        }
    }
}
template <typename T, size_t WIDTH, size_t HEIGHT>
template <typename E, size_t WIDTH2, size_t HEIGHT2>
Grid<T, WIDTH, HEIGHT>& Grid<T, WIDTH, HEIGHT>::operator=(
    const Grid<E, WIDTH2, HEIGHT2>& rhs)
{
    // No need to check for self-assignment because this version of
    // assignment is never called when T and E are the same
    // No need to free any memory first
```

```
        // Copy the new memory.
        copyFrom(rhs);
        return *this;
    }
```

Code snippet from MethodTemplatesNonType\Grid.h

Template Class Specialization

You can provide alternate implementations of class templates for specific types. For example, you might decide that the Grid behavior for char*s (C-style strings) doesn't make sense. The grid currently stores shallow copies of pointer types. For char*'s, it might make sense to do a deep copy of the string.

Alternate implementations of templates are called *template specializations*. Again, the syntax is a little weird. When you write a template class specialization, you must specify that it's a template, and that you are writing the version of the template for that particular type. Here is the syntax for specializing the original version of the Grid for char*s:

Available for
download on
Wrox.com

```
// When the template specialization is used, the original template must be
// visible too. #including it here ensures that it will always be visible
// when this specialization is visible.
#include "Grid.h"
template <>
class Grid<char*>
{
    public:
        Grid(size_t inWidth = kDefaultWidth, size_t inHeight = kDefaultHeight);
        Grid(const Grid<char*>& src);
        virtual ~Grid();
        Grid<char*>& operator=(const Grid<char*>& rhs);
        void setElementAt(size_t x, size_t y, const char* inElem);
        char* getElementAt(size_t x, size_t y) const;
        size_t getHeight() const { return mHeight; }
        size_t getWidth() const { return mWidth; }
        static const size_t kDefaultWidth = 10;
        static const size_t kDefaultHeight = 10;
    protected:
        void copyFrom(const Grid<char*>& src);
        char*** mCells;
        size_t mWidth, mHeight;
};
```

Code snippet from GridSpecialization\GridString.h

Note that you don't refer to any type variable, such as T, in the specialization: You work directly with char*s. One obvious question at this point is why this class is still a template. That is, what good is the following syntax?

```
template <>
class Grid<char*>
```

This syntax tells the compiler that this class is a `char*` specialization of the `Grid` class. Suppose that you didn't use that syntax and just tried to write this:

```
class Grid
```

The compiler wouldn't let you do that because there is already a class named `Grid` (the original template class). Only by specializing it can you reuse the name. The main benefit of specializations is that they can be invisible to the user. When a user creates a `Grid` of `int`s or `SpreadsheetCell`s, the compiler generates code from the original `Grid` template. When the user creates a `Grid` of `char*`s, the compiler uses the `char*` specialization. This can all be "behind the scenes."

```
Grid<int> myIntGrid;                  // Uses original Grid template
Grid<char*> stringGrid1(2, 2);       // Uses char* specialization
string dummy = "dummy";
stringGrid1.setElementAt(0, 0, "hello");
stringGrid1.setElementAt(0, 1, dummy.c_str());
stringGrid1.setElementAt(1, 0, dummy.c_str());
stringGrid1.setElementAt(1, 1, "there");
Grid<char*> stringGrid2(stringGrid1);
```

Code snippet from GridSpecialization\GridTest.cpp

When you specialize a template, you don't "inherit" any code: Specializations are not like subclasses. You must rewrite the entire implementation of the class. There is no requirement that you provide methods with the same names or behavior. In fact, you could write a completely different class with no relation to the original. Of course, that would abuse the template specialization ability, and you shouldn't do it without good reason. Here are the implementations for the methods of the `char*` specialization. Unlike in the template definitions, you do not repeat the `template<>` syntax before each method or static member definition:

```
Grid<char*>::Grid(size_t inWidth, size_t inHeight) :
    mWidth(inWidth), mHeight(inHeight)
{
    mCells = new char** [mWidth];
    for (size_t i = 0; i < mWidth; i++) {
        mCells[i] = new char* [mHeight];
        for (size_t j = 0; j < mHeight; j++) {
            mCells[i][j] = nullptr;
        }
    }
}
Grid<char*>::Grid(const Grid<char*>& src)
{
    copyFrom(src);
}
Grid<char*>::~Grid()
{
```

```
    // Free the old memory.
    for (size_t i = 0; i < mWidth; i++) {
        for (size_t j = 0; j < mHeight; j++) {
            delete [] mCells[i][j];
        }
        delete [] mCells[i];
    }
    delete [] mCells;
    mCells = nullptr;
}
void Grid<char*>::copyFrom(const Grid<char*>& src)
{
    mWidth = src.mWidth;
    mHeight = src.mHeight;
    mCells = new char** [mWidth];
    for (size_t i = 0; i < mWidth; i++) {
        mCells[i] = new char* [mHeight];
    }
    for (size_t i = 0; i < mWidth; i++) {
        for (size_t j = 0; j < mHeight; j++) {
            if (src.mCells[i][j] == nullptr) {
                mCells[i][j] = nullptr;
            } else {
                size_t len = strlen(src.mCells[i][j]) + 1;
                mCells[i][j] = new char[len];
                strncpy(mCells[i][j], src.mCells[i][j], len);
            }
        }
    }
}
Grid<char*>& Grid<char*>::operator=(const Grid<char*>& rhs)
{
    // Check for self-assignment.
    if (this == &rhs) {
        return *this;
    }
    // Free the old memory.
    for (size_t i = 0; i < mWidth; i++) {
        for (size_t j = 0; j < mHeight; j++) {
            delete [] mCells[i][j];
        }
        delete [] mCells[i];
    }
    delete [] mCells;
    mCells = nullptr;
    // Copy the new memory.
    copyFrom(rhs);
    return *this;
}
void Grid<char*>::setElementAt(size_t x, size_t y, const char* inElem)
{
    delete [] mCells[x][y];
    if (inElem == nullptr) {
        mCells[x][y] = nullptr;
```

```
        } else {
            size_t len = strlen(inElem) + 1;
            mCells[x][y] = new char[len];
            strncpy(mCells[x][y], inElem, len);
        }
    }
    char* Grid<char*>::getElementAt(size_t x, size_t y) const
    {
        if (mCells[x][y] == nullptr) {
            return nullptr;
        }
        size_t len = strlen(mCells[x][y]) + 1;
        char* ret = new char[len];
        strncpy(ret, mCells[x][y], len);
        return ret;
    }
```

Code snippet from GridSpecialization\GridString.h

getElementAt() returns a deep copy of the string, so you don't need an overload that returns a const char*. However, since it does return a deep copy, the caller is responsible to free the memory returned by getElementAt() with delete[].

This section discussed how to use template class specialization. It allows you to write a special implementation for a template with the template types replaced by specific types. The next chapter continues the discussion of specialization with a more advanced feature called *partial specialization*.

Subclassing Template Classes

You can write subclasses of template classes. If the subclass inherits from the template itself, it must be a template as well. Alternatively, you can write a subclass to inherit from a specific instantiation of the template class, in which case your subclass does not need to be a template. As an example of the former, suppose you decide that the generic Grid class doesn't provide enough functionality to use as a game board. Specifically, you would like to add a move() method to the game board that moves a piece from one location on the board to another. Here is the class definition for the GameBoard template:

Available for download on Wrox.com

```
template <typename T>
class GameBoard : public Grid<T>
{
    public:
        GameBoard(size_t inWidth = Grid<T>::kDefaultWidth,
            size_t inHeight = Grid<T>::kDefaultHeight);
        void move(size_t xSrc, size_t ySrc, size_t xDest, size_t yDest);
};
```

Code snippet from GridSubclass\GameBoard.h

This GameBoard template subclasses the Grid template, and thereby inherits all its functionality. You don't need to rewrite setElementAt(), getElementAt(), or any of the other methods. You also don't need to add a copy constructor, operator=, or destructor, because you don't have any dynamically allocated memory in the GameBoard. The dynamically allocated memory in the Grid superclass will be taken care of by the Grid copy constructor, operator=, and destructor.

The inheritance syntax looks normal, except that the superclass is Grid<T>, not Grid. The reason for this syntax is that the GameBoard template doesn't really subclass the generic Grid template. Rather, each instantiation of the GameBoard template for a specific type subclasses the Grid instantiation for that type. For example, if you instantiate a GameBoard with a ChessPiece type, then the compiler generates code for a Grid<ChessPiece> as well. The ": public Grid<T>" syntax says that this class subclasses from whatever Grid instantiation makes sense for the T type parameter. Note that the C++ name lookup rules for template inheritance require you to specify that kDefaultWidth and kDefaultHeight are declared in, and thus dependent on, the Grid<T> superclass.

Here are the implementations of the constructor and the move() method. Again, note the use of Grid<T> in the call to the superclass constructor. Additionally, although many compilers don't enforce it, the name lookup rules require you to use the this pointer to refer to data members and methods in the superclass:

```
template <typename T>
GameBoard<T>::GameBoard(size_t inWidth, size_t inHeight) :
    Grid<T>(inWidth, inHeight)
{
}
template <typename T>
void GameBoard<T>::move(size_t xSrc, size_t ySrc, size_t xDest, size_t yDest)
{
    this->mCells[xDest][yDest] = this->mCells[xSrc][ySrc];
    this->mCells[xSrc][ySrc] = T(); // default construct the src cell
}
```

Code snippet from GridSubclass\GameBoard.h

As you can see, move() uses the syntax T() described in the section on "Method Templates with Non-Type Parameters."

You can use the GameBoard template as follows:

```
GameBoard<ChessPiece> chessBoard;
ChessPiece pawn;
chessBoard.setElementAt(0, 0, pawn);
chessBoard.move(0, 0, 0, 1);
```

Code snippet from GridSubclass\GameBoardTest.cpp

Inheritance versus Specialization

Some programmers find the distinction between template inheritance and template specialization confusing. The following table summarizes the differences:

	INHERITANCE	SPECIALIZATION
Reuses code?	**Yes:** Subclasses contain all superclass members and methods.	**No:** You must rewrite all code in the specialization.
Reuses name?	**No:** The subclass name must be different from the superclass name.	**Yes:** The specialization must have the same name as the original.
Supports polymorphism?	**Yes**: Objects of the subclass can stand in for objects of the superclass.	**No:** Each instantiation of a template for a type is a different type.

Use inheritance for extending implementations and for polymorphism. Use specialization for customizing implementations for particular types.

C++11 Template Aliases

Chapter 9 introduces the concept of a `typedef`. It allows you to give another name to specific types. For example you could write the following `typedef`:

```
typedef int MyInt;
```

With the preceding `typedef` you have given another name to type `int` allowing you to define integers by using type `MyInt` instead of `int` as follows:

```
MyInt i = 123;
```

Of course, the original type `int` still exists and can still be used as type specification. Similarly, you could use a `typedef` to give another name to a templatized class. However, C++ requires you to specify concrete types for **each** template type. An example will make it clearer. Suppose you have the following class using templates:

```
template<typename T1, typename T2>
class MyTemplateClass {/* ... */};
```

If you want to use a `typedef` to define another name for `MyTemplateClass`, you have to give concrete types for `T1` and `T2`. For example:

```
typedef MyTemplateClass<int, double> OtherName;
```

Specifying only one of the types, like the following example, is not valid in C++:

```
template<typename T1>
typedef MyTemplateClass<T1, double> OtherName;  // Error
```

C++11 removes this limitation by introducing *template aliases,* which can be used as follows:

```
template<typename T1>
using OtherName = MyTemplateClass<T1, double>;
```

Pay special attention to the syntax. The new type name OtherName should be at the beginning with the template alias syntax, while it should be at the end for the typedef syntax. This template/type alias syntax can be used to replace the earlier typedef syntax, whether a template is involved or not. For example:

```
using MyInt = int;
```

This is exactly the same as:

```
typedef int MyInt;
```

C++11 Alternative Function Syntax

The *alternative function syntax* is discussed in Chapter 9 and is mentioned again here because it is a very useful C++11 feature in combination with templates. The problem solved with the alternative function syntax is that you don't always know the exact return type at the beginning of your function prototype. Take the following templatized function as example:

```
template<typename Type1, typename Type2>
RetType myFunc(const Type1& t1, const Type2& t2) {return t1 + t2;}
```

In this example, RetType should be the type of the expression t1+t2, which isn't known yet at the beginning of the prototype line. t1 and t2 become known once the semantic analyzer reaches the end of the parameter list. Chapter 1 introduces the C++11 decltype feature. decltype(T) returns the type of its argument T. With this knowledge, you might try to solve the previous return type issue by using the decltype feature as follows:

```
template<typename Type1, typename Type2>
decltype(t1+t2) myFunc(const Type1& t1, const Type2& t2) {return t1 + t2;}
```

Unfortunately, this is also not valid in C++11 because t1 and t2 are still not yet defined when the compiler is parsing decltype(t1+t2).

C++11 solves this problem with the alternative function syntax as follows. Note that in the new syntax, the return type is specified after the parameter list, hence the names of the parameters (and their types, and consequently the type t1+t2) are known:

Available for download on Wrox.com

```
template<typename Type1, typename Type2>
auto myFunc(const Type1& t1, const Type2& t2) -> decltype(t1+t2)
    {return t1 + t2;}
```

Code snippet from AlternativeFunctionSyntax\AlternativeFunctionSyntax.cpp

The auto *keyword here instructs the compiler that the prototype is using the alternative function syntax, which is a completely different meaning than the* auto *keyword that is introduced in Chapter 1 to let the compiler automatically deduce the type of an expression.*

FUNCTION TEMPLATES

You can also write templates for stand-alone functions. For example, you could write a generic function to find a value in an array and return its index:

Available for download on Wrox.com

```cpp
static const size_t NOT_FOUND = (size_t)(-1);
template <typename T>
size_t Find(T& value, T* arr, size_t size)
{
    for (size_t i = 0; i < size; i++) {
        if (arr[i] == value) {
            return i; // Found it; return the index
        }
    }
    return NOT_FOUND; // Failed to find it; return NOT_FOUND
}
```

Code snippet from FunctionTemplate\FindTemplate.cpp

The `Find()` function template can work on arrays of any type. For example, you could use it to find the index of an `int` in an array of `int`s or a `SpreadsheetCell` in an array of `SpreadsheetCell`s.

You can call the function in two ways: explicitly specifying the type with angle brackets or omitting the type and letting the compiler *deduce* it from the arguments. Here are some examples:

Available for download on Wrox.com

```cpp
int x = 3, intArr[] = {1, 2, 3, 4};
size_t sizeIntArr = sizeof(intArr) / sizeof(int);
size_t res;
res = Find(x, intArr, sizeIntArr);        // calls Find<int> by deduction
res = Find<int>(x, intArr, sizeIntArr);   // calls Find<int> explicitly
if (res != NOT_FOUND)
    cout << res << endl;
else
    cout << "Not found" << endl;

double d1 = 5.6, dArr[] = {1.2, 3.4, 5.7, 7.5};
size_t sizeDoubleArr = sizeof(dArr) / sizeof(double);
res = Find(d1, dArr, sizeDoubleArr);         // calls Find<double> by deduction
res = Find<double>(d1, dArr, sizeDoubleArr); // calls Find<double> explicitly
if (res != NOT_FOUND)
    cout << res << endl;
else
    cout << "Not found" << endl;
```

```
//res = Find(x, dArr, sizeDoubleArr); // DOES NOT COMPILE!
                                      // Arguments are different types.

SpreadsheetCell c1(10), c2Arr[2] =
        {SpreadsheetCell(4), SpreadsheetCell(10)};
size_t sizeC2Arr = sizeof(c2Arr) / sizeof(SpreadsheetCell);
res = Find(c1, c2Arr, sizeC2Arr);
res = Find<SpreadsheetCell>(c1, c2Arr, sizeC2Arr);
```

Code snippet from FunctionTemplate\FindTemplate.cpp

Like class templates, function templates can take non-type parameters. For brevity, only an example of a type parameter for function templates is shown.

 The C++ standard library provides a templatized find() *function that is much more powerful than the one above. See Chapter 13 for details.*

Function Template Specialization

Just as you can specialize class templates, you can specialize function templates. For example, you might want to write a Find() function for char* C-style strings that compares them with strcmp() instead of operator==. Here is a specialization of the Find() function to do this:

Available for
download on
Wrox.com

```
template<>
size_t Find<char*>(char*& value, char** arr, size_t size)
{
    cout << "Specialization" << endl;
    for (size_t i = 0; i < size; i++) {
        if (strcmp(arr[i], value) == 0) {
            return i; // Found it; return the index
        }
    }
    return NOT_FOUND; // Failed to find it; return NOT_FOUND
}
```

Code snippet from FunctionTemplate\FindTemplateSpecialization.cpp

You can omit the <char*> in the function name when the parameter type can be deduced from the arguments, making your prototype look like this:

```
template<>
size_t Find(char*& value, char** arr, size_t size)
```

However, the deduction rules are tricky when you involve overloading as well (see next section), so, in order to avoid mistakes, it's better to note the type explicitly.

Although the specialized find() function could take just char* instead of char*& as its first parameter, it's best to keep the arguments parallel to the non-specialized version of the function for the deduction rules to function properly.

You can use the specialization as follows:

```
char* word = "two";
char* arr[] = {"one", "two", "three", "four"};
size_t sizeArr = sizeof(arr) / sizeof(arr[0]);
size_t res;
res = Find<char*>(word, arr, sizeArr); // Calls the char* specialization
res = Find(word, arr, sizeArr);        // Calls the char* specialization
```

Code snippet from FunctionTemplate\FindTemplateSpecialization.cpp

Function Template Overloading

You can also overload template functions with non-template functions. For example, instead of writing a Find() template specialization for char*, you could write a non-template Find() function that works on char*s:

```
size_t Find(char*& value, char** arr, size_t size)
{
    cout << "overload" << endl;
    for (size_t i = 0; i < size; i++) {
        if (strcmp(arr[i], value) == 0) {
            return i; // Found it; return the index
        }
    }
    return NOT_FOUND; // Failed to find it; return NOT_FOUND
}
```

Code snippet from FunctionTemplate\FindTemplateOverload.cpp

This function is identical in behavior to the specialized version in the previous section. However, the rules for when it is called are different:

```
char* word = "two";
char* arr[] = {"one", "two", "three", "four"};
size_t sizeArr = sizeof(arr) / sizeof(arr[0]);
size_t res;
res = Find<char*>(word, arr, sizeArr); // Calls the Find template with T=char*
res = Find(word, arr, sizeArr);        // Calls the Find non-template function!
```

Code snippet from FunctionTemplate\FindTemplateOverload.cpp

Thus, if you want your function to work both when char* is explicitly specified and via deduction when it is not, you should write a specialized template version instead of a non-template, overloaded version.

Like template class method definitions, function template definitions (not just the prototypes) must be available to all source files that use them. Thus, you should put the definitions in header files if more than one source file uses them.

Function Template Overloading and Specialization Together

It's possible to write both a specialized `Find()` template for `char*`s and a stand-alone `Find()` function for `char*`s. The compiler always prefers the non-template function to a templatized version. However, if you specify the template instantiation explicitly, the compiler will be forced to use the template version:

Available for
download on
Wrox.com

```
char* word = "two";
char* arr[] = {"one", "two", "three", "four"};
size_t sizeArr = sizeof(arr) / sizeof(arr[0]);
size_t res;
res = Find<char*>(word, arr, sizeArr); // Calls the char* specialization of
                                       // the template
res = Find(word, arr, sizeArr);        // Calls the Find non-template function
```

Code snippet from FunctionTemplate\FindTemplateSpecialOverload.cpp

Friend Function Templates of Class Templates

Function templates are useful when you want to overload operators in a class template. For example, you might want to overload the insertion operator (`operator<<`) for the `Grid` class template to stream a grid.

> *If you are unfamiliar with the mechanics for overloading* `operator<<`, *consult Chapter 18 for details.*

As discussed in Chapter 18, you can't make `operator<<` a member of the `Grid` class: It must be a stand-alone function template. The definition, which should go directly in `Grid.h`, looks as follows:

Available for
download on
Wrox.com

```
template <typename T>
ostream& operator<<(ostream& ostr, const Grid<T>& grid)
{
    for (size_t i = 0; i < grid.mHeight; i++) {
        for (size_t j = 0; j < grid.mWidth; j++) {
            // Add a tab between each element of a row.
            ostr << grid.mCells[j][i] << "\t";
        }
        ostr << std::endl; // Add a newline between each row.
    }
    return ostr;
}
```

Code snippet from FriendFunctionTemplates\Grid.h

This function template will work on any `Grid`, as long as there is an insertion operator for the elements of the grid. The only problem is that `operator<<` accesses `protected` members of the `Grid` class. Therefore, it must be a `friend` of the `Grid` class. However, both the `Grid` class and the `operator<<` are templates. What you really want is for each instantiation of `operator<<` for a particular type `T` to be a friend of the `Grid` template instantiation for that type. The syntax looks like this:

```
// Forward declare Grid template.
template <typename T> class Grid;

// Prototype for templatized operator<<.
template<typename T>
ostream& operator<<(ostream& ostr, const Grid<T>& grid);

template <typename T>
class Grid
{
    public:
        // Omitted for brevity
        friend ostream& operator<< <T>(ostream& ostr, const Grid<T>& grid);
        // Omitted for brevity
};
```

Code snippet from FriendFunctionTemplates\Grid.h

This friend declaration is tricky: You're saying that, for an instance of the template with type `T`, the `T` instantiation of `operator<<` is a `friend`. In other words, there is a one-to-one mapping of friends between the class instantiations and the function instantiations. Note particularly the explicit template specification `<T>` on `operator<<` (the space after `operator<<` is optional, but in the interest of readability it should always be there). This syntax tells the compiler that `operator<<` is itself a template.

SUMMARY

This chapter started a discussion on using templates for generic programming. You saw the syntax on how to write templates and examples where templates are really useful. It explained how to write class templates, how to organize your code in different files, how to use template parameters, and how to templatize methods of a class. It further discussed how to use template class specialization to write special implementations of a template where the template types are replaced with specific types. The chapter finished with an explanation of function templates.

The next chapter continues the discussion on templates with some more advanced features such as variadic templates and metaprogramming.

20

Advanced Templates

WHAT'S IN THIS CHAPTER?

➤ What the details are of the different kinds of template parameters

➤ How to use partial specialization

➤ How to write recursive templates

➤ How to write type-safe variable arguments functions using variadic templates

➤ What metaprogramming is and how to use it

The previous chapter covered the most widely used features of class and function templates. If you are interested in only a basic knowledge of templates so that you can better understand how the STL works, or perhaps write your own simple classes, you can skip this chapter on advanced templates. However, if templates interest you and you want to uncover their full power, continue reading this chapter to learn about some of the more obscure, but fascinating, details.

MORE ABOUT TEMPLATE PARAMETERS

There are actually three kinds of template parameters: type, non-type, and template template (no, you're not seeing double: that really is the name). You've seen examples of type and non-type parameters in the previous chapter, but not template template parameters yet. There are also some tricky aspects to both type and non-type parameters that are not covered in the previous chapter.

More about Template Type Parameters

Type parameters to templates are the main purpose of templates. You can declare as many type parameters as you want. For example, you could add to the grid template a second type parameter specifying another templatized class container on which to build the grid. The standard template library defines several templatized container classes, including vector and deque, which are introduced in Chapter 12. In your original grid class you might want to have an array of vectors or an array of deques instead of just an array of arrays. With another template type parameter, you can allow the user to specify whether she wants the underlying container to be a vector or a deque. Here is the class definition with the additional template parameter:

```cpp
template <typename T, typename Container>
class Grid
{
    public:
        Grid(size_t inWidth = kDefaultWidth,
            size_t inHeight = kDefaultHeight);
        Grid(const Grid<T, Container>& src);
        virtual ~Grid();
        Grid<T, Container>& operator=(const Grid<T, Container>& rhs);
        void setElementAt(size_t x, size_t y, const T& inElem);
        T& getElementAt(size_t x, size_t y);
        const T& getElementAt(size_t x, size_t y) const;
        size_t getHeight() const { return mHeight; }
        size_t getWidth() const { return mWidth; }
        static const size_t kDefaultWidth = 10;
        static const size_t kDefaultHeight = 10;
    protected:
        void copyFrom(const Grid<T, Container>& src);
        Container* mCells;
        size_t mWidth, mHeight;
};
```

Code snippet from GridTemplateContainer\Grid.h

This template now has two parameters: T and Container. Thus, wherever you previously referred to Grid<T> you must now refer to Grid<T, Container> to specify both template parameters. The only other change is that mCells is now a pointer to a dynamically allocated array of Containers instead of a pointer to a dynamically allocated two-dimensional array of T elements.

Here is the constructor definition. It assumes that the Container type has a resize() method. If you try to instantiate this template by specifying a type that has no resize() method, the compiler will generate an error:

```cpp
template <typename T, typename Container>
Grid<T, Container>::Grid(size_t inWidth, size_t inHeight) :
    mWidth(inWidth), mHeight(inHeight)
{
    // Dynamically allocate the array of mWidth containers
    mCells = new Container[mWidth];
    for (size_t i = 0; i < mWidth; i++) {
        // Resize each container so that it can hold mHeight elements.
        mCells[i].resize(mHeight);
    }
}
```

Code snippet from GridTemplateContainer\Grid.h

Here is the destructor definition. There's only one call to new in the constructor, so only one call to delete in the destructor.

```
template <typename T, typename Container>
Grid<T, Container>::~Grid()
{
    delete [] mCells;
    mCells = nullptr;
}
```

Code snippet from GridTemplateContainer\Grid.h

The code in copyFrom() assumes that you can access elements in the container by using array [] notation. Chapter 18 explains how to overload the [] operator to implement this feature in your own container classes. Both vector and deque from the STL support this syntax.

```
template <typename T, typename Container>
void Grid<T, Container>::copyFrom(const Grid<T, Container>& src)
{
    mWidth = src.mWidth;
    mHeight = src.mHeight;
    mCells = new Container[mWidth];
    for (size_t i = 0; i < mWidth; i++) {
        // Resize each element, as in the constructor.
        mCells[i].resize(mHeight);
    }
    for (size_t i = 0; i < mWidth; i++) {
        for (size_t j = 0; j < mHeight; j++) {
            mCells[i][j] = src.mCells[i][j];
        }
    }
}
```

Code snippet from GridTemplateContainer\Grid.h

Here are the implementations of the remaining methods:

```
template <typename T, typename Container>
Grid<T, Container>::Grid(const Grid<T, Container>& src)
{
    copyFrom(src);
}
template <typename T, typename Container>
Grid<T, Container>& Grid<T, Container>::operator=(
    const Grid<T, Container>& rhs)
{
    // Check for self-assignment.
    if (this == &rhs) {
        return *this;
    }
    // Free the old memory.
```

```
        delete [] mCells;
        mCells = nullptr;
        // Copy the new memory.
        copyFrom(rhs);
        return *this;
}
template <typename T, typename Container>
void Grid<T, Container>::setElementAt(size_t x, size_t y, const T& inElem)
{
        mCells[x][y] = inElem;
}
template <typename T, typename Container>
T& Grid<T, Container>::getElementAt(size_t x, size_t y)
{
        return mCells[x][y];
}
template <typename T, typename Container>
const T& Grid<T, Container>::getElementAt(size_t x, size_t y) const
{
        return mCells[x][y];
}
```

Code snippet from GridTemplateContainer\Grid.h

Now you can instantiate and use Grid objects like this:

```
Grid<int, vector<int>> myIntGrid;
Grid<int, deque<int>> myIntGrid2;
myIntGrid.setElementAt(3, 4, 5);
cout << myIntGrid.getElementAt(3, 4);
Grid<int, vector<int>> grid2(myIntGrid);
grid2 = myIntGrid;
```

Code snippet from GridTemplateContainer\GridTest.cpp

The use of the word Container for the parameter name doesn't mean that the type really must be a container. You could try to instantiate the Grid class with an int instead:

```
Grid<int, int> test; // WILL NOT COMPILE
```

This line will not compile, but it might not give you the error you expect. It won't complain that the second type argument is an int instead of a container. Instead it will tell you that left of '.resize' must have class/struct/union type. That's because the compiler attempts to generate a Grid class with int as the Container. Everything works fine until it tries to compile this line:

```
mCells[i].resize(mHeight);
```

At that point, the compiler realizes that mCells[i] is an int, so you can't call the resize() method on it.

This approach is used in the STL. The stack, queue, and priority_queue class templates all take a template type parameter specifying the underlying container, which can be a vector, deque, or list.

Default Values for Template Type Parameters

You can give template parameters default values. For example, you might want to say that the default container for your Grid is a vector. The template class definition would look like this:

```
template <typename T, typename Container = vector<T>>
class Grid
{
    public:
        // Everything else is the same as before.
};
```

Code snippet from GridTemplateContainer\GridDefault.h

You can use the type T from the first template parameter as the argument to the vector template in the default value for the second template parameter. In versions of C++ earlier than C++11, there must be a space between the two closing angle brackets. C++11 does not require this space anymore.

The C++ syntax requires that you do not repeat the default value in the template header line for method definitions.

With this default parameter, clients can now instantiate a grid with or without specifying an underlying container:

```
Grid<int, vector<int>> myIntGrid;
Grid<int> myIntGrid2;
```

Code snippet from GridTemplateContainer\GridDefaultTest.cpp

Introducing Template Template Parameters

There is one problem with the Container parameter in the previous section. When you instantiate the class template, you write something like this:

```
Grid<int, vector<int>> myIntGrid;
```

Note the repetition of the int type. You must specify that it's the element type both of the Grid and of the vector. What if you wrote this instead?

```
Grid<int, vector<SpreadsheetCell>> myIntGrid;
```

That wouldn't work very well. It would be nice to be able to write the following, so that you couldn't make that mistake:

```
Grid<int, vector> myIntGrid;
```

The `Grid` class should be able to figure out that it wants a `vector` of `int`s. The compiler won't allow you to pass that argument to a normal type parameter though, because `vector` by itself is not a type, but a template.

If you want to take a template as a template parameter, you must use a special kind of parameter called a *template template parameter*. The syntax is crazy, but, if you're still interested, read on.

Specifying a template template parameter is sort of like specifying a function pointer parameter in a normal function. Function pointer types include the return type and parameter types of a function. Similarly, when you specify a template template parameter, the full specification of the template template parameter includes the parameters to that template.

Containers in the STL have a template parameter list that looks something like this:

```
template <typename E, typename Allocator = allocator<E> >
class vector
{
    // Vector definition
};
```

The `E` parameter is the element type. The `Allocator` parameter is covered in Chapter 12.

Given the preceding template specification, here is the template class definition for the `Grid` class that takes a container template as its second template parameter:

```
template <typename T,
    template <typename E, typename Allocator = allocator<E>> class Container
        = vector>
class Grid
{
    public:
        // Omitted code that is the same as before
    protected:
        Container<T>* mCells;
        // Omitted code that is the same as before
};
```

Code snippet from GridTemplateContainer\GridTemplateTemplate.h

What is going on here? The first template parameter is the same as before: the element type `T`. The second template parameter is now a template itself for a container such as `vector` or `deque`. As you saw earlier, this "template type" must take two parameters: an element type `E` and an allocator `Allocator`. Note the repetition of the word `class` after the nested template parameter list. The name of this parameter in the `Grid` template is `Container` (as before). The default value is now `vector`, instead of `vector<T>`, because the `Container` is a template instead of an actual type.

The syntax rule for a template template parameter more generically is this:

```
template <..., template <TemplateTypeParams> class ParameterName, ...>
```

Now that you've suffered through the syntax to declare the template, the rest is easy. Instead of using `Container` by itself in the code, you must specify `Container<T>` as the container type you use. For example, the constructor now looks like this (you don't repeat the default template template parameter argument in the template specification for the method definition):

Available for
download on
Wrox.com

```
template <typename T,
  template <typename E, typename Allocator = allocator<E>> class Container>
Grid<T, Container>::Grid(size_t inWidth, size_t inHeight) :
  mWidth(inWidth), mHeight(inHeight)
{
    mCells = new Container<T>[mWidth];
    for (size_t i = 0; i < mWidth; i++) {
        mCells[i].resize(mHeight);
    }
}
```

Code snippet from GridTemplateContainer\GridTemplateTemplate.h

After implementing all the methods, you can use the template as follows:

Available for
download on
Wrox.com

```
Grid<int, vector> myGrid;
myGrid.setElementAt(1, 2, 3);
myGrid.getElementAt(1, 2);
Grid<int, vector> myGrid2(myGrid);
```

Code snippet from GridTemplateContainer\GridTemplateTemplateTest.cpp

This C++ syntax is a bit convoluted because it is trying to allow for maximum flexibility. Try not to bog down in the syntax here, and keep the main concept in mind: You can pass templates as parameters to other templates.

More about Non-Type Template Parameters

You might want to allow the user to specify an empty (not in the literal sense) element that is used to initialize each cell in the grid. Here is a perfectly reasonable approach to implement this goal:

Available for
download on
Wrox.com

```
template <typename T, const T EMPTY>
class Grid
{
    public:
        Grid(size_t inWidth = kDefaultWidth,
            size_t inHeight = kDefaultHeight);
        Grid(const Grid<T, EMPTY>& src);
        virtual ~Grid();
        Grid<T, EMPTY>& operator=(const Grid<T, EMPTY>& rhs);
        // Omitted for brevity
    protected:
        void copyFrom(const Grid<T, EMPTY>& src);
        T** mCells;
        size_t mWidth, mHeight;
};
```

Code snippet from GridEmpty\Grid.h

This definition is legal. You can use the type T from the first parameter as the type for the second parameter, and non-type parameters can be const just like function parameters. You can use this initial value for T to initialize each cell in the grid:

```
template <typename T, const T EMPTY>
Grid<T, EMPTY>::Grid(size_t inWidth, size_t inHeight) :
    mWidth(inWidth), mHeight(inHeight)
{
    mCells = new T* [mWidth];
    for (size_t i = 0; i < mWidth; i++) {
        mCells[i] = new T[mHeight];
        for (size_t j = 0; j < mHeight; j++) {
            mCells[i][j] = EMPTY;
        }
    }
}
```

Code snippet from GridEmpty\Grid.h

The other method definitions stay the same, except that you must add the second type parameter to the template lines, and all the instances of Grid<T> become Grid<T, EMPTY>. After making those changes, you can then instantiate an int Grid with an initial value for all the elements:

```
Grid<int, 0> myIntGrid;
Grid<int, 10> myIntGrid2;
```

Code snippet from GridEmpty\GridTest.cpp

The initial value can be any integer you want. However, suppose that you try to create a SpreasheetCell Grid:

```
SpreadsheetCell emptyCell;
Grid<SpreadsheetCell, emptyCell> mySpreadsheet; // WILL NOT COMPILE
```

Code snippet from GridEmpty\GridTest.cpp

That line leads to a compiler error because you cannot pass objects as arguments to non-type parameters.

 Non-type parameters cannot be objects, or even doubles *or* floats. *They are restricted to integral types,* enums, *pointers, and references.*

This example illustrates one of the vagaries of template classes: They can work correctly on one type but fail to compile for another type.

Reference and Pointer Non-Type Template Parameters

A more comprehensive way of allowing the user to specify an initial empty element for the grid uses a reference to a T as the non-type template parameter. Here is the new class definition:

Available for download on Wrox.com

```
template <typename T, const T& EMPTY>
class Grid
{
    // Everything else is the same as the previous example, except the
    // template lines in the method definitions specify const T& EMPTY
    // instead of const T EMPTY.
};
```

Code snippet from GridEmpty\GridRefNonType.h

Now you can instantiate this template class for any type. However, the reference you pass as the second template argument must refer to a global variable with *external linkage*. Chapter 9 discusses *external linkage*, which can be thought of as the opposite of *static linkage*, and just means that the variable is available in source files outside the one in which it is defined. You can declare that a variable has external linkage with the `extern` keyword:

```
extern const int x = 0;
```

Note that this line occurs outside of any function or method body. Here is a program that declares `int` and `SpreadsheetCell` grids with initialization parameters:

Available for download on Wrox.com

```
extern const int emptyInt = 0;
extern const SpreadsheetCell emptyCell(0);
int main()
{
    Grid<int, emptyInt> myIntGrid;
    Grid<SpreadsheetCell, emptyCell> mySpreadsheet;
    Grid<int, emptyInt> myIntGrid2(myIntGrid);
    return 0;
}
```

Code snippet from GridEmpty\GridTestRefNonType.cpp

> *Reference and pointer template arguments must refer to global variables that are available from all translation units. The technical term for these types of variables is data with* external linkage.

Using Zero-Initialization of Template Types

Neither of the options presented so far for providing an initial empty value for the cells is very attractive. Instead, you may simply want to initialize each cell to a reasonable default value that you choose (instead of allowing the user to specify). Of course, the immediate question is: What's a reasonable value for any possible type? For objects, a reasonable value is an object created with the default constructor. In fact, that's exactly what you're already getting when you create an array of objects. However, for simple data types like integral types (int, short, ...), a reasonable initial value is 0; for floating point types, a reasonable initial value is 0.0; and for pointers, a reasonable initial value is nullptr. Therefore, what you really want to be able to do is assign this initial value to non-objects and use the default constructor on objects. You actually saw the syntax for this behavior in the section on "Method Templates with Non-Type Parameters" in the previous chapter. Here is the implementation of the Grid template constructor using the zero-initialization syntax:

Available for
download on
Wrox.com

```
template <typename T>
Grid<T>::Grid(size_t inWidth, size_t inHeight) :
    mWidth(inWidth), mHeight(inHeight)
{
    mCells = new T* [mWidth];
    for (size_t i = 0; i < mWidth; i++) {
        mCells[i] = new T[mHeight];
        for (size_t j = 0; j < mHeight; j++) {
            mCells[i][j] = T();
        }
    }
}
```

Code snippet from GridEmpty\GridZeroInitialized.h

Given this ability, you can revert to the original Grid class (without an EMPTY non-type parameter) and just initialize each cell element to its zero-initialized "reasonable value."

TEMPLATE CLASS PARTIAL SPECIALIZATION

The char* class specialization shown in the previous chapter is called *full template class specialization* because it specializes the Grid template for every template parameter. There are no template parameters left in the specialization. That's not the only way you can specialize a class; you can also write a *partial class specialization*, in which you specialize some template parameters but not others. For example, recall the basic version of the Grid template with width and height non-type parameters:

Available for
download on
Wrox.com

```
template <typename T, size_t WIDTH, size_t HEIGHT>
class Grid
{
    public:
        void setElementAt(size_t x, size_t y, const T& inElem);
        T& getElementAt(size_t x, size_t y);
        const T& getElementAt(size_t x, size_t y) const;
        size_t getHeight() const { return HEIGHT; }
        size_t getWidth() const { return WIDTH; }
    protected:
        T mCells[WIDTH][HEIGHT];
};
```

Code snippet from GridPartialString\Grid.h

You could specialize this template class for `char*` C-style strings like this:

```
#include "Grid.h" // The file containing the Grid template definition
template <size_t WIDTH, size_t HEIGHT>
class Grid<char*, WIDTH, HEIGHT>
{
    public:
        Grid();
        Grid(const Grid<char*, WIDTH, HEIGHT>& src);
        virtual ~Grid();
        Grid<char*, WIDTH, HEIGHT>& operator=(
            const Grid<char*, WIDTH, HEIGHT>& rhs);
        void setElementAt(size_t x, size_t y, const char* inElem);
        char* getElementAt(size_t x, size_t y) const;
        size_t getHeight() const { return HEIGHT; }
        size_t getWidth() const { return WIDTH; }
    protected:
        void copyFrom(const Grid<char*, WIDTH, HEIGHT>& src);
        char* mCells[WIDTH][HEIGHT];
};
```

Code snippet from GridPartialString\GridString.h

In this case, you are not specializing all the template parameters. Therefore, your template line looks like this:

```
template <size_t WIDTH, size_t HEIGHT>
class Grid<char*, WIDTH, HEIGHT>
```

Note that the template has only two parameters: WIDTH and HEIGHT. However, you're writing a Grid class for three arguments: T, WIDTH, and HEIGHT. Thus, your template parameter list contains two parameters, and the explicit Grid<char*, WIDTH, HEIGHT> contains three arguments. When you instantiate the template, you must still specify three parameters. You can't instantiate the template with only height and width:

```
Grid<int, 2, 2> myIntGrid;       // Uses the original Grid
Grid<char*, 2, 2> myStringGrid; // Uses the partial specialization for char *s
Grid<2, 3> test;                 // DOES NOT COMPILE! No type specified.
```

Code snippet from GridPartialString\GridTestString.cpp

Yes, the syntax is confusing. And it gets worse. In partial specializations, unlike in full specializations, you include the template line in front of every method definition:

```
template <size_t WIDTH, size_t HEIGHT>
Grid<char*, WIDTH, HEIGHT>::Grid()
{
    for (size_t i = 0; i < WIDTH; i++) {
        for (size_t j = 0; j < HEIGHT; j++) {
```

```
            mCells[i][j] = nullptr; // Initialize each element to nullptr.
        }
    }
}
```

Code snippet from GridPartialString\GridString.h

You need this template line with two parameters to show that this method is parameterized on those two parameters. Note that wherever you refer to the full class name, you must use `Grid<char*, WIDTH, HEIGHT>`.

You can find the rest of the method definitions in the downloadable source code archive for this book on `www.wrox.com`.

Another Form of Partial Specialization

The previous example does not show the true power of partial specialization. You can write specialized implementations for a subset of possible types without specializing individual types. For example, you can write a specialization of the `Grid` class for all pointer types. This specialization might perform deep copies of objects to which pointers point instead of storing shallow copies of the pointers in the grid.

Here is the class definition, assuming that you're specializing the initial version of the `Grid` with only one parameter:

```
#include "Grid.h"
template <typename T>
class Grid<T*>
{
    public:
        Grid(size_t inWidth = kDefaultWidth,
            size_t inHeight = kDefaultHeight);
        Grid(const Grid<T*>& src);
        virtual ~Grid();
        Grid<T*>& operator=(const Grid<T*>& rhs);
        void setElementAt(size_t x, size_t y, T* inElem);
        T* getElementAt(size_t x, size_t y) const;
        size_t getHeight() const { return mHeight; }
        size_t getWidth() const { return mWidth; }
        static const size_t kDefaultWidth = 10;
        static const size_t kDefaultHeight = 10;
    protected:
        void copyFrom(const Grid<T*>& src);
        T*** mCells;
        size_t mWidth, mHeight;
};
```

Code snippet from GridPartialPtr\GridPtr.h

As usual, these two lines are the crux of the matter:

```
template <typename T>
class Grid<T*>
```

The syntax says that this class is a specialization of the Grid template for all pointer types. At least that's what it's telling the compiler. What it's telling you and me is that the C++ standards committee should have come up with a better syntax. Unless you've been working with it for a long time, it's quite jarring.

You are providing the implementation only in cases where T is a pointer type. Note that if you instantiate a grid like this: Grid<int*> myIntGrid, then T will actually be int, not int*. That's a bit unintuitive, but unfortunately, the way it works. Here is a code example:

Available for
download on
Wrox.com

```
Grid<int> myIntGrid;      // Uses the non-specialized grid
Grid<int*> psGrid(2, 2); // Uses the partial specialization for pointer types

int x = 3, y = 4;
psGrid.setElementAt(0, 0, &x);
psGrid.setElementAt(0, 1, &y);
psGrid.setElementAt(1, 0, &y);
psGrid.setElementAt(1, 1, &x);

Grid<int*> psGrid2(psGrid);
Grid<int*> psGrid3;
psGrid3 = psGrid2;

const Grid<int*>& psGrid4 = psGrid2;
cout << *(psGrid4.getElementAt(1, 1)) << endl;
x=6;
cout << *(psGrid4.getElementAt(1, 1)) << endl;
```

Code snippet from GridPartialPtr\GridPtrTest.cpp

The psGrid4 grid is storing pointers, so psGrid4.getElementAt(1, 1) will return a pointer to x. Changing the value of the variable x will change the result of dereferencing the pointer returned by getElementAt(1, 1). The output of the above code should be as follows:

```
3
6
```

At this point, you're probably wondering whether this really works. We sympathize with your skepticism. One of the authors was so surprised by this syntax when he first read about it that he didn't believe it actually worked until he was able to try it out. If you don't believe us, try it out yourself. Here are the method implementations. Pay close attention to the template line syntax before each method:

Available for
download on
Wrox.com

```
template <typename T>
Grid<T*>::Grid(size_t inWidth, size_t inHeight) :
    mWidth(inWidth), mHeight(inHeight)
{
    mCells = new T** [mWidth];
```

```cpp
        for (size_t i = 0; i < mWidth; i++) {
            mCells[i] = new T*[mHeight];
        }
}
template <typename T>
Grid<T*>::Grid(const Grid<T*>& src)
{
    copyFrom(src);
}
template <typename T>
Grid<T*>::~Grid()
{
    // Free the old memory.
    for (size_t i = 0; i < mWidth; i++) {
        delete [] mCells[i];
    }
    delete [] mCells;
    mCells = nullptr;
}
template <typename T>
void Grid<T*>::copyFrom(const Grid<T*>& src)
{
    mWidth = src.mWidth;
    mHeight = src.mHeight;
    mCells = new T** [mWidth];
    for (size_t i = 0; i < mWidth; i++) {
        mCells[i] = new T*[mHeight];
    }
    for (size_t i = 0; i < mWidth; i++) {
        for (size_t j = 0; j < mHeight; j++) {
            mCells[i][j] = src.mCells[i][j];
        }
    }
}
template <typename T>
Grid<T*>& Grid<T*>::operator=(const Grid<T*>& rhs)
{
    // Check for self-assignment.
    if (this == &rhs) {
        return *this;
    }
    // Free the old memory.
    for (size_t i = 0; i < mWidth; i++) {
        delete [] mCells[i];
    }
    delete [] mCells;
    mCells = nullptr;
    // Copy the new memory.
    copyFrom(rhs);
    return *this;
}
template <typename T>
void Grid<T*>::setElementAt(size_t x, size_t y, T* inElem)
{
```

```
    mCells[x][y] = inElem;
}
template <typename T>
T* Grid<T*>::getElementAt(size_t x, size_t y) const
{
    return mCells[x][y];
}
```

> *For brevity, this example is not implementing any deep copying of the pointers.*
> *This would be a good exercise for the reader.*

EMULATING FUNCTION PARTIAL SPECIALIZATION WITH OVERLOADING

The C++ standard does not permit partial template specialization of functions. Instead, you can overload the function with another template. The difference is subtle. Suppose that you want to write a specialization of the Find() function, presented in the previous chapter, that dereferences the pointers to use operator== directly on the objects pointed to. Following the syntax for class template partial specialization, you might be tempted to write this:

```
template <typename T>
size_t Find<T*>(T*& value, T** arr, size_t size)
{
    for (size_t i = 0; i < size; i++) {
        if (*arr[i] == *value) {
            return i; // Found it; return the index
        }
    }
    return NOT_FOUND; // failed to find it; return NOT_FOUND
}
```

However, that syntax declares a partial specialization of the function template, which the C++ standard does not allow. The standard way to implement the behavior you want is to write a new template for Find():

```
template <typename T>
size_t Find(T*& value, T** arr, size_t size)
{
    for (size_t i = 0; i < size; i++) {
        if (*arr[i] == *value) {
```

```
                return i; // Found it; return the index
        }
    }
    return NOT_FOUND; // failed to find it; return NOT_FOUND
}
```

Code snippet from FunctionTemplatePtr\FindTemplatePtr.cpp

The difference might seem trivial and academic, but it makes the difference between portable standard code and code that is not standard compliant.

More on Deduction

You can define in one program the original `Find()` template, the overloaded `Find()` for partial specialization on pointer types, the complete specialization for `char*`s, and the overloaded `Find()` just for `char*`s. The compiler will choose the appropriate version to call based on its deduction rules.

> *The compiler always chooses the "most specific" version of the function, with non-template versions being preferred over template versions.*

The following code calls the specified versions of `Find()`:

```
size_t res = NOT_FOUND;

int x = 3, intArr[] = {1, 2, 3, 4};
size_t sizeArr = sizeof(intArr) / sizeof(int);
res = Find(x, intArr, sizeArr);       // calls Find<int> by deduction
res = Find<int>(x, intArr, sizeArr); // calls Find<int> explicitly

double d1 = 5.6, dArr[] = {1.2, 3.4, 5.7, 7.5};
sizeArr = sizeof(dArr) / sizeof(double);
res = Find(d1, dArr, sizeArr);        // calls Find<double> by deduction
res = Find<double>(d1, dArr, sizeArr); // calls Find<double> explicitly

char* word = "two";
char* arr[] = {"one", "two", "three", "four"};
sizeArr = sizeof(arr) / sizeof(arr[0]);
res = Find<char*>(word, arr, sizeArr);// calls template specialization for char*s
res = Find(word, arr, sizeArr);       // calls overloaded Find for char*s

int *px = &x, *pArr[] = {&x, &x};
sizeArr = sizeof(pArr) / sizeof(pArr[0]);
res = Find(px, pArr, sizeArr);    // calls the overloaded Find for pointers

SpreadsheetCell c1(10), c2[] = {SpreadsheetCell(4), SpreadsheetCell(10)};
sizeArr = sizeof(c2) / sizeof(c2[0]);
res = Find(c1, c2, sizeArr);      // calls Find<SpreadsheetCell> by deduction
```

```
// calls Find<SpreadsheetCell> explicitly
res = Find<SpreadsheetCell>(c1, c2, sizeArr);

SpreadsheetCell *pc1 = &c1;
SpreadsheetCell *psa[] = {&c1, &c1};
sizeArr = sizeof(psa) / sizeof(psa[0]);
res = Find(pc1, psa, sizeArr);     // Calls the overloaded Find for pointers
```

Code snippet from FunctionTemplatePtr\FindTemplatePtr.cpp

TEMPLATE RECURSION

Templates in C++ provide capabilities that go far beyond the simple classes and functions you have seen so far in this and the previous chapter. One of these capabilities is *template recursion*. This section first provides a motivation for template recursion, and then shows how to implement it.

 This section employs some operator overloading features which are discussed in Chapter 18. If you skipped that chapter or are unfamiliar with the syntax for overloading `operator[]`*, consult Chapter 18 before continuing.*

An N-Dimensional Grid: First Attempt

The `Grid` template example up to now supports only two dimensions, which limits its usefulness. What if you wanted to write a 3-D Tic-Tac-Toe game or write a math program with four-dimensional matrices? You could, of course, write a template or non-template class for each of those dimensions. However, that would repeat a lot of code. Another approach is to write only a single-dimensional grid. Then, you could create a `Grid` of any dimension by instantiating the `Grid` with another `Grid` as its element type. This `Grid` element type could itself be instantiated with a `Grid` as its element type, and so on. Here is the implementation of the `OneDGrid` class template. It's simply a one-dimensional version of the `Grid` template from the earlier examples, with the addition of a `resize()` method, and the substitution of `operator[]` for `setElementAt()` and `getElementAt()`. Production code, of course, would do bounds-checking on the array access, and would throw an exception if something were amiss.

Available for
download on
Wrox.com

```
template <typename T>
class OneDGrid
{
    public:
        OneDGrid(size_t inSize = kDefaultSize);
        OneDGrid(const OneDGrid<T>& src);
        virtual ~OneDGrid();
        OneDGrid<T>& operator=(const OneDGrid<T>& rhs);
        void resize(size_t newSize);
        T& operator[](size_t x);
        const T& operator[](size_t x) const;
```

```cpp
        size_t getSize() const { return mSize; }
        static const size_t kDefaultSize = 10;
    protected:
        void copyFrom(const OneDGrid<T>& src);
        T* mElems;
        size_t mSize;
};
template <typename T>
OneDGrid<T>::OneDGrid(size_t inSize) : mSize(inSize)
{
    mElems = new T[mSize];
}
template <typename T>
OneDGrid<T>::OneDGrid(const OneDGrid<T>& src)
{
    copyFrom(src);
}
template <typename T>
OneDGrid<T>::~OneDGrid()
{
    delete [] mElems;
    mElems = nullptr;
}
template <typename T>
void OneDGrid<T>::copyFrom(const OneDGrid<T>& src)
{
    mSize = src.mSize;
    mElems = new T[mSize];
    for (size_t i = 0; i < mSize; i++) {
        mElems[i] = src.mElems[i];
    }
}
template <typename T>
OneDGrid<T>& OneDGrid<T>::operator=(const OneDGrid<T>& rhs)
{
    // Check for self-assignment.
    if (this == &rhs) {
        return *this;
    }
    // Free the old memory.
    delete [] mElems;
    mElems = nullptr;
    // Copy the new memory.
    copyFrom(rhs);
    return *this;
}
template <typename T>
void OneDGrid<T>::resize(size_t newSize)
{
    T* newElems = new T[newSize]; // Allocate the new array of the new size
    // Handle the new size being smaller or bigger than the old size.
    for (size_t i = 0; i < newSize && i < mSize; i++) {
        // Copy the elements from the old array to the new one.
        newElems[i] = mElems[i];
    }
```

```
        mSize = newSize; // Store the new size.
        delete [] mElems; // Free the memory for the old array.
        mElems = newElems; // Store the pointer to the new array.
}
template <typename T>
T& OneDGrid<T>::operator[](size_t x)
{
    return mElems[x];
}
template <typename T>
const T& OneDGrid<T>::operator[](size_t x) const
{
    return mElems[x];
}
```

Code snippet from OneDGrid\OneDGrid.h

With this implementation of the `OneDGrid`, you can create multidimensional grids like this:

Available for download on Wrox.com

```
OneDGrid<int> singleDGrid;
OneDGrid<OneDGrid<int>> twoDGrid;
OneDGrid<OneDGrid<OneDGrid<int>>> threeDGrid;
singleDGrid[3] = 5;
twoDGrid[3][3] = 5;
threeDGrid[3][3][3] = 5;
```

Code snippet from OneDGrid\OneDGridTest.cpp

This code works fine, but the declarations are messy. We can do better.

A Real N-Dimensional Grid

You can use template recursion to write a "real" N-dimensional grid because dimensionality of grids is essentially recursive. You can see that in this declaration:

```
OneDGrid<OneDGrid<OneDGrid<int>>> threeDGrid;
```

You can think of each nesting `OneDGrid` as a recursive step, with the `OneDGrid` of `int` as the base case. In other words, a three-dimensional grid is a single-dimensional grid of single-dimensional grids of single-dimensional grids of `int`s. Instead of requiring the user to do this recursion, you can write a template class that does it for you. Then, you can create N-dimensional grids like this:

```
NDGrid<int, 1> singleDGrid;
NDGrid<int, 2> twoDGrid;
NDGrid<int, 3> threeDGrid;
```

The `NDGrid` template class takes a type for its element and an integer specifying its "dimensionality." The key insight here is that the element type of the `NDGrid` is not the element type specified in the template parameter list, but is in fact another `NDGrid` of dimensionality one less than the current. In other words, a three-dimensional grid is an array of two-dimensional grids; the two-dimensional grids are each arrays of one-dimensional grids.

With recursion, you need a base case. You can write a partial specialization of the NDGrid for dimensionality of 1, in which the element type is not another NDGrid, but is in fact the element type specified by the template parameter.

Here is the general NDGrid template definition, with highlights showing where it differs from the OneDGrid shown in the previous section:

Available for
download on
Wrox.com

```cpp
template <typename T, size_t N>
class NDGrid
{
    public:
        NDGrid();
        NDGrid(size_t inSize);
        NDGrid(const NDGrid<T, N>& src);
        virtual ~NDGrid();
        NDGrid<T, N>& operator=(const NDGrid<T, N>& rhs);
        void resize(size_t newSize);
        NDGrid<T, N-1>& operator[](size_t x);
        const NDGrid<T, N-1>& operator[](size_t x) const;
        size_t getSize() const { return mSize; }
        static const size_t kDefaultSize = 10;
    protected:
        void copyFrom(const NDGrid<T, N>& src);
        NDGrid<T, N-1>* mElems;
        size_t mSize;
};
```

Code snippet from NDGrid\NDGrid.h

Note that mElems is a pointer to an NDGrid<T, N-1>: This is the recursive step. Also, operator[] returns a reference to the element type, which is again NDGrid<T, N-1>, not T.

Here is the template definition for the base case:

Available for
download on
Wrox.com

```cpp
template <typename T>
class NDGrid<T, 1>
{
    public:
        NDGrid(size_t inSize = kDefaultSize);
        NDGrid(const NDGrid<T, 1>& src);
        virtual ~NDGrid();
        NDGrid<T, 1>& operator=(const NDGrid<T, 1>& rhs);
        void resize(size_t newSize);
        T& operator[](size_t x);
        const T& operator[](size_t x) const;
        size_t getSize() const { return mSize; }
        static const size_t kDefaultSize = 10;
    protected:
        void copyFrom(const NDGrid<T, 1>& src);
        T* mElems;
        size_t mSize;
};
```

Code snippet from NDGrid\NDGrid.h

Here the recursion ends: The element type is T, not another template instantiation.

The trickiest aspect of the implementations, other than the template recursion itself, is appropriately sizing each dimension of the array. This implementation creates the N-dimensional array with every dimension of equal size. It's significantly more difficult to specify a separate size for each dimension. However, even with this simplification, there is still a problem: The user should have the ability to create the array with a specified size, such as 20 or 50. Thus, one constructor takes an integer size parameter. However, when you dynamically allocate the nested array of grids, you cannot pass this size value on to the grids because arrays create objects using their default constructor. Thus, you must explicitly call resize() on each grid element of the array. That code follows, with the default and one-argument constructors separated for clarity.

The base case doesn't need to resize its elements because the elements are Ts, not grids.

Here are the implementations of the main NDGrid template, with highlights showing the differences from the OneDGrid:

```cpp
template <typename T, size_t N>
NDGrid<T, N>::NDGrid(size_t inSize) : mSize(inSize)
{
    mElems = new NDGrid<T, N-1>[mSize];
    // Allocating the array above calls the 0-argument
    // constructor for the NDGrid<T, N-1>, which constructs
    // it with the default size. Thus, we must explicitly call
    // resize() on each of the elements.
    for (size_t i = 0; i < mSize; i++) {
        mElems[i].resize(inSize);
    }
}
template <typename T, size_t N>
NDGrid<T, N>::NDGrid() : mSize(kDefaultSize)
{
    mElems = new NDGrid<T, N-1>[mSize];
}
template <typename T, size_t N>
NDGrid<T, N>::NDGrid(const NDGrid<T, N>& src)
{
    copyFrom(src);
}
template <typename T, size_t N>
NDGrid<T, N>::~NDGrid()
{
    delete [] mElems;
    mElems = nullptr;
}
template <typename T, size_t N>
void NDGrid<T, N>::copyFrom(const NDGrid<T, N>& src)
{
    mSize = src.mSize;
    mElems = new NDGrid<T, N-1>[mSize];
    for (size_t i = 0; i < mSize; i++) {
```

```
            mElems[i] = src.mElems[i];
        }
    }
    template <typename T, size_t N>
    NDGrid<T, N>& NDGrid<T, N>::operator=(const NDGrid<T, N>& rhs)
    {
        // Check for self-assignment.
        if (this == &rhs) {
            return *this;
        }
        // Free the old memory.
        delete [] mElems;
        mElems = nullptr;
        // Copy the new memory.
        copyFrom(rhs);
        return *this;
    }
    template <typename T, size_t N>
    void NDGrid<T, N>::resize(size_t newSize)
    {

        // Allocate the new array with the new size.
        NDGrid<T, N - 1>* newElems = new NDGrid<T, N - 1>[newSize];
        // Copy all the elements, handling the cases where newSize is
        // larger than mSize and smaller than mSize.
        for (size_t i = 0; i < newSize && i < mSize; i++) {
            newElems[i] = mElems[i];
            // Resize the nested Grid elements recursively.
            newElems[i].resize(newSize);
        }
        // Store the new size and pointer to the new array.
        // Free the memory for the old array first.
        mSize = newSize;
        delete [] mElems;
        mElems = newElems;

    }
    template <typename T, size_t N>
    NDGrid<T, N-1>& NDGrid<T, N>::operator[](size_t x)
    {
        return mElems[x];
    }
    template <typename T, size_t N>
    const NDGrid<T, N-1>& NDGrid<T, N>::operator[](size_t x) const
    {
        return mElems[x];
    }
```

Code snippet from NDGrid\NDGrid.h

Here are the implementations of the partial specialization (base case). Note that you must rewrite a lot of the code because you don't inherit any implementations with specializations. Highlights show the differences from the non-specialized NDGrid:

```
template <typename T>
NDGrid<T, 1>::NDGrid(size_t inSize) : mSize(inSize)
{
    mElems = new T[mSize];
}
template <typename T>
NDGrid<T, 1>::NDGrid(const NDGrid<T, 1>& src)
{
    copyFrom(src);
}
template <typename T>
NDGrid<T, 1>::~NDGrid()
{
    delete [] mElems;
    mElems = nullptr;
}
template <typename T>
void NDGrid<T, 1>::copyFrom(const NDGrid<T, 1>& src)
{
    mSize = src.mSize;
    mElems = new T[mSize];
    for (size_t i = 0; i < mSize; i++) {
        mElems[i] = src.mElems[i];
    }
}
template <typename T>
NDGrid<T, 1>& NDGrid<T, 1>::operator=(const NDGrid<T, 1>& rhs)
{
    // Check for self-assignment.
    if (this == &rhs) {
        return *this;
    }
    // Free the old memory.
    delete [] mElems;
    mElems = nullptr;
    // Copy the new memory.
    copyFrom(rhs);
    return *this;
}
template <typename T>
void NDGrid<T, 1>::resize(size_t newSize)
{
    T* newElems = new T[newSize];
    for (size_t i = 0; i < newSize && i < mSize; i++) {
        newElems[i] = mElems[i];
        // Don't need to resize recursively, because this is the base case.
    }
    mSize = newSize;
    delete [] mElems;
    mElems = newElems;
}
template <typename T>
T& NDGrid<T, 1>::operator[](size_t x)
{
    return mElems[x];
}
```

```
template <typename T>
const T& NDGrid<T, 1>::operator[](size_t x) const
{
    return mElems[x];
}
```

Now, you can write code like this:

```
NDGrid<int, 3> my3DGrid;
my3DGrid[2][1][2] = 5;
my3DGrid[1][1][1] = 5;
cout << my3DGrid[2][1][2] << endl;
```

C++11 TYPE INFERENCE

Type inference is new in C++11 and allows the compiler to automatically deduce the exact type of an expression. There are two new keywords for type inference: `auto` and `decltype`. Type inference turns out to be very useful in combination with templates. This section goes into more detail on their use in a template context.

The auto Keyword

The new `auto` keyword has two completely different meanings. The first meaning is to tell the compiler to automatically deduce the type of a variable at compile time. The following line shows the simplest use of the `auto` keyword in that context:

```
auto x = 123;    // x will be of type int
```

In this example you don't win much by typing `auto` instead of `int`; however, it becomes useful for more complicated types. Suppose you have a `map` that maps an `int` to a `vector` of `strings`:

```
std::map<int, std::vector<std::string>> m;
```

Before C++11, if you wanted a constant iterator to the beginning of this `map`, you had to type the following:

```
std::map<int, std::vector<std::string>>::const_iterator citer = m.begin();
```

With the `auto` keyword it becomes:

```
auto citer = m.cbegin();
```

The second use of the `auto` keyword is when using the new C++11 *alternative function syntax*, which is mentioned in Chapter 9. Basically, it allows you to put the return type at the end of the function prototype instead of at the beginning. For example, take the following function:

```
int func(int i)
{
    return i + 2;
}
```

This can be rewritten by using the alternative function syntax as follows:

```
auto func(int i) -> int
{
    return i + 2;
}
```

The `auto` keyword here has a completely different meaning. It states that this function prototype is using the alternative function syntax. If you look at the preceding example you might think that this alternative function syntax doesn't really add any new value to the language. However, the new syntax becomes important in the context of templates together with the new `decltype` keyword, as you will see in the next sections.

The decltype Keyword

The `decltype` keyword takes an expression as argument, and computes the type of that expression. For example:

```
int x = 123;
decltype(x) y = 456;
```

In this example, the compiler will make `y` of type `int` because that's the type of `x`. Just like the `auto` keyword for the alternative function syntax, the `decltype` keyword doesn't seem to add much value on first sight. However, in the context of templates, `auto` and `decltype` become pretty powerful.

auto and decltype with Templates

The use of the `auto` and `decltype` keywords in combination with templates is best illustrated with an example. The following example defines two classes: `MyInt` and `MyString`. These are simple wrappers for an `int` and a `std::string`, respectively. Their constructors accept a single value used for initialization. Both classes also have an `operator+` as member method. Here is the header file:

Available for
download on
Wrox.com

```
#include <string>
// Forward class declarations
class MyInt;
class MyString;

class MyInt
{
    public:
```

```
        MyInt(int i) : m_i(i) {}
        MyInt operator+(const MyString& rhs) const;
        int getInt() const { return m_i; }
    protected:
        int m_i;
};

class MyString
{
    public:
        MyString(std::string str) : m_str(str) {}
        MyString operator+(const MyInt& rhs) const;
        const std::string& getString() const { return m_str; }
    protected:
        std::string m_str;
};
```

Code snippet from TypeInference\TypeInference.h

The implementation is as follows. This code uses two other new features of C++11: `stoi()` and `to_string()`, both of them are discussed in the "Numeric Conversions" section in Chapter 14:

```
MyInt MyInt::operator+(const MyString& rhs) const
{
    return m_i + stoi(rhs.getString());
}
MyString MyString::operator+(const MyInt& rhs) const
{
    string str = m_str;
    str.append(to_string(rhs.getInt()));
    return str;
}
```

Code snippet from TypeInference\TypeInference.cpp

With this implementation you will get a different result depending on the order of the arguments to the addition operator. For example:

```
MyInt i(4);
MyString str("5");
MyInt a = i + str;
MyString b = str + i;
```

Code snippet from TypeInference\TypeInference.cpp

In this case, the type of variable a should be `MyInt` and the type of variable b should be `MyString`.

Imagine that you want to write a function template to perform the addition. You can write the
following:

```
template<typename T1, typename T2, typename Result>
Result DoAddition(const T1& t1, const T2& t2)
{
    return t1 + t2;
}
```

Code snippet from TypeInference\TypeInference.cpp

As you can see, it requires you to specify three template parameters: the type of the first operand,
the type of the second operand, and the type of the result of performing the addition. You can call
this function template as follows:

```
auto c = DoAddition<MyInt, MyString, MyInt>(i, str);
```

Code snippet from TypeInference\TypeInference.cpp

This is obviously not that elegant because you need to manually specify the type of the return value.
After reading about the `decltype` keyword, you might want to try to fix this issue as follows:

```
template<typename T1, typename T2>
decltype(t1 + t2) DoAddition(const T1& t1, const T2& t2)
{
    return t1 + t2;
}
```

However, this will not work because at the time of parsing the `decltype` keyword, the compiler
doesn't know `t1` and `t2` yet. They become known later in the function prototype. The correct
solution is to combine the alternative function syntax with the `decltype` keyword as shown in the
following implementation:

```
template<typename T1, typename T2>
auto DoAddition2(const T1& t1, const T2& t2) -> decltype(t1 + t2)
{
    return t1 + t2;
}
```

Code snippet from TypeInference\TypeInference.cpp

With this implementation you can call `DoAddition2()` as follows:

```
auto d = DoAddition2(i, str);
auto e = DoAddition2(str, i);
```

Code snippet from TypeInference\TypeInference.cpp

You can see that you need not specify any function template parameters anymore because the compiler will deduce the two template parameter types based on the arguments given to `DoAddition2()`, and will automatically calculate the type of the return value. In this example, d will be of type `MyInt` and e will be of type `MyString`.

C++11 VARIADIC TEMPLATES

Normal templates can take only a fixed number of template parameters. For example, the following code defines a template that requires three template parameters:

```
template<typename T1, typename T2, typename T3>
class MyTemplate { }
```

C++11 introduces the notion of *variadic templates*. These are templates that can take a variable number of template parameters. For example, the following code defines a template that can accept any number of template parameters, using a *parameter pack* called `Types`:

```
template<typename... Types>
class MyVariadicTemplate { }
```

 The three dots behind typename *are not an error. This is the syntax for variadic templates. You are allowed to put spaces before and after the three dots. Thus, the previous variadic template can also be written as follows:*

```
template<typename   ...  Types>
class MyVariadicTemplate { }
```

You can instantiate the `MyVariadicTemplate` with any number of types. For example:

```
MyVariadicTemplate<int> temp1;
MyVariadicTemplate<string, double, list<int>> temp2;
```

The `MyVariadicTemplate` can even be instantiated with zero template arguments:

```
MyVariadicTemplate<> temp3;
```

To avoid instantiating a variadic template with zero template arguments, you can write your template as follows:

```
template<typename T1, typename... Types>
class MyVariadicTemplate { }
```

With this new definition, trying to instantiate `MyVariadicTemplate` with zero template arguments will result in a compiler error:

```
error: wrong number of template arguments (0, should be 1 or more)
```

It is not possible to directly iterate over the different arguments given to a variadic template. The only way you can do this is with the aid of template recursion. The following sections show two examples on how to use variadic templates.

Type-Safe Variable-Length Argument Lists

Variadic templates allow you to create type-safe variable-length argument lists. The following example defines a function called processValues() that uses this feature to allowing it to accept a variable number of arguments with different types in a type-safe way. The function processValues() will process each value in the variable-length argument list and will execute a function called handleValue() for each single argument. This means that you have to write a handleValue() function for each type that you want to handle; int, double and string in the following example:

Available for download on Wrox.com

```
void handleValue(int value) { cout << "Integer: " << value << endl; }
void handleValue(double value) { cout << "Double: " << value << endl; }
void handleValue(const char* value) { cout << "String: " << value << endl; }
template<typename T>
void processValues(T arg) // Base case
{
    handleValue(arg);
}
template<typename T1, typename... Tn>
void processValues(T1 arg1, Tn... args)
{
    processValues(arg1);
    processValues(args...);
}
```

Code snippet from VarArgs\VarArgsWithVariadicTemplates.cpp

What the preceding example also demonstrates is the double use of the triple dots . . . operator. This operator appears in two places. First, it is used behind typename to denote that this parameter can accept a variable number of arguments. The official name for typename... Tn is a *parameter pack*. The second use of the . . . operator is behind args. In this case, the operator will unpack/expand the parameter pack args. Take the following line from the preceding example:

```
processValues(args...);
```

This line will *unpack* or *expand* the args parameter pack into its separate arguments, separated by commas, and then call the processValues() function with those expanded arguments. The template always requires at least one template parameter, T1. The act of recursively calling processValues() with args... is that on each call there will be one template parameter less.

Since the implementation of the processValues() function is recursive, you need to have a way to stop the recursion. This is done by implementing a partial specialization of the processValues() template function, which accepts just a single template argument.

You can test the `processValues()` variadic template as follows:

```
processValues(1, 2, 3.56, "test", 1.1f);
```

The recursive calls generated by this example are:

```
processValues(1, 2, 3.56, "test", 1.1f);
  processValues(1);
    handleValue(1);
  processValues(2, 3.56, "test", 1.1f);
    processValues(2);
      handleValue(2);
    processValues(3.56, "test", 1.1f);
      processValues(3.56);
        handleValue(3.56);
      processValues("test", 1.1f);
        processValues("test");
          handleValue("test");
        processValues(1.1f);
          handleValue(1.1f);
```

It is important to remember that this method of variable-length argument lists is fully type-safe. The `processValues()` function will automatically call the correct `handleValue()` overload based on the actual type. Automatic casting can happen as usual in C++. For example, the `1.1f` in the preceding example is of type `float`. The `processValues()` function will call `handleValue(double value)` because conversion from `float` to `double` is without any loss. However, the compiler will issue an error when you call `processValues()` with an argument of a certain type for which there is no `handleValue()` function defined.

There is one small problem with the preceding implementation. Since it's a recursive implementation, the parameters will be copied for each recursive call to `processValues()`. This can become costly depending on the type of the arguments. You might think that you can avoid this copying by passing references to the `processValues()` function instead of using pass-by-value. Unfortunately that also means that you cannot call `processValues()` with constant values anymore, because a reference to a constant value is not allowed.

To use references and still allow constant values, you can leverage another C++11 feature called rvalue references, which are discussed in Chapter 9. Doing that results in the following implementation:

```
template<typename T>
void processValuesRValueRefs(T&& arg)
{
    handleValue(arg);
}
template<typename T1, typename... Tn>
void processValuesRValueRefs(T1&& arg1, Tn&&... args)
```

```
    {
        processValuesRValueRefs(arg1);
        processValuesRValueRefs(args...);
    }
```

Code snippet from VarArgs\VarArgsWithVariadicTemplates.cpp

Inside the body of a function using a parameter pack you can retrieve the number of arguments in the pack as follows:

```
    int numOfArgs = sizeof...(args);
```

A practical example of using variadic templates is to write a secure and type-safe version of `printf()`.

Variable Number of Mix-In Classes

Parameter packs can be used almost everywhere. For example, the following code uses a parameter pack to define a variable number of mix-in classes for the `MyClass` class. Chapter 3 discusses the concept of mix-in classes.

```
class Mixin1
{
    public:
        Mixin1(int i) : m_i(i) {}
        virtual void Mixin1Func() {cout << "Mixin1: " << m_i << endl;}
    protected:
        int m_i;
};
class Mixin2
{
    public:
        Mixin2(int i) : m_i(i) {}
        virtual void Mixin2Func() {cout << "Mixin2: " << m_i << endl;}
    protected:
        int m_i;
};
template<typename... Mixins>
class MyClass : public Mixins...
{
    public:
        MyClass(const Mixins&... mixins) : Mixins(mixins)... {}
};
```

Code snippet from VariadicMixins\VariadicMixins.cpp

This code first defines two mix-in classes `Mixin1` and `Mixin2`. They are kept pretty simple for this example. Their constructor accepts an integer, which is stored, and they have a function to print information about that specific instance of the class. The `MyClass` variadic template uses a parameter pack `typename... Mixins` to accept a variable number of mix-in classes. The class then inherits from all those mix-in classes and the constructor accepts the same number of arguments to initialize each inherited mix-in class. The class can be used as follows:

```
MyClass<Mixin1, Mixin2> a(Mixin1(11), Mixin2(22));
a.Mixin1Func();
a.Mixin2Func();

MyClass<Mixin1> b(Mixin1(33));
b.Mixin1Func();
//b.Mixin2Func();    // Error: does not compile.
```

Code snippet from VariadicMixins\VariadicMixins.cpp

When you try to call `Mixin2Func()` on `b` you will get a compiler error because `b` is not inheriting from the `Mixin2` class. The output of this program is as follows:

```
Mixin1: 11
Mixin2: 22
Mixin1: 33
```

METAPROGRAMMING

This section touches on *template metaprogramming*. It is a very complicated subject and there are books written about it explaining all the little details. This book doesn't have the space to go into all the details of metaprogramming. Instead, this section explains the most important concepts, with the aid of a couple of examples.

The goal of template metaprogramming is to perform some computation at compile time instead of at run time. It is basically a mini programming language on top of C++. The following section starts the discussion with a simple demonstration that calculates the factorial of a number at compile time and makes the result available as a simple constant at run time.

Factorial at Compile Time

Template metaprogramming allows you to perform calculations at compile time instead of at run time. The following code is a small example that calculates the factorial of a number at compile time:

```
template<long long f>
class Factorial
{
    public:
        static const long long val = (f*Factorial<f-1>::val);
};
template<>
class Factorial<1>
{
```

```
    public:
        static const long long val = 1;
};
int main()
{
    cout << Factorial<6>::val << endl;
    return 0;
}
```

Code snippet from Factorial\Factorial.cpp

This will calculate the factorial of 6, mathematically written as 6!, which is 1×2×3×4×5×6 or 720. The code is using template recursion as explained earlier in this chapter, which requires the general recursive template and the base template to stop the recursion.

 It is important to remember that the factorial calculations are happening at compile time. At run time you access the compile time calculated value through ::val, *which is just a constant value.*

Loop Unrolling

A second example of template metaprogramming is to unroll loops at compile time instead of executing the loop at run time. Take a look at the following example:

Available for download on Wrox.com

```
template<int i, typename FuncType>
class Loop
{
    public:
        static inline void Do(FuncType func) {
            Loop<i-1, FuncType>::Do(func);
            func(i);
        }
};
template<typename FuncType>
class Loop<-1, FuncType>
{
    public:
        static inline void Do(FuncType func) { }
};
```

Code snippet from LoopUnrolling\LoopUnrolling.cpp

This example uses template recursion because it needs to do something in a loop at compile time. For template recursion you need the recursive implementation of the template and a base template that will stop the recursion. On each recursion, the Loop template will instantiate itself with `i-1`. When it hits `-1`, the base template is used, which stops the recursion. The `Loop` template can be used as follows:

```
void DoWork(int i) { cout << "DoWork(" << i << ")" << endl; }
int main()
{
    Loop<3, function<void(int)>>::Do(DoWork);
}
```

Code snippet from LoopUnrolling\LoopUnrolling.cpp

This code will cause the compiler to unroll the loop and will call the function `DoWork()` four times in a row (0-3). Note that this example is using the C++11 `std::function` feature, which is explained in Chapter 16. The output of the program is:

```
DoWork(0)
DoWork(1)
DoWork(2)
DoWork(3)
```

This already looks interesting, but we can do better, and make the call even easier to write by using `decltype`:

```
Loop<3, decltype(DoWork)>::Do(DoWork);
```

Code snippet from LoopUnrolling\LoopUnrolling.cpp

This code will output exactly the same as the first version. However, here you ask the compiler to deduce the type of the `DoWork()` function automatically by using the `decltype` keyword so that you don't need to write the exact type yourself.

To further demonstrate the power of the new C++11 features in combination with template metaprogramming, take the following call for the `Loop` template:

```
double DoWork2(string str, int i)
{
    cout << "DoWork2(" << str << ", " << i << ")" << endl;
    return 0.0;
}
int main()
{
    auto a = bind(DoWork2, "TestStr", placeholders::_1);
    Loop<2, decltype(a)>::Do(a);
}
```

Code snippet from LoopUnrolling\LoopUnrolling.cpp

This is using quite a number of C++11 features. The code first implements a function that accepts a `string` and an `int` and returns a `double`. The `main()` function uses `std::bind()` to bind the first parameter of `DoWork2()` to a fixed string, `"TestStr"`. See Chapter 13 for details on `std::bind()`. The result of `std::bind()` is assigned to `a`, and because of the `auto` keyword, the compiler will automatically deduce the type of `a`. The code then instantiates the `Loop` template and uses `decltype` to let the compiler deduce the type of `a` and use it as the second template parameter. If you compile and run this code, the output should be as follows:

```
DoWork2(TestStr, 0)
DoWork2(TestStr, 1)
DoWork2(TestStr, 2)
```

You can go one step further and remove the need to specify the type of the function as the second parameter for the `Loop` template altogether by defining a function template that will deduce the type automatically:

Available for download on Wrox.com

```
template<int i, typename FuncType>
void loopFunc(FuncType f)
{
    Loop<i, FuncType>::Do(f);
}
int main()
{
    loopFunc<2>(bind(DoWork2, "TestStr", placeholders::_1));
}
```

Code snippet from LoopUnrolling\LoopUnrolling.cpp

The output will be the same as before. As you can see in the `main()` function, you don't need to specify the type of the `DoWork2()` function anymore. The `loopFunc()` function template will automatically deduce this type and use it to instantiate the `Loop` template.

C++11 Printing Tuples

This example will use template metaprogramming to print the individual elements of a C++11 `std::tuple`. Tuples are explained in Chapter 16. They allow you to store any number of values, each with its own specific type. A `tuple` has a fixed size and fixed value types, determined at compile time. However, tuples don't have any built-in mechanism to iterate over their elements. The following example shows how you could use template metaprogramming to iterate over the elements of a `tuple` at compile time:

Available for download on Wrox.com

```
template<int n, typename TupleType>
class tuple_print
{
    public:
        tuple_print(TupleType t) {
            tuple_print<n-1, TupleType> tp(t);
            cout << get<n-1>(t) << endl;
        }
};
```

```
template<typename TupleType>
class tuple_print<0, TupleType>
{
    public:
        tuple_print(TupleType t) {}
};
int main()
{
    typedef tuple<int, string, bool> MyTuple;
    MyTuple t1(16, "Test", true);
    tuple_print<tuple_size<MyTuple>::value, MyTuple> tp(t1);
}
```

Code snippet from PrintTuple\PrintTuple.cpp

Like it is often the case with template metaprogramming, this example is again using template recursion. There is a `tuple_print` template class that accepts a size integer and the type of the `tuple`. It then recursively instantiates itself in the constructor and decrements the size on every call. A partial specialization of the `tuple_print` class for a zero sized `tuple` stops the recursion. The `main()` function shows how this `tuple_print` template class could be used.

If you look at the `main()` function, you can see that the line to use the `tuple_print` template looks a bit complicated because it requires the size of the `tuple` and the exact type of the `tuple` as template arguments. This can be simplified a lot by introducing a template helper function that will automatically deduce the template parameters. The simplified implementation is as follows:

Available for
download on
Wrox.com

```
template<int n, typename TupleType>
class tuple_print_helper
{
    public:
        tuple_print_helper(TupleType t) {
            tuple_print_helper<n-1, TupleType> tp(t);
            cout << get<n-1>(t) << endl;
        }
};
template<typename TupleType>
class tuple_print_helper<0, TupleType>
{
    public:
        tuple_print_helper(TupleType t) {}
};
template<typename T>
void tuple_print(T t)
{
    tuple_print_helper<tuple_size<T>::value, T> tph(t);
}
int main()
{
    auto t1 = make_tuple(167, "Testing", false, 2.3);
    tuple_print(t1);
}
```

Code snippet from PrintTuple\PrintTupleSimplified.cpp

The first change made here is to rename the original `tuple_print` template class to `tuple_print_helper`. The code then implements a small function template called `tuple_print()`, which accepts the type of the `tuple` as a template argument and accepts the `tuple` itself as a function argument. The body of that function instantiates the `tuple_print_helper` template class. The `main()` function shows how to use this simplified version. Since you don't need to know the exact type of the `tuple` yourself anymore, you can use the recommended `make_tuple()` together with the `auto` keyword to avoid having to write the `tuple` type yourself. The call to the `tuple_print()` function template is very simple:

```
tuple_print(t1);
```

You don't need to specify the function template argument because the compiler can deduce this automatically from the supplied argument.

C++11 Type Traits

Type traits allow you to make decisions based on types at compile time. For example, you can write a template that requires a type that is derived from a certain type, or a type that is convertible to a certain type, or a type that is integral, and so on. The standard defines several helper classes for this. The following list gives a few examples of the available type traits-related classes in the C++11 standard. See the Reference resource on the website (www.wrox.com) for a complete list.

➤ Primary type categories

➤ `is_void`

➤ `is_integral`

➤ `is_floating_point`

➤ `is_pointer`

➤ ...

➤ Composited type categories

➤ `is_reference`

➤ `is_object`

➤ `is_scalar`

➤ ...

➤ Type properties

➤ `is_const`

➤ `is_literal_type`

➤ `is_polymorphic`

➤ `is_unsigned`

➤ `is_constructible`

➤ `is_copy_constructible`

➤   `is_move_constructible`

➤   `is_assignable`

➤   . . .

➤ Type relations

    ➤   `is_same`

    ➤   `is_base_of`

    ➤   `is_convertible`

➤ const-volatile modifications

    ➤   `remove_const`

    ➤   `add_const`

    ➤   . . .

➤ Reference modifications

    ➤   `remove_reference`

    ➤   `add_lvalue_reference`

    ➤   `add_rvalue_reference`

➤ Sign modifications

    ➤   `make_signed`

    ➤   `make_unsigned`

➤ Other transformations

    ➤   `enable_if`

    ➤   `conditional`

    ➤   . . .

Type traits is a pretty advanced and complicated feature. By just looking at the preceding list, which is already a shortened version of the list in the standard itself, it is clear that this book cannot explain all details about type traits. This section explains just a couple of use cases to show you how type traits could be used.

Using Type Categories

Type traits requires the `<type_traits>` header file. Before an example can be given for a template using type traits, you first need to know a bit more on how classes like `is_integral` work.

The standard defines an `integral_constant` class that looks as follows:

```
template <class T, T v>
struct integral_constant {
    static constexpr T value = v;
    typedef T value_type;
```

```
        typedef integral_constant<T,v> type;
        constexpr operator value_type() { return value; }
    };
    typedef integral_constant<bool, true> true_type;
    typedef integral_constant<bool, false> false_type;
```

What this defines is two types: `true_type` and `false_type`. When you call `true_type::value` you will get the value `true` and when you call `false_type::value` you will get the value `false`. You can also call `true_type::type`, which will return the type of `true_type`. The same holds for `false_type`. Classes like `is_integral` and `is_class` inherit from `integral_constant`. For example, `is_integral` can be specialized for type `bool` as follows:

```
    template<> struct is_integral<bool> : true_type { };
```

This allows you to write `is_integral<bool>::value`, which will return the value `true`. Note that you don't need to write these specializations yourself; they are part of the standard library.

The following code shows the simplest example of how type categories can be used:

```
if (is_integral<int>::value) {
    cout << "int is integral" << endl;
} else {
    cout << "int is not integral" << endl;
}
if (is_class<string>::value) {
    cout << "string is a class" << endl;
} else {
    cout << "string is not a class" << endl;
}
```

Code snippet from TypeTraits\basic.cpp

This example is using `is_integral` to check whether `int` is an integral type or not, and uses `is_class` to check whether `string` is a class or not. The output is as follows:

```
int is integral
string is a class
```

Of course, you will likely never use type traits in this way. They become more useful in combination with templates to generate code based on some properties of a type. The following template example demonstrates this:

```
template<typename T>
void process_helper(const T& t, true_type)
{
    cout << t << " is an integral type." << endl;
}
template<typename T>
void process_helper(const T& t, false_type)
{
    cout << t << " is a non-integral type." << endl;
}
```

```
template<typename T>
void process(const T& t)
{
    process_helper(t, typename is_integral<T>::type());
}
int main()
{
    process(123);
    process(2.2);
    process(string("Test"));
    return 0;
}
```

Code snippet from TypeTraits\is_integral.cpp

The output of this example is as follows:

```
123 is an integral type.
2.2 is a non-integral type.
Test is a non-integral type.
```

The preceding code defines an overloaded function template `process_helper()` that accepts a type as template argument. The first argument to this function is a value and the second argument is either an instance of `true_type` or `false_type`. The `process()` function template accepts a single argument and will call the `process_helper()` function with the second parameter defined as follows:

```
typename is_integral<T>::type()
```

This uses `is_integral` to see if `T` is an integral type. Calling `::type` will return the resulting `integral_constant`, which can be a `true_type` or a `false_type`. The `process_helper()` function needs an instance of `true_type` or `false_type` as second parameter, so that is the reason for the two empty brackets behind `::type`. Note that the two overloaded `process_helper()` functions use nameless parameters of type `true_type` or `false_type`. They are nameless because they don't use those parameters inside their function body. If you don't like this syntax, you might as well write the following:

```
void process_helper(const T& t, true_type tt)
```

However, because `tt` will not be used in the body of the function, this will most likely trigger a warning from your compiler saying that `tt` is unused.

Using Type Relations

There are three type relations available: `is_same`, `is_base_of` and `is_convertible`. They all work similarly. This section gives an example of how to use `is_same`.

The following example defines a `same_helper()` function template. It accepts two constant references and one Boolean value. The function prints the two values followed by a specific string depending on the value of the Boolean parameter. The `same()` function template uses the `is_same` type traits feature to figure out whether the two given arguments are of the same type or not and then calls the `same_helper()` function. It uses `::value` because the `same_helper()` function requires a Boolean value `true` or `false`. Using the `same()` function template is very easy as is shown in the `main()` function:

```cpp
template<typename T1, typename T2>
void same_helper(const T1& t1, const T2& t2, bool b)
{
    cout << "'" << t1 << "' and '" << t2 << "' are ";
    cout << (b ? "the same types." : "different types.") << endl;
}
template<typename T1, typename T2>
void same(const T1& t1, const T2& t2)
{
    same_helper(t1, t2, is_same<T1, T2>::value);
}
int main()
{
    same(1, 32);
    same(1, 3.01);
    same(3.01, string("Test"));
}
```

Code snippet from TypeTraits\is_same.cpp

The output should be as follows:

```
'1' and '32' are the same types.
'1' and '3.01' are different types
'3.01' and 'Test' are different types
```

Using enable_if

First, a little warning before continuing with `enable_if`. Using `enable_if` requires knowledge of a feature called *Substitution Failure Is Not An Error* (SFINAE), a complicated and obscure feature of C++. This section explains the basics of SFINAE with an example.

The previous example with the `same()` and `same_helper()` function templates can be rewritten into one overloaded `check_type()` function template by using the `enable_if` type traits transformation as follows:

```cpp
template<typename T1, typename T2>
void check_type(const T1& t1, const T2& t2,
    typename enable_if<is_same<T1, T2>::value>::type* p = nullptr)
{
    cout << "'" << t1 << "' and '" << t2 << "' ";
    cout << "are the same types." << endl;
}
template<typename T1, typename T2>
void check_type(const T1& t1, const T2& t2,
```

```
        typename enable_if<!is_same<T1, T2>::value>::type* p = nullptr)
    {
        cout << "'" << t1 << "' and '" << t2 << "' ";
        cout << "are different types." << endl;
    }
    int main()
    {
        check_type(1, 32);
        check_type(1, 3.01);
        check_type(3.01, string("Test"));
    }
```

> *Code snippet from TypeTraits\enable_if.cpp*

The output will be:

```
'1' and '32' are the same types.
'1' and '3.01' are different types.
'3.01' and 'Test' are different types.
```

This example defines one function called `check_type()`, which is overloaded on its third parameter. The third parameter for the first overload looks as follows:

```
typename enable_if<is_same<T1, T2>::value>::type* p = nullptr
```

It first uses `is_same` to check whether the two types are the same or not and gets the value of that result with `::value`. This value is given to `enable_if`, and `::type` is used to get the resulting type. When the argument to `enable_if` is `true`, calling `::type` will return some valid type. It is not important to know what exacty this returned type is; it's only important to know that it will return some valid type. However, when the argument to `enable_if` is `false`, the result will not have a wrapped type so calling `::type` will fail. This is where SFINAE comes into play.

When the compiler starts to compile the first line of the `main()` function, it tries to find a function `check_type()` that accepts two integer values. It will find the first `check_type()` function template overload in the source code and will deduce that it can use an instance of this by making `T1` and `T2` both integers. It will then try to process the third parameter. Since both types are integers and thus the same, `is_same<T1, T2>::value` will return `true`, which will cause `enable_if<true>::type` to return some valid type. With this instantiation, everything is fine and the compiler can use that version of `check_type()`.

However, when the compiler tries to compile the second line in the `main()` function, it will again try to find a suitable `check_type()` function. It starts with the first overload and decides it can use that overload by setting `T1` to type integer and `T2` to type `double`. It will then try to process the third parameter. This time, `T1` and `T2` are different types, which means that `is_same<T1, T2>::value` will return `false`. Because of this, `enable_if<false>` will not have a wrapped type and calling `enable_if<false>::type` will fail. The compiler will notice this error but will not yet generate a real compilation error because of SFINAE. The compiler will gracefully backtrack and try to find another `check_type()` function. In this case the second `check_type()` overload will work out perfectly because `!is_same<T1, T2>::value` will be `true` and thus `enable_if<true>::type` will be some valid type.

 As mentioned before, relying on SFINAE can become tricky and complicated. It is recommended to use it judiciously.

Conclusion

As you have seen in this section, template metaprogramming can be a very powerful tool, but it can also get quite complicated. One problem with template metaprogramming, not yet mentioned before, is that everything happens at compile time so you cannot use a debugger to pinpoint a problem. If you decide to use template metaprogramming in your code, make sure you write good comments to explain exactly what is going on and why you are doing something a certain way. If you don't properly document your template metaprogramming code, it might be very difficult for someone else to understand your code, and it might even make it difficult for yourself to understand your own code in the future.

SUMMARY

This and the previous chapter show you how to use templates for generic programming and template metaprogramming for compile time computations. We hope that you gained an appreciation for the power and capabilities of these features, and an idea of how you could apply these concepts to your own code. Don't worry if you didn't understand all the syntax, or follow all the examples, on your first reading. The concepts can be difficult to grasp when you are first exposed to them, and the syntax is tricky whenever you want to write somewhat complicated templates. When you actually sit down to write a template class or function, you can consult this chapter and the previous one for a reference on the proper syntax.

21

Effective Memory Management

WHAT'S IN THIS CHAPTER?

➤ What the different ways are to use and manage memory

➤ What the often perplexing relationship is between arrays and pointers

➤ A low-level look at working with memory

➤ What smart pointers are and how to use them

➤ Solutions to a few memory related problems

In many ways, programming in C++ is like driving without a road. Sure, you can go anywhere you want, but there are no lines or traffic lights to keep you from injuring yourself. C++, like the C language, has a hands-off approach towards its programmers. The language assumes that you know what you're doing. It allows you to do things that are likely to cause problems because C++ is incredibly flexible and sacrifices safety in favor of performance.

Memory allocation and management is a particularly error-prone area of C++ programming. To write high-quality C++ programs, professional C++ programmers need to understand how memory works behind the scenes. This chapter explores the ins and outs of memory management. You will learn about the pitfalls of dynamic memory and some techniques for avoiding and eliminating them.

WORKING WITH DYNAMIC MEMORY

When learning to program, dynamic memory is often the first major stumbling block that novice programmers face. Memory is a low-level component of the computer that unfortunately rears its head even in a high-level programming language like C++. Many programmers only understand enough about dynamic memory to get by. They shy away from data structures that use dynamic memory, or get their programs to work by trial and error.

There are two main advantages to using dynamic memory in your programs:

➤   Dynamic memory can be shared between different objects and functions.

➤   The size of dynamically-allocated memory can be determined at run time.

A solid understanding of how dynamic memory really works in C++ is essential to becoming a professional C++ programmer.

How to Picture Memory

Understanding dynamic memory is much easier if you have a mental model for what objects look like in memory. In this book, a unit of memory is shown as a box with a label next to it. The label indicates a variable name that corresponds to the memory. The data inside the box displays the current value of the memory.

For example, Figure 21-1 shows the state of memory after the following line is executed. The line should be in a function, so that i is a local variable:

```
int i = 7;
```

Since i is a local variable, it is allocated on the stack because it is declared as a simple type, not dynamically using the new keyword.

When you use the new keyword, memory is allocated on the heap. The following code creates a variable ptr on the stack, and then allocates memory on the heap to which ptr points.

```
int* ptr;
ptr = new int;
```

Figure 21-2 shows the state of memory after this code is executed. Notice that the variable ptr is still on the stack even though it points to memory on the heap. A pointer is just a variable and can live either on the stack or the heap, although this fact is easy to forget. Dynamic memory, however, is always allocated on the heap.

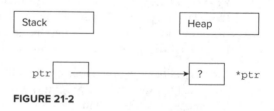

FIGURE 21-2

The next example shows that pointers can exist both on the stack and on the heap.

```
int** handle;
handle = new int*;
*handle = new int;
```

The preceding code first declares a pointer to a pointer to an integer as the variable handle. It then dynamically allocates enough memory to hold a pointer to an integer, storing the pointer to that new memory in handle. Next, that memory (*handle) is assigned a pointer to another section of dynamic memory that is big enough to hold the integer. Figure 21-3 shows the two levels of pointers with one pointer residing on the stack (`handle`) and the other residing on the heap (`*handle`).

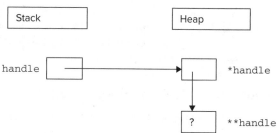

Allocation and Deallocation

You should already be familiar with the basics of dynamic memory from earlier chapters in this

FIGURE 21-3

book. To create space for a variable, you use the `new` keyword. To release that space for use by other parts of the program, you use the `delete` keyword. Of course, it wouldn't be C++ if simple concepts such as `new` and `delete` didn't have several variations and intricacies.

Using new and delete

When you want to allocate a block of memory, you call `new` with the type of the variable for which you need space. `new` returns a pointer to that memory, although it is up to you to store that pointer in a variable. If you ignore the return value of `new`, or if the pointer variable goes out of scope, the memory becomes *orphaned* because you no longer have a way to access it.

For example, the following code orphans enough memory to hold an `int`. Figure 21-4 shows the state of memory after the code is executed. When there are blocks of data on the heap with no access, direct or indirect, from the stack, the memory is orphaned.

```
void leaky()
{
    new int;    // BUG! Orphans memory!
    cout << "I just leaked an int!" << endl;
}
```

| Stack | | Heap | |

| ? | [leaked integer] |

FIGURE 21-4

Until they find a way to make computers with an infinite supply of fast memory, you will need to tell the compiler when the memory associated with an object can be released and used for another purpose. To free memory on the heap, simply use the `delete` keyword with a pointer to the memory, as shown here:

```
int* ptr;
ptr = new int;
delete ptr;
```

As a rule of thumb, every line of code that allocates memory with new should correspond to another line of code that releases the same memory with delete.

What about My Good Friend malloc?

If you are a C programmer, you may be wondering what was wrong with the malloc() function. In C, malloc() is used to allocate a given number of bytes of memory. For the most part, using malloc() is simple and straightforward. The malloc() function still exists in C++, but we recommend avoiding it. The main advantage of new over malloc() is that new doesn't just allocate memory, it constructs objects.

For example, consider the following two lines of code, which use a hypothetical class called Foo:

```
Foo* myFoo = (Foo*)malloc(sizeof(Foo));
Foo* myOtherFoo = new Foo();
```

After executing these lines, both myFoo and myOtherFoo will point to areas of memory on the heap that are big enough for a Foo object. Data members and methods of Foo can be accessed using both pointers. The difference is that the Foo object pointed to by myFoo isn't a proper object because it was never constructed. The malloc() function only sets aside a piece of memory of a certain size. It doesn't know about or care about objects. In contrast, the call to new will allocate the appropriate size of memory and will also properly construct the object. Chapter 18 describes these two duties of new in more detail.

A similar difference exists between the free() function and the delete operator. With free(), the object's destructor will not be called. With delete, the destructor will be called and the object will be properly cleaned up.

You should never use malloc() and free() in C++. Only use new and delete.

When Memory Allocation Fails

Many, if not most, programmers write code with the assumption that new will always be successful. The rationale is that if new fails, it means that memory is very low and life is very, very bad. It is often an unfathomable state to be in because it's unclear what your program could possibly do in this situation.

By default, your program will terminate if new fails. In many programs, this behavior is acceptable. The program exits when new fails because new throws an exception if there is not enough memory available for the request. Chapter 10 explains approaches to recover gracefully from an out-of-memory situation.

There is also an alternative version of new which will not throw an exception. Instead, it will return nullptr (or NULL if your compiler doesn't support nullptr yet), similar to the behavior of malloc() in C. The syntax for using this version is shown here:

```
int* ptr = new(nothrow) int;
```

Of course, you still have the same problem as the version that throws an exception — what do you do when the result is `nullptr`? The compiler doesn't require you to check the result, so the `nothrow` version of `new` is more likely to lead to other bugs than is the version that throws an exception. For this reason, we suggest that you use the standard version of `new`. If out-of-memory recovery is important to your program, the techniques covered in Chapter 10 give you all the tools you need.

Arrays

Arrays package multiple variables of the same type into a single variable with indices. Working with arrays quickly becomes natural to a novice programmer because it is easy to think about values in numbered slots. The in-memory representation of an array is not far off from this mental model.

Arrays of Basic Types

When your program allocates memory for an array, it is allocating *contiguous* pieces of memory, where each piece is large enough to hold a single element of the array. For example, a local array of five `int`s would be declared on the stack as follows:

```
int myArray[5];
```

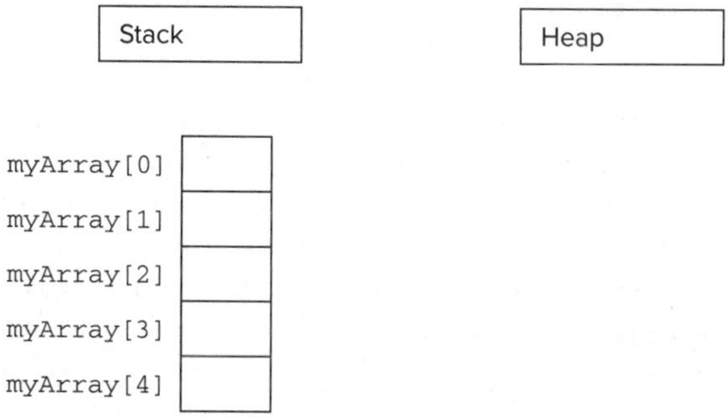

FIGURE 21-5

Figure 21-5 shows the state of memory after the array is declared. Declaring arrays on the heap is no different, except that you use a pointer to refer to the location of the array. The following code allocates memory for an array of five `int`s and stores a pointer to the memory in a variable called `myArrayPtr`.

```
int* myArrayPtr = new int[5];
```

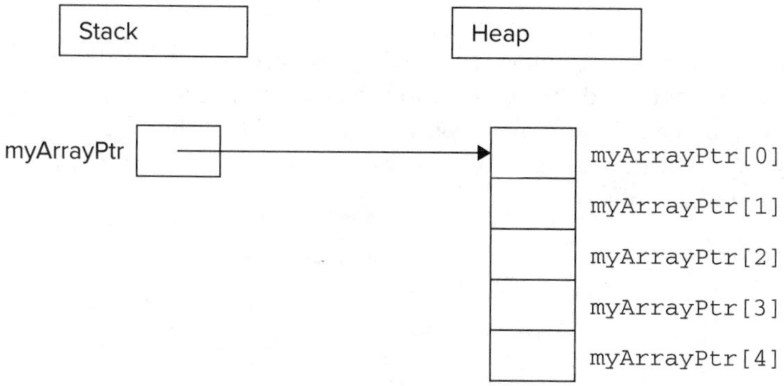

FIGURE 21-6

As Figure 21-6 illustrates, the heap-based array is similar to the stack-based array, but in a different location. The `myArrayPtr` variable points to the 0th element of the array. The advantage of putting an array on the heap is that you can use dynamic memory to define its size at run time. For example, the following function receives a desired number of documents from a hypothetical function named `askUserForNumberOfDocuments()` and uses that result to create an array of `Document` objects.

```
Document* createDocArray()
{
    int numDocs = askUserForNumberOfDocuments();
    Document* docArray = new Document[numDocs];
    return docArray;
}
```

 Some compilers allow variable-sized arrays on the stack. This is not a standard feature of C++, so we recommend cautiously backing away when you see it.

In the preceding function, `docArray` is a dynamically allocated array. Do not get this confused with a *dynamic array*. The array itself is not dynamic because its size does not change once it is allocated. Dynamic memory lets you specify the size of an allocated block at run time, but it does not automatically adjust its size to accommodate the data. There are data structures that do dynamically adjust in size to their data, such as the STL built-in `vector` class. It is recommended to use these STL containers like `vector` instead of standard arrays because they are much safer to use.

There is a function in C++ called `realloc()`, which is a holdover from the C language. Don't use it! In C, `realloc()` is used to effectively change the size of an array by allocating a new block of memory of the new size and moving all of the old data to the new location. This approach is extremely dangerous in C++ because user-defined objects will not respond well to bitwise copying.

 Do not use `realloc()` *in C++. It is not your friend.*

Arrays of Objects

Arrays of objects are no different than arrays of simple types. When you use `new[N]` to allocate an array of *N* objects, enough space is allocated for *N* contiguous blocks where each block is large enough for a single object. Using `new`, the zero-argument constructor for each of the objects will automatically be called. In this way, allocating an array of objects using `new[]` will return a pointer to an array of fully formed and initialized objects.

For example, consider the following class:

```
class Simple
{
    public:
        Simple() { cout << "Simple constructor called!" << endl; }
        virtual ~Simple() { cout << "Simple destructor called!" << endl; }
};
```

Code snippet from ArrayDelete\ArrayDelete.cpp

If you were to allocate an array of four `Simple` objects, the `Simple` constructor would be called four times.

Available for
download on
Wrox.com

```
Simple* mySimpleArray = new Simple[4];
```

Code snippet from ArrayDelete\ArrayDelete.cpp

The output of this code is:

```
Simple constructor called!
Simple constructor called!
Simple constructor called!
Simple constructor called!
```

The memory diagram for this array is shown in Figure 21-7. As you can see, it is no different than an array of basic types.

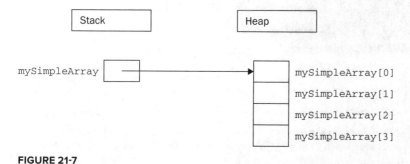

FIGURE 21-7

Deleting Arrays

When you allocate memory with the array version of `new` (`new[]`), you must release it with the array version of `delete` (`delete[]`). This version will automatically destruct the objects in the array in addition to releasing the memory associated with them. If you do not use the array version of `delete`, your program may behave in odd ways. In some compilers, only the destructor for the 0th element of the array will be called because the compiler only knows that you are deleting a pointer to an object, and all the other elements of the array will become orphaned objects. In others, memory corruption may occur because `new` and `new[]` can use completely different memory allocation schemes.

Available for
download on
Wrox.com

```
Simple* mySimpleArray = new Simple[4];
// Use mySimpleArray...
delete [] mySimpleArray;
mySimpleArray = nullptr;
```

Code snippet from ArrayDelete\ArrayDelete.cpp

> *Always use* `delete` *on anything allocated with* `new`, *and always use* `delete[]` *on anything allocated with* `new[]`.

Of course, the destructors are only called if the elements of the array are objects. If you have an array of pointers, you will still need to delete each object pointed to individually just as you allocated each object individually, as shown in the following code:

Available for download on Wrox.com

```
size_t arrSize = 4;
Simple** mySimplePtrArray = new Simple*[arrSize];
// Allocate an object for each pointer.
for (size_t i = 0; i < arrSize; i++) {
    mySimplePtrArray[i] = new Simple();
}
// Use mySimplePtrArray...
// Delete each allocated object.
for (size_t i = 0; i < arrSize; i++) {
    delete mySimplePtrArray[i];
}
// Delete the array itself.
delete [] mySimplePtrArray;
mySimplePtrArray = nullptr;
```

Code snippet from ArrayDelete\ArrayDelete.cpp

> *Instead of storing plain old dumb pointers in your data structures like the arrays above, it is recommended to store smart pointers in your data structures. These smart pointers will automatically deallocate memory associated with them. Smart pointers are discussed in detail later in this chapter.*

Multi-Dimensional Arrays

Multi-dimensional arrays extend the notion of indexed values to use multiple indices. For example, a Tic-Tac-Toe game might use a two-dimensional array to represent a three-by-three grid. The following example shows such an array declared on the stack and accessed with some test code:

Available for download on Wrox.com

```
char board[3][3];
// Test code
board[0][0] = 'X';    // X puts marker in position (0,0).
board[2][1] = '0';    // 0 puts marker in position (2,1).
```

Code snippet from tictactoe\tictactoe.cpp

You may be wondering whether the first subscript in a two-dimensional array is the x-coordinate or the y-coordinate. The truth is that it doesn't really matter, as long as you are consistent. A four-by-seven grid could be declared as `char board[4][7]` or `char board[7][4]`. For most applications, it is easiest to think of the first subscript as the x-axis and the second as the y-axis.

Multi-Dimensional Stack Arrays

In memory, a stack-based two-dimensional array looks like Figure 21-8. Since memory doesn't have two axes (addresses are merely sequential), the computer represents a two dimensional array just like a one-dimensional array. The difference is the size of the array and the method used to access it.

The size of a multi-dimensional array is all of its dimensions multiplied together, then multiplied by the size of a single element in the array. In Figure 21-8, the three-by-three board is 3×3×1 = 9 bytes, assuming that a character is 1 byte. For a four-by-seven board of characters, the array would be 4×7×1 = 28 bytes.

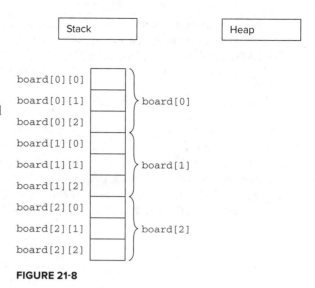

FIGURE 21-8

To access a value in a multi-dimensional array, the computer treats each subscript as accessing another subarray within the multi-dimensional array. For example, in the three-by-three grid, the expression board[0] actually refers to the subarray highlighted in Figure 21-9. When you add a second subscript, such as board[0][2], the computer is able to access the correct element by looking up the second subscript within the subarray, as shown in Figure 21-10.

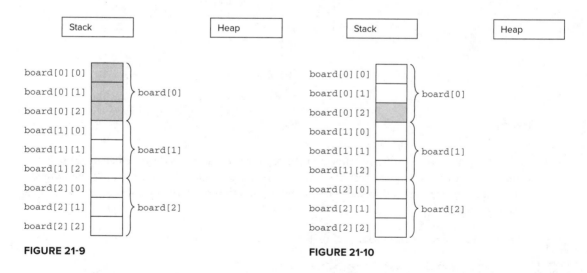

FIGURE 21-9   **FIGURE 21-10**

These techniques are extended to N-dimensional arrays, though dimensions higher than three tend to be difficult to conceptualize and are rarely useful in everyday applications.

Multi-Dimensional Heap Arrays

If you need to determine the dimensions of a multi-dimensional array at run time, you can use a heap-based array. Just as a single-dimensional dynamically allocated array is accessed through a pointer, a multi-dimensional dynamically allocated array is also accessed through a pointer. The only difference is that in a two-dimensional array, you need to start with a pointer-to-a-pointer; and in an *N*-dimensional array, you need *N* levels of pointers. At first, it might seem like the correct way to declare and allocate a dynamically allocated multi-dimensional array is as follows:

```
char** board = new char[i][j]; // BUG! Doesn't compile
```

This code doesn't compile because heap-based arrays don't work like stack-based arrays. Their memory layout isn't contiguous, so allocating enough memory for a stack-based multi-dimensional array is incorrect. Instead, you can start by allocating a single contiguous array for the first subscript dimension of a heap-based array. Each element of that array is actually a pointer to another array that stores the elements for the second subscript dimension. This layout for a two-by-two dynamically allocated board is shown in Figure 21-11.

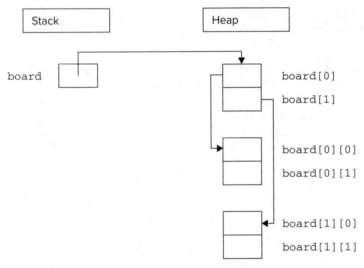

FIGURE 21-11

Unfortunately, the compiler doesn't allocate memory for the subarrays on your behalf. You can allocate the first dimension array just like a single-dimensional heap-based array, but the individual subarrays must be explicitly allocated. The following function properly allocates memory for a two-dimensional array:

```
char** allocateCharacterBoard(size_t xDimension, size_t yDimension)
{
    char** myArray = new char*[xDimension]; // Allocate first dimension
    for (size_t i = 0; i < xDimension; i++) {
        myArray[i] = new char[yDimension];  // Allocate ith subarray
    }
    return myArray;
}
```

Code snippet from CharacterBoard\CharacterBoard.cpp

When you wish to release the memory associated with a multi-dimensional heap-based array, the array `delete[]` syntax will not clean up the subarrays on your behalf. Your code to release an array should mirror the code to allocate it, as in the following function:

```
void releaseCharacterBoard(char** myArray, size_t xDimension)
{
    for (size_t i = 0; i < xDimension; i++) {
        delete [] myArray[i];      // Delete ith subarray
    }
    delete [] myArray;             // Delete first dimension
}
```

Code snippet from CharacterBoard\CharacterBoard.cpp

 Now that you know all the details to work with arrays, it is recommended to avoid old C-style arrays as much as possible because they do not provide any memory safety. Instead, use the C++ STL containers like `std::array`, `std::vector`, `std::list`, *and so on. For example, use* `vector<T>` *for a one dimensional dynamic array. Use* `vector<vector<T>>` *for a two dimensional dynamic array and so on.*

Working with Pointers

Pointers get their bad reputation from the relative ease with which you can abuse them. Because a pointer is just a memory address, you could theoretically change that address manually, even doing something as scary as the following line of code:

```
char* scaryPointer = (char*)7;
```

The previous line builds a pointer to the memory address 7, which is likely to be random garbage or memory that is used elsewhere in the application. If you start to use areas of memory that weren't set aside on your behalf with `new`, eventually you will corrupt the memory associated with an object, or the memory involved with the management of the heap, and your program will malfunction. Such a malfunction can manifest itself in several ways. For example, it can manifest itself as invalid results because the data has been corrupted, or as hardware exceptions being triggered due to accessing non-existent memory or attempting to write to protected memory. If you are lucky, you will get one of the serious errors that usually results in program termination by the operating system or the C++ run-time library; if you are unlucky, you will just get a wrong result.

A Mental Model for Pointers

There are two ways to think about pointers. More mathematically minded readers might view pointers simply as addresses. This view makes pointer arithmetic, covered later in this chapter, a bit easier to understand. Pointers aren't mysterious pathways through memory; they are simply numbers that happen to correspond to a location in memory. Figure 21-12 illustrates a two-by-two grid in the address-based view of the world.

Stack

board | 1000

Heap

2000	1000
5000	1001

	2000
	2001

	5000
	5001

FIGURE 21-12

 The addresses in Figure 21-12 are just for illustrative purposes. Addresses on a real system are highly dependent on your hardware and operating system.

Readers who are more comfortable with spatial representations might derive more benefit from the "arrow" view of pointers. A pointer is simply a level of indirection that says to the program "Hey! Look over there." With this view, multiple levels of pointers simply become individual steps on the path to data. Figure 21-11 showed a graphical view of pointers in memory.

When you *dereference* a pointer, by using the * operator, you are telling the program to look one level deeper in memory. In the address-based view, think of a dereference as a jump in memory to the address indicated by the pointer. With the graphical view, every dereference corresponds to following an arrow from its base to its head.

When you take the address of a location, using the & operator, you are adding a level of indirection in memory. In the address-based view, the program is simply noting the numerical address of the location, which can be stored as a pointer. In the graphical view, the & operator creates a new arrow whose head ends at the location designated by the expression. The base of the arrow can be stored as a pointer.

Casting with Pointers

Since pointers are just memory addresses (or arrows to somewhere), they are somewhat weakly typed. A pointer to an XML Document is the same size as a pointer to an integer. The compiler will let you easily cast any pointer type to any other pointer type using a C-style cast:

```
Document* documentPtr = getDocument();
char* myCharPtr = (char*)documentPtr;
```

A static cast offers a bit more safety. The compiler will refuse to perform a static cast on pointers to different data types:

```
Document* documentPtr = getDocument();
char* myCharPtr = static_cast<char*>(documentPtr);    // BUG! Won't compile
```

If the two pointers you are casting are actually pointing to objects that are related through inheritance, the compiler will permit a static cast. However, a dynamic cast is a safer way to accomplish a cast within an inheritance hierarchy. Consult Chapter 8 for details on dynamic casts.

const with Pointers

The interaction between the const keyword and pointers is a bit confusing because it is unclear to what you are applying const. If you dynamically allocate an array of integers and apply const to it, is the array address protected with const, or are the individual values protected? The answer depends on the syntax.

If const occurs before the type, it means that the pointed-to value is protected. In the case of an array, the individual elements of the array are const. The following function receives a pointer to a const integer. The first line will not compile because the actual value is protected by const. The second line would compile, because the pointer itself is unprotected:

```
void test(const int* inProtectedInt, int* anotherPtr)
{
    *inProtectedInt = 7;   // BUG! Attempts to write to const value
    inProtectedInt = anotherPtr;  // Works fine
}
```

To protect the pointer itself, the const keyword immediately precedes the variable name, as shown in the following code. This time, both the pointer and the pointed-to value are protected, so neither line would compile:

```
void test(const int* const inProtectedInt, int* anotherPtr)
{
    *inProtectedInt = 7;   // BUG! Attempts to write to const value
    inProtectedInt =  anotherPtr;  // BUG! Attempts to write to const value
}
```

In practice, protecting the pointer is rarely necessary. If a function is able to change the value of a pointer that you pass it, it makes little difference. The effect will only be local to the function, and the pointer will still point to its original address as far as the caller is concerned. Marking a pointer as const is more useful in documenting its purpose than for any actual protection. Protecting the pointed-to value(s), however, is quite common to protect against overwriting shared data, and to' allow the compiler to perform more powerful optimizations.

ARRAY-POINTER DUALITY

You have already seen some of the overlap between pointers and arrays. Heap-allocated arrays are referred to by a pointer to their first element. Stack-based arrays are referred to by using the array syntax ([]) with an otherwise normal variable declaration. As you are about to learn, however, the overlap doesn't end there. Pointers and arrays have a complicated relationship.

Arrays Are Pointers!

A heap-based array is not the only place where you can use a pointer to refer to an array. You can also use the pointer syntax to access elements of a stack-based array. The address of an array is really the address of the 0th element. The compiler knows that when you refer to an array in its entirety by its variable name, you are really referring to the address of the 0th element. In this way, the pointer works just like a heap-based array. The following code creates an array on the stack, but uses a pointer to access the array:

```
int main()
{
    int myIntArray[10];
    int* myIntPtr = myIntArray;
    // Access the array through the pointer.
    myIntPtr[4] = 5;
}
```

The ability to refer to a stack-based array through a pointer is useful when passing arrays into functions. The following function accepts an array of integers as a pointer. Note that the caller will need to explicitly pass in the size of the array because the pointer implies nothing about size. In fact, C++ arrays of any form, pointer or not, have no built-in notion of size.

Available for
download on
Wrox.com

```
void doubleInts(int* theArray, size_t inSize)
{
    for (size_t i = 0; i < inSize; i++) {
        theArray[i] *= 2;
    }
}
```

Code snippet from ArraysAndPointers\ArraysAndPointers.cpp

The caller of this function can pass a stack-based or heap-based array. In the case of a heap-based array, the pointer already exists and is simply passed by value into the function. In the case of a stack-based array, the caller can pass the array variable, and the compiler will automatically treat the array variable as a pointer to the array, or you can explicitly pass the address of the first element. All three forms are shown here:

Available for
download on
Wrox.com

```
size_t arrSize = 4;
int* heapArray = new int[arrSize];
heapArray[0] = 1;
heapArray[1] = 5;
heapArray[2] = 3;
heapArray[3] = 4;
doubleInts(heapArray, arrSize);
delete [] heapArray;
heapArray = nullptr;

int stackArray[] = {5, 7, 9, 11};
```

```
arrSize = sizeof(stackArray) / sizeof(stackArray[0]);
doubleInts(stackArray, arrSize);
doubleInts(&stackArray[0], arrSize);
```

Code snippet from ArraysAndPointers\ArraysAndPointers.cpp

Even if the function doesn't explicitly have a parameter that is a pointer, the parameter-passing semantics of arrays are uncannily similar to that of pointers, because the compiler treats an array as a pointer when it is passed to a function. A function that takes an array as an argument and changes values inside the array is actually changing the original array, not a copy. Just like a pointer, passing an array effectively mimics pass-by-reference functionality because what you really pass to the function is the address of the original array, not a copy. The following implementation of doubleInts() changes the original array even though the parameter is an array, not a pointer:

```
void doubleInts(int theArray[], size_t inSize)
{
    for (size_t i = 0; i < inSize; i++) {
        theArray[i] *= 2;
    }
}
```

Code snippet from ArraysAndPointers\ArraysAndPointers.cpp

You may be wondering why things work this way. Why doesn't the compiler just copy the array when array syntax is used in the function definition? This is done for efficiency — it takes time to copy the elements of an array, and they potentially take up a lot of memory. By always passing a pointer, the compiler doesn't need to include the code to copy the array.

To summarize, arrays declared using array syntax can be accessed through a pointer. When an array is passed to a function, it is always passed as a pointer.

Not All Pointers Are Arrays!

Since the compiler lets you pass in an array where a pointer is expected, as in the doubleInts() function shown earlier, you may be lead to believe that pointers and arrays are the same. In fact there are subtle, but important, differences. Pointers and arrays share many properties and can sometimes be used interchangeably (as shown earlier), but they are not the same.

A pointer by itself is meaningless. It may point to random memory, a single object, or an array. You can always use array syntax with a pointer, but doing so is not always appropriate because pointers aren't always arrays. For example, consider the following code:

```
int* ptr = new int;
```

The pointer ptr is a valid pointer, but it is not an array. You can access the pointed-to value using array syntax (ptr[0]), but doing so is stylistically questionable and provides no real benefit. In fact, using array syntax with non-array pointers is an invitation for bugs. The memory at ptr[1] could be anything!

Arrays are automatically referenced as pointers, but not all pointers are arrays.

LOW-LEVEL MEMORY OPERATIONS

One of the great advantages of C++ over C is that you don't need to worry quite as much about memory. If you code using objects, you just need to make sure that each individual class properly manages its own memory. Through construction and destruction, the compiler helps you manage memory by telling you when to do it. Hiding the management of memory within classes makes a huge difference in usability, as demonstrated by the STL classes.

With some applications, however, you may encounter the need to work with memory at a lower level. Whether for efficiency, debugging, or curiosity, knowing some techniques for working with raw bytes can be helpful.

Pointer Arithmetic

The C++ compiler uses the declared types of pointers to allow you to perform *pointer arithmetic*. If you declare a pointer to an int and increase it by 1, the pointer moves ahead in memory by the size of an int, not by a single byte. This type of operation is most useful with arrays, since they contain homogeneous data that is sequential in memory. For example, assume you declare an array of ints on the heap:

```
int* myArray = new int[8];
```

You are already familiar with the following syntax for setting the value in position 2:

```
myArray[2] = 33;
```

With pointer arithmetic, you can equivalently use the following syntax, which obtains a pointer to the memory that is "2 ints ahead" of myArray and then dereferences it to set the value:

```
*(myArray + 2) = 33;
```

As an alternative syntax for accessing individual elements, pointer arithmetic doesn't seem too appealing. Its real power lies in the fact that an expression like myArray + 2 is still a pointer to an int, and thus can represent a smaller int array. Suppose you had the following wide string:

```
const wchar_t* myString = L"Hello, World!";
```

Suppose you also had a function that took in a string and returned a new string that contains a capitalized version of the input:

```
wchar_t* toCaps(const wchar_t* inString);
```

You could capitalize myString by passing it into this function. However, if you only wanted to capitalize *part* of myString, you could use pointer arithmetic to refer to only a latter part of the string. The following code calls `toCaps()` on the `World` part of the string by just adding 7 to the pointer, even though `wchar_t` is usually more than 1 byte:

```
toCaps(myString + 7);
```

Another useful application of pointer arithmetic involves subtraction. Subtracting one pointer from another of the same type gives you the number of elements of the pointed-to type between the two pointers, not the absolute number of bytes between them.

Custom Memory Management

For 99 percent of the cases you will encounter (some might say 100 percent of the cases), the built-in memory allocation facilities in C++ are adequate. Behind the scenes, `new` and `delete` do all the work of handing out memory in properly sized chunks, maintaining a list of available areas of memory, and releasing chunks of memory back to that list upon deletion.

When resource constraints are extremely tight, or under very special conditions, such as managing shared memory, implementing custom memory management may be a viable option. Don't worry — it's not as scary as it sounds. Basically, managing memory yourself generally means that classes allocate a large chunk of memory and dole out that memory in pieces as it is needed.

How is this approach any better? Managing your own memory can potentially reduce overhead. When you use `new` to allocate memory, the program also needs to set aside a small amount of space to record how much memory was allocated. That way, when you call `delete`, the proper amount of memory can be released. For most objects, the overhead is so much smaller than the memory allocated that it makes little difference. However, for small objects or programs with enormous numbers of objects, the overhead can have an impact.

When you manage memory yourself, you might know the size of each object a priori, so you might be able to avoid the overhead for each object. The difference can be enormous for large numbers of small objects. The syntax for performing custom memory management is described in Chapter 18.

Garbage Collection

At the other end of the memory hygiene spectrum lies *garbage collection*. With environments that support garbage collection, the programmer rarely, if ever, explicitly frees memory associated with an object. Instead, objects to which there are no references anymore will be cleaned up automatically at some point by the run-time library.

Garbage collection is not built into the C++ language as it is in C# and Java. Most C++ programs manage memory at the object level through `new` and `delete`. It is possible to implement garbage collection in C++, but freeing yourself from the task of releasing memory would probably introduce new headaches.

One approach to garbage collection is called *mark and sweep*. With this approach, the garbage collector periodically examines every single pointer in your program and annotates the fact that the referenced memory is still in use. At the end of the cycle, any memory that hasn't been marked is deemed to be not in use and is freed.

A mark and sweep algorithm could be implemented in C++ if you were willing to do the following:

1. Register all pointers with the garbage collector so that it can easily walk through the list of all pointers.

2. Subclass all objects from a mix-in class, perhaps `GarbageCollectible`, that allows the garbage collector to mark an object as in-use.

3. Protect concurrent access to objects by making sure that no changes to pointers can occur while the garbage collector is running.

As you can see, this simple approach to garbage collection requires quite a bit of diligence on the part of the programmer. It may even be more error-prone than using `delete`! Attempts at a safe and easy mechanism for garbage collection have been made in C++, but even if a perfect implementation of garbage collection in C++ came along, it wouldn't necessarily be appropriate to use for all applications. Among the downsides of garbage collection:

➤ When the garbage collector is actively running, the program will likely be unresponsive.

➤ With garbage collectors, you have so called non-deterministic destructors. Because an object is not destroyed until it is garbage collected, the destructor is not executed immediately when the object leaves its scope. This means that cleaning up resources (such as closing a file, releasing a lock, etc.), which is done by the destructor, is not performed until some indeterminate time in the future.

Object Pools

Garbage collection is like buying plates for a picnic and leaving any used plates out in the yard where the wind will conveniently blow them into the neighbor's yard. Surely, there must be a more ecological approach to memory management.

Object pools are the analog of recycling. You buy a reasonable number of plates, and after using a plate, you clean it so that it can be reused later. Object pools are ideal for situations where you need to use many objects of the same type over time, and creating each one incurs overhead.

Chapter 24 contains further details about using object pools for performance efficiency.

Function Pointers

You don't normally think about the location of functions in memory, but each function actually lives at a particular address. In C++, you can use *functions as data*. In other words, you can take the address of a function and use it like you use a variable.

Function pointers are typed according to the parameter types and return type of compatible functions. One way to work with function pointers is to use the `typedef` mechanism to assign a type name to the family of functions that have the given characteristics. For example, the following line declares a type called `YesNoFcn` that represents a pointer to any function that has two `int` parameters and returns a `bool`:

```
typedef bool(*YesNoFcn)(int, int);
```

Code snippet from FunctionPointers\FunctionPointers.cpp

C++11 introduces the type alias feature which you can use instead of a `typedef` and which might be more readable. Type aliases are discussed in Chapter 9. The following line is basically the same as the previous `typedef` line:

```
using YesNoFcn = bool(*)(int, int);
```

Now that this new type exists, you could write a function that takes a `YesNoFcn` as a parameter. For example, the following function accepts two `int` arrays and their size, as well as a `YesNoFcn`. It iterates through the arrays in parallel and calls the `YesNoFcn` on corresponding elements of both arrays, printing a message if the `YesNoFcn` function returns `true`. Notice that even though the `YesNoFcn` is passed in as a variable, it can be called just like a regular function:

```
void findMatches(int values1[], int values2[], size_t numValues, YesNoFcn inFunc)
{
    for (size_t i = 0; i < numValues; i++) {
        if (inFunc(values1[i], values2[i])) {
            cout << "Match found at position " << i <<
                " (" << values1[i] << ", " << values2[i] << ")" << endl;
        }
    }
}
```

Code snippet from FunctionPointers\FunctionPointers.cpp

To call the `findMatches()` function, all you need is any function that adheres to the defined `YesNoFcn` type — that is, any type that takes in two `int`s and returns a `bool`. For example, consider the following function, which returns `true` if the two parameters are equal:

```
bool intEqual(int inItem1, int inItem2)
{
    return inItem1 == inItem2;
}
```

Code snippet from FunctionPointers\FunctionPointers.cpp

Because the `intEqual()` function matches the `YesNoFcn` type, it can be passed as the final argument to `findMatches()`, as follows:

```
int arr1[] = {2, 5, 6, 9, 10, 1, 1};
int arr2[] = {4, 4, 2, 9, 0, 3, 4};
int arrSize = sizeof(arr1) / sizeof(arr1[0]);
cout << "Calling findMatches() using intEqual():" << endl;
findMatches(arr1, arr2, arrSize, &intEqual);
```

Code snippet from FunctionPointers\FunctionPointers.cpp

Notice that the `intEqual()` function is passed into the `findMatches()` function by taking its address. Technically, the `&` character is optional — if you simply put the function name, the compiler will know that you mean to take its address. The output is as follows:

```
Calling findMatches() using intEqual():
Match found at position 3 (9, 9)
```

The benefit of function pointers lies in the fact that `findMatches()` is a generic function that compares parallel values in two arrays. As it is used above, it compares based on equality. However, since it takes a function pointer, it could compare based on other criteria. For example, the following function also adheres to the definition of a `YesNoFcn`:

```
bool bothOdd(int inItem1, int inItem2)
{
    return inItem1 % 2 == 1 && inItem2 % 2 == 1;
}
```

Code snippet from FunctionPointers\FunctionPointers.cpp

The following code calls `findMatches()` using `bothOdd`:

```
cout << "Calling findMatches() using bothOdd():" << endl;
findMatches(arr1, arr2, arrSize, &bothOdd);
```

Code snippet from FunctionPointers\FunctionPointers.cpp

The output will be:

```
Calling findMatches() using bothOdd():
Match found at position 3 (9, 9)
Match found at position 5 (1, 3)
```

By using function pointers, a single function, `findMatches()`, was customized to different uses based on a parameter, `inFunc`.

Instead of using these old-style function pointers, you can also use the C++11 `std::function` which is explained in Chapter 16.

Pointers to Methods and Members

You can create and use pointers to both variables and functions. Now, consider pointers to class members and methods. It's perfectly legitimate in C++ to take the addresses of class members and methods in order to obtain pointers to them. However, you can't access a non-`static` member or call a non-`static` method without an object. The whole point of class members and methods is that they exist on a per-object basis. Thus, when you want to call the method or access the member via the pointer, you must dereference the pointer in the context of an object. Here is an example:

Available for download on Wrox.com

```
SpreadsheetCell myCell(123);
double (SpreadsheetCell::*methodPtr) () const = &SpreadsheetCell::getValue;
cout << (myCell.*methodPtr)() << endl;
```

Code snippet from PtrsToMethodsAndMembers\SpreadsheetCellTest.cpp

Don't panic at the syntax. The second line declares a variable called `methodPtr` of type pointer to a non-`static const` method that takes no arguments and returns a `double`. At the same time, it initializes this variable to point to the `getValue()` method of the `SpreadsheetCell` class. This syntax is quite similar to declaring a simple function pointer, except for the addition of `SpreadsheetCell::` before the `*methodPtr`. Note also that the `&` is required in this case.

The third line calls the `getValue()` method (via the `methodPtr` pointer) on the `myCell` object. Note the use of parentheses surrounding `myCell.*methodPtr`. They are needed because `()` has higher precedence than `*`.

Most of the time C++ programmers simplify the second line by using a `typedef`:

Available for download on Wrox.com

```
SpreadsheetCell myCell(123);
typedef double (SpreadsheetCell::*PtrToGet) () const;
PtrToGet methodPtr = &SpreadsheetCell::getValue;
cout << (myCell.*methodPtr)() << endl;
```

Code snippet from PtrsToMethodsAndMembers\SpreadsheetCellTest.cpp

Pointers to methods and members usually won't come up in your programs. However, it's important to keep in mind that you can't dereference a pointer to a non-`static` method or member without an object. Every so often, you'll find yourself wanting to try something like passing a pointer to a non-`static` method to a function such as `qsort()` that requires a function pointer, which simply won't work .

 Note that C++ permits you to dereference a pointer to a `static` member or method without an object.

SMART POINTERS

Memory management in C++ is a perennial source of errors and bugs. Many of these bugs arise from the use of dynamic memory allocation and pointers. When you extensively use dynamic memory allocation in your program and pass many pointers between objects, it's difficult to remember to call `delete` on each pointer exactly once and at the right time. The consequences of getting it wrong are severe: When you free dynamically allocated memory more than once you can cause memory corruption or a fatal run-time error, and when you forget to free dynamically allocated memory you cause memory leaks.

Smart pointers help you manage your dynamically allocated memory and are the recommended technique for avoiding memory leaks. Smart pointers are a notion that arose from the fact that most memory-related issues are avoidable by putting everything on the stack. The stack is much safer than the heap because stack variables are automatically destructed and cleaned up when they go out of scope. Smart pointers combine the safety of stack variables with the flexibility of heap variables. There are several kinds of smart pointers. The most simple type of smart pointer takes sole ownership of the memory and when the smart pointer goes out of scope, it will free the referenced memory, for example, `unique_ptr` in C++11.

However, managing pointers presents more problems than just remembering to delete them when they go out of scope. Sometimes several objects or pieces of code contain copies of the same pointer. This problem is called *aliasing*. In order to free all memory properly, the last piece of code to use the memory should call `delete` on the pointer. However, it is often difficult to know which piece of code uses the memory last. It may even be impossible to determine the order when you code because it might depend on run-time inputs. Thus, a more sophisticated type of smart pointer implements reference counting to keep track of its owners. When all owners are finished using the pointer, the number of references drops to 0 and the smart pointer calls `delete` on its underlying dumb pointer. The standard C++11 `shared_ptr` smart pointer discussed later includes reference counting. It is important to be familiar with this concept.

Some languages provide garbage collection so that programmers are not responsible for freeing any memory. In these languages, all pointers can be thought of as smart pointers because you don't need to remember to free any of the memory to which they point. Although some languages, such as Java, provide garbage collection as a matter of course, it is very difficult to write a garbage collector for C++. Thus, smart pointers are simply a technique to make up for the fact that C++ exposes memory management without garbage collection.

C++ provides several language features that make smart pointers attractive. First, you can write a type-safe smart pointer class for any pointer type using templates. Second, you can provide an interface to the smart pointer objects using operator overloading that allows code to use the smart pointer objects as if they were dumb pointers. Specifically, you can overload the * and -> operators such that the client code can dereference a smart pointer object the same way it dereferences a normal pointer.

The Old Deprecated auto_ptr

The old, pre-C++11 standard template library included a basic implementation of a smart pointer, called `auto_ptr`. Unfortunately, `auto_ptr` has some serious shortcomings. One of these shortcomings is that it does not work correctly when used inside STL containers like `vectors`. C++11 has officially deprecated `auto_ptr` and replaced it with `shared_ptr` and `unique_ptr`, discussed in the next section. `auto_ptr` is mentioned here to make sure you know about it and to make sure you never use it.

 *Do **not** use the old* `auto_ptr` *smart pointer anymore. Instead use the new C++11* `shared_ptr` *or* `unique_ptr`*!*

C++11 The New C++11 Smart Pointers

C++11 introduces two new smart pointer classes: shared_ptr and unique_ptr. The difference between the two is that shared_ptr is a reference counted smart pointer, while unique_ptr is not reference counted. This means that you can have several shared_ptr instances pointing to the same dynamically allocated memory and the memory will only be deallocated when the last shared_ptr goes out of scope. For this reason, shared_ptr is safer/easier to use compared to unique_ptr. Most of the remainder of this section focuses on the shared_ptr template.

As a rule of thumb, always store dynamically allocated objects in stack-based instances of shared_ptr. For example, consider the following function that blatantly leaks memory by allocating a Simple object on the heap and neglecting to release it:

```
void leaky()
{
    Simple* mySimplePtr = new Simple();  // BUG! Memory is never released!
    mySimplePtr->go();
}
```

Using the shared_ptr template, the object is still not explicitly deleted; but when the shared_ptr instance goes out of scope (at the end of the function) it automatically deallocates the Simple object in its destructor:

```
void notLeaky()
{
    shared_ptr<Simple> mySimpleSmartPtr(new Simple());
    mySimpleSmartPtr->go();
}
```

You need to include the <memory> header file which defines these smart pointer templates. One of the greatest characteristics of smart pointers is that they provide enormous benefit without requiring the user to learn a lot of new syntax. As you can see in the preceding code, the smart pointer can still be dereferenced (using * or ->) just like a standard pointer.

Sometimes you might think that your code is properly deallocating dynamically allocated memory. Unfortunately, it most likely is **not correct** in all situations. Take the following function:

```
void couldBeLeaky()
{
    Simple* mySimplePtr = new Simple();
    mySimplePtr->go();
    delete mySimplePtr;
}
```

The above function dynamically allocates a Simple object, uses the object, and then properly calls delete. However, you can still have memory leaks in this example! If the go() method throws an exception, the call to delete will never be executed, causing a memory leak. So, also in this case it is recommended to use smart pointers.

Never assign the result of a memory allocation to a dumb pointer. Whether you use new *or* malloc() *or any other memory allocation method, always immediately give the resulting memory pointer to a smart pointer,* shared_ptr *or* unique_ptr.

If you use old C-style arrays, you cannot use shared_ptr to manage their memory. Instead of using the old C-style arrays, you should switch to modern memory safe containers like the std::array, std::vector and so on, or give the C-style array to a unique_ptr which is allowed.

 Never use a shared_ptr *to manage a pointer to a C-style array. Use* unique_ptr *to manage the C-style array, or use STL containers instead of C-style arrays.*

A shared_ptr can be created in two ways. With the first way, you have to mention the type you want to allocate twice: once as template parameter for shared_ptr and once as parameter to the new operator:

```
shared_ptr<Simple> mySimpleSmartPtr(new Simple());
```

The second syntax is as follows:

```
auto mySimpleSmartPtr = make_shared<Simple>();
```

This syntax uses the auto keyword and uses make_shared(), so you only have to specify the allocated type (Simple) once. If the Simple constructor requires parameters, you put them in between the parentheses of the make_shared() call. In fact, using make_shared() not only requires less typing, but the compiler can also generate more efficient code than using the longer syntax. For example, with Microsoft Visual C++ if you define your shared_ptr with the syntax shown in the following line, VC++ needs to allocate memory for the object and then allocate memory for a so called *reference count control block* that stores the reference count. The details of the reference count control block are specific to VC++ and are not important for this discussion.

```
shared_ptr<Simple> mySimpleSmartPtr(new Simple());
```

However, by using make_shared() as follows, VC++ optimizes this memory allocation and allocates enough memory for both the object and the reference count control block with a single memory allocation call:

```
auto mySimpleSmartPtr = make_shared<Simple>();
```

By default, shared_ptr will use the standard new and delete operators to allocate and deallocate memory. You can change this behavior as follows:

```
int* malloc_int(int value)
{
    int* p = (int*)malloc(sizeof(int));
    *p = value;
    return p;
}
int main()
{
    shared_ptr<int> myIntSmartPtr(malloc_int(42), free);
    return 0;
}
```

Code snippet from shared_ptr\shared_ptr_malloc_int.cpp

This will allocate the memory for the integer with `malloc_int()`, and the `shared_ptr` will deallocate the memory using the standard `free()` function. As mentioned earlier, in C++ you should never use `malloc()` but `new` instead. However, this feature of `shared_ptr` is available because it is very useful to manage other resources instead of just memory. For example, it can be used to automatically close a file or network socket or anything when the `shared_ptr` goes out of scope. The following example uses a `shared_ptr` to store a file pointer. When the `shared_ptr` goes out of scope, the file pointer is automatically closed with a call to the `CloseFile()` function. Remember that C++ has proper object oriented classes to work with files (see Chapter 15). Those classes will already automatically close their files when they go out of scope. This example using the old C `fopen()` and `fclose()` functions is just to give a demonstration for what `shared_ptrs` can be used for besides pure memory:

```
void CloseFile(FILE* filePtr)
{
    if (filePtr == nullptr)
        return;
    fclose(filePtr);
    cout << "File closed." << endl;
}
int main()
{
    shared_ptr<FILE> filePtr(fopen("data.txt", "w"), CloseFile);
    if (filePtr == nullptr) {
        cerr << "Error opening file." << endl;
    } else {
        cout << "File opened." << endl;
        // Use filePtr
    }
    return 0;
}
```

Code snippet from shared_ptr\shared_ptr_file.cpp

Both `shared_ptr` and `unique_ptr` support the C++11 move semantics remove discussed in Chapter 9 to make them very efficient. Because of this, it is also efficient to return a `shared_ptr` or a `unique_ptr` from a function. For example, you can write the following function `func()` and use it as demonstrated in the `main()` function:

```
// ... definition of Simple not shown for brevity
shared_ptr<Simple> func()
{
    auto ptr = make_shared<Simple>();
    return ptr;
}
int main()
{
    shared_ptr<Simple> mySmartPtr = func();
    return 0;
}
```

Code snippet from shared_ptr\shared_ptr_return_from_function.cpp

This will be efficient because C++11 will automatically call `std::move()` on the return statement in the `func()` function, which will trigger the move semantics of the `shared_ptr`. The same happens if you would use `unique_ptr` instead of `shared_ptr`. The `unique_ptr` does not support the normal copy assignment operator and copy constructor, but it does support the move assignment operator and move constructor, and that is why you can return a `unique_ptr` from a function. Take the following `unique_ptr` assignments:

```
unique_ptr<int> p1(new int(42));
unique_ptr<int> p2 = p1;         // Error: does not compile
unique_ptr<int> p3 = move(p1);   // OK
```

The line defining `p2` will not compile because it is trying to use the copy constructor, which is not available for `unique_ptr`. The definition of `p3` is good because `std::move()` (defined in the `<utility>` header file, see Chapter 9) is used to trigger the move constructor of `unique_ptr`. After `p3` is defined, `p1` will be reset to `nullptr` and you will only be able to access the integer 42 through `p3`; ownership has been moved from `p1` to `p3`.

There is one more class in C++11 that is related to the `shared_ptr` template; the `weak_ptr`. A `weak_ptr` can contain a reference to memory that is managed by a `shared_ptr`. The `weak_ptr` does not own the memory, so the `shared_ptr` is not prevented from deallocating the memory. A `weak_ptr` will not destroy the pointed to memory when it goes out of scope; however, it can be used to determine if the memory has been deallocated by the associated `shared_ptr` or not. The constructor of a `weak_ptr` requires a `shared_ptr` or another `weak_ptr` as argument. To get access to the pointer stored in the `weak_ptr` you need to convert it to a `shared_ptr`. There are two ways to do this: Use the `lock()` method on the `weak_ptr` instance, which will return a `shared_ptr`, or create a new `shared_ptr` instance and give the `weak_ptr` as argument to the `shared_ptr` constructor. The `weak_ptr` is a rather advanced feature of the C++11 smart pointers. It is rarely used and not further discussed in this book, but it is good to know its existence.

Writing Your Own Smart Pointer Class

It is highly recommended to use the standard `shared_ptr` or `unique_ptr` classes. However, sometimes you need some functionality not provided by these standard implementations, or your compiler might not yet support `shared_ptr` in which case you can implement your own reference-counted smart pointer. This section explains how you can implement your own reference-counted smart pointer. Chapter 18 provides an initial version of a smart pointer class called `Pointer` which is using operator overloading so the user can use the `Pointer` class just like a normal dumb pointer. This section enhances this `Pointer` class to include reference counting which is missing from the initial version.

The Need for Reference Counting

As a general concept, *reference counting* is the technique for keeping track of the number of instances of a class or particular object that are in use. A reference-counting smart pointer is one that keeps track of how many smart pointers have been built to refer to a single real pointer, or single object. This way, smart pointers can avoid double deletion.

The double deletion problem is easy to provoke. Consider the following class, `Nothing`, which simply prints out messages when an object is created or destroyed:

Available for download on Wrox.com

```cpp
class Nothing
{
    public:
        Nothing() { cout << "Nothing::Nothing()" << endl; }
        ~Nothing() { cout << "Nothing::~Nothing()" << endl; }
};
```

Code snippet from shared_ptr\shared_ptr_double_delete.cpp

If you were to create two standard `shared_ptrs` and have them both refer to the same `Nothing` object as follows, both smart pointers would attempt to delete the same object when they go out of scope:

Available for download on Wrox.com

```cpp
void doubleDelete()
{
    Nothing* myNothing = new Nothing();
    shared_ptr<Nothing> smartPtr1(myNothing);
    shared_ptr<Nothing> smartPtr2(myNothing);
}
```

Code snippet from shared_ptr\shared_ptr_double_delete.cpp

The output of the previous function would be:

```
Nothing::Nothing()
Nothing::~Nothing()
Nothing::~Nothing()
```

Yikes! One call to the constructor and two calls to the destructor? You will get exactly the same result with the `unique_ptr` template and with the old deprecated `auto_ptr` smart pointer. You might be surprised that even the reference-counted `shared_ptr` class behaves this way. However, this is correct behavior according to the C++11 standard. You should not use `shared_ptr` like in the previous `doubleDelete()` function to create two `shared_ptrs` pointing to the same object. Instead, you should simply use the assignment operator as follows:

```
void noDoubleDelete()
{
    Nothing* myNothing = new Nothing();
    shared_ptr<Nothing> smartPtr1(myNothing);
    shared_ptr<Nothing> smartPtr2 = smartPtr1;
}
```

Code snippet from shared_ptr\shared_ptr_double_delete.cpp

The output of this code is:

```
Nothing::Nothing()
Nothing::~Nothing()
```

Even though there are two `shared_ptrs` pointing to the same `Nothing` object, the `Nothing` object is only destroyed once. Remember that `unique_ptr` is not reference counted. In fact, `unique_ptr` will not allow you to use the assignment operator as in the `noDoubleDelete()` function. That's another reason to prefer `shared_ptr` instead of `unique_ptr`.

If your program uses smart pointers by copying them, assigning them, or passing them as arguments to functions, the `shared_ptr` *is the perfect solution.*

If you really need to write code as shown in the previous `doubleDelete()` function, you will need to implement your own smart pointer to prevent double deletion. You can also implement your own reference-counted smart pointer in case your compiler does not yet support `shared_ptr`. How to do this is shown in the next section. But again, it is recommended to use the standard `shared_ptr` template and simply avoid code as in the `doubleDelete()` function, and use assignment instead:

```
shared_ptr<Nothing> smartPtr2 = smartPtr1;
```

The SuperSmartPointer

This section explains how to write your own reference-counting smart pointer that you can use to solve the double deletion problem from the `doubleDelete()` function in the previous section.

The approach for the `SuperSmartPointer`, a reference-counting smart pointer implementation is to keep a static map for reference counts. Each key in the map is the memory address of a traditional pointer that is referred to by one or more `SuperSmartPointers`. The corresponding value is the number of `SuperSmartPointers` that refer to that object.

The implementation of `SuperSmartPointer` that follows is based on the smart pointer code shown in Chapter 18. You may want to review that code before continuing. The major changes occur when a new pointer is set (through the single argument constructor, the copy constructor, or `operator=`)

and when a `SuperSmartPointer` is finished with an underlying pointer (upon destruction or reassignment with `operator=`).

On initialization of a new pointer, the `initPointer()` method checks the static map to see if the pointer is already contained by an existing `SuperSmartPointer`. If it is not, the count is initialized to 1. If it is already in the map, the count is bumped up. When the pointer is reassigned or the containing `SuperSmartPointer` is destroyed, the `finalizePointer()` method is called. This method throws an exception if the pointer is not found in the map. If the pointer is found, its count is decremented by one. If this brings the count down to zero, the underlying pointer can be safely released. At that time, the key/value pair is explicitly removed from the map to keep the map size down:

```cpp
template <typename T>
class SuperSmartPointer
{
    public:
        explicit SuperSmartPointer(T* inPtr);
        virtual ~SuperSmartPointer();
        SuperSmartPointer(const SuperSmartPointer<T>& src);
        SuperSmartPointer<T>& operator=(const SuperSmartPointer<T>& rhs);
        const T& operator*() const;
        const T* operator->() const;
        T& operator*();
        T* operator->();
        operator void*() const { return mPtr; }
    protected:
        T* mPtr;
        static std::map<T*, int> sRefCountMap;
        void finalizePointer();
        void initPointer(T* inPtr);
};
template <typename T>
std::map<T*, int> SuperSmartPointer<T>::sRefCountMap;
template <typename T>
SuperSmartPointer<T>::SuperSmartPointer(T* inPtr)
{
    initPointer(inPtr);
}
template <typename T>
SuperSmartPointer<T>::SuperSmartPointer(const SuperSmartPointer<T>& src)
{
    initPointer(src.mPtr);
}
template <typename T>
SuperSmartPointer<T>&
    SuperSmartPointer<T>::operator=(const SuperSmartPointer<T>& rhs)
{
    if (this == &rhs) {
        return *this;
    }
    finalizePointer();
    initPointer(rhs.mPtr);
    return *this;
}
```

```
template <typename T>
SuperSmartPointer<T>::~SuperSmartPointer()
{
    finalizePointer();
}
template<typename T>
void SuperSmartPointer<T>::initPointer(T* inPtr)
{
    mPtr = inPtr;
    if (sRefCountMap.find(mPtr) == sRefCountMap.end()) {
        sRefCountMap[mPtr] = 1;
    } else {
        sRefCountMap[mPtr]++;
    }
}
template<typename T>
void SuperSmartPointer<T>::finalizePointer()
{
    if (sRefCountMap.find(mPtr) == sRefCountMap.end()) {
        throw std::runtime_error("ERROR: Missing entry in map!");
    }
    sRefCountMap[mPtr]--;
    if (sRefCountMap[mPtr] == 0) {
        // No more references to this object--delete it and remove from map
        sRefCountMap.erase(mPtr);
        delete mPtr;
        mPtr = nullptr;
    }
}
template <typename T>
const T* SuperSmartPointer<T>::operator->() const
{
    return mPtr;
}
template <typename T>
const T& SuperSmartPointer<T>::operator*() const
{
    return *mPtr;
}
template <typename T>
T* SuperSmartPointer<T>::operator->()
{
    return mPtr;
}
template <typename T>
T& SuperSmartPointer<T>::operator*()
{
    return *mPtr;
}
```

Code snippet from SuperSmartPointer\SuperSmartPointer.cpp

Unit Testing the SuperSmartPointer

The Nothing class defined earlier can be employed for a simple unit test for SuperSmartPointer. One modification is needed to determine if the test passed or failed. Two static members are added to the `Nothing` class, which track the number of allocations and the number of deletions. The constructor and destructor modify these values instead of printing a message. If the `SuperSmartPointer` works, the numbers should always be equivalent when the program terminates. Here is the adapted `Nothing` class:

```
class Nothing
{
    public:
        Nothing() { sNumAllocations++; }
        virtual ~Nothing() { sNumDeletions++; }
        static int sNumAllocations;
        static int sNumDeletions;
};
int Nothing::sNumAllocations = 0;
int Nothing::sNumDeletions = 0;
```

Code snippet from SuperSmartPointer\SuperSmartPointer.cpp

Following is the actual test. Note that an extra set of curly braces is used to keep the `SuperSmartPointers` in a smaller scope, so the example can show automatic allocation and deallocation self-contained within one block:

```
Nothing* myNothing = new Nothing();
{
    SuperSmartPointer<Nothing> ptr1(myNothing);
    SuperSmartPointer<Nothing> ptr2(myNothing);
}
if (Nothing::sNumAllocations != Nothing::sNumDeletions) {
    std::cout << "TEST FAILED: " << Nothing::sNumAllocations <<
            " allocations and " << Nothing::sNumDeletions <<
            " deletions" << std::endl;
} else {
    std::cout << "TEST PASSED" << std::endl;
}
```

Code snippet from SuperSmartPointer\SuperSmartPointer.cpp

A successful execution of this test program will result in the following output:

```
TEST PASSED
```

You should also write additional tests for the `SuperSmartPointer` class. For example, you should test the copy construction and `operator=` functionality. This is left as an exercise for the reader.

Enhancing This Implementation

The previous `SuperSmartPointer` implementation is not completely free of problems. Templates exist on a per-type basis. In other words, if you have some `SuperSmartPointers` that store pointers to integers and others that store pointers to characters, there are actually two classes generated at compile time: `SuperSmartPointer<int>` and `SuperSmartPointer<char>`. Because the reference count map is stored statically within the class, two maps will be generated. In most cases, this won't cause a problem, but you could cast a `char*` to an `int*` resulting in two `SuperSmartPointer`s of two different template classes that refer to the same allocated memory. Because the table data is separate, double deletion would occur, as demonstrated by the following code:

```
char* ch = new char;
SuperSmartPointer<char> ptr1(ch);
SuperSmartPointer<int> ptr2((int*)ch);   // BUG! Double deletion will occur!
```

One solution to this problem is to make the reference map a global variable, though globals are often frowned upon. Another solution would be to wrap the map in a non-template singleton class, perhaps called `MapManager`, which is referenced by the `SuperSmartPointer` template classes. The singleton pattern is discussed in Chapter 29.

The other issue with this implementation is that it is not thread safe. As Chapter 22 explains, threads are a new feature of C++11. Threads are very common in modern programming so you should be aware of thread safety. Access to the static map should be protected by a lock so that concurrent additions and deletions do not conflict with each other. Chapter 22 gives you all the details about how to protect access to data in multithreaded programs.

 Remember, the `SuperSmartPointer` *class is given here for illustrative purposes only. You should use the standard C++11* `shared_ptr` *or* `unique_ptr` *in your programs unless you have a valid reason and you know exactly what you are doing.*

COMMON MEMORY PITFALLS

It is difficult to pinpoint the exact situations that can lead to a memory-related bug. Every memory leak or bad pointer has its own nuances. There is no magic bullet for resolving memory issues, but there are several common categories of problems and some tools you can use to detect and resolve them.

Underallocating Strings

The most common problem with C-style strings is *underallocation*. In most cases, this arises when the programmer fails to allocate an extra character for the trailing `'\0'` sentinel. Underallocation of strings also occurs when programmers assume a certain fixed maximum size. The basic built-in string functions will not adhere to a fixed size — they will happily write off the end of the string into uncharted memory.

The following code reads data off a network connection and puts it in a C-style string. This is done in a loop because the network connection only receives a small amount of data at a time. On each loop, `getMoreData()` is called, which returns a pointer to dynamically allocated memory. When `nullptr` is returned from `getMoreData()`, all of the data has been received.

```
char buffer[1024] = {0};   // Allocate a whole bunch of memory.
while (true) {
    char* nextChunk = getMoreData();
```

```
        if (nextChunk == nullptr) {
            break;
        } else {
            strcat(buffer, nextChunk); // BUG! No guarantees against buffer overrun!
            delete [] nextChunk;
        }
    }
```

There are three ways to resolve the possible underallocation problem. In decreasing order of preference, they are:

1. Use C++-style strings, which will handle the memory associated with concatenation on your behalf.

2. Instead of allocating a buffer as a global variable or on the stack, allocate it on the heap. When there is insufficient space left, allocate a new buffer large enough to hold at least the current contents plus the new chunk, copy the original buffer into the new buffer, append the new contents, and delete the original buffer.

3. Create a version of getMoreData() that takes a maximum count (including the '\0' character) and will return no more characters than that; then track the amount of space left and the current position in the buffer.

Memory Leaks

Finding and fixing memory leaks can be one of the more frustrating parts of programming in C or C++. Your program finally works and appears to give the correct results. Then, you start to notice that your program gobbles up more and more memory as it runs. Your program has a memory leak. The use of smart pointers to avoid memory leaks is a good first approach to solving the problem.

Memory leaks occur when you allocate memory and neglect to release it. At first, this sounds like the result of careless programming that could easily be avoided. After all, if every new has a corresponding delete in every class you write, there should be no memory leaks, right? Actually, that's not always true. In the following code, the Simple class is properly written to release any memory that it allocates. However, when the doSomething() function is called, the pointer is changed to another Simple object without deleting the old one. The doSomething() function doesn't delete the old object on purpose to demonstrate memory leaks. Once you lose a pointer to an object, it's nearly impossible to delete it.

Available for
download on
Wrox.com

```
class Simple
{
    public:
        Simple() { mIntPtr = new int(); }
        ~Simple() { delete mIntPtr; }
        void setIntPtr(int inInt) { *mIntPtr = inInt; }
    protected:
        int* mIntPtr;
};
void doSomething(Simple*& outSimplePtr)
{
    outSimplePtr = new Simple(); // BUG! Doesn't delete the original.
}
```

```
int main()
{
    Simple* simplePtr = new Simple(); // Allocate a Simple object.
    doSomething(simplePtr);
    delete simplePtr; // Only cleans up the second object
    return 0;
}
```

Code snippet from Leaky\Leaky.cpp

In cases like the preceding example, the memory leak probably arose from poor communication between programmers or poor documentation of code. The caller of doSomething() may not have realized that the variable was passed by reference and thus had no reason to expect that the pointer would be reassigned. If they did notice that the parameter is a non-const reference to a pointer, they may have suspected that something strange was happening, but there is no comment around doSomething() that explains this behavior.

Finding and Fixing Memory Leaks in Windows with Visual C++

Memory leaks are hard to track down because you can't easily look at memory and see what objects are not in use and where they were originally allocated. However, there are programs that can do this for you. Memory leak detection tools range from expensive professional software packages to free downloadable tools. If you already work with Microsoft Visual C++, its debug library has built-in support for memory leak detection. This memory leak detection is not enabled by default, unless you create an MFC project. To enable it in other projects, you need to include the following three lines at the beginning of your code:

Available for download on Wrox.com

```
#define _CRTDBG_MAP_ALLOC
#include <stdlib.h>
#include <crtdbg.h>
```

Code snippet from Leaky\Leaky MS VC++.cpp

These lines should be in the exact order as shown above. Next, you need to redefine the new operator as follows:

Available for download on Wrox.com

```
#ifdef _DEBUG
    #ifndef DBG_NEW
        #define DBG_NEW new ( _NORMAL_BLOCK , __FILE__ , __LINE__ )
        #define new DBG_NEW
    #endif
#endif  // _DEBUG
```

Code snippet from Leaky\Leaky MS VC++.cpp

Note that this is within a "#ifdef _DEBUG" statement so the redefinition of new will only be done when compiling a debug version of your application. This is what you normally want. Release builds usually do not do any memory leak detection.

The last thing you need to do is to add the following line as the first line in your `main()` function:

```
_CrtSetDbgFlag(_CRTDBG_ALLOC_MEM_DF | _CRTDBG_LEAK_CHECK_DF);
```

Code snippet from Leaky\Leaky MS VC++.cpp

This tells the Visual C++ CRT (C Run Time) library to write all detected memory leaks to the debug output console when the application exits. For the previous leaky program, the debug console will contain lines similar to the following:

```
Detected memory leaks!
Dumping objects ->
c:\leaky\leaky.cpp(19) : {59} normal block at 0x007E3330, 4 bytes long.
 Data: <    > 00 00 00 00
c:\leaky\leaky.cpp(37) : {58} normal block at 0x007E32F0, 4 bytes long.
 Data: <03~ > 30 33 7E 00
Object dump complete.
```

The output clearly shows in which file and on which line memory was allocated but never deallocated. The line number is between parentheses immediately behind the filename. The number between the curly brackets is a counter for the memory allocations. For example, {59} means the 59th allocation in your program since it started. You can use the VC++ `_CrtSetBreakAlloc()` function to tell the VC++ debug runtime to break into the debugger when a certain allocation is performed. For example, add the following line to the beginning of your `main()` function to let the debugger break on the 59th allocation:

```
_CrtSetBreakAlloc(59);
```

In this leaky program, there are two leaks — the first `Simple` object that is never deleted and the heap-based integer that it creates. In the Visual C++ debugger output window, you can simply double click on one of the memory leaks and it will automatically jump to that line in your code.

Of course, programs like Microsoft Visual C++ discussed in this section, and Valgrind discussed in the next section can't actually fix the leak for you — what fun would that be? These tools provide information that you can use to find the actual problem. Normally, that involves stepping through the code to find out where the pointer to an object was overwritten without the original object being released. Some debuggers, like Visual C++, provide "watch point" functionality that can break execution of the program when this occurs.

Finding and Fixing Memory Leaks in Linux with Valgrind

Valgrind is an example of a free open-source tool for Linux that, amongst other things, pinpoints the exact line in your code where a leaked object was allocated.

The following output, generated by running Valgrind on the previous leaky program, pinpoints the exact locations where memory was allocated but never released. Valgrind finds the same two memory leaks — the first `Simple` object that is never deleted and the heap-based integer that it creates:

```
==15606== ERROR SUMMARY: 0 errors from 0 contexts (suppressed: 0 from 0)
==15606== malloc/free: in use at exit: 8 bytes in 2 blocks.
==15606== malloc/free: 4 allocs, 2 frees, 16 bytes allocated.
==15606== For counts of detected errors, rerun with: -v
==15606== searching for pointers to 2 not-freed blocks.
==15606== checked 4455600 bytes.
==15606==
==15606== 4 bytes in 1 blocks are still reachable in loss record 1 of 2
==15606==    at 0x4002978F: __builtin_new (vg_replace_malloc.c:172)
==15606==    by 0x400297E6: operator new(unsigned) (vg_replace_malloc.c:185)
==15606==     by 0x804875B: Simple::Simple() (leaky.cpp:8)
==15606==    by 0x8048648: main (leaky.cpp:24)
==15606==
==15606==
==15606== 4 bytes in 1 blocks are definitely lost in loss record 2 of 2
==15606==    at 0x4002978F: __builtin_new (vg_replace_malloc.c:172)
==15606==    by 0x400297E6: operator new(unsigned) (vg_replace_malloc.c:185)
==15606==     by 0x8048633: main (leaky.cpp:24)
==15606==    by 0x4031FA46: __libc_start_main (in /lib/libc-2.3.2.so)
==15606==
==15606== LEAK SUMMARY:
==15606==    definitely lost: 4 bytes in 1 blocks.
==15606==    possibly lost:   0 bytes in 0 blocks.
==15606==    still reachable: 4 bytes in 1 blocks.
==15606==         suppressed: 0 bytes in 0 blocks.
```

 It is strongly recommended to use smart pointers as much as possible to avoid memory leaks.

Double-Deleting and Invalid Pointers

Once you release memory associated with a pointer using `delete`, the memory is available for use by other parts of your program. Nothing stops you, however, from attempting to continue to use the pointer, which is now a *dangling pointer*. Double deletion is also a problem. If you use `delete` a second time on a pointer, the program could be releasing memory that has since been assigned to another object.

Double deletion and use of already released memory are both hard problems to track down because the symptoms may not show up immediately. If two deletions occur within a relatively short amount of time, the program might work indefinitely because the associated memory is not reused that quickly. Similarly, if a deleted object is used immediately after being deleted, most likely it will still be intact.

Of course, there is no guarantee that such behavior will work or continue to work. The memory allocator is under no obligation to preserve any object once it has been deleted. Even if it does work, it is extremely poor programming style to use objects that have been deleted.

Many memory leak checking programs, such as Microsoft Visual C++ and Valgrind, will also detect double deletion and use of released objects.

If you disregard the recommendation for using smart pointers and instead still use dumb pointers, at least set your pointers to `nullptr` after deallocating their memory. This will prevent you from accidentally deleting the same pointer twice or to use an invalid pointer. It's worth noting that you are allowed to call `delete` on a `nullptr` pointer; it simply will not do anything.

Accessing Out-of-Bounds Memory

Earlier in this chapter, you read that since a pointer is just a memory address, it is possible to have a pointer that points to a random location in memory. Such a condition is quite easy to fall into. For example, consider a C-style string that has somehow lost its `'\0'` termination character. The following function, which attempts to fill the string with all `'m'` characters, would instead continue to fill the contents of memory following the string with `'m'`s:

```
void fillWithM(char* inStr)
{
    int i = 0;
    while (inStr[i] != '\0') {
        inStr[i] = 'm';
        i++;
    }
}
```

If an improperly terminated string were handed to this function, it would only be a matter of time before an essential part of memory is overwritten and the program crashes. Consider what might happen if the memory associated with the objects in your program is suddenly overwritten with `'m'`s. It's not pretty!

Bugs that result in writing to memory past the end of an array are often called *buffer overflow errors*. Such bugs have been exploited by several high-profile malware programs, for example viruses and worms. A devious hacker can take advantage of the ability to overwrite portions of memory to inject code into a running program.

Many memory checking tools detect buffer overflows as well. Also, using higher-level constructs like C++ `strings` and `vectors` will help prevent numerous bugs associated with writing to C-style strings and arrays.

 Avoid using old C-style strings and arrays that offer no protection whatsoever. Instead, use modern and safe constructs like C++ `strings` *and* `vectors` *that manage all their memory for you.*

SUMMARY

In this chapter, you learned the ins and outs of dynamic memory. Aside from memory checking tools and careful coding, there are two keys to avoiding dynamic memory-related problems. First, you need to understand how pointers work under the hood. In reading about two different mental models for pointers, we hope you are confident that you know how the compiler doles out memory. Second, you can avoid all sorts of dynamic memory issues by obscuring pointers with stack-based objects, like the C++ `string` class, `vector` class, smart pointers, and so on.

If there is one thing that you should have learned from this chapter it is that you should try to avoid the use of old C-style constructs and functions as much as possible, and use the safe C++ alternatives.

22

C++11 Multithreaded Programming with C++

WHAT'S IN THIS CHAPTER?

➤ What multithreaded programming is and how to write multithreaded code

➤ What deadlocks and race conditions are, and how to use mutual exclusion to prevent them

➤ How to use atomic types and atomic operations

➤ What thread pools are

Multithreaded programming is important on computer systems with multiple processors. It allows you to write a program to utilize all those processors in parallel. Systems with multiple processors already exist for a long time; however, they were rarely used in consumer systems. Today, all major CPU vendors are selling multicore processors. A multicore processor physically looks like a single processor, but inside it contains several parallel CPU processors, also called cores. Nowadays, multicore processors are being used for everything from servers to consumer computers. Even the latest smartphones have multicore processors. Because of this proliferation of multicore processors, writing multithreaded applications is becoming more and more important. A Professional C++ programmer needs to know how to write correct multithreaded code to take full advantage of all the available processors and cores. Writing multithreaded applications used to rely on platform- and operating system-specific APIs. This makes it difficult to write platform independent multithreaded code. C++11 solves this problem with the introduction of a standard threading library.

Multithreaded programming is a complicated subject. This chapter introduces you to multithreaded programming using the new C++11 library, but it cannot go into all details due to space constraints. There are entire books written about developing multithreaded programs. If you are interested in more details, consult one of the references in the multithreaded section in Appendix B.

If your compiler does not yet support the C++11 threading library, you might use other third-party libraries available that try to make multithreaded programming more platform independent. There are, for example, the `pthreads` library and the `boost::thread` library. However, since they are not part of the C++ standard, these are not discussed in this book.

INTRODUCTION

Multithreaded programming allows you to perform multiple calculations in parallel. This way you can take advantage of the multiple processors and cores inside most CPUs these days. Years ago, the CPU market was racing for the highest frequency, which is perfect for single threaded applications. This race has stopped due to a combination of power management and heat management problems. Today the CPU market is racing toward the most cores on a single CPU. Dual- and quad-core CPUs are already common at the time of this writing, and announcements have already been made about 12-, 16-, 32-, and even 80-core CPUs. They are still in an experimental stage, but you can be sure they will come out sooner than you might expect.

Similarly, if you look at the processing units on graphics cards, called GPUs, you'll see that they are massively parallel computing units. Today, high-end graphics cards already have more than 2,000 cores and this will only increase rapidly. These graphics cards are not only used for gaming anymore, but also to perform computationally intense tasks. Examples are image and video manipulation, protein folding (useful for discovering new drugs), processing signals as part of the SETI project (Search for Extra-Terrestrial Intelligence), and so on.

C++98/03 did not have support for multithreaded programming, and you had to resort to third-party libraries or to the multithreading APIs of your target operating system. C++11 now includes a multithreading library, making it easier to write cross-platform multithreaded applications. There are two reasons to start writing multithreaded code. First, if you have a computational problem and you manage to separate it into small pieces that can be run in parallel independently from each other, you can expect a huge performance boost running it on modern multi-core GPUs and CPUs. Second, you can modularize computations along orthogonal axes; for example, doing long computations in a thread instead of blocking the GUI thread, so the user interface remains responsive while a long computation occurs in the background.

Figure 22-1 shows an example of a problem perfectly suited to run in parallel. An example could be the processing of pixels of an image by an algorithm that does not require information about neighboring pixels. The algorithm could split the image into four parts. On a single-core CPU, each part is processed sequentially; on a dual-core CPU, two parts are processed in parallel; and on a quad-core CPU, four parts are processed in parallel resulting in an almost linear scaling of the performance with the number of cores.

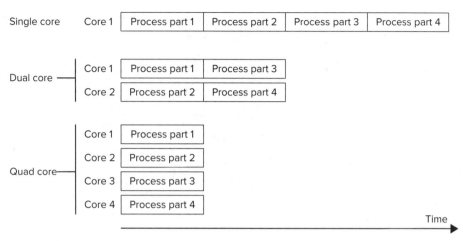

FIGURE 22-1

Of course, it's not always possible to split the problem into parts that can be executed independently of each other in parallel. But often it can be parallelized at least partially, resulting in a performance increase.

A difficult part in multithreaded programming is to parallelize your algorithm, which is highly dependent on the type of your algorithm. Other difficult parts are preventing race conditions and deadlocks. These will be discussed in the following section.

Race Conditions and Deadlocks

Race conditions can occur when multiple threads want to read/write to a shared memory location. For example, suppose you have a shared variable and one thread increments this value while another thread decrements it. Incrementing and decrementing the value means that the current value needs to be retrieved from memory, incremented or decremented, and stored back in memory. On older architectures, for example PDP-11 and VAX, this used to be implemented with an INC processor instruction which was atomic. On multicore x86 processors, the INC instruction is not atomic anymore, meaning that the CPU could execute other instructions in the middle of this operation, which might cause the code to retrieve a wrong value.

The following table shows the result when the increment is finished executing before the decrement starts, and assumes that the initial value is 1:

THREAD 1 (INCREMENT)	THREAD 2 (DECREMENT)
load value (value = 1)	
increment value (value = 2)	
store value (value = 2)	
	load value (value = 2)
	decrement value (value = 1)
	store value (value = 1)

The final value stored in memory is 1. When the decrement thread is finished before the increment thread starts, the final value is also 1, as seen in the following table:

THREAD 1 (INCREMENT)	THREAD 2 (DECREMENT)
	load value (value = 1)
	decrement value (value = 0)
	store value (value = 0)
load value (value = 0)	
increment value (value = 1)	
store value (value = 1)	

However, when the instructions get interleaved on the CPU, the result is different:

THREAD 1 (INCREMENT)	THREAD 2 (DECREMENT)
load value (value = 1)	
increment value (value = 2)	
	load value (value = 1)
	decrement value (value = 0)
store value (value = 2)	
	store value (value = 0)

The final result in this case is 0. In other words, the effect of the increment operation is lost. This is a race condition.

 To prevent race conditions try to design your programs so that multiple threads do not need to read or write to shared memory locations. You can also use a synchronization method as described in the Mutual Exclusion section later in this chapter, or if possible, use atomic operations described in the next section.

If you opt to solve the race condition by using a synchronization method such as mutual exclusion, you might run into another common problem with multithreaded programming: *deadlocks*. Deadlocks are threads blocking indefinitely because they are waiting to acquire access to resources currently locked by other blocked threads.

For example, suppose you have two threads and two resources, A and B. Both threads require a lock on both resources, but they acquire the locks in different order. The following table shows this situation in pseudo code:

THREAD 1	THREAD 2
Lock A	Lock B
Lock B	Lock A
// ... compute	// ... compute
Release B	Release A
Release A	Release B

Now, imagine that the code in the two threads is executed in the following order:

Thread 1: Lock A

Thread 2: Lock B

Thread 1: Lock B (waits, because lock held by Thread 2)

Thread 2: Lock A (waits, because lock held by Thread 1)

Both threads are now waiting indefinitely, a deadlock situation. Figure 22-2 shows a graphical representation of this deadlock situation. Thread 1 is holding a lock on resource A and is waiting to get a lock on resource B. Thread 2 is holding a lock on resource B and is waiting to get a lock on resource A.

In this graphical representation, you see a cycle that depicts the deadlock situation. Both threads will wait indefinitely, unless you include mechanisms in your program to break these kinds of deadlocks. One possible solution is to try for a certain time to acquire a lock on a resource. If the lock could not be obtained within a certain time interval, the thread stops waiting and possibly releases other locks it is currently holding. The thread might then sleep for a little bit and try again later to acquire all the resources it needs. This method might give other threads the opportunity to acquire necessary locks and continue their execution. Whether this method works or not depends heavily on your specific deadlock case.

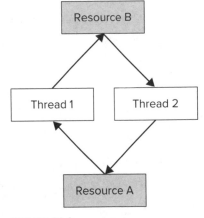

FIGURE 22-2

Instead of using a workaround as described in the previous paragraph, you should try to avoid any possible deadlock situation altogether. If you need to acquire multiple locks, the recommended way is to use the standard std::lock() or std::try_lock() methods described later in the section on mutual exclusion. These methods will obtain or try to obtain a lock on several resources, doing their best to prevent deadlocks.

ATOMIC OPERATIONS LIBRARY

C++11 introduces atomic types on which atomic operations can be applied. These allow atomic accesses, which means that concurrent reading and writing without additional synchronization is allowed. Reads will never result in undefined behavior.

The increment race condition example given in the previous section can be solved by using an atomic type. For example, the following code is not thread-safe and can show race condition behavior as explained earlier:

```
int counter = 0;    // Global variable
...
++counter;          // Executed in multiple threads
```

To make this thread-safe without explicitly using any locks, use an atomic type:

```
atomic<int> counter(0) ;  // Global variable
...
++counter;                // Executed in multiple threads
```

You need to include the `<atomic>` header to use these atomic types. The standard defines the following named integral atomic types:

NAMED ATOMIC TYPE	EQUIVALENT ATOMIC TYPE	INTEGRAL TYPE
atomic_char	atomic<char>	char
atomic_schar	atomic<signed char>	signed char
atomic_uchar	atomic<unsigned char>	unsigned char
atomic_short	atomic<short>	short
atomic_ushort	atomic<unsigned short>	unsigned short
atomic_int	atomic<int>	int
atomic_uint	atomic<unsigned int>	unsigned int
atomic_long	atomic<long>	long
atomic_ulong	atomic<unsigned long>	unsigned long
atomic_llong	atomic<long long>	long long
atomic_ullong	atomic<unsigned long long>	unsigned long long
atomic_char16_t	atomic<char16_t>	char16_t
atomic_char32_t	atomic<char32_t>	char32_t
atomic_wchar_t	atomic<wchar_t>	wchar_t

Atomic Type Example

This section explains why you should use atomic types. Suppose you have a function called `func()` that increments an integer given as a reference parameter in a loop:

Available for download on Wrox.com

```cpp
void func(int& counter)
{
    for (int i = 0; i < 10000; ++i) {
        ++counter;
    }
}
```

Code snippet from atomic\inc_func_non_atomic.cpp

Now, you would like to run several threads in parallel, all executing this `func()` function. By implementing this naively without atomic types, you introduce a race condition. The following `main()` function launches several threads with the `std::thread` class defined in the `<thread>` header file. The constructor of the `thread` class requires a pointer to a function to execute in the new thread, and the arguments for the function. After having launched 10 threads, the `main()` function waits for all threads to finish, by calling `join()` on each thread. The details of how to use `std::thread` and `join()` are not important at this point and are discussed later in this chapter.

Available for download on Wrox.com

```cpp
#include <iostream>
#include <vector>
#include <thread>
#include <functional>
int main()
{
    int counter = 0;
    std::vector<std::thread> threads;
    for (int i = 0; i < 10; ++i) {
        threads.push_back(std::thread{func, std::ref(counter)});
    }
    for (auto& t : threads) {
        t.join();
    }
    std::cout << "Result = " << counter << std::endl;
    return 0;
}
```

Code snippet from atomic\inc_func_non_atomic.cpp

Since `func()` increments the integer 10.000 times, and `main()` launches 10 background threads, each of which executes `func()`, the expected result is 100.000. If you execute this program several times, you might get the following output:

```
Result = 86044
Result = 100000
Result = 99726
Result = 90780
Result = 100000
```

```
Result = 85054
Result = 84157
Result = 77133
Result = 74325
```

This code is clearly showing race condition behavior. In this example, the best and recommended solution is to use the new atomic types. The following code highlights the required changes:

```
#include <iostream>
#include <vector>
#include <thread>
#include <functional>
#include <atomic>
void func(std::atomic<int>& counter)
{
    for (int i = 0; i < 10000; ++i) {
        ++counter;
    }
}
int main()
{
    std::atomic<int> counter(0);
    std::vector<std::thread> threads;
    for (int i = 0; i < 10; ++i) {
        threads.push_back(std::thread{func, std::ref(counter)});
    }
    for (auto& t : threads) {
        t.join();
    }
    std::cout << "Result = " << counter << std::endl;
    return 0;
}
```

Code snippet from atomic\inc_func_atomic.cpp

The changes add the `<atomic>` header file, and change the type of the shared counter to `std::atomic<int>` instead of `int`. When you run the new example, you will always get 100.000 as the result:

```
Result = 100000
Result = 100000
Result = 100000
Result = 100000
Result = 100000
```

Without explicitly adding any locks to your code, you have made it thread-safe and race condition free because the `++counter` operation on an atomic type will load the value, increment the value, and store the value in one atomic transaction, which cannot be interrupted.

If you want to compile multithreaded code with GCC, you have to link with the `pthread` *library. For example:*

```
> gcc -lstdc++ -lpthread inc_func_atomic.cpp
```

Atomic Operations

The C++11 standard defines a number of atomic operations. This section describes a few of those operations. For a full list, consult the Standard Library Reference resource on the website, www.wrox.com.

An example of an atomic operation is:

```
bool atomic_compare_exchange_strong(atomic<C>* object, C* expected, C desired);
```

This operation can also be called as a member of atomic<C>:

```
bool atomic<C>::compare_exchange_strong(C* expected, C desired);
```

This operation implements the following logic atomically:

```
if (memcmp(object, expected, sizeof(*object)) == 0) {
    memcpy(object, &desired, sizeof(*object));
    return true;
} else {
    memcpy(expected, object, sizeof(*object));
    return false;
}
```

A second example is atomic<T>::fetch_add(), which fetches the current value of an atomic type, adds the given increment to the atomic value, and returns the original non-incremented value. For example:

Available for download on Wrox.com

```
atomic<int> value(10);
cout << "Value = " << value << endl;
int fetched = value.fetch_add(4);
cout << "Fetched = " << fetched << endl;
cout << "Value = " << value << endl;
```

Code snippet from atomic\fetch_add.cpp

If no other threads are touching the contents of the fetched and value variables, the output is as follows:

```
Value = 10
Fetched = 10
Value = 14
```

Atomic integral types support the following atomic operations: fetch_add(), fetch_sub(), fetch_and(), fetch_or(), fetch_xor(), ++, --, +=, -=, &=, ^= and |=. Atomic pointer types support fetch_add(), fetch_sub(), ++, --, += and -=.

Most of the atomic operations can accept an extra parameter specifying the memory ordering that you would like. For example:

```
T atomic<T>::fetch_add(T value, memory_order = memory_order_seq_cst);
```

You may change the default `memory_order`. The standard provides: `memory_order_relaxed`, `memory_order_consume`, `memory_order_acquire`, `memory_order_release`, `memory_order_acq_rel` and `memory_order_seq_cst`, all defined in the `std` namespace. However, it is rare that you will want to use them instead of the default. While another memory order may perform better than the default, according to some metric, if you use them slightly wrong you will again introduce race conditions or other difficult-to-track threading-related problems. If you do need to know more about memory ordering, consult one of the multithreading references in Appendix B.

THREADS

The C++11 threading library, defined in the `<thread>` header file, makes it very easy to launch new threads. Specifying what needs to be executed in the new thread can be done in several ways. You can let the new thread execute a global function, the `operator()` of a function object, a lambda expression, or even a member function of an instance of some class. The following sections give small examples of all these methods.

Thread with Function Pointer

Functions like `CreateThread()`, `_beginthread()`, and so on, on Windows, and `pthread_create()` with the `pthreads` library, require that the thread function only has one parameter. On the other hand, a function that you want to use with the C++11 `std::thread` class can have as many parameters as you want.

Suppose you have the following function. The `counter()` function accepts two integers: the first representing an ID and the second representing the number of iterations that the function should loop. The body of the function is a single loop that loops the given number of iterations. On each iteration, a message is printed to standard output:

Available for download on Wrox.com

```
void counter(int id, int numIterations)
{
    for (int i = 0; i < numIterations; ++i) {
        cout << "Counter " << id << " has value ";
        cout << i << endl;
    }
}
```

Code snippet from thread\ThreadFunction.cpp

You can launch multiple threads executing this function using `std::thread`. You can create a thread `t1`, executing `counter()` with arguments 1 and 6 as follows:

```
thread t1(counter, 1, 6);
```

The constructor of the `thread` class is a variadic template, which means that it accepts any number of arguments. Variadic templates are discussed in detail in Chapter 20. The first argument is the name of the function to execute in the new thread. The subsequent variable number of arguments are passed to this function when execution of the thread starts.

If you want to run the `counter()` function in parallel in several threads, you need to make sure that access to `cout` is thread-safe. To make this thread-safe, you need to call:

```
cout.sync_with_stdio(true);
```

Without calling `sync_with_stdio(true)`, accessing the stream from multiple threads might cause race conditions.

The following code launches two threads executing the `counter()` function. After launching the threads, `main()` calls `join()` on both threads. This is to make sure that the main thread keeps running until both threads are finished. A call to `t1.join()` blocks until the thread `t1` is finished. Without these two `join()` calls, the `main()` function would finish immediately after launching the two threads. This will trigger the application to shut down; causing all other threads spawned by the application to be terminated as well, whether these threads are finished or not.

These `join()` calls are necessary in these small examples. In real-world applications, you should try to avoid the use of `join()`, because it causes the thread calling `join()` to block. Often there are better ways. For example, in a GUI application, a thread that finishes can post a message to the UI thread. The UI thread itself has a message loop processing messages like mouse moves, button clicks and so on. This message loop can also receive the messages from the thread, and you can react to them how you want, all without blocking the UI thread with a `join()` call.

Available for download on Wrox.com

```cpp
#include <iostream>
#include <thread>
using namespace std;
int main()
{
    cout.sync_with_stdio(true); // Make sure cout is thread-safe
    thread t1(counter, 1, 6);
    thread t2(counter, 2, 4);
    t1.join();
    t2.join();
    return 0;
}
```

Code snippet from thread\ThreadFunction.cpp

A possible output of this example looks as follows:

```
Counter 2 has value 0
Counter 1 has value 0
Counter 1 has value 1
Counter 1 has value 2
Counter 1 has value 3
Counter 1 has value 4
```

```
Counter 1 has value 5
Counter 2 has value 1
Counter 2 has value 2
Counter 2 has value 3
```

The output on your system will be different and it will most likely be different every time you run it. This is because two threads are executing the `counter()` function at the same time, so the output depends on the number of processing cores in your system and on the thread scheduling of the operating system.

Since this example is calling `cout.sync_with_stdio(true)`, accessing `cout` is thread-safe, however, output from different threads can still be interleaved. This means that the output of the previous example can be mixed together as in:

```
Counter Counter 2 has value 0
1 has value 0
Counter 1 has value 1
Counter 1 has value 2
```

Instead of:

```
Counter 1 has value 0
Counter 2 has value 0
Counter 1 has value 1
Counter 1 has value 2
```

This can be fixed by using synchronization methods, which are discussed later in this chapter.

 Thread function arguments are always copied into some internal storage for the thread. Use `std::ref()` *from the* `<functional>` *header to pass them by reference.*

Thread with Function Object

The previous section demonstrated how to create a thread and tell it to run a specific function in the new thread by passing a pointer to the function to execute. You can also use a function object, as shown in the following example. With the function pointer technique discussed earlier, the only way to pass information to the thread is by passing arguments to the function. With function objects you can add member variables to your function object class, which you can initialize and use however you want. The example first defines a class called `Counter`. It has two member variables: an ID and the number of iterations for the loop. Both of these member variables are initialized with the class constructor. To make the `Counter` class a function object, you need to implement `operator()`, as discussed in Chapter 13. The implementation of `operator()` is the same as the `counter()` function in the previous section:

```cpp
class Counter
{
    public:
        Counter(int id, int numIterations)
            : mId(id), mNumIterations(numIterations)
        {
        }
```

```
        void operator()() const
        {
            for (int i = 0; i < mNumIterations; ++i) {
                cout << "Counter " << mId << " has value ";
                cout << i << endl;
            }
        }
    protected:
        int mId;
        int mNumIterations;
};
```

Code snippet from thread\ThreadFunctionObject.cpp

Three methods for initializing threads with a function object are demonstrated in the following main(). The first uses the C++11 uniform initialization syntax. You create an instance of the Counter class with its constructor arguments and give it to the thread constructor between curly braces.

The second defines a named instance of the Counter class and gives this named instance to the constructor of the thread class.

The third looks similar to the first; it creates an instance of the Counter class and gives it to the constructor of the thread class, but uses parentheses instead of curly braces. The ramifications of this are discussed after the code.

```
int main()
{
    cout.sync_with_stdio(true); // Make sure cout is thread-safe
    // Using C++11 initialization syntax
    thread t1{Counter(1, 20)};
    // Using named variable
    Counter c(2, 12);
    thread t2(c);
    // Using temporary
    thread t3(Counter(3, 10));
    // Wait for threads to finish
    t1.join();
    t2.join();
    t3.join();
    return 0;
}
```

Code snippet from thread\ThreadFunctionObject.cpp

If you compare the creation of t1 with the creation of t3, it looks like the only difference seems to be that the first method uses curly braces while the third method uses brackets. However, when your function object constructor doesn't require any parameters, the third method as written above will not work. For example:

```
class Counter
{
    public:
        Counter() {}
```

```
                void operator()() const { /* Omitted for brevity */ }
    };
    int main()
    {
        cout.sync_with_stdio(true); // Make sure cout is thread-safe
        thread t1(Counter());    // Error!
        t1.join();
        return 0;
    }
```

This will result in a compilation error because C++ will interpret the second line in the main()
function as a declaration of a function called t1, which returns a thread object and accepts
a pointer to a function without parameters returning a Counter object. For this reason, it's
recommended to use the C++11 uniform initialization syntax:

```
thread t1{Counter()};    // OK
```

If your compiler does not support this new syntax you have to add an extra set of parentheses to
prevent the compiler from interpreting the line as a function declaration:

```
thread t1((Counter()));   // OK
```

> *Function objects are always copied into some internal storage for the thread.*
> *If you want to execute* operator() *on a specific instance of your function*
> *object instead of copying it, you should use* std::ref() *from the* <functional>
> *header to pass your instance by reference.*

Thread with Lambda

Because the threading library is new in C++11, the C++11 lambda expression feature fits nicely with
it, as demonstrated in the following example:

```
int main()
{
    cout.sync_with_stdio(true); // Make sure cout is thread-safe
    thread t1([](int id, int numIterations) {
                    for (int i = 0; i < numIterations; ++i) {
                        cout << "Counter " << id << " has value ";
                        cout << i << endl;
                    }
                }, 1, 5);
    t1.join();
    return 0;
}
```

Code snippet from thread\ThreadLambda.cpp

Thread with Member Function

The previous examples illustrate different methods of specifying the thread code:

➤ A global function

➤ A function object using `operator()`

➤ A lambda expression

However, these are not the only techniques available; you can also specify a member function of a class.

The following example defines a basic `Request` class with a `process()` method. The `main()` function creates an instance of the `Request` class and launches a new thread, which will execute the `process()` member function of the `Request` instance, `req`:

```cpp
class Request
{
    public:
        Request(int id) : mId(id) { }
        void process()
        {
            cout << "Processing request " << mId << endl;
        }
    protected:
        int mId;
};
int main()
{
    cout.sync_with_stdio(true); // Make sure cout is thread-safe
    Request req(100);
    thread t{&Request::process, &req};
    t.join();
    return 0;
}
```

Code snippet from thread\ThreadMemFunc.cpp

With this technique you are executing a method on a specific object in a separate thread. If other threads are accessing the same object, you need to make sure this happens in a thread-safe way to avoid race conditions. Mutual exclusion, discussed later in this chapter, can be used as synchronization mechanism to make it thread-safe.

Thread Local Storage

C++11 supports the concept of *thread local storage*. With a new keyword called `thread_local`, you can mark any variable as thread local, which means that each thread will have its own unique copy of the variable and it will last for the entire duration of the thread. For each thread, the variable is initialized exactly once. This is very similar to a `static` variable, except that each thread will have its own unique instance of the thread local variable. For example, in the following code, every thread shares one-and-only-one copy of k, while each thread has its own unique copy of n:

```
thread_local int n;
int k;
void doWork()
{
    // perform some computation
}
```

Note that if the `thread_local` variable is declared in the scope of a function, its behavior is as if it were declared `static`, except that every thread has its own unique copy and it is initialized exactly once per thread, no matter how many times that function is called in that thread.

Cancelling Threads

The standard does not include any mechanism for cancelling a running thread from inside another thread. The best way to achieve this is to provide some communication mechanism that the two threads agree on. The simplest mechanism is to have a shared variable which the target thread checks periodically to determine if it should terminate. Other threads can set this shared variable to indirectly instruct the thread to shut down.

A second method is to use condition variables, discussed later in this chapter.

Retrieving Results from Threads

As you saw in the previous examples, launching a new thread is pretty easy. However, in most cases you are probably interested in results produced by the thread. For example, if your thread performs some mathematical calculations, you really would like to get the results out of the thread once the thread is finished. One way is to pass a pointer or reference to a result variable to the thread in which the thread will store the results. Another method is to store the results inside a class member variable, which you can retrieve later once the thread has finished executing.

However, there is another and easier method to obtain a result from threads: *futures*. They also make it easier to handle errors that occur inside your threads. Futures are discussed later in this chapter.

Copying and Rethrowing Exceptions

The whole exception mechanism in C++ works perfectly, as long as it stays within one single thread. Every thread can throw its own exceptions, but they need to be caught within their own thread. Exceptions thrown in one thread cannot be caught in another thread. This introduces quite a few problems when you would like to use exception handling in combination with multithreaded programming.

Without C++11 it's very difficult if not impossible to gracefully handle exceptions across threads. C++11 solves this issue with the following new exception-related functions:

```
exception_ptr current_exception() noexcept;
```

This function returns an exception_ptr object that refers to the exception currently being handled, or a copy of the currently handled exception, or a null exception_ptr object if no exception is being handled. This referenced exception object remains valid for as long as there is an object of type exception_ptr that is referencing it. exception_ptr is of type NullablePointer, which means it can easily be tested with a simple if statement as the example later in this section demonstrates.

```
[[noreturn]] void rethrow_exception(exception_ptr p);
```

This function rethrows the exception referenced by the exception_ptr parameter. Rethrowing the referenced exception does not have to be done in the same thread that generated the referenced exception in the first place, which makes this feature perfectly suited for handling exceptions across different threads. The [[noreturn]] attribute makes it clear that this function will never return normally and is introduced in Chapter 9.

```
template<class E> exception_ptr make_exception_ptr(E e) noexcept;
```

This function creates an exception_ptr object that refers to a copy of the given exception object. This is basically a shorthand notation for the following code:

```
try {
    throw e;
} catch(...) {
    return current_exception();
}
```

Let's see how handling exceptions across different threads can be implemented by using these new features.

The following code defines a function that does some work and throws an exception. This function will ultimately be running in a separate background thread:

```
void doSomeWork() throw(runtime_error)
{
    for (int i = 0; i < 5; ++i)
        cout << i << endl;
    cout << "Thread throwing a runtime_error exception..." << endl;
    throw runtime_error("Exception from thread");
}
```

Code snippet from ExceptionsWithThreads\ExceptionsWithThreads.cpp

The following threadFunc() function wraps the call to the preceding function in a try/catch block, which will catch all exceptions that doSomeWork() might throw. A single argument is supplied to threadFunc(), which is of type exception_ptr&. Once an exception is caught, the function current_exception() is used to get a reference to the exception being handled, which is then assigned to the exception_ptr parameter. After that, the thread exits normally:

```
void threadFunc(exception_ptr& err)
{
    try {
        doSomeWork();
```

```
        } catch (...) {
            cout << "Thread caught exception, returning exception..." << endl;
            err = current_exception();
        }
    }
```

Code snippet from ExceptionsWithThreads\ExceptionsWithThreads.cpp

The following `doWorkInThread()` function is called from within the main thread. Its responsibility is to create a new thread and start executing the preceding `threadFunc()` function in it. A reference to an object of type `exception_ptr` is given as argument to `threadFunc()`. Once the thread is created, the `doWorkInThread()` function waits for the thread to finish by using the `join()` method, after which the error object is examined. Since `exception_ptr` is of type `NullablePointer`, you can easily check it by using `if (error)`. If it's a non-null value, the exception is rethrown in the current thread, which is the main thread in this example. By rethrowing the exception in the main thread, the exception has been transferred from one thread to another thread.

Available for
download on
Wrox.com

```
void doWorkInThread() throw(runtime_error)
{
    exception_ptr error;
    // Launch background thread
    thread t{threadFunc, ref(error)};
    // Wait for thread to finish
    t.join();
    // See if thread has thrown any exception
    if (error)
    {
        cout << "Main thread received exception, rethrowing it..." << endl;
        rethrow_exception(error);
    }
    else
        cout << "Main thread did not receive any exception." << endl;
}
```

Code snippet from ExceptionsWithThreads\ExceptionsWithThreads.cpp

The `main()` function is pretty straightforward. It calls `doWorkInThread()` and wraps the call in a `try/catch` block to catch exceptions thrown by any thread spawned by `doWorkInThread()`:

Available for
download on
Wrox.com

```
int main()
{
    cout.sync_with_stdio(true); // Make sure cout is thread-safe
    try {
        doWorkInThread();
    } catch (const exception& e) {
        cout << "Main function caught: '" << e.what() << "'" << endl;
    }
    return 0;
}
```

Code snippet from ExceptionsWithThreads\ExceptionsWithThreads.cpp

The output is as follows:

```
0
1
2
3
4
Thread throwing a runtime_error exception...
Thread caught exception, returning exception...
Main thread received exception, rethrowing it...
Main function caught: 'Exception from thread'
```

To keep this example compact and easier to understand, the `doWorkInThread()` function is using `join()` to block and wait until the thread is finished. Of course, in real-world applications you will not want to block your main thread. For example, in a GUI application, you might let `threadFunc()` send a message to the UI thread with as argument a copy of the result of `current_exception()`.

MUTUAL EXCLUSION

If you are writing multithreaded applications, you have to be sensitive to sequencing of operations. If your threads read and write shared data, this can be a problem. There are many ways to avoid this problem, such as never actually sharing data between threads. However, if you can't avoid sharing data, you must provide for synchronization so that only one thread at a time can change the data.

The real problem arises when there are two or more units of data (hardware-level units) which have to be changed as a single atomic action. A simple assignment to a simple scalar variable typically requires no synchronization. For example, on the x86, a 32-bit aligned value is handled atomically at the hardware level and a single transaction requires no explicit synchronization. For example, setting a Boolean variable to `false` to stop a thread requires no synchronization, but an operation like `++`, `--`, or `op=` for any given `op` requires synchronization. Scalars can often be synchronized properly by using the `fetch_xyz()` operations described earlier in this chapter, but when your data is more complex, and you need to use that data from multiple threads, you must provide synchronization.

C++11 has support for mutual exclusion in the form of *mutex* and *lock* classes. These can be used to implement synchronization between threads and are discussed in the next sections.

Mutex Classes

The mutual exclusion classes are all defined in the `<mutex>` header file and are in the `std` namespace. The basic mechanism of using a mutex is as follows:

➤ A thread that wants to read/write to memory shared with other threads tries to lock a mutex object. If another thread is currently holding this lock, the new thread that wants to gain access will block until the lock is released, or until a timeout interval expires.

➤ Once the thread has obtained the lock, it is free to read and write memory which is shared with other threads because at this point it is working under the assumption that no other threads are attempting to read or write the same data.

➤ After the thread is finished with reading/writing to the shared memory it releases the lock to give some other thread an opportunity to obtain the lock to the shared memory. If two or more threads are waiting on the lock, there are no guarantees as to which thread will be granted the lock and thus allowed to proceed.

The standard provides *non-timed mutex* classes and *timed mutex* classes discussed in the following sections.

Non-Timed Mutex Classes

The library has two non-timed mutex classes: `std::mutex` and `std::recursive_mutex`. Each supports the following methods:

➤ `lock()`: The calling thread will try to obtain the lock and will block until the lock has been acquired. It will block indefinitely. If there is a desire to limit the amount of time the thread blocks, you should use a time mutex, discussed in the next section.

➤ `try_lock()`: The calling thread will try to obtain the lock. If the lock is currently held by another thread, the call will return immediately. If the lock has been obtained, `try_lock()` returns `true`, otherwise it returns `false`.

➤ `unlock()`: Releases the lock held by the calling thread, making it available for another thread.

`std::mutex` is a standard mutual exclusion class with exclusive ownership semantics. There can be only one thread owning the mutex. If another thread wants to obtain ownership of this mutex, it will either block when using `lock()`, or fail when using `try_lock()`. A thread already having ownership of a mutex is not allowed to call `lock()` or `try_lock()` again on that mutex. This might lead to a deadlock!

`std::recursive_mutex` behaves almost identically to `std::mutex`, except that a thread already having ownership of a recursive mutex is allowed to call `lock()` or `try_lock()` again on the same mutex. The calling thread should call the `unlock()` method as many times as it obtained a lock on the recursive mutex.

Timed Mutex Classes

The library provides a `std::timed_mutex` and a `std::recursive_timed_mutex`; both are timed mutex classes supporting the normal `lock()`, `try_lock()` and `unlock()` methods. Additionally they support:

➤ `try_lock_for(rel_time)`: The calling thread will try to obtain the lock for a certain relative time. If the lock could not be obtained after the given timeout, the call fails and returns `false`. If the lock could be obtained within the timeout, the call succeeds and returns `true`.

➤ `try_lock_until(abs_time)`: The calling thread will try to obtain the lock until the system time equals or exceeds the specified absolute time. If the lock could be obtained before this time, the call returns `true`. If the system time passes the given absolute time, the function stops trying to obtain the lock and returns `false`.

A thread already having ownership of a `timed_mutex` is not allowed to call one of the previous lock calls again on that mutex. This might lead to a deadlock!

`recursive_timed_mutex` behaves almost identically to `timed_mutex`, except that a thread already having ownership of a recursive mutex is allowed to call one of the previous lock calls again on the same mutex. The calling thread should call the `unlock()` method as many times as it obtained a lock on the recursive mutex.

Locks

A *lock* class is a wrapper class that makes it easier to obtain and release a lock on a mutex; the destructor of the lock class will automatically release the associated mutex. The standard defines two types of locks: a simple lock, `std::lock_guard`, whose constructor always acquires the mutex and will block until the lock is acquired; and a more sophisticated `std::unique_lock`, which allows you to defer lock acquisition until later in the computation, long after the declaration. `unique_lock` has several constructors:

➤ A constructor accepting a reference to a mutex. This one tries to obtain a lock on the mutex and blocks until the lock is obtained. The keyword `explicit` for constructors is discussed in Chapter 7.

```
explicit unique_lock(mutex_type& m);
```

➤ A constructor accepting a reference to a mutex and an instance of the `std::defer_lock_t` struct. The `unique_lock` stores the reference to the mutex, but does not immediately try to obtain a lock. A lock can be obtained later.

```
unique_lock(mutex_type& m, defer_lock_t) noexcept;
```

➤ A constructor accepting a reference to a mutex and an instance of the `std::try_to_lock_t` struct. The lock tries to obtain a lock to the referenced mutex, but if it fails it does not block.

```
unique_lock(mutex_type& m, try_to_lock_t);
```

➤ A constructor accepting a reference to a mutex and an instance of the `std::adopt_lock_t` struct. The lock assumes that the calling thread already has obtained a lock on the referenced mutex and will manage this lock.

```
unique_lock(mutex_type& m, adopt_lock_t);
```

➤ A constructor accepting a reference to a mutex and an absolute time. The constructor tries to obtain a lock until the system time passes the given absolute time. The Chrono library is discussed in Chapter 16.

```
template <class Clock, class Duration>
unique_lock(mutex_type& m, const chrono::time_point<Clock, Duration>& abs_time);
```

➤ A constructor accepting a reference to a mutex and a relative time. The constructor tries to get a lock on the mutex with the given relative timeout.

```
template <class Rep, class Period>
unique_lock(mutex_type& m, const chrono::duration<Rep, Period>& rel_time);
```

The `unique_lock` class also has the following methods: `lock()`, `try_lock()`, `try_lock_for()` and `try_lock_until()`, which behave as explained in the section on timed mutex classes earlier in this chapter. You can use the `owns_lock()` method to see if the lock has been acquired.

C++11 also has support for obtaining locks on multiple mutex objects at once. For this, you can use the generic `lock()` variadic template function. Variadic template functions are discussed in Chapter 20.

```
template <class L1, class L2, class... L3> void lock(L1&, L2&, L3&...);
```

This generic function locks all the mutex objects in order. If one of the mutex lock calls throws an exception, `unlock()` is called on all locks that have already been obtained.

There is also a generic `try_lock()` function:

```
template <class L1, class L2, class... L3> int try_lock(L1&, L2&, L3&...);
```

`try_lock()` tries to obtain a lock on all the given mutex objects by calling `try_lock()` on each of them in sequence. It returns -1 if all calls to `try_lock()` succeed. If any `try_lock()` fails, `unlock()` is called on all locks that have already been obtained, and the return value is the zero-based index of the parameter position of the mutex on which `try_lock()` failed.

 When your threads need to acquire multiple locks at once, it is recommended to use the generic `try_lock()` or `lock()`, always using the same order for the mutex arguments. If you don't use the same order for the mutex arguments, deadlocks might occur.

The following example demonstrates how to use the generic `lock()` function. The `process()` function first creates two locks, one for each mutex, and gives an instance of `std::defer_lock_t` as second argument to tell `unique_lock` not to acquire the lock during construction. The call to `lock()` will then acquire both locks:

```
mutex mut1;
mutex mut2;
void process()
{
    unique_lock<mutex> lock1(mut1, defer_lock_t());
    unique_lock<mutex> lock2(mut2, defer_lock_t());
    lock(lock1, lock2);
    // Locks acquired
}
```

```
int main()
{
    process();
    return 0;
}
```

Code snippet from mutex\multiple_locks.cpp

By always calling `lock()` in all threads with the `lock1` and `lock2` arguments in the same order, `lock()` will not cause any deadlocks. However, if you do call `lock()` from another thread, for example as follows, deadlocks might occur:

```
lock(lock2, lock1);
```

std::call_once

You can use `std::call_once()` in combination with `std::once_flag` to make sure a certain function or method is called exactly one time no matter how many threads try to call `call_once()`.

Only one `call_once()` invocation will actually call the given function or method; this invocation is called the *effective* `call_once()` invocation. This effective invocation on a specific `once_flag` instance finishes before all subsequent `call_once()` invocations on the same `once_flag` instance. Other threads calling `call_once()` on the same `once_flag` instance will block until the effective call is finished. Figure 22-3 illustrates this with three threads. Thread 1 performs the effective `call_once()` invocation, Thread 2 blocks until the effective invocation is finished, and Thread 3 doesn't block because the effective invocation from Thread 1 has already finished.

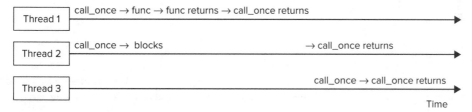

FIGURE 22-3

The following example demonstrates the use of `call_once()`. The example defines a class called `Data`, which has a dynamically allocated block of memory called `mMemory`. The `mutable` keyword is discussed in Chapter 7. Multiple threads can execute `operator()`; however, for this example, `mMemory` should be initialized only once. To accomplish this, the class includes a member `mOnceFlag` of type `once_flag`. The `operator()` uses `call_once()` together with this `once_flag` to call the `init()` method. The result is that only one thread will execute this `init()` method exactly one time. While this `call_once()` call is in progress, other threads will block until the `init()` method returns:

```
class Data
{
    public:
        void operator()()
        {
```

```
            call_once(mOnceFlag, &Data::init, this);
            // Do work
            cout << "Work" << endl;
        }
    protected:
        void init()
        {
            cout << "init()" << endl;
            mMemory = new char[24];
        }
        mutable once_flag mOnceFlag;
        mutable char* mMemory;
};
int main()
{
    cout.sync_with_stdio(true); // Make sure cout is thread-safe
    Data d;
    thread t1{ref(d)};
    thread t2{ref(d)};
    thread t3{ref(d)};
    t1.join();
    t2.join();
    t3.join();
    return 0;
}
```

Code snippet from mutex\call_once.cpp

The output of this code is as follows:

```
init()
Work
Work
Work
```

The example omits the code for deallocation of the memory. Of course, in this example, you could also allocate the memory for mMemory in the constructor of the Data class. It is done using the init() method to demonstrate the use of call_once().

Mutex Usage Examples

Thread-Safe Writing to Streams

Earlier in this chapter, in the section about threads, you saw an example with a class called Counter. That example mentioned that C++ streams are thread-safe when you call sync_with_stdio(true), but the output from different threads can still be interleaved. To solve this issue, you can use a mutual exclusion object to make sure that only one thread at a time is reading/writing to the stream object.

The following example synchronizes all accesses to cout in the Counter class. For this, a static mutex object is added to the class. It should be static, because all instances of the class should use the same `mutex` instance. Before writing to `cout`, the updated example uses a `lock_guard` to obtain a lock on the `mutex`. Changes compared to the earlier version are highlighted:

```cpp
class Counter
{
    public:
        Counter(int id, int numIterations)
            : mId(id), mNumIterations(numIterations)
        {
        }
        void operator()() const
        {
            for (int i = 0; i < mNumIterations; ++i) {
                lock_guard<mutex> lock(mMutex);
                cout << "Counter " << mId << " has value ";
                cout << i << endl;
            }
        }
    protected:
        int mId;
        int mNumIterations;
        static mutex mMutex;
};
mutex Counter::mMutex;
int main()
{
    // Omitted for brevity.
}
```

Code snippet from mutex\ThreadFunctionObjectWithMutex.cpp

Using Timed Locks

The following example demonstrates how to use a timed mutex. It is the same `Counter` class as before, but this time it uses a `timed_mutex` in combination with a `unique_lock`. A relative time of 200 milliseconds is given to the `unique_lock` constructor, causing it to try to obtain a lock for 200 milliseconds. If the lock could not be obtained within this timeout interval, the constructor returns. Afterwards you can check whether or not the lock has been acquired, which can be done with an `if` statement on the `lock` variable because the `unique_lock` class defines a `bool()` conversion operator. The timeout is specified by using the C++11 Chrono library, which is discussed in Chapter 16.

```cpp
class Counter
{
    public:
        Counter(int id, int numIterations)
            : mId(id), mNumIterations(numIterations)
        {
        }
        void operator()() const
        {
            for (int i = 0; i < mNumIterations; ++i) {
                unique_lock<timed_mutex> lock(mTimedMutex,
                    chrono::milliseconds(200));
```

```
                        if (lock) {
                            cout << "Counter " << mId << " has value ";
                            cout << i << endl;
                        } else {
                            // Lock not acquired in 200 ms
                        }
                    }
                }
    protected:
        int mId;
        int mNumIterations;
        static timed_mutex mTimedMutex;
};
timed_mutex Counter::mTimedMutex;
int main()
{
    // Omitted for brevity.
}
```

Code snippet from mutex\ThreadFunctionObjectWithTimedMutex.cpp

Double-Checked Locking

You can use locks to implement the *double-checked locking algorithm*. This can, for example, be used to make sure that a variable is initialized exactly once as an alternative to using `call_once()`. The following example shows how you can implement this. It is called the double-checked locking algorithm because it is checking the value of the `initialized` variable twice, once before acquiring the lock and once right after acquiring the lock. The first `initialized` check is to prevent obtaining a lock when it is not needed and will increase performance. The second check is required to make sure that no other thread performed the initialization between the first `initialized` check and acquiring the lock:

```
class MyClass
{
    public:
        void init() {cout << "Init" << endl;}
};
MyClass var;
bool initialized = false;
mutex mut;
void func()
{
    if (!initialized) {
        unique_lock<mutex> lock(mut);
        if (!initialized) {
            var.init();
            initialized = true;
        }
    }
    cout << "OK" << endl;
}
```

```
int main()
{
    cout.sync_with_stdio(true); // Make sure cout is thread-safe
    vector<thread> threads;
    for (int i = 0; i < 5; ++i)
        threads.push_back(thread{func});
    for (auto& t : threads)
        t.join();
    return 0;
}
```

Code snippet from mutex\double_checked_locking.cpp

The output of this program is as follows:

```
Init
OK
OK
OK
OK
OK
```

This output clearly shows that only one thread has initialized the MyClass instance.

CONDITION VARIABLES

Condition variables allow a thread to block until a certain condition is set by another thread or until the system time reaches a specified time. They allow for explicit inter-thread communication. If you are familiar with multithreaded programming using the Win32 API, you can compare condition variables with *event objects* in Windows.

You need to include the <condition_variable> header file to use condition variables. There are two kinds of condition variables available in the standard:

➤   std::condition_variable: A condition variable that can only wait on a unique_lock<mutex>, which, according to the standard, allows for maximum efficiency on certain platforms.

➤   std::condition_variable_any: A condition variable that can wait on any kind of object, including custom lock types.

The condition_variable class supports the following methods:

```
notify_one();
```

Wake up one of the threads waiting on this condition variable. This is similar to an auto-reset event in Windows.

```
notify_all();
```

Wake up all threads waiting on this condition variable.

```
wait(unique_lock<mutex>& lk);
```

The thread calling `wait()` should already have acquired a lock on `lk`. The effect of calling `wait()` is that it will atomically call `lk.unlock()` and then block the thread, waiting for a notification. When the thread is unblocked by a `notify_one()` or `notify_all()` call in another thread, the function will call `lk.lock()` again, possibly blocking on the lock and then returns.

```
wait_for(unique_lock<mutex>& lk,
    const chrono::duration<Rep, Period>& rel_time);
```

Similar to the previous `wait()` method, except that the thread will be unblocked by a `notify_one()` call, a `notify_all()` call, or when the given timeout has expired.

```
wait_until(unique_lock<mutex>& lk,
    const chrono::time_point<Clock, Duration>& abs_time);
```

Similar to the previous `wait()` method, except that the thread will be unblocked by a `notify_one()` call, a `notify_all()` call, or when the system time passes the given absolute time.

There are also versions of `wait()`, `wait_for()`, and `wait_until()` that accept an extra predicate parameter. For example, `wait()` accepting an extra predicate is equivalent to:

```
while (!predicate())
    wait(lk);
```

The `condition_variable_any` class supports the same methods as the `condition_variable` class except that it accepts any kind of `Lock` class instead of only a `unique_lock<mutex>`.

Condition variables can, for example, be used for background threads processing items from a queue. You can define a queue in which you insert items to be processed. A background thread waits until there are items in the queue. When an item is inserted into the queue, the thread wakes up, processes the item, and goes back to sleep, waiting for the next item. Suppose you have the following queue:

```
std::queue<std::string> mQueue;
```

You need to make sure only one thread is modifying this queue at any given time. You can do this with a mutex:

```
std::mutex mMutex;
```

To be able to notify a background thread when an item is added, you need a condition variable:

```
std::condition_variable mCondVar;
```

A thread that wants to add an item to the queue first acquires a lock on the mutex, adds the item to the queue, and notifies the background thread:

```
// Lock mutex and add entry to the queue.
unique_lock<mutex> lock(mMutex);
mQueue.push(entry);
// Notify condition variable to wake up thread.
mCondVar.notify_all();
```

The background thread waits for notifications in an infinite loop as follows:

```
unique_lock<mutex> lock(mMutex);
while (true) {
    // Wait for a notification.
    mCondVar.wait(lock);
    // Condition variable is notified, so something is in the queue.
    // Process queue item...
}
```

The section "Example: Multithreaded Logger Class" toward the end of this chapter provides a complete example of how to use condition variables to send notifications to other threads.

The standard also defines a helper function called `std::notify_all_at_thread_exit(cond, lk)` where `cond` is a condition variable and `lk` is a `unique_lock<mutex>` instance. A thread calling this function should already have acquired the lock `lk`. When the thread exits, it will automatically execute the following:

```
lk.unlock();
cond.notify_all();
```

 The lock `lk` stays locked until the thread exits. So, you need to make sure that this does not cause any deadlocks in your code, for example due to wrong lock ordering. Lock ordering is discussed earlier in this chapter.

FUTURES

As discussed earlier in this chapter, using `std::thread` to launch a thread that calculates a single result does not make it easy to get the computed result back once the thread has finished executing. Another problem with `std::thread` is handling errors like exceptions. If a thread throws an exception and this exception is not handled by the thread itself, the C++ runtime will call `std::terminate`, which usually will terminate the whole application. You can avoid this by using `std::future`, which is able to transport an uncaught exception to another thread, which can then handle the exception however it wants. Of course, you should always try to handle exceptions in the threads themselves as much as possible, preventing them from leaving the thread.

`std::future` and `std::promise` work together to make it easier to retrieve a result from a function that ran in the same thread or in another thread. Once a function, running in the same thread or in another thread, has calculated the value that it wants to return, it puts this value in a `promise`. This value can then be retrieved through a `future`. You can think of a `future/promise` pair as an inter-thread communication channel for a result.

A thread that launched another thread to calculate a value can get this value as follows. `T` is the type of the calculated result:

```
future<T> fut = ...;    // Is discussed later
T res = fut.get();
```

The call to `get()` will retrieve the result and store it in the variable `res`. If the other thread has not yet finished calculating the result, the call to `get()` will block until the value becomes available. You can avoid blocking by first asking the `future` if there is a result available:

```
if (fut.wait_for(0)) {  // Value is available
    T res = fut.get();
} else {                // Value is not yet available
    ...
}
```

A `promise` is the input side for the result; `future` is the output side. A `promise` is something where a thread will store its calculated result. The following code demonstrates how a thread might do this:

```
promise prom = ...; // Is discussed later
T val = ...;        // Calculate result value
prom.set_value(val);
```

If a thread encounters some kind of error during its calculation, it could store an exception in the `promise` instead of the value:

```
prom.set_exception(runtime_error("message"));
```

A thread that launches another thread to calculate something should give the `promise` to the newly launched thread, so that it can store the result in it. This is made easy by using `std::packaged_task`, which will automatically link a `future` and a `promise`. The following code demonstrates this. It creates a `packaged_task`, which will execute the given lambda expression in a separate thread. The lambda expression accepts two arguments and returns the sum of them as the result. The `future` is retrieved from the `packaged_task` by calling `get_future()`. The thread is started by the third line, and the last line uses the `get()` function to wait and retrieve the result from the launched thread:

```
packaged_task<int(int, int)> task([](int i1, int i2) {return i1+i2;});
auto fut = task.get_future();  // Get the future
task(2, 3);                    // Launch the task
int res = fut.get();           // Retrieve the result
```

Code snippet from future\packaged_task.cpp

This code is just for demonstration purposes. Currently, it launches a separate thread and then calls `get()` which blocks until the result is calculated. This sounds like a very expensive function call. In real-world applications you can use the `promise`/`future` model by periodically checking if there is a result available in the `future` (using `wait_for()` as discussed earlier). When the result is not yet available, you can do something else in the mean time, instead of blocking.

If you want to give the C++ runtime more control over whether or not a thread is created to calculate something, you can use `std::async()`. It accepts a function to be executed and returns a `future` that you can use to retrieve the result. There are two ways in which `async()` can call your function:

➤ Creating a new thread to run your function asynchronously

➤ Running your function at the time you call `get()` on the returned `future`

If you call `async()` without additional arguments, the run-time library will automatically choose one of the two methods depending on factors like the number of processors in your system. You can force the runtime to use one or the other method by specifying a `launch::async` or `launch::deferred` policy argument, respectively. The following example demonstrates the use of `async()`:

```cpp
int calculate()
{
    return 123;
}
int main()
{
    auto fut = async(calculate);
    //auto fut = async(launch::async, calculate);
    //auto fut = async(launch::deferred, calculate);

    // Do some more work...

    // Get result
    int res = fut.get();
    cout << res << endl;
    return 0;
}
```

Code snippet from future\async.cpp

As you can see in this example, `std::async()` is one of the easiest methods to perform some calculations in another thread or the same thread, and retrieve the result afterwards.

EXAMPLE: MULTITHREADED LOGGER CLASS

This section demonstrates how to use threads, the mutex and lock classes, and condition variables to write a multithreaded `Logger` class. The class allows log messages to be added to a queue from different threads. The `Logger` class itself will process this queue in another background thread that serially writes the log messages to a file. The class will be designed in three iterations.

It is obvious that you will have to protect access to the queue with a mutex to prevent multiple threads from reading/writing to the queue at the same time. Based on that, you might define the `Logger` class as follows:

```cpp
class Logger
{
    public:
        // Starts a background thread writing log entries to a file.
```

```
        Logger();
        // Add log entry to the queue.
        void log(const std::string& entry);
    protected:
        void processEntries();
        // Mutex and condition variable to protect access to the queue.
        std::mutex mMutex;
        std::condition_variable mCondVar;
        std::queue<std::string> mQueue;
        // The background thread.
        std::thread mThread;
    private:
        // Prevent copy construction and assignment.
        Logger(const Logger& src);
        Logger& operator=(const Logger& rhs);
};
```

Code snippet from logger\Version1\Logger.h

The implementation is as follows. Note that this initial design has a couple of problems and when you try to run it, it might behave strangely or even crash, as discussed and solved after the example. The inner while loop in the processEntries() method is also worth looking at. It processes all messages in the queue one at a time, and acquires and releases the lock on each iteration. This is done to make sure the loop doesn't keep the lock for too long, blocking other threads.

```
Logger::Logger()
{
    // Start background thread.
    mThread = thread{&Logger::processEntries, this};
}
void Logger::log(const std::string& entry)
{
    // Lock mutex and add entry to the queue.
    unique_lock<mutex> lock(mMutex);
    mQueue.push(entry);
    // Notify condition variable to wake up thread.
    mCondVar.notify_all();
}
void Logger::processEntries()
{
    // Open log file.
    ofstream ofs("log.txt");
    if (ofs.fail()) {
        cerr << "Failed to open logfile." << endl;
        return;
    }
    // Start processing loop.
    unique_lock<mutex> lock(mMutex);
    while (true) {
        // Wait for a notification.
        mCondVar.wait(lock);
        // Condition variable is notified, so something is in the queue.
        lock.unlock();
        while (true) {
```

```
            lock.lock();
            if (mQueue.empty()) {
                break;
            } else {
                ofs << mQueue.front() << endl;
                mQueue.pop();
            }
            lock.unlock();
        }
    }
}
```

Code snippet from logger\Version1\Logger.cpp

This `Logger` class can be tested by using the following test code, which launches a number of background threads, all logging a few messages to the same `Logger` instance:

```
void logSomeMessages(int id, Logger& logger)
{
    for (int i = 0; i < 10; ++i) {
        stringstream ss;
        ss << "Log entry " << i << " from thread " << id;
        logger.log(ss.str());
    }
}
int main()
{
    Logger logger;
    vector<thread> threads;
    // Create a few threads all working with the same Logger instance.
    for (int i = 0; i < 10; ++i) {
        threads.push_back(thread{logSomeMessages, i, ref(logger)});
    }
    // Wait for all threads to finish.
    for (auto& t : threads) {
        t.join();
    }
    return 0;
}
```

Code snippet from logger\Version1\main.cpp

If you build and run this naïve initial version, you will notice a couple of problems with it, especially when you run it on a multicore machine.

The first problem is that the background `Logger` thread will be terminated abruptly when the main() function finishes. This means that messages still in the queue will not be written to the file on disk. Some run-time libraries will even issue an error or generate a crash dump when the background `Logger` thread is abruptly terminated. You need to add a mechanism to gracefully shut down the background thread and wait until the background thread is completely shut down before terminating the application itself. This can be done by adding a Boolean member variable to the class. The destructor of the `Logger` class will set this Boolean to `true`, notify the background thread, and wait until the thread is shut down. The notification will trigger the background thread to wake up, check this Boolean value and, if it's `true`, write all messages in the queue to the file and terminate the processing loop. The new definition of the class is as follows:

```cpp
class Logger
{
    public:
        // Starts a background thread writing log entries to a file.
        Logger();
        // Gracefully shut down background thread.
        virtual ~Logger();
        // Add log entry to the queue.
        void log(const std::string& entry);
    protected:
        void processEntries();
        bool mExit;
        // Remaining of the class omitted for brevity
};
```

Code snippet from logger\Version2\Logger.h

The `Logger` constructor needs to initialize the `mExit` variable:

```cpp
Logger::Logger() : mExit(false)
{
    // Start background thread.
    mThread = thread{&Logger::processEntries, this};
}
```

Code snippet from logger\Version2\Logger.cpp

The destructor sets the Boolean variable, wakes up the thread, and then waits until the thread is shut down:

```cpp
Logger::~Logger()
{
    // Gracefully shut down the thread by setting mExit
    // to true and notifying the thread.
    mExit = true;
    // Notify condition variable to wake up thread.
    mCondVar.notify_all();
    // Wait until thread is shut down.
    mThread.join();
}
```

Code snippet from logger\Version2\Logger.cpp

The `processEntries()` method needs to check this Boolean variable and terminate the processing loop when it's `true`:

```cpp
void Logger::processEntries()
{
    // Open log file.
    ofstream ofs("log.txt");
```

```cpp
if (ofs.fail()) {
    cerr << "Failed to open logfile." << endl;
    return;
}
// Start processing loop.
unique_lock<mutex> lock(mMutex);
while (true) {
    // Wait for a notification.
    mCondVar.wait(lock);
    // Condition variable is notified, so something is in the queue
    // and/or we need to shut down this thread.
    lock.unlock();
    while (true) {
        lock.lock();
        if (mQueue.empty()) {
            break;
        } else {
            ofs << mQueue.front() << endl;
            mQueue.pop();
        }
        lock.unlock();
    }
    if (mExit)
        break;
}
```

Code snippet from logger\Version2\Logger.cpp

A second problem with the first naïve implementation is that sometimes the program might just block indefinitely in a deadlock situation where the main thread is blocking on the following line in the Logger destructor:

```cpp
mThread.join();
```

And the Logger background thread is blocking on the following line in the processEntries() method:

```cpp
mCondVar.wait(lock);
```

That is because the code contains a race condition. The main thread launches the processEntries() background thread in the Logger constructor, but immediately continues executing the remaining code in the main() function. This remaining code is rather small in this example. It can happen that this remaining code from the main() function, including the Logger destructor, is executed before the Logger background thread has started its processing loop. When that happens, the Logger destructor will already have called notify_all() before the background thread is waiting for the notification, and thus the background thread will miss this notification from the destructor.

To solve this race condition, the Logger constructor should wait after launching the background thread until the background thread is ready to process entries. You can implement this by adding a Boolean variable (mThreadStarted), a mutex (mMutexStarted), and a condition variable (mCondVarStarted) to the Logger class. Here is the final definition:

```cpp
class Logger
{
    public:
        // Starts a background thread writing log entries
        // to a file.
        Logger();
        // Gracefully shut down background thread.
        virtual ~Logger();
        // Add log entry to the queue.
        void log(const std::string& entry);
    protected:
        void processEntries();
        bool mThreadStarted;
        bool mExit;
        // Mutex and condition variable to protect access to the queue.
        std::mutex mMutex;
        std::condition_variable mCondVar;
        std::queue<std::string> mQueue;
        // The background thread.
        std::thread mThread;
        // Mutex and condition variable to detect when the thread
        // starts executing its loop.
        std::mutex mMutexStarted;
        std::condition_variable mCondVarStarted;
    private:
        // Prevent copy construction and assignment.
        Logger(const Logger& src);
        Logger& operator=(const Logger& rhs);
};
```

Code snippet from logger\FinalVersion\Logger.h

The final implementation of the Logger class is as follows. Note that the constructor is using the wait() method accepting a predicate.

```cpp
Logger::Logger() : mThreadStarted(false), mExit(false)
{
    // Start background thread.
    mThread = thread{&Logger::processEntries, this};
    // Wait until background thread starts its processing loop.
    unique_lock<mutex> lock(mMutexStarted);
    mCondVarStarted.wait(lock, [&](){return mThreadStarted == true;});
}
Logger::~Logger()
{
    // Gracefully shut down the thread by setting mExit
    // to true and notifying the thread.
    mExit = true;
    // Notify condition variable to wake up thread.
    mCondVar.notify_all();
```

```
        // Wait until thread is shut down.
        mThread.join();
}
void Logger::log(const std::string& entry)
{
        // Lock mutex and add entry to the queue.
        unique_lock<mutex> lock(mMutex);
        mQueue.push(entry);
        // Notify condition variable to wake up thread.
        mCondVar.notify_all();
}
void Logger::processEntries()
{
        // Open log file.
        ofstream ofs("log.txt");
        if (ofs.fail()) {
            cerr << "Failed to open logfile." << endl;
            return;
        }
        // Start processing loop.
        unique_lock<mutex> lock(mMutex);
        // Notify listeners that thread is starting processing loop.
        mThreadStarted = true;
        mCondVarStarted.notify_all();
        while (true) {
            // Wait for a notification.
            mCondVar.wait(lock);
            // Condition variable is notified, so something is in the queue
            // and/or we need to shut down this thread.
            lock.unlock();
            while (true) {
                lock.lock();
                if (mQueue.empty()) {
                    break;
                } else {
                    ofs << mQueue.front() << endl;
                    mQueue.pop();
                }
                lock.unlock();
            }
            if (mExit)
                break;
        }
}
```

Code snippet from logger\FinalVersion\Logger.cpp

THREAD POOLS

Instead of creating and deleting threads dynamically throughout your program lifetime, you can create a pool of threads that can be used as needed. This technique is often used in programs that want to handle some kind of event in a thread. In most environments, the ideal number of threads to have is equal to the number of processing cores. If there are more threads than cores, threads will have to be suspended to allow other threads to run, and this will ultimately add overhead. However, the rate of arrival of events may mean that, at some times there are more events per unit time than can be processed. The solution in this case is to use the producer/consumer model, where a number of pre-created threads are waiting for something to do.

Since not all processing is identical, it is not uncommon to have a thread that receives, as part of its input, a function object that represents the computation to be done.

Because all the threads are pre-existing, it is vastly more efficient for the operating system to schedule one to run than it is for the operating system to create one in response to an input. Furthermore, the use of a thread pool allows you to manage the number of threads that are created, so depending on the platform, you may have as few as one thread or as many as 64.

Note that while the ideal number of threads is equal to the number of cores, this applies only in the case where the thread is compute bound and cannot block for any other reason, including I/O. When a thread can block, it is often appropriate to run more threads than there are cores. Determining the optimal number of threads in such cases may involve doing throughput measurements with the system under normal load conditions.

You can implement a thread pool in a similar way as an object pool. Chapter 24 gives an example implementation of an object pool. The implementation of a thread pool is left as an exercise for the reader.

THREADING DESIGN AND BEST PRACTICES

This section briefly mentions a couple of best practices related to multithreaded programming.

> **Before terminating the application, always use `join()` to wait for background threads to finish:** Make sure you use `join()` on all background threads before terminating your application. This will make sure all those background threads have the time to do proper cleanup. Background threads for which there is no `join()` will terminate abruptly when the main thread is terminated.

> **The best synchronization is no synchronization:** Multithreaded programming becomes much easier if you manage to design your different threads in such a way that all threads working on shared data read only from that shared data and never write to it, or only write to parts never read by other threads. In that case there is no need for any synchronization and you cannot have problems like race conditions or deadlocks.

> **Try to use the single-thread ownership pattern:** This means that a block of data is owned by no more than one thread at a time. Owning the data means that no other thread is allowed to read/write to the data. When the thread is finished with the data, the data can be passed off to another thread, which now has sole and complete responsibility/ownership of the data. No synchronization is necessary in this case.

> **Use atomic types and operations when possible:** Atomic types and atomic operations make it easier to write race condition and deadlock free code, because they handle synchronization automatically. If atomic types and operations are not possible in your multithreaded design, and you need shared data, you have to use a mutual exclusion mechanism to ensure proper synchronization.

➤ **Use locks to protect mutable shared data:** If you need mutable shared data to which multiple threads can write to, and you cannot use atomic types and operations, you have to use a locking mechanism to make sure reads and writes between different threads are synchronized.

➤ **Release locks as soon as possible:** When you need to protect your shared data with a lock, make sure you release the lock as soon as possible. While a thread is holding a lock, it is blocking other threads waiting for the same lock, possibly hurting performance.

➤ **Make sure to acquire multiple locks in the same order:** If multiple threads need to acquire multiple locks, they must be acquired in the same order in all threads to prevent deadlocks. You can use the generic `std::lock()` specifying the locks in the same order to minimize the chance that you will violate lock ordering restrictions.

➤ **Use a multithreading aware profiler:** Use a multithreading aware profiler to find performance bottlenecks in your multithreaded applications and to find out if your multiple threads are indeed utilizing all available CPU cores in your system. An example of a multithreading aware profiler is the profiler in Visual Studio 2010 Premium or Ultimate.

➤ **Understand the multithreading support features of your debugger:** Most debuggers have at least basic support for debugging multithreaded applications. You should be able to get a list of all running threads in your application and you should be able to switch to any of those threads to inspect their call stack. You can use this, for example, to inspect deadlocks because you can see exactly what each thread is doing.

➤ **Use thread pools instead of creating and destroying a lot of threads dynamically:** Your performance decreases if you dynamically create and destroy a lot of threads. In that case it's better to use a thread pool to reuse existing threads.

SUMMARY

This chapter gave a brief overview of multithreaded programming using the C++11 threading library. It explained how you can use atomic types and atomic operations to operate on shared data without you having to use explicit locks. In case you cannot use these atomic types and operations, you learned how to use a mutual exclusion mechanism to ensure proper synchronization between different threads that need read/write access to shared data. You also saw how promises and futures represent a simple inter-thread communication channel; you can use futures to more easily get a result from a background thread. The chapter finished with a number of best practices for multithreaded application design.

As mentioned in the introduction, this chapter tried to touch on all the functionality provided by the C++11 threading library, but due to space constraints, it cannot go into all the details of multithreaded programming. There are books available that discuss nothing but multithreading. See Appendix B for a few references.

PART IV
C++ Software Engineering

▶ **CHAPTER 23:** Maximizing Software Engineering Methods

▶ **CHAPTER 24:** Writing Efficient C++

▶ **CHAPTER 25:** Developing Cross-Platform and Cross-Language Applications

▶ **CHAPTER 26:** Becoming Adept at Testing

▶ **CHAPTER 27:** Conquering Debugging

▶ **CHAPTER 28:** Incorporating Design Techniques and Frameworks

▶ **CHAPTER 29:** Applying Design Patterns

23

Maximizing Software Engineering Methods

WHAT'S IN THIS CHAPTER?

➤ What a software life cycle model is, with examples of the Stagewise Model, the Waterfall Model, the Spiral Model, and RUP

➤ What software engineering methodologies are, with examples of Agile, Scrum, XP, and Software Triage

➤ What Source Code Control means

Chapter 23 starts the last part of this book, which is about *software engineering*. This part describes software engineering methods, code efficiency, cross-platform development, software testing, software debugging, design techniques, and design patterns.

When you first learned how to program, you were probably on your own schedule. You were free to do everything at the last minute if you wanted to, and you could radically change your design during implementation. When coding in the professional world, however, programmers rarely have such flexibility. Even the most liberal engineering managers admit that some amount of process is necessary. Knowing the software engineering process is as important these days as knowing how to code.

This chapter surveys various approaches to software engineering. It does not go into great depth on any one approach — there are plenty of excellent books on software engineering processes. The idea is to cover the different types of processes in broad strokes so you can compare and contrast them. We try not to advocate or discourage any particular methodology. Rather, we hope that by learning about the tradeoffs of several different approaches, you'll be able to construct a process that works for you and the rest of your team. Whether you're a contractor working alone on projects, or your team consists of hundreds of engineers on several continents, understanding the different approaches to software development will help your job on a daily basis.

The last part of this chapter discusses Source Code Control solutions which make it easier to manage source code and keep track of its history. A Source Code Control solution is mandatory in every company to avoid a source code maintenance nightmare.

THE NEED FOR PROCESS

The history of software development is filled with tales of failed projects. From over-budget and poorly marketed consumer applications to grandiose mega-hyped operating systems, it seems that no area of software development is free from this trend.

Even when software successfully reaches users, bugs have become so commonplace that end users are forced to endure constant updates and patches. Sometimes the software does not accomplish the tasks it is supposed to or doesn't work the way the user would expect. These issues all point to a common truism of software — writing software is hard.

One wonders why software engineering seems to differ from other forms of engineering in its frequency of failures. While cars do have their share of bugs, you rarely see them stop suddenly and demand a reboot due to a buffer overflow (though as more auto components become software-driven, you just may.) Your TV may not be perfect, but you don't have to upgrade to version 2.3 to get Channel 6 to work.

Is it the case that other engineering disciplines are just more advanced than software? Is a civil engineer able to construct a working bridge by drawing upon the long history of bridge building? Are chemical engineers able to build a compound successfully because most of the bugs were worked out in earlier generations?

 Is software too new, or is it really a different type of discipline with inherent qualities contributing to the occurrence of bugs, unusable results, and doomed projects?

It certainly seems as if there's something different about software. For one thing, technology changes rapidly in software, creating uncertainty in the software development process. Even if an earth-shattering breakthrough does not occur during your project, the pace of the industry leads to problems. Software often needs to be developed quickly because competition is fierce.

Software development schedules can also be unpredictable. Accurate scheduling is nearly impossible when a single gnarly bug can take days or even weeks to fix. Even when things seem to be going according to schedule, the widespread tendency of product definition changes (*feature creep*) can throw a wrench in the process.

Software is complex. There is no easy and accurate way to prove that a program is bug-free. Buggy or messy code can have an impact on software for years if it is maintained through several versions. Software systems are often so complex that when staff turnover occurs, nobody wants to get anywhere near the messy code that forgotten engineers have left behind. This leads to a cycle of endless patching, hacks, and workarounds.

Of course, standard business risks apply to software as well. Marketing pressures and miscommunication get in the way. Many programmers try to steer clear of corporate politics, but it's not uncommon to have adversity between the development and product marketing groups.

All of these factors working against software engineering products indicate the need for some sort of process. Software projects are big, complicated, and fast-paced. To avoid failure, engineering groups need to adopt a system to control this unwieldy process.

SOFTWARE LIFE CYCLE MODELS

Complexity in software isn't new. The need for a formalized process was recognized decades ago. Several approaches to modeling the *software life cycle* have attempted to bring some order to the chaos of software development by defining the software process in terms of steps from the initial idea to the final product. These models, refined over the years, guide much of software development today.

The Stagewise Model and Waterfall Model

The classic life cycle model for software is often referred to as the *Stagewise Model*. This model is based on the idea that software can be built almost like following a recipe. There is a set of steps that, if followed correctly, will yield a mighty fine chocolate cake, or program as the case may be. Each stage must be completed before the next stage can begin, as shown in Figure 23-1.

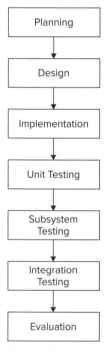

The process starts with formal planning, including gathering an exhaustive list of requirements. This list defines feature completeness for the product. The more specific the requirements are, the more likely that the project will succeed. Next, the software is designed and fully specified. The design step, like the requirements step, needs to be as specific as possible to maximize the chance of success. All design decisions are made at this time, often including pseudocode and the definition of specific subsystems that will need to be written. Subsystem owners work out how their code will interact, and the team agrees on the specifics of the architecture. Implementation of the design occurs next. Because the design has been fully specified, the code needs to adhere strongly to the design or else the pieces won't fit together. The final four stages are reserved for unit testing, subsystem testing, integration testing, and evaluation.

The main problem with the Stagewise Model is that, in practice, it is nearly impossible to complete one stage without at least exploring the next stage. A design cannot be set in stone without at least writing *some* code. Furthermore, what is the point of testing if the model doesn't provide a way to go back to the coding phase?

FIGURE 23-1

A number of refinements to the Stagewise Model were formalized as the *Waterfall Model* in the early 1970s. This model continues to be highly influential, if not downright dominant, in modern software engineering organizations. The main advancement that the Waterfall Model brought was a notion of feedback between stages. While it still stresses a rigorous process of planning, designing, coding, and testing, successive stages can overlap in part. Figure 23-2 shows an example of the Waterfall Model, illustrating the feedback and overlapping refinements. Feedback allows lessons learned in one phase to result in changes to the previous phase. Overlap permits activity in two phases to occur simultaneously.

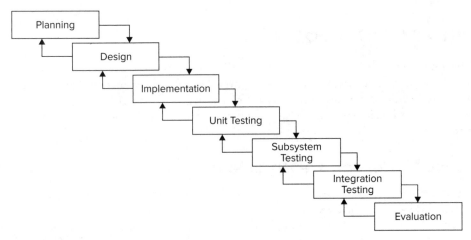

FIGURE 23-2

Various incarnations of the Waterfall Model have refined the process in different ways. For example, some plans include a "feasibility" step where experiments are performed before formal requirements are even gathered.

Benefits of the Waterfall Model

The value of the Waterfall Model lies in its simplicity. You, or your manager, may have followed this approach in past projects without formalizing it or recognizing it by name. The underlying assumption behind the Stagewise Model and Waterfall Model is that as long as each step is accomplished as completely and accurately as possible, subsequent steps will go smoothly. As long as all of the requirements are carefully specified in the first step, and all the design decisions and problems are hashed out in the second step, implementation in the third step should be a simple matter of translating the designs into code.

The simplicity of the Waterfall Model makes project plans based on this system organized and easy to manage. Every project is started the same way: by exhaustively listing all the features that are necessary. Managers using this approach can require that by the end of the design phase, for example, all engineers in charge of a subsystem submit their design as a formal design document or a functional subsystem specification. The benefit for the manager is that by having engineers specify requirements and design upfront, risks are, hopefully, minimized.

From the engineer's point of view, the Waterfall Model forces resolution of major issues upfront. All engineers will need to understand their project and design their subsystem before writing a significant amount of code. Ideally, this means that code can be written once instead of hacked together or rewritten when the pieces don't fit.

For small projects with very specific requirements, the Waterfall Model can work quite well. Particularly for consulting arrangements, it has the advantage of specifying specific metrics for success at the start of the project. Formalizing requirements helps the consultant to produce exactly what the client wants and forces the client to be specific about the goals for the project.

Drawbacks of the Waterfall Model

In many organizations, and almost all modern software engineering texts, the Waterfall Model has fallen out of favor. Critics disparage its fundamental premise that software development tasks happen in discrete linear steps. While the Waterfall Model allows for the overlapping of phases, it does not allow backward movement to a large degree. In many projects today, requirements come in throughout the development of the product. Often, a potential customer will request a feature that is necessary for the sale, or a competitor's product will have a new feature that requires parity.

The upfront specification of all requirements makes the Waterfall Model unusable for many organizations because it is not dynamic enough.

Another drawback is that in an effort to minimize risk by making decisions as formally and early as possible, the Waterfall Model may actually be hiding risk. For example, a major design issue might be undiscovered, glossed over, forgotten, or purposely avoided in the design phase. By the time integration testing reveals the mismatch, it may be too late to save the project. A major design flaw has arisen but, according to the Waterfall Model, the product is one step away from shipping! A mistake anywhere in the waterfall process will likely lead to failure at the end of the process. Early detection is difficult and rare.

While the Waterfall Model is still quite common and can be an effective way of visualizing the process, it is often necessary to make it more flexible by taking cues from other approaches.

The Spiral Model

The *Spiral Model* was proposed by Barry W. Boehm in 1988 in recognition of the occurrence of unexpected problems and changing requirements in the software development process. This method is part of a family of techniques known as *iterative processes*. The fundamental idea is that it's okay if something goes wrong because you'll fix it the next time around. A single spin through the spiral Model is shown in Figure 23-3.

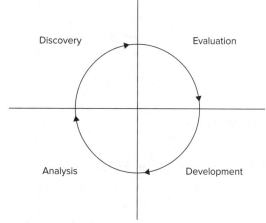

FIGURE 23-3

The phases of the Spiral Model are similar to the steps of the Waterfall Model. The discovery phase involves building requirements and determining objectives. During the evaluation phase, implementation alternatives are considered and prototypes may be built. In the Spiral Model, particular attention is paid to evaluating and resolving risks in the evaluation phase. The tasks deemed most risky are the ones that are implemented in the current cycle of the spiral. The tasks in the development phase are determined by the risks identified in the evaluation phase. For example, if evaluation reveals a risky algorithm that may be impossible to implement, the main task for development in the current cycle will be modeling, building, and testing that algorithm. The fourth phase is reserved for analysis and planning. Based on the results of the current cycle, the plan for the subsequent cycle is formed. Each iteration is expected to be fairly short in duration, taking only a few key features and risks into consideration.

Figure 23-4 shows an example of three cycles through the spiral in the development of an operating system. The first cycle yields a plan containing the major requirements for the product. The second cycle results in a prototype showing the user experience. The third cycle builds a component that is determined to be a high risk.

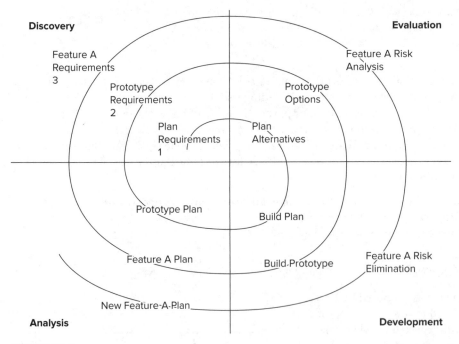

FIGURE 23-4

Benefits of the Spiral Model

The Spiral Model can be viewed as the application of an iterative approach to the best that the Waterfall Model has to offer. Figure 23-5 shows the Spiral Model as a waterfall process that has been modified to allow iteration. Hidden risks and a linear development path, the main drawbacks of the Waterfall Model, are resolved through short iterative cycles.

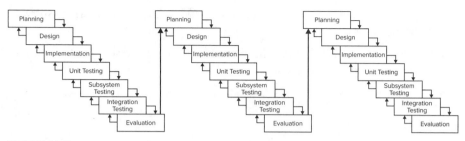

FIGURE 23-5

Performing the riskiest tasks first is another benefit. By bringing risk to the forefront and acknowledging that new conditions can arise at any time, the Spiral Model avoids the hidden time bombs that can occur in the Waterfall Model. When unexpected problems arise, they can be dealt with by using the same four-stage approach that works for the rest of the process.

This iterative approach also allows for incorporating feedback from testers. For example, an early version of the product can be released for internal or even external evaluation. These testers could, for example, say that a certain feature is missing, or an existing feature is not working as expected. The Spiral Model has a built-in mechanism to react to such input.

Finally, by repeatedly analyzing after each cycle and building new designs, the practical difficulties with the design-then-implement approach are virtually eliminated. With each cycle, there is more knowledge of the system that can influence the design.

Drawbacks of the Spiral Model

The main drawback of the Spiral Model is that it can be difficult to scope each iteration small enough to gain real benefit. In a worst-case scenario, the Spiral Model can degenerate into the Waterfall Model because the iterations are too long. Unfortunately, the Spiral Model only *models* the software life cycle. It cannot prescribe a specific way to break down a project into single-cycle iterations because that division varies from project to project.

Other possible drawbacks are the overhead of repeating all four phases for each cycle and the difficulty of coordinating cycles. Logistically, it may be difficult to assemble all the group members for design discussions at the right time. If different teams are working on different parts of the product simultaneously, they are probably operating in parallel cycles, which can get out of synch. For example, the user interface group could be ready to start the discovery phase of the Window Manager cycle, but the core OS group could still be in the development phase of the memory subsystem.

The Rational Unified Process

The *Rational Unified Process (RUP)* is a disciplined and formal approach to managing the software development process. The most important characteristic of the RUP is that, unlike the Spiral Model or the Waterfall Model, RUP is more than just a theoretical process model. RUP is actually a software product, marketed and sold by Rational Software, a division of IBM. Treating the process as software is compelling for a number of reasons:

➤ The process itself can be updated and refined, just as software products periodically have updates.

> ➤ Rather than simply suggesting a development framework, RUP includes a set of software tools for working with that framework.

> ➤ As a product, RUP can be rolled out to the entire engineering team so that all members are using the exact same processes and tools.

> ➤ Like many software products, RUP can be customized to the needs of the users.

RUP as a Product

As a product, the RUP takes the form of a suite of software applications that guides developers through the software development process. The product also offers specific guidance for other Rational products, such as the Rational Rose visual modeling tool and the Rational ClearCase configuration management tool. Extensive groupware communication tools are included as part of the "marketplace of ideas" that allow developers to share knowledge.

One of the basic principles behind RUP is that each iteration on a development cycle should have a tangible result. During the Rational Unified Process, users will create numerous designs, requirement documents, reports, and plans. The RUP software provides visualization and development tools for the creation of these artifacts.

RUP as a Process

Defining an accurate model is the central principle of RUP. Models, according to RUP, help explain the complicated structures and relationships in the software development process. In RUP, models are often expressed in Unified Modeling Language (UML) format.

RUP defines each part of the process as an individual *workflow*. Workflows represent each step of a process in terms of who is responsible for it, what tasks are being performed, the artifacts or results of these tasks, and the sequence of events that drives the tasks. Almost everything about RUP is customizable, but several *core process workflows* are defined "out of the box" by RUP.

The core process workflows bear some resemblance to the stages of the Waterfall Model, but each one is iterative and more specific in definition. The *business modeling workflow* models business processes, usually with the goal of driving software requirements forward. The *requirements workflow* creates the requirements definition by analyzing the problems in the system and iterating on its assumptions. The *analysis and design workflow* deals with system architecture and subsystem design. The *implementation workflow* covers the modeling, coding, and integration of software subsystems. The *test workflow* models the planning, implementation, and evaluation of software quality tests. The *deployment workflow* is a high-level view on overall planning, releasing, supporting, and testing workflows. The *configuration management workflow* goes from new project conception to iteration and end-of-product scenarios. Finally, the *environment workflow* supports the engineering organization through the creation and maintenance of development tools.

RUP in Practice

RUP is aimed mainly at larger organizations and offers several advantages over the adoption of traditional life cycle models. Once the team has gotten over the learning curve to use the software, all members will be using a common platform for designing, communicating, and implementing their ideas. The process can be customized to the needs of the team, and each stage reveals a wealth of valuable artifacts that document each phase of the development.

A product like RUP can be too heavyweight for some organizations. Teams with diverse development environments or tight engineering budgets might not want to or be able to standardize on a software-based development system. The learning curve can also be a factor — new engineers that aren't familiar with the process software will have to learn how to use it while getting up to speed on the product and the existing code base.

SOFTWARE ENGINEERING METHODOLOGIES

Software life cycle models provide a formal way of answering the question "What do we do next?" but are rarely (with the exception of formalized systems like RUP) able to contribute an answer to the logical follow-up question, "How do we do it?" To provide some answers to the "how" question, a number of methodologies have been developed that provide practical rules of thumb for professional software development. Books and articles on software methodologies abound, but a few innovations deserve particular attention: *Agile, Scrum, Extreme Programming,* and *Software Triage.*

Agile

To address the shortcomings of the Waterfall Model, the *Agile Methodology* was introduced in 2001 in the form of an *Agile Manifesto*. The entire manifesto reads as follows (`http://agilemanifesto.org/`):

MANIFESTO FOR AGILE SOFTWARE DEVELOPMENT

We are uncovering better ways of developing software by doing it and helping others do it. Through this work we have come to value:

➤ **Individuals and interactions** over processes and tools

➤ **Working software** over comprehensive documentation

➤ **Customer collaboration** over contract negotiation

➤ **Responding to change** over following a plan

That is, while there is value in the items on the right, we value the items on the left more.

As can be understood from this manifesto, the term *Agile* is only a high-level description. Basically, it tells you to make the process flexible so that customers' changes can easily be incorporated into the project during development.

Scrum

Agile is just a high-level foundation; it does not specify exactly how this should be implemented in real life. That's where *Scrum* comes into play; it's an Agile methodology with precise descriptions on how to use it on a daily base.

Just like the Spiral Model, Scrum is an iterative process. It is becoming more and more popular as a means to manage software development projects. In Scrum, each iteration is called a *sprint cycle*. The sprint cycle is the central part of the Scrum process. The length of sprints, which should be decided at the beginning of the project, is typically between two and four weeks. At the end of each sprint, the goal is to have a version of the software available that is fully working and tested, and which represents a subset of the customers' requirements. Scrum recognizes that customers will often change their minds during the development and thus allows the result of each sprint to be shipped to the customer. This gives customers the opportunity to see iterative versions of the software and allows them to give feedback to the development team about potential issues.

Roles

The *Product Owner* (PO) is the connection to the customer and to other people. The PO writes high-level *user stories* based on input from the customer, gives each user story a priority, and puts the stories in the Scrum product backlog. Actually, everyone on the team is allowed to write high-level user stories for the product backlog, but the Product Owner decides which user stories are kept and which are removed.

The *Scrum Master* (SM) is responsible for keeping the process running and can be part of the team, although not the team leader, because with Scrum the team leads itself. The SM is the contact person for the team so that the rest of the team members can concentrate on their tasks. The SM ensures that the Scrum process is followed correctly by the team; for example, by organizing the Daily Scrum meetings, which are discussed later. The Scrum Master and Product Owner should be two different persons.

The third and final role in the Scrum process is the *Team* itself. Teams, which develop the software, should be kept small, preferably fewer than 10 members.

The Process

The Scrum process enforces a daily meeting called the *Daily Scrum* or *Standup*. In this meeting, all team members sit together with the Scrum Master. According to the Scrum process, this meeting should start every day at exactly the same time and location, and should be no longer than 15 minutes. During this meeting, all team members get to answer three questions:

> ➤ What did you do since the last Daily Scrum?

> ➤ What are you planning to do after the current Daily Scrum?

> ➤ What problems are you facing to reach your goal?

Problems faced by team members should be noted by the Scrum Master who will try to solve them after the Daily Scrum meeting.

Before the start of each sprint cycle there is a *Sprint Planning* meeting in which team members must decide which product features they will implement in the new sprint. This is formalized in a sprint *backlog.* The features are selected from a *product backlog* containing prioritized user stories, which are high-level requirements of new features. User stories from the product backlog are broken down into smaller tasks with an *effort estimation* and are put in the sprint backlog. Once a sprint is in progress, the sprint backlog is frozen and cannot be changed during that sprint. The Sprint Planning should not take more than eight hours and is usually split into two parts: meeting with the Product Owner and the team to discuss the priority of product backlog items; and meeting with the team only to complete the sprint backlog.

In a Scrum team you will often find a physical board with three columns: *To Do, In Progress,* and *Done.* Every task for the sprint is written on a small paper and stuck on the board in the correct column. Tasks are not assigned to people during a meeting; instead, every team member can go to the board, pick one of the To Do tasks, and move that paper to the In Progress column. When the team member is finished with that task, the paper is moved to the Done column. This method makes it easy for team members to quickly get an overview of the work that still needs to be done and what tasks are in progress or finished. Although a number of software solutions are available to work with a virtual Scrum board, it's recommended to have a physical board because it visualizes the process much better.

Usually, a burn-down chart is also created every day to display the days of the sprint on the horizontal axis and the remaining development hours on the vertical axis. This gives a quick overview of the progress made and can be used to determine whether all planned tasks can be completed during the sprint.

Once a sprint cycle is finished, there are two meetings: the *Sprint Review* and the *Sprint Retrospective.* The Sprint Review should be less than four hours and should discuss the results of the sprint cycle, including what tasks were completed and what tasks were not completed and why. This meeting also includes a *Demo* to demonstrate the implemented features. The Sprint Retrospective should also have a four-hour maximum and should allow the team to think about how the last sprint cycle was executed. For example, the team can identify shortcomings in the process and adapt the process for the next sprint.

Benefits of Scrum

Scrum is resilient to unforeseen problems that come up during the development. When a problem pops up, it can be handled in one of the following sprints. The team is involved in every step of the project. It discusses user stories from the product backlog with the Product Owner and converts user stories into smaller tasks for inclusion in a sprint backlog. The team autonomously assigns work to its members with the aid of the physical Scrum tasks board. This board makes it easy to quickly see which team member is working on which task. And finally, the Daily Scrum meeting makes sure that everyone knows what is happening.

A huge benefit to the paying customer is a Demo that follows each sprint, which demonstrates the new iterative version of the project. The customer gets a quick sense of how the development is progressing and can make changes to requirements, which usually can be incorporated into a future sprint.

Drawbacks of Scrum

Some companies might find it difficult to accept that the team itself decides who is doing what. Tasks are not assigned to team members by a manager or a team leader. All members pick their own tasks from the Scrum tasks board.

The Scrum Master is a key person to make sure the team stays on track. It is very important that the SM trusts the team. Having too tight control over the team members will cause the Scrum process to fail.

A possible problem with Scrum is called *feature creep*. Scrum allows new user stories to be added to the product backlog during the development. The danger exists that project managers keep adding new features to the product backlog. This problem is best solved by deciding on a final release date, or the end date of the last sprint.

Extreme Programming (XP)

When one of the authors arrived home from work a few years ago and told his wife that his company had adopted some of the principles of Extreme Programming, she joked, "I hope you wear a safety harness for that." Despite the somewhat hokey name, Extreme Programming effectively bundles up the best of existing software development guidelines and new material into an increasingly popular methodology.

XP, popularized by Kent Beck in *eXtreme Programming eXplained* (Addison-Wesley, 1999), claims to take the best practices of good software development and turn them up a notch. For example, most programmers would agree that testing is a good thing. In XP, testing is deemed so good that you're supposed to write the tests before you write the code.

XP in Theory

The Extreme Programming methodology is made up of 12 main guiding principles. These principles are manifested throughout all phases of the software development process and have a direct impact on the daily tasks of engineers.

Plan as You Go

In the Waterfall Model, planning happened once, at the beginning of the process. Under the Spiral Model, planning was the first phase of each iteration. In RUP, planning is an integral step in most of the workflows. Under XP, planning is more than just a step — it's a never-ending task. XP teams start with a rough plan that captures the major points of the product being developed. Throughout the development process, the plan is refined and modified as necessary. The theory is that conditions are constantly changing and new information is obtained all the time.

Under XP, estimates for a given feature are always made by the person who will be implementing that particular feature. This helps to avoid situations where the implementer is forced to adhere to an unrealistic and artificial schedule. Initially, estimates are very rough, perhaps on the order of weeks for a feature. As the time horizon shortens, the estimates get more granular. Features are broken down into tasks taking no more than five days.

Build Small Releases

One of the theories of XP is that software projects grow risky and unwieldy when they try to accomplish too much at one time. Instead of massive software releases that involve core changes and several pages of release notes, XP advocates smaller releases with a timeframe closer to two months than 18 months. With such a short release cycle, only the most important features can make it into the product. This forces engineering and marketing to agree on what features are truly important.

Share a Common Metaphor

XP uses the term *metaphor* as other methodologies might use *architecture*. The idea is that all members of the team should share a common high-level view of the system. This isn't necessarily the specifics of how objects will communicate, or the exact APIs that will be written. Rather, the metaphor is the mental model for the components of the system. Team members should use the metaphor to drive shared terminology when discussing the project.

Simplify Your Designs

A mantra frequently sung by XP-savvy engineers is "avoid speculative generality." This goes against the natural inclinations of many programmers. If you are given the task of designing a file-based object store, you may start down the path of creating the be-all, end-all solution to all file-based storage problems. Your design might quickly evolve to cover multiple languages and any type of object. XP says you should lean towards the other end of the generality continuum. Instead of making the ideal object store that will win awards and be celebrated by your peers, design the simplest possible object store that gets the job done. You should understand the current requirements and write your code to those specifications to avoid overly complex code.

It may be hard to get used to simplicity in design. Depending on the type of work you do, your code may need to exist for years and be used by other parts of the code that you haven't even dreamed of. As discussed in Chapter 4, the problem with building in functionality that *may* be useful in the future is that you don't know what those hypothetical use cases are, and there is no way to craft a good design that is purely speculative. Instead, XP says you should build something that is useful today and leave open the opportunity to modify it later.

Test Constantly

According to *eXtreme Programming eXplained*, "Any program feature without an automated test simply doesn't exist." Extreme Programming is zealous about testing. Part of your responsibility as an XP engineer is to write the unit tests that accompany your code. A unit test is generally a small piece of code that makes sure that an individual piece of functionality works. For example, individual unit tests for a file-based object store may include `testSaveObject`, `testLoadObject`, and `testDeleteObject`.

XP takes unit testing one step further by suggesting that unit tests should be written before the actual code is written. Of course, the tests won't pass because the code hasn't been written yet. In theory, if your tests are thorough, you should know when your code is done because all the tests will complete successfully. We told you it was "extreme."

Refactor When Necessary

Most programmers *refactor* their code from time to time. Refactoring is the process of redesigning existing working code to take into account new knowledge or alternate uses that have been discovered since the code was written. Refactoring is difficult to build into a traditional software engineering schedule because its results are not as tangible as implementing a new feature. Good managers, however, recognize its importance for long-term code maintainability.

The extreme way of refactoring is to recognize situations during development when refactoring is useful and to do the refactoring at that time. Instead of deciding at the start of a release which existing parts of the product need design work, XP programmers learn to recognize the signs of code that is ready to be refactored. While this practice will almost certainly result in unexpected and unscheduled tasks, restructuring the code when appropriate should make future development easier.

Code in Pairs

XP suggests that all production code should be written by two people working side-by-side simultaneously, called *pair programming*. Obviously, only one person can actually be in control of the keyboard. The other person takes a high-level approach, thinking about issues such as testing, necessary refactoring, and the overall model of the project.

As an example, if you are in charge of writing the user interface for a particular feature of your application, you might want to ask the original author of the feature to sit down with you. She can advise you about the correct use of the feature, warn you about any "gotchas" you should watch out for, and help oversee your efforts at a high level. Even if you can't acquire the help of the original author, just grabbing another member of the team can help. The theory is that working in pairs builds shared knowledge, ensures proper design, and puts an informal system of checks and balances in place.

Share the Code

In many traditional development environments, code ownership is strongly defined and often enforced. One of the authors worked previously in an environment where the manager explicitly forbade checking in changes to code written by any other member of the team. XP takes the extreme opposite approach by declaring that the code is collectively owned by everybody.

Collective ownership is practical for a number of reasons. From a management point of view, it is less detrimental when a single engineer leaves suddenly because there are others who understand that part of the code. From an engineer's point of view, collective ownership builds a common view of how the system works. This helps design tasks and frees the individual programmer to make any change that will add value to the overall project.

One important note about collective ownership is that it is not necessary for every programmer to be familiar with every single line of code. It is more of a mindset that the project is a team effort, and there is no reason for any one person to hoard knowledge.

Integrate Continuously

All programmers are familiar with the dreaded chore of integrating code. This is the task when you discover that your view of the object store is a complete mismatch with the way it was actually written. When subsystems come together, problems are exposed. XP recognizes this phenomenon and advocates integrating code into the project frequently as it is being developed.

XP suggests a specific method for integration. Two programmers (the pair that developed the code) sit down at a designated "integration station" and merge the code in together. The code is not checked in until it passes 100 percent of the tests. By having a single station, conflicts are avoided and integration is clearly defined as a step that must occur before a check-in.

A similar approach can still work on an individual level. Engineers run tests individually or in pairs before checking code into the repository. A designated machine continually runs automated tests.

When the automated tests fail, the team receives an email indicating the problem and listing the most recent check-ins.

Work Sane Hours

XP has a thing or two to say about the hours you've been putting in. The claim is that a well-rested programmer is a happy and productive programmer. XP advocates a work week of approximately 40 hours and warns against putting in overtime for more than two consecutive weeks.

Of course, different people need different amounts of rest. The main idea, though, is that if you sit down to write code without a clear head, you're going to write poor code and abandon many of the XP principles.

Have a Customer on Site

Since an XP-savvy engineering group constantly refines its product plan and builds only what is currently necessary, having a customer contribute to the process is very valuable. Although it is not always possible to convince a customer to be physically present during development, the idea that there should be communication between engineering and the end user is clearly a valuable notion. In addition to assisting with the design of individual features, customers can help prioritize tasks by conveying their individual needs.

Share Common Coding Standards

Due to the collective ownership guideline and the practice of pair programming, coding in an extreme environment can be difficult if each engineer has her own naming and indenting conventions. XP doesn't advocate any particular style, but supplies the guideline that if you can look at a piece of code and immediately identify the author, your group probably needs better definition of its coding standards.

For additional information on various approaches to coding style, see Chapter 5.

XP in Practice

XP purists claim that the 12 tenets of Extreme Programming are so intertwined that adopting some of them without others would largely ruin the methodology. For example, pair programming is vital to testing because if you can't determine how to test a particular piece of code, your partner can help. Also, if you're tired one day and decide to skip the testing, your partner will be there to evoke feelings of guilt.

Some of the XP guidelines, however, can prove difficult to implement. To some engineers, the idea of writing tests before code is too abstract. For those engineers, it may be sufficient to *design* the tests without actually writing them until there is code to test. Many of the XP principles are rigidly defined, but if you understand the theory behind it, you may be able to find ways to adapt the guidelines to the needs of your project.

The collaborative aspects of XP can be challenging as well. Pair programming has measurable benefits, but it may be difficult for a manager to rationalize having half as many people actually writing code each day. Some members of the team may even feel uncomfortable with such close collaboration, perhaps finding it difficult to type while others are watching. Pair programming also has obvious challenges if the team is physically spread out or if members tend to telecommute regularly.

For some organizations, Extreme Programming may be too radical. Large established companies with formal policies in place for engineering may be slow to adopt new approaches like XP. However, even if your company is resistant to the implementation of XP, you can still improve your own productivity by understanding the theory behind it.

Software Triage

In the fatalistically-named book *Death March* (Prentice Hall, 2003) Edward Yourdon describes the frequent and scary condition of software that is behind schedule, short on staff, over budget, or poorly designed. Yourdon's theory is that when software projects get into this state, even the best modern software development methodologies will no longer apply. As you have learned in this chapter, many approaches to software development are built around formalized documents or taking a user-centered approach to design. In a project that's already in "death march" mode, there simply isn't time for these approaches.

The idea behind software triage is that when a project is already in a bad state, resources are scarce. Time is scarce, engineers are scarce, and money may be scarce. The main mental obstacle that managers and developers need to overcome when a project is way behind schedule is that it will be impossible to satisfy the original requirements in the allotted time. The task then becomes organizing remaining functionality into "must-have," "should-have," and "nice-to-have" lists.

Software triage is a daunting and delicate process. It often requires the leadership of a seasoned veteran of "death march" projects to make the tough decisions. For the engineer, the most important point is that in certain conditions, it may be necessary to throw familiar processes out the window (along with some existing code, unfortunately) to finish a project on time.

BUILDING YOUR OWN PROCESS AND METHODOLOGY

There is one software development methodology that we wholeheartedly endorse, and it's not necessarily any of the above. It's unlikely that any book or engineering theory will perfectly match the needs of your project or organization. We recommend that you learn from as many approaches as you can and design your own process. Combining concepts from different approaches may be easier than you think. For example, RUP optionally supports an XP-like approach. Here are some tips for building the software engineering process of your dreams.

Be Open to New Ideas

Some engineering techniques seem crazy at first or unlikely to work. Look at new innovations in software engineering methodologies as a way to refine your existing process. Try things out when you can. If XP sounds intriguing, but you're not sure if it will work in your organization, see if you can work it in slowly, taking a few of the principles at a time or trying it out with a smaller pilot project.

Bring New Ideas to the Table

Most likely, your engineering team is made up of people from varying backgrounds. You may have people who are veterans of startups, long-time consultants, recent graduates, and PhDs on your team. You all have a different set of experiences and your own ideas of how a software project should be run. Sometimes the best processes turn out to be a combination of the way things are typically done in these very different environments.

Recognize What Works and What Doesn't Work

At the end of a project (or better yet, during the project, like with the Sprint Retrospective of the Scrum methodology), get the team together to evaluate the process. Sometimes there's a major problem that nobody notices until the whole team stops to think about it. Perhaps there's a problem that *everybody* knows about but nobody has discussed.

Consider what isn't working and see how those parts can be fixed. Some organizations require formal code reviews prior to any source code check-in. If code reviews are so long and boring that nobody does a good job, discuss code-reviewing techniques as a group. For example, consider reviewing only the interface files. Your group might even decide that changing an interface file after the interface is finalized with a review will be marked as a failure. This might help your team members to quickly learn how to write good interfaces.

Also consider what is going well and see how those parts can be extended. For example, if maintaining the feature tasks as a group-editable website is working, then maybe devote some time to making the website better.

Don't Be a Renegade

Whether a process is mandated by your manager or custom-built by the team, it's there for a reason. If your process involves writing formal design documents, make sure you write them. If you think that the process is broken or too complex, see if you can talk to your manager about it. Don't just avoid the process — it will come back to haunt you.

SOURCE CODE CONTROL

Managing all source code is very important for any company, big or small, even for personal developers. A software solution is required to manage all source code in a central place. In a company for example, it would be very impractical to store all the source code on the machines of the individual developers. This would result in a maintenance nightmare because not everyone will always have the latest code. All source code should be stored in a central place and should be managed by *Source Code Control* software. There are three kinds of Source Code Control software solutions:

➤ **Local:** These solutions store all source code files and their history locally on your machine and are not really suitable for use in a team. These are solutions from the 70s and 80s and shouldn't be used anymore. They are not discussed further.

➤ **Client/Server:** These solutions are split into a client component and a server component. For a personal developer, the client and server components can run on the same machine, but the separation makes it easy to move the server component to a dedicated physical server machine.

➤ **Distributed:** These solutions go one step further than the client/server model. With a distributed solution, the developers don't need to be connected to the same company network. They can work on the same source code from anywhere in the world over the Internet.

Both the client/server and the distributed solutions consist of two parts. The first part is the server software, which is software running on the central server and which is responsible for keeping track of all source code files and their history. The second part is the client software. This client software should be installed on every developer's machine and is responsible to communicate with the server software to get the latest version of a source file, get a previous version of a source file, commit local changes back to the server, rollback changes to a previous version and so on.

Most Source Code Control systems have a special terminology, but unfortunately, not all systems use exactly the same terms. The following list explains a number of terms that are commonly used:

➤ **Branch:** The source code can be *branched,* which means that multiple versions can be developed side-by-side. For example, one branch could be created for every released version. On those branches, bug fixes could be implemented for those released versions, while new features are added to the main branch. Bug fixes created for released versions can also be merged back to the main branch.

➤ **Checkout:** This is the action of creating a local copy on the developer's machine based on a specified version of the source code on the central server.

➤ **Checkin, Commit, or Merge:** A developer should make changes to the local copy of the source code. When everything works correctly on the local machine, the developer can checkin/commit/merge those local changes back to the central server.

➤ **Conflict:** When multiple developers make changes to the same source file, a conflict might occur during checkin of that source file. The Source Code Control software often will try to automatically resolve these conflicts. If that is not possible, the client software will ask the user to resolve any conflicts manually.

➤ **Label or Tag:** A label or tag can be attached to all files at any given time. This makes it easy to jump back to the version of those files at that time.

➤ **Repository:** The collection of files on the central server is called the repository. This also includes metadata about those files, such as checkin comments.

➤ **Resolve:** When checkin conflicts occur, the user will have to resolve them before checkin can continue.

➤ **Revision or Version:** A revision or version is a snapshot of the contents of a file at a specific point in time. Versions represent specific points to which the code can be reverted to, or compared against.

➤ **Update or Sync:** Updating or synchronizing means that the local copy on the developer's machine is synchronized with a version on the central server. Note that this may require a merge, which may result in a conflict that needs to be resolved.

➤ **Working Copy:** The working copy is the local copy on the individual developer's machine.

Several Source Code Control software solutions are available. Some of them are free, some of them are commercial. The following table lists a few available solutions:

	FREE/OPEN-SOURCE	COMMERCIAL
LOCAL ONLY	SCCS, RCS	PVCS
CLIENT/SERVER	CVS, Subversion	IBM Rational ClearCase, Microsoft Visual SourceSafe, Microsoft Team Foundation Server
DISTRIBUTED	Git, Mercurial	TeamWare, BitKeeper, Plastic SCM

 The preceding list is definitely not an exhaustive list. It's just a small selection to give you an idea of what's available.

The authors are not recommending one or the other software solution. Most software companies these days have a Source Code Control solution already in place, which every developer needs to adopt. If this is not the case, the company should definitely invest some time for doing research on the available solutions, and to pick one that suits them. The bottom line is that it will be a maintenance nightmare without any Source Code Control solution in place. Even for your personal projects you might want to investigate the available solutions. If you find one that you like to work with, it will make your life easier. It will automatically keep track of different versions and a history of your changes. This makes it easy for you to change back to an older version if a change didn't work out the way it was supposed to.

SUMMARY

This chapter has introduced you to several models and methodologies for the software development process. There are certainly many other ways of building software, both formalized and informal. There probably isn't a single correct method for developing software except the method that works for your team. The best way to find this method is to do your own research, learn what you can from various methods, talk to your peers about their experiences, and iterate on your process. Remember, the only metric that matters when examining a process methodology is how much it helps your team to write code.

The last part of this chapter briefly touched on the concept of Source Code Control. This should be an integral part of any software company, big or small, and can even be beneficial for personal projects at home. There are several Source Code Control software solutions available, so it is recommended that you try out a few and see which of them work for you.

24

Writing Efficient C++

WHAT'S IN THIS CHAPTER?

➤ What "efficiency" and "performance" mean

➤ What kind of language-level optimizations you can use

➤ Which design-level guidelines you can follow to design efficient programs

➤ What profiling tools are

The efficiency of your programs is important regardless of your application domain. If your product competes with others in the marketplace, speed can be a major differentiator: Given the choice between a slower and a faster program, which one would you choose? No one would buy an operating system that takes two weeks to boot up, unless it was the only option. Even if you don't intend to sell your products, they will have users. Those users will not be happy with you if they end up wasting time waiting for your programs to complete tasks.

Now that you understand the concepts of Professional C++ design and coding, and have tackled some of the more complex facilities that the language provides, you are ready to incorporate performance into your programs. Writing efficient programs involves thought at the design level, as well as details at the implementation level. Although this chapter falls late in this book, remember to consider performance from the beginning of your program life cycle.

OVERVIEW OF PERFORMANCE AND EFFICIENCY

Before delving further into the details, it's helpful to define the terms performance and efficiency, as used in this book. The *performance* of a program can refer to several areas, such as speed, memory usage, disk access, and network use. This chapter focuses on speed performance. The term *efficiency*, when applied to programs, means running without wasted effort. An efficient program completes its tasks as quickly as possible within the given circumstances. A program can be efficient without being fast, if the application domain is inherently prohibitive to quick execution.

 An efficient, or high-performance, *program runs as fast as is possible for the particular tasks.*

Note that the title of this chapter, "Writing Efficient C++," means writing programs that run efficiently, not efficiently writing programs. That is, the time you learn to save by reading this chapter will be your users', not your own!

Two Approaches to Efficiency

The traditional approach to writing efficient programs is to aim for *optimizing*, or improving the performance of, pre-existing code. This technique usually involves only *language-level efficiency*: specific, independent, code changes such as passing objects by reference instead of by value. That approach will only get you so far. If you want to write truly high-performance applications, you must think about efficiency from the beginning of your design. This *design-level efficiency* includes choosing efficient algorithms, avoiding unnecessary steps and computations, and selecting appropriate design optimizations.

Two Kinds of Programs

As noted, efficiency is important for all application domains. Additionally, there is a small subset of programs, such as system-level software, embedded systems, intensive computational applications, and real-time games, which require extremely high levels of efficiency. Most programs don't. Unless you write those types of high-performance applications, you probably don't need to worry about squeezing every ounce of speed out of your C++ code. Think of it as the difference between building normal family cars and building sports cars. Every car must be reasonably efficient, but sports cars require extremely high performance. You wouldn't want to waste your time optimizing family cars for speed when they'll never go faster than 70 miles per hour.

Is C++ an Inefficient Language?

C programmers often resist using C++ for high-performance applications. They claim that the language is inherently less efficient than C or a similar procedural language because C++ includes high-level concepts, such as exceptions and virtual methods. However, there are problems with this argument.

First, you cannot ignore the effect of compilers. When discussing the efficiency of a language, you must separate the performance capabilities of the language itself from the effectiveness of its compilers at optimizing it. Recall that the C or C++ code you write is not the code that the computer executes. A compiler first translates that code into machine language, applying optimizations in the process. This means that you can't simply run benchmarks of C and C++ programs and compare the result. You're really comparing the compiler optimizations of the languages, not the languages themselves. C++ compilers can "optimize away" many of the high-level constructs in the language to generate machine code similar to that generated from a comparable C program.

Critics, however, still maintain that some features of C++ cannot be optimized away. For example, as Chapter 8 explains, virtual methods require the existence of a vtable and an additional level of indirection at run time, possibly making them slower than regular non-virtual function calls. However, when you really think about it, this argument is still unconvincing. Virtual method calls provide more than just a function call: They also give you a run-time choice of which function to call. A comparable non-virtual function call would need a conditional statement to decide which function to call. If you don't need those extra semantics, you can use a non-virtual function (although for safety and style reasons, we recommend you don't). A general design rule in the C++ language is, "if you don't use it, you don't need to pay for it." If you don't use virtual methods, you pay no performance penalty for the fact that you could use them. Thus, non-virtual function calls in C++ are identical to function calls in C in terms of performance. However, since virtual function calls have such a tiny overhead, we recommend making all your class methods, including destructors but not constructors, virtual.

Also important, the high-level constructs of C++ enable you to write cleaner programs that are more efficient at the design level, are more easily maintained, and avoid accumulating unnecessary and dead code.

Finally, the authors of this book have used C++ for successful system-level software where high performance was required. We believe that you will be better served in your development, performance, and maintenance by choosing C++ instead of a procedural language.

LANGUAGE-LEVEL EFFICIENCY

Many books, articles, and programmers spend a lot of time trying to convince you to apply language-level optimizations to your code. These tips and tricks are important, and can speed up your programs in some cases. However, they are far less important than the overall design and algorithm choices in your program. You can pass-by-reference all you want, but it won't ever make your program fast if you perform twice as many disk writes as you need. It's easy to get bogged down in references and pointers and forget about the big picture.

Furthermore, some of these language-level tricks can be performed automatically by good optimizing compilers. Check your compiler documentation for details before spending time optimizing a particular area yourself.

In this book, we've tried to present a balance of strategies. Thus, we've included here what we feel are the most useful language-level optimizations. This list is not comprehensive, but should give you a good start if you want to optimize your code. However, make sure to read, and practice, the design-level efficiency advice described later in this chapter as well.

 Apply language-level optimizations judiciously.

Handle Objects Efficiently

C++ does a lot of work for you behind the scenes, particularly with regard to objects. You should always be aware of the performance impact of the code you write. If you follow a few simple guidelines, your code will become significantly more efficient.

Pass-by-Reference

This rule is discussed elsewhere in this book, but it's worth repeating here.

> *Objects should rarely be passed by value to a function or method.*

Pass-by-value incurs copying costs that are avoided with pass-by-reference. One reason why this rule can be difficult to remember is that on the surface there doesn't appear to be any problem when you pass-by-value. Consider a class to represent a person that looks like this:

```cpp
class Person
{
    public:
        Person();
        Person(const string& inFirstName, const string& inLastName, int inAge);
        string getFirstName() const { return mFirstName; }
        string getLastName() const { return mLastName; }
        int getAge() const { return mAge; }
    protected:
        string mFirstName, mLastName;
        int mAge;
};
```

Code snippet from Person\Person.cpp

You could write a function that takes a `Person` object as follows:

```cpp
void processPerson(Person p)
{
    // Process the person.
}
```

Code snippet from Person\Person.cpp

You might call it like this:

```cpp
Person me("Marc", "Gregoire", 32);
processPerson(me);
```

Code snippet from Person\Person.cpp

This doesn't look like there's any more code than if you wrote the function like this instead:

```
void processPerson(const Person& p)
{
    // Process the person.
}
```

Code snippet from Person\Person.cpp

The call to the function remains the same. However, consider what happens when you pass-by-value in the first version of the function. In order to initialize the p parameter of processPerson(), me must be copied with a call to its copy constructor. Even though you didn't write a copy constructor for the Person class, the compiler generates one that copies each of the data members. That still doesn't look so bad: there are only three data members. However, two of those are strings, which are themselves objects with copy constructors. So, each of their copy constructors will be called as well. The version of processPerson() that takes p by reference incurs no such copying costs. Thus, pass-by-reference in this example avoids three function calls when the code enters the function.

And you're still not done. Remember that p in the first version of processPerson() is a local variable to the processPerson() function, and so must be destroyed when the function exits. This destruction requires a call to the Person destructor, which will call the destructor of all of the data members. strings have destructors, so exiting this function (if you passed by value) incurs calls to three destructors. None of those calls are needed if the Person object is passed by reference.

 If a function must modify an object, you can pass the object by reference. If the function should not modify the object, you can pass it by const reference, as in the preceding example. See Chapter 9 for details on references and const.

 Avoid using pass-by-pointer, which is a relatively obsolete method for pass-by-reference, and is a throwback to the C language, rarely suitable for C++ (unless passing nullptr has meaning in your design).

Return-by-Reference

Just as you should pass objects by reference to functions, you should also return them by reference from functions in order to avoid copying the objects unnecessarily. Unfortunately, it is sometimes impossible to return objects by reference, such as when you write overloaded operator+ and other similar operators. You should never return a reference or a pointer to a local object that will be destroyed when the function exits.

Catch Exceptions by Reference

As noted in Chapter 10, you should catch exceptions by reference in order to avoid an extra copy. Throwing exceptions is heavy in terms of performance, so any little thing you can do to improve their efficiency will help.

C++11 Use Move Semantics

You should implement a move constructor and move assignment operator for your objects, which allow the C++ compiler to use move semantics. With move semantics for your objects, returning them by value from a function will be efficient without incurring large copying costs. Consult Chapter 9 for details on move semantics.

Avoid Creating Temporary Objects

The compiler creates temporary, unnamed objects in several circumstances. Chapter 7 explains that after writing a global `operator+` for a class, you can add objects of that class to other types, as long as those types can be converted to objects of that class. For example, the `SpreadsheetCell` class definition looks in part like the following:

```
class SpreadsheetCell
{
    public:
        // Other constructors omitted for brevity
        SpreadsheetCell(double initialValue);
        friend const SpreadsheetCell operator+(const SpreadsheetCell& lhs,
            const SpreadsheetCell& rhs);
        // Remainder omitted for brevity
};
```

The constructor that takes a `double` allows you to write code like this:

```
SpreadsheetCell myCell(4), aThirdCell;
aThirdCell = myCell + 5.6;
aThirdCell = myCell + 4;
```

The first addition line constructs a temporary `SpreadsheetCell` object from the `5.6` argument; then calls the `operator+` with `myCell` and the temporary object as arguments. The result is stored in `aThirdCell`. The second addition line does the same thing, except that `4` must be coerced to a `double` in order to call the `double` constructor of the `SpreadsheetCell`.

The important point in this example is that the compiler generates code to create an extra, unnamed `SpreadsheetCell` object for each addition line. That object must be constructed and destructed with calls to its constructor and destructor. If you're still skeptical, try inserting `cout` statements in your constructor and destructor and watching the printout.

In general, the compiler constructs a temporary object whenever your code converts a variable of one type to another type for use in a larger expression. This rule applies mostly to function calls. For example, suppose that you write a function with the following prototype:

```
void doSomething(const SpreadsheetCell& s);
```

You can call it like this:

```
doSomething(5.56);
```

The compiler constructs a temporary `SpreadsheetCell` object from `5.56` using the `double` constructor, which it passes to `doSomething()`. Note that if you remove the `const` from the `s` parameter, you can no longer call `doSomething()` with a constant; you must pass a variable. You can use C++11 rvalue references, discussed in Chapter 9, to allow passing a constant to `doSomething()`.

You should generally attempt to avoid cases in which the compiler is forced to construct temporary objects. Although it is impossible to avoid in some situations, you should at least be aware of the existence of this "feature" so you aren't surprised by performance and profiling results.

C++11 move semantics are also used by the compiler to make working with temporary objects more efficient. That's another reason to add move semantics to your classes.

The Return-Value Optimization

A function that returns an object by value can cause the creation of a temporary object. Continuing with the `Person` example, consider this function:

```
Person createPerson()
{
    Person newP;
    return newP;
}
```

Code snippet from Person\Person.cpp

Suppose that you call it like this (assuming that `operator<<` is implemented for the `Person` class):

```
cout << createPerson();
```

Code snippet from Person\Person.cpp

Even though this call does not store the result of `createPerson()` anywhere, the result must be stored somewhere in order to pass it to `operator<<`. In order to generate code for this behavior, the compiler is allowed to create a temporary variable in which to store the `Person` object returned from `createPerson()`.

Even if the result of the function is not used anywhere, the compiler might still generate code to create the temporary object. For example, suppose that you have this code:

```
createPerson();
```

The compiler might generate code to create a temporary object for the return value, even though it is not used.

However, you usually don't need to worry about this issue because the compiler will optimize away the temporary variable in most cases. This optimization is called the *return-value optimization*.

Use Inline Methods and Functions

As described in Chapter 7, the code for an `inline` method or function is inserted directly into the code where it is called, avoiding the overhead of a function call. You should mark as `inline` all functions and methods that you think can qualify for this optimization. However, remember that inlining requests by the programmer are only a recommendation to the compiler, which is allowed to refuse them.

On the other hand, some compilers inline appropriate functions and methods during their optimization steps, even if those functions aren't marked with the `inline` keyword. Thus, you should read your compiler documentation before wasting a lot of effort deciding which functions to inline.

DESIGN-LEVEL EFFICIENCY

The design choices in your program affect its performance far more than do language details such as pass-by-reference. For example, if you choose an algorithm for a fundamental task in your application that runs in $O(n^2)$ time instead of a simpler one that runs in $O(n)$ time, you could potentially perform the square of the number of operations that you really need. To put numbers on that, a task that uses an $O(n^2)$ algorithm and performs one million operations would perform only one thousand with an $O(n)$ algorithm. Even if that operation is optimized beyond recognition at the language level, the simple fact that you perform one million operations when a better algorithm would use only one thousand will make your program very inefficient. However, for small inputs, big-O time can be very misleading. An $O(n^2)$ algorithm might actually perform better than an $O(\log n)$ algorithm on small input sizes. Consider your likely input sizes before making a decision. Big-O notation also ignores constant factors, so it's not always the most valid guideline. Nonetheless, you should choose your algorithms carefully. Refer to Part I, specifically Chapter 2, of this book for a detailed discussion of algorithm design choices and big-O notation.

In addition to your choice of algorithms, design-level efficiency includes specific tips and tricks. The remainder of this section presents two design techniques for optimizing your program: caching, and object pools.

Cache as Much as Possible

Caching means storing items for future use in order to avoid retrieving or recalculating them. You might be familiar with the principle from its use in computer hardware. Modern computer processors are built with memory caches that store recently and frequently accessed memory values in a location that is quicker to access than main memory. Most memory locations that are accessed at all are accessed more than once in a short time period, so caching at the hardware level can significantly speed up computations.

Caching in software follows the same approach. If a task or computation is particularly slow, you should make sure that you are not performing it more than necessary. Store the results in memory the first time you perform the task so that they are available for future needs. Here is a list of tasks that are usually slow:

➤ **Disk access:** You should avoid opening and reading the same file more than once in your program. If memory is available, save the file contents in RAM if you need to access it frequently.

➤ **Network communication:** Whenever you need to communicate over a network, your program is subject to the vagaries of the network load. Treat network accesses like file accesses, and cache as much static information as possible.

➤ **Mathematical computations:** If you need the result of a computation in more than one place in your program, perform the calculation once and share the result.

➤ **Object allocation:** If you need to create and use a large number of short-lived objects in your program, consider using an object pool, which is described later in this chapter.

➤ **Thread creation:** This task can also be slow. You can "cache" threads in a thread-pool as discussed in Chapter 22.

Cache Invalidation

One common problem with caching is that the data you store are often only copies of the underlying information. The original data might change during the lifetime of the cache. For example, you might want to cache the values in a configuration file so that you don't need to read it repeatedly. However, the user might be allowed to change the configuration file while your program is running, which would make your cached version of the information obsolete. In cases like this, you need a mechanism for *cache invalidation:* When the underlying data change, you must either stop using your cached information, or repopulate your cache.

One technique for cache invalidation is to request that the entity managing the underlying data notifies your program of the data change. It could do this through a *callback* that your program registers with the manager. Alternatively, your program could poll for certain events that would trigger it to repopulate the cache automatically. Regardless of your specific cache invalidation technique, make sure you think about these issues before relying on a cache in your program.

Use Object Pools

Object pools are a technique for avoiding the creation and deletion of a large number of objects throughout the lifetime of your program. If you know that your program needs a large number of short-lived objects of the same type, you can create a *pool,* or cache, of those objects. Whenever you need an object in your code, you ask the pool for one. When you are done with the object, you return it to the pool. The object pool creates the objects only once, so their constructor is called only once, not each time they are used. Thus, object pools are appropriate when the constructor performs some setup actions that apply to many uses of the object, and when you can set instance-specific parameters on the object through non-constructor method calls.

An Object Pool Implementation

This section provides an implementation of a pool class template that you can use in your programs. The pool allocates a *chunk* of objects of the specified class when it is constructed and hands them out via the `acquireObject()` method. When the client is done with the object, she returns it via the `releaseObject()` method. If `aquireObject()` is called but there are no free objects, the pool allocates another chunk of objects.

The most difficult aspect of an object pool implementation is keeping track of which objects are free and which are in use. This implementation takes the approach of storing free objects in a queue. Each time a client requests an object, the pool gives that client the top object from the queue. The pool does not explicitly track objects that are in use. It trusts the clients to return them correctly to the pool when the clients are finished with them.

The code uses the `queue` class from the Standard Template Library (STL), discussed in Chapter 12. Memory for allocated objects is handled by `shared_ptr` smart pointers; see Chapter 21. When the pool allocates a new object, the new object is managed by a new `shared_ptr` which is added to the queue.

Here is the class definition, with comments that explain the details. Note that the template is parameterized on the class type from which the objects in the pool are to be constructed.

```cpp
#include <queue>
#include <stdexcept>
#include <memory>
using std::queue;
using std::shared_ptr;

// Provides an object pool that can be used with any class that provides a
// default constructor.
//
// The object pool constructor creates a pool of objects, which it hands out
// to clients when requested via the acquireObject() method. When a client is
// finished with the object it calls releaseObject() to put the object back
// into the object pool.
//
// The constructor and destructor on each object in the pool will be called only
// once each for the lifetime of the program, not once per acquisition and release.
//
// The primary use of an object pool is to avoid creating and deleting objects
// repeatedly. The object pool is most suited to applications that use large
// numbers of objects for short periods of time.
//
// For efficiency, the object pool doesn't perform sanity checks.
// It expects the user to release every acquired object exactly once.
// It expects the user to avoid using any objects that he or she has released.
template <typename T>
class ObjectPool
{
    public:
        // Creates an object pool with chunkSize objects.
        // Whenever the object pool runs out of objects, chunkSize
        // more objects will be added to the pool. The pool only grows:
        // objects are never removed from the pool (freed), until
        // the pool is destroyed.
        //
        // Throws invalid_argument if chunkSize is 0.
        // Throws bad_alloc if allocation fails.
```

```
ObjectPool(size_t chunkSize = kDefaultChunkSize)
    throw(std::invalid_argument, std::bad_alloc);

// Reserves an object for use. Clients must not free the object!
shared_ptr<T> acquireObject();

// Returns the object to the pool. Clients must not use the object after
// it has been returned to the pool.
void releaseObject(shared_ptr<T> obj);
protected:
// mFreeList stores the objects that are not currently in use by clients.
queue<shared_ptr<T>> mFreeList;
size_t mChunkSize;
static const size_t kDefaultChunkSize = 10;
// Allocates mChunkSize new objects and adds them to mFreeList.
void allocateChunk();
private:
// Prevent assignment and pass-by-value
ObjectPool(const ObjectPool<T>& src);
ObjectPool<T>& operator=(const ObjectPool<T>& rhs);
};
```

Code snippet from ObjectPool\ObjectPool.h

Note that the user of the object pool specifies through the template parameter the name of the class from which objects can be created, and through the constructor the allocation "chunk size." This "chunk size" controls the number of objects created at one time. Here is the code that defines the kDefaultChunkSize:

```
template<typename T> const size_t ObjectPool<T>::kDefaultChunkSize;
```

Code snippet from ObjectPool\ObjectPool.h

The default of 10, given in the class definition, is probably too small for most uses. If your program requires thousands of objects at once, you should use a larger, more appropriate, value.

The constructor validates the chunkSize parameter, and calls the allocateChunk() helper method to obtain a starting allocation of objects:

```
template <typename T> ObjectPool<T>::ObjectPool(size_t chunkSize)
    throw(std::invalid_argument, std::bad_alloc)
{
    if (chunkSize == 0) {
        throw std::invalid_argument("chunk size must be positive");
    }
    mChunkSize = chunkSize;
    // Create mChunkSize objects to start.
    allocateChunk();
}
```

Code snippet from ObjectPool\ObjectPool.h

The `allocateChunk()` method allocates `mChunkSize` elements. It stores a `shared_ptr` to each object in the `queue`:

```
// Allocates mChunkSize new objects.
template <typename T> void ObjectPool<T>::allocateChunk()
{
    for (size_t i = 0; i < mChunkSize; ++i) {
        mFreeList.push(std::make_shared<T>());
    }
}
```

Code snippet from ObjectPool\ObjectPool.h

`acquireObject()` returns the top object from the free list, first calling `allocateChunk()` if there are no free objects:

```
template <typename T> shared_ptr<T> ObjectPool<T>::acquireObject()
{
    if (mFreeList.empty()) {
        allocateChunk();
    }
    auto obj = mFreeList.front();
    mFreeList.pop();
    return obj;
}
```

Code snippet from ObjectPool\ObjectPool.h

Finally, `releaseObject()` returns the object to the tail of the free list:

```
template <typename T> void ObjectPool<T>::releaseObject(shared_ptr<T> obj)
{
    mFreeList.push(obj);
}
```

Code snippet from ObjectPool\ObjectPool.h

Using the Object Pool

Consider an application that is structured around obtaining requests for actions from users and processing those requests. This application would most likely be the middleware between a graphical front-end and a back-end database. For example, it could be part of an airline reservation system or an online banking application. You might want to encode each user request in an object, with a class that looks something like this:

```
class UserRequest
{
    public:
        UserRequest() {}
```

```
            virtual ~UserRequest() {}
                // Methods to populate the request with specific information.
                // Methods to retrieve the request data.
                // (not shown)
        protected:
                // Data members (not shown)
    };
```

Code snippet from ObjectPool\ObjectPoolTest.cpp

Instead of creating and deleting large numbers of requests throughout the lifetime of your program, you could use an object pool. Your program structure would then be something as follows:

```
shared_ptr<UserRequest> obtainUserRequest(ObjectPool<UserRequest>& pool)
{
    // Obtain a UserRequest object from the pool.
    auto request = pool.acquireObject();
    // Populate the request with user input. (not shown)
    return request;
}
void processUserRequest(ObjectPool<UserRequest>& pool,
    shared_ptr<UserRequest> req)
{
    // Process the request. (not shown)
    // Return the request to the pool.
    pool.releaseObject(req);
}
int main()
{
    ObjectPool<UserRequest> requestPool(10);
    cout << "Loop starting." << endl;
    for (size_t i = 0; i < 100; ++i) {
        auto req = obtainUserRequest(requestPool);
        processUserRequest(requestPool, req);
    }
    cout << "Loop finished." << endl;
    return 0;
}
```

Code snippet from ObjectPool\ObjectPoolTest.cpp

PROFILING

Although we urge you to think about efficiency as you design and code, you should accept that not every finished application will perform as well as it could. It is easy for efficiency to fall by the wayside in an attempt to generate a functional program; in our experience, most efficiency optimization is performed on already working programs. Even if you did consider efficiency in your development, you might not have optimized the right parts of the program. Chapter 2 introduces the "90/10" rule: 90 percent of the running time of most programs is spent in only 10 percent of the code (Hennessy and Patterson, *Computer Architecture, A Quantitative Approach, Fourth Edition,* (Morgan Kaufmann, 2006)). This means that you could optimize 90 percent of your code out of existence, but still only improve the running time of the program by 10 percent. Obviously, you want to optimize the parts of the code that are exercised the most for the specific workload that you expect the program to run.

Consequently, it is often helpful to *profile* your program to determine which parts of the code require optimization. There are many *profiling tools* available that analyze programs as they run in order to generate data about their performance. Most profiling tools provide analysis at the function level by specifying the amount of time (or percent of total execution time) spent in each function in the program. After running a profiler on your program, you can usually tell immediately which parts of the program need optimization. Profiling before and after optimizing is also useful to prove that your optimizations had an effect.

If you are using Microsoft Visual C++ 2010 Premium or Ultimate, you already have a great built-in profiler, which is discussed later in this chapter. Another good profiling tool is Rational PurifyPlus from IBM. Both of these products require license fees, but you should check if your company or academic institution has a site license for their use. If the license restriction is prohibitive, there are several free profiling tools. One of the most well-known is gprof (GNU profiler), which can be found on most Unix systems, including Solaris and Linux.

Profiling Example with gprof

The power of profiling can best be seen with a real coding example. As a disclaimer, the performance bugs in the first attempt shown are not subtle. Real efficiency issues would probably be more complex, but a program long enough to demonstrate them would be too lengthy for this book.

Suppose that you work for the United States Social Security Administration. Every year the administration puts up a website that allows users to look up the popularity of new baby names from the previous year. Your job is to write the back-end program that looks up names for users. Your input is a file containing the name of every new baby. This file will obviously contain redundant names. For example, in the file for boys for 2003, the name Jacob was the most popular, showing up 29,195 times. Your program must read the file to construct an in-memory database. A user may then request the absolute number of babies with a given name, or the rank of that name among all the babies.

First Design Attempt

A logical design for this program consists of a `NameDB` class with the following public methods:

```cpp
#include <string>
#include <stdexcept>
using std::string;
class NameDB
{
    public:
        // Reads the list of baby names in nameFile to populate the database.
        // Throws invalid_argument if nameFile cannot be opened or read.
        NameDB(const string& nameFile) throw (std::invalid_argument);
```

```
            // Returns the rank of the name (1st, 2nd, etc).
            // Returns -1 if the name is not found.
            int getNameRank(const string& name) const;
            // Returns the number of babies with this name.
            // Returns -1 if the name is not found.
            int getAbsoluteNumber(const string& name) const;
            // Protected and private members and methods not shown
};
```

Code snippet from NameDB\FirstAttempt\NameDB.h

The hard part is choosing a good data structure for the in-memory database. A first attempt might be an array, or a `vector` from the STL, of name/count `pair`s. Each entry in the `vector` would store one of the names, along with a count of the number of times that name shows up in the raw data file. Here is the complete class definition with such a design:

```
#include <string>
#include <stdexcept>
#include <vector>
#include <utility>
using std::string;
class NameDB
{
    public:
        NameDB(const string& nameFile) throw (std::invalid_argument);
        int getNameRank(const string& name) const;
        int getAbsoluteNumber(const string& name) const;
    protected:
        std::vector<std::pair<string, int>> mNames;
        // Helper methods
        bool nameExists(const string& name) const;
        void incrementNameCount(const string& name);
        void addNewName(const string& name);
};
```

Code snippet from NameDB\FirstAttempt\NameDB.h

Note the use of the STL `vector` and `pair`, discussed in Chapter 12. A `pair` is a utility class that combines two variables of different types.

Here are the implementations of the constructor and the helper methods `nameExists()`, `incrementNameCount()`, and `addNewName()`. If you're unfamiliar with the STL, you might be confused by the loops in `nameExists()` and `incrementNameCount()`. They iterate over all the elements of the `vector`.

```
// Reads the names from the file and populates the database.
// The database is a vector of name/count pairs, storing the
// number of times each name shows up in the raw data.
NameDB::NameDB(const string& nameFile) throw (invalid_argument)
{
    // Open the file and check for errors.
```

```cpp
    ifstream inFile(nameFile.c_str());
    if (!inFile) {
        throw invalid_argument("Unable to open file");
    }
    // Read the names one at a time.
    string name;
    while (inFile >> name) {
        // Look up the name in the database so far.
        if (nameExists(name)) {
            // If the name exists in the database, just increment the count.
            incrementNameCount(name);
        } else {
            // If the name doesn't yet exist, add it with a count of 1.
            addNewName(name);
        }
    }
    inFile.close();
}
// Returns true if the name exists in the database, false otherwise.
bool NameDB::nameExists(const string& name) const
{
    // Iterate through the vector of names looking for the name.
    for (auto it = mNames.cbegin(); it != mNames.cend(); ++it) {
        if (it->first == name) {
            return true;
        }
    }
    return false;
}
// Precondition: name exists in the vector of names.
// Postcondition: the count associated with name is incremented.
void NameDB::incrementNameCount(const string& name)
{
    for (auto it = mNames.begin(); it != mNames.end(); ++it) {
        if (it->first == name) {
            it->second++;
            return;
        }
    }
}
// Adds a new name to the database
void NameDB::addNewName(const string& name)
{
    mNames.push_back(make_pair(name, 1));
}
```

Code snippet from NameDB\FirstAttempt\NameDB.cpp

Note that in the preceding example, you could use an algorithm like find_if() to accomplish the same thing as the loops in nameExists() and incrementNameCount(). We show the loops explicitly in order to emphasize the performance problems.

The savvy reader might notice some performance problems already. What if there are hundreds of thousands of names? The many linear searches involved in populating the database might become slow.

In order to complete the example, here are the implementations of the two public methods:

```cpp
// Returns the rank of the name.
// First looks up the name to obtain the number of babies with that name.
// Then iterates through all the names, counting all the names with a higher
// count than the specified name. Returns that count as the rank.
int NameDB::getNameRank(const string& name) const
{
    // Make use of the getAbsoluteNumber() method.
    int num = getAbsoluteNumber(name);
    // Check if we found the name.
    if (num == -1) {
        return -1;
    }
    // Now count all the names in the vector that have a
    // count higher than this one. If no name has a higher count,
    // this name is rank number 1. Every name with a higher count
    // decreases the rank of this name by 1.
    int rank = 1;
    for (auto it = mNames.cbegin(); it != mNames.cend(); ++it) {
        if (it->second > num) {
            rank++;
        }
    }
    return rank;
}
// Returns the count associated with this name
int NameDB::getAbsoluteNumber(const string& name) const
{
    for (auto it = mNames.cbegin(); it != mNames.cend(); ++it) {
        if (it->first == name) {
            return it->second;
        }
    }
    return -1;
}
```

Code snippet from NameDB\FirstAttempt\NameDB.cpp

Profile of the First Attempt

In order to test the program, you need a `main()` function:

```cpp
#include "NameDB.h"
#include <iostream>
using namespace std;
int main()
{
    NameDB boys("boys_long.txt");
    cout << boys.getNameRank("Daniel") << endl;
```

```
    cout << boys.getNameRank("Jacob") << endl;
    cout << boys.getNameRank("William") << endl;
    return 0;
}
```

Code snippet from NameDB\FirstAttempt\NameDBTest.cpp

This `main()` function creates one `NameDB` database called `boys`, telling it to populate itself with the file `boys_long.txt`, which contains 500,500 names.

There are three steps to using gprof:

1. Compile your program with a special flag that causes it to log raw execution information next time it is run. When using GCC as your compiler, the flag is -pg, for example:

   ```
   > gcc -lstdc++ -std=c++0x -pg -o namedb NameDB.cpp NameDBTest.cpp
   ```

   See Bonus Chapter 2 on the website (www.wrox.com) for more information on the `-std=c++0x` flag.

2. Next, run your program. This run should generate a file called `gmon.out` in the working directory. Be patient when you run the program because this first version is very slow.

3. The final step is to run the gprof command in order to analyze the `gmon.out` profiling information and produce a (somewhat) readable report. gprof outputs to standard out, so you should redirect the output to a file:

   ```
   > gprof namedb gmon.out > gprof_analysis.out
   ```

Now you can analyze the data. Unfortunately, the output file is somewhat cryptic and intimidating. It takes a little while to learn how to interpret it. gprof provides two separate sets of information. The first set summarizes the amount of time spent executing each function in the program. The second, and more useful, set summarizes the amount of time spent executing each function *and its descendants*, and is also called a *call graph*. Here is some of the output from the `gprof_analysis` `.out` file, edited to make it more readable. Note that the numbers will be different on your machine.

```
index  %time    self  children    called    name
[1]    100.0    0.00   14.06                 main [1]
                0.00   14.00      1/1             NameDB::NameDB [2]
                0.00    0.04      3/3             NameDB::getNameRank [25]
                0.00    0.01      1/1             NameDB::~NameDB [28]
```

The following list explains the different columns:

➤ `index`: an index to be able to refer to this entry in the call graph.

➤ `%time`: the percentage of the total execution time of the program required by this function and its descendants.

➤ `self`: how many seconds the function itself was executing.

➤ `children`: how many seconds the descendants of this function were executing.

➤ `called`: how often this function was called.

➤ `name`: the name of the function. If the name of the function is followed by a number between square brackets, that number refers to another index in the call graph.

The preceding extract tells us that `main()` and its descendants took 100 percent of the total execution time of the program, for a total of 14.06 seconds. The second line shows that the `NameDB` constructor took 14.00 seconds of the total 14.06 seconds. So it's immediately clear where the performance issue is situated. To track down which part of the constructor is taking so long, you need to jump to the call graph entry with index 2, because that's the index in square brackets behind the name in the last column. The call graph entry with index 2 is as follows on my test laptop:

```
[2] 99.6   0.00   14.00      1           NameDB::NameDB [2]
           1.20    6.14   500500/500500      NameDB::nameExists [3]
           1.24    5.24   499500/499500      NameDB::incrementNameCount [4]
           0.00    0.18    1000/1000         NameDB::addNewName [19]
           0.00    0.00       1/1            vector::vector [69]
```

The nested entries below `NameDB::NameDB` show which of its descendants took the most time. Here you can see that `nameExists()` took 6.14 seconds, and `incrementNameCount()` took 5.24 seconds. Remember that these times are the sums of all the calls to the functions. The fourth column in those lines shows the number of calls to the function (500,500 to `nameExists()` and 499,500 to `incrementNameCont()`). No other function took a significant amount of time.

Without going any further in this analysis, two things should jump out at you:

1. 14 seconds to populate the database of approximately 500,000 names is slow. Perhaps you need a better data structure.

2. `nameExists()` and `incrementNameCount()` take almost identical time, and are called almost the same number of times. If you think about the application domain, that makes sense: Most names in the text file input are duplicates, so the vast majority of the calls to `nameExists()` are followed by a call to `incrementNameCount()`. If you look back at the code, you can see that these functions are almost identical; they could probably be combined. In addition, most of what they are doing is searching the `vector`. It would probably be better to use a sorted data structure to reduce the searching time.

Second Attempt

With these two observations from the gprof output, it's time to redesign the program. The new design uses a `map` instead of a `vector`. Chapter 12 explains that the STL `map` keeps the entries sorted, and provides $O(\log n)$ lookup instead of the $O(n)$ searches in the `vector`.

The new version of the program also combines `nameExists()` and `incrementNameCount()` into one `nameExistsAndIncrement()` method.

Here is the new class definition:

```cpp
#include <string>
#include <stdexcept>
#include <map>
using std::string;
class NameDB
{
    public:
        NameDB(const string& nameFile) throw (std::invalid_argument);
```

```
        int getNameRank(const string& name) const;
        int getAbsoluteNumber(const string& name) const;
    protected:
        std::map<string, int> mNames;
        bool nameExistsAndIncrement(const string& name);
        void addNewName(const string& name);
};
```

Code snippet from NameDB\SecondAttempt\NameDB.h

Here are the new method implementations:

```
// Reads the names from the file and populates the database.
// The database is a map associating names with their frequency.
NameDB::NameDB(const string& nameFile) throw (invalid_argument)
{
    // Open the file and check for errors.
    ifstream inFile(nameFile.c_str());
    if (!inFile) {
        throw invalid_argument("Unable to open file");
    }
    // Read the names one at a time.
    string name;
    while (inFile >> name) {
        // Look up the name in the database so far.
        if (!nameExistsAndIncrement(name)) {
            // If the name exists in the database, the
            // method incremented it, so we just continue.
            // We get here if it didn't exist, in which case
            // we add it with a count of 1.
            addNewName(name);
        }
    }
    inFile.close();
}
// Returns true if the name exists in the database, false
// otherwise. If it finds it, it increments it.
bool NameDB::nameExistsAndIncrement(const string& name)
{
    // Find the name in the map.
    auto res = mNames.find(name);
    if (res != mNames.end()) {
        res->second++;
        return true;
    }
    return false;
}
// Adds a new name to the database
void NameDB::addNewName(const string& name)
{
    mNames[name] = 1;
}
```

```
// Returns the rank of the name.
// First looks up the name to obtain the number of babies with that name.
// Then iterates through all the names, counting all the names with a higher
// count than the specified name. Returns that count as the rank.
int NameDB::getNameRank(const string& name) const
{
    int num = getAbsoluteNumber(name);
    // Check if we found the name.
    if (num == -1) {
        return -1;
    }
    // Now count all the names in the map that have
    // count higher than this one. If no name has a higher count,
    // this name is rank number 1. Every name with a higher count
    // decreases the rank of this name by 1.
    int rank = 1;
    for (auto it = mNames.cbegin(); it != mNames.cend(); ++it) {
        if (it->second > num) {
            rank++;
        }
    }
    return rank;
}
// Returns the count associated with this name.
int NameDB::getAbsoluteNumber(const string& name) const
{
    auto res = mNames.find(name);
    if (res != mNames.end()) {
        return res->second;
    }
    return -1;
}
```

Code snippet from NameDB\SecondAttempt\NameDB.cpp

Profile of the Second Attempt

By following the same steps shown earlier, you can obtain the gprof performance data on the new version of the program. The data are quite encouraging:

```
index %time  self  children    called       name
[1]    100.0 0.00    0.21                    main [1]
                     0.02    0.18   1/1           NameDB::NameDB [2]
                     0.00    0.01   1/1           NameDB::~NameDB [13]
                     0.00    0.00   3/3           NameDB::getNameRank [28]
[2]     95.2 0.02    0.18      1           NameDB::NameDB [2]
                     0.02    0.16 500500/500500   NameDB::nameExistsAndIncrement [3]
                     0.00    0.00 1000/1000       NameDB::addNewName [24]
                     0.00    0.00   1/1           map::map [87]
```

If you run this on your machine, the output will be different. It's even possible that you will not see the data for NameDB methods in your output. Because of the efficiency of this second attempt, the timings are getting so small that you might see more map methods in the output than NameDB methods.

On my test laptop, `main()` now takes only 0.21 seconds: a 67-fold improvement! There are certainly further improvements that you could make on this program. For example, the current constructor performs a lookup to see if the name is already in the `map`, and if not, adds it to the `map`. You could combine these two operations. You could always use the `insert()` method of the `map` without first checking if the name already exists. The `insert()` method returns a `pair<iterator, bool>`. The Boolean will be `true` if it added the name to the `map`, and `false` if the name was already present. When the name is already in the `map`, you increment its count, which you can reach through the `iterator` in the returned `pair`. This `iterator` is a `map` entry, so to access the count, you use `res.first->second`. To implement this improvement, you can remove the `nameExistsAndIncrement()` and `addNewName()` methods, and change the constructor as follows:

```
NameDB::NameDB(const string& nameFile) throw (invalid_argument)
{
    // Open the file and check for errors
    ifstream inFile(nameFile.c_str());
    if (!inFile) {
        throw invalid_argument("Unable to open file");
    }
    // Read the names one at a time.
    string name;
    while (inFile >> name) {
        auto res = mNames.insert(make_pair(name, 1));
        if (res.second == false) {
            res.first->second++;  // Already in the map, increment count
        }
    }
    inFile.close();
}
```

Another improvement could be to use caching to cache ranking of names, but this is left as an exercise for the reader.

Profiling Example with Visual C++ 2010

Microsoft Visual C++ 2010 Premium and Ultimate come with a great built-in profiler, which is briefly discussed in this section. The VC++ profiler has a complete graphical user interface. We are not recommending one or the other profiler, but it is always good to have an idea of what a command-line based profiler like gprof can provide in comparison to a GUI-based profiler like the one included with VC++.

Profile of the First Design Attempt

To start profiling an application in Visual C++ 2010, you first need to open the project in Visual Studio. This example uses the same `NameDB` code as in the first inefficient design attempt earlier. This code is not repeated here. Once your project is opened in Visual Studio, click on the "Analyze" menu and then choose "Profiler ⇨ New Performance Session." A new docked window should appear. Figure 24-1 shows a screenshot of this window.

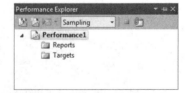

FIGURE 24-1

In this new window, click the first button on the toolbar at the top which is the "Launch Performance Wizard" button. This will start a wizard. The first page of this wizard is shown in Figure 24-2.

The VC++ 2010 profiler has four different kinds of profiling methods:

➤ **CPU Sampling:** Used to monitor applications with low overhead. This means that the act of profiling the application will not have a big performance impact on the target application.

➤ **Instrumentation:** This method will add extra code to the application to be able to accurately count the number of function calls and to time individual function calls.

FIGURE 24-2

However, this method has a much bigger performance impact on the application. It is recommended to use the CPU Sampling method first to get an idea about the bottlenecks in your application. If this method does not give you enough information, you can try the Instrumentation method.

➤ **.NET Memory Allocation:** This method is not relevant to native C++ applications.

➤ **Concurrency:** This allows you to monitor multithreaded applications. It allows you to graphically see which threads are running, which threads are waiting for something, and so on.

For this profiling example, leave the default CPU Sampling method and click the "Next" button. The next page of the wizard will ask you to select the application that you want to profile. Here you should select your NameDB project and click the "Next" button. On the last page of the wizard you can enable the "Launch profiling after the wizard finishes" and then click the "Finish" button. Now you need to be patient, as Visual C++ will start building your project, and when building is finished,

the program will automatically be executed and profiled. Since the first design attempt is so inefficient, this will take a long time. It is possible that you will get a message saying that you don't have the right credentials for profiling, and whether you would like to upgrade your credentials. If you get this message, you should allow VC++ to upgrade your credentials otherwise the profiler will not work properly.

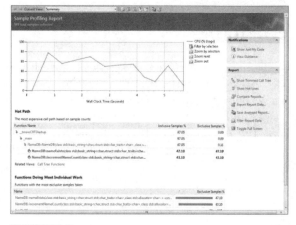

When the program execution is finished, Visual Studio will automatically open the profiling report. Figure 24-3 shows how this report might look when profiling the first attempt of the NameDB application.

FIGURE 24-3

From this report you can immediately see the hot path. Just like with gprof, it shows that `nameExists()` and `incrementNameCount()` are taking up most of the running time of the program, 47.1 and 43.1 percent of the running time on my testing laptop. The Visual Studio profiling report is interactive. For example, you can drill down the `nameExists()` method by clicking on it. This will result in a drill-down report for that function, which looks like Figure 24-4.

This drill-down view of the `nameExists()` method shows a graphical breakdown at the top, and the actual code of the method at

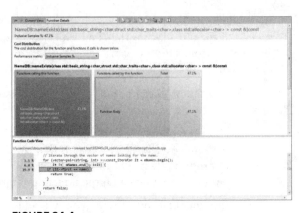

FIGURE 24-4

the bottom. The code view shows the percentage of the running time that a line needed. The line using up most of the time is shown in red, and the line using up second most of the time is shown in yellow. When you are interactively browsing the profiling report, you can always go back by using the back arrow at the top-left of the report.

At the top of the report there is also a drop-down menu, which you can use to quickly jump to certain summary or details pages. If you go back to the "Summary" of the profiling report, you can see that there is a "Show Trimmed Call Tree" link on the right. Clicking that link will display a trimmed call tree showing you an alternative view of the hot path in your code. This is shown in Figure 24-5.

FIGURE 24-5

Also in this view, you immediately see that `main()` is calling the `NameDB` constructor, which is calling `nameExists()` and `incrementNameCount()`, which are using up most of the time.

SUMMARY

This chapter discussed the key aspects of efficiency and performance in C++ programs, and provided several specific tips and techniques for designing and writing more efficient applications. We hope you gained an appreciation for the importance of performance and for the power of profiling tools. The most important thing to remember from this chapter is to think about performance and efficiency from the beginning of your program life cycle: *Design-level efficiency is far more important than language-level efficiency.*

25

Developing Cross-Platform and Cross-Language Applications

WHAT'S IN THIS CHAPTER?

➤   How to write code that runs on multiple platforms

➤   How to mix different programming languages together

C++ programs can be compiled to run on a variety of computing platforms and the language has been rigorously defined to ensure that programming in C++ for one platform is very similar to programming in C++ for another. Yet, despite the standardization of the language, platform differences eventually come into play when writing professional-quality programs in C++. Even when development is limited to a particular platform, small differences in compilers can elicit major programming headaches. This chapter examines the necessary complication of programming in a world with multiple platforms and multiple programming languages.

The first part of this chapter surveys the platform-related issues that C++ programmers encounter. A *platform* is the collection of all of the details that make up your development and/or run-time system. For example, your platform may be the Microsoft Visual C++ 2010 compiler running on Windows 7 on an Intel Core i7 processor. Alternatively, your platform might be the GCC 4.6 compiler running on Linux on a PowerPC processor. Both of these platforms are able to compile and run C++ programs, but there are significant differences between them.

The second part of this chapter looks at how C++ can interact with other programming languages. While C++ is a general-purpose language, it may not always be the right tool for the job. Through a variety of mechanisms, you can integrate C++ with other languages that may better serve your needs.

CROSS-PLATFORM DEVELOPMENT

There are several reasons why the C++ language encounters platform issues. Even though C++ is a high-level language, its definition includes low-level implementation details. For example, C++ arrays are defined to live in contiguous blocks of memory. Such a specific implementation detail exposes the language to the possibility that not all systems arrange and manage their memory in the same way. C++ also faces the challenge of providing a standard language and a standard library without a standard implementation. Varying interpretations of the specification among C++ compiler and library vendors can lead to trouble when moving from one system to another. Finally, C++ is selective in what the language provides as standard. Despite the presence of a standard library, sophisticated programs often need functionality that is not provided by the language or the standard library. This functionality generally comes from third-party libraries or the platform, and can vary greatly.

Architecture Issues

The term *architecture* generally refers to the processor, or family of processors, on which a program runs. A standard PC running Windows or Linux generally runs on the x86 architecture, and older versions of Mac OS were usually found on the PowerPC architecture. As a high-level language, C++ shields you from the differences between these architectures. For example, a Pentium processor may have a single instruction that performs the same functionality as six PowerPC instructions. As a C++ programmer, you don't need to know what this difference is or even that it exists. One advantage to using a high-level language is that the compiler takes care of converting your code into the processor's native assembly code format.

Processor differences do, however, rise up to the level of C++ code at times. You won't face most of these issues unless you are doing particularly low-level work, but you should be aware that they exist.

Binary Compatibility

As you probably already know, you cannot take a program written and compiled for a Pentium computer and run it on a PowerPC-based Mac. These two platforms are not *binary compatible* because their processors do not support the same set of instructions. When you compile a C++ program, your source code is turned into binary instructions that the computer executes. That binary format is defined by the platform, not by the C++ language.

One solution to support platforms that are not binary compatible is to build each version separately with a compiler on each target platform.

Another solution is *cross-compiling*. When you are using platform X for your development, but you want your program to run on platforms Y and Z, you can use a cross-compiler on your platform X that generates binary code for platform Y and Z.

You can also make your program *open source*. By making your source available to the end user, she can compile it natively on her system and build a version of the program that is in the correct binary format for her machine. As discussed in Chapter 2, open-source software has become increasingly popular. One of the major reasons is that it allows programmers to collaboratively develop software and increase the number of platforms on which it can run.

Address Sizes

When someone describes an architecture as *32-bit*, they most likely mean that the *address* size is 32 bits, or 4 bytes. In general, a system with a larger address size can handle more memory and might operate more quickly on complex programs.

Since pointers are memory addresses, they are inherently tied to address sizes. Many programmers are taught that pointers are always 4 bytes, but this is wrong. For example, consider the following program, which outputs the size of a pointer:

```
int *ptr;
cout << "ptr size is " << sizeof(ptr) << " bytes" << endl;
```

Code snippet from PtrSize\PtrSize.cpp

If this program is compiled and run on a 32-bit x86 system, such as the Pentium architecture, the output will be:

```
ptr size is 4 bytes
```

If you compile it with a 64-bit compiler and run it on a 64-bit x86 system, like the Intel Core i7, the output will be:

```
ptr size is 8 bytes
```

From a programmer's point of view, the upshot of varying pointer sizes is that you cannot equate a pointer with 4 bytes. More generally, you need to be aware that most sizes are not prescribed by the C++ standard. The standard only says that a short integer has as much, or less, space as an integer, which has as much, or less, space as a long integer.

The size of a pointer is also not necessarily the same as the size of an integer. For example, on a 64-bit platform, pointers will be 64 bit, but integers could be 32 bit. Casting a 64-bit pointer to a 32-bit integer will result in losing 32 critical bits!

 Never assume that a pointer is 32 bits or 4 bytes, and never cast a pointer to an integer.

Byte Order

All modern computers store numbers in a binary representation, but the representation of the same number on two platforms may not be identical. This sounds contradictory, but as you'll see, there are two approaches to reading numbers that both make sense.

A single slot in your computer's memory is usually a byte because most computers are *byte addressable*. Number types in C++ are usually multiple bytes. For example, a `short` may be 2 bytes. Imagine that your program contains the following line:

```
short myShort = 513;
```

In binary, the number 513 is 0000 0010 0000 0001. This number contains 16 ones and zeros, or 16 bits. Because there are 8 bits in a byte, the computer would need 2 bytes to store the number. Because each individual memory address contains 1 byte, the computer needs to split the number up into multiple bytes. Assuming that a `short` is 2 bytes, the number will get split into two even parts. The higher part of the number is put into the *high-order byte* and the lower part of the number is put into the *low-order byte*. In this case, the high-order byte is 0000 0010 and the low-order byte is 0000 0001.

Now that the number has been split up into memory-sized parts, the only question that remains is how to store them in memory. Two bytes are needed, but the order of the bytes is unclear and in fact depends on the architecture of the system in question.

One way to represent the number is to put the high-order byte first in memory and the low-order byte next. This strategy is called *big-endian ordering* because the bigger part of the number comes first. PowerPC and Sparc processors use a big-endian approach. Some other processors, such as x86, order the bytes in the opposite order, putting the low-order byte first in memory. This approach is called *little-endian ordering* because the smaller part of the number comes first. An architecture may choose one approach or the other, usually based on backward compatibility. For the curious, the terms "big-endian" and "little-endian" predate modern computers by several hundred years. Jonathan Swift coined the terms in his eighteenth-century novel *Gulliver's Travels* to describe the opposing camps of a debate about the proper end on which to break an egg.

Regardless of the *ordering* a particular architecture uses, your programs can continue to use numerical values without paying any attention to whether the machine uses big-endian ordering or little-endian ordering. The ordering only comes into play when data moves between architectures. For example, if you are sending binary data across a network, you may need to consider the ordering of the other system. A solution is to use the standard Network Byte Ordering, which is always big-endian. So, before sending data across a network, convert it to big-endian, and whenever you receive data from a network, convert it from big-endian to the byte ordering of your system.

Similarly, if you are writing binary data to a file, you may need to consider what will happen when that file is opened on a system with opposite byte ordering.

Implementation Issues

When a C++ compiler is written, it is designed by a human being who attempts to adhere to the C++ standard. Unfortunately, the C++ standard is more than a thousand pages long and written in a combination of prose, language grammars, and examples. Two human beings implementing a compiler according to such a standard are unlikely to interpret every piece of prescribed information in the exact same way or to catch every single edge case. As a result, compilers will have bugs.

Compiler Quirks and Extensions

There is no simple rule for finding or avoiding compiler bugs. The best you can do is stay up-to-date on compiler updates and perhaps subscribe to a mailing list or newsgroup for your compiler. If you suspect that you have encountered a compiler bug, a simple web search for the error message or condition you have witnessed could uncover a workaround or patch.

One area that compilers are notorious for having trouble with is language additions that were not in the initial standard. For example, some of the template and run-time type features in C++ weren't originally part of the language, and as a result, some compilers still don't properly support these features. You will also encounter the same issues with the new features in C++11. Not all compilers support every single new feature yet.

Another issue to be aware of is that compilers often include their own language extensions without making it obvious to the programmer. For example, variable-sized stack-based arrays are not part of the C++ language, yet the following compiles and runs as expected with the g++ compiler:

```
int i = 4;
char myStackArray[i];  // Not a standard language feature!
```

Code snippet from VariableArray\VariableArray.cpp

Some compiler extensions may be useful, but if there is a chance that you will switch compilers at some point, you should see if your compiler has a strict mode where it will avoid such extensions. For example, compiling the previous code with the -pedantic flag passed to g++ will yield the following warning:

```
warning: ISO C++ forbids variable length array 'myStackArray' [-Wvla]
```

The C++ specification allows for a certain type of compiler-defined language extension through the #pragma mechanism. #pragma is a precompiler directive whose behavior is defined by the implementation. If the implementation does not understand the directive, it ignores it. For example, some compilers allow the programmer to turn compiler warnings off temporarily with #pragma.

Library Implementations

Most likely, your compiler includes an implementation of the C++ Standard Library, including the Standard Template Library. Since the STL is written in C++, however, you aren't required to use the one that came bundled with your compiler. You could use a third-party STL that, for example, has been optimized for speed, or you could even write your own.

Of course, STL implementers face the same problem that compiler writers face — the standard is subject to interpretation. In addition, certain implementations may make tradeoffs that are incompatible with your needs. For example, one implementation may optimize for speed, while another implementation may focus on using as little memory as possible for containers.

When working with an STL implementation, or indeed any third-party library, it is important to consider the tradeoffs that the designer made during development. Chapter 2 contains a more detailed discussion of the issues involved in using libraries.

Platform-Specific Features

C++ is a great general-purpose language. With the addition of the Standard Library, the language is packed full of so many features that a casual programmer could happily code in C++ for years without going beyond what is built in. However, professional programs require facilities that C++ does not provide. This section lists several important features that are provided by the platform, not by the C++ language.

➤ **Graphical user interfaces:** Most commercial programs today run on an operating system that has a graphical user interface, containing such elements as clickable buttons, movable windows, and hierarchical menus. C++, like the C language, has no notion of these elements. To write a graphical application in C++, you need to use platform-specific libraries that allow you to draw windows, accept input through the mouse, and perform other graphical tasks.

➤ **Networking:** The Internet has changed the way we write applications. These days, most applications check for updates through the web, and games provide a networked multiplayer mode. C++ does not provide a mechanism for networking, though several standard libraries exist. The most common means of writing networking software is through an abstraction called *sockets*. A socket library implementation can be found on most platforms and it provides a simple procedure-oriented way to transfer data over a network. Some platforms support a streams-based networking system that operates like I/O streams in C++. Since IPv4 is running out of IP addresses, its successor, IPv6, will soon take over. Therefore, choosing a networking library that is IPv-independent would be a better choice than choosing one that only supports IPv4.

➤ **OS Events and application interaction:** In pure C++ code, there is little interaction with the surrounding operating system and other applications. The command-line arguments are about all you get in a standard C++ program without platform extensions. For example, operations such as copy and paste are not directly supported in C++ and require platform-provided libraries.

➤ **Low-level files:** Chapter 15 explains standard I/O in C++, including reading and writing files. Many operating systems provide their own file APIs, which are sometimes incompatible with the standard file classes in C++. These libraries often provide OS-specific file tools, such as a mechanism to get the home directory of the current user.

➤ **Threads:** Concurrent threads of execution within a single program are not directly supported in C++03 or earlier. C++11 does include a threading library, explained in Chapter 22. If your compiler does not yet support the C++11 threading library, you need to use a third-party library. The most commonly used third-party thread library is called `pthreads`. Many operating systems and object-oriented frameworks also provide their own threading models.

CROSS-LANGUAGE DEVELOPMENT

For certain types of programs, C++ may not be the best tool for the job. For example, if your Unix program needs to interact closely with the shell environment, you may be better off writing a shell script than a C++ program. If your program performs heavy text processing, you may decide that the Perl language is the way to go. Sometimes what you want is a language that blends the general features of C++ with the specialized features of another language. Fortunately, there are some techniques you can use to get the best of both worlds — the flexibility of C++ combined with the unique specialty of another language.

Mixing C and C++

As you already know, the C++ language is a superset of the C language. All C programs will compile and run in C++ with a few minor exceptions. These exceptions usually have to do with reserved words. In C, for example, the term *class* has no particular meaning. Thus, it could be used as a variable name, as in the following C code:

```
int class = 1; // Compiles in C, not C++
printf("class is %d\n", class);
```

Code snippet from MixingC\MixingC.cpp

This program will compile and run in C, but will yield an error when compiled as C++ code. When you translate, or *port*, a program from C to C++, these are the types of errors you will face. Fortunately, the fixes are usually quite simple. In this case, rename the class variable to classID and the code will compile.

The ease of incorporating C code in a C++ program comes in handy when you encounter a useful library or legacy code that was written in C. Functions and classes, as you've seen many times in this book, work just fine together. A class method can call a function, and a function can make use of objects.

Shifting Paradigms

One of the dangers of mixing C and C++ is that your program may start to lose its object-oriented properties. For example, if your object-oriented web browser is implemented with a procedural networking library, the program will be mixing these two paradigms. Given the importance and quantity of networking tasks in such an application, you might consider writing an *object-oriented wrapper* around the procedural library.

For example, imagine that you are writing a web browser in C++, but you are using a C networking library that contains the functions declared in the following code. Note that the HostRecord and Connection data structures have been omitted for brevity.

```
// netwrklib.h
#include "hostrecord.h"
#include "connection.h"
// Gets the host record for a particular Internet host given
// its hostname (i.e. www.host.com)
HostRecord* lookupHostByName(char* inHostName);
// Connects to the given host
Connection* connectToHost(HostRecord* inHost);
// Retrieves a web page from an already-opened connection
char* retrieveWebPage(Connection* inConnection, char* page);
```

The `netwrklib.h` interface is fairly simple and straightforward. However, it is not object-oriented, and a C++ programmer who uses such a library is bound to feel *icky*, to use a technical term. This library isn't organized into a cohesive class and it isn't even `const`-correct. Of course, a talented C programmer could have written a better interface, but as the user of a library, you have to accept what you are given. Writing a wrapper is your opportunity to customize the interface.

Before we build an object-oriented wrapper for this library, take a look at how it might be used as is to gain an understanding of actual usage. In the following program, the `netwrklib` library is used to retrieve the web page at www.wrox.com/index.html:

```
#include <iostream>
#include "netwrklib.h"
using namespace std;
int main()
{
    HostRecord* myHostRecord = lookupHostByName("www.wrox.com");
    Connection* myConnection = connectToHost(myHostRecord);
    char* result = retrieveWebPage(myConnection, "/index.html");
    cout << "The result is " << result << endl;
    return 0;
}
```

A possible way to make the library more object-oriented is to provide a single abstraction that recognizes the links between looking up a host, connecting to the host, and retrieving a web page. A good object-oriented wrapper could hide the unnecessarily complexity of the `HostRecord` and `Connection` types.

This example follows the design principles described in Chapters 3 and 4: The new class should capture the common use case for the library. The previous example shows the most frequently used pattern — first a host is looked up, then a connection is established, then a page is retrieved. It is also likely that subsequent pages will be retrieved from the same host so a good design will accommodate that mode of use as well.

Following is the `public` portion of the definition for the `WebHost` class. This class makes the common case easy for the client programmer:

```
// WebHost.h
class WebHost
{
    public:
        // Constructs a WebHost object for the given host
        WebHost(const string& inHost);
        // Obtains the given page from this host
        string getPage(const string& inPage);
};
```

Consider the way a client programmer would use this class:

```
#include <iostream>
#include "WebHost.h"
```

```
int main()
{
    WebHost myHost("www.wrox.com");
    string result = myHost.getPage("/index.html");
    cout << "The result is " << result << endl;
    return 0;
}
```

The `WebHost` class effectively encapsulates the behavior of a host and provides useful functionality without unnecessary calls and data structures. The class even provides a useful new piece of functionality — once a `WebHost` is created, it can be used to obtain multiple web pages, saving code and possibly making the program run faster.

The implementation of the `WebHost` class makes extensive use of the `netwrklib` library without exposing any of its workings to the user. To enable this abstraction, the class needs a data member:

```
// WebHost.h
#include "netwrklib.h"
class WebHost
{
    // Omitted for brevity
    protected:
        Connection* mConnection;
};
```

The corresponding source file puts a new face on the functionality contained in the `netwrklib` library. First, the constructor builds a `HostRecord` for the specified host. Because the `WebHost` class deals with C++ strings instead of C-style strings, it uses the `c_str()` method on `inHost` to obtain a `const char*`, then performs a `const` cast to make up for `netwrklib`'s const-incorrectness. The resulting `HostRecord` is used to create a `Connection`, which is stored in the `mConnection` data member for later use:

```
WebHost::WebHost(const string& inHost)
{
    const char* host = inHost.c_str();
    HostRecord* theHost = lookupHostByName(const_cast<char*>(host));
    mConnection = connectToHost(theHost);
}
```

Subsequent calls to `getPage()` pass the stored connection to the `netwrklib`'s `retrieveWebPage()` function and return the value as a C++ string:

```
string getPage(const string& inPage)
{
    const char* page = inPage.c_str();
    string result = retrieveWebPage(mConnection, const_cast<char*>(page));
    return result;
}
```

 Networking-savvy readers may note that keeping a connection open to a host indefinitely is considered bad practice and doesn't adhere to the HTTP specification. We've chosen elegance over etiquette in this example.

As you can see, the `WebHost` class provides an object-oriented wrapper around the C library. By providing an abstraction, you can change the underlying implementation without affecting client code, and you can provide additional features. These features can include connection reference counting, parsing of pages, or automatically closing connections after a specific time to adhere to the HTTP specification and automatically reopening the connection on the next `getPage()` call.

Linking with C Code

In the previous example, we assumed that you had the raw C code to work with. The example took advantage of the fact that most C code will successfully compile with a C++ compiler. If you have only compiled C code, perhaps in the form of a library, you can still use it in your C++ program, but you need to take a few extra steps.

In order to implement function overloading, the complex C++ namespace is "flattened." For example, if you have a C++ program, it is legitimate to write:

```
void MyFunc(double);
void MyFunc(int);
void MyFunc(int, int);
```

However, this would mean that the linker would see several different names, all called `MyFunc`, and would not know which one you want to call. Therefore, all C++ compilers perform an operation which is referred to as *name mangling* and is the logical equivalent of generating names as follows:

```
MyFunc_double
MyFunc_int
MyFunc_int_int
```

To avoid conflicts with other names you might have defined, the generated names usually have some characters which are legal to the linker but not legal in C++ source code. For example, Microsoft VC++ generates names as follows:

```
?MyFunc@@YAXN@Z
?MyFunc@@YAXH@Z
?MyFunc@@YAXHH@Z
```

This encoding is complex and often vendor-specific. The C++ standard does not specify how function overloading should be implemented on a given platform, so there is no standard for name mangling algorithms.

In C, function overloading is not supported (the compiler will complain about duplicate definitions). So, names generated by the C compiler are quite simple; for example `_MyFunc`.

Now, if you compile a simple program with the C++ compiler, even if it has only one instance of the `MyFunc` name, it will still generate a request to link to a mangled name. But, when you link with the C library, it cannot find the desired mangled name, and the linker will complain. Therefore, it is necessary to tell the C++ compiler to not mangle that name. This is done by using the `extern "language"` qualification in both the header file (to instruct the client code to create a name compatible with the specified language) and, if your library source is in C++, at the definition site (to instruct the library code to generate a name compatible with the specified language).

The syntax of extern "language" is as follows:

```
extern "language" declaration1();
extern "language" declaration2();
```

Or:

```
extern "language" {
    declaration1();
    declaration2();
}
```

The C++ standard says that any language specification can be used, so in principle the following could be supported by a compiler:

```
extern "C" MyFunc(int i);
extern "FORTRAN" MatrixInvert(Matrix* M);
extern "Pascal" SomeLegacySubroutine(int n);
extern "Ada" AimMissileDefense(double angle);
```

In practice, many compilers only support "C". Each compiler vendor will inform you which language designators they support.

For example, in the following code, the function prototype for doCFunction() is specified as an external C function:

```
extern "C" {
    void doCFunction(int i);
}
int main()
{
    doCFunction(8); // Call the C function.
    return 0;
}
```

The actual definition for doCFunction() is provided in a compiled binary file attached in the link phase. The extern keyword informs the compiler that the linked-in code was compiled in C.

A more common pattern for using extern is at the header level. For example, if you are using a graphics library written in C, it probably came with a .h file for you to use. You can write another header file that wraps the original one in an extern block to specify that the entire header defines functions written in C. The wrapper .h file is often named with .hpp to distinguish it from the C version of the header:

```
// graphicslib.hpp
extern "C" {
    #include "graphicslib.h"
}
```

Another common model is to write a single header file, which is conditioned on whether it is being compiled for C or C++. A C++ compiler predefines the symbol __cplusplus if you are compiling for C++. The symbol is not defined for C compilations. So you will often see header files in the following form:

```
#ifdef __cplusplus
    extern "C" {
#endif
        declaration1();
        declaration2();
#ifdef __cplusplus
    } // matches extern "C"
#endif
```

This means that declaration1() and declaration2() are functions that are in a library compiled by the C compiler. Using this technique, the same header file can be used in both C and C++ clients.

Whether you are including C code in your C++ program or linking against a compiled C library, remember that even though C++ is essentially a superset of C, they are different languages with different design goals. Adapting C code to work in C++ is quite common, but providing an object-oriented C++ wrapper around procedural C code is often much better.

Mixing C# with C++

Even though this is a C++ book, we won't pretend that there aren't newer and snazzier languages out there. One example is C#. By using the *Interop services* from C#, it's pretty easy to call C++ code from within your C# applications. An example scenario could be that you develop parts of your application, like the graphical user interface, in C#, but use C++ to implement certain performance-critical components. To make Interop work, you need to write a library in C++, which will be called from C#. On Windows, the library will be in a .DLL file. The following C++ example defines a FunctionInDLL() function that will be compiled into a library. The function accepts a Unicode string and returns an integer. The implementation writes the received string to the console and returns the value 42 to the caller:

Available for
download on
Wrox.com

```
#include <iostream>
using namespace std;
extern "C"
{
    __declspec(dllexport) int FunctionInDLL(const wchar_t* p)
    {
        wcout << L"The following string was received by C++:\n      '";
        wcout << p << L"'" << endl;
        return 42;    // Return some value...
    }
}
```

Code snippet from CSharp\HelloCpp.cpp

Keep in mind that you are implementing a function in a library, not writing a program; so, you will not need a `main()` function. Compiling this code depends on your environment. If you are using Microsoft Visual C++, you need to go to the properties of your project and select "Dynamic Library (.dll)" as the configuration type. Note that the example uses `__declspec(dllexport)` to tell the linker that this function should be made available to clients of the library. How to do this depends on your compiler. `__declspec(dllexport)` is the way you do this with Microsoft Visual C++.

Once you have the library, you can call it from C# by using Interop services. First, you need to include the Interop namespace:

```
using System.Runtime.InteropServices;
```

Next, you define the function prototype, and tell C# where it can find the implementation of the function. This is done with the following line, assuming you have compiled the library as `HelloCpp.dll`:

```
[DllImport("HelloCpp.dll", CharSet = CharSet.Unicode)]
public static extern int FunctionInDLL(String s);
```

The first part of this line is saying that C# should import this function from a library called `HelloCpp.dll`, and that it should use Unicode strings. The second part specifies the actual prototype of the function, which is a function accepting a string as parameter and returning an integer. The following code shows a complete example on how to use the C++ library from C#:

```csharp
using System;
using System.Runtime.InteropServices;
namespace HelloCSharp
{
    class Program
    {
        [DllImport("HelloCpp.dll", CharSet = CharSet.Unicode)]
        public static extern int FunctionInDLL(String s);
        static void Main(string[] args)
        {
            Console.WriteLine("Writen by C#.");
            int res = FunctionInDLL("Some string from C#.");
            Console.WriteLine("C++ returned the value " + res);
        }
    }
}
```

Code snippet from CSharp\HelloCSharp.cs

The output will be as follows:

```
Writen by C#.
The following string was received by C++:
    'Some string from C#.'
C++ returned the value 42
```

The details of the C# code are outside the scope of this C++ book, but the general idea should be clear with this example.

Mixing Java and C++ with JNI

The *Java Native Interface*, or JNI, is a part of the Java language that allows the programmer to access functionality that was not written in Java. Because Java is a cross-platform language, the original intent was to make it possible for Java programs to interact with the operating system. JNI also allows programmers to make use of libraries written in other languages, such as C++. Access to C++ libraries may be useful to a Java programmer who has a performance-critical piece of his application, or who needs to use legacy code.

JNI can also be used to execute Java code within a C++ program, but such a use is far less common. Because this is a C++ book, we do not include an introduction to the Java language. This section is targeted at readers who already know Java and wish to incorporate C++ code into their Java code.

To begin your Java cross-language adventure, start with the Java program. For this example, the simplest of Java programs will suffice:

```
public class HelloCpp {
    public static void main(String[] args)
    {
        System.out.println("Hello from Java!");
    }
}
```

Code snippet from JNI\HelloCpp.java

Next, you need to declare a Java method that will be written in another language. To do this, you use the `native` keyword and leave out the implementation:

```
public class HelloCpp {
    // This will be implemented in C++.
    public native void callCpp();
    // Remainder omitted for brevity
}
```

Code snippet from JNI\HelloCpp.java

C++ code will eventually be compiled into a shared library that gets dynamically loaded into the Java program. You need to load this library inside a Java static block so that it is loaded when the Java program begins executing. The name of the library can be whatever you want, for example `hellocpp.so` on Unix systems, or `hellocpp.dll` on Windows systems.

```
public class HelloCpp {
    static {
        System.loadLibrary("hellocpp");
    }
    // Remainder omitted for brevity
}
```

Code snippet from JNI\HelloCpp.java

Finally, you need to actually call the C++ code from within the Java program. The `callCpp()` Java method serves as a placeholder for the not-yet-written C++ code. Because `callCpp()` is a method of the `HelloCpp` class, you need to create a new `HelloCpp` object and call the `callCpp()` method on it:

Available for download on Wrox.com

```java
public class HelloCpp {
    static {
        System.loadLibrary("hellocpp");
    }
    // This will be implemented in C++.
    public native void callCpp();
    public static void main(String[] args)
    {
        System.out.println("Hello from Java!");
        HelloCpp cppInterface = new HelloCpp();
        cppInterface.callCpp();
    }
}
```

Code snippet from JNI\HelloCpp.java

That's all for the Java side. Now, just compile the Java program as you normally would:

```
javac HelloCpp.java
```

Then use the `javah` program (the authors like to pronounce it *jav-AHH!*) to create a header file for the native method:

```
javah HelloCpp
```

After running `javah`, you will find a file named `HelloCpp.h`, which is a fully working (if somewhat ugly) C/C++ header file. Inside of that header file is a C function definition for a function called `Java_HelloCpp_callCpp()`. Your C++ program will need to implement this function. The full prototype is:

```
JNIEXPORT void JNICALL Java_HelloCpp_callCpp(JNIEnv* env, jobject javaobj);
```

Your C++ implementation of this function can make full use of the C++ language. This example outputs some text from C++. First, you need to include the `jni.h` header file and the `HelloCpp.h` file that was created by `javah`. You will also need to include any C or C++ headers that you intend to use:

Available for download on Wrox.com

```cpp
#include <jni.h>
#include "HelloCpp.h"
#include <iostream>
```

Code snippet from JNI\HelloCpp.cpp

The C++ function is written as normal. The parameters to the function allow interaction with the Java environment and the object that called the native code. They are beyond the scope of this example.

```
JNIEXPORT void JNICALL Java_HelloCpp_callCpp(JNIEnv* env, jobject javaobj)
{
    std::cout << "Hello from C++!" << std::endl;
}
```

Code snippet from JNI\HelloCpp.cpp

Compiling this code into a library depends on your environment, but you will most likely need to tweak your compiler's settings to include the JNI headers. Using the GCC compiler on Linux, your compile command might look like this:

```
g++ -shared -I/usr/java/jdk/include/ -I/usr/java/jdk/include/linux HelloCpp.cpp \
-o hellocpp.so
```

The output from the compiler is the library used by the Java program. As long as the shared library is somewhere in the Java class path, you can execute the Java program normally:

```
java HelloCpp
```

You should see the following result:

```
Hello from Java!
Hello from C++!
```

Of course, this example just scratches the surface of what is possible through JNI. You can use JNI to interface with OS-specific features or hardware drivers. For complete coverage of JNI, you should consult a Java text.

Mixing C++ with Perl and Shell Scripts

C++ contains a built-in general-purpose mechanism to interface with other languages and environments. You've already used it many times, probably without paying much attention to it — it's the arguments to and return value from the `main()` function.

C and C++ were designed with command-line interfaces in mind. The `main()` function receives the arguments from the command line, and returns a status code that can be interpreted by the caller. In a scripting environment, arguments to and status codes from your program can be a powerful mechanism that allows you to interface with the environment.

Scripting versus Programming

Before delving into the details of mixing C++ and scripts, consider whether your project is an *application* or a *script*. The difference is subtle and subject to debate. The following descriptions are just guidelines. Many so-called scripts are just as sophisticated as full-blown applications. The question isn't whether or not something can be done as a script, but whether or not a scripting language is the best tool.

An application is a program that performs a particular task. Modern applications typically involve some sort of user interaction. In other words, applications tend to be driven by the user, who directs the application to take certain actions. Applications often have multiple capabilities. For example, a user can use a photo editing application to scale an image, paint over an image, or print an image. Most of the software you would buy in a box is an application. Applications tend to be relatively large and often complex programs.

A script generally performs a single task, or a set of related tasks. You might have a script that automatically sorts your email, or backs up your important files. Scripts often run without user interaction, perhaps at a particular time each day or triggered by an event, such as the arrival of new mail. Scripts can be found at the OS level (such as a script that compresses files every night) or at the application level (such as a script that automates the process of shrinking and printing images). Automation is an important part of the definition of a script — scripts are usually written to codify a sequence of steps that a user would otherwise perform manually.

Now, consider the difference between a *scripting language* and a *programming language*. Not all scripts are necessarily written in scripting languages. You could write a script that sorts your email by using the C programming language, or you could write an equivalent script by using the Perl scripting language. Similarly, not all applications are written in programming languages. A suitably motivated coder could write a web browser in Perl if she really wanted to. The line is blurry.

In the end, what matters most is which language provides the functionality you need. If you are going to be interacting extensively with the operating system, you might consider a scripting language because scripting languages tend to have better support for OS interaction. If your project is going to be larger in scope and involve heavy user interaction, a programming language will probably be easier in the long run.

Using Scripts

The original Unix OS included a rather limited C library, which did not support certain common operations. Unix programmers therefore developed the habit of launching *shell scripts* from applications to accomplish tasks that should have had API or library support.

Today, many of these Unix programmers still insist on using scripts as a form of subroutine call. Usually, they execute the `system()` C library call with a string which is the script to execute. There are significant risks to this approach. For example, if there is an error in the script, the caller may or may not get a detailed error indication. The `system()` call is also exceptionally heavy-duty, since it has to create an entire new process to execute the script. This may ultimately be a serious performance bottleneck in your application.

In general, you should explore the features of the C++ library to see if there are better ways to do something. There are some platform-independent wrappers around a lot of platform-specific libraries; for example, the Boost `<filesystem>` library. Concepts like launching a Perl script by using `system()` to process some textual data may not be the best choice. Using techniques like the regular expression library of C++11 might be a better choice for your string processing needs.

A Practical Example — Encrypting Passwords

Assume that you have a system that writes everything a user sees and types to a file for auditing purposes. The file can be read only by the system administrator so that she can figure out who to blame if something goes wrong. An excerpt of such a file might look like this:

```
Login: bucky-bo
Password: feldspar
bucky-bo> mail
bucky-bo has no mail
bucky-bo> exit
```

While the system administrator may want to keep a log of all user activity, she may wish to obscure everybody's passwords in case the file is somehow obtained by a hacker. A script seems like the natural choice for this project because it should happen automatically, perhaps at the end of every day. There is, however, one piece of the project that might not be best suited for a scripting language. Encryption libraries tend to exist mainly for high-level languages such as C and C++. Therefore, one possible implementation is to write a script that calls out to a C++ program to perform the encryption.

The following script uses the Perl language, though almost any scripting language could accomplish this task. If you don't know Perl, you will still be able to follow along. The most important element of Perl syntax for this example is the ` character. The ` character instructs the Perl script to *shell out* to an external command. In this case, the script will shell out to a C++ program called `encryptString`.

> *Launching an external process causes a big overhead because a complete new process has to be created. You shouldn't use it when you need to call the external process often. In this password encryption example, it is OK, because you can assume that a log file will only contain a few password lines.*

The strategy for the script is to loop over every line of a file looking for lines that contain a password prompt. The script will write a new file, `userlog.out`, which contains the same text as the source file, except that all passwords are encrypted. The first step is to open the input file for reading and the output file for writing. Then, the script needs to loop over all the lines in the file. Each line in turn is placed in a variable called `$line`.

```perl
open (INPUT, "userlog.txt") or die "Couldn't open input file!";
open (OUTPUT, ">userlog.out") or die "Couldn't open output file!";
while ($line = <INPUT>) {
```

Code snippet from Perl\processLog.pl

Next, the current line is checked against a *regular expression* to see if this particular line contains the `Password:` prompt. If it does, Perl will store the password in the variable `$1`.

```perl
if ($line =~ m/^Password: (.*)/) {
```

Since a match has been found, the script calls the `encryptString` program with the detected password to obtain an encrypted version of it. The output of the program is stored in the `$result` variable, and the result status code from the program is stored in the variable `$?`. The script checks `$?` and quits immediately if there is a problem. If everything is okay, the password line is written to the output file with the encrypted password instead of the original one.

```
$result = `./encryptString $1`;
if ($? != 0) { exit(-1) }
print OUTPUT "Password: $result\n";
```

If the current line is not a password prompt, the script writes the line as is to the output file. At the end of the loop, it closes both files and exits.

```
    } else {
        print OUTPUT "$line";
    }
}
close (INPUT);
close (OUTPUT);
```

That's it. The only other required piece is the actual C++ program. Implementation of a cryptographic algorithm is beyond the scope of this book. The important piece is the `main()` function because it accepts the string that should be encrypted as an argument.

Arguments are contained in the `argv` array of C-style strings. You should always consult the `argc` parameter before accessing an element of `argv`. If `argc` is 1, there is one element in the argument list and it is accessible as `argv[0]`. The 0th element of the `argv` array is generally the name of the program, so actual parameters begin at `argv[1]`.

Following is the `main()` function for a C++ program that encrypts the input string. Notice that the program returns 0 for success and non-0 for failure, as is standard in Unix:

Available for download on Wrox.com

```
int main(int argc, char* argv[])
{
    if (argc < 2) {
        cerr << "Usage: " << argv[0] << " string-to-be-encrypted" << endl;
        return -1;
    }
    cout << encrypt(argv[1]);
    return 0;
}
```

Code snippet from Perl\encryptString.cpp

 There is actually a blatant security hole in this code. When the to-be-encrypted string is passed to the C++ program as a command-line argument, it may be visible to other users through the process table. A more secure way to get the information into the C++ program would be to send it through standard input, which is the forte of the expect *scripting language.*

Now that you've seen how easily C++ programs can be incorporated into scripting languages, you can combine the strengths of the two languages for your own projects. You can use a scripting language to interact with the OS and control the flow of the script, and a traditional programming language for the heavy lifting.

 This example is just to demonstrate how to use Perl and C++ together. C++11 includes a regular expression library, which makes it very easy to convert this Perl/C++ solution into a pure C++ solution. This pure C++ solution will run much faster because it avoids calling an external program. See Chapter 14 for details on this regular expression library.

Mixing C++ with Assembly Code

C++ is considered a fast language, especially relative to other object-oriented languages. Yet, in some rare cases, you might want to use raw assembly code when speed is absolutely critical. The compiler generates assembly code from your source files, and this generated assembly code is fast enough for virtually all purposes. Both the compiler and the linker (when it supports link time code generation like VC++ 2010) use optimization algorithms to make the generated assembly code as fast as possible. These optimizers are getting more and more powerful by using special processor instruction sets such as MMX and SSE. These days, it's very hard to write your own assembly code that will outperform the code generated by the compiler, unless you know all the little details of these enhanced instruction sets.

However, in case you do need it, the keyword asm can be used by a C++ compiler to allow the programmer to insert raw assembly code. The keyword is part of the C++ standard, but its implementation is compiler-defined. In some compilers, you can use asm to drop from C++ down to the level of assembly right in the middle of your program. Sometimes, the support for the asm keyword depends on your target architecture. For example, Microsoft VC++ 2010 supports the asm keyword when compiling in 32-bit mode, but asm is not supported when compiling in 64-bit mode.

Inline assembly can be useful in some applications, but we don't recommend it for most programs. There are several reasons to avoid inline assembly code:

➤ Your code is no longer portable to another processor once you start including raw assembly code for your platform.

➤ Most programmers don't know assembly languages and won't be able to modify or maintain your code.

➤ Assembly code is not known for its readability. It can hurt your program's use of style.

➤ Most of the time, it is not necessary. If your program is slow, look for algorithmic problems or consult some of the other performance suggestions in Chapter 24.

When you encounter performance issues in your application, first look into algorithmic speed-ups, and use raw assembly code only as a last resort.

Practically, if you have a computationally expensive block of code, you should move it to its own C++ function. If you determine, using performance profiling (see Chapter 24), that this function is a performance bottleneck, and there is no way to write the code smaller and faster, you might use raw assembly to try to increase performance.

In such a case, one of the first things you will want to do is declare the function extern "C" so the C++ name mangling is suppressed. Then, write a separate module in assembly code which performs the function more efficiently. The advantage of a separate module is that there is a "reference implementation" in C++ which is platform-independent; and, there is a platform-specific high-performance implementation, in raw assembly code. The use of extern "C" means that the assembly code can use a simple naming convention (otherwise, you have to reverse-engineer your compiler's name mangling algorithm). Then, you can link with either the C++ version, or the assembly code version.

You would write this module in assembly code and run it through an assembler, rather than using inline asm directives in C++; this is particularly true in many of the popular x86-compatible-64-bit compilers, where the inline asm keyword is not supported.

However, using raw assembly code should only be done if there are significant performance improvement factors. A factor of 2 might justify the effort. A factor of 10 is compelling. A factor of 10% is not worth the effort.

SUMMARY

If you take away one point from this chapter, it should be that C++ is a flexible language. It exists in the sweet spot between languages that are too tied to a particular platform and languages that are too high-level and generic. Rest assured that when you develop code in C++, you aren't locking yourself into the language forever. C++ can be mixed with other technologies and has a solid history and code base that help guarantee its relevance in the future.

26

Becoming Adept at Testing

WHAT'S IN THIS CHAPTER?

➤ What software quality control is and how to track bugs

➤ What unit testing means and how to use it in practice

➤ What integration, system and regression testing means

A programmer has overcome a major hurdle in her career when she realizes that testing is a part of the software development process. Bugs are not an occasional occurrence. They are found in *every* project of significant size. A good *quality-assurance* (QA) team is invaluable, but the full burden of testing cannot be placed on QA alone. Your responsibility as a programmer is to write code that works and tests to prove its correctness.

A distinction is often made between *white box testing*, in which the tester is aware of the inner workings of the program, and *black box testing*, which tests the program's functionality without concern for its implementation. Both forms of testing are important to professional-quality projects. Black box testing is the most fundamental approach because it typically models the behavior of a user. For example, a black box test can examine interface components like buttons. If the tester clicks the button and nothing happens, there is obviously a bug in the program.

Black box testing cannot cover everything. Modern programs are too large to employ a simulation of clicking every button, providing every kind of input, and performing all combinations of commands. White box testing is necessary because it is easier to ensure test coverage when tests are written at the object or subsystem level. White box tests are often easier to write and automate than black box tests. This chapter focuses on topics that would generally be considered white box testing techniques because the programmer can use these techniques during development.

This chapter begins with a high-level discussion of quality control, including some approaches to viewing and tracking bugs. A section on unit testing, one of the simplest and most useful types of testing, follows this introduction. You will read about the theory and practice of unit testing, as well as several examples of unit tests in action. Next, higher-level tests are covered, including integration tests, system tests, and regression tests. Finally, this chapter ends with a list of tips for successful testing.

QUALITY CONTROL

Large programming projects are rarely finished when a feature-complete goal is reached. There are always bugs to find and fix, both during and after the main development phase. Understanding the shared responsibility of quality control and the life cycle of a bug is essential to performing well in a group.

Whose Responsibility Is Testing?

Software development organizations have different approaches to testing. In a small startup, there may not be a group of people whose full-time job is testing the product. Testing may be the responsibility of the individual developers, or all the employees of the company may be asked to lend a hand and try to break the product before its release. In larger organizations, a full-time quality assurance staff probably qualifies a release by testing it according to a set of criteria. Nonetheless, some aspects of testing may still be the responsibility of the developers. Even in organizations where the developers have no role in formal testing, you still need to be aware of what your responsibilities are in the larger process of quality assurance.

The Life Cycle of a Bug

All good engineering groups recognize that bugs will occur in software both before and after its release. There are many different ways to deal with these problems. Figure 26-1 shows a formal bug process, expressed as a flow chart. In this particular process, a bug is always filed by a member of the QA team. The bug reporting software sends a notification to the development manager, who sets the priority of the bug and assigns the bug to the appropriate module owner. The module owner can accept the bug or explain why the bug actually belongs in a different module or is invalid, giving the development manager the opportunity to assign it to someone else.

Once the bug has found its rightful owner, a fix is made and the developer marks the bug as "fixed." At this point, the QA engineer verifies that the bug no longer exists and marks the bug as "closed" or reopens the bug if it is still present.

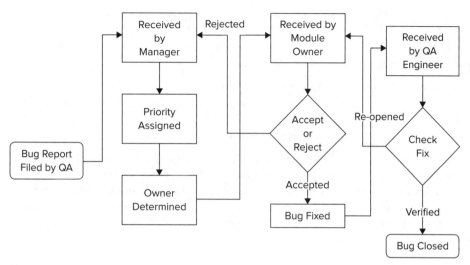

FIGURE 26-1

A less formal approach is shown in Figure 26-2. In this workflow, anybody can file a bug and assign an initial priority and a module. The module owner receives the bug report and can either accept it or reassign it to another engineer or module. When a correction is made, the bug is marked as "fixed." Toward the end of the testing phase, all the implementation and QA engineers divide up the fixed bugs and verify that each bug is no longer present in the current build. The release is ready when all bugs are marked as "closed."

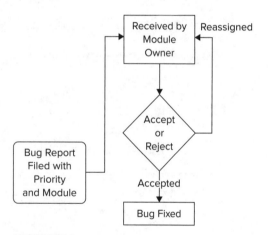

Bug-Tracking Tools

FIGURE 26-2

There are many ways to keep track of software bugs, from informal e-mail- or spreadsheet-based schemes to expensive third-party bug-tracking software. The appropriate solution for your organization depends on the group's size, the nature of the software, and the level of formality you wish to build around bug fixing.

There are also a number of free open-source bug-tracking solutions available. One of the more popular free tools for bug tracking is *Bugzilla*, written by the authors of the Mozilla web browser. As an open-source project, Bugzilla has gradually accumulated a number of useful features to the point where it now rivals expensive bug-tracking software packages. Among its many features are:

➤ Customizable settings for a bug, including its priority, associated component, status, and so on

➤ E-mail notification of new bug reports or changes to an existing report

➤ Tracking of dependencies between bugs and resolution of duplicate bugs

➤ Reporting and searching tools

➤ A web-based interface for filing and updating bugs

Figure 26-3 shows a bug being entered into a Bugzilla project that was set up for this book. For our purposes, each chapter was input as a Bugzilla component. The filer of the bug can specify the severity of the bug (how big of a deal it is). A summary and description are included to make it possible to search for the bug or list it in a report format.

Bug-tracking tools like Bugzilla are becoming essential components of a professional software development environment. In addition to supplying a central list of currently open bugs, bug-tracking tools provide an important archive of previous bugs and their fixes. A support engineer, for instance, might use Bugzilla to search for a problem similar to one reported by a customer. If a fix was made, the support person will be able to tell the customer which version they need to update to or how to work around the problem.

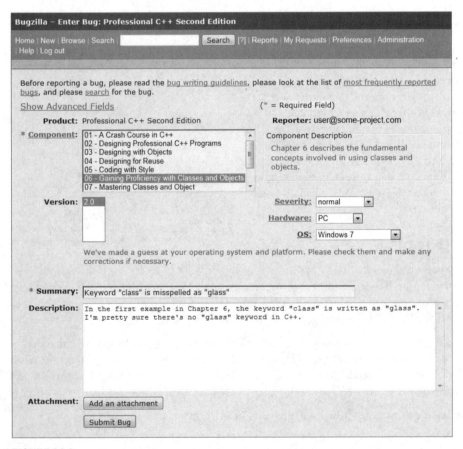

FIGURE 26-3

UNIT TESTING

The only way to find bugs is through testing. One of the most important types of tests from a developer's point of view is the *unit test*. Unit tests are pieces of code that exercise specific functionality of a class or subsystem. These are the finest-grained tests that you could possibly write. Ideally, one or more unit tests should exist for every low-level task that your code can perform. For example, imagine that you are writing a math library that can perform addition and multiplication. Your suite of unit tests might contain the following tests:

- Basic test of addition
- Test addition of large numbers
- Test addition of negative numbers
- Test addition of zero to a number
- Test the commutative property of addition
- Basic test of multiplication
- Test multiplication of large numbers
- Test multiplication of negative numbers
- Test multiplication with zero
- Test the commutative property of multiplication

Well-written unit tests protect you in many ways. First, they prove that a piece of functionality actually works. Until you have some code that actually makes use of your class, its behavior is a major unknown. Second, they provide a first alert when a recently introduced change breaks something. This specific usage, called a *regression test*, is covered later in this chapter. Third, when used as part of the development process, they force the developer to fix problems from the start. If you are prevented from checking in your code with failed unit tests, you're forced to address problems right away. Fourth, unit tests let you try out code before other code is in place. When you first started programming, you could write a whole program and then run it for the first time. Professional programs are too big for that approach, so you need to be able to test components in isolation. Last, but certainly not least, they provide an example of usage.

Almost as a side effect, unit tests make great reference code for other programmers. If a co-worker wants to know how to perform matrix multiplication by using your math library, you can point her to the appropriate test.

Approaches to Unit Testing

It's hard to go wrong with unit tests, unless you don't write them or write them poorly. In general, the more tests you have, the more coverage you have. The more coverage you have, the less likely it is for bugs to fall through the cracks and for you to have to tell your boss, or worse, your customer, "Oh, we never tested that."

There are several methodologies for writing unit tests most effectively. The Extreme Programming methodology, explained in Chapter 23, instructs its followers to write unit tests *before* writing code.

In theory, writing tests first helps you solidify the requirements for the component and provide a metric that can be used to determine when it is done.

Writing tests first can be tricky and requires diligence on the part of the programmer. For some programmers, it simply doesn't mesh well with their coding style. A less rigid approach is to *design* the tests before coding, but *implement* them later in the process. This way, the programmer is still forced to understand the requirements of the module but doesn't have to write code that makes use of nonexistent classes.

In some groups, the author of a particular subsystem doesn't write the unit tests for that subsystem. The theory is that if you write the tests for your own code, you might subconsciously work around problems that you know about, or only cover certain cases that you know your code handles well. In addition, it's sometimes difficult to get excited about finding bugs in code you just wrote, so you might only put in a half-hearted effort. In practice, having one developer write unit tests for another developer's code requires a lot of extra overhead and coordination. When such coordination is accomplished, however, this approach helps guarantee more-effective tests.

Another way to ensure that unit tests are actually testing the right parts of the code is to write them so that they maximize *code coverage*. You can use a code coverage tool, such as gcov, that will tell you what percentage of public methods are called by unit tests. In theory, a properly tested class has unit tests for all of its public methods.

The Unit Testing Process

The process of providing unit tests for your code begins before the code is written. Even if you do not subscribe to the methodology of writing unit tests before you write code, you should take the time to consider what sorts of tests you will provide. This way, you can break the task up into well-defined chunks, each of which has its own test-validated criteria. For example, if your task is to write a database access class, you might first write the functionality that inserts data into the database. Once that is fully tested with a suite of unit tests, you can continue to write the code to support updates, deletes, and selects, testing each piece as you go.

The following list of steps is a suggested approach for designing and implementing unit tests. As with any programming methodology, the best process is the one that yields the best results. We suggest that you experiment with different ways of using unit tests to discover what works best for you.

Define the Granularity of Your Tests

Before you start designing the individual tests, you need to do a reality check. Given the requirements of your component, its complexity, and the amount of time available, what level of unit testing can you provide? In an ideal world, you would write more tests than code to thoroughly validate the functionality of a program (though if it were truly an ideal world, we probably wouldn't need tests because everything would work). In reality, you are probably already crunched for time, and your initial task is to maximize the effectiveness of unit tests given the constraints placed upon you.

The *granularity* of tests refers to their scope. As the following table illustrates, you can unit test a database class with just a few test functions, or you can go nuts and really ensure that everything works as it should.

LARGE-GRAINED TESTS	MEDIUM-GRAINED TESTS	FINE-GRAINED TESTS
testConnection()	[all of the large-grained tests]	[all large- and medium-grained tests]
testInsert()	testConnectionDropped()	testConnectionThroughHTTP()
testUpdate()	testInsertBadData()	testConnectionLocal()
testDelete()	testInsertStrings()	testConnectionErrorBadHost()
testSelect()	testInsertIntegers()	testConnectionErrorServerBusy()
	testUpdateStrings()	testInsertWideCharacters()
	testUpdateIntegers()	testInsertLargeData()
	testDeleteNonexistentRow()	testInsertMalformed()
	testSelectComplicated()	testUpdateWideCharacters()
	testSelectMalformed()	testUpdateLargeData()
		testUpdateMalformed()
		testDeleteWithoutPermissions()
		testDeleteThenUpdate()
		testSelectNested()
		testSelectWideCharacters()
		testSelectLargeData()

As you can see, each successive column brings in more-specific tests. As you move from large-grained tests to more finely grained tests, you start to consider error conditions, different input data sets, and different modes of operation.

Of course, the decision you make initially when choosing the granularity of your tests is not set in stone. Perhaps the database class is just being written as a proof-of-concept and might not even be used. A few simple tests may be adequate now, and you can always add more later. Or perhaps the use cases change at a later date. The database class might not initially have been written with international characters in mind. Once such features are added, they should be tested with specific targeted unit tests.

If you plan to revisit or refine the tests at a later date, you should make every effort to actually do so. Consider the unit tests to be part of the actual implementation. When you make a modification, don't just modify the tests so that they continue to work, write new tests and re-evaluate the existing ones.

 Unit tests are part of the subsystem that they are testing. As you enhance and refine the subsystem, enhance and refine the tests.

Brainstorm the Individual Tests

Over time, you will gain an intuition for which aspects of a piece of code should turn into a unit test. Certain methods or inputs just feel like they should be tested. This intuition is gained through trial and error and by looking at unit tests that other people in your group have written. It should be pretty easy to pick out which programmers are the best unit testers. Their tests tend to be organized and frequently modified.

Until unit test creation becomes second nature, approach the task of figuring out which tests to write by brainstorming. To get some ideas flowing, consider the following questions:

1. What are the things that this piece of code was written to do?
2. What are the typical ways each method would be called?
3. What preconditions of the methods could be violated by the caller?
4. How could each method be misused?
5. What kinds of data are you expecting as input?
6. What kinds of data are you *not* expecting as input?
7. What are the edge cases or exceptional conditions?

You don't need to write formal answers to those questions (unless your manager is a particularly fervent devotee of this book or of certain testing methodologies), but they should help you generate some ideas for unit tests. The table of tests for the database class contained test functions, each of which arose from one of these questions.

Once you have generated ideas for some of the tests you would like to use, consider how you might organize them into categories, and the breakdown of tests will fall into place. In the database class example, the tests could be split into the following categories:

➤ Basic tests

➤ Error tests

➤ Localization tests

➤ Bad input tests

➤ Complicated tests

Splitting your tests into categories makes them easier to identify and augment. It might also make it easier to realize which aspects of the code are well tested and which could use a few more unit tests.

 It's easy to write a massive number of simple tests, but don't forget about the more complicated cases!

Create Sample Data and Results

The most common trap to fall into when writing unit tests is to match the test to the behavior of the code instead of using the test to validate the code. If you write a unit test that performs a database select for a piece of data that is definitely in the database, and the test fails, is it a problem with the code or a problem with the test? It's often easier to assume that the code is right and to modify the test to match. This approach is usually wrong.

To avoid this pitfall, you should understand the inputs to the test and the expected output before you try it out. This is sometimes easier said than done. For example, say you wrote some code to encrypt an arbitrary block of text using a particular key. A reasonable unit test would take a fixed string of text and pass it in to the encryption module. Then, it would examine the result to see if it was correctly encrypted.

When you go to write such a test, it is tempting to try out the behavior with the encryption module first and see the result. If it looks reasonable, you might write a test to look for that value. Doing so really doesn't prove anything, however. You haven't actually tested the code — you've just written a test that guarantees it will continue to return that same value. Often times, writing the test requires some real work — you would need to encrypt the text independently of your encryption module to get an accurate result.

 Decide on the correct output for your test before you ever run the test.

Write the Tests

The exact code behind a test will vary depending on what type of test framework you have in place. One framework, cppunit, is discussed later in this chapter. Independent of the actual implementation, however, the following guidelines will help ensure effective tests:

- ➤ Make sure that you're testing only one thing in each test. That way, if a test fails, it will point to a specific piece of functionality.

- ➤ Be specific inside the test. Did the test fail because an exception was thrown or because the wrong value was returned?

- ➤ Use logging extensively inside of test code. If the test fails some day, you will have some insight into what happened.

- ➤ Avoid tests that depend on earlier tests or are otherwise interrelated. Tests should be as atomic and isolated as possible.

- ➤ If the test requires the use of other subsystems, consider writing *stub versions* of those subsystems that simulate the modules' behavior so that changes in loosely related code don't cause the test to fail.

- ➤ Ask your code reviewers to look at your unit tests as well. When you do a code review, tell the other engineer where you think additional tests could be added.

As you will see later in this chapter, unit tests are usually very small and simple pieces of code. In most cases, writing a single unit test will take only a few minutes, making them one of the most productive uses of your time.

Run the Tests

When you're done writing a test, you should run it right away before the anticipation of the results becomes too much to bear. The joy of a screen full of passing unit tests shouldn't be minimized. For most programmers, this is the easiest way to see quantitative data that declare your code useful and correct.

Even if you adopt the methodology of writing tests before writing code, you should still run the tests immediately after they are written. This way, you can prove to yourself that the tests fail initially. Once the code is in place, you have tangible data that shows that it accomplished what it was supposed to accomplish.

It's unlikely that every test you write will have the expected result the first time. In theory, if you are writing tests before writing code, all of your tests should fail. If one passes, either the code magically appeared or there is a problem with a test. If the code is done and tests still fail (some would say that if the tests fail, the code is actually *not* done), there are two possibilities. The code could be wrong or the test could be wrong.

Unit Testing in Action

Now that you've read about unit testing in theory, it's time to actually write some tests. The following example draws on the object pool example from Chapter 24. As a brief recap, the object pool is a class that can be used to avoid excessive object creation. By keeping track of already created objects, the pool acts as a broker between code that needs a certain type of object and such objects that already exist.

The public interface for the ObjectPool class is as follows. Note that comments have been removed for brevity; consult Chapter 24 for details on the ObjectPool class:

```
template <typename T>
class ObjectPool
{
    public:
        ObjectPool(size_t chunkSize = kDefaultChunkSize)
            throw(std::invalid_argument, std::bad_alloc);
        shared_ptr<T> acquireObject();
        void releaseObject(shared_ptr<T> obj);
    // [Private/Protected methods and data omitted.]
};
```

Code snippet from ObjectPoolTest\ObjectPool.h

If the notion of an object pool is new to you, you may wish to peruse Chapter 24 before continuing with this example.

Introducing cppunit

cppunit is an open-source unit testing framework for C++ that is based on a Java package called junit. The framework is fairly lightweight (in a good way), and it is very easy to get started. The advantage of using a framework such as cppunit is that it allows the developer to focus on writing tests instead of dealing with setting up tests, building logic around tests, and gathering results. cppunit includes a number of helpful utilities for test developers, and automatic output in various formats. The full breadth of features is not covered here. We suggest you read up on cppunit at http://cppunit.sourceforge.net.

The most common way of using cppunit is to subclass the CppUnit::TestFixture class (note that CppUnit is the namespace and TestFixture is the class). A *fixture* is a logical group of tests. A TestFixture subclass can override the setUp() method to perform any tasks that need to happen prior to the tests running, as well as the tearDown() method, which can be used to clean up after the tests have run. A fixture can also maintain state with member variables. A skeleton implementation of ObjectPoolTest, a class for testing the ObjectPool class, is shown here:

```
#include <cppunit/TestFixture.h>
class ObjectPoolTest : public CppUnit::TestFixture
{
    public:
        void setUp();
        void tearDown();
};
```

Code snippet from ObjectPoolTest\ObjectPoolTest.h

Because the tests for ObjectPool are relatively simple and isolated, empty definitions will suffice for setUp() and tearDown(). The beginning stage of the source file is shown here:

```
#include "ObjectPoolTest.h"
void ObjectPoolTest::setUp() { }
void ObjectPoolTest::tearDown() { }
```

Code snippet from ObjectPoolTest\ObjectPoolTest.cpp

That's all the initial code we need to start developing unit tests.

Writing the First Test

Since this may be your first exposure to cppunit, or to unit tests at large, the first test will be a very simple one. It tests whether 0 < 1.

An individual unit test in cppunit is just a method of the fixture class. To create a simple test, add its declaration to the ObjectPoolTest.h file:

```
#include <cppunit/TestFixture.h>
class ObjectPoolTest : public CppUnit::TestFixture
{
    public:
        void setUp();
        void tearDown();
        void testSimple();   // Our first test!
};
```

Code snippet from ObjectPoolTest\ObjectPoolTest.h

The test definition uses the CPPUNIT_ASSERT macro to perform the actual test. CPPUNIT_ASSERT, like other assert macros you may have used, surrounds an expression that *should* be true. Chapter 27 explains asserts in more detail. In this case, the test claims that 0 is less than 1, so it surrounds the statement 0 < 1 in a CPPUNIT_ASSERT macro call. This macro is defined in the <cppunit/TestAssert.h> file:

```cpp
#include "ObjectPoolTest.h"
#include <cppunit/TestAssert.h>
void ObjectPoolTest::setUp() { }
void ObjectPoolTest::tearDown() { }
void ObjectPoolTest::testSimple()
{
    CPPUNIT_ASSERT(0 < 1);
}
```

Code snippet from ObjectPoolTest\ObjectPoolTest.cpp

That's it. Of course, most of your unit tests will do something a bit more interesting than a simple assert. As you will see, the common pattern is to perform some sort of calculation and assert that the result is the value you expected. With cppunit, you don't even need to worry about exceptions — the framework will catch and report them as necessary.

Building a Suite of Tests

There are a few more steps before the simple test can be run. cppunit runs a group of tests as a *suite*. A suite tells cppunit which tests to run, as opposed to a fixture, which groups tests together logically. The common pattern is to give your fixture class a static method that builds a suite containing all of its tests. In the updated versions of ObjectPoolTest.h and ObjectPoolTest.cpp, the suite() method is used for this purpose:

```cpp
#include <cppunit/TestFixture.h>
#include <cppunit/TestSuite.h>
#include <cppunit/Test.h>
class ObjectPoolTest : public CppUnit::TestFixture
{
    public:
        void setUp();
        void tearDown();
        void testSimple();  // Our first test!
        static CppUnit::Test* suite();
};
```

Code snippet from ObjectPoolTest\ObjectPoolTest.h

```cpp
#include "ObjectPoolTest.h"
#include <cppunit/TestAssert.h>
#include <cppunit/TestCaller.h>
void ObjectPoolTest::setUp() { }
void ObjectPoolTest::tearDown() { }
```

```
void ObjectPoolTest::testSimple()
{
    CPPUNIT_ASSERT(0 < 1);
}
CppUnit::Test* ObjectPoolTest::suite()
{
    CppUnit::TestSuite* suiteOfTests =
            new CppUnit::TestSuite("ObjectPoolTest");
    suiteOfTests->addTest(new CppUnit::TestCaller<ObjectPoolTest>(
                                        "testSimple",
                                        &ObjectPoolTest::testSimple));
    return suiteOfTests; // Note that Test is a superclass of TestSuite
}
```

Code snippet from ObjectPoolTest\ObjectPoolTest.cpp

The template syntax for creating a `TestCaller` is a bit dense, but just about every single test you write will follow this exact pattern, so you can ignore the implementation of `TestSuite` and `TestCaller` for the most part.

To actually run the suite of tests and see the results, you will need a *test runner*. `cppunit` is a flexible framework. It contains several different runners that operate in different environments, such as the MFC Runner, which is designed to run within a program written with the Microsoft Foundation Classes. For a text-based environment, you should use the Text Runner, which is defined in the `CppUnit::TextUi` namespace.

The code to run the suite of tests defined by the `ObjectPoolTest` fixture follows. It creates a runner, adds the tests returned by the `suite()` method, and calls `run()`.

```
#include "ObjectPoolTest.h"
#include <cppunit/ui/text/TestRunner.h>
int main()
{
    CppUnit::TextUi::TestRunner runner;
    runner.addTest(ObjectPoolTest::suite());
    runner.run();
    return 0;
}
```

Code snippet from ObjectPoolTest\ObjectPoolTest.cpp

To compile and run these unit tests, you will need to download, build, and install `cppunit`. Please consult the `cppunit` documentation on their website for installation instructions specific to your platform. After `cppunit` is installed, the code can be built. For example, on Linux, this can be done as follows:

```
> export LD_LIBRARY_PATH=/usr/local/lib
> g++ -I/usr/local/include/cppunit -L/usr/local/lib -lcppunit \
    -ldl -std=C++0x *.cpp
```

See Bonus Chapter 2 on the website (www.wrox.com) for more information on the `-std=c++0x` flag.

This command is for a default `cppunit` installation on Linux using the GCC compiler. If you are working on another platform or with another compiler, please consult the `cppunit` website for instructions. After the code is compiled, linked, and run, you should see output similar to the following:

```
OK (1 tests)
```

If you modify the code to assert that 1 < 0, the test will fail; `cppunit` will report the failure as follows:

```
!!!FAILURES!!!
Test Results:
Run:  1    Failures: 1    Errors: 0
1) test: testSimple (F) line: 21 ObjectPoolTest.cpp
assertion failed
- Expression: 1 < 0
```

Note that by using the `CPPUNIT_ASSERT` macro, the framework was able to pinpoint the exact line on which the test failed — a useful piece of information for debugging.

Adding the Real Tests

Now that the framework is all set up and a simple test is working, it's time to turn your attention to the `ObjectPool` class and write some code that actually tests it. All of the following tests will be added to `ObjectPoolTest.h` and `ObjectPoolTest.cpp`, just like the earlier simple test.

Before you can write the tests, you'll need a helper object to use with the `ObjectPool` class. The `ObjectPool` creates *chunks* of objects of a certain type and hands them out to the caller as requested. Some of the tests will need to check if a retrieved object is the same as a previously retrieved object. One way to do this is to create a pool of serial objects — objects that have a monotonically increasing serial number. The following code defines such a class:

Available for download on Wrox.com

```cpp
#include <cstddef>  // For size_t
class Serial
{
    public:
        Serial();
        size_t getSerialNumber() const;
    protected:
        static size_t sNextSerial;
        size_t mSerialNumber;
};
```

Code snippet from ObjectPoolTest\Serial.h

Available for download on Wrox.com

```cpp
#include "Serial.h"
Serial::Serial()
{
    mSerialNumber = sNextSerial++; // A new object gets the next serial number.
}
```

```
size_t Serial::getSerialNumber() const
{
    return mSerialNumber;
}
size_t Serial::sNextSerial = 0;   // The first serial number is 0.
```

Code snippet from ObjectPoolTest\Serial.cpp

On to the tests! As an initial sanity check, you might want a test that creates an object pool. If any exceptions are thrown during creation, cppunit will report an error:

```
void ObjectPoolTest::testCreation()
{
    ObjectPool<Serial> myPool;
}
```

Code snippet from ObjectPoolTest\ObjectPoolTest.cpp

The next test is a *negative test* because it is doing something that *should* fail. In this case, the test tries to create an object pool with an invalid chunk size of 0. The object pool constructor should throw an exception. Normally, cppunit would catch the exception and report an error. However, since that is the desired behavior, the test catches the exception explicitly and sets a flag. The final step of the test is to assert that the flag was set. Thus, if the constructor does *not* throw an exception, the test will fail:

```
void ObjectPoolTest::testInvalidChunkSize()
{
    bool caughtException = false;
    try {
        ObjectPool<Serial> myPool(0);
    } catch (const invalid_argument& ex) {
        caughtException = true;  // OK. We were expecting an exception.
    }
    CPPUNIT_ASSERT(caughtException);
}
```

Code snippet from ObjectPoolTest\ObjectPoolTest.cpp

testAcquire() tests a specific piece of public functionality — the ability of the ObjectPool to give out an object. In this case, there is not much to assert. To prove validity of the resulting Serial reference, the test asserts that its serial number is greater than or equal to zero:

```
void ObjectPoolTest::testAcquire()
{
    ObjectPool<Serial> myPool;
    shared_ptr<Serial> serial = myPool.acquireObject();
    CPPUNIT_ASSERT(serial->getSerialNumber() >= 0);
}
```

Code snippet from ObjectPoolTest\ObjectPoolTest.cpp

The next test is a bit more interesting. The ObjectPool should not give out the same Serial object twice (unless it is explicitly released). This test checks the exclusivity property of the ObjectPool by creating a pool with a fixed chunk size and retrieving exactly that many objects. If the pool is properly dishing out unique objects, none of their serial numbers should match. Note that this test only covers objects created as part of a single chunk. A similar test for multiple chunks would be an excellent idea.

```
void ObjectPoolTest::testExclusivity()
{
    const size_t poolSize = 5;
    ObjectPool<Serial> myPool(poolSize);
    set<size_t> seenSerials;
    for (size_t i = 0; i < poolSize; i++) {
        shared_ptr<Serial> nextSerial = myPool.acquireObject();
        // Assert that this number hasn't been seen before.
        CPPUNIT_ASSERT(seenSerials.find(nextSerial->getSerialNumber()) ==
                       seenSerials.end());
        // Add this number to the set.
        seenSerials.insert(nextSerial->getSerialNumber());
    }
}
```

Code snippet from ObjectPoolTest\ObjectPoolTest.cpp

This implementation uses the set container from the STL. Consult Chapter 12 for details if you are unfamiliar with this container.

The final test (for now) checks the release functionality. Once an object is released, the ObjectPool can give it out again. The pool shouldn't create additional chunks until it has *recycled* all released objects. This test first retrieves a Serial from the pool and records its serial number. Then, the object is immediately released back into the pool. Next, objects are retrieved from the pool until either the original object is recycled (identified by its serial number) or the chunk has been used up. If the code gets all the way through the chunk without seeing the recycled object, the test fails.

```
void ObjectPoolTest::testRelease()
{
    const size_t poolSize = 5;
    ObjectPool<Serial> myPool(poolSize);
    shared_ptr<Serial> originalSerial = myPool.acquireObject();
    size_t originalSerialNumber = originalSerial->getSerialNumber();
    // Return the original object to the pool.
    myPool.releaseObject(originalSerial);
    // Now make sure that the original object is recycled before
    // a new chunk is created.
    bool wasRecycled = false;
    for (size_t i = 0; i < poolSize; i++) {
        shared_ptr<Serial> nextSerial = myPool.acquireObject();
        if (nextSerial->getSerialNumber() == originalSerialNumber) {
            wasRecycled = true;
```

```
            break;
        }
    }
    CPPUNIT_ASSERT(wasRecycled);
}
```

Code snippet from ObjectPoolTest\ObjectPoolTest.cpp

Once these tests are added to the suite, you should be able to run them, and they should all pass. Of course, if one or more tests fails, you are presented with the quintessential issue in unit tests — is it the test or the code that is broken?

Basking in the Glorious Light of Unit Test Results

The tests in the previous section should have given you a good idea of how to get started writing actual professional-quality tests for real code. It's just the tip of the iceberg though. The previous examples should help you think of additional tests that you could write for the `ObjectPool` class. For example, none of the tests deal with allocation of multiple chunks — there should definitely be coverage of that functionality. There also weren't complex tests that acquired and released the same object multiple times.

There is no end to the number of unit tests you could write for a given piece of code, and that's the best thing about unit tests. If you find yourself wondering how your code might react to a certain situation, that's a unit test. If a particular aspect of your subsystem seems to be presenting problems, increase unit test coverage of that particular area. Even if you simply want to put yourself in the client's shoes to see what it's like to work with your class, writing unit tests is a great way to get a different perspective.

HIGHER-LEVEL TESTING

While unit tests are the best first line of defense against bugs, they are only part of the larger testing process. Higher-level tests focus on how pieces of the product work together, as opposed to the relatively narrow focus of unit tests. In a way, higher-level tests are more challenging to write because it's less clear what tests need to be written. Yet, you cannot really claim that the program works until you have tested how its pieces work together.

Integration Tests

An *integration test* covers areas where components meet. Unlike a unit test, which generally acts on the level of a single class, an integration test usually involves two or more classes. Integration tests excel at testing interactions between two components, often written by two different programmers. In fact, the process of writing an integration test often reveals important incongruities in designs.

Sample Integration Tests

Since there are no hard-and-fast rules to determine what integration tests you should write, some examples might help you get a sense of when integration tests are useful. The following scenarios depict cases where an integration test is appropriate, but they do not cover every possible case. Just as with unit tests, over time you will refine your intuition for useful integration tests.

An XML-Based File Serializer

Suppose that your project includes a persistence layer that is used to save certain types of objects to disk and to read them back in. The hip way to serialize data is to use the XML format, so a logical breakdown of components might include an XML conversion layer sitting on top of a custom file API. Both of these components can be thoroughly unit tested. The XML layer would have unit tests that ensure that different types of objects are correctly converted to XML and populated from XML. The file API would have tests that read, write, update, and delete files on disk.

When these modules start to work together, integration tests are appropriate. At the very least, you should have an integration test that saves an object to disk through the XML layer, then reads it back in and does a comparison to the original. Because the test covers both modules, it is a basic integration test.

Readers and Writers to a Shared Resource

Imagine a program that contains a data space shared by different components. For example, a stock-trading program might have a queue of buy-and-sell requests. Components related to receiving stock transaction requests would add orders to the queue, and components related to performing stock trades would take data off the queue. You could unit test the heck out of the queue class, but until it is tested with the actual components that will be using it, you really don't know if any of your assumptions are wrong.

A good integration test would use the stock request components and the stock trade components as clients of the queue class. You would write some sample orders and make sure that they successfully entered and exited the queue through the client components.

Wrapper around a Third-Party Library

Integration tests do not always need to occur at integration points in your own code. Many times, integration tests are written to test the interaction between your code and a third-party library.

For example, you may be using a database connection library to talk to a relational database system. Perhaps you built an object-oriented wrapper around the library that adds support for connection caching or provides a friendlier interface. This is a very important integration point to test because, even though the wrapper probably provides a more useful interface to the database, it introduces possible misuse of the original library.

In other words, writing a wrapper is a good thing, but writing a wrapper that introduces bugs is going to be a disaster.

Methods of Integration Testing

When it comes to actually writing integration tests, there is often a fine line between integration and unit tests. If a unit test is modified so that it touches another component, is it suddenly an integration test? In a way, the answer is moot because a good test is a good test regardless of the type of test. We recommend that you use the concepts of integration and unit testing as two *approaches* to testing, but avoid getting caught up in labeling the category of every single test.

In terms of implementation, integration tests are often written by using a unit testing framework, further blurring their distinction. As it turns out, unit testing frameworks provide an easy way to write a yes/no test and produce useful results. Whether the test is looking at a single unit of functionality or the intersection of two components hardly makes a difference from the framework's point of view.

However, for performance and organizational reasons, you may wish to attempt to separate unit tests from integration tests. For example, your group may decide that everybody must run integration tests before checking in new code, but be a bit more lax on running unrelated unit tests. Separating the two types of tests also increases the value of results. If a test failure occurs within the XML class tests, it will be clear that it's a bug in that class, not in the interaction between that class and the file API.

System Tests

System tests operate at an even higher level than integration tests. These tests examine the program as a whole. System tests often make use of a *virtual user* that simulates a human being working with the program. Of course, the virtual user must be programmed with a script of actions to perform. Other system tests rely on scripts or a fixed set of inputs and expected outputs.

Much like unit and integration tests, an individual system test performs a specific test and expects a specific result. It is not uncommon to use system tests to make sure that different features work in combination with one another.

In theory, a fully system-tested program would contain a test for every permutation of every feature. This approach quickly grows unwieldy, but you should still make an effort to test many features in combination. For example, a graphics program could have a system test that imports an image, rotates it, performs a blur filter, converts it to black and white, and then saves it. The test would compare the saved image to a file that contains the expected result.

Unfortunately, few specific rules can be stated about system tests because they are highly dependent on the actual application. For applications that process files with no user interaction, system tests can be written much like unit and integration tests. For graphical programs, a virtual user approach may be best. For server applications, you might need to build stub clients that simulate network traffic. The important part is that you are actually testing real use of the program, not just a piece of it.

Regression Tests

Regression testing is more of a testing concept than a specific type of test. The idea is that once a feature works, developers tend to put it aside and assume that it will continue to work. Unfortunately, new features and other code changes often conspire to break previously working functionality.

Regression tests are often put in place as a sanity check for features that are, more or less, complete and working. If the regression test is well written, it will cease to pass when a change is introduced that breaks the feature.

If your company has an army of quality-assurance testers, regression testing may take the form of manual testing. The tester acts as a user would and goes through a series of steps, gradually testing every feature that worked in the previous release. This approach is thorough and accurate if carefully performed, but not particularly scalable.

At the other extreme, you could build a completely automated system that performs each function as a virtual user. This would be a scripting challenge, though several commercial and noncommercial packages exist to ease the scripting of various types of applications.

A middle ground is known as *smoke testing*. Some tests will only test the subset of the most important features that should work. The idea is that if something is broken, it should show up right away. If smoke tests pass, they could be followed by more rigorous manual or automated testing. The term *smoke testing* was introduced a long time ago, in electronics. After a circuit was built, with different components like vacuum tubes, resistors, etc., the question was, "Is it assembled correctly?" A solution was to "plug it in, turn it on, and see if smoke comes out." If smoke came out, the design might be wrong, or the assembly might be wrong. By seeing what part went up in smoke, the error could be determined.

Some bugs are like the dream where you show up for school in your underwear — they are both terrifying and recurring. Recurring bugs are frustrating and a poor use of engineering resources. Even if, for some reason, you decide not to write a suite of regression tests, you should *still* write regression tests for bugs that you fix.

By writing a test for a bug fix, you both prove that the bug is fixed and set up an alert that is triggered if the bug ever comes back (for example, if your change is rolled back or otherwise undone or if two branches are not merged correctly into the main development branch). When a regression test of a previously fixed bug fails, it should be easy to fix because the regression test can refer to the original bug number and describe how it was fixed the first time.

TIPS FOR SUCCESSFUL TESTING

As a software engineer, your role in testing may range anywhere from basic unit testing responsibility to complete management of an automated test system. Because testing roles and styles vary so much, we have assembled several tips from our experiences that may help you in various testing situations:

➤ Spend some time designing your automated test system. A system that runs constantly throughout the day will detect failures quickly. A system that sends emails to engineers automatically, or sits in the middle of the room loudly playing show tunes when a failure occurs, will result in increased visibility of problems.

➤ Don't forget about stress testing. Even though a full suite of unit tests passes for your database access class, it could still fall down when used by several dozen threads simultaneously. You should test your product under the most extreme conditions it could face in the real world.

➤ Test on a variety of platforms or a platform that closely mirrors the customer's system. One method of testing on multiple operating systems is to use a virtual machine environment that allows you to run several different operating systems on the same machine.

➤ Some tests can be written to intentionally inject faults in a system. For example, you could write a test that deletes a file while it is being read, or simulates a network outage during a network operation.

➤ Bugs and tests are closely related. Bug fixes should be proven by writing regression tests. The comment with a test should refer to the original bug number.

➤ Don't remove tests that are failing. When a co-worker is slaving over a bug and finds out you removed tests, he will come looking for you.

The most important tip we can give you is to remember that testing is a part of software development. If you agree with that and accept it before you start coding, it won't be quite as unexpected when the feature is finished, but there is still more work to do to prove that it works.

SUMMARY

This chapter has covered the basic information that all professional programmers should know about testing. Unit testing in particular is the easiest and most effective way to increase the quality of your own code. Higher-level tests provide coverage of use cases, synchronicity between modules, and protection against regressions. No matter what your role is with regard to testing, you should now be able to confidently design, create, and review tests at various levels.

Now that you know how to find bugs, it's time to learn how to fix them. To that end, Chapter 27 covers techniques and strategies for effective debugging.

27

Conquering Debugging

WHAT'S IN THIS CHAPTER?

➤ What the Fundamental Law of Debugging, and bug taxonomies are

➤ Tips for avoiding bugs

➤ How to plan for bugs

➤ The different kinds of memory errors

➤ How to use a debugger to pinpoint code causing a bug

Your code will contain bugs. Every professional programmer would like to write bug-free code, but the reality is that few software engineers succeed in this endeavor. As computer users know, bugs are endemic in computer software. The software that you write is probably no exception. Therefore, unless you plan to bribe your co-workers into fixing all your bugs, you cannot be a Professional C++ programmer without knowing how to debug C++ code. One factor that often distinguishes experienced programmers from novices is their debugging skills.

Despite the obvious importance of debugging, it is rarely given enough attention in courses and books. Debugging seems to be the type of skill that everyone wants you to know, but no one knows how to teach. This chapter attempts to provide you with concrete guidelines and techniques for debugging even the most galling problems.

The contents include an introduction to the Fundamental Law of Debugging and bug taxonomies, followed by tips for avoiding bugs. Techniques for planning for bugs include error logging, debug traces, and asserts. The chapter concludes with specific tips for debugging the problems that arise, including techniques for reproducing bugs, debugging reproducible bugs, debugging nonreproducible bugs, debugging memory errors, and debugging multithreaded programs. The chapter concludes with a step-by-step debugging example.

THE FUNDAMENTAL LAW OF DEBUGGING

The first rule of debugging is to be honest with yourself and admit that your program will contain bugs. This realistic assessment enables you to put your best effort into preventing bugs from crawling into your program in the first place while you simultaneously include the necessary features to make debugging as easy as possible.

 The Fundamental Law of Debugging: Avoid bugs when you're coding, but plan for bugs in your code.

BUG TAXONOMIES

A *bug* in a computer program is incorrect run-time behavior. This undesirable behavior includes both *catastrophic bugs* and *noncatastrophic bugs*. Examples of catastrophic bugs are program death, data corruption, operating system failures, or some other similarly horrific outcome. A catastrophic bug can also manifest itself external to the software or computer system running the software, for example, a piece of medical software might contain a catastrophic bug causing a massive radiation overdose to a patient. Noncatastrophic bugs are bugs that cause the program to behave incorrectly in more subtle ways, for example, a web browser might return the wrong web page, or a spreadsheet application might calculate the standard deviation of a column incorrectly.

There are also so-called *cosmetic bugs*, where something is visually not correct, but otherwise works correctly. For example, a button in a user interface is left-enabled when it shouldn't be, but clicking it does nothing. All computations are perfectly correct, the program does not crash, but it doesn't look as "nice" as it should.

The underlying cause, or *root cause*, of the bug is the mistake in the program that causes this incorrect behavior. The process of debugging a program includes both determining the root cause of the bug and fixing the code so that the bug will not occur again.

AVOIDING BUGS

It's impossible to write completely bug-free code, so debugging skills are important. However, a few tips can help you to minimize the number of bugs:

➤ **Read this book from cover to cover:** Learn the C++ language intimately, especially pointers and memory management. Then, recommend this book to your friends and coworkers so they avoid bugs too.

➤ **Design *before* you code:** Designing *while* you code tends to lead to convoluted designs that are harder to understand and are more error-prone. It also makes you more likely to omit possible edge cases and error conditions.

➤ **Use code reviews:** At least two people should look at every line of code that you write. Sometimes it takes a fresh perspective to notice problems.

➤ **Test, test, and test again:** Follow the guidelines in Chapter 26.

➤ **Expect error conditions, and handle them appropriately:** In particular, plan for and handle out-of-memory conditions. They will occur. See Chapter 10.

➤ **Last, and probably most important, use smart pointers to avoid memory leaks:** See Chapter 21 for details.

PLANNING FOR BUGS

Your programs should contain features that enable easier debugging when the inevitable bugs arise. This section describes these features and presents sample implementations that you can incorporate into your own programs.

Error Logging

Imagine this scenario: You have just released a new version of your flagship product, and one of the first users reports that the program "stopped working." You attempt to pry more information from the user, and eventually discover that the program died in the middle of an operation. The user can't quite remember what he was doing, or if there were any error messages. How will you debug this problem?

Now imagine the same scenario, but in addition to the limited information from the user, you are also able to examine the error log on the user's computer. In the log you see a message from your program that says "Error: unable to allocate memory." Looking at the code near the spot where that error message was generated, you find a line in which you dereferenced a pointer without checking for NULL. You've found the root cause of your bug!

Error logging is the process of writing error messages to persistent storage so that they will be available following an application, or even machine, death. Despite the example scenario, you might still have doubts about this strategy. Won't it be obvious by your program's behavior if it encounters errors? Won't the user notice if something goes wrong? As the preceding example shows, user reports are not always accurate or complete. In addition, many programs, such as the operating system kernel and long-running daemons like `inetd` or `syslogd` on Unix, are not interactive and run unattended on a machine. The only way these programs can communicate with users is through error logging.

Thus, your program should log errors as it encounters them. That way, if a user reports a bug, you will be able to examine the log files on the machine to see if your program reported any errors prior to encountering the bug. Unfortunately, error logging is platform dependent: C++ does not contain a standard logging mechanism. Examples of platform-specific logging mechanisms include the `syslog` facility in Unix and the event reporting API in Windows. You should consult the documentation for your development platform. There are also some open-source implementations of cross-platform logging classes, including `log4cpp`, available at `http://log4cpp.sourceforge.net/`.

Now that you're convinced that error logging is a great feature to add to your programs, you might be tempted to log error messages every few lines in your code, so that, in the event of any bug, you'll be able to trace the code path that was executing. These types of error messages are appropriately called "traces."

However, you should not write these traces to error logs for two reasons. First, writing to persistent storage is slow. Even on systems that write the logs asynchronously, logging that much information will slow down your program. Second, and most important, most of the information that you would put in your traces is not appropriate for the end user to see. It will just confuse the user, leading to unwarranted service calls. That said, tracing is an important debugging technique under the correct circumstances, as described in the next section.

Here are some specific guidelines for the types of errors your programs should log:

➤ Unrecoverable errors, such as an inability to allocate memory or a system call failing unexpectedly.

➤ Errors for which an administrator can take action, such as low memory, an incorrectly formatted data file, an inability to write to disk, or a network connection being down.

➤ Unexpected errors such as a code path that you never expected to take or variables with unexpected values. Note that your code should "expect" users to enter invalid data and should handle it appropriately. An unexpected error would represent a bug in your program.

➤ Potential security breaches such as a network connection attempted from an unauthorized address, or too many network connections attempted (denial of service).

Additionally, most APIs allow you to specify a *log level* or *error level*. You can log nonerror conditions under a log level that is less severe than "error." For example, you might want to log significant state changes in your application, or startup and shutdown of the program. You also might consider giving your users a way to adjust the log level of your program at run time so that they can customize the amount of logging that occurs.

Debug Traces

When debugging complicated problems, public error messages generally do not contain enough information. You often need a complete trace of the code path taken, or values of variables before the bug showed up. In addition to basic messages, it's sometimes helpful to include the following information in debug traces:

➤ The thread ID, if it's a multithreaded program

➤ The name of the function that generates the trace

➤ The name of the source file in which the code that generates the trace lives

You can add this tracing to your program through a special debug mode, or via a *ring buffer*. Both of these methods are explained in detail in the next sections.

Debug Mode

The first technique to add debug traces is to provide a debug mode for your program. In debug mode, the program writes trace output to standard error or to a file, and perhaps does extra checking during execution. There are several ways to add a debug mode to your program.

Compile-Time Debug Mode

You can use preprocessor #ifdefs to selectively compile the debug code into your program. The advantage of this method is that your debug code is not compiled into the "release" binary, and so does not increase its size. The disadvantages are that there is no way to enable debugging at a customer site for testing or following the discovery of a bug.

The rest of this section shows an example of a simple program instrumented with a compile-time debug mode. This program doesn't do anything useful: It is only for demonstrating the technique.

In order to generate a debug version of this program, it should be compiled with the symbol DEBUG_ MODE defined. Your compiler should allow you to define symbols during compilation; consult your compiler's documentation for details. For example, GCC allows you to specify -Dsymbol through the command-line; and Microsoft VC++ allows you to specify the symbols through the Visual Studio IDE, or if you use the VC++ command-line, /D symbol.

This example uses the C++11 variadic function template feature, which is discussed in Chapter 20. It also uses __func__, defined by the C++ standard, which is a function-local predefined variable with a definition similar to:

```
static const char __func__[] = "function-name";
```

If your compiler doesn't support this standard __func__ yet, you should check its documentation. Maybe it supports __FUNCTION__ instead, or something similar.

The code first defines a Logger class with a static public log() method. This class is only defined when the DEBUG_MODE symbol is defined. It also defines a helper macro to make it easy to log something. Logging something in this program should be done using this macro, because it will automatically remove all logging code when DEBUG_MODE is not defined. How exactly the macro is working is explained after the code.

The log file is opened, flushed and closed on each call to log(). This might lower performance a little bit; however, it does guarantee correct logging, which is more important.

Available for download on Wrox.com

```
#ifdef DEBUG_MODE
    class Logger
    {
        public:
            template<typename... Args>
            static void log(const Args&... args)
            {
                ofstream ofs(msDebugFileName, ios_base::app);
                if (ofs.fail()) {
                    cerr << "Unable to open debug file!" << endl;
                    return;
                }
                logHelper(ofs, args...);
                ofs << endl;
            }
        protected:
```

```
            template<typename T1>
            static void logHelper(ofstream& ofs, const T1& t1)
            {
                ofs << t1;
            }
            template<typename T1, typename... Tn>
            static void logHelper(ofstream& ofs, const T1& t1, const Tn&... args)
            {
                ofs << t1;
                logHelper(ofs, args...);
            }
            static const char* msDebugFileName;
    };
    const char* Logger::msDebugFileName = "debugfile.out";

    #define log(...) Logger::log(__func__, "(): ", __VA_ARGS__)
#else
    #define log(...)
#endif

class ComplicatedClass
{
    public:
        ComplicatedClass() {}
};
class UserCommand
{
    public:
        UserCommand() {}
};

ostream& operator<<(ostream& ostr, const ComplicatedClass& src);
ostream& operator<<(ostream& ostr, const UserCommand& src);
UserCommand getNextCommand(ComplicatedClass* obj);
void processUserCommand(UserCommand& cmd);
void trickyFunction(ComplicatedClass* obj) throw(exception);

int main(int argc, char* argv[])
{
#ifdef DEBUG_MODE
    // Print the command-line arguments to the trace
    for (int i = 0; i < argc; i++) {
        log(argv[i]);
    }
#endif
    ComplicatedClass obj;
    trickyFunction(&obj);
    // Rest of the function not shown
    return 0;
}
ostream& operator<<(ostream& ostr, const ComplicatedClass& src)
{
    ostr << "ComplicatedClass";
    return ostr;
}
```

```
ostream& operator<<(ostream& ostr, const UserCommand& src)
{
    ostr << "UserCommand";
    return ostr;
}
UserCommand getNextCommand(ComplicatedClass* obj)
{
    UserCommand cmd;
    return cmd;
}
void processUserCommand(UserCommand& cmd)
{
    // details omitted for brevity
}
void trickyFunction(ComplicatedClass* obj) throw(exception)
{
    log("given argument: ", *obj);
    for (size_t i = 0; i < 100; ++i) {
        UserCommand cmd = getNextCommand(obj);
        log("retrieved cmd ", i, ": ", cmd);
        try {
            processUserCommand(cmd);
        } catch (const exception& e) {
            log("received exception from processUserCommand(): ", e.what());
            throw;
        }
    }
}
```

Code snippet from CompileTimeDebugMode\CTDebug.cpp

This implementation uses the following macro:

```
#ifdef DEBUG_MODE
    #define log(...) Logger::log(__func__, "(): ", __VA_ARGS__)
#else
    #define log(...)
#endif
```

In debug mode, every call to log() in your code will be replaced with a call to the Logger::log() method. The macro automatically includes the function name, __func__, as first argument to the Logger::log() method.

When the DEBUG_MODE symbol is not defined, log() is defined as being empty, which will basically remove all log() calls in your code. For example, take the following line:

```
log("given argument: ", *obj);
```

If DEBUG_MODE is defined, the macro will replace this with:

```
Logger::log(__func__, "(): ", "given argument: ", *obj);
```

However, if DEBUG_MODE is not defined, the macro will replace the line with:

```
;
```

> Be careful not to put any code that must be executed for correct program functioning inside your log() calls. For example, a line like this is probably asking for trouble: log("Result: ", myFunctionCall()). If DEBUG_MODE is not defined, the preprocessor will strip all log() calls, which means the call to myFunctionCall() will be stripped as well.

> Macros in C++ should be avoided as much as possible because they can be hard to debug. However, for logging purposes, using a simple macro is acceptable and it makes using the logging code much easier.

Start-Time Debug Mode

Start-time debug mode is an alternative to #ifdefs that is just as simple to implement. A command-line argument to the program can specify whether it should run in debug mode. Unlike compile-time debug mode, this strategy includes the debug code in the "release" binary, and allows debug mode to be enabled at a customer site.

However, it still requires users to restart the program in order to run it in debug mode, which is not always an attractive alternative for customers, and which may prevent you from obtaining useful information about bugs.

The following example of start-time debug mode uses the same program as that shown for compile-time debug mode so that you can directly compare the differences. Changes are highlighted.

One aspect of this program needs further comment: There is no standard library functionality in C++ for parsing command-line arguments. This program uses a simple function isDebugSet() to check for the debug flag among all the command-line arguments, but a function to parse all command-line arguments would need to be more sophisticated.

```cpp
class Logger
{
    public:
        static void enableLogging(bool enable) { msLoggingEnabled = enable; }
        static bool isLoggingEnabled() { return msLoggingEnabled; }
        template<typename... Args>
        static void log(const Args&... args)
        {
            if (!msLoggingEnabled)
                return;
            ofstream ofs(msDebugFileName, ios_base::app);
            if (ofs.fail()) {
                cerr << "Unable to open debug file!" << endl;
                return;
            }
            logHelper(ofs, args...);
```

```
                ofs << endl;
            }
    protected:
        template<typename T1>
        static void logHelper(ofstream& ofs, const T1& t1)
        {
            ofs << t1;
        }
        template<typename T1, typename... Tn>
        static void logHelper(ofstream& ofs, const T1& t1, const Tn&... args)
        {
            ofs << t1;
            logHelper(ofs, args...);
        }
        static const char* msDebugFileName;
        static bool msLoggingEnabled;
};
const char* Logger::msDebugFileName = "debugfile.out";
bool Logger::msLoggingEnabled = false;

#define log(...) Logger::log(__func__, "(): ", __VA_ARGS__)

class ComplicatedClass
{
    public:
        ComplicatedClass() {}
};
class UserCommand
{
    public:
        UserCommand() {}
};

bool isDebugSet(int argc, char* argv[]);
ostream& operator<<(ostream& ostr, const ComplicatedClass& src);
ostream& operator<<(ostream& ostr, const UserCommand& src);
UserCommand getNextCommand(ComplicatedClass* obj);
void processUserCommand(UserCommand& cmd);
void trickyFunction(ComplicatedClass* obj) throw(exception);

int main(int argc, char* argv[])
{
    Logger::enableLogging(isDebugSet(argc, argv));
    if (Logger::isLoggingEnabled()) {
        // Print the command-line arguments to the trace
        for (int i = 0; i < argc; i++) {
            log(argv[i]);
        }
    }
    ComplicatedClass obj;
    trickyFunction(&obj);
    // Rest of the function not shown
    return 0;
}
```

```
bool isDebugSet(int argc, char* argv[])
{
    for (int i = 0; i < argc; i++) {
        if (strcmp(argv[i], "-d") == 0) {
            return true;
        }
    }
    return false;
}
ostream& operator<<(ostream& ostr, const ComplicatedClass& src)
{
    ostr << "ComplicatedClass";
    return ostr;
}
ostream& operator<<(ostream& ostr, const UserCommand& src)
{
    ostr << "UserCommand";
    return ostr;
}
UserCommand getNextCommand(ComplicatedClass* obj)
{
    UserCommand cmd;
    return cmd;
}
void processUserCommand(UserCommand& cmd)
{
    // details omitted for brevity
}
void trickyFunction(ComplicatedClass* obj) throw(exception)
{
    log("given argument: ", *obj);
    for (size_t i = 0; i < 100; ++i) {
        UserCommand cmd = getNextCommand(obj);
        log("retrieved cmd ", i, ": ", cmd);
        try {
            processUserCommand(cmd);
        } catch (const exception& e) {
            log("received exception from processUserCommand(): ", e.what());
            throw;
        }
    }
}
```

Code snippet from StartTimeDebugMode\STDebug.cpp

There are two ways to run this application:

```
> STDebug
> STDebug -d
```

Debug mode will be activated only when the -d argument is specified on the command line.

Run-Time Debug Mode

The most flexible way to provide a debug mode is to allow it to be enabled or disabled at run time. One way to provide this feature is to supply an asynchronous interface that controls debug mode on-the-fly. In a GUI program, this interface could take the form of a menu command. In a CLI (Command Line Interface) program, this interface could be an asynchronous command that makes an interprocess call into the program (using sockets, signals, or remote procedure calls for example). C++ provides no standard way to perform interprocess communication or GUIs, so an example of this technique is not shown.

Ring Buffers

Debug mode is useful for debugging reproducible problems and for running tests. However, bugs often appear when the program is running in nondebug mode, and by the time you or the customer enables debug mode, it is too late to gain any information about the bug. One solution to this problem is to enable tracing in your program at all times. You usually need only the most recent traces to debug a program, so you should store only the most recent traces at any point in a program's execution. One way to provide this limitation is through careful use of log file rotations.

However, in order to avoid the problems with logging traces described earlier in the "Error Logging" section, it is better if your program doesn't log these traces continuously to disk; instead it should store them in memory. Then, it should provide a mechanism to dump all the trace messages to standard error or to a log file if the need arises.

A common technique is to use a *ring buffer* to store a fixed number of messages, or messages in a fixed amount of memory. When the buffer fills up, it starts writing messages at the beginning of the buffer again, overwriting the older messages. This cycle can repeat indefinitely. The following sections provide an implementation of a ring buffer and show you how you can use it in your programs.

Ring Buffer Interface

The following `RingBuffer` class provides a simple debug ring buffer. The client specifies the number of entries in the constructor and adds messages with the `addEntry()` method. Once the number of entries exceeds the number allowed, new entries overwrite the oldest entries in the buffer.

The buffer also provides the option to print entries as they are added to the buffer. The client can specify an output stream in the constructor, and can reset it with the `setOutput()` method.

Finally, the buffer supports streaming to an output stream.

```
class RingBuffer
{
    public:
        // Constructs a ring buffer with space for numEntries.
        // Entries are written to *ostr as they are queued.
        RingBuffer(size_t numEntries = kDefaultNumEntries,
            ostream* ostr = nullptr);
```

```
        virtual ~RingBuffer();
        // Adds the string to the ring buffer, possibly overwriting the
        // oldest string in the buffer (if the buffer is full).
        void addEntry(const string& entry);
        // Streams the buffer entries, separated by newlines, to ostr.
        friend ostream& operator<<(ostream& ostr, const RingBuffer& rb);
        // Sets the output stream to which entries are streamed as they are added.
        // Returns the old output stream.
        ostream* setOutput(ostream* newOstr);
    protected:
        vector<string> mEntries;
        ostream* mOstr;
        size_t mNumEntries, mNext;
        bool mWrapped;
        static const size_t kDefaultNumEntries = 500;
};
```

Code snippet from RingBuffer\RingBuffer.h

Ring Buffer Implementation

This implementation of the ring buffer stores a fixed number of strings. Each of these strings must be copied into the ring buffer, requiring dynamic allocation of memory. This approach certainly is not the most efficient solution. Other possibilities would be to provide a fixed number of bytes of memory for the buffer. However, that requires mucking with low-level C-strings and memory management, which you should avoid whenever possible. This implementation should be sufficient unless you're writing a high-performance application.

This ring buffer uses the STL vector to store the string entries. The use of the STL is straightforward except for the implementation of operator<< for the RingBuffer, which employs some fancy iterators. Consult Chapters 11 through 17 for details on the STL.

```
// Initialize the vector to hold exactly numEntries. The vector size
// does not need to change during the lifetime of the object.
// Initialize the other members.
RingBuffer::RingBuffer(size_t numEntries, ostream* ostr) : mEntries(numEntries),
    mOstr(ostr), mNumEntries(numEntries), mNext(0), mWrapped(false)
{
}
RingBuffer::~RingBuffer()
{
}
// The addEntry algorithm is pretty simple: add the entry to the next
// free spot, then reset mNext to indicate the free spot after
// that. If mNext reaches the end of the vector, it starts over at 0.
//
// The buffer needs to know if the buffer has wrapped or not so
// that it knows whether to print the entries past mNext in operator<<
void RingBuffer::addEntry(const string& entry)
{
    // Add the entry to the next free spot and increment
    // mNext to point to the free spot after that.
```

```
        mEntries[mNext++] = entry;
        // Check if we've reached the end of the buffer. If so, we need to wrap.
        if (mNext >= mNumEntries) {
            mNext = 0;
            mWrapped = true;
        }
        // If there is a valid ostream, write this entry to it.
        if (mOstr != nullptr) {
            *mOstr << entry << endl;
        }
    }
    ostream* RingBuffer::setOutput(ostream* newOstr)
    {
        ostream* ret = mOstr;
        mOstr = newOstr;
        return ret;
    }
    // operator<< uses an ostream_iterator to "copy" entries directly
    // from the vector to the output stream.
    //
    // operator<< must print the entries in order. If the buffer has wrapped,
    // the earliest entry is one past the most recent entry, which is the entry
    // indicated by mNext. So first print from entry mNext to the end.
    //
    // Then (even if the buffer hasn't wrapped) print from the beginning to mNext-1.
    ostream& operator<<(ostream& ostr, const RingBuffer& rb)
    {
        if (rb.mWrapped) {
            // If the buffer has wrapped, print the elements from
            // the earliest entry to the end.
            copy(rb.mEntries.begin() + rb.mNext, rb.mEntries.end(),
                ostream_iterator<string>(ostr, "\n"));
        }
        // Now, print up to the most recent entry.
        // Go up to begin() + mNext because the range is not inclusive on the
        // right side.
        copy(rb.mEntries.begin(), rb.mEntries.begin() + rb.mNext,
            ostream_iterator<string>(ostr, "\n"));
        return ostr;
    }
```

Code snippet from RingBuffer\RingBuffer.cpp

Using the Ring Buffer

In order to use the ring buffer, you can declare an object and start adding messages to it. When you want to print the buffer, just use `operator<<` to print it to the appropriate `ostream`. Here is the earlier start-time debug mode program modified to show use of a ring buffer instead:

```
RingBuffer debugBuf;

class ComplicatedClass
{
    public:
```

```cpp
        ComplicatedClass() {}
};
class UserCommand
{
    public:
        UserCommand() {}
};

ostream& operator<<(ostream& ostr, const ComplicatedClass& src);
ostream& operator<<(ostream& ostr, const UserCommand& src);
UserCommand getNextCommand(ComplicatedClass* obj);
void processUserCommand(UserCommand& cmd);
void trickyFunction(ComplicatedClass* obj) throw(exception);

int main(int argc, char* argv[])
{
    // Print the command-line arguments.
    for (int i = 0; i < argc; i++) {
        debugBuf.addEntry(argv[i]);
    }
    ComplicatedClass obj;
    trickyFunction(&obj);
    // Print the current contents of the debug buffer to cout.
    cout << debugBuf;
    return 0;
}
ostream& operator<<(ostream& ostr, const ComplicatedClass& src)
{
    ostr << "ComplicatedClass";
    return ostr;
}
ostream& operator<<(ostream& ostr, const UserCommand& src)
{
    ostr << "UserCommand";
    return ostr;
}
UserCommand getNextCommand(ComplicatedClass* obj)
{
    UserCommand cmd;
    return cmd;
}
void processUserCommand(UserCommand& cmd)
{
    // Details omitted for brevity
}
void trickyFunction(ComplicatedClass* obj) throw(exception)
{
    // Trace log the values with which this function starts.
    ostringstream ostr;
    ostr << __func__ << "(): given argument: " << *obj;
    debugBuf.addEntry(ostr.str());
    for (size_t i = 0; i < 100; ++i) {
        UserCommand cmd = getNextCommand(obj);
```

```
        ostringstream ostr;
        ostr << __func__ << "(): retrieved cmd " << cmd;
        debugBuf.addEntry(ostr.str());
        try {
            processUserCommand(cmd);
        } catch (const exception& e) {
            string msg = __func__;
            msg += "(): received exception from processUserCommand():";
            msg += e.what();
            debugBuf.addEntry(msg);
            throw;
        }
    }
}
```

Code snippet from RingBuffer\RingBufferTest.cpp

Note that this interface to the ring buffer sometimes requires you to construct strings by using `ostringstream`s or `string` concatenation before adding entries to the buffer. The following section explains how you can avoid this.

C++11 ## Ring Buffer with Variadic Function Template

To avoid the need to use `ostringstream`s or `string` concatenation, you can use the C++11 variadic function template feature, discussed in Chapter 20. The new `RingBuffer` definition is as follows. Comments have been removed to save space.

```
class RingBuffer
{
    public:
        RingBuffer(size_t numEntries = kDefaultNumEntries,
            ostream* ostr = nullptr);
        virtual ~RingBuffer();
        template<typename... Args>
        void addEntry(const Args&... args)
        {
            ostringstream os;
            addEntryHelper(os, args...);
            addStringEntry(os.str());
        }
        friend ostream& operator<<(ostream& ostr, const RingBuffer& rb);
        ostream* setOutput(ostream* newOstr);
    protected:
        vector<string> mEntries;
        ostream* mOstr;
        size_t mNumEntries, mNext;
        bool mWrapped;
        static const size_t kDefaultNumEntries = 500;
        template<typename T1>
        void addEntryHelper(ostringstream& os, const T1& t1)
        {
            os << t1;
        }
```

```
template<typename T1, typename... Tn>
void addEntryHelper(ostringstream& os, const T1& t1, const Tn&... args)
{
    os << t1;
    addEntryHelper(os, args...);
}
void addStringEntry(const string& entry);
};
```

Code snippet from RingBufferVariadicTemplates\RingBuffer.h

The implementation of this new `RingBuffer` class is identical to the first version, except for the following line:

```
void RingBuffer::addEntry(const string& entry)
```

In the new implementation, this line should be changed to:

`void RingBuffer::addStringEntry(const string& entry)`

This new ring buffer is used a little bit differently compared to the first version, but the result is much more readable and more compact. The new `trickyFunction()` implementation is as follows:

```
void trickyFunction(ComplicatedClass* obj) throw(exception)
{
    // trace log the values with which this function starts
    debugBuf.addEntry(__func__, "(): given argument: ", *obj);
    for (size_t i = 0; i < 100; ++i) {
        UserCommand cmd = getNextCommand(obj);
        debugBuf.addEntry(__func__, "(): retrieved cmd ", cmd);
        try {
            processUserCommand(cmd);
        } catch (const exception& e) {
            debugBuf.addEntry(__func__,
                "(): received exception from processUserCommand():", e.what());
            throw;
        }
    }
}
```

Code snippet from RingBufferVariadicTemplates\RingBufferTest.cpp

There is no need any more for using `ostringstream`s or `string` concatenation. You can call the `addEntry()` variadic method template and specify as many arguments as you want. Since this is using the C++11 variadic template feature, this variable argument method is completely type-safe. Variadic templates are discussed in detail in Chapter 20.

Displaying the Ring Buffer Contents

Storing trace debug messages in memory is a great start, but in order for them to be useful, you need a way to access these traces for debugging.

Your program should provide a "hook" to tell it to print the messages. This hook could be similar to the interface you would use to enable debugging at run time. Additionally, if your program encounters a fatal error that causes it to exit, it should print the ring buffer to standard error or to a log file before exiting.

Another way to retrieve these messages is to obtain a memory dump of the program. Each platform handles memory dumps differently, so you should consult a book or expert on your platform.

Asserts

The <cassert> library defines an assert macro. It takes a Boolean expression and, if the expression evaluates to false, prints an error message and terminates the program. If the expression evaluates to true, it does nothing.

 You should try to avoid any library functions or macros that can terminate your program. It's recommended to write your own assert function or macro that, for example, throws an exception, or in which you handle failed asserts in a way that suits your application, without terminating the program. However, the <cassert> library is sometimes used, so you need to know about its existence.

Although the behavior of an assert may not sound particularly helpful, it turns out to be quite useful in some cases. It allows you to "force" your program to exhibit a bug at the exact point where that bug originates. If you didn't assert at that point, your program might proceed with those incorrect values, and the bug might not show up until much later. Thus, asserts allow you to detect bugs earlier than you otherwise would. Though, as said in the previous warning, it's highly recommended to write your own version of assert that does not terminate the application.

 The behavior of the standard assert macro depends on the NDEBUG preprocessor symbol: If the symbol is not defined, the assertion takes place, otherwise it is ignored. Compilers often define this symbol when compiling "release" builds. If you want to leave asserts in release builds, you must change your compiler settings, or, as recommended, write your own version of assert that isn't affected by the value of NDEBUG.

You could use asserts in your code whenever you are "assuming" something about the state of your variables. For example, if you call a library function that is supposed to return a pointer and claims never to return nullptr, throw in an assert after the function call to make sure that the pointer isn't nullptr.

Note that you should assume as little as possible. For example, if you are writing a library function, don't assert that the parameters are valid. Instead, check the parameters and return an error code or throw an exception if they are invalid.

For example, in the start-time debugging example, the function `trickyFunction()` takes a parameter of type `ComplicatedClass*`. Instead of assuming that the argument is valid, it might be a good idea to assert it like this:

```
void trickyFunction(ComplicatedClass* obj) throw(exception)
{
    assert(obj != nullptr);
    // Remainder of the function omitted for brevity
}
```

 Be careful not to put any code that must be executed for correct program functioning inside asserts. For example, a line like this is probably asking for trouble: `assert(myFunctionCall() != nullptr)`. *If a release build of your code strips asserts, then the call to* `myFunctionCall()` *will be stripped as well.*

C++11 Static Asserts

The asserts discussed in the previous section are evaluated at run time. C++11 introduces the `static_assert` feature, which is an assert that is evaluated at compile time.

A `static_assert` requires two parameters: an expression to evaluate and a string. When the expression evaluates to `false`, the compiler will issue an error that contains the given string. A simple example is to check `INT_MAX`:

```
static_assert(INT_MAX >= 0x7FFFFFFF,
    "Code requires INT_MAX to be at least 0x7FFFFFFF.");
```

If you compile this with a compiler where `INT_MAX` is less than `0x7FFFFFFF`, the compiler will issue an error that looks as follows:

```
test.cpp(3): error C2338: Code requires INT_MAX to be at least 0x7FFFFFFF.
```

Another example where `static_asserts` are pretty powerful is in combination with type traits. Type traits are discussed in Chapter 20. For example, if you write a function template or class template, you could use `static_asserts` together with type traits to issue compiler errors when template types don't satisfy certain conditions.

The following example requires that the template type for the `process()` function template has `Base1` as its base class:

Available for download on Wrox.com

```
#include <type_traits>
using namespace std;

class Base1 {};
class Base1Child : public Base1 {};
class Base2 {};
```

```
class Base2Child : public Base2 {};

template<typename T>
void process(const T& t)
{
    static_assert(is_base_of<Base1, T>::value, "Base1 should be a base for T.");
}
int main()
{
    process(Base1());
    process(Base1Child());
    //process(Base2());        // Error
    //process(Base2Child());   // Error
    return 0;
}
```

Code snippet from StaticAssert\StaticAssert.cpp

If you try to call the process() function template with an instance of Base2 or Base2Child, the compiler will issue an error that looks as follows:

```
1>test.cpp(13): error C2338: Base1 should be a base for T.
1>          test.cpp(21) : see reference to function template
1>          instantiation 'void process<Base2>(const T &)' being compiled
1>          with
1>          [
1>              T=Base2
1>          ]
```

DEBUGGING TECHNIQUES

Debugging a program can be incredibly frustrating. However, with a systematic approach it becomes significantly easier. Your first step in trying to debug a program should always be to reproduce the bug. Depending on whether or not you can reproduce the bug, your subsequent approach will differ. The next three sections explain how to reproduce bugs, how to debug reproducible bugs, and how to debug nonreproducible bugs. Additional sections explain details about debugging memory errors and debugging multithreaded programs.

Reproducing Bugs

If you can reproduce the bug consistently, it will be much easier to determine the root cause. Finding the root cause of bugs that are not reproducible is difficult, if not impossible.

As a first step to reproduce the bug, run the program with exactly the same inputs as the run when the bug first appeared. Be sure to include all inputs, from the program's startup to the time of the bug's appearance. A common mistake is to attempt to reproduce the bug by performing only the triggering action. This technique may not reproduce the bug because the bug might be caused by an entire sequence of actions.

For example, if your web browser program dies when you request a certain web page, it may be due to memory corruption triggered by that particular request's network address. On the other hand, it may be because your program records all requests in a queue, with space for one million entries, and this entry was number one million and one. Starting the program over and sending one request certainly wouldn't trigger the bug in that case.

Sometimes it is impossible to emulate the entire sequence of events that leads to the bug. Perhaps the bug was reported by someone who can't remember everything that he or she did. Alternatively, maybe the program was running for too long to emulate every input. In that case, do your best to reproduce the bug. It takes some guesswork, and can be time-consuming, but effort at this point will save time later in the debugging process. Here are some techniques you can try:

➤ Repeat the triggering action in the correct environment and with as many inputs as possible similar to the initial report.

➤ Run automated tests that exercise similar functionality. Reproducing bugs is one benefit of automated tests. If it takes 24 hours of testing before the bug shows up, it's preferable to let those tests run on their own rather than spend 24 hours of your time trying to reproduce it.

➤ If you have the necessary hardware available, running slight variations of tests concurrently on different machines can sometimes save time.

➤ Run stress tests that exercise similar functionality. If your program is a web server that died on a particular request, try running as much browsers as possible simultaneously that make that request.

After you are able to reproduce the bug consistently, you should attempt to find the smallest sequence that triggers the bug. You can start with the minimum sequence, containing only the triggering action, and slowly expand the sequence to cover the entire sequence from startup, until the bug is triggered. This will result in the simplest and most efficient test case to reproduce it, which makes it simpler to find the root cause of the problem, and easier to verify the fix.

Debugging Reproducible Bugs

When you can reproduce a bug consistently and efficiently, it's time to figure out the problem in the code that causes the bug. Your goal at this point is to find the exact lines of code that trigger the problem. You can use two different strategies:

1. **Logging debug messages:** By adding enough debug messages to your program and watching its output when you reproduce the bug, you should be able to pinpoint the exact lines of code where the bug occurs. If you have a debugger at your disposal, adding debug messages is usually not recommended because it requires modifications to the program and can be time-consuming. However, if you have already instrumented your program with debug messages as described earlier, you might be able to find the root cause of your bug by running your program in debug mode while reproducing the bug.

2. **Using a debugger:** Hopefully you are familiar with debuggers, which allow you to step through the execution of your program and to view the state of memory and the values of

variables at various points. If you have not yet used debuggers, you should learn to use them as soon as possible. They are often indispensable tools for finding the root cause of bugs. When you have access to the source code, you will use a *symbolic debugger*: a debugger that utilizes the variable names, class names, and other symbols in your code. In order to use a symbolic debugger you must instruct your compiler to generate debug symbols.

The debugging example at the end of this chapter demonstrates both these approaches.

Debugging Nonreproducible Bugs

Fixing bugs that are not reproducible is significantly more difficult than fixing reproducible bugs. You often have very little information and must employ a lot of guesswork. Nevertheless, a few strategies can aid you:

1. Try to turn a nonreproducible bug into a reproducible bug. By using educated guesses, you can often determine approximately where the bug lies. It's worthwhile to spend some time trying to reproduce the bug. Once you have a reproducible bug you can figure out its root cause by using the techniques described earlier.

2. Analyze error logs. Easily done if you have instrumented your program with error log generation as described earlier. You should sift through this information because any errors that were logged directly before the bug occurred are likely to have contributed to the bug itself. If you're lucky (or if you coded your program well), your program will have logged the exact reason for the bug at hand.

3. Obtain and analyze traces. Again, easily done if you have instrumented your program with tracing output, for example via a ring buffer as described earlier. At the time of the bug's occurrence, you hopefully obtained a copy of the traces. These traces should lead you right to the location of the bug in your code.

4. Examine a *memory dump* file, if it exists. Some platforms generate memory dump files of applications that terminate abnormally. On Unix and Linux these memory dumps are called *core files*. Each platform provides tools for analyzing these memory dumps. They can, for example, be used to generate a stack trace of the application, or to view the contents of its memory before the application died.

5. Inspect the code. Unfortunately, this is often the only strategy to determine the cause of a nonreproducible bug. Surprisingly, it often works. When you examine code, even code that you wrote yourself, with the perspective of the bug that just occurred, you can often find mistakes that you overlooked previously. We don't recommend spending hours staring at your code, but tracing through the code path by hand will often lead you directly to the problem.

6. Use a memory-watching tool, such as one of those described in the "Debugging Memory Problems" section, which follows. Such tools will often alert you to memory errors that don't always cause your program to misbehave, but could potentially be the cause of the bug at hand.

7. File or update a bug report. Even if you can't find the root cause of the bug right away, the report will be a useful record of your attempts if the problem is encountered again. Consult Chapter 26 for details on bug-tracking systems.

Once you have found the root cause of a nonreproducible bug, you should create a reproducible test case and move it to the "reproducible bugs" category. It is important to be able to reproduce a bug before you actually fix it. Otherwise, how will you test the fix? A common mistake when debugging nonreproducible bugs is to fix the wrong problem in the code. Because you can't reproduce the bug, you don't know if you've really fixed it, so don't be surprised when it shows up again a month later.

Debugging Memory Problems

Most catastrophic bugs, such as application death, are caused by memory errors. Many noncatastrophic bugs are triggered by memory errors as well. Some memory bugs are obvious: If your program attempts to dereference a `nullptr` pointer, the default action is to terminate the program. However, nearly every platform gives you the capability of responding to catastrophic errors and taking remedial action. The amount of effort you devote to this depends on the importance of this kind of recovery to your end users. For example, a text editor really needs to make a best-attempt to save the modified buffers (possibly under a "recovered" name), while for other programs, users can find the default behavior acceptable, even if it is unpleasant.

Some memory bugs are more insidious. If you write past the end of an array in C++, your program will probably not crash directly at that point. However, if that array was on the stack, you may have written into a different variable or array, changing values that won't show up until later in the program. Alternatively, if the array was on the heap, you could cause memory corruption in the heap, which will cause errors later when you attempt to allocate or free more memory dynamically.

Chapter 21 introduces some of the common memory errors from the perspective of what to avoid when you're coding. This section discusses memory errors from the perspective of identifying problems in code that exhibits bugs. You should be familiar with the discussion in Chapter 21 before continuing with this section.

Categories of Memory Errors

In order to debug memory problems you should be familiar with the types of errors that can occur. This section describes the major categories of memory errors. Each memory error includes a small code example demonstrating the error and a list of possible *symptoms* that you might observe. Note that a symptom is not the same thing as a bug itself: A symptom is an observable behavior caused by a bug.

Memory Freeing Errors

The following table summarizes five major errors involving freeing memory.

ERROR TYPE	SYMPTOMS	EXAMPLE
| Memory leak | Process memory usage grows over time. Process runs slower over time. Eventually, operations and system calls fail because of lack of memory. | ```cpp
void memoryLeak()
{
    int* p = new int[1000];
    return; // BUG! Not freeing p.
}
``` |
| Using mismatched allocation and free operations | Does not usually cause a program crash immediately. Can cause memory corruption on some platforms, which might show up as a program crash (segmentation violation) later in the program. | ```cpp
void mismatchedFree()
{
    int* p1 = (int*)malloc(sizeof(int));
    int* p2 = new int;
    int* p3 = new int[1000];
    delete p1;    // BUG! Should use free
    delete[] p2;  // BUG! Should use delete
    free(p3);     // BUG! Should use delete[]
}
``` |
| Freeing memory more than once | Can cause a program crash (segmentation violation) if the memory at that location has been handed out in another allocation between the two calls to delete. | ```cpp
void doubleFree()
{
    int* p1 = new int[1000];
    delete[] p1;
    int* p2 = new int[1000];
    delete[] p1; // BUG! freeing p1 twice
}
``` |
| Freeing unallocated memory | Will usually cause a program crash (segmentation violation or bus error). | ```cpp
void freeUnallocated()
{
    int* p = reinterpret_cast<int*>(10000);
    delete p; // BUG! p not a valid pointer.
}
``` |

continues

(*continued*)

ERROR TYPE	SYMPTOMS	EXAMPLE
| Freeing stack memory | Technically a special case of freeing unallocated memory. Will usually cause a program crash. | ```cpp
void freeStack()
{
    int x;
    int* p = &x;
    delete p; // BUG! Freeing stack memory
}
``` |

As you can see, some of the memory free errors do not cause immediate program termination. These bugs are more subtle, leading to problems later in the run of the program.

 Most of the preceding problems can be avoided by using smart pointers instead of dumb pointers. Smart pointers are discussed in Chapter 21.

Memory Access Errors

The second category of memory errors involves the actual reading and writing of memory.

ERROR TYPE	SYMPTOMS	EXAMPLE
| Accessing Invalid Memory | Almost always causes program to crash immediately. | ```cpp
void accessInvalid()
{
    int* p = reinterpret_cast<int*>(10000);
    *p = 5; // BUG! p is not a valid pointer.
}
``` |
| Accessing Freed Memory | Does not usually cause a program crash.<br><br>If the memory has been handed out in another allocation, can cause "strange" values to appear unexpectedly. | ```cpp
void accessFreed()
{
    int* p1 = new int;
    delete p1;
    int* p2 = new int;
    *p1 = 5; // BUG! The memory pointed to
             // by p1 has been freed.
}
``` |
```

ERROR TYPE	SYMPTOMS	EXAMPLE

Accessing Memory in a Different Allocation	Does not cause a program crash. Can cause "strange" values to appear unexpectedly.	```cpp
		void accessElsewhere()
		{
		    int x, y[10], z;
		    x = 0;
		    z = 0;
		    for (int i = 0; i <= 10; i++) {
		        y[i] = 5; // BUG for i==10! element 10
		                  // is past end of array.
		    }
		}
		``

Reading Uninitialized Memory	Does not cause a program crash unless you use the uninitialized value as a pointer and dereference it (as in the example). Even then, it will not always cause a program crash.	```cpp
		void readUninitialized()
		{
		    int* p;
		    cout << *p; // BUG! p is uninitialized
		}
		``

Memory access errors are more likely than memory free errors to cause program crashes. However, they don't always do so. They can instead lead to subtle errors, in which the program does not terminate but instead produces erroneous results. Erroneous results can lead to serious consequences, for example when external devices (such as robotic arms, X-ray machines, radiation treatments, life support systems, etc.) are being controlled by the computer.

Note that the discussed symptoms for memory freeing errors and memory access errors are the default symptoms for release builds of your program. Debug builds will most likely behave differently, and when run inside a debugger, the debugger might break into the code when an error occurs.

Tips for Debugging Memory Errors

Memory-related bugs often show up in slightly different places in the code each time you run the program. This is usually the case with heap memory corruption. Heap memory corruption is like a time bomb, ready to explode at some attempt to allocate, free, or use memory on the heap. So, when you see a bug that is reproducible, but shows up in slightly different places, suspect memory corruption.

If you suspect a memory bug, your best option is to use a memory-checking tool for C++. Debuggers often provide options to run the program while checking for memory errors. Additionally, there are some excellent third-party tools such as *purify* from Rational Software (now owned by IBM) or *valgrind* for Linux (discussed in Chapter 21). Microsoft provides a free download called *Application Verifier* which can be used in a Windows environment. It is a run-time verification tool to help you in finding subtle programming errors like the previously discussed memory errors. These debuggers and tools work by interposing their own memory allocation and freeing routines in order to check for any misuse of dynamic memory, such as freeing unallocated memory, dereferencing unallocated memory, or writing off the end of an array.

If you don't have a memory-checking tool at your disposal, and the normal strategies for debugging are not helping, you may need to resort to code inspection. Here are some specific items to look for, once you've narrowed down the part of the code containing the bug.

Object and Class-related Errors

➤ Verify that your classes with dynamically allocated memory have destructors that free exactly the memory that's allocated in the object: no more, and no less.

➤ Ensure that your classes handle copying and assignment correctly with copy constructors and assignment operators, as described in Chapter 7.

➤ Check for suspicious casts. If you are casting a pointer to an object from one type to another, make sure that it's valid. When possible, use `dynamic_casts`.

General Memory Errors

➤ Make sure that every call to `new` is matched with exactly one call to `delete`. Similarly, every call to `malloc`, `alloc`, or `calloc` should be matched with one call to `free`. And every call to `new[]` should be matched with one call to `delete[]`. To avoid double freeing memory or using freed memory, it's recommended to set your pointer to `nullptr` after freeing its memory.

➤ Check for buffer overruns. Anytime you iterate over an array or write into or read from a C-style string, verify that you are not accessing memory past the end of the array. These problems can often be avoided by using STL containers and strings.

➤ Check for dereferencing of invalid pointers.

➤ When declaring a pointer on the stack, make sure you always initialize it as part of its declaration, for example:

```
T* p = nullptr;
```
or
```
T* p = new T;
```
but never:
```
T* p;
```

➤ Similarly, make sure your classes always initialize pointer data members in their constructors, by either allocating memory in the constructor or setting the pointers to `nullptr`.

Debugging Multithreaded Programs

C++11 includes a threading library that provides mechanisms for threading and synchronization between threads. This threading library is discussed in Chapter 22. Multithreaded C++ programs are common, so it is important to think about the special issues involved in debugging a multithreaded program. Bugs in multithreaded programs are often caused by variations in timings in the operating system scheduling, and can be difficult to reproduce. Thus, debugging multithreaded programs takes a special set of techniques:

1. **Use message-based debugging:** When debugging multithreaded programs, message-based debugging can be more effective than using a debugger. Depending on your application, you can implement message-based debugging by writing messages to `cout`, a log file, a GUI control and so on. Add debug statements to your program before and after critical sections, and before acquiring and after releasing locks. Often by watching this output, you will be able to detect deadlocks and race conditions because you will be able to see that two threads are in a critical section at the same time or that one thread is stuck waiting for a lock.

2. **Insert forced sleeps and context switches:** If you are having trouble reproducing the problem consistently, or have a hunch about the root cause but want to verify it, you can force certain thread-scheduling behavior by making your threads sleep for specified amounts of time. The C++11 `<thread>` header defines `sleep_until()` and `sleep_for()` in the `std::this_thread` namespace, which you can use to sleep. Sleeping for several seconds right before releasing a lock, immediately before signaling a condition variable, or directly before accessing shared data can reveal race conditions that would otherwise go undetected. If this debugging technique reveals the root cause, it must be fixed, so that it works correctly after removing these forced sleeps and context switches. Leaving these forced sleeps and context switches in place to 'fix' the problem is wrong.

Debugging Example: Article Citations

This section presents a buggy program and shows you the steps to take in order to debug it and fix the problem.

Suppose that you're part of a team writing a web page that allows users to search for the research articles that cite a particular paper. This type of service is useful for authors who are trying to find work similar to their own. Once they find one paper representing a related work, they can look for every paper that cites that one to find other related work.

In this project, you are responsible for the code that reads the raw citations data from text files. For simplicity, assume that the citation info for each paper is found in its own file. Furthermore, assume that the first line of each file contains the author, title, and publication info for the paper; the second line is always empty; and all subsequent lines contain the citations from the article (one on each line). Here is an example file for one of the most important papers in Computer Science:

```
Alan Turing,"On Computable Numbers with an Application to the Entscheidungsproblem",
Proceedings of the London Mathematical Society, Series 2, Vol.42 (1936 - 37) pages
230 to 265.

Godel, "Uber formal unentscheidbare Satze der Principia Mathernatica und verwant der
Systeme, I", Monatshefte Math. Phys., 38 (1931). 173-198.
Alonzo Church. "An unsolvable problem of elementary number theory", American J of
Math., 58(1936), 345 363.
```

Alonzo Church. "A note on the Entscheidungsproblem", J. of Symbolic logic, 1 (1930), 40 41.
Cf. Hobson, "Theory of functions of a real variable (2nd ed., 1921)", 87, 88.
Proc. London Math. Soc (2) 42 (1936 7), 230 265.

Buggy Implementation of an ArticleCitations Class

You decide to structure your program by writing an `ArticleCitations` class that reads the file and stores the information. This class stores the article info from the first line in one string, and the citations' info in an array of strings. Please note that this design decision is not the best possible. You should opt for one of the STL containers to store the citations. However, for the purpose of illustrating buggy applications, it's perfect. The class definition looks like this:

```cpp
#include <string>
using std::string;
class ArticleCitations
{
    public:
        ArticleCitations(const string& fileName);
        virtual ~ArticleCitations();
        ArticleCitations(const ArticleCitations& src);
        ArticleCitations& operator=(const ArticleCitations& rhs);
        string getArticle() const { return mArticle; }
        size_t getNumCitations() const { return mNumCitations; }
        string getCitation(size_t i) const { return mCitations[i]; }
    protected:
        void readFile(const string& fileName);
        string mArticle;
        string* mCitations;
        size_t mNumCitations;
};
```

Code snippet from ArticleCitations\FirstAttempt\ArticleCitations.h

The implementation follows. This program is buggy! Don't use it verbatim or as a model.

```cpp
ArticleCitations::ArticleCitations(const string& fileName)
{
    // All we have to do is read the file.
    readFile(fileName);
}
ArticleCitations::ArticleCitations(const ArticleCitations& src)
{
    // Copy the article name, author, etc.
    mArticle = src.mArticle;
    // Copy the number of citations.
    mNumCitations = src.mNumCitations;
    // Allocate an array of the correct size.
    mCitations = new string[mNumCitations];
    // Copy each element of the array.
    for (size_t i = 0; i < mNumCitations; i++) {
        mCitations[i] = src.mCitations[i];
    }
}
```

```
ArticleCitations& ArticleCitations::operator=(const ArticleCitations& rhs)
{
    // Check for self-assignment.
    if (this == &rhs) {
        return *this;
    }
    // Free the old memory.
    delete [] mCitations;
    // Copy the article name, author, etc.
    mArticle = rhs.mArticle;
    // Copy the number of citations.
    mNumCitations = rhs.mNumCitations;
    // Allocate a new array of the correct size.
    mCitations = new string[mNumCitations];
    // Copy each citation.
    for (size_t i = 0; i < mNumCitations; i++) {
        mCitations[i] = rhs.mCitations[i];
    }
    return *this;
}
ArticleCitations::~ArticleCitations()
{
    delete [] mCitations;
}
void ArticleCitations::readFile(const string& fileName)
{
    // Open the file and check for failure.
    ifstream istr(fileName.c_str());
    if (istr.fail()) {
        throw invalid_argument("Unable to open file");
    }
    // Read the article author, title, etc. line.
    getline(istr, mArticle);
    // Skip the white space before the citations start.
    istr >> ws;
    size_t count = 0;
    // Save the current position so we can return to it.
    ios_base::streampos citationsStart = istr.tellg();
    // First count the number of citations.
    while (!istr.eof()) {
        string temp;
        getline(istr, temp);
        // Skip white space before the next entry.
        istr >> ws;
        count++;
    }
    if (count != 0) {
        // Allocate an array of strings to store the citations.
        mCitations = new string[count];
        mNumCitations = count;
        // Seek back to the start of the citations.
        istr.seekg(citationsStart);
```

```
        // Read each citation and store it in the new array.
        for (count = 0; count < mNumCitations; count++) {
            string temp;
            getline(istr, temp);
            mCitations[count] = temp;
        }
    }
}
```

Code snippet from ArticleCitations\FirstAttempt\ArticleCitations.cpp

Testing the ArticleCitations class

Following the advice of Chapter 26, you decide to unit test your `ArticleCitations` class before proceeding, though for simplicity in this example, the unit test does not use a test framework. The following program asks the user for a filename, constructs an `ArticleCitations` class with that filename, and passes the object by value to the `processCitations()` function, which prints out the info using the public accessor methods on the object.

```
#include "ArticleCitations.h"
#include <iostream>
using namespace std;
void processCitations(ArticleCitations cit);
int main()
{
    string fileName;
    while (true) {
        cout << "Enter a file name (\"STOP\" to stop): ";
        cin >> fileName;
        if (fileName == "STOP") {
            break;
        }
        // Test constructor
        ArticleCitations cit(fileName);
        processCitations(cit);
    }
    return 0;
}
void processCitations(ArticleCitations cit)
{
    cout << cit.getArticle() << endl;
    size_t num = cit.getNumCitations();
    for (size_t i = 0; i < num; i++) {
        cout << cit.getCitation(i) << endl;
    }
}
```

Code snippet from ArticleCitations\ArticleCitationsTest.cpp

Message-Based Debugging

You decide to test the program on the Alan Turing example (stored in a file called `paper1.txt`). Here is the output:

```
Enter a file name ("STOP" to stop): paper1.txt
Alan Turing."On Computable Numbers with an Application to the Entscheidungsproblem",
Proceedings of the London Mathematical Society, Series 2, Vol.42 (1936 - 37) pages
230 to 265.




Enter a file name ("STOP" to stop): STOP
```

That doesn't look right. There are supposed to be five citations printed instead of five blank lines.

For this bug, you decide to try message-based debugging, and since this is a console example, you decide to print messages to `cout`. In this case, it makes sense to start by looking at the function that reads the citations from the file. If that doesn't work right, then obviously the object won't have the citations. You can modify `readFile()` as follows:

```cpp
void ArticleCitations::readFile(const string& fileName)
{
    // Code omitted for brevity
    // First count the number of citations.
    cout << "readFile(): counting number of citations" << endl;
    while (!istr.eof()) {
        string temp;
        getline(istr, temp);
        // Skip white space before the next entry.
        istr >> ws;
        cout << "Citation " << count << ": " << temp << endl;
        count++;
    }
    cout << "Found " << count << " citations" << endl;
    cout << "readFile(): reading citations" << endl;
    if (count != 0) {
        // Allocate an array of strings to store the citations.
        mCitations = new string[count];
        mNumCitations = count;
        // Seek back to the start of the citations.
        istr.seekg(citationsStart);
        // Read each citation and store it in the new array.
        for (count = 0; count < mNumCitations; count++) {
            string temp;
            getline(istr, temp);
            cout << temp << endl;
            mCitations[count] = temp;
        }
    }
}
```

Running the same test on this program gives the following output:

```
Enter a file name ("STOP" to stop): paper1.txt
readFile(): counting number of citations
Citation 0: Godel, "Uber formal unentscheidbare Satze der Principia Mathernatica und
verwant der Systeme, I", Monatshefte Math. Phys., 38 (1931). 173-198.
Citation 1: Alonzo Church. "An unsolvable problem of elementary number theory",
American J of Math., 58(1936), 345 363.
Citation 2: Alonzo Church. "A note on the Entscheidungsproblem", J. of Symbolic
logic, 1 (1930), 40 41.
Citation 3: Cf. Hobson, "Theory of functions of a real variable (2nd ed., 1921)",
87, 88.
Citation 4: Proc. London Math. Soc (2) 42 (1936 7), 230 265.
Found 5 citations
readFile(): reading citations
[ 5 empty lines omitted for brevity ]
Alan Turing,"On Computable Numbers with an Application to the Entscheidungsproblem",
Proceedings of the London Mathematical Society, Series 2, Vol.42 (1936 - 37) pages
230 to 265.
[ 5 empty lines omitted for brevity ]
Enter a file name ("STOP" to stop): STOP
```

As you can see from the output, the first time the program reads the citations from the file, in order to count them, they are read correctly. However, the second time, they are not read correctly. Why not? One way to delve deeper into this issue is to add some debugging code to check the state of the file stream after each attempt to read a citation:

```cpp
void printStreamState(const istream& istr)
{
    if (istr.good()) {
        cout << "stream state is good" << endl;
    }
    if (istr.bad()) {
        cout << "stream state is bad" << endl;
    }
    if (istr.fail()) {
        cout << "stream state is fail" << endl;
    }
    if (istr.eof()) {
        cout << "stream state is eof" << endl;
    }
}
void ArticleCitations::readFile(const string& fileName)
{
    // Code omitted for brevity
    // First count the number of citations.
    cout << "readFile(): counting number of citations" << endl;
    while (!istr.eof()) {
        string temp;
        getline(istr, temp);
        // Skip white space before the next entry.
        istr >> ws;
        printStreamState(istr);
        cout << "Citation " << count << ": " << temp << endl;
```

```
                count++;
        }
        cout << "Found " << count << " citations" << endl;
        cout << "readFile(): reading citations" << endl;
        if (count != 0) {
            // Allocate an array of strings to store the citations.
            mCitations = new string[count];
            mNumCitations = count;
            // Seek back to the start of the citations.
            istr.seekg(citationsStart);
            // Read each citation and store it in the new array.
            for (count = 0; count < mNumCitations; count++) {
                string temp;
                getline(istr, temp);
                printStreamState(istr);
                cout << temp << endl;
                mCitations[count] = temp;
            }
        }
    }
}
```

Code snippet from ArticleCitations\CoutDebugging\ArticleCitations.cpp

When you run your program this time, you find some interesting information:

```
Enter a file name ("STOP" to stop): paper1.txt
readFile(): counting number of citations
stream state is good
Citation 0: Godel, "Uber formal unentscheidbare Satze der Principia Mathernatica und
verwant der Systeme, I", Monatshefte Math. Phys., 38 (1931). 173-198.
stream state is good
Citation 1: Alonzo Church. "An unsolvable problem of elementary number theory",
American J of Math., 58(1936), 345 363.
stream state is good
Citation 2: Alonzo Church. "A note on the Entscheidungsproblem", J. of Symbolic
logic, 1 (1930), 40 41.
stream state is good
Citation 3: Cf. Hobson, "Theory of functions of a real variable (2nd ed., 1921)",
87, 88.
stream state is eof
Citation 4: Proc. London Math. Soc (2) 42 (1936 7), 230 265.
Found 5 citations
readFile(): reading citations
stream state is fail
stream state is eof
stream state is fail
stream state is eof
stream state is fail
stream state is eof
stream state is fail
stream state is eof
stream state is fail
stream state is eof
```

```
Alan Turing,"On Computable Numbers with an Application to the Entscheidungsproblem",
Proceedings of the London Mathematical Society, Series 2, Vol.42 (1936 - 37) pages
230 to 265.
[ 5 empty lines omitted for brevity ]
Enter a file name ("STOP" to stop):
```

It looks like the stream state is good until after the final citation is read for the first time. Then, the stream state is eof, because the end-of-file has been reached. That is expected. What is not expected is that the stream state is both fail and eof after all attempts to read the citations a second time. That doesn't appear to make sense at first: The code uses seekg() to seek back to the beginning of the citations before reading them a second time, so the file shouldn't still be at the end.

However, Chapter 15 explains that streams maintain their error and eof states until you clear them explicitly. seekg() doesn't clear the eof state automatically. When in an error or eof state, streams fail to read data correctly, which explains why the stream state is fail also after trying to read the citations a second time. A closer look at your method reveals that it fails to call clear() on the istream after reaching the end of the file. If you modify the method by adding a call to clear(), it will read the citations properly.

Here is the corrected readFile() method without the debugging cout statements:

```
void ArticleCitations::readFile(const string& fileName)
{
    // Code omitted for brevity
    if (count != 0) {
        // Allocate an array of strings to store the citations.
        mCitations = new string[count];
        mNumCitations = count;
        // Clear the previous eof.
        istr.clear();
        // Seek back to the start of the citations.
        istr.seekg(citationsStart);
        // Read each citation and store it in the new array.
        for (count = 0; count < mNumCitations; count++) {
            string temp;
            getline(istr, temp);
            mCitations[count] = temp;
        }
    }
}
```

Code snippet from ArticleCitations\AfterCoutDebugging\ArticleCitations.cpp

Using the GDB Debugger on Linux

Now that your ArticleCitations class seems to work well on one citations file, you decide to blaze ahead and test some special cases, starting with a file with no citations. The file looks like this, and is stored in a file named paper2.txt:

```
Author with no citations
```

When you try to run your program on this file, you get the following result:

```
Enter a file name ("STOP" to stop): paper1.txt
[ correct output of reading paper1.txt omitted for brevity ]
Enter a file name ("STOP" to stop): paper2.txt
Author with no citations
Segmentation fault (core dumped)
```

The segmentation fault means that the program crashed. This time you decide to give the debugger a shot. The Gnu DeBugger (gdb) is widely available on Unix and Linux platforms. First, you must compile your program with debugging info (-g with g++). After that, you can launch the program under gdb. Here's an example session using the debugger to find the root cause of this problem. This example assumes your compiled executable is called buggyprogram. Text that you have to type is shown in bold.

```
> gdb buggyprogram
[ Start-up messages omitted for brevity ]
Reading symbols from /home/marc/c++/gdb/buggyprogram...done.
(gdb) run
Starting program: buggyprogram
Enter a file name ("STOP" to stop): paper1.txt
[ correct output of reading paper1.txt omitted for brevity ]
Enter a file name ("STOP" to stop): paper2.txt
Program received signal SIGSEGV, Segmentation fault.
0x06a87bdc in std::basic_string<char, std::char_traits<char>, std::allocator<char>
>::assign(std::basic_string<char, std::char_traits<char>, std::allocator<char> >
const&) () from /usr/lib/libstdc++.so.6
(gdb)
```

When the program crashes, the debugger breaks the execution, and allows you to poke around in the state of the program at that time. The bt command shows the current stack trace. Such a stack trace shows the last operation at the top, with frame number zero, #0:

```
(gdb) bt
#0  0x06a87bdc in std::basic_string<char, std::char_traits<char>, std::::
allocator<char> >::assign(std::basic_string<char, std::char_traits<char>, std::::
allocator<char> > const&) () from /usr/lib/libstdc++.so.6
#1  0x06a87cb5 in std::basic_string<char, std::char_traits<char>, std::::
allocator<char> >::operator=(std::basic_string<char, std::char_traits<char>, std::::
allocator<char> > const&) () from /usr/lib/libstdc++.so.6
#2  0x080492ba in ArticleCitations::ArticleCitations (this=0xbffff2c4, src=...) at
ArticleCitations.cpp:24
#3  0x080499ba in main (argc=1, argv=0xbffff384) at ArticleCitationsTest.cpp:20
```

When you get a stack trace like this, you should try to find the first stack frame from the top that is in your own code. In this example, this is stack frame #2. From this frame you can see that there seems to be some sort of problem in the ArticleCitations copy constructor. This copy constructor is invoked because the main() function calls processCitations() and the argument is passed by value. Of course, in production code you should pass a const reference, but pass-by-value is used for this example of a buggy program. You can tell the debugger to switch to stack frame #2 with the up command, which requires an argument specifying how many frames to go up:

```
(gdb) up 2
#2  0x080492ba in ArticleCitations::ArticleCitations (this=0xbffff2c4, src=...) at
ArticleCitations.cpp:24
24          mCitations[i] = src.mCitations[i];
```

This output shows that the following line caused a problem:

```
mCitations[i] = src.mCitations[i];
```

Now, use the `list` command to show the code in the current stack frame around the offending line:

```
(gdb) list
19          mNumCitations = src.mNumCitations;
20          // Allocate an array of the correct size
21          mCitations = new string[mNumCitations];
22          // Copy each element of the array
23          for (size_t i = 0; i < mNumCitations; i++) {
24            mCitations[i] = src.mCitations[i];
25          }
26      }
27
28      ArticleCitations& ArticleCitations::operator=(const ArticleCitations& rhs)
```

In gdb, you can print values available in the current scope with the `print` command. In order to find the root cause of the problem, you can try printing some of the object member variables. The error happens inside the copy constructor, so checking the value of the `src` parameter is a good start:

```
(gdb) print src
$3 = (const ArticleCitations &) @0xbffff2b4: {mArticle = "Author with no citations",
mCitations = 0x804c00c, mNumCitations = 5}
```

Ah-ha! Here's the problem. This article isn't supposed to have any citations. Why is `mNumCitations` set to 5? Take another look at the code in `readFile()` for the case that there are no citations. In that case, it looks like it never initializes `mNumCitations` and `mCitations`! They are left with whatever junk is already in those memory locations. In this case, the previous `ArticleCitations` object had the value 5 in `mNumCitations`. The second `ArticleCitations` object must have been placed in the same location in memory and so received that same value. You need to initialize `mCitations` and `mNumCitations`, whether or not you actually find any citations in the file. Here is the fixed code:

```
void ArticleCitations::readFile(const string& fileName)
{
    // Code omitted for brevity
    mCitations = nullptr;
    mNumCitations = 0;
    if (count != 0) {
        // Allocate an array of strings to store the citations.
        mCitations = new string[count];
        mNumCitations = count;
        // Clear the previous eof.
        istr.clear();
```

```
            // Seek back to the start of the citations.
            istr.seekg(citationsStart);
            // Read each citation and store it in the new array.
            for (count = 0; count < mNumCitations; count++) {
                string temp;
                getline(istr, temp);
                mCitations[count] = temp;
            }
        }
    }
```

Code snippet from ArticleCitations\FinalVersion\ArticleCitations.cpp

As this example shows, memory errors don't always show up right away. It often takes a debugger and some persistence to figure them out.

 If you attempt to replicate this debugging session on a different platform, you may find that, due to the vagaries of memory errors, the program crashes in a different place than this example shows.

Using the Code::Blocks Debugger

The previous section gives a demonstration of how you can use the popular gdb debugger on Linux. This is a command-line debugger. Code::Blocks on the other hand is a free open-source graphical IDE (Integrated Development Environment), which includes a debugger. Basically, Code::Blocks is a graphical user interface on top of the GCC compiler and the gdb debugger, and is available for several different platforms. This section demonstrates how you can use this graphical debugger to debug the same ArticleCitations example from the previous section.

This example assumes that Code::Blocks is installed properly on your system. Consult the Code::Blocks website for instructions. The first thing you have to do is start Code::Blocks and create a new project. Select Console Application as your new project type and click on the Go button. You will be asked if you want to use C or C++; choose C++ and continue. On the next page of the wizard you need to specify a name for the new project. Choose "ArticleCitations" and select the folder where you want Code::Blocks to save your new project. On the last page of the wizard you need to select your C++ compiler. Select GNU GCC Compiler and click the Finish button. Code:: Blocks will now create your new project.

Once the project has been created, you will see a Management tree on the left. This tree contains your source code files. Initially it contains a file called main.cpp. Delete that file from the list. Then right-click the ArticleCitations project in the Management tree and choose Add Files. Add ArticleCitations.cpp and ArticleCitations.h from the DebuggerDebugging folder in the downloadable code archive, and add ArticleCitationsTest.cpp. Figure 27-1 shows how the Management tree should look after this step.

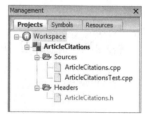

FIGURE 27-1

Now you can compile the project by choosing Build from the Build menu. If everything was set up correctly, the compilation should succeed without errors.

To test the application you first need to copy `paper1.txt` and `paper2.txt` to the `ArticleCitations` project folder. The two text files should be in the same folder as the `ArticleCitations.cbp` Code::Blocks project file. To start debugging the program, click on Debug and then Start. First, type `paper1.txt` and press enter. The paper1 citations will be shown. Next, type `paper2.txt` and press enter. The application crashes and Code::Blocks will

automatically break into the debugger. To find out where the crash happened, go to the Debug menu, click on Debugging Windows and then on Call Stack. This will show you the call stack at the time of the crash. This call stack might look like Figure 27-2.

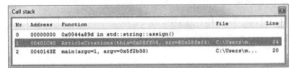

FIGURE 27-2

> If you run this on a different platform, your call stack might look different due to the vagaries of memory errors.

The first frame that is in your code is frame #1, the `ArticleCitations` copy constructor. When you double-click that frame, Code::Blocks will jump to it, and will mark the current source code line with a little arrow on the left like in Figure 27-3.

FIGURE 27-3

From this, you notice that the following assignment is causing the problem:

```
mCitations[i] = src.mCitations[i];
```

At the bottom of the Code::Blocks window there should be a Debugger tab that looks like Figure 27-4.

In this Debugger tab you can type gdb commands like in the previous section. To debug the crash in the copy constructor, you can inspect the `src` parameter by typing the following in the Debugger tab:

FIGURE 27-4

```
print src
```

From the output you will see that `mNumCitations` is five. However, paper2 doesn't have any citations so `mNumCitations` should be zero. The reason and the fix is exactly the same as in the previous section.

Using the Visual C++ 2010 Debugger

This section explains the same debugging procedure as described in the previous section, but uses the Microsoft Visual C++ 2010 debugger instead of Code::Blocks.

First, you need to create a project. Start VC++ and click on File ⇨ New ⇨ Project. In the project template tree on the left, select Visual C++ ⇨ Win32. Then select the Win32 Console Application template in the list in the middle of the window. At the bottom you can give a name for the project and a location where to save it. Specify ArticleCitations as the name, choose a folder where to save the project, and click the OK button. A wizard will open. Click the Next button, select Empty Project, and click Finish.

Once your new project is loaded, you can see a list of project files in the Solution Explorer. If this docking window is not visible, go to View ⇨ Solution Explorer. Right click the ArticleCitations project in the Solution Explorer and click Add ⇨ Existing Item. Add all the files from the `ArticleCitations\VisualStudio` folder in the downloadable code archive to the project. Your Solution Explorer should look similar to Figure 27-5.

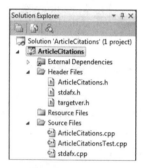

FIGURE 27-5

Now you can compile the program; click on Build ⇨ Build Solution.

Copy the `paper1.txt` and `paper2.txt` test files to your ArticleCitations project folder, which is the folder containing the `ArticleCitations.vcxproj` file.

Run the application with Debug ⇨ Start Debugging, and test the program by first specifying the `paper1.txt` file. It should properly read the file and output the result to the console. Then, type `paper2.txt`, which causes the VC++ debugger to break the execution. You will get a message saying "Unhandled exception" in which you need to click the Break button.

At this point, you should inspect the call stack, Debug ⇨ Windows ⇨ Call Stack. In this call stack, you need to find the first line that contains code that you wrote. This is shown in Figure 27-6.

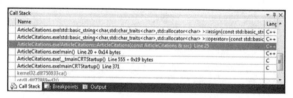

FIGURE 27-6

Just as with gdb and Code::Blocks, you see that the problem is in the ArticleCitations copy constructor. You can double click that line in the call stack window to jump to the right place in the code. Then click on Debug ⇨ Windows ⇨ Autos to inspect variables. In the list of variables you can find the `src` parameter. Click on the plus sign to expand the data members of the `src` variable. Figure 27-7 shows how it looks.

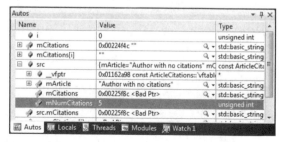

FIGURE 27-7

From this window, you see that `src.mNumCitations` is five, while it should be zero. The reason and the fix is exactly the same as earlier.

Lessons from the ArticleCitations Example

You might be inclined to disregard this example as too small to be representative of real debugging. Although the buggy code is not lengthy, many classes that you write will not be much bigger, even in large projects. Thus, this example corroborates the message from Chapter 26 about the importance of unit testing. Imagine if you had failed to test this example thoroughly before integrating it with the rest of the project. If these bugs showed up later, you and other engineers would have to spend more time narrowing down the problem before you could debug it as shown here. Additionally, the techniques shown in this example apply to all debugging, large scale or small.

SUMMARY

The most important concept in this chapter was the Fundamental Law of Debugging: *Avoid bugs when you're coding, but plan for bugs in your code.* The reality of programming is that bugs will appear. If you've prepared your program properly, with error logging, debug traces, asserts, and static asserts, then the actual debugging will be significantly easier.

In addition to these techniques, this chapter also presented specific approaches for debugging bugs. The most important rule when actually debugging is to reproduce the problem. Then, you can use message-based debugging or a symbolic debugger to track down the root cause. Memory errors present particular difficulties, and account for the majority of bugs in C++ code. This chapter described the various categories of memory bugs and their symptoms, and showed examples of debugging errors in a program.

28

Incorporating Design Techniques and Frameworks

WHAT'S IN THIS CHAPTER?

➤ An overview of C++ language features that are common but involve easy-to-forget syntax

➤ What the double dispatch technique is and how to use it

➤ How to use mix-in classes

➤ What frameworks are

One of the major themes of this book has been the adoption of reusable techniques and patterns. As a programmer, you tend to face similar problems repeatedly. With an arsenal of diverse approaches, you can save yourself time by applying the proper technique to a given problem.

A *design technique* is a standard approach for solving a particular problem in C++. Often, a design technique aims to overcome an annoying feature or language deficiency. Other times, a design technique is a piece of code that you use in many different programs to solve a common C++ problem.

This chapter focuses on design techniques — C++ idioms that aren't necessarily built-in parts of the language, but are nonetheless frequently used. The first part of this chapter covers the language features in C++ that are common but involve easy-to-forget syntax. Most of this material is a review, but it is a useful reference tool when the syntax escapes you. The topics covered include:

➤ Starting a class from scratch

➤ Extending a class with a subclass

➤ Throwing and catching exceptions

➤ Reading from a file

➤ Writing to a file

➤ Defining a template class

The second part of this chapter focuses on higher-level techniques that build upon C++ language features. These techniques offer a better way to accomplish everyday programming tasks. Topics include:

➤ The double dispatch technique

➤ Mix-in classes

This chapter concludes with an introduction to frameworks, a coding technique that greatly eases the development of large applications.

"I CAN NEVER REMEMBER HOW TO ..."

Chapter 1 compares the size of the C standard to the size of the C++ standard. It is possible, and somewhat common, for a C programmer to memorize the entire C language. The keywords are few, the language features are minimal, and the behaviors are well defined. This is not the case with C++. Even the authors of this book need to look things up. With that in mind, this section presents examples of coding techniques that are used in almost all C++ programs. When you remember the concept but forget the syntax, turn to these pages for a refresher.

... Write a Class

Don't remember how to get started? No problem — here is the definition of a simple class:

```cpp
#ifndef _simple_h_
#define _simple_h_
// A simple class that illustrates class definition syntax.
class Simple
{
    public:
        Simple();                           // Constructor
        virtual ~Simple();                  // Destructor
        virtual void publicMethod();        // Public method
        int mPublicInteger;                 // Public data member
    protected:
        int mProtectedInteger;              // Protected data member
        static const int mConstant = 2;     // Protected constant
        static int sStaticInt;              // Protected static data member
    private:
        int mPrivateInteger;                // Private data member
        // Disallow assignment and pass-by-value
        Simple(const Simple& src);
        Simple& operator=(const Simple& rhs);
};
#endif
```

Code snippet from Simple\Simple.h

Note that this class definition shows what is possible. However, in your own class definitions, you should try to avoid having `public` data members. Instead, you should make them `protected` and provide `public` getter and setter methods. You should also try to minimize `private` data members, and instead opt for `protected` data members so that you don't prevent subclasses from using them. You can make the copy constructor and assignment operator `private` to prevent assignment and pass-by-value.

Next, here is the implementation, including the initialization of the static data member:

Available for download on Wrox.com

```cpp
#include "Simple.h"
int Simple::sStaticInt = 0;    // Initialize static data member.
Simple::Simple()
{
    // Implementation of constructor
}
Simple::~Simple()
{
    // Implementation of destructor
}
void Simple::publicMethod()
{
    // Implementation of public method
}
```

Code snippet from Simple\Simple.cpp

Note that with C++11, you can initialize `sStaticInt` within the class definition as explained in Chapter 6.

Chapters 6 and 7 provide all the details for writing your own classes.

... Subclass an Existing Class

To subclass, you declare a new class that is a *public* extension of another class. Here is the definition for a sample subclass called `SubSimple`:

Available for download on Wrox.com

```cpp
#ifndef _subsimple_h_
#define _subsimple_h_
#include "Simple.h"
// A subclass of the Simple class
class SubSimple : public Simple
{
    public:
        SubSimple();                    // Constructor
        virtual ~SubSimple();           // Destructor
        virtual void publicMethod();    // Overridden method
        virtual void anotherMethod();   // Added method
};
#endif
```

Code snippet from Simple\SubSimple.h

The implementation:

```
#include "SubSimple.h"
SubSimple::SubSimple() : Simple()
{
    // Implementation of constructor
}
SubSimple::~SubSimple()
{
    // Implementation of destructor
}
void SubSimple::publicMethod()
{
    // Implementation of overridden method
}
void SubSimple::anotherMethod()
{
    // Implementation of added method
}
```

Code snippet from Simple\SubSimple.cpp

Consult Chapter 8 for details on inheritance techniques.

... Throw and Catch Exceptions

If you've been working on a team that doesn't use exceptions (for shame!) or if you've gotten used to Java-style exceptions, the C++ syntax may escape you. Here's a refresher, which uses the built-in exception class `std::runtime_error`. In most large programs, you will write your own exception classes.

```
#include <stdexcept>
#include <iostream>
void throwIf(bool inShouldThrow) throw (std::runtime_error)
{
    if (inShouldThrow) {
        throw std::runtime_error("Here's my exception");
    }
}
int main()
{
    try {
        throwIf(false); // doesn't throw
        throwIf(true);  // throws!
    } catch (const std::runtime_error& e) {
        std::cerr << "Caught exception: " << e.what() << std::endl;
    }
    return 0;
}
```

Code snippet from Exceptions\Exceptions.cpp

Chapter 10 discusses exceptions in more detail.

... Read from a File

Complete details for file input are included in Chapter 15. Here is a quick sample program for file reading basics. This program reads its own source code and outputs it one token at a time.

```cpp
#include <iostream>
#include <fstream>
#include <string>
using namespace std;
int main()
{
    ifstream inFile("FileRead.cpp");
    if (inFile.fail()) {
        cerr << "Unable to open file for reading." << endl;
        return 1;
    }
    string nextToken;
    while (inFile >> nextToken) {
        cout << "Token: " << nextToken << endl;
    }
    inFile.close();
    return 0;
}
```

Code snippet from FileRead\FileRead.cpp

... Write to a File

The following program outputs a message to a file, then reopens the file and appends another message. Additional details can be found in Chapter 15.

```cpp
#include <iostream>
#include <fstream>
using namespace std;
int main()
{
    ofstream outFile("FileWrite.out");
    if (outFile.fail()) {
        cerr << "Unable to open file for writing." << endl;
        return 1;
    }
    outFile << "Hello!" << endl;
    outFile.close();

    ofstream appendFile("FileWrite.out", ios_base::app);
    if (appendFile.fail()) {
        cerr << "Unable to open file for appending." << endl;
        return 2;
    }
    appendFile << "Append!" << endl;
    appendFile.close();
    return 0;
}
```

Code snippet from FileWrite\FileWrite.cpp

... Write a Template Class

Template syntax is one of the messiest parts of the C++ language. The most-forgotten piece of the template puzzle is that code that uses the template needs to be able to see the method implementations as well as the class template definition. The usual technique to accomplish this is to `#include` the source file in the header file so that clients can `#include` the header file as they normally do. The following program shows a class template that wraps a reference to an object and adds *get* and *set* semantics to it.

```cpp
template <typename T>
class SimpleTemplate
{
    public:
        SimpleTemplate(T& inObject);
        const T& get() const;
        void set(T& inObject);
    protected:
        T& mObject;
};
#include "SimpleTemplate.cpp" // Include the implementation!
```

Code snippet from Template\SimpleTemplate.h

```cpp
template<typename T>
SimpleTemplate<T>::SimpleTemplate(T& inObject) : mObject(inObject)
{
}
template<typename T>
const T& SimpleTemplate<T>::get() const
{
    return mObject;
}
template<typename T>
void SimpleTemplate<T>::set(T& inObject)
{
    mObject = inObject;
}
```

Code snippet from Template\SimpleTemplate.cpp

```cpp
#include <iostream>
#include <string>
#include "SimpleTemplate.h"
using namespace std;
int main()
{
    // Try wrapping an integer.
    int i = 7;
    SimpleTemplate<int> intWrapper(i);
    i = 2;
    cout << "wrapper value is " << intWrapper.get() << endl;
```

```
    // Try wrapping a string.
    string str = "test";
    SimpleTemplate<string> stringWrapper(str);
    str += "!";
    cout << "wrapper value is " << stringWrapper.get() << endl;
    return 0;
}
```

Code snippet from Template\TemplateTest.cpp

Details about templates can be found in Chapters 19 and 20.

THERE MUST BE A BETTER WAY

As you read this paragraph, thousands of C++ programmers throughout the world are solving problems that have already been solved. Someone in a cubicle in San Jose is writing a smart pointer implementation from scratch that uses reference counting. A young programmer on a Mediterranean island is designing a class hierarchy that could benefit immensely from the use of mix-in classes.

As a Professional C++ programmer, you need to spend less of your time reinventing the wheel, and more of your time adapting reusable concepts in new ways. The following techniques are general-purpose approaches that you can apply directly to your own programs or customize for your needs.

Double Dispatch

Double dispatch is a technique that adds an extra dimension to the concept of polymorphism. As described in Chapter 3, polymorphism lets the program determine behavior based on run-time types. For example, you could have an `Animal` class with a `move()` method. All `Animal`s move, but they differ in terms of *how* they move. The `move()` method is defined for every subclass of `Animal` so that the appropriate method can be called, or dispatched, for the appropriate animal at run time without knowing the type of the animal at compile time. Chapter 8 explains how to use virtual methods to implement this run-time polymorphism.

Sometimes, however, you need a method to behave according to the run-time type of two objects, instead of just one. For example, suppose that you want to add a method to the `Animal` class that returns `true` if the animal eats another animal and `false` otherwise. The decision is based on two factors — the type of animal doing the eating, and the type of animal being eaten. Unfortunately, C++ provides no language mechanism to choose a behavior based on the run-time type of more than one object. Virtual methods alone are insufficient for modeling this scenario because they determine a method, or behavior, depending on the run-time type of only the receiving object.

Some object-oriented languages provide the ability to choose a method at run time based on the run-time types of two or more objects. They call this feature *multi-methods*. In C++, however, there is no core language feature to support multi-methods, but you can use the *double dispatch* technique, which provides a technique to make functions virtual for more than one object.

> Double dispatch *is really a special case of* multiple dispatch, *in which a behavior is chosen depending on the run-time types of two or more objects. In practice, double dispatch, which chooses a behavior based on the run-time types of exactly two objects, is usually sufficient.*

Attempt #1: Brute Force

The most straightforward way to implement a method whose behavior depends on the run-time types of two different objects is to take the perspective of one of the objects and use a series of if/else constructs to check the type of the other. For example, you could implement a method called eats() on each Animal subclass that takes the other animal as an argument. The method would be declared pure virtual in the base class as follows:

```
class Animal
{
    public:
        virtual bool eats(const Animal& inPrey) const = 0;
};
```

Code snippet from DoubleDispatch\DoubleDispatchBruteForce.cpp

Each subclass would implement the eats() method and return the appropriate value based on the type of the argument. The implementation of eats() for several subclasses follows. Note that the Dinosaur subclass avoids the series of if/else constructs because (according to the authors) dinosaurs eat anything.

```
bool Bear::eats(const Animal& inPrey) const
{
    if (typeid(inPrey) == typeid(Bear&)) {
        return false;
    } else if (typeid(inPrey) == typeid(Fish&)) {
        return true;
    } else if (typeid(inPrey) == typeid(Dinosaur&)) {
        return false;
    }
    return false;
}
bool Fish::eats(const Animal& inPrey) const
{
    if (typeid(inPrey) == typeid(Bear&)) {
        return false;
    } else if (typeid(inPrey) == typeid(Fish&)) {
        return true;
    } else if (typeid(inPrey) == typeid(Dinosaur&)) {
        return false;
    }
    return false;
}
```

```
bool Dinosaur::eats(const Animal& inPrey) const
{
    return true;
}
```

Code snippet from DoubleDispatch\DoubleDispatchBruteForce.cpp

This brute force approach works, and it's probably the most straightforward technique for a small number of classes. However, there are several reasons why you might want to avoid such an approach:

➤ OOP purists often frown upon explicitly querying the type of an object because it implies a design that is lacking in proper object-oriented structure.

➤ As the number of types grows, such code can grow messy and repetitive.

➤ This approach does not force subclasses to consider new types. For example, if you added a Donkey subclass, the Bear class would continue to compile, but would return false when told to eat a Donkey, even though everybody knows that bears eat donkeys.

Attempt #2: Single Polymorphism with Overloading

You could attempt to use polymorphism with overloading to circumvent all of the cascading if/else constructs. Instead of giving each class a single eats() method that takes an Animal reference, why not overload the method for each Animal subclass? The base class definition would look like this:

```
class Animal
{
    public:
        virtual bool eats(const Bear& inPrey) const = 0;
        virtual bool eats(const Fish& inPrey) const = 0;
        virtual bool eats(const Dinosaur& inPrey) const = 0;
};
```

Because the methods are pure virtual in the superclass, each subclass would be forced to implement the behavior for every other type of Animal. For example, the Bear class would contain the following methods:

```
class Bear : public Animal
{
    public:
        virtual bool eats(const Bear& inPrey) const { return false; }
        virtual bool eats(const Fish& inPrey) const { return true; }
        virtual bool eats(const Dinosaur& inPrey) const { return false; }
};
```

This approach initially appears to work, but it really solves only half of the problem. In order to call the proper eats() method on an Animal, the compiler needs to know the compile-time type of the animal being eaten. A call such as the following will be successful because the compile-time types of both the eater and the eaten animals are known:

```
Bear myBear;
Fish myFish;
cout << myBear.eats(myFish) << endl;
```

The missing piece is that the solution is only polymorphic in one direction. You could access `myBear` in the context of an `Animal` and the correct method would be called:

```
Bear myBear;
Fish myFish;
Animal& animalRef = myBear;
cout << animalRef.eats(myFish) << endl;
```

However, the reverse is not true. If you accessed `myFish` in the context of the `Animal` class and passed that to the `eats()` method, you would get a compile error because there is no `eats()` method that takes an `Animal`. The compiler cannot determine, at compile time, which version to call. The following example will not compile:

```
Bear myBear;
Fish myFish;
Animal& animalRef = myFish;
cout << myBear.eats(animalRef) << endl; // BUG! No method Bear::eats(Animal&)
```

Because the compiler needs to know which overloaded version of the `eats()` method is going to be called at compile time, this solution is not truly polymorphic. It would not work, for example, if you were iterating over an array of `Animal` references and passing each one to a call to `eats()`.

Attempt #3: Double Dispatch

The *double dispatch* technique is a truly polymorphic solution to the multiple type problem. In C++, polymorphism is achieved by overriding methods in subclasses. At run time, methods are called based on the actual type of the object. The preceding single polymorphic attempt didn't work because it attempted to use polymorphism to determine which overloaded version of a method to call instead of using it to determine on which class to call the method.

To begin, focus on a single subclass, perhaps the `Bear` class. The class needs a method with the following declaration:

```
virtual bool eats(const Animal& inPrey) const;
```

The key to double dispatch is to determine the result based on a method call on the argument. Suppose that the `Animal` class had a method called `eatenBy()`, which took an `Animal` reference as a parameter. This method would return `true` if the current `Animal` gets eaten by the one passed in. With such a method, the definition of `eats()` becomes very simple:

```
bool Bear::eats(const Animal& inPrey) const
{
    return inPrey.eatenBy(*this);
}
```

At first, it looks like this solution adds another layer of method calls to the single polymorphic method. After all, each subclass will still have to implement a version of `eatenBy()` for every subclass of `Animal`. However, there is a key difference. Polymorphism is occurring twice! When you call the `eats()` method on an `Animal`, polymorphism determines whether you are calling `Bear::eats()`, `Fish::eats()`, or one of the others. When you call `eatenBy()`, polymorphism again determines which class's version of the method to call. It calls `eatenBy()` on the run-time type of the `inPrey` object. Note that the run-time type of `*this` is always the same as the compile-time type so that the compiler can call the correct overloaded version of `eatenBy()` for the argument (in this case `Bear`).

Following are the class definitions for the `Animal` hierarchy using double dispatch. Note that forward class declarations are necessary because the base class uses references to the subclasses.

```cpp
// forward declarations
class Fish;
class Bear;
class Dinosaur;
class Animal
{
    public:
        virtual bool eats(const Animal& inPrey) const = 0;
        virtual bool eatenBy(const Bear& inBear) const = 0;
        virtual bool eatenBy(const Fish& inFish) const = 0;
        virtual bool eatenBy(const Dinosaur& inDinosaur) const = 0;
};
class Bear : public Animal
{
    public:
        virtual bool eats(const Animal& inPrey) const;
        virtual bool eatenBy(const Bear& inBear) const;
        virtual bool eatenBy(const Fish& inFish) const;
        virtual bool eatenBy(const Dinosaur& inDinosaur) const;
};
class Fish : public Animal
{
    public:
        virtual bool eats(const Animal& inPrey) const;
        virtual bool eatenBy(const Bear& inBear) const;
        virtual bool eatenBy(const Fish& inFish) const;
        virtual bool eatenBy(const Dinosaur& inDinosaur) const;
};
class Dinosaur : public Animal
{
    public:
        virtual bool eats(const Animal& inPrey) const;
        virtual bool eatenBy(const Bear& inBear) const;
        virtual bool eatenBy(const Fish& inFish) const;
        virtual bool eatenBy(const Dinosaur& inDinosaur) const;
};
```

Code snippet from DoubleDispatch\DoubleDispatch.cpp

The implementations follow. Note that each `Animal` subclass implements the `eats()` method in the same way, but it cannot be factored up into the parent class. The reason is that if you attempt to do so, the compiler won't know which overloaded version of the `eatenBy()` method to call because `*this` would be an `Animal`, not a particular subclass. Method overload resolution is determined according to the compile-time type of the object, not its run-time type.

```cpp
bool Bear::eats(const Animal& inPrey) const
{
    return inPrey.eatenBy(*this);
}
bool Bear::eatenBy(const Bear& inBear) const
{
    return false;
}
bool Bear::eatenBy(const Fish& inFish) const
{
    return false;
}
bool Bear::eatenBy(const Dinosaur& inDinosaur) const
{
    return true;
}


bool Fish::eats(const Animal& inPrey) const
{
    return inPrey.eatenBy(*this);
}
bool Fish::eatenBy(const Bear& inBear) const
{
    return true;
}
bool Fish::eatenBy(const Fish& inFish) const
{
    return true;
}
bool Fish::eatenBy(const Dinosaur& inDinosaur) const
{
    return true;
}


bool Dinosaur::eats(const Animal& inPrey) const
{
    return inPrey.eatenBy(*this);
}
bool Dinosaur::eatenBy(const Bear& inBear) const
{
    return false;
}
bool Dinosaur::eatenBy(const Fish& inFish) const
{
    return false;
}
bool Dinosaur::eatenBy(const Dinosaur& inDinosaur) const
{
    return true;
}
```

Code snippet from DoubleDispatch\DoubleDispatch.cpp

Double dispatch is a concept that takes a bit of getting used to. We suggest playing with this code to adapt to the concept and its implementation.

Mix-In Classes

Chapters 3 and 8 introduce the technique of using multiple inheritance to build *mix-in classes*. Mix-in classes add a small piece of extra behavior to a class in an existing hierarchy. You can usually spot a mix-in class by its name ending in "-able", such as `Clickable`, `Drawable`, `Printable`, or `Lovable`.

Designing a Mix-In Class

Mix-in classes come in several forms. Because mix-in classes are not a formal language feature, you can write them however you want without breaking any rules. Some mix-in classes indicate that a class supports a certain behavior, such as a hypothetical `Drawable` mix-in class. Any class that mixes in the `Drawable` class must implement the method `draw()`. The mix-in class itself contains no functionality — it just marks an object as supporting the `draw()` behavior. This usage is similar to Java's notion of an interface — a list of prescribed behaviors without their implementation.

Other mix-in classes contain actual code. You might have a mix-in class called `Playable` that is mixed into certain types of media objects. The mix-in class could, for example, contain most of the code to communicate with the computer's sound drivers. By mixing in the class, the media object would get that functionality for free.

When designing a mix-in class, you need to consider what behavior you are adding and whether it belongs in the object hierarchy or in a separate class. Using the previous example, if all media classes are playable, the base class should descend from `Playable` instead of mixing the `Playable` class into all of the subclasses. If only certain media classes are playable and they are scattered throughout the hierarchy, a mix-in class makes sense.

One of the cases where mix-in classes are particularly useful is when you have classes organized into a hierarchy on one axis, but they also contain similarity on another axis. For example, consider a war simulation game played on a grid. Each grid location can contain an `Item` with attack and defense capabilities and other characteristics. Some items, such as a `Castle`, are stationary. Others, such as a `Knight` or `FloatingCastle`, can move throughout the grid. When initially designing the object hierarchy, you might end up with something like Figure 28-1, which organizes the classes according to their attack and defense capabilities.

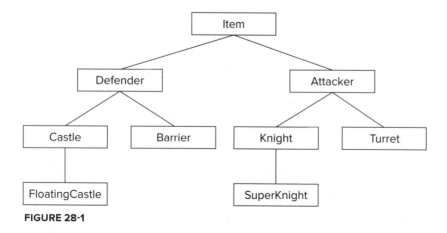

FIGURE 28-1

The hierarchy in Figure 28-1 ignores the movement functionality that certain classes contain. Building your hierarchy around movement would result in a structure similar to Figure 28-2.

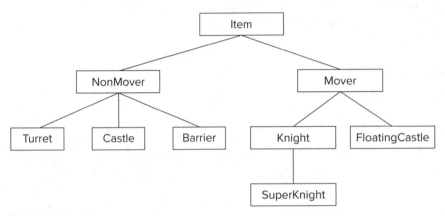

FIGURE 28-2

Of course, the design of Figure 28-2 throws away all the organization of Figure 28-1. What's a good object-oriented programmer to do?

There are two common solutions for this problem. Assuming that you go with the first hierarchy, organized around attackers and defenders, you need some way to work movement into the equation. One possibility is that, even though only a portion of the subclasses support movement, you *could* add a move() method to the Item base class. The default implementation would do nothing. Certain subclasses would override move() to actually change their location on the grid.

The other approach is to write a Movable mix-in class. The elegant hierarchy from Figure 28-1 could be preserved, but certain classes in the hierarchy would subclass Movable in addition to their parent in the diagram. Figure 28-3 shows this design.

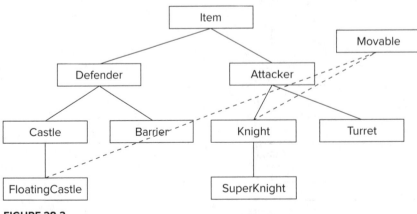

FIGURE 28-3

Implementing a Mix-In Class

Writing a mix-in class is no different from writing a normal class. In fact, it's usually much simpler. Using the earlier war simulation, the `Movable` mix-in class might look as follows:

```
class Movable
{
    public:
        virtual void move() = 0;
};
```

This `Movable` mix-in class doesn't contain any actual functionality. However, it does two very important things. First, it provides a type for `Items` that can be moved. This allows you to create, for example, an array of all movable items without knowing or caring what actual subclass of `Item` they belong to. The `Movable` class also declares that all movable items must implement a method called `move()`. This way, you could iterate over all of the `Movable` objects and tell each of them to move.

Using a Mix-In Class

The code for using a mix-in class is syntactically equivalent to multiple inheritance. In addition to subclassing your parent class in the main hierarchy, you also subclass the mix-in class:

```
class FloatingCastle : public Castle, public Movable
{
    public:
        virtual void move();
    // Other methods and members not shown here
};
```

The only remaining task is to provide a definition of the `move()` method for `FloatingCastle`. Once that is done, you'll have a class that exists in the most logical place in the hierarchy, but still shares commonality with objects elsewhere in the hierarchy.

OBJECT-ORIENTED FRAMEWORKS

When graphical operating systems first came on the scene in the 1980s, procedural programming was the norm. At the time, writing a GUI application usually involved manipulating complex data structures and passing them to OS-provided functions. For example, to draw a rectangle in a window, you might populate a `Window` struct with the appropriate information and pass it to a `drawRect()` function.

As object-oriented programming grew in popularity, programmers looked for a way to apply the OO paradigm to GUI development. The result is known as an *Object-Oriented Framework*. In general, a framework is a set of classes that are used collectively to provide an object-oriented interface to some underlying functionality. When talking about frameworks, programmers are usually referring to large class libraries that are used for general application development. However, a framework can really represent functionality of any size. If you write a suite of classes that provides database functionality for your application, those classes could be considered a framework.

Working with Frameworks

The defining characteristic of a framework is that it provides its own set of techniques and patterns. Frameworks usually require a bit of learning to get started with because they have their own mental model. Before you can work with a large application framework, such as the Microsoft Foundation Classes (MFC), you need to understand its view of the world.

Frameworks vary greatly in their abstract ideas and in their actual implementation. Many frameworks are built on top of legacy procedural APIs, which may affect various aspects of their design. Other frameworks are written from the ground up with object-oriented design in mind. Some frameworks might ideologically oppose certain aspects of the C++ language, such as the BeOS framework, which consciously shunned the notion of multiple inheritance.

When you start working with a new framework, your first task is to find out what makes it tick. To what design principles does it subscribe? What mental model are its developers trying to convey? What aspects of the language does it use extensively? These are all vital questions, even though they may sound like things that you'll pick up along the way. If you fail to understand the design, model, or language features of the framework, you will quickly get into situations where you overstep the bounds of the framework. For example, if the framework has its own string class, e.g., MFC's CString, and you choose to use another string class, e.g., std::string, you will end up with a lot of unnecessary conversion work that could have been easily avoided.

An understanding of the framework's design will also make it possible for you to extend it. For example, if the framework omits a feature, such as support for printing, you could write your own printing classes using the same model as the framework. By doing so, you retain a consistent model for your application, and you have code that can be reused by other applications.

The Model-View-Controller Paradigm

As mentioned, frameworks vary in their approaches to object-oriented design. One common paradigm is known as *model-view-controller*, or MVC. This paradigm models the notion that many applications commonly deal with a set of data, one or more views on that data, and manipulation of the data.

In MVC, a set of data is called the *model*. In a race car simulator, the model would keep track of various statistics, such as the current speed of the car and the amount of damage it has sustained. In practice, the model often takes the form of a class with many getters and setters. The class definition for the model of the race car might look as follows:

```
class RaceCar
{
    public:
        RaceCar();
        int getSpeed() const;
        void setSpeed(int inValue);
        int getDamageLevel() const;
        void setDamageLevel(int inValue);
    protected:
        int mSpeed;
        int mDamageLevel;
};
```

A *view* is a particular visualization of the model. For example, there could be two views on a `RaceCar`. The first view could be a graphical view of the car, and the second could be a graph that shows the level of damage over time. The important point is that both views are operating on the same data — they are different ways of looking at the same information. This is one of the main advantages of the MVC paradigm — by keeping data separated from its display, you can keep your code more organized, and easily create additional views.

The final piece to the MVC paradigm is the *controller.* The controller is the piece of code that changes the model in response to some event. For example, when the driver of the race car simulator runs into a concrete barrier, the controller would instruct the model to bump up the car's damage level and reduce its speed.

The three components of MVC interact in a feedback loop. Actions are handled by the controller, which adjusts the model, resulting in a change to the view(s). This interaction is shown in Figure 28-4.

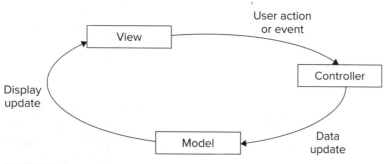

FIGURE 28-4

The model-view-controller paradigm has gained widespread support within many popular frameworks. Even nontraditional applications, such as web applications, are moving in the direction of MVC because it enforces a clear separation between data, the manipulation of data, and the displaying of data.

SUMMARY

In this chapter, you have read about some of the common techniques that Professional C++ programmers use consistently in their projects. As you advance as a software developer, you will undoubtedly form your own collection of reusable classes and libraries. Discovering design techniques opens the door to developing and using *patterns*, which are higher-level reusable constructs. You will experience the many applications of patterns next in Chapter 29.

29

Applying Design Patterns

WHAT'S IN THIS CHAPTER?

➤ What a pattern is and what the difference is with a design technique

➤ How to use the following patterns:

  ➤ Iterator

  ➤ Singleton

  ➤ Factory

  ➤ Proxy

  ➤ Adapter

  ➤ Decorator

  ➤ Chain of Responsibility

  ➤ Observer/Listener

A *design pattern* is a standard approach to program organization that solves a general problem. C++ is an object-oriented language, so the design patterns of interest to C++ programmers are generally object-oriented patterns, which describe strategies for organizing objects and object relationships in your programs. These patterns are usually applicable to any object-oriented language, such as for example C++, C#, Java, or Smalltalk. In fact, if you are familiar with C# or Java programming, you will recognize many of these patterns.

Design patterns are less language specific than are techniques. The difference between a pattern and a technique is admittedly fuzzy, and different books employ different definitions. This book defines a technique as a strategy particular to the C++ language, while a pattern is a more general strategy for object-oriented design applicable to any object-oriented language.

Note that many patterns have several different names. The distinctions between the patterns themselves can be somewhat vague, with different sources describing and categorizing them slightly differently. In fact, depending on the books or other sources you use, you may find the same name applied to different patterns. There is even disagreement as to which design approaches qualify as patterns. With a few exceptions, this book follows the terminology used in the seminal book *Design Patterns: Elements of Reusable Object-Oriented Software*, by Erich Gamma et al. (Addison-Wesley Professional, 1994) However, other pattern names and variations are noted when appropriate.

The design pattern concept is a simple, but powerful, idea. Once you are able to recognize the recurring object-oriented interactions that occur in a program, finding an elegant solution becomes a matter of merely selecting the appropriate pattern to apply. This chapter describes several design patterns in detail and presents sample implementations.

Certain patterns go by different names or are subject to different interpretations. Any aspect of design is likely to provoke debate among programmers, and the authors believe that is a good thing. Don't simply accept these patterns as the only way to accomplish a task — draw on their approaches and ideas to refine them and form new patterns.

THE ITERATOR PATTERN

The *iterator* pattern provides a mechanism for separating algorithms or operations from the data on which they operate. At first glance, this pattern seems to contradict the fundamental principle in object-oriented programming of grouping together in objects data and the behaviors that operate on that data. While that argument is true on a certain level, the iterator pattern does not advocate removing fundamental behaviors from objects. Instead, it solves two problems that commonly arise with tight coupling of data and behaviors.

The first problem with tightly coupling data and behaviors is that it precludes generic algorithms that work on a variety of objects, not all of which are in the same class hierarchy. In order to write generic algorithms, you need some standard mechanism to access the contents of the objects.

The second problem with tightly coupled data and behaviors is that it's sometimes difficult to add new behaviors. At the very least, you need access to the source code for the data objects. However, what if the object hierarchy of interest is part of a third-party framework or library that you cannot change? It would be nice to be able to add an algorithm or operation that works on the data without modifying the original object hierarchy of data.

You've already seen an example of the iterator pattern in the STL. Conceptually, *iterators* provide a mechanism for an operation or algorithm to access a container of elements in a sequence. The name comes from the English word *iterate*, which means "repeat." It applies to iterators because they repeat the action of moving forward in the sequence to reach each new element. In the STL, the generic algorithms use iterators to access the elements of the containers on which they operate. By defining a standard iterator interface, the STL allows you to write algorithms that can work on any container that supplies an iterator with the appropriate interface. Thus, iterators allow you to write generic algorithms without modifying the classes that hold the data. Figure 29-1 shows an iterator as an assembly line that sends the elements of a data object to an "operation."

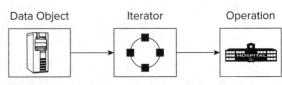

FIGURE 29-1

Chapter 17 illustrates a detailed example on how to implement an iterator for a class that conforms to the STL requirements, which means that its iterator can be used by the generic STL algorithms.

THE SINGLETON PATTERN

The *singleton* is one of the simplest design patterns. In English the word "singleton" means "one of a kind" or "individual." It has a similar meaning in programming. The singleton pattern is a strategy for enforcing the existence of exactly one instance of a class in a program. Applying the singleton pattern to a class guarantees that only one object of that class will ever be created. The singleton pattern also specifies that that one object is globally accessible from anywhere in the program. Programmers usually refer to a class following the singleton pattern as a *singleton class*.

If your program relies on the assumption that there will be exactly one instance of a class, you should enforce that assumption with the singleton pattern.

Example: A Logging Mechanism

Singletons are particularly useful for utility classes. Many applications have a notion of a logger — a class that is responsible for writing status information, debugging data, and errors to a central location. The ideal logging class has the following characteristics:

➤ It is available at all times.

➤ It is easy to use.

➤ It provides a set of useful features.

The singleton pattern is a good match for a logger because, even though the logger could be used in many different contexts and for many different purposes, it is conceptually a single instance. Implementing the logger class as a singleton also makes it easier to use because you never have to worry about *which* logger is the current one or how to get a hold of the current logger; there's only one, so it's a moot point!

Implementation of a Singleton

There are two basic ways to implement a singleton in C++. The first approach uses static methods to form a class that needs no instantiation. The second uses access control levels to regulate the creation and access of one single instance.

Both approaches are shown here, using a simple Logger class as an example. This Logger class provides the following features:

➤ It can log a single string or a vector of strings.

➤ Each log message has an associated log level, which is prefixed to the log message.

➤ Every log message is flushed to disk so that it will appear in the file immediately.

Static Class Singleton

Technically, a class that uses all static methods isn't really a singleton: It's a *nothington*, to coin a new term. The term *singleton* implies that there is exactly one instance of the class. If all of the methods are static and the class is never instantiated at all, can you call it a singleton? The authors claim that, because design patterns exist to help you build a mental model of object-oriented structures, you can call a static class a singleton if you please. However, you should recognize that a static class as a singleton lacks polymorphism and a built-in mechanism for construction and destruction. For cases like the Logger class, these may be acceptable losses.

The interface to the Logger static class follows. Note that it uses all static methods for access, so there is no need ever to instantiate a Logger object. In fact, the constructor has been made private to enforce this behavior.

```cpp
#include <iostream>
#include <fstream>
#include <vector>
#include <string>
// Definition of a singleton logger class, implemented with static methods.
class Logger
{
    public:
        static const std::string kLogLevelDebug;
        static const std::string kLogLevelInfo;
        static const std::string kLogLevelError;
        // Logs a single message at the given log level
        static void log(const std::string& inMessage,
                        const std::string& inLogLevel);
        // Logs a vector of messages at the given log level
        static void log(const std::vector<std::string>& inMessages,
                        const std::string& inLogLevel);
        // Closes the log file
        static void teardown();
    protected:
        static void init();
        static const char* const kLogFileName;
        static bool sInitialized;
        static std::ofstream sOutputStream;
    private:
        Logger() {}
};
```

Code snippet from StaticLogger\Logger.h

The implementation of the Logger class is fairly straightforward. The sInitialized static member is checked within each logging call to make sure that the init() method has been called to open the log file. Once the log file has been opened, each log message is written to it with the log level prepended.

```cpp
#include <stdexcept>
#include "Logger.h"
using namespace std;

const string Logger::kLogLevelDebug = "DEBUG";
const string Logger::kLogLevelInfo = "INFO";
const string Logger::kLogLevelError = "ERROR";
```

```
const char* const Logger::kLogFileName = "log.out";
bool Logger::sInitialized = false;
ofstream Logger::sOutputStream;

void Logger::log(const string& inMessage, const string& inLogLevel)
{
    if (!sInitialized) {
        init();
    }
    // Print the message and flush the stream with endl.
    sOutputStream << inLogLevel << ": " << inMessage << endl;
}
void Logger::log(const vector<string>& inMessages, const string& inLogLevel)
{
    for (size_t i = 0; i < inMessages.size(); i++) {
        log(inMessages[i], inLogLevel);
    }
}
void Logger::teardown()
{
    if (sInitialized) {
        sOutputStream.close();
        sInitialized = false;
    }
}
void Logger::init()
{
    if (!sInitialized) {
        sOutputStream.open(kLogFileName, ios_base::app);
        if (!sOutputStream.good()) {
            throw runtime_error("Unable to initialize the Logger!");
        }
        sInitialized = true;
    }
}
```

Code snippet from StaticLogger\Logger.cpp

 To focus on the actual singleton pattern, this implementation uses a hardcoded file name. Of course, in production quality software, this file name should be configurable by the user, and you should not use relative paths, but fully qualified paths, for example, by retrieving the temporary directory for your OS.

Access-Controlled Singleton

Object-oriented purists (Warning: They are out there, and they may work at your company!) might scoff at the static class solution to the singleton problem. Since you can't instantiate a Logger object, you can't build a hierarchy of loggers and make use of polymorphism. Such a hierarchy is rarely employed in the singleton case, but it is a valid drawback. Perhaps more significantly, as a result of using entirely static methods, there is no object orientation at all. This also means that there is no way to invoke a destructor. The static version of the `Logger` class requires the programmer to explicitly call the `teardown()` method. This is a serious defect. The class built in the previous example is essentially a collection of C-style functions, not a cohesive class.

To build a true singleton in C++, you can use the access control mechanisms as well as the `static` keyword. With this approach, an actual `Logger` object exists at run time, and the class enforces that exactly one exists. Clients can always get a hold of that object through a static method called `instance()`. The class definition looks like this:

```cpp
#include <iostream>
#include <fstream>
#include <vector>
#include <string>
// Definition of a true singleton logger class.
class Logger
{
    public:
        static const std::string kLogLevelDebug;
        static const std::string kLogLevelInfo;
        static const std::string kLogLevelError;
        // Returns a reference to the singleton Logger object
        static Logger& instance();
        // Logs a single message at the given log level
        void log(const std::string& inMessage,
                const std::string& inLogLevel);
        // Logs a vector of messages at the given log level
        void log(const std::vector<std::string>& inMessages,
                const std::string& inLogLevel);
    protected:
        // Static variable for the one-and-only instance
        static Logger sInstance;
        // Constant for the filename
        static const char* const kLogFileName;
        // Data member for the output stream
        std::ofstream mOutputStream;
    private:
        Logger();
        virtual ~Logger();
};
```

Code snippet from SingletonLogger\Logger.h

One advantage of this approach is already apparent. Because an actual object will exist, the `init()` and `teardown()` methods present in the static solution can be omitted in favor of a constructor and destructor. This is a big win, because the previous solution required the client to explicitly call `teardown()` to close the file. Now that the logger is an object, the file can be closed when the object is destructed, which will happen when the program ends.

The implementation follows. Notice that the actual `log()` methods remain almost unchanged, except for the fact that they are no longer static, and that they no longer have to check if the logger has been initialized. The constructor and destructor are called automatically because the class contains an instance of itself as a static member. Because they are private, no external code can create or delete a `Logger`.

```cpp
#include <stdexcept>
#include "Logger.h"
using namespace std;

const string Logger::kLogLevelDebug = "DEBUG";
const string Logger::kLogLevelInfo = "INFO";
const string Logger::kLogLevelError = "ERROR";
const char* const Logger::kLogFileName = "log.out";
// The static instance will be constructed when the program starts and
// destructed when it ends.
Logger Logger::sInstance;

Logger& Logger::instance()
{
    return sInstance;
}
Logger::~Logger()
{
    mOutputStream.close();
}
Logger::Logger()
{
    mOutputStream.open(kLogFileName, ios_base::app);
    if (!mOutputStream.good()) {
        throw runtime_error("Unable to initialize the Logger!");
    }
}
void Logger::log(const string& inMessage, const string& inLogLevel)
{
    mOutputStream << inLogLevel << ": " << inMessage << endl;
}
void Logger::log(const vector<string>& inMessages, const string& inLogLevel)
{
    for (size_t i = 0; i < inMessages.size(); i++) {
        log(inMessages[i], inLogLevel);
    }
}
```

Code snippet from SingletonLogger\Logger.cpp

Using a Singleton

The following two pieces of code display the usage of the two different versions of the `Logger` class:

```cpp
Logger::log("test message", Logger::kLogLevelDebug);
vector<string> items = {"item1", "item2"};
Logger::log(items, Logger::kLogLevelError);
Logger::teardown();
```

Code snippet from StaticLogger\TestStaticLogger.cpp

```
Logger::instance().log("test message", Logger::kLogLevelDebug);
vector<string> items = {"item1", "item2"};
Logger::instance().log(items, Logger::kLogLevelError);
```

Code snippet from SingletonLogger\TestTrueSingletonLogger.cpp

Both programs have the same functionality. After executing, the file log.out should contain the following lines:

```
DEBUG: test message
ERROR: item1
ERROR: item2
```

Singletons and Multithreading

The implementation of the singleton pattern in the previous section has a few issues. The first problem has to do with file static dependencies. The C++ standard does not define the order of initialization of static variables across translation units. Because of this, it can happen that some code is accessing the singleton class before it has been constructed, which leads to undefined behavior that is difficult to track. A second problem is that destruction of static objects is not guaranteed to occur in the order that you desire.

These problems can be solved by moving the static instance into the instance() method as follows:

```
Logger& Logger::instance()
{
    static Logger sInstance;
    return sInstance;
}
```

However, this solution is not safe in a multithreaded scenario, because there can be a race condition between the two lines in the new instance() method. To fix this race condition, the following implementation uses a static pInstance pointer to the single instance of the class. This static pointer will be initialized within a thread-safe block of code using a mutex for thread synchronization. The copy constructor and assignment operator are declared as private. The reason for the Cleanup class is discussed later in this section.

```
#include <iostream>
#include <fstream>
#include <vector>
#include <string>
#include <mutex>
// Definition of a multithread safe singleton logger class
class Logger
{
    public:
        static const std::string kLogLevelDebug;
        static const std::string kLogLevelInfo;
        static const std::string kLogLevelError;
```

```
            // Returns a reference to the singleton Logger object
            static Logger& instance();
            // Logs a single message at the given log level
            void log(const std::string& inMessage,
                    const std::string& inLogLevel);
            // Logs a vector of messages at the given log level
            void log(const std::vector<std::string>& inMessages,
                    const std::string& inLogLevel);
        protected:
            // Static variable for the one-and-only instance
            static Logger* pInstance;
            // Constant for the filename
            static const char* const kLogFileName;
            // Data member for the output stream
            std::ofstream mOutputStream;
            // Embedded class to make sure the single Logger
            // instance gets deleted on program shutdown.
            friend class Cleanup;
            class Cleanup
            {
                public:
                    ~Cleanup();
            };
            // Logs message. The thread should own a lock on sMutex
            // before calling this function.
            void logHelper(const std::string& inMessage,
                        const std::string& inLogLevel);
        private:
            Logger();
            virtual ~Logger();
            Logger(const Logger&);
            Logger& operator=(const Logger&);
            static std::mutex sMutex;
    };
```

Code snippet from ThreadSafeLogger\Logger.h

The new implementation is as follows:

```
#include <stdexcept>
#include "Logger.h"
using namespace std;

const string Logger::kLogLevelDebug = "DEBUG";
const string Logger::kLogLevelInfo = "INFO";
const string Logger::kLogLevelError = "ERROR";
const char* const Logger::kLogFileName = "log.out";
Logger* Logger::pInstance = nullptr;
mutex Logger::sMutex;

Logger& Logger::instance()
{
    static Cleanup cleanup;
```

```
        lock_guard<mutex> guard(sMutex);
        if (pInstance == nullptr)
            pInstance = new Logger();
        return *pInstance;
    }
    Logger::Cleanup::~Cleanup()
    {
        lock_guard<mutex> guard(Logger::sMutex);
        delete Logger::pInstance;
        Logger::pInstance = nullptr;
    }
    Logger::~Logger()
    {
        mOutputStream.close();
    }
    Logger::Logger()
    {
        mOutputStream.open(kLogFileName, ios_base::app);
        if (!mOutputStream.good()) {
            throw runtime_error("Unable to initialize the Logger!");
        }
    }
    void Logger::log(const string& inMessage, const string& inLogLevel)
    {
        lock_guard<mutex> guard(sMutex);
        logHelper(inMessage, inLogLevel);
    }
    void Logger::log(const vector<string>& inMessages, const string& inLogLevel)
    {
        lock_guard<mutex> guard(sMutex);
        for (size_t i = 0; i < inMessages.size(); i++) {
            logHelper(inMessages[i], inLogLevel);
        }
    }
    void Logger::logHelper(const std::string& inMessage,
        const std::string& inLogLevel)
    {
        mOutputStream << inLogLevel << ": " << inMessage << endl;
    }
```

Code snippet from ThreadSafeLogger\Logger.cpp

The Cleanup class is there to make sure the single Logger instance gets deleted properly on program shutdown. This is necessary because this implementation is dynamically allocating the Logger instance by using the new operator in a block of code protected with a mutex. A static instance of the Cleanup class will be created the first time the instance() method is called. When the program terminates, the C++ runtime will destroy this static Cleanup instance, which will trigger the deletion of the Logger object and a call to the Logger destructor to close the file.

 This version uses the C++11 threading library for its lock_guard *and* mutex *classes, discussed in Chapter 22. If you do not have support for this C++11 threading library, you can replace those with any other kind of* lock_guard *and* mutex *available on your platform.*

THE FACTORY PATTERN

A factory in real life constructs tangible objects, such as tables or cars. Similarly, a *factory* in object-oriented programming constructs objects. When you use factories in your program, portions of code that want to create a particular object ask the factory for an instance of the object instead of calling the object constructor themselves. For example, an interior decorating program might have a `FurnitureFactory` object. When part of the code needs a piece of furniture such as a table, it would call the `createTable()` method of the `FurnitureFactory` object, which would return a new table.

At first glance, factories seem to lead to complicated designs without clear benefits. It appears that you're only adding another layer of complexity to the program. Instead of calling `createTable()` on a `FurnitureFactory`, you could simply create a new `Table` object directly. However, factories can actually be quite useful. Instead of creating various objects all over the program, you centralize the object creation for a particular domain. This localization is often a better model of real-world creation of objects.

Another benefit of factories is that you can use them alongside class hierarchies to construct objects without knowing their exact class. As you'll see in the following example, factories can run parallel to class hierarchies.

The main benefit is that factories abstract the object creation process; you can easily substitute a different factory in your program. Just as you can use polymorphism with the created objects, you can use polymorphism with factories. The following example demonstrates this.

Example: A Car Factory Simulation

In the real world, when you talk about driving a car, you can do so without referring to the specific type of car. You could be discussing a Toyota or a Ford. It doesn't matter, because both Toyotas and Fords are drivable. Now, suppose that you want a new car. You would then need to specify whether you wanted a Toyota or a Ford, right? Not always. You could just say "I want a car," and depending on where you were, you would get a specific car. If you said, "I want a car" in a Toyota factory, chances are you'd get a Toyota. (Or you'd get arrested, depending on how you asked). If you said, "I want a car" in a Ford factory, you'd get a Ford.

The same concepts apply to C++ programming. The first concept, of a generic car that's drivable, is nothing new; it's standard polymorphism, described in Chapter 3. You could write an abstract `Car` class that defines a `drive()` method. Both `Toyota` and `Ford` could be subclasses of the `Car` class, as shown in Figure 29-2.

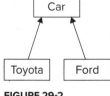

FIGURE 29-2

Your program could drive `Car`s without knowing whether they were really `Toyota`s or `Ford`s. However, with standard object-oriented programming, the one place that you'd need to specify `Toyota` or `Ford` is when you create the car. Here, you would need to call the constructor for one or the other. You can't just say, "I want a car." However, suppose that you also had a parallel class hierarchy of car factories. The `CarFactory` superclass could define a virtual `buildCar()` method. The `ToyotaFactory` and `FordFactory` subclasses would override the `buildCar()` method to build a Toyota or a Ford. Figure 29-3 shows the `CarFactory` hierarchy.

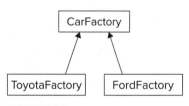

FIGURE 29-3

Now, suppose that there is one `CarFactory` object in a program. When code in the program, such as a car dealer, wants a new car, it calls `buildCar()` on the `CarFactory` object. Depending on whether that car factory was really a `ToyotaFactory` or a `FordFactory`, the code would get either a `Toyota` or a `Ford`. Figure 29-4 shows the objects in a car dealer program using a `ToyotaFactory`.

Requests "Car"   ToyotaFactory

Returns "Car"   Builds Toyota

CarDealer

FIGURE 29-4

Figure 29-5 shows the same program, but with a `FordFactory` instead of a `ToyotaFactory`. Note that the `CarDealer` object and its relationship with the factory stay the same.

Requests "Car"   FordFactory

Returns "Car"   Builds Ford

CarDealer

FIGURE 29-5

This example demonstrates the main benefit: You can use polymorphism with factories. When you ask the car factory for a car, you might not know whether it's a Toyota factory or a Ford factory, but either way it will give you a `Car` that you can drive. This approach leads to easily extensible programs; simply changing the factory instance can allow the program to work on a completely different set of objects and classes.

Implementation of a Factory

One reason for using factories is if the type of the object you want to create depends on some condition. For example, if you are a dealer who needs a car right away, you might want to put your order into the factory that has the fewest requests, regardless of whether the car you eventually get is a `Toyota` or a `Ford`. The following implementation shows how to write such factories in C++.

The first thing you'll need is the hierarchy of cars. To keep this example simple, the `Car` class simply has an abstract method that returns a description of the car. Both `Car` subclasses are also defined in the following example:

```
#include <iostream>
class Car
{
    public:
        virtual void info() = 0;
};
```

```cpp
class Ford : public Car
{
    public:
        virtual void info() { std::cout << "Ford" << std::endl; }
};
class Toyota : public Car
{
    public:
        virtual void info() { std::cout << "Toyota" << std::endl; }
};
```

Code snippet from CarFactory\Car.h

The `CarFactory` base class is a bit more interesting. Each factory keeps track of the number of cars in production. When the public `requestCar()` method is called, the number of cars in production at the factory is increased by one, and calling the pure virtual `createCar()` method returns a new car. The idea is that individual factories will override `createCar()` to return the appropriate type of car. The `CarFactory` itself implements `requestCar()`, which takes care of updating the number of cars in production. `CarFactory` also provides a `public` method to query the number of cars being produced at each factory.

The class definitions for the `CarFactory` class and subclasses are shown here:

```cpp
#include "Car.h"
class CarFactory
{
    public:
        CarFactory();
        Car* requestCar();
        int getNumCarsInProduction() const;
    protected:
        virtual Car* createCar() = 0;
    private:
        int mNumCarsInProduction;
};
class FordFactory : public CarFactory
{
    protected:
        virtual Car* createCar();
};
class ToyotaFactory : public CarFactory
{
    protected:
        virtual Car* createCar();
};
```

Code snippet from CarFactory\CarFactory.h

As you can see, the subclasses simply override `createCar()` to return the specific type of car that they produce. The implementation of the `CarFactory` hierarchy is as follows:

```
#include "CarFactory.h"
// Initialize the count to zero when the factory is created.
CarFactory::CarFactory() : mNumCarsInProduction(0) {}
// Increment the number of cars in production and return the new car.
Car* CarFactory::requestCar()
{
    mNumCarsInProduction++;
    return createCar();
}
int CarFactory::getNumCarsInProduction() const
{
    return mNumCarsInProduction;
}
Car* FordFactory::createCar()
{
    return new Ford();
}
Car* ToyotaFactory::createCar()
{
    return new Toyota();
}
```

Code snippet from CarFactory\CarFactory.cpp

The implementation approach used in this example is called an *abstract factory* because the type of object created depends on which *concrete* subclass of the factory class is being used. A similar pattern can be implemented in a single class instead of a class hierarchy. In that case, a single `create()` method takes a type or string parameter from which it decides which object to create. For example, a `CarFactory` object would provide a `buildCar()` method that takes a string representing the type of car and constructs the appropriate type. The Microsoft MFC library uses such a concept. MFC has a function called `CRuntimeClass::CreateObject()` which accepts one parameter, a string which is the name of the class of which you want to create an object. The `CreateObject()` method is compiled into the MFC library in binary form, but still, due to the factory pattern, it is able to create objects of types unknown at the time the library was compiled.

Factory methods are one way to implement virtual constructors: *methods that create objects of different types. For example, the* `buildCar()` *method creates both* Toyotas *and* Fords, *depending on the concrete factory object on which it is called.*

Using a Factory

The simplest way to use a factory is to instantiate it and to call the appropriate method, as in the following piece of code:

```
ToyotaFactory myFactory;
Car* myCar = myFactory.requestCar();
```

A more interesting example makes use of the virtual constructor idea to build a car in the factory that has the fewest cars in production. To do this, you will need a function that looks at several factories and chooses the least busy one, such as the following function:

```cpp
shared_ptr<CarFactory> getLeastBusyFactory(
    const vector<shared_ptr<CarFactory>>& inFactories)
{
    if (inFactories.size() == 0)
        return nullptr;
    shared_ptr<CarFactory> bestSoFar = inFactories[0];
    for (size_t i = 1; i < inFactories.size(); i++) {
        if (inFactories[i]->getNumCarsInProduction() <
            bestSoFar->getNumCarsInProduction()) {
            bestSoFar = inFactories[i];
        }
    }
    return bestSoFar;
}
```

Code snippet from CarFactory\CarTest.cpp

The following code makes use of this function to build 10 cars, whatever brand they might be, from the currently least busy factory.

```cpp
vector<shared_ptr<CarFactory>> factories;
// Create 3 Ford factories and 1 Toyota factory.
auto factory1 = make_shared<FordFactory>();
auto factory2 = make_shared<FordFactory>();
auto factory3 = make_shared<FordFactory>();
auto factory4 = make_shared<ToyotaFactory>();
// To get more interesting results, preorder some cars.
factory1->requestCar();
factory1->requestCar();
factory2->requestCar();
factory4->requestCar();
// Add the factories to a vector.
factories.push_back(factory1);
factories.push_back(factory2);
factories.push_back(factory3);
factories.push_back(factory4);
// Build 10 cars from the least busy factory.
for (size_t i = 0; i < 10; i++) {
    shared_ptr<CarFactory> currentFactory = getLeastBusyFactory(factories);
    shared_ptr<Car> theCar(currentFactory->requestCar());
    theCar->info();
}
```

Code snippet from CarFactory\CarTest.cpp

When executed, the program will print out the make of each car produced:

```
Ford
Ford
```

```
Ford
Toyota
Ford
Ford
Ford
Toyota
Ford
Ford
```

The results are rather predictable because the loop effectively iterates through the factories in a round-robin fashion. However, one could imagine a scenario where multiple dealers are requesting cars, and the current status of each factory isn't quite so predictable.

Other Uses of Factories

You can also use the factory pattern for more than just modeling real-world factories. For example, consider a word processor in which you want to support documents in different languages, where each document uses a single language. There are many aspects of the word processor in which the choice of document language requires different support: the character set used in the document (whether or not accented characters are needed), the spellchecker, the thesaurus, and the way the document is displayed to name a few. You could use factories to design a clean word processor by writing an abstract `LanguageFactory` superclass and concrete factories for each language of interest, such as `EnglishLanguageFactory` and `FrenchLanguageFactory`. When the user specifies a language for a document, the program instantiates the appropriate language factory and attaches it to the document. From then on, the program doesn't need to know which language is supported in the document. When it needs a language-specific piece of functionality, it can just ask the `LanguageFactory`. For example, when it needs a spellchecker, it can call the `createSpellchecker()` method on the factory, which will return a spellchecker in the appropriate language.

THE PROXY PATTERN

The *proxy* pattern is one of several patterns that divorce the abstraction of a class from its underlying representation. A proxy object serves as a stand-in for a real object. Such objects are generally used when using the real object would be time-consuming or impossible. For example, take a document editor. A document could contain several big objects, such as images. Instead of loading all those images when opening the document, the document editor could substitute all images with image proxies. These proxies don't immediately load the images. Only when the user scrolls down in the document and reaches an image, the document editor will ask the image proxy to draw itself. Then, the proxy will delegate the work to the real image class, which will load the image.

Example: Hiding Network Connectivity Issues

Consider a networked game with a `Player` class that represents a person on the Internet who has joined the game. The `Player` class would include functionality that requires network connectivity, such as an instant messaging feature. In the event that a player's connection becomes slow or unresponsive, the `Player` object representing that person can no longer receive instant messages.

Because you don't want to expose network problems to the user, it may be desirable to have a separate class that hides the networked parts of a `Player`. This `PlayerProxy` object would substitute for the actual `Player` object. Clients of the class would either use the `PlayerProxy` class at all times as a gatekeeper to the real `Player` class, or the system would substitute a `PlayerProxy` when a `Player` became unavailable. During a network failure, the `PlayerProxy` object could still display the player's name and last-known state, and could continue to function when the original `Player` object cannot. Thus, the proxy class hides some undesirable semantics of the underlying `Player` class.

Implementation of a Proxy

The public interface for a `Player` class follows. The `sendInstantMessage()` method requires network connectivity to properly function:

```
class Player
{
    public:
        virtual string getName();
        // Sends an instant message to the player over the network and
        // returns the reply as a string. Network connectivity is required.
        virtual string sendInstantMessage(const string& inMessage) const;
};
```

Proxy classes often evoke the is-a versus has-a debate. You *could* implement `PlayerProxy` as a completely separate class that contains a `Player` object. This design would make most sense if the `PlayerProxy` is always used by the program when it wants to talk to a `Player` object. Alternatively, you could implement `PlayerProxy` as a subclass that overrides functionality that requires network connectivity. This design makes it easy to swap out a `Player` for a `PlayerProxy` when network connectivity ceases. This example uses the latter approach by subclassing `Player`, as shown here:

```
class PlayerProxy : public Player
{
    public:
        virtual string sendInstantMessage(const string& inMessage) const;
};
```

The implementation of the `PlayerProxy`'s `sendInstantMessage()` method simply cuts out the network functionality and returns a string indicating that the player has gone offline.

```
string PlayerProxy::sendInstantMessage(const string& inMessage)
{
    return "The player could not be contacted.";
}
```

Another solution could be for the `PlayerProxy`'s `sendInstantMessage()` method to check the network connectivity, and either return a default string or forward the request. For example:

```
string PlayerProxy::sendInstantMessage(const string& inMessage)
{
    if (hasNetworkConnectivity())
```

```
            return Player::sendInstantMessage(inMessage);
        else
            return "The player could not be contacted.";
    }
```

Using a Proxy

If a proxy is well written, using it should be no different from using any other object. For the `PlayerProxy` example, the code that uses the proxy could be completely unaware of its existence. The following function, designed to be called when the `Player` has won, could be dealing with an actual `Player` or a `PlayerProxy`. The code is able to handle both cases in the same way because the proxy ensures a valid result.

```
bool informWinner(const Player* inPlayer)
{
    string result;
    result = inPlayer->sendInstantMessage("You have won! Play again?");
    if (result == "yes") {
        cout << inPlayer->getName() << " wants to play again" << endl;
        return true;
    } else {
        // The player said no, or is offline.
        cout << inPlayer->getName() << " does not want to play again" << endl;
        return false;
    }
}
```

THE ADAPTER PATTERN

The motivation for changing the abstraction given by a class is not always driven by a desire to hide functionality or protect against performance concerns. Sometimes, the underlying abstraction cannot be changed but it doesn't suit the current design. In this case, you can build an *adapter* or *wrapper* class. The adapter provides the abstraction that the rest of the code uses and serves as the bridge between the desired abstraction and the actual underlying code. Chapter 12 discusses how the STL uses the adapter pattern to implement containers like `stack` and `queue` in terms of other containers, such as `deque` and `list`.

Example: Adapting a Logger Class

For this adapter pattern example, let's assume a very basic `Logger` class. Methods are shown with their implementations directly in the header file. This is not Best Practice, but is done to save space.

```
#include <string>
#include <iostream>
class Logger
{
    public:
        static const std::string kLogLevelDebug;
```

```
            static const std::string kLogLevelInfo;
            static const std::string kLogLevelError;
            Logger() { std::cout << "Logger constructor" << std::endl; }
            void log(const std::string& level, const std::string& str) {
                std::cout << level << ": " << str << std::endl;
            }
    };
    const std::string Logger::kLogLevelDebug = "DEBUG";
    const std::string Logger::kLogLevelInfo = "INFO";
    const std::string Logger::kLogLevelError = "ERROR";
```

Code snippet from LoggerAdapter\LoggerAdapter.h

The Logger class has a constructor, which outputs a line of text to the standard console, and a method called log() that writes the given line of text to the console prefixed with a log level.

One reason why you might want to write a wrapper class around this basic Logger class is to change the interface of it. Maybe you are not interested in the log level and you would like to call the log() method with only one parameter, the message itself.

Implementation of an Adapter

The first step in implementing the adapter pattern is to define the new interface for the underlying functionality. This new interface is called NewLoggerInterface and looks as follows:

```
class NewLoggerInterface
{
    public:
        virtual void log(const std::string& str) = 0;
};
```

Code snippet from LoggerAdapter\LoggerAdapter.h

This class is an abstract class, which declares the desired interface that you want for your new logger. It only defines one abstract method which needs to be implemented by any class inheriting from this interface. You can think of NewLoggerInterface as a mix-in class. Mix-in classes are discussed in Chapter 28.

The next step is to write the actual new logger class, NewLoggerAdapter, which inherits from the NewLoggerInterface so that it has the interface that you designed. It also privately inherits from the original Logger class. It is inherited privately so that no functionality from the original Logger class will be publicly available in the NewLoggerAdapter class. The constructor of the new class writes a line to standard output to keep track of which constructors are being called. The code then implements the abstract log() method from the NewLoggerInterface interface by forwarding the call to the original log() method and specifying kLogLevelInfo as log level:

```
class NewLoggerAdapter : public NewLoggerInterface, private Logger
{
    public:
```

```
        NewLoggerAdapter() {
            std::cout << "NewLoggerAdapter constructor" << std::endl;
        }
        virtual void log(const std::string& str) {
            Logger::log(Logger::kLogLevelInfo, str);
        }
};
```

Code snippet from LoggerAdapter\LoggerAdapter.h

Using an Adapter

Since adapters exist to provide a more appropriate interface for the underlying functionality, their use should be straightforward and specific to the particular case. Given the previous example, the following program uses the new simplified interface for the Logger class:

Available for
download on
Wrox.com

```
#include "LoggerAdapter.h"
int main()
{
    NewLoggerAdapter logger;
    logger.log("Testing the logger.");
    return 0;
}
```

Code snippet from LoggerAdapter\TestLoggerAdapter.cpp

When you compile and run this example, it will produce the following output:

```
Logger constructor
NewLoggerAdapter constructor
INFO: Testing the logger.
```

THE DECORATOR PATTERN

The *decorator* pattern is exactly what it sounds like — a "decoration" on an object. The pattern is used to change the behavior of an object at run time. Decorators are a lot like subclasses, but their effects can be temporary. For example, if you have a stream of data that you are parsing and you reach data that represents an image, you could temporarily decorate the stream object with an ImageStream object. The ImageStream constructor would take the stream object as a parameter and would have built-in knowledge of image parsing. Once the image is parsed, you could continue using the original object to parse the remainder of the stream. The ImageStream acts as a decorator because it adds new functionality (image parsing) to an existing object (a stream).

Example: Defining Styles in Web Pages

As you may already know, web pages are written in a simple text-based structure called HyperText Markup Language (HTML). In HTML, you can apply styles to a text by using style tags, such as

<B> and </B> for bold and <I> and </I> for italic. The following line of HTML will display the message in bold:

```
<B>A party? For me? Thanks!</B>
```

The following line will display the message in bold italic:

```
<I><B>A party? For me? Thanks!</B></I>
```

Assume that you are writing an HTML editing application. Your users will be able to type in paragraphs of text and apply one or more styles to them. You *could* make each type of paragraph a new subclass, as shown in Figure 29-6, but that design could be cumbersome and would grow exponentially as new styles were added.

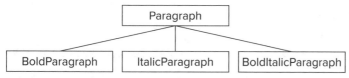

FIGURE 29-6

The alternative is to consider styled paragraphs not as *types* of paragraphs, but as *decorated* paragraphs. This leads to situations like the one shown in Figure 29-7, where an `ItalicParagraph` operates on a `BoldParagraph`, which in turn operates on a `Paragraph`. The recursive decoration of objects nests the styles in code just as they are nested in HTML.

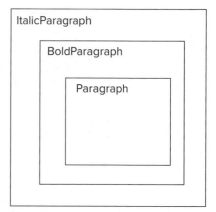

FIGURE 29-7

Implementation of a Decorator

To decorate the `Paragraph` class with zero or more styles, you will need a hierarchy of styled `Paragraph` classes. Each of the styled `Paragraph` classes will be constructible from an existing `Paragraph`. This way, they can all decorate a `Paragraph` or a styled `Paragraph`. The most convenient way to implement the styled classes is as subclasses of `Paragraph`. Here is the `Paragraph` base class:

```cpp
class Paragraph
{
    public:
        Paragraph(const string& inInitialText) : mText(inInitialText) {}
        virtual string getHTML() const { return mText; }
    protected:
        string mText;
};
```

Code snippet from Decorator\Decorator.cpp

The `BoldParagraph` class will be a subclass of `Paragraph` so that it can override `getHTML()`. However, because we intend to use it as a decorator, its only public non-copy constructor takes a `const` reference to a `Paragraph`. Note that it passes an empty string to the `Paragraph` constructor because `BoldParagraph` doesn't make use of the `mText` data member — its only purpose in subclassing `Paragraph` is to override `getHTML()`.

```cpp
class BoldParagraph : public Paragraph
{
    public:
        BoldParagraph(const Paragraph& inParagraph) :
            Paragraph(""), mWrapped(inParagraph) {}
        virtual string getHTML() const {
            return "<B>" + mWrapped.getHTML() + "</B>";
        }
    protected:
        const Paragraph& mWrapped;
};
```

Code snippet from Decorator\Decorator.cpp

The `ItalicParagraph` class is almost identical:

```cpp
class ItalicParagraph : public Paragraph
{
    public:
        ItalicParagraph(const Paragraph& inParagraph) :
            Paragraph(""), mWrapped(inParagraph) {}
        virtual string getHTML() const {
            return "<I>" + mWrapped.getHTML() + "</I>";
        }
    protected:
        const Paragraph& mWrapped;
};
```

Code snippet from Decorator\Decorator.cpp

Again, remember that `BoldParagraph` and `ItalicParagraph` only subclass `Paragraph` so that they can override `getHTML()`. The content of the paragraph comes from the wrapped object, not from the `mText` data member.

Using a Decorator

From the user's point of view, the decorator pattern is appealing because it is very easy to apply, and is transparent once applied. The client doesn't need to know that a decorator has been employed at all. A `BoldParagraph` behaves just like a `Paragraph`.

Here is a quick example that creates and outputs a paragraph, first in bold, then in bold and italic:

```cpp
Paragraph p("A party? For me? Thanks!");
// Bold
cout << BoldParagraph(p).getHTML() << endl;
```

```
// Bold and Italic
cout << ItalicParagraph(BoldParagraph(p)).getHTML() << endl;
```

Code snippet from Decorator\Decorator.cpp

The output will be as follows:

```
<B>A party? For me? Thanks!</B>
<I><B>A party? For me? Thanks!</B></I>
```

There is an interesting side effect of this implementation that just happens to work correctly for HTML. If you applied the same style twice in a row, the effect would only occur once:

```
cout << BoldParagraph(BoldParagraph(p)).getHTML() << endl;
```

The result of this line is:

```
<B>A party? For me? Thanks!</B>
```

If you can see the reason why, you've mastered C++! What's happening here is that instead of using the `BoldParagraph` constructor that takes a `const Paragraph` reference, the compiler is using the built-in copy constructor for `BoldParagraph`! In HTML, that's fine — there's no such thing as double-bold. However, other decorators built using a similar framework may need to implement the copy constructor to properly set the reference.

THE CHAIN OF RESPONSIBILITY PATTERN

A *chain of responsibility* is used when you want each class in an object-oriented hierarchy to get a crack at performing a particular action. The technique generally employs polymorphism so that the most specific class gets called first and can either handle the call or pass it up to its parent. The parent then makes the same decision — it can handle the call or pass it up to its parent. A chain of responsibility does not necessarily have to follow a class hierarchy, but it typically does.

Chains of responsibility are perhaps most commonly used for event handling. Many modern applications, particularly those with graphical user interfaces, are designed as a series of events and responses. For example, when a user clicks on the *File* menu and selects *Open*, an open event has occurred. When the user moves the mouse over the drawable area of a paint program, mouse move events are generated continuously. If the user presses down a button on the mouse, a mouse down event for that button-press is generated. The program will then start paying attention to the mouse move events, allowing the user to "draw" some object, and continue doing this until the mouse up event occurs. Each operating system has its own way of naming and using these events, but the overall idea is the same: When an event occurs, it is somehow communicated to the program, which takes appropriate action.

As you know, C++ does not have any built-in facilities for graphical programming. It also has no notion of events, event transmission, or event handling. A chain of responsibility is a reasonable approach to event handling because in an object-oriented hierarchy, the processing of events often maps to the class/subclass structure.

Example: Event Handling

Consider a drawing program, which has a hierarchy of Shape classes, as in Figure 29-8.

The leaf nodes handle certain events. For example, Square or Circle can receive mouse down events that will select the chosen shape. The parent class handles events that have the same effect regardless of the particular shape. For example, a delete event is handled the same way, regardless

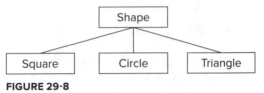

FIGURE 29-8

of the type of shape being deleted. The ideal algorithm for handling a particular event is to start at the leaf nodes and walk up the hierarchy until the message is handled. In other words, if a mouse down event occurs on a Square object, first the Square will get a chance to handle the event. If it doesn't recognize the event, the Shape class gets a chance. This approach is an example of a chain of responsibility because each subclass may pass the message up to the next class in the chain.

Implementation of a Chain of Responsibility

The code for a chained messaging approach will vary based on how the operating system handles events, but it tends to resemble the following code, which uses integers to represent types of events:

```
void Square::handleMessage(int inMessage)
{
    switch (inMessage) {
        case kMessageMouseDown:
            handleMouseDown();
            break;
        case kMessageInvert:
            handleInvert();
            break;
        default:
            // Message not recognized--chain to superclass
            Shape::handleMessage(inMessage);
    }
}
void Shape::handleMessage(int inMessage)
{
    switch (inMessage) {
        case kMessageDelete:
            handleDelete();
            break;
        default:
        {
            stringstream ss;
            ss << __func__ << ": Unrecognized message received: " << inMessage;
            throw invalid_argument(ss.str());
        }
    }
}
```

When the event-handling portion of the program or framework receives a message, it finds the corresponding shape and calls handleMessage(). Through polymorphism, the subclass's version of handleMessage() is called. This gives the leaf node first crack at handling the message. If it doesn't know how to handle it, it passes it up to its superclass, which gets the next chance. In this example, the final recipient of the message throws an exception if it is unable to handle the event. You could also have your `handleMessage()` method return a boolean indicating success or failure.

Note that while event chains usually correlate with the class hierarchy, they do not have to. In the preceding example, the `Square` class could have just as easily passed the message to an entirely different object. The chained approach is flexible and has a very appealing structure for object-oriented hierarchies. The downside is that it requires diligence on the part of the programmer. If you forget to chain up to the superclass from a subclass, events will effectively get lost. Worse, if you chain to the wrong class, you could end up in an infinite loop!

Using a Chain of Responsibility

For a chain of responsibility to respond to events, there must be another class that *dispatches* the events to the correct object. Because this task varies greatly by framework or platform, the following example shows pseudocode for handling a mouse down event, in lieu of platform-specific C++ code:

```
MouseLocation loc = getClickLocation();
Shape* clickedShape = findShapeAtLocation(loc);
if (clickedShape)
    clickedShape->handleMessage(kMessageMouseDown);
```

THE OBSERVER PATTERN

The other common model for event handling is known as *observer*, *listener messaging*, or *publish and subscribe*. This is a more prescriptive model that is often less error-prone than message chains. With the publish and subscribe technique, individual objects *register* the events they are able to understand with a central event handling registry. When an event is received, it is transmitted to the list of subscribed objects.

Example: Event Handling

Just as with the earlier chain of responsibility pattern, observers are often used to handle events. The main difference between the two patterns is that the chain of responsibility works best for logical hierarchies where you need to find the correct class to handle the event. Observers work best when events can be handled by multiple objects, or are unrelated to a hierarchy.

Implementation of an Observer

First, a `Listener` mix-in class is defined. Any object that wants to subscribe to one or more events should inherit from this mix-in class:

Available for
download on
Wrox.com

```
class Listener
{
    public:
        virtual void handleMessage(int inMessage) = 0;
};
```

Code snippet from Observer\Listener.h

The definition of a simple event registry class is shown next. It allows any object that extends the mix-in class `Listener` to subscribe to one or more events. It maintains a directory of `Listeners` and their corresponding events. It also contains a method for the program to call when an event is received, which will dispense the event to all subscribed `Listeners`.

To simplify this example, a few assumptions are made. These assumptions are not necessarily going to be valid in all contexts. To focus the example on demonstrating the observer pattern, the event registry just uses static methods and a static `map`, meaning there is only one `map` during the run time of the program. If you need multiple separate event registries, you'll have to adapt the `EventRegistry` class. Support for unregistering listeners is also not included. Normally, the destructor of a listener may want to unregister all subscriptions for that object. The given implementation also allows an object to register itself twice, which may be undesirable depending on your use case. You might also need to register objects with an implied ordering (for example, Z-axis for graphical objects) in which events are processed; in the following example, there is no implied ordering, so an `std::map` is used, which imposes its own order on event handling. Note that the model has many variants depending on the needs of the design. Thus, you should read this code for the overall structure, and not think of it as an exact model that is universally applicable in all circumstances.

```cpp
#include "Listener.h"
#include <vector>
#include <map>
class EventRegistry
{
    public:
        static void registerListener(int inMessage, Listener* inListener);
        static void handleMessage(int inMessage);
    protected:
        static std::map<int, std::vector<Listener*>> sListenerMap;
};
```

Code snippet from Observer\EventRegistry.h

The implementation of the `EventRegistry` class follows. When a new `Listener` is registered, it is added to the `vector` of `Listeners` stored in the listener `map` for the given event. When an event is received, the registry simply retrieves the `vector` and passes the event to each `Listener`:

```cpp
// Define the static map.
map<int, vector<Listener*>> EventRegistry::sListenerMap;

void EventRegistry::registerListener(int inMessage, Listener* inListener)
{
    // Chapter 12 explains std::map. Note that if you specify a key
    // using [] to access it, and there is not yet an entry in the map for
    // that key, a new entry is created.
    sListenerMap[inMessage].push_back(inListener);
}
void EventRegistry::handleMessage(int inMessage)
{
    // Check to see if the message has *any* listeners. This check is required
    // because otherwise, accessing sListenerMap[inMessage] would create
```

```
    // a new entry when it's not yet in the map. See Chapter 12.
    if (sListenerMap.find(inMessage) == sListenerMap.end())
        return;
    for (auto iter = sListenerMap[inMessage].begin();
            iter != sListenerMap[inMessage].end(); ++iter) {
        (*iter)->handleMessage(inMessage);
    }
}
```

Code snippet from Observer\EventRegistry.cpp

Using an Observer

Following is a very simple unit test that demonstrates how to use the *publish and subscribe* technique. The class `TestListener` subscribes to message 0 in its constructor. Subscribing to a message in a constructor is a common pattern for objects that are `Listeners`. The class contains two flags that keep track of whether message 0 was successfully received, and whether any unknown messages were received. If message 0 was received and no unknowns were received, the test passes.

Available for
download on
Wrox.com

```
class TestListener : public Listener
{
    public:
        TestListener();
        void handleMessage(int inMessage);
        bool bMessage0Received;
        bool bUnknownMessageReceived;
};
```

Code snippet from Observer\TestListener.h

Available for
download on
Wrox.com

```
TestListener::TestListener() :
    bMessage0Received(false),
    bUnknownMessageReceived(false)
{
    // Subscribe to event 0.
    EventRegistry::registerListener(0, this);
}
void TestListener::handleMessage(int inMessage)
{
    switch (inMessage) {
        case 0:
            bMessage0Received = true;
            break;
        default:
            bUnknownMessageReceived = true;
            break;
    }
}
```

Code snippet from Observer\TestListener.cpp

```cpp
int main()
{
    TestListener tl;
    EventRegistry::handleMessage(0);
    EventRegistry::handleMessage(1);
    EventRegistry::handleMessage(2);
    if (!tl.bMessage0Received) {
        cout << "TEST FAILED: Message 0 was not received" << endl;
    } else if (tl.bUnknownMessageReceived) {
        cout << "TEST FAILED: TestListener received unknown message" << endl;
    } else {
        cout << "TEST PASSED" << endl;
    }
    return 0;
}
```

Code snippet from Observer\TestObserver.cpp

Of course, an actual implementation in your program would vary from the implementation shown here based on the services provided by the environment and your individual needs.

SUMMARY

This chapter has given you just a taste of how patterns can help you organize object-oriented concepts into high-level designs. There is a seemingly infinite supply of design patterns cataloged and discussed on the Portland Pattern Repository Wiki at www.c2.com. It's easy to get carried away and spend all your time trying to find the specific pattern that applies to your task. We recommend that you focus on a few patterns that interest you and focus your learning on how patterns are developed, not just the small differences between similar ones. After all, to paraphrase the old saying, "Teach me a design pattern, and I'll code for a day. Teach me how to *create* design patterns, and I'll code for a lifetime."

Design patterns are a terrific way to end your journey through *Professional C++ Programming* because they are a perfect example of how good C++ programmers can become great C++ programmers. By thinking through your designs, experimenting with different approaches in object-oriented programming, and selectively adding new techniques to your coding repertoire, you'll be able to take your C++ skills to the Professional level.

C++ Interviews

Reading this book will surely give your C++ career a kick-start, but employers will want you to prove yourself before they offer the big bucks. Interview methodologies vary from company to company, but many aspects of technical interviews are predictable. A thorough interviewer will want to test your basic coding skills, your debugging skills, your design and style skills, and your problem-solving skills. The set of questions you might be asked is quite large. In this appendix, you'll read about some of the different types of questions you may encounter and the best tactics for landing that high-paying C++ programming job you're after.

This appendix iterates through the chapters of the book, discussing the aspects of each chapter that are likely to come up in an interview situation. Each section also includes a discussion of the types of questions that could be designed to test those skills, and the best ways to deal with those questions.

CHAPTER 1: A CRASH COURSE IN C++

A technical interview will often include some basic C++ questions to weed out the candidates who put C++ on their resume simply because they've heard of the language. These questions might be asked during a *phone screen*, when a developer or recruiter calls you before bringing you in for an in-person interview. They could also be asked via e-mail or in person. When answering these questions, remember that the interviewer is just trying to establish that you've actually learned and used C++. You generally don't need to get every detail right to earn high marks.

Things to Remember

➤ `main()` and its parameters

➤ When you are applying for a platform specific job, check what kind of `main()` function and which parameters that platform might use, for example, on Windows, your program might use `WinMain()`, `_tmain()`, `wmain()`, and a few others.

➤ Use of functions

➤ Header file syntax, including the omission of ".h" for standard library headers

➤ Basic use of namespaces

➤ Language basics, such as loop syntax, the ternary operator, and variables

➤ The difference between the stack and the heap

➤ Dynamically allocated arrays

➤ Use of `const`

➤ What references are

➤ The C++11 `auto` and `decltype` keywords

Types of Questions

Basic C++ questions will often come in the form of a vocabulary test. The interviewer may ask you to define C++ terms, such as `const` or `static`. He or she may be looking for the textbook answer, but you can often score extra points by giving sample usage or extra detail. For example, in addition to saying that one of the uses of `const` is to specify that a reference argument cannot be changed, you can also say that a `const` reference is more efficient than a copy when passing an object into a function or method.

The other form that basic C++ competence questions can take is a short program that you write in front of the interviewer. An interviewer may give you a warm-up question, such as, "Write *Hello, World* in C++." When you get a seemingly simple question like this, make sure that you score all the extra points you can by showing that you are namespace-savvy, you use streams instead of `printf()`, and you know which standard headers to include.

CHAPTER 2: DESIGNING PROFESSIONAL C++ PROGRAMS

Your interviewer will want to make sure that in addition to knowing the C++ language, you are skilled at applying it. You may not be asked a design question explicitly, but good interviewers have a variety of techniques to sneak design into other questions, as you'll see.

A potential employer will also want to know that you're able to work with code that you didn't write yourself. If you've listed specific libraries on your resume, you should be prepared to answer questions on those. If you didn't list specific libraries, a general understanding of the importance of libraries will probably suffice.

Things to Remember

➤ Design is subjective — be prepared to defend design decisions you make during the interview.

➤ Recall the details of a design you've done in the past prior to the interview in case you are asked for an example.

➤ Be prepared to define *abstraction* and give an example.

➤ Be prepared to sketch out a design visually, including class hierarchies.

➤ Be prepared to tout the benefits of code reuse.

➤ The concept of libraries

➤ The tradeoffs between building from scratch and reusing existing code

➤ The basics of big-O notation, or at least remember that $O(n \log n)$ is better than $O(n^2)$

➤ The functionality that is included in the C++ Standard Library

➤ The high-level definition of design patterns

Types of Questions

Design questions are hard for an interviewer to come up with — any program that you could design in an interview setting is probably too simple to demonstrate real-world design skills. Design questions may come in a more fuzzy form, such as, "Tell me the steps in designing a good program," or "Explain the principle of abstraction." They can also be less explicit. When discussing your previous job, the interviewer can say, "Can you explain the design of that project to me?"

If the interviewer is asking you about a specific library, he or she will probably focus on the high-level aspects of the library as opposed to technical specifics. For example, you can be asked to explain what the strengths and weaknesses of the STL are from a library design point of view. The best candidates talk about the STL's breadth and standardization as strengths, and its steep learning curve as the major drawback.

You may also be asked a design question that initially doesn't sound as if it's related to libraries. For example, the interviewer could ask how you would go about creating an application that downloads MP3 music from the web and plays it on the local computer. This question isn't explicitly related to libraries, but that's what it's getting at; the question is really asking about process.

You should begin by talking about how you would gather requirements and do initial prototypes. Because the question mentions two specific technologies, the interviewer would like to know how you would deal with them. This is where libraries come into play. If you tell the interviewer that you would write your own web classes and MP3 playing code, you won't fail the test, but you will be challenged to justify the time and expense of reinventing these tools.

A better answer would be to say that you would survey existing libraries that perform web and MP3 functionality to see if one exists that suits the project. You might want to name some technologies that you would start with, such as libcurl for web retrieval in Linux or the Windows Media library for music playback in Windows.

Mentioning some websites with free libraries, and some ideas of what those websites provide, might also get you extra points. For example, www.codeguru.com and www.codeproject.com for Windows libraries; www.boost.org for C++ libraries; and www.sourceforge.org for Linux libraries. Explaining the major differences between some licenses, such as the GPL license, Boost license, Creative Commons license, CodeGuru license, OpenBSD license, and so on, might score you extra credit. Don't stress GNU/GPL too much; you might get negative points because you might be seen as an active hazard to the company's Intellectual Property (IP).

CHAPTER 3: DESIGNING WITH OBJECTS

Object-oriented design questions are used to weed out C programmers who merely know what a reference is, from C++ programmers who actually use the object-oriented features of the language. Interviewers don't take anything for granted; even if you've been using object-oriented languages for years, they may still want to see evidence that you understand the methodology.

Things to Remember

➤ The differences between the procedural and object-oriented paradigms

➤ The differences between a class and an object

➤ Expressing classes in terms of components, properties, and behaviors

➤ Is-a and has-a relationships

➤ The tradeoffs involved in multiple inheritance

Types of Questions

There are typically two ways to ask object-oriented design questions. You can be asked to define an object-oriented concept, or you can be asked to sketch out an object-oriented hierarchy. The former is pretty straightforward. Remember that examples might earn you extra credit.

If you're asked to sketch out an OO hierarchy, the interviewer will usually provide a simple application, such as a card game, for which you should design a class hierarchy. Interviewers often ask design questions about games because they are applications with which most people are already familiar. They also help lighten the mood a bit when compared to questions about things like database implementations. The hierarchy you generate will, of course, vary based on the game or application they are asking you to design. Here are some points to consider:

➤ The interviewer wants to see your thought process. Think aloud, brainstorm, engage the interviewer in a discussion, and don't be afraid to erase and go in a different direction.

➤ The interviewer may assume that you are familiar with the application. If you've never heard of Blackjack and you get a question about it, ask the interviewer to clarify or change the question.

➤ Unless the interviewer gives you a specific format to use when describing the hierarchy, we recommend that your class diagrams take the form of inheritance trees with rough lists of methods and data members for each class.

➤ You may have to defend your design or revise it to take added requirements into consideration. Try to gauge whether the interviewer sees actual flaws in your design, or whether she just wants to put you on the defensive to see your skills of persuasion.

CHAPTER 4: DESIGNING FOR REUSE

Interviewers rarely ask questions about designing reusable code. This omission is unfortunate because having programmers on staff who can write only single-purpose code can be detrimental to a programming organization. Occasionally, you'll find a company that is savvy on code reuse and asks about it in their interviews. Such a question is an indication that it might be a good company to work for.

Things to Remember

➤ The principle of abstraction

➤ The creation of subsystems and class hierarchies

➤ The general rules for good interface design, which are interfaces with only `public` methods and no implementation details

➤ When to use templates and when to use inheritance

Types of Questions

Questions about reuse will almost certainly be about previous projects on which you have worked. For example, if you worked at a company that produced both consumer and professional video-editing applications, the interviewer may ask how code was shared between the two applications. Even if you aren't explicitly asked about code reuse, you might be able to sneak it in. When you're describing some of your past work, tell the interviewer if the modules you wrote were used in other projects. Even when answering apparently straight coding questions, make sure to consider and mention the interfaces involved.

CHAPTER 5: CODING WITH STYLE

Anybody who's coded in the professional world has had a co-worker who codes as if they learned C++ from the back of a cereal box. Nobody wants to work with someone who writes messy code, so interviewers sometimes attempt to determine a candidate's style skills.

Things to Remember

➤ Style matters, even during interview questions that aren't explicitly style related.

➤ Well-written code doesn't need extensive comments.

➤ Comments can be used to convey metainformation.

➤ The principle of decomposition

➤ The principle of refactoring

➤ Naming techniques

Types of Questions

Style questions can come in a few different forms. One of the authors was once asked to write the code for a relatively complex algorithm on a whiteboard. As soon as he wrote the first variable name, the interviewer stopped him and told him he passed. The question wasn't about the algorithm; it was just a red herring to see how well he named his variables. More commonly, you may be asked to submit code that you've written, or to give your opinions on style.

You need to be careful when a potential employer asks you to submit code. You probably cannot legally submit code that you wrote for a previous employer. You also have to find a piece of code that shows off your skills without requiring too much background knowledge. For example, you wouldn't want to submit your master's thesis on high-speed image rendering to a company that is interviewing you for a database administration position.

If the company gives you a specific program to write, that's a perfect opportunity to show off what you've learned in this book. How many other candidates will include unit tests with their program, or extensive comments? Even if the potential employer doesn't specify the program, you should consider writing a small program specifically to submit to the company. Instead of selecting some code you've already written, start from scratch to produce code that is relevant to the job and highlights good style.

Also, if you have documentation that you have written and that can be released, meaning it is not proprietary, use it to show your skills to *communicate*, it will give you extra points. Websites you have built or maintained, articles you have submitted to places like CodeGuru, CodeProject, SourceForge, and so on, are very useful; it says you can not only *write code*, but you can *communicate* to others how to effectively *use* that code. Of course, having a book title attached to your name is also a big plus.

CHAPTERS 6 AND 7: CLASSES AND OBJECTS

There are no bounds to the types of questions you can be asked about classes and objects. Some interviewers are syntax-fixated and might throw some complicated code at you. Others are less concerned with the implementation and more interested in your design skills.

Things to Remember

- ➤ Basic class definition syntax
- ➤ Access specifiers for methods and data members
- ➤ The use of the `this` pointer
- ➤ How name resolution works, which resolves a name first by local scope, then class scope (implying `this->`) and then global scope
- ➤ Object creation and destruction, both on the stack and the heap
- ➤ Cases when the compiler generates a constructor for you
- ➤ Constructor initializers

- ➤ Copy constructor and assignment operator

- ➤ The `mutable` keyword

- ➤ Method overloading and default parameters

- ➤ Friend classes and methods

- ➤ Managing dynamically allocated memory in objects

- ➤ `static` methods and members

- ➤ Inline methods and the fact that the `inline` keyword is just a hint for the compiler which can ignore the hint

- ➤ The key idea of separating interface and implementation classes, which says that interfaces should only contain `public` methods, and should be as stable as possible; they should not contain any data members or `private/protected` methods; thus, interfaces can remain stable while implementations are free to change under them.

- ➤ C++11 initializer lists

- ➤ C++11 in-class member initializers

- ➤ C++11 explicitly defaulted and deleted special member functions

Types of Questions

Questions such as, "What does the keyword `mutable` mean?" make great phone screening questions. A recruiter may have a list of C++ terms and will move candidates to the next stage of the process based on the number that they get right. You may not know all of the terms that are thrown at you, but keep in mind that other candidates are facing the same questions and it's one of the few metrics available to a recruiter.

The *find-the-bug* style of questions is popular among interviewers and course instructors alike. You will be presented with some nonsense code and asked to point out its flaws. Interviewers struggle to find quantitative ways to analyze candidates, and this is one of the few ways to do it. In general, your approach should be to read each line of code and voice your concerns, brainstorming aloud. The types of bugs can fall into these categories:

- ➤ **Syntax errors:** These are rare — interviewers know you can find compile-time bugs with a compiler.

- ➤ **Memory problems:** These include problems such as leaks and double deletion.

- ➤ **"You wouldn't do that" problems:** This category includes things that are technically correct but are not recommended. For example, don't use C-style character arrays, use `std::string` instead.

- ➤ **Style errors:** Even if the interviewer doesn't count it as a bug, point out poor comments or variable names.

Here's a find-the-bug problem that demonstrates each of these areas:

```cpp
class Buggy
{
        Buggy(int param);
        ~Buggy();
        double fjord(double inVal);
        int fjord(double inVal);
    protected:
        void turtle(int i = 7, int j);
        int param;
        double* mGraphicDimension;
};
Buggy::Buggy(int param)
{
    param = param;
    mGraphicDimension = new double;
}
Buggy::~Buggy()
{
}
double Buggy::fjord(double inVal)
{
    return inVal * param;
}
int Buggy::fjord(double inVal)
{
    return (int)fjord(inVal);
}
void Buggy::turtle(int i, int j)
{
    cout << "i is " << i << ", j is " << j << endl;
}
```

Take a careful look at the code, and then consult the following corrected version for the answers:

```cpp
#include <iostream>            // Streams are used in the implementation.
class Buggy
{
    public:                    // These should most likely be public.
        Buggy(int inParam);    // Parameter naming.
        virtual ~Buggy();      // Recommended to make destructors virtual.
        Buggy(const Buggy& src);              // Provide copy ctor and operator=
        Buggy& operator=(const Buggy& rhs); // when the class has dynamically
                                             // allocated memory.
        Buggy(Buggy&& src);                  // C++11: provide move ctor and operator=
        Buggy& operator=(Buggy&& rhs); // when the class has dynamically
                                       // allocated memory to increase
                                       // performance. (See Chapter 9).
        double fjord(double inVal); // int version won't compile. Overloaded
                                    // methods cannot differ only in return type.
    protected:
        void turtle(int i, int j);  // Only last arguments can have defaults.
        int mParam;                 // Data member naming
        double* mGraphicDimension;
};
```

```cpp
Buggy::Buggy(int inParam) : mParam(inParam)
{
    mGraphicDimension = new double;
}
Buggy::~Buggy()
{
    delete mGraphicDimension;  // Avoid memory leak.
    mGraphicDimension = nullptr;
}
Buggy::Buggy(const Buggy& src)
{
    mParam = src.mParam;
    mGraphicDimension = new double;
    *mGraphicDimension = *(src.mGraphicDimension);
}
Buggy& Buggy::operator=(const Buggy& rhs)
{
    if (this == &rhs) {
        return *this;
    }
    mParam = rhs.mParam;
    delete mGraphicDimension;
    mGraphicDimension = new double;
    *mGraphicDimension = *(rhs.mGraphicDimension);
    return *this;
}
Buggy::Buggy(Buggy&& src)
{
    mParam = src.mParam;
    mGraphicDimension = src.mGraphicDimension;
    src.mGraphicDimension = nullptr;
}
Buggy& Buggy::operator=(Buggy&& rhs)
{
    if (this == &rhs) {
        return *this;
    }
    mParam = rhs.mParam;
    mGraphicDimension = rhs.mGraphicDimension;
    rhs.mGraphicDimension = nullptr;
    return *this;
}
double Buggy::fjord(double inVal)
{
    return inVal * mParam;     // Changed data member name
}
void Buggy::turtle(int i, int j)
{
    std::cout << "i is " << i << ", j is " << j << std::endl; // Namespaces
}
```

For this example, you should also mention that it's recommended to use a smart pointer, such as the C++11 `shared_ptr`, instead of the dumb `mGraphicDimension` pointer, and include an explanation of why a smart pointer is recommended.

CHAPTER 8: DISCOVERING INHERITANCE TECHNIQUES

Questions about inheritance usually come in the same forms as questions about classes. The interviewer might also ask you to implement a class hierarchy to show that you have worked with C++ enough to subclass without looking it up in a book.

Things to Remember

➤ The syntax for subclassing a class

➤ The difference between `private` and `protected` from a subclass point of view

➤ Method overriding and `virtual`

➤ The reason why destructors should be `virtual`

➤ Chained constructors

➤ The ins and outs of upcasting and downcasting

➤ The principle of polymorphism

➤ Pure `virtual` methods and abstract base classes

➤ Multiple inheritance

➤ Run Time Type Information (RTTI)

➤ C++11 inherited constructors

➤ The C++11 `final` keyword on classes

➤ The C++11 `override` and `final` keywords on methods

Types of Questions

Many of the pitfalls in inheritance questions are related to getting the details right. When you are writing a base class, don't forget to make the methods `virtual`. If you mark all methods `virtual`, be prepared to justify that decision. You should be able to explain what `virtual` means and how it works. Also, don't forget the `public` keyword before the name of the parent class in the subclass definition (e.g., `class Sub : public Super`). It's unlikely that you'll be asked to perform nonpublic inheritance during an interview.

More challenging inheritance questions have to do with the relationship between a superclass and a subclass. Be sure you know how the different access levels work, and the difference between `private` and `protected`. Remind yourself of the phenomenon known as *slicing*, when certain types of casts cause a class to lose its subclass information.

CHAPTER 9: UNDERSTANDING C++ QUIRKS AND ODDITIES

Many interviewers tend to focus on the more obscure cases because that way experienced C++ programmers can demonstrate that they have conquered the unusual parts of C++. Sometimes interviewers have difficulty coming up with interesting questions and end up asking the most obscure question they can think of.

Things to Remember

➤ References must be bound to a variable when they are declared and the binding cannot be changed.

➤ The advantages of pass-by-reference over pass-by-value

➤ The many uses of `const`

➤ The many uses of `static`

➤ The different types of casts in C++

➤ The difference between rvalues and lvalues

➤ How `typedefs` work

➤ C++11 rvalue references

➤ C++11 move semantics with move constructors and move assignment operators

➤ C++11 type aliasing using the template alias feature

➤ C++11 uniform initialization

➤ C++11 alternative function syntax

➤ C++11 `nullptr`

Types of Questions

Asking a candidate to define `const` and `static` is a classic C++ interview question. Both keywords provide a sliding scale with which an interviewer can assess an answer. For example, a fair candidate will talk about `static` methods and `static` data members. A good candidate will give good examples of `static` methods and `static` data members. A great candidate will also know about `static` linkage and `static` variables in functions.

The edge cases described in this chapter also come in find-the-bug type problems. Be on the lookout for misuse of references. For example, imagine a class that contains a reference as a data member:

```
class Gwenyth
{
    public:
        int& mCaversham;
};
```

Because `mCaversham` is a reference, it needs to be bound to a variable when the class is constructed. To do that, you'll need to use a constructor initializer. The class could take the variable to be referenced as a parameter to the constructor:

```
class Gwenyth
{
    public:
        Gwenyth(int& i);
        int& mCaversham;
};
```

```
Gwenyth::Gwenyth(int& i) : mCaversham(i)
{
}
```

CHAPTER 10: HANDLING ERRORS

Managers sometimes shy away from hiring recent graduates or novice programmers for vital (and high-paying) jobs because it is assumed that they don't write production-quality code. You can prove to an interviewer that your code won't keel over randomly by demonstrating your error-handling skills during an interview.

Things to Remember

➤ Syntax of exceptions

➤ Catch exceptions as `const` references.

➤ For production code, hierarchies of exceptions are preferable to a few generic ones.

➤ Throw lists in C++ are not like throw lists in Java.

➤ Smart pointers help avoid memory leaks when exceptions are thrown.

➤ The basics of how stack unwinding works when an exception gets thrown

➤ How to handle errors in constructors and destructors

➤ Why you should never use the C functions `setjmp()` and `longjmp()` in C++

Types of Questions

Interviewers will be on the lookout to see how you report and handle errors. When you are asked to write a piece of code, make sure you implement proper error handling.

You might be asked to give a high-level overview of how stack unwinding works when an exception is thrown, without implementation details.

Of course, not all programmers understand or appreciate exceptions. Some may even have a completely unfounded bias against them for performance reasons. If the interviewer asks you to do something without exceptions, you'll have to revert to traditional `nullptr` checks and error codes. That would be a good time to demonstrate your knowledge of `nothrow new`.

An interviewer can also ask questions in the form of *"Would you use this?"* One example question could be *"Would you use* `setjmp()`/`longjmp()` *in C++, since they are more efficient than exceptions?"* Your answer should be a big no, because `setjmp()`/`longjmp()` cannot possibly work in C++ because they bypass scoped destructors, and the fact that exceptions have a big performance penalty is a misconception. On modern compilers, exceptions have close to zero cost.

CHAPTERS 11, 12, 13 AND 17: THE STANDARD TEMPLATE LIBRARY

As you've seen, certain aspects of the STL can be difficult to work with. Few interviewers would expect you to recite the details of STL classes unless you claim to be an STL expert. If you know that the job you're interviewing for makes heavy use of the STL, you might want to write some STL code the day before to refresh your memory. Otherwise, recalling the high-level design of the STL and its basic usage should suffice.

Things to Remember

➤ The different types of containers and their relationships with iterators

➤ Basic usage of `vector`, which is probably the most frequently used STL class

➤ Usage of associative containers, such as `map`

➤ Usage of C++11 unordered associative containers, such as `unordered_map`, and the differences with associative containers

➤ The purpose of STL algorithms and some of the built-in algorithms

➤ The ways in which you can extend the STL (details are most likely unnecessary)

➤ Usage of C++11 lambda expressions in combination with STL algorithms

➤ The remove-erase-idiom

➤ Your own opinions about the STL

Types of Questions

If interviewers are dead set on asking detailed STL questions, there really are no bounds to the types of questions they could ask. If you're feeling uncertain about syntax though, you should state the obvious during the interview — "In real life, of course, I'd look that up in *Professional C++*, but I'm pretty sure it works like this . . ." At least that way the interviewer is reminded that he or she should forgive the details as long as you get the basic idea right.

High-level questions about the STL are often used to gauge how much you've used the STL without making you recall all the details. For example, casual users of the STL are familiar with associative and non-associative containers. A slightly more advanced user would be able to define an iterator and describe how iterators work with containers. An even more advanced user should be familiar with the remove-erase-idiom and should be able to explain in which cases you can use it and what its benefits are. An interviewer might also gauge your knowledge about lambda expressions which are new in C++11. Other high-level questions could ask you about your experience with STL algorithms or whether you've customized the STL.

CHAPTER 14: USING STRINGS AND REGULAR EXPRESSIONS

Strings are very important, in every kind of application. An interviewer will most likely ask at least one question related to string handling in C++.

Things to Remember

➤ The `std::string` class

➤ Differences between the C++ `std::string` class and C-style strings, including why C-style strings should be avoided

➤ Conversion of strings to numeric types like integers and floating point numbers, and vice versa

➤ C++11 raw string literals

➤ The importance of localization

➤ Ideas behind Unicode

➤ The concepts of locales and facets

➤ What regular expressions are

Types of Questions

An interviewer could ask you to explain how you can append two strings together. With this question he or she wants to find out whether you are thinking as a professional C++ programmer or as a C programmer. If you get such a question, you should explain the `std::string` class, and show how to use it to append two strings. It's also worth mentioning that the `string` class will handle all memory management for you automatically and contrast this to C-style strings.

Your interviewer may not ask specifically about localization, but you can show your worldwide interest by using `wchar_t` instead of `char` during the interview. If you do receive a question about your experience with localization, be sure to mention the importance of considering worldwide use from the beginning of the project.

You may also be asked about the general idea behind locales and facets. You probably will not have to explain the exact syntax, but you should explain that they allow you to format text and numbers according to the rules of a certain language/country.

You might get a question about Unicode, but most likely it will be a question to explain the ideas and the basic concepts behind Unicode instead of implementation details. So, make sure you understand the high-level concepts of Unicode and that you can explain their use in the context of localization. You should also know about the different options for encoding Unicode characters, such as UTF-8 and UTF-16, without specific details.

As seen in this chapter, regular expressions can have a daunting syntax. It is unlikely that an interviewer will ask you about little details of regular expressions. However, you should be able to explain the concept of regular expressions and what kind of string manipulations you can do with them.

CHAPTER 15: DEMYSTIFYING C++ I/O

If you're interviewing for a job writing GUI applications, you probably won't get too many questions about I/O streams because GUI applications tend to use other mechanisms for I/O. However, streams can come up in other problems and, as a standard part of C++, they are fair game as far as the interviewer is concerned.

Things to Remember

➤ The definition of a stream

➤ Basic input and output using streams

➤ The concept of manipulators

➤ Types of streams (console, file, string, etc.)

➤ Error-handling techniques

Types of Questions

I/O may come up in the context of any question. For example, the interviewer could ask you to read in a file containing test scores and put them in a `vector`. This question tests basic C++ skills, basic STL, and basic I/O. Even if I/O is only a small part of the problem you're working on, be sure to check for errors. If you don't, you're giving the interviewer an opportunity to say something negative about your otherwise perfect program.

CHAPTER 16: ADDITIONAL LIBRARY UTILITIES

Chapter 16 describes a number of new features and libraries in the C++11 standard. An interviewer might touch on a few of those topics to see whether you are keeping up-to-date with the latest developments in the C++ world.

Things to Remember

➤ The use of `std::function`

➤ The Chrono library to work with durations, clocks, and time points

➤ The C++11 method of generating random numbers

➤ `std::tuple` as a generalization of `std::pair`

Types of Questions

You don't need to expect detailed questions about these topics. A possible question could be to explain the usage of `std::function`. You might also get a question to explain the basic ideas and concepts of the new Chrono and random number generation libraries, but without going into syntax details. If the interviewer starts focusing on random numbers, it is important to explain the differences between true random numbers and pseudo random numbers.

CHAPTER 18: OVERLOADING C++ OPERATORS

It's possible, though somewhat unlikely, that you would have to perform something more difficult than a simple operator overload during an interview. Some interviewers like to have an advanced question on hand that they don't really expect anybody to answer correctly. The intricacies of operator overloading make great nearly-impossible questions because few programmers get the syntax right without looking it up. That means it's a great area to review before an interview.

Things to Remember

➤ Overloading stream operators, because they are the most commonly overloaded operators, and are conceptually unique

➤ What a functor is and how to create one

➤ Choosing between a method operator or a global friend function

➤ Some operators can be expressed in terms of others, i.e., `operator<=` can be written by complementing the result of `operator>`.

➤ The use of C++11 rvalue references to implement move assignment operators

Types of Questions

Let's face it — operator overloading questions (other than the simple ones) are cruel. Anybody who is asking such questions knows this and is going to be impressed when you get it right. It's impossible to predict the exact question that you'll get, but the number of operators is finite. As long as you've seen an example of overloading each operator that makes sense to overload, you'll do fine!

Besides asking you to implement an overloaded operator, you could be asked high-level questions about overloaded operators. A find-the-bug question could contain an operator that is overloaded to do something that is conceptually wrong for that particular operator. In addition to syntax, keep the use cases and theory of operator overloading in mind.

CHAPTERS 19 AND 20: TEMPLATES

As one of the most arcane parts of C++, templates are a good way for interviewers to separate the C++ novices from the pros. While most interviewers will forgive you for not remembering some of the advanced template syntax, you should go into the interview knowing the basics.

Things to Remember

➤ How to write a basic templatized class

➤ How to use a templatized class

➤ The C++11 alternative function syntax and its use for calculating the type of the return value (type inference)

➤ C++11 template aliases and why they are better than `typedefs`

➤ The concept of C++11 variadic templates

➤ The ideas behind metaprogramming

Types of Questions

Many interview questions start out with a simple problem and gradually add complexity. Often, interviewers have an endless amount of complexity that they are prepared to add, and they simply want to see how far you get. For example, an interviewer might begin a problem by asking you to create a class that provides sequential access to a fixed number of `ints`. Next, the class will need to grow to accommodate an arbitrary sized array. Then, it will need arbitrary data types, which is where templates come in. From there, the interviewer could take the problem in a number of directions, asking you to use operator overloading to provide array-like syntax, or continuing down the template path by asking you to provide a default type.

Templates are more likely to be employed in the solution of another coding problem than to be asked about explicitly. You should brush up on the basics in case the subject comes up. However, most interviewers understand that the template syntax is difficult, and asking someone to write complex template code in an interview is rather cruel.

The interviewer might ask you high-level questions related to metaprogramming to find out whether you have heard about it or not. While explaining, you could give a small example such as compile-time loop unrolling. Don't worry if the syntax for your example is not entirely correct. As long as you explain what it is supposed to do, you should be fine.

CHAPTER 21: EFFECTIVE MEMORY MANAGEMENT

You can be sure that an interviewer will ask you some questions related to memory management, including your knowledge of smart pointers. Besides smart pointers, you will also get more low-level questions. The goal is to determine whether the object-oriented aspects of C++ have distanced you too much from the underlying implementation details. Memory management questions will give you a chance to prove that you know what's really going on.

Things to Remember

➤ Drawing the stack and the heap can help you understand what's going on.

➤ Use `new` and `delete` instead of `malloc()` and `free()`.

➤ Use `new[]` and `delete[]` for arrays.

➤ If you have an array of pointers to objects, you still need to allocate memory for each individual pointer and delete the memory — the array allocation syntax doesn't take care of pointers.

➤ The existence of memory allocation problem detectors, such as Valgrind, to expose memory problems

➤ Smart pointers and specifically the new C++11 `std::shared_ptr` and `std::unique_ptr`, and why you should not use the old `std::auto_ptr`

➤ Use `std::make_shared()` to create a `std::shared_ptr`.

Types of Questions

Find-the-bug questions often contain memory issues, such as double-deletion, `new`/`new[]` mix-up, and memory leaks. When you are tracing through code that makes heavy use of pointers and arrays, you should draw and update the state of memory as you process each line of code. Even if you see the answer right away, it will let the interviewer know that you're able to draw the state of memory.

Another good way to find out if a candidate understands memory is to ask how pointers and arrays differ. At this point, the differences may be so tacit in your mind that the question catches you off-guard for a moment. If that's the case, skim Chapter 21 again for the discussion.

When answering questions about memory allocation, it's always a good idea to mention the concept of smart pointers and their benefits for automatically cleaning up memory or other resources. You definitely should also mention that it's much better to use STL containers like `std::vector` instead of C-style arrays because the STL containers handle memory management for you automatically.

CHAPTER 22: MULTITHREADED PROGRAMMING WITH C++

Multithreaded programming is becoming more and more important with the release of multicore processors for everything from servers to consumer computers. Even the latest smartphones have multicore processors. An interviewer might ask you a couple of multithreading questions. C++11 includes a standard threading library, so it's a good idea to know how it works.

Things to Remember

➤ Race conditions and deadlocks and how to prevent them

➤ The atomic types and atomic operations for possible lock-free programming

➤ `std::thread` to spawn threads

➤ The concept of mutual exclusion, including the usage of the different mutex and lock classes, to provide synchronization between threads

➤ Condition variables and how to use them to signal other threads

➤ What futures and promises are

➤ Copying and rethrowing of exceptions across thread boundaries

Types of Questions

Since the multithreading library is only available since C++11, you don't need to expect detailed questions, unless you are interviewing for a specific multithreading programming position.

An interviewer might ask you high-level questions, such as asking you to explain the general concepts behind multithreaded programming. This is a very broad question but allows the interviewer to get an idea of your multithreaded knowledge.

CHAPTER 23: MAXIMIZING SOFTWARE ENGINEERING METHODS

You should be suspicious if you go through the complete interview process with a company, and the interviewers do *not* ask any process questions — it may mean that they don't have any process or that they don't care about it. Alternatively, they might not want to scare you away with their process behemoth.

Source code control is also an important aspect of any development process.

Most of the time, you'll get a chance to ask questions regarding the company. We suggest you consider asking about engineering processes and source code control solutions as one of your standard questions.

Things to Remember

> ➤ Traditional life-cycle models
>
> ➤ The tradeoffs of formal models, such as the Rational Unified Process
>
> ➤ The main principles of Extreme Programming
>
> ➤ Scrum as an example of an agile process
>
> ➤ Other processes you have used in the past
>
> ➤ Principles behind source code control solutions

Types of Questions

The most common question you'll be asked is to describe the process that your previous employer used. When answering, you should mention what worked well and what failed, but try not to denounce any particular methodology. The methodology you criticize could be the one that your interviewer uses.

The authors spend a dizzying amount of their time reading resumes and one trend is clear — everybody is listing Extreme Programming as a skill these days. While there's little hard data on the subject, it certainly seems unlikely that strict adherence to XP is commonplace in programming environments. What we've found is that many organizations have started to look into XP and have adopted some of its principles without subscribing to it in any formal way.

If the interviewer asks you about XP, he or she probably doesn't want you to simply recite the textbook definition — the interviewer knows that you can read the table of contents of an XP book. Instead, pick a few ideas from XP that you find appealing. Explain each to the interviewer along with your thoughts on them. Try to engage the interviewer in a conversation, proceeding in a direction in which he or she is interested based on the cues that person gives.

If you get a question regarding source code control it will most likely be a high-level question. You should explain the general principles behind source code control solutions, mention the fact that there are commercial and free open-source solutions available, and explain how source code control happened at your previous employer.

CHAPTER 24: WRITING EFFICIENT C++

Efficiency questions are quite common in interviews because many organizations are facing scalability issues with their code and need programmers who are savvy about performance.

Things to Remember

➤ Language level efficiency is important, but it can only go so far; design-level choices are ultimately more significant.

➤ Reference parameters are more efficient because they avoid copying.

➤ Object pools can help avoid the overhead of creating and destroying objects.

➤ Profiling is vital to determine which operations are really consuming the most running time.

Types of Questions

Often, the interviewer will use their own product as an example to drive efficiency questions. Sometimes the interviewer will describe an older design and some performance-related symptoms they experienced. The candidate is supposed to come up with a new design that alleviates the problem. Unfortunately, there is a major problem with a question like this — what are the odds that you're going to come up with the same solution that the company did when the problem was actually solved? Because the odds are slim, you need to be extra careful to justify your designs. You may not come up with the actual solution, but you can still have an answer that is correct or even better than the company's newer design.

Other types of efficiency questions may ask you to tweak some C++ code for performance or iterate on an algorithm. For example, the interviewer could show you code that contains extraneous copies or inefficient loops.

The interviewer might also ask you for a high-level description of profiling tools and what their benefits are.

CHAPTER 25: DEVELOPING CROSS-PLATFORM AND CROSS-LANGUAGE APPLICATIONS

Few programmers submit resumes that list only a single language or technology, and few large applications rely on only a single language or technology. Even if you're interviewing for only a C++ position, the interviewer can still ask questions about other languages, especially as they relate to C++.

Things to Remember

➤ The ways in which platforms can differ (architecture, sizes, etc.)

➤ The fine line between programming and scripting

➤ The interactions between C++ and other languages

Types of Questions

The most popular cross-language question is to compare and contrast two different languages. You should avoid saying just positive or just negative things about a particular language, even if you really love or hate that other language. The interviewer wants to know that you are able to see tradeoffs and make decisions based on them.

Cross-platform questions are more likely to be asked while discussing previous work. If your resume indicates that you once wrote C++ applications that ran on a custom hardware platform, you should be prepared to talk about the compiler you used and the challenges of that platform.

CHAPTER 26: BECOMING ADEPT AT TESTING

Potential employers value strong testing abilities. Because your resume probably doesn't indicate your testing skills, unless you have explicit QA experience, you might face interview questions about testing.

Things to Remember

> ➤ The difference between black box and white box testing

> ➤ The concept of unit testing, integration testing, system testing, regression testing and writing tests along with code

> ➤ Techniques for higher-level tests

> ➤ Testing and QA environments in which you've worked before: What worked and what didn't?

Types of Questions

An interviewer could ask you to write some tests during the interview, but it's unlikely that a program presented during an interview would contain the depth necessary for interesting tests. It's more likely that you will be asked high-level testing questions. Be prepared to describe how testing was done at your last job, and what you liked and didn't like about it. After you answer, this is a good question for you to ask the interviewer. It might start a conversation about testing and give you a better idea of the environment at your potential job.

CHAPTER 27: CONQUERING DEBUGGING

Engineering organizations look for candidates who are able to debug both their own code as well as code that they've never seen before. Technical interviews often attempt to size up your debugging muscles.

Things to Remember

> ➤ Debugging doesn't start when bugs appear; you should instrument your code ahead of time, so you're prepared for the bugs when they arrive.

> ➤ Logs and debuggers are your best tools.

> ➤ Asserts and the reason why you should avoid the standard `assert()` macro from `<cassert>`

➤ How to use the C++11 static asserts

➤ The symptoms that a bug exhibits may appear to be unrelated to the actual cause.

➤ Object diagrams can be helpful in debugging, especially during an interview.

Types of Questions

During an interview, you might be challenged with an obscure debugging problem. Remember that the process is the most important thing, and the interviewer probably knows that. Even if you don't find the bug during the interview, make sure that the interviewer knows what steps you would go through to track it down. If the interviewer hands you a function and tells you that it crashes during execution, he or she should award just as many points to a candidate who properly discusses the sequence of steps to find the bug, as to a candidate who finds it right away.

CHAPTER 28: INCORPORATING DESIGN TECHNIQUES AND FRAMEWORKS

Each of the techniques presented in Chapter 28 makes a fine interview question. Rather than repeat what you already read in the chapter, we suggest that you skim back over Chapter 28 prior to an interview to make sure that you are able to understand each of the techniques.

If you are being interviewed for a GUI-based job, you should know about the existence of frameworks such as MFC, Qt, and possibly others.

CHAPTER 29: APPLYING DESIGN PATTERNS

Because design patterns are very popular in the professional world (many candidates even list them as skills), it's likely that you'll encounter an interviewer who wants you to explain a pattern, give a use case for a pattern, or implement a pattern.

Things to Remember

➤ The basic idea of a pattern as a reusable object-oriented design concept

➤ The patterns you have read about in this book, as well as others that you've used in your work

➤ There are hundreds of patterns with often-conflicting names, so you and your interviewer may use different words for the same pattern.

Types of Questions

Answering questions about design patterns is usually a walk in the park, unless the interviewer expects you to know the details of every single pattern known to humankind. Luckily, most interviewers who appreciate design patterns will just want to chat with you about them and get your opinions. After all, looking up concepts in a book or online instead of memorizing them is a good pattern itself.

B

Annotated Bibliography

This appendix contains a list of books and online resources on various C++-related topics that were either consulted while writing this book, or are recommended for further or background reading.

C++

Beginning C++

➤ Harvey M. Deitel and Paul J. Deitel, C++ *How to Program (Seventh Edition)*, Prentice Hall, 2009, ISBN: 0-136-11726-0.

Known as the "Deitel" book, this text assumes no prior programming experience.

➤ Bruce Eckel, *Thinking in C++, Volume 1: Introduction to Standard C++ (Second Edition)*, Prentice Hall, 2000, ISBN: 0-139-79809-9.

An excellent introduction to C++ programming that expects the reader to know C already. Available at no cost online at www.bruceeckel.com.

➤ Stanley B. Lippman, Josée Lajoie, and Barbara E. Moo, C++ *Primer (Fourth Edition)*, Addison-Wesley, 2005, ISBN: 0-201-72148-1.

Requires no knowledge of C++, but assumes experience with high-level object-oriented languages.

➤ Steve Oualline, *Practical C++ Programming (Second Edition)*, O'Reilly, 2003, ISBN: 0-596-00419-2.

An introductory C++ text that assumes no prior programming experience.

➤ Walter Savitch, *Problem Solving with C++ (Eighth Edition)*, Addison-Wesley, 2011, ISBN: 0-132-16273-3.

This book assumes no prior programming experience. It is often used as a textbook in introductory programming courses.

General C++

➤ Marshall Cline, C++ *FAQ LITE*, `www.parashift.com/c++-faq-lite`.

➤ Marshall Cline, Greg Lomow, and Mike Girou, C++ *FAQs (Second Edition)*, Addison-Wesley, 1998, ISBN: 0-201-30983-1.

This compilation of frequently asked questions from the `comp.lang.c++` newsgroup is useful for quickly looking up a specific point about C++. The printed version contains more information than the online version, but the material available online should be sufficient for most professional C++ programmers.

➤ Stephen C. Dewhurst, C++ *Gotchas*, Addison-Wesley, 2002, ISBN: 0-321-12518-5.

Provides 99 specific tips for C++ programming.

➤ Bruce Eckel and Chuck Allison, *Thinking in C++, Volume 2: Practical Programming*, Prentice Hall, 2003, ISBN: 0-130-35313-2.

The second volume of Eckel's book covers more advanced C++ topics. It's also available at no cost online at `www.bruceeckel.com`.

➤ Ray Lischner, C++ *in a Nutshell*, O'Reilly, 2003, ISBN: 0-596-00298-X.

A C++ reference covering everything from the basics to more-advanced material.

➤ Scott Meyers, *Effective C++ (Third Edition): 55 Specific Ways to Improve Your Programs and Designs*, Addison-Wesley, 2005, ISBN: 0-321-33487-6.

➤ Scott Meyers, *More Effective C++: 35 New Ways to Improve Your Programs and Designs*, Addison-Wesley, 1996, ISBN: 0-201-63371-X.

These two books provide excellent tips and tricks on commonly misused and misunderstood features of C++.

➤ Stephen Prata, C++ *Primer Plus (Fifth Edition)*, Sams Publishing, 2004, ISBN: 0-672-32697-4.

One of the most comprehensive C++ books available.

➤ Bjarne Stroustrup, *The C++ Programming Language (Special Third Edition)*, Addison-Wesley, 2000, ISBN: 0-201-70073-5.

The "Bible" of C++ books, written by the designer of C++ himself. Every C++ programmer should own a copy of this book, but it can be a bit obscure in places for the C++ novice.

➤ British Standards Institute, *The C++ Standard: Incorporating Technical Corrigendum No. 1*, Wiley, 2003, ISBN: 0-470-84674-7.

This book is almost 800 pages of dense standardese. It doesn't explain how to use C++, only what the formal rules are. We don't recommend this book unless you really want to understand every detail of C++.

➤ Newsgroups at `http://groups.google.com`, including `comp.lang.c++.moderated` and `comp.std.c++`.

The newsgroups contain a lot of useful information if you're willing to wade through the flame wars, insults, and misinformation that appear as well.

➤ *The C++ Resources Network* at www.cplusplus.com.

This site contains a lot of information related to C++.

I/O Streams and Strings

➤ Cameron Hughes and Tracey Hughes, *Mastering the Standard C++ Classes: An Essential Reference*, Wiley, 1999, ISBN: 0-471-32893-6.

A good book for learning how to write custom istream and ostream classes.

➤ Cameron Hughes and Tracey Hughes, *Stream Manipulators and Iterators in C++*, www.informit.com/articles/article.aspx?p=171014.

This well-written article by the authors of *Mastering the Standard C++ Classes* takes the mystery out of defining custom stream manipulators in C++.

➤ Philip Romanik and Amy Muntz, *Applied C++: Practical Techniques for Building Better Software*, Addison-Wesley, 2003, ISBN: 0-321-10894-9.

In addition to a unique blend of software development advice and C++ specifics, this book provides one of the best explanations we've read of locale and Unicode support in C++.

➤ Joel Spolsky, *The Absolute Minimum Every Software Developer Absolutely, Positively Must Know About Unicode and Character Sets (No Excuses!)*, www.joelonsoftware.com/articles/Unicode.html.

After reading Joel's treatise on the importance of localization, you'll want to check out his other entries on *Joel on Software*.

➤ The Unicode Consortium, *The Unicode Standard 5.0*, Addison-Wesley, 2006, ISBN: 0-321-48091-0.

This is the definitive book on Unicode, which all developers using Unicode must have.

➤ Unicode, Inc., *Where is my Character?*, www.unicode.org/standard/where.

The best resource for finding Unicode characters, charts, and tables.

➤ *Wikipedia Universal Character Set*, http://en.wikipedia.org/wiki/Universal_Character_Set.

An explanation of what the Universal Character Set (UCS) is, including the Unicode standard.

The C++ Standard Library

➤ Nicolai M. Josuttis, *The C++ Standard Library: A Tutorial and Reference*, Addison-Wesley, 1999, ISBN: 0-201-37926-0.

This book covers the entire standard library, including I/O streams and strings as well as the containers and algorithms. It's an excellent reference.

➤ Scott Meyers, *Effective STL: 50 Specific Ways to Improve Your Use of the Standard Template Library*, Addison-Wesley, 2001, ISBN: 0-201-74962-9.

Meyers wrote this book in the same spirit as his "*Effective C++*" books. It provides targeted tips for using the STL, but is not a reference or tutorial.

➤ David R. Musser, Gillmer J. Derge, and Atul Saini, *STL Tutorial and Reference Guide (Second Edition)*, Addison-Wesley, 2001, ISBN: 0-321-70212-3.

This book is similar to the Josuttis text, but covers only the STL part of the standard library.

➤ Pete Becker, *The C++ Standard Library Extensions: A Tutorial and Reference*, Addison-Wesley, 2006, ISBN: 0-321-41299-0.

This book explains the new features added to the C++ Standard Library with the Technical Report 1 (TR1).

➤ Stephan T. Lavavej, *Standard Template Library (STL)*, `http://channel9.msdn.com/Shows/Going+Deep/C9-Lectures-Introduction-to-STL-with-Stephan-T-Lavavej`.

An interesting video lecture series on the C++ Standard Template Library.

C++ Templates

➤ Herb Sutter, *Sutter's Mill: Befriending Templates*, C/C++ User's Journal, `http://drdobbs.com/cpp/184403853`.

The best explanation we could find about making function templates friends of classes.

➤ David Vandevoorde and Nicolai M. Josuttis, *C++ Templates: The Complete Guide*, Addison-Wesley, 2002, ISBN: 0-201-73484-2.

Everything you ever wanted to know (or didn't want to know) about C++ templates. It assumes significant background in general C++.

➤ David Abrahams and Aleksey Gurtovoy, *C++ Template Metaprogramming: Concepts, Tools, and Techniques from Boost and Beyond*, Addison-Wesley, 2004, ISBN: 0-321-22725-5.

This book delivers practical metaprogramming tools and techniques into the hands of the everyday programmer.

C++11

➤ *C++ Standards Committee Papers*, `www.open-std.org/jtc1/sc22/wg21/docs/papers`.

Access a wealth of papers written by the C++ standards committee.

➤ Scott Meyers, *Presentation Materials: Overview of the New C++ (C++0x)*, Artima, 2011, `www.artima.com/shop/overview_of_the_new_cpp`.

This contains the presentation materials from Scott Meyers' three-day training course on the new C++ standard, and is an excellent reference to get a list of all new C++11 features.

➤ *Wikipedia C++11*, http://en.wikipedia.org/wiki/C%2B%2B11.

A description of all new features added to C++11.

➤ *ECMAScript Language Specification*, www.ecma-international.org/publications/ files/ECMA-ST/ECMA-262.pdf.

The syntax of the regular expressions in C++11 is the same as the regular expressions in the ECMAScript language, described in this specification document.

C

➤ Brian W. Kernighan and Dennis M. Ritchie, *The C Programming Language (second edition)*, Prentice Hall, 1998, ISBN: 0-131-10362-8.

"K&R," as this book is known, is a reference on the C language, but it's not so useful for learning it the first time.

➤ Samuel P. Harbison III and Guy L. Steele Jr., *C: A Reference Manual, Fifth Edition*, Prentice Hall, 2002, ISBN: 0-130-89592-X.

This book can be considered a replacement for the K&R book. Instead of a narrative style, where knowledge is embedded in the text, it is done as a more formal reference manual. Every C programmer should own a copy.

➤ Peter Prinz, Tony Crawford (Translator), Ulla Kirch-Prinz, *C Pocket Reference*, O'Reilly, 2002, ISBN: 0-596-00436-2.

A concise reference to all things C.

➤ Eric S. Roberts, *The Art and Science of C: A Library Based Introduction to Computer Science*, Addison-Wesley, 1994, ISBN: 0-201-54322-2.

➤ Eric S. Roberts, *Programming Abstractions in C: A Second Course in Computer Science*, Addison-Wesley, 1997, ISBN: 0-201-54541-1.

These two books provide a great introduction to programming in C with good style. They are often used as textbooks in introductory programming courses.

➤ Peter Van Der Linden, *Expert C Programming: Deep C Secrets,* Prentice Hall, 1994, ISBN: 0-131-77429-8.

An enlightening and often hysterical look at the C language, its evolution, and its inner workings.

INTEGRATING C++ AND OTHER LANGUAGES

➤ Ian F. Darwin, *Java Cookbook (Second Edition)*, O'Reilly, 2004, ISBN: 0-596-00701-9.

This book provides step-by-step instructions for using JNI to integrate Java with other languages, including C++.

ALGORITHMS AND DATA STRUCTURES

➤ Thomas H. Cormen, Charles E. Leiserson, Ronald L. Rivest, and Clifford Stein, *Introduction to Algorithms (Third Edition)*, The MIT Press, 2009, ISBN: 0-262-03384-4.

This text is one of the most popular introductory algorithms books, covering all the common data structures and algorithms.

➤ Donald E. Knuth, *The Art of Computer Programming Volume 1: Fundamental Algorithms (Third Edition)*, Addison-Wesley, 1997, ISBN: 0-201-89683-4.

➤ Donald E. Knuth, *The Art of Computer Programming Volume 2: Seminumerical Algorithms (Third Edition)*, Addison-Wesley, 1997, ISBN: 0-201-89684-2.

➤ Donald E. Knuth, *The Art of Computer Programming Volume 3: Sorting and Searching (Second Edition)*, Addison-Wesley, 1998, ISBN: 0-201-89685-0.

➤ Donald E. Knuth, *The Art of Computer Programming Volume 4A: Combinatorial Algorithms Part 1*, Addison-Wesley, 2011, ISBN: 0-201-03804-8.

For those of you who enjoy mathematical rigor, there is no better algorithms and data structures text than Knuth's four-volume tome. But, it is probably inaccessible without undergraduate knowledge of mathematics or theoretical computer science.

➤ Kyle Loudon, *Mastering Algorithms with C,* O'Reilly, 1999, ISBN: 1-565-92453-3.

An approachable reference to data structures and algorithms.

RANDOM NUMBERS

➤ Eric Bach and Jeffrey Shallit, *Algorithmic Number Theory, Vol. 1: Efficient Algorithms*, The MIT Press, 1996, ISBN: 0-262-02405-5.

➤ Oded Goldreich, *Modern Cryptography, Probalistic Proofs and Pseudorandomness*, Springer, 2010, ISBN: 3-642-08432-X.

Both of these books explain the theory of computational pseudo randomness.

➤ *Wikipedia Mersenne Twister,* http://en.wikipedia.org/wiki/Mersenne_twister.

A mathematical explanation of the Mersenne Twister to generate pseudo-random numbers.

OPEN-SOURCE SOFTWARE

➤ The Open Source Initiative at www.opensource.org.

➤ The GNU Operating System — Free Software Foundation at www.gnu.org.

These web pages for the two main open-source movements explain their philosophies and provide information about obtaining open-source software and contributing to its development.

➤ SourceForge at www.sourceforge.net.

This website hosts many open-source projects. It's a great resource for finding useful open-source software.

➤ www.codeguru.com and www.codeproject.com.

Excellent resources to find free libraries and code for reuse in your own projects.

SOFTWARE ENGINEERING METHODOLOGY

➤ Barry W. Boehm, TRW Defense Systems Group, *A Spiral Model of Software Development and Enhancement*, IEEE Computer, 21(5): 61–72, 1988.

This landmark paper described the state of software development at the time and proposed the Spiral Model.

➤ Kent Beck and Cynthia Andres, *Extreme Programming Explained: Embrace Change (Second Edition)*, Addison-Wesley, 2004, ISBN: 0-321-27865-8.

One of several books in a series that promote Extreme Programming as a new approach to software development.

➤ Robert T. Futrell, Donald F. Shafer, and Linda Isabell Shafer, *Quality Software Project Management*, Prentice Hall, 2002, ISBN: 0-130-91297-2.

A guidebook for anybody who is responsible for the management of software development processes.

➤ Robert L. Glass, *Facts and Fallacies of Software Engineering*, Addison-Wesley, 2002, ISBN: 0-321-11742-5.

This book discusses various aspects of the software development process and exposes hidden truisms along the way.

➤ Philippe Kruchten, *The Rational Unified Process: An Introduction (Third Edition)*, Addison-Wesley, 2003, ISBN: 0-321-19770-4.

Provides an overview of RUP, including its mission and processes.

➤ Edward Yourdon, *Death March (Second Edition)*, Prentice Hall, 2003, ISBN: 0-131-43635-X.

A wonderfully enlightening book about the politics and realities of software development.

➤ Rational Unified Process from IBM, www3.software.ibm.com/ibmdl/pub/software/rational/web/demos/viewlets/rup/runtime/index.html.

The IBM website contains a wealth of information about RUP, including the interactive presentation at the preceding URL.

➤ Mike Cohn, *Succeeding with Agile: Software Development Using Scrum*, Addison-Wesley, 2009, ISBN: 0-321-57936-4.

An excellent guide to start with the Scrum methodology.

➤ *Wikipedia Scrum*, http://en.wikipedia.org/wiki/Scrum_(development).

A detailed discussion of the Scrum methodology.

➤ *Manifesto for Agile Software Development*, http://agilemanifesto.org/.

The complete agile software development manifesto.

➤ *Wikipedia Revision control*, http://en.wikipedia.org/wiki/Revision_control.

Explains the concepts behind revision control systems, and what kinds of solutions there are available.

PROGRAMMING STYLE

➤ Martin Fowler, Kent Beck, John Brant, William Opdyke, and Don Roberts, *Refactoring: Improving the Design of Existing Code*, Addison-Wesley, 1999, ISBN: 0-201-48567-2.

This classic book espouses the practice of recognizing and improving bad code.

➤ James Foxall, *Practical Standards for Microsoft Visual Basic .NET*, Microsoft Press, 2002, ISBN: 0-735-61356-7.

Exhibits the tenets of Microsoft Windows coding style, using Visual Basic .NET.

➤ Diomidis Spinellis, *Code Reading: The Open Source Perspective*, Addison-Wesley, 2003, ISBN: 0-201-79940-5.

This unique book turns the issue of programming style upside down by challenging the reader to learn to read code properly in order to become a better programmer.

➤ Dimitri van Heesch, *Doxygen*, www.stack.nl/~dimitri/doxygen/index.html.

A highly configurable program that generates documentation from source code and comments.

➤ John Aycock, *Reading and Modifying Code*, John Aycock, 2008, ISBN 0-980-95550-5.

A nice little book with advice about how to perform the most common operations on code: reading, modifying, testing, debugging, and writing.

➤ *Wikipedia Code Refactoring*, http://en.wikipedia.org/wiki/Refactoring.

A discussion on what code refactoring means, including a number of techniques for refactoring.

COMPUTER ARCHITECTURE

➤ David A. Patterson and John L. Hennessy, *Computer Organization and Design: The Hardware/ Software Interface (Fourth Edition)*, Morgan Kaufmann, 2008, ISBN: 0-123-74493-8.

➤ John L. Hennessy and David A. Patterson, *Computer Architecture: A Quantitative Approach (Fourth Edition)*, Morgan Kaufmann, 2006, ISBN: 0-123-70490-1.

These two books provide all the information most software engineers ever need to know about computer architecture.

EFFICIENCY

➤ Dov Bulka and David Mayhew, *Efficient C++: Performance Programming Techniques*, Addison-Wesley, 1999, ISBN: 0-201-37950-3.

One of the few books to focus exclusively on efficient C++ programming, it covers both language-level and design-level efficiency.

➤ GNU gprof, `www.gnu.org/software/binutils/`.

Information about the gprof profiling tool.

TESTING

➤ Elfriede Dustin, *Effective Software Testing: 50 Specific Ways to Improve Your Testing*, Addison-Wesley, 2002, ISBN: 0-201-79429-2.

While this book is aimed at quality assurance professionals, any software engineer will benefit from its discussion of the software-testing process.

DEBUGGING

➤ The GNU DeBugger (GDB), at `www.gnu.org/software/gdb/gdb.html`.

GDB is an excellent symbolic debugger.

➤ Valgrind, at `http://valgrind.org/`.

An open-source memory-debugging tool for Linux.

➤ Microsoft Application Verifier, at `http://msdn.microsoft.com/en-us/library/aa480483.aspx`.

A run-time verification tool for C++ code that assists in finding subtle programming errors and security issues that can be difficult to identify with normal application testing techniques.

DESIGN PATTERNS

➤ Andrei Alexandrescu, *Modern C++ Design: Generic Programming and Design Patterns Applied*, Addison-Wesley, 2001, ISBN: 0-201-70431-5.

Offers an approach to C++ programming employing highly reusable code and patterns.

➤ Cunningham and Cunningham, *The Portland Pattern Repository*, `www.c2.com/cgi/wiki?WelcomeVisitors`.

You could spend all day browsing through this community-edited website about design patterns.

➤ Erich Gamma, Richard Helm, Ralph Johnson, and John Vlissides, *Design Patterns: Elements of Reusable Object-Oriented Software*, Addison-Wesley, 1994, ISBN: 0-201-63361-2.

Called the "Gang of Four" book (because of its four authors), this text is the seminal work on design patterns.

➤ *Wikipedia Design Patterns*, `http://en.wikipedia.org/wiki/Design_pattern_` `(computer_science)`.

Contains a description of a large number of design patterns used in computer programming.

OPERATING SYSTEMS

➤ Abraham Silberschatz, Peter B. Galvin, and Greg Gagne, *Operating System Concepts (Eighth Edition)*, Wiley, 2008, ISBN: 0-470-12872-0.

A great discussion on operating systems, including multithreading issues such as deadlocks and race conditions.

MULTITHREADED PROGRAMMING

➤ Anthony Williams, *C++ Concurrency in Action: Practical Multithreading*, Manning Publications, 2011, ISBN: 1-933-98877-0.

An excellent book on practical multithreaded programming, including the new C++11 threading library.

➤ Cameron Hughes and Tracey Hughes, *Professional Multicore Programming: Design and Implementation for C++ Developers*, Wrox, 2008, ISBN: 0-470-28962-7.

This book is for developers of various skill levels who are making the move into multicore programming.

➤ Maurice Herlihy and Nir Shavit, *The Art of Multiprocessor Programming*, Morgan Kaufmann, 2008, ISBN: 0-123-70591-6.

A great book on writing code for multiprocessor and multicore systems.

➤ *Wikipedia POSIX Threads*, `http://en.wikipedia.org/wiki/POSIX_Threads`.

➤ *Boost Threads*, `www.boost.org`.

Explains how to work with POSIX threads or Boost threads in case your compiler does not yet support the C++11 threading library.

Standard Library Header Files

The interface to the C++ Standard Library consists of 78 header files, 26 of which present the C standard library. It's often difficult to remember which header files you need to include in your source code, so this material provides a brief description of the contents of each header, organized into eight categories:

- The C Standard Library
- Containers
- Algorithms, iterators, and allocators
- General utilities
- Mathematical utilities
- Exceptions
- I/O Streams
- Threading library

THE C STANDARD LIBRARY

The C++ Standard Library includes the entire C Standard Library. The header files are generally the same, except for two points:

- The header names are `<cname>` instead of `<name.h>`.
- All the names declared in the header files are in the `std` namespace.

 For backward compatibility, you can still include `<name.h>` if you want. However, that puts the names into the global namespace instead of the `std` namespace. We recommend avoiding this feature.

The following table provides a summary of the most useful functionality:

HEADER FILE NAME	CONTENTS
`<cassert>`	`assert()` macro.
C++11 `<ccomplex>`	Utilities to work with complex numbers.
`<cctype>`	Character predicates and manipulation functions, such as `isspace()` and `tolower()`.
`<cerrno>`	Defines `errno` expression.
C++11 `<cfenv>`	Supports the floating-point environment, such as floating-point exceptions, rounding, and so on.
`<cfloat>`	C-style defines related to floating-point arithmetic, such as `FLT_MAX`.
C++11 `<cinttypes>`	Defines a number of macros to use with the `printf()`, `scanf()` and similar functions. Also includes a few functions to work with `intmax_t`.
`<ciso646>`	In C, the `<iso646.h>` file defines macros `and`, `or`, etc. In C++, those are keywords, so they are not in this header.
`<climits>`	C-style limit defines, such as `INT_MAX`.
`<clocale>`	A few localization macros and functions like `LC_ALL` and `setlocale()`.
`<cmath>`	Math utilities, including trigonometric functions, `sqrt()`, `fabs()`, and others.
`<csetjmp>`	`setjmp()` and `longjmp()`. Never use these in C++!
`<csignal>`	`signal()` and `raise()`. Avoid these in C++.
C++11 `<cstdalign>`	Alignment related macro `__alignas_is_defined`.
`<cstdarg>`	Macros and types for processing variable-length argument lists.
C++11 `<cstdbool>`	Boolean type related macro `__bool_true_false_are_defined`.
`<cstddef>`	Important constants such as `NULL`, and important types such as `size_t`.
C++11 `<cstdint>`	Defines a number of standard integer types such as `int8_t`, `int64_t` and so on. It also includes macros specifying minimum and maximum values of those types.
`<cstdio>`	File operations, including `fopen()` and `fclose()`. Formatted I/O: `printf()`, `scanf()`, and family. Character I/O: `getc()`, `putc()`, and family. File positioning: `fseek()`, `ftell()`.

HEADER FILE NAME	CONTENTS
`<cstdlib>`	Random numbers with `rand()` and `srand()`. The `abort()` and `exit()` functions, which you should avoid. C-style memory allocation functions: `calloc()`, `malloc()`, `realloc()`, `free()`. C-style searching and sorting with `qsort()` and `bsearch()`. String to number conversions: `atof()`, `atoi()`, etc.
`<cstring>`	Low-level memory management functions, including `memcpy()` and `memset()`. C-style string functions, such as `strcpy()` and `strcmp()`. Secure versions such as `strcpy_s()`. Defines `NULL` and `size_t` as well.
`<ctgmath>`	Just includes `<ccomplex>` and `<cmath>`.
`<ctime>`	Time-related functions, including `time()` and `localtime()`.
`<cuchar>`	Defines a number of Unicode-related macros, and functions like `mbrtoc16()`.
`<cwchar>`	Versions of string, memory, and I/O functions for wide characters.
`<cwctype>`	Versions of functions in `<cctype>` for wide characters: `iswspace()`, `towlower()`, and so on.

(C++11 markers appear beside `<ctgmath>` and `<cuchar>`.)

CONTAINERS

The definitions for the STL containers can be found in 12 header files:

HEADER FILE NAME	CONTENTS
`<array>`	The `array` class template.
`<bitset>`	The `bitset` class template.
`<deque>`	The `deque` class template.
`<forward_list>`	The `forward_list` class template.
`<list>`	The `list` class template.
`<map>`	The `map` and `multimap` class templates.
`<queue>`	The `queue` and `priority_queue` class templates.
`<set>`	The `set` and `multiset` class templates.
`<stack>`	The `stack` class template.
`<unordered_map>`	The `unordered_map` and `unordered_multimap` class templates.
`<unordered_set>`	The `unordered_set` and `unordered_multiset` class templates.
`<vector>`	The `vector` class template and the `vector<bool>` specialization.

(C++11 markers appear beside `<array>`, `<forward_list>`, `<unordered_map>`, and `<unordered_set>`.)

Each of these header files contains all the definitions you need to use the specified container, including iterators. Chapter 12 describes these containers in detail.

ALGORITHMS, ITERATORS, AND ALLOCATORS

The "rest" of the STL can be found in five different header files:

HEADER FILE NAME	CONTENTS
`<algorithm>`	Prototypes for most of the algorithms in the STL.
`<functional>`	Defines the built-in function objects, negators, binders, and adaptors.
`<iterator>`	Definitions of `iterator_traits`, iterator tags, `iterator`, `reverse_iterator`, insert iterators (such as `back_inserter`), and stream iterators.
`<memory>`	Defines the default allocator, some utility functions for dealing with uninitialized memory inside containers, and the important C++11 `shared_ptr` and `unique_ptr` smart pointer class templates.
`<numeric>`	Prototypes for some numerical algorithms: `accumulate()`, `inner_product()`, `partial_sum()`, `adjacent_difference()`, and a few others.

GENERAL UTILITIES

The Standard Library contains some general-purpose utilities in several different header files:

	HEADER FILE NAME	CONTENTS
C++11	`<chrono>`	Defines the Chrono library. See Chapter 16.
C++11	`<codecvt>`	Provides code conversion facets for various character encodings.
C++11	`<initializer_list>`	Defines the `initializer_list` class. See Chapter 9.
	`<limits>`	Defines the `numeric_limits` class template, and specializations for most built-in types. See Chapter 11.
	`<locale>`	Defines the `locale` class, the `use_facet()` and `has_facet()` template functions, and the various facet families. See Chapter 14.
	`<new>`	Defines the `bad_alloc` exception and `set_new_handler()` function. Prototypes for all six forms of `operator new` and `operator delete`. See Chapter 18.
C++11	`<random>`	Defines the random number generation library. See Chapter 16.
C++11	`<ratio>`	Defines the Ratio library to work with compile-time rational numbers. See Chapter 16.

HEADER FILE NAME	CONTENTS
C++11 <regex>	Defines the regular expression library. See Chapter 14.
<string>	Defines the `basic_string` class template and the `typedef` instantiations of `string` and `wstring`.
C++11 <system_error>	Defines error categories and error codes.
C++11 <tuple>	Defines the `tuple` class template as a generalization of the `pair` class template. See Chapter 16.
C++11 <type_traits>	Defines type traits for use in template metaprogramming. See Chapter 20.
C++11 <typeindex>	Defines a simple wrapper for `type_info`, which can be used as an index type in associative containers and in unordered associative containers.
<typeinfo>	Defines the `bad_cast` and `bad_typeid` exceptions. Defines the `type_info` class, objects of which are returned by the `typeid` operator. See Chapter 8 for details on `typeid`.
<utility>	Defines the `pair` class template. See Chapter 12.

MATHEMATICAL UTILITIES

C++ provides some facilities for numeric processing. These capabilities are not described in detail in this book; for details, consult one of the Standard Library references listed in the Annotated Bibliography.

HEADER FILE NAME	CONTENTS
<complex>	Defines the `complex` class template for processing complex numbers.
<valarray>	Defines `valarray` and related classes and class templates for processing mathematical vectors and matrices.

EXCEPTIONS

Exceptions and exception support are covered in Chapter 10. Two header files provide most of the requisite definitions, but some exceptions for other domains are defined in the header file for that domain.

HEADER FILE NAME	CONTENTS
<exception>	Defines the `exception` and `bad_exception` classes, and the `set_unexpected()`, `set_terminate()`, and `uncaught_exception()` functions.
<stdexcept>	Non-domain-specific exceptions not defined in `<exception>`.

I/O STREAMS

The following table lists all the header files related to I/O streams in C++. However, normally your applications only need to include `<fstream>`, `<iomanip>`, `<iostream>`, `<istream>`, `<ostream>`, and `<sstream>`. Consult Chapter 15 for details.

HEADER FILE NAME	CONTENTS
`<fstream>`	Defines the `basic_filebuf`, `basic_ifstream`, `basic_ofstream`, and `basic_fstream` classes. Declares the `filebuf`, `wfilebuf`, `ifstream`, `wifstream`, `ofstream`, `wofstream`, `fstream`, and `wfstream` typedefs.
`<iomanip>`	Declares the I/O manipulators not declared elsewhere (mostly in `<ios>`).
`<ios>`	Defines the `ios_base` and `basic_ios` classes. Declares most of the stream manipulators. You rarely have to include this header directly.
`<iosfwd>`	Forward declarations of the templates and `typedefs` found in the other I/O stream header files. You rarely need to include this header directly.
`<iostream>`	Declares `cin`, `cout`, `cerr`, `clog`, and the wide-character counterparts. Note that it's not just a combination of `<istream>` and `<ostream>`.
`<istream>`	Defines the `basic_istream` and `basic_iostream` classes. Declares the `istream`, `wistream`, `iostream`, and `wiostream` typedefs.
`<ostream>`	Defines the `basic_ostream` class. Declares the `ostream` and `wostream` typedefs.
`<sstream>`	Defines the `basic_stringbuf`, `basic_istringstream`, `basic_ostringstream`, and `basic_stringstream` classes. Declares the `stringbuf`, `wstringbuf`, `istringstream`, `wistringstream`, `ostringstream`, `wostringstream`, `stringstream`, and `wstringstream` typedefs.
`<streambuf>`	Defines the `basic_streambuf` class. Declares the `typedefs` `streambuf` and `wstreambuf`. You rarely have to include this header directly.
`<strstream>`	Deprecated.

C++11 THREADING LIBRARY

C++11 includes a threading library, which allows you to write platform-independent multithreaded applications. See Chapter 22 for details. The threading library consists of the following header files:

HEADER FILE NAME	CONTENTS
`<atomic>`	Defines the atomic types, `atomic<T>`, and atomic operations.
`<condition_variable>`	Defines the `condition_variable` and `condition_variable_any` classes.
`<future>`	Defines `future`, `promise`, `packaged_task` and `async()`.
`<mutex>`	Defines the different mutex and lock classes, and `call_once()`.
`<thread>`	Defines the `thread` class.

INDEX

Symbols

16-bit characters, 10
32-bit characters, 10
! operator, 11
%= operator, 12
& operator, 12
&= operator, 12
*= operator, 12
+= operator, 12
<< operator, 6, 12
<<= operator, 12
= operator, 11
>> operator, 12
>>= operator, 12
^ operator, 12
^= operator, 12
| operator, 12
|= operator, 12
+ operator, string class, 513–514
/= operator, 12
-= operator, 12
+ addition operator, 11
- - decrement operator, 11
~ in destructors, 172
# in directives, 5
/ division operator, 11
++ increment operator, 11
% mod operator, 11
* multiplication operator, 11
- subtraction operator, 11
* (quotation mark), 7
\ (backslash character), 7
\n (escape character), 6–7
\r (carriage return), 7
\t (tab), 7

A

abstract base classes, 232–233
abstract superclasses, 85
abstraction, 92, 206–207
    benefits, 54
    classes, 100
    design and, 54–55

design success, 95
interface
    exposed, 93–95
    versus implementation, 93
    reusable code, 99–100
access-controlled singleton
    patterns, 989–991
access specifiers, 135–136
    private, 136
    protected, 136
    public, 136
accumulate( ) function,
    461–462, 486
ad hoc comments, 119
adapter design pattern, 1002–1004
adapters
    containers
        priority_queue, 424
            example, 425–427
            operations, 425
        queue, 421
            example, 422–424
            operations, 422
        stack
            example, 427–428
            operations, 427
    function objects
        bind2nd( ), 475–476
        std::bind( ), 473–475
add( ) method, overloading,
    197–198
addition operator (+), 11
addOne( ) function, 30
address sizes, 885
aggregation, 83–84
    reusable code, 102
Agile Methodology, 847
algorithms. See also functions
    binary_search( ), 484
    C++ standard library, 361
    callbacks, 457
    comparison algorithms,
        486–488
    count_if( ), 468
    equal_range( ), 484

examples, voter registration
    audits, 503–507
extending STL, 602–605
for_each( ), 469
generate( ), 468–469
header files, 1048
interface, 370
iterator invalidation and, 406
iterators, 481
lower_bound( ), 484
modifying algorithms,
    490–491
        copy( ), 493–495
        erase( ), 497
        iota( ), 491
        move( ), 496–497
        replace( ), 497
        reverse( ), 499
        transform( ), 491–493
        unique( ), 498–499
move semantics, 462
non-modifying, search
    algorithms, 483–486
numerical processing, 486
operational algorithms,
    488–490
overview, 457–458
set algorithms, 501–503
sorting algorithms, 499–501
STL (standard template
    library), 376–378
        comparison, 380
        modifying, 381–382
        non-modifying, 378–381
        numerical processing, 380
        operational, 381
        search algorithms,
            378–379
        sorting, 382–383
        utility algorithms, 378
upper_bound( ), 484
utility, 482–483
aliasing, 780
    template aliases, 708–709
    type aliases, 295–296
alignment, curly braces, 126–127

allocate( ) method, 596
allocation operators, 675–682
Allocator parameter, 393
Allocator type, 596
allocators, 627
    header files, 1048
allTrue( ) function, 472
alternation (ECMAScript), 525
alternative function syntax,
    709–710, 739
ambiguity in naming, 240–241
    base classes, 242
analysis and design workflow, 846
anchors (ECMAScript), 525
angle brackets, C++11, 305–306
anonymous namespaces, 290
API (application programming
    interface), 58
    exposed interface, 94
applications
    description, 898–899
    platform and, 888
architecture
    address sizes, 885
    binary compatibility, 884–885
    byte order, 885–886
arguments
    iterator template arguments,
      482
    iterators, 458
    superclass method, 255–256
    type-safe variable-length
      argument lists, 743–745
    types, operator overloading,
      648
    variable-length argument lists,
      312–314
arithmetic function objects,
    470–471
arithmetic operators, 470
    increment/decrement, 655–656
    overloading, 202–203
      shorthand operators,
        203–204
      unary minus and unary
        plus, 654–655
array class, 418
array container, 371
arrays, 20–21
    associative arrays, 663–664
    constant expressions, 20
    deleting, 26
    dynamic memory, 25–27
      deleting, 765–766
      types, 763–764
    dynamically allocated, 764
    heap, multi-dimensional,
      767–769

    of objects, 764–765
    pointers, 772–773
    stack, multi-dimensional, 767
    standard C-style arrays, 450
    std::array, 21–22
    vector container and, 370
ASCII (American Standard Code
    for Information Interchange),
    517–518
assembly code, 902–903
assert macro, 943–944
    static_assert, 944–945
assign( ) method, 398
assigning object value to objects,
    162–165
assignment
    bitwise, 172
    disallowing, 180
    self-assignment, 178
    shallow, 172
assignment compared to copying,
    165–166
assignment operator, 162
    declaring, 163
    defining, 164
    helper routines, 179–180
    initializer-lists, 635
    move assignment operator,
      278–279
    Spreadsheet class, 177–179
associative arrays, 663–664
associative containers, 386, 428
    hashmaps as, 628–641
    map
      constructing, 430–431
      element lookup, 434–435
      element remove, 435
      example, 436–438
      insert( ) method,
        431–432
      iterators, 433–434
      operator[ ], 432–433
      types, 430
    method requirements, 629–633
    multimap
      element lookup, 438
      example, 439–441
    multiset, 444
    set, 441–444
    typedefs, 628–629
    unordered, 444–449
      unordered_map, 445–449
      unordered_multimap,
        449
      unordered_multiset,
        449–450
      unordered_set, 449–450
at( ) method, 363

atomic operations, 805–806
    library, 802
atomic types, 803–804
attributes, C++11, 308
auditVoterRolls( ) function,
    504–505
auto keyword, 402, 570, 710,
    738–739
    templates, 739–742
auto variable, 10
auto_ptr, 780

B

back references, 526, 529
back_insert_iterator class,
    599–600
bad( ) method, 550
bad_alloc exception, 347–348
base classes
    abstract, 232–233
    ambiguity, 242
    source code, 233
    virtual base, 242
    virtual base classes, 265
begin( ) method, 451
behaviors, 80
    overriding, 85
bibliography, 1035–1044
bidirectional I/O, 566–567
big-endian ordering, 886
big-O notation, 61–62
binary compatibility, 884–885
binary logical operators,
    overloading, 656–657
binary operators, 11
binary_search( ) function, 484
bind2nd( ) method, 475–476
bitset, 452
    bitwise operators, 453
    example, 453–456
bitset container, 373–374
bitwise copying, 172
bitwise function objects, 473
bitwise operators, 453
    overloading, 656–657
black box testing, 905
bool, vector and, 412–413
bool( ) conversion operator, 321
bool variable, 10
Boolean expressions, conversion
    operators, 672–674
bounded repeats, 525
brackets for deleting arrays, 26
break keyword, 19
buffer overflow errors, 795
buffered streams, 546, 549

buffers, packet buffers, 422–424
bugs
    avoiding, 928–929
    catastrophic bugs, 928
    cosmetic bugs, 928
    debug traces, 930–943
    error logging, 929–930
    inheritance, 212
    noncatastrophic bugs, 928
    planning for, 929–945
    reporting, 906–907
    reproducing, 945–946
        debugging nonreproducible, 947–948
        debugging reproduced, 946–947
    root cause, 928
    tracking tools, 907–908
Bugzilla, 907–908
built-in classes, vectors, 396
business modeling workflow, 846
byte addressability, 886
byte order, 885–886

C

C
    linking with, 892–894
    porting to C++, 889
C#, 894–895
C++
    as object-oriented language, 33–35
    Stroustrup, Bjarne, 3
C++11, 301
    angle brackets, 305–306
    attributes, 308
    containers, changes, 391–392
    conversion operators, 306–308
    emplace operations, 392
    function syntax, 304
    initialization, uniform, 302–303
    initializer lists, 306
    literals, user-defined, 308–310
    null pointers, 304–305
C++ design
    abstraction, 54–55
    differences, 52–53
    reuse, 55–57
C standard library, 67–68
C++ Standard Library, 361
    compile-time rational arithmetic, 369
    exceptions, 367
    header files, 1045–1047
        algorithms, 1048
        allocators, 1048

containers, 1047–1048
        exceptions, 1049
        general utilities, 1048–1049
        I/O streams, 1050
        iterators, 1048
        mathematical utilities, 1049
        threading library, 1051
    I/O streams, 366
    localization, 367
    mathematical utilities, 368
    random numbers, 368
    regular expressions, 369
    smart pointers, 367
    STL (standard template library), containers, 369–376
    strings, 366
    time utilities, 368
    tuples, 369
C-style arrays, 450
C-style comments, 4
C-style strings, 28, 510–512
cache invalidation, 867
caching, design-level efficiency, 866–867
callbacks, 457
    predicate function callbacks, 460
calling copy constructors, explicitly, 155
calling methods, from methods, 138–139
call_once( ), 819
capitalization in naming, 124
capture blocks, lambda expressions, 463, 465
capture groups, 526
capturing, 465
cascading if statement, 16
casting
    downcasting, 229
    pointers, 770–771
    upcasting, 229
casting variables, 10
casts
    const_cast, 296
    dynamic_cast, 298–299
    reinterpret_cast, 298
    situations for use, 300
    static_cast, 296–297
catastrophic bugs, 928
catch statements, 338, 354
catching exceptions, 30–31, 318, 321–324, 970
    multiple, 326–329
    stack unwinding and, 346–347
cbegin( ) method, 625–626
cend( ) method, 625–626
chain of responsibility pattern, 1007–1009

chaining constructors, 224
char exception, 325
char16_t variable, 10
char32_t variable, 10
char variable, 10
character classes, 527
character sets
    encodings, 519
    matches, 526–528
    non-Western, 519–521
    UCS (Universal Character Set), 519
    wide characters, 518–519
    word boundaries, 528
characters, 10
    code points, 519
chess program, 69–74
Chrono library
    clocks, 578–580
    duration, 574–578
    time_point class, 580–581
class templates, 684
    friend function templates, 713–714
    grid classes, 687–691
    partial class specialization, 724–729
    writing, 685–692
classes, 78–79
    abstraction, 100
    access specifiers, 135–136
    array, 418
    back_insert_iterator, 599–600
    base classes
        abstract, 232–233
        virtual, 242
    built-in, vectors, 396
    character classes, 527
    condition_variable, 823
    data members, 33
        access, 137–138
    declaring, 33–35
    DefaultHash, 607
    definitions, 134–137
    derived, 212
    DoubleSpreadsheetCell, 233
    duration, 574–578
    enumerated types, 194–195
    exception, writing, 339–342
    exending, 212–215
    friends, 195–197
    fstream, 566–567
    generic template class, 364
    hash class definition, 606–607
    HashIterator, 620–621
    hierarchies, 71–72
        diamond-shaped, 242

classes *(continued)*
  exceptions, 337–339
  reusable code and, 101
implementation, 207
insert_iterator, 599–600
instantiation, 365
interface, 207
iterator_traits, 604–605
lock classes, 817–819
Matrix, 350–351
members, 135
methods, 135
mix-in, 92, 979–981
  variadic templates, 745–746
nested, 192–194
nested_exception mix-in class, 342
opaque, 99
ostream_iterator, 598
pair, 428–429
parent classes, 212
reverse_iterator, 596–598
smart pointers, writing, 784–790
Spreadsheet, 134 *(See Spreadsheet class)*
SpreadsheetCell, 134
stand-alone, reuse and, 57
standard library, 36
static data members, 181
std::pair, 590–594
std::vector, 36
string, 366, 513–516
StringSpreadsheetCell, 233
stringstream, 567
subclassing, 969–970
SubObject, 353–354
templates
  subclassing
  writing, 972–973
time_point, 580–581
user-defined, vectors, 396
valarray, 368
WeatherPrediction, 219
WebHost, 891
writing, 968–969
clear( ) method, 639
clients, inheritance and, extending classes, 213–214
clocks, 578–580
code
  compiling, 5
  decomposing, 22
  reusable
    advantages, 59
    design, 98–110
    ease of use, 109–110
    generality, 109–110
    writing, 56

reusing
  C standard library, 67–68
  capabilities, 60–61
  categories of available code, 57
  disadvantages, 59–60
  frameworks, 58
  libraries, 58
  licensing, 64
  limitations, 60–61
  open source libraries, 66–67
  performance, 61–64
  platform limitations, 64
  polymorphism and, 86
  prototype, 65
  stand-alone functions/ classes, 57
  strategies, 60–65
  support, 64
  third-party application bundles, 65–66
code points, 519
Code::Blocks debugger, 963–964
coding, templates, 362–366
  coding without, 685–687
coercing variables, 10
comments, 4
  C-style, 4
  code reuse design, 108
  reasons for
    complicated code explanation, 114–115
    metainformation conveyance, 115–116
    usage explanation, 112–114
  style
    ad hoc, 119
    every line, 116–117
    fixed-format, 118–119
    prefix comments, 117–118
    self-documenting, 119–120
comparison algorithms, 380, 486–488
comparison function objects, 471–472
comparison operators, overloading, 204–206
comparisons, vectors, 398–399
compile-time debug mode, 931–934
compile-time rational arithmetic, 369
compiler, template processing, 693
compiler-generated constructors, 160
compiler-generated default constructors, 148–149
compilers
  bugs, 887
  language extensions, 887

compiling code, 5
components, 79
condition variables, 823–825
conditional operators, 17–18
conditionals
  conditional operators, 17–18
  if/else statements, 16
  switch statements, 17
  ternary operator, 17
condition_variable class, 823
configuration management workflow, 846
const characters, string literals and, 512
const data members, 181, 183–184
const iterator, 625
const keyword, 31–32, 187, 282–283
  methods, 286
  parameters, 32, 282–286
  pointers, 283–285, 771
  references, 285–286
  variables, 282–286
const methods, 186–188
const reference data members, 181, 185
const reference parameters, 32–33
constant expressions, arrays
constants, 125
  const keyword, 32
  namespaced, 124
const_cast, 296
constexpr keyword, 286–288
constructor inheritance, 247–251
constructor initializers. *See* ctor-initializer
constructors, 34
  chaining, 224
  compiler-generated, 160
  copy constructors, 154–157
    calling explicitly, 155
    subclasses, 258–259
  default, 146–151
    compiler-generated, 148–149
    explicitly defaulted, 150
    explicitly deleted, 150–151
  delegating, 146
  delegating constructors, 159
  DoubleSpreadsheetCell constructor, 235
  error handling, 350–352
  function-try-blocks, 352–354
  hashmap class, 610–611, 634
  on heap, 145
  initializer-list constructors, 157–158
  move constructors, 278–279
  multiple, 145–146

parent constructors, 223–224
on stack, 144
vectors, 396–397
writing, 143–144
zero-initialization, 396
containers, 386–387
adapters, 386
queue, 421–424
associative, 386, 428
map, 430–438
multimap, 438–441
multiset, 444
set, 441–444
bitset, 452
bitwise operators, 453
example, 453–456
C++11 changes, 391–392
C++ standard library, 361
forward_list, forward
interators, 458
hash tables, 386
header files, 1048
interface, 370
methods, 617–619
reversible, 628
sequential, 386
array class, 418
deque, 413
forward_list,
418–421
hashmap, 641
list, 413–417, 419–420
vector, 393–412
standard C-style arrays, 450
STL (standard template library),
369–376
array, 371
bitset, 373–374
deque, 371
forward_list,
371–372
hash tables, 374
list container, 370–371
map, 373
multimap, 373
multiset, 372–373
priority_queue, 372
set, 372–373
stack, 372
table listing, 375–376
unordered associative
containers, 374
vector, 370
streams, 451–452
strings, 451
typedefs, 616
vector, 276
writing, hashmap, 605–615
continue keyword, 19

conversion
implicit, 199–200
numeric, 515–516
operators, C++11
conversion operators
ambiguity, 671–672
bool( ), 321
Boolean expressions, 672–674
writing, 669–671
copy( ) function, 493–495
copy constructors, 154–157
assignment comparison,
165–166
calling explicitly, 155
ctor-initializers, 154
helper routines, 179–180
object members and, 166
Spreadsheet class, declaration,
177
subclasses, 258–259
copy_backward( ) function,
493–494
copying
bitwise, 172
shallow, 172
copyString( ) function, 510–511
core process workflows, 846
cosmetic bugs, 928
counters
naming conventions, 123
static data members, 181
count_if( ) algorithm, 468, 570
cout stream, 548
covariant return types, 243
cppunit, 914–916
CPUs, 798
cross-compiling, 884
cross-language development,
888–889
assembly code, 902–903
C# and C++, 894–895
JNI (Java Native Interface),
896–898
linking with C-code, 892–894
paradigm shifts, 889–892
Perl, 898–902
shell scripts, 899
cross-platform development
architecture
address sizes, 885
binary compatibility,
884–85
byte order, 885–886
implementation, 886
compiler and, 887
library implementations, 887
platform-specific features, 888
.cruft, 121
c_str( ) method, 891

ctor-initializers, 133, 151–152
copy constructors, 154
data member initialization, 153
curly braces, alignment and, 126–127

D

d-char-sequence, 516
dangling pointers, 174, 367, 794
data members, 33
access, 137–138
ambiguity, 241
const, 181, 183–184
const reference data members,
185
const reference members, 181
mutable, 188
reference data members,
184–185
reference members, 181
references, 271
static, 181, 288
accessing, 181–183
methods, 181–182
deadlocks, 800–801
deallocate( ) method, 596
deallocation operators, 675–682
debug mode
compile-time, 931–934
ring buffers, 937–943
run-time, 937
start-time, 934–936
debugging
article citation example,
953–966
Code::Blocks, 963–964
debug traces, debug mode,
930–937
Fundamental Law of
Debugging, 928
introduction, 927
Linux, GDB debugger,
960–963
memory
class-related errors, 952
error categories, 948–951
general errors, 952
object errors, 952
multithreaded programs,
952–953
reproducing bugs, 945–946
debugging nonreproducible,
947–948
debugging reproduced,
946–947
symbolic debugger, 947
Visual C++ 2010 debugger,
965–966

decltype keyword, 739
declarations, 5
    assignment operators, 163
    classes, 33–35
    forward declaration, 184
    functions, 23
    methods, order, 136–137
    pointers, 25
declaring variables, 8–9
decltype keyword, templates, 739–742
decltype variable, 10
decomposing code, 22
decomposition, 120
    modular, 121
    refactoring, 121
decorator design pattern, 109, 1004–1007
decrement( ) method, 622–623
decrement operator (--), 11
decrement operators, overloading, 655–656
deduction rules, 730–731
default constructors, 146–151
    compiler-generated, 148–149
    explicit defaulted, 150
    explicit deleted, 150–151
default parameters, 190–191
DefaultHash class, 607
#define directive, 5
definitions, 5
    classes, 134–137
delegating constructors, 146, 159
delete-expression, 675
delete keyword, 761
demote( ) method, 38
deployment workflow, 846
deque container, 371, 413
dereferencing operators, 666–669
dereferencing pointers, 27, 770
derived classes, 212
design. See also C++ design; programming design; software design
    abstraction and, 54–55
    chess program, 69–74
    reusable code, 98–99
        abstraction, 99–100
        aggregation, 102
        checks and safeguards, 104
        class hierarchies, 101
        comments, 108
        documentation, 108
        interfaces, 104–109
        separate concepts, 100–102
        subsystems, 100–101
        templates, 102–104
        user interface dependencies, 102
    threading, 834–835

design-level efficiency, 860
    caching, 866–867
    object pools, 867–871
design patterns, 68, 985–986
    adapter pattern, 1002–1004
    chain of responsibility pattern, 1007–1009
    decorator pattern, 109, 1004–1007
    factory pattern, 995–1000
    iterator pattern, 986–987
    observer pattern, 1009–1012
    proxy pattern, 1000–1002
    singleton pattern, 987–994
design techniques, 68, 967–968
    classes
        subclassing, 969–970
        template, writing, 972–973
        writing, 968–969
    double dispatch, 973–978
    files
        reading from, 971
        writing to, 971
    mix-in classes, 979–981
    throwing/catching exceptions, 970
destination ranges, 490–491
destructors, 160–162
    error handling and, 354–355
    freeing memory, 172
    ifstream, 562
    ofstream, 562
    vectors, 396–397
    virtual, 225
        method templates, 698
diamond-shaped hierarchies, 242
directives
    preprocessor, 5–6
    using, 8
distributions, random numbers, 587–590
division operator (/), 11
DLL (Dynamic Link Libraries), 294
do/while loop, 19
doCFunction( ) method, 893
documentation
    code reuse design, 108
    comments
        reasons for, 112–116
        styles, 116–120
double-checked locking algorithm, 822–823
double deletion, 794–795
    smart pointers, 785
double dispatch, 973–978
double-ended queue. See deque container
double-freeing, 367
double precision numbers, 10
double variable, 10

doubleDelete( ) function, 785–786
DoubleSpreadsheetCell class, 233
    constructor, 235
DoubleSpreadsheetCell constructor, 235
doubleToDouble( ) method, 186
doubly linked list structures, 370–371
downcasting, 229
doWorkInThread( ) function, 814
dumb pointers, memory allocation results, 782
duration class, 574–578
dynamic arrays versus dynamically allocated arrays, 764
dynamic-length vectors, 395–396
dynamic memory, 759
    advantages, 760
    allocation, 169–180
        delete keyword, 761
        failure, 762–763
        malloc( ) function, 762
        new keyword, 761
    arrays, 25–27
        deleting, 765–766
        multi-dimensional, 766–769
        types, 763–764
    freeing, 172
    mental model, 760–761
    pointers, 24–28
dynamic strings
    C-style strings, 510–512
    raw string literals, 516–517
    string class, 513–516
    string literals, 512
dynamically allocated arrays, 764
dynamic_cast, 298–299

E

ease of use, 109–110
ECMAScript, 524–525
    alternation, 525
    anchors, 525
    back references, 529
    character sets, matches, 526–528
    grouping, 526
    precedence, 526
    raw string literals, 529
    regular expressions, 529
    repetition, 525
    wildcards, 525
    word boundaries, 528
efficiency, 859–860
    design-level, 860, 866–867
        caching, 866–867
        object pools, 867–871

language-level, 860, 861–862
    catching exceptions by
        reference, 864
    move semantics, 864
    pass-by-reference, 862–863
    return by reference, 863
    temporary objects,
        864–865
elements
    list container, 414
    map associative container,
        434–435
    multimap associative container,
        438
    objects, fields, 401–402
    requirements, 387–388
    value semantics, 387
    vectors
        access methods, 394–395
        appending to, 404–406
        initial value, 394–395
        user-defined classes, 396
emplace( ) method, 422
emplace operations, 392
    hashmap class, 637–638
employee records system sample
    program
    Database class
        Database.cpp file, 42–43
        Database.h file, 41–42
        DatabaseTest.cpp file, 44
    Employee class
        Employee.cpp file, 39–40
        Employee.h file, 37–38
        EmployeeTest.cpp file,
            40–41
    user interface, UserInterface.
        cpp file, 44–47
empty( ) function, 477
emulation, function partial
    specialization, 729–731
enable_if, 755–757
encryption, passwords, 900–902
end( ) method, 451
end-of-file, 557
end-of-line sequence, 6
#endif directive, 5
endl manipulator, 551
enumerated types, 13–14
    in classes, 194–195
    strongly typed enumerations,
        14–15
    type-safe, 15
eof( ) method, 558
equal( ) function, 486–488
equal_range( ) function, 484
erase( ) function, 497
erase( ) method, 441
error categories, 948–951

error checking, 388
error handling, 74
    constructors, 350–352
        function-try-blocks,
            352–354
    destructors, 354–355
    exceptions, 317–318
    input, 557–558
    memory allocation errors,
        347–350
    new handler callback function,
        348
    output, 549–550
error level, 930
error logging, 929–930
ErrorCorrelator, 426
escape character, \n, 6–7
event objects, 823
events, platform and, 888
exception classes, writing, 339–342
exception handling, 323
    unexpected_handler, 333
    unhandled exceptions, 329–330
exception_ptr, 813
exceptions, 30–31, 388
    bad_alloc, 347–348
    benefits, 318–319
    C++, 320
    C++ standard library, 367
    catching, 318, 321–324, 970
        multiple, 326–329
        by reference, 864
        stack unwinding and,
            346–347
    char, 325
    class hierarchy and, 337–339
    custom, 126
    header files, 1049
    hierarchy, 336–337
    introduction, 317
    invalid_argument, 322
    lambda expressions, 463
    matching, 328–329
    multithreaded programming,
        812–815
    nested, 342–344
    nested_exception mix-in class,
        342
    polymorphism and, 336–337
    runtime_error, 328
    specifications, 331–336
    throw lists, 331–336
    throwing, 318, 321–324, 970
        multiple, 326–329
        stack unwinding and,
            346–347
    types, 324–325
    unexpected, 332
    unhandled, 329–330

execution order of operators, 13
explicitly calling copy constructors,
    155
explicity defaulted constructors, 150
exposed interface, 93–95
    API (application programming
        interface), 94
    audience considerations, 93
    subsystem interface, 94
    utility classes versus libraries,
        94
expressions
    regular expressions, 369,
        523–524
    short-circuit logic, 18
extending, 84
    classes, inheritance and,
        213–214
extending classes, 212–215
extern keyword, 290–291
external linkage, 288, 723
extraction operators, overloading,
    657–659

F

facets, 522–523
factorials at compile time, 746–747
factory design pattern, 995–1000
fail( ) method, 550
feature creep, 840
file streams, 562–563
    ifstream destructor, 562
    ofstream destructor, 562
    seek( ) method, 563–565
    tell( ) method, 563–565
files
    header files, 310–312
    objects, linking, 5
    reading from, 971
    writing to, 971
FILO (first-in, last-out), 372
final keyword, 215
find( ) algorithm, 602–603
find( ) function, 458–461,
    483–486
    reverse_iterator, 597
Find( ) function, template, 710
find_all( ) algorithm, 602–603
findElement( ) method, 612
find_if( ) function, 460–461, 475
fixed-format comments, 118–119
fixed-length arrays, vectors,
    393–395
fixed-length vectors, 393–395
float variable, 9
floating-point numbers, 9
flush( ) method, 549, 566

flush-on-access, 565–566
for loop, 19
    range-based, 20, 401
for_each( ) function, 469,
    488–490
formatting
    alignment, curly braces,
        126–127
    parentheses, 128
    spaces, 128
    tabs, 128
forward declaration, 184
forward_list container, 371–372,
    418–421
    forward iterators, 458
frameworks
    code reuse, 58
    object oriented, 981
        MVC (Model-View-
            Controller), 982–983
free software, 66
freeing memory, destructors and,
    172
friend function templates to class
    templates, 713–714
friend keyword, 196
friends, 195–197
fstream class, 566–567
func( ) method, 335
function adapters, binders
    bind2nd( ), 475–476
    std::bind( ), 473–475
function-call operator, 664–665
function objects, 457, 469, 665
    adapters, binders, 473–475
    adapting functions, 479–480
    arithmetic function objects,
        470–471
    bitwise function objects, 473
    comparison function objects,
        471–472
    logical function objects,
        472–473
    member functions, 477–478
    negators, 476
    threads, 808–810
    writing, 480–481
function pointers, 776–778
    implementing, 570
    threads, 806–808
    typedefs, 294–295
function templates, 710–711
    overloading, 712–713
    specialization, 711–712
function-try-blocks, 352–354
functional relationships, 89–90
functionality
    adding, 85

replacing, 85
required, user interface,
    106–107
functions, 22–23, 684. *See also*
    algorithms
    accumulate( ), 486
    addOne( ), 30
    allTrue( ), 472
    alternative function syntax,
        709, 739
    auditVoterRolls( ), 504–505
    binary_search( ), 486
    C++11 syntax, 304
    callbacks, predicate function
        callbacks, 460
    copy_backward( ), 493–494
    copyString( ), 510–511
    as data, 776–778
    declarations, 23
    doubleDelete( ), 785–786
    doWorkInThread( ), 814
    empty( ), 477
    equal( ), 486–488
    equal_range( ), 486
    Find( ), 710
    find( ), 458–461, 602–603
    find_all( ), 602–603
    find_if( ), 460–461
    for_each( ), 488–490
    friends, 195–197
    funcTwo( ), 345
    getDuplicates( ), 505–506
    hash functions, 444–445
    includes( ), 501
    incr( ), 278
    lexicographal_compare( ),
        486–488
    lower_bound( ), 486
    main( ), 6
    make_move_iterator( ), 601
    malloc( ), 762
    malloc_int( ), 783
    max( ), 482
    mem_fn( ), 477–478
    min( ), 482
    minmax( ), 482
    mismatch( ), 486–488
    namespaces and, 7
    operator( ), 664–665
    parameters, 23
    partial specialization,
        overloading and, 729–731
    printVector( ), 405
    procedures and, 78
    process( ), 571
    processValues( ), 743–745
    prototypes, 22
    ptr_fun( ), 479

random_shuffle( ), 501
readName( ), 554
realloc( ), 764
sizeof( ), 511
sort( ), 499–500
stand-alone, reuse and, 57
static, 291
strcat( ), 29, 511
strcopy( ), 511
strlen( ), 511
swap( ), 482, 619
testCallback( ), 467
threadFunc( ), 813
throw_with_nested( ), 343
unexpected( ), 333
upper_bound( ), 486
functors, 665
funcTwo( ) function, 345
Fundamental Law of Debugging,
    928
futures, 825–827

G

garbage collection, 775–776
GDB debugger, 960–963
generality, 109–110
generate( ) algorithm, 468–469
generating random numbers,
    581–582, 585–587
    random number engines,
        582–584
        predefined, 584–585
generic programming, 362
    reusable code and, 683
    templates and, 683
generic template class, 364
get( ) method, 554–555
getDuplicates( ) function,
    505–506
getline( ) method, 557
getSize( ) method, 363
getString( ) method, 234
    renaming, 189
getters/setters, 124
getValue( ) method, 135
    renaming, 189
global functions, operators, 647–648
GNU project, 66
good( ) method, 550, 558
GPL (GNU Public License), 66
gprof, 872–880
granularity of testing, 910–911
graphical user interface, 888
graphics cards, cores, 798
greedy repeats, 525
grouping (ECMAScript), 526

H

handles, 99
has-a relationship, 83–84
　is-a relationship comparison,
　　86–89
hash( ) function, implementation,
　607–608
hash functions, 444–445, 605
　DefaultHash class, 607
　hash class definition, 606–607
hash tables, 374, 386, 444–449, 605.
　See also unordered associative
　containers
　unordered_map, 445–447
HashIterator class, 620–621
　methods, 621–625
hashmap, interface, 608–610
hashmap class
　accessor operations, 640
　as associative container,
　　628–641
　clear operation, 639
　constructor, 610–611, 634
　emplace operations, 637–638
　erase operations, 638–639
　implementation, 610
　initializer list assignment
　　operator, 635
　initializer list constructor,
　　634–635
　insertion operations, 635–637
　sequential containers, 641
　as STL container, 616–627
　template demonstration, 615
　templates, 608–609
　typedefs, 609
header files, 310–312
　algorithms, 1048
　allocators, 1048
　containers, 1047–1048
　exceptions, 1049
　general utilities, 1048–1049
　I/O streams, 1050
　interators, 1048
　mathematical utilities, 1049
　template definitions, 694
　threading library, 1051
heap, 24, 25
　constructors on, 145
　objects on, 141–142
　vector allocation, 397
heap arrays, multi-dimensional,
　767–769
Hello, World
　arrays, 20–21
　　std::array, 21–22
　comments, 4

conditionals
　conditional operators,
　　17–18
　if/else statements, 16
　switch statements, 17
　ternary operator, 17
functions, 22–23
I/O streams, 6–7
loops
　do/while, 19
　for loop, 19–20
　while loop, 19
main( ) function, 6
namespaces, 7–8
operators, 11–13
preprocessor directives, 5–6
types
　enumerated, 13–14
　structs, 15–16
variables, 8–11
helper methods, 138
helper routines
　assignment operator, 179–180
　copy constructors, 179–180
hierarchies, 90–91
　classes, 71–72
　　exceptions, 337–339
　diamond shaped, 242
　exceptions, 336–337
　parallel, 243
　reusable code and, 101
high-order bytes, 886
homogenous elements, 369
Hungarian Notation, 124–125

I

I/O
　bidirectional, 566–567
　overview, 545–546
　streams, 6–7, 366
　　header files, 1050
　　user input, 7
if/else statements, 16
　cascading if statement, 16
#ifdef directive, 5
#ifndef directive, 5
ifstream destructor, 562
ifstream object, bool( )
　conversion operator, 321
implementation
　cross-platform development
　　and, 886
　　compiler and, 887
　　library implementations,
　　　887

implementation class, 207
implementation workflow, 846
　versus interface, 93
implicit conversion, 199–200
In-class member initializers, 158–159
in-memory streams, 560–561
#include directive, 5
includes, preprocessor directives, 6
includes( ) function, 501
incr( ) function, 278
increment( ) method, 622–623
increment operator (++), 11
　overloading, 655–656
indexing, iterators and, 404
inheritance, 84, 211–212
　bug fixes and, 212
　clients and, extending classes,
　　213–214
　constructors, 247–251
　derived classes, 212
　functionality
　　adding, 85
　　replacing, 85
　multiple, 91–92, 239–240
　　uses, 242–243
　non-public, 264
　parent classes, 212
　pointers, 214
　polymorphism, spreadsheet,
　　229–230
　preventing, 215
　properties, 85
　　replacing, 85
　reuse
　　subclasses and, 220–222
　　WeatherPrediction class,
　　　219
　specialization comparison, 708
　subclasses, 214–215
　superclasses, 212
　templates comparison, 103–104
initialization
　constructors, 151–153 (*See also*
　　ctor-initializers)
　lists (C++11), 306
　n-class member initializers,
　　158–159
　nonlocal variables, 292
　references, 268
　uniform in C++, 302–303, 397
　zero-initialization, template
　　types, 723–724
initializer-list constructors, 157–158
　assignment operators, 635
　hashmap class, 634–635
initializer_list, 397
inline keyword, 191–192
inline methods, 191–192

input
  error handling, 557–558
  locale awareness, 559
  manipulators, 558–559
  objects, 559–560
  streams, 552–553
    get( ) method, 554–555
    getline( ), 557
    peek( ), 556–557
    putback( ), 556
    readName( ) function, 554
    unget( ), 555–556
input stream iterator, 599
inRange( ) method, 171
insert( ) method, map associative container, 431–432
insert iterators, 599–600
insertion operators, overloading, 657–659
insert_iterator class, 599–600
instantiation, 365
  selective, 693
int variable, 9
integer non-type parameters, 697–698
integers, 9
  enumerated types, 13
integration tests, 921–923
  methods, 922–923
interface, 206
  algorithms, 370
  API (Application Programming Interface), 94
  containers, 370
  exposed, 93–95
    audience considerations, 93
    subsystem interface, 94
    utility classes versus libraries, 94
  versus implementation, 93
  implementation class, 207
  interface class, 207
  usability, 104–109
interface class, 207
internal linkage, 288
Interop services, 894
interviews, 1013–1034
intVector, 398
invalid_argument exception, 322
invalidation of iterators, 406
ios_base::out, 562
iostream subclass, 566–567
is-a relationship, 84–86
  has-a relationship comparison, 86–89
  polymorphism, 86
iterator adapters (STL)
  insert iterators, 599–600

move iterators, 600–602
reverse iterators, 596–598
stream iterators, 598–599
iterator design pattern, 986–987
iterators, 377, 388–389
  arguments, 458
  categories, 389
  const, 625
  generate( ) algorithm, 468–469
  header files, 1048
  indexing and, 404
  input stream iterator, 599
  invalidation, 406
  list container, 414
  map associative container, 433–434
  methods, 390–391
  operations, 403–404
  output stream iterator, 598
  regular expressions, 530
  safety, 402–403
  template arguments, 482
  traits, 604–605
  typedefs, 390–391, 625–626
  types, 481
  vector, 399–401
  writing, 619–620
iterator_traits class, 604–605

J–K

JNI (Java Native Interface), 896–898
keywords
  auto, 402, 570, 710, 738–739, 739–742
  break, 19
  const, 31–32, 187, 282–283
    methods, 286
    parameters, 32, 282–286
    pointers, 283–285, 771
    references, 285–286
    variables, 282–286
  constexpr, 286–288
  continue, 19
  decltype, 739–742
  delete, 761
  extern, 290–291
  final, 215
  friend, 196
  inline, 191–192
  new, 761
  noexcept, 331
  override, 246
  static
    functions, 291
    variables, 291

throw, 322
typename, 613
using, 246
virtual, 216

L

lambda expressions
  capture block, 465
  as parameters, 467
  return types, 465–466
  syntax, 463–464
  threading, 810
language extensions, 887
language-level efficiency, 860, 861–862
  catching exceptions by reference, 864
  move semantics, 864
  pass-by-reference, 862–863
  return by reference, 863–864
  temporary objects, 864
lexicographical_compare( ) function, 486–488
libraries
  atomic operations, 802–806
  C standard library, 67–68
  C++ standard library (See C++ standard library)
  Chrono
    clocks, 578–580
    duration, 574–578
    time_point class, 580–581
  code reuse, 58
  implementations, 887
  library handles, 294
  netwrklib, 890
  open source, 66–67
    finding, 66–67
    using, 66–67
  procedural, object-oriented wrapper, 889–890
  Ratio, 571–574
  regex, 530–531
    regex_iterator( ), 536–537
    regex_match( ), 531–534
    regex_replace( ), 540–543
    regex_search( ), 534–536
    regex_token_iterator( ), 537–539
  regular expressions library, 509
  standard library, 35
    classes, 36

life cycles of objects, 142
    assigning to objects, 162–165
    creation, 143–160
    destruction, 160–162
LIFO (last-in, first-out), 372
linear congruential engine, 583
linkage
    doubly linked list structures,
      370–371
    external, 288, 723
    internal, 288
    static, 723
    static keyword, 288–290
linking
    object files, 5
    streams, 565–566
Linux, GDB debugger, 960–963
list container, 370–371, 413–414
    elements
        accessing, 414
        adding/removing, 414
    enrollment, 416–417
    forward_list comparison,
      419–420
    iterators, 414
    merge( ) method, 416
    remove( ) method, 416
    remove_if( ) method, 416
    reverse( ) method, 416
    size, 414
    sort( ) method, 416
    special operations, 414–417
    unique( ) method, 416
literals
    literal pooling, 512
    string literals, 512
      localizing, 518
      raw string literals, 516–517,
        529
    user-defined, C++11, 308–310
little-endian ordering, 886
locales, 521
    classic, 522
    input and, 559
    Windows, 521–522
localization, 367, 517–518
    string literals, 518
locks
    double-checked locking
      algorithm, 822
    multithreading, 817–819
log( ) method, 931–934
log level, 930
Logger::log( ) method, 933
logical function objects, 472–473
long double variable, 10
long long variable, 9
long variable, 9
longjmp( ), 319

loops
    do/while loop, 19
    for loop, 19
      range-based, 20
    loop unrolling, 747–749
    while loop, 19
low-level files, platform and, 888
low-order bytes, 886
lower_bound( ) function, 484

M

macros, preprocessor macros,
    314–315
main( ) function, 6
make_move_iterator( ) function,
    601
make_pair( ) template, 429
make_shared( ) method, 782
malloc( ) function, 762
malloc_int( ) function, 783
map associative container
    constructing, 430–431
    elements
        insert( ) method,
          431–432
        lookup, 434–435
        removing, 435
    example, 436–438
    iterators, 433–434
    operator[ ], 432–433
    types, 430
    unordered_map comparison,
      446–447
map container, 373
mark and sweep garbage collection,
    775
mathematical utilities, 368
    header files, 1049
Matrix class, 350–351
max( ) function, 482
member functions, 477–478
    threads, 811
members, 135
    pointers to, 778–779
mem_fn( ) function, 477–478
memory
    aliasing, 780
    allocation
        contiguous pieces, 763
        dumb pointers, 782
        failure behavior, 348–350
        null pointers, 348
        vectors, 406–407
    allocation errors, 347–350
    class-related errors, 952
    double deletion, 794–795
    dynamic, 759

    advantages, 760
    allocation, 169–180,
      761–763
    arrays, 763–766
    mental model, 760–761
    multi-dimensional arrays,
      766–769
    pointers, 24–28
    errors, categories, 948–951
    freeing, destructors and, 172
    function pointers, 776–778
    garbage collection, 775–776
    general errors, 952
    heap, 24, 25
    object errors, 952
    object pools, 776
    orphaned, 176
    out-of-bounds access, 795
    pointer arithmetic, 774–775
    pointers, 769
      smart pointers, 779–790
    stack, 24
    strings, underallocating,
      790–791
memory access errors, 950–951
memory freeing errors, 948–949
memory leaks, 367, 791–794
    Linux, 793–794
    Valgrind, 793–794
    Windows, 792–793
memory management, custom, 775
merge( ) method, 416
Mersenne twister, 583
metaprogramming. See template
    metaprogramming
method calls, 106
method templates, 698–701
    non-type parameters, 701–703
methods, 135
    add( ), overloading, 197–198
    allocate( ), 596
    assign( ), 398
    associative containers, 629–633
    at( ), 363
    bad( ), 550
    begin( ), 451
    bind2nd( ), 475–476
    calling from methods, 138–139
    cbegin( ), 625–626
    cend( ), 625–626
    clear( ), 639
    const, 186–188
    const keyword, 286
    constructors, 34
    containers, 617–619
    c_str( ), 891
    deallocate( ), 596
    declarations, ordering, 136–137
    decrement( ), 622–623

methods *(continued)*
  defining, 137–140
  demote( ), 38
  doCFunction( ), 893
  doubleToDouble( ), 186
  emplace( ), 422
  end( ), 451
  eof( ), 558
  erase( ), 441
  fail( ), 550
  findElement( ), 612
  flush( ), 549, 566
  func( ), 335
  get( ), 554–555
  getSize( ), 363
  getString( ), 189, 234
  getValue( ), 135, 189
  good( ), 550, 558
  helper methods, 138
  increment( ), 622–623
  inline, 191–192
  inRange( ), 171
  insert( ), 431–432
  iterators, 390–391
  log( ), 931–934
  Logger::log( ), 933
  make_shared( ), 782
  multi, 973
  namespaces and, 7
  output, raw output methods,
    548–549
  overloaded
    add( ), 197–198
    deleting, 189
    operator+ method,
      198–200
  overloading, 188–190
  overriding, 215–216
    changing parameters,
      245–247
    chaning return type,
      243–245
    clients and, 217–218
    overloaded superclass
      method, 252–254
    preventing, 219
    private superclass
      method, 254–255
    static methods, 251–252
    superclass method access
      level, 256–258
    superclass method
      arguments, 255–256
    throw list, 334–335
    virtual, 259–263
  pointers to, 778–779
  promote( ), 38
  pure virtual methods, 232–233
  push( ), 422

push_back( ), 320
put( ), 548–549
rbegin( ), 597, 628
refcall( ), 274
rend( ), 597, 628
set( ), 189
setValue( ), 135
static, 186, 288
stringToDouble( ), 186
testAcquire( ), 919
tie( ), 565–566
virtual, 216
  pure, 232–233
wait( ), 824
what( ), 340, 550
write( ), 548–549
MFC (Microsoft Foundation
  Classes), 982
min( ) function, 482
minmax( ) function, 482
mismatch( ) function, 486–488
mix-in classes, 92, 979–981
  variadic templates, 745–746
mod operator (%), 11
modifying algorithms, 381–382,
  490–491
  copy( ), 493–495
  erase( ), 497
  iota( ), 491
  move( ), 496–497
  replace( ), 497
  reverse( ), 499
  transform( ), 491–493
  unique( ), 498–499
modular decomposition, 121
move( ) function, 496–497
move assignment operator, 278–279,
  653
move constructor, 278–279
move iterators, 600–602
move semantics, 278–279
  algorithms, 462
  language-level efficiency and,
    864
  move iterators, 600–602
MoveableClass instances, 601
move_backward( ) function,
  496–497
moving ownership, 279
multi-dimensional arrays, dynamic
  memory, 766–769
multi-methods, 973
multimap container, 373
  element lookup, 438
  example, 439–441
multiple inheritance, 91–92,
  239–240
  uses, 242–243
multiplication operator (*), 11

multiset associative
  container, 444
multithreaded programming, 797
  cancelling threads, 812
  condition variables, 823–825
  deadlocks, 800–801
  debugging, 952–953
  exceptions, 812–815
  futures, 825–827
  introduction, 798–799
  lambda expression, 810
  locks, 817–819
  logger class example, 827–833
  member functions, 811
  mutual exclusion, mutex
    classes, 815–817
  race conditions, 799–800
  results retrieval, 812
  std::call_once( ), 819–820
  thread local storage, 811–812
  thread pools, 833–834
  threading design, 834–835
  threads
    function object, 808–810
    function pointers,
      806–808
multithreading
  singleton design pattern and,
    992–994
  threading models, 71
mutability, lambda expressions, 463
mutable data members, 188
mutex classes, 815–817
  timed, 821–822
  writing to streams, 820–821
mutual exclusion, mutex classes,
  815–817
MVC (Model-View-Controller), 70
  object-oriented frameworks,
    982–983
MyEnum, 15

N

N-dimensional grids, template
  recursion and, 733–738
name mangling, 892
namespaces, 7–8
  anonymous, 290
  functions, 7
  methods, 7
  namespaced constants, 124
naming
  ambiguity, 240–241
    base classes, 242
  conventions
    capitalization, 124
    counters, 123

Hungarian Notation,
124–125
namespaced constants, 124
prefixes, 123
getters, 124
selecting, 122–123
setters, 124
narrowing, uniform initialization,
303
negative tests, 919
negators, 476
nested classes, 192–194
nested exceptions, 342–344
nested_exception mix-in class,
342
networking, platform and, 888
netwrklib library, 890
new-expression, 675
new keyword, 761
NGrid template class, 733–738
noexcept keyword, 331
non-integral array indices, 663–664
non-modifying alorigthms, search
algorithms, 483–486
non-public inheritance, 264
non-type template parameters,
695–697, 721–724
method templates, 701–703
pointers, 723
reference, 723
non-Western character sets, 519–521
noncatastrophic bugs, 928
nonlocal variables, order of
initialization, 292
nonstandard strings, 29
nothrow, 348
null pointers
C++11, 304–305
dereferencing, 27
memory allocation routines,
348
numbers, rational, 572
numeric conversion, 515–516
numerical processing algorithms,
380, 486

object-oriented frameworks, 981
MVC (Model-View-Controller),
982–983
object-oriented languages
C++ as, 33–35
philosophy
behaviors, 80
classes, 78–79
components, 79
properties, 79

object-oriented wrappers, 889–890
object pools, 776
design-level efficiency, 867–871
objects, 81–83, 684
aggregation, 83–84
arrays of, 764–765
constructors, writing, 143–144
elements, fields, 401–402
even objects, 823
files, linking, 5
function objects, 111, 457
adapters, 473–480
adapting functions,
479–480
arithmetic function objects,
470–471
comparison function
objects, 471–472
logical function objects,
472–473
member functions,
477–478
negators, 476
writing, 480–481
on heap, 141–142
inheritance, multiple, 91–92
input, 559–560
life cycles, 142
assigning to objects,
162–165
creation, 143–160
destruction, 160–162
memory, dynamic allocation,
169–180
output, 559–560
passing by reference, 155–156
relationships
has-a, 83–84, 86–89
hierarchies, 90–91
is-a, 84–86, 86–89
mix-in classes, 92
not-a, 89–90
as return values, 165–166
on stack, 141
destruction, 161
out of scope, 161
temporary, 864–865
observer design pattern, 1009–1012
ofstream destructor, 562
OOP (object-oriented programming),
33
opaque classes, 99
open source libraries, 66–67
finding, 66–67
using, 66–67
open source programs, 884–885
operational algorithms, 381,
488–490
operator*, 667–668

operator->, 668–669
operator->*, 669
operator[ ], 662–663
map associative container,
432–433
operator( ) function, 664–665
operator delete, 676–677
overloading, 677–679
operator+ method, 198–200
global, 200–202
operator new, 676
overoading, 677–679
operator overloading, 106, 145–146,
362
add( ) method, 197–198
allocation/deallocation
operators, 675–682
argument types, 648
arithmetic, 202–203
increment/decrement,
655–656
shorthand operators,
203–204
unary minus and unary
plus, 654–655
behavior choices, 649
binary logical operators,
656–657
bitwise operators, 656–657
comparison, 204–206
dereferencing operators,
666–669
extraction operators, 657–659
function-call operator,
664–665
implementing overloaded, 238
insertion operators, 657–659
limitations, 646–647
methods versus global
functions, 647–648
operator delete, 676–677
operator+ method, 198–200
global, 200–202
operators not to overload, 649
overloadable operators,
650–653
placement new, 676
reasons for, 646
return types, 648–649
subscripting operator, 659–662
non-integral array indices,
663–664
read-only access, 662–663
type building, 206
use, 366
operators
%=, 12
&, 12
&=, 12

operators *(continued)*
  *=, 12
  +=, 12
  <<, 12
  <<=, 12
  >>, 12
  >>=, 12
  ^, 12
  ^=, 12
  |, 12
  |=, 12
  -=, 12
  /=, 12
  arithmetic, 470
  arity, 646
  assignment operator, 162
    declaring, 163
    defining, 164
    move assignment operator,
      278–279
    Spreadsheet class, 177–179
  associativity, 647
  binary, 11
  bitwise, 453
  conditional, 17–18
  conversion
    ambiguity, 671–672
    bool( ), 321
    Boolean expressions,
      672–674
    C++11, 306–308
    writing, 669–671
  dereferencing, 666–669
  execution order, 13
  function-call, 664–665
  global functions, 648
  overloading, 559–560
  placement new, 676
  precedence, 647
  scope resolution, 137
  sequencing operator, 649
  string class, 513–514
  ternary, 11, 17
  unary, 11
orphaned memory, 176
ostream_iterator class, 598
out scope (objects on stack), 161
output
  error handling, 549–550
  manipulators, 550–552
  objects, 559–560
  overview, 547–548
  raw output methods, 548–549
  standard output, 548
  streams, 547–552
    buffered, 549
    flush( ) method, 549
    put( ) method, 548–549
    write( ) method, 548–549

output stream iterator, 598
overload resolution, 189
overloading
  function partial specialization
    and, 729–731
  function templates, 712
  methods, 188–190
    deleting overloaded, 189
    operator+ method,
      198–200
    operator+ method
      (global), 200–202
  operators
    arithmetic, 202–204
    implementing overloaded,
      238
  single polymorphism with,
    975–976
  superclass method, 252–254
overloading operators, 106,
  145–146, 559–560
  allocation/deallocation
    operators, 675–682
  argument types, 648
  arithmetic operators
    increment/decrement,
      655–656
    unary minus and unary
      plus, 654–655
  behavior choices, 649
  binary logical operators, 656–657
  bitwise operators, 656–657
  comparison operators, 204–206
  dereferencing operators,
    666–669
  extraction operators, 657–659
  function-call operator,
    664–665
  insertion operators, 657–659
  limitations, 646–647
  operator delete, 676–677
  operators not to overload, 649
  overloadable operators,
    650–653
  placement new, 676
  reasons for, 646
  return types, 648–649
  subscripting operator, 659–662
    non-integral array indices,
      663–664
    read-only access, 662–663
  type building, 206
  use, 366
override keyword, 246
overriding
  behaviors, 85
  methods, 213–214
    changing parameters2,
      245–247

changing return type,
  243–245
clients and, 217–218
overloaded superclass
  method, 252–254
preventing, 219
private superclass
  method, 254–255
static methods, 251–252
superclass method access
  level, 256–258
superclass method
  arguments, 255–256
syntax, 216–217
throw list, 334–335
virtual, 259–263
what( ), 340

P

packets, buffers, 422–424
pair class, 428–429
parallel hierarchies, 243
parameter packs, 742
parameters, 684
  Allocator, 393
  const keyword, 282–286
  const keyword and, 32
  const reference parameters,
    32–33
  default, 190–191
  functions, 23, 806
  lambda expressions, 463, 467
  overridden methods, 245–247
  references, 271–273, 275
  template template parameters,
    719–721
  templates, 684
    integer non-type
      parameters, 697–698
    method templates,
      701–703
    non-type parameters,
      695–697, 721–724
    parameter packs, 742
    type parameters, 715–719
  vector, 393
parent classes, 212
  parent constructors, 223–224
  private, 264
  protected, 264
  references, 226–229
parent constructors, 223–224
parent destructors, 224–226
parenthese in code, 128
partial specialization
  classes, 724–729
  functions, 729–731

pass-by-reference, efficiency, 862–863
passing
  objects, by reference, 155–156
  by value, disallowing, 180
  variables
    by reference, 28
    by value, 28
passwords, encrypting, 900–902
pattern-matching, 369
patterns. *See* design patterns
  subsitution pattern, 524
peek( ) method, 556–557
performance, 859–860
  reuse and, 61–64
Perl, password encryption, 900–902
placement new operators, 676
platform, definition, 883
platform-specific features, 888
pointer arithmetic, 774–775
pointers, 769
  arrays, 772–773
  casting and, 770–771
  const keyword, 283–285, 771
  dangling, 174, 367, 794
  declaring, 25
  dereferencing, 27, 770
  dynamic memory, 24–28
  function pointers, 776–778
    threads, 806–808
  inheritance and, 214
  to members, 778–779
  mental model, 770
  to methods, 778–779
  non-type template parameters,
    723
  null, C++11, 304–305
  to references, 270
  versus references, 125–126,
    273–276
  references from, 272
  references to, 270
  smart pointers, 26, 779–780
    auto_ptr, 780
    C++ standard library, 367
    class writing, 784–790
    reference counting, 785
    shared_ptr, 781–784
    stack unwinding and, 346
    SuperSmartPointer, 786,
      788–790
    unique_ptr, 781–784
  structures, 27
  this, 139–140
  typedefs, 294–295
  variables, 27
polymorphism, 86
  exceptions and, 336–337
  inheritance, spreadsheet,
    229–230

single, with overloading,
    975–976
  SpreadsheetCell hierarchy,
    236–237
POSIX, initializing semaphores, 319
#pragma directive, 5
precedence, ECMAScript, 526
precision numbers, double precision
    numbers, 10
predicate function callbacks, 460
prefix comments, 117–118
preprocessor directives, 5–6
  #define, 5
  #endif, 5
  #ifdef, 5
  #ifndef, 5
  #include, 5
  includes, 6
  #pragma, 5
preprocessor macros, 314–315
printf( ), 545
printing, tuples, 749–751
printVector( ) function, 405
priority_queue container adapter,
    424
  example, 425–427
  operations, 425
private, superclasses, 254–255
procedural library, object-oriented
    wrapper, 889–890
procedures, 684
  functions and, 78
process( ) function, 571
processValues( ) function,
    743–745
profiling, 871–872
  gprof example, 872–880
  Visual C++ 2010 example,
    880–882
programming
  generic, 362
  multithreaded (*See*
    multithreaded programming)
  scripting comparison, 898–899
programming design, 50
  importance of, 50–52
programming languages, 899
programs, employee records sample
    program, 37–47
promote( ) method, 38
properties, 79
  inheritance and, 85
  replacing, 85
protected methods, inheritance,
    214
proxy design pattern, 1000–1002
ptr_fun( ) function, 479
public extensions, 969–970
public methods, inheritance, 214

pure virtual methods, 232–233
push( ) method, 422
push_back( ) method, 320, 392
put( ) method, 548–549
putback( ) method, 556

Q

QA (quality assurance), 905
queue container adapter, 421
  example, 422–424
  operations, 422

R

r-char-sequence, 517
race conditions, 799–800
random number engine adapter, 368,
    584
random number engines, 368,
    582–584
  linear congruential engine, 583
  Mersenne twister, 583
  predefined, 584–585
  subtract with carry engine, 583
random numbers
  C++ standard library, 368
  distribution, 582, 587–590
  generating, 581–582, 585–587
random_device engine, 582–584
random_shuffle( ) function, 501
range-based for loop, 20
range specification, 527
ranges
  destination, 490–491
  source, 490–491
Ratio library, 571–574
rational numbers, 572
raw output methods, 548–549
raw string literals, 516–517, 529
rbegin( ) method, 597, 628
read-only access, 662–663
reading from files, 971
readName( ) function, 554
realloc( ) function, 764
recursion, templates, 731–738
refactoring, decomposition
    and, 121
refcall( ) method, 274
reference counting smart pointers,
    785–786
reference data members, 181,
    184–185
  const reference data members,
    185
reference parameters, 275
  const, 32–33

references, 29–30
back references, 526, 529
const keyword, 285–286
data members, 271
initializing, 268
modifying, 269
non-type template parameters, 723
parameters, 271–273
parent classes, 226–229
passing objects by, 155–156
passing variables by, 28, 272–273
from pointers, 272
to pointers, 270
versus pointers, 125–126, 273–276
pointers to, 270
reference variables, 268–270
return values, 273
rvalue, 277–282
unnamed values, 268
regex library, 530–531
regex_iterator( ), 536–537
regex_iterator algorithm, 536–537
regex_match( ), 531–534
regex_replace( ), 540–543
regex_search( ), 534–536
regex_token_iterator( ), 537–539
typedefs, 530–531
regression testing, 909, 923–924
regular expressions, 369, 523–524
ECMAScript, 524–529
iterators, 530
raw string literals, 529
regex library, 530–531
regular expressions library, 509
reinterpret_cast, 298
relationships
functional, 89–90
has-a, 83–84, 86–89
hierarchies, 90–91
inheritance, multiple, 91–92
is-a, 84–86, 86–89
mix-in classes, 92
not-a, 89–90
remove( ) method, 416
remove-erase-idiom, 405, 497–498
remove_if( ) method, 416
rend( ) method, 597, 628
repeats, greedy, 525
repetition (ECMAScript), 525
replace( ) function, 497
replace operations, 526
required functionality, user interface, 106–107
requirements on elements, 387–388

requirements workflow, 846
return by reference, 863–864
return types
lambda expressions, 463, 465–466
operator overloading, 648–649
return values
objects as, 165–166
references, 273
returning values, 23
reusable code
abstraction, 99–100
aggregation, 102
checks and safeguards, 104
class hierarchies, 101
comments, 108
design, 98–99
documentation, 108
ease of use, 109–110
generality, 109–110
generic programming, 683
interfaces, usability, 104–109
separate concepts, 100–102
subsystems, 100–101
templates, 102–104
user interface dependencies, 102
reuse
advantages, 58–59
C standard library, 67–68
capabilities, 60–61
categories of available code, 57
disadvantages, 59–60
frameworks, 58
ideas, 57
inheritance and
subclasses and, 220–222
WeatherPrediction class, 219
libraries, 58
open source, 66–67
licensing, 64
limitations, 60–61
performance and, 61–64
philosophy, 97–98
platform limitations, 64
prototype, 65
stand-alone functions/classes, 57
strategies, 60–65, 97
support, 64
third-party application bundles, 65–66
writing reusable code, 56
reverse( ) functions, 416, 499
reverse iterators, 596–598
reverse_iterator class, 596–598
reversible containers, 628
ring buffers, 937–943

round-robin scheduling with
vector, 407–412
RTTI (Run Time Type Information), 263–264
run-time debug mode, 937
runtime_error exception, 328
RUP (Rational Unified Process) of
software development, 845–847
rvalue references, 277–282
move assignment operator, 653

S

sample programs, employee records
system, 37–47
scanf( ), 545
scope, resolution, 300–301
scope resolution operator, 137
scripting
languages, 899
password encryption, 900–902
programming comparison, 898–899
script definition, 899
shell scripts, 899
Scrum, 848–850
search algorithms, 378–379, 483–486
seek( ) method, 563–565
self-assignment, 178
self-documenting comments, 119–120
semantics. *See* move semantics
semaphores, initializing, 319
sequencing operator, 649
sequential containers, 386
array class, 418
deque, 413
forward_list, 418–421
hashmap, 641
list, 413–414
adding/removing elements, 414
element access, 414
enrollment, 416–417
forward_list
comparison, 419–420
iterators, 414
merge( ) method, 416
remove( ) method, 416
remove_if( ) method, 416
reverse( ) method, 416
size, 414
sort( ) method, 416
special operations, 414–417
unique( ) method, 416
vector, type parameters, 393

serialization, XML format, 922
set( ) method, 189
set algorithms, 501–503
set associative container, 441–444
setjmp( ), 319
setValue( ) method, 135
SFINAE (Substitution Failure Is Not An Error), 755–757
shallow copying, 172
shared_ptr, 367, 781–784
shell scripts, 899
short-circuit logic, 18
short variable, 9
single polymorphism with overloading, 975–976
singleton design pattern
    access-controlled, 989–991
    implementation, 987–991
    multithreading and, 992–994
    static class singletons, 988–989
sizeof( ) function, 511
slicing, 229
smart pointers, 26, 779–780
    auto_ptr, 780
    C++ standard library, 367
    classes, writing, 784–790
    double deletion and, 785
    reference cointing, 785–786
    shared_ptr, 781–784
    stack unwinding and, 346
    SuperSmartPointer, 786–788
        enhancing, 789–790
        unit testing, 788–789
    unique_ptr, 781–784
smoke testing, 924
software, life cycle
    RUP (Rational Unified Process), 845–847
    Spiral Model, 843–845
    Stagewise Model, 841
    Waterfall Model, 841–843
software design, 50
    feature creep, 840
software engineering, 839
    Agile Methodology, 847
    Scrum, 848–850
    XP (Extreme Programming), 850–854
software triage, 854
sort( ) function, 499–500
sort( ) method, 416
sorting algorithms, 382–383, 499–501
Source Code Control software, 855–857
source files, template definitions, 694–695
source ranges, 490–491
spaces in code, 128

specialization
    function templates, 711–712
    inheritance comparison
    partial specialization
        classes, 724–729
        functions, 729–731
splicing, 414–415
Spreadsheet class, 134
    assignment operator, 177–179
    copy constructors, declaration, 177
    definition, 170
SpreadsheetCell base class, 231–232
SpreadsheetCell class, 134
    subclassing, 234
spreadsheets
    application example
        Spreadsheet class, 134
        SpreadsheetCell base class, 231–232
        SpreadsheetCell class, 134
    inheritance and, polymorphism, 229–230
stack, 24
    constructors on, 144
    objects on, 141
        destruction, 161
        out of scope, 161
    unwinding, 344–346
    variables, exceptions, 31
stack arrays, multi-dimensional, 767
stack container, 372
stack container adapter
    example, 427–428
    operations, 427
stack frame, 24
stand-alone functions/classes, reuse and, 57
standard library, 35
    classes, 36
standard output, 548
start-time debug mode, 934–936
statements
    catch, 338, 354
    class definitions, 134
    throw, 321
static class singletons, 988–989
static data members, 181
    access, 181–183
    counters, 181
static keyword
    data members, 288
    functions, 291
    linkage, 288–290
    methods, 288
    variables, 291
static linkage, 723

static methods, 186
    overridden methods, 251–252
static_assert macro, 944–945
static_cast, 296–297
std::array, 21–22
std::bind( ), 473–475
std::call_once( ), 819–820
std::cerr, 6
std::cout, 6
std::endl, 6
std::function, 569
    function pointers, implementing, 570
std::pair class, 590–594
std::swap( ), 619
std::vector class, 36
STL (standard template library), 65, 102, 361
    algorithms, 376–378
        comparison, 380
        modifying, 381–382
        non-modifying, 378–381
        numerical processing, 380
        operational, 381
        search algorithms, 378–379
        sorting, 382–383
        utility algorithms, 378
    Allocator type, 596
    containers, 369–376
        array, 371
        bitset, 373–374
        deque, 371
        forward_list, 371–372
        hash tables, 374
        list, 370–371
        map, 373
        multimap, 373
        multiset, 372–373
        priority_queue, 372
        set, 372–373
        stack, 372
        table listing, 375–376
        unordered associative containers, 374
        vector, 370
        writing, 605–641
    extending, algorithm writing, 602–605
    iterator adapters
        insert iterators, 599–600
        move iterators, 600–602
        reverse iterators, 596–598
        stream iterators, 598–599
    iterator traits, 604–605
    omissions, 384
    vector container, 276
strcat( ) function, 29, 511
strcopy( ) function, 511

stream iterators, 598–599
    input stream iterator, 599
    output stream iterators, 598
streams, 451–452, 545, 546–547.
    See also I/O streams
    buffered, 546
    cout, 548
    current position, 546
    destinations, 547
    file streams, 562–563
        ifstream destructor, 562
        ofstream destructor, 562
        seek( ) method, 563–565
        tell( ) method, 563–565
    fstream class, 567
    in-memory, 560–561
    input, 552–553
        error handling, 557–558
        get( ) method, 554–555
        getline( ), 557
        peek( ), 556–557
        putback( ), 556
        readName( ) function,
            554
        unget( ), 555–556
    linking, 565–566
    output
        buffered, 549
        flush( ) method, 549
        put( ) method, 548–549
        write( ) method,
            548–549
    sources, 547
    string streams, 560–562
    unbuffered, 546
    writing to, mutex classes,
        820–821
string class, 366, 513–516
    numeric conversion, 515–516
    operators, 513–514
string literals, 512
    const characters, 512
    localizing, 518
    raw string literals, 529
string streams, 560–562
string type, 28
strings, 366
    C-style, 28
    dynamic
        C-style strings, 510–512
        raw string literals, 516–517
        string class, 513–516
        string literals, 512
    nonstandard, 29
    numeric conversions, 515–516
    strcat( ), 29
    underallocating, 790–791
    wide characters, 518–519
    wide strings

strings, 451
StringSpreadsheetCell class, 233
stringstream class, 567
stringToDouble( ) method, 186
strlen( ) function, 511
strongly typed enumerations, 14–15
Stroustrup, Bjarne, 3
structs, 15–16, 136
structures, pointers to, 27
subclasses, 969–970
        copy constructors, 258–259
        equals operator, 258–259
        inheritance, reuse and,
            220–222
        parent classes, parent
            constructors, 223–224
        protected methods, 214
        public methods, 214
        replacing functionality,
            222–223
    SpreadsheetCell class, 234
subclassing, 84
SubObject class, 353–354
subscripting operator, 659–662
    non-integral array indices,
        663–664
    read-only access, 662–663
substitution pattern, 524
subsystems, code reuse and, 100–101
subtract with carry engine, 583
subtraction operator (-), 11
superclasses, 85
    abstract, 85
    inheritance, 212
    methods
        access level, 256–258
        arguments, 255–256
        private, 254–255
SuperSmartPointer, 786–788
    enhancing, 789–790
    unit testing, 788–789
swap( ) function, 482, 619
switch statements, 17
symbolic debugger, 947
system tests, 923
system_clock, 578

T

tabs in code, 128
tell( ) method, 563–565
template classes, writing, 972–973
template metaprogramming
    factorials at compile time,
        746–747
    loop unrolling, 747–749
    tuple printing, 749–751
    type traits, 751–757

template specializations, 703–706
    inheritance comparison, 708
template template parameters,
    719–721
templates, 362, 683
    aliases, 708–709
    benefits, 103
    class templates, 684
        friend function templates,
            713–714
        partial specialization,
            724–729
    classes, subclassing, 706–707
    code reuse, 102–104
    coding without, 685–687
    cons, 103
    function templates, 710–711
        overloading, 712–713
        specialization, 711–712
    generic programming, 362
    generic template class, 364
    grid class, 687–691
    hashmap class, 608–609
    header files, 694
    inheritance comparison,
        103–104
    instantiation, 687, 691
        selective, 693
    iterator template arguments,
        482
    keywords
        auto, 739–742
        decltype, 739–742
    make_pair( ), 429
    method templates, 698–701
        nont-type parameters
    names, 688
    NGrid template class, 733–738
    parameterization, 684
    parameters
        integer non-type
            parameters, 697–698
        non-type, 695–697,
            721–724
        parameter packs, 742
        type, 715–719
    processing, 693
    recursion, 731–738
    source files, 694–695
    templated types (regex library),
        530
    types, 693
        zero-initialization,
            723–724
    variadic, 742–743
        mix-in classes, 745–746
        type-safe variable-length
            argument lists, 743–745
ternary operators, 11, 17

test runners, 917
test workflow, 846
testAcquire( ) method, 919
testCallback( ) function, 467
testing
    black box, 905
    integration tests, 921–923
        methods, 922–923
    QA (quality assurance), 905
    regression testing, 909,
        923–924
    responsibility for, 906
    smoke testing, 924
    system tests, 923
    tips, 924–925
    unit testing, 909–910
        cppunit, 915–916
        methods, 909–910
        negative tests, 919
        process, 910–914
        running tests, 914
        sample data, 912–913
        suites, 916–918
        test runners, 917
        writing tests, 913
    white box, 905
The C++ Programming Language
    (Bjarne), 3
The C Programming Language
    (Kernighan and Ritchie), 3–4
third-party applications, bundling,
    reuse and, 65–66
this pointer, 139–140
thread pools, 833–834
threadFunc( ) function, 813
threading
    design, 834–835
    library, 1051
    models, 71
threads
    cancelling, 812
    function objects, 808–810
    function pointers, 806–808
    lambda expression, 810
    local storage
    member functions, 811
    parameters, 806
    platform and, 888
    results retrieval, 812
throw keyword, 322
throw lists, 331–336
    usefulness, 336
throw statement, 321
throwing exceptions, 30, 318,
    321–324, 970
    multiple, 326–329
    stack unwinding and, 346–347
throw_with_nested( ) function,
    343

tick period, 574
ticks, 574
tie( ) method, 565–566
tilde (~) in destructors, 172
time utilities, 368
timed mutexes
time_point class, 580–581
time_point type, 578
tokenizing values, 553
try/catch construct, 321
tuples, 369, 590–594
    printing, 749–751
type inference
    auto keyword, 738–739
    decltype keyword, 739
type parameters, templates, 715–719
type-safe enumerations, 15
type-safe variable-length argument
    lists, 743–745
type traits, 751–757
typedefs, 292–293
    associative containers, 628–629
    container requirements, 616
    function pointers, 294–295
    hashmap class, 609
    iterators, 390–391, 625–626
    regex library, 530–531
    string library, 520
typeid operator, virtual methods,
    263
typename keyword, 613
types, 684
    aliases, 295–296
    atomic types, 803–804
    categories, 751–754
    covariant return types, 243
    enumerated, 13–14
        classes, 194–195
        strongly typed
            enumerations, 14–15
    operator overloading and, 206
    overridden methods, 243–245
    relations, 754–755
    string, 28
    structs, 15–16
    templates, 693

U

UCS (Universal Character Set),
    519
unary operators, 11
    overloading, 654–655
unbuffered streams, 546
unexpected( ) function, 333
unexpected_handler, 333
unget( ) method, 555–556
uniform initialization, 397

uniform random number generator,
    368
uninitialized pointers, derefencing,
    27
unions, 136
unique( ) function, 416, 498–499
unique_ptr, 367, 781–784
unit testing, 909–910
    cppunit, 915–916
    granularity, 910–911
    methods, 909–910
    negative tests, 919
    process, 910–914
    running tests, 914
    sample data, 912–913
    suites, 916–918
    test runners, 917
    writing tests, 913
unordered associative containers,
    374, 444–449, 605–615. *See
    also* hash tables
    unordered_map, 445–447
        example, 448–449
        map comparison,
            446–447
    unordered_multimap, 449
    unordered_multiset, 449–450
    unordered_set, 449–450
unordered_map associative
    container, 445–447
    example, 448–449
    map comparison, 446–447
unordered_multimap associative
    container, 449
unordered_multiset associative
    container, 449–450
unordered_set associative
    container, 449–450
unsigned int variable, 9
unsigned long long variable, 9
unsigned long variable, 9
unsigned short variable, 9
unwinding stack, 344–346
upcasting, 229
    ambiguities and, 241
upper_bound( ) function, 484
user-defined classes, vectors, 396
user-defined literals (C++11),
    308–310
user interface, dependencies, code
    reuse and, 102
using directive, 8
using keyword, 246
utilities
    mathematical, 368
    time, 368
utility algorithms, 378, 482–483
utiltities, variable-length argument
    lists, 312–314

V

valarray class, 368
value semantics, 387
values, 684
    parameterizing, 684
    passing by, 272–273
        disallowing, 180
    passing variables by, 28
    return values, references, 273
    returning, 23
variable-length argument lists, 312–314
variables, 8–9
    auto, 10
    bool, 10
    casting, 10
    char, 10
    char16_t, 10
    char32_t, 10
    coercing, 10
    condition variables, 823–825
    const keyword, 282–286
    converting, 10
    declaring, 8–9
    decltype, 10
    double, 10
    float, 9
    int, 9
    long, 9
    long double, 10
    long long, 9
    nonlocal, order of initialization, 292
    passing
        by reference, 28, 272–273
        by value, 28
        by values, 272–273
    pointers, 27
    reference variables, 268–270
    short, 9
    stack, exceptions, 31
    static, 291
    string literals, 512
    type changing, 10
    unsigned int, 9
    unsigned long, 9
    unsigned long long, 9
    unsigned short, 9
    wchar_t, 10
variadic templates, 742–743
    mix-in classes, 745–746
    ring buffer and, 941–942
    type-safe variable-length argument lists, 743–745
vector, 279
    assigning, 398
    built-in classes, 396
    comparing, 398–399
    constructors, 396–397
    copying, 398
    destructors, 396–397
    dynamic-length, 395–396
    elements
        access methods, 394–395
        appending, 404–406
        initial value, 394–395
        user-defined classes, 396
    fixed-length, 393–395
    heap, allocation, 397
    intVector, 398
    iterators, 399–401
    memory allocation scheme, 406–407
    printVector( ) function, 405
    push_back( ) method, 320
    round-robin scheduling, 407–412
    type parameters, 393
    vectorbool, 412–413
vector container, 276, 370
virtual base classes, 242, 265
virtual destructors, 225
    method templates, 698
    need for, 262–263
virtual keyword, 216
    implementing virtual, 260–261
    justification for, 262
virtual methods, 216
    method templates, 698
    overriding, 259–263
    pure, 232–233
    typeid operator, 263
Visual C++ 2010 debugger, 965–966
voter registration auditing algorithm example, 503–507

W

wait( ) method, 824
wchar_t variable, 10
WeatherPrediction class, 219
    MyWeatherPrediction class, 220–222
WebHost class, 891
what( ) method, 550
    overriding, 340
while loop, 19
white box testing, 905
wide characters, 518–519
wide strings
wildcards, ECMAScript
Windows, memory leaks, 792–793
word boundaries, 528
workflows, 846
write( ) method, 548–549
writing classes, 968–969
writing to files, 971

X–Y–Z

zero-initialization, 396
    template types, 723–724